Statements on Auditing Standards (AICPA)

SAS No.*

SAS No.	Year	Title
1	1972	Codification of Auditing Standards and Procedures
8	1975	Other Information in Documents Containing Audited Financial Statements
12	1976	Inquiry of a Client's Lawyer Concerning Litigation, Claims, and Assessments
21	1977	Segment Information
22	1978	Planning and Supervision
25	1979	The Relationship of Generally Accepted Auditing Standards to Quality Control Standards
26	1979	Association with Financial Statements
29	1980	Reporting on Information Accompanying the Basic Financial Statements in Auditor-Submitted Documents
31	1980	Evidential Matter
32	1980	Adequacy of Disclosure of Financial Statements
37	1981	Filings Under Federal Securities Statutes
39	1981	Audit Sampling
41	1982	Working Papers
42	1982	Reporting on Condensed Financial Statements and Selected Financial Data
43	1982	Omnibus Statement on Auditing Standards
45	1983	Omnibus Statement on Auditing Standards—1983
46	1983	Consideration of Omitted Procedures After the Report Date
47	1983	Audit Risk and Materiality in Conducting an Audit
48	1984	The Effects of Computer Processing on the Examination of Financial Statements
50	1986	Reports on the Application of Accounting Principles
51	1986	Reporting on Financial Statements Prepared for Use in Other Countries
52	1988	Omnibus Statement on Auditing Standards—1987
54	1988	Illegal Acts by Clients
55	1988	Consideration of the Internal Control Structure in a Financial Statement Audit
56	1988	Analytical Procedures
57	1988	Auditing Accounting Estimates
58	1988	Reports on Audited Financial Statements
59	1988	The Auditor's Consideration of an Entity's Ability to Continue as a Going Concern
60	1988	Communication of Internal Control Structure Related Matters Noted in an Audit
61	1988	Communication With Audit Committees
62	1989	Special Reports
64	1990	Omnibus Statement on Auditing Standards—1990
65	1991	The Auditor's Consideration of the Internal Audit Function in an Audit of Financial Statements
67	1991	The Confirmation Process
69	1992	The Meaning of "Present Fairly in Conformity With Generally Accepted Accounting Principles" in the Independent Auditor's Report
70	1992	Service Organizations
71	1992	Review of Interim Financial Information
72	1993	Letters for Underwriters and Certain Other Requesting Parties
73	1994	Using the Work of a Specialist
74	1995	Compliance Auditing Considerations in Audits of Governmental Entities and Recipients of Governmental Financial Assistance
76	1995	Amendments to SAS No. 72, "Letters for Underwriters and Certain Other Requesting Parties"
77	1995	Amendments to SAS No. 22 ("Planning and Supervision"), SAS No. 59 ("Auditor's Consideration of an Entity's Ability to Continue as a Going Concern"), and SAS No. 62 ("Special Reports")
78	1995	Consideration of Internal Control in a Financial Statement Audit: Amendment to SAS No. 55
79	1995	Amendment to SAS No. 58, "Reports on Audited Financial Statements"
80	1996	Amendment to SAS No. 31, "Evidential Matter"
82	1997	Consideration of Fraud in a Financial Statement Audit
83	1997	Establishing an Understanding with the Client
84	1997	Communications Between Predecessor and Successor Auditors
85	1997	Management Representations
86	1998	Amendment to SAS No. 72, "Letters for Underwriters and Certain Other Requesting Parties"
87	1998	Restricting the Use of an Auditor's Report
88	1999	Service Organizations and Reporting on Consistency
89	1999	Audit Adjustments
90	1999	Audit Committee Communications
91	1999	Federal GAAP Hierarchy
92	2000	Auditing Derivative Instruments, Hedging Activities, and Investments in Securities
93	2000	Omnibus Statement on Auditing Standards—2000

*Does not include superseded statements.

Auditing and Assurance Services

Tenth Edition

Jack C. Robertson, PhD
Certified Public Accountant
Certified Fraud Examiner
C.T. Zlatkovich Centennial Professor of Accounting
The University of Texas at Austin

Timothy J. Louwers, PhD
Certified Public Accountant
Certified Internal Auditor
Certified Information Systems Auditor
Associate Professor of Accounting
Louisiana State University

Boston   Burr Ridge, IL   Dubuque, IA   Madison, WI   New York   San Francisco   St. Louis
Bangkok   Bogotá   Caracas   Kuala Lumpur   Lisbon   London   Madrid   Mexico City
Milan   Montreal   New Delhi   Santiago   Seoul   Singapore   Sydney   Taipei   Toronto

McGraw-Hill Higher Education

A Division of The **McGraw-Hill** *Companies*

AUDITING AND ASSURANCE SERVICES

Published by McGraw-Hill, an imprint of The McGraw-Hill Companies, Inc. 1221 Avenue of the Americas, New York, NY, 10020. Copyright © 2002, 1999, 1996, 1993, 1990, 1988, 1985, 1982, 1979, 1976 by The McGraw-Hill Companies, Inc. All rights reserved. No part of this publication may be reproduced or distributed in any form or by any means, or stored in a data base or retrieval system, without the prior written consent of The McGraw-Hill Companies, Inc., including, but not limited to, in any network or other electronic storage or transmission, or broadcast for distance learning.

Some ancillaries, including electronic and print components, may not be available to customers outside the United States.

This book is printed on acid-free paper.

domestic   2 3 4 5 6 7 8 9 0 KGP/KGP 0 9 8 7 6 5 4 3 2
international 1 2 3 4 5 6 7 8 9 0 KGP/KGP 0 9 8 7 6 5 4 3 2 1

ISBN 0-07-241050-7

Publisher: *Brent Gordon*
Senior sponsoring editor: *Stewart Mattson*
Developmental editor: *Erin Cibula*
Editorial coordinator: *Heather Sabo*
Marketing manager: *Ryan Blankenship*
Project manager: *Natalie J. Ruffatto*
Senior production supervisor: *Lori Koetters*
Senior producer, media technology: *Ed Przyzycki*
Coordinator of freelance design: *Mary Kazak*
Associate supplement producer: *Joyce J. Chappetto*
Cover design: *Joanne Schopler*
Cover illustration: *Tom White*
Interior Design: *Lucy Lesiak*
Typeface: *10.5/12 Goudy*
Compositor: *GAC / Indianapolis*
Printer: *Quebecor World Kingsport Inc.*

Library of Congress Cataloging-in-Publication Data

Robertson, Jack C.
    Auditing and assurance services / Jack C. Robertson, Timothy J. Louwers.—10th ed.
        p.   cm.
    Rev. ed. of: Auditing / Jack C. Robertson, Timothy J. Louwers. 9th ed. Boston: Irwin/McGraw-Hill, c1999.
    Includes index.
    ISBN 0-07-241050-7 (alk. paper)
    1. Auditing.   I. Louwers, Timothy J.   II. Robertson, Jack C. Auditing   III. Title.
HF5667.R72   2002
657'.45—dc21   2001032955

INTERNATIONAL EDITION   ISBN 0-07-112115-3

Copyright © 2002. Exclusive rights by The McGraw-Hill Companies, Inc. for manufacture and export.
This book cannot be re-exported from the country to which it is sold by McGraw-Hill. The International Edition is not available in North America.

www.mhhe.com

Auditors are assumed to have knowledge of the philosophy and practice of auditing; to have the degree of training, experience, and skill common to the average independent auditor; to have the ability to recognize indications of irregularities; and to keep abreast of developments in the perpetration and detection of irregularities.

R. K. Mautz and H. A. Sharaf
The Philosophy of Auditing

The very existence of the accounting profession depends on public confidence in the determination of certified public accountants to safeguard the public interest.

J. L. Carey
Professional Ethics of Public Accounting

This book is dedicated to
Charles T. Zlatkovich
Professor Emeritus
C. Aubrey Smith Professorship
Educator
Mentor
The University of Texas at Austin

ABOUT THE AUTHORS

Jack C. Robertson is the C.T. Zlatkovich Centennial Professor at The University of Texas at Austin, where he has been a member of the faculty since 1970. In 1975–76, he was the academic fellow on the staff of the managing partner of Coopers & Lybrand; in 1982–83, he served as the Academic Fellow in the SEC Office of the Chief Accountant; in 1988, he was the Visiting Erskine Fellow in the Department of Accountancy at the University of Canterbury in Christchurch, New Zealand. He has given invited presentations in Jerusalem, Tel Aviv, Christchurch, Dunedin, Wellington, Kyoto, Kobe, and Vilnius.

He is a member of the American Institute of CPAs (AICPA), the Texas Society of CPAs (TSCPA), the American Accounting Association (AAA), the Institute of Internal Auditors, and the Association of Certified Fraud Examiners. He has served on committees and task forces of the AICPA and TSCPA, and he has been active in the AAA—serving as secretary, vice-chairman, chairman, and historian of the Auditing Section. In the TSCPA, he is active on the Professional Ethics Committee and has received a presidential citation for meritorious service in the field of ethics. He was a member of the Board of Regents that created the Certified Fraud Examiner program for the Association of Certified Fraud Examiners.

His publications consist of books and articles on auditing, financial reporting, professional ethics, and fraud examination. His artistic avocation is playing trumpet in a mariachi music group.

At The University of Texas, Professor Robertson has developed three new auditing courses that have served as national models for courses elsewhere. Prior to his appointment as the C.T. Zlatkovich Centennial Professor, he held the Price Waterhouse Auditing Professorship (1979–1984).

Timothy J. Louwers is an Associate Professor at Louisiana State University where he teaches auditing and information systems auditing. He received his Ph.D. in accounting from Florida State University where his dissertation was named the 1994 American Accounting Association Outstanding Auditing Dissertation. Prior to beginning his academic career, he spent a number of years in public accounting with KPMG.

Professor Louwers' research interests include auditors' reporting decisions and ethical issues in the accounting profession. He has written over 30 academic and practitioner articles appearing in such journals as *Journal of Accounting Research*, *Journal of Accountancy*, *Behavioral Research in Accounting*, *Decision Sciences*, *Research on Accounting Ethics*, *CPA Journal*, and *Internal Auditing*.

He remains active in the business and academic community through participation in the American Accounting Association (serving as the 2000–2001 Chairman of the Professionalism and Ethics Committee), the American Institute of Certified Public Accountants, the Institute of Internal Auditors, and the Information Systems Audit and Control Association. He has received numerous teaching and research awards, including two Halliburton Teaching Fellow awards while at the University of Houston.

PREFACE

As we enter the new millennium, the practice of accounting and auditing has evolved and expanded its horizons. The tenth edition of *Auditing and Assurance Services* emphasizes three important aspects of this expansion—assurance services, fraud auditing, and computer assisted audit tools and techniques (CAATTs). We have attempted to integrate these three aspects throughout the textbook. We prominently feature assurance services in this new edition, with coverage both in the introductory chapter (Chapter 1) and in a module (Module A) devoted to assurance and other accounting services. We dedicate a chapter (Chapter 7) to fraud auditing and integrate fraud cases throughout the audit process chapters (Chapters 4 through 12). Finally, just as computer auditing is now a way of life in the auditing community, we integrate audit technology throughout the textbook, through early discussion of CAATTS, *Electronic Workpapers* available on the textbook website, and Internet exercises.

Auditing and Assurance Services reflects the challenges inherent in accounting and auditing practice, particularly in public accounting firms. Clients who pay the fees expect value in the form of consulting advice, recommendations for improvements in the business, and an audit report. On the other hand, public users of these clients' financial statements expect effective service; that is, they expect auditors to be objective skeptics working to monitor the business management and blow the whistle on fraudulent financial statements. These dual challenges of service to clients and service to the public merge the business and professional aspects of public accounting practice.

This tenth edition maintains an emphasis on financial auditors' decision-making processes: (1) recognizing problems and developing audit objectives, (2) gathering evidence with audit procedures, and (3) making judgments about control risk and the fair presentation of financial statement assertions. We wrote the textbook to bridge the gap between students' knowledge of accounting principles and the professional practice of accounting and auditing in the working world. The text covers both the concepts and the procedures of auditing. On the conceptual level, students learn about the social role of auditing; the services offered in internal, governmental, and public accounting practice; and the professional standard for behavioral and technical competence. On the technical level, they learn about the programs and procedures for defining audit objectives, gathering evidence, making decisions, and exercising professional skepticism.

In our dual roles of both textbook authors and instructors, we are uniquely sensitive to the costs incurred by our students. With this in mind, we have bundled a separate audit practice set with the textbook at no additional cost. The integrated fraud cases eliminate the necessity of a separate audit casebook. Finally, we have attempted to streamline the book without sacrificing readability.

Important Features and Supplements

We designed the textbook to guide and direct students' study. As authors, we are continually motivated by our desire to produce the very best source of information on auditing and assurance services. We have always been open to constructive criticism, and that openness to others' creative ideas and pedagogical innovations has resulted in several changes from the previous edition of this textbook. While the constant evolution of business, technology, and the public accounting profession ensures that we will never achieve our quest of creating the perfect auditing and assurance textbook, we do believe that we are getting closer. The features described below enhance students' ability to comprehend basic concepts and apply them in real case situations.

Fraud Auditing
The tenth edition contains full-chapter coverage of fraud auditing, until now unavailable in introductory auditing books. The basic purpose of the chapter is to create awareness of, and sensitivity to, the signs and signals of potential errors and frauds. The chapter contains some unique insights on extended audit and investigation procedures.

Apollo Shoes Audit Practice Case
The Apollo Shoes case is a stand-alone audit practice set. The case carries all the topics found in other similar cases, and more. Case assignments connect many of the technical topics in a logical sequence of audit engagement activities.

"Modular Format"
In a break from textbook tradition, all the chapters in this tenth edition of the text are not numbered sequentially. The first 12 chapters in Parts I and II present an order of topics for an introduction to the profession and to the process of auditing financial statements from beginning to end. We present these chapters first to facilitate your "getting into auditing" right away.

The next eight entries are called "Modules" in Parts III. Labeled Module A, Module B, etc., these are the topics for which professors have a variety of preferences for placement in courses. They cover assurance and other accounting services, statistics, government and internal auditing, ethics, information systems auditing, and legal liability. The Modules stand alone and instructors can insert them in a course syllabus wherever they best suit the course plan.

Electronic Workpapers
Students can complete many of the homework assignments on electronic spreadsheets. The *Electronic Workpapers* files are posted on the textbook website where students and instructors can easily retrieve them.

Internet Website
Because of the time constraints associated with textbook publishing, we are often hindered in our attempts to provide the most current information on events affecting the auditing profession. To address our concerns, we have created an Internet website (www.mhhe.com/business/robertson10e). This site contains up-to-date information on recent pronouncements, trends in the auditing profession, and other hot topics. The website also contains a special student area, where students can download *Electronic Workpapers*, access authoritative accounting resources, and browse the "archive of accounting humor."

Learning Aids
Each chapter and module in *Auditing and Assurance Services* contains features that enhance readability, study, and learning.

Professional Standards References.   Each chapter opens with a list of professional standards references from the AICPA, GAO, and IIA standards relevant to the chapter topics. The inside front and back covers list these standards and other library resources used by professional auditors.

Learning Objectives.   Each chapter begins with the presentation of several learning objectives. These are repeated as marginal notes within the chapters.

Auditing Insights.   All the chapters contain illustrative auditing insights, some of which are in the flow of the chapter text, while others stand alone to add realism and interest. These notes bring the real world into the textbook treatment of auditing.

Review Checkpoints.   Instead of placing a long list of review questions at the end of each chapter, review checkpoints (questions) are placed inside each chapter in several sections so students can test themselves as they proceed through a chapter. These checkpoint islands make the text user-friendly by effectively breaking each chapter into smaller sections.

Cases. The case stories in Chapters 7 through 12 are short stories structured to reveal error or fraud in an account. An audit approach section follows each story. The audit approach describes an audit objective, desirable controls, test of controls procedures, and audit of balance procedures that can result in discovering the situation.

The purpose of these case stories is to enliven the study of auditing. They replace the typical lengthy exposition of audit fundamentals (often tedious and boring) with illustrative situations based on real events. Twenty-five cases with audit approaches are in Chapters 7–11. Another 20 cases are in the end-of-chapter discussion cases section. There, the case story is told, and the students' assignment is to write the audit approach section.

Subject Titles on Exercises and Problems. Each of the exercises, problems, and discussion cases at the end of the chapter is identified with a topic title. The titles enable students and instructors to select problems on topics of interest.

Key Terms. Throughout the book, key terms are highlighted in boldface print. An alphabetical key terms reference list with definitions is in the back of the book.

Apollo Shoes, Inc. Casebook (ISBN 007247680x)

New to this edition, the Apollo Shoes Inc. Case has been consolidated for ease in one supplement packaged for free with each new textbook. This case was created to expose students to an integrated audit engagement. Assignments related to Apollo connect many of the technical topics in a logical sequence of audit engagement activities.

Instructor's Manual (ISBN 0072476761)

The Instructor's Manual contains some sample course syllabi, an index to the cases in Chapters 7–11, a few extra cases and explanations, and summaries of the chapter learning objectives. These summaries are prepared for reproduction in a student package where they can serve as guides to lectures and notetaking. The instructor's manual also contains numerous transparency masters for instructor and student use.

Solutions Manual (ISBN 0072476796)

The Solutions Manual contains solutions to all the review checkpoints, multiple choice questions, exercises, problems, and discussion cases.

Study Guide (ISBN 0072476753)

The study guide was prepared by Lawrence P. Kalbers of Long Island University—C.W. Post Campus. It contains a guide for CPA Examination study, an outline of each chapter, questions for study and review, and an outline of AICPA statements on auditing standards.

Test Bank (ISBN 0072476788 print and ISBN 007247677X computer)

The test bank available to instructors contains numerous objective, short-answer, and essay questions. It is available in hard copy as well as through the secured instructor section of the textbook web site. A computerized version of the test bank is available on CD and allows editing of questions, provides up to 99 versions of each test, and permits question selection based on type of question and level of difficulty.

Acknowledgments

The American Institute of Certified Public Accountants has generously given permission for liberal quotations from official pronouncements and other AICPA publications, all of which lend authoritative sources to the text. In addition, several publishing houses, professional associations, and accounting firms have granted permission to quote and extract from their copyrighted material. Their cooperation is much appreciated because a great amount of significant auditing thought exists in this wide variety of sources.

A special acknowledgment is due Mr. Joseph T. Wells, founder and chairman of the Association of Certified Fraud Examiners. He created the Certified Fraud Examiner (CFE) designation. Mr. Wells is a nationally known authority in the field of fraud examination education, and his entrepreneurial spirit has captured the interest of fraud examination professionals throughout the United States. Professor Robertson was privileged to have been a member of the inaugural CFE Board of Regents that produced the first CFE handbook and managed the initial CFE Symposium. Mr. Wells and the Association of Certified Fraud Examiners have been generous contributors to the fraud auditing material in this text.

The excellent suggestions provided by several professors have been a significant help in completing this book. Sincere appreciation is due to

Barbara Apostolou, Louisiana State University
Jack Armitage, University of Nebraska at Omaha
Richard Asebrook, University of Massachusetts
Michael Bamber, University of Georgia
Thelda Barron, University of Tennessee at Martin
Mary Ann Boughnou, Webster University
Scott Boyland, Washington and Lee University
Gary Braun, University of Texas at El Paso
Barry Byran, University of Mississippi
Kate Campbell, University of Maryland
William Cargill, Texas A&M International University
James Cashwell, Miami University of Ohio
William Dent, University of Texas at Dallas
James Hopkins, Morningside College
Stanley Earl Jenne, University of Montana
Lawrence Kalbers, Long Island University—C. W. Post
Chip Klemstine, University of Michigan at Ann Arbor
Joseph Lisciandro, Slippery Rock University of Pennsylvania
William Morris, University of North Texas
Denise Patterson, California State University at Fresno
Kenny Reynolds, Louisiana State University
Elmer Rider, Delaware Valley College
Richard Roscher, University of North Carolina at Wilmington
David Sinason, Northern Illinois University
Brett Stone, State University College—New Paltz
William Stout, University of Louisville
Jay Thibodeau, Bentley College
Paul Warner, Hofstra University
Don Watne, Portland State University
Scott Whisenant, Georgetown University
Tom Wilson, University of Southwestern Louisiana
James Yardley, Virginia Polytechnic University

Their suggestions greatly enhanced several portions of the text. However, we remain responsible for all errors of commission and omission.

In addition, we would like to recognize our outstanding editorial staff at McGraw-Hill/Irwin: Stewart Mattson, Heather Sabo, Erin Cibula, Natalie Ruffatto, Lori Koetters, Mary Kazak, and Joyce Chappetto for their encouragement, assistance, and guidance in the production of this book.

Professor Robertson owes a great debt of gratitude to professional accountants in all walks of life. The first five editions of Auditing (beginning in 1976) were dedicated to two accountants who were truly professional in every meaning of the word: Jim Tom Barton, a CPA and author of Texana literature, and Albert L. Wade, a CPA of the "old school." These gentlemen have both passed away, but are remembered well. Still among the living is Professor Emeritus Charles T. Zlatkovich—exemplar, mentor, and friend—to whom this edition is dedicated.

Saving the best to the end, words cannot express the extent of support freely given by Susan Robertson and Barbara Louwers. They have endured the agony and ecstasy of revision and have lent their own hand to producing the manuscript and the supplements. Behind these authors, they are a force saying, "Get it finished so we can go out for a celebration dinner!"

Jack C. Robertson   Timothy J. Louwers
Austin, Texas   Baton Rouge, Louisiana

CONTENTS IN BRIEF

TABLE OF CONTENTS

PART I
AUDITING AND ASSURANCE SERVICES

PART II

THE AUDIT PROCESS

PART III

SPECIAL TOPICS

Chapter 1

Auditing and
Assurance Services

Professional Standards References

Learning Objectives

Learning objectives are statements of what you should be able to do after you have studied each chapter of this textbook, examined related professional standards, answered the review checkpoints in each chapter, and completed assigned homework problems. For example, in an auto mechanic school one learning objective would be: "Be able to take a carburetor apart and put it back together in 15 minutes."

Learning objectives for auditing, however, are not this task specific. The learning objectives are given at the beginning of each chapter and are duplicated within the chapter at appropriate places. As you study each part of the chapter, you can use them as points of reference.

Chapter 1 gives you an introduction to professional accounting practice. Other accounting courses helped you learn the principles and methods of accounting. Now you are starting a study of the ways and means of practicing accounting, auditing, and assurance services outside the classroom. Your objectives are to be able to:

1. Define information risk and explain how auditing and assurance services play a role in reducing this business risk.

2. Define and contrast accounting, auditing, and assurance services.

3. Describe and define the five principal management assertions embodied in financial statements, and why auditors use them as a focal point of the audit.

4. Explain some characteristics of "professional skepticism."

5. Describe the organization of public accounting firms and identify the various services they offer.

6. List and explain the requirements for becoming a CPA.

7. Describe the audits and auditors in governmental, internal, and operational auditing.

USER DEMAND FOR RELIABLE INFORMATION

LEARNING OBJECTIVE
1. Define information risk and explain how auditing and assurance services play a role in reducing this business risk.

In today's competitive economy, almost all companies and organizations use some form of electronic commerce. For example, many companies market their products to customers and record orders from them directly through the Internet (B2C (business-to-consumer)). For significant customer-supplier relationships (B2B (business-to-business)), company computers are directly linked to each other through Internet-based virtual private networks (VPNs). Transactions that once took several weeks to complete manually (from customer purchase order generation to final payment being deposited to the supplier's bank account) now take only as long as it takes to ship and receive the goods. Purchase orders for goods are made via computer and payment is made automatically through electronic funds transfer (EFT) directly to the vendor's bank. In grocery and discount retail stores, clerks use optical scanners at the checkout counter (point of sale) to keep track of inventory and to determine when more inventory should be ordered. Time clock cards are no longer necessary because employees record work hours electronically when they pass their identification cards through an optical scanner. Many employees are no longer paid by check; their employers deposit the paychecks electronically into the employee's checking accounts.

As you can imagine, economic activity in this electronic environment takes place in an atmosphere fraught with risk. For example, **business risk** is the chance a company takes that customers will buy from competitors, that product lines will become obsolete, that taxes will increase, that government contracts will be lost, or that employees will go on strike. To minimize these risks and take advantage of other opportunities presented in today's competitive economy, decision makers, such as chief executive officers (CEOs), demand timely, relevant, and reliable information. Decisions to purchase or sell goods or services, lend money, enter into employment agreements, buy or sell investments, and other kinds of economic decisions depend in large part on the timeliness of useful information. Information professionals (such as accountants, auditors, and information assurance providers) help satisfy the demand for timely, accurate information.

Information and Information Risk

Four environmental conditions create user demand for relevant, reliable information:

1. *Complexity.* Events and transactions in today's economy are numerous and often very complicated. Decision makers are not trained to collect and compile the information themselves. They need the services of information professionals.
2. *Remoteness.* Decision makers are usually separated from current and potential business partners by distance and time, as well as by lack of expertise. They need to employ full-time information professionals to do the work they cannot do for themselves.
3. *Time-sensitivity.* Decision makers in today's ultra-competitive economy often must make decisions on a moment's notice. They may not have the luxury of waiting several months for all of the relevant information to be disclosed.
4. *Consequences.* Decisions affect individuals' (as well as companies') financial security and well-being. Decisions can involve significant investments of time and money. The consequences are so important that reliable information, obtained and verified by information professionals, is an absolute necessity.

A further complication to effective decision-making is the presence of information risk. **Information risk** is the risk (probability) that the information (mainly financial) disseminated by a company will be materially false or misleading. Decision makers usually obtain their information from companies or organizations with which they want to conduct business, to obtain (or provide) loans, or to buy or sell stock. Since the primary source of information is the target company itself, an incentive exists for that company's management to make their business or service appear to be better than it actually may be. For example, preparers and issuers of financial information (directors, managers, accountants, and other people employed in a business) might benefit by giving false, misleading, or overly optimistic information. This potential **conflict of interest** is a condition that creates society's demand for audit and assurance services. Users need more than just information; they need reliable information. Internet buyers rely on website information when purchasing online. Financial analysts and investors depend on financial reports for making stock purchase and sale decisions. Creditors (suppliers, banks, and so on) use financial reports to decide whether to give trade credit and bank loans. Labor organizations use financial reports to help determine a company's ability to pay wages. Government agencies and Congress use financial information in preparing analyses of the economy and in making laws concerning taxes, subsidies, and the like. These various users cannot take it on themselves to determine whether information is reliable and, therefore, low on the information risk-scale. Thus, they hire independent information assurers such as auditors to reduce the information risk. Auditors (and other information assurance providers) assume the social role of certifying (or *attesting* to) published financial information, thereby offering users the valuable service of assurance that the information risk is low.

Auditing and Assurance Services

The potential conflict between information preparers and users has become real often enough to create a natural skepticism on the part of users. Thus, they depend on information professionals to serve as objective intermediaries who will lend some credibility to the information. This "lending of credibility" to information is known as **assurance.** When the assurance is provided for specific assertions made by management (usually about financial information), we often refer to the assurance provided as **attestation.**

E X H I B I T 1–1   THE RELATIONSHIPS AMONG AUDITING, ATTESTATION, AND ASSURANCE SERVICES

Assurance Services
Any Information

Attestation Services
Primarily Financial Information

Auditing
Financial Statements

When the assertions are embodied in a company's financial statements, we refer to the attestation as **auditing**. Exhibit 1–1 depicts the relationships among assurance, attestation, and auditing services.

From your earlier studies, you know that accounting is the process of recording, classifying, and summarizing into financial statements a company's transactions that create assets, liabilities, equities, revenues, and expenses. It is the means of satisfying users' demands for financial information that arise from the forces of complexity, remoteness, time-sensitivity, and consequences. The function of **financial reporting** is to provide statements of financial position (balance sheets), statements of results of operations (income statements), statements of changes in financial position (cash flow statements), and accompanying disclosure notes (footnotes) to outside decision makers who have no internal source of information like the management of the company has.

Auditing and assurance services do not include the function of financial report production. A company's accountants under the direction of its management perform that function. Auditors obtain evidence that enables them to determine whether the information in the financial statements is reliable. Auditors then report to the users that the information is reliable by expressing an opinion that the company's presentation of financial position, results of operations, and changes in financial position, is in accordance with generally accepted accounting principles. This is the attestation of the attest function, as it relates to the traditional financial statements.

Reliable information helps make capital markets efficient and helps people know the consequences of a wide variety of economic decisions. However, CPAs practicing the assurance function are not the only information professionals at work in the economy. Bank examiners, IRS auditors, state regulatory agency auditors (e.g., auditors in a state's insurance department), internal auditors employed by a company, and federal government agency auditors all practice information assurance in one form or another.

R E V I E W
C H E C K P O I N T S

1.1 What is business risk? What is information risk?

1.2 What conditions create demand for useful information?

1.3 What is assurance? What is attestation? What condition creates demand for attestation and assurance services?

1.4 What is the difference between auditing and accounting?

AUDITING INSIGHT

INDEPENDENT AUDITORS: GUARDIANS OF INFORMATION RISK

Financial statement users have reason to be wary of unaudited financial statements. They can contain overstatements of assets and income based on managers' enthusiastic optimism or on desires to mislead decision makers. Nine research studies covering 1,562 audits during the years 1975–1988 showed a general tendency: Independent auditors frequently discovered, and management corrected, material errors of asset and income overstatement before annual audited financial statements were released for public use.

Source: Kinney, W. R., Jr., and R. D. Martin. "Does Auditing Reduce Bias in Financial Reporting? A Review of Audit-Related Adjustment Studies." *Auditing: A Journal of Practice and Theory.*

DEFINITIONS OF ASSURANCE SERVICES AND FINANCIAL AUDITING

LEARNING OBJECTIVE
2. Define and contrast accounting, auditing, and assurance services.

As the business environment is changing, so too is the accounting profession. In this section, we define auditing and assurance services and explain their role in today's "information economy."

Definition and Examples of Assurance Services

In the mid-1990's, members of the American Institute of CPAs (AICPA), the public accounting community's professional association, perceived a general decline in the demand for their services. Member clients had expressed concerns that the traditional services were no longer relevant in today's fast-moving economy. In response, the Special Committee on Assurance Services (SCAS) was established to examine the current state of affairs, as well as environmental trends affecting the profession. In addition to identifying skills necessary to compete in the new economy, the committee also identified several overlooked opportunities for information professionals, such as risk identification, business process measurement, and website assurance. The Committee's final report (AICPA 1996) fundamentally changed the focus of the accounting profession, expanding the profession's traditional focus on accounting information to all types of information, both financial and non-financial in nature. The expanded services are collectively referred to as **assurance services**:

> Assurance services are independent professional services that improve the quality of information, or its context, for decision makers.

You are right if you think this definition is so broad that a large class of activities can fit within it! However, the definition contains some boundaries. The SCAS maintains that assurance services are natural extensions of attestation services that earlier evolved from financial statement audit services. Even so, attestation and audit services are highly structured and intended to be useful for large groups of decision makers (e.g., investors, lenders). On the other hand, assurance services are more customized and intended to be useful to smaller, targeted groups of decision makers. In this sense, assurance services bear resemblance to consulting services. The major elements, and boundaries, of the definition are these:

- *Independence*. CPAs want to preserve their attestation and audit reputations and competitive advantages by preserving integrity and objectivity when performing assurance services.
- *Professional Services*. Virtually all work performed by CPAs (accounting, auditing, data management, taxation, management, marketing, finance) is defined as

"professional services" as long as it involves some element of judgment based on education and experience.

- *Improving the Quality of Information.* The emphasis is on "information"—CPAs' traditional stock in trade. CPAs can enhance quality by assuring users about the reliability and relevance of information, and these two features are closely related to the familiar credibility-lending products of attestation and audit services.
- *Improving the Context of Information.* "Context" is relevance in a different light. For assurance services, improving the context of information refers to improving its usefulness when targeted to particular decision makers in the surroundings of particular decision problems. CPAs will need time and experience in various assurance services to develop more fully this concept of context.
- *For Decision Makers.* They are the "consumers" for assurance services, and they personify the consumer focus of new and different professional work. They may or may not be the "client" that pays the fee, and they may or may not be one of the parties to an assertion or other information. The decision makers are the beneficiaries of the assurance services. Depending upon the assignment, decision makers may be a very small, targeted group (e.g., managers of a data base) or a large targeted group (e.g., potential investors interested in a mutual fund manager's performance).

Examples of Assurance Services

The SCAS conducted surveys and found hundreds of examples of current and potential assurance services. Here are a few of them presented for the purpose of adding some definite examples to the generalities you have studied so far. Some will look familiar, and others may defy imagination. Be aware, however, that the possibilities for assurance services may lie within the expertise of some but not all CPA firms—nobody maintains that all CPA firms will want or be able to provide all the assurance services (unlike audit services that people generally expect all CPAs to be able to perform).

- Internet website certification (CPA WebTrust)
- Accounts receivable review and cash enhancement
- Third-party reimbursement maximization
- Rental property operations review
- Customer satisfaction surveys
- Benchmarking/best practices
- Evaluation of investment management policies
- Fraud and illegal acts prevention and deterrence

AUDITING INSIGHT

CPA WEBTRUST

One of the psychological barriers to Internet business transactions is people's anxiety about entering private information, such as a credit card number, to make payment in a purchase transaction. So, assurance practitioners developed the CPA WebTrust service that is an examination of the information security devices in operation on a commercial website. When the business offered on the website has engaged the service and the practitioners have completed a review of the security, the business is entitled to display a "CPA WebTrust" icon. A user can click on the icon and read the assurance service report that gives comfort about the transaction security. You may want to find such a business on an Internet site and read the CPA WebTrust report.

Source: **CPA Letter**

AUDITING INSIGHT

FORE!

Wilson Sporting Goods Company is using CPAs to prove that amateur golfers can hit Wilson's Ultra golf ball farther than they can hit competitors' golf balls. Wilson says the CPAs certify that Wilson's Ultra outdistances its competitors by an average of 5.7 yards per drive. Wilson's accountants don't impress competitors. "I can walk off a golf ball's distance as well as any accountant," says Harry Groome, an account executive with Ayer, Inc., the ad agency for the Maxfli gold balls made by Dunlop Slazenger Corporation. "Using a CPA is an odd way to measure a golf drive." Marlene Baddeloo, the engagement manager for the accounting firm that oversees Wilson's golf-ball competitions, agrees "that anyone could pace off a golf driving range to see how far a ball goes." But she says firm staffers since last May have checked that Wilson employees haven't doctored the results at more than 30 driving ranges. "We also make sure the amateurs participating aren't affiliated with Wilson or its competitors and haven't been paid to participate," she adds. The use of accountants may upset Wilson's competitors, but it sure makes the accountants happy. "Our personnel love . . . [to] wear shorts and spend the day out in the air," says Ms. Baddeloo. "I get a lot of volunteers."

Source: Lee Berton, "After This, CPAs May Take Over Instant-Replay Duties for Football." *The Wall Street Journal.*

- Information systems security reviews (SysTrust)
- Internal audit strategic review

While attestation and audit services are special types of assurance services, consulting services are not. In consulting services CPAs use their professional skills and experiences to produce recommendations to a client for outcomes like information system design and operation; in assurance services, the focus is entirely on the information that decision makers use. (As time and experience passes in the development of the assurance services, this distinction may prove to be an extremely fine line in dividing consulting and assurance.) However, like consulting services, assurance services have a "customer focus," and CPAs will need to develop and sell assurance services that add value for customers (decision makers).

Definition of Auditing

While assurance services include many areas of information, auditing refers specifically to the certification of financial statements. The most general definition of auditing is from a committee of the American Accounting Association (AAA)—the organization of accounting professors. The AAA Committee on Basic Auditing Concepts (1971) defined auditing as follows:

> Auditing is a systematic process of objectively obtaining and evaluating evidence regarding assertions about economic actions and events to ascertain the degree of correspondence between the assertions and established criteria and communicating the results to interested users.

This definition contains several ideas important in a wide variety of audit practices. Auditing is a *systematic process.* It is purposeful and logical and is based on the discipline of a structured approach to decision making. It is not haphazard, unplanned, or unstructured.

The process involves obtaining and evaluating *evidence.* Evidence consists of all the influences that ultimately guide auditors' decisions, and relates to *assertions about economic actions and events.* When beginning an audit engagement, an independent auditor is given financial statements and other disclosures by management and thus obtains management's explicit assertions about economic actions and events (assets, liabilities, revenue, expense).

EXHIBIT 1–2	OVERVIEW OF FINANCIAL STATEMENT AUDITING

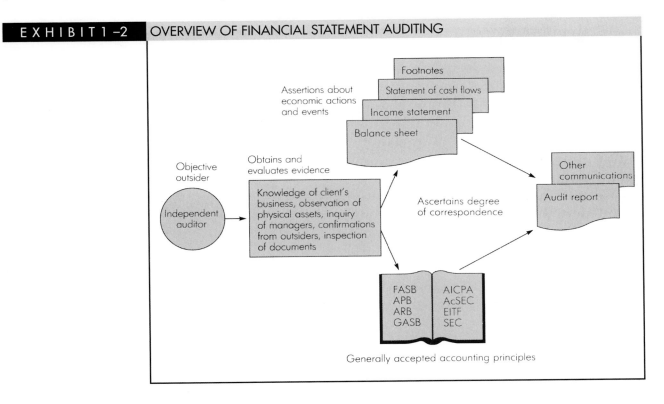

Independent auditors generally begin work with explicit representations from management—assertions of financial statement numbers and information disclosed in footnotes—and they set out to obtain evidence to prove or disprove these representations. Other auditors, however, are not so well provided with explicit representations. An internal auditor may be assigned to "evaluate the cost effectiveness of the company's policy to lease, rather than to purchase, heavy equipment." A governmental auditor may be assigned to "determine whether goals of providing equal educational opportunity" have been achieved with federal grant funds. Oftentimes, these latter two types of auditors must develop the explicit standards of performance for themselves.

The purpose of obtaining and evaluating evidence is to *ascertain the degree of correspondence between the assertions and established criteria*. Auditors will ultimately *communicate their findings to interested users*. To communicate in an efficient and understandable manner, auditors and users must have a common basis for measuring and describing financial information. This basis is the established criteria essential for effective communication.

Established criteria may be found in a variety of sources. For independent auditors, the criteria largely consist of the generally accepted accounting principles (GAAP). IRS agents rely heavily on criteria specified in the Internal Revenue Code. Governmental auditors may rely on criteria established in legislation or regulatory agency rules. Bank examiners and state insurance board auditors look to definitions and rules of law. Internal and governmental auditors rely a great deal on financial and managerial models of efficiency and economy. All auditors rely to some extent on elusive criteria of general truth and fairness. Exhibit 1–2 depicts an overview of financial statement auditing.

The American Accounting Association definition is broad and general enough to encompass independent, internal, and governmental auditing. The viewpoint of auditors in public accounting practice is reflected in the AICPA statement of the main objective of a financial statement audit. *Statement on Auditing Standards No. 1 (AU 110)* states:

> The objective of the ordinary examination of financial statements by the independent auditor is the expression of an opinion on the fairness with which they present, in all material respects, financial position, results of operations, and cash flows in conformity with generally accepted accounting principles. The auditor's report is the medium through which he expresses his opin-

EXIBIT 1–3	STANDARD AUDIT REPORT

Independent Auditors' Report

To the Board of Directors and Stockholders of Microsoft Corporation:

We have audited the accompanying consolidated balance sheets of Microsoft Corporation and subsidiaries as of June 30, 1999 and 2000, and the related consolidated statements of income, cash flows, and stockholders' equity for each of the three years in the period ended June 30, 2000. These financial statements are the responsibility of the Company's management. Our responsibility is to express an opinion on these financial statements based on our audits.

We conducted our audits in accordance with auditing standards generally accepted in the United States of America. Those standards require that we plan and perform the audit to obtain reasonable assurance about whether the financial statements are free of material misstatement. An audit includes examining, on a test basis, evidence supporting the amounts and disclosures in the financial statements. An audit also includes assessing the accounting principles used and significant estimates made by management, as well as evaluating the overall financial statement presentation. We believe that our audits provide a reasonable basis for our opinion.

In our opinion, such consolidated financial statements present fairly, in all material respects, the financial position of Microsoft Corporation and subsidiaries as of June 30, 1999 and 2000, and the results of their operations and their cash flows for each of the three years in the period ended June 30, 2000 in conformity with accounting principles generally accepted in the United States of America.

Deloitte & Touche LLP
Seattle, Washington
July 18, 2000

ion or, if circumstances require, disclaims an opinion. In either case, he states whether his examination has been made in accordance with generally accepted auditing standards.[1]

The expression of opinion on financial statements is given in the last paragraph of the audit report. A standard report is shown in Exhibit 1–3. As your study of auditing continues, you will find that auditors perform many tasks designed to reduce the risk of giving an inappropriate opinion on financial statements. Auditors are careful to work for trustworthy clients, to gather and analyze evidence about the assertions in financial statements, and to take steps to assure that audit personnel report properly on the financial statements when adverse information is known.

AUDITOR'S ROLE ACCORDING TO MOTHER-IN-LAW

Mother-in-Law: Jack, what do you do?
Jack: I'm an auditor.

Friend to Mother-in-Law: What does Jack do?
Mother-in-Law: He snoops around in other peoples' books.

R E V I E W
CHECKPOINTS

1.5 In what ways are assurance services similar in general to attestation services (including audits of financial statements)?

1.6 What are the five major elements of the broad definition of assurance services?

1.7 Why do you think the AICPA is so interested in developing CPAs' expertise in assurance services?

1.8 Define and explain auditing. What would you answer if asked by an anthropology major: "What do auditors do?"

1.9 Who cares about information risk reduction?

---

[1] The Statements on Auditing Standards (SAS) are authoritative AICPA pronouncements on auditing theory and practice. Statements on Auditing Procedure (SAP) number 1–54 were codified in SAS 1 in 1972. Statements on Auditing Standards are issued periodically. Your instructor can tell you the number of the most recently issued SAS. Throughout this text, SAS references are followed by parenthetical section numbers, which refer to the SAS volumes published by AICPA.

MANAGEMENT'S ASSERTIONS EMBODIED IN THE FINANCIAL STATEMENTS

LEARNING OBJECTIVE

3. Describe and define the five principal management assertions embodied in financial statements, and why auditors use them as a focal point of the audit.

As noted earlier, the management of the company is responsible for preparing the financial statements, thus they contain management's assertions about economic actions and events. As you study this section, keep in mind this scheme of things. The purpose of the audit is to obtain and evaluate evidence about these five assertions management makes in financial statements (SAS 31, AU 326):

1. Existence or occurrence.
2. Completeness.
3. Rights and obligations.
4. Valuation or allocations.
5. Presentation and disclosure.

Exhibit 1–4 illustrates the five principal assertions in some detail with relation to the inventory in the statement of financial position. The sections that follow describe and define the assertions more fully.

Existence or Occurrence

The audit objective related to **existence or occurrence** is to establish with evidence that assets, liabilities, and equities actually exist and that revenue and expense transactions actually occurred. Thus, auditors count cash and inventory, confirm receivables and insurance policies, and perform other procedures to obtain evidence related to their

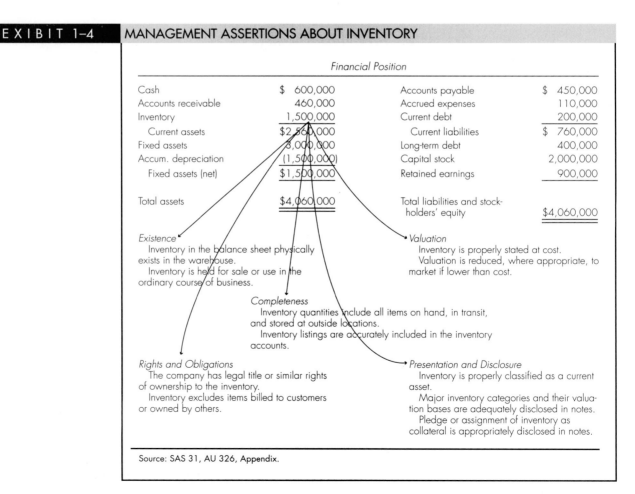

EXIBIT 1–4   MANAGEMENT ASSERTIONS ABOUT INVENTORY

Financial Position

Cash	$ 600,000	Accounts payable	$ 450,000
Accounts receivable	460,000	Accrued expenses	110,000
Inventory	1,500,000	Current debt	200,000
Current assets	$2,560,000	Current liabilities	$ 760,000
Fixed assets	3,000,000	Long-term debt	400,000
Accum. depreciation	(1,500,000)	Capital stock	2,000,000
Fixed assets (net)	$1,500,000	Retained earnings	900,000
Total assets	$4,060,000	Total liabilities and stockholders' equity	$4,060,000

Existence
Inventory in the balance sheet physically exists in the warehouse.
Inventory is held for sale or use in the ordinary course of business.

Completeness
Inventory quantities include all items on hand, in transit, and stored at outside locations.
Inventory listings are accurately included in the inventory accounts.

Rights and Obligations
The company has legal title or similar rights of ownership to the inventory.
Inventory excludes items billed to customers or owned by others.

Valuation
Inventory is properly stated at cost.
Valuation is reduced, where appropriate, to market if lower than cost.

Presentation and Disclosure
Inventory is properly classified as a current asset.
Major inventory categories and their valuation bases are adequately disclosed in notes.
Pledge or assignment of inventory as collateral is appropriately disclosed in notes.

Source: SAS 31, AU 326, Appendix.

specific objectives of determining whether cash, inventory, receivables, insurance in force, and other assets actually exist. You must be careful at this point, however, because the finding of existence alone generally proves little about the other four assertions.

A special aspect of existence or occurrence is *cutoff*. **Cutoff** refers to recognizing assets and liabilities as of a *proper date* and accounting for revenue, expense, and other transactions in the *proper period*. Simple cutoff errors can occur: (1) when a company records late December sales invoices for goods not actually shipped until January or (2) when a company records cash receipts through the end of the week (e.g., Friday, January 4) and the last batch for the year should have been processed on December 31. In auditor's jargon, the **cutoff date** refers to the client's year-end balance sheet date. Proper cutoff means accounting for all transactions that occurred during a period and neither postponing some recordings to the next period nor accelerating next-period transactions into the current-year accounts.

Completeness

The objective related to completeness is to establish with evidence that all transactions and accounts that should be presented in the financial reports are included. Thus, auditors' specific objectives include obtaining evidence to determine whether, for example, all the inventory on hand is included, all the inventory consigned out is included, all the inventory consigned in is excluded, all the notes payable are reported, and so forth. A verbal or written management representation saying that all transactions are included in the accounts is not considered a sufficient basis for deciding whether the completeness assertion is true. Auditors need to obtain persuasive evidence about completeness.

The completeness assertion also has a special cutoff aspect. Both completeness and cutoff mean that *all* the transactions of a period should be recorded in the proper period and not shifted to another. Incomplete accounting and coincident cutoff errors include such things as: (1) failure to record accruals for expenses incurred but not yet paid, thus understating both expenses and liabilities; (2) failure to record purchases of materials not yet received and, therefore, not included in the ending inventory, thus understating both inventory and accounts payable; and (3) failure to accrue unbilled revenue through the fiscal year-end for customers on a cycle billing system, thus understating both revenue and accounts receivable.

Rights and Obligations

The objective related to rights and obligations is to establish with evidence that amounts reported as assets of the company represent its property rights and that the amounts reported as liabilities represent its obligations. In plainer terms, the objective is to obtain evidence about *ownership* and *owership*. You should be careful about *ownership*, however, because the idea includes assets (rights) for which a company does not actually hold title. For example, an auditor will have a specific objective of obtaining evidence about the amounts capitalized for leased property. Likewise, the *owership* idea includes "accounting liabilities" a company may not yet be legally obligated to pay. For example, specific objectives would include obtaining evidence about the obligations under a capitalized lease or the estimated liability for product guarantees.

Valuation or Allocation

The objective related to valuation or allocation is to determine whether proper values have been assigned to assets, liabilities, equities, revenue, and expense. Auditors obtain evidence about specific valuations and mathematical accuracy by reconciling bank accounts, comparing vendors' invoices to inventory prices, obtaining lower-of-cost-or-market data, evaluating collectibility of receivables, and so forth. Many valuation and allocation decisions amount to decisions about the proper application of GAAP.

Presentation and Disclosure

Auditors also must determine whether accounting principles are properly selected and applied and whether disclosures are adequate. This objective relates to the presentation and disclosure assertion. Specific objectives include proper current and long-term balance sheet classification, mathematical accuracy of figures, and footnote disclosure of accounting policies. The presentation and disclosure objective is the meeting place for accounting principles and audit reporting standards.

A Compliance Assertion

Although not one of the five AICPA assertions, *compliance* with laws and regulations is very important for a business, and disclosure of known noncompliance is usually necessary for presentation of financial statements in conformity with generally accepted accounting principles. Auditors gather evidence about specific objectives related to financial laws and regulations, such as federal and state securities acts, tax withholding regulations, minimum wage laws, wage and price guidelines, credit allocation regulations, income tax laws, and specialized industry regulations. Compliance with legal terms of the company's private contracts (e.g., merger agreements and bond indentures) is also important for financial statement presentations.

Compliance with laws and regulations is a required characteristic of governmental audits, such as those by GAO, IRS, and state auditors. It is generally an objective for internal auditors with respect to managerial policies.

Importance of Assertions

Financial statement assertions are important and fairly complicated. They are the management assertions subject to audit and the focal points for audit procedures. When evidence-gathering procedures are specified, you should be able to relate the evidence produced by each procedure to one or more specific objectives tailored to specific assertions. The secret to writing and reviewing a list of audit procedures is to ask: "Which assertion(s) does this procedure produce evidence about?" Then, "Does the list of procedures (the audit program) cover all the assertions?"

You can simplify the five AICPA assertions by remembering them as **presentation**, **existence**, **rights** (ownership), **completeness**, and **valuation**—a good mnemonic is **PERCV**. Just do not forget that each of them has additional aspects.

R E V I E W
CHECKPOINTS

1.10 List and briefly explain the five major assertions that can be made in financial statements and auditors' objectives related to each.

1.11 Why should auditors think about a "compliance assertion" that is not listed in the auditing standards about assertions (SAS 31, AU 326)?

PROFESSIONAL SKEPTICISM

LEARNING OBJECTIVE
4. Explain some characteristics of "professional skepticism."

Professional skepticism is an auditor's tendency not to believe management assertions, a tendency to ask management to "prove it" (with evidence). The occurrence of errors and fraud in financial reports dictates this basic aspect of professional skepticism: *A potential conflict of interest always exists between the auditor and the management of the enterprise under audit.*

Holding a belief that a potential conflict of interest always exists causes auditors to perform procedures to search for errors and frauds that could have a material effect on financial statements. The extra work is not needed in the vast majority of audits where no errors or frauds exist. Nevertheless, auditors have responded in all audits to do something because of misdeeds perpetrated by a few people.

Persuading a skeptical auditor is not impossible, just somewhat more difficult than persuading a normal person in an everyday context. Skepticism is a manifestation of objectivity—holding no special concern for preconceived conclusions on any side of an issue. Skepticism is not an attitude of being cynical, hypercritical, or scornful. The properly skeptical auditor asks these questions (1) What do I need to know? (2) How well do I know it? (3) Does it make sense?

Professional skepticism should lead auditors to appropriate inquiry about every clue of errors and frauds. Clues should lead to thinking about the evidence needed, wringing out all the implications from the evidence, then arriving at the most suitable and supportable explanation. Time pressure to complete an audit is no excuse for failing to exercise professional skepticism. Too many auditors have gotten themselves into trouble by accepting a manager's glib explanation and stopping too early in an investigation without seeking facts.

Even so, auditors must be careful. Once an audit is under way and procedures designed to search for errors and frauds have found none, the audit team must be willing to accept the apparent fact there is no evidence that the potential conflict is a real one.

Still, due audit care requires a disposition to question all material assertions made by management whether oral or written. This attitude must be balanced with an open mind about the integrity of management. Auditors should neither blindly assume that every management is dishonest nor thoughtlessly assume management to be perfectly honest. The key lies in auditors' attitude toward gathering the evidence necessary to reach reasonable and supportable audit decisions.

AUDITING INSIGHT

AUDITOR SKEPTICISM

Management Explanations

Explanations received from an entity's management are merely the first step in an audit process, not the last. Listen to the explanation, then examine or test it by looking at sufficient competent evidential matter. The familiar phrase *healthy skepticism* should be viewed as a show-me attitude and not a predisposition to accepting unsubstantiated explanations.

Dealing with Former Co-Workers

If a close relationship previously existed between the auditor and a former colleague now employed by a client, the auditor must guard against being too trusting in accepting representations about the client's financial statements. Otherwise, the auditor may rely too heavily on the word of a former associate, overlooking that a common interest no longer exists.

Source: AICPA, Audit Risk Alert (1993, 1994)

REVIEW
CHECKPOINTS

1.12 Why should auditors act as though there is always a potential conflict of interest between the auditor and the management of the enterprise under audit?

PUBLIC ACCOUNTING

LEARNING OBJECTIVE

5. Describe the organization of public accounting firms and identify the various services they offer.

Many people think of public accounting and financial statement auditing in terms of the largest international accounting firms (collectively called the "Big 5"). Notwithstanding this perception, public accounting is practiced in thousands of practice units ranging in size from sole proprietorships (individuals who "hang out the shingle") to the Big 5 firms with thousands of professionals. Further, many public accounting firms no longer designate themselves "CPA firms." Many of them describe their businesses and their organizations as "business and management advisory" firms, or some variation on these terms. The public accounting firms promote themselves as full-service advisory organizations, and their business consulting practices are generally becoming a large proportion of their revenues. However, this is not to say that auditing and taxation service revenues are actually declining, only that the consulting business is growing and becoming a larger proportion of the revenue pie. Exhibit 1–5 shows an organization for a public accounting firm. However, some firms differ in their organization. Some have other departments, such as small-business advisory and forensic accounting. Some firms have other names for their staff and management positions. The exhibit shows one form of organization structure.

Audit Services

Most of the large, international accounting firms were founded around the turn of the 20th Century (late 1800's/early 1900's) during the industrial revolution and before income taxes even existed in the United States. As such, the primary focus of their practice has been traditional accounting and auditing services. Audits of traditional financial statements remain the most frequent type of attest services public companies and for most large and medium nonpublic companies demand. Despite significant increases in consulting services, auditing amounts to around 25–50 percent of the business of most large public accounting firms. Most of this textbook is about the audit of traditional financial statements.

Non-Audit Services (Other Attestation Engagements)

Accounting and review services are "non-audit" services, performed frequently for medium and small businesses and not-for-profit organizations. Smaller accounting firms

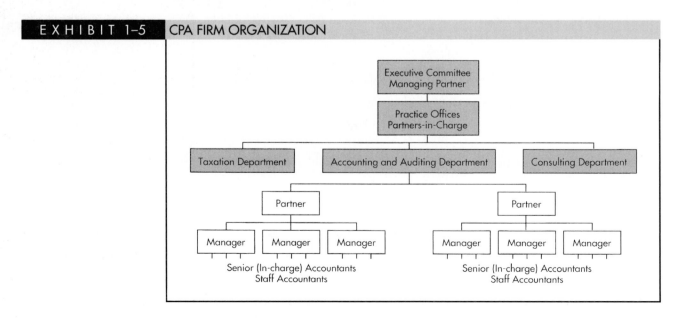

EXHIBIT 1–5   CPA FIRM ORGANIZATION

perform a great deal of nonaudit work. For example, CPAs can perform a compilation, which consists of writing up the financial statements from a client's books and records, without performing any evidence-gathering work. They also can perform a review, a semiaudit service in which some evidence-gathering work is performed, but which is lesser in scope than an audit.

Assurance Services

As defined earlier, "Assurance services are independent professional services that improve the quality of information or its context for decisionmakers." Assurance services involve the lending of credibility to information, whether financial or non-financial. CPAs have assured vote counts (Academy Awards), dollar amounts of prizes sweepstakes have claimed to have awarded, advertisements, investment performance statistics, and characteristics claimed for computer software programs. While assurance services (separate and distinct from auditing) currently represent a fairly small part of a normal firm's operating revenues, the Special Committee on Assurance Services (1996) estimates a market for CPAs for assurance services at around $30 billion. (The Committee estimated current audit revenues to be approximately $7 billion).

Taxation Services

Local, state, national, and international tax laws are often called "accountant and attorney full-employment acts!" The laws are complex, and CPAs perform services of tax planning and tax return preparation in the areas of income, gift, estate, property, and other taxation. A large proportion of the practice in small accounting firms is tax practice. Tax laws change frequently, and tax practitioners must spend considerable time in continuing education and self-study to keep current.

Consulting Services

All accounting firms handle a great deal of consulting. Consulting and management advisory services are the great "open end" of public accounting practice, placing accountants in direct competition with the non-CPA consulting firms. The field is virtually unlimited, and a list of consulting activities could not possibly do justice to all of them. Indeed, accounting firms have created consulting units with professionals from other fields—doctors, actuaries, engineers, advertising executives, to name a few. Many of the large accounting firms have tried to become "one-stop shopping centers" for clients' auditing, taxation, and business advice needs.

The Securities and Exchange Commission (SEC), the governmental agency charged with investor protection, has expressed some reservations as to whether the performance of non-audit services impairs a CPA firm's ability to conduct an independent audit. The SEC's concern is that the large amount of revenues generated from consulting services may sway the auditor's opinion on the company's financial statements. Audit firms, on the other hand, claim that the provision of consulting services allows them a closer look at the client's operations, providing a synergistic, positive effect on the audit.

R E V I E W
CHECKPOINTS

1.13 What are some examples of assurance services performed on non-financial information?

1.14 What are the five major areas of public accounting services?

How to Become a CPA

Education, the Uniform CPA Examination, experience, and a state certificate and license are the four basic requirements for becoming a CPA.

Education

The state boards of accountancy—regulatory agencies in each state—set the education requirements for taking the CPA examination and receiving a CPA certificate. Most states presently require 150 semester hours of college education as a condition for sitting for the CPA examination.

In addition to entry-level education requirements, the AICPA and most states have regulations about *continuing professional education* (CPE). At present, the AICPA and most states require 120 contact hours (not semester or quarter college hours) over three-year reporting periods, with no less than 20 hours in any one year. CPAs obtain CPE hours in a variety of ways—AICPA continuing-education courses, state CPA society-sponsored courses, in-house training in CPA firms and industry, college courses, and private-provider courses. These types of courses range in length from one hour to two weeks, depending on the subject. Many CPE providers offer courses online.

CPA Examination

The Examinations Division of the AICPA administers the Uniform CPA Examination in May and November each year. The two-day examination covers business law and professional responsibilities, auditing, financial accounting and reporting, and other accounting and reporting (e.g., cost accounting, governmental accounting, and personal and corporate tax). General information about the examination can be obtained from the AICPA pamphlet entitled, "Information for CPA Candidates." Because qualifications for taking the CPA examination vary from state to state, you should contact your state board of accountancy for an application or more information. Many states make this information available through their Internet websites. You can find your state board of accountancy website through the National Association of State Boards of Accountancy (NASBA) website (www.nasba.org).

TOPIC	Question Types	DURATION
Business Law and Professional Responsibilities	Essay and objective	3.0 hours
Auditing	Essay and objective	4.5 hours
Accounting and Reporting	100% objective	3.5 hours
Financial Accounting and Reporting	Essay and objective	4.5 hours

Experience

Most states and territories require a person who has attained the education level and passed the CPA Examination to have a period of experience working under a practicing CPA before awarding a CPA certificate. Experience requirements vary across states, but the most common system requires two years for holders of bachelor's degrees and one year for holders of master's degrees. While a few states require that the experience be obtained in a public accounting firm, most of them accept experience in other organizations (GAO, internal audit, management accounting, Internal Revenue Service, and the like) as long as the applicant performs work requiring accounting judgment and is supervised by a competent accountant, preferably a CPA.

State Certificate and License

The AICPA does not issue CPA certificates or licenses to practice. While NASBA and the AICPA are making efforts, we currently have no national or international CPA certificate. All the states and territories have state accountancy laws and state licensing boards to administer them. These agencies make physical arrangements to give the CPA examination, collect the examinations, receive the grades from the AICPA grading service, and notify candidates whether they passed or failed. After satisfying state requirements for education and experience, successful candidates receive their CPA certificate from their state board of accountancy. At the same time, new CPAs must pay a fee to obtain a state license to practice. Thereafter, state boards of accountancy regulate the behavior of CPAs under their jurisdiction (enforcing state codes of ethics) and supervise the continuing education requirements.

After becoming a CPA licensed in one state, a person can obtain a CPA certificate and license in another state. The process is known as *reciprocity*. CPAs can file the proper application with another state board of accountancy, meet the state's requirements, and obtain another CPA certificate. Many CPAs hold certificates and licenses in several states. Efforts are currently underway through NASBA to streamline the reciprocity process so that CPAs can practice across state lines without having to have 50 different licenses.

From a global perspective, individuals must be licensed in each country. Similar to CPAs in the United States, "Chartered Accountants" (CAs) practice in Canada, Australia, and Great Britain. To alleviate the problems of practicing across international borders, in 2000, the AICPA proposed a new "XYZ" (as yet to be named) designation that would be recognized internationally.

Skills Sets and Your Education

The requirements to become a CPA are pretty strenuous, but they may not be enough! Let the authors take you on a brief tour of the core competencies capabilities listed by the Special Committee on Assurance Services, the Accounting Education Change Commission, and other guidance-providing groups: history, international culture, psychology, economics, mathematics (calculus and statistics), national and international political science, art, literature, inductive and deductive reasoning, ethics, group dynamic processes, legal-political-social forces impinging on business, finance, capital markets, managing change, history of accounting, regulation, information systems, taxation, and (oh yes) accounting and auditing standards. And—administrative capability, analytical skills, business knowledge, communication skills (writing and speaking), efficiency,

---

AUDITING INSIGHT

DEFINING THE "XYZ" DESIGNATION

In September 2000, the AICPA announced a new global "XYZ" (until a name is chosen) designation. The designation is defined by four critical characteristics that are intended to make it uniquely positioned in the global business community:

- Globally recognized and respected.
- Based on a wide range of disciplines beyond that of accounting.
- Bound by a common global standard of ethics.
- Based on a global standard of competency, with a commitment to continuous learning and periodic assessment to ensure currency of knowledge and skills.

Source: *The CPA Letter*

intellectual capability, marketing and selling, model building, people development, capacity for putting client needs first, and more.

We hope you are suitably impressed by this recitation of virtually all the world's knowledge. Join with us if you think it is truly mind-boggling! You will be very old when you accomplish a fraction of the skills development and education suggested by these topics. Now the good news: (1) not everyone needs to be complete in all these areas upon graduation from college, (2) learning and skill development proceed over a lifetime, and (3) professional practice is conducted by teams in which some people specialize in some areas while others specialize in other areas—no one expects you to know everything and operate as a "Lone Ranger."

R E V I E W
CHECKPOINTS

1.15 Why is continuing education required of CPAs?

1.16 Why do you think experience is required by most states to be a CPA?

1.17 What are some of the functions of a state board of public accountancy?

1.18 What are some of the limitations to auditing across state and national boundaries? What initiatives are being taken to remove some of the restrictions?

OTHER KINDS OF AUDITS AND AUDITORS

LEARNING OBJECTIVE
7. Describe the audits and auditors in governmental, internal, and operational auditing.

The American Accounting Association and the AICPA definitions clearly apply to the financial audit practice of independent external auditors who practice auditing in public accounting firms. The word audit, however, is used in other contexts to describe broader kinds of work.

The variety of audit work performed by different kinds of auditors causes some problems with terminology. In this textbook, "independent auditor," "external auditor," and "CPA" will refer to people doing audit work with public accounting firms. In the governmental and internal contexts discussed below, auditors are identified as governmental auditors, operational auditors, and internal auditors. While many of these auditors are certified public accountants, the term CPA in this book will refer to auditors in public practice.

Operational and Internal Auditing

In 1999, the Board of Directors of the Institute of Internal Auditors (IIA) redefined internal auditing and stated its objective as follows:

> Internal auditing is an independent, objective assurance and consulting activity that adds value to and improves an organization's operations. It helps an organization accomplish its objectives by bringing a systematic, disciplined approach to evaluate and improve the effectiveness of risk management, control, and governance processes.

Internal auditors are employed by organizations, such as a banks, hospitals, city governments, or industrial companies. Some internal auditing activity is known as operational auditing. **Operational auditing** refers to the study of business operations for the purpose of making recommendations about the economic and efficient use of resources, effective achievement of business objectives, and compliance with company policies. The goal of operational auditing is to help managers discharge their management responsibilities and improve profitability.

Operational and internal auditors also perform audits of financial reports for internal use, much like external auditors audit financial statements distributed to outside users. Thus, some internal auditing work is similar to the auditing described elsewhere in this textbook. In addition, the expanded-scope of services provided by internal auditors include: (1) reviews of control systems that ensure compliance with company policies, plans, and procedures and with laws and regulations; (2) appraisals of the economy and efficiency of operations; and (3) reviews of effectiveness in achieving program results in comparison to pre-established objectives and goals.

Operational auditing is included in the definition of internal auditing cited above. In a similar context, an AICPA committee defined operational auditing performed by independent CPA firms as a distinct type of management consulting service whose goal is to help a client improve the use of its capabilities and resources to achieve its objectives. So, internal auditors consider operational auditing integral to internal auditing, and external auditors define it as a type of management consulting service offered by public accounting firms.

Governmental Auditing

The U.S. General Accounting Office (GAO) is an accounting, auditing, and investigating agency of the U.S. Congress, headed by the U.S. Comptroller General. In one sense, GAO auditors are the highest level of internal auditors for the federal government. Many states have audit agencies similar to the GAO. These agencies answer to state legislatures and perform the same types of work described in the GAO definition below. In another sense, GAO and similar state agencies are really external auditors with respect to government agencies they audit because they are organizationally independent.

Many government agencies have their own internal auditors and inspectors general. Well-managed local governments also have internal audit departments. For example, most federal agencies (Department of Defense, Department of Human Resources, Department of the Interior), state agencies (education, welfare, controller), and local governments (cities, counties, tax districts) have internal audit staffs. Governmental and internal auditors have much in common.

The U.S. General Accounting Office shares with internal auditors the same elements of *expanded-scope* services. The GAO, however, emphasizes the accountability of public officials for the efficient, economical, and effective use of public funds and other resources. The generally accepted government auditing standards (GAGAS) define and describe *expanded-scope* governmental auditing as follows:

> The term "audit" includes both financial and performance audits. . . . Financial related audits include determining whether (1) financial information is presented in accordance with established . . . criteria [e.g. GAAP], (2) the entity has adhered to specific financial compliance requirements [with laws and regulations], and (3) the entity's internal control structure over financial reporting and/or safeguarding assets is suitably designed and implemented to achieve the control objectives. . . . Performance audits include economy and efficiency audits and program audits.

In this definition, you can see the attest function applied to financial reports and a compliance audit function applied with respect to laws and regulations. All government organizations, programs, activities, and functions are created by law and are surrounded by regulations that govern the things they can and cannot do. For example, a program established to provide school meals to low-income students must comply with regulations about the eligibility of recipients. A compliance audit of such a program involves a study of schools' policies, procedures, and performance in determining eligibility and handing out meal tickets.

Also in this definition, you see *performance audits*, a category that includes two types: (1) economy and efficiency audits and (2) program audits. Contrary to some opinions, the U.S. Government is concerned about accountability for taxpayers' resources, and performance audits are a means of seeking to improve accountability for the efficient and economical use of resources and the achievement of program goals. Performance audits, like internal auditors' operational audits, involve studies of the management of government organizations, programs, activities, and functions.

Expanded-scope governmental auditing is auditing that goes beyond an audit of financial reports and compliance with laws and regulations to include economy and efficiency and program results audits. The GAO elaborations on the elements of expanded-scope auditing are consistent with internal auditors' view.

Regulatory Auditors

For the sake of clarity, other kinds of auditors deserve separate mention. The U.S. Internal Revenue Service employs auditors. They take the "economic assertions" of taxable income made by taxpayers in tax returns and determine their correspondence with the standards found in the Internal Revenue Code. They also audit for fraud and tax evasion. Their reports can either clear a taxpayer's return or claim that additional taxes are due.

State and federal bank examiners audit banks, savings and loan associations, and other financial institutions for evidence of solvency and compliance with banking and other related laws and regulations. In the 1980s and early 1990s, these examiners made news as a result of the large number of failures of U.S. financial institutions.

SOME GAO ENGAGEMENT EXAMPLES

- *Anti-Drug Media Campaign: ONDCP Met Most Mandates, but Evaluations of Impact Are Inconclusive (GGD/HEHS-00-153)*
- *Aviation Safety: Safer Skies Initiative Has Taken Initial Steps to Reduce Accident Rates by 2007 (GAO/RCED-00-111)*
- *Battlefield Automation: Army Needs to Update Fielding Plan for First Digitized Corps (NSIAD-00-167)*
- *Government Records: Results of a Search for Records Concerning the 1947 Crash Near Roswell, New Mexico (GAO/NSIAD-95-187)*

REVIEW CHECKPOINTS

1.19 What is *operational* auditing? How does the AICPA view operational auditing?

1.20 What are the elements of *expanded-scope* auditing, according to the GAO?

1.21 What is *compliance* auditing?

1.22 Name some other types of auditors in addition to external, internal, and governmental auditors.

SUMMARY

This chapter begins by defining information risk, and explains how auditing and assurance services play a role in minimizing this risk. The financial statements are explained in terms of the primary assertions management makes in them, and these assertions are identified as the focal points of the auditors' procedural evidence-gathering work. Auditing is practiced in numerous forms by various practice units including public accounting firms, the Internal Revenue Service, the U.S. General Accounting Office, internal audit departments in companies, and several other types of regulatory auditors. Fraud examiners, many of whom are internal auditors and inspectors, have found a niche in auditing-related activities.

In 1997, the AICPA embarked on a program to promote the development of assurance services. This broad category of information-enhancement services builds upon CPAs' auditing, attestation, accounting, and consulting skills to create products useful to a wide range of decision makers (customers). Many leaders see assurance services as the wave of the future for the business and professionalism of accountants' public practice. The AICPA created an Assurance Services Executive Committee to develop practice aids and guidance for CPAs.

Most auditors aspire to become certified public accountants, which involves passing a rigorous examination, obtaining practical experience, and maintaining competence through continuing professional education. Auditors also obtain credentials as Certified Internal Auditors, Certified Management Accounts, Certified Information Systems Auditors, and Certified Fraud Examiners. Each of these fields has large professional organizations that govern the professional standards and quality of practice of its members.

When you begin a study of auditing, you may be eager to attack the nitty-gritty of doing financial statement audit work. Although the textbook will enable you to learn about auditing, instructors are seldom able to duplicate a practice environment in a classroom setting. You may feel frustrated about knowing "how to do it." This frustration is natural because auditing is done in the field under pressure of time limits and in the surroundings of accounting information systems, client personnel, and electronic workpapers. The textbook can provide a foundation and framework for understanding auditing, but nothing can substitute for the first few months of work when the classroom study comes alive in the field.

MULTIPLE-CHOICE QUESTIONS FOR PRACTICE AND REVIEW

1.23 Which of the following would be considered an assurance engagement?
- *a.* Giving an opinion on a prize promoter's claims about the amount of sweepstakes prizes awarded in the past.
- *b.* Giving an opinion on the conformity of the financial statements of a university with generally accepted accounting principles.
- *c.* Giving an opinion on the fair presentation of a newspaper's circulation data.
- *d.* Giving assurance about the average drive length achieved by golfers with a client's golf balls.
- *e.* All of the above.

1.24 It is always a good idea for auditors to begin an audit with the professional skepticism characterized by the assumption that
- *a.* A potential conflict of interest always exists between the auditor and the management of the enterprise under audit.
- *b.* In audits of financial statements, the auditor acts exclusively in the capacity of an auditor.
- *c.* The professional status of the independent auditor imposes commensurate professional obligations.
- *d.* Financial statements and financial data are verifiable.

1.25 In an attestation engagement, a CPA practitioner is engaged to
- *a.* Compile a company's financial forecast based on management's assumptions without expressing any form of assurance.
- *b.* Prepare a written report containing a conclusion about the reliability of a management assertion.
- *c.* Prepare a tax return using information the CPA has not audited or reviewed.
- *d.* Give expert testimony in court on particular facts in a corporate income tax controversy.

1.26 A determination of cost savings obtained by outsourcing cafeteria services is most likely to be an objective of
- *a.* Environmental auditing.
- *b.* Financial auditing.
- *c.* Compliance auditing.
- *d.* Operational auditing.

1.27 The primary difference between operational auditing and financial auditing is that in operational auditing
- *a.* The auditor is not concerned with whether the audited activity is generating information in compliance with financial accounting standards.

    b. The auditor is seeking to help management use resources in the most effective manner possible.

    c. The auditor starts with the financial statements of an activity being audited and works backward to the basic processes involved in producing them.

    d. The auditor can use analytical skills and tools that are not necessary in financial auditing.

1.28 According to the AICPA, the objective of an audit of financial statements is

    a. An expression of opinion on the fairness with which they present financial position, results of operations, and cash flows in conformity with generally accepted accounting principles.

    b. An expression of opinion on the fairness with which they present financial position, results of operations, and cash flows in conformity with accounting standards promulgated by the Financial Accounting Standards Board.

    c. An expression of opinion on the fairness with which they present financial position, result of operations, and cash flows in conformity with accounting standards promulgated by the U.S. Securities and Exchange Commission.

    d. To obtain systematic and objective evidence about financial assertions and report the results to interested users.

1.29 Bankers who are processing a loan application from companies seeking large loans will probably ask for financial statements audited by an independent CPA because

    a. Financial statements are too complex to analyze themselves.

    b. They are too far away from company headquarters to perform accounting and auditing themselves.

    c. The consequences of making a bad loan are very undesirable.

    d. They generally see a potential conflict of interest between company managers who want to get loans and the bank's needs for reliable financial statements.

1.30 Operational audits of a company's efficiency and economy of managing projects and of the results of programs are conducted by whom? (Two answers.)

    a. Management advisory services departments of CPA firms in public practice.

    b. The company's internal auditors.

    c. Governmental auditors employed by the U.S. General Accounting Office.

    d. All of the above.

1.31 Independent auditors of financial statements perform audits that reduce and control

    a. Business risks faced by investors.

    b. Information risk faced by investors.

    c. Complexity of financial statements.

    d. Timeliness of financial statements

1.32 The primary objective of compliance auditing is to

    a. Give an opinion on financial statements.

    b. Develop a basis for a report on internal control.

    c. Perform a study of effective and efficient use of resources.

    d. Determine whether auditee personnel are following laws, rules, regulations, and policies.

1.33 What requirements are usually necessary to become licensed as a Certified Public Accountant?

    a. Successful completion of the Uniform CPA Examination.

    b. Experience in the accounting field.

    c. Education.

    d. All of the above.

1.34 The organization primarily responsible for ensuring that public officials are using public funds efficiently, economically, and effectively is the

    a. Governmental Internal Audit Agency (GIAA).

    b. Central Internal Auditors (CIA).

    c. The Securities and Exchange Commission (SEC)

    d. General Accounting Organization (GAO)).

1.35 Performance audits usually include (two answers)

    a. Financial audits.

    b. Economy and efficiency audits.

    c. Compliance audits.

    d. Program audits.

1.36 The objective in an auditor's review of credit ratings of a client's customers is to obtain evidence related to management's assertion about

    a. Compliance.

    b. Existence or occurrence.

    c. Rights and obligations.

    d. Valuation or allocation.

EXERCISE AND PROBLEMS

1.37 Audit, Attestation, and Assurance Services. Below is a list of various professional services. Identify each by its apparent characteristics as "audit service," "attestation service," or "assurance service."

Real estate demand studies

Ballot for awards show

Utility rates applications

Newspaper circulation audits

Third-party reimbursement maximization

Annual financial report to stockholders

Rental property operation review

Examinations of financial forecasts and projections

Customer satisfaction surveys

Compliance with contractual requirements

Benchmarking/best practices

Evaluation of investment management policies

Information systems security reviews

Productivity statistics

Internal audit strategic review

Financial statements submitted to a bank loan officer

1.38 Controller as Auditor. The chairman of the board of Hughes Corporation proposed that the board hire as controller a CPA who had been the manager on the corporation's audit performed by a firm of independent accountants. The chairman thought that hiring this person would make the annual audit unnecessary and would consequently result in saving the professional fee paid to the auditors. The chairman proposed to give this new controller a full staff to conduct such investigations of accounting and operating data as necessary. Evaluate this proposal.

1.39 Operational Auditing. Bigdeal Corporation manufactures paper and paper products and is trying to decide whether to purchase Smalltek Company. Smalltek has developed a process for manufacturing boxes that can replace other containers that use flourocarbons for expelling a liquid product. The price may be as high as $45 million. Bigdeal prefers to buy Smalltek and integrate its products, while leaving the Smalltek management in charge of day-to-day operations. A major consideration is the efficiency and effectiveness of the Smalltek management. Bigdeal wants to obtain a report on the operational efficiency and effectiveness of the Smalltek sales, production, and research and development departments.

Required:
Who can Bigdeal engage to produce this operational audit report? Several possibilities exist. Are there any particular advantages or disadvantages in choosing among them?

1.40 Auditor as Guarantor. Your neighbor Loot Starkin invited you to lunch yesterday. Sure enough, it was no "free lunch" because Loot wanted to discuss the annual report of the Dodge Corporation. He owns Dodge stock and just received the annual report. Loot says: "PriceWaterhouseCoopers prepared the audited financial statements and gave an unqualified opinion, so my investment must be safe."

Required:
What misconceptions does Loot Starkin seem to have about the auditor's role with respect to Dodge Corporation?

1.41 Identification of Audits and Auditors. Audits may be characterized as: (a) financial statement audits, (b) compliance audits —audits of compliance with control policies and procedures and with laws and regulations, (c) economy and efficiency audits, and (d) program results audits. The work can be done by independent (external) auditors, internal auditors, or governmental auditors (including IRS auditors and federal bank examiners). Below is a list of the purposes or products of various audit engagements:

1. Analyze proprietary schools' spending to train students for oversupplied occupations.

2. Determine the fair presentation in conformity with GAAP of an advertising agency's financial statements.

3. Study the Department of Defense's expendable launch vehicle program.

4. Determine costs of municipal garbage pickup services compared to comparable service subcontracted to a private business.

5. Audit tax shelter partnership financing terms.

6. Study a private aircraft manufacturer's test pilot performance in reporting on the results of test flights.

7. Conduct periodic U.S. Comptroller of Currency examination of a national bank for solvency.

8. Evaluate the promptness of materials inspection in a manufacturer's receiving department.

9. Report on the need for the States to consider reporting requirements for chemical use data.

10. Render a public report on the assumptions and compilation of a revenue forecast by a sports stadium/racetrack complex.

Required:

Prepare a three-column schedule showing: (1) Each of the engagements listed above; (2) the type of audit (financial statement, compliance, economy and efficiency, or program results); and (3) the kind of auditors you would expect to be involved.

1.42   Analysis and Judgment. As part of your regular year-end audit of a publicly held client, you must estimate the probability of success of its proposed new product line. The client has experienced financial difficulty during the last few years and—in your judgment—a successful introduction of the new product line is necessary for the client to remain a going concern.

Five steps are necessary for successful introduction of the product: (1) successful labor negotiations between the construction firms contracted to build the necessary addition to the present plant and the building trades unions; (2) successful defense of patent rights; (3) product approval by the FDA; (4) successful negotiation of a long-term raw material contract with a foreign supplier; and (5) successful conclusion of distribution contract talks with a large national retail distributor.

In view of the circumstances, you contact experts who have provided your audit firm with reliable estimates in the past. The labor relations expert estimates that there is an 80 percent chance of successfully concluding labor negotiations before the strike deadline. Legal counsel advises that there is a 90 percent chance of successfully defending patent rights. The expert on FDA product approvals estimates a 95 percent chance of approval. The experts in the remaining two areas estimate the probability of successfully resolving (a) the raw materials contract and (b) the distribution contract talks to be 90 percent in each case. Assume these estimates are reliable.

Required:

What is your assessment of the probability of successful product introduction? (Hint: You can assume the five steps are independent of each other.)

1.43   Internet Exercise: Professional Certification. Each state has unique rules for certification concerning education, work experience, and residency. Visit the website for your state board of accountancy and download a list of the requirements for becoming a CPA in your state. Although not all of the state boards of accountancy have websites, you might be able to find your state's website by accessing the National Association of State Boards of Accountancy (NASBA) at its website (**http://www.nasba.org**).

1.44   Internet Exercise: Visit the AICPA! The American Institute of CPAs provides the primary means of professional support for most practicing CPAs. Visit the AICPA website (**http://www.aicpa.org**) and find five ways that the AICPA can help CPAs continue to provide quality service to their clients.

Chapter 2

Professional Standards: "The Rules of the Road"

Professional Standards References

Compendium Section	Document Reference	Topic
AU 150	SAS 1	Generally Accepted Auditing Standards (GAAS)
AU 161	SAS 25	Relationship of GAAS to Quality Control Standards
AU 201	SAS 1	Nature of the General Standards
AU 210	SAS 1	Training and Proficiency of the Independent Auditor
AU 220	SAS 1	Independence
AU 230	SAS 1	Due Care in the Performance of Work
AU 310	SAS 1	Relationship between Auditor's Appointment and Planning
AU 311	SAS 22	Planning and Supervision
AU 9311		Interpretation: Responsibility of Assistants for Resolution of Accounting and Auditing Issues
AU 9311		Interpretation: Communications between Auditors and Firm Personnel for Non-Audit Services
AU 312	SAS 47	Audit Risk and Materiality in Conducting an Audit
AU 319	SAS 78	Internal Control Structure in a Financial Statement Audit
AU 326	SAS 80	Evidential Matter
AU 410	SAS 1	Adherence to Generally Accepted Accounting Principles
AU 411	SAS 69	The Meaning of "Present Fairly in Conformity with GAAP" in the Independent Auditor's Report
AU 411	SAS 91	Amendment to SAS No. 69, The Meaning of "Present Fairly in Conformity with GAAP" in the Independent Auditor's Report
AU 420	SAS 1	Consistency of Application of GAAP
AU 9420		Interpretations on Consistent Application of GAAP
AU 431	SAS 32	Adequacy of Disclosure in Financial Statements
AU 504	SAS 26	Association with Financial Statements
AU 508	SAS 58	Reports on Audited Financial Statements
AU 530	SAS 1	Dating the Independent Auditor's Report
AT 101	SSAE 10	Attestation Engagements
QC 20	SQCS 2	System of Quality Control for a CPA Firm's Accounting and Auditing Practice
PR 100		Standards for Performing and Reporting on Peer Reviews

Learning Objectives

Chapter 1 gave you a general introduction to professional accounting practice. Chapter 2 explains three sets of interrelated practice standards for audit services offered by CPAs in public practice—generally accepted auditing standards, attestation and assurance standards, and quality control standards. Your objectives are to be able to:

1. Name the various practice standards for internal, governmental, independent auditors, and auditing firms, and identify their sources.

2. Write and explain the 10 AICPA generally accepted auditing standards (GAAS), and explain how GAAS was or was not followed in specific fact situations.

3. Describe the standard unqualified audit report in terms of its communication of audit standards and other messages.

4. Explain audit evidence in terms of its competence and relative strength of persuasiveness.

5. List the reasons for having general attestation and assurance standards and provide examples of representative engagements.

6. List and explain the important features of quality control standards for a CPA firm.

PRACTICE STANDARDS

LEARNING OBJECTIVE

1. Name the various practice standards for internal, governmental, independent auditors, and auditing firms, and identify their sources.

Just as highway laws govern Interstate highway driving, practice standards serve as general guides to the conduct of auditing and other assurance engagements. The accounting and auditing profession has several sets of standards ("rules of the road") governing the quality of professional work. This chapter deals directly with three topics: generally accepted auditing standards (issued by the AICPA Auditing Standards Board (ASB)); attestation and assurance standards for CPAs performing non-audit engagements (also issued by the ASB); and quality control standards for CPA firms as a whole (issued by the SEC practice section of the AICPA Division for Firms). Generally accepted governmental audit standards (issued primarily by the U.S. General Accounting Office), internal audit standards (issued by the Institute of Internal Auditors), and Professional Standards and Practices for Certified Fraud Examiners (Association of Certified Fraud Examiners) will be discussed later.

Another set of auditing standards is known as the International Standards on Auditing (ISA), issued by the International Auditing Practices Committee of the International Federation of Accountants. In the international community, accountants and regulators have a great interest in **harmonization**—that is, making the standards coordinated, if not uniform, throughout the world. The ISAs are a first step in this direction. They are not cited specifically in this textbook because many of them are the same as U.S. generally accepted auditing standards. However, some differences exist. The AICPA publishes books of standards, and the ISAs reproduced in them are accompanied by summaries of the points on which they are more demanding or conflict with U.S. generally accepted auditing standards.

R E V I E W
CHECKPOINTS

2.1 What are the practice standards, and who issues them for: independent auditors of financial statements? governmental auditors? internal auditors? fraud auditors? auditing firms? auditors in other countries?

GENERALLY ACCEPTED AUDITING STANDARDS (GAAS)

The AICPA Generally Accepted Auditing Standards (GAAS) were first written as a short statement of 10 standards. Since 1939, these 10 standards have been augmented by additional explanations and requirements in *Statements on Auditing Procedures* (1939–72) and in *Statements on Auditing Standards* (1972–present). The 10 basic standards are classified as *general standards, field work standards,* and *reporting standards.* (See Exhibit 2–1)

The *Statements on Auditing Standards* (SASs) are issued from time to time in a numbered series. Officially they are considered "interpretations" of the 10 basic standards, but, for all practical purposes, they are also GAAS. Any auditor who does not follow SAS directives can be judged to have performed a deficient audit. The auditing standards literature also includes a series of *Interpretations*. Although officially considered less authoritative and less binding than the SASs, auditors still must justify any departures from them. For the most part, interpretations give technical help.

Auditing standards are quite different from *auditing procedures*. **Auditing procedures** are the particular and specialized actions auditors take to obtain evidence in a specific audit engagement. **Auditing standards**, on the other hand, are audit quality guides that remain the same through time and for all audits, including audits of complex electronic accounting systems. Procedures may vary, depending on the complexity of an accounting system, on the type of company, and on other situation-specific factors. For example, loans are liabilities for most companies, but are assets for financial institutions. Auditors must use different procedures to audit loans depending on the type of client they are auditing. This difference is the reason audit reports refer to an audit "conducted in accordance with generally accepted auditing standards," rather than in accordance with auditing procedures.

EXHIBIT 2-1   AUDITING STANDARDS

AICPA GENERALLY ACCEPTED AUDITING STANDARDS

General Standards

1. The audit is to be performed by a person or persons having adequate technical training and proficiency as an auditor.
2. In all matters relating to the assignment, an independence in mental attitude is to be maintained by the auditor or auditors.
3. Due professional care is to be exercised in the performance of the audit and the preparation of the report.

Field Work Standards

1. The work is to be adequately planned, and assistants, if any, are to be properly supervised.
2. A sufficient understanding of internal control is to be obtained to plan the audit and to determine the nature, timing, and extent of tests to be performed.
3. Sufficient competent evidential matter is to be obtained through inspection, observations, inquiries, and confirmations to afford a reasonable basis for an opinion regarding the financial statements under audit.

Reporting Standards

1. The report shall state whether the financial statements are presented in accordance with generally accepted accounting principles.
2. The report shall identify those circumstances in which such principles have not been consistently observed in the current period in relation to the preceding period.
3. Informative disclosures in the financial statements are to be regarded as reasonably adequate unless otherwise stated in the report.
4. The report shall either contain an expression of opinion regarding the financial statements, taken as a whole, or an assertion to the effect that an opinion cannot be expressed. When an overall opinion cannot be expressed, the reasons therefore should be stated. In all cases where an auditor's name is associated with financial statements, the report should contain a clear-cut indication of the character of the auditor's work, if any, and the degree of responsibility the auditor is taking.

GAAS General Standards

The three general standards of GAAS relate to the personal integrity and professional qualifications of auditors (SAS 1, AU 201).

Competence

The first general standard requires competence—adequate technical training and proficiency—as an auditor. This competence starts with education in accounting, because auditors hold themselves out as experts in accounting standards and financial reporting. It continues with on-the-job training in developing and applying professional judgment in real-world audit situations. Auditors learn to: (1) recognize the underlying assertions being made by the management of a company in each element (account) in the financial statements, (2) decide the evidence that is relevant for supporting or refuting the truth of the assertions, (3) select and perform procedures for obtaining the evidence, and (4) evaluate the evidence and decide whether the management assertions correspond to reality and GAAP. Auditors must be thoughtfully prepared to encounter a wide range of judgment on the part of management accountants, varying from true objective judgment to the occasional extreme of deliberate misstatement (SAS 1, AU 210).

Independence

The second general standard requires *independence in mental attitude*—intellectual honesty. Auditors are expected to be unbiased and impartial with respect to the financial statements and other information they audit. They are expected to be fair both to the companies and executives who issue financial information and to the outside persons who use it. *Independence in appearance* is another matter and is addressed in more detail later when we discuss the AICPA Code of Professional Conduct. The appearance of independence—avoiding financial and managerial relationships with clients—is important because the appearance is all the public users of audit reports can see. They cannot see inside auditors' heads to detect the "mental attitude." Independence must be zealously guarded because the general public will grant social recognition of professional status to auditors only as long as they are perceived to be independent (SAS 1, AU 220).

The notion of *individual independence* is more specific in the conduct of each audit engagement. In essence, an individual auditor must not subordinate his or her judgment to others and must stay away from influences that might bias judgment.

AUDITING INSIGHT

THREE ASPECTS OF PRACTICAL INDEPENDENCE

1. *Programming Independence.* Auditors must remain free from interference by client managers who try to restrict, specify, or modify the procedures auditors want to perform, including any attempt to assign personnel or otherwise control the audit work. Occasionally, client managers try to limit the numbers of auditors permitted in a location.
2. *Investigative Independence.* Auditors must have free access to books, records, correspondence, and other evidence. They must have the cooperation of management without any attempt to interpret or screen evidence. Sometimes, client managers refuse auditors' requests for access to necessary information.
3. *Reporting Independence.* Auditors must not let any feelings of loyalty to the client or auditee interfere with their obligation to report fully and fairly. Neither should the client management be allowed to overrule auditors' judgments on the appropriate content of an audit report. Disciplinary actions have been taken against auditors who go to a client management conference with a preliminary estimate for a financial adjustment and emerge after agreeing with management to a smaller adjustment.

Due Professional Care

The exercise of due professional care requires observance of all the general standards and the field work standards, but adds an additional element of professionalism. Auditors must properly plan and supervise the audit in order to complete the engagement on a timely basis. The hierarchical review process, in which firm auditors continually review each other's work, also contributes to the exercise of due professional care.

AUDITING INSIGHT

LESSONS AUDITORS IGNORE AT THEIR OWN RISK

Litigation is an exacting and uncompromising teacher, but it provides auditors with some hard and useful lessons. The tuition is the high cost of malpractice insurance, legal fees, adverse court decisions, embarrassing publicity, and stress.

- There is no substitute for knowledge of the client's business
- There is no substitute for effective, ongoing substantial supervision of the work of people assigned to the engagement.
- The partner in charge of the engagement must constantly emphasize the importance of integrity, objectivity, and professional skepticism.

Source: Hall and Renner, "Lessons That Auditors Ignore at Their Own Risk," *Journal of Accountancy*.

REVIEW CHECKPOINTS

2.2 What is the difference between auditing standards and auditing procedures?

2.3 By what standard can a judge determine the quality of due professional care? Explain.

2.4 What are the three specific aspects of practical independence an auditor should carefully guard in the course of a financial statement audit?

GAAS Field Work Standards

The three field work standards set forth general quality criteria for conducting an audit. Auditors cannot effectively satisfy the general standards requiring due professional care if they have not also satisfied the standards of field work.

Planning and Supervision

SAS 22 (AU 311) contains several lists of considerations for planning and supervising an audit. They are all concerned with (1) preparing an audit program and supervising the audit work, (2) obtaining knowledge of the client's business, and (3) dealing with differences of opinion among the audit firm's own personnel.

A written audit program is required (SAS 22, AU 311). An **audit program** is a list of the audit procedures the auditors need to perform to produce evidence for good audit decisions. The procedures in an audit program should be stated in enough detail to instruct the assistants about the work to be done. (You will see detailed audit programs later in this textbook.)

An understanding of the client's business is an absolute necessity. This knowledge helps auditors identify areas for special attention (the places where errors or frauds might exist), evaluate the reasonableness of accounting estimates made by management, evaluate management's answers to inquiries, and make judgments about the appropriateness of accounting principles choices (SAS 22, AU 311). An auditor gains this understanding of a business by conducting interviews with management and other client personnel;

through experience with other companies in the same industry; and by reading extensively—AICPA accounting and audit guides, industry publications, other companies' financial statements, business periodicals, and textbooks (SAS 22, AU 311).

Auditors on an audit team may sometimes disagree among themselves on audit decisions ranging from inclusion or omission of procedures to conclusions about the fair presentation of an account or the whole financial statements. When differences of opinion arise, audit personnel should consult with one another and with experts in the firm to try to resolve the disagreement. If resolution is not achieved, the audit firm should have procedures to allow an audit team member to document the disagreement and to dissociate himself or herself from the matter. In this case, the basis for the final audit decision on the matter also should be documented in the working papers for later reference (SAS 22, AU 311).

Timing is important for audit planning. To have time to plan an audit, auditors should be engaged before the client's fiscal year-end (SAS 1, AU 310). The more advance notice auditors can have, the better they are able to provide enough time for planning. The audit team may be able to perform part of the audit at an **interim date**—a date some weeks or months before the fiscal year-end—and thereby make the rest of the audit work more efficient. At an interim date, auditors can perform preliminary analytical procedures, do a preliminary assessment of internal control risk, and audit some account balances. Advance knowledge of problems can enable auditors to alter the audit program as necessary so that year-end work (performed on and after the fiscal year-end date) can be more efficient. Advance planning for the observation of physical inventory and for the confirmation of accounts receivable is particularly important.

AUDITING INSIGHT

TOO LATE

FastTrak Corporation got mad at its auditor because the partner in charge of the engagement would not agree to let management use operating lease accounting treatment for some heavy equipment whose leases met the criteria for capitalization. FastTrak fired the auditors 10 weeks after the company's balance sheet date, then started contacting other audit firms to restart the audit. However, the audit report was due at the SEC in two weeks. Every other audit firm contacted by FastTrak refused the audit because it could not be planned and performed properly on such short notice with such a tight deadline.

Internal Control

The second field standard requires an understanding of the internal controls inherent in the client's accounting information systems that ultimately produce the client's financial statements. Satisfactory internal control reduces the probability of errors and frauds in the accounts. This basic belief provides the foundation for the work auditors do in an assessment of control risk. **Control risk** is the probability that a material misstatement (error or fraud) could occur and not be prevented or detected on a timely basis by the company's internal controls (SAS 47, AU 312).

Internal control may be defined simply as a system's capability to prevent or detect material accounting errors and provide for their correction on a timely basis. Auditors need to know enough about the client's control to assess the control risk.

The primary purpose of control risk assessment is to help the auditors develop the audit program, which specifies the *nature, timing, and extent of the audit procedures* for gathering evidence about the account balances that will go into the financial statements. The second field work standard presumes two necessary relationships: (a) good internal control reduces the control risk, and an auditor thus has a reasonable basis for minimizing the extent of subsequent audit procedures; (b) conversely, poor internal control produces greater control risk, and an auditor must increase the extent of subsequent audit procedures. If auditors were to assume no relationship between the quality of controls and the accuracy of output, then an assessment of control risk would be pointless.

AUDITING INSIGHT

CONTROL LAPSE CONTRIBUTES TO DUPLICATE PAYMENTS

Allstate Trucking processed insurance claims on damages to shipments in transit on its trucks, paying them in a self-insurance plan. After payment, the claims documents were not marked "paid." Later, the same documents were processed again for duplicate payments to customers who kicked back 50 percent to a dishonest Allstate employee. The auditors learned that the documents were not marked "paid," concluded that the specific control risk of duplicate payments was high, extended their procedures to include a search for duplicate payments in the damage expense account, found them, and traced the problem to the dishonest employee. Embezzlements of $35,000 per year were stopped.

Sufficient, Competent Evidential Matter

Evidence is the heart of attest function work. The third field work standard requires auditors to obtain enough evidence to justify the decision about an opinion on financial statements. **Evidence** is *all the influences upon the minds of auditors that ultimately guide their decisions.* Evidence includes the underlying accounting data and all available corroborating information (SAS 31, AU 326). Competent evidence—evidence that is valid and relevant—may be quantitative or qualitative; it may be objective or subjective; it may be absolutely compelling to a decision or it may only be mildly persuasive. The audit team's task is to collect and evaluate sufficient competent evidence to afford a reasonable and logical basis for audit decisions.

The standard refers to "sufficient," rather than "absolute," evidence. Auditors do not audit all of a company's transactions and events. They audit data samples and make audit decisions by inference, in most cases.

R E V I E W
CHECKPOINTS

2.5 What three elements of planning and supervision are considered essential in audit practice?

2.6 Why does the timing of an auditor's appointment matter in the conduct of a financial statement audit?

2.7 For what reasons does an auditor obtain an understanding of a client's internal control?

2.8 Define audit evidence.

LEARNING OBJECTIVE

3. Describe the standard unqualified audit report in terms of its communication of audit standards and other messages.

GAAS Reporting Standards

The ultimate objective of independent auditors—the report on the audit—is guided by the four GAAS reporting standards. These four deal with generally accepted accounting principles (GAAP), consistency, adequate disclosure, and report content. Auditing standards dictate use of a "standard report." (The standard unqualified audit report is shown in Exhibit 2–2, and you should review it in relation to the discussion below.)

"Unqualified," in the name of the report, means "good" in the sense that the auditors are not calling attention to anything wrong with the audit work or the financial statements. "Qualified" means "bad" in the sense that the financial statements contain a departure from GAAP or that there was a problem with conducting the audit in accordance with GAAS. All standard **unqualified reports** contain these features:

1. **Title.** The title should contain the word **independent,** as in "independent auditor" or "independent accountant."

EXHIBIT 2–2 STANDARD UNQUALIFIED AUDIT REPORT

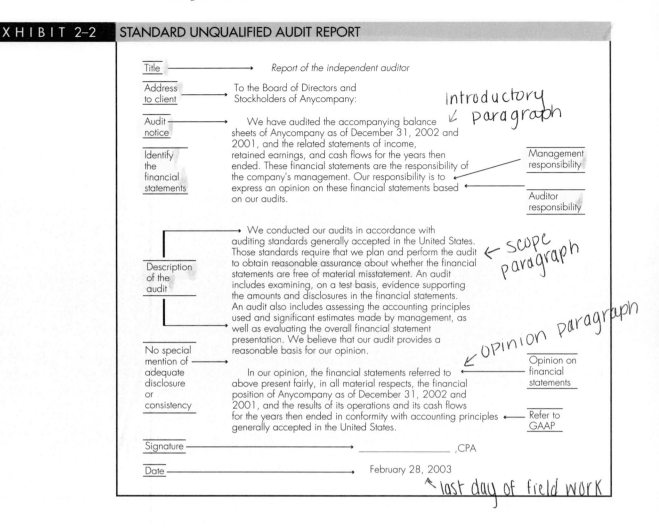

2. **Address**. The report should be addressed to the client, which occasionally may be different from the auditee. A **client** is the person (company, board of directors, agency, or some other person or group) who retains the auditor and pays the fee. In financial audits the client and the auditee usually are the same economic entity. **Auditee** is the actual designation of the company or other entity whose financial statements are being audited. Occasionally the client and the auditee are different. For example, if Conglomerate Corporation hires and pays the auditors to audit Newtek Company in connection with a proposed acquisition, Conglomerate is the client and Newtek is the auditee.

3. **Notice of audit**. A sentence should identify the financial statements and declare that they were audited. This appears in the *introduction paragraph*.

4. **Responsibilities**. The report should state management's responsibility for the financial statements and the auditor's responsibility for the audit report. These statements are also in the *introduction paragraph*.

5. **Description of the audit**. The second paragraph (*scope paragraph*) should declare that the audit was conducted in accordance with generally accepted auditing standards and describe the principal characteristics of an audit, including a statement of belief that the audit provided a reasonable basis for the opinion.

6. **Opinion**. The report should contain an opinion (*opinion paragraph*) regarding conformity with generally accepted accounting principles.

7. **Signature**. The auditor should sign the report, manually or otherwise.

8. Date. The report should be dated with the date when all significant field work was completed.

Generally Accepted Accounting Principles (GAAP)

The first reporting standard is a straightforward directive. In the audit report, it is carried out with the opinion sentence in the opinion paragraph: "In our opinion, the financial statements . . . present fairly in all material respects the financial position . . . and the results of operations and cash flows . . . *in conformity with generally accepted accounting principles.*"

However, determining the appropriate GAAP in a company's circumstances is not always an easy matter. Students often think of FASB statements on accounting standards as the complete body of GAAP. Not so. GAAP consists of all the accounting methods and procedures that have *substantial authoritative support*. FASB (or GASB, for governmental entities) is only one source of such support, albeit usually the highest and most powerful. The auditing standard concerning "the meaning of 'present fairly in conformity with GAAP' in the audit report" sets forth a hierarchy of authoritative support for various sources of GAAP (*SAS 69 and SAS 91, AU 411*). Exhibit 2–3 is a summary of the GAAP hierarchy. Some parts of it deserve explanation.

FASB/GASB statements cover many accounting issues and problems. When FASB/GASB have spoken on an issue, their standards are considered generally compelling. However, FASB/GASB have not covered all conceivable accounting matters.

EXHIBIT 2–3   GAAP HIERARCHY SUMMARY

	Nongovernmental Entities	Federal Entities	State and Local Entities
a.	FASB Statements and Interpretations, APB Opinions, and AICPA Accounting Research Bulletins.	FASAB Statements and Interpretations, plus AICPA and FASB pronouncements specifically made applicable to state and local governmental entities by FASAB Statements or Interpretations.	GASB Statements and Interpretations, plus AICPA and FASB pronouncements specifically made applicable to state and local governmental entities by GASB Statements or Interpretations.
b.	FASB Technical Bulletins, AICPA Industry Audit and Accounting Guides, and AICPA Statements of Position.	FASAB Technical Bulletins and the following pronouncements, if specifically made applicable to state and local governmental entities by the AICPA, AICPA Industry Audit and Accounting Guides, and AICPA Statements of Position.	GASB Technical Bulletins and the following pronouncements, if specifically made applicable to state and local governmental entities by the AICPA, AICPA Industry Audit and Accounting Guides and AICPA Statements of Position.
c.	Consensus positions of the FASB Emerging Issues Task Force. And AICPA (AcSEC) Practice Bulletins.	AICPA AcSEC Practice Bulletins.if applicable to federal governmental entities.	Consensus positions of the GASB Emerging Issues Task Force and AICPA AcSEC Practice Bulletins if applicable to state and local governmental entities.
d.	AICPA accounting interpretations, "Qs and As" published by the FASB staff, as well as industry practices widely recognized and prevalent.	"Qs and As" published by the FASAB staff, as well as industry practices widely recognized and prevalent.	"Qs and As" published by the GASB staff, as well as industry practices widely recognized and prevalent.
e.	Other accounting literature, including FASB Concepts Statements; AICPA Issues Papers; International Accounting Standards Committee Statements; GASB Statements,Interpretations, and Technical Bulletins;pronouncements of other professional associations or regulatory agencies; AICPA Technical Practice Aids; and **accounting textbooks,** handbooks, and articles.	Other accounting literature, including FASAB Concepts Statements; the pronouncements referred to in categories (a) through (d) of the hierarchy of nongovernmental entities when not specifically made applicable to federal governmental entities; FASB Concepts Statements; GASB Statements, Interpretations, Technical Bulletins, and Concepts Statements; AICPA Issues Papers; International Accounting Standards Committee Statements; pronouncements of other professional associations or regulatory agencies; AICPA Technical Practice Aids; and **accounting textbooks,** handbooks, and articles.	Other accounting literature, including GASB Concepts Statements; the pronouncements referred to in categories (a) through (d) of the hierarchy of nongovernmental entities when not specifically made applicable to state and local governments; FASB Concepts Statements; AICPA Issues Papers; International Accounting Standards Committee Statements; pronouncements of other professional associations or regulatory agencies; AICPA Technical Practice Aids; and **accounting textbooks,** handbooks, and articles.

When a conclusion about GAAP cannot be found in FASB/GASB statements, auditors must go down the hierarchy to find the next highest source of support for a client's accounting solution to a financial reporting problem.

The unqualified opinion sentence contains these implicit messages: (a) the accounting principles in the financial statements have general acceptance (authoritative support); (b) the accounting principles used by the company are appropriate in the circumstances; (c) the financial statements and notes are informative of matters that may affect their use, understanding, and interpretation (full disclosure accounting principle); (d) the classification and summarization in the financial statements is neither too detailed nor too condensed for users; and (e) the financial statements are accurate within practical materiality limits (SAS 69, AU 411). This last feature refers to materiality and accuracy. Auditors and users do not expect financial account balances to be absolutely accurate to the penny. Accounting is too complicated, and too many estimates are used in financial statements to expect absolute accuracy. After all, many financial reports use numbers rounded to the thousands, even millions, of dollars! Everyone agrees that financial figures are "fair," as long as they are not "materially" misstated—that is, misstated by enough to make a difference in users' decisions.

Consistency

The second reporting standard calls for *implicit (or "exception-based") reporting*, not like the *explicit reporting* on GAAP conformity required by the first reporting standard. An official accounting pronouncement (*APB 20*, "Accounting Changes") governs the accounting and disclosure of a company's change of accounting principles.

The second reporting standard allows the audit report to be silent (i.e., *implicit*) about consistency when no accounting changes have been made. Users are entitled to believe that the company has not changed its accounting principles when the audit report contains no reference to a change. However, when a company has made a change (i.e., an exception occurs), a sentence must be added to the audit report to alert users to the fact. This added sentence is the *explicit report* required when a change has been made.

Adequate Disclosure

The third reporting standard is also an *implicit report* element. This standard requires auditors to use professional judgment to decide whether the financial statements and related disclosures contain all the important accounting information users need for their decisions (SAS 32, AU 431). Auditors may need to disclose information not specified completely in authoritative sources. For example, auditors might need to deal with a rare and unusual fact situation that no one has encountered before. Using this standard, auditors have latitude for determining whether disclosures are adequate. Likewise, users of financial statements have the right to claim that certain information is necessary for adequate disclosure. In fact, many lawsuits are brought forward on the issue that certain necessary information was not disclosed, and auditors must show reasons for lack of disclosure.

When auditors believe some information is necessary for adequate disclosure, yet the company refuses to disclose it, a departure from GAAP exists. A "qualified opinion" is usually written, and the reason for the departure (missing disclosure) is described *in the audit report*. Sometimes the missing disclosure is added to the audit report itself (SAS 32, AU 431).

Report Content

The fourth reporting standard is the most complex. It contains three important elements:

1. The report shall contain either an expression of opinion regarding the financial statements, taken as a whole, or an assertion to the effect that an opinion cannot be expressed.

The first sentence divides opinion statements into two classes: (a) opinions (i.e., unqualified, adverse, and qualified) on the financial statements *taken as a whole* and (b) the disclaimer of opinion. An **adverse opinion** is the opposite of an unqualified opinion—it states that the financial statements are *not* in conformity with GAAP. A **disclaimer of opinion** is an auditor's declaration that no opinion is given (SAS 58, AU 508). The reference to statements taken as a whole applies equally to a set of financial statements and footnotes and to each individual financial statement and footnote. The second sentence adds to the idea of statements "taken as a whole" as follows:

2. When an overall opinion cannot be expressed, the reasons therefore should be stated.

An "overall opinion" here refers to the unqualified opinion. Thus, when an adverse opinion, qualified opinion, or disclaimer of opinion is rendered, all the substantive reasons for doing so must be explained. An additional paragraph is generally used for such an explanation.

The last sentence refers both to the audit description and the opinion paragraph.

3. In all cases where an auditor's name is associated with financial statements, the report should contain a clear-cut indication of:
   a. The character of the auditor's work.
   b. The degree of responsibility the auditor is taking.

This last sentence means precisely what it says when referring to "in all cases." Every time CPAs (even when acting as accountants associated with unaudited financial statements) are associated by name or by action with financial statements, they must report on their work and responsibility (SAS 26, AU 504). The character of the work is usually described by the standard reference to an audit in accordance with generally accepted auditing standards. But if an audit has been restricted in some way or if the statements are simply unaudited, the auditor must say so.

The "degree of responsibility" is indicated by the form of the opinion. Auditors take full responsibility for their opinion about conformity with GAAP when they give either an unqualified or an adverse opinion. They take no responsibility whatsoever when they give a disclaimer of opinion. They take responsibility when they give the qualified opinions for all matters except those stated as the reasons for the qualification.

AUDITING INSIGHT

ASSOCIATION WITH FINANCIAL STATEMENTS

As a CPA, you are **associated with financial statements** when: (1) you have consented to the use of your name in connection with the statements or (2) you have prepared the statements, even if your name is not used in any written report (SAS 26, AU 504).

The concept of association is far reaching. CPAs are associated with financial statements and must render reports even in such cases as these: (1) financial statements are merely reproduced on an accountant's letterhead, (2) financial statements are produced by the accountant's computer as part of a bookkeeping service, and (3) a document containing financial statements merely identifies an accountant as the auditor for the company. The reason a report is required is that most users of financial statements assume an audit has been conducted and "everything is OK" whenever an independent accountant is known to be involved with financial statements. Consequently, accountants must inform the users about the nature of the work performed and the conclusions expressed on the financial statements.

2.9 What are the eight important elements of a standard unqualified audit report?

2.10 What is the highest level of authoritative support for GAAP? the lowest level?

2.11 Do auditors take any responsibility for clients' choices of accounting principles?

2.12 What messages are usually implicit in a standard audit report?

2.13 What four kinds of audit opinion statements are identified in this chapter? What is the message of each one?

2.14 Why should public accountants issue a report whenever they are associated with financial statements?

SUFFICIENT COMPETENT EVIDENCE IN AUDITING

LEARNING OBJECTIVE

4. Explain audit evidence in terms of its competence and relative strength of persuasiveness.

After obtaining the financial statements, auditors proceed to the task of specifying procedures for gathering evidence about the assertions in them. However, before studying these procedures, you need to understand some features of *evidence* in auditing.

The third fieldwork standard requires auditors to obtain sufficient competent evidential matter. The accounting records (journals, ledgers, accounting policy manuals, computer files, and the like) are evidence of the bookkeeping-accounting process, but they are not sufficient competent supporting evidence for the financial statements. Evidence corroborating these records must be obtained through auditors' direct personal knowledge, examination of documents, and the inquiry of company personnel.

Competence of Evidence

To be considered **competent**, evidence must be valid, relevant, and unbiased. The following *hierarchy* of evidential matter will help you understand the relative competence and persuasive power of different kinds of evidence. The hierarchy starts with the strongest form of evidence and proceeds to the weakest.

1. An auditor's **direct, personal knowledge**, obtained through **physical observation** and his or her own **mathematical computations**, is generally considered the most competent evidence.

2. Documentary evidence obtained directly from independent external sources (**external evidence**) is considered competent.

3. Documentary evidence that has originated outside the client's data processing system but which has been received and processed by the client (**external-internal evidence**) is generally considered competent when internal control is strong.

4. **Internal evidence** consisting of documents that are produced, circulated, and finally stored within the client's information system is generally considered low in competence. However, internal evidence is used extensively when it is produced under satisfactory conditions of internal control. Sometimes, internal evidence is the only kind available.

5. **Verbal and written representations** given by the client's officers, directors, owners, and employees are generally considered the least competent evidence. Such representations should be corroborated with other types of evidence.

Auditors must be careful about the competence of evidence. When specifying audit procedures for gathering evidence, the best approach is to seek the evidence of the highest competence. If physical observation and mathematical calculation are not relevant to

---

AUDITING INSIGHT

EVIDENCE GATHERING: FOOLING THE AUDITORS

John S. Jordan, president of Jordan Concepts, Inc., overstated the company's receivables by more than $10 million to provide false collateral for a $24 million loan. How did he fool the auditors? He allegedly planted a listening device in the auditors' workroom! Thus, he had advance knowledge of the documents the auditors planned to request. He gave them false documents, including shipping documents, checks, bank statements, and remittance advices printed by a local printer at his request. The scheme unraveled when other officers of the company informed the FBI. Jordan was convicted on charges of conspiracy, bank fraud, mail fraud, and wire fraud.

OBSERVATION: A client's use of a hidden listening device is an extreme case, but auditors ought to be careful and suitably skeptical of documents delivered by client personnel.

Source: Association of Certified Fraud Examiners.

---

the account or are impossible or too costly, then move down the hierarchy to obtain the best evidence available.

Sufficiency of Evidence

The third standard of fieldwork states that the auditor should gather enough evidence to support an opinion on the financial statements, but *how much competent evidence is enough?* The auditing profession has no official standard, leaving the matter of sufficiency to auditors' *professional judgment*. Realistically, however, audit decisions must be based on enough evidence to stand the scrutiny of other auditors (supervisors and reviewers) and outsiders (such as critics, judges, and jurors). The real test of sufficiency is whether you can persuade someone else that your evidential base is strong enough to reach the same conclusions you have reached. The fact that important evidence is difficult or costly to obtain is not an acceptable reason for failing to obtain it.

R E V I E W
CHECKPOINTS

2.15 How are external, external-internal, and internal documentary evidence generally defined?

2.16 How does the source of evidence affect its competence?

ATTESTATION AND ASSURANCE STANDARDS

LEARNING OBJECTIVE

5. List the reasons for having general attestation and assurance standards and provide examples of representative engagements.

Many people appreciate the value of auditors' attestations to historical financial statements, and they have found other financial and non-financial information for CPAs to attest. The all-inclusive definition of an *attest engagement* is:

> An engagement in which a practitioner is engaged to issue or does issue a report on subject matter or an assertion about the subject matter that is the responsibility of another party.

Examples of attestation engagements accepted by CPAs appear in the box on the next page. As you can see, several of the attestation engagements are very similar to assurance services discussed earlier in the text, and to be truthful, the line separating the two types of engagements is fuzzy.

The **attestation standards** are a general set of standards intended to guide attestation work in areas other than audits of financial statements. They were first published in the

EXAMPLES OF ATTESTATION ENGAGEMENTS

Financial
- Supplementary financial statistics.
- Financial forecasts and projections.
- Pro forma financial information.
- Cost-plus-fixed-fee contract costs.

Nonfinancial
- Compliance with contractual requirements.
- Descriptions of internal control systems.
- Inventory quantities and location.
- Computer software performance characteristics.
- Utility rate applications.
- Ad valorem and realty tax bases.
- Productivity statistics.

Sources: Stilwell, M.C., Elliot, R.K. "A Model for Expanding the Attest Function," *Journal of Accountancy;* and Brackney, K.S. and Helms, G.L. "A Survey of Attestation Practices" *Auditing: A Journal of Practice and Theory.*

1986 Statement on Standards for Attestation Engagements. Because assurance services are constantly evolving, there are currently no specific assurance standards. However, because of their similarity to attestation engagements, CPAs often rely on attestation standards for guidance in the conduct of assurance engagements. The attestation standards were written long after the generally accepted auditing standards for financial statement audits (GAAS), and you can see in Exhibit 2–4 the ideas borrowed from the existing GAAS.

The major differences lie in the areas of practitioner competence, internal control, and reporting. With respect to practitioner competence, the GAAS presume knowledge of accounting and require training and proficiency as an auditor (meaning an auditor of financial statements, since that was the only kind of attestation being performed when the GAAS were written). On the other hand, the attestation standards are more general, requiring training and proficiency in the "attest function" and knowledge of the "subject matter of the assertions." The *attest function* refers to the ability to recognize the information being asserted, to determine the evidence relevant to the assertions, and to make decisions about the correspondence of the information asserted with suitable criteria. The "knowledge of the subject matter" is not confined to accounting and financial assertions because attestations may cover a wide variety of information.

The attestation standards, unlike GAAS, have no requirement regarding an understanding of the internal control structure for an information system. Considerations of internal control are implicit in the task of obtaining sufficient evidence. Anyway, some kinds of attested information may not have an underlying information control system in the same sense as a financial accounting and reporting system.

Reporting is different because attestations on nonfinancial information do not depend upon generally accepted accounting principles. These are the only criteria for financial statement audits. The attestation standards speak of "evaluation against reasonable criteria" and "conformity with established or stated criteria," and they leave the door open for attestations on a wide variety of informational assertions.

The AICPA's main objective in publishing the attestation standards was to provide guidance and establish a broad framework for a wide variety of attestation engagements. The relationship between attestation and yet-to-be determined assurance standards remains to be seen. Before the attestation standards were published, CPAs used the

EXHIBIT 2–4	COMPARISON OF ATTESTATION AND AUDIT STANDARDS

Attestation Standards	Generally Accepted Auditing Standards
1. The engagement shall be performed by a practitioner or practitioners having adequate technical training and proficiency in the attest function.	1. The audit is to be performed by a person or persons having adequate technical training and proficiency as an auditor.
2. The engagement shall be performed by a practitioner or practitioners having adequate knowledge of the subject matter.	
3. The practitioner shall perform an engagement only if . . . the subject matter is capable of capable of evaluation against reasonable criteria.	
4. In all matters relating to the engagement, an independence in mental attitude shall be maintained by the practitioner.	2. In all matters relating to the assignment, an independence in mental attitude is to be maintained by the auditor or auditors.
5. Due professional care shall be exercised in the planning and performance of the engagement.	3. Due professional care is to be exercised in the performance of the audit and the preparation of the report.
6. The work shall be adequately planned, and assistants, if any, shall be properly supervised.	4. The work is to be adequately planned, and assistants, if any, shall be properly supervised.
	5. A sufficient understanding of internal control is to be obtained to plan the audit and to determine the nature, timing, and extent of tests to be performed.
7. Sufficient evidence shall be obtained to provide a reasonable basis for the conclusion that is expressed in the report.	6. Sufficient competent evidential matter is to be obtained through inspection, observation, inquiries, and confirmations to afford a reasonable basis for an opinion regarding the financial statements under audit.
8. The report shall state the practitioner's conclusion about whether the subject matter is presented in conformity with the established or stated criteria against which it is measured.	7. The report shall state whether the financial statements are presented in accordance with generally accepted accounting principles.
*. the practitioner shall perform an engagement only if...the subject matter is capable of reasonably consistent estimation of measurement using [reasonable] criteria.	8. The report shall identify those circumstances in which such principles have not been consistently observed in the current period in relation to the preceding period.
9. The report shall state all of the practitioner's significant reservations about the engagement, the subject matter, and if applicable, the assertion and the presentation of the assertion.	9. Information disclosures in the financial statements are to be regarded as reasonably adequate unless otherwise stated in the report.
10. The report shall identify the subject matter or the assertion being reported on and state the character of the engagement.	10. The report shall either contain an expression of opinion regarding the financial statements, taken as a whole, or an assertion to the effect that an opinion cannot be expressed. When an overall opinion cannot be expressed, the reasons therefore should be stated. In all cases where an auditor's name is associated with financial statements, the report should contain a clear-cut indication of the character of the auditor's work, if any, and the degree of responsibility the auditor is taking.
11. Under certain circumstances, the report shall state that the use of the report is restricted to specified parties.	

* The concept of consistent measurement is part of standard number 3.

GAAS audit standards as a point of departure for other attestations. New assurance opportunities may well be accepted, only now with the attestation standards as the point of departure until the ASB publishes specific assurance standards.

2.17 What is an "attest engagement"? What is an "assurance engagement"?

2.18 What is the purpose served by the attestation standards?

2.19 What are the major differences between the attestation standards and the generally accepted auditing standards?

STANDARDS FOR CPA FIRMS

LEARNING OBJECTIVE

6. List and explain the important features of quality control standards for a CPA firm.

Public accounting firms do business in a competitive environment. They are in business to make a profit, yet they are also in the profession to perform public accounting services in the public/social interest. This duality—profit motive and professional responsibility—creates tensions to perform quality services and make a profit. There are several organizations, including specifically the AICPA and the SEC, that are very interested in the accounting profession's maintenance of high standards. Toward this end, both the AICPA and the SEC work together to provide guidance to firms engaged in the practice of public accounting.

Accounting firms can volunteer to join one or both of the AICPA Division for Firms' Private Companies Practice Section (PCPS) and the SEC Practice Section (SECPS). The Division and its sections form the backbone of the AICPA's "self-regulation" system. Rules for membership include requirements for an average of 40 hours of continuing professional education (CPE) each year for professional employees and a *peer review* every three years. A **peer review** is a study of a firm's quality control policies and procedures, followed by a report on the firm's quality of audit practice in accordance with the quality control standards. Both the PCPS and the SECPS have peer review committees that review the work and reports of the peer reviewers.

Elements of Quality Control

Statement on Quality Control Standards No. 2 (SQCS 2), entitled "System of Quality Control for a CPA Firm's Accounting and Auditing Practice," sets the stage for CPA firms. This standard establishes the criteria examined in the peer reviews. *SQCS 2* gives five elements of quality control for a CPA firm. These are listed and explained briefly in Exhibit 2–5. When a peer review or a quality review is conducted, the reviewers "audit" the CPA firm's statement of policies and procedures designed to ensure compliance with the five elements. These statements vary in length and complexity, depending on the size of the CPA firm. (Students who wish to know these policies and procedures in detail when interviewing for a job should ask for a copy of the firm's "quality control document.")

Other Firm-Specific Guidance

Auditors of SEC-registered companies are *required* to be members of the SEC Practice Section of the AICPA. (Professionals working in accounting firms that audit public companies and are not members of SECPS cannot remain members of the AICPA.) The goal of this requirement is to ensure the high quality of audits of public companies. The SECPS membership consists of about 1,000 accounting firms that employ about 127,000 professionals and audit the 15,000 public companies.

EXHIBIT 2–5   ELEMENTS OF QUALITY CONTROL

With respect to the following elements of quality control, CPA firms are required to establish and document policies and procedures, communicate them to their personnel, and assign responsibility for managing the firm's quality control to a person or committee.

1. Independence, Integrity, and Objectivity.

   People at all organizational levels must maintain independence in fact and appearance according to the rules of conduct of the AICPA, perform professional work honestly, and be impartial, intellectually honest, and free of conflicts of interest in professional relationships.

2. Personnel Management.

   (a) Personnel management starts with hiring people who can perform competently.

   (b) People should then be assigned to engagements duties according to their abilities and experience. The quality of a firm's work ultimately depends on the integrity, competence, and motivation of personnel who perform and supervise the work.

   (c) Professional development continuing education should be provided so that personnel will have the knowledge required to enable them to fulfill their responsibilities.

   (d) Advancement and promotion policies should ensure that persons selected for higher positions and responsibilities have the necessary qualifications, including character, intelligence, judgment, and motivation.

3. Acceptance and Continuance of Clients.

   Decisions of whether to accept or continue a client should minimize the likelihood of association with a client whose management lacks integrity. Prudence suggests that a firm be selective in determining its professional relationships and the services it provides. When accepting and continuing client relationships, firms should consider their own competence, the risks inherent in the circumstances, and should obtain an understanding with the client of the nature of the services (i.e., an engagement agreement).

4. Engagement Performance.

   Professional work should be performed to meet standards established in professional standards, in regulatory requirements, and in the firm's own policies in the areas of planning, performing, supervising, reviewing, documenting, and communicating results. Supervision appropriate for the competencies of the personnel assigned to the work is important, as is consultation for assistance with difficult accounting and auditing problems from persons having appropriate levels of knowledge, competence, judgment, and authority.

5. Monitoring.

   A program should be organized for continual consideration and evaluation of the firm's policies, procedures, and guidance materials that affect the other four elements of quality control, especially the effectiveness of professional development (continuing education) activities. Also, the firm should periodically assess and document actual compliance with its quality control policies and procedures (i.e., an internal peer review).

The **Public Oversight Board (POB)** of the SECPS is like a board of outside directors. Its members are prominent persons from professions other than public accounting. In the past, members have been lawyers, former SEC commissioners, professors, foreign service professionals, and industry executives. The POB reviews the peer review process in the SECPS. (Annually, the Office of the Chief Accountant of the SEC reviews the POB review process and reports its findings to the SEC commissioners.)

The **Quality Control Inquiry Committee (QCIC)** is a special committee of the SECPS. Member firms are required to report to the QCIC any litigation against the firm or its personnel alleging audit deficiencies involving public companies or regulated financial institutions. The QCIC obtains lawsuit documents related to the litigation, but it does not try the case. The QCIC's goal is to determine whether the litigation has any bearing on quality control deficiencies in the CPA firm.

From its inception in 1979 through 1996, the QCIC has taken numerous actions to improve firms' quality of practice. Over this 17-year span: 65 special or accelerated peer reviews have been ordered; 105 firms were advised and took corrective measures related to the causes of the litigation; on 45 occasions, suggestions were made to the Auditing Standards Board and other AICPA technical committees, some of which resulted in new standards; and 28 cases were referred to the AICPA Professional Ethics Division for investigation into the work of specific individuals.

In 1997 the AICPA and the U.S. Securities and Exchange Commission (SEC) created the **Independence Standards Board**. The board was formed to deal specifically with the tasks of creating, codifying, amending, and preserving independence standards for auditors of public companies (the SEC's jurisdiction). The board's goal is to ensure that audit quality is not compromised and that auditor performance continues to meet public expectations. The membership of the board consists of four public members (business executives, investment analysts) and four CPAs in public practice.

R E V I E W
CHECKPOINTS

2.20 What is the meaning of quality control as it relates to a CPA firm?

2.21 Consider the following quality control policy and identify the quality control element to which it relates: "Designate individuals as specialists to serve as authoritative resources; provide procedures for resolving differences of opinion between audit personnel and specialists."

2.22 What roles are played by the SEC Practice Section (SECPS), the Public Oversight Board (POB), the Independence Standards Board (ISB), and the Quality Control Inquiry Committee (QCIC) in connection with the self-regulation of CPA firms?

SUMMARY

Financial statement auditors are most concerned with the 10 GAAS standards because they are the direct guides for the quality of everyday audit practice. The three general standards set requirements for auditors' competence, independence, and due professional care. The three field work standards set requirements for planning and supervising each audit, obtaining an understanding of the client's internal controls, and obtaining sufficient competent evidence to serve as a basis for an audit report. The theory of sufficient, competent evidence is introduced with an explanation of the relative strengths of persuasiveness of various types of evidence. The four reporting standards cover requirements for GAAP, consistency, adequate disclosure, and report content.

The attestation standards are the general framework for applying the "attest function" to a wide range of subjects. They are the quality guides for general attestation work. Theoretically, they could serve as quality guides for independent audits of financial statements. However, they were created long after the GAAS for audits of financial statements, and the AICPA cannot reasonably get rid of GAAS. Until specific assurance standards are established, the attestation standards provide guidance on the performance of assurance services. Later when you study Governmental and Internal Auditing, you will see that the GAO and internal audit standards incorporate all the GAAS and most of the ideas from the attestation standards. All auditors have some common ground in generally accepted auditing standards.

While the AICPA attestation standards and auditing standards govern the quality of work on each individual engagement, the quality control standards govern a CPA firm's audit and accounting practice taken as a whole. Quality control standards are the foundation of the self-regulatory system of peer and quality review conducted by the private companies' practice section and the SEC practice section of the AICPA Division for Firms. The five elements of quality control are supposed to be the objects for a firm's policies and procedures for assuring that attestation standards and auditing standards are followed faithfully in all aspects of the firm's accounting and auditing practice. The Public Oversight Board, its Quality Control Inquiry Committee, and the U.S. Securities and Exchange Commission monitor these aspects of quality control.

MULTIPLE-CHOICE QUESTIONS FOR PRACTICE AND REVIEW

2.23 When people speak of the attest function, they are referring to the work of auditors in
a. Lending credibility to a client's financial statements.
b. Detecting fraud and embezzlement in a company.
c. Lending credibility to an auditee's financial statements.
d. Performing a program results audit in a government agency.

2.24 After the auditors learned of Client Company's failure to record an expense for obsolete inventory, they agreed to a small adjustment to the financial statements because the Client president told them the company would violate its debt agreements if the full amount were recorded. This is an example of a lack of
a. Auditors' training and proficiency.
b. Planning and supervision.
c. Audit investigative independence.
d. Audit reporting independence.

2.25 The primary purpose for obtaining an understanding of the company's internal control in a financial statement audit is
a. To determine the nature, timing, and extent of auditing procedures to be performed.
b. To make consulting suggestions to the management.
c. To obtain direct sufficient competent evidential matter to afford a reasonable basis for an opinion on the financial statements.
d. To determine whether the company has changed any accounting principles.

2.26 When auditing financial statements, the minimum work an auditor must perform in connection with a company's internal control is best described by which of the following statements
a. Perform exhaustive tests of accounting controls and evaluate the company's control system effectiveness.
b. Determine whether the company's control policies are designed well enough to prevent material errors.
c. Prepare auditing working papers documenting the understanding of the company's internal control.
d. Design procedures to search for significant deficiencies in the actual operation of the company's internal control.

2.27 Where will you find an auditor's own responsibility for expressing the opinion on financial statements
a. Stated explicitly in the introductory paragraph of the standard unqualified report.
b. Unstated but understood in the introductory paragraph of the standard unqualified report.
c. Stated explicitly in the opinion paragraph of the standard unqualified report.
d. Stated explicitly in the scope paragraph of the standard unqualified report.

2.28 Company A hired Sampson & Delila, CPAs, to audit the financial statements of Company B and deliver the audit report to Megabank. Which is the client?
a. Megabank.
b. Sampson & Delila.
c. Company A.
d. Company B.

2.29 Which of the following is not found in the standard unqualified audit report on financial statements?
a. An identification of the financial statements that were audited.
b. A general description of an audit.
c. An opinion that the financial statements present financial position in conformity with GAAP.
d. An emphasis paragraph commenting on the effect of economic conditions on the company.

2.30 The attestation standards do not contain a requirement that auditors obtain
a. Adequate knowledge in the subject matter of the assertions being examined.
b. An understanding of the auditee's internal control structure.
c. Sufficient evidence for the conclusions expressed in an attestation report.
d. Independence in mental attitude.

2.31 Auditor Jones is studying a company's accounting treatment of a series of complicated transactions in exotic financial instruments. She should look for the highest level of authoritative support for proper accounting in
a. Consensus positions of the FASB Emerging Issues Task Force (EITF).
b. AICPA industry audit and accounting guides.
c. FASB statements on accounting standards.
d. FASB statements on financial accounting concepts.

2.32 The evidence considered most competent by auditors is best described as
a. Internal documents, such as sales invoice copies produced under conditions of strong internal control.
b. Written representations made by the president of the company.
c. Documentary evidence obtained directly from independent external sources.
d. Direct personal knowledge obtained through physical observation and mathematical recalculation.

2.33   An auditor's understanding of the control system in an auditee's organization contributes information for
  a. Determining whether members of the audit team have the required technical training and proficiency to perform the audit.
  b. Ascertaining the independence in mental attitude of members of the audit team.
  c. Planning the professional development courses the audit staff needs to keep up to date with new auditing standards.
  d. Planning the nature, timing, and extent of subsequent substantive audit procedures on an audit.

EXERCISES AND PROBLEMS

2.34   Audit Engagement Independence. You are meeting with executives of Cooper Cosmetics Corporation to arrange your firm's engagement to audit the corporation's financial statements for the year ending December 31. One executive suggests the audit work to be divided among three staff members. One person would examine asset accounts, a second would examine liability accounts, and the third would examine income and expense accounts to minimize audit time, avoid duplication of staff effort, and curtail interference with company operations.

Advertising is the corporation's largest expense, and the advertising manager suggests that a staff member of your firm, whose uncle owns the advertising agency that handles the corporation's advertising, be assigned to examine the Advertising Expense account because the staff member has a thorough knowledge of the complex contact between Cooper Cosmetics and the advertising agency.

Required:

a. To what extent should a CPA follow the client's suggestions for the conduct of an audit? Discuss.

b. List and discuss the reasons why audit work should not be assigned solely according to asset, liability, and income and expense categories.

c. Should the staff member of your CPA firm whose uncle owns the advertising agency be assigned to examine advertising costs? Discuss.

2.35   Field Work Standards. You have accepted the engagement of auditing the financial statements of the C. Reis Company, a small manufacturing firm that has been your client for several years. Because you were busy writing the report for another engagement, you sent a staff accountant to begin the audit, with the suggestion that she start with the accounts receivable. Using the prior year's working papers as a guide, the auditor prepared a trial balance of the accounts, aged them, prepared and mailed positive confirmation requests, examined underlying support for charges and credits, and performed other work she considered necessary to obtain evidence about the validity and collectibility of the receivables. At the conclusion of her work, you reviewed the working papers she prepared and found she had carefully followed the prior year's working papers.

Required:

The opinion rendered by a CPA states that the audit was made in accordance with generally accepted auditing standards. List the three generally accepted standards of field work. Relate them to the above illustration by indicating how they were fulfilled or, if appropriate, how they were not fulfilled.

(AICPA adapted)

2.36   Time of Appointment and Planning. Your public accounting practice is located in a city of 15,000 population. Your work, conducted by you and two assistants, consists of compiling clients' monthly statements and preparing income tax returns for individuals from cash data and partnership returns from books and records. You have a few corporate clients; however, service to them is limited to preparation of income tax returns and assistance in year-end closings where bookkeeping is deficient.

One of your corporate clients is a retail hardware store. Your work for this client has been limited to preparing the corporation income tax return from a trial balance submitted by the bookkeeper.

On December 26, you receive from the president of the corporation a letter containing the following request:

We have made arrangements with the First National Bank to borrow $500,000 to finance the purchase of a complete line of appliances. The bank has asked us to furnish our auditor's certified statement as of December 31, which is the closing date of our accounting year. The trial balance of the general ledger should be ready by January 10, which should allow ample time to prepare your report for submission to the bank by January 20. In view of the importance of this certified report to our financing program, we trust you will arrange to comply with the foregoing schedule.

Required:
From a theoretical viewpoint, discuss the difficulties that are caused by such a short-notice audit request.

(AICPA adapted)

2.37   Reporting Standards. CPA Musgrave and his associates audited the financial statements of North Company, a computer equipment retailer. Musgrave conducted the audit in accordance with the general and field work standards of generally accepted auditing standards and therefore wrote a standard audit description in his audit report. Then he received an emergency call to fill in as a substitute tenor in his barbershop quartet.

No one else was in the office that Saturday afternoon, so he handed you the completed financial statements and footnotes and said: "Make sure it's OK to write an unqualified opinion on these statements. The working papers are on the table. I'll check with you on Monday morning."

Required:
In general terms, what must you determine in order to write an unqualified opinion paragraph for Musgrave's signature?

2.38   GAAS in an Electronic Environment. The Lovett Corporation uses an IBM mainframe computer system with peripheral optical reader and high-speed laser printer equipment. Transaction information is initially recorded on paper documents (e.g., sales invoices) and then read by optical equipment that produces a magnetic disk containing the data. These data file disks are processed by a computer program, and printed listings, journals, and general ledger balances are produced on the high-speed printer equipment.

Required:
Explain how the audit standard requiring "adequate technical training and proficiency" is important for satisfying the general and field work standards in the audit of Lovett Corporation's financial statements.

2.39   Authoritative Support. Auditors' reports on financial statements contain an opinion on the conformity of the statements with generally accepted accounting principles (GAAP). An audit decision on GAAP includes the determination of whether an accounting treatment is "generally accepted," and this determination is made by finding the authoritative support for the accounting treatment.

Required:
List in order of priority the sources of authoritative support an auditor can consult when faced with a decision about GAAP.

2.40   Deficiencies and Omissions in an Audit Report. On completion of all field work on September 23, 2002, the following report was written by Betsy Ross to the directors of Continental Corporation.

To Whom It May Concern

The accompanying balance sheet of Continental Corporation and the related statements of income and retained earnings as of July 31, 2002, are the responsibility of management. In accordance with your instructions, we have conducted a complete audit. We planned and performed the audit to obtain reasonable assurance about whether the financial statements are free of material misstatement. An audit includes examining, on a test basis, evidence supporting the amounts and disclosures in the financial statements. An audit also includes assessing the accounting principles used and significant estimates made by management, as well as evaluating the overall financial statement presentation. We believe that our audit provides a reasonable basis for our opinion.

In many respects this was an unusual year for the Continental Corporation. The weakening of the economy in the early part of the year and the strike of plant employees in the summer led to a decline in sales and net income. After making several tests of the sales records, nothing came to our attention that would indicate sales have not been properly recorded.

In our opinion, with the explanation given above, and with the exception of some minor errors we consider immaterial, the aforementioned financial statements present the financial position of Continental Corporation at July 31, 2002, and the results of its operations, and its cash flows for the year then ended in conformity with pronouncements of the Financial Accounting Standards Board.

Betsy Ross & Co., CPA
July 31, 2002

Required:
List and explain the deficiencies and omissions in Ross's audit report.

2.41   Association with Financial Statements. For each of the situations described below, state whether the CPA is or is not associated with the financial statements. What is the consequence of being associated with financial statements?

a. CPA audits financial statements and his or her name is in the corporate annual report containing them.

b. CPA prepares the financial schedules in the partnership tax return.

c. CPA uses the computer to process client-submitted data and delivers financial statement output.

d. CPA uses the computer to process client-submitted data and delivers a general ledger printout.

e. CPA lets client copy client-prepared financial statements on the CPA's letterhead.

f. Client issues quarterly financial statements and prints the CPA's name in the document.

g. CPA renders consulting advice about the system to prepare interim financial statements but does not review the statements prior to their release.

DISCUSSION CASES

2.42   Investment Performance Attestation. Nancy Drew is the president of Mystery Capital Management, Inc. Mystery manages $1.2 billion in two mutual funds, one a stock fund and the other a bond fund. Competition for investors' money is fierce, and hundreds of money management companies compete by advertising their funds' performance statistics. The U.S. Securities and Exchange Commission has criticized the advertisements for misrepresenting the returns investors can actually earn. In addition to the investment performance statistics, money management firms also advertise the amounts of their fees, usually representing no-load or low-fee arrangements, but they often do not advertise the Rule 12(b) expenses allowed under SEC rules.

Ms. Drew has retained your CPA firm to give an opinion on the fair presentation of Mystery Capital Management's investment performance statistics and expense ratios used in its advertisements. The plan is to present your report in the company's advertisements.

Required:
For each of the attestation standards, state its applicability in relation to the engagement.

2.43   Auditing Standards Case Study. Ray, the owner of a small company, asked Holmes, CPA, to conduct an audit of the company's records. Ray told Holmes that the audit was to be completed in time to submit audited financial statements to a bank as part of a loan application. Holmes immediately accepted the engagement and agreed to provide an auditor's report within three weeks. Ray agreed to pay Holmes a fixed fee plus a bonus if the loan was granted.

Holmes hired two accounting students to conduct the audit and spent several hours telling them exactly what to do. Holmes told the students not to spend time reviewing the controls but, instead, to concentrate on proving the mathematical accuracy of the ledger accounts and on summarizing the data in the accounting records that support Ray's financial statements. The students followed Holmes' instructions and after two weeks gave Holmes the financial statements, which did not include footnotes. Holmes studied the statements and prepared an unqualified auditor's report. The report, however, did not refer to generally accepted accounting principles or to the fact that Ray had changed to the accounting standard for capitalizing interest.

Required:
Briefly describe each of the generally accepted auditing standards and indicate how the action(s) of Holmes resulted in a failure to comply with each standard.

(AICPA adapted)

2.44   Quality Control Standards.   Each of the following quality control policies and procedures are typical of ones that can be found in CPA firms' quality control documents. Identify each of them with one of the elements of quality control required by the AICPA Quality Control Standards.

a. Review semiannual performance reports with individuals and assess their progress in relation to job performance, future objectives, assignment preferences, and career opportunities.

b. Publish guidelines for review of each audit report, including determination of the adequacy of evidence shown in the working papers, conformity of the report with professional standards, and review of the report by a partner not otherwise connected with the audit engagement.

c. Maintain or provide access to adequate reference libraries and designated experts by (1) maintaining technical manuals and internal technical newsletters and (2) advising staff personnel of the degree of authority accorded internal experts' opinions and the procedures to be followed for resolving disagreements with experts.

d. Consider the experience and training of the engagement personnel in relation to the complexity or other requirements of the engagement and the extent of supervision to be provided.

e. Review recruiting results annually to determine whether goals and personnel needs are being achieved.

f. Distribute new professional pronouncements (FASB, ASB, IRS, others), and encourage personnel at all levels to join the professional organizations (AICPA, state society of CPAs, others).

g. A special team will review a selection of completed audits for compliance with professional standards, including generally accepted auditing standards, generally accepted accounting principles, and the firm's quality control policies and procedures.

h. Obtain from personnel periodic, written representations listing their investments, outside business relationships, and employment of their close relatives.

i. A firm management committee shall annually review client relationships in light of changes in management, directors, ownership, legal counsel, financial condition, litigation status, nature of client's business, and scope of the engagement.

2.45 Relative Competence of Evidence. The third generally accepted standard of audit field work requires that auditors obtain sufficient competent evidential matter to afford a reasonable basis for an opinion regarding the financial statements under examination. In considering what constitutes sufficient competent evidential matter, a distinction should be made between underlying accounting data and all corroborating information available to the auditor.

Required:
What presumptions can be made about:

a. The relative competence of evidence obtained from external and internal sources.

b. The role of internal control with respect to internal evidence produced by a client's data processing system.

c. The relative persuasiveness of auditor observation and recalculation evidence compared to external, external-internal, and internal documentary evidence.

2.46 Sources of Professional Standards. Listed below are 17 descriptions of professional standards or parts thereof.

a. Definition of a financial statement audit

b. Guidance for reporting on internal control

c. Standards for the practice of internal auditing

d. Generally accepted government auditing standards

e. Education requirements for becoming a CPA

f. Contents of the Uniform CPA Examination

g. Requirements for obtaining a reciprocal CPA certificate

h. Standards of financial accounting

i. Generally accepted auditing standards

j. Interpretations and rulings for the Code of Conduct

k. Standards for involvement with unaudited financial statements of nonpublic companies

l. Standards for consulting practice in CPA firms

m. Statements on auditing standards

n. Statements on responsibilities in tax practice

o. Guidance for lending credibility to nonfinancial information

p. Standards for peer review and quality review

q. Statements on responsibilities in personal financial planning practice

Required:
Name the AICPA committee or other authoritative source of each of the professional standards. Choose from these: AICPA Auditing Standards Board, Institute of Internal Auditors (IIA), state board of accountancy, AICPA Examinations Division, Financial Accounting Standards Board (FASB), AICPA Continuing Professional Education Division, AICPA Professional Ethics Executive Committee, AICPA Accounting and Review Services Committee (ARSC), U.S. General Accounting Office (GAO), AICPA Consulting Services Executive Committee, AICPA Personal Financial Planning Executive Committee, and AICPA Federal Taxation Executive Committee.

2.47 Internet Exercise: GAAS and the Internet. Chapter 2 includes a discussion of the 10 Generally Accepted Auditing Standards (GAAS). What are the implications of the Internet on an auditor's adherence to GAAS? How do the general standards of generally accepted auditing standards apply to the auditor's (or client's) use of the Internet? field work standards? reporting standards? To find the answer to this question, we suggest that you check out a brief discussion of this issue under "Hot Topics" contained on our Internet Site: http://www.mhhe.com/business/accounting/robertson.

2.48. Internet Exercise: Independence and the Independence Standards Board (ISB). Given the auditor's role of watchdog to safeguard public interests, the importance of independence can not be underestimated. Despite its importance, there are several unresolved issues relating to current independence rules and practices. For example, the SEC and the AICPA have different independence rules. Second, critics of the current system have argued that the AICPA independence rules have evolved in a piecemeal fashion, not linked to any underlying principles. Critics have also expressed concern that the current rules reflect some outdated assumptions. Finally, regulators were finding it difficult to reconcile U.S. and foreign independence rules. To resolve these issues, the AICPA created an Independence Standards Board in 1997 to develop a conceptual framework that will facilitate the promulgation of principle-based standards and to develop a process for addressing emerging independence issues.

After visiting the Independence Standards Board's site (**http://www.cpaindependence.org**), answer the following questions:

1. How much progress has the ISB made on establishing an independence conceptual framework since its inception in 1997?

2. What resources are available through the ISB to resolve independence-related issues?

Chapter 3

Reports on Audited Financial Statements

Professional Standards References

Compendium Section	Document Reference	Topic
AU 341	SAS 59	Auditor's Consideration of an Entity's Ability to Continue as a Going Concern
AU 410	SAS 1	Adherence to Generally Accepted Accounting Principles
AU 9410		Interpretation: Impact of FASB Statement Prior to Effective Date
AU 411	SAS 69	The Meaning of "Present Fairly in Conformity with GAAP" in the Independent Auditor's Report
AU 420	SAS 1	Consistency of Application of Generally Accepted Accounting Principles
AU 420	SAS 88	Service Organizations and Reporting on Consistency
AU 9420		Interpretations: Consistency of Application of GAAP
AU 431	SAS 32	Adequacy of Disclosure in Financial Statements
AU 435	SAS 21	Segment Information
AU 504	SAS 26	Association with Financial Statements
AU 9504		Interpretation: Interim and Condensed Information, Lack of Independence
AU 508	SAS 58	Reports on Audited Financial Statements
AU 9508		Interpretations: Reports on Audited Financial Statements
AU 530	SAS 1	Dating of the Independent Auditor's Report
AU 543	SAS 1	Part of Examination by Other Independent Auditors
AU 9543		Interpretations: Other Auditors
AU 544	SAS 1	Lack of Conformity with GAAP (Regulated Companies)
AU 550	SAS 8	Other Information in Documents Containing Audited Financial Statements
AU 9550		Interpretation: Other Information in Electronic Sites
AU 552	SAS 42	Condensed Financial Statements and Selected Financial Data
AU 558	SAS 52	Required Supplementary Information
AU 9558		Interpretation: Supplementary Oil and Gas Reserve Information

Learning Objectives

Management has the primary responsibility for the fair presentation of financial statements in conformity with generally accepted accounting principles. Auditors have primary responsibility for expressing an opinion on those financial statements, based on their audit, in an audit report. While most companies receive "clean" (unqualified) reports, the main body of this chapter covers the most frequent variations in audit reports. You must know the standard unqualified report as a starting place, since this chapter explains reasons for changing the standard language when auditors cannot give this so-called "clean opinion." Your objectives, with respect to variations in audit reports, are to be able to:

1. List three general functions of the auditor's report.

2. Explain the significance of each of the three paragraphs in a standard unqualified audit report.

3. Describe the type of reports that may be written if the client's financial statements contain a departure from generally accepted accounting principles.

4. List any unusual aspects that may affect the conduct of the audit and describe the type of reports that may be written to address the circumstances.

5. Write an audit report with an unqualified opinion but containing additional explanation for a given description of accounting facts and audit circumstances.

6. List other circumstances affecting auditor's reporting responsibilities and explain how they affect audit reporting.

THE PURPOSE OF THE AUDIT REPORT

LEARNING OBJECTIVE
1. List three general functions of the auditor's report.

The American Accounting Association definition of auditing concludes with the phrase ". . . communicating those results [of the auditor's evidence collection and corroboration procedures] to interested users." The auditor's report serves to communicate to users three specific statements with respect to the financial statements, the conduct of the audit, and the client in general.

First, the auditor's report indicates whether the financial statements are presented in conformity with generally accepted accounting principles (GAAP). If the client's financial statements do not conform, the auditor must provide an indication of how the financial statements would appear if they did. Additionally, the auditor must disclose any client omissions from the financial statements. For example, if the client omits a footnote, the auditor must disclose the GAAP departure in the report.

Second, auditors use their report to indicate any unusual aspects of the audit examination. They may not have been able to examine all facets of the company due to the timing of the audit, due to the nature of the client, or due to client-imposed restrictions. For example, if the client has never been audited before, the auditor has the near impossible task of recreating financial statements from the previous year. In a more ominous scenario, the client may not allow the auditor access to all relevant information, thereby prohibiting the auditor from gathering enough evidence to express an opinion on the financial statements. Auditors may also use their report to divide responsibility, indicating that auditors from another firm conducted a significant portion of the audit.

Third, even if the financial statements are fairly presented and no problems were noted in the conduct of the audit, the auditor can use the report to communicate information useful to decision makers that may not appear on the face of the financial statements. Auditors, for example, can highlight a change in the client's accounting principles that may result in a comparability problem when comparing last year's numbers with those of the current year. When a client is experiencing significant financial difficulties, auditors can express their concerns ("substantial doubt") about the client's ability to continue as a going concern. Auditors can also use their report to emphasize matters such as *subsequent events*, significant *related party* transactions, or other events and transactions that they believe are material to financial statement users. In the following sections of this chapter, we will discuss how the various conditions, events, and transactions mentioned above affect the auditor's report.

R E V I E W
CHECKPOINTS

3.1 What are three general functions of
    the auditor's report?

STANDARD UNQUALIFIED REPORT AND VARIATIONS

LEARNING OBJECTIVE

2. Explain the significance of each of the three paragraphs in a standard unqualified audit report.

An auditor issues a standard unqualified report when the financial statements present fairly the financial condition of the company, there were no unusual issues related to the conduct of the audit, and the auditor does not need to highlight any company transactions or events to financial users. The standard report contains three basic segments: (1) the introductory paragraph, (2) the scope paragraph, and (3) the opinion paragraph. An example is given in Exhibit 3–1.

Introductory Paragraph

The introductory paragraph declares that an audit has been conducted and identifies the financial statements the auditor examined. These identifications are important because the opinion paragraph at the end is an opinion on these financial statements. If one or more of the basic financial statements is not identified in the introductory paragraph, the opinion paragraph likewise should not offer any opinion on it (them). Sometimes clients hire auditors to audit and report on only one of the financial statements and not on the others. Most often, such an engagement is for the audit of the balance sheet only. Audit standards make a special exception for this type of engagement referred to as a "limited reporting engagement" (SAS 58, AU 508). An unqualified report on only one financial

---

EXHIBIT 3–1   STANDARD UNQUALIFIED AUDIT REPORT

Report of Independent Auditors

The Board of Directors and Shareholders
McDonald's Corporation

We have audited the accompanying consolidated balance sheet of McDonald's Corporation as of December 31, 1999 and 1998, and the related consolidated statements of income, shareholders' equity and cash flows for each of the three years in the period ended December 31, 1999. These financial statements are the responsibility of McDonald's Corporation management. Our responsibility is to express an opinion on these financial statements based on our audits.

We conducted our audits in accordance with auditing standards generally accepted in the United States. Those standards require that we plan and perform the audit to obtain reasonable assurance about whether the financial statements are free of material misstatement. An audit includes examining, on a test basis, evidence supporting the amounts and disclosures in the financial statements. An audit also includes assessing the accounting principles used and significant estimates made by management, as well as evaluating the overall financial statement presentation. We believe that our audits provide a reasonable basis for our opinion.

In our opinion, the financial statements referred to above present fairly, in all material respects, the consolidated financial position of McDonald's Corporation at December 31, 1999 and 1998, and the consolidated results of its operations and its cash flows for each of the three years in the period ended December 31, 1999, in conformity with accounting principles generally accepted in the United States.

ERNST & YOUNG LLP
Chicago, Illinois
January 26, 2000

statement is permitted. In the introductory paragraph, the auditor states that only one statement (e.g., balance sheet or income statement) has been audited. In the opinion paragraph, the opinion is limited to one presentation (e.g., financial position or results of operations).

The introductory paragraph also explicitly states that the financial statements are the responsibility of management. This statement was added to ensure that users did not mistakenly attribute responsibility for the preparation of the financial statements to the auditors. Instead, the auditor's responsibility is to express an opinion on the financial statements based on the audit work performed (SAS 58, AU 508).

Scope Paragraph

The scope paragraph is the auditor's report of the character of the work in the audit. The sentence "We conducted our audits in accordance with generally accepted auditing standards" refers primarily to the general and fieldwork standards. Its message is: (1) The auditors were trained and proficient, (2) the auditors were independent, (3) due professional care was exercised, (4) the work was planned and supervised, (5) the auditor obtained a sufficient understanding of the client's internal controls, and (6) the auditor obtained sufficient competent evidential matter. Because of the growth in international business and differences in auditing regulations across international boundaries, auditors must also specify which country's generally accepted auditing standards were employed in the conduct ot the audit (e.g., auditing standards generally accepted in the United States).

To the extent that one or more of these general and field work standards is not actually satisfied during an audit, the scope paragraph must be *qualified*. A qualification in this paragraph means the addition of words explaining exactly which standard was not satisfied. Such qualifications may be caused by lack of independence, lack of sufficient competent evidence, or restrictions on procedures imposed by the client (SAS 58, AU 508). In practice, auditors always change the standard opinion paragraph language when the scope paragraph is qualified.

Opinion Paragraph

Users of audited financial statements are generally most interested in the opinion paragraph. This long sentence contains the auditors' conclusions about the financial statements. It is the public manifestation of the private audit decision process.

The reporting standards are incorporated in the opinion sentence (SAS 58, AU 508):

1. The standard report states that the financial statements are presented in conformity with generally accepted accounting principles of a specified country.
2. The standard report identifies those circumstances, if any, in which such principles have not been consistently observed in the current period in relation to the preceding period.
3. The standard report identifies and describes omitted or inadequate disclosures, if any.
4. The standard report contains an expression of opinion regarding the financial statements taken as a whole. An "overall opinion" is expressed in the standard report, so no reasons for not doing so need to be stated. The scope paragraph gives the "clear-cut indication of the character of the audit examination," and the degree of responsibility is unqualified positive assurance.

With regard to the fourth reporting standard, other examples later in this chapter will show how auditors assert that an opinion cannot be expressed (*disclaimer of opinion*) and how audit responsibility can be limited (*qualified opinion*).

When reading the reporting standards, you should understand the term *financial statements* include not only the traditional balance sheet, income statement, and statement of cash flows but also all the footnote disclosures and additional information (e.g., earnings per share calculations) that are integral elements of the basic financial presentation required by GAAP.

Reports Other than the Standard Unqualified Report

Subsequent sections of this chapter explain the major variations on the standard report. There are three basic reasons for giving a report other than the standard unqualified audit report.

- When the financial statements contain a *departure from GAAP*, including inadequate disclosure, the auditor must choose between an *unqualified opinion*, a *qualified opinion*, or an *adverse opinion*. The choice depends on the nature and materiality (significance) of the effect of the GAAP departure.

- If audit-related issues affect the conduct of the audit, the auditor may need to deviate from the standard report format. For example, when the audit has a *scope limitation* (*a departure from GAAS*, in which the extent of audit work was limited), and the auditor has not been able to obtain sufficient competent evidence on a particular account balance or disclosure, the auditor must choose between a *qualified opinion* and a *disclaimer of opinion*. The choice again depends on the materiality (significance) of the matter for which evidence is not sufficient. Another audit-related issue may be an auditor's *lack of independence* (*a departure from GAAS*), which would result in a disclaimer of opinion. This special kind of disclaimer is not directly related to financial statement materiality. The use of other auditors in the conduct of the audit is a third audit-related issue resulting in a change from the standard audit report.

- When the auditor believes it is important to bring certain company information to financial statement users' attention, the auditor may highlight the information by adding an additional explanatory paragraph to an otherwise standard report. For example, if the client changes its inventory method from FIFO to LIFO, the auditor mentions this change in the audit report because it affects the comparability of the financial statements. If the client is suffering financial difficulties, the auditor may highlight the deteriorating financial condition in the report in this additional paragraph. Lastly, the auditor may use the additional paragraph to *emphasize a matter*, such as an impending merger or the loss of a significant customer.

R E V I E W
CHECKPOINTS

3.2 Think about the standard unqualified introductory and scope paragraphs: (a) What do they identify as the objects of the audit? (b) What is meant by the sentence: "We conducted our audit in accordance with auditing standards generally accepted in the United States"?

3.3 Describe the type of report issued when an audit engagement is limited.

3.4 What are the major reasons for deviating from the standard unqualified report?

GAAP DEPARTURE REPORTS

LEARNING OBJECTIVE

3. Describe the type of reports that may be written if the client's financial statements contain a departure from generally accepted accounting principles.

A company's management can decide to present financial statements containing an accounting treatment or disclosure that is not in conformity with GAAP. The reasons vary. Management may not wish to capitalize leases and show the related debt, may calculate earnings per share using a different formula, may not accrue unbilled revenue at the end of a period, may make unreasonable accounting estimates, or may be reluctant to disclose all the known details of a contingency (*SAS 58, AU 508*). Whatever the reason, the fact is a departure from GAAP exists in the financial statements. Now the auditor must decide the type of opinion to render.

Unjustified GAAP Departure Reports

If the departure is immaterial, the auditor can treat the departure as if it did not exist. The audit opinion can be unqualified.

If the departure is material enough to affect users' decisions based on the financial statements, the auditor must *qualify* the opinion. In this case, the qualification takes the "except-for" language form (SAS 58, AU 508). The opinion sentence begins: "In our opinion, except for the [nature of the GAAP departure explained in the report], the financial statements present fairly, in all material respects . . . in conformity with accounting principles generally accepted in the United States." This except-for form of GAAP departure qualification isolates a particular departure, but says that the financial statements are otherwise in conformity with GAAP. The nature of the GAAP departure must be explained in a separate paragraph in the audit report (SAS 58, AU 508).

In the except-for qualified report, the introductory and scope paragraphs are the same as the standard unqualified report. After all, the audit has been performed without limitation, and the auditors have sufficient competent evidence about the financial statements, including the GAAP departure.

GAAP-departure report examples are hard to find in published financial statements. Most published statements come under the jurisdiction of the U.S. Securities and Exchange Commission, which requires public companies to file financial statements in conformity with GAAP without any departures. Exhibit 3–2 shows a special kind of GAAP departure. The SEC permits foreign companies to omit the segment disclosures required by U.S. GAAP. Nevertheless, the omission is a GAAP departure, so noted in the except-for qualified opinion.

However, if the GAAP departure is (1) more than material ("super-material") or (2) pervasive, affecting numerous accounts and financial statement relationships, the auditor must issue an *adverse* opinion. An adverse opinion is exactly the opposite of the unqualified opinion. In this type of opinion, auditors say the financial statements *do not* present financial position, results of operations, and cash flows in conformity with generally accepted accounting principles. The introductory and scope paragraphs should not be qualified because, in order to decide to use the adverse opinion, the audit team must possess all evidence necessary to reach the decision. When this opinion is given, all the

---

EXHIBIT 3–2   OPINION QUALIFIED WITH AN EXCEPTION FOR A DEPARTURE FROM GENERALLY ACCEPTED ACCOUNTING PRINCIPLES

Independent Auditors' Report

The Board of Directors
Rifle, Inc. (Japanese):

(Standard introductory paragraph here)
(Standard scope paragraph here)

The segment information required to be disclosed in financial statements under United States generally accepted accounting principles is not presented in the accompanying consolidated financial statements. Foreign issuers are presently exempted from such disclosure requirements in Securities and Exchange Act filings with the United States Securities and Exchange Commission.

In our opinion, except that the omission of the segment information results in an incomplete presentation as explained in the preceding paragraph, the consolidated financial statements referred to above present fairly, in all material respects, the financial position of Rifle, Inc., and subsidiaries at December 31, 1998 and 1997, and the reults of their operations and their cash flows for each of the years in the three-year period ended December 31, 1998, in conformity with the United States generally accepted accounting principles.

/s/SHW Cole Marsden
February 15, 1999

EXHIBIT 3–3   ADVERSE REPORT

Report of Independent Auditor

The Board of Directors and Stockholders,
Last National Bank:

(Standard introductory paragraph here)
(Standard scope paragraph here)

As discussed in Note 16, an additional provision in the amount of $30,000,000 for possible loan losses on nonperforming loans in the Bank's portfolio at December 31, 2000, was charged to operations during the year ended December 31, 2001, which, in our opinion, should have been reflected in the financial statements for 2000. Had this provision been properly recorded in the 2000 financial statements, the net loss in that year and deficit in undivided profits would have been increased by $30,000,000 and stockholders' equity would have been decreased by that amount, and the Bank would have reported net earnings of $700,000 for the year ended December 31, 2001 rather than the net loss of $29,300,000 as reflected in the statements of operations, stockholders' equity, and cash flows for that period.

In our opinion, because of the effects of the matters discussed above, the aforementioned balance sheet as of December 31, 2000, and the statements of operations, stockholders' equity, and cash flows for the years ended December 31, 2000 and 2001, do not present fairly, in conformity with generally accepted accounting principles, the financial position of Last National Bank as of December 31, 2000, or the results of its operations or its cash flows for the two years ended December 31, 2000 and 2001.

However, in our opinion, the balance sheet as of December 31, 2001, presents fairly, in all material respects, the financial position of Last National Bank as of December 31, 2001, in conformity with accounting principles generally accepted in the United States.

/s/Auditor signature
January 31, 2002

substantive reasons must be disclosed in the report in explanatory paragraphs (SAS 58, AU 508).

Because of the SEC requirement, adverse opinions are hard to find. The example in Exhibit 3–3 is a disguised version of an actual report. In this situation, the auditors were firmly convinced that the bank should have recorded a larger provision for loan losses in 2000. Instead, the bank recorded the loan losses in 2001. This caused the income and cash flow statements to be materially wrong for both the years 2000 and 2001, overstating income in 2000 and understating income in 2001. Likewise, the balance sheet for 2000 was wrong because assets were overstated. The adverse opinions relate to the results of operations for 2000 and 2001 and to the financial position as of December 31, 2000. However, as noted in the last paragraph, the balance sheet for 2001 was in conformity with GAAP. This report illustrates the fact that auditors can give different opinions on different financial statements in the same report (SAS 58, AU 508).

Auditors do not like to be bearers of bad news. However, audit standards are quite clear on the point that if an auditor has a basis for an adverse opinion, giving a disclaimer of opinion is not an option—the auditor must give an adverse opinion.

Justified GAAP Departures: Rule 203 Reports

The unqualified opinion depends upon GAAP for standards of financial accounting. However, Rule 203 of the AICPA Code of Professional Conduct provides for the possibility that adherence to promulgated pronouncements of accounting principles (FASB statements, APB opinions, accounting research bulletins) might create misleading financial statements:

Rule 203. A member [auditor] shall not (1) express an opinion or state affirmatively that financial statements or other financial data of an entity are presented in conformity with generally accepted accounting principles or (2) state that he or she is not aware of any material modifications that should be made to such statements or data in order for them to be in conformity with generally accepted accounting principles, if such statements or data contain any departure from an accounting principle promulgated by bodies designated by Council to establish such principles that has a material effect on the statements taken as a whole. *If, however, the statements or data*

EXHIBIT 3-4	REPORT CONFORMING TO RULE 203

Report of Independent Public Accountants

To the Stockholders and Board of Directors
of Walnut Industries, Inc.:

(Standard introductory paragraph here)
(Standard scope paragraph here)

As described in Note 3, in May 2001, the Company exchanged shares of its common stock for $5,060,000 of its outstanding public debt. The fair value of the common stock issued exceeded the carrying amount of the debt by $466,000, which has been shown as an extraordinary loss in the 2001 statement of operations. Because a portion of the debt exchanged was convertible debt, a literal application of Statement of Financial Accounting Standards No. 84, "Induced Conversions of Convertible Debt," would have resulted in a further reduction in net income of $3,611,000, which would have been offset by a corresponding $3,611,000 credit to additional paid-in capital; accordingly, there would have been no net effect on stockholders' investment. In the opinion of Company management, with which we agree, a literal application of accounting literature would have resulted in misleading financial statements that do not properly portray the economic consequences of the exchange.

In our opinion, the consolidated financial statements referred to above present fairly, in all material respects, the financial position of Walnut Industries, Inc., and Subsidiaries as of December 31, 2001 and 2000, and the results of their operations and their cash flows for each of the three years in the period ended December 31, 2001, in conformity with generally accepted accounting principles.

/s/ CPA Firm
February 10, 2002

contain such a departure and the member can demonstrate that due to unusual circumstances the financial statements or data would otherwise have been misleading, the member can comply with the rule by describing the departure, its approximate effects, if practicable, and the reasons why compliance with the principle would result in a misleading statement. [Emphasis added.]

Rule 203 has the effect of allowing financial statements to contain a departure from an FASB or GASB (or their predecessors) statement on accounting standards, permitting the auditors to explain why the departure was necessary, and then allowing the departure to be "in conformity with generally accepted accounting principles," as indicated by the unqualified opinion. An example of such a report that refers to an FASB statement is presented in Exhibit 3–4.

REVIEW CHECKPOINTS

3.5 Explain the effect of greater or lesser materiality on an auditor's report when the client uses an accounting method that departs from generally accepted accounting principles.

3.6 What is the purpose of Code of Professional Conduct Rule 203? How does the rule affect audit reporting?

REPORTING ON UNUSUAL ASPECTS OF THE AUDIT

LEARNING OBJECTIVE

4. List any unusual aspect that may affect the conduct of the audit and describe the type of reports that may be written to address the circumstances.

Not only do auditors use audit reports to document unusual issues (i.e., GAAP departures) related to the client's financial statements, but they also use the report to document unusual aspects related to the conduct of the audit. In this section, we discuss four unusual aspects of the audit that may be highlighted in the auditor's report.

Scope Limitation Reports (GAAS Departure)

Auditors are most comfortable when they have all the evidence they need to make a report decision, whether the opinion is to be unqualified, adverse, or qualified for a GAAP

| EXHIBIT 3–5 | SCOPE LIMITATION REPORTS |

Panel A: Qualified Opinion

Independent Auditor's Report

To the Board of Directors,
X Company:

(Standard introductory paragraph here)

Except as discussed in the following paragraph, we conducted our audits in accordance with generally accepted auditing standards. . . . (Remainder of paragraph the same as the standard unqualified scope paragraph) . . .

The Company did not make a count of its physical inventory in 2001 or 2000, stated in the accompanying financial statements at $10 million as of December 31, 2001 and at $15 million as of December 31, 2000, and we were unable to observe the physical quantities on hand. The Company's records do not permit the application of other auditing procedures to the audit of the inventories.

In our opinion, except for the effects of such adjustments, if any, as might have been determined to be necessary had we been able to examine evidence regarding the inventories described above, the financial statements referred to above present fairly, in all material respects, the financial position of X Company at December 31, 2001 and 2000, and the results of operations and cash flows for the years then ended in conformity with generally accepted accounting principles.

/s/ Auditor signature
January 29, 2002

Panel B: Disclaimer of Opinion

Independent Auditor's Report

To The Board of Directors,
X Company:

We were engaged to audit the accompanying balance sheets of X Company as of December 31, 2001 and 2000, and the related statements of income, retained earnings, and cash flows for the years then ended. These financial statements are the responsibility of the Company's management.

(Scope paragraph omitted)

The Company did not make a count of its physical inventory in 2001 or 2000, stated in the accompanying financial statements at $10 million as of December 31, 2001 and at $15 million as of December 31, 2000, and we were unable to observe the physical quantities on hand. The Company's records do not permit the application of other auditing procedures to the audit of the inventories.

Since the Company did not take physical inventories and we were not able to apply other auditing procedures to satisfy ourselves as to inventory quantities and cost, the scope of our work was not sufficient to enable us to express, and we do not express, an opinion on these financial statements.

/s/ Auditor signature
January 29, 2002

departure. However, two kinds of situations can create **scope limitations**—conditions in which the auditors are unable to obtain sufficient competent evidence. The two arise from (1) management's deliberate refusal to let auditors perform some procedures and (2) circumstances, such as late appointment as auditor, in which some procedures cannot be performed (SAS 58, AU 508).

If management's refusal or the circumstance affect the audit in a minor, immaterial way, the audit can be considered unaffected, and the report can be unqualified as if the limitation never occurred.

Management's deliberate refusal to give access to documents or otherwise limit the application of audit procedures is the most serious condition. It casts doubt on management's integrity. (Why does management refuse access or limit the work?) In most such cases, the audit report is qualified or an opinion is disclaimed, depending upon the materiality of the financial items affected.

Exhibit 3–5 shows two reports that illustrate the auditors' alternatives. The illustrated failure to take physical counts of inventory might have been deliberate management actions, or it might have resulted from other circumstances (such as the company not anticipating the need for an audit and appointing the auditor after the latest year-end).

EXHIBIT 3–6	DISCLAIMER ON UNAUDITED FINANCIAL STATEMENTS

Report of Independent Accountant

To Board of Directors
United Whidgette Company, Inc.:

The accompanying balance sheet of United Whidgette Company, Inc., as of December 31, 2001, and the related statements of income, retained earnings, and cash flows for the year then ended were not audited by us and, accordingly, we do not express an opinion or any other form of assurance on them.

/s/ CPA signature
January 15, 2002

In Panel A, the opinion is qualified, using the except-for language form. In this case, the lack of evidence is considered material but not "super-material" to overwhelm the meaning of a qualified audit opinion and the usefulness of the unaffected parts of the financial statements. The proper qualification phrase is "In our opinion, *except for the effects of adjustments, if any, as might have been determined to be necessary had we been able to examine evidence regarding the inventories*, the financial statements present fairly, in all material respects, . . . in conformity with generally accepted accounting principles." This report "carves out" the inventory from the audit reporting responsibility, taking no audit responsibility for this part of the financial statements.

Notice that the introductory paragraph in Panel A is the same as for an unqualified report. However, the scope paragraph is *qualified* because the audit was not entirely completed in accordance with generally accepted auditing standards. Specifically, the audit team was unable to obtain sufficient competent evidence about the inventories. Whenever the scope paragraph is qualified for an important omission of audit work, the opinion paragraph should also be qualified.

In Panel B, the situation is fatal to the audit opinion. The auditors believe that the inventories are too large and too important in this case to say "except for adjustments, if any." The audit report then must be a disclaimer of opinion. Notice that the introductory paragraph in Panel B is different from the standard unqualified introduction. This report says "*We were engaged to audit* . . . ," instead of "*We have audited*. . . ." The introductory paragraph omits the last sentence in which the auditors normally take responsibility for an opinion; in this case, there is no opinion. Notice also that the scope paragraph is entirely *omitted*. The standard scope paragraph says the audit was in conformity with generally accepted auditing standards (GAAS), and that the audit was a reasonable basis for the opinion. These statements are simply not true in this case.

In the extreme, the limitations can be so many and so severe that the statements are basically unaudited. In this case, the disclaimer of opinion on the financial statements of public companies takes the form shown in Exhibit 3–6.

Reporting with Lack of Independence (GAAS Departure)

Independence is the foundation of the attest function. When auditors lack independence an audit in accordance with generally accepted auditing standards is impossible. An audit is not just the application of tools, techniques, and procedures of auditing but also the independence in mental attitude of the auditors. This idea is set forth clearly in the following excerpt from SAS 26, "Association with Financial Statements" (AU 504):

> When an accountant is not independent, any procedures he might perform would not be in accordance with generally accepted auditing standards, and he would be precluded from expressing an opinion on such statements. Accordingly, he should disclaim an opinion with respect to the financial statements and should state specifically that he is not independent.

AUDITING INSIGHT

OTHER RESPONSIBILITIES WITH A DISCLAIMER

A disclaimer of opinion because of severe scope limitation or because of association with unaudited financial statements carries some additional reporting responsibilities. In addition to the disclaimer, these guides should be followed:

1. If the CPA should learn that the statements are not in conformity with generally accepted accounting principles (including adequate disclosures), the departures should be explained in the disclaimer.
2. If prior years' unaudited statements are presented, the disclaimer should cover them as well as the current-year statement.
3. Each page of the statements should be clearly labeled "unaudited."

This standard applies to the financial statements of public companies. In keeping with this standard, evidence gathered by an auditor who is not independent is not considered sufficient competent evidence. In such cases, a disclaimer like the one shown in Exhibit 3–7 is appropriate.

In addition, these guides should be followed:

1. The report should not mention any reasons for not being independent because the readers might erroneously interpret them as unimportant.
2. The report should make no mention of any audit procedures applied because readers might erroneously conclude that they were sufficient.
3. If the CPA should learn that the statements are not in conformity with generally accepted accounting principles (including adequate disclosures), the departures should be explained in the disclaimer.
4. Each page of the financial statements should be labeled clearly as being unaudited.

This required report for nonindependence situations exists to provide guidance for unusual situations. Clearly, a public company would not hire a nonindependent auditor to give such a disclaimer. Several years ago, a bank's management became irate with its auditors over the auditors' insistence on providing for large loan losses. The bank management filed a lawsuit against the auditors. Under ethics interpretations, such circumstances render the auditors nonindependent, and the disclaimer described above would be the required report. The bank needed to have the audit report to meet a reporting deadline. Since there was no time to engage a new auditor, the bank had to give up its lawsuit, and the auditor was able to give a standard report. (The bank recorded additional charges for loan losses as the auditors believed necessary.)

EXHIBIT 3–7	DISCLAIMER WHEN A CPA IS NOT INDEPENDENT

Board of Directors,
The Metropolitan Corporation:

We are not independent with respect to the Metropolitan Corporation and the accompanying balance sheet as of June 30, 2002, and the related statements of revenues and expenditures and changes in fund balances for the year then ended were not audited by us. Accordingly, we do not express an opinion on them.

/s/ Auditor signature
November 8, 2002

Using the Work and Reports of Other Independent Auditors

Often a principal auditor audits a material portion of a company's assets, liabilities, revenues, and expenses. At the same time, other independent auditors may be engaged to audit subsidiaries, divisions, branches, components, or investments that are included in the company's financial statements. However, the principal auditor is the one whose signature appears in the audit report on the financial statements of a consolidated or parent company. The auditor of the company must first determine who is the principal auditor—that is, who audits the major portions of the financial statements and knows the most about the entity (SAS 1, AU 543). Then, the principal auditor must make other decisions regarding use of the work and reports of the other independent auditor(s). These rules relate to one or more other auditors' concurrent work on financial statement for the same year. They do not apply to other independent auditors who audited last year's financial statements (predecessor auditors) or newly engaged auditors for the current year (successor auditors).

The principal auditor must first obtain information about the independence and professional reputation of the other auditor(s). If the principal auditor is satisfied with these qualities, he or she must next communicate with the other auditor and decide whether to make reference to the other auditor in the audit report (SAS 1, AU 543). The principal auditor may decide to make no reference, and the audit report will follow the form and wording of the standard unqualified report. In this case, the principal auditor takes responsibility for the other auditor's work.

On the other hand, the principal auditor may decide to refer to the work and reports of other auditors. Such a reference is not in itself a scope or an opinion qualification, and the report is not inferior to a standard unqualified report that does not contain a reference (SAS 1, AU 543). The decision to refer to the other auditor(s) shows *divided responsibility* for the audit work, and the explanation should show very clearly the extent of the divided responsibility by disclosing the percent or amount of assets, revenues, and expenses covered by other auditors' work (SAS 58, AU 508). However, the opinion paragraph must be consistent with the sufficiency and competency of evidence gathered by all the auditors. If other auditors have rendered opinions qualified in some way, the the principal auditor must consider the circumstances when deciding whether to qualify, modify, or expand the report on the consolidated financial statements.

When the principal auditor refers to the other auditors' work, the other auditor is ordinarily not identified by name. (See the example in Exhibit 3–8.) In fact, the other auditor can be named in the principal auditor's report only by express permission and with publication of the audit report along with the report of the principal auditor (SAS 1, AU 543).

R E V I E W
CHECKPOINTS

3.7   What are the differences among a report qualified for a scope limitation, a report in which the opinion is disclaimed because of scope limitation, and a standard unqualified report?

3.8   What are unaudited statements? In connection with unaudited statements, which general reporting guides should the auditor follow for public companies?

3.9   If an auditor is not independent with respect to a public company client, what type of opinion must be issued? Why?

3.10   Is the reference in an audit report to work performed by another auditor a scope qualification? Explain.

EXHIBIT 3–8   REFERENCE TO WORK AND REPORT OF OTHER AUDITORS

Report of Independent Auditors

To the Board of Directors and Shareholders
of Templeton, Inc.:

We have audited the accompanying consolidated balance sheets of Templeton, Inc., and subsidiaries as of December 31, 2001, and 2000, and the related consolidated statements of income, shareholders' equity, and cash flows for each of the three years in the period ended December 31, 2001. These financial statements are the responsibility of the Company's management. Our responsibility is to express an opinion on these financial statements based on our audits. We did not audit the financial statements of American Reserve Company, a consolidated subsidiary, which statements reflect total assets constituting 35 percent in 2001 and 36 percent in 2000, and total revenues constituting 13 percent in 2001, 14 percent in 2000, and 17 percent in 1999 of the related consolidated totals, or the 2000 and 1999 financial statements of Georgia Company, used as a basis for recording the company's equity in net income of that corporation. Those statements were audited by other auditors whose reports have been furnished to us, and our opinion, insofar as it relates to the amounts included for American Reserve Company and Georgia Company, is based solely on the reports of the other auditors.

(Standard scope paragraph here, with a revised closing sentence: We believe that our audits *and the reports of other auditors* provide a reasonable basis for our opinion.)

In our opinion, based upon our audits and the reports of other auditors, the financial statements referred to above present fairly, in all material respects, the consolidated financial position of Templeton, Inc., and subsidiaries at December 31, 2001 and 2000, and the consolidated results of their operations and their cash flows for each of the three years in the period ended December 31, 2001, in conformity with generally accepted accounting principles.

/s/ CPA Firm
February 17, 2002

UNQUALIFIED OPINION WITH EXPLANATION

LEARNING OBJECTIVE
5. Write an audit report with an unqualified opinion but containing additional explanation for a given description of accounting facts and audit circumstances.

Several circumstances may permit an unqualified opinion paragraph, but raise the need to add an additional paragraph to the standard report. Three such situations are covered in this section:

- *Consistency.* An explanatory sentence about a change in accounting principles.
- *Going Concern.* Paragraph that draws attention to problems related to the client's ability to continue as a going concern.
- *Emphasis Paragraph(s).* Additional explanatory paragraphs that "emphasize a matter" of importance.

Because the only change is the addition of a fourth paragraph appended to an otherwise standard report, these reports are commonly referred to as "standard plus" reports. While it is not unusual to see an unqualified audit report with an additional explanatory paragraph (most commonly for a consistency exception), Exhibit 3–9 presents an actual unqualified report with *three(!)* additional explanatory paragraphs (a standard plus, plus, plus report?). The following sections describe the circumstances in which auditors consider such disclosures necessary.

Consistency

The second standard of reporting (the "consistency standard") requires that the audit report shall make reference to the consistent application of accounting principles only when the company has changed accounting principles. The objective is to ensure that the auditor will give users appropriate notice if the comparability of a company's financial statements from year to year has been materially affected by a change (*SAS 1*, AU 420).

Accounting Principles Board Opinion No. 20 ("Accounting Changes") contains the accounting principles regarding changes in principles, estimates, the accounting entity, and correction of errors. Auditing standards track the requirements of APB 20 and require a notification be added to the audit report for changes in accounting principles and

EXHIBIT 3-9   UNQUALIFIED REPORT EXPLAINING GOING-CONCERN PROBLEMS, EMPHASIS OF A MATTER, AND CONSISTENCY EXCEPTIONS

To the Board of Directors and Shareholders of
Eagle Food Centers, Inc.:

We have audited the accompanying consolidated balance sheets of Eagle Food Centers, Inc. and subsidiaries as of January 29, 2000 and January 30, 1999, and the related consolidated statements of operations, equity, and cash flows for each of the three years in the period ended January 29, 2000. These financial statements are the responsibility of the Company's management. Our responsibility is to express an opinion on these financial statements based on our audits.

We conducted our audits in accordance with auditing standards generally accepted in the United States of America. Those standards require that we plan and perform the audit to obtain reasonable assurance about whether the financial statements are free of material misstatement. An audit includes examining, on a test basis, evidence supporting the amounts and disclosures in the financial statements. An audit also includes assessing the accounting principles used and significant estimates made by management, as well as evaluating the overall financial statement presentation. We believe that our audits provide a reasonable basis for our opinion.

In our opinion, such consolidated financial statements present fairly, in all material respects, the financial position of Eagle Food Centers, Inc. and subsidiaries as of January 29, 2000 and January 30, 1999 and the results of their operations and their cash flows for each of the three years in the period ended January 29, 2000 in conformity with accounting principles generally accepted in the United States of America.

The accompanying consolidated financial statements for the year ended January 29, 2000 have been prepared assuming that the Company will continue as a going concern. As discussed in Note B to the consolidated financial statements, the Company filed for Chapter 11 Bankruptcy on February 29, 2000 in order to reorganize the Company's operations and restructure the Company's Senior Notes. The Company is uncertain about if or when it will emerge from Chapter 11 Bankruptcy, which raises substantial doubt about the Company's ability to continue as a going concern. Management's plans concerning this matter are also discussed in Note B. The financial statements do not include adjustments that might result from the outcome of this uncertainty.

The accompanying consolidated financial statements do not purport to reflect or provide for the consequences of the bankruptcy proceedings. In particular, such financial statements do not purport to show (a) as to assets, their realizable value on a liquidation basis or their availability to satisfy liabilities; (b) as to prepetition liabilities, the amounts that may be allowed for claims or contingencies, or the status and priority thereof; (c) as to stockholder accounts, the effect of any changes that may be made in the capitalization of the Company; or (d) as to operations, the effect of any changes that may be made in its business.

As discussed in Note C to the financial statements, the Company changed its method of accounting for goodwill.

DELOITTE & TOUCHE LLP
Davenport, Iowa
April 14, 2000

discretionary changes in the accounting entity. A report with a consistency reference is in Exhibit 3–9.

Certain changes do not require consistency references in the audit report, namely: (1) changes in accounting estimates, (2) error corrections that do not involve a change in accounting principles, (3) changes in the classification or aggregation of financial statement amounts, (4) changes in the format or basis of the statement of cash flows (e.g., from a balancing format to a net change format), (5) changes in the reporting entity resulting from a transaction or event, and (6) changes in the subsidiaries included in consolidated financial statements as a result of forming a new subsidiary, buying another company, spinning off or liquidating a subsidiary, or selling a subsidiary (*SAS 1*, AU 420). However, failure to disclose any of these changes could amount to a GAAP departure and could present a different reason for qualifying the opinion.

When evaluating a change in accounting principle, auditors must be satisfied that management's justification for the change is reasonable. *APB Opinion No. 20*, "Accounting Changes," states:

> The presumption that an entity should not change an accounting principle may be overcome only if the enterprise justifies the use of an alternative acceptable accounting principle on the basis that it is preferable.

A change from accelerated depreciation to straight-line "to increase profits" may be preferable from management's viewpoint, but such a reason is not reasonable justification for most auditors. If the auditors cannot agree that a change is to a preferable accounting principle, then an opinion qualification based on a departure from GAAP is appropriate

(SAS 58, AU 508). (The SEC requires auditors to submit a letter stating whether a change is to a preferable principle—one that provides a better measure of business operations.)

In audit reports on subsequent years' financial statements, an appropriate consistency reference should be stated as long as the financial statements for the year of the change are included in the years presented (SAS 1, AU 420).

Reporting on "Going-Concern" Problems

Generally accepted accounting principles are based on the going-concern concept, which means the entity is expected to continue in operation and meet its obligations as they become due, without substantial disposition of assets outside the ordinary course of business, restructuring of debt, externally forced revisions of its operations (e.g., a bank reorganization forced by the FDIC), or similar actions. Hence, an opinion that financial statements are in conformity with GAAP means that continued existence may be presumed for a "reasonable time" not to exceed one year beyond the date of the financial statements (SAS 59, AU 341).

Dealing with questions of going concern is difficult because auditors are forced to evaluate matters of financial analysis, business strategy, and financial forecasting. Most managements are unwilling to give up and close their businesses without strong attempts to survive. Sometimes, survival optimism prevails until the creditors force bankruptcy proceedings and liquidation. Auditors are generally reluctant to puncture any balloons of optimism. Managers and auditors view news of financial troubles in an audit report (an attention-directing paragraph or a disclaimer based on going-concern doubt) as a *"self-fulfilling prophecy"* that causes bankruptcy because of the disclosure's effect on investors, suppliers, and creditors. However fallacious this view might be, it still prevails and sometimes inhibits auditors' consideration of going-concern questions.

Auditors are responsible for determining any substantial doubt about a company's ability to continue as a going concern. Careful auditors should not ignore signs of financial difficulty and operate entirely on the assumption that the company is a going concern. Financial difficulties, labor problems, loss of key personnel, litigation, and other such things may be important signals. Likewise, elements of financial flexibility (salability of assets, lines of credit, debt extension, dividend elimination) may be available as survival strategies. (In the auditing standards these elements of financial flexibility and management strategy are known as **mitigating factors** that may reduce the financial difficulty problems (SAS 59, AU 341).)

Accounting and finance research efforts have produced several bankruptcy prediction models. These models use publicly available financial information to classify companies in "fail" and "nonfail" categories. At least one auditing firm uses such a model as an analytical review tool. Auditing standards, however, make no mention of research models, specifying instead many company-specific considerations and elements of internal information for analysis. Several types of audit reports may be used for going-concern problems, but the most common report is a standard report with an unqualified opinion paragraph and an additional explanatory paragraph(s) to direct attention to management's disclosures about the problems (in Exhibit 3–9, notice the reference to Note B). The report in Exhibit 3–9 demonstrates the requirement that the words *"substantial doubt"* and *"going concern"* must appear in the explanatory paragraph (SAS 77, AU 341). Auditing standards recommend this warning paragraph when the auditors conclude that the company may not be able to continue in existence as a going concern (SAS 59, AU 341). However, in practice, a company in financial distress may present explanatory notes describing its financial problems, and its auditors may decide that they are not serious enough to put a warning in the audit report.

Auditors may choose other types of reports when auditing a client with going-concern difficulties. Other report choices include a disclaimer of opinion, resulting from massive uncertainty about the ability of the business to continue as a going-concern; an adverse report or a report qualified for a GAAP departure if the auditor believes the company's disclosures about financial difficulties and going-concern problems are inadequate; or a report qualified for a scope limitation if available evidence is not given to the auditors, leading to the "except for adjustments, if any" type of qualified opinion explained earlier in this chapter.

Emphasis Paragraph

Beyond the standard unqualified report wording, auditors have one avenue for enriching the information content in an audit report. They can add one or more paragraphs to emphasize something they believe readers should consider important or useful. In the auditing standards, this type of addition to the audit report is known as the **emphasis of a matter** paragraph. An emphasis paragraph can be added when the auditor intends to write an unqualified opinion paragraph. Indeed, the matter emphasized is not supposed to be mentioned in the standard unqualified opinion sentence.

Although auditing standards place no official limits on the content of an emphasis paragraph (SAS 58, AU 508), auditors often use them to describe circumstances that present some business or information risk. In the example presented in Exhibit 3–9, the auditing firm is emphasizing the fact that, given that the client has filed for bankruptcy, financial statement users should be especially cautious when reading the financial statements because they do not take the bankruptcy into account. Other examples of matters that can be emphasized include a description of the auditee as a subsidiary of a larger entity, the effects of business events on the comparability of financial statements, the interaction of the auditee with related parties, and the effect of events that occur after the balance sheet date.

R E V I E W
CHECKPOINTS

3.11 What circumstances cause auditors to recognize inconsistent applications of GAAP in an audit report?

3.12 What circumstances are not considered inconsistencies?

3.13 What circumstances may lead an auditor to have substantial doubts about an entity's ability to continue as a going concern?

3.14 List some circumstances, events, or transactions that auditors may want to emphasize to financial statement users.

OTHER REPORTING TOPICS

LEARNING OBJECTIVE

6. List other circumstances affecting auditor's reporting responsibilities and explain how they affect the audit reporting.

A great deal of financial information is distributed publicly in annual reports and in other documents containing audited financial statements. The company president's letter to shareholders, management's discussion and analysis of results of operations, interim financial statements, and supplementary schedules all contain financial information that is not mentioned explicitly in the auditors' reports. Yet, auditors have professional responsibilities with regard to much of this information. When something is wrong or unusual, auditors should expand the audit report. In this section, we discuss this topic and several other topics in audit reporting that are somewhat outside the mainstream of the basic report modification topics covered so far in Chapter 3.

Reporting on Comparative Statements

The SEC requires public companies to present comparative balance sheets for two years and comparative income statements and cash flow statements for three years. Financial statement footnotes contain disclosures in comparative form for two or three years.

Altogether, these comparative financial statements and footnotes are the "financial statements as a whole" mentioned in the fourth GAAS reporting standard (SAS 58, AU 508).

When auditors issue a report on the current-year financial statements, they update the report they previously issued on the prior-year financial statements. For example, the auditors in Exhibit 3–1 issued a report (not shown in the exhibit) on the 1998 and 1997 financial statements; later, after the most recent audit, they issued the report dated January 26, 2000, on the 1999 financial statements and on the 1998 statements presented in comparative form. The updated report on the 1998 financial statements is based not only on the prior-year audit but also on information that has come to light since then (particularly in the course of the most recent audit work). An updated report may be the same as previously issued, or it may be different depending on whether current information causes a retroactive change in the auditor's reporting decision. An updated report carries the date of the end of the most recent fieldwork and the auditors' responsibility now runs to the more recent date (SAS 58, AU 508).

An updated report differs from the *reissuance* of a previous report. A reissuance amounts to providing more copies of the report or giving permission to use it in another document sometime after its original delivery date. The report date of a reissued report is the original date of the end of field work on that year's audit, indicating a cutoff date for the auditors' responsibility (SAS 1, AU 530).

Exhibit 3–1 shows a common situation in which the same auditor audited both years' financial statements. If the company had changed auditors, the introductory paragraph would have identified only the current-year statements as the ones audited by the new (successor) auditor. A sentence would be added giving facts about the former (predecessor) auditor's report: "The financial statements of the company as of December 31, 1998, were audited by other auditors whose report dated February 4, 1999, expressed an unqualified opinion on those statements." The opinion paragraph would cite only the current-year financial statements audited by the successor auditor.

Auditors can give different opinions on different financial statements in the same report. Exhibit 3–3 shows the situation in which the prior-year financial statements were considered materially misstated, but the most recent balance sheet was in conformity with GAAP. You can see that the opinion on the misstated financial statements is an adverse opinion, and the opinion on the most recent balance sheet is unqualified.

Auditors can also change the opinion given on last-year's financial statements. In audit standards, this is known as an "opinion on prior period financial statements different from the opinion previously expressed." The auditors must have good reasons for such a change, which must be explained in the report (SAS 58, AU 508). For example, consider the Last National Bank situation shown in Exhibit 3–3. Suppose the bank originally failed to record the additional $30 million loan loss reserve in the 2000 financial statements, and the auditors gave the adverse opinion last year. This year, assume the bank restated its 2000 financial statements, recording the additional loan loss reserve in the proper period. The report on the 2001 and 2000 comparative financial statements should contain the explanation shown in Exhibit 3–10.

Reporting on Condensed Financial Statements

Published financial statements are lengthy and complicated. Companies sometimes have occasion to present the financial statements in considerably less detail (SAS 42, AU 552). Generally, such condensed financial statements are derived directly from full-scale audited financial statements. However, condensed financial statements are not a fair presentation of financial position, results of operations, and cash flows in conformity with GAAP. Auditors who report on such statements cannot render the standard unqualified report, even if this report was given on the full-scale financial statements.

Auditors can give a special kind of report on condensed financial statements derived from full-scale financial statements that have been audited. The report must refer to the audit report on the full financial statements, giving the date and the type of opinion, and

EXHIBIT 3–10   COMPARATIVE STATEMENT OPINION CHANGED FROM ADVERSE
TO UNQUALIFIED

Report of Independent Auditor

To the Board of Directors and Shareholders,
Last National Bank:

(Standard introductory paragraph here)
(Standard scope paragraph here)

In our report dated January 30, 2001, we expressed an opinion that the balance sheet as of December 31, 2000, and the statements of income, retained earnings, and cash flows for the year then ended did not fairly present financial position, results of operations, and cash flows in conformity with generally accepted accounting principles because the Bank did not record an additional $30,000,000 provision for possible loan losses on nonperforming loans in the Bank's portfolio as of December 31, 2000. As described in Note 2 in these financial statements, the Bank has restated its 2000 financial statements to record the additional loan loss provision in conformity with generally accepted accounting principles. Accordingly, our present opinion on the 2000 financial statements, as presented herein, is different from the opinion we expressed in our previous report.

In our opinion, the financial statements referred to above present fairly, in all material respects, the financial position of Last National Bank as of December 31, 2001 and 2000, and the results of its operations and its cash flows for the years then ended in conformity with generally accepted accounting principles.

/s/ Auditor signature
January 31, 2002

EXHIBIT 3–11   REPORT ON CONDENSED FINANCIAL STATEMENTS DERIVED FROM AUDITED
FINANCIAL STATEMENTS

Independent Auditor's Report

To the Stockholders
of X Company:

We have audited, in accordance with generally accepted auditing standards, the balance sheet of X Company as of December 31, 2001, and the related statements of income, retained earnings, and cash flows for the year then ended (not presented herein); and in our report dated February 15, 2002, we expressed an unqualified opinion on those financial statements.

In our opinion, the information set forth in the accompanying condensed financial statements is fairly stated, in all material respects, in relation to the financial statements from which it has been derived.

/s/ Auditor signature
August 21, 2002

---

state whether the information in the condensed financial statements is fairly stated in all material respects in relation to the complete financial statements. A hypothetical example is shown in Exhibit 3–11.

Other Information Accompanying Audited Financial Statements

"Other information" standards are found in *SAS 8* (AU 550), entitled "Other Information in Documents Containing Audited Financial Statements." These standards contain the general framework for auditor involvement with information outside the basic financial statements. The involvement is limited to review procedures and exception-basis reporting. All annual reports to shareholders and SEC filings contain such sections as a president's letter and management's discussion and analysis of operations. These sections are separate from the audited financial statements and are not covered by the audit opinion. Nevertheless, auditors have an obligation to read (study) the other information and determine whether it is inconsistent with the audited financial statements. However, auditors are not obligated to review press releases, analysts' interviews, or other forms of irregular financial news releases unless specifically engaged by the client. In addition, a client's financial statements and other information placed on a website are

| EXHIBIT 3–12 | ACTION WHEN OTHER INFORMATION IS MATERIALLY INCONSISTENT (*SAS 8, AU 550*) |

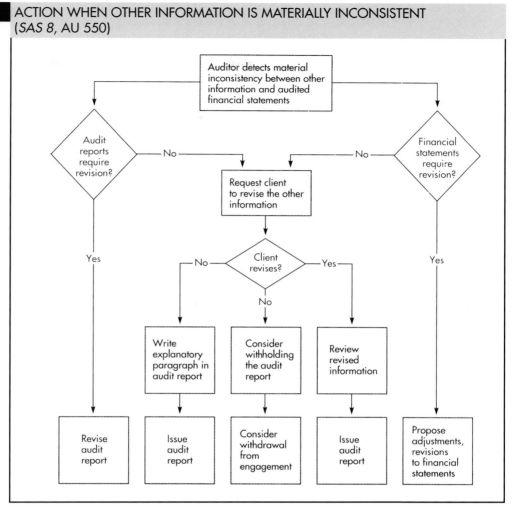

not considered "documents," and consequently, auditors are not required to review them for inconsistencies or material misstatements (AU 9550). This interpretation is likely to change as publication of financial statements on corporate websites becomes more commonplace.

If auditors decide a material inconsistency exists in other information, such as the president's selective use of audited financial statement numbers, action is required. The appropriate actions are diagrammed in Exhibit 3–12.

An example of other information is a president's letter remark: "Earnings increased from $1 million to $2 million, an increase of 50 cents per share." This statement can be corroborated by comparison to the audited financial statements. The president's comment would be considered inconsistent if the $1 million was income before an extraordinary loss and the $2 million was income after an extraordinary gain, or if the 50-cent change in EPS was the difference between last year's fully diluted EPS and this year's primary EPS. The president may have selected numbers without due regard to their meaningful comparison.

Other kinds of other information, however, might not be so directly related to audited figures. For example, the marketing vice president might write: "This year's sales represent a 20 percent share of the total market for our product." If auditors detect a material misstatement of fact (not necessarily a direct inconsistency with audited financial statement numbers), the information should be discussed with the client. One example would be the marketing vice president's comment about market shares. Auditors must decide whether they have the expertise to evaluate the information in question, whether management has experts who developed the information, and whether consultation with some other expert is needed. This last step would be taken only if there is a valid basis for pursuing the matter and if it concerns information that is particularly important.

If a misstatement of material fact exists, auditing standards provide the following: (1) notify the client in writing of the auditor's views, (2) consult with legal counsel about appropriate action to take, and (3) take the action indicated by professional judgment in the particular circumstances. These three points are vague, mainly because there is no catalog of "other information" that is not under the auditor's opinion. Auditors have latitude to decide what to do about material misstatements of other information, providing an analogy to the third AICPA reporting standard. (Informative disclosures in the financial statements are to be regarded as reasonably adequate unless otherwise stated in the report.)

The reporting obligation is exception reporting. The standard report is silent about other information unless an inconsistency or a material misstatement of fact exists. When something is wrong, the report is expanded with an explanatory paragraph. This treatment is identical to the emphasis of a matter paragraph—there is nothing wrong either with the financial statements or with the conduct of the audit, but the auditor needs to emphasize that the other information accompanying the audited financial statements is not consistent.

Quarterly and Supplementary Information

Accounting principles do not require interim (quarterly) financial information as a basic and necessary element of financial statements conforming to GAAP. When interim information is presented, however, it should conform to the accounting principles in *APB Opinion No. 28*. The SEC, on the other hand, requires the presentation of interim information as supplementary information outside the basic financial statements. Thus, interim information is voluntary insofar as FASB is concerned, but is required insofar as the SEC is concerned. However, the FASB and GASB may require supplementary information to be presented outside the basic financial statements. Oil and gas and other mineral reserve information is currently required to be presented as supplementary information.

Problems arise when: (1) required information is omitted, (2) the information departs materially from GAAP guidelines, (3) the review procedures that auditors should perform cannot be completed, (4) management's presentation of the information indicates the auditor performed review procedures without also saying the auditor does not express an opinion on it, and (5) management places the information close to, or within, the basic financial statements (e.g., in a financial statement footnote) and does not label it unaudited. When these problems arise, auditors should expand the audit report or give a disclaimer on the information. The expanded report for the first three cases calls attention to omission, departure from GAAP guides, or failure to review. In the latter two cases, a disclaimer of opinion on the supplementary information is added to the standard report so readers can be well informed that the auditors are not expressing an audit opinion that covers the information.

AUDITING INSIGHT

REPORTING IN AN ELECTRONIC ENVIRONMENT

The eXtensible Business Reporting Language (or XBRL) is a new language to express financial reporting and other business reporting information on the Internet. The language, a successor to the web-based Hypertext Markup Language (HTML), requires that companies use standard specified codes to tag financial data. Similar to using an Internet search engine, users will be able to quickly find and download financial information from a range of companies, industries and time frames by searching for the XBRL tags.

3.15 What is an updated audit report? What is a reissued audit report?

3.16 What two kinds of disclosure problems must an auditor be alert to detect when reading "other information" in an annual report? Explain them.

3.17 Why do you think auditors are prohibited from giving a standard unqualified audit report on condensed financial statements?

3.18 When must an auditor give a disclaimer of opinion on supplementary information in financial statements?

SUMMARY

The purpose of the audit report is clearly stated in the definition of auditing—to communicate the results of the audit to interested users. The "results of the audit" generally refers to the financial statements' adherence to GAAP, but the auditor can also communicate other matters as well, such as unusual aspects of the audit, going-concern difficulties, or other matters which financial statement users should be aware. As discussed in this chapter, depending on the circumstances, auditors have a wide variety of reports from which to choose.

Throughout the explanation of the auditors' choices of reports in this chapter, the materiality dimension plays an important role. When an auditor makes decisions about the audit report, immaterial or unimportant information can be ignored and treated as if it did not exist. However, when inaccuracies, departures from GAAP, accounting changes, and going concern uncertainties have a large enough financial impact, the standard audit report must be changed. In practice, when an auditor decides a matter is material enough to make a difference, a further distinction must be made between "lesser materiality" and "greater materiality." Lesser materiality means that the item in question is important and needs to be disclosed or the opinion needs to be qualified for it. The information cannot simply be ignored. Greater materiality means the item in question is very important and has an extreme effect on the reporting decision.

Auditing standards refer to several basic circumstances that cause departures from the standard unqualified audit report. These circumstances are shown in Exhibit 3–13 in

EXHIBIT 3–13   INFLUENCE OF MATERIALITY ON AUDIT REPORTS

Circumstances for Departure from Standard Report	Required Type of Report	
	Lesser Materiality	Greater Materiality
Departure from an official pronouncement (e.g., FASB, GASB, APB, ARB)	Qualified "except for": Separate paragraph discloses reasons and effects.*	Adverse Opinion: Separate paragraph discloses reasons and effects.*
Departure from GAAP	Qualified "except for": Separate paragraph discloses reasons and effects.	Adverse Opinion: Separate paragraph discloses reasons and effects.
Auditor is not independent	Disclaimer of opinion: Report states explicitly that the auditor is not independent.	
Scope limitation (lack of evidence)	Qualified Opinion: Refers to possible effects on financials.	Disclaimer of Opinion: Separate paragraph explains limitation.
Going Concern Uncertainty	Unqualified Opinion: Separate paragraph directs attention to management's notes.	Disclaimer of Opinion: Separate paragraph discloses reasons.

* Where the departure is necessary to make the financials not misleading, an unqualified opinion is issued with an explanation of the circumstances (Rule 203).

relation to the influence of materiality. You can see that each report qualified when the item is of lesser materiality becomes a disclaimer or an adverse report when the item involves greater materiality. The exception is the lack of independence issue where materiality does not make a difference.

In addition to the qualifications and disclaimers of audit opinions, audit reports can be modified and expanded with additional paragraphs. Such additions to the audit report arise from lack of consistent application of GAAP, the need for an "emphasis of a matter" paragraph, and going-concern problems. The chapter concludes with discussions of other report-related topics that are outside the mainstream of audit report modifications, but important nonetheless as evidenced by their frequent appearance on the Uniform CPA examination.

MULTIPLE-CHOICE QUESTIONS FOR PRACTICE AND REVIEW

3.19 Some of the GAAS reporting standards require certain statements in all audit reports ("explicit") and others require statements only under certain conditions ("implicit" basis). Which combination shown below correctly describes these features of the reporting standards?

Standards	(a)	(b)	(c)	(d)
1. GAAP	Explicit	Explicit	Implicit	Implicit
2. Consistency	Implicit	Explicit	Explicit	Implicit
3. Disclosure	Implicit	Implicit	Explicit	Explicit
4. Report	Explicit	Explicit	Implicit	Implicit

3.20 A CPA found that the client has not capitalized a material amount of leases in the financial statements. When considering the materiality of this departure from GAAP, the CPA's reporting options are
a. Unqualified opinion or disclaimer of opinion.
b. Unqualified opinion or qualified opinion.
c. Emphasis paragraph with unqualified opinion or an adverse opinion.
d. Qualified opinion or adverse opinion.

3.21 An auditor has found that the client is suffering financial difficulty and the going-concern status is seriously in doubt. Even though the client has placed good disclosures in the financial statements, the CPA must choose between the following audit report alternatives:
a. Unqualified report with a going-concern explanatory paragraph or disclaimer of opinion.
b. Standard unqualified report or a disclaimer of opinion.
c. Qualified opinion or adverse opinion.
d. Standard unqualified report or adverse opinion.

3.22 A company accomplished an early extinguishment of debt, and the auditors believe literal application of *APB Opinion No. 26* would cause recognition of a huge loss that would materially distort the financial statements and cause them to be misleading. The auditors' reporting choices are
a. Explain the situation and give an adverse opinion.
b. Explain the situation and give a disclaimer of opinion.
c. Explain the situation and give an unqualified opinion, relying on Rule 203 of the AICPA Code of Professional Conduct.
d. Give the standard unqualified audit report.

3.23 Which of these situations would require an auditor to insert an explanatory paragraph about consistency in an unqualified audit report?
a. Client changed its estimated allowance for uncollectible accounts receivable.
b. Client corrected a prior mistake in accounting for interest capitalization.
c. Client sold one of its subsidiaries and consolidated six this year compared to seven last year.
d. Client changed its inventory costing method from FIFO to LIFO.

3.24 Wolfe became the new auditor for Royal Corporation, succeeding Mason, who audited the financial statements last year. Wolfe needs to report on Royal's comparative financial statements and should write in his report an explanation about another auditor having audited the prior year
a. Only if Mason's opinion last year was qualified.

b. Describing the prior audit and the opinion but not naming Mason as the predecessor auditor.

c. Describing the audit but not revealing the type of opinion Mason gave.

d. Describing the audit and the opinion and naming Mason as the predecessor auditor.

3.25   When other independent auditors are involved in the current audit of parts of the client's business, the principal auditor can write an audit report that (two answers)

a. Mentions the other auditor, describes the extent of the other auditor's work, and gives an unqualified opinion.

b. Does not mention the other auditor and gives an unqualified opinion in a standard unqualified report.

c. Places primary responsibility for the audit report on the other auditors.

d. Names the other auditors, describes their work, and presents only the principal auditor's report.

3.26   An "emphasis of a matter" paragraph inserted in a standard audit report causes the report to be characterized as

a. Unqualified opinion report.

b. Divided responsibility.

c. Adverse opinion report.

d. Disclaimer of opinion.

3.27   Under which of the following conditions can a disclaimer of opinion never be given?

a. Going-concern problems are overwhelming the company.

b. The client does not let the auditor have access to evidence about important accounts.

c. The auditor owns stock in the client corporation.

d. The auditor has found that the client has used the NIFO (next-in, first-out) inventory costing method.

3.28   For which of the following accounting changes would an auditor's report normally contain a reference to consistency?

a. A change in principle that does not result in inconsistent statements because the previous year's statements are not presented.

b. An immaterial change to a principle required by a new FASB pronouncement.

c. A change in an accounting estimate.

d. A change in the classification or aggregation of financial statement amounts.

EXERCISES AND PROBLEMS

3.29   Unqualified   Report,   Accounting Change, and Uncertainty.   The audit report below was drafted by Moore, a staff accountant with Tyler & Tyler, CPAs, at the completion of the audit of the financial statements of Park Publishing Company, for the year ended September 30, 2001. The engagement partner reviewed the audit working papers and properly decided to issue an unqualified opinion. In drafting the report, Moore considered the following:

- During fiscal year 2001, Park changed its depreciation method. The engagement partner concurred with this change in accounting principles and its justification and Moore included an explanatory paragraph in the report.

- The 2001 financial statements are affected by an uncertainty concerning a lawsuit, the outcome of which cannot presently be estimated. Moore included an explanatory emphasis paragraph in the report.

- The financial statements for the year ended September 30, 2000, are to be presented for comparative purposes. Tyler & Tyler previously audited these statements and expressed an unqualified opinion.

Independent Auditors' Report

To the Board of Directors of Park Publishing Company:

We have audited the accompanying balance sheets of Park Publishing Company as of September 30, 2001, and 2000, and the related statements of income and cash flows for the years then ended. These financial statements are the responsibility of the company's management.

We conducted our audits in accordance with generally accepted auditing standards. Those standards require that we plan and perform the audit to obtain reasonable assurance about whether the financial statements are fairly presented. An audit includes examining, on a test basis, evidence supporting the amounts and disclosures in the financial statements. An audit also includes assessing significant estimates made by management, as well as evaluating the overall financial statement presentation. We believe that our audits provide a basis for determining whether any material modifications should be made to the accompanying financial statements.

As discussed in Note X to the financial statements, the company changed its method of computing depreciation in fiscal 2001.

In our opinion, except for the accounting change, with which we concur, the financial statements referred to above present fairly, in all material respects, the financial position of Park Publishing Company as of September 30, 2001, and the results of its operations and its cash flows for the year then ended in conformity with generally accepted accounting principles.

As discussed in Note Y to the financial statements, the company is a defendant in a lawsuit alleging infringement of certain copyrights. The company has filed a counteraction, and preliminary hearings on both actions are in progress. Accordingly, any provision for liability is subject to adjudication of this matter.

Tyler & Tyler, CPAs
November 5, 2001

Required:
Identify the deficiencies in the audit report as drafted by Moore. Group the deficiencies by paragraph and in the order in which the deficiencies appear. Do not rewrite the report.

(AICPA adapted)

3.30 Reports and the Effect of Materiality. The concept of materiality is important to CPAs in audits of financial statements and expressions of opinion on these statements.

How will materiality influence an auditor's reporting decision in the following circumstances?

a. The client prohibits confirmation of accounts receivable, and sufficient, competent evidence cannot be obtained using alternative procedures.

b. The client is a gas and electric utility company that follows the practice of recognizing revenue when it is billed to customers. At the end of the year, amounts earned but not yet billed are not recorded in the accounts or reported in the financial statements.

c. The client leases buildings for its chain of transmission repair shops under terms that qualify as capital leases under SFAS 13. These leases are not capitalized as leased property assets and lease obligations.

d. The client company has lost a lawsuit in federal district court. The case is on appeal in an attempt to reduce the amount of damages awarded to the plaintiffs. No loss amount is recorded.

3.31 Errors in an Adverse Report. The board of directors of Cook Industries, Inc. engaged Brown & Brown, CPAs, to audit the financial statements for the year ended December 31, 2001. Joe Brown has decided an adverse report is appropriate. He also became aware of a March 14, 2002, subsequent event, which the Cook financial vice president properly disclosed in the notes to the financial statements. Brown wants responsibility for subsequent events to be limited to this specific event after the field work was completed on March 7.

Required:
Identify the deficiencies in the draft of the report presented below. Do not rewrite the report.

Report of Independent Accountants
To the President of Cook Industries, Inc.:

We have audited the financial statements of Cook Industries, Inc., for the year ended December 31, 2001. We conducted our audits in accordance with generally accepted auditing standards. Those standards require that we plan and perform the audit to obtain reasonable assurance about whether the financial statements are free of material misstatement. An audit includes examining, on a test basis, evidence supporting the amounts and disclosures in the financial statements. An audit also includes assessing the accounting principles used and significant estimates made by management, as well as evaluating the overall financial statement presentation. We believe that our audit provides a reasonable basis for our opinion.

As discussed in Note K to the financial statements, the Company has properly disclosed a subsequent event dated March 14, 2002.

As discussed in Note G to the financial statements, the Company carries its property and equipment at appraisal values, and provides depreciation on the basis of such values. Further, the Company does not provide for income taxes with respect to differences between financial income and taxable income arising from the use, for income tax purposes, of the installment method of reporting gross profit from certain types of sales.

In our opinion, the financial statements referred to above do not present fairly the financial position of Cook Industries, Inc., as of December 31, 2001, and the results of its operations and its cash flows for the year then ended in conformity with generally accepted accounting principles.

/s/ Brown & Brown
Certified Public Accountants
March 14, 2002

(AICPA adapted)

3.32 Reporting on Consistency. Various types of "accounting changes" can affect the second reporting standard of the generally accepted auditing standards. This standard reads: "The report shall identify those circumstances in which such principles (generally accepted accounting principles) have not been consistently observed in the current period in relation to the preceding period."

Assume that the list below describes changes which have a material effect on a client's financial statements for the current year:

1. A change from the completed contract method to the percentage-of-completion method of accounting for long-term, construction-type contracts.

2. A change in the estimated useful life of previously recorded fixed assets based on newly acquired information.

3. Correction of a mathematical error in inventory pricing made in a prior period.

4. A change from prime costing to full absorption costing for inventory valuation.

5. A change from presentation of statements of individual companies to presentation of consolidated statements.

6. A change from deferring and amortizing pre-production costs to recording such costs as an expense when incurred because future benefits of the costs have become doubtful. The new accounting method was adopted in recognition of the change in estimated future benefits.

7. A change to including the employer share of FICA taxes in "retirement benefits" on the income statement from including it in "other taxes."

8. A change from the FIFO method of inventory pricing to the LIFO method of inventory pricing.

Required:

Identify the type of change described in each item above. (The types are: change in accounting principle, change in the reporting entity, error correction, combined error correction and change in principle, and change in an accounting estimate.) State whether any explanatory paragraph is required in the auditor's report as it relates to the second standard of reporting. Organize your answer sheet as shown in Exhibit 3.32–1. For example, a change from the LIFO method of inventory pricing to the FIFO method of inventory pricing would appear as shown in Exhibit 3.32–1.

EXHIBIT 3.32–1

Item No.	Type of Change	Should Auditor's Report Be Modified?
Example	An accounting change from one generally accepted accounting principle to another generally accepted accounting principle.	Yes

3.33   Errors in a Comparative Report with Change from Prior Year   The following audit report was drafted by an assistant at the completion of the audit of Cramdon, Inc., on March 1, 2002. The partner in charge of the engagement has decided the opinion on the 2001 financial statements should be modified only with reference to the change in the method of computing the cost of inventory. In 2000, Cramdon used the NIFO method, which is not accepted under generally accepted accounting principles, but in 2001 changed to FIFO and restated the 2000 financial statements. (The audit report on the 2000 financial statement contained an adverse opinion.) The 2000 audit report (same audit firm) was dated March 5, 2001.

Report of Independent Auditor

To the Board of Directors
of Cramdon, Inc.:

We have audited the accompanying financial statements of Cramdon, Inc., as of December 31, 2001 and 2000. These financial statements are the responsibility of the Company's management. Our responsibility is to express an opinion on these financial statements based on our audits.

We conducted our audits in accordance with generally accepted auditing standards. Those standards require that we plan and perform the audit to obtain reasonable assurance about whether the financial statements are free of material misstatement. An audit includes examining, on the test basis, evidence supporting the amounts and disclosures in the financial statements. An audit also includes assessing the accounting principles used and significant estimates made by management, as well as evaluating the overall financial statement presentation. We believe that our audit provides a reasonable basis for our opinion.

As discussed in Note 7 to the financial statements, the company changed its method of accounting for inventory cost from NIFO to FIFO. The 2000 financial statements have been restated to reflect this change. Accordingly, our present opinion on the 2000 financial statements, as presented herein, is different from the opinion we expressed in our previous report dated December 31, 2000.

In our opinion, based on the preceding, the financial statements referred to above present fairly, in all material respects, the financial position of Cramdon, Inc., as of December 31, 2001, and the results of its operations and its cash flows for the period then ended in conformity with generally accepted accounting principles consistently applied, except for the changes in the method of computing inventory cost as described in Note 7 to the financial statements.

/s/ CPA Firm
March 5, 2002

Required:
Identify the deficiencies and errors in the draft report and write an explanation of the reasons they are errors and deficiencies. Do not rewrite the report.

3.34   Using the Work and Report of Another Auditor.   Lando Corporation is a domestic company with two wholly owned domestic subsidiaries. Michaels, CPA, has been engaged to audit the financial statements of the parent company and one of the subsidiaries and to act as the principal auditor. Thomas, CPA, has audited the financial statements of the other subsidiary whose operations are material in relation to the consolidated financial statements.

The work performed by Michaels is sufficient for Michaels to serve as the principal auditor and to report as such on the financial statements. Michaels has not yet decided whether to make reference to the part of the audit performed by Thomas.

Required:

a. What are the reporting requirements with which Michaels must comply if Michaels decides to name Thomas and make reference to the audit work done by Thomas?

b. What report should be issued if Michaels can neither assume responsibility for Thomas' work nor divide responsibility by referring to his work?

3.35   Reference to Another Auditor in Principal Auditor's Report   and Other Operating Matters. Presented below is Rex Wolf's independent auditor's report that contains deficiencies. Bonair Corporation is profit oriented and publishes general-purpose financial statements for distribution to owners, creditors, potential investors, and the general public:

Report of Independent Auditor
To the Board of Directors and Shareholders
Bonair Corporation

We have audited the accompanying consolidated balance sheet of Bonair Corporation and subsidiaries as of December 31, 2001, and the related statements of income and retained earnings for the year then ended. Our responsibility is to express an opinion on these financial statements based on our audit. We did not examine the financial statements of Caet Company, a major consolidated subsidiary. These statements were examined by Nero Stout, CPA, whose report thereon has been furnished to us, and our opinion expressed herein, insofar as it relates to Caet Company, is based solely upon the other auditor's report on Caet Company.

Except as stated in the paragraph above, we conducted our audit in accordance with generally accepted auditing standards. Those standards require that we plan and perform the audit to obtain reasonable assurance about whether the financial statements are free of material misstatement. An audit includes assessing control risk, examining on a test basis evidence supporting the amounts and disclosures in the financial statements. An audit also includes assessing the accounting principles used and significant estimates made by management, as well as evaluating the overall financial statement presentation. We believe that our audit provides a reasonable basis for our opinion.

In our opinion, except for the matter of the report of the other auditors, the financial statements referred to above present fairly, in all material respects, the financial position of Bonair Corporation and subsidiaries December 31, 2001, and the results of their operations and their cash flows for the year then ended.

Rex Wolf, CPA

Required:
Describe the reporting deficiencies, and explain why they are considered deficiencies. Organize your response according to each of the paragraphs in the standard unqualified audit report.

3.36   Reporting on Supplementary and Other Information.   For the separate fact situations given below, specify the appropriate form and content of the audit report on the related financial statements.

a. Mona Corporation voluntarily presented the interim financial information described in *APB Opinion No. 28.* This year, however, time ran short, and the controller's staff was unable to present everything specified by *APB 28.*

b. When Kinky Korp Company presented its interim financial figures in a footnote to the financial statements, the footnote was labeled "Interim Financial Results," and the closing sentence of the narrative introduction was: "Grey & Fox, CPAs, reviewed the interim financial results in accordance with standards established by the American Institute of Certified Public Accountants."

c. Kaviar, Inc.'s president, Sharon Kaviar, wrote a management discussion and analysis section in the annual report to shareholders, in which she said: "Research and development expenses increased this year by 20 percent." Consulting the R&D expense disclosure in the financial statements, you see that the expense for last year is reported to be $3 million and for this year $3.75 million.

3.37   Various Report Situations   Assume the auditors encountered the following separate situations when deciding upon the report to issue for the current-year financial statements.

1. The auditor decided that sufficient competent evidence could not be obtained to complete the audit of significant investments the company held in a foreign company.

2. The company failed to capitalize lease assets and obligations, but explained them fully in the notes to the financial statements.

3. The company is defending a lawsuit on product liability claims. (Customers allege that power saw safety guards were improperly installed.) All the facts about the lawsuit are disclosed in notes to the financial statement, but the auditors believe the company ought to record a minimum probable settlement loss the lawyers say is likely.

4. The company hired the auditors after the December 31 inventory-taking. The accounting records and other evidence are not reliable enough to enable the auditors to have sufficient evidence about the proper inventory amount.

5. The oil company client is required by FASB to present supplementary oil and gas reserve information outside the basic financial statements. The auditors find that this information, which is not required as a part of the basic financial statements, is omitted.

6. The auditors are principal auditors of the parent company, but they decide not to take responsibility for the work done by other auditors on three subsidiary companies included in the consolidated financial statements. The principal auditors reviewed the other auditors' work and reputation, but they still do not want to take responsibility for the other auditors' portion, which amounts to 32 percent of the consolidated assets and 39 percent of the consolidated revenues.

7. The company changed its depreciation method from units-of-production to straight-line, and the auditor believes the straight-line method is the most appropriate in the circumstances. The change, fully explained in the notes to the financial statements, has a material effect on the year-to-year comparability of the comparative financial statements.

8. Because the company has experienced significant operating losses and has had to obtain waivers of debt payment requirements from its lenders, the auditors decide that there is substantial doubt that the company can continue in existence as a going concern. Even so, the auditors want to render a positive assurance report because the company has fully described all the problems in a note in the financial statements.

Required:

a. What kind of opinion should the auditors write for each separate case?

b. What other modification(s) or addition(s) to the standard report is (are) required for each separate case?

3.38   Explain Deficiencies in an Opinion Disclaimer.   Your partner wrote the following audit report yesterday. You need to describe the reporting deficiencies, explain the reasons for them, and discuss with him how the report should be corrected. This may be a hard job because he has always felt somewhat threatened because you were the first woman partner in the firm. You have decided to write up a three-column worksheet showing the deficiencies, reasons, and corrections needed. This was his report:

I made my examination in accordance with generally accepted auditing standards. However, I am not independent with respect to Mavis Corporation because my wife owns 5 percent of the outstanding common stock of the company. The accompanying balance sheet as of December 31, 2001, and the related statements of income and retained earnings and cash flows for the year then ended were not audited by me. Accordingly, I do not express an opinion on them.

Required:
Prepare the worksheet described above.

3.39   Evidence Required for Various Audit Reports.   Auditors' alternatives for reporting on financial statements offer many choices among unqualified, qualified, disclaimed, modified, and expanded report language.

Required:

a. List the reports that require fully sufficient competent evidence.

b. List the reports that result from pervasive and massive evidence deficiencies.

c. List the reports that result from isolated evidence deficiencies.

REPORT-WRITING CASES

These cases require a written audit report. The *Electronic Workpapers* (available on the textbook website listed on the back of the text) has an ASCII file (filename AUDIT) containing the standard unqualified audit report, which can be used as the starting place for a nonstandard report requirement. You can read this file into many word processing programs to make your report-writing task easier and more professional.

3.40   Other Information in a Financial Review Section of an Annual Report.   Mr. Humphreys (chairman of the board) and Ms. VanEns (vice president, finance) prepared the draft of the financial review section of the annual report. You are reviewing it for consistency with the audited financial statements. The draft contains the following explanation about income coverage of interest expense:

Last year, operating income before interest and income taxes covered interest expense by a ratio of 6:1. This year, on an incremental basis, the coverage of interest expense increased to a ratio of 6.588:1.

The relevant portion of the audited financial statements showed the following:

	Current Year	Prior Year
Operating income	$400,000	$360,000
Extraordinary gain from realization of tax benefits	100,000	
Interest expense	(81,250)	(60,000)
Income taxes	(127,500)	(120,000)
Net income	$291,250	$180,000

Required:

a. Determine whether the financial review section statement about coverage of interest is or is not consistent with the audited financial statements. Be able to show your conclusion with calculations.

b. Assume you find an inconsistency, and the officers disagree with your conclusions. Write the explanatory paragraph you should put in your audit report.

3.41   Departures from GAAP.   On January 1, Graham Company purchased land (the site of a new building) for $100,000. Soon thereafter, the Highway Department announced a new feeder roadway route that would run alongside the site. The effect was a dramatic increase in local property values. Nearby comparable land sold for $700,000 in December of the current year. Graham shows the land at $700,000 in its accounts, and, after reduction for implicit taxes at 33 percent, the fixed asset total is $400,000 larger, with the same amount shown separately in a stockholder equity account titled "Current value increment." The valuation is fully disclosed in a footnote to the financial statements, along with a

letter from a certified property appraiser attesting to the $700,000 value.

Required:

a. Write the appropriate audit report, assuming you believe the departure from GAAP is material but not enough to cause you to give an adverse opinion.

b. Write the appropriate report, assuming you believe an adverse opinion is necessary.

c. For discussion: Should you (could you) issue a report conforming to Rule 203 of the AICPA Code of Professional Conduct?

3.42   Reporting on an Accounting Change.   In December of the current year, Williams Company changed its method of accounting for inventory and cost of goods sold from LIFO to FIFO. The account balances shown in the trial balance have already been recalculated and adjusted retroactively, as required by *APB Opinion No. 20*. The accounting change and the financial effects are described in Note 2 in the financial statements.

a. Assume you believe the accounting change is justified, as required by *APB Opinion No. 20*. Write the audit report appropriate in the circumstances.

b. Assume you believe the accounting change is not justified and causes the financial statements to be materially distorted. Inventories that would have been reported at $1.5 million (LIFO) are reported at $1.9 million (FIFO); operating income before tax that would have been $130,000 is reported at $530,000; current assets are revised upward 17 percent and total assets 9 percent; stockholder equity is 14 percent greater. Write the audit report appropriate in the circumstances.

3.43   Financial Difficulty—The "Going-Concern" Problem.   The Pitts Company has experienced significant financial difficulty. Current liabilities exceed current assets by $1 million, cash is down to $10,000, the interest on the long-term debt has not been paid, and a customer has sued for $500,000 on a product liability claim. Significant questions concerning the going-concern status of the company exist.

Required:

a. Write the appropriate audit report, assuming you decide that an audit opinion instead of a disclaimer is appropriate in the circumstances.

b. Write the appropriate audit report, assuming you decide the uncertainties are so overwhelming that you do not want to express an opinion.

3.44   Arguments with Auditors.   Officers of the company do not want to disclose information about the product liability lawsuit filed by a customer asking $500,000 in damages. They believe the suit is frivolous and without merit. Outside counsel is more cautious. The auditors insist upon disclosure. Angered, the Richnow Company chairman of the board threatens to sue the auditors if a standard unqualified report is not issued within three days.

Required:

Write the audit report appropriate in the circumstances.

3.45   Late Appointment of Auditor.   Dalton Wardlaw, CPA, has completed the field work for the audit of the financial statements of Musgrave Company, for the year ended December 31, and is now preparing the audit report.

Wardlaw has audited the financial statements for several years, but this year Musgrave delayed the start of the audit work, and Wardlaw was busy anyway, so he was not present to observe the taking of the physical inventory on December 31. However, he performed alternative procedures, including: (1) examination of shipping and receiving documents with regard to transactions since the year-end, (2) extensive review of the inventory count sheets, and (3) discussion of the physical inventory procedures with responsible company personnel. He also satisfied himself about the propriety of the inventory valuation calculations and the consistency of the valuation method. Musgrave determines year-end inventory quantities solely by means of physical count.

Required:

Write Wardlaw's audit report on the balance sheet at the end of the current year under audit, and on the statements of operations, retained earnings,

and cash flows for the one year then ended. (Hint: Did the alternative procedures produce sufficient, competent evidence?)

3.46   Using Work of Other Independent Auditors.   You (Anderson, Olds, & Watershed) are the principal auditor on the December 31 consolidated financial statements of Ferguson Company and subsidiaries. However, other auditors do the work on certain subsidiaries for the year under audit amounting to:

	2001	2000
Total assets	29%	31%
Total revenues	36%	41%

Mr. Wardlaw investigated the other auditors, as required by auditing standards, and they furnished him with their audit reports. Wardlaw has decided to rely on their work and to refer to the other auditors in the AOW audit report. None of the audit work showed any reason to qualify any of the audit opinions.

Required:

Write the AOW audit report referring to the work and reports of the other auditors.

3.47   Internet Exercise—Company Audit Reports.   One of the great resources on the World Wide Web for auditors is the SEC's EDGAR database **(http://www.sec.gov/).** EDGAR stands for Electronic Data Gathering, Analysis and Retrieval system. Most publicly traded companies file SEC-required documents electronically. The SEC makes this information available on its web page. Some of the more useful filings for accountants include the following:

Form	Description
Annual Report to Shareholders	The Annual Report to Shareholders is the principal document used by most public companies to disclose corporate information to shareholders. It usually includes financial data, results of continuing operations, market segment information, new product plans, subsidiary activities and research and development activities. Sometimes, companies include the annual report by reference in their Form 10-K filed with the SEC, and the actual report may not be present.
Form 10-K or 10-KSB	This report is the annual report that most reporting companies file with the Commission. It provides a comprehensive overview of the registrant's business. The report must be filed within 90 days after the end of the company's fiscal year.
Form 10-Q	The Form 10-Q is a report filed quarterly by most reporting companies. It includes unaudited financial statements and provides a continuing view of the company's financial position during the year. The report must be filed for each of the first three fiscal quarters of the company's fiscal year and is due within 45 days of the close of the quarter.
Form 8-K	This "current events report" is used to report the occurrence of any material events or corporate changes which are of importance to investors or security holders and previously have not been reported by the registrant. It provides more current information on certain specified events than would Forms 10-Q or 10-K.
Form S-1	This report is the basic registration form used to register public securities offerings.

Required:

Choose five publicly traded companies with which you are familiar. After accessing the EDGAR database, download copies of the auditors' reports from the Form 10-K filings and check the boxes in the table below that apply. The first has been done for you. (**Hint:** Search the 10-K filings. Once you've accessed the 10-K filing, use the "Find in page" function in your Internet browser to locate the auditor's report using the key word "independent," as in "Report of Independent Auditors").

| Company Name | Type of Opinion | | | | Additional Explanatory Paragraph? | | |
	Unqualified Opinion	Qualified Opinion	Disclaimer of Opinion	Adverse Opinion	Consistency	Going Concern	Emphasize a matter
Universal Seismic (1997)	✔					✔	

Chapter 4
Materiality and Risk

Professional Standards References

Compendium Section	Document Reference	Topic
AU 310	SAS 83	*Establishing an Understanding with the Client*
AU 311	SAS 22	*Planning and Supervision*
AU 9311		*Interpretations: Communication with Non-Audit Personnel, Responsibility of Assistants*
AU 312	SAS 47	*Audit Risk and Materiality in Conducting an Audit*
AU 313	SAS 45	*Substantive Tests Prior to the Balance Sheet Date*
AU 316	SAS 82	*Consideration of Fraud in a Financial Statement Audit*
AU 326	SAS 80	*Evidential Matter*
AU 9326		*Interpretation: Auditor's Consideration of the Completeness Assertion*
AU 329	SAS 56	*Analytical Procedures*
AU 330	SAS 67	*The Confirmation Process*
AU 331	SAS 1	*Inventories*
AU 332	SAS 81	*Auditing Investments*
AU 334	SAS 45	*Related Parties*
AU 9334		*Interpretations: Related Parties*
AU 336	SAS 73	*Using the Work of a Specialist*
AU 339	SAS 41	*Working Papers*
AU 9339		*Interpretation: Providing Working Papers to a Regulator*
AU 342	SAS 57	*Auditing Accounting Estimates*
AU 9342		*Interpretation: Auditing Accounting Estimates*

Learning Objectives

This chapter deals with some of the tools of planning— materiality determination, the assessment of risks with reference to the audit risk model, and tolerable misstatement assignment decisions—all leading up to the preparation of audit programs. An audit program is a list of audit procedures used to gather enough evidence to express an opinion on the financial statements. The chapter concludes with an examination of the use of the personal computer (PC) as an audit tool, with an emphasis on the use of computer-assisted audit tools and techniques (CAATTs) to improve audit efficiency and effectiveness. After studying Chapter 4, you should be able to:

1. Analyze a materiality determination case and decide upon a maximum amount of misstatement acceptable in a company's financial statements.

2. Describe the conceptual audit risk model and explain the meaning and importance of its components in terms of professional judgment and audit planning.

3. Describe the content and purpose of audit programs.

4. List and describe seven general types of audit procedures for gathering evidence.

5. Discuss the effectiveness of various audit procedures.

6. Describe how a computer can be used as an audit tool.

MATERIALITY

In the first three chapters, the word *"material"* has shown up several times. For example, **internal control** was defined as a system's capability to prevent or detect *material* accounting errors and provide for their correction on a timely basis. With respect to reporting, the decision to issue an adverse or qualified report depends on the *materiality* of the GAAP departure. So *what* is materiality, and *how* can you deal with it? We discuss materiality and its effect on financial statement auditing in this section.

Financial Statement Materiality

The concept of materiality pervades financial accounting and reporting: *Information is material and should be disclosed if it is likely to influence the economic decisions of financial statement users.* The emphasis is on the users' point of view, not on accountants' and managers' points of view. Thus, *material information* is a synonym for *important information*.

Financial statement measurements and information in some footnote disclosures are not perfectly accurate. As recognized in the scope paragraph of the auditor's standard report, the financial statements are a function of the "accounting principles used and significant estimates made by management." The choices of depreciation method (straight-line versus accelerated), inventory valuation method (e.g., FIFO, LIFO, weighted average cost), classification of marketable securities (available for sale, trading, or held to maturity) all affect final financial statement numbers. Furthermore, many financial measurements are based on estimates, such as the estimated depreciable lives of fixed assets or the estimated amount of uncollectible accounts receivable. Thus, you must think of net income not as one "true" figure, but as one possible measure in a range of potential net income figures allowable under generally accepted accounting principles.

Auditors are limited by the very complex nature of accounting. Some amount of inaccuracy is permitted in financial statements because: (1) unimportant inaccuracies do not affect users' decisions and hence are not material, (2) the cost of finding and correcting small errors is too great, and (3) the time taken to find them would delay issuance

AUDITING INSIGHT

AUDIT CONSIDERATIONS FOR ACCOUNTING ESTIMATES

An accounting estimate is an approximation of a financial statement number, and estimates are often included in financial statements (SAS 57, AU 342).

Examples include net realizable value of accounts receivable, market if (lower than cost) value of inventory, depreciation expense, property and casualty insurance loss reserves, percentage-of-completion contract revenues, pension expense, warranty liabilities, and many more.

Management is responsible for making accounting estimates. Auditors are responsible for determining that all appropriate estimates have been made, that they are reasonable, and that they are presented in conformity with GAAP and adequately disclosed.

Part of the audit process includes the auditors producing their own estimate and comparing it to management's estimate. Often, consideration of a range for an amount is involved. For example, management may estimate an allowance for doubtful accounts to be $50,000, and the auditors may estimate that the allowance could be $40,000 to $55,000. In this case, management's estimate is within the auditors' range of reasonableness. However, the auditors should take note that the management estimate leans toward the conservative side (more than the auditors' $40,000 lower estimate, but not much less than the auditors' higher $55,000 estimate). If other estimates exhibit the same conservatism, and the effect is material, the auditors will need to evaluate the overall reasonableness of the effect of all estimates taken together.

If the auditors develop an estimate that differs (e.g., a range of $55,000 to $70,000 for the allowance that management estimated at $50,000), the preferred treatment is to consider the difference between management's estimate and the closest end of the auditors' range as an error (in this case, error = $5,000 = auditors' $55,000 minus management's $50,000). The remaining difference to the farthest end of the range ($15,000 = $70,000 − $55,000) is noted and reconsidered in combination with the findings on all management's estimates (SAS 47, AU 312).

The best evidence of the reasonableness of estimates is the actual subsequent experience of the company with the financial amounts estimated at an earlier date.

of financial statements. Accounting numbers are not perfectly accurate, but accountants and auditors want to maintain that financial reports are *materially* accurate and do not contain *material* misstatements.

Auditors use materiality three ways: (1) as a guide to *planning the audit program*—directing attention and audit work to the important, uncertain, or error-prone items and accounts; (2) as a guide to *evaluation of the evidence*; and (3) as a guide for making *decisions about the audit report*. An important point is that materiality in auditing is perceived in terms of both potential misstatement (in a planning sense) and known or estimated misstatement (in an evaluation and reporting decision sense). An account, such as inventory, is not necessarily material in an audit context because of its size or its place in the financial statements. The importance derives from the potential for, and effect of, misstatements that might exist in the account.

Materiality Judgment Criteria

Many accountants wish that definitive, quantitative materiality guides could be issued, but many fear the rigidity such guides would impose. The best rules of thumb seem to be that anything less than 5 percent is probably not material and anything greater than 10 percent probably is material. (A legitimate question, therefore, is 5 percent or 10 percent of *what?*) In *Staff Accounting Bulletin No. 99–"Materiality"* (1999), however, the SEC cautions auditors about over-reliance on certain quantitative benchmarks to assess materiality, noting that "misstatements are not immaterial simply because they fall beneath a numerical threshold." Thus, auditors must examine both *quantitative* and *qualitative* factors when assessing materiality. Some of the more common factors auditors use in making materiality judgments are these:

Absolute Size

An amount of potential misstatement may be important regardless of any other considerations. Not many auditors use absolute size alone as a criterion because a given amount, say $50,000, may be appropriate in one case and too large or too small in another. Yet, some auditors have been known to say: "$1 million [or some other large number] is material, no matter what."

Relative Size

The relation of potential misstatement to a relevant base number is often used (usually with reference to the 5 percent–10 percent rule of thumb). Potential misstatements in income statement accounts usually are related to net income either before or after taxes. If income fluctuates widely, a "normalized" or average income over recent years may be substituted for the current-year net income, or the relation may be to the trend change of income. The base for nonprofit entities may be gross revenue or contributions or a figure important in the statement of cash flows. Potential misstatements in balance sheet accounts may be related to a subtotal number, such as current assets or net working capital. Some auditors prefer the total gross margin as a uniform base because it is less subject to year-to-year fluctuations than the net income number. We want to emphasize that normally, auditors choose one measure of materiality for the entire audit, not separate measures for each of the financial statements. The reason is that all adjusting entries affect at least one balance sheet and one income statement account; what may be immaterial to the balance sheet may be very material to the income statement.

AUDITING INSIGHT

RELATIVE SIZE MATERIALITY DETERMINATION ILLUSTRATED

Suppose the auditors take the influence of earnings per share (EPS) on stock price as an important consideration in determining materiality. For illustrative purposes, suppose the model for stock price determination is a simple EPS multiple. (This is not to suggest that stock prices actually are determined by such a simple method as multiplying the EPS in all cases. Analysts and investors use many other valuation models beyond the scope of this illustration.)

Assume that Alpha.com, Inc. has 100,000 shares outstanding and its stock trades at a 14 × price-earning multiple, thus indicating a stock price of $51.80. (Stock price = EPS ($3.70 = $370,000/100,000) × 14 = $51.80.) The auditors must make a judgment about how much investors could overpay for the stock, yet it would not make any difference to them, say 5 percent to 10 percent.

	Low (5%)	High (10%)
Indicated stock price (14 × $3.70)	$ 51.80	$ 51.80
Price materiality judgment	2.59	5.18
Adjusted stock price	49.21	46.62
Adjusted earnings per share (divide by 14 multiple)	3.52	3.33
Indicated net income (multiply by 100,000 shares)	352,000	333,000
Add pretax accounts that can be audited completely:		
Interest expense	40,000	40,000
Income tax expense (40%)	234,667	222,000
Indicated pretax income*	626,667	595,000
Unaudited pretax income	666,000	666,000
Indicated planning materiality based on pretax income	39,333	71,000

* Calculate the pretax income, which, when reduced by interest expense and 40 percent income taxes, produces the indicated net income (after-tax).

Nature of the Item or Issue

An important qualitative factor is the descriptive nature of the item or issue. An illegal payment is important primarily because of its nature as well as its absolute or relative amount. A misstatement in segment information may be small in relation to the total business but important for analysis of the segment (*SAS 21*, AU 435). Generally, potential errors in more liquid assets (cash, receivables, and inventory) are considered more important than potential errors in other accounts (such as fixed assets and deferred charges). Materiality may be either qualitative or quantitative.

Circumstances

Auditors generally place extra emphasis on detection of misstatement in financial statements that will be widely used (publicly held companies) or used by important outsiders (bank loan officers). Auditors' liability is a relevant consideration. When management can exercise discretion over an accounting treatment, auditors tend to exercise more care and use a more stringent materiality criterion. Troublesome political events in foreign countries also can cause auditors to try to be more accurate with measurements and disclosures.

Uncertainty

Matters surrounded by uncertainty about the outcome of future events usually come under more stringent materiality considerations.

Cumulative Effects

Auditors must evaluate the sum of known or potential misstatements. Considering five different $15,000 mistakes that all increase net income as immaterial is inappropriate when the net income-based materiality limit is $50,000.

Financial Statement Accounts and Materiality Assignment

To plan the audit of various accounts, auditors need to assign part of the planning materiality to each account. The amount assigned to an account is called the *tolerable misstatement* for that account. The **tolerable misstatement** is the amount by which a particular account may be misstated (error not discovered by auditors!), yet still not cause the financial statements taken as a whole to be materially misleading. Thus, tolerable misstatement for each account is based on the overall financial statement materiality.

The extent to which tolerable misstatement is "based on" the overall materiality amount may vary from auditor to auditor. One method assigns tolerable misstatement amounts that add up to twice the overall materiality. The theory is that actual financial misstatements in accounts can be both overstatements and understatements, and the two directions will tend to balance out. Another is to assign tolerable misstatement in amounts such that the square root of the sum of the squared tolerable misstatements is equal to the overall materiality. The theory here is that the different misstatements behave like random errors in a calculation of statistical variance. Another method, used later as an illustration, is to assign tolerable misstatement amounts that exactly add up to materiality. This method assumes that the worst case is that all the errors in the account balances have the same directional effect on income (i.e., overstatement or understatement, but not some of both).

You should not be surprised that there are different methods for assigning overall materiality to tolerable misstatements for accounts. The auditing standards do not even require that the overall materiality judgment be expressed as a dollar amount, much less assigned to individual accounts in dollar amounts. You will find many different thought processes and methods used in practice.

When materiality is quantified, some accountants prefer a **bottoms-up approach**—judging materiality amounts in each account separately, and then combining them to see what the overall effect might be. Other accountants prefer a **top-down approach**—judging an overall material amount for the financial statements, and then allocating it to particular accounts (e.g., receivables, inventory) to help determine the amount of work in each area.

A top-down approach may be considered theoretically preferable. It requires auditors to think first about the financial statements taken altogether. Then, it forces the planning for each account into the context of the financial statements taken as a whole. The top-down approach helps to avoid the problem of "being surprised" when judgments about separate accounts (the bottoms-up approach) add up to more than a material amount appropriate for the income statement, balance sheet, or statement of cash flows.

Consider a top-down approach to the materiality judgment for the current-year financial information of Alpha.com, Inc., shown in Exhibit 4–1. The judgment involves centering attention on the most important financial decisions that may be related to the use of the financial statements. The net income number may be the most important because the company is growing and issuing stock to the public. The illustration boxed earlier (Relative Size Materiality Determination Illustrated) shows a calculation of overall materiality based on an assumed effect of income misstatement on the stock price. If the auditors decide the stock could be mispriced by 10 percent, and nobody would care, then the income before taxes and interest could be overstated (or understated) by as much as $71,000.

The problem now is to assign the materiality number ($71,000) to different accounts. Different auditors can reach different allocation decisions even when using the same

---

| EXHIBIT 4–1 | ILLUSTRATIVE ASSIGNMENTS OF OVERALL MATERIALITY |

Account/SUBTOTAL	CASE A	CASE B	CASE C
Sales	$21,000	$15,000	$10,000
Cost of goods sold	35,000	38,000	46,000
Gross margin	56,000	53,000	56,000
Expenses	15,000	18,000	15,000
Total materiality	$71,000	$71,000	$71,000

Allocation in Case A (Exhibit 4–1)

1. If the gross margin is misstated by $56,000 and the expenses by $15,000 (in the same direction—e.g., overstatement of income), the result is a misstatement of operating income before taxes of $71,000.
2. If the misstatement of gross margin is $56,000, the sales number can account for $21,000.
   a. Sales overstatement can be investigated by auditing the accounts receivable within a tolerable misstatement of $21,000. If sales are overstated, then a "dangling" debit must be somewhere in the double-entry bookkeeping, and the most likely place is in the accounts receivable.
   b. Sales understatement can be investigated by auditing the control over sales completeness, and possibly by searching for unrecorded accounts receivable, both to a tolerable misstatement of $21,000.
3. If the misstatement of gross margin is $56,000, the cost of goods sold number can account for $35,000.
   a. Cost of goods sold understatement can be investigated by auditing the inventory for overstatement within a tolerable misstatement of $35,000. If the beginning inventory is accurate and purchases for the year are accurate, then overstatement of the ending inventory causes understatement of the cost of goods sold and overstatement of income.
   b. Cost of goods sold overstatement can be investigated by auditing the inventory for understatement, again with a tolerable misstatement of $35,000. The cost of goods sold may even be misstated from recording purchases for nonbusiness purposes (a favorite way to embezzle funds), but the audit of control over validity of purchases will produce related evidence.
4. The expenses number can account for $15,000 of misstatement.
   a. Expenses can be audited for understatement by "searching for unrecorded liabilities" in the accounts payable within a tolerable misstatement of $15,000. This search is a difficult set of audit procedures, and it involves knowledge of all the accrued expenses the company should have recognized but may have forgotten (e.g., accrued rent, payroll, property taxes, and so forth).
   b. Expenses can be audited for overstatement by selecting samples of the recorded expenses and investigating them for accounting errors, again within tolerable misstatement of $15,000. An example of an accounting error is a repair expense that should have been capitalized.
5. Depreciation is not mentioned because, in this company's case, the number of fixed assets is small, the additions were acquired in a small number of transactions, and all the depreciation calculations can be recalculated. Even though the equipment asset number is large and the depreciation is an estimate, the balances can be audited completely, with no sampling risk of missing material misstatements.
6. Cash, loans payable, interest expense, and income tax expense can also be audited completely, so no tolerable misstatement is assigned to these accounts.

method. Consider the three allocations shown in Exhibit 4–1. The discussion that follows takes Case A as an example.

Cases B and C are given in Exhibit 4–1 to show that other allocations could be made. Each of them could be explained in the same manner as the six numbered items in the Exhibit 4–1 box. Indeed, some auditors might assign some tolerable misstatement to cash, loans, equipment, interest expense, and depreciation.

In the boxed explanation accompanying Exhibit 4–1, each materiality assignment starts with an expression of *tolerable misstatement* for an income statement number, and then the number is related to one or more balance sheet accounts. The reason for this phenomenon is that income misstatements in the double-entry bookkeeping system leave a "dangling debit" or a "dangling credit" loose somewhere in the balance sheet accounts, and the audit challenge is to find it. A "dangling debit" is the other side of a credit overstatement; for example, if sales revenue is overstated, a debit-balance account—accounts receivable or cash—is also overstated. A "dangling credit" is the other side of a debit overstatement; for example, if expenses are overstated, a credit-balance account—accounts payable or accrued expenses—is also overstated. This relation becomes tricky when expenses are understated; for example, if cost of goods sold is understated, some debits that should be in cost of goods sold remain in inventory, and the "dangling debit" resides in an inventory overstatement. Even trickier: if expenses are understated by omission of an accrual, the "dangling credit" is not even in the balance sheet. It is an unrecorded liability (credit) that *should* be among the liabilities but is not.

Throughout these explanations, you can see part of the materiality number described as *tolerable misstatement* with relation to one account at a time. Tolerable misstatement is the part of the overall materiality number assigned to an account. You will see tolerable misstatement used more later in connection with audit sampling applications.

R E V I E W
CHECKPOINTS

4.1 What is "material information" in accounting and auditing? What is "planning materiality" in an audit context?

4.2 Do auditing standards require auditors to express planning materiality as a specific dollar amount?

4.3 What do you think is the best objective evidence of the reasonableness of an accounting estimate? Use the allowance for doubtful accounts receivable as an example.

THE AUDIT RISK MODEL

LEARNING OBJECTIVE

2. Describe the conceptual audit risk model and explain the meaning and importance of its components in terms of professional judgment and audit planning.

We defined **information risk** as the probability that the financial statements distributed by a company will be *materially* false and misleading. Auditors' evidence-gathering and reporting reduce this risk to financial statement users, but auditors themselves face the risk of giving the wrong opinion on the financial statements—giving the unqualified audit opinion when unknown material misstatements (errors and frauds) actually exist in the statements. Auditing standards require auditors to design audits to provide reasonable assurance of detecting material errors and frauds (SAS 82, AU 316).

This overall risk is known as **audit risk**. It contains three major components—**inherent risk**, **control risk**, and **detection risk**. Since several adjectives are used to describe "risk" in auditing, you should always speak of risk with a modifier (audit, inherent, control, and detection) to specify the one you mean.

Audit Risk

In an overall sense, **audit risk** is the probability that an auditor will give an inappropriate opinion on financial statements. For example, the worst manifestation of this risk is giving an unqualified opinion on financial statements that are misleading because of material misstatements the auditors failed to discover. Such a risk always exists, even when audits are well planned and carefully performed. The risk is much greater in poorly planned and carelessly performed audits.

Audit risk is a conceptual *quality criterion* for audit performance. The auditing profession has no official standard for an acceptable level of overall audit risk, except that it should be "acceptably low." However, auditors would be appalled to think that even 1 percent of their audits would be bad. For a large firm with 2,000 audit clients, 1 percent would mean 20 bad audits per year! Conceptually, the overall audit risk ought to be less than 1 percent.

Audit risk is most often utilized in practice with regard to individual balances and disclosures. You should keep this context in mind when you study the risk model summary presented at the end of this section. In the overall sense and for an individual account or disclosure, the audit risk cannot be too high (e.g., 50 percent, the flip of a coin) or too low (e.g., zero). Some audit risk is allowable under GAAS, but not too much. Auditors specify it by professional judgment and firm policy.

Inherent Risk

Inherent risk is the probability that material errors or frauds have occurred in transactions entering the accounting system used to develop financial statements (SAS 39, AU 350; SAS 47, AU 312). You can think of inherent risk as the *susceptibility* of the account to misstatement. Inherent risk is a characteristic of the client's business, the major types of transactions, and the effectiveness of its accountants. Auditors do not create or control inherent risk. They can only try to assess its magnitude.

External auditors' basis for assessing a client's inherent risk is found in their familiarity with the types of errors, frauds, and misstatements that can occur in any account balance or class of transactions. Clearly, hundreds of innocent errors and not-so-innocent fraud schemes are possible. Instead of trying to learn hundreds of possible errors and frauds, it is better to start with seven general categories of them. In a sense, these categories answer the audit question: What can go wrong?" Exhibit 4–2 shows a typology of the seven categories, with some examples.

| EXHIBIT 4–2 | GENERAL CATEGORIES AND EXAMPLES OF ERRORS AND FRAUDS |

1. Invalid transactions are recorded: Fictitious sales are recorded and charged to nonexistent customers. (existence)
2. Valid transactions are omitted from the accounts: Shipments to customers never get recorded. (completeness)
3. Unauthorized transactions are executed and recorded: A customer's order is not approved for credit, yet the goods are shipped, billed, and charged to the customer without requiring payment in advance. (existance)
4. Transaction amounts are inaccurate: A customer is billed and the sale is recorded in the wrong amount because the quantity shipped and the quantity billed is not the same and the unit price is for a different product. (evaluation)
5. Transactions are classified in the wrong accounts: Sales to a subsidiary company are recorded as sales to outsiders instead of intercompany sales, or the amount is charged to the wrong customer account receivable record. (presentation / disclosure)
6. Transaction accounting and posting is incorrect: Sales are posted in total to the accounts receivable control account, but some are not posted to individual customer account records. (presentation or valuation)
7. Transactions are recorded in the wrong period: Shipments made in January (next year) are backdated and recorded as sales and charges to customers in December. Shipments in December are recorded as sales and charged to customers in January. (presentation, existance)

An assessment of inherent risk can be based on a variety of information. Auditors may know that material misstatements were discovered during the last year's audit, so inherent risk will be considered higher than it would be if last year's audit had shown no material misstatements. Auditors might believe the client's accounting clerks tend to misunderstand GAAP and the company's own accounting policies, thus suggesting a significant probability of mistakes in transaction processing. The nature of the client's business may produce complicated transactions and calculations generally known to be subject to data processing and accounting treatment error. For example, real estate, franchising, and oil and gas transactions are frequently complicated and subject to accounting error. Some kinds of inventories are harder than others to count, value, and keep accurately in perpetual records.

The concept of *relative* risk is closely related to inherent risk. In audit practice, **relative risk** refers to conditions of more or less inherent risk. Some accounts (e.g., cash and inventory) are more susceptible to embezzlement, theft, or other loss than are other accounts (e.g., land or prepaid expenses). The important relationship you should understand is that audit care and attention should be greater where relative risk and inherent risk are higher.

Control Risk

Control risk is the probability that the client's internal control activities will *fail* to detect material misstatements, provided any enter the accounting system in the first place (SAS 39, AU 350; SAS 47, AU 312). Auditors do not create or control the control risk. They can only evaluate a company's control system and assess the probability of failure to detect material misstatements.

The external auditors' task of control risk assessment starts with learning about a company's controls designed to prevent, detect, and correct the potential errors and frauds illustrated in Exhibit 4–2. The auditors then observe and test the controls, if necessary, to determine their effectiveness.

Control effectiveness conclusions and risk assessments may be made on a preliminary basis for planning purposes. Auditors often carry over preconceived notions about

---

AUDITING INSIGHT

INHERENT RISK ARISING FROM ECONOMIC CONDITIONS

Implications of an Economic Downturn

Auditors should be aware of the effects economic distress and slow recovery may have on their clients. The following reminders are particularly significant and pervasive:

- Asset valuations should be challenged in considering whether amounts are recoverable and the bases of accounting are appropriate.
- Inappropriate offsetting of assets and liabilities should be carefully evaluated.
- Changes in cost-deferral policies and the reasonableness of amortization periods should be carefully evaluated.
- Allowances for doubtful accounts, in general, and loan-loss allowances for financial institutions, in particular, should be evaluated carefully and thoroughly.
- Compliance with financial covenants and the necessity to obtain waivers from lending institutions to meet current requirements should be carefully reviewed.
- Changes in sales practices or terms that may require a change in accounting should be identified and considered.

Source: AICPA, Audit Risk Alert.

control risk when they perform the audit on a client year after year. This carryover is known as **anchoring** the control risk assessment (starting with knowledge of last year's conclusions), and it represents: (1) a useful continuity of experience with a particular client and (2) a potential pitfall if conditions change for the worse and the auditor fails to acknowledge the deterioration of control.

Control risk should not be assessed so low that auditors place complete reliance on controls and do not perform any other audit work.

Detection Risk

Detection risk is the probability that audit procedures will *fail* to produce evidence of material misstatements, provided any have entered the accounting system in the first place and have not been detected and corrected by the client's control activities (SAS 39, AU 350; SAS 47, AU 312). In contrast to inherent risk and control risk, auditors are responsible for performing the evidence-gathering procedures that manage and control detection risk. These audit procedures represent the auditors' opportunity to detect material misstatements that can cause financial statements to be misleading.

Later in this chapter, you will study substantive procedures. These are the procedures used to detect material misstatements in dollar amounts and disclosures presented in the financial statements and footnotes. The two categories of *substantive procedures* are: (1) audit of the *details of transactions and balances* and (2) *analytical procedures* applied to produce circumstantial evidence about dollar amounts in the accounts. Detection risk is realized when procedures in these two categories fail to detect material misstatements.

Risk Model—A Summary

The foregoing components of audit risk can be expressed in a model that assumes that each of the elements is *independent*. Thus, the risks are *multiplied* as follows:

Audit risk (AR) = Inherent risk (IR) $\times$ Control risk (CR) $\times$ Detection risk (DR)

Auditors want to perform an audit of a particular balance or disclosure well enough to hold the audit risk (AR) to a relatively low level (e.g., 0.05, which means that on average 5 percent of audit decisions will be wrong). As such, AR is a quality criterion based on professional judgment. All the other risk assessments are estimates based on professional judgment and evidence.

For example, suppose an auditor thought a particular inventory balance was subject to great inherent risk of material misstatement (say, IR = 0.90) and that the client's internal control was not very effective (say, CR = 0.70). If the auditor wanted to control audit risk at a low level (say, AR = 0.05), according to the model, this example would produce the following results:

$$AR = IR \times CR \times DR$$
$$0.05 = 0.90 \times 0.70 \times DR$$
$$\text{Solving for DR: } DR = 0.08$$

You should notice that detection risk (DR) depends upon the other risks. DR is derived from the others by solving the risk model equation. It is not an independent judgment. Hence:

$$DR = AR/(IR \times CR)$$
$$DR = .08 = 0.05/(0.90 \times 0.70)$$

While detection risk is defined as the risk that the auditors' procedures *fail* to discover material misstatements, it is important that you understand that the operationalization of DR is different. There is not an eight percent risk of the auditors' failing to detect a material misstatement, because the auditors have complete control of the procedures that they perform. The auditors can decide to audit everything and reduce detection risk to a negligible amount. Rather, the eight percent is the amount of risk the auditors can *allow* and still maintain overall audit risk at .05. In other words, the other procedures would need to be so designed that detection risk (DR) did not exceed 0.08 (approximately).

Based upon the allowable detection risk, auditors modify the *nature*, the *timing*, and the *extent* of their audit procedures. The nature of the tests refers to their overall *effectiveness* at detecting misstatements. While inquiring of management as to whether they are aware of any frauds occurring in the past year is an audit procedure, it certainly is not an *effective* one. Timing refers to when the audit procedures take place. The closer the procedures are performed to year-end (the date of the financial statements), the more effective they are considered. Finally, extent refers to the number of tests performed. Clearly the more accounts receivable confirmations that are mailed out to customers, the more effective the procedure.

The practical problem here is knowing whether the audit has been planned and performed well enough to hold the detection risk as low as 0.08. Despite the simplicity of the risk model, it is only a conceptual tool. Auditors have few ways to calculate detection risk, so the model represents more of a way to think about audit risks than a way to calculate them. However, several accounting firms use this model to calculate risks and the related sample sizes.

The model produces some insights, including these:

1. Auditors cannot rely entirely on an estimate of zero inherent risk to the exclusion of other evidence-gathering procedures. Thus, you cannot have the condition:

$$AR = IR\ (=0) \times CR \times DR = 0$$

2. Auditors cannot place complete reliance on internal control to the exclusion of other audit procedures. Thus, you cannot have the condition:

$$AR = IR \times CR\ (=0) \times DR = 0$$

3. Audits would not seem to exhibit due audit care if the risk of failure to detect material misstatements were too high, for example:

$$AR = IR\ (=0.80) \times CR\ (=0.80) \times DR\ (=0.50) = 0.32$$

4. Auditors can choose to rely almost exclusively on evidence produced by substantive procedures, even if they think inherent risk and control risk are high. For example, this combination is acceptable (provided AR = 0.05 is acceptable):

$$AR = IR\ (=1.00) \times CR\ (=1.00) \times DR\ (=0.05) = 0.05$$

Audit risk and detection risk go hand-in-hand with materiality. You cannot think usefully about audit risk and detection risk without also thinking about the size of misstatements.

R E V I E W
CHECKPOINTS

4.4 What are the four audit risks an auditor must consider? What does each involve?

4.5 What is anchoring with regard to auditors' judgments about the quality or effectiveness of internal control?

4.6 What are some of the effects of bad economic times that produce risks that auditors should be alert to detect in clients' financial statements?

4.7 What is the difference between "audit risk in an overall sense" and "audit risk applied to individual account balances"?

4.8 What is meant by the terms *nature*, *timing*, and *extent* of audit procedures?

Audit Programs

LEARNING OBJECTIVE

3. Describe the content and purpose of audit programs.

An **audit program** is a specification (list) of procedures designed to produce evidence directed toward achieving a particular objective. Auditors use two kinds of audit programs, each with a different objective. One contains the specification of procedures for obtaining an understanding of the client's business and management's control system and for assessing the inherent risk and the control risk related to the financial account balances. For identification purposes, we will call this program the "internal control program." The other contains the specification of substantive procedures for gathering direct evidence on the assertions (i.e., existence, completeness, valuation, rights and obligations, presentation and disclosure) about dollar amounts in the account balances. For identification, we will call this one the "balance-audit program."

These audit programs are the result of many considerations previously discussed, such as:

- Assertions and objectives embodied in the client's financial statements.
- Persuasive strengths of evidence.
- Preliminary risk assessments.
- Preliminary materiality decisions and tolerable misstatement assignments.

In actual field situations, these audit programs are very lengthy. Special program documents may contain separate listings of procedures and questionnaires on the company's internal control environment, internal control activities, management control, and computer control. The audit programs contain numerous detailed specifications of procedures the auditors intend to perform as the work progresses. The following two boxes abstract elements of audit programs for illustrative purposes.

INTERNAL CONTROL PROGRAM

Understand the Business, Inherent Risk, Control Risk

- Communicate with predecessor auditors. Study the company's 8-K report regarding auditor changes.
- Study prior-year audit working papers, AICPA audit and accounting guides, and industry publications concerning the company and its industry.
- Interview management with regard to business and accounting policies.
- Evaluate the competence and independence of the company's internal auditors.
- Determine the need for specialists on the engagement.
- Determine the extent of significant computer applications in the company's accounting system.
- Obtain the financial statements and make decisions about the planning materiality appropriate in the circumstances.
- Perform preliminary analytical procedures to identify risk areas in the financial statement accounts.
- Assess the inherent risk in general and with respect to particular accounts.

*****

- Obtain an understanding of the company's control system through interviews, observations, and tests of controls
- Perform detail test of control procedures, if necessary.
- Assess the control risk.
- Assess the risk of material misstatement due to fraud.
- Use the control risk assessment to design the nature, timing, and extent of substantive audit procedures.

BALANCE-AUDIT PROGRAM

Accounts Receivable

- Prepare and send confirmations on a sample of customers' accounts receivable. Analyze the responses.
- Obtain an aged trial balance of the receivables. Calculate and analyze the age status of the accounts and the allowance for uncollectible accounts.
- Interview the credit manager concerning the past-due accounts. Obtain credit reports and financial statements for independent analysis of overdue accounts.
- Vouch receivables balances to cash received after the confirmation date.
- Study loan agreements and make note of any pledge of receivables, sales with recourse, or other restrictions or contingencies related to the receivables.
- Study sales contracts for evidence of customers' rights of return or price allowance terms.
- Obtain written representations from the client concerning pledges for collateral, related party receivables, collectibility, and other matters related to accounts receivable.

The technical parts of internal control risk assessment programs are too detailed to cover at this stage. They are explained more fully in subsequent chapters.

The balance-audit program contains brief specifications of procedures for auditing accounts receivable. You can see the elements of general procedures (e.g., confirmation, recalculation, inquiry, examination of documents) and the assertions toward which they are directed. The balance-audit program approach typically consists of several audit programs, each applicable to a particular account or *cycle*.

Accounting Cycles

To simplify the audit plan, auditors typically group the accounts into several *cycles*. A **cycle** is a set of accounts that go together in an accounting system. This book uses these four cycles: (1) Revenue and collection cycle; (2) Acquisition and expenditure cycle; (3) Production and conversion cycle; and (4) Finance and investment cycle.

Using the revenue and collection cycle as an example, the idea of the cycle organization is to group together accounts related to one another by the transactions that normally affect them all. This cycle starts with a sale to a customer and a charge to cost of goods sold, along with recording an account receivable, which is later collected in cash or provided in an allowance for doubtful accounts. Auditors find it easier to audit such related accounts with a coordinated set of procedures instead of attacking each account as if it existed alone.

In Exhibit 4–3, the Kingston accounts are rearranged into *cycle* order. You can see that some accounts are in more than one cycle. For example, the cash account is represented in all the cycles, because: (a) cash receipts are involved in cash sales and collections of accounts receivable (revenue and collection cycle), (b) cash receipts are involved in deposit of stock issuance and loan proceeds (finance and investment cycle), (c) cash disbursements are involved in buying inventory and fixed assets and paying for expenses (acquisition and expenditure cycle), and (d) cash disbursements are involved in paying wages and overhead expenses (production and conversion cycle).

R E V I E W
CHECKPOINTS

4.9 Two kinds of audit programs have been identified. What are they? What is the objective of each?

4.10 What are four of the major "cycles" in an accounting system? What accounts can be identified with them?

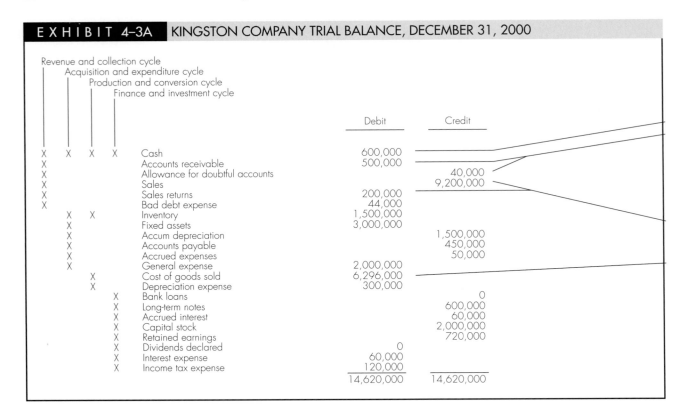

EXHIBIT 4–3A   KINGSTON COMPANY TRIAL BALANCE, DECEMBER 31, 2000

Revenue and collection cycle
    Acquisition and expenditure cycle
        Production and conversion cycle
            Finance and investment cycle

					Debit	Credit
X	X	X	X	Cash	600,000	
X				Accounts receivable	500,000	
X				Allowance for doubtful accounts		40,000
X				Sales		9,200,000
X				Sales returns	200,000	
X				Bad debt expense	44,000	
	X	X		Inventory	1,500,000	
	X			Fixed assets	3,000,000	
	X			Accum depreciation		1,500,000
	X			Accounts payable		450,000
	X			Accrued expenses		50,000
	X			General expense	2,000,000	
		X		Cost of goods sold	6,296,000	
		X		Depreciation expense	300,000	
			X	Bank loans		0
			X	Long-term notes		600,000
			X	Accrued interest		60,000
			X	Capital stock		2,000,000
			X	Retained earnings		720,000
			X	Dividends declared	0	
			X	Interest expense	60,000	
			X	Income tax expense	120,000	
					14,620,000	14,620,000

GENERAL AUDIT PROCEDURES

LEARNING OBJECTIVE

4. List and describe seven general types of audit procedures for gathering evidence.

An **account balance (substantive) audit program** is a specification (list) of procedures designed to produce evidence about the assertions in financial statements. Auditors use seven general procedures to gather evidence. One or more of these procedures may be used no matter what account balance, control procedure, class of transactions, or other information is under audit. Exhibit 4–4 shows seven types of evidence and the procedures most closely related to each.

1. Recalculation

Auditor recalculation of calculations previously performed by a client personnel produces compelling mathematical evidence. A client calculation is either right or wrong. Client calculations performed by computer programs can be recalculated using computer-assisted audit tools and techniques (CAATTs), with differences printed out for further audit investigation. Mathematical evidence can serve the objectives of both *existence* and *valuation* for financial statement amounts that exist principally as calculations (for example, depreciation, pension liabilities, actuarial reserves, statutory bad debt reserves, and product guarantee liabilities). Recalculation, in combination with other procedures, also is used to provide evidence of *valuation* for all other financial data.

2. Physical Observation

Physical inspection of tangible assets provides compelling evidence of *existence* and may provide tentative evidence of condition and *valuation*. In a strict sense, physical observation is limited to tangible assets and formal documents, such as securities certificates. In a broader sense, the procedure of physical observation is utilized whenever auditors

EXHIBIT 4-3B   KINGSTON COMPANY UNAUDITED FINANCIAL STATEMENTS

FINANCIAL POSITION

Cash	$ 600,000	Accounts payable	$ 450,000
Accounts receivable	460,000	Accrued expenses	110,000
Inventory	1,500,000	Current debt	200,000
Current Assests	$2,560,000	Current Liabilities	$ 760,000
Fixed assets (net)	$3,000,000	Long-term debt	$ 400,000
Accum. depreciation	(1,500,000)	Capital stock	$2,000,000
Fixed assets (net)	$1,500,000	Retained earnings	900,000
		Total Liabilities	
Total Assets	$4,060,000	and Stockholder Equity	$4,060,000

RESULTS OF OPERATIONS

Sales (net)	$9,000,000
Cost of goods sold	6,296,000
Gross Profit	$2,704,000
General expenses	$2,044,000
Depreciation expense	300,000
Interest expense	60,000
Operating Income Before Taxes	$ 300,000
Income Tax Expense	120,000
Net income	$ 180,000

CASH FLOWS

Operations:	
Net Income	$ 180,000
Depreciation	300,000
Increase in Accounts Receivable	(141,500)
Decrease in Inventory	50,000
Decrease in Accounts Payable	(25,000)
Decrease in Accrued Expenses	(15,000)
Decrease in Accrued Interest	(20,500)
Cash Flow from Operations	$(328,500)
Investing Activities:	
Purchase Fixed Assets	$ 0
Financing Activities:	
Repay Bank Loan	$(275,000)
Repay Notes Payable	(200,000)
Financing Activities	$(475,000)
Increase (Decrease) in Cash	$(146,500)
Beginning Balance	746,500
Ending Balance	$ 600,000

NOTES TO FINANCIAL STATEMENTS

1. Accounting Policies
2. Inventories
3. Plant and Equipment
4. Long-term Debt
5. Stock Options
6. Income Taxes
7. Contingencies
Etc.

EXHIBIT 4-4   TYPES OF EVIDENCE AND RELATED AUDIT PROCEDURES

Types of Evidence	Evidence-Gathering Procedures
1. Auditor's calculations.	1. Recalculation by the auditor. (valuation)
2. Physical observation, inspection.	2. Observation and examination by the auditor. (valuation, exis)
3. Statements by independent parties.	3. Confirmation by letter. (existence, rights)
4. Statements by client personnel.	4. Verbal inquiry and written representations. (all of them)
5. Documents prepared by independent parties.	5. Examination of documents (vouching or tracing). (existance, completeness)
6. Documents prepared by the client.	5. Examination of documents (vouching or tracing).
7. Data interrelationships.	6. Scanning.
	7. Analytical procedures.

view the client's physical facilities and personnel on an inspection tour, when they watch personnel carry out accounting and control activities, and when they participate in a surprise payroll distribution. Physical observation also can produce a general awareness of events in the client's offices.

3. Confirmation

Confirmation by direct correspondence with independent parties is a procedure widely used in auditing (SAS 67, AU 330). It can produce evidence of existence and ownership and sometimes of *valuation* and *cutoff*. Most transactions involve outside parties and, theoretically, written correspondence could be conducted even on such items as individual paychecks. However, auditors limit their use of confirmation to major transactions and balances about which outside parties could be expected to provide information. A selection of confirmation applications includes:

- Banks—account balances.
- Customers—receivables balances.
- Borrowers—note terms and balances.
- Agents—inventory on consignment or in warehouses.
- Lenders—note terms and balances.
- Policyholders—life insurance contracts.
- Vendors—accounts payable balances.
- Registrar—number of shares of stock outstanding.
- Attorneys—litigation in progress.
- Trustees—securities held, terms of agreements.
- Lessors—lease terms.

The important general points about confirmations are these:

- Confirmation letters should be printed on the client's letterhead, and signed by a client officer.
- Auditors should be very careful that the recipient's address is reliable and not subject to alteration by the client in such a way as to misdirect the confirmation.
- The request should seek information the recipient can supply, like the amount of a balance or the amounts of specified invoices or notes.
- Confirmations should be controlled by the audit firm, not given to client personnel for mailing. Auditing standards require direct communication.
- Responses should be returned directly to the audit firm, not to the client.

Confirmations of receivables and payables may take several forms. Two widely used forms are *positive confirmation* and *negative confirmation*. The **positive confirmation** requests a reply in all cases. The **negative confirmation** requests a reply only if the recipient considers the account balance to be incorrect. Auditors should try to obtain replies from all positive confirmations by sending second and third requests to nonrespondents. If there is no response to positive confirmations, or if the response to either positive or negative confirmations specifies an exception to the client's records, the auditors should investigate with other audit procedures.

4. Verbal Inquiry

Verbal inquiry is a procedure that generally involves the collection of oral evidence from independent parties and client officials. Statements must be obtained in a written representation letter for all important inquiries. Auditors use inquiry procedures during the early office and plant tour and when conferences are conducted. Evidence gathered by

AUDITING INSIGHT

Verbal Inquiry = Interview

Auditors conduct interviews almost every day. Sometimes they seem more like casual conversations than "interviews." Nevertheless, the following guides for the inquiry/interview procedure can help you obtain good information and maintain good relations with client personnel.

1. **Prepare.** Think about the information you want to obtain, the questions to ask, and the best person to interview.

2. **Make an Appointment.** Call in advance for a time or at least ask permission to interrupt: "Do you have time to talk with me about [subject]?" Introduce yourself and make enough conversation to warm up the person without wasting time.

3. **Don't Ask the Questions.** Try to get the person to describe the accounting, the controls, or whatever the subject in his or her own words. You will get more information. Just firing off questions makes the meeting an interrogation. Most auditors find it hard to think of all the right questions ahead of time anyway. Do not exhibit a questionnaire or checklist; doing so makes the interview too mechanical. You can take informal notes to remember the substance of the interview.

4. **Ask Questions.** Fill in the gaps in the person's description or explanation by asking prompting questions to elicit additional descriptions and explanations.

5. **Be Noncommittal.** Refrain from expressing your own value judgments or criticisms while you talk with the client person. Do not reveal any audit-sensitive information.

6. **Close Gracefully.** Thank the person for the time and information. Ask permission to return later for "anything I forgot."

7. **Document the Interview.** Write a memorandum for the audit working papers. Now you can get out the questionnaire or checklist, complete it, and see whether you overlooked anything important.

AUDITING INSIGHT

WHO'S LYING NOW?

This news item was released at the time of the U.S. Senate hearings on the Clarence Thomas nomination to the U.S. Supreme Court, after the Anita Hill information about sexual harassment became public (1991).

*****

Psychologist Paul Ekman has spent 30 years studying the art of lying. He knows the averted eyes, fleeting facial expressions and hesitations that characterize a person at war with the truth.

After viewing the Thomas-Hill contradictory testimony, Ekman concluded: "Whichever one started out lying is now totally convinced of what they are saying. People who have an enormous stake in distorting the truth can . . . convince themselves that what they prefer to believe truly happened. Most people think they can tell when someone is lying, but they can't." A study showed that police, judges, and even FBI agents cannot reliably separate truth-tellers from liars.

Source: News item from Los Angeles Times Service.

*****

So, what can most auditors do? The best strategy is first to distinguish new assertions from "evidence." Most responses to inquiries produce more management assertions about facts, estimates, or judgments. Second, verify the new assertions with other, independent evidence.

formal and informal inquiry generally cannot stand alone as convincing, and auditors must corroborate responses with independent findings based on other procedures. An exception to this general rule is a negative statement where someone volunteers adverse information, such as an admission of theft, fraud, or use of an accounting policy that is misleading.

5. Examination of Documents

Much auditing work involves gathering evidence by examining authoritative documents prepared by independent parties and by the client. Such documents can provide evidence regarding all five assertions.

Documents Prepared by Independent Outside Parties

A great deal of documentary evidence is external-internal. The most convincing documentation is that prepared by other parties and sent to the client. The signatures, seals, engraving, or other distinctive artistic attributes of formal authoritative documents make such sources more reliable (less susceptible to alteration) than ordinary documents prepared by outsiders. Some examples of both types of documents are listed below:

Formal Authoritative Documents	Ordinary Documents
1. Bank statements	1. Vendors' invoices
2. Canceled checks	2. Customers' purchase orders
3. Insurance policies	3. Loan applications
4. Notes receivable (on unique forms)	4. Notes receivable (on standard bank forms)
5. Securities certificates	5. Insurance policy applications
6. Indenture agreements	6. Simple contracts
7. Elaborate contracts	7. Correspondence
8. Title papers (e.g., autos)	

Documents Prepared and Processed within the Entity under Audit

Documentation of this type is internal evidence. Some of these documents may be quite informal and not very authoritative or reliable. As a general proposition, the reliability of these documents depends on the quality of internal control under which they were produced and processed. Some of the most common of these documents are:

Internal Documents	
1. Sales invoice copies	7. Shipping documents
2. Sales summary reports	8. Receiving reports
3. Cost distribution reports	9. Requisition slips
4. Loan approval memos	10. Purchase orders
5. Budgets and performance reports	11. Credit memoranda
6. Documentation of transactions with subsidiary or affiliated companies	12. Transaction logs
	13. Batch control logs (computer)

Vouching—Examination of Documents

The important point about *vouching* in the examination of documents is the *direction* of the search for audit evidence. In **vouching**, an item of financial information is selected from an account (e.g., the posting of a sales invoice in a customer's master file record), then the auditor goes *backward (downward)* through the accounting and control system to find the source documentation that supports the item selected. The auditor finds the journal entry or data input list, the sales summary, the sales invoice copy, and the shipping documents, and, finally, the customer's purchase order. Vouching of documents can help auditors decide whether all recorded data are adequately supported (the *existence/occurrence assertion*), but vouching does not provide evidence to show whether all events were recorded. (*Tracing* covers this problem.)

Tracing—Examination of Documents

Tracing in the examination of documents takes the *opposite* direction from vouching. When an auditor performs **tracing**, he or she selects sample items of basic source documents and proceeds *forward (upward)* through the accounting and control system (whether computer or manual) to find the final recording of the accounting transactions. For example, samples of payroll payments are traced to cost and expense accounts, sales invoices to the sales accounts, cash receipts to the accounts receivable subsidiary accounts, and cash disbursements to the accounts payable subsidiary accounts.

Using tracing, an auditor can decide whether all events were recorded (the *completeness assertion*), and complement the evidence obtained by vouching. However, you must be alert to events that may not have been captured in the source documents and not entered into the accounting system. For example, the search for unrecorded liabilities for raw materials purchases must include examination of invoices received in the period following the fiscal year-end and examination of receiving reports dated near the year-end. In practice, the terms vouch and trace are often used interchangeably. The important concept is the direction of the test.

6. Scanning   — not very competent evidence

Scanning is the way auditors exercise their general alertness to unusual items and events in clients' documentation. A typical scanning directive in an audit program is: "Scan the expense accounts for credit entries; vouch any to source documents."

In general, scanning is an "eyes-open" approach of looking for anything unusual. The scanning procedure usually does not produce direct evidence itself, but it can raise questions for which other evidence must be obtained. Scanning can be accomplished on computer records using computer audit software to select records to be printed out for further audit investigation. Typical items discovered by the scanning effort include debits in revenue accounts, credits in expense accounts, unusually large accounts receivable write-offs, unusually large paychecks, unusually small sales volume in the month following the year-end, and large cash deposits just prior to year-end. Scanning can contribute some evidence related to the existence of assets and the completeness of accounting records, including the proper cutoff of material transactions.

Scanning is valuable when sampling methods are applied in audit decisions. When a sample is the basis for selecting items for audit, the detection risk of choosing a sample that does not reflect the entire population of items always exists. Such an event may cause a decision error. Auditors subjectively reduce this detection risk by scanning items not selected in the sample and thus guard against decision error.

7. Analytical Procedures

Auditors can evaluate financial statement accounts by studying and comparing relationships among financial and nonfinancial data. The methods of study and comparison are known as **analytical procedures**. Auditors are required to use them when planning the audit (i.e., at the beginning) and when performing the final review of the financial statements before the audit report is issued (i.e., at the end of the audit). Auditors may use them to find evidence about management's assertions at other times during the audit work. (SAS 56, AU 329)

Analytical procedures are the "other" category in the list of general procedures. They are "everything else an auditor can think to do" that does not meet the definitions of recalculation, physical observation, confirmation, structured verbal inquiry, examination of documents, or scanning. The procedures themselves range from simple comparisons to applications of complex mathematical estimation models. They can be used to obtain evidence on any of the management assertions.

According to auditing standards, analytical procedures take the five general forms shown below. Auditors need to be careful to use independent, reliable information for analyses. Thus the sources of information shown for the analytical procedures are very important (SAS 56, AU 329).

Analytical Procedures	Sources of Information
1. Comparison of current-year account balances to balances of one or more comparable periods.	Financial account information for comparable period(s).
2. Comparison of the current-year account balances to anticipated results found in the company's budgets and forecasts.	Company budgets and forecasts.
3. Evaluation of the relationships of current-year account balances to other current-year balances for conformity with predictable patterns based on the company's experience.	Financial relationships among accounts in the current period.
4. Comparison of current-year account balances and financial relationships (e.g., ratios) with similar information for the industry in which the company operates.	Industry statistics.
5. Study of the relationships of current-year account balances with relevant nonfinancial information (e.g., physical production statistics).	Nonfinancial information, such as physical production statistics.

Because analytical procedures are loosely defined, many auditors consider the evidence they produce to be "soft." Therefore, auditors, professors, and students tend to concentrate on recalculation, observation, confirmation, and vouching of documents that are perceived to produce "hard" evidence. However, you should resist this distinction. Analytical procedures are, in fact, quite effective.

Hylas and Ashton collected evidence on misstatements requiring financial statement adjustment in a large number of audits.[1] They were interested primarily in describing the audit procedures used to detect the misstatements. Their definition of analytical procedures was broad. It included data comparisons, predictions based on outside data, analyses of interrelationships among account balances, "reasonableness tests," "estimates," and cursory review of financial statements in the audit planning stage. They also had two procedure categories called expectations from prior years (which involves the carryover of analytical and detail knowledge about continuing audit clients), and discussions with client personnel.

They found that auditors gave credit for misstatement discovery to analytical procedures for 27.1 percent of all misstatements. They gave credit to "expectations" and "discussions" for another 18.5 percent. Altogether, the so-called soft procedures accounted for detection of 45.6 percent of the misstatements. All of these procedures typically are applied early in the audit, so you should not infer that other kinds of audit procedures would or would not have detected the same misstatements. The detection success of other procedures depends on the results of the early applied procedures because, as this study was designed, even a good physical observation procedure did not get credit for "discovery" of a misstatement that already had been discovered using analytical procedures.

Auditors must consider the value of analytical procedures, especially since they are usually less costly than more detailed, document-oriented procedures. The "hard evidence" procedures, however, have their own pitfalls. Auditors might not be competent to "see" things they are supposed to observe. Clients can manipulate confirmations by giving auditors the addresses of conspirators or by asking customers just to "sign it and

[1] R. E. Hylas and R. H. Ashton, "Audit Detection of Financial Statement Errors," *Accounting Review*, October 1982, pp. 751–65.

send it back." An audit program consists of several different types of procedures, and analytical procedures deserve a prominent place.

4.11 What is meant by "vouching"? by "tracing"? by "scanning"?

4.12 What are the seven guides for performing an effective inquiry-interview procedure? Why should an auditor not start an interview with a set of prepared questions?

4.13 What can auditors do to improve the effectiveness of confirmation requests?

4.14 What are the five types of general analytical procedures?

4.15 Are analytical procedures very effective for discovering errors and misstatements?

EFFECTIVENESS OF AUDIT PROCEDURES

LEARNING OBJECTIVE

5. Discuss the effectiveness of various audit procedures.

Audits are supposed to be designed to provide reasonable assurance of detecting errors and frauds that are material to the financial statements (SAS 82, AU 316). When errors and frauds exist, and auditors do a good job of detecting them, adjustments will be made to management's unaudited financial statements before an audit report is issued. How often does this happen? Wright and Ashton obtained information on 186 audits performed by KPMG.[2] The reported frequency of audit adjustments is shown in Exhibit 4–5.

What kinds of misstatements did the auditors find? Wright and Ashton reported the data for 23 accounts. A selection of them is shown in Exhibit 4–6. The misstatements consisted of both understatements and overstatements. (However, you should remember that these are not "good" or "bad" descriptions. Overstatement of assets and understatement of liabilities both cause stockholders' equity to be overstated.) Since they come from respondents in one CPA firm, these data may not be generalizable to all audits. In this case, however, the overstatements/understatements look mixed in the current assets, understatements are in the majority in the noncurrent assets, understatements appear to be in the majority in the liabilities, and understatements appear to be in the majority in the expense accounts.

As you can see, discovery of misstatements in management's unaudited financial statements is not unusual. How do the auditors do it? What procedures do they find effective?

EXHIBIT 4–5	FREQUENCY OF AUDIT ADJUSTMENTS (Sample of audits from one CPA firm)

Number of Audit Adjustments*	Number of Audits	Percent of Audits
Zero or 1	22	12%
2–5	30	16
6–10	45	24
More than 10	89	48
Total	186	100%

*Total number of adjustments detected regardless of size or nature.

---

[2] Data for Exhibit 4–5 and the other related exhibits come from: A. Wright and R.H. Ashton, "Identifying Audit Adjustments with Attention-Directing Procedures," *The Accounting Review*, October 1989, pp. 710–28.

EXHIBIT 4–6   SUMMARY OF MISSTATEMENTS
(Selected Accounts)

Number of Misstatements

Account	Overstatement	Understatement
Cash	6	10
Securities	21	17
Accounts receivable	48	22
Inventory	24	32
Property, plant	14	23
Other noncurrent	11	24
Accounts payable	21	25
Accrued liabilities	17	40
Other current liabilities	10	13
Long-term liabilities	12	24
Revenue	32	30
Cost of goods sold	38	45
Selling expense	11	16
Gen. & admin. expense	39	52

Note: The effect of adjustments on income was that 43 percent of the adjustments reduced the reported income, while 28 percent increased the reported income. The other 29 percent of the adjustments were reclassifications that neither reduced nor increased income.

Wright and Ashton compiled data on seven "initial events" that identified misstatements in financial statements. They are called "initial events" instead of "audit procedures" because they were the first work that identified misstatements, and all of them do not correspond exactly with specific procedures auditors would list in an audit program. Exhibit 4–7 shows the initial events that indicated misstatements that required adjustment. The so-called soft information from expectations based on prior-year experience, analytical procedures, and client inquiry accounted for an overall 50 percent of the discovered misstatements. (These data are consistent with the earlier Hylas-Ashton study. See footnote 1.)

EXHIBIT 4–7   INITIAL EVENTS THAT IDENTIFIED ADJUSTMENTS
(Sample of audits from one CPA firm)

Initial Event	Number of Adjustments	Percent
Tests of details: examination of transaction amounts and descriptions, account balance details, workups to support account balances, data on various reconciliations	104	28.7%
*Expectations from the prior year	78	21.5
*Analytical procedures: comparison of current unaudited balances with balances of prior years, predictions of current balances based on exogenous data, analyses of interrelationships	56	15.5
*Client inquiry	48	13.3
Test of detail: checks for mathematical accuracy	35	9.7
General audit procedures	8	2.2

* These were the three "attention-directing procedures" that accounted for 50.3 percent of the identified adjustments.

Nevertheless, detail audit procedures also were effective. Wright and Ashton note that the "ordering effect" (the fact that the attention-directing procedures come first) biases the results against showing that detail procedures *might* have detected the misstatements if they had not already been detected. They note further that (1) few

POTHOLES IN THE AUDIT PROCEDURE ROAD

Recalculation

An auditor calculated inventory valuations (quantities x price), thinking the measuring unit was gross (144 units each), when the client had actually recorded counts in dozens (12 units each), thus causing the inventory valuation to be 12 times the proper measure.

Physical Observation

While observing the fertilizer tank assets in ranch country, the auditor was fooled when the manager was able to move them to other locations and place new numbers on them. The auditor "observed" the same tanks many times.

Confirmation

The insurance company executive gave the auditor a false address for a marketable securities confirmation, intercepted the confirmation, and then returned it with no exceptions noted. The company falsified $20 million in assets.

Verbal Inquiry

Seeking evidence of the collectibility of accounts receivable, the auditors "audited by conversation" and took the credit manager's word about the collection probabilities on the over-90-day past due accounts. They sought no other evidence.

Examination of Documents

The auditors did not notice that the bank statement had been crudely altered. (Can you find the alteration in the bank statement in Exhibit 7–3 in Chapter 7?)

Scanning

The auditors extracted a computer list of all the bank's loans over $1,000. They neglected to perform a similar scan for loans with negative balances, a condition that should not occur. The bank had data processing problems that caused many loan balances to be negative, although the trial balance balanced!

adjustments were initially signaled by confirmations or inventory observation and (2) simple methods of comparison and client inquiry detected many misstatements.

R E V I E W
CHECKPOINTS

4.16 Is there any pattern in auditors' experience in finding overstatements and understatements in accounts?

4.17 List several types of audit work (initial events, audit procedures) in their order of apparent effectiveness for identifying financial statement misstatements. Where would you put accounts receivable confirmation and inventory observation on this list?

AUDITING WITH COMPUTERS

LEARNING OBJECTIVE

6. Describe how a computer can be used as an audit tool.

Personal computers (PCs) are widely used in applications for planning, testing internal controls, and evidence collection. The role of PCs in revolutionizing auditing warrants a complete section devoted to the auditor-developed applications that have served to increase audit efficiency and effectiveness. You already know how to prepare accounting schedules with spreadsheet software and to use word processing software to prepare your class papers. Auditing software makes use of these same computer software tools to prepare auditing working papers, audit programs, and audit memos.

Computer-Assisted Audit Tools and Techniques

Auditors use personal computers regularly in small and large public accounting firms to perform such clerical steps as preparing the working trial balance, posting adjusting entries, grouping accounts that represent one line item on the financial statement into lead schedules, computing comparative financial statements and common ratios for analytical procedures, preparing supporting workpaper schedules, and producing draft financial statements. Many firms also use personal computers to assess control risk, perform sophisticated analytical functions on individual accounts, access public and firm databases for analysis of unusual accounting and auditing problems, and utilize decision support software to make complex evaluations. Exhibit 4–8 illustrates the different phases a typical public accounting firm or internal audit department might experience when developing expertise in using personal computers as audit tools.

Following assessment of control risk in a computer environment, the auditor's task is to gain access to machine-readable detail records, to select samples of items for manual or computer audit procedures, to perform calculations and analyses of entire data files, and to produce audit working papers of the work performed. **Computer-assisted audit tools and techniques (CAATTs)** include programs that may be utilized to read,

EXHIBIT 4–8   USING THE COMPUTER AS AN AUDIT TOOL

Applications	Goals and Objectives	Software Available
Phase 1: Automating the Audit Process		
Trial balance and working papers.	Overall audit efficiency.	Automated work papers vendor supplied, developed by CPA firms and others.
Adjusting and updating financial data.	Automation of time-consuming activities.	Firm developed or vendor supplied.
Time and budget data.	Improved control.	Firm developed or vendor supplied.
Audit program, memo, and report generation.	Efficient and more readable.	Word processing.
Financial statement and consolidation preparation.	Efficient automation.	Firm developed or vendor supplied.
Tax return preparation and analysis.	Efficient automation.	Firm developed or vendor supplied.
Phase 2: Basic Auditing Functions		
Spreadsheet analysis working papers.	Efficiency in common working papers.	Vendor supplied, firm-developed uses.
Analytical procedures.	Improved overall analysis of ratios, fluctuations.	Part of automated workpaper packages.
Sampling planning, selection, and evaluation.	Evidence collection and evaluation efficiency.	Statistical, firm developed.
Text retrieval.	Search GAAP and GAAS pronouncements.	Public resources (e.g., Compact Disclosure, LEXUS-NEXIS, FARS, ReSOURCE) or firm developed.
Phase 3: Advanced Auditing Functions		
Analytical procedures for specific accounts.	Improved auditor analysis.	Firm developed.
Access to client files on larger computers.	Ability to download directly into automated workpaper software.	Vendor supplied or firm developed.
Access to firm and public databases.	Provide auditor with reference information.	Personal computer as a terminal, Internet.
Modeling and decision support systems.	Improved auditor decisions.	Firm-developed decision support systems.
Continuous monitoring.	Improved audit effectiveness.	Firm developed or vendor supplied.

compute, and operate on machine-readable records. These software packages provide access to audit evidence that otherwise would be unavailable. You need to know about CAATTS because they are used on most audits in which the client's accounting records are stored in computer files or in a database. While the use of CAATTs was once reserved for the information system auditor, the programs have evolved to become much more user friendly to the point that if you understand spreadsheet software, you can use most of the audit-specific functions.

For the most part, the widely used CAATTS packages are very similar. Most have been developed from standard spreadsheet and database applications with which you are already familiar. The applications, however, have been modified so that auditors can perform common audit tasks at the touch of a button by accessing predeveloped macros (subroutines). The essential advantages of CAATTs include:

- Original programming is not required. CAATTs packages consist of a set of preprogrammed editing, operating, and output subroutines.
- The same software can be used on various clients' computer systems.
- Training time is short. About one week of intensive training is sufficient to learn how to use a CAATTS package.

Audit Procedures Performed by CAATTS

Computer accounting applications capture and generate voluminous amounts of data that usually are available only on machine-readable records. CAATTS can be used to access the data and organize it into a format useful to the audit team. Audit software can be used to accomplish five basic types of audit procedures:

1. *Recalculation.* The computer can verify calculations with more speed and accuracy than can be done by hand. The audit software can be used to test the accuracy of client computations and to perform analytical procedures to evaluate the reasonableness of account balances. Examples of this use are to (a) recalculate depreciation expense, (b) recalculate extensions on inventory items, (c) compute file totals, and (d) compare budgeted, standard, and prior-year data with current-year data.

2. *Confirmation.* Auditors can program statistical or judgmental criteria for selecting customers' accounts receivable, loans, and other receivables for confirmation. The CAATTS can be used to print the confirmations and get them ready for mailing. It can do everything except carry them to the post office!

3. *Document Examination* (limited). CAATTS can compare audit evidence from other sources to company records efficiently. The audit evidence must be converted to machine-readable form and then can be compared to the company records on computer files. Examples are (a) comparing inventory test counts with perpetual records, (b) comparing adjusted audit balances on confirmed accounts receivable to the audit file of the book balances, and (c) comparing vendor statement amounts to the company's record of accounts payable.

4. *Scanning.* Auditors can use CAATTS to examine records to determine quality, completeness, consistency, and correctness. This is the computer version of scanning the records for exceptions to the auditors' criteria. For example, scan (a) accounts receivable balances for amounts over the credit limit, (b) inventory quantities for negative balances or unreasonably large balances, (c) payroll files for terminated employees, or (d) loan files for loans with negative balances.

5. *Analytical Procedures.* CAATTS functions can match data in separate files to determine whether comparable information is in agreement. Differences can be printed out for investigation and reconciliation. Examples are comparing (a) payroll details with personnel records, (b) current and prior inventory to details of purchases and sales, (c) paid vouchers to check disbursements, and (d) current- and prior-year fixed asset records to identify dispositions. CAATTS can also

summarize and sort data in a variety of ways. Examples are (a) preparing general ledger trial balances, (b) sorting inventory items by location to facilitate observations, and (c) summarizing inventory turnover statistics for obsolescence analysis.

6. *Fraud Investigation.* CAATTS can be used in a variety of ways to search for fraudulent activities. For example, lists of vendor addresses can be compared to employee address files to see whether employees are paying invoices to companies that they own or operate. Duplicate payments can be found by sorting payments by invoice number and amount paid. Telephone records can be quickly sorted and scanned to ensure that employees are not misusing company telephones.

CAATTs Software Limitations

Notwithstanding the powers of the computer, several general auditing procedures are outside its reach. The computer cannot observe and count physical things (inventory, for example), but it can compare auditor-made counts to the computer records. The computer cannot examine external and internal documentation; thus, it cannot vouch accounting output to sources of basic evidence. An exception would exist in a computer system that stores the basic source documents on magnetic media. Auditors need to test the controls over creation of the files but then have no choice but to treat the file as a basic "document" source. However, when manual vouching is involved, computer-assisted selection of sample items is a great efficiency. Finally, CAATTS can never take the place of the auditor's professional judgment (determining the reasonableness of the allowance for doubtful accounts, for example).

R E V I E W
CHECKPOINTS

4.18 What are computer assisted audit tools and techniques (CAATTs)?

4.19 What audit tasks can be accomplished with word processing software? Spreadsheet software?

4.20 What are some audit procedures that can be performed using CAATTs?

4.21 What advantages are derived from using CAATTs to perform recalculations? To select samples and print confirmations?

SUMMARY

Chapter 4 begins a series of audit planning topics by explaining several technical tools of planning. While classified as planning tools, they provide a fundamental basis for many of the decisions made throughout the audit process.

The technical planning tools include auditors' determination of materiality with relation to the financial statements taken as a whole. Materiality in this sense is defined as the largest amount of uncorrected dollar misstatement that could exist in published financial statements, yet the statements would still fairly present the company's financial position and results of operations in conformity with GAAP. A method of calculating materiality based on judgments about acceptable misstatement is presented to connect income misstatement to earnings-per-share misstatements and an effect on stock prices. The "second leg" of materiality determination is assigning the overall materiality to the tolerable misstatement acceptable in particular accounts. The tolerable misstatement is the amount by which an account can be misstated without exceeding the overall materiality criterion for the whole audit.

Risk assessment is the common language of auditing. The SAS 39 "audit risk model" is explained, and its components of audit risk, inherent risk, control risk, and detection risk are defined. Implications of the risk model are explored in relation to limits on the risks permitted in practical applications.

Solving for detection risk in the audit risk model yields guidance for the *nature, timing,* and *extent* of audit procedures to be performed. Audit procedures are intended to enable auditors to conduct the work in accordance with the three AICPA fieldwork standards concerning planning and supervision of the audit, obtaining an understanding of the internal control, and obtaining sufficient competent evidence to serve as a basis for the audit report. The exact specification of the procedures, the arrangement for their timing (i.e., *when* they are performed), and the determination of their extent (i.e., the *sample sizes* of data examined, such as the number of customer accounts receivable to confirm) all depend upon the activities, concepts, and tools of audit planning. This explanation of procedures is enriched with additional notes about the ways in which procedures can be misapplied. Analytical procedures are introduced, and their power is illustrated with some empirical research findings based on actual audit results.

Audit programs are lists of audit procedures to be performed, and are categorized as "internal control programs" and "balance-audit programs." The illustrations are not complete programs for conducting any particular audit, but they show the general nature and content of audit programs.

Computer auditing is not something for future consideration. It is encountered in almost every audit today. Computer usage in audit fieldwork is explained in terms of its efficiency for using spreadsheets and word processors. The advantages of using the computer to obtain substantive evidence are explained in the context of computer-assisted audit tools and techniques (CAATTS). The future no doubt holds significant promise for development in decision aids and expert systems.

MULTIPLE-CHOICE QUESTIONS FOR PRACTICE AND REVIEW

4.22 Auditors are not responsible for accounting estimates with respect to
a. Making the estimates.
b. Determining the reasonableness of estimates.
c. Determining that estimates are presented in conformity with GAAP.
d. Determining that estimates are adequately disclosed in the financial statements.

4.23 Tolerable misstatement in the context of audit planning means
a. Amounts that should be disclosed if they are likely to influence the economic decisions of financial statement users.
b. The largest amount of uncorrected dollar misstatement that could exist in published financial statements, yet they would still fairly present the company's financial position and results of operations in conformity with GAAP.
c. Part of the overall materiality amount for the financial statements assigned to a particular account.
d. A dollar amount assigned to an account as required by auditing standards.

4.24 The risk that the auditors' own work will lead to the decision that material misstatements do not exist in the financial statements, when in fact such misstatements do exist is
a. Audit risk.
b. Inherent risk.
c. Control risk.
d. Detection risk.

4.25 Auditors are responsible for the quality of the work related to management and control of
a. Inherent risk.
b. Relative risk.
c. Control risk.
d. Detection risk.

4.26 The auditors assessed a combined inherent risk and control risk at 0.50 and said they wanted to achieve a 0.05 risk of failing to detect misstatements in an account equal to the $17,000 tolerable misstatement assigned to the account. What detection risk do the auditors plan to use for planning the remainder of the audit work?
a. 0.20.
b. 0.10.
c. 0.75.
d. 0.00.

4.27   An audit program contains
   a. Specifications of audit standards relevant to the financial statements being audited.
   b. Specifications of procedures the auditors believe appropriate for the financial statements under audit.
   c. Documentation of the assertions under audit, the evidence obtained, and the conclusions reached.
   d. Reconciliation of the account balances in the financial statements with the account balances in the client's general ledger.

4.28   The revenue cycle of a company generally includes these accounts
   a. Inventory, accounts payable, and general expenses.
   b. Inventory, general expenses, and payroll.
   c. Cash, account receivable, and sales.
   d. Cash, notes payable, and capital stock.

4.29   When auditing the existence assertion for an asset, auditors proceed from the
   a. Financial statement numbers back to the potentially unrecorded items.
   b. Potentially unrecorded items forward to the financial statement numbers.
   c. General ledger back to the supporting original transaction documents.
   d. Supporting original transaction documents to the general ledger.

4.30   Which of the following is not a benefit claimed for the practice of determining materiality in the initial planning stage of starting an audit?
   a. Being able to fine-tune the audit work for effectiveness and efficiency.
   b. Avoiding the problem of doing more work than necessary (overauditing).
   c. Being able to decide early what kind of audit opinion to give.
   d. Avoiding the problem of doing too little work (underauditing).

4.31   Jones, CPA, is planning the audit of Rhonda's Company. Rhonda verbally asserts to Jones that all the expenses for the year have been recorded in the accounts. Rhonda's representation in this regard
   a. Is sufficient evidence for Jones to conclude that the completeness assertion is supported for the expenses.
   b. Can enable Jones to minimize his work on the assessment of control risk for the completeness of expenses.
   c. Should be disregarded because it is not in writing.
   d. Is not considered a sufficient basis for Jones to conclude that all expenses have been recorded.

4.32   It is appropriate and acceptable under generally accepted auditing standards for an auditor to
   a. Assess both inherent and control risk at 100 percent and achieve an acceptably low audit risk by performing extensive detection work.
   b. Assess control risk at zero and perform a minimum of detection work.
   c. Assess inherent risk at zero and perform a minimum of detection work.
   d. Decide that audit risk can be 40 percent.

4.33   Confirmations of accounts receivable provide evidence primarily about these two assertions
   a. Completeness and valuation.
   b. Valuation and rights and obligations.
   c. Rights and obligations and existence.
   d. Existence and completeness.

4.34   Spreadsheet software would be most useful for which of the following audit activities?
   a. Testing internal controls over computerized accounting applications.
   b. Preparing an audit program.
   c. Preparing a comparison of current year expenses with those from the previous year.
   d. Drafting a planning memo.

4.35   Which of the following is an advantage of computer-assisted audit tools and techniques (CAATTs)?
   a. The CAATTS programs are all written in one identical computer language.
   b. The software can be used for audits of clients that use differing computer equipment and file formats.
   c. CAATTS has reduced the need for the auditor to study input controls for computer-related procedures.
   d. The use of CAATTS can be substituted for a relatively large part of the required testing.

4.36   A primary advantage of using computer-assisted audit tools and techniques in the audit of an advanced computer system is that it enables the auditor to
   a. Substantiate the accuracy of data through self-checking digits and hash totals.
   b. Utilize the speed and accuracy of the computer.

c. Verify the performance of machine operations which leave visible evidence of occurrence.

d. Gather and store large quantities of supportive evidential matter in machine-readable form.

4.37 With respect to the concept of materiality, which one of the following statements is correct?

a. Materiality depends only on the dollar amount of an item relative to other items in the financial statements.

b. Materiality depends on the nature of a transaction rather than the dollar amount of the transaction.

c. Materiality is determined by reference to AICPA guidelines.

d. Materiality is a matter of professional judgment.

4.38 If tests of controls induce the auditor to change the assessed level of control risk for PP&E from 0.4 to 1.0, and audit risk (.05) and inherent risk remain constant, the acceptable level of detection risk is most likely to

a. Change from .1 to .04.

b. Change from .2 to .3.

c. Change from .25 to .1.

d. Be unchanged.

EXERCISES AND PROBLEMS

4.39 General Audit Procedures and Financial Statement Assertions. The seven general audit procedures produce evidence about the principal management assertions in financial statements. However, some procedures are useful for producing evidence about certain assertions, while other procedures are useful for producing evidence about other assertions. The assertion being audited may influence the auditors' choice of procedures.

Required:
Prepare a two-column table with the seven general procedures listed on the right. Opposite each one, write the management assertions most usefully audited by using each procedure.

4.40 Financial Assertions and Audit Objectives. You were engaged to examine the financial statements of Spillane Company for the year ended December 31.

Assume that, on November 1, Spillane borrowed $500,000 from Second National Bank to finance plant expansion. The long-term note agreement provided for the annual payment of principal and interest over five years. The existing plant was pledged as security for the loan.

Due to the unexpected difficulties in acquiring the building site, the plant expansion did not begin on time. To make use of the borrowed funds, management decided to invest in stocks and bonds, and on November 16 the $500,000 was invested in securities.

Required:
What are the audit objectives for the audit of the investments in securities at December 31?

Approach: Develop specific assertions related to securities (assets) based on the five general assertions.

4.41 Calculate a Planning Materiality Amount. The auditors were planning the work on the financial statements of the Mary Short Cosmetics Company. The unaudited financial statements showed $515,000 net income after providing an allowance of 35 percent for income taxes. The company had no debt and no interest expense. Mary Short's stock is traded over the counter, and investors have generally assigned a price-earnings multiple of 16 to the stock. Press releases by the company have enabled analysts to estimate the income for the year at about $515,000, which was forecast by the company at the beginning of the year. There are 750,000 shares outstanding, and the last quoted price for the stock was $11.

The auditors have decided that a 6 percent mispricing error in the stock would not cause investors to change their buying and selling decisions.

Required:
Calculate the "planning materiality" the auditors could allow, based on the income before income taxes.

4.42 Audit Risk Model. Audit risks for particular accounts and disclosures can be conceptualized in the model: Audit risk (AR) = Inherent risk (IR) = Internal control risk (CR) = Detection risk (DR). Use this model as a framework for considering the following situations and deciding whether the auditor's conclusion is appropriate.

1. Paul, CPA, has participated in the audit of Tordik Cheese Company for five years, first as an assistant accountant and the last two years as the senior accountant. He has never seen an accounting adjustment recommended. He believes the inherent risk must be zero.

2. Hill, CPA, has just (November 30) completed an exhaustive study and evaluation of the internal control system of Edward Foods, Inc. (fiscal year ending December 31). She believes the control risk must be zero because no material errors could possibly slip through the many error-checking procedures and review layers used by Edward.

3. Fields, CPA, is lazy and does not like audit jobs in Philadelphia, anyway. On the audit of Philly Manufacturing Company, he decided to use detail procedures to audit the year-end balances very thoroughly to the extent that his risk of failing to detect material errors and irregularities should be 0.02 or less. He gave no thought to inherent risk and conducted only a very limited review of Philly's internal control system.

4. Shad, CPA, is nearing the end of a "dirty" audit of Allnight Protection Company. Allnight's accounting personnel all resigned during the year and were replaced by inexperienced people. The comptroller resigned last month in disgust. The journals and ledgers were a mess because the one computer specialist was hospitalized for three months during the year. Thankfully, Shad thought, "I've been able to do this audit in less time than last year when everything was operating smoothly."

(AICPA adapted)

4.43   Audit Procedures.   Auditors frequently refer to the terms standards and procedures. Standards deal with measures of the quality of performance. Standards specifically refer to the generally accepted auditing standards expressed in the Statements on Auditing Standards. Procedures relate to the acts performed by auditors to gather evidence. Procedures specifically refer to the methods or techniques used by auditors in the conduct of the examination. Procedures are also expressed in the Statements on Auditing Standards.

Required:
List seven different types of procedures auditors can use during an audit of financial statements and give an example of each.

4.44   Confirmation Procedure.   A CPA accumulates various kinds of evidence on which to base the opinion on financial statements. Among this evidence are confirmations from third parties.

Required:
a. What is an audit confirmation?

b. What characteristics of the confirmation process and the recipient are important if a CPA is to consider the confirmation evidence competent?

4.45   Auditing an Accounting Estimate. Suppose management estimated the lower-of-cost-or-market valuation of some obsolete inventory at $99,000, and wrote it down from $120,000, recognizing a loss of $21,000. The auditors obtained the following information: The inventory in question could be sold for an amount between $78,000 and $92,000. The costs of advertising and shipping could range from $5,000 to $7,000.

Required:
a. Would you propose an audit adjustment to the management estimate? Write the appropriate accounting entry.

b. If management's estimate of inventory market (lower than cost) had been $80,000, would you propose an audit adjustment? Write the appropriate accounting entry.

DISCUSSION CASES

4.46   Risk Assessment.   This question consists of 15 items pertaining to an auditor's risk analysis for a company. Your task is to tell how each item affects overall audit risk—the probability of giving an unqualified audit report on materially misleading financial statements.

Bond, CPA, is considering audit risk at the financial statement level in planning the audit of Toxic Waste Disposal (TWD) Company's financial statements for the year ended December 31, 2001. TWD is a privately owned company that contracts with municipal governments to remove environmental wastes. Audit risk at the overall financial statement level is influenced by the risk of material misstatements, which may be indicated by a combination of factors related to management, the industry, and the company.

Required:
Based only on the following information, indicate whether each of the following factors (Items 1 through 15) would most likely increase overall audit risk, decrease overall audit risk, or have no effect on overall audit risk. Discuss your reasoning.

Company Profile

1. This was the first year TWD operated at a profit since 1996 because the municipali-

ties received increased federal and state funding for environmental purposes.

2. TWD's board of directors is controlled by Mead, the majority stockholder, who also acts as the chief executive officer.

3. The internal auditor reports to the controller and the controller reports to Mead.

4. The accounting department has experienced a high rate of turnover of key personnel.

5. TWD's bank has a loan officer who meets regularly with TWD's CEO and controller to monitor TWD's financial performance.

6. TWD's employees are paid biweekly.

7. Bond has audited TWD for five years.

Recent Developments

8. During 2001, TWD changed its method of preparing its financial statements from the cash basis to generally accepted accounting principles.

9. During 2001, TWD sold one half of its controlling interest in United Equipment Leasing (UEL) Co. TWD retained significant interest in UEL.

10. During 2001, litigation filed against TWD in 1996 alleging that TWD discharged pollutants into state waterways was dropped by the state. Loss contingency disclosures that TWD included in prior years' financial statements are being removed for the 2001 financial statements.

11. During December 2001, TWD signed a contract to lease disposal equipment from an entity owned by Mead's parents. This related party transaction is not disclosed in TWD's notes to its 2001 financial statements.

12. During December 2001, TWD completed a barter transaction with a municipality. TWD removed waste from a municipally owned site and acquired title to another contaminated site at below-market price. TWD intends to service this new site in 2002.

13. During December 2001, TWD increased its casualty insurance coverage on several pieces of sophisticated machinery from historical cost to replacement cost.

14. Inquiries about the substantial increase in revenue TWD recorded in the fourth quarter of 2001 disclosed a new policy. TWD guaranteed several municipalities that it would refund the federal and state funding paid to TWD if any municipality fails federal or state site clean-up inspection in 2002.

15. An initial public offering of TWD's stock is planned for late 2002.

4.47 Discovering Intentional Financial Misstatements in Transactions and Account Balances—Using the Computer. AMI International was a large office products company. Headquarters management imposed pressure on operating division managers to meet profit forecasts. The division managers met these profit goals using several accounting manipulations involving the recordkeeping system that maintained all transactions and account balances on computer files. Employees who operated the computer accounting system were aware of the modifications of policy the managers ordered to accomplish the financial statement manipulations. The management and employees carried out these activities:

1. Inventory write-downs for obsolete and damaged goods were deferred.

2. The sales entry system was kept open after the quarterly and annual cutoff dates, recording sales of goods shipped after the cutoff dates.

3. Transactions coded as leases of office equipment were recorded as sales.

4. Shipments to branch offices were recorded as sales.

5. Vendors' invoices for parts and services were not recorded until later, but the actual invoice date was faithfully entered according to accounting policy.

Required:

Describe one or more procedures that could be performed with computer assisted audit tools and techniques (CAATTs) to detect signs of each of these transaction manipulations. Limit your answer to the actual work accomplished by the computer software.

4.48 Potential Audit Procedure Failures. For each of the general audit procedures of (a) recalculation, (b) physical observation, (c) confirmation (accounts receivable, securities, or other assets), (d) verbal inquiry, (e) examination of internal documents, and (f) scanning, discuss one way the procedure could be misapplied or the auditors could be misled in such a way as to render the work (audit evidence) misleading or irrelevant. Give examples different from the examples in Chapter 4.

4.49 Risk of Misstatement in Various Accounts. Based on information you have available in Chapter 4:

a. Which accounts may be most susceptible to overstatement? To understatement?

b. Why do you think a company might permit asset accounts to be understated?

c. Why do you think a company might permit liability accounts to be overstated?

d. Which direction of misstatement is most likely: income overstatement or income understatement?

4.50.   Internet Exercise: Audit Programs on the Internet.   Auditnet **(www.auditnet.org)** is a website that provides support for practicing internal and external auditors. One of its resources is Auditors Sharing Audit Programs (ASAP), a library of audit programs for a number of different audit areas. If you need an audit program, you can simply visit the sites, download a program, and modify it to meet the needs of your client's engagement.

Required

Access the Auditnet website, browse through the programs, and download an audit program that interests you.

Chapter 5
Audit Planning

Professional Standards References

Compendium Section	Document Reference	Topic
AU 310	SAS 83	*Establishing an Understanding with the Client*
AU 311	SAS 22	*Planning and Supervision*
AU 9311		*Interpretations: Communication with Non-Audit Personnel, Responsibility of Assistants*
AU 312	SAS 47	*Audit Risk and Materiality in Conducting an Audit*
AU 313	SAS 45	*Substantive Tests Prior to the Balance Sheet Date*
AU 315	SAS 84	*Communication between Predecessor and Successor Auditors*
AU 316	SAS 82	*Consideration of Fraud in a Financial Statement Audit*
AU 322	SAS 65	*Auditor's Consideration of Internal Audit Function*
AU 326	SAS 80	*Evidential Matter*
AU 9326		*Interpretation: Auditor's Consideration of the Completeness Assertion*
AU 329	SAS 56	*Analytical Procedures*
AU 330	SAS 67	*The Confirmation Process*
AU 331	SAS 1	*Inventories*
AU 334	SAS 45	*Related Parties*
AU 9334		*Interpretations: Related Parties*
AU 336	SAS 73	*Using the Work of a Specialist*
AU 339	SAS 41	*Working Papers*
AU 9339		*Interpretation: Providing Working Papers to a Regulator*
AU 341	SAS 59	*Auditor's Consideration of an Entity's Ability to Continue as a Going Concern*

Learning Objectives

Chapter 5 covers the role of planning in an independent audit of financial statements beginning with preengagement arrangements. Other planning topics covered in this chapter include gaining an understanding of the client's business and industry, analytic procedures, and the role of computers in planning an audit. The chapter concludes with format and content of audit workpapers. After studying Chapter 5, you should be able to:

1. List and describe the activities auditors undertake before beginning an audit.

2. Identify the procedures and sources of information auditors can use to obtain knowledge of a client's business and industry.

3. Perform analytical procedures using unaudited financial statements to identify potential problems in the accounts.

4. List and discuss matters of planning auditors should consider for clients who use computers.

5. Review an audit working paper for proper form and content.

PREENGAGEMENT ARRANGEMENTS

LEARNING OBJECTIVE

1. List and describe the activities auditors undertake before beginning an audit.

Auditors undertake several activities before beginning any audit work on a client's financial statements. In general, these activities can be called *risk management activities*. Risk in an audit engagement generally refers to the probability of something going wrong. Auditors try to reduce risk by carefully managing the engagement. The flip side of risk management is *quality management*, which was discussed previously under the title of "Quality Control Standards." The topics discussed next can best be understood in the context of risk management and quality management.

Client Selection and Retention

An important element of an accounting firm's quality control policies and procedures is a system for deciding to accept a new client and, on a continuing basis, deciding whether to resign from audit engagements. Accounting firms are not obligated to accept undesirable clients, nor are they obligated to continue to audit clients when relationships deteriorate or when the management comes under a cloud of suspicion.

Client acceptance and retention policies and procedures include: (1) obtaining and reviewing financial information about the prospective client—annual reports, interim statements, registration statements, Form 10-Ks, and reports to regulatory agencies; (2) inquiring of the prospective client's banker, legal counsel, underwriter, or other persons who do business with the company for information about the company and its management; (3) communicating with the predecessor auditor, if any, for information on the integrity of management, on disagreements with management about accounting principles, auditing procedures, or similar matters, and on the reasons for a change of auditors; (4) considering whether the engagement would require special attention or involve unusual risks; (5) evaluating the accounting firm's independence with regard to the prospective client; and (6) considering the need for special skills (e.g., computer auditing or specialized industry knowledge).

One large accounting firm often requires a search of business press and legal files on the Lexis-Nexis system. The firm searches for news articles, lawsuits and bankruptcy court outcomes naming the company, the chairman of the board, the CEO, the CFO, and other high-ranking officers. The firm engages an outside search firm (private investigators) to conduct additional searches for information when the prospective clients are financial institutions, companies accused of fraud, companies under SEC or other regulatory investigation, companies that have changed auditors frequently, and companies showing recent losses. These characteristics are "red flags" for the auditors, and they intend to be careful to know as much as they can about the companies and their officers.

Decisions to continue auditing a client are similar to acceptance decisions, except that the accounting firm will have more firsthand experience with the company. Retention reviews may be done periodically (say, annually) or upon occurrence of major events, such as changes in management, directors, ownership, legal counsel, financial condition, litigation status, nature of the client's business, or scope of the audit engagement. In general, conditions which would have caused an accounting firm to reject a prospective client may develop and lead to a decision to discontinue the engagement. For example, a client company may expand and diversify on an international scale so that a small accounting firm may not have the competence to continue the audit. It is not unusual to see newspaper stories about accounting firms dropping clients after directors or officers admit to falsification of financial statements or to theft and misuse of corporate assets.

Communication between Predecessor and Successor Auditors

When companies change auditors, the former auditor is the *predecessor*, and the new auditor is the *successor*. Experience has shown that managements have fired their auditors because of arguments about the scope of the audit or the acceptability of accounting principles. Sometimes, these arguments involve auditors' access to necessary evidence, questions of early revenue recognition, or disputes over deferral of expenses and losses.

A successor auditor is required to initiate contact with, and *attempt* to obtain basic information directly from, the predecessor (SAS 84, AU 315). However, the AICPA Code of Professional Conduct does not permit the predecessor to give information obtained during the terminated engagement without the explicit consent of the client. Confidentiality remains even when the auditor-client relationship ends. Therefore, auditing

AUDITING INSIGHT

MORE ACCOUNTING FIRMS ARE DUMPING RISKY CLIENTS

A growing number of high-level executives are suffering from rejection—by their accountants.

Hoping to protect themselves, the company's most prestigious accounting firms are turning more aggressive in dumping audit clients they deem to be high–risk.

Accounting industry officials say the crackdown on potential problem clients is only beginning. All the largest firms have taken dramatic steps to mitigate risk in their client base.

One Big 5 firm booted 74 public companies in the period 1994–1997, another firm ditched 47. A partner explained the trend: "When we looked back at the lawsuits we've had, we realize that a large number could have been avoided if we had been more careful about the clients we selected."

The firms say they have to boot clients because shareholder and creditors of troubled companies have sued them so often in the recent years over allegedly faulty audits.

To ferret out potential lemons, accounting firms have increased their scrutiny of information that prospective clients submit about everything from finance to management changes. Accountants are grilling former auditors about management integrity.

On top of their other problems, companies that have trouble with their auditors may have a tough time getting new auditors. "Now, we won't take a client that has fired its previous accounting firm over an accounting dispute, because it indicates a greater risk."

Source: *Wall Street Journal*

standards require the successor auditor to ask that the consent be given to permit the predecessor auditor to speak. If this consent is refused, the successor auditor should be wary.

To reduce the risk of accepting a new client that represents a business and lawsuit risk, auditing standards require the successor to inquire specifically about these topics (SAS 84, AU 315):

- Facts that might bear on the integrity of management.
- Disagreements the predecessor may have had with management about accounting principles and auditing procedures.
- Communications the predecessor gave the former client about:
  - Fraud.
  - Illegal acts.
  - Internal control recommendations.
- The predecessor's understanding about the reasons for the change of auditors (particularly about the predecessor's termination).

Engagement Letters

When a new audit client is accepted, and when an auditor continues to audit a company from year to year, an **engagement letter** should be prepared. This letter sets forth the understanding with the client, including in particular (a) the objectives of the engagement, (b) management's responsibilities, (c) the auditor's responsibilities, and (d) any limitations of the engagement. Other matters of understanding like the ones shown in Exhibit 5–1 can be included in the letter. Auditing standards require auditors to document the understanding in the audit working papers, preferably in the form of a written letter (SAS 83, AU 310). In effect, the engagement letter is the audit contract. Thus, it serves as a means for reducing the risk of misunderstandings with the client and as a means of avoiding legal liability for claims that the auditors did not perform the work promised.

Many accounting firms also have policies about sending a **termination letter** to former clients. Such a letter is a good idea because it provides an opportunity to deal with the subject of future services, in particular: (a) access to working papers by a successor auditor (refer to the preceding discussion about predecessor and successor auditors), (b) reissuance of an audit report when required for SEC reporting or comparative financial reporting, and (c) fee arrangements for such future services. The termination letter can also contain a report of the auditor's understanding of the circumstances of termination (e.g., disagreements about accounting principles and auditing procedures, fees, or other conflicts). These matters may be of great interest to a prospective successor auditor who knows to ask for a copy of the termination letter.

Staff Assignment

When a new client is obtained, most accounting firms assign a full-service team. This team usually consists of the audit engagement partner (the person with final responsibility for the audit); the audit manager; an industry specialist; one or more senior audit staff members; statistics and computer specialists (if needed); a tax partner; a consulting services partner; and a second audit partner. The tax and consulting partners are consultants to the audit team if the engagement does not include other specific tax and consulting work contracted by the client.

The **second audit partner** is one who reviews the work of the audit team. This partner is supposed to have a detached professional point of view because he or she is not directly responsible for "keeping the client happy." A second audit partner is required for audits of financial statements filed with the U.S. Securities and Exchange Commission. On SEC engagements, the audit engagement partner is required to rotate to other clients so he or she does not remain in charge of a particular client for more than seven years.

EXHIBIT 5–1 ENGAGEMENT LETTER

Anderson, Olds, and Watershed
Certified Public Accounts
Chicago, Illinois

July 15, 2000

Mr. Larry Lancaster
Kingston Company
Chicago, Illinois

Dear Mr. Lancaster:

This will confirm our understanding of the arrangements for auditing the Kingston Company financial statements for 2000.

We will audit the balance sheet at December 31, 2000, and the related statements of income, retained earnings, and cash flows for the year ending that date. Our audit will be made in accordance with generally accepted auditing standards and will include such tests of the accounting records and such other auditing procedures as we consider necessary.

Our audit will be based on samples of recorded transactions. We will plan the audit to detect material errors and frauds that may affect your financial statements. However, our work is subject to the unavoidable risk that errors, frauds, and illegal acts, if they exist, will not be detected. We expect to obtain reasonable but not absolute assurance that major misstatements do not exist in the financial statements. Our findings regarding your system of internal control, including information about reportable control conditions and material weaknesses, will be reported to the audit committee of your board of directors in a separate letter at the close of the audit.

At your request, we will perform the following other services: (1) timely preparation of all required federal tax returns and (2) a review and report on the company's methods for estimating current cost information on your real estate assets.

We will provide your staff with a package of blank schedules needed by our staff during the audit. The delivery dates have been discussed and mutually agreed upon. We understand that your staff will prepare all the schedules in the package, all the financial statements and notes thereto, and the Form 10-K for our review. The scope of our services does not include preparation of any of these financial statements.

Mr. Dalton Wardlaw will be the partner in charge of all work performed for you. He will inform you immediately if we encounter any circumstances that could significantly affect our fee estimate of $60,000 discussed with you on July 1, 2000. He is aware of the due date for the audit report, February 15, 2001. You should feel free to call on him at any time.

If the specifications above are in accordance with your understanding of the terms of our engagement, please sign below and return the duplicate copy to us. We look forward again to serving you as independent public accountants.

Sincerely yours,

Arnold Anderson, CPA

Accepted by _____   Date _____

Time Budget

The partner and manager in charge of the audit prepare a plan for the timing of the work and set the number of hours that each segment of the audit is expected to take. Time budgets are used to maintain control of the audit by identifying problem areas early in the engagement, thereby ensuring that the audit is completed on a timely basis. Time budgets are usually based on last year's performance for continuing clients, taking changes in the client's business into account. In a first-time audit, the budget may be based on a predecessor auditor's experience or on general experience with similar companies. A simple time budget is shown on the following page.

The time budget is illustrative. Real time budgets are much more detailed. Some specify the expected time by level of staff people on the team (partner, manager, in-charge accountant, staff assistant, specialist). The illustration shows time at *interim* and at *year-end*. **Interim audit work** refers to procedures performed several weeks or months before the balance sheet date. **Year-end audit work** refers to procedures performed shortly before and after the balance sheet date. Audit firms typically spread the workload out during the

	Audit Time Budget (hours)	
	Interim	Year-end
Knowledge of the business	15	
Internal audit familiarization	10	
Internal control evaluation	30	10
Audit program planning	25	
Related parties investigation	5	10
Client conferences	10	18
Cash	10	15
Accounts receivable	15	5
Inventory	35	20
Accounts payable	5	35
Representation letters		20
Financial statement review		25
Report preparation		12

year by scheduling interim audit work so they will have enough time and people available when several audits have year-ends on the same date (December 31 is common). For many audit firms, the audit "busy season" runs from October through April of the following year. The interim work can consist of both internal control risk assessment work (SAS 55, AU 319) and audit of balances as they exist at the early date (SAS 45, AU 313).

Everyone who works on the audit reports the time taken to perform procedures for each segment of the audit. These time reports are recorded by budget categories for the purposes of (1) evaluating the efficiency of the audit team members, (2) compiling a record for billing the client, and (3) compiling a record for planning the next audit. Time budgets create job pressures. Staff members are under pressure to "meet the budget," and beginning auditors often experience frustration over learning how to do audit work efficiently.

R E V I E W
CHECKPOINTS

5.1 What sources of information can a CPA use in connection with deciding whether to accept a new client? What methods can a CPA use?

5.2 Why does a predecessor auditor need to obtain the client's consent to give information to a successor auditor? What information should a successor auditor try to obtain from a predecessor auditor?

5.3 What benefits are obtained by having an engagement letter? What is a termination letter?

5.4 What persons and skills are normally assigned to a "full-service" audit team?

UNDERSTANDING THE CLIENT'S BUSINESS

LEARNING OBJECTIVE

2. Identify the procedures and sources of information auditors can use to obtain knowledge of a client's business and industry.

Knowledge and understanding of the client's business in the context of the client's industry is absolutely essential in an audit. Auditing standards require the audit team to obtain a thorough understanding of the business to plan and perform the audit work (SAS 22, AU 311). The understanding and planning culminates in an **audit program**, which is a list of the audit procedures necessary to obtain sufficient, competent evidence that will serve as the basis for the audit report. Auditing standards require a *written* audit program (*SAS 22*, AU 311). A mental program "in my head" is not sufficient.

Auditors must understand the broad economic environment in which the client operates, including such things as the effects of national economic policies (e.g., price regulations and import/export restrictions), the geographic location and its economy (northeastern states versus Sunbelt states), and developments in taxation and regulatory areas (e.g., energy industry deregulation, approval processes in the drug and chemical industries). Industry characteristics are important. There is a great deal of difference in the production and marketing activities of banks, insurance companies, mutual funds, supermarkets, hotels, oil and gas, agriculture, manufacturing, and so forth. Few auditors are experts in all these businesses. Audit firms typically have people who are expert in one or two industries and rely on them to manage audits in those industries. Indeed, some CPA firms have reputations for having many audit clients in a particular industry, while other CPA firms have a larger presence in other industries.

Methods and Sources of Information

Numerous sources of information are available for obtaining the understanding of the client's business and industry. They can be categorized by the methods auditors use in practice.

Inquiry and Observation of Client Personnel
Interviews with the company's management, directors, and audit committee can bring auditors up to date on changes in the business and the industry. Such inquiries of client personnel have the multiple purposes of building personal working relationships, observing the competence and integrity of client personnel, obtaining general understanding, and probing gently for problem areas that might harbor financial misstatements. Other early information-gathering activities include (a) review of the corporate charter and bylaws or partnership agreement; (b) review of contracts, agreements, and legal proceedings, and (c) reading and study of the minutes of the meetings of directors and committees of the board of directors. The minutes provide a history of the company, identifying key *related parties*, critical events and transactions, and future company intentions. A company's failure to provide minutes is a significant scope limitation that may result in the audit firm disclaiming an opinion on the company's financial statements.

At the same time that inquiries and interviews take place, the audit team can take a tour of the company's physical facilities. Auditors use this time to look for activities and issues that should be reflected in the accounting records. For example, an auditor might notice a jumbled pile of materials and parts in the warehouse and make a note to check for its inventory condition and valuation. The tour is the time to see company personnel in their normal workplaces. Later, the auditors will meet these same people in direct evidence-gathering circumstances.

Review of Prior Working Papers
For continuing audits, specific information about the client is available in prior year audit working papers and in the client *permanent files*. Personnel who worked on the audit in prior years are available to convey their understanding of the business. In addition, auditing research has found that client errors are often repeated one year to the next, so auditors review prior year proposed adjustments to identify recurring problem areas. For example, accounting firms often develop client income tax provisions once the audit is complete, thus the income tax adjusting entry would show up as an adjustment every year.

Study Industry Accounting and Auditing Practices
Numerous sources for reading material are available. The AICPA industry accounting and auditing guides are a good place to start. (Their titles are listed on the inside back

---

AUDITING INSIGHT

WHAT'S IN THE MINUTES OF MEETINGS?

Boards of directors are supposed to monitor the client's business. The minutes of their meetings and the meetings of their committees (e.g., executive committee, finance committee, compensation committee, audit committee) frequently contain information of vital interest to the independent auditors. Some examples:

- Amount of dividends declared.
- Authorization of officers' salaries.
- Authorization of stock options and other "perk" compensation.
- Acceptance of contracts, agreements, lawsuit settlements.
- Approval of major purchases of property and investments.
- Discussions of merger and divestiture progress.
- Authorization of financing by stock issues, long-term debt, and leases.
- Approval to pledge assets as security for debts.
- Discussion of negotiations on bank loans and payment waivers.
- Approval of accounting policies and accounting for estimates and unusual transactions.
- Authorizations of individuals to sign bank checks.

Auditors take notes or make copies of important parts of these minutes and compare them to information in the accounts and disclosures (e.g., compare the amount of dividends declared to the amount paid, compare officers' authorized salaries to amounts paid, compare agreements to pledge assets to proper disclosure in the notes to financial statements).

---

cover of this book.) These guides explain the typical transactions and accounts used by various kinds of businesses and not-for-profit organizations. In addition, most industries have specialized trade magazines and journals. You may not choose to read *Grocer's Spotlight* for pleasure, but magazines of this special type are very valuable for learning and maintaining an industry expertise. Specific information about public companies can be found in registration statements and 10-K reports filed with the SEC.

In addition, many companies present "company story" information on World Wide Web pages. A visit to the site can provide a wealth of information about products, markets, and strategies.

General business magazines and newspapers often contribute insights about an industry, a company, and individual corporate officers. Many are available, including such leaders as *Business Week, Forbes, Fortune, Harvard Business Review, Barron's,* and *The Wall Street Journal.* Practicing auditors typically read several of these regularly.

Other Aspects of Planning

The general understanding discussed above can lead to some specific areas for further investigation and planning.

Materiality and Planning

The major reason for thinking about materiality at the planning stage is to try to fine-tune the audit for effectiveness and efficiency. Thinking about it in advance helps to avoid surprises. Suppose near the end of an audit, the partner decided that individual and aggregate misstatements over $40,000 should be considered material, but then realized that the nature, timing, and extent of audit procedures resulted in an acceptable audit risk only at the $70,000 level! More work should be done, and now it is very late to do it. Conversely, an audit team might **overaudit**—perform more audit work than is necessary, thinking in terms of detecting $70,000 in total misstatement when accuracy to the nearest $100,000 is satisfactory.

AUDITING INSIGHT

SOURCES OF BUSINESS AND INDUSTRY INFORMATION

General Information

Dun & Bradstreet Principal International Businesses.
Standard & Poor's Register of Corporations, Directors, and Executives.
Value Line Investment Survey.
Moody's manuals (various industries).
Standard & Poor's Corporation Records.
Statistical Abstract of the United States.
Dun & Bradstreet, Key Business Ratios.

Communications Media

Broadcasting-Cablecasting Yearbook (annual).
Advertising Age (twice weekly).
Broadcasting (weekly).
Publishers Weekly (weekly).
Variety (weekly).

Source: CPA firm compendium of "Sources of Industry Data."

First-Time Audits

A first audit requires more work than a repeat engagement. If an existing company has been operating for a while but has never been audited, the additional work includes an audit of the beginning balances in the balance sheet accounts. The starting place for the audited accounting must be established with reliable account balances. Such accounts as inventory, fixed assets, and intangible assets affect the current-year income and cash flow statements. This work may involve going back to audit several years' transactions that make up the balance sheet accounts.

Internal Auditors

Audit efficiency can be realized by working in tandem with internal auditors. Independent auditors should understand a company's internal audit activities as they relate to the system of internal control. Internal auditors can also assist with performance of parts of the audit under the supervision of the independent audit team. Prior to using internal auditors, external auditors should consider internal auditors' objectivity (to whom do they report) and competence. Competence can be gauged by reviewing internal auditor qualifications and workpapers. Finally, internal auditors should never be given tasks that require the external auditors' professional judgment. Thus, while internal auditors may perform bank reconciliations, they normally would not be involved in assessing the reasonableness of the company's allowance for doubtful accounts.

Identification of Related Parties

During planning, auditors take measures to identify **related parties**, those individuals or organizations that are closely tied to the auditee, possibly by familial or investment relationships. Since one of the basic assumptions of historical cost accounting is that transactions are valued at prices agreed upon by two *objective* parties, *valuation* of related party transactions are particularly troublesome. Auditing standards (*SAS 45, AU 334,* "Related Parties") state that "The auditor should be aware that the substance of a particular transaction could be significantly different from its form and that financial statements should recognize the substance of particular transactions, rather than merely their legal form." Auditors strive to identify related party relationships and transactions during planning so as to be able to obtain evidence that the financial accounting and disclosure for them are proper.

A second concern with related parties is that evidence obtained from them should not be considered highly competent in terms of persuasiveness. The source of the evidence may be biased. Hence, auditors should obtain evidence of the purpose, nature, and extent of related party transactions and their effect on financial statements, and the evidence should extend beyond inquiry of management.

Specialists

The understanding of the business can lead to information that indicates the need to employ *specialists* on the audit. **Specialists** are persons skilled in fields other than accounting and auditing—actuaries, appraisers, attorneys, engineers, and geologists—who are not members of the audit team. Auditors are not expected to be expert in all fields of knowledge that may contribute information to the financial statements. When a specialist is engaged, auditors must know about his or her professional qualifications, experience, and reputation. A specialist should be unrelated to the company under audit, if possible. Auditors must obtain an understanding of a specialist's methods and assumptions. Provided some additional auditing work is done on the data used by the specialist, auditors may rely on the specialist's work in connection with audit decisions (SAS 73, AU 336).

Analytical Procedures

The auditors' own analyses of the client's financial statements can contribute a significant understanding of the business, and how it has operated for the period covered by the financial statements. Analytical procedures (e.g., ratio and comparison analyses) applied at the beginning of the audit can point out specific areas of audit risk. These applications are explained in more detail later in this chapter.

Planning Memorandum

Auditors usually prepare a **planning memorandum** summarizing the preliminary analytical procedures and the materiality assessment with specific directions about the effect on the audit. This planning memo also usually includes information about: (1) investigation or review of the prospective or continuing client relationship, (2) needs for special technical or industry expertise, (3) staff assignment and timing schedules, (4) the assessed level of control risk, (5) significant industry or company risks, (6) computer system control environment, (7) utilization of the company's internal auditors, (8) identification of unusual accounting principles problems, and (9) schedules of work periods, meeting dates with client personnel, and completion dates. The memo summarizes all the important overall planning information.

All the planning becomes a basis for preparing the *audit program*. An **audit program** is a specification of procedures that auditors use to guide the work of inherent and control risk assessment and to obtain sufficient competent evidence that serves as a basis for the audit report. An illustrative excerpt from a planning memorandum is shown on the next page. It connects a tolerable misstatement assignment to a preliminary analytical observation and an audit program procedural plan suggestion.

The next section deals with preliminary analytical procedures and their usefulness for providing auditors insights about where potential material misstatements might lie in the unaudited accounts. The preliminary analytical work performed in the planning stage of an audit is sometimes called *specific risk analysis*, meaning that potentially troublesome accounts are identified for special audit attention. The concept of *materiality* is used to distinguish significant potential problem areas from unimportant ones.

Alpha.com, Inc.

Planning Memo (excerpt)

Inventory

We need to pay particular attention to the audit of physical inventory on hand and the valuation of inventory.

Our materiality assessment analysis assigned $35,000 tolerable misstatement to the inventory presented in the unaudited amount of $1,600,000. However, the preliminary analytical procedures showed a potential inventory overstatement in the amount of $225,000 (if the prior-year cost of goods sold ratio of 75% is again appropriate to the current year).

In our audit program, we should be careful to provide procedures to: (1) interview production managers and inquire about purchase price experience, physical volume of products sold and inventoried, and accounting procedures for transferring costs from inventory to cost of goods sold; (2) schedule our observation of the physical inventory for the year-end date and perform extensive test-counting of quantities on hand selected from the perpetual inventory records; and (3) select a large sample of items for price-testing and lower-of-cost-or-market analysis.

R E V I E W CHECKPOINTS

5.5 What are some of the types of knowledge and understanding about a client's business and industry an auditor is expected to obtain?

5.6 What are some of the methods and sources of information for understanding a client's business and industry?

5.7 What's the problem with evidence obtained from related parties?

5.8 What is the primary benefit for auditors' preliminary assessment of materiality as a matter of audit planning?

PRELIMINARY ANALYTICAL PROCEDURES

LEARNING OBJECTIVE

3. Perform analytical procedures using unaudited financial statements to identify potential problems in the accounts.

According to auditing standards, analytical procedures must be applied in the beginning planning stages of each audit (SAS 56, AU 329). The purpose of this work is "attention directing"—to alert the audit team to problems (errors, frauds) in the account balances and disclosures. Analytical procedures were introduced earlier and described in terms of five general types of procedures. For review, they are:

1. Comparison of current-year account balances to balances for one or more comparable periods.
2. Comparison of the current-year account balances to anticipated results found in the company's budgets and forecasts.
3. Evaluation of the relationships of current-year account balances to other current-year balances for conformity with predictable patterns based on the company's experience.
4. Comparison of current-year account balances and financial relationships (e.g., ratios) with similar information for the industry in which the company operates.
5. Study of the relationships of current-year account balances with relevant nonfinancial information (e.g., physical production statistics).

Analytical procedures can take many forms, ranging from simple to complex. Auditors look for relationships that do not make sense as indicators of problems in the accounts,

AUDITING INSIGHT

SOME EXAMPLES OF ANALYTICAL PROCEDURES

Auditors noticed large quantities of rolled steel in the company's inventory. Several 60,000-pound rolls were entered in the inventory list. The false entries were detected because the auditor knew the company's fork-lift trucks had a 20,000-pound lifting capacity.

*****

Auditors could have compared the total quantity of vegetable oils the company claimed to have inventoried in its tanks to the storage capacity reported in national export statistics. The company's "quantity on hand" amounted to 90 percent of the national supply and greatly exceeded its own tank capacity.

*****

Last year's working papers showed that the company employees had failed to accrue wages payable at the year-end date. A search for the current accrual entry showed it had again been forgotten.

*****

Auditors programmed a complex regression model to estimate the electric utility company's total revenue. They used empirical relations of fuel consumption, meteorological reports of weather conditions, and population census data in the area. The regression model estimated revenue within close range of the reported revenue.

and they use such indicators to plan further audit work. **Horizontal analysis** refers to changes of financial statement numbers and ratios across two or more years. **Vertical analysis** refers to financial statement amounts expressed each year as proportions of a base, such as sales for the income statement accounts and total assets for the balance sheet accounts. Other analytical procedures can be complex, including mathematical time series and regression calculations, complicated comparisons of multiyear data, and trend and ratio analyses.

Attention Directing

In the planning stage, analytical procedures are used to identify potential problem areas so subsequent audit work can be designed to reduce the risk of missing something important. The application thus can be described as *attention directing*—pointing out accounts that may contain errors and frauds. The insights derived from *preliminary* analytical procedures do not provide direct evidence about the numbers in the financial statements. They only help the audit team plan the audit program.

An Organized Approach

With an organized approach—a standard starting place—preliminary analytical procedures can provide considerable familiarity with the client's business. Many auditors start with comparative financial statements and calculate common-size statements (vertical analysis) and year-to-year change in balance sheet and income statement accounts (horizontal analysis). This is the start of describing the financial activities for the current year under audit. Exhibit 5–2 contains financial balances for the prior year (consider them audited) and the current year (consider them unaudited at this stage). Common-size statements (vertical) are shown in parallel columns, and the dollar amount and percentage change (horizontal) are shown in the last two columns. These are some basic beginning analytical data.

EXHIBIT 5–2	ALPHA.COM, INC.—PRELIMINARY ANALYTICAL PROCEDURES DATA					
	Prior Year		Current Year		Change	
Income	Balance	Common Size	Balance	Common Size	Amount	Percent Change
Sales (net)	$9,000,000	100.00%	$9,000,000	100.00%	$ 900,000	10.00%
Cost of goods sold	6,750,000	75.00	7,200,000	72.73	450,000	6.67
Gross margin	2,250,000	25.00	2,700,000	27.27	450,000	20.00
General expense	1,590,000	17.67	1,734,000	17.52	144,000	9.06
Depreciation	300,000	3.33	300,000	3.03	0	0.00
Operating income	360,000	4.00	666,000	6.46	306,000	85.00
Interest expense	60,000	0.67	40,000	0.40	(20,000)	−33.33
Income taxes (40%)	120,000	1.33	256,000	2.59	136,000	113.33
Net income	$ 180,000	2.00%	$ 370,000	3.74%	$ 190,000	105.56%
Assets						
Cash	$ 600,000	14.78%	$ 200,000	4.12%	($ 400,000)	−66.67%
Accounts receivable	500,000	12.32	900,000	18.56	400,000	80.00
Allowance doubtful accounts	(40,000)	−0.99	(50,000)	−1.03	(10,000)	25.00
Inventory	1,500,000	36.95	1,600,000	32.99	100,000	6.67
Total current assets	2,560,000	63.05	2,650,000	54.63	90,000	3.52
Equipment	3,000,000	73.89	4,000,000	82.47	1,000,000	33.33
Accumulated depreciation	(1,500,000)	−36.95	(1,800,000)	−37.11	(300,000)	20.00
Total assets	$4,060,000	100.00%	$4,850,000	100.00%	$ 790,000	19.46%
Liabilities and Equity						
Accounts payable	$ 500,000	12.32%	$ 400,000	8.25%	($ 100,000)	−20.00%
Bank loans, 11%	0	0.00	750,000	15.46	750,000	
Accrued interest	60,000	1.48	40,000	0.82	(20,000)	−33.33
Total current liabilities	560,000	13.79	1,190,000	24.53	630,000	112.50
Long-term debt, 10%	600,000	14.78	400,000	8.25	(200,000)	−33.33
Total liabilities	1,160,000	28.57	1,590,000	32.78	430,000	37.07
Capital stock	2,000,000	49.26	2,000,000	41.24	0	0.00
Retained earnings	900,000	22.17	1,260,000	25.98	360,000	40.00
Total liabilities and equity	$4,060,000	100.00%	$4,850,000	100.00%	$ 790,000	19.46%

Describe the Financial Activities

After generating these basic financial data, the next step is to describe the financial changes and relationships you can see in the data. According to the current-year unaudited financial statements in Exhibit 5–2, the company increased the net income by increasing sales 10 percent, reducing cost of goods sold as a proportion of sales, and controlling other expenses. At least some of the sales growth appears to have been prompted by easier credit (larger accounts receivable) and more service (more equipment in use). The company also used much of its cash and borrowed more to purchase the equipment, to make its payment on the long-term debt, and to pay dividends.

Ask Relevant Questions

The next step is to ask: "What could be wrong?" and "What errors and frauds, as well as legitimate explanations, could account for these financial results?" For this explanation, we will limit attention to the accounts receivable and inventory accounts. At this point, some other ratios can help support the analysis. Exhibit 5–3 contains several familiar ratios. (Appendix 5A at the end of this chapter contains these ratios and their formulas.)

   Question: Are the accounts receivable collectible? (*Alternative:* Is the allowance for doubtful accounts large enough?) Easier credit can lead to more bad debts. The company

EXHIBIT 5–3	ALPHA.COM, INC.—SELECTED FINANCIAL RATIOS

	Prior Year	Current Year	Percent Change
Balance Sheet Ratios			
Current ratio	4.57	2.23	–51.29%
Days' sales in receivables	18.40	30.91	67.98
Doubtful accounts ratio	0.0800	0.0556	–30.56
Days' sales in inventory	80.00	80.00	0.00
Debt/equity ratio	0.40	0.49	21.93
Operations Ratios			
Receivables turnover	19.57	11.65	–40.47
Inventory turnover	4.50	4.50	0.00
Cost of goods sold/sales	75.00%	72.73%	–3.03
Gross margin percentage	25.00%	27.27%	9.09
Return on beginning equity	6.62%	12.76%	92.80
Financial Distress Ratios (Altman)			
Working capital/total assets	0.49	0.30	–38.89
Retained earnings/total assets	0.22	0.26	17.20
EBIT/total assets	0.09	0.14	54.87
Market value of equity/total debt	2.59	1.89	–27.04
Net sales/total assets	2.22	2.04	–7.92
Discriminant Z score	4.96	4.35	–12.32

has a much larger amount of receivables (Exhibit 5–2), the days' sales in receivables has increased significantly (Exhibit 5–3), the receivables turnover has decreased (Exhibit 5–3), and the allowance for doubtful accounts is smaller in proportion to the receivables (Exhibit 5–3). If the prior-year allowance for bad debts at 8 percent of receivables was appropriate, and conditions have not become worse, maybe the allowance should be closer to $72,000 than $50,000. The auditors should work carefully on the evidence related to accounts receivable valuation.

Question: Could the inventory be overstated? (*Alternative:* Could the cost of the goods sold be understated?) Overstatement of the ending inventory would cause the cost of goods sold to be understated. The percentage of cost of goods sold to sales shows a decrease (Exhibits 5–2 and 5–3). If the 75 percent of the prior year represents a more accurate cost of goods sold, then the income before taxes might be overstated by $225,000 (75 percent of $9.9 million minus $7.2 million unaudited cost of goods sold). The days' sales in inventory and the inventory turnover remained the same (Exhibit 5–3), but you might expect them to change in light of the larger volume of sales. Careful work on the physical count and valuation of inventory appears to be needed.

Other questions can be asked and other relationships derived when industry statistics are available. Industry statistics can be obtained from such services as Dun & Bradstreet and Robert Morris Associates. These statistics include industry averages for important financial yardsticks, such as gross profit margin, return on sales, current ratio, debt/net worth, and many others. A comparison with client data may reveal out-of-line statistics, indicating a relatively strong feature of the company, a weak financial position, or possibly an error or misstatement in the client's financial statements. However, care must be taken with industry statistics. A particular company may or may not be well represented by industry averages.

Comparing reported financial results with internal budgets and forecasts also can be useful. If the budget or forecast represents management's estimate of probable future outcomes, planning questions can arise for items that fall short of or exceed the budget. If a company expected to sell 10,000 units of a product but sold only 5,000 units, the auditors would want to plan a careful lower-of-cost-or-market study of the inventory of unsold units. If 15,000 were sold, an auditor would want to audit for sales validity. Budget comparisons can be tricky, however. Some companies use budgets and forecasts as goals, rather than as expressions of probable outcomes. Also, meeting the budget with little or no shortfall or excess can result from managers manipulating the numbers to "meet the budget." Auditors must be careful to know something about a company's business conditions from sources other than the internal records when analyzing comparisons with budgets and forecasts.

Cash Flow Analysis

If the client has not already prepared the cash flow statement, the auditors can use the comparative financial statements to prepare one. Cash flow analysis enables the auditors to see the crucial information of cash flow from operating, investment, and financing activities. A cash flow deficit from operations may signal financial difficulty. Companies fail when they run out of cash (no surprise) and are unable to pay their debts when they become due. Since auditors must study the going-concern status of the client (SAS 59, AU 341), cash flow analysis is a good starting place.

You can use the information in Exhibit 5–2 to prepare a cash flow statement. This is an exercise in a technique you learned in earlier accounting courses.

Analytical Procedures Requirements

Even though particular analytical procedures are not required by audit standards, the *timing of required application* is specified in two instances. Analytical procedures applicable in the circumstances are required (1) at the beginning of an audit—the planning stage application of analytical procedures discussed in this chapter and (2) at the end of an audit when the partners in charge review the overall quality of the work and look for apparent problems.

R E V I E W
CHECKPOINTS

5.9 What are the five types of general analytical procedures?

5.10 What is the purpose of performing preliminary analytical procedures in the audit planning stage?

5.11 What are the steps auditors can use to apply comparison and ratio analysis to unaudited financial statements?

5.12 What are some of the ratios that can be used in preliminary analytical procedures?

5.13 Is anything questionable about the relation of retained earnings and income as shown in Exhibit 5–2?

PLANNING IN AN ELECTRONIC ENVIRONMENT

LEARNING OBJECTIVE

4. List and discuss matters of planning auditors should consider for clients who use computers.

Although the term *electronic environment* has a certain mystique, audits performed in clients' complex electronic environments are conceptually the same as audits of less sophisticated systems. To be more specific, even though a client uses computers to process transactions:

- The definition of auditing is not changed.
- The purposes of auditing are not changed.
- The generally accepted auditing standards are not changed.

AUDITING INSIGHT

EXTENT OF COMPUTER PROCESSING APPLICATIONS

Transactions Typically Computerized	Transactions Typically Not Computerized
Characteristics:	Characteristics:
Frequent, repetitive, large number.	Infrequent, occasional, small number.
Examples:	Examples:
Credit sales and billing.	Income tax expense and liability.
Cash receipts.	Bank loan transactions.
Accounts receivable charges and credits.	Bonds payable transactions.
Purchases.	Deferred charges and credits.
Cash disbursements.	Prepaid expenses.
Accounts payable charges and credits.	Investment purchases and sales.
Manufacturing cost accounting.	Capital stock sales and repurchases.
Inventory accounting.	Merger and acquisition transactions.
Fixed asset acquisitions and disposals.	
Payroll.	

- The assertions of management embodied in financial statements are not changed.
- The requirement to gather sufficient competent evidence is not changed.
- The independent auditor's report on financial statements is not changed.

Therefore, everything you have learned from previous chapters is valid; only the method of recording, processing, and storing accounting data is different. In the box above are some common applications for computers in business.

Effect of Computer Processing on Transactions

The method used to process accounting transactions will affect a company's organizational structure and will influence the procedures and techniques used to accomplish the organization's objectives. The following are characteristics that distinguish computer processing from manual processing:

- *Unconventional or temporary transaction trails.* Some computer systems are designed so that a complete transaction trail useful for audit purposes might exist only for a short time or only in computer-readable form. (An **audit trail** is a chain of evidence provided through coding, cross-references, and documentation connecting account balances and other summary results with the original transaction documents calculations.) The audit trail of frequent printouts in simple system and hard-copy source documents supporting keyed data entry gradually disappear as systems become more advanced. These documents are replaced by sensor-based data collection input and microfilm or machine-readable output. All information systems need an audit trail in case of transmission interruption or power surge; however, the retention period may be short and the information available only in machine-readable form. The loss of hard-copy documents and reports and the temporary nature of the audit trail may require external auditors to alter both the timing and nature of audit procedures. Greater cooperation and coordination are required between external and internal auditors.

- *Uniform processing of transactions.* Computer processing subjects similar transactions to the same processing instructions. Consequently, computer processing virtually eliminates the occurrence of random errors normally associated with manual processing. Conversely, programming errors (or other similar systematic errors in either the computer hardware or software) will result in all like transactions being processed incorrectly when those transactions are processed under the same conditions.

- *Potential for errors and frauds.* The potential for individuals to gain unauthorized access or alter data without visible evidence, as well as to gain access (direct or indirect) to assets, may be greater in computerized accounting systems than in manual systems. Employees have more access to computer information through numerous terminals hooked together in a common computer network. Less human involvement in handling transactions processed by computers can reduce the potential for observing errors and frauds. Errors or fraud made in designing or changing application programs can remain undetected for long periods.

- *Potential for increased management supervision.* Computer systems offer management a wide variety of analytical tools to review and supervise the operations of the company. The availability of these additional controls may enhance the entire system of internal control and, therefore, reduce the control risk. For example, traditional comparisons of actual operating ratios with those budgeted, as well as reconciliation of accounts, frequently are available for management review on a more timely basis when such information is computerized. Additionally, some programmed applications provide computer operating statistics that may be used to monitor the actual processing of transactions.

- *Initiation or subsequent execution of transactions by computer.* With automatic transaction initiation, certain transactions may be initiated or executed automatically by a computer system without human review. Computer-initiated transactions include the generation of invoices, checks, shipping orders, and purchase orders. Without a human-readable document indicating the transaction event, the correctness of automatic transactions is difficult to judge. The authorization of these transactions may not be documented in the same way as those in a manual accounting system, and management's authorization of these transactions may be implicit in its acceptance of the design of the system. For example, authorization of transactions occurs when certain flags are installed in programs or records (e.g., inventory quantity falling below reorder point). Therefore, authorization is more difficult to trace to the proper person. Control procedures must be designed into the system to ensure the genuineness and reasonableness of automatic transactions and to prevent or detect erroneous transactions.

Effect of Client Computer Processing on Audit Planning

All organizations use computers in data processing to some extent. One very important aspect of the inquiry-based familiarization is obtaining information for planning the computer-based audit work. The extent to which computer processing is used in significant accounting applications as well as the complexity of the processing may influence the nature, timing, and extent of audit procedures. Accordingly, when evaluating the effect of a client's computer processing on an audit of financial statements, auditors should consider such matters as (*SAS 22,* AU 311):

- The extent to which the computer is used in each significant accounting application (e.g., sales and billing, payroll).
- The complexity of the computer operations used by the entity (e.g., batch processing, online processing, outside service centers).
- The organizational structure of the computer processing activities.
- The availability of data required by the auditor.

- The computer-assisted audit techniques available to increase the efficiency of audit procedures.
- The need for specialized skills.

Extent to Which Computers Are Used

When planning the audit, auditors should consider the extent to which computers are used in each significant accounting application. Significant accounting applications are those relating to accounting information that can materially affect the financial statements. When the client uses computers to process significant accounting applications, the audit team may need computer-related skills to understand the flow of these transactions. The extent of computer use may also affect the nature, timing, and extent of audit procedures.

Complexity of Computer Operations

Auditors should consider the complexity of the client's computer operations, including the use of an outside service center. When assessing the complexity of computer processing, the audit manager should consider his or her training and experience relative to the methods of data processing. If the client outsources significant accounting applications (e.g., payroll), the auditors will need to coordinate audit procedures with service auditors at the processing center.

Auditors can consider other matters when assessing the complexity of computer processing. The computer hardware utilized by the entity may show the extent of complexity involved. The extent to which various computerized systems share common files or are otherwise integrated affects the complexity of computer operations because these characteristics may cause all such integrated systems to be considered significant accounting applications. In some computerized systems, a transaction trail may be available only in computer-readable form for short periods and possibly in a complex form.

Organizational Structure of Computer Processing

The organizational structure of a client's computer processing can have significant effects on how the auditor plans to conduct the work. Clients may have great differences in the way these activities are organized. The degree of centralization inherent in the organizational structure especially may vary.

A highly centralized organizational structure generally will have all significant computer processing controlled and supervised at a central location. The control environment, the computer hardware, and the computer systems may be uniform throughout the company. Auditors may be able to obtain most of the necessary computer processing information by visiting the central location. At the other extreme, a highly decentralized organizational structure generally allows various departments, divisions, subsidiaries, or geographical locations to develop, control, and supervise computer processing in an autonomous fashion. In this situation, the computer hardware and the computer systems usually will not be uniform throughout the company. Thus, auditors may need to visit many locations to obtain the necessary audit information.

Availability of Data

Computer systems provide an ability to store, retrieve, and analyze large quantities of data. Input data, certain computer files, and other data the audit team needs may exist only for short periods or only in computer-readable form. In some computer systems, hard-copy input documents may not exist at all because information is entered directly. For example, electronic signatures have replaced manual signatures on electronic purchase orders sent directly to vendors via electronic data interchange, with the consequence that the auditors will not be able to examine a hard-copy signature. The client's data retention policies may require auditors to arrange for some information to be retained for review. Alternatively, auditors may need to plan to perform audit procedures at a time when the information is still available.

In addition, certain information generated by the computer system for management's internal purposes may be useful in performing analytical procedures. For example, since storage is easy, the client may save larger quantities of operating information (data warehousing), such as sales information by month, by product, and by salesman. Such information can be accessed (data mining) for use in analytical procedures to determine whether the revenue amounts are reasonable. Auditors may also drill down to examine individual transactions that comprise a general ledger account balance.

Use of Computer-Assisted Audit Tools and Techniques (CAATTs)

Auditors may use computer-assisted audit techniques to increase the efficiency of certain audit procedures and to provide opportunities to apply certain procedures to an entire population of accounts or transactions. Recent innovations have allowed auditors with little or no computer background to perform tasks that used to be reserved for information system auditors.

Need for Specialized Skills

When the automation of transactions is complex, auditing firms need to employ audit specialists who understand computer technology and who are aware of basic audit objectives. These "information system auditors" are members of the audit team and are called upon when the need for their skills arises, just as statistical sampling specialists or SEC specialists are available when their expertise is needed. To determine the need for specialized computer skills, the auditors should consider all aspects of a client's computer processing. When planning the engagement, the audit manager may find the need for certain specialized skills to consider the effect of computer processing on the audit, to understand the flow of transactions, or to design and perform audit procedures. For example, the audit team many need specialized skills relating to various methods of data processing, programming languages, software packages, or computer-assisted audit techniques. Audit managers and partners should possess sufficient computer knowledge to know when to call on specialists and to understand and supervise their work.

R E V I E W
CHECKPOINTS

5.14 What are the general characteristics of transactions that are typically computerized? Typically not computerized?

5.15 Define a transaction audit trail. How might a computer system transaction audit trail in an advanced system differ from one in a simple system or a manual system?

5.16 What are some other important differences between manual and computer accounting systems?

5.17 In addition to the planning matters considered in a manual accounting system, what additional ones should be considered when computer processing is involved?

AUDIT WORKPAPERS

LEARNING OBJECTIVE
5. Review an audit working paper for proper form and content.

An audit is not complete without preparation of proper working paper documentation. **Workpapers** are the auditors' record of compliance with generally accepted auditing standards (*SAS 41, AU 339*). They should contain support for the decisions regarding procedures necessary in the circumstances and all other important decisions made during the audit. Even though the auditor legally owns the working papers, professional ethics require that they not be transferred without consent of the client because of the confidential information recorded in them.

Workpapers can be classified in three categories: (1) *permanent file* papers, (2) audit administrative papers, and (3) audit evidence papers. The last two categories are often called the *current file* because they relate to the audit of one year.

The Permanent File

The *permanent file* contains information of *continuing audit significance* over many years' audits of the same client. The audit team can use this file year after year, while each year's current audit evidence papers are filed away after they have served their purpose. Documents of permanent interest and applicability include: (1) copies or excerpts of the corporate charter and bylaws, or partnership agreements; (2) copies or excerpts of continuing contracts, such as leases, bond indentures, and royalty agreements; (3) a history of the company, its products, and its markets; (4) copies or excerpts of stockholders, directors, and committee minutes on matters of lasting interest; and (5) continuing schedules of accounts whose balances are carried forward for several years, such as owners' equity, retained earnings, partnership capital, and the like. Copies of prior years' financial statements and audit reports also may be included. The permanent file is a ready source of information for familiarization with the client by new personnel on the engagement.

Audit Administrative Papers

Administrative papers contain the documentation of the early planning phases of the audit. They usually include the engagement letter, staff assignment notes, conclusions related to understanding the client's business, results of preliminary analytical procedures, initial assessments of audit risks, and the initial assessments of audit materiality. Many accounting firms follow the practice of summarizing these data in an *engagement planning memorandum*.

Audit planning and administration also include work on the preliminary assessment of control risk and preparation of a written audit program. In general, the following items are usually among the administrative workpapers in each year's current working paper file:

1. Engagement letter.
2. Staff assignments.
3. Client organization chart.
4. Memoranda of conferences with management.
5. Memoranda of conferences with the directors' audit committee.
6. Preliminary analytical review notes.
7. Initial risk assessment notes.
8. Initial materiality assessment notes.
9. Engagement planning memorandum.
10. Audit engagement time budget.
11. Internal control questionnaire and control analyses.
12. Management controls questionnaire.
13. Computer controls questionnaire.
14. Internal control system flowcharts.
15. Audit program.

Audit Evidence Papers

The current-year audit evidence workpapers contain the specific assertions under audit, the record of the procedures performed, the evidence obtained, and the decisions made in the course of the audit. (See Exhibit 5–4.) These papers communicate the quality of the audit, so they must be clear, concise, complete, neat, well indexed, and informative. Each separate working paper (or multiple pages that go together) must be complete in the sense that it can be removed from the working paper file and considered on its own,

EXHIBIT 5–4 CURRENT WORKPAPER FILE

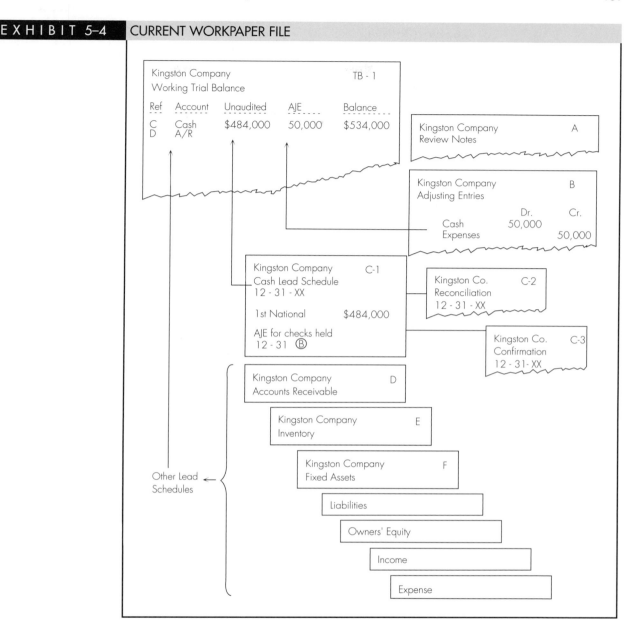

with proper *cross-references* available to show how the paper coordinates with other working papers. Working papers may be in the form of magnetic tape or disks, film, and photographs as well as on computer or handwritten paper.

The most important facet of the current audit evidence papers is the requirement that they show the auditors' decision problems and conclusions. (See Exhibit 5–5.) The papers must record the management assertions that were audited (book values or qualitative disclosures), the evidence gathered about them, and final conclusions. Auditing standards (SAS 41, AU 339) require the working papers show that: (1) the client's accounting records agree or reconcile with the financial statements, (2) the work was adequately planned and supervised, (3) a sufficient understanding of the control structure was obtained, and (4) sufficient competent evidential matter was obtained as a reasonable basis for an audit opinion. Common sense also dictates that the working papers be sufficient to show that the financial statements conform to GAAP and that the disclosures are adequate. The working papers also should explain how exceptions and unusual

EXHIBIT 5–5   ILLUSTRATIVE WORKING PAPER

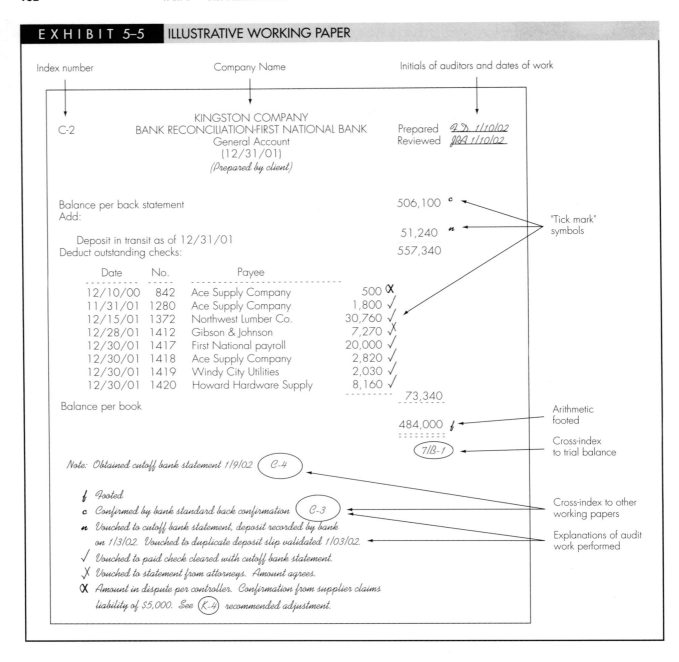

accounting questions were resolved or treated. (Notice in Exhibit 5–5 the auditor's confirmation of the disputed account payable liability.) Taken altogether, these features should demonstrate that all the auditing standards were observed.

Workpaper Arrangement and Indexing

Every auditing organization has a different method of arranging and indexing workpapers. In general, however, the papers are grouped in order behind the trial balance according to balance sheet and income statement captions. Usually, the current assets appear first, followed by fixed assets, other assets, liabilities, equities, income, and expense accounts. The typical arrangement is shown in Exhibit 5–4.

Several workpaper preparation techniques are quite important for the quality of the finished product. The points explained on the next page are illustrated in Exhibit 5–5.

- *Indexing.* Each paper is given an index number, like a book page number, so it can be found, removed, and replaced without loss.
- *Cross-referencing.* Numbers or memoranda related to other papers carry the index of other paper(s) so the connections can be followed.
- *Heading.* Each paper is titled with the name of the company, the balance sheet date, and a descriptive title of the contents of the working paper.
- *Signatures and initials.* The auditor who performs the work and the supervisor who reviews it must sign the papers so personnel can be identified.
- *Dates of audit work.* The dates of performance and review are recorded on the working papers so reviewers of the papers can tell when the work was performed.
- *Audit marks and explanations.* Audit marks (or "tick marks") are the auditor's shorthand for abbreviating comments about work performed. Audit marks always must be accompanied by a full explanation of the auditing work.

Electronic Workpapers

We use the term *workpapers* quite a bit in this section, but the term is becoming anachronistic. Audit firms rarely use *paper* to document their findings anymore; more commonly, firms are using electronic workpapers. For example, auditors prepare memos using word processing software and financial schedules (such as bank reconciliations and depreciation schedules) using spreadsheet software.

Auditors' automated workpapers can result in improved utilization of auditor time and reduced storage costs. Electronic workpapers create great efficiency because workpapers can be easily updated and modified from year to year. Additionally, electronic workpapers can reduce the time spent on numbering, referencing, initialing, dating, reviewing ("ticking and tying"), and approving workpapers by automating these tasks through the use of macro programs. These tasks have traditionally consumed large quantities of audit effort, which can be directed more productively to more critical aspects of the audit. Finally, while an audit report barely covers a page, audit workpapers can easily fill many binders. Those binders usually end up in a numbered box in a storage facility with numerous similar boxes containing audit workpapers from other engagements, rarely to be seen again. Automated workpaper software allows auditors to create, share, edit, review, correct, approve, and finalize workpapers without the "paper," thereby reducing the storage space requirements of hard-copy workpapers.

R E V I E W
CHECKPOINTS

5.18 What information would you expect to find in a permanent audit file? In the front of a current working paper file?

5.19 What is considered the most important content of the auditor's current audit working papers?

5.20 How can computer word processing and spreadsheet packages be used to generate support in work papers?

SUMMARY

Many of the concepts (*materiality*, *audit risk*) discussed in the previous chapter are part of the *theoretical* foundation for performing audits. This chapter contains the specific set of *practical* planning activities auditors undertake when beginning an audit engagement. *Preengagement activities* start with the work of deciding whether to accept a new client and become its auditor and, on an annual basis, deciding whether to continue as auditor on existing clients. CPA firms are not obligated to provide audits to every organization that asks for one, and they regularly exercise discretion about the organizations with which they wish to associate. The investigation may involve the cooperative task of communicating with the former (predecessor) auditor of the organization. Once a client is accepted, the preengagement work continues with the preparation of an engagement letter, assignment of partners, managers, and staff to the job and with the preparation of a time budget for the audit.

The activities part of the chapter also covers the important process of *obtaining an understanding* of the client's business and industry. Methods and sources of information are explained. One of the most important activities is the performance of *preliminary analytical procedures* applied to the client's unaudited financial statements. The analytical process includes: getting the financial data, calculating common-size and comparative financial statements, calculating ratios, describing the company's financial activities, and asking relevant questions. This analysis enables auditors to look for problem areas and signs of potential misstatement in the financial statements. Detecting signs of problems enables the auditors to plan procedures for the audit program to follow up and to determine whether misstatements, errors, or frauds have affected the fair presentation of the financial balances.

Even though computer technology changes the accounting system and the environment in which it operates, technology does not change the basic auditing standards. Qualities of competence, independence, due care, planning, control risk assessment, and sufficient competent evidence are not changed. However, the nuances and aspects of achieving them must be tailored to a world of computers. Auditors must consider several factors when planning in an electronic environment.

The closing topic is a brief preview of workpapers, with some basic pointers about their form, content, and purpose. Now the stage is set to take up a more detailed explanation of the theory and process of auditing internal control. The next chapter deals with the task of control risk assessment.

MULTIPLE-CHOICE QUESTIONS FOR PRACTICE AND REVIEW

5.21 Analytical procedures are generally used to produce evidence from
a. Confirmations mailed directly to the auditors by client customers.
b. Physical observation of inventories.
c. Relationships among current financial balances and prior balances, forecasts, and nonfinancial data.
d. Detailed examination of external, external-internal, and internal documents.

5.22 Which of the following matchups of types of analytical procedures and sources of information below makes the most sense?

5.23 Auditors perform analytical procedures in the planning stage of an audit for the purpose of
a. Deciding the matters to cover in an engagement letter.
b. Identifying unusual conditions that deserve more auditing effort.
c. Determining which of the financial statement assertions are the most important for the client's financial statements.
d. Determining the nature, timing, and extent of audit procedures for auditing the inventory.

Type of Analytical Procedure	Source of Information
a. Comparison of current account balances with prior periods	i. Physical production statistics.
b. Comparison of current account balances with expected balances	ii. Company's budgets and forecasts.
c. Evaluation of current account balances with relation to predictable historical patterns	iii. Published industry ratio.
d. Evaluation of current account balances in relation to nonfinancial	iv. Company's own comparative information financial statements.

5.24 Analytical procedures can be used in which of the following ways?
  a. As a means of overall review at the end of an audit.
  b. As "attention directing" methods when planning an audit at the beginning.
  c. As substantive audit procedures to obtain evidence during an audit.
  d. All of the above.

5.25 Analytical procedures used when planning an audit should concentrate on
  a. Weaknesses in the company's internal control activities.
  b. Predictability of account balances based on individual transactions.
  c. Five major management assertions in financial statements.
  d. Accounts and relationships that may represent specific potential problems and risks in the financial statements.

5.26 When a company that has $5 million current assets and $3 million current liabilities pays $1 million of its accounts payable, its current ratio will
  a. Increase.
  b. Decrease.
  c. Remain unchanged.

5.27 When a company that has $3 million current assets and $5 million current liabilities pays $1 million of its accounts payable, its current ratio will
  a. Increase.
  b. Decrease.
  c. Remain unchanged.

5.28 When a company that has $5 million current assets and $5 million current liabilities pays $1 million of its accounts payable, its current ratio will
  a. Increase.
  b. Decrease.
  c. Remain unchanged.

5.29 When a company that sells its products for a (gross) profit increases its sales by 15 percent and its cost of goods sold by 7 percent, the cost of goods sold ratio will
  a. Increase.
  b. Decrease.
  c. Remain unchanged.

5.30 An audit engagement letter should normally include the following matter of agreement between the auditor and the client
  a. Schedules and analyses to be prepared by the client's employees.
  b. Methods of statistical sampling the auditor will use.
  c. Specification of litigation in progress against the client.
  d. Client representations about availability of all minutes of meetings of the board of directors.

5.31 When a successor auditor initiates communications with a predecessor auditor, the successor should expect
  a. To take responsibility for obtaining the client's consent for the predecessor to give information about prior audits.
  b. To conduct interviews with the partner and manager in charge of the predecessor audit firm's engagement.
  c. To obtain copies of some or all of the predecessor auditor's working papers.
  d. All of the above.

5.32 Generally accepted auditing standards require that auditors always prepare and use
  a. A written planning memo explaining the auditors' understanding of the client's business.
  b. Written client consents to discuss audit matters with successor auditors.
  c. A written audit program.
  d. Written time budgets and schedules for performing each audit.

5.33 When planning an audit, which of the following is not a factor that affects auditors' decisions about the quantity, type, and content of audit working papers?
  a. The auditors' need to document compliance with generally accepted auditing standards.
  b. The existence of new sales contracts important for the client's business.
  c. The auditors' judgment about their independence with regard to the client.
  d. The auditors' judgments about materiality.

5.34 An audit working paper that shows the detailed evidence and procedures regarding the balance in the accumulated depreciation account for the year under audit will be found in the
  a. Current file evidence working papers.
  b. Permanent file working papers.
  c. Administrative working papers in the current file.
  d. Planning memorandum in the current file.

5.35 An auditor's permanent file working papers most likely will contain
  a. Internal control analysis for the current year.
  b. The latest engagement letter.
  c. Memoranda of conference with management.
  d. Excerpts of the corporate charter and by-laws.

EXERCISES AND PROBLEMS

5.36   Communications between Predecessor and Successor Auditors.   Assume that the Kingston Company was audited last year by CPA Diggs. Now, Larry Lancaster wishes to engage Anderson, Olds, and Watershed, CPAs, to audit its annual financial statements. Lancaster is generally pleased with the services provided by Diggs, but he thinks the audit work was too detailed and interfered excessively with normal office routines. Anderson has asked Lancaster to inform Diggs of the decision to change auditors, but he does not wish to do so.

Required:

List and discuss the steps Anderson should follow with regard to dealing with a predecessor auditor and a new client before accepting the engagement. (Hint: Use SAS 84 (AU 315) and interpretations of the independence rules of conduct for a complete response to this requirement.)

5.37   Understand the Business—Transactions and Accounts.   In the left column of the table below are several classes of transactions. The right column names several general ledger accounts.

Required:

Identify the general ledger accounts that are affected by each class of transactions.

Approach: Match the classes of transactions with the general ledger accounts where their debits and credits are usually entered.

Classes of Transactions	General Ledger Accounts
Cash receipts	Cash
Cash disbursements	Accounts receivable
Credit sales	Allowance for doubtful accounts
Sales returns and allowances	Inventory
	Fixed assets
Purchases on credit	Accounts payable
Purchase returns	Long-term debt
Uncollectible account write-offs	Sales revenue
	Investment income
	Expenses

5.38   Analytical Review Ratio Relationships.   The following situations represent errors and frauds that could occur in financial statements. Your requirement is to state how the ratio in question would compare (greater, equal, or less) to what the ratio "should have been" had the error or fraud not occurred.

a.   The company recorded fictitious sales with credits to sales revenue accounts and debits to accounts receivable. Inventory was reduced and cost of goods sold was increased for the profitable "sales." Is the current ratio greater than, equal to, or less than what it should have been?

b.   The company recorded cash disbursements paying trade accounts payable but held the checks past the year-end date—meaning that the "disbursements" should not have been shown as credits to cash and debits to accounts payable. Is the current ratio greater than, equal to, or less than what it should have been? Consider cases in which the current ratio before the improper "disbursement" recording was (1) greater than 1:1, (2) equal to 1:1, and (3) less than 1:1.

c.   The company uses a periodic inventory system for determining the balance sheet amount of inventory at year-end. Very near the year-end, merchandise was received, placed in the stockroom, and counted, but the purchase transaction was neither recorded nor paid until the next month. What was the effect on inventory, cost of goods sold, gross profit, and net income? How were these ratios affected, compared to what they would have been without the error: current ratio (remember three possible cases), gross margin ratio, cost of goods sold ratio, inventory turnover, and receivables turnover?

d.   The company is loathe to write off customer accounts receivable, even though the financial vice president makes entirely adequate provision for uncollectible amounts in the allowance for bad debts. The gross receivables and the allowance both contain amounts that should have been written off long ago. How are these ratios affected compared to what they would be if the old receivables were properly written off: current ratio, days' sales in receivables, doubtful account ratio, receivables turnover, return on beginning equity, working capital/total assets?

e.   Since last year, the company has reorganized its lines of business and placed more emphasis on its traditional products while selling off some marginal businesses merged by the previous management. Total assets are 10 percent less than they were last year, but working capital has increased. Retained earnings remained the same because the disposals created no gains, and the net income after taxes is still near zero, the same as last year. Earnings before interest and taxes remained the same, a small positive EBIT. The total market value of the company's equity has not increased, but that is better than the declines of the past several years. Proceeds from the disposals have been used to retire long-term debt. Net sales have decreased 5 percent because the sales decrease resulting from the disposals has not been overcome by increased sales of the traditional products. Is the discriminant Z score of the current year higher or lower than the prior year? (See Appendix 5A for the Z score formula.)

5.39   Audit Working Papers   The preparation of workpapers is an integral part of a CPA's audit of financial statements. On a recurring engagement, CPAs review the audit programs and workpapers from the prior audit while planning the current audit to determine their usefulness for the current-year work.

Required:

a. (1)What are the purposes or functions of audit working papers?

(2)What records may be included in audit working papers?

b. What factors affect the CPA's judgment of the type and content of the working papers for a particular engagement?

c. To comply with generally accepted auditing standards, a CPA includes certain evidence in the working papers; for example, "evidence that the audit was planned and work of assistants was supervised and reviewed." What other evidence should a CPA include in audit working papers to comply with generally accepted auditing standards?

d. How can a CPA make the most effective use of the preceding year's audit programs in a recurring audit?

(AICPA adapted)

5.40   Analytical Procedures and Interest Expense.   Weyman Z. Wannamaker is the Chief Financial Officer of Cogburn Company. He prides himself on being able to manage the cash resources of the company to maximize the interest expense. Consequently, on the second business day of each month, Weyman pays down or draws cash on the company's revolving line of credit at First National Bank in accordance with his cash requirements forecast.

You are the auditor. You find the general ledger of notes payable on this line of credit as shown below. You inquired at First National Bank and learned that Cogburn Company's loan agreement specifies payment on the first day of each month for the interest due on the previous month's outstanding balance at the rate of "prime plus 1.5 percent." The bank gave you a report that showed the prime rate of interest was 8.5 percent for the first six months of the year and 8.0 percent for the last six months.

Cogburn Company
Notes Payable Balances

Date	Balance
Jan 1	$150,000
Feb 1	$200,000
Apr 1	$225,000
May 1	$285,000
Jun 1	$375,000
Aug 1	$430,000
Sep 1	$290,000
Oct 1	$210,000
Nov 1	$172,000
Dec 1	$ 95,000

Required:

a. Prepare an audit estimate of the amount of interest expense you expect to find as the balance of the interest expense account related to these notes payable.

b. Which of the types of analytical procedures did you use to determine this estimate?

c. Suppose that you find that the interest expense account shows expense of $23,650 related to these notes. What could be wrong?

d. Suppose that you find that the interest expense account shows expense of $24,400 related to these notes. What could be wrong?

e. Suppose that you find that the interest expense account shows expense of $25,200 related to these notes. What could be wrong?

5.41   Competence of Evidence and Related Parties.   Johnson & Company, CPAs, audited the Guaranteed Savings & Loan Company. M. Johnson had the assignment of evaluating the collectibility of real estate loans. Johnson was working on two particular loans: (1) a $4 million loan secured by the Smith Street Apartments and (2) a $5.5 million construction loan on the Baker Street Apartments now being built. The appraisals performed by the Guaranteed Appraisal Partners, Inc., showed values in excess of the loan amounts. Upon inquiry, Mr. Bumpus, the S&L vice president for loan acquisition, stated: "I know the Smith Street loan is good because I myself own 40 percent of the partnership that owns the property and is obligated on the loan."

Johnson then wrote in the working papers: (1) the Smith Street loan appears collectible. Mr. Bumpus personally attested to knowledge of the collectibility as a major owner in the partnership obligated on the loan, (2) the Baker Street loan is assumed to be collectible because it is new and construction is still in progress, (3) the appraised values all exceed the loan amounts.

Required:

a. Do you perceive any problems with related party involvement in the evidence used by M. Johnson? Explain.

b. Do you perceive any problems with M. Johnson's reasoning or the competence of evidence used in that reasoning?

DISCUSSION CASES

5.42   Analytical Review.   Kermit Griffin, an audit manager, had begun a preliminary analytical review of selected statistics related to the Majestic Hotel. His objective was to obtain an understanding of this hotel's business in order to draft a preliminary audit program. He wanted to see whether he could detect any troublesome areas or questionable accounts that might require special audit attention. Unfortunately, Mr. Griffin caught the flu and was hospitalized. From his sickbed, he sent you the schedule he had prepared (Exhibit 5.42–1). He has asked you to write a memoran-

---

EXHIBIT 5.42–1

AP-6   Prepared by _____

                                                                   Reviewed by _____

MAJESTIC HOTEL
Preliminary Analytical Procedures
FYE 3/31/02

The Majestic Hotel, East Apple, New Jersey, compiles operating statistics on a calendar-year basis. Hotel statistics, below, were provided by the controller, A.J. Marcello, for 2002. The parallel column contains industry average statistics obtained from the National Hotel Industry Guide.

	Majestic (percent)	Industry (percent)
Sales:		
Rooms	60.4%	63.9%
Food and beverage	35.7	32.2
Other	3.9	3.9
Costs:		
Rooms department	15.2%	17.3%
Food and beverage	34.0	27.2
Administrative and general	8.0	8.9
Management fee	3.3	1.1
Advertising	2.7	3.2
Real estate taxes	3.5	3.2
Utilities, repairs, maintenance	15.9	13.7
Profit per sales dollar	17.4%	25.4%
Rooms dept. ratios to room sales dollars:		
Salaries and wages	18.9%	15.7%
Laundry	1.1	3.7
Other	5.3	7.6
Profit per rooms sales dollar	74.8%	73.0%
Food/beverage ratios to F/B sales dollars:		
Cost of food sold	42.1%	37.0%
Food gross profit	57.9	63.0
Cost of beverages sold	43.6	29.5
Beverages gross profit	56.4	70.5
Combined gross profit	57.7	64.6
Salaries and wages	39.6	32.8
Music and entertainment	—	2.7
Other	13.4	13.8
Profit per F/B sales dollar	4.7	15.3
Average annual percent of rooms occupied	62.6	68.1
Average room rate per day	$160	$120
Number of rooms available per day	200	148

dum identifying areas of potential misstatements or other matters that the preliminary audit program should cover.

Required:

Write a memorandum describing Majestic's operating characteristics compared to the "industry average" insofar as you can tell from the statistics. Does this analytical review identify any areas that might present problems in the audit?

5.43   Preliminary   Analytical   Procedures. ALPHA.COM, INC. wanted to expand its manufacturing and sales facilities. The company applied for a loan from First Bank, presenting the prior-year audited financial statements and the forecast for the current year shown in Exhibit 5.43–1. (ALPHA.COM, INC.'S fiscal year-end is December 31.) The bank was impressed with the business prospects and granted a $1,750,000 loan at 8 percent interest to finance working capital and

the new facilities that were placed in service July 1 of the current year. Since ALPHA.COM, INC. planned to sell stock for permanent financing, the bank made the loan due on December 31 of the following year. Interest is payable each calendar quarter on October 1 of the current year, and January 1, April 1, July 1, October 1, and December 31 of the following year.

The auditors' interviews with ALPHA.COM, INC. management near the end of the current year produced the following information: The facilities did not cost as much as previously anticipated. However, sales were slow and the company granted more liberal return privilege terms than in the prior year. Officers wanted to generate significant income to impress First Bank and to preserve the company dividend ($120,000 paid in the prior year). The production managers had targeted inventory levels for a 4.0 turnover ratio and were largely successful even though prices of materials

---

EXHIBIT 5.43–1   ALPHA.COM, INC. PRIOR YEAR (AUDITED), FORECAST CURRENT YEAR, CURRENT YEAR ACTUAL (UNAUDITED)

	Prior Year	Forecast	Current Year
REVENUE AND EXPENSE:			
Sales (net)	$9,000,000	9,900,000	9,720,000
Cost of goods sold	6,296,000	6,926,000	7,000,000
Gross margin	2,704,000	2,974,000	2,720,000
General expense	2,044,000	2,000,000	2,003,000
Depreciation	300,000	334,000	334,000
Operating income	$ 360,000	$ 640,000	$ 383,000
Interest expense	60,000	110,000	75,000
Income taxes (40%)	120,000	212,000	123,200
Net income	$ 180,000	$ 318,000	$ 184,800
ASSETS:			
Cash	$ 600,000	$ 880,000	$ 690,800
Accounts receivable	500,000	600,000	900,000
Allowance doubtful accounts	(40,000)	(48,000)	(90,000)
Inventory	1,500,000	1,500,000	1,350,000
Total current assets	$2,560,000	$2,932,000	$2,850,800
Fixed assets	3,000,000	4,700,000	4,500,000
Accum. depreciation	(1,500,000)	(1,834,000)	(1,834,000)
Total assets	$4,060,000	$5,798,000	$5,516,800
LIABILITIES AND EQUITY:			
Accounts payable	$ 450,000	$ 450,000	$ 330,000
Bank loans, 8%	0	1,750,000	1,750,000
Accrued interest	60,000	40,000	40,000
Accruals and other	50,000	60,000	32,000
Total current liabilities	$ 560,000	$2,300,000	$2,152,000
Long-term debt, 10%	600,000	400,000	400,000
Total liabilities	$1,160,000	$2,700,000	$2,552,000
Capital stock	2,000,000	2,000,000	2,000,000
Retained earnings	900,000	1,098,000	964,800
Total liabilities and equity	$4,060,000	$5,798,000	$5,516,800

and supplies had risen about 2 percent relative to sales dollar volume. The new facilities were depreciated using a 25-year life from the date of opening.

ALPHA.COM, INC. has now produced the current-year financial statements (Exhibit 5.43–1, column labeled "current year") for the auditors' work on the current audit.

Required:

Perform preliminary analytical procedures analysis on the current-year unaudited financial statements for the purpose of identifying accounts that might contain errors or frauds. Use your knowledge of ALPHA.COM, INC. and the forecast in Exhibit 5.43–1. Use also the comparative,

common size financial data in Exhibit 5.43–2 and the ratios in Exhibit 5.43–3. You should (a) identify the accounts that might be misstated, and (b) calculate preliminary amounts of potential misstatement.

5.44 Predecessor and Successor Auditors. The president of Allpurpose Loan Company had a genuine dislike for external auditors. Almost any conflict generated a towering rage. Consequently, the company changed auditors often.

Wells & Ratley, CPAs, was recently hired to audit the 1998 financial statements. The W&R firm succeeded the firm of Canby & Company, which had obtained the audit after Albrecht & Hubbard had been fired. A&H audited the 1997

EXHIBIT 5.43–2   ALPHA.COM, INC. PRELIMINARY ANALYTICAL PROCEDURES DATA COMPARATIVE, COMMONSIZE FINANCIAL STATEMENTS

	Prior Year (Audited)		Current Year (Unaudited)		Change	
	Balance	Common Size	Balance	Common Size	Amount	Percent Change
REVENUE AND EXPENSE:						
Sales (net)	$9,000,000	100.00%	$9,720,000	100.00%	$ 720,000	8.00%
Cost of goods sold	6,296,000	69.96	7,000,000	72.02	704,000	11.18
Gross margin	2,704,000	30.04%	2,720,000	27.98%	16,000	0.59%
General expense	2,044,000	22.71	$2,003,000	20.61	(41,000)	−2.01
Depreciation	300,000	3.33	334,000	3.44	34,000	11.33
Operating income	$ 360,000	4.00%	$ 383,000	3.94%	$ 23,000	6.39%
Interest expense	60,000	0.67	75,000	0.77	15,000	25.00
Income taxes (40%)	120,000	1.33	123,200	1.27	3,200	2.67
Net income	$ 180,000	2.00%	$ 184,800	1.90%	$ 4,800	2.67%
ASSETS:						
Cash	$ 600,000	14.78%	690,800	12.52%	90,800	15.13%
Accounts receivable	500,000	12.32	900,000	16.31	400,000	80.00
Allowance doubtful accounts	(40,000)	−0.99	(90,000)	−1.63	(50,000)	125.00
Inventory	1,500,000	36.95	1,350,000	24.47	(150,000)	−10.00
Total current assets	$2,560,000	63.05%	$2,850,800	51.67%	$ 290,800	11.36%
Fixed assets	3,000,000	73.89	4,500,000	81.57	1,500,000	50.00
Accum depreciation	(1,500,000)	−36.95	(1,834,000)	−33.24	(334,000)	22.27
Total assets	$4,060,000	100.00%	$5,516,800	100.00%	$1,456,800	35.88%
LIABILITIES AND EQUITY:						
Accounts payable	$ 450,000	11.08%	$ 330,000	5.98%	($ 120,000)	−26.67%
Bank loans, 8%	0	0.00	1,750,000	31.72	1,750,000	
Accrued interest	60,000	1.48	40,000	0.73	(20,000)	−33.33
Accruals and other	50,000	1.23	32,000	0.58	(18,000)	−36.00
Total current liabilities	$ 560,000	13.79%	$2,152,000	39.01%	$1,592,000	284.29%
Long-term debt, 10%	600,000	14.78	400,000	7.25	(200,000)	−33.33
Total liabilities	$1,160,000	28.57%	$2,552,000	46.26%	$1,392,000	120.00%
Capital stock	2,000,000	49.26	2,000,000	36.25		0.00
Retained earnings	900,000	22.17	964,800	17.49	64,800	7.20
Total liabilities and equity	$4,060,000	100.00%	$5,516,800	100.00%	$1,456,800	35.88%

financial statements and rendered a report that contained an additional paragraph explaining an uncertainty about Allpurpose Loan Company's loan loss reserve. Goodbye A&H! The president then hired Canby & Company to audit the 1998 financial statements, and Art Canby started the work. But before the audit could be completed, Canby was fired, and W&R was hired to complete the audit. Canby & Company did not issue an audit report because the audit was not finished.

Required:

Does the Wells & Ratley firm need to initiate communications with Canby & Company? With Albrecht & Hubbard? With both? Explain your response in terms of the purposes of communications between predecessor and successor auditors.

5.45   Client Selection.   You are a CPA in a regional accounting firm that has 10 offices in three states. Mr. Shine has approached you with a request for an audit. He is president of Hitech Software and Games, Inc., a five-year-old company that has recently grown to $500 million in sales and $200 million in total assets. Mr. Shine is thinking about going public with a $25 million issue of common stock, of which $10 million would be a secondary issue of shares he holds. You are

very happy about this opportunity because you know Mr. Shine is the new president of the Symphony Society board and has made quite a civic impression since he came to your medium-size city seven years ago. Hitech is one of the growing employers in the city.

Required:

a. Discuss the sources of information and the types of inquiries you and the firm's partners can make in connection with accepting Hitech as a new client.

b. Does the AICPA require any investigation of prospective clients?

c. Suppose Mr. Shine has also told you that 10 years ago his closely held hamburger franchise business went bankrupt, and upon investigation you learn from its former auditors (your own firm) that Shine played "fast and loose" with franchise-fee income recognition rules and presented such difficulties that your office in another city resigned from the audit (before the bankruptcy). Do you think the partner in charge of the audit practice should accept Hitech as a new client?

EXHIBIT 5.43–3   ALPHA.COM, INC. SELECTED FINANCIAL RATIOS

	Prior Year	Current Year	Percent Change
Balance Sheet Ratios			
Current ratio	4.57	1.32	−71.02%
Days' sales in receivables	18.40	30.00	63.04%
Doubtful accounts ratio	0.0800	0.1000	25.00%
Days' sales in inventory	85.77	69.43	−19.05%
Debt/equity ratio	0.40	0.86	115.19%
Operations Ratios			
Receivables turnover	19.57	12.00	−38.67%
Inventory turnover	4.20	5.19	23.54%
Cost of goods sold/sales	69.96%	72.02%	2.95%
Gross margin %	30.04%	27.98%	−6.86%
Return on beginning equity	6.62%	6.37%	−3.71%
Financial Distress Ratios (Altman)			
Working capital/Total assets	0.49	0.13	−74.29%
Retained earnings/Total assets	0.22	0.17	−21.11%
EBIT/Total assets	0.09	0.07	−21.70%
Market value equity/Total debt	2.59	1.18	−54.55%
Net sales/Total assets	2.22	1.76	−20.52%
Discriminant Z Score	4.96	3.09	−37.67%
Market value of equity	$3,000,000	$3,000,000	

In the ALPHA.COM example in Exhibits 5–2 and 5–3, the market value of the equity in the calculations is $3 million.

APPENDIX 5A   SELECTED FINANCIAL RATIOS

Balance Sheet Ratios	Formula*
Current Ratio	$\dfrac{\text{Current assets}}{\text{Current liabilities}}$
Days' sales in receivables	$\dfrac{\text{Ending net receivables}}{\text{Credit sales}} \times 360$
Doubtful account ratio	$\dfrac{\text{Allowance for doubtful accounts}}{\text{Ending gross receivables}}$
Days' sales in inventory	$\dfrac{\text{Ending inventory}}{\text{Cost of goods sold}} \times 360$
Debt ratio	$\dfrac{\text{Current and long-term debt}}{\text{Total debt} + \text{Stockholder equity}}$

Operations Ratio	
Receivables turnover	$\dfrac{\text{Credit sales}}{\text{Ending net receivables}}$
Inventory turnover	$\dfrac{\text{Cost of goods sold}}{\text{Ending inventory}}$
Cost of goods sold ratio	$\dfrac{\text{Cost of goods sold}}{\text{Net sales}}$
Gross margin ratio	$\dfrac{\text{Net sales} - \text{Cost of goods sold}}{\text{Net sales}}$
Return on beginning equity	$\dfrac{\text{Net income}}{\text{Stockholder equity (beginning)}}$

Financial Distress Ratios (Altman)	
(X_1) Working capital ÷ Total assets	$\dfrac{\text{Current assets} - \text{Current liabilities}}{\text{Total assets}}$
(X_2) Retained earnings ÷ Total assets	$\dfrac{\text{Retained earnings (ending)}}{\text{Total assets}}$
(X_3) Earnings before interest and taxes ÷ Total assets	$\dfrac{\text{Net income} + \text{Interest expense} + \text{Income tax expense}}{\text{Total assets}}$
(X_4) Market value of equity ÷ Total debt	$\dfrac{\text{Market value of common and preferred stock}}{\text{Current liabilities and long-term debt}}$
(X_5) Net sales ÷ Total assets	$\dfrac{\text{Net sales}}{\text{Total assets}}$
Discriminant Z score (Altman)	$1.2 \times X_1 + 1.4 \times X_2 + 3.3 \times X_3 + 0.6 \times X_4 + 1.0 \times X_5$

*These ratios are shown to be calculated using year-end, rather than, year-average, numbers for such balances as accounts receivable and inventory. Other accounting and finance reference books may contain formulas using year-average numbers. As long as no dramatic changes have occurred during the year, the year-end numbers can have much audit relevance because they reflect the most current balance data. For comparative purposes, the ratios should be calculated on the same basis for all the years being compared.

In the Alpha.com example in Exhibits 5–3 and 5–4, the market value of the equity in the calculations is $3 million.

The discriminant Z score is an index of a company's "financial health." The higher the score, the healthier the company. The lower the score, the closer financial failure approaches. The score that predicts financial failure is a matter of dispute. Research suggests that companies with scores above 3.0 never go bankrupt. Generally, companies with scores below 1.0 experience financial difficulty of some kind. The score can be a negative number.

Chapter 6
Internal Control Evaluation: Assessing Control Risk

Professional Standards References

Compendium Section	Document Reference	Topic
AU 150	SAS 1	*Generally Accepted Auditing Standards (GAAS)*
AU 319	SAS 78	*Consideration of Internal Control in a Financial Statement Audit*
AU 325	SAS 60	*Communication of Internal Control Related Matters Noted in an Audit*
AU 9325		*Interpretation: Reporting on Existence of Material Weakness*
AU 380	SAS 61	*Communications with Audit Committees*
AU 380	SAS 90	*Audit Committee Communications*
AU 9380		*Interpretation: Applicability of SAS 61*
AU 326	SAS 80	*Evidential Matter*
AU 339	SAS 41	*Working Papers*

Learning Objectives

This chapter presents a general introduction to the theory and definitions you will find useful for internal control evaluation and control risk assessment. Internal control evaluation and control risk assessment are a very important part of the work in every audit of financial statements. Generally accepted auditing standards (GAAS) emphasize internal control in the second field work standard:

> A sufficient understanding of internal control is to be obtained to plan the audit and to determine the nature, timing, and extent of tests to be performed (*SAS 1*, AU 150; *SAS 78*, AU 319).

The key idea in the audit standard is that the "understanding of a client's internal control" need be only *sufficient* "to plan the audit" (i.e., determine the nature, timing, and extent of subsequent audit procedures). The audit standard does not require auditors to evaluate controls exhaustively in every audit. However, as you study this chapter, you will encounter aspects of auditors' involvement with controls that go beyond this limited purpose. After studying Chapter 6, you should be able to:

1. Define and describe internal control according to the COSO Report.

2. Define and describe the five basic components of internal control, and specify some of their characteristics.

3. Distinguish between management's and auditors' responsibility regarding a company's internal control.

4. Explain the phases of an evaluation of control and risk assessment and the documentation and extent of audit work required.

5. Explain the limitations of all internal control systems.

INTERNAL CONTROLS—THE COSO REPORT

LEARNING OBJECTIVE
1. Define and describe internal control according to the COSO Report.

In 1995, the AICPA Auditing Standards Board amended the auditing standards to make them consistent with a popular report on internal control known under the title of *Internal Control—Integrated Framework*. This report was produced in 1992 by the Committee of Sponsoring Organizations of the Treadway Commission (hereafter abbreviated as the "COSO Report").[1]

Definition

The COSO Report defined internal control as follows:

> Internal control is a process, effected by an entity's board of directors, management and other personnel, designed to provide reasonable assurance regarding the achievement of objectives in the following three categories:
>
> • Reliability of financial reporting.
> • Effectiveness and efficiency of operations.
> • Compliance with applicable laws and regulations.

Fundamental Concepts

Internal control is designed to achieve *objectives in three categories*. In the *financial reporting* category, the objectives are reliable published financial reports (e.g., annual financial statements, interim financial reports) and safeguarding assets from unauthorized use (e.g., embezzlement, theft, damage, unauthorized purchase or disposition). Another

---

[1] The National Commission on Fraudulent Financial Reporting (Treadway Commission) produced a 1987 report on problems in financial reporting. The sponsoring organizations (COSO) of the Treadway Commission were: the American Institute of CPAs, the American Accounting Association, the Institute of Internal Auditors, the Institute of Management Accountants, and the Financial Executives Institute.

useful, though unofficial, definition of internal control related to a company's financial reporting objectives is: "All the control methods a company uses to prevent, detect, and correct errors and frauds that might get into financial statements." You can properly infer that such control enables a company to safeguard its assets from unauthorized disposition and prepare financial statements in conformity with generally accepted accounting principles. In the *operations* category, some examples of objectives are: good business reputation, return on investment, market share, new product introduction, and safeguarding assets in the context of their effective and efficient use. The operations control objectives, internal auditors' primary focus, cover business strategy and tactics. In the *compliance* category, the broad objective is compliance with laws and regulations that affect the company. Internal and external auditors are also concerned with evaluation of compliance objective controls.

People are the key component of an entity's internal control. A company may have policy manuals, forms, computer-controlled information and accounting, and other features of control, but people make the system work at every level of company management. People establish the objectives, put control mechanisms in place, and operate them.

Internal control provides *reasonable assurance*, not absolute assurance, that category control objectives will be achieved. Since people operate the controls, breakdowns can occur. Human error, deliberate circumvention, management override, and improper collusion among people who are supposed to act independently can cause failure to achieve objectives. Internal control can help prevent and detect these people-caused failures, but it cannot guarantee that they will never happen. In auditing standards, the concept of **reasonable assurance** recognizes that the costs of controls should not exceed the benefits that are expected from the controls. Hence, a company can decide that certain controls are too costly in light of the risk of loss that may occur.

Internal control is a *process*, not an end in itself, but a means to ends (i.e., the category objectives). It is a dynamic function (process) operating every day within a company's framework (structure).

REVIEW CHECKPOINTS

6.1 What are the three categories of control objectives according to the COSO Report?

6.2 Review the "fundamental concepts" of control according to COSO. Which concept do you believe is the most important?

6.3 What four types of control breakdowns can cause failure to achieve control objectives?

COMPONENTS OF INTERNAL CONTROL

LEARNING OBJECTIVE

2. Define and describe the five basic components of internal control, and specify some of their characteristics.

The COSO Report states that internal control consists of five interrelated *components* (Exhibit 6–1)—management's control environment, management's risk assessment, management's control activities, management's monitoring, and the management information and communication systems that link all the components. COSO wrote the report to be a guide for managements of organizations (directors, officers, internal auditors, and employees). Hence, *management* is used to describe all the components. The COSO Report is not a guide for external auditors' procedural control evaluation and control risk assessment responsibilities. However, the components provide the focus for auditors' attention.

| E X H I B I T   6–1 | INTERRELATED INTERNAL CONTROL COMPONENTS |

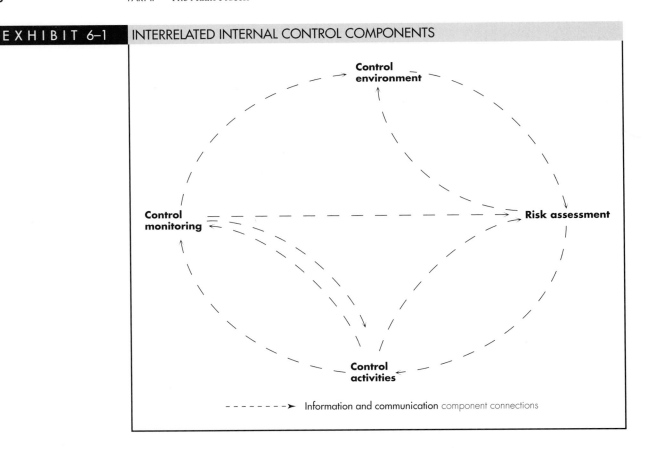

The COSO Report defined each of the three categories and stated that management should enact the five components in each of them. The control components are relevant for each of the control objectives categories. Exhibit 6–2 diagrams this scheme. The financial reporting objectives (shaded area of Exhibit 6–2) are of most direct concern to external auditors and will be the focus of the rest of the material in this chapter.

Control Environment

Since management fraud in financial statements became a topic for acceptable discussion in the late 1980s, the "tone at the top" has become a buzzword for the necessary condition for good internal control. The "tone" is virtually identical to the *control environment* component.

The control environment sets the tone of the organization. It is the foundation for all other components of internal control. It provides discipline and structure. Control environment factors include the integrity, ethical values, and competence of the company's people. The following are general elements of an internal control environment:

- Management's philosophy and operating style
- Management and employee integrity and ethical values
- Company organization structure
- Company commitment to competence—job skills and knowledge
- Functioning of the board of directors, particularly its audit committee
- Methods of assigning authority and responsibility
- Presence of an internal audit function
- Human resource policies and practices

EXHIBIT 6–2	INTERNAL CONTROL—INTEGRATED FRAMEWORK (COSO)

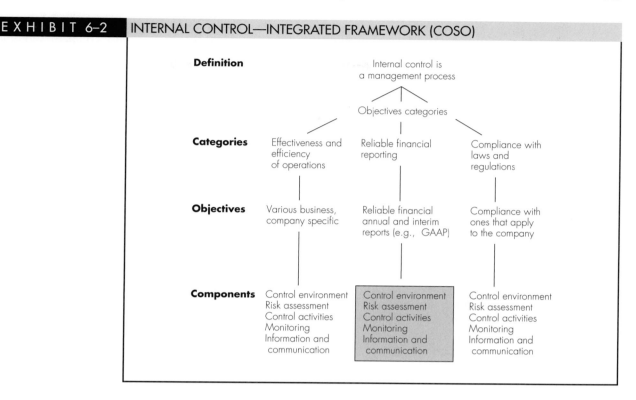

As you can see, one of the most important features of the control environment is the people who make the system work. A company's personnel problems sometimes create internal control problems. High turnover in accounting jobs means that inexperienced people are doing the accounting and control tasks, and they generally make more mistakes than experienced people. New accounting officers and managers (financial vice president, controller, chief accountant, plant accountant, data processing manager) may not be familiar enough with company accounting and may make technical and judgmental errors. Sometimes, accounting officers and employees are fired because they refuse to go along with improper accounting procedures desired by a higher level of management. In general, high turnover among accounting personnel may be a warning signal.

Risk Assessment

Using the ill-fated White Star liner *Titanic* as an analogy, management (and auditors for that matter) have often been accused of spending too much time making sure that the deck chairs are properly aligned, rather than peering over the bow looking for icebergs. "Icebergs" represent **business risk**—those factors, events, and conditions that may prevent the organization from achieving its business objectives. Given the quickly changing environment in which today's businesses operate, management, internal auditors, and external auditors must focus on the risks to entity's operations and ensure controls are in place to eliminate, mitigate, or compensate for those risks. For example, adequate insurance levels protect against losses from theft or fire. Derivative securities are used to hedge against changes in interest rates or changes in the prices of raw materials.

Risk assessment also includes the risks present in the financial reporting category. All companies face the risk that their financial statements may be unreliable. They may report assets that do not exist or ones that are not owned by the company. Asset and liability amounts may be improperly valued. They may fail to report liabilities and expenses. They may present information that does not conform to GAAP. Management needs to assess financial reporting risks in terms of its own business. Financial accounting and reporting problems are different for manufacturers, banks, insurance companies, hospitals, churches, charities, and a wide range of other organizations.

Information and Communication

The information and communication component of internal control is a necessary prerequisite for achieving management's objectives. To make effective decisions, managers must have access to timely, reliable, and relevant information. All information systems consist of four essential functions—data identification, data entry, transaction processing, and report production and distribution.

Data identification is the analysis of events, transactions, and conditions, and their "capture" for decision-making purposes. In an accounting context, the "capture" amounts to creation of *source documents*, such as sales invoices, credit memos, cash receipts listings, purchase orders, receiving reports, negotiable checks, and the like. These source documents provide the information for data entry. However, in some computerized accounting systems, the paper source documents are not produced first. Transactions may be entered directly on a keyboard, or electronic equipment may capture the transaction information. Telephone company computers capture your telephone number, the location called, and the duration of the call to determine your long-distance telephone charges. Checkout clerks in grocery stores scan package bar codes when ringing up your groceries.

Data description and entry may also consist of personnel using source documents to enter transaction information on a keyboard into a computer software program. Data may be entered in real-time or in batches. **Batch processing** is characterized by grouping like transactions to be processed in a batch at a time, using the same program. Simple batch computer systems deal with one component of an organization at a time, such as payroll or billing. For example, all payroll records are run at one time and the input is in the form of a batch of time cards or magnetic tape containing employees' identification numbers and hours worked.

In advanced paperless systems, electronic equipment may enter the accounting information automatically without producing an intermediate journal. Your long-distance telephone call is entered automatically into the telephone company's revenue and receivable accounts. Your monthly telephone bill is later produced from the accounting information.

More advanced information systems perform simultaneous multiple functions in different organizational components. Advanced systems, for example, typically update companywide databases as soon as transactions occur. These systems are described by terms such as *online* or *real time*. Because of advances in computer technology (many of today's small computers have the same processing capacity as older mainframe computers developed 20 years ago), many companies have linked personal computers (or microcomputers) together in a local area network (LAN). Thus, end-users can directly access information rather than having to request the information from a centralized information processing department.

Complex information systems are said to be *transaction driven* (or *event driven*) because the individual transaction triggers the processing activity and updates all relevant files. In contrast, a batch system could be said to be *program driven* because a specific program must be loaded into the computer to process all transactions that fit the program and its related files.

Auditors often encounter combinations of simple batch systems and advanced systems. For example, terminals and workstations are commonly used for transaction data entry, and this hardware is always used in advanced systems. However, the same hardware is also used in a simple-advanced hybrid system to collect transaction data on disks for batch update. Computer terminals may be used only for inquiry about the status of balances (e.g., perpetual inventory updated periodically by batch) instead of being used to

COMPUTER TERMINOLOGY

Online

Online is used with two different meanings. Data files are said to be online if they are electronically available to the central processor and can be accessed without operator intervention. Online also refers to a user who is connected to the central processor. Data processing also is termed online (or direct access or random) when transactions can be input into computer processing from the point of origin without first being sorted.

Real Time

Real time has a variety of meanings. Real time can refer to a quick response, such as is necessary for airline reservations. Real time in an accounting and production sense means that the system evaluates information and feeds back (return signals) in time to take action.

Networks

Networks refer to systems of interconnected computers. Computers linked at one location are commonly referred to as a local area network (LAN). Computers linked across distances via telecommunication lines are referred to as a wide area network (WAN). When different companies link their computers together to speed order processing, a value-added network (VAN) is created.

enter transactions and update records. A company can have some parts of its information system involved in immediate update processing (e.g., sale order entry) while some other applications in the same company can be batch processed (e.g., payroll that has a natural periodic cycle).

Transaction measurement and processing usually refers to posting the journals to the general ledger accounts, using the debits and credits you learned in other accounting courses. The posting operation updates the account balances. When all data are entered and processed, the account balances are ready for placement in reports. Returning to the payroll example, after validating the input and matching transactions against the employee master file for pay rate and deduction information, software programs compute the payroll, print checks, update year-to-date records, and summarize payroll information for management.

Report production and distribution is the object of the information system. The account balances are put into internal management reports and external financial statements. The internal reports are management's feedback for monitoring operations. The external reports are the financial information for outside investors, creditors, and others. Completing the payroll example, after completion of the payroll program run, the programs and data files are returned to storage (magnetic), and the output of checks and reports are distributed.

The information system produces a trail of computer operations, from data identification to reports. Often, this is called the *audit trail*. You can visualize that it starts with the source documents and proceeds through to the financial reports. Auditors often follow this trail frontwards and backwards! They will follow it backwards from the financial reports to the source documents to determine whether everything in the financial reports is supported by appropriate source documents. They will follow it forward from source documents to reports to determine whether everything that happened (transactions) was recorded in the accounts and reported in the financial statements.

An information and communication system processes transactions and produces management reports without necessarily guaranteeing their accuracy. Nevertheless, the information system contains important elements of control.

R E V I E W
CHECKPOINTS

6.4 What are the five components of management's control?

6.5 What is the purpose of risk assessment for a company?

6.6 What financial reporting risks do managements in all kinds of companies face?

6.7 What is the audit trail? Of what use is it in the audit process?

6.8 Why are some computer systems said to be "transaction driven," while others (primarily batch systems) are said to be "program driven?"

Control Activities

While the "tone at the top" (control environment) is pervasive, **control activities** are specific actions taken by a client's management and employees to help ensure that management directives are carried out. Control activities (both computerized and manual) are imposed on the accounting system for the purpose of preventing, detecting, and correcting errors and frauds that might enter and flow through to the financial statements. Control activities include: (1) *Performance reviews*—management's continuous supervision of operations, (2) *Segregation of duties* designed to reduce opportunities for a person to be in a position to perpetrate and conceal errors and frauds when performing normal duties, (3) *Physical controls* designed to ensure safeguarding and security of assets and records, and (4) *Information processing controls*, including approvals, authorizations, verifications, and reconciliations. We discuss each of these control activities in the following sections.

Performance Reviews

Management has primary responsibility for ensuring the organization's objectives are being met. Performance reviews require management's active participation in the supervision of operations. Management study of budget variances with follow-up action is an example of a performance review.

Managers should also provide for periodic comparison of the recorded amounts with independent evidence of existence and valuation. Periodic comparisons may include counts of cash on hand, reconciliation of bank statements, counts of securities, inventory counting, confirmation of accounts receivable and accounts payable, and other such comparison operations undertaken to determine whether accounting records—the recorded accountability—represent real assets and liabilities.

A management that performs frequent performance reviews has more opportunities to detect errors in the records than a management that does not. The frequency, of course, is governed by the costs and benefits. One should not try to count, compare, or confirm assets with great frequency (say, weekly) unless they are especially susceptible to loss or error or unless they are unusually valuable.

Subsequent action to investigate further or correct differences is also important. Periodic comparison and action to correct errors lowers the risk that material misstatements remain in the accounts. Such comparisons are frequently assigned to internal auditors and other employees. Research has shown that companies with active internal auditors have fewer account errors.

Segregation of Duties

A very important characteristic of effective internal control is an appropriate segregation of functional responsibilities. Four kinds of functional responsibilities should be performed by different departments, or at least by different persons on the company's accounting staff:

1. *Authorization to execute transactions.* This duty belongs to people who have authority and responsibility for initiating the recordkeeping for transactions. Authoriza-

tion may be general, referring to a class of transactions (e.g., all purchases), or it may be specific (e.g., sale of a major asset).

2. *Recording transactions.* This duty refers to the accounting and recordkeeping function (bookkeeping) which, in most organizations, is delegated to a computer system. (People who control the computer processing are the recordkeepers.)

3. *Custody of assets involved in the transactions.* This duty refers to the actual physical possession or effective physical control of property.

4. *Periodic reconciliation of existing assets to recorded amounts.* This duty refers to making comparisons at regular intervals and taking appropriate action with respect to any differences.

Incompatible responsibilities are combinations of responsibilities that place a person alone in a position to create and conceal errors, frauds, and misstatements in his or her normal job. Duties should be so divided that no one person can control two or more of these responsibilities. If different departments or persons are forced to deal with these different facets of transactions, then two benefits are obtained: (1) Frauds are more difficult because they would require *collusion* of two or more persons, and most people hesitate to seek the help of others to conduct wrongful acts, and (2) by acting in a coordinated manner (handling different aspects of the same transaction), innocent errors are more likely to be found and flagged for correction. The old saying is: "Two heads are better than one."

Physical Controls

Physical access to assets and important records, documents, and blank forms should be limited to authorized personnel. Such assets as inventory and securities should not be available to persons who have no need to handle them. Likewise, access to cost records and accounts receivable records should be denied to people who do not have a recordkeeping responsibility for them. Some blank forms are very important for accounting and control, and their availability should be restricted. Someone not involved in accounting for sales should not be able to pick up blank sales invoices and blank shipping orders. A person should not be able to obtain blank checks (including computer-paper blank checks) unless he or she is involved in cash disbursement activities. Sometimes, access to blank forms is the equivalent of access to, or custody of, an important asset. For example,

AUDITING INSIGHT

HOW COMPUTERS AFFECT INTERNAL CONTROL

Many internal control activities once performed by different individuals in manual systems may be concentrated in computer systems. The number of people who handle a transaction is typically reduced, often to just the individual employee who enters the data into the computer. Therefore, individuals who have access to the computer may be in a position to perform incompatible functions. As a result, other control activities may be required in computer systems to achieve the degree of control ordinarily accomplished by segregating functions in manual systems. These may include such techniques as password control procedures to prevent incompatible functions from being performed by individuals who have access to assets and access to records through an online terminal or by limiting the types of transactions that may be performed from certain computers.

In a simple environment, an individual manager can be responsible for managing and ensuring the quality of gathering, processing, and using data. In more complex environments, an individual manager may be responsible for only a portion of the processing and control. Unless carefully defined and monitored, this sharing of control responsibilities can result in loss of overall control.

someone who has access to blank checks has a measure of actual custody and access to cash.

Physical security of computer equipment and limited access to computer program files and data files are as important as restricting access to blank checks or inventory. Access controls help prevent improper use or manipulation of data files, unauthorized or incorrect use of computer programs, and improper use of the computer equipment. Locked doors, security passes, passwords, and check-in logs (including logs produced by the computer) can be used to limit access to the computer system hardware. Having definite schedules for running computer applications is another way to detect unauthorized access because the computer system software can produce reports that can be compared to the planned schedule. Variations then can be investigated for unauthorized use of computer resources.

Since magnetic storage media can be erased or written over, controls are necessary to ensure that the proper file is being used and that the files and programs are appropriately backed up. Backup involves a retention system for files, programs, and documentation, so master files can be reconstructed in case of accidental loss and so processing can continue at another site if the computer center is lost to fire or flood. Thus, backup files must be stored offsite, away from the main computer.

Weaknesses or absences of access controls decrease the overall integrity of the computer system. The audit team should be uncomfortable when such deficiencies exist and should weigh their impact in the overall evaluation of control risk.

Information processing controls

Information processing controls are organized under three categories—input controls, processing controls, and output controls.

The weakest point in computer systems is input—the point at which transaction data are transformed from hard-copy source documents into machine-readable tape or disk, or when direct entry is made with a communication device such as a remote terminal. When undetected errors are entered originally, they may not be detected during processing, and, if detected, they are troublesome to correct. Processing control refers to error-condition check routines written into the computer program. Output control refers primarily to control over the distribution of reports, but feedback on errors and comparison of input totals to output totals also are part of this "last chance" control point.

Input Control Activities.   **Input controls** (also commonly referred to as "application controls") are designed to provide reasonable assurance that data received for processing by the computer department have been authorized properly and converted into machine-sensible form, and that data have not been lost, suppressed, added, duplicated, or improperly changed. These controls also apply to correction and resubmission of data initially rejected as erroneous. The following controls are particularly important:

- **Input Authorized and Approved.** Only properly authorized and approved input should be accepted for processing by the computer center. Authorization usually is a clerical (noncomputer) procedure involving a person's signature or stamp on a transaction document. However, some authorizations can be general (e.g., a management policy of automatic approval for sales under $1,000), and some authorizations can be computer controlled (e.g., automatic production of a purchase order when an inventory item reaches a predetermined reorder point).

- **Check Digits.** Numbers often are used in computer systems in lieu of customer names, vendor names, and so forth. One common type of number validation procedure is the calculation of a *check digit*. A **check digit** is an extra number, precisely calculated, that is tagged onto the end of a basic identification number such as an employee number. The basic code with its check digit sometimes is called a **self-checking number**. An electronic device can be installed on a data input device or the calculation can be programmed. The device or the program calculates the correct check digit and compares it to the one on the input data. When the digits do not match, an error message is indicated on the device or printed out on an input error report. Check digits are used only on identification numbers (not quantity or value fields) to detect coding errors or keying errors such as the transposition of digits (e.g., coding 387 as 837).[2]

- **Record counts.** Counts of records are tallies of the number of transaction documents submitted for data conversion. The known number submitted can be compared to the count of records produced by the data-conversion device (e.g., the number of sales transactions or count of magnetic records coded). A count mismatch indicates a lost item or one converted twice. Record counts are used as batch control totals and also are used during processing and at the output stage—whenever the comparison of a known count can be made with a computer-generated count.

- **Batch financial totals.** These totals are used in the same way as record counts, except the batch total is the sum of some important quantity or amount (e.g., the total sales dollars in a batch of invoices). Batch totals are also useful during processing and at the output stage.

- **Batch hash totals.** These totals are similar to batch number totals, except the hash total is not meaningful for accounting records (e.g., the sum of all the invoice numbers on invoices submitted to the data input operator).

- **Valid character tests.** These tests are used to check input data fields to see if they contain numbers where they are supposed to have numbers and alphabetic letters where they are supposed to have letters.

- **Valid sign tests.** Sign tests check data fields for appropriate plus or minus signs.

- **Missing data tests.** These edit tests check data fields to see if any are blank when they must contain data for the record entry to be correct.

- **Sequence tests.** These test the input data for numerical sequence of documents when sequence is important for processing, as in batch processing. This validation routine also can check for missing documents in a prenumbered series.

- **Limit or reasonableness tests.** These tests are computerized checks to see whether data values exceed or fall below some predetermined limit. For example, a payroll application may have a limit test to flag or reject any weekly payroll time record of 50 or more hours. The limit tests are a computerized version of scanning—the general audit procedure of reviewing data for indication of anything unusual that might turn out to be an error.

- **Error Correction and Resubmission.** Errors should be subject to special controls. Usually, the computer department itself is responsible only for correcting its own errors (data conversion errors, for example). Other kinds of errors, such as those due to improper coding, should be referred to and handled by the user departments. It is a good idea to have a control group log the contents of error reports in order to monitor the nature, disposition, and proper correction of rejected data. Unless properly supervised and monitored, the error-correction process itself can become a source of data input errors.

---

[2] One check digit algorithm is the "Modulus 11 Prime Number" method:

a. Begin with a basic number: 814973.

b. Multiply consecutive prime number weights of 19, 17, 13, 7, 5, 3 to each digit in the basic code number:

$$
\begin{array}{cccccc}
8 & 1 & 4 & 9 & 7 & 3 \\
\times 19 & \times 17 & \times 13 & \times 7 & \times 5 & \times 3 \\
\hline
= 152 & + 17 & + 52 & + 63 & + 35 & + 9 = 328
\end{array}
$$

Note: the sequence of weights is the same for all codes in a given system.

c. Add the result of the multiplication = 328.

d. Determine the next higher multiple of 11, which is 330.

e. Subtract the sum of the multiplication $(330 - 328 = 2)$. This is the check digit.

f. New account number: 8149732.

Now if this number is entered incorrectly, say it is keypunched as 8419732, the check digit will not equal 2 and an error will be indicated. [See J.G. Burch, Jr., F.R. Strater, Jr., and G. Grudniski, *Information Systems: Theory and Practice*, 5th ed. (New York: John Wiley & Sons)]

AUDITING INSIGHT

WHEN GOOD CONTROLS GO BAD

Zondervan Corporation announced a $5 million pretax write-down for the year. The problem was in the accounting controls at its Family Bookstore division. Ten percent of the inventory was "missing." The company had unsalable finished products and $1 million in "overlooked liabilities."

Zondervan's workers were not putting purchasing records into their computers correctly. Only 20 percent of the bookstore managers were using the system correctly. The system was capable of handling 7,000 individual product identifiers for 30 store locations; but the company was processing 10,000 products for 87 stores. Employees improvised by bunching more than one product onto one identifier code. This activity made record-tracking virtually impossible.

Source: *Forbes.*

Processing Control Activities.   Processing controls are designed to provide reasonable assurance that data processing has been performed as intended without any omission or double-counting of transactions. Many of the processing controls are the same as the input controls, but they are used in the actual processing phases, rather than at the time input is checked. Other important controls are the following:

- **Run-to-Run Totals.** Movement of data from one department to another or one processing program to another should be controlled. One useful control is run-to-run totals. Run-to-run refers to sequential processing operations—runs—on the same data. These totals may be batch record counts, financial totals, and/or hash totals obtained at the end of one processing run. The totals are passed to the next run and compared to corresponding totals produced at the end of the second run.

- **Control Total Reports.** Control totals—record counts, financial totals, hash totals, and run-to-run totals—should be produced during processing operations and printed out on a report. Someone (the control group, for example) should have the responsibility for comparing and/or reconciling them to input totals or totals from earlier processing runs. Loss or duplication of data thus may be detected. For example, the total of the balances in the accounts receivable master file from the last update run, plus the total of the credit sales from the current update transactions, should equal the total of the balances at the end of the current processing.

- **File and Operator Controls.** External and internal labels are means of assuring that the proper files are used in applications. The systems software should produce a log to identify instructions entered by the operator and to make a record of time and use statistics for application runs. Supervisory personnel should review these logs on a periodic basis.

- **Limit and Reasonableness Tests.** These tests should be programmed to ensure that illogical conditions do not occur; for example, depreciating an asset below zero or calculating a negative inventory quantity. These conditions, and others considered important, should generate error reports for supervisory review. Other logic and validation checks also can be used during processing.

Output Control Activities.   Output controls are the final check on the accuracy of the results of computer processing. These controls should be designed to ensure that only authorized persons receive reports or have access to files produced by the system. Typical output controls are the following:

- **Control Totals.** Control totals produced as output should be compared and/or reconciled to input and run-to-run control totals produced during processing. An independent control group should be responsible for the review of output control totals and investigation of differences.

AUDITING INSIGHT

WALLOPING WATER BILL

Patricia and Thomas received an unexpected welcome from the City of Austin—a $3,200 water utility bill for 30 days of service in their three-bedroom house.

Said Patricia, "I thought at that rate I could live off the most expensive scotch they make."

City water officials were very nice about fixing the glitch. A city official said, "The bill apparently slipped through the cracks. This is the first billing mistake this large since 1991."

Fifty-five water meter readers check 445,000 meters each month in the service area. The average monthly error rate is nine per 10,000 (0.09 percent). The city catches mistakes on about 396 bills before they are mailed each month. That leaves about four undetected mistakes on 445,000 meters per month (0.0009 percent).

The city utility computer system controls and its limit and reasonableness tests are designed to detect these billing errors, and the controls are effective 99.91 percent of the time.

Source: *Austin American-Statesman*

- **Master File Changes.** These changes should be reported in detail back to the user department from which the request for change originated because an error can be pervasive. For example, changing selling prices incorrectly can cause all sales to be priced wrong. Someone should compare computer-generated change reports to original source documents for assurance that the data are correct.

- **Output Distribution.** Systems output should be distributed only to persons authorized to receive it. A distribution list should be maintained and used to deliver report copies. The number of copies produced should be restricted to the number needed.

Monitoring

Internal control systems need to be monitored. Management should assess the quality of its control performance on a timely basis. Monitoring includes regular management and supervisory activities and other actions personnel take in performing their duties. Errors, frauds, and internal control deficiencies should be reported to top management and to the audit committee of the board of directors.

Monitoring helps ensure that internal control continues to operate effectively. Everyday monitoring of the types shown below are part of the internal control process:

- Operating managers compare internal reports and published financial statements with their knowledge of the business.
- Customer complaints of amounts billed are analyzed.
- Vendor complaints of amounts paid are analyzed.
- Regulators report to the company on compliance with laws and regulations (e.g., bank examiners' reports, IRS audits).
- Accounting managers supervise the accuracy and completeness of transaction processing.
- Recorded amounts are periodically compared to actual assets and liabilities (e.g., internal auditors' inventory counts, receivables and payables confirmations, bank reconciliations).
- External auditors report on control performance and give recommendations for improvement.
- Training sessions for management and employees heighten awareness of the importance of controls.

These elements of the monitoring component have a great deal in common with the controls included in the control activities component. Indeed, some of the control activities explained earlier in this chapter are monitoring activities as well (e.g., periodic comparison).

Supervision is an important element of monitoring. You can readily imagine a company having clerks and computers to carry out the accounting and control. Equally important is management's provision for supervision of the work. A supervisor could, for example, oversee the credit manager's performance or could periodically compare the sum of customers' balances to the accounts receivable control account total. Supervisors or department heads can correct errors found by the clerical staff and make or approve accounting decisions.

R E V I E W
CHECKPOINTS

6.9 What is a control activity?

6.10 What are some of the characteristics that distinguish among control environment, information and communication system, and control activities in an internal control system?

6.11 What four general kinds of functional responsibilities should be performed by different departments or persons in a control system with good division of duties?

6.12 Describe five input controls that could be used to ensure that a customer payment has been correctly posted to their account.

6.13 What is a self-checking number? Can you give an example of one of your own?

6.14 Give some examples of everyday work a company's management can use to enact the monitoring component of internal control.

MANAGEMENT VERSUS AUDITOR RESPONSIBILITY FOR INTERNAL CONTROL

Just as management is responsible for an organization's financial statements, management is also responsible for the components of its internal control. Management establishes a control environment, assesses risks it wishes to control, specifies information and communication channels and content (including the accounting system and its reports), designs and implements control activities, and monitors, supervises, and maintains the controls.

While the objective of internal control is to produce reliable financial statement assertions, principally in account balances, the overriding objective of control activities is to process transactions correctly. Correctly processed transactions produce correct account balances, which in turn help produce accurate and reliable assertions in the financial statements. These connections are shown in Exhibit 6–3.

Control Objectives

The presentation in Exhibit 6–4 summarizes seven objectives, with a general statement of the objective and a specific example (accounts receivable/sales transaction processing context). The explanations that follow tell you some more about these objectives and give some examples of client control activities designed to accomplish them.

Validity refers to ensuring that recorded transactions are ones that *should* have been recorded. The client can require an employee to match shipping documents with sales invoices before a sale is recorded. This activity is supposed to prevent recording undocumented (possibly fictitious) sales.

EXHIBIT 6–3	TRANSACTION PROCESSING CONTROL OBJECTIVES AND FINANCIAL STATEMENT ASSERTIONS

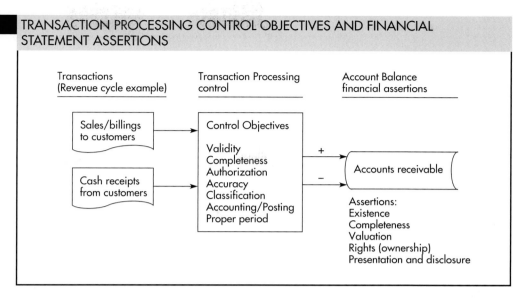

EXHIBIT 6–4	TRANSACTION PROCESSING INTERNAL CONTROL OBJECTIVES

Objectives	General	Specific Example (accounts receivable/sales)
Validity	Recorded transactions are valid and documented.	Recorded sales are supported by invoices, shipping documents, and customer orders.
Completeness	All valid transactions are recorded, and none are omitted.	All shipping documents are prenumbered and matched with sales invoices daily.
Authorization	Transactions are authorized according to company policy.	Credit sales over $1,000 are given prior approval by the credit manager.
Accuracy	Transaction dollar amounts are properly calculated.	Sales invoices contain correct quantities and are mathematically correct.
Classification	Transactions are properly classified in the accounts.	Sales to subsidiaries and affiliates are classified as intercompany transactions.
Accounting/Posting	Transaction accounting is complete.	All sales on credit are charged to customers' individual accounts.
Proper period	Transactions are recorded in the proper period.	Sales of the current period are charged to customers in the current period, and sales of the next period are charged in the next period.

Completeness refers to ensuring that valid transactions are *not omitted entirely* from the accounting records. If sales are represented by shipments, then no shipping documents should be left unmatched with sales invoices. Transaction documents (e.g., shipping documents) are often prenumbered. Accounting for the numerical sequence of prenumbered shipping documents is a control activity designed to achieve the completeness objective.

Authorization refers to ensuring that transactions are approved before they are recorded. Credit approval for a sale transaction is an example. Sometimes, you may need to ponder the nature of authorization for some transactions. For example, what "authorization" is needed to record a cash receipt? Usually none—companies are happy to accept payments—but a sales manager may need to approve a good customer taking a discount after the discount period has elapsed.

Management must establish criteria for *recognizing* transactions in the accounting system and for supervisory *approval* of transactions. A control system should permit accounting to proceed only for authorized transactions and should bar unauthorized transactions.

Authorization may be general and may be delegated to a fairly low level of management. For example, (1) all shipments amounting to more than $1,000 in value require credit approval and (2) all sales can be recorded in the accounting department upon receipt of a copy of a shipping ticket. Some authorizations may be quite tacit. For example, listing the payments received on account when the mail is opened may be sufficient authorization to accept and record cash receipts. Some authorizations may be very important and defined specifically by the board of directors. For example, sales of major assets or responsibility for signing the company name to a loan agreement may be authorized specifically in the minutes of the board of directors.

Accuracy refers to ensuring that dollar amounts are figured correctly. A manual or computer check for billing the same quantity shipped, at the correct list price, with correct multiplication and addition of the total, is intended to control for accuracy. (This objective, rather than the completeness one, covers errors of billing at too low a price or for a smaller quantity than shipped.)

Classification refers to ensuring that transactions are recorded in the right accounts, charged or credited to the right customers (including classification of sales to subsidiaries and affiliates, as mentioned in Exhibit 6–4), entered in the correct segment product line or inventory description, and so forth. Classification might be confused with accuracy, but remember that accuracy refers to the accounting numbers.

Accounting/Posting is a general category concerned with ensuring that the accounting process for a transaction is completely performed and in conformity with GAAP. For example, a clerk can balance the total of individual customers' receivables with the control account to determine whether all charges and credits to the control account also have been entered in individual customers' accounts. (Classification is the control over whether the entries got into the right customers' accounts, and accuracy is the control category related to use of correct numbers.)

Proper period refers to ensuring that the accounting for transactions is in the period in which they occur. This control objective is very closely related to the *cutoff* aspect of the *existence* and *completeness* assertions. Procedurally, the client's accountants must be alert to the dates of transactions in relation to month-, quarter-, and year-end. Proper period accounting (cutoff) is a pervasive problem. You will see it mentioned in relation to all kinds of transactions—sales, purchases, inventories, expense accruals, income accruals, and others.

Control Objectives and Management's Assertions

The transaction processing control objectives are closely connected to management's assertions in financial statements. An association of the control objectives with the five assertions is shown in Exhibit 6–5. The Xs in the exhibit show the primary relevance of control objectives to assertions.

To interpret Exhibit 6–5, associate the achievement of control objectives with the probability that an assertion may be materially misstated. For example, if a company has strong control over the validity of recorded sales and cash receipts transactions, if it has an effective system of credit authorization, and if it ensures that sales transactions are correctly recorded in the proper period, then the auditor can assess a low control risk related to the existence/occurrence assertions for sales and accounts receivables balances.

EXHIBIT 6–5	ASSOCIATION OF CONTROL OBJECTIVES AND FINANCIAL STATEMENT ASSERTIONS

Control Objectives	Existence, Occurrence	Completeness	Valuation	Rights, Obligations	Presentation and Disclosure
Validity	X			X	
Completeness		X		X	
Authorization	X		X		
Accuracy			X		
Classification					X
Accounting					X
Proper Period	X	X			

Financial Statement Assertions

Auditors' Internal Control Responsibilities

External auditors are responsible for *evaluating* existing internal controls and *assessing* the control risk in them for the period under audit. **Control risk**, a function of the client's controls, is the probability that a company's controls will fail to detect errors and frauds, provided any enter the accounting system in the first place. The auditors' assessment task is to assign an evaluation to the control risk. Many auditors conclude the internal control risk assessment decision with a descriptive assessment (e.g., maximum, slightly below maximum, high, moderate, low), and some auditors put probability numbers on it (e.g., 1.0, 0.90, 0.70, 0.50, 0.30).

The primary reason under GAAS for conducting an evaluation of a company's internal control and assessing control risk is to give the auditors a basis for planning the audit and determining the nature, timing, and extent of audit procedures for the account balance (substantive) audit program.

If auditors assess control risk as "maximum" (i.e., poor control), they will tend to perform a great deal of substantive balance-audit work with large sample sizes (extent), at or near the company's fiscal year-end (timing), using procedures designed to obtain high-quality external evidence (nature). On the other hand, if auditors assess control risk as "low" (i.e., effective control), they can perform a lesser quantity of substantive balance-audit work with small sample sizes (extent), at an interim date before the company's fiscal year-end (timing), using a mixture of procedures designed to obtain high-quality external evidence and lower quality internal evidence (nature). Of course, auditors may assess control risk between "low" and "maximum" (e.g., "moderate," "high," or "slightly below maximum") and adjust the substantive audit work accordingly.

A secondary reason for evaluating internal control is to provide information useful to management and directors for carrying out the company's control mission. Regulators, Congress, and the public have been concerned about auditors' communication of internal control and other matters to high levels in public corporations, especially in banks and other financial institutions. In response, the AICPA Auditing Standards Board issued two pronouncements that address auditors' responsibilities to (1) communicate internal control matters noted in an audit (SAS 60, AU 325), and (2) communicate certain matters to the audit committee of the board of directors (SAS 61, AU 380).

When performing an audit, auditors may notice *reportable conditions* and *material weaknesses*. **Reportable conditions** are defined as *matters the auditors believe should be communicated to the client's audit committee because they represent significant deficiencies in the design or operation of the internal controls that could adversely affect the organization's ability to record, process, summarize, and report financial data in the financial statements* (SAS 60, AU 325). Examples include:

- Absence of appropriate segregation of duties.
- Absence of appropriate reviews and approvals of transactions.
- Evidence of failure of control procedures.
- Evidence of intentional management override of control procedures by persons in authority to the detriment of control objectives.
- Evidence of willful wrongdoing by employees or management, including manipulation, falsification, or alteration of accounting records.

Reportable conditions include the more serious condition called a **material weakness** in internal control, which is defined as *a condition in which the design or operation of internal control does not reduce to a relatively low level the risk that errors or frauds in amounts that would be material to the financial statements being audited may occur and may not be detected within a timely period by employees in the normal course of performing their assigned functions.* This long and involved definition describes a more serious version of a reportable condition.

Although auditors are not obligated to search for or identify reportable conditions and material weaknesses, they must communicate ones that come to their attention in the normal performance of the audit. The report, preferably in writing, is to be addressed to the management, the board of directors, or its audit committee. An illustration of a report is in Exhibit 6–6.

While written communications are preferred, auditing standards permit auditors to communicate reportable conditions orally, in which case a memorandum of the oral report should be placed in the working papers (SAS 60, AU 325). However, because the potential for misinterpretation is great, auditors should not issue reports stating that no reportable conditions were noted during an audit (AU 9325). A manager receiving such a report could conclude (incorrectly) that the auditors are stating positively that the company has no internal control problems.

Auditors' communications of reportable conditions and material weaknesses are intended to help management carry out its responsibilities for internal control monitoring and change. However, external auditors' observations and recommendations are usually

---

EXHIBIT 6–6	INTERNAL CONTROL STRUCTURE-RELATED LETTER

Anderson, Olds, and Watershed
Certified Public Accountants
Chicago, Illinois
January 31, 2002

Board of Directors
Kingston Company
Chicago, Illinois
Gentlemen:

In planning and performing our audit of the financial statements of Kingston Company for the year ended December 31, 2001, we considered its internal control in order to determine our auditing procedures for the purpose of expressing our opinion on the financial statements and not to provide assurance on the internal control system. However, we noted a certain matter involving the internal control and its operation that we consider to be a reportable condition under standards established by the American Institute of Certified Public Accountants. A reportable condition involves a matter coming to our attention relating to a significant deficiency in the design or operation of the internal control that, in our judgment, could adversely affect the company's ability to record, process, summarize, and report financial data consistent with the assertions of management in the financial statements.

The matter noted is that shipping personnel have both transaction-initiation and alteration authority and custody of inventory assets. If invoice/shipping copy documents are altered to show shipment of smaller quantities than actually shipped, customers or accomplices can receive your products without charge. The sales revenue and accounts receivable could be understated, and the inventory could be overstated. This deficiency caused us to spend more time auditing your inventory quantities.

This report is intended solely for the information and use of the board of directors and its audit committee.

Respectfully yours,
/s/ Anderson, Olds, and Watershed

limited to external financial reporting matters. While external auditors are not responsible for designing effective controls for audit clients, auditing firms often undertake control design as consulting engagements and consider such work to be separate and apart from the audit engagement responsibility.

The concern about reporting control-related matters within a company has spilled over into a set of other important matters that auditors are required to report to companies' audit committees (SAS 61, AU 380). The purpose of these communications is to enhance the audit committees' ability to oversee the audit functions (external and internal) in a company. The auditors are responsible for informing the audit committee about these matters:

- Independent auditors' responsibilities regarding financial statements and other information in documents that include the audited financial statements (e.g., the annual report to shareholders, the annual 10-K report filed with the SEC).
- The *quality* and *acceptability* of the company's accounting principles and underlying estimates in its financial statements.
- Significant audit adjustments recommended by the auditors.
- Disagreements with management about accounting principles, accounting estimates, the scope of the audit, disclosures in the notes, and the wording of the audit report.
- The auditor's view on accounting matters on which management has consulted with other accountants.
- Major accounting and auditing issues discussed with management in connection with beginning or continuing an auditor-client relationship.
- Difficulties with management encountered while performing the audit—delays in starting the audit or providing information, unreasonable time schedule, unavailability of client personnel, and failure of client personnel to complete data schedules.

Internal auditors also have responsibilities for reporting to a company's board of directors. *Statement on Internal Auditing Standards No. 7* ("Communicating with the Board of Directors") states that the director of internal auditing should have direct communication with the board. In particular, significant findings about frauds, illegal acts, errors, inefficiency, waste, ineffectiveness, conflicts of interest, and control weaknesses should be reviewed with the management, then communicated to the board of directors and its audit committee. As with the external auditors, these communications are designed to inform the board and the audit committee so they can fulfill their responsibilities.

Auditors often issue another type of report to management called a *management letter*. This letter may contain commentary and suggestions on a variety of matters in addition to internal control matters. Examples are operational and administrative efficiency, business strategy, and profit-making possibilities. While not required by auditing standards, management letters are a type of management advice rendered as a part of an audit.

6.15 What are managements' and auditors' respective responsibilities regarding internal control?

6.16 Define control risk and explain the role of control risk assessment in audit planning.

6.17 What are the primary and secondary reasons for conducting an evaluation of an audit client's internal control?

6.18 What is a reportable condition regarding internal control?

6.19 What is material weakness?

6.20 What reports on control and other matters are auditors required to give to a company's management, board of directors, or audit committee?

INTERNAL CONTROL EVALUATION

LEARNING OBJECTIVE

4. Explain the phases of an evaluation of control and risk assessment and the documentation and extent of audit work required.

The five components of internal control are considered to be criteria for evaluating a company's financial reporting controls and the bases for auditors' assessment of control risk as it relates to financial statements. Thus, auditors must consider the five components in terms of (1) understanding a client's financial reporting controls and documenting that understanding, (2) preliminarily assessing the control risk, and (3) testing the controls, reassessing control risk, and using that assessment to plan the remainder of the audit work.

Exhibit 6–7 puts the internal control evaluation phases in perspective. In Phase 1, auditors are required to document their understanding of the client's internal control. The audit team can halt the control evaluation process for the *efficiency* or *effectiveness* reasons explained below. However, if the auditors want to justify a low risk assessment to restrict the substantive audit procedures, the evaluation must be continued in Phase 3, the testing phase.

Phase 1: Understand and Document the Client's Internal Control

A major goal in audits is to be *efficient*. This means performing the work in minimum time and with minimum cost while still doing high-quality work to obtain sufficient, competent evidence. The allocation of work times between control evaluation and "year-end audit work" is a cost-benefit trade-off. Generally, the more auditors know about good controls, the less substantive year-end work they need to do. However, auditors do not necessarily need to determine the actual quality of a company's internal control. They only need to know enough to plan the other audit work. They can obtain only a minimum understanding of a client's control, assess a high control risk, and perform extensive substantive balance-audit work. Alternatively, they can perform a complete evaluation of control, assess control risk to be lower, and minimize the balance-audit work.

Obtaining an Understanding

The Phase 1 obtaining-an-understanding work should occur early. It gives auditors an overall acquaintance with the control environment and management's risk assessment, the flow of transactions through the accounting system, and the design of some client control activities. Each of these elements of the control system may be affected by computer processing. The Phase 1 work should produce general knowledge of the control environment along these lines:

- Existence and implementation of a company code of conduct
- Degree of emphasis on meeting performance targets
- Formal and informal job descriptions
- Assignment of responsibilities and delegation of authority
- Membership and operation of the board's audit committee
- Financial reporting attitudes (e.g., conservative, liberal)
- Information flow to managers
- Nature of employee candidate background checks
- Type of actions taken when employee misconduct (e.g., theft, embezzlement, fraudulent reporting) is discovered
- Work assignments of internal auditors, if any
- A description of the company's computer resources
- A description of the organizational structure of information processing operations as it relates to personnel within the information processing department, and the interaction with personnel in other departments.

EXHIBIT 6–7   PHASES OF INTERNAL CONTROL EVALUATION

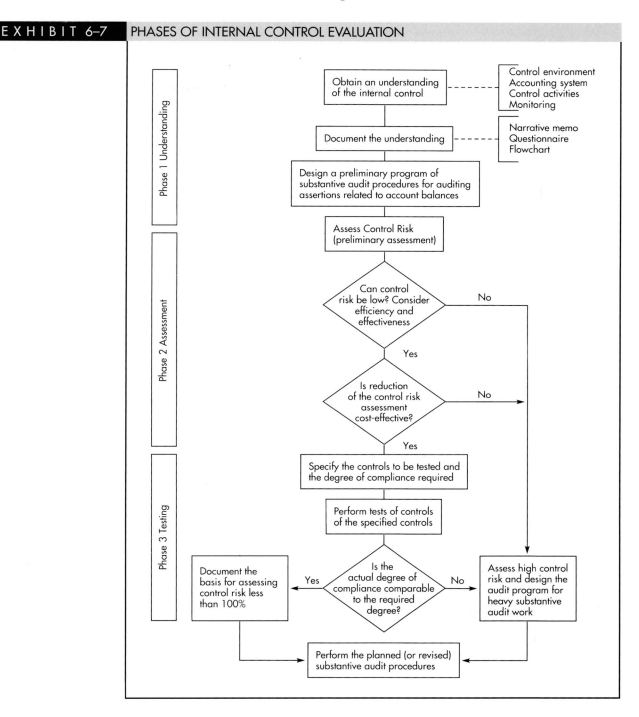

After the audit team gains an understanding of the control environment, its next task is to obtain an understanding of the accounting system—the flow of transactions. This review should produce general knowledge along the following lines:

- The various classes of significant accounting transactions
- The types of material errors and frauds that could occur
- Methods by which each significant class of transactions is:
     Authorized and initiated
     Documented and recorded

Processed in the accounting system

Placed in financial reports and disclosures

Auditors obtain an understanding of internal control from several sources of information. Minimum requirements for a good control-oriented accounting system include a chart of accounts and some written definitions and instructions about measuring and classifying transactions. In most organizations, such material is incorporated in computer systems documentation, computer program documentation, systems and procedures manuals, flowcharts of transaction processing, and various paper forms. The description of computer resources should give auditors (1) an overview of information processing activities, (2) knowledge of access to computer resources used to process accounting information, and (3) knowledge of company policies regarding access only by authorized personnel. Auditors should inquire about the division of responsibilities between systems and programming staff and operation personnel to assess the segregation of duties. They should understand the existence and organization of the control function and its assigned responsibilities. Auditors should identify the position the information processing function has in the overall organization structure, as well as understand the interaction between user departments and the computer department.

Accounting manuals should contain statements of objectives and policies. Management should approve statements of specific accounting and control objectives and assure that appropriate steps are taken to accomplish them. A company's internal auditors and systems staff often review and evaluate this documentation. Independent auditors may review and study their work instead of doing the same tasks over again. Other sources of information include: (1) previous experience with the company as found in last year's audit, (2) responses to inquiries directed to client personnel, (3) inspection of documents and records, and (4) observation of activities and operations made in a "walk-through" of one or a few transactions.

Auditors can decide to stop the evaluation work in Phase 1 for either of two reasons, both of them coordinated with the final audit program. First, the audit team might conclude that no more evidence is needed to show that control is too poor to justify restrictions of subsequent audit procedures. This conclusion is equivalent to assessing control risk at 1.0 (100 percent) and specifying extensive account balance-audit procedures, such as confirmation of all customer accounts as of December 31. Essentially, this decision is a matter of *audit effectiveness*.

Second, the audit team might decide that more time and effort would be spent evaluating controls to lower the control risk assessment than could be saved by being able to

AUDITING INSIGHT

UNDERSTANDING THE AUDITABILITY OF THE ACCOUNTS

Bad Books Block Audit for County: Travis County commissioners kept such poor financial records for four nonprofit corporations they controlled that an audit cannot be done, commissioners were told Tuesday. The four corporations are conduits for more than $630 million in low-interest financing for businesses. CPA D. Holliday of Holliday & Associates struggled to find words to describe the corporations' records. "To say they are horrid is stretching it, because there weren't any records," Holliday told Commissioners Court members.

Among the findings were: (1) No records were kept of purchase and redemption of certificates of deposit for hundreds of thousands of dollars, (2) there may be certificates of deposit the county officials do not know exist, (3) bank statements were not kept, (4) checking accounts were not reconciled.

The former treasurer of the corporations said: "We had a very simple bookkeeping system. Money went in and went out. The system wasn't sophisticated because it wasn't needed."

Source: *Austin American Statesman.*

AUDITING INSIGHT

EFFECT OF COMPUTERS ON INTERNAL CONTROL EVALUATION

According to auditing standards, the establishment and maintenance of internal control is an important responsibility of management (SAS 78, AU 319). The policies and procedures included as elements of a computer-based system are part of that responsibility. The audit team's responsibility is to make an assessment of the control risk in the system. Management can meet its responsibility and assist auditors in the following ways: (1) by ensuring that documentation of the system is complete and up to date, (2) by maintaining a system of transaction processing that includes an audit trail, and (3) by making computer resources and knowledgeable personnel available to the auditors to help them understand and audit the system.

justify less account balance work (providing the controls turn out to be working well). The cost of obtaining a low control risk assessment may be high. In this case, the conclusion is also equivalent to assessing control risk at 1.0, but this time because the auditors lack knowledge about the controls and not because they have decided controls are poor. However, the result is the same: extensive year-end account balance-audit procedures are specified. For example, suppose the extensive evaluation of controls over the validity of charges to customers would take 40 hours. If controls were excellent, suppose then the sample confirmation as of November 1 (with subsequent review of the December 31 trial balance) would take 30 hours less to perform than confirmation of all accounts as of December 31. The additional work on controls is not economical. The decision to stop work on control risk assessment in this case is a matter of *audit efficiency*—deciding not to work 40 hours to save 30 hours.

Document the Internal Control Understanding

Working paper documentation of a decision to assess control risk as 1.0 (no reliance on internal control to restrict procedures) can consist only of a memorandum of that fact. However, for future reference in next year's audit, the memorandum should contain an explanation of the effectiveness-related or efficiency-related reasons.

Working paper documentation is required and should include records showing the audit team's understanding of the controls. The understanding can be summarized in the form of *questionnaires*, *narratives*, and *flowcharts*.

Internal Control Questionnaires   The most efficient means of gathering evidence about the control structure is to conduct a formal interview with knowledgeable managers, using the checklist type of **internal control questionnaire** illustrated in Exhibit 6–8. This questionnaire is organized under headings that identify the control environment questions and the questions related to each of the seven control objectives. All questionnaires are not organized like this, so auditors need to know the general transaction control objectives in order to know whether the questionnaire is complete. Likewise, if you are assigned to write a questionnaire, you will need to be careful to include questions about each transaction control objective.

Internal control questionnaires are designed to help the audit team obtain evidence about the control environment and about the accounting and control activities that are considered good error-checking routines. Answers to the questions, however, should not be taken as final and definitive evidence about how well control actually functions. Evidence obtained through the interview-questionnaire process is hearsay evidence because its source is generally a single person who, while knowledgeable, is still not the person who actually performs the control work. This person may give answers that reflect what he or she believes the system should be, rather than what it really is. The person may be unaware of informal ways in which duties have been changed or may be innocently ignorant

EXHIBIT 6–8 INTERNAL CONTROL QUESTIONNAIRE—SALES TRANSACTION PROCESSING

Client _____ Audit Date _____
Client Personnel Interviewed _____

Auditor _____ Date Completed _____
Reviewed by _____ Date Reviewed _____

have controls *do not have controls in place*

Question	NA	Yes	No	Answer — Remarks
Environment:				
1. Is the credit department independent of the marketing department?				
2. Are sales of the following types controlled by the same procedures described below? Sales to employees, COD sales, disposals of property, cash sales, and scrap sales.				
Validity Objective				
3. Is access to sales invoice blanks restricted?				
4. Are prenumbered bills of lading or other shipping documents prepared or completed in the shipping department?				
Completeness Objective				
5. Are sales invoice blanks prenumbered?				
6. Is the sequence checked for missing invoices?				
7. Is the shipping document numerical sequence checked for missing bills of lading numbers?				
Authorization Objective				
8. Are all credit sales approved by the credit department prior to shipment?				
9. Are sales and terms based on approved standards?				
10. Are returned sales credits and other credits supported by documentation as to receipt, condition, and quantity, and approved by a responsible officer?				
Accuracy Objective				
11. Are shipped quantities compared to invoice quantities?				
12. Are sales invoices checked for error in quantities, prices, extensions and footing, freight allowances, and checked with customers' orders?				
13. Is there an overall check on arithmetic accuracy of period sales data by a statistical or product-line analysis?				
14. Are periodic sales data reported directly to general ledger accounting independent of accounts receivable accounting?				
Classification Objective				
15. Does the accounting manual contain instructions for classifying sales?				
Accounting/Posting Objective				
16. Are summary journal entries approved before posting?				
Proper Period Objective				
17. Does the accounting manual contain instructions to date sales invoices on the shipment date?				

of the system details. Nevertheless, interviews and questionnaires are useful when a manager tells of a weak feature. An admission of weak control is fairly convincing.

A strong point about questionnaires is that an auditor is less likely to forget to cover some important point. Questions generally are worded such that a "no" answer points out some weakness or control deficiency, thus making analysis easier. Naturally, company personnel know that yes answers are "good" and no answers are "bad," so they tend to tell auditors "yes" all the time.

Narrative Descriptions.   One way to tailor these inquiry procedures to a particular company is to write a **narrative description** of each important control subsystem. Such a narrative would simply describe all the environmental elements, the accounting system, and the control activities. The narrative description may be efficient in audits of very small businesses.

Accounting and Control System Flowcharts.   Another widely used method for documenting the auditors' understanding of accounting and control is to construct a flowchart. Many control-conscious companies will have their own flowcharts, and the auditors can use them instead of constructing their own. The advantages of flowcharts can be summarized by an old cliché: "A picture is worth a thousand words." Flowcharts can enhance auditors' evaluations, and annual updating of a chart is relatively easy with additions or deletions to the symbols and lines.

Construction of a flowchart takes time because an auditor must learn about the operating personnel involved in the system and gather samples of relevant documents. Thus, the information for the flowchart, like the narrative description, involves a lot of legwork and observation. When the flowchart is complete, however, the result is an easily evaluated, informative description of the system.

For any flowcharting application, the chart must be understandable to an audit supervisor. A flowchart should be drawn with a template and ruler or with computer software. A messy chart is hard to read. The starting point in the system should, if possible, be placed at the upper left-hand corner. The flow of procedures and documents should be from left to right and from top to bottom, as much as is possible. Narrative explanations should be written on the face of the chart as annotations or in a readily available reference key.

The flowchart should communicate all relevant information and evidence about segregation of responsibilities, authorization, and accounting and control activities in an understandable, visual form. Exhibit 6–9 contains a flowchart representation of the beginning stages of a sales and delivery processing system. This is a partial flowchart. The outconnectors shown by the circled A and B indicate continuation on other flowcharts. Ultimately, the flowchart ends showing entries in accounting journals and ledgers.

In Exhibit 6–9, you can see some characteristics of flowchart construction and some characteristics of this accounting system. By reading down the columns headed for each department, you can see that transaction initiation authority (both credit approval and sales invoice preparation) and custody of assets are separated. Notice that all documents have an intermediate or final resting place in a file. (Some of these files are in the flowcharts connected to A and B.) This flowchart feature gives auditors information about where to find audit evidence later.

AUDITING INSIGHT

ANALYZING AND DOCUMENTING INTERNAL CONTROL

We can bring to bear a variety of techniques and tools to assist clients in strengthening internal control. The most exciting of these methodologies is INFOCUS, our microcomputer package for analyzing portions of an entity's internal controls and graphically portraying potential weaknesses. INFOCUS harnesses the microcomputer to combine flowcharting and narratives, blending attributes of both to achieve a unique approach to documenting and evaluating internal controls that is applicable regardless of size, complexity, type of business, or nature of the entity.

Source: Grant Thornton open letter to clients.

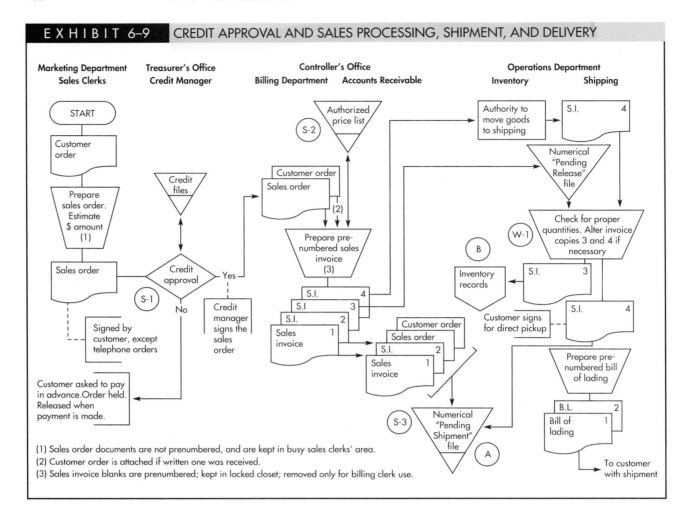

EXHIBIT 6–9   CREDIT APPROVAL AND SALES PROCESSING, SHIPMENT, AND DELIVERY

(1) Sales order documents are not prenumbered, and are kept in busy sales clerks' area.
(2) Customer order is attached if written one was received.
(3) Sales invoice blanks are prenumbered; kept in locked closet; removed only for billing clerk use.

Phase 2: Assess the Control Risk (preliminary)

After completing Phase 1—obtaining an understanding of control and designing a preliminary audit program—the audit team should be able to make a preliminary assessment of the control risk. One way to make the assessment is to analyze the control strengths and weaknesses. **Strengths** are specific features of good general and application controls. **Weaknesses** are the lack of controls in particular areas. The auditors' findings and preliminary conclusions should be written up for the working paper files.

Strengths and weaknesses should be documented in a working paper sometimes called a *bridge working paper*, so called because it connects (bridges) the control evaluation to subsequent audit procedures. The major strengths and weaknesses apparent in the flow chart (Exhibit 6–9) can be summarized as shown in Exhibit 6–10. On the flowchart, the strengths are indicated by the circled **S-#** and the weaknesses by **W-#.** In the bridge working paper, the "audit program" column contains *test of controls procedures* for auditing the control strengths and suggestions about *substantive account balance audit procedures* related to the weaknesses (the last column in Exhibit 6–10). Auditors do not need to perform test of controls audit procedures on weaknesses just to prove they are weaknesses. Doing so would be inefficient.

In terms of control risk assessment, at this stage the control risk related to the inventory balance might be set very high (e.g., 0.95 or 1.00). The three control strengths, however, relate to good control over sales validity and accounts receivable accuracy. The auditors probably will want to rely on these controls to reduce the accounts receivable balance audit work. Test of controls procedures ought to be performed to obtain evidence

EXHIBIT 6–10	BRIDGE WORKING PAPER

Index

By_____ Date_____
Reviewed_____ Date_____

KINGSTON COMPANY
Credit Approval, Sales Processing, Shipment, and Delivery Control
December 31, 2001

	Strength/Weakness	Audit Implication	Audit Program
S-1	Credit approval on sales order.	Credit authorization reduces risk of bad debt loss and helps check on validity of customer identification.	Select a sample of recorded sales invoices, and look for credit manager signature on attached sales order.
S-2	Unit prices are taken from an authorized list.	Prices are in accordance with company policy, minimizing customer disputes.	Using the S-1 sample of sales invoices, vouch prices used thereon to the price lists.
S-3	Sales are not recorded until goods are shipped.	Cutoff will be proper and sales will not be recorded too early.	Using the S-1 sample of sales invoices, compare the recording date to the shipment date on attached bill of lading or copy 4. (Also, scan the "pending shipment" file for old invoices that might represent unrecorded shipments.)
W-1	Shipping personnel have transaction alteration (initiation) authority to change the quantities on invoices, as well as custody of the goods.	Dishonest shipping personnel can alone let accomplices receive large quantities and alter the invoice to charge them for small quantities. In this system, sales and accounts receivable would be understated, and inventory could be overstated.	The physical count of inventory will need to be observed carefully (extensive work) to detect material overstatement.

about whether the apparent strengths actually are performed well. The "audit program" segment of Exhibit 6–10 for each of the strengths is a statement of a *test of controls audit procedure*. Test of controls auditing (Phase three) consists of procedures designed to produce evidence of how well the controls worked in practice. If they pass the auditor's criteria (the required degree of compliance), control risk can be assessed below the maximum. If they fail the test, the final conclusion is to assess a high or maximum control risk, revise the account balance audit plan to take the control weakness into account, and then proceed with the audit work.

The distinction between the *understanding and documenting phase* and the *preliminary control risk assessment phase* is useful for understanding the audit work. However, most auditors in practice do the two together, not as separate and distinct audit tasks.

Preliminary Control Risk Assessment in Information Systems

Preliminary control risk assessment, when a computer is used, involves:

- Identifying specific control objectives based on the types of misstatements that may be present in significant accounting applications.
- Identifying the points in the flow of transactions where specific types of misstatements could occur.
- Identifying specific control activities designed to prevent or detect these misstatements.
- Identifying the control activities that must function to prevent or detect the misstatements.
- Evaluating the design of control activities to determine whether it suggests a low control risk and whether test of controls audit procedures on them might be cost effective.

E X H I B I T 6–11   COMPUTER ACCOUNTING: POINTS OF VULNERABILITY TO MISSTATEMENT ERRORS

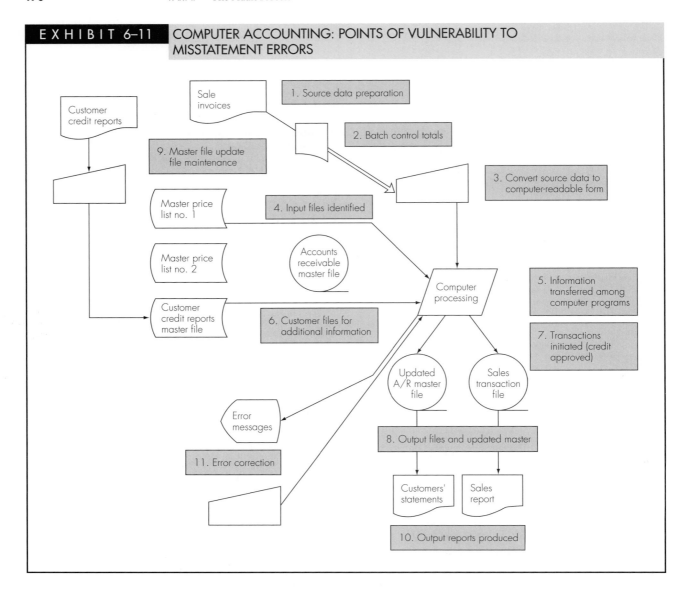

Identifying specific control objectives is no different than in a manual data processing system. However, the process of identifying the points in the flow of transactions where misstatements could occur is different in a computer system in comparison to a manual system. For example, when a computer is used, these points (see Exhibit 6–11) are places where misstatements could occur:

1. Activities related to source data preparation are performed, causing the flow of transactions to include authorization and initial execution.
2. Noncomputerized procedures are applied to source data, such as a manual summarization of accounting data (preparation of batch totals).
3. Source data are converted into computer-readable form.
4. Input files are identified for use in processing.
5. Information is transferred from one computer program to another.
6. Computer-readable files are used to supply additional information relating to individual transactions (e.g., customer credit reports).
7. Transactions are initiated by the computer.

8. Output files are created or master files are updated.
9. Master files are changed (records added, deleted, or modified) outside the normal flow of transactions within each cycle through file maintenance procedures.
10. Output reports or files are produced.
11. Errors identified by control activities are corrected.

Once the audit team identifies the points where a misstatement might occur, specific control objectives can be related to such points. For example, one possible misstatement might involve billing customers with incorrect prices because a wrong file was used. One way to state a control objective relating to this type of misstatement is: "Appropriate price information should be used during the billing process."

When points where misstatements could occur in the flow of transactions are identified, auditors should focus on specific control activities that may prevent or detect such misstatements. Control activities should be considered in terms of specific control objectives. For example, for the objective of using appropriate price information, one control procedure might be "The billing application program should identify the correct price file by matching the file name in the program to the name on the header label."

In an electronic environment, control activities may have characteristics that differ from manual control activities designed to accomplish the same control objectives. For example, in a manual system, credit approval usually is indicated by an authorized signature on a source document, such as a customer's order or invoice. In an electronic environment, however, approval can be accomplished by utilizing a **digitized signature,** an approved encrypted password that releases a credit sale transaction by assigning a special code to it. The electronic signature provides access to programs that permit initiating a specific type of transaction or changing master files. In such a case, although the control objective is identical in the manual and computerized systems, the methods used to achieve the objective and the visible evidence of conformity with authorized activities differ considerably and the audit approach may be significantly different.

Apparent weakness in any of the input, processing, and output controls are matters of concern. However, absence of a control at the input stage may be offset by other controls at later stages. For example, if check digits are not calculated when the input is prepared, but transaction numbers are compared to master file numbers and nonmatches are rejected and printed in an error report, the control is likely to be satisfactory and effective. Of course, it usually is more efficient to catch errors early rather than late; but control still can be considered effective for the accounting records and financial statements. Internal auditors, however, may be very interested in when controls are applied, since they are concerned about the efficiency of computer operations.

Material weaknesses in manual and computer controls become a part of independent auditors' assessment of control risk. Lack of input controls may permit data to be lost or double-counted and poor processing controls can permit accounting calculation, allocation, and classification errors to occur. Poor output controls over distribution of reports and other output (negotiable checks, for example) can be the source of misstatements that could make financial statements materially misleading.

Phase 3: Perform Test of Controls Audit Procedures and Reassess Control Risk

When auditors reach the third phase of an evaluation of internal control, they will have identified specific controls on which risk could be assessed very low (e.g., the strengths shown in Exhibit 6–10). To reduce the final risk assessment to a low level, auditors must determine (1) the required degree of company compliance with the control policies and procedures and (2) the actual degree of company compliance. The **required degree of compliance** is the auditors' decision criterion for good control performance. Knowing that compliance cannot realistically be expected to be perfect, auditors might decide, for example, that evidence of using bills of lading (shipping documents) to validate sales

AUDITING INSIGHT

TEST OF CONTROLS NECESSARY FOR ASSESSING LOW CONTROL RISK

Inquiry alone generally will not provide sufficient evidential matter to support a conclusion about the effectiveness of design or operation of a specific [client] control. When the auditor determines that a specific [client] control may have a significant effect in reducing control risk to a low level for a specific assertion, he or she ordinarily needs to perform additional tests [of controls] to obtain sufficient evidential matter to support the conclusion about the effectiveness of the design or operation of that [client] control.

Source: *SAS 78,* AU 319.69.

invoice recordings 96 percent of the time is sufficient to assess a low control risk for the audit of accounts receivable (looking for overstatement in receivables and sales).

Perform Test of Controls Audit Procedures

Now the auditors can perform **test of controls procedures** to determine how well the company's controls actually functioned during the period under audit. A test of controls audit procedure is a two-part statement. Part one is an *identification of the data population* from which a sample of items will be selected for audit. Part two is an *expression of an action* taken to produce relevant evidence. In general, the action is: (1) determine whether the selected items correspond to a standard (e.g., mathematical accuracy), and (2) determine whether the selected items agree with information in another data population. The test of controls procedures in Exhibit 6–10 show this two-part design.

One other important aspect of these audit procedures is known as the direction of the test. The procedures described in Exhibit 6–10 provide evidence about control over the validity of sales transactions. However, they do not provide evidence about control over completeness of recording all shipments. Another data population—the shipping documents—can be sampled to provide evidence about completeness. The direction of the test idea is illustrated in Exhibit 6–12. If completeness control is found to be strong, the auditors can limit the year-end procedures of searching for unrecorded assets.

Some test of controls procedures involve **reperformance**—the auditors perform again the arithmetic calculations and the comparisons the company people were supposed to have performed. Some accountants, however, believe mere **inspection** is enough—the auditors just look to see whether the documents were marked with an initial, signature, or stamp to indicate they had been checked. They maintain that reperformance is not necessary.

EXHIBIT 6–12 DIRECTION OF THE TEST OF CONTROLS AUDIT PROCEDURES

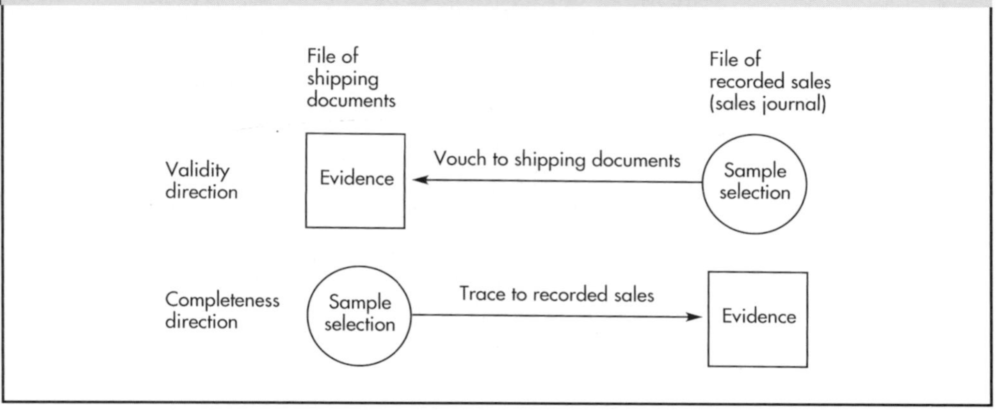

Some test of controls procedures depend on *documentary evidence*, like a sales entry supported by a bill of lading. Documentary evidence in the form of signatures, initials, checklists, reconciliation working papers, and the like provides better evidence than procedures that leave no documentary tracks. Some controls, such as segregation of employees' duties, may leave no documents behind. In this case, the best kind of procedures—reperformance of control activities—cannot be done, and the second procedure—inquiry and observation—must be used. This procedure amounts to an auditor's unobtrusive eyewitness observation of employees at their jobs performing control activities.

Test of controls procedures, when performed, should be applied to samples of transactions and control activities executed throughout the period under audit. The reason for this requirement is that the conclusions about controls will be generalized to the whole period under audit.

Reassess the Control Risk

Final control risk assessment is complicated. In the sampling modules, you will find explanations of sampling methods for performing test of controls procedures of the type illustrated in Exhibit 6–10. Further discussion of "assessing control risk" will be saved for these modules. However, for an advance peek at the result, recognize that the final evaluation of a company's internal control is the assessment of the control risk (CR) related to each assertion. Control risk is the CR element in the audit risk model: $AR = IR \times CR \times DR$. These assessments are an auditor's expression of the effectiveness of internal control for preventing, detecting, and correcting specific errors and frauds in management's financial statement assertions. Each of these final control risk assessments can be qualitative or quantitative. Audit organizations generally use qualitative labels to identify their control risk assessments. Nevertheless, audit theory places control risk on a probability continuum, and the qualitative control categories (Exhibit 6–13) are points with underlying control risk probabilities.

An assessment of control risk should be coordinated with the final audit plan. The final account balance audit plan includes the specification (list) of **substantive audit procedures** to detect material misstatements in account balances and footnote disclosures.

You have studied tests of controls and substantive balance-audit procedures as if they were easily distinguishable. Be advised, however, that general audit procedures can be used both as test of controls procedures and as substantive procedures. Actually, you would be better advised to think in terms of test of controls and substantive **purposes** of a procedure instead of test of controls and substantive procedures. A single procedure may produce both control and substantive evidence and, thus, serve both purposes (hence the name **dual-purpose** tests). For example, a selection of recorded sales entries could be used (1) to vouch sales to supporting bills of lading and (2) to calculate the correct dollar amount of sales. The first datum is relevant information about control compliance. The second is dollar-value information that may help measure an amount of misstatement in the book balance of sales. Another example is the confirmation of accounts receivable procedure. This procedure has a primary substantive purpose, but,

E X H I B I T 6–13	QUALITATIVE AND QUANTITATIVE CONTROL RISKS

Control Risk Categories (Qualitative)	Control Risk Probabilities (Quantitative)
Low control risk	0.10–0.45
Moderate control risk	0.40–0.70
Control risk slightly below the maximum	0.60–0.95
Maximum control risk	1.00

when confirmation replies tell about significant or systematic errors, the evidence is relevant to control evaluation as well as to dollar-value measurement. Most audit procedures serve dual purposes and yield evidence both about controls and about financial statement assertions.

6.21 Must the Phase 1 obtaining-an-understanding work of an evaluation of internal control always be followed by assessment and testing phases? Explain.

6.22 Where can an auditor find a client's documentation of the accounting system?

6.23 What are the advantages and disadvantages of documenting internal control by using: (1) an internal control questionnaire, (2) a narrative memorandum, and (3) a flowchart?

6.24 What is a bridge working paper? Describe its content and its connection to the test of controls and account balance audit programs.

6.25 What is a test of controls audit procedure? What two parts are important in a written procedure?

6.26 What is the difference between inspection and reperformance in test of controls audit procedures?

6.27 What purposes are served by a "dual-purpose test"?

INTERNAL CONTROL LIMITATIONS

As noted at the beginning of the chapter, internal control provides *reasonable assurance*, not absolute assurance, that category control objectives will be achieved. There are several limitations to internal control systems that prevent management (and auditors for that matter) from obtaining complete assurance that company controls are absolutely effective. These limitations include human error, deliberate circumvention, management override, and improper collusion. Internal control can help prevent and detect many errors, but it cannot guarantee that they will never happen. Hence, control systems generally do not provide absolute assurance that the objectives of internal control are satisfied.

Most internal controls are directed at lower-level employees, not management. Therefore it is often possible for *management to override controls* by force of authority. Similarly, while segregation of duties is an extremely effective control, *collusion* among people who are supposed to act independently can cause failure to achieve objectives.

Additionally, control systems are subject to cost-benefit considerations. Controls possibly could be made perfect, or nearly so, at great expense. An inventory could be left unlocked and unguarded (no control against theft and no control expenses), or a fence could be used; locks could be installed; lighting could be used at night; television monitors could be put in place; armed guards could be hired. Each of these successive safeguards costs money, as does extensive supervision of clerical personnel in an office. At some point, the cost of protecting the inventory from theft (or of supervisors' catching every clerical error) exceeds the benefit of control. Hence, a company can decide that certain controls are too costly in light of the risk of loss that may occur. **Reasonable assurance** is thought to be enough, and has been defined: "The concept of reasonable assurance recognizes that the cost of an entity's internal control should not exceed the benefits that are expected to be derived."

The explanations of control characteristics in this chapter contain an underlying thread of bureaucratic organization theory and a large-business orientation. A company must be large and employ several people (about 10 or more) to have a theoretically appropriate segregation of functional responsibilities and its accompanying high degree of specialization of work. Supervision requires people. The paperwork and computer control necessary in most large systems is extensive. Control theory also suggests that people perform in accounting and control roles and do not engage in frequent personal interaction across functional responsibility boundaries. None of these theoretical dimensions fit small and midsized businesses very well. Auditors should be careful to recognize the bureaucratic, large-business orientation of internal control theory. When the business under audit is small, auditors must make allowances for (1) the number of people employed, and (2) the control attitude of important managers and owners.

The key person in internal control in a small business with few employees is the owner-manager. A diligent owner-manager may be able to oversee and supervise all the important authorization, record keeping, and custodial functions. He or she also may be able to assure satisfactory transaction processing accuracy. Thus, an auditor evaluating control risk will study the extent of the owner-manager's involvement in the operation of the accounting and control system and evaluate the owner-manager's competence and integrity.

R E V I E W
CHECKPOINTS

6.28 What are some of the limitations of any system of internal control?

6.29 What is the concept of reasonable assurance? Who is responsible for assessing it?

6.30 What audit problems can arise over management's beliefs about reasonable assurance?

6.31 Is the general theory of internal control embodied in the basic characteristics of reliable internal control equally applicable to large and small enterprises? Discuss.

SUMMARY

This chapter explains the theory and practice of auditors' involvement with a client's control process. The purposes of auditor involvement are to assess the control risk in order to plan the substantive audit program and to report control deficiencies to management and the board of directors.

In theory, a financial reporting control system consists of five components—management's control environment, management's risk assessment, management's information and communication (accounting) system, management's control activities, and management's monitoring of the control system. Each of these is evaluated and documented in the audit working papers. The control environment and management's risk assessment is explained in terms of understanding the client's business. Elements of the accounting system are explained in conjunction with control activities designed to prevent, detect, and correct misstatements that occur in transactions. The explanations of these controls integrate computerized accounting systems with control practice.

Documentation of a control system is explained with reference to control questionnaires, flowcharts, and narratives. Questionnaires and flowcharts are demonstrated. The understanding and the documentation is taken one step further to the test of controls phase and the cost reduction reasons for doing work to obtain a low control risk assessment. The assessed control risk is connected to the CR in the control risk model.

Control evidence is linked to audit programs with a "bridge working paper" presentation. The nature of test of controls procedures is explained in terms of a two-part statement that dictates identification of the data population, from which control evidence is drawn, and the action taken to produce the relevant evidence. You should be careful to distinguish the "client's control activities" from the "auditors' test of control procedures." Control activities are part of the internal control designed and operated by the company. The auditors' procedures are the auditors' own evidence-gathering work performed to obtain evidence about the client's control activities.

The chapter closes with a section on the limitations of internal control systems, including cost-benefit and reasonable assurance considerations.

MULTIPLE-CHOICE QUESTIONS FOR PRACTICE AND REVIEW

6.32 Which one of these events is an auditor not required to communicate to a company's audit committee or board of directors?

  a. Management's significant accounting policies.

  b. Management judgments about accounting estimates used in the financial statements.

  c. Immaterial errors in processing transactions discovered by the auditors.

  d. Disagreements with management about accounting principles.

6.33 Which of the following is likely to be of least importance to an auditor when obtaining an understanding of the computer controls in a company with a computerized accounting system?

  a. The segregation of duties within the computer function.

  b. The controls over source documents.

  c. The documentation maintained for accounting applications.

  d. The cost/benefit ratio of computer operations.

6.34 After obtaining a preliminary understanding of a client's computer controls, an auditor may decide not to perform test of controls auditing related to the controls within the computerized portion of the client's control system. Which of the following would not be a valid reason for choosing to omit test of controls auditing?

  a. The client's computer controls duplicate manual controls existing elsewhere in the system.

  b. There appear to be major weaknesses that indicate a high control risk.

  c. The time and dollar costs of testing exceed the time and dollar savings in substantive work if the tests of computer controls show the controls to operate effectively.

  d. The client's controls appear adequate enough to justify a low control risk assessment.

6.35 What is the computer process called when data processing is performed concurrently with a particular activity and the results are available soon enough to influence the particular course of action being taken or the decision being made?

  a. Batch processing.

  b. Real-time processing.

  c. Integrated data processing.

  d. Random access processing.

6.36 Which of the following is not a characteristic of a batch-processed computer system?

  a. The collection of like transactions that are sorted and processed sequentially against a master file.

  b. Keyboard input of transactions, followed by machine processing.

  c. The production of numerous printouts.

  d. The posting of a transaction, as it occurs, to several files, without intermediate printouts.

6.37 In the weekly computer run to prepare payroll checks, a check was printed for an employee who had been terminated the previous week. Which of the following controls, if properly utilized, would have been most effective in preventing the error or ensuring its prompt detection?

  a. A control total for hours worked, prepared from time cards collected by the timekeeping department.

  b. Requiring the treasurer's office to account for the numbers of the prenumbered checks issued to the computer department for the processing of the payroll.

  c. Use of the check digit for employee numbers.

  d. Use of a header label for the payroll input sheet.

6.38 The most important fundamental concept involved in a company's internal control is

  a. Effectiveness and efficiency of operations.

  b. People operate the control system.

  c. Reliability of financial reporting.

  d. Compliance with applicable laws and regulations.

6.39 The primary purpose for obtaining an understanding of an audit client's internal control is to

  a. Provide a basis for making constructive suggestions in a management letter.

b. Determine the nature, timing, and extent of tests to be performed in the audit.

c. Obtain sufficient competent evidential matter to afford a reasonable basis for an opinion on the financial statements under examination.

d. Provide information for a communication of internal control-related matters to management.

6.40 Restrictions of audit procedures can be characterized by

a. Selecting larger sample sizes for audit.

b. Moving audit procedures to the fiscal year-end date.

c. Deciding to obtain external evidence instead of internal evidence.

d. Selecting smaller sample sizes for audit.

6.41 Which of the following can an auditor observe as a general control activity used by companies:

a. Segregation of functional responsibilities.

b. Management philosophy and operating style.

c. Open lines of communication to the audit committee of the board of directors.

d. External influences such as federal bank examiner audits.

6.42 A client's control activity is

a. An action taken by auditors to obtain evidence.

b. An action taken by client personnel for the purpose of preventing, detecting, and correcting errors and frauds in transactions.

c. A method for recording, summarizing, and reporting financial information.

d. The functioning of the board of directors in support of its audit committee.

6.43 The control objective intended to reduce the probability that fictitious transactions get recorded in the accounts is

a. Completeness.

b. Authorization.

c. Proper period.

d. Validity.

6.44 The control objective intended to reduce the probability that a credit sale transaction will get debited to cash instead of accounts receivable is

a. Validity.

b. Classification.

c. Accuracy.

d. Completeness.

6.45 When planning an audit, an auditor's prior experience with the client's internal control activities can be used to

a. Identify the errors and frauds that could occur in the business.

b. Assess the operational efficiency this year of the internal controls in general.

c. Find evidence of whether management has circumvented controls by collusion.

d. Prepare working papers documenting the decision about the control risk this year.

6.46 Choose one of the following descriptions as the best example of a validity check transaction processing control activity:

a. The client's computer is programmed to detect whether a numerical amount in a transaction exceeds a predetermined amount.

b. After computer-detected transaction errors are successfully resubmitted, the system prints a report of the causes of the errors.

c. The client's computer is programmed to print an error report when a transaction numerical amount does not match a corresponding amount in a master file record.

d. After transaction data are entered, the client's computer processes transactions, then sends transaction identification data back to the entry terminal for comparison with the data originally entered.

6.47 Totals of amounts in computer-record data fields that are not usually added but are used only for data processing control purposes are called

a. Record totals.

b. Hash totals.

c. Processing data totals.

d. Field totals.

6.48 In updating a computerized accounts receivable file, which one of the following would be used as a batch control to verify the accuracy of the posting of cash receipts remittances?

a. The sum of the cash deposits plus the discounts less the sales returns.

b. The sum of the cash deposits.

c. The sum of the cash deposits less the discounts taken by customers.

d. The sum of the cash deposits plus the discounts taken by customers.

6.49 In most audits of large companies, internal control risk assessment contributes to audit efficiency, which means

a. The cost of year-end audit work will exceed the cost of control evaluation work.

b. Auditors will be able to reduce the cost of year-end audit work by an amount more than the control evaluation costs.

c. The cost of control evaluation work will exceed the cost of year-end audit work.

d. Auditors will be able to reduce the cost of year-end audit work by an amount less than the control evaluation costs.

6.50   Which of the following is a device designed to help the audit team obtain evidence about the control environment and about the accounting and control activities of an audit client:

a. A narrative memorandum describing the control system.

b. An internal control questionnaire.

c. A flowchart of the documents and procedures used by the company.

d. A well-indexed file of working papers.

6.51   A bridge working paper shows the connection between

a. Control evaluation findings and subsequent audit procedures.

b. Control objectives and accounting system procedures.

c. Control objectives and company control activities.

d. Financial statement assertions and test of control procedures.

6.52   Test of control audit procedures are required for

a. Obtaining evidence about the financial statement assertions.

b. Accomplishing control over the validity of recorded transactions.

c. Analytical review of financial statement balances.

d. Obtaining evidence about the operating effectiveness of client control activities.

EXERCISES AND PROBLEMS

6.53   Internal Control Audit Standards. Auditors are required to obtain a sufficient understanding of each of the components of a client's internal control system. This understanding is used to assess control risk and plan the audit of the client's financial statements.

Required:

a. For what purposes should an auditor's understanding of the internal control components be used in planning an audit?

b. What is required for an auditor to assess control risk below the maximum level?

c. What should an auditor consider when seeking a further reduction in the planned assessed level of control risk to a level below the maximum?

d. What are the documentation requirements concerning an client's internal control components and the assessed level of control risk?

(AICPA adapted)

6.54   Costs and Benefits of Control.   The following questions and cases deal with the subject of cost-benefit analysis of internal control. Some important concepts in cost-benefit analysis are:

1. Measurable benefit. Benefits or cost savings may be measured directly or may be based on estimates of expected value. An expected

loss is an estimate of the amount of a probable loss multiplied by the frequency or probability of the loss-causing event. A measurable benefit can arise from the reduction of an expected loss.

2. Qualitative benefit. Some gains or cost savings may not be measurable, such as company public image, reputation for regulatory compliance, and customer satisfaction.

3. Measurable costs. Controls may have direct costs such as wages and equipment expenses.

4. Qualitative cost factors. Some costs may be indirect, such as lower employee morale created by overcontrolled work restrictions.

5. Marginal analysis. Each successive control feature may have marginal cost and benefit effects on the control problem.

Case A:

Porterhouse Company has numerous bank accounts. Why might management hesitate to spend $10,000 (half of a clerical salary) to assign someone the responsibility of reconciling each account every month for the purpose of catching the banks' accounting errors? Do other good reasons exist to justify spending $10,000 each year to reconcile bank accounts monthly?

Case B:

Harper Hoe Company keeps a large inventory of hardware products in a warehouse. Last year,

$500,000 was lost to thieves who broke in through windows and doors. Josh Harper figures that installing steel doors with special locks and burglar bars on the windows at a cost of $25,000 would eliminate 90 percent of the loss. Hiring armed guards to patrol the building 16 hours a day at a current annual cost of $75,000 would eliminate all the loss, according to officials of the Holmes Security Agency. Should Josh arrange for one, both, or neither of the control measures?

Case C:

The Merry Mound Cafeteria formerly collected from each customer at the end of the food line. A cashier, seated at a cash register, rang up the amount (displayed on a digital screen) and collected money. Management changed the system, and now a clerk at the end of the line operates an adding machine and gives each customer a paper tape. The adding machine accumulates a running total internally. The customer presents the tape at the cash register on the way out and pays.

The cafeteria manager justified the direct cost of $10,000 annually for the additional salary and $500 for the new adding machine by pointing out that he could serve 4 more people each weekday (Monday through Friday) and 10 more people on Saturday and Sunday. The food line now moves faster and customers are more satisfied. (The average meal tab is $6, and total costs of food and service are considered fixed.) "Besides," he said, "my internal control is better." Evaluate the manager's assertions.

6.55   Cash Receipts and Billing Control.

The narrative description (below) of a company's cash receipts and billing system is in the auditors' working papers.

Rural Building Supplies, Inc., is a single-store retailer that sells a variety of tools, garden supplies, lumber, small appliances, and electrical fixtures. About half of the sales are to walk-in customers and about half to construction contractors. Rural employs 12 salaried sales associates, a credit manager, three full-time clerical workers, and several part-time cash register clerks and assistant bookkeepers. The full-time clerical workers are: the cashier who handles the cash and the bank deposits, the accounts receivable supervisor who prepares invoices and does the accounts receivable work, and the bookkeeper who keeps journals and ledgers and sends customer statements. Their work is described more fully in the narrative.

Control Narrative

Rural's retail customers pay for merchandise by cash or credit card at cash registers when they purchase merchandise. A building contractor can purchase merchandise on account if approved by the credit manager. The credit manager bases approvals on general knowledge of the contractor's reputation. After credit is approved, the sales associate files a prenumbered charge form with the accounts receivable (A/R) supervisor to set up the contractor's account receivable.

The A/R supervisor independently verifies the pricing and other details on the charge form by reference to a management-authorized price list, corrects any errors, prepares the sales invoice, and supervises a part-time employee who mails the invoice to the contractor. The A/R supervisor electronically posts the details of the invoice in the A/R subsidiary ledger, and the computer system simultaneously transmits the transaction details to the bookkeeper. The A/R supervisor also prepares (1) a monthly computer-generated A/R subsidiary ledger without a reconciliation to the A/R control account, and (2) a monthly report of overdue accounts.

The cashier performs the cash receipts functions, including supervising the cash register clerks. The cashier opens the mail, compares each check with the enclosed remittance advice, stamps each check "for deposit only," and lists the checks for the deposit slip. The cashier then gives the remittance advices to the bookkeeper for recording. The cashier deposits the checks each day and prepares a separate deposit of the cash from the cash registers. The cashier retains the verified bank deposit slips (stamped and dated at the bank) to use in reconciling the monthly bank statements. The cashier sends to the bookkeeper a copy of the daily cash register summary. The cashier does not have access to the bookkeeper's journals or ledgers.

The bookkeeper receives information for journalizing and posting to the general ledger from the A/R supervisor (details of credit transactions) and from the cashier (cash reports). After recording the remittance advices received from the cashier, the bookkeeper electronically transmits the information to the A/R supervisor for subsidiary ledger updating. Upon receipt of the A/R supervisor's report of overdue balances, the bookkeeper sends monthly statements of account to contractors with unpaid balances. The bookkeeper authorizes the A/R supervisor to write off accounts as uncollectible six months after sending the first overdue notice. At this time, the bookkeeper notifies the credit manager not to approve additional credit to that contractor.

Required:

Take the role of the supervising auditor on the Rural engagement. Your assistants prepared the narrative description. Now, you must analyze it and identify the internal control weaknesses. Organize them under the heading of employee job functions: Credit manager, Accounts receivable supervisor, Cashier, and Bookkeeper. (Do not give advice about correcting the weaknesses.)

Optional Requirement:

Discuss the possibilities for fraud you notice in this control system.

6.56   Test of Controls Procedures and Errors/Frauds.   The four questions below are taken from an internal control questionnaire. For each question, state (a) one test of controls procedure you could use to find out whether the control technique was really used, and (b) what error or fraud could occur if the question were answered "no," or if you found the control was not effective.

1. Are blank (sales) invoices available only to authorized personnel?

2. Are (sales) invoices checked for the accuracy of quantities billed? Prices used? Mathematical calculations?

3. Are the duties of the accounts receivable bookkeeper separate from any cash functions?

4. Are customer accounts regularly balanced with the control account?

6.57   Control Objectives and Procedures Associations.   Exhibit 6.57–1 contains an arrangement of examples of transaction errors (lettered a–g) and a set of client control activities and devices (numbered 1–15). You should photocopy the Exhibit page or obtain a full-size copy from your instructor for the following requirements.

Required:

a. Opposite the examples of transaction errors lettered a–g, write the name of the control objective clients wish to achieve to prevent, detect, or correct the error.

b. Opposite each numbered control activity, place an "X" in the column that identifies the error(s) the activity is likely to control by prevention, detection, or correction.

EXHIBIT 6.57–1

a.	2, 3, 8, 15	Sales recorded, goods not shipped
b.	2, 3, 4, 5, 8	Goods shipped, sales not recorded
c.	1, 14, 15	Goods shipped to a bad credit risk customer
d.	3, 6, 15	Sales billed at the wrong price or wrong quantity
e.	7, 8	Product line A sales recorded as Product line B
f.	9, 12, 13	Failure to post charges to customers for sales
g.	10, 11, 15	January sales recorded in December

Control Activities

1. Sales order approved for credit

2. Prenumbered shipping doc prepared, sequence checked

3. Shipping document quantity compared to sales invoice

4. Prenumbered sales invoices, sequence checked

5. Sales invoice checked to sales order

6. Invoiced prices compared to approved price list

7. General ledger code checked for sales product lines

8. Sales dollar batch totals compared to sales journal

9. Periodic sales total compared to same period accounts receivable postings

10. Accountants have instructions to date sales on the date of shipment

11. Sales entry date compared to shipping document date

12. Accounts receivable subsidiary totaled and reconciled to accounts receivable control account

13. Intercompany accounts reconciled with subsidiary company records

14. Credit files updated for customer payment history

15. Overdue customer accounts investigated for collection

6.58   Control Objectives and Assertion Associations.   Exhibit 6.57–1 contains an arrangement of examples of transaction errors (lettered a–g) and a set of client control activities and devices (numbered 1–15).

Required:

For each error/control objective, identify the financial statement assertion most benefited by the control.

6.59   Client Control Procedures and Audit Test of Control Procedures.   Exhibit 6.57–1 contains an arrangement of examples of transaction errors (lettered a–g) and a set of client control activities and devices (numbered 1–15).

Required:

For each client control activity numbered 1–15, write an auditor's test of control procedure that could produce evidence on the question of whether the client's control activity has been installed and is in operation.

DISCUSSION CASES

6.60   Obtaining a "Sufficient" Understanding of Internal Control.   The 12 partners of a regional-sized CPA firm met in special session to discuss audit engagement efficiency. Jones spoke up, saying: "We all certainly appreciate the firmwide policies set up by Martin and Smith, especially in connection with the audits of the large clients that have come our way recently. Their experience with a large accounting firm has helped build up our practice. But I think the standard policy of conducting reviews and tests of internal control on all audits is raising our costs too much. We can't charge our smaller clients fees for all the time the staff spends on this work. I would like to propose that we give engagement partners discretion to decide whether to do a lot of work on assessing control risk. I may be old-fashioned, but I think I can finish a competent audit without it." Discussion on the subject continued but ended when Martin said, with some emotion: "But we can't disregard generally accepted auditing standards like Jones proposes!"

What do you think of Jones' proposal and Martin's view of the issue? Discuss.

6.61   Starting the "Logical Approach." One of the things you can do in a "logical approach" to the evaluation of internal control is to imagine what types of errors or frauds could occur with regard to each significant class of transactions. Assume a company has the significant classes of transactions listed below. For each one, identify one or more errors or frauds that could occur and specify the accounts that would be affected if proper controls were not specified or were not followed satisfactorily.

1. Credit sales transactions.
2. Raw materials purchase transactions.
3. Payroll transactions.
4. Equipment acquisition transactions.
5. Cash receipts transactions.
6. Leasing transactions.
7. Dividend transactions.
8. Investment transactions (short term).

6.62   Restricting Account Balance Audit Procedures.   Below is a list of audit procedures for the audit of accounts receivable. They differ in their timing and extent.

Required:

Sort the procedures into two substantive audit programs: (1) One assuming the auditors assessed control risk low, and (2) the other assuming the auditors assessed control risk high (maximum). Discuss the reasons for putting procedures in one or the other program.

Procedures:

- Confirm a sample of 75 customer accounts receivable balances as of October 31 for a company with a December 31 balance sheet date.
- Confirm a sample of 165 customer accounts receivable balances as of December 31.
- Perform an analytical comparison of the December 31 customer accounts balances to the October 31 balances.
- Vouch the last 5 days' recorded sales (December 27–31) to bills of lading for cutoff evidence.
- Vouch the last 15 days' sales (December 17–31) to bills of lading for cutoff evidence.
- Trace the last 5 days' shipments (December 27–31) to recorded sales invoices for cutoff evidence.
- Trace the last 15 days' shipments (December 17–31) to recorded sales invoices for cutoff evidence.

6.63   Irregularity Opportunities.   The Simon Blfpstk Construction Company has two divisions. The president (Simon) manages the roofing division. Simon delegated authority and responsibility for management of the modular manufacturing division to John Gault. The company has a competent accounting staff and a full-time internal auditor. Unlike Simon, however, Gault and his secretary handle all the bids for manufacturing jobs, purchase all the materials without competitive bids, control the physical inventory of materials, contract for shipping by truck, supervise the construction activity, bill the customer when the job is finished, approve all bid changes, and collect the payment from the customer. With Simon's tacit approval, Gault has asked the internal auditor not to interfere with his busy schedule.

Required:

Discuss this fact situation in terms of internal control and identify frauds that could occur.

Chapter 7

Fraud Awareness Auditing: SAS No. 82 and Beyond

Professional Standards References

Compendium Section	Document Reference	Topic
AU 110	SAS 1	*Responsibilities and Functions of the Independent Auditor*
AU 230	SAS 1	*Due Care in the Performance of Work*
AU 316	SAS 82	*Consideration of Fraud in a Financial Statement Audit*
AU 317	SAS 54	*Illegal Acts by Clients*
AU 342	SAS 57	*Auditing Accounting Estimates*
AU 380	SAS 61	*Communication with Audit Committees*
AU 801	SAS 74	*Compliance Auditing Applicable to Governmental Entities and Recipients of Governmental Financial Assistance*
	SIAS 3	*Deterrence, Detection, Investigation, and Reporting of Fraud*
	GAO	*Government Auditing Standards (1994 Revision)*
AU 8240	ISA	*Fraud and Error*

Learning Objectives

Fraud auditing can be very exciting. It has the aura of detective work—finding things people want to keep hidden. However, fraud auditing and fraud examination are not easy and are not activities to be pursued without training, experience, and care. Fraud *awareness* and independent auditor's consideration of fraud in a financial statement audit are the focus of this chapter, enabling you to get an introduction, so you can accomplish these learning objectives:

1. Define and explain the differences among several kinds of errors, frauds, and illegal acts that might occur in an organization.

2. Explain the various auditing standards regarding external, internal, and governmental auditors' responsibilities with respect to detecting and reporting errors, frauds, and illegal acts.

3. List and explain some conditions that can lead to frauds.

4. Describe ways and means for preventing frauds.

5. Describe some common employee fraud schemes and explain some audit and investigation procedures for detecting them.

6. Describe some common financial reporting fraud features and explain some audit and investigation procedures for detecting them.

7. Explain the use of some extended audit procedures for finding fraud.

8. Describe the ways CPAs can assist in prosecuting fraud perpetrators.

INTRODUCTION

Independent auditors' responsibilities regarding fraud in financial statements begin with an attitude of *professional skepticism* (SAS 82, amending SAS I, AU 230):

> The auditor neither assumes that management is dishonest nor assumes unquestioned honesty. In exercising professional skepticism, the auditor should not be satisfied with less than persuasive evidence because of a belief that management is honest.

Users of audited financial statements generally believe that one of the main objectives of audits is fraud detection. The goal in this chapter is to enhance your familiarity with the nature, signs, prevention, detection, and reaction to fraud that can help you perform financial statement audits with awareness of fraud possibilities. In this fashion, this chapter will enable you to understand the auditing standards regarding *Consideration of Fraud in a Financial Statement Audit* (SAS 82, AU 316), but it goes considerably beyond SAS 82

AUDITING INSIGHT

EXCERPTS: PUBLIC OVERSIGHT BOARD
PANEL ON AUDIT EFFECTIVENESS (AUGUST 2000)

(3.28) The Panel accepts the premise that a GAAS audit is not, and should not become, a fraud audit.

(3.51) [GAAS should require] . . . a "forensic-type fieldwork phase." . . . to convey an attitudinal shift in the auditor's degree of skepticism [wherein] auditors . . . should presume the possibility of dishonesty at various levels of management, including collusion, override of internal control and falsification of documents. [Asking] . . . "Where is the entity vulnerable to financial statement fraud if management were inclined to perpetrate it?"

(3.52) The Panel recommends that audit firms . . . Develop or expand training programs for auditors at all levels oriented toward responsibilities and procedures for fraud detection.

and gives you insights into white collar criminals' motivations and auditors' procedures for detecting their coverups.

Auditors are supposed to know enough about fraud to notice its signs and signals and know when to call upon more experienced investigators. Financial statement auditors need to understand fraud and potential fraud situations, and they need to know how to ask the right kinds of questions during an audit.

DEFINITIONS RELATED TO FRAUD

LEARNING OBJECTIVE

1. Define and explain the differences among several kinds of errors, frauds, and illegal acts that might occur in an organization.

Several kinds of "fraud" are defined in laws, while others are matters of general understanding. Exhibit 7–1 shows some acts and devices often involved in financial frauds. Collectively, these are known as **white-collar crime**—the misdeeds done by people who wear ties to work and steal with a pencil or a computer terminal. White-collar crime produces ink stains instead of bloodstains.

Fraud consists of knowingly making material misrepresentations of fact, with the intent of inducing someone to believe the falsehood and act upon it and, thus, suffer a loss or damage. This definition encompasses all the ways people can lie, cheat, steal, and dupe other people.

Employee fraud is the use of fraudulent means to take money or other property from an employer. It usually involves falsifications of some kind—false documents, lying, exceeding authority, or violating an employer's policies. It consists of three phases: (1) the fraudulent act, (2) the conversion of the money or property to the fraudster's use, and (3) the coverup.

Embezzlement is a type of fraud involving employees' or nonemployees' wrongfully taking money or property entrusted to their care, custody, and control, often accompanied by false accounting entries and other forms of lying and coverup.

EXHIBIT 7–1	AN ABUNDANCE OF FRAUDS

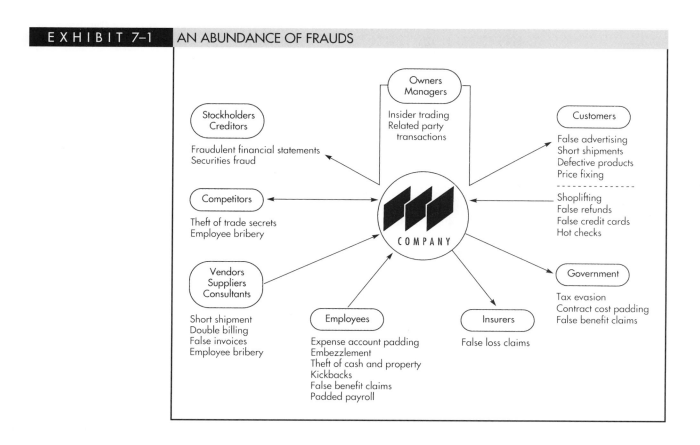

Larceny is simple theft—for example, an employee taking an employer's money or property that has not been entrusted to the custody of the employee.

Defalcation is another name for employee fraud, embezzlement, and larceny. *SAS 82* also calls it "misappropriation of assets."

Management fraud is deliberate fraud committed by management that injures investors and creditors through materially misleading financial statements. The class of perpetrators is management; the class of victims is investors and creditors; and the instrument of perpetration is financial statements.[1] Management fraud is also called "fraudulent financial reporting."

Fraudulent financial reporting was defined by the National Commission on Fraudulent Financial Reporting (1987) as *intentional or reckless conduct, whether by act or omission, that results in materially misleading financial statements*.

Errors are unintentional misstatements or omissions of amounts or disclosures in financial statements.

Direct-effect illegal acts are violations of laws or government regulations by the company or its management or employees that produce direct and material effects on dollar amounts in financial statements.

Fraud auditing has been defined in courses conducted by the Association of Certified Fraud Examiners as: A proactive approach to detect financial frauds using accounting records and information, analytical relationships, and an awareness of fraud perpetration and concealment schemes.

Characteristics of Fraudsters

White-collar criminals are not like typical bank robbers, who are often described as "young and dumb." Bank robbers and other strongarm artists often make comic mistakes like writing the holdup note on the back of a probation identification card, leaving the getaway car keys on the convenience store counter, using a zucchini as a holdup weapon, and timing the holdup to get stuck in rush hour traffic. Then there's the classic about the robber who ran into his own mother at the bank (she turned him in!).

Burglars and robbers average about $400–$500 for each hit. Employee frauds average $20,000, on up to $500,000. Yet, employee frauds are not usually the intricate, well-disguised ploys you find in espionage novels. Who are these thieves wearing ties? What do they look like? Unfortunately, they "look like" most everybody else, including you and me. They have these characteristics:

- Likely to be married.
- Probably not tattooed.
- Educated beyond high school.
- Range in age from teens to over 60.
- Employment tenure from 1 to 20 or more years.

- Not likely to be divorced.
- Member of a church.
- No arrest record.
- Socially conforming.
- Usually act alone (70 percent of incidents).

White-collar criminals do not make themselves obvious, although there may be telltale signs—described later as "red flags." Unfortunately, the largest frauds are committed by people who hold high executive positions, have long tenure with an organization, and are respected and trusted employees. After all, these are the people who have access to the largest amounts of money and have the power to give orders and override controls.

The Art of Fraud Awareness Auditing

Fraud examination work combines the expertise of auditors and criminal investigators. Fraud examiners are fond of saying that their successes are the result of accident, hunches, or luck. Nothing can be further from the reality. Successes come from experience, logic, and the ability to see things that are not obvious (as Sherlock Holmes

---

[1] R. K. Elliott and J. J. Willingham, *Management Fraud: Detection and Deterrence* (New York: Petrocelli Books, Inc., 1980), p. 4.

AUDITING INSIGHT

WHO DOES IT?

Alex W was a 47-year-old treasurer of a credit union. Over a seven-year period, he stole $160,000. He was a good husband and the father of six children, and he was a highly reputed official of the credit union. His misappropriations came as a stunning surprise to his associates. He owed significant amounts on his home, cars, college for two children, two side investments, and five different credit cards. His monthly payments significantly exceeded his take-home pay.

Source: Association of Certified Fraud Examiners (ACFE), "Auditing for Fraud."

noticed the dog that did not bark). Fraud awareness auditing, broadly speaking, involves familiarity with many elements: the human element, organizational behavior, knowledge of common fraud schemes, evidence and its sources, standards of proof, and sensitivity to red flags.[2]

Independent auditors of financial statements and fraud examiners approach their work differently. While many differences exist, these are some of the most important and obvious ones:

- Financial auditors follow a program/procedural approach designed to accomplish a fairly standard job, while fraud examiners float in a mind-set of sensitivity to the unusual where nothing is standard.

- Financial auditors make note of errors and omissions, while fraud examiners focus as well on exceptions, oddities, and patterns of conduct.

- Financial auditors assess control risk in general and specific terms to design other audit procedures, while fraud examiners habitually "think like a crook" to imagine ways controls might be subverted for fraudulent purposes.

- Financial auditors use a concept of materiality (dollar size big enough to matter) that is usually much higher than the amounts that fraud examiners consider worth pursuing. Financial auditors use materiality as a measure of importance one year at a time, whereas fraud examiners think of a cumulative materiality. (Theft of $20,000 per year may not loom large each year, but after a 15-year fraud career, $300,000 is a considerable loss.)

- Financial audits are based on theories of financial accounting and auditing logic, while fraud examination has a theory of behavioral motive, opportunity, and integrity.

External and internal auditors get credit for finding about 20 percent of discovered frauds. Larger percentages are discovered by voluntary confessions, anonymous tips, and other haphazard means. Fraud examiners have a higher success rate because they are called in for a specific purpose when fraud is known or highly suspected.

Some aspects of audit methodology make a big difference for fraud discovery. Fraud examiners often enjoy the expensive luxury of utilizing deductive reasoning—that is, after being tipped off that a certain type of loss occurred, they can identify the suspects, make clinical observations (stakeouts), conduct interviews and interrogations, eliminate

[2] These and other aspects of the art of fraud auditing are more fully developed in: G. J. Bologna and R. J. Lindquist, *Fraud Auditing and Forensic Accounting* (New York: John Wiley & Sons, 1995); W. S. Albrecht, M. B. Romney, D. J. Cherrington, I. R. Payne, and A. J. Roe, *How to Detect and Prevent Business Fraud* (New York: Prentice Hall, 1982); R. White and W. G. Bishop, III, *The Role of the Internal Auditor in the Deterrence, Detection, and Reporting of Fraudulent Financial Reporting* (The Institute of Internal Auditors); M. J. Barrett and R. N. Carolus, *Control and Internal Auditing* (The Institute of Internal Auditors); W. S. Albrecht, G. W. Wernz, and T. L. Williams, *Fraud—Bringing Light to the Dark Side of Business* (Burr Ridge, IL.: Richard D. Irwin, Inc., 1995); and Jack C. Robertson, *Fraud Examination for Managers and Auditors* (Viesca Books, 2000).

AUDITING INSIGHT

THE CASE OF THE EXTRA CHECKOUT

The district grocery store manager could not understand why receipts and profitability had fallen and inventory was hard to manage at one of the largest stores in her area. She hired an investigator who covertly observed the checkout clerks and reported that no one had shown suspicious behavior at any of the nine checkout counters. Nine? That store only has eight, she exclaimed! (The store manager had installed another checkout aisle, not connected to the cash receipts and inventory maintenance central computer, and was pocketing all the receipts from that register.)

Source: ACFE, "Auditing for Fraud."

dead-end results, and concentrate on running the fraudster to ground. They can conduct covert activities that usually are not in the financial auditors' tool kit. The "expensive luxury" of the deductive approach involves surveying a wide array of information and information sources, eliminating the extraneous, and retaining the selection that proves the fraud.

R E V I E W
CHECKPOINTS

7.1 What are the defining characteristics of: White-collar crime? Employee fraud? Embezzlement? Larceny? Defalcation? Management fraud? Errors? Illegal acts?

7.2 What does a fraud perpetrator look like? How does one act?

7.3 Compare and contrast the type of work performed by external auditors (auditing financial statements to render an audit report) and fraud examiners.

AUDITORS' AND INVESTIGATORS' RESPONSIBILITIES

LEARNING OBJECTIVE
2. Explain the various auditing standards regarding external, internal, and governmental auditors' responsibilities with respect to detecting and reporting errors, frauds, and illegal acts.

Audit standards from several sources explain the responsibilities for errors, frauds, and illegal acts. The term **external auditors** refers to independent CPAs who audit financial statements for the purpose of rendering an opinion; **internal auditors** and **Certified Internal Auditors** are references to persons employed within organizations; **government auditors** refers to auditors whose work is governed by the generally accepted government audit standards (GAGAS—the GAO audit standards); and **fraud examiners** refers to people engaged specifically for fraud investigation work.

External Auditors' Responsibilities

The AICPA auditing standards are very rigorous. Relevant standards concern frauds (SAS 82, AU 316), illegal acts by clients (SAS 54, AU 317), auditing accounting estimates (SAS 57, AU 342), and communication with audit committees (SAS 61, AU 380).

Consideration of Fraud in a Financial Statement Audit
SAS 82 presents an extensive array of audit responsibilities. The details are in Appendix 7A. Basically, SAS 82 requires auditors to understand fraud, assess fraud risks, design

audits to provide reasonable assurance of detecting material management fraud and employee fraud that could have a material effect on financial statements, and report on findings to management, directors, users of financial statements (sometimes), and outside agencies (certain conditions).

Illegal Acts by Clients

SAS 54 deals with two kinds of "illegal acts:" (1) **Direct-effect illegal acts** affect financial statement amounts (e.g., violations of tax laws and government contracting regulations for cost and revenue recognition), and they come under the same responsibilities as errors and frauds; and (2) **Illegal acts** is the term used to refer to violations of laws and regulations that are *far removed* from financial statement effects (e.g., violations relating to insider securities trading, occupational health and safety, food and drug administration, environmental protection, and equal employment opportunity). The far-removed illegal acts come under a responsibility for general awareness, particularly in matters of contingent liability disclosure, but not routine responsibility for detection and reporting. Details of *SAS 54* are in Appendix 7A.

Auditing Accounting Estimates

SAS 57 is related to fraudulent financial reporting because numerous fraud cases have involved manipulation of estimates. This area is difficult because an **accounting estimate** is *management's approximation* of a financial statement element, item, or account. (Examples include: allowance for loan losses, net realizable value of inventory, percentage-of-completion revenue, and fair value in nonmonetary exchanges.)

Management is responsible for making the accounting estimates, and auditors are responsible for evaluating their reasonableness in the context of the financial statements taken as a whole. Auditors are supposed to keep track of the differences between: (1) management's estimates and (2) the closest reasonable estimates supported by the audit evidence. And they are supposed to evaluate: (1) the differences taken altogether for indications of a systematic bias and (2) the combination of differences with other likely misstatements in the financial statements.

Communication with Audit Committees

SAS 61 sets forth requirements intended to assure that auditors inform the clients' audit committees about the scope and results of the independent audit. The auditing standards place great faith in audit committees and boards of directors. All companies with securities traded on the exchanges (e.g., New York, American, NASDAQ) are required to have audit committees. *SAS 61* requires auditors to make oral or written communications on numerous topics, some of which are listed in Appendix 7A.

Internal Auditors' Responsibilities

Internal auditors' attitudes about fraud responsibilities cannot be usefully generalized. Some hesitate to get involved because they believe a watchdog role will damage their image and effectiveness as internal consultants. Many attend the fraud investigation education programs offered by the Association of Certified Fraud Examiners because they want to add fraud expertise to their skills.

In the ordinary course of performing internal audit assignments, internal auditors review the reliability and integrity of financial and operating information; review the systems established to ensure compliance with policies, plans, procedures, laws, and regulations; and review the means of safeguarding assets and verify the existence of assets. This work is expanded in *Statement on Internal Auditing Standards No. 3*, entitled *Deterrence, Detection, Investigation, and Reporting of Fraud*. An abbreviated list of some specifications from *SIAS 3* is in Appendix 7A.

Generally Accepted Government Auditing Standards (U.S. General Accounting Office)

The GAO standards (GAGAS) apply to audits conducted by government employees and to public accounting firms engaged to perform audits on governmental organizations, programs, activities, and functions. The basic governmental audit requirements are to know the applicable laws and regulations, design the audit to detect abuse and illegal acts, and report to the proper level of authority. A few more details about these requirements are in Appendix 7A.

Auditors are supposed to prepare a written report on their tests of compliance with applicable laws and regulations, including all material instances of noncompliance and all instances or indications of illegal acts that could result in criminal prosecution. Reports should be directed to the top official of an organization and, in some cases, to an appropriate oversight body, including other government agencies and audit committees. Persons receiving the audit reports are responsible for reporting to law enforcement agencies.

Fraud Examiner Responsibilities

Fraud examiners have the strongest spirit of fraud detection and investigation. They differ significantly from other kinds of auditors. When they take an assignment, fraud is already known or strongly suspected. They do not fish around for fraud while performing "normal" work. In fact, the Association of Certified Fraud Examiners teaches that assignments are begun only with **predication,** which means a reason to believe fraud may have occurred. (The Professional Standards and Practices for Certified Fraud Examiners are reproduced in Appendix 7B.)

Fraud examiners' attitudes and responsibilities differ from those of other auditors in two additional respects—internal control and materiality. Their interest in internal control policies and procedures lies not so much in evaluating their strengths but in evaluating their weaknesses. Fraud examiners "think like crooks" to imagine fraud schemes that get around an organization's internal controls.

Fraud examiners have a different attitude about "materiality." While other auditors may have a large dollar amount as a criterion for an error that is big enough to matter, fraud examiners have a much lower threshold. An oddity is an oddity no matter the amount of money involved, and small oddities ought not be ignored just because "$5,000 isn't material to the financial statements taken as a whole." External auditors comprehend materiality in relation to each year's financial statements, where, for example, a $50,000 misstatement of income might not be big enough to matter. Fraud examiners think of materiality as a *cumulative amount*. A fraud loss of $20,000 this year may not be material to an external auditor, but $20,000 each year for a 15-year fraud career amounts to $300,000 in the fraud examiner's eyes—and it is big enough to matter!

AUDITING INSIGHT

NO SEPARATION OF DUTIES

An electronic data processing employee instructed the company's computer to pay his wife rent for land she allegedly leased to the company by assigning her an alphanumeric code as a lessor and then ordering the payments. The control lesson: Never let a data entry clerk who processes payment claims also have access to the approved vendor master file for additions or deletions.

Source: G. J. Bologna and R. J. Lindquist, *Fraud Auditing and Forensic Accounting* (New York: John Wiley & Sons)

AUDITING INSIGHT

FOLLOWING UP A SINGLE TRANSACTION

A California welfare department compliance unit supervisor and one of her clerks falsified dozens of welfare claims over a period of a year and collected unauthorized payments. They were caught when a data entry clerk discovered incomplete information on an input document authorizing a claim payment. The clerk then checked with the eligibility worker whose name had been forged on the document, and the worker denied authorizing the claim or signing the document. An investigation was launched, and the input falsification fraud was estimated at $300,000.

Source: G. J. Bologna and R. J. Lindquist, *Fraud Auditing and Forensic Accounting*, (New York: John Wiley & Sons).

R E V I E W
CHECKPOINTS

7.4 What are the AICPA auditing standards requirements regarding: (*a*) awareness of fraud, (*b*) procedural audit work, (*c*) professional skepticism, and (*d*) reporting? Do these standards differ for (1) errors, frauds, and direct-effect illegal acts; and (2) far-removed-effect illegal acts? (Refer to Appendix 7A.)

7.5 To what extent would you say internal auditors include fraud detection responsibility in their normal audit assignments? (Refer to Appendix 7A.)

7.6 How does the requirement for design of audit procedures differ in GAGAS audit work from external auditors' work on financial statement audits (not involving governmental auditing)? Consider both error/frauds and illegal acts aspects. (Refer to Appendix 7A.)

7.7 In fraud examiners' terminology, what is *predication*?

7.8 Why might fraud examiners have attitudes about control systems and materiality different from other auditors?

CONDITIONS THAT MAKE FRAUD POSSIBLE, EVEN EASY

LEARNING OBJECTIVE
3. List and explain some conditions that can lead to frauds.

When can fraud occur? Imagine the probability of fraud being a function of three factors—motive, opportunity, and lack of integrity. When one or two of these factors weigh heavily in the direction of fraud, the probability increases. When three of them lean in the direction of fraud, it almost certainly will occur.[3] As Bologna and Lindquist put it: Some people are honest all the time, some people (fewer than the honest ones) are dishonest all the time, most people are honest all the time, and some people are honest most of the time.[4]

Motive

A **motive** is some kind of pressure a person experiences and believes unshareable with friends and confidants. *Psychotic* motivation is relatively rare; but it is characterized by the "habitual criminal," who steals simply for the sake of stealing. *Egocentric* motivations drive people to steal to achieve more personal prestige. *Ideological* motivations are held

---

[3] For further reference, see: D. R. Cressey, "Management Fraud, Accounting Controls, and Criminological Theory," pp. 117–47, and Albrecht et al., "Auditor Involvement in the Detection of Fraud," pp. 207–61, both in R. K. Elliott and J. J. Willingham, *Management Fraud: Detection and Deterrence* (New York: Petrocelli Books, Inc., 1980); J. K. Loebbecke; M. M. Eining; and J. J. Willingham, "Auditors' Experience with Material Irregularities: Frequency, Nature, and Detectability," *Auditing: A Journal of Practice and Theory*, Fall 1989, pp. 1–28.

[4] Bologna and Lindquist, *Fraud Auditing*, p. 8.

by people who think their cause is morally superior, and they are justified in making someone else a victim. However, *economic* motives are far more common in business frauds than the other three.

The economic motive is simply a need for money, and at times it is intertwined with egocentric and ideological motivations. Ordinarily honest people can fall into circumstances where they have a new or unexpected need for money, and the normal options for talking about it or going through legitimate channels seem to be closed. Consider these needs to:

- Pay college tuition.
- Pay hospital bills for a parent with cancer.
- Pay gambling debts.
- Pay for drugs.
- Pay alimony and child support.
- Pay for high lifestyle (homes, cars, boats).
- Finance business or stock speculation losses.
- Report good financial results.

Opportunity

An **opportunity** is an open door for solving the unshareable problem in secret by violating a trust. The violation may be a circumvention of internal controls or a simple chance to take advantage of a lapse of control. Everyone has some degree of trust conferred for a job, even if it is merely the trust not to shirk and procrastinate. The higher the position in an organization, the greater the degree of trust; and, hence, the greater the opportunity for larger frauds. Here are some examples:

- Nobody counts the inventory, so losses are not known.
- The petty cash box is often left unattended.
- Supervisors set a bad example by taking supplies home.
- Upper management considered a written statement of ethics but decided not to publish one.
- Another employee was caught and fired, but not prosecuted.
- The finance vice president has investment authority without any review.
- Frequent emergency jobs leave a lot of excess material just lying around.

Lack of Integrity

Practically everyone, even the most violent criminal, knows the difference between right and wrong. Unimpeachable **integrity** is the ability to act in accordance with the highest

Auditing Insight

She Can Do Everything

Mrs. Lemon was the only bookkeeper for an electrical supply company. She wrote the checks and reconciled the bank account. In the cash disbursements journal, she coded some checks as inventory, but she wrote the checks to herself, using her own true name. When the checks were returned with the bank statement, she simply destroyed them. She stole $416,000 over five years. After being caught and sentenced to prison, she testified to having continuous guilt over doing something she knew was wrong.

Source: ACFE, "Auditing for Fraud."

AUDITING INSIGHT

THEY DESERVE EVERYTHING THEY GOT!

A controller of a small fruit packing company in California stole $112,000 from the company. When asked why, he said: "Nobody at the company, especially the owners, ever talked to me. They treated me unfairly, they talked down to me, and they were rude."

Source: ACFE, "Auditing for Fraud."

moral and ethical values all the time. Thus, lapses and occasional lack of integrity permit motive and opportunity to take form as fraud. People normally do not make deliberate decisions to "lack integrity today while I steal some money." They find a way to describe (rationalize) the act in words that make it acceptable for their self-image. Here are some of these rationalizations:

- I need it more than the other person (Robin Hood theory).
- I'm borrowing the money and will pay it back.
- Nobody will get hurt.
- The company is big enough to afford it.
- A successful image is the name of the game.
- Everybody is doing it.

R E V I E W
CHECKPOINTS

7.9 What are some of the pressures that can cause honest people to contemplate theft? List some egocentric and ideological ones as well as economic ones.

7.10 What kinds of conditions provide opportunities for employee fraud? For financial statement fraud?

7.11 Give some examples of "rationalizations" that people have used to excuse fraud. Can you use them?

FRAUD PREVENTION

LEARNING OBJECTIVE

4. Describe ways and means for preventing frauds.

Accountants and auditors have often been exhorted to be the leaders in fraud prevention by employing their skills in designing "tight" control systems. This strategy is, at best, a short-run solution to a large and pervasive problem. Business activity is built on the trust that people at all levels will do their jobs properly. Control systems limit trust and, in the extreme, can strangle business in bureaucracy. Managers and employees must have freedom to do business, which means giving them freedom to commit frauds as well. Effective long-run prevention measures are complex and difficult, involving the elimination of the causes of fraud by mitigating the effect of motive, opportunity, and lack of integrity.

Managing People Pressures in the Workplace

From time to time, people will experience financial and other pressures. The pressures cannot be eliminated, but the facilities for sharing them can be created. Some companies have "ethics officers" to serve this purpose. Their job is to be available to talk over the ethical dilemmas faced in the workplace and help people adopt legitimate responses.

AUDITING INSIGHT

HOW TO ENCOURAGE FRAUD

- Practice autocratic management.
- Manage by power with little trust in people.
- Manage by crisis.
- Centralize authority in top management.
- Measure performance on a short-term basis.
- Make profits the only criterion for success.
- Make rewards punitive, stingy, and political.
- Give feedback that is always critical and negative.
- Create a highly hostile, competitive workplace.
- Insist everything be documented with a rule for everything.

Source: Adapted from G. J. Bologna and R. J. Lindquist, *Fraud Auditing and Forensic Accounting* (New York: John Wiley & Sons).

Many companies have "hot lines" for anonymous reporting of ethical problems. Reportedly, the best kind of hot line arrangement is to have the responding party be an agency outside the organization. In the United States, some organizations are in the business of being the recipients of hot line calls, coordinating their activities with the management of the organization.

The most effective long-run prevention, however, lies in the practice of management by caring for people. Managers and supervisors at all levels can exhibit a genuine concern for the personal and professional needs of their subordinates and fellow managers, and subordinates can show the same concern for each other and their managers. Many companies facilitate this caring attitude with an organized Employee Assistance Program (EAP). EAPs offer a range of counseling referral services dealing with substance abuse, mental health, family problems, crisis help, legal matters, health education, retirement, career paths, job loss troubles, AIDS education, and family financial planning.

External auditors must obtain an understanding of the company's "control environment," which relates to the overall scheme of management activity in the company. Managements that consider carefully the people pressures in the workplace, using some of the devices mentioned above, have good control environments and the beginnings of good control systems.

Control Procedures and Employee Monitoring

Auditors would be aghast at an organization that had no controls. Controls in the form of job descriptions and performance specifications are indeed needed to help people know the jobs they are supposed to accomplish. Almost all people need some structure for their working hours. An organization whose only control is "trustworthy employees" has no control.[5] Unfortunately, "getting caught" is an important consideration for many people when coping with their problems. Controls provide the opportunity to get caught.

Without going into much detail about controls, let it be noted that procedures for recognizing and explaining red flags are important for nipping frauds in the bud before they get bigger. Companies need controls that reveal the following kinds of symptoms :[6]

- Missing documents.
- Second endorsements on checks.

---

[5] W. S. Albrecht, "How CPAs Can Help Clients Prevent Employee Fraud," *Journal of Accountancy*, December 1988, pp. 110–14.

[6] Ibid., p. 113–14.

- Unusual endorsements on checks.
- Unexplained adjustments to inventory balances.
- Unexplained adjustments to accounts receivable.
- Old items in bank reconciliations.
- Old outstanding checks.
- Customer complaints.
- Unusual patterns in deposits in transit.

The problem with control systems is that they are essentially negative restrictions on people. The challenge is to have a bare minimum of useful controls and to avoid picky rules that are "fun to beat." The challenge of "beating the system," which can lead to bigger and better things, is an invitation to fraudulent types of behavior. (How many college students find ways to get into course registration before their scheduled times?)

Integrity by Example and Enforcement

The key to integrity in business is "accountability"—that is, each person must be willing to put his or her decisions and actions in the sunshine. Many organizations begin by publishing codes of conduct. Some of these codes are simple, and some are very elaborate. Government agencies and defense contractors typically have the most elaborate rules for employee conduct. Sometimes they work, sometimes they do not. A code can be effective if the "tone at the top" supports it. When the chairman of the board and the president make themselves visible examples of the code, other people will then believe it is real. Subordinates tend to follow the boss's lead.

Hiring and firing are important. Background checks on prospective employees are advisable. A new employee who has been a fox in some other organization's hen house will probably be a fox in a new place. Organizations have been known to hire private investigators to make these background checks. Fraudsters should be fired and, in most cases, prosecuted. They have a low rate of recidivism (repeat offenses) if they are prosecuted,

---

R E V I E W
CHECKPOINTS

7.12 Make a two-column list with fraud-prevention management-style characteristics in one column and, opposite each of these, management-style characteristics that might lead to fraud.

AUDITING INSIGHT

WHERE DID HE COME FROM?

The controller defrauded the company for several million dollars. As it turned out, he was no controller at all. He didn't know a debit from a credit. The fraudster had been fired from five previous jobs where money had turned up missing. He was discovered one evening when the president showed up unexpectedly at the company and found a stranger in the office with the controller. The stranger was doing all of the accounting for the bogus controller.

Source: ACFE, "Auditing for Fraud."

---

but they have a high rate if not.[7] Prosecution delivers the message that management does not believe that "occasional dishonesty" is acceptable.

FRAUD DETECTION

Since an organization cannot prevent all fraud, its auditors, accountants, and security personnel must be acquainted with some detection techniques. Frauds consist of the fraud act itself, the conversion of assets to the fraudster's use, and the coverup. Catching people in the fraud act is difficult and unusual. The act of conversion is equally difficult to observe, since it typically takes place in secret away from the organization's offices (e.g., fencing stolen inventory). Auditors and fraud examiners investigate frauds by noticing signs and signals of fraud, then following the trail of missing, mutilated, or false documents that are part of the accounting records coverup.

This chapter has already mentioned signs and signals in terms of red flags, oddities, and unusual events. Being able to notice them takes some experience, but this book can give some starting places.[8]

Red Flags

Employee Fraud

LEARNING OBJECTIVE

5. Describe some common employee fraud schemes and explain some audit and investigation procedures for detecting them.

Employee fraud can involve high-level executives and people below the top executive levels. Observation of persons' habits and lifestyle and *changes* in habits and lifestyles may reveal some red flags. Fraudsters of the past have exhibited these characteristics:

- Lose sleep.
- Take drugs.
- Can't relax.
- Can't look people in the eye.
- Go to confession (e.g., priest, psychiatrist).
- Work standing up.

- Drink too much.
- Become irritable easily.
- Get defensive, argumentative.
- Sweat excessively.
- Find excuses and scapegoats for mistakes.
- Work alone, work late.

Personality red flags are difficult because (1) honest people sometimes show them and (2) they often are hidden from view. It is easier to notice *changes*, especially when a

---

[7] Ibid., p.114.

[8] Long lists of red flags can be found in Bologna and Lindquist, *Fraud Auditing*, pp. 49–56; Albrecht et. al., in *Management Fraud*, pp. 223–26; *Statements on Auditing Standards 82 and 54*; "Auditing for Fraud" courses of the Association of Certified Fraud Examiners; courses offered by other organizations, such as the AICPA and The Institute of Internal Auditors.

AUDITING INSIGHT

HIGH STYLE IN THE MAILROOM

A female mailroom employee started wearing designer clothes (and making a big deal about it). She drove a new BMW to work. An observant manager, who had known her as an employee for seven years and knew she had no outside income, became suspicious. He asked the internal auditors to examine her responsibilities extra carefully. They discovered she had taken $97,000 over a two-year period.

Source: ACFE, "Auditing for Fraud."

AUDITING INSIGHT

A LARGE HOUSEHOLD

A benefit analyst with C.G. Insurance used her remote terminal in a Dade County, Florida, field claims office to defraud the company of $206,000 in 18 months. She used her position of trust and her knowledge of the claims system to execute the fraud by using false names to submit fictitious claims using the address of herself, her father, and her boyfriend. The repetition of the same claimant addresses eventually tipped off the insurance company's security department.

Source: G. J. Bologna and R. J. Lindquist, *Fraud Auditing and Forensic Accounting* (New York: John Wiley & Sons).

person changes his or her lifestyle or spends more money than the salary justifies—for example, on homes, furniture, jewelry, clothes, boats, autos, vacations, and the like.

Often, auditors can notice telltale hints of the coverup. These generally appear in the accounting records. The key is to notice exceptions and oddities, such as transactions that are: at odd times of the day, month, season; too many or too few; in the wrong branch location; in amounts too high, too low, too consistent, too different. Exceptions and oddities like these can appear:

- Missing documents.
- Excessive voids and credit memos.
- Common names or addresses for refunds.
- General ledger does not balance.
- Inventory shortages.
- Alterations on documents.
- Employees cannot be found.
- Documents photocopied.

- Cash shortages and overages.
- Customer complaints.
- Adjustments to receivables and payables.
- Increased past due receivables.
- Increased scrap.
- Duplicate payments.
- Second endorsements on checks.
- Dormant accounts become active.

LEARNING OBJECTIVE

6. Describe some common financial reporting fraud features and explain some audit and investigation procedures for detecting them.

Management Fraud (Fraudulent Financial Reporting)

Fraud that affects financial statements and causes them to be materially misleading often arises from the perceived need to "get through a difficult period." The difficult period may be characterized by cash shortage, increased competition, cost overruns, and similar events that cause financial difficulty. Managers usually view these conditions as "temporary," believing they can be overcome by getting a new loan, selling stock, or otherwise buying time to recover. In the meantime, falsified financial statements are used to "benefit the company." These conditions and circumstances ("fraud risk factors") have existed along with frauds in the past:

- Management decisions are dominated by an individual or small group.
- Managers' accounting attitudes are unduly aggressive.
- Managers place much emphasis on meeting earnings projections.
- Management's business reputation is poor.
- Management has engaged in opinion shopping.
- Managers are evasive responding to auditors' inquiries.
- Managers engage in frequent disputes with auditors.
- Managers display significant disrespect for regulatory bodies.
- Company has a weak internal control environment.
- Company accounting personnel are lax or inexperienced in their duties.
- Company employs inexperienced managers.
- Company is in a period of rapid growth.
- Company profit lags the industry.
- Company has going concern problems (near bankruptcy).
- Company is decentralized without adequate monitoring.
- Company has many difficult accounting measurement and presentation issues.

By both fraud and "creative accounting," companies have caused financial statements to be materially misleading by (1) overstating revenues and assets, (2) understating expenses and liabilities, and (3) giving disclosures that are misleading or that omit important information. Generally, fraudulent financial statements show financial performance and ratios that are better than current industry experience or better than the company's own history. Sometimes the performance meets exactly the targets announced by management months earlier.

Because of the double-entry bookkeeping system, fraudulent accounting entries always affect two accounts and two places in financial statements. Since many management frauds involve improper recognition of assets, we have the theory of the "dangling debit," which is an asset amount that can be investigated and found to be false or questionable. Frauds may involve the omission of liabilities, but the matter of finding and investigating the "dangling credit" is normally very difficult. It "dangles" off the books. Misleading disclosures also present difficulty, mainly because they involve words and messages instead of numbers. Omissions may be hard to notice, and misleading inferences may be very subtle.

AUDITING INSIGHT

OVERSTATED REVENUE, RECEIVABLES, AND DEFERRED COSTS

Cali Computer Systems, Inc., sold franchises enabling local entrepreneurs to open stores and sell Cali products. The company granted territorial franchises; in one instance recording revenue of $800,000 and in another $580,000. Unfortunately, the first of these "contracts" for a territorial franchise simply did not exist, and the second was not executed and Cali had not performed its obligations by the time it was recorded. In both cases, the imaginary revenue was about 40 percent of reported revenues. These franchises were more in the nature of business hopes than completed transactions.

Cali was supposed to deliver computer software in connection with the contracts and had deferred $277,000 of software development cost in connection with the programs. However, this software did not work, and the contracts were fulfilled with software purchased from other suppliers.

Source: SEC Accounting and Auditing Enforcement Release 190.

A client's far-removed illegal acts may cause financial statements to be misleading, and external auditors are advised to be aware of circumstances that might indicate them. The AICPA has given these signs and signals of the potential for illegal acts (SAS 54, AU 317):

- Unauthorized transactions.
- Government investigations.
- Regulatory reports of violations.
- Payments to consultants, affiliates, employees for unspecified services.
- Excessive sales commissions and agent's fees.
- Unusually large cash payments.
- Unexplained payments to government officials.
- Failure to file tax returns, to pay duties and fees.

R E V I E W
CHECKPOINTS

7.13 Is there anything odd about these situations? (1) Auditors performed a surprise payroll distribution, and J. Jones, S. Smith, and D. Douglas were absent from work. (2) A check to Larson Lectric Supply was endorsed with "Larson Lectric" above the signature of "Eloise Garfunkle." (3) Numerous checks were issued dated September 3, November 22, December 25, January 1, May 8, and July 4, 2001.

7.14 What account could you audit to determine whether a company had recorded fictitious sales?

AUDITING INSIGHT

THE TRUSTED EMPLOYEE

A small business owner hired his best friend to work as his accountant. The friend was given full unlimited access to all aspects of the business and was completely responsible for the accounting. Five years later, the owner finally terminated the friend because the business was not profitable. Upon taking over the accounting, the owner's wife found that cash receipts from customers were twice the amounts formerly recorded by the accountant "friend." An investigation revealed that the friend had stolen $450,000 in cash sales receipts from the business, while the owner had never made more than $16,000 a year. (The friend had even used the stolen money to make loans to the owner and to keep the business going!)

NO LOCKS ON THE DOOR

Perini Corporation kept blank checks in an unlocked storeroom, where every clerk and secretary had access. Also in the storeroom was the automatic check signing machine. The prenumbered checks were not logged and restricted to one person. The bookkeeper was very surprised to open the bank statement one month and find that $1.5 million in stolen checks had been paid on the account.

Source: ACFE, "Auditing for Fraud."

Internal Control

An important feature of internal control is the separation of these duties and responsibilities: (1) transaction authorization, (2) recordkeeping, (3) custody of, or access to, assets, and (4) reconciliation of actual assets to the accounting records. Generally, a person who, acting alone or in a conspiracy, can perform two or more of these functions also can commit a fraud by taking assets, converting them, and covering up.

Fraud awareness auditing involves perceptions of the controls installed (or not installed) by a company, plus "thinking like a crook" to imagine ways and means of stealing. When controls are absent, the ways and means may be obvious. Otherwise, it might take some scheming to figure out how to steal from an organization.

R E V I E W
CHECKPOINTS

7.15 What could happen if a person could authorize medical insurance claims and enter them into the system for payment without supervisory review?

7.16 What could happen if the inventory warehouse manager also had responsibility for making the physical inventory observation and reconciling discrepancies to the perpetual inventory records?

SCHEMES AND DETECTION PROCEDURES

In this section of the chapter, we will try a new approach. Instead of discussing lists of schemes and detection procedures in the abstract, we will have a series of cases. They will follow a standard format in two major parts: (1) Case Situation, and (2) Audit Approach. Some problems at the end of the chapter will give the case situation, and you will be assigned to write the audit approach section. The first three cases deal with employee fraud, and the last two deal with management fraud. With the first three cases, you can practice on learning objective five: *Describe some common employee fraud schemes and explain some audit and investigation procedures for detecting them.* With the last two cases, you can practice on learning objective six: *Describe some common financial reporting fraud features and explain some audit and investigation procedures for detecting them.*

CASE 7.1
CASE OF THE MISSING PETTY CASH

PROBLEM

Petty cash embezzlement.

METHOD

The petty cash custodian (1) brought postage receipts from home and paid them from the fund, (2) persuaded the supervisor to sign blank authorization slips the custodian could use when the supervisor was away, and used these to pay for fictitious meals and minor supplies, (3) took cash to get through the weekend, replacing it the next week.

PAPER TRAIL

Postage receipts were from a distant post office station the company did not use. The blank authorization slips were dated on days the supervisor was absent. The fund was cash short during the weekend and for a few days the following week.

AMOUNT

The fund was small ($500), but the custodian replenished it about every two working days, stealing about $50 each time. With about 260 working days per year and 130 reimbursements, the custodian was stealing about $6,500 per year. The custodian was looking forward to getting promoted to general cashier and bigger and better things!

AUDIT APPROACH

OBJECTIVE

Obtain evidence of the existence of the petty cash fund and validity of petty cash transactions.

CONTROL

A supervisor is assigned to approve petty cash disbursements by examining them for validity and signing an authorization slip.

TEST OF CONTROLS

Audit for transaction authorization and validity. Select a sample of petty cash reimbursement check copies with receipts and authorization slips attached; study them for evidence of authorization and validity (vouching procedure). Notice the nature and content of the receipts. Obtain supervisor's vacation schedule and compare dates to authorization slip dates.

AUDIT OF BALANCE

On Friday, count the petty cash and receipts to see that they add up to $500. Then, count the fund again later in the afternoon. (Be sure the second count is a surprise and that the custodian and supervisor sign off on the count working paper so the auditor will not be accused of theft.)

DISCOVERY SUMMARY

Knowing the location of the nearby post office branch used by the company, the auditor noticed the pattern of many receipts from a distant branch, which was near the custodian's apartment. Several authorizations were dated during the supervisor's vacation, and he readily admitted signing the forms in blank so his own supervisor "wouldn't be bothered." The second count on the same day was a real surprise, and the fund was found $65 short.

CASE 7.2
THE LAUNDRY MONEY SKIM

PROBLEM

Cash receipts skimmed from collections.

Albert owned and operated 40 coin laundries around town. As the business grew, he could no longer visit each one, empty the cash boxes, and deposit the receipts. Each location grossed about $140 to $160 per day, operating 365 days per year. (Gross income about $2 million per year.)

METHOD

Four part-time employees each visited 10 locations, collecting the cash boxes and delivering them to Albert's office, where he would count the coins and currency (from the change machine) and pre-pare a bank deposit. One of the employees skimmed $5 to $10 from each location visited each day.

PAPER TRAIL

None, unfortunately. The first paper that gets produced is Albert's bank deposit, and the money is gone by then.

AMOUNT

The daily theft does not seem like much, but at an average of $7.50 per day from each of 10 locations, it was about $27,000 per year. If all four of the employees had stolen the same amount, the loss could have been about $100,000 per year.

AUDIT APPROACH

OBJECTIVE

Obtain evidence of the completeness of cash receipts—that is, that all the cash received is delivered to Albert for deposit.

CONTROL

Albert had no controls over the part-time employee collectors. He conducted no overt or covert surprise observation and at no time two people went to collect cash (thereby needing to agree, in collusion, to steal). Albert did not rotate locations among the collectors or give any other indications to the employees that he was concerned about control.

TEST OF CONTROLS

With no controls, auditors cannot perform test of control procedures. Obviously, however, "thinking like a crook" leads to the conclusion that the employees could simply pocket money.

AUDIT OF BALANCE

The "balance" in this case is the total revenue that should have been deposited, and auditing for completeness is always difficult. Albert marked a quantity of coins with an etching tool and marked some $1 and $5 bills with ink. Unknown to the employees, he put these in all the locations, carefully noting the coins and bills in each.

DISCOVERY SUMMARY

Sure enough, over several months a pattern of missing money emerged. When confronted, the employee confessed.

CASE 7.3
THE WELL-PADDED PAYROLL

PROBLEM

Embezzlement with fictitious people on the payroll.

METHOD

Maybelle was responsible for preparing personnel files for new hires, approving wages, verifying time cards, and distributing payroll checks. She "hired" fictitious employees, faked their records, and ordered checks through the payroll system. She deposited some checks in several personal bank accounts and cashed others, endorsing all of them with the names of the fictitious employees and her own.

PAPER TRAIL

Payroll creates a large paper trail with individual earnings records, W-2 tax forms, payroll deductions for taxes and insurance, and Form 941 payroll tax reports. She mailed all the W-2 forms to the same post office box.

AMOUNT

Maybelle stole $160,000 by creating some "ghosts," usually 3 to 5 out of 112 people on the payroll and paying them an average of $256 per week for three years. Sometimes the ghosts quit and were later replaced by others. But she stole "only" about 2 percent of the total payroll during the period.

AUDIT APPROACH

OBJECTIVE

Obtain evidence of the existence and validity of payroll transactions.

CONTROL

Different people should be responsible for hiring (preparing personnel files), approving wages, and distributing payroll checks. "Thinking like a crook" leads an auditor to see that Maybelle could put people on the payroll and obtain their checks.

TEST OF CONTROLS

Audit for transaction authorization and validity. Random sampling might not work because of the small number of ghosts. Look for the obvious. Select several weeks' check blocks, account for numerical sequence (to see whether any checks have been removed), and examine canceled checks for two endorsements. Examine the checks to determine when and where they were deposited or cashed.

AUDIT OF BALANCE

Payroll processing usually produces no "balance" to audit for existence/occurrence, other than the accumulated total of payroll transactions, and the total may not appear out of line with history because the fraud is small in relation to total payroll and has been going on for years. Conduct a surprise payroll distribution, then follow up by examining prior canceled checks for the missing employees. Scan personnel files for common addresses.

DISCOVERY SUMMARY

Both the surprise distribution and the scan for common addresses provided the names of 2 or 3 exceptions. Both led to canceled checks (which Maybelle had not removed and the bank reconciler had not noticed), which carried Maybelle's own name as endorser. Confronted, she confessed.

CASE 7.4
FALSE SALES, ACCOUNTS RECEIVABLE, AND INVENTORY

PROBLEM

Overstated sales and accounts receivable caused overstated net income, retained earnings, current assets, working capital, and total assets.

METHOD

Q. T. Wilson was a turnaround specialist who took the challenge at Mini Marc Corporation, a manufacturer of computer peripheral equipment. He set high goals for sales and profits. To meet these goals, managers shipped bricks to distributors and recorded some as sales of equipment to retail distributors and some as inventory out on consignment. No real products left the plant for these "sales." The theory was that actual sales would grow, and the bricks would be replaced later with real products. In the meantime, the distributors may have thought they were holding consignment inventory in the unopened cartons.

PAPER TRAIL

All the paperwork was in order because the managers had falsified the sales and consignment invoices, but they did not have customer purchase orders for all the false sales. Shipping papers were in order, and several shipping employees knew the boxes did not contain disk drives.

AMOUNT

Prior to the manipulation, annual sales were $135 million. During the two falsification years, sales were $185 million and $362 million. Net income went up from a loss of $20 million to $23 million (income), then to $31 million (income); and the gross profit margin percent went from 6 percent to 28 percent. The revenue and profit figures outpaced the industry performance. The accounts receivable collection period grew to 94 days, while it was 70 days elsewhere in the industry.

AUDIT APPROACH

OBJECTIVE

Obtain evidence about the existence and valuation of sales, accounts receivable, and inventory.

CONTROL

Company accounting and control procedures required customer purchase orders or contracts evidencing real orders. A sales invoice was supposed to indicate the products and their prices, and shipping documents were supposed to indicate actual shipment. Sales were always charged to a customer's account receivable.

TEST OF CONTROLS

The company had no glaring control omissions that "thinking like a crook" would have pointed to fraud possibilities. Sensitive auditors might have noticed the high tension created by concentration on meeting profit goals. Normal selection of sales transactions with vouching to customer orders and shipping documents might turn up a missing customer order. Otherwise, the paperwork would seem to be in order. The problem lay in the managers' power to override controls and instruct shipping people to send bricks. Auditors ought to ask the question: "Have you shipped anything, other than company products, this year?"

AUDIT OF BALANCE

Confirmations of distributors' accounts receivable may have elicited exception responses. The problem was to have a large enough confirmation sample to pick up some of these distributors or to be skeptical enough to send a special sample of confirmations to distributors who took the "sales" near the end of the accounting period.

DISCOVERY SUMMARY

The overstatements were not detected. The confirmation sample was small and did not contain any of the false shipments. Tests of detail transactions did not turn up any missing customer orders. The inventory out on consignment was audited by obtaining a written confirmation from the holders, who apparently had not opened the boxes. The remarkable financial performance was attributed to good management.

CASE 7.5
OVERSTATE THE INVENTORY, UNDERSTATE THE COST OF GOODS SOLD

PROBLEM

Overstated inventory caused understated cost of goods sold; overstated net income and retained earnings; overstated current assets, working capital, and total assets.

METHOD

A division manager at Doughboy Foods wanted to meet his profit goals and simply submitted overstated quantities in inventory reports. The manager (a) inserted fictitious count sheets in the independent auditors' working papers, (b) handed additional count sheets to the independent auditors after the count was completed saying "these got left out of your set," and (c) inserted false data into the computer system that produced a final inventory compilation

(even though this ploy caused the computer-generated inventory not to match with the count sheets).

PAPER TRAIL

In general, management reports should correspond to accounting records. The manager's inventory reports showed amounts larger than shown in the accounts. He fixed the problem by showing false inventory that was "not recorded on the books."

AMOUNT

The food products inventory was overstated by $650,000. Through a two-year period, the false reports caused an income overstatement of 15 percent in the first year and would have caused a 39 percent overstatement the second year.

AUDIT APPROACH

OBJECTIVE

Obtain evidence of the existence, completeness, and valuation of inventory.

CONTROL

Inventory counts should be taken under controlled conditions, but not under the control of managers who might benefit from manipulation. (However, if these managers are present, auditors should nevertheless be prepared to perform the audit work.) Inventory-takers should be trained and follow instructions for recording quantities and condition.

TEST OF CONTROLS

Auditors should attend the inventory-taker training sessions and study the instructions for adequacy. Observation of the inventory-taking should be conducted by managers and by auditors to ensure compliance with the instructions.

AUDIT OF BALANCE

For evidence of existence, select a sample of inventory items from the perpetual records and test-count them in the warehouse. For evi-

dence of completeness, select a sample of inventory items in the warehouse, test-count them, and trace them to the final inventory compilation. For evidence of valuation, find the proper prices of inventory for one or both of the samples, calculate the total cost for the items, and compare to their amounts recorded in the books. Compare book inventory amounts to management reports. Control the working papers so only members of the audit team have access.

Analytical procedures gave some signals. The particular manager's division had the lowest inventory turnover rate (6.3) among all the company divisions (comparable turnover about 11.1) and its inventory had consistently increased from year to year (227 percent over the two-year period).

DISCOVERY SUMMARY

In the second year, when the manager handed over the count sheets "that got left out of your set," the auditor thanked him, then went to the warehouse to check them out. Finding them inaccurate, she compared book inventories to his management reports and found an overstatement in the reports. This prompted further comparison of the computer-generated inventory with the count sheets and more evidence of overstated quantities on 22 of the 99 count sheets.

R E V I E W CHECKPOINTS

7.17 If the petty cash custodian were replaced and the frequency of fund reimbursement decreased from every two days to every four days, what might you suspect?

7.18 Give some examples of control omissions that would make it easy to "think like a crook" and see opportunities for fraud.

7.19 If sales and income were overstated by recording a false cash sale at the end of the year, what "dangling debit" might give the scheme away?

7.20 What three general descriptions can be given to manipulations that produce materially misleading financial statements?

DOCUMENTS, SOURCES, AND "EXTENDED PROCEDURES"

The auditing literature often refers to "extended procedures," *SAS 82* calls them "specific responses to fraud risk factors," and lists a few. (The details are in Appendix 7A.) An exhaustive list could be very lengthy. However, authorities fear that a definitive list might limit the range of such procedures, so "extended procedures" is generally left as an open-ended set to refer vaguely to "whatever is necessary in the circumstances." This section describes some of the "extended procedures" and warns that (1) some auditors may consider them ordinary and (2) other auditors may consider them unnecessary in any circumstances. They are useful detective procedures in either event.

Content of Common Documents

Auditing textbooks often advise beginner auditors to "examine checks," and to "check the employees on a payroll." It helps to know something about these common documents and the information that can be seen on them.

Information on a Check

Exhibit 7–2 describes the information found on a typical check. Knowledge of the codes for federal reserve districts, offices, states, and bank identification numbers could enable an auditor to spot a crude check forgery. Similarly, a forger's mistakes with the optional identification printing or the magnetic check number might supply a tipoff. If the amount of a check is altered after it has cleared the bank, the change would be noted by comparing the magnetic imprint of the amount paid to the amount written on the check face. The back of a check carries the endorsement(s) of the payees and holders in due course; the date and the name and routing number of the bank where the check was deposited; and the date, identification of the federal reserve office, and its routing number for the federal reserve check clearing. (Sometimes there is no federal reserve clearing identification when local checks are cleared locally without going through a federal reserve office.) Auditors can follow the path of a canceled check by following the banks where it was deposited and cleared. This route may or may not correspond with the characteristics of the payee. (For example, ask why a check to a local business in Texas was deposited in a small Missouri bank and cleared through the St. Louis federal reserve office.)

Information on a Bank Statement

Most of the information shown on the bank statement in Exhibit 7–3 is self-explanatory. However, auditors should not overlook the usefulness of some of the information: the bank's count and dollar amount of deposits and checks can be compared to the detail data on the statement; the account holder's federal business identification number is on the statement, and this can be used in other data bases (you might find a person's Social Security number in the bank statement); and the statement itself can be studied for alterations. (Study the statement in Exhibit 7-3. Any alterations?)

Valid Social Security Numbers

In the United States, Social Security numbers have become a universal identification number. They can be useful to auditors when checking the personnel files and the validity of people on the payroll. Here are some characteristics of SSNs:[9]

- Every SSN consists of three groups of digits, three digits followed by two, followed by four (XXX–XX–XXXX). No group contains consecutive zeros, so 000–XX–XXXX, XXX–00–XXXX, and XXX–XX–0000 are not valid numbers.

---

[9] Caution: The Social Security Administration periodically adds numbers that have been issued and may use numbers assigned to one geographic area for another. If the validity of a SSN becomes important in an audit, check with the Social Security Administration to ascertain the current status of numbers issued. For further reference, see M. L. Levy, "Financial Fraud: Schemes and Indicia," *Journal of Accountancy*, August 1985, p. 85; E. J. Pankau, *Check It Out* (Chicago: Contemporary Books, 1992).

EXHIBIT 7–2   HOW TO READ A CANCELED CHECK AND ENDORSEMENT

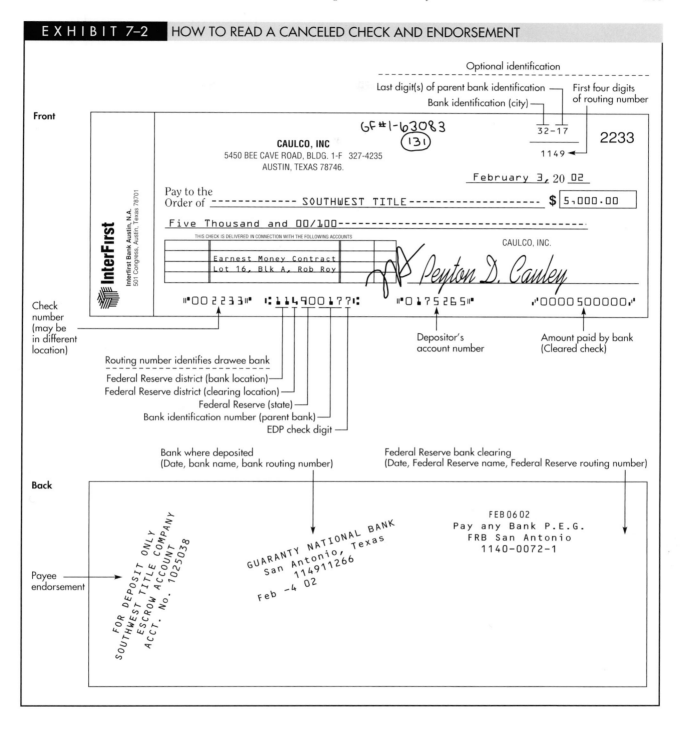

- The first three digits gives the "area," usually indicating the state or territory where the number was issued. Numbers are usually issued at an early age, so the number might identify the state of birth. By reference to Appendix 7C, you can see that certain three-digit area numbers have not been assigned (as of 2000): the ones in the ranges 729–749 and 766–999. The numbers from 700 to 728 were issued for the Railroad Retirement system years ago and probably belong to older workers.
- The middle two digits are the "group number," which could be from 01 to 99. However, many two-digit combinations have not been assigned. By reference to Appendix 7C, you can see that the SSN numbers 001–98–9876, 004–08–9876, and

EXHIBIT 7–3	SMALL BUSINESS BANK STATEMENT

```
                                                              27

   ✕ First RepublicBank

      FIRST REPUBLICBANK AUSTIN, N.A.                   ACCOUNT
      P.O. BOX 908                    ---         604017-526-5
      AUSTIN, TEXAS  78781            ---    ---

                                      ---               PAGE
                                           ---             1


      CAULCO INC                             SSN/TAX ID
      BLDG 1 OFFICE F                        74-2076251
      5450 BEE CAVE RD
      AUSTIN,  TX                            CYC MC FREQ
      78746                                  01 01 M0000


      **  YOUR CHECKING ACCOUNT      01-29-02 THRU 02-28-02  **

   TO YOUR PREVIOUS BALANCE OF - - - - - - - -        7,559.06
   YOU ADDED           1 DEPOSITS FOR  - - - - -       5,654.16
   YOU SUBTRACTED   26 WITHDRAWALS FOR - - - - -      10,838.29
   GIVING YOU A CURRENT BALANCE OF - - - - - - -       7,374.93

   NUMBER OF DAYS USED FOR AVERAGES  - - - - - -             31
   YOUR AVERAGE LEDGER BALANCE - - - - - - - - -       4,014.67
   YOUR LOW BALANCE OCCURRED ON 02-22 AND WAS  -       2,374.93

              THANK YOU


   ----------------------------------------------------------
   ----------------------------------------------------------
                 DEPOSITS AND OTHER ADDITIONS

        DATE      AMOUNT  ✓
        0204    5654.16 ✓
   ----------------------------------------------------------
                 CHECKS AND OTHER WITHDRAWALS

   CHECK DATE   AMOUNT CHECK DATE    AMOUNT CHECK DATE    AMOUNT
   2201 0211    57.83✓ 2214 0203    403.92✓ 2225 0217   ✓ 182.77
     **                2215 0203    135.59✓   **
   2205 0222    16.72✓ 2216 0216      6.16✓ 2231 0205   ✓ 254.37
   2206 0203   533.28✓ 2217 0217    138.43✓ 2232 0210   ✓  60.61
   2207 0203  1312.15✓ 2218 0217    131.92✓
     **                2219 0217     82.97✓ 2234 0217   ✓  64.69
   2209 0203   247.10✓ 2220 0217     87.49✓ 2235 0218   ✓ 279.97
   2210 0203   249.98✓ 2221 0217     85.68✓   **
   2211 0203   255.26✓ 2222 0217     84.69✓ 2238 0219   ✓  90.00
   2212 0203   242.09✓   **
   2213 0203   384.91✓ 2224 0217    449.71✓
```

008–11–9876 are fictitious because the group numbers 98, 08, and 11 in combination with those areas have not been used (as of 2000). (Levy pointed out that, in SSNs issued before 1965, group numbers of 10 or higher should be even numbers; and in SSNs issued in or after 1965, the group number can be odd or even. This feature can be correlated with a person's reported birthdate.)

• The last four digits can be 0001 to 9999. The only invalid one is 0000.

Some social security numbers in the range of issued numbers actually are not valid because the owner died. Question: How can the manager of a company pension plan determine whether the plan is making payments to dead people? Answer: Obtain a copy of the Social Security Administration's "death file" and match the pension plan file of payees' SSNs to the SSNs on the tape. The tape contains the SSNs known to be invalid because of death.

R E V I E W
CHECKPOINTS

7.21 How can you tell whether the amount on a check had been raised after it was paid by a bank?

7.22 If a false Social Security number of a new employee is entered in the payroll system, and the employee receives a paycheck, what control in the system is not being used? What's wrong with this number: 585–81–1234 for Byron Middleton, born July 4, 1950, in Cheyenne, Wyoming?

Sources of Information

A wide variety of records and information is available for various kinds of investigations ranging from personal background checks to business inquiries. Our concern here is with public records and ways to get them. A few of the hundreds of sources are described briefly below. Many databases and information sources are available on the Internet.

General Business Sources

City and county tax assessor-collectors keep files on real property by address and legal description, owner, taxable value, improvements, amount of taxes and delinquencies. State (and some city) regulatory agencies have directories of liquor licenses, and various professionals (e.g., CPAs, dentists, doctors, plumbers, electricians). The U.S. Department of Housing and Urban Development (HUD) has a central index file of appraisers, real estate brokers, and most components of the building industry. The U.S. Department of State has data on companies that apply for import and export licenses. The Federal Aviation Administration maintains files on the chain of ownership of all civil aircraft in the United States. The U.S. Securities and Exchange Commission has extensive financial information on about 15,000 registered companies and their properties, principle officers, directors, and owners. Local Better Business Bureaus keep information about criminal rackets, cons, and their operators, and can provide information about the business reputation of local businesses. Standard & Poor's *Register of Corporations, Directors, and Executives* lists about 37,000 public and private companies and the names and titles of over 400,000 officials.[10]

Business and Asset Identification Sources

Each county and state has a system for registering businesses—corporations, joint ventures, sole proprietorships, partnerships. They keep files on registered "assumed names" (DBA, or "Doing Business As" names). Some businesses may be registered with a state and not a county, or with a county and not a state. All real corporations are chartered by a state, and each state's secretary of state keeps corporate record information, such as the date of registration and the initial officers and owners. (Using these sources, you can find the assets or business "hidden" in the spouse's name.) Crooks often work through a labyrinth of business entities, and you can find all the registered ones in these sources. You can find phony vendor companies created by real employees to bilk employers with false billings. Banks, finance companies, and other creditors often file Uniform Commercial Code (UCC) records to record the interest of the creditor in assets used as

---

[10] Hundreds of sources and directories under the categories of business, finance, people, property, and electronic data bases are listed and described in the U.S. General Accounting Office publication entitled *Investigators' Guide to Sources of Information* (GAO/OSI-88-1, March 1988, updated periodically).

collateral for a loan, so other parties cannot claim interest in the assets (e.g., boats, business equipment, appliances). UCCs are in county clerks' offices and in a state's office of the secretary of state or commercial department of the state records office. (They are also online in some commercial databases.)[11]

Federal and State Revenue Agencies

Ever wonder how revenue agents find tax evaders? One accountant described the following sources of tips for possible big audit findings. (1) Police and Drug Enforcement Agency arrest records point to people who may have illicit unreported income. (2) Real estate sales records may identify people who "forget" to put their sales in a tax return. (3) Auto registrations of expensive cars point to people who have a lot of money to spend, maybe some unreported income. (4) Comparison of state sales tax returns with income tax revenue amounts may reveal discrepancies (depending on which tax collector is feared the most). (5) Agents have used college-town newspaper rental ads to identify people who rent rooms, garage apartments, duplex halves, and the like, but forget to report the income.

R E V I E W
CHECKPOINTS

7.23 Where could you find information about: Real estate valuation? Aircraft ownership? Names of licensed doctors? Assumed (fictitious) business names? Liens on personal property?

Extended Procedures

The nature of extended procedures is limited only by an auditor's imagination and, sometimes, the willingness of management to cooperate in extraordinary audit activities. Next is a short series of extended procedures, with some brief explanations.[12]

Count the Petty Cash Twice in a Day

The second count is unexpected, and you might catch an embezzling custodian short.

Investigate Suppliers (Vendors)

Check the Better Business Bureau for reputation, the telephone book for a listing and address, the state and county corporation records for owners and assumed names. You may find fictitious vendors being used to make false billings or companies related to purchasing department employees.

Investigate Customers

As with vendors, investigation may reveal companies set up by insiders, with billings at below-list prices so the insiders can "buy" goods and resell them at a profit.

Examine Endorsements on Canceled Checks

Look for second endorsements, especially the names of employees. Most business payments are deposited with one endorsement. Be sure to include checks payable to "cash" or to a bank for purchase of cashiers' checks. The second endorsee indicates that the payee may not have received the benefit of the payment.

---

[11] These and other sources of business and personal information are described in Pankau, *Check It Out.*

[12] Further explanation of these and other procedures can be found in the books and articles cited in preceding footnotes and in these sources: AICPA *Technical Practice Aids* (TPA 8200.02); D. Churbuck, "Desktop Forgery," *Forbes*, November 27, 1989, pp. 246–54; O. Hilton, *Scientific Examination of Questioned Documents*, rev. ed. (New York: Elsevier North Holland, 1982); A. C. Levinston, "40 Years of Embezzlement Tracking," *Internal Auditor*, April 1991, pp. 51–55.

Add Up the Accounts Receivable Subsidiary
Cash payments on customer accounts have been stolen, with receipts given, credit entry to the customer account, but no cash deposit and no entry to the control account.

Audit General Journal Entries
Experience has shown that the largest number of accounting errors requiring adjustment are found in nonroutine, nonsystematic journal entries. (Systematic accounting is the processing of large volumes of day-to-day ordinary transactions.)

Match Payroll to Life and Medical Insurance Deductions
Ghosts on the payroll seldom elect these insurance coverages. Doing so reduces the embezzler's take and complicates the coverup.

Match Payroll to Social Security Numbers
Fictitious SSNs may be chosen at random, making the mistake of using an unissued number or one that does not match with the birthdate. Sort the payroll SSNs in numerical order and look for false, duplicate, or unlikely (e.g., consecutive) numbers.

Match Payroll with Addresses
Look for multiple persons at the same address.

Retrieve Customers' Checks
If an employee has diverted customer payments, the canceled checks showing endorsements and deposits to a bank where the company has no account are not available because they are returned to the issuing organization (customer). Ask the customer for originals, copies, or for examination access.

Use Marked Coins and Currency
Plant marked money in locations where cash collections should be gathered and turned over for deposit.

Measure Deposit Lag Time
Compare the dates of cash debit recording and deposit slip dates to dates credited by the bank. Someone who takes cash, then holds the deposit for the next cash receipts to make up the difference, causes a delay between the date of recording and the bank's date of deposit.

Document Examination
Look for erasures, alterations, copies where originals should be filed, telltale lines from a copier when a document has been pieced together, handwriting, and other oddities. Auditors should always insist on seeing original documents instead of photocopies. Professional document examination is a technical activity that requires special training, but crude alterations may be observed, at least enough to bring them to specialists' attention.

Inquiry, Ask Questions
Be careful not to discuss fraud possibilities with the managers who might be involved. It gives them a chance to cover up or run. Wells described fraud audit questioning (FAQ) as a nonaccusatory method of asking key questions of personnel during a regular audit to give them an opportunity to furnish information about possible misdeeds. Fraud possibilities are addressed in a direct manner, so the FAQ approach must have the support of management. Example questions are: "Do you think fraud is a problem for business in general?" "Do you think this company has any particular problem with fraud?" "In your department, who is beyond suspicion?" "Is there any information you would like to furnish regarding possible fraud within this organization?"[13]

---

[13] Joseph T. Wells, "From the Chairman: Fraud Audit Questioning," *The White Paper*, National Association of Certified Fraud Examiners, May–June 1991, p. 2. This technique must be used with extreme care and practice.

AUDITING INSIGHT

WANT TO FUDGE YOUR TAX DEDUCTIONS?

Don't try to turn that $300 receipt into $800 with the stroke of a ballpoint pen. The IRS has ultraviolet scanners, ink chromatographers, densitometers, and argon-ion lasers that can identify the brand of pen, the age of the paper, and the source of the paper. Something printed on a laser printer is harder, but they're working on it.

Source: D. Churbuck, "Desktop Forgery," *Forbes*.

Covert Surveillance

Observe activities while not being seen. External auditors might watch employees clocking onto a work shift, observing whether they use only one time card. Traveling hotel auditors may check in unannounced, use the restaurant and entertainment facilities, and watch the employees skimming receipts and tickets. (Trailing people on streets and maintaining a "stake-out" should be left to trained investigators.)

Horizontal and Vertical Analyses

This is analytical review ratio analysis. Horizontal analysis refers to changes of financial statement numbers and ratios across several years. Vertical analysis refers to commonsize financial statement amounts expressed each year as proportions of a base, such as sales for the income statement accounts and total assets for the balance sheet accounts. Auditors look for relationships that do not make sense as indicators of potential large misstatement and fraud.

Net Worth Analysis

This is used when fraud has been discovered or strongly suspected, and the information to calculate a suspect's net worth can be obtained (e.g., asset and liability records, bank accounts). The method is to calculate the suspect's net worth (known assets minus known liabilities) at the beginning and end of a period (months or years), then try to account for the difference as (1) known income less living expenses and (2) unidentified difference. The unidentified difference may be the best available approximation of the amount of a theft.

Expenditure Analysis

This is similar to net worth analysis, except the data is the suspect's spending for all purposes compared to known income. If spending exceeds legitimate and explainable income, the difference may be the amount of a theft.

R E V I E W
CHECKPOINTS

7.24 What is the difference between a "normal procedure" and an "extended procedure?"

7.25 What might be indicated by two endorsements on a canceled check?

7.26 What three oddities might be found connected with ghosts on a padded payroll?

7.27 What can an auditor find using horizontal analysis? Vertical analysis? Net worth analysis? Expenditure analysis?

AFTER DISCOVERING A FRAUD

Building a case against a fraudster is a task for trained investigators. Most internal and external auditors take roles as assistants to fraud examiners, who know how to conduct interviews and interrogations, perform surveillance, use informants, and obtain usable confessions. In almost all cases, the postdiscovery activity proceeds with a special prosecutorial assignment under the cooperation or leadership of management. A district attorney and police officials may be involved. Prosecution of fraudsters is advisable because, if left unpunished, they often go on to steal again. This is no place for "normal" auditing, but auditors have been given some guidelines related to relevant communications.

AICPA and Internal Audit Standards

Standards for external auditors (*SAS 82*, AU 316) contain materiality thresholds related to auditors' reporting their knowledge of frauds. Auditors may consider some minor frauds "inconsequential" especially when they involve misappropriations of assets by employees at low organizational levels (i.e., embezzlement defalcations). Auditors should report these to management at least one level above the people involved. The idea is that small matters can be kept in the management family. On the other hand, frauds involving senior managers and any frauds that cause material misstatement in the financial statements should be reported directly to the organization's audit committee of the board of directors. These matters are never "inconsequential." (These reports are specified in *SAS 60*, AU 325—*Communication of Internal Control Matters Noted in an Audit*, and in *SAS 61*, AU 380—*Communication with Audit Committees*, as detailed in Appendix 7A.)

Clients' illegal acts also come under a "clearly inconsequential" materiality standard. Illegal acts that amount to more than this should be reported to the organization's audit committee, and the financial statements should contain adequate disclosures about the organization's illegal acts (*SAS 54*, AU 317). External auditors always have the option to withdraw from the engagement if management and directors do not take action satisfactory in the circumstances.

Under the AICPA audit standards, disclosures of frauds and clients' illegal acts to outside agencies are limited (*SAS 82* and *SAS 54*). If the auditors get fired, the firm can cite these matters in the letter attached to SEC Form 8-K, which requires explanation of an organization's change of auditors. A fired auditor can tell the successor auditor about them when the successor makes the inquiries required by audit standards (*SAS 84*, AU 315). Auditors must respond when answering a subpoena issued by a court or other agency with authority. When performing work under GAO audit standards (GAGAS), auditors are required to report frauds and illegal acts to the client agency under the audit contract.

In addition, another reporting obligation was imposed by Private Securities Litigation Reform Act of 1995 (amending the Securities and Exchange Act of 1934). Under this law, when auditors believe an illegal act that is more than "clearly inconsequential" has or may have occurred, the auditors must inform the organization's board of directors. When the auditors believe the illegal act has a material effect on the financial statements, the board of directors has one business day to inform the U.S. Securities and Exchange Commission (SEC). If the board does not inform the SEC, the auditors must (*a*) within one business day, give the SEC the same report they gave the board of directors, or (*b*) resign from the engagement, and within one business day give the SEC the report. If the auditors do not fulfill this legal obligation, the SEC can impose a monetary fine.

As for the internal auditors, *Statement on Internal Audit Standards No. 3* requires them to inform management of suspected wrongdoing. They are expected to report fraud findings to management, the board of directors, or the audit committee of the board, being careful not to report to persons who might be involved in a fraud scheme.

Consulting and Assisting

LEARNING OBJECTIVE

8. Describe the ways CPAs can assist in prosecuting fraud perpetrators.

While engaged in the audit work, auditors should know how to preserve the **chain of custody** of evidence. The chain of custody is the crucial link of the evidence to the suspect, called the "relevance" of evidence by attorneys and judges. If documents are lost, mutilated, coffee-soaked, compromised (so a defense attorney can argue that they were altered to frame the suspect), they can lose their effectiveness for the prosecution. Auditors should learn to mark the evidence, writing an identification of the location, condition, date, time, and circumstances as soon as it appears to be a signal of fraud. This marking should be on a separate tag or page, the original document should be put in a protective envelope (plastic) for preservation, and audit work should proceed with copies of the documents instead of originals. A record should be made of the safekeeping and of all persons who use the original. Any eyewitness observations should be timely recorded in a memorandum or on tape (audio or video), with corroboration of colleagues, if possible. Other features of the chain of custody relate to interviews, interrogations, confessions, documents obtained by subpoena, and other matters, but these activities usually are not conducted by auditors.

Independent CPAs often accept engagements for litigation support and expert witnessing. This work can be termed **forensic accounting,** which means the application of accounting and auditing skills to legal problems, both civil and criminal. **Litigation support** can take several forms, but it usually amounts to consulting in the capacity of helping attorneys document cases and determine damages. **Expert witness** work involves testifying to findings determined during litigation support and testifying about accounting principles and auditing standards applications. The AICPA and the Institute of Internal Auditors conduct continuing education courses for auditors who want to become experts in these fields.

7.28 Why is prosecution of fraud perpetrators generally a good idea?

7.29 What are the AICPA and SEC materiality guidelines for reporting frauds and illegal acts?

7.30 Why must care be taken with evidence of fraudulent activity?

SUMMARY

According to the AICPA generally accepted auditing standards, fraud-detection audit procedures are *conditional*. GAAS states this: "Auditors should specifically assess the risk of material misstatement due to fraud and should consider this assessment in designing the audit procedures to be performed. Auditors should consider fraud risk factors that relate to both (*a*) misstatements arising from fraudulent financial reporting, and (*b*) misstatements arising from misappropriations of assets" (SAS 82, AU 316). The fraud risk assessment comes first. It must show the auditors reasons to suspect frauds in the accounts. This risk assessment demands audit skills for noticing the "red flags" signs of fraud and deciding whether they are significant for planning subsequent procedures. Thus, according to GAAS, performance of fraud-detection procedures is conditional upon (1) the existence of red flags, (2) the auditors' skill in noticing them and assessing the fraud risk, and (3) the auditors' willingness to follow them with fraud-detecting procedures.

The AICPA auditing standards concentrate on management fraud—the production of materially false and misleading financial statements (i.e., fraudulent financial reporting). However, *SAS 82* also requires auditors to pay some attention to employee fraud perpetrated against a client organization. Attention to employee fraud is important in the context that the coverup may create financial statement misstatements (e.g., over-stating an inventory to disguise unauthorized removal of valuable products).

Independent auditors traditionally regard fraud-detecting procedures as "not normal." GAAS supports this view by making such procedures conditional upon the fraud risk assessment. However, "normality" is in the eyes of the beholder. In the 1930s, confirmation of receivables and observation of inventories were not widely regarded as normal procedures. Under SEC pressure after the McKesson and Robbins affair, these two procedures were written into the auditing standards and made normal for all audits. Today, auditors regard confirmation and observation as standard procedures. Auditors perform them to try to detect errors and frauds, but they are not conditional. They are performed in all audits. Tomorrow, other procedures may become "normal" either through client demand or through external regulatory pressure.

Fraud awareness auditing starts with knowledge of the types of errors, frauds, and illegal acts that can be perpetrated. External, internal, and governmental auditors all have standards for care, attention, planning, detection, and reporting of some kinds of errors, frauds, and illegal acts. Fraud examiners, on the other hand, have little in the way of standard programs or materiality guidelines to limit their attention to fraud possibilities. They float on a sea of observations of exceptions and oddities that may be the tip of a fraud iceberg.

Fraud may be contemplated when people have motives, usually financial needs, for stealing money or property. Motive, combined with opportunity and a lapse of integrity, generally makes the probability of fraud or theft very high. Opportunities arise when an organization's management has lax attitudes about setting examples for good behavior and about maintenance of a supportive control environment. The fear of getting caught by controls deters some fraudsters. Otherwise, attentive management can ease the pressures people feel and, thus, reduce the incidence of fraud.

Auditors need to know about the red flags, those telltale signs and indications that have accompanied many frauds. When studying a business operation, auditors' ability to "think like a crook" to devise ways to steal can help in planning procedures designed to determine whether it happened. Often, imaginative "extended procedures" can be employed to unearth evidence of fraudulent activity. However, auditors must always exercise technical and personal care because accusations of fraud are always taken very seriously. For this reason, after preliminary findings indicate fraud possibilities, auditors should enlist the cooperation of management and assist fraud examination professionals when bringing an investigation to a conclusion.

MULTIPLE CHOICE QUESTIONS FOR PRACTICE AND REVIEW

7.31   Embezzlement is a type of fraud that involves
   a. An employee taking an employer's money or property not entrusted to the employee's control in the employee's normal job.
   b. A manager's falsification of financial statements for the purpose of misleading investors and creditors.
   c. An employee's mistaken representation of opinion that causes incorrect accounting entries.
   d. An employee taking an employer's money or property entrusted to the employee's control in the employee's normal job.

7.32   One of the typical characteristics of management fraud is
   a. Falsification of documents in order to steal money from an employer.
   b. Victimization of investors through the use of materially misleading financial statements.
   c. Illegal acts committed by management to evade laws and regulations.
   d. Conversion of stolen inventory to cash deposited in a falsified bank account.

7.33   AICPA auditing standards do not require auditors of financial statements to:
   a. Understand the nature of errors and frauds

b. Assess the risk of occurrence of errors and frauds.

c. Design audits to provide reasonable assurance of detecting errors and frauds.

d. Report all finding of errors and frauds to police authorities.

7.34   Under the Private Securities Litigation Reform Act, independent auditors are required to

a. Report in writing all instances of illegal acts to the client's board of directors.

b. Report to the SEC all instances of illegal acts they believe have a material effect on financial statements if the board of directors does not first report to the SEC.

c. Report clearly inconsequential illegal acts to the audit committee of the client's board of directors.

d. Resign from the audit engagement and report the instances of illegal acts to the SEC.

7.35   Which two of the following characterize the work of fraud examiners and are different from the typical attitude of external auditors?

a. Analysis of control weaknesses for opportunities to commit fraud.

b. Analysis of control strengths as a basis for planning other audit procedures.

c. Determination of a materiality amount that represents a significant misstatement of the current-year financial statements.

d. Thinking of a materiality amount in cumulative terms—that is, becoming large over a number of years.

7.36   When auditing with "fraud awareness," auditors should especially notice and follow up employee activities under which of these conditions?

a. The company always estimates the inventory but never takes a complete physical count.

b. The petty cash box is always locked in the desk of the custodian.

c. Management has published a company code of ethics and sends frequent communication newsletters about it.

d. The board of directors reviews and approves all investment transactions.

7.37   Two of the major differences between the attitudes of financial statement auditors (in a "normal audit") and fraud examiners are

a. Financial statement auditors consider the criminology of motive, opportunity, and integrity while fraud examiners base their work on financial accounting and auditing logic.

b. Financial statement auditors usually follow a standard program while fraud examiners are sensitive to oddities where nothing is standard.

c. Financial statement auditors consider materiality as an amount large enough to make financial statements misleading while fraud examiners think in terms of cumulative materiality over a number of years.

d. Financial statement auditors take note of exceptions and oddities in transactions while fraud examiners are sensitive to errors, omissions, and control weaknesses.

7.38   The best way to enact a broad fraud-prevention program is to

a. Install airtight control systems of checks and supervision.

b. Name an "ethics officer" who is responsible for receiving and acting upon fraud tips.

c. Place dedicated "hotline" telephones on walls around the workplace with direct communication to the company ethics officer.

d. Practice management "of the people and for the people" to help them share personal and professional problems.

7.39   Which of the following gives the least indication of fraudulent activity?

a. Numerous cash refunds have been made to different people at the same post office box address.

b. Internal auditor cannot locate several credit memos to support reductions of customers' balances.

c. Bank reconciliation has no outstanding checks or deposits older than 15 days.

d. Three people were absent the day the auditors handed out the paychecks and have not picked them up four weeks later.

7.40   When financial statement auditors decide to carry out a response to a particular fraud risk in an account balance or class of transactions, they are most likely to (refer to Appendix 7A)

a. Exercise more professional skepticism.

b. Carefully avoid conducting interviews with people in the fraud rich areas.

c. Perform procedures like inventory observation and cash counts on a surprise or unannounced basis.

d. Study more carefully management's selection and application of accounting principles.

7.41 Which of the following combinations is a good means of hiding employee fraud but a poor means of carrying out management (financial reporting) fraud?

a. Overstating sales revenue and overstating customer accounts receivable balances.

b. Overstating sales revenue and overstating bad debt expense.

c. Understating interest expense and understating accrued interest payable.

d. Omit the disclosure information about related party sales to the president's relatives at below-market prices.

7.42 Which of these arrangements of duties could most likely lead to an embezzlement or theft?

a. Inventory warehouse manager has responsibility for making the physical inventory observation and reconciling discrepancies to the perpetual inventory records.

b. Cashier prepared the bank deposit, endorsed the checks with a company stamp, and took the cash and checks to the bank for deposit (no other bookkeeping duties).

c. Accounts receivable clerk received a list of payments received by the cashier so she could make entries in the customers' accounts receivable subsidiary accounts.

d. Financial vice president received checks made out to suppliers and the supporting invoices, signed the checks, and put them in the mail to the payees.

7.43 If sales and income were overstated by recording a false credit sale at the end of the year, where could you find the false "dangling debit?" In the

a. Inventory?

b. Cost of goods sold?

c. Bad debt expense?

d. Accounts receivable?

7.44 Which of these is an invalid Social Security number?

a. 462–00–3358.

b. 473–09–7787.

c. 506–98–5529.

d. 700–05–1358.

7.45 Public records from which of these sources could be used to find the owner of an office building?

a. U.S. Department of State export/import license files.

b. Federal Aviation Administration records.

c. City and county tax assessor-collector files.

d. Securities and Exchange Commission filings.

7.46 Experience has shown that the largest number of accounting errors requiring adjustment is found in

a. Systematic processing of large volumes of day-to-day ordinary transactions.

b. Payroll fraudsters' mistakes in using unissued Social Security numbers.

c. Petty cash embezzlements.

d. Nonroutine, nonsystematic journal entries.

7.47 The type of financial analysis that expresses balance sheet accounts as percentages of total assets is known as

a. Horizontal analysis.

b. Vertical analysis.

c. Net worth analysis.

d. Expenditure analysis.

7.48 When dealing with several estimates management made preparing financial statements, auditors should consider

a. The closest reasonable estimates supported by the audit evidence.

b. The differences between management's estimates and the closest reasonable estimates supported by the audit evidence taken altogether for indications of systematic bias.

c. The care management exercised designing the control system over processing management estimate transactions.

d. Each estimate alone in relation to the difference between management's estimate and the closest reasonable estimate supported by the audit evidence.

7.49 The auditors most likely to be most concerned about an auditee's compliance with laws and regulations are

a. GAO (government) auditors.

b. CPAs practicing independent auditing of financial statements.

c. Internal auditors.

d. Operational auditors.

7.50   In business, not-for-profit, and governmental settings, the most common motive for embezzlement is
    a. Psychotic (persons who are habitual white-collar criminals).
    b. Egocentric (persons who need to achieve personal prestige).
    c. Ideological (persons who think their causes are morally superior).
    d. Economic (persons who need money).

7.51   An enlightened management can make progress toward preventing internal employee fraud by first
    a. Installing and enforcing strong internal controls.
    b. Performing background checks on new hires for positions charged with custody of money and property.
    c. Installing employee assistance programs to enable employees to share their problems with counselors of various types.
    d. Performing continuing background checks on successful executives as they are promoted to higher positions.

7.52   If a management attempts financial statement manipulation by failing to record cost of goods sold for actual sales, auditors are most likely to discover the effect by auditing the
    a. Accounts receivable.
    b. Cost of goods sold.
    c. Inventory.
    d. Cash.

7.53   The client company operates 254 retail stores in the United States and 15 stores in Mexico, all of them selling groceries, clothing, and household maintenance products. In the United States each store maintains electronic perpetual inventory records, and the annual inventory-takers use handheld electronic devices connected to the perpetual system to count and reconcile inventory differences. In Mexico, the inventory balances are determined on the periodic method by actual count, and the inventory-takers use preprinted product lists to record inventory on hand for subsequent computer compilation. Absent any obvious fraud risk factors, a preferable approach to the independent auditors' observation of the inventory-taking is
    a. Inform management in advance and send auditors to the 240 largest stores in the United States and to all 15 stores in Mexico to observe the inventory-taking.
    b. Inform management in advance of the selection of a sample of stores in the U.S. and a sample of stores in Mexico where auditors will observe inventory-taking.
    c. Inform management in advance of a selection of a sample of stores in the U.S. and a sample of stores in Mexico where auditors will observe inventory-taking; and in addition visit other stores in both countries without notifying management in advance.
    d. Inform management in advance of a selection of a sample of stores in the U.S. and a sample of stores in Mexico where auditors will observe inventory-taking; and also inform management that the inventory-taking will be observed in other unspecified stores in both countries.

7.54   The type of analysis that can enable auditors to estimate the amount an embezzler's scheme took from an organization is
    a. Expenditure analysis.
    b. Horizontal analysis.
    c. Vertical analysis.
    d. Time series analysis.

EXERCISES AND PROBLEMS

7.55   **Give Examples of Errors and Frauds.** This is an exercise concerning financial reporting misstatements, not employee theft. Give an example of an error or fraud that would misstate financial statements to affect the accounts as follow, taken one case at a time. (Note: "overstate" means the account has a higher value than would be appropriate under GAAP, and "understate" means it has a lower value.)

    a. Overstate an asset, understate another asset.
    b. Overstate an asset, overstate stockholder equity.
    c. Overstate an asset, overstate revenue.
    d. Overstate an asset, understate an expense.
    e. Overstate a liability, overstate an expense.
    f. Understate an asset, overstate an expense.
    g. Understate a liability, understate an expense.

7.56   Overall Analysis of Accounting Estimates.   Oak Industries, a manufacturer of radio and cable TV equipment and an operator of subscription TV systems, had a multitude of problems. Subscription services in a market area, for which $12 million cost had been deferred, were being terminated, and the customers were not paying on time ($4 million receivables in doubt). The chances are 50–50 that the business will survive another two years.

An electronic part turned out to have defects that needed correction. Warranty expenses are estimated to range from $2 million to $6 million. The inventory of this part ($10 million) is obsolete, but $1 million can be recovered in salvage; or, the parts in inventory can be rebuilt at a cost of $2 million (selling price of the inventory on hand would then be $8 million, with 20 percent of selling price required to market and ship the products, and the normal profit expected is 5 percent of the selling price). If the inventory were scrapped, the company could manufacture a replacement inventory at a cost of $6 million, excluding marketing and shipping costs and normal profit.

The company has defaulted on completion of a military contract, and the government is claiming a $2 million refund. Company attorneys think the dispute might be settled for as little as $1 million.

The auditors had previously determined that an overstatement of income before taxes of $7 million would be material to the financial statements. These items were the only ones left for audit decisions about possible adjustment. Management has presented the analysis below for the determination of loss recognition:

Write-off deferred subscription costs	$ 3,000,000
Provide allowance for bad debts	4,000,000
Provide for expected warranty expense	2,000,000
Lower of cost or market inventory write-down	2,000,000
Loss on government contract refund	—
Total write-offs and losses	$11,000,000

Required:
Prepare your own analysis of the amount of adjustment to the financial statements. Assume that none of these estimates have been recorded yet, and give the adjusting entry you would recommend. Give any supplementary explanations you believe necessary to support your recommendation.

7.57   Select Effective Extended Procedures.   Given below are some "suspicions," and you have been requested to select some effective extended procedures designed to confirm or deny the suspicions.

Required:
Write the suggested procedures for each case in definite terms so another person can know what to do.

a. The custodian of the petty cash fund may be removing cash on Friday afternoon to pay for weekend activities.

b. A manager noticed that eight new vendors were added to the purchasing department approved list after the assistant purchasing agent was promoted to chief agent three weeks ago. She suspects all or some of them might be phony companies set up by the new chief purchasing agent.

c. The payroll supervisor may be stealing unclaimed paychecks of people who quit work and don't pick up the last check.

d. Although no customers have complained, cash collections on accounts receivable are down, and the counter clerks may have stolen customers' payments.

e. The cashier may have "borrowed" money, covering it by holding each day's deposit until cash from the next day(s) collection is enough to make up the shortage from an earlier day, then sending the deposit to the bank.

7.58   Horizontal and Vertical Analysis.   Horizontal analysis refers to changes of financial statement numbers and ratios across two or more years. Vertical analysis refers to financial statement amounts expressed each year as proportions of a base, such as sales for the income statement accounts, and total assets for the balance sheet accounts. Exhibit 7.58–1 contains the Retail Company's prior year (audited) and current year (unaudited) financial statements, along with amounts and percentages of change from year to year (horizontal analysis) and common-size percentages (vertical analysis). Exhibit 7.58–2 contains selected financial ratios based on these financial statements. Analysis of these data may enable auditors to discern relationships that raise questions about misleading financial statements.

Required:
Study the data in Exhibits 7.58–1 and 7.58–2. Write a memo identifying and explaining potential problem areas where misstatements in the current year financial statements might exist.

EXHIBIT 7.58–1 | RETAIL COMPANY

	Prior Year Audited Balance	Prior Year Audited Common Size	Current Year Balance	Current Year Common Size	Change Amount	Change Percent
Assets:						
Cash	$ 600,000	14.78%	$ 484,000	9.69%	(116,000)	−19.33%
Accounts receivable	500,000	12.32	400,000	8.01	(100,000)	−20.00
Allowance doubt. accts.	(40,000)	−0.99	(30,000)	−0.60	10,000	−25.00
Inventory	1,500,000	36.95	1,940,000	38.85	440,000	29.33
Total current assets	2,560,000	63.05	2,794,000	55.95	234,000	9.14
Fixed assets	3,000,000	73.89	4,000,000	80.10	1,000,000	33.33
Accum. depreciation	(1,500,000)	−36.95	(1,800,000)	−36.04	(300,000)	20.00
Total assets	$4,060,000	100.00%	$4,994,000	100.00%	934,000	23.00%
Liabilities and equity:						
Accounts payable	$ 450,000	11.08%	$ 600,000	12.01%	150,000	33.33%
Bank loans, 11%	0	0.00	750,000	15.02	750,000	NA
Accrued interest	50,000	1.23	40,000	0.80	(10,000)	−20.00
Accruals and other	60,000	1.48	10,000	0.20	(50,000)	−83.33
Total current liab.	560,000	13.79	1,400,000	28.03	840,000	150.00
Long-term debt, 10%	500,000	12.32	400,000	8.01	(100,000)	−20.00
Total liabilities	1,060,000	26.11	1,800,000	36.04	740,000	69.81
Capital stock	2,000,000	49.26	2,000,000	40.05	0	0
Retained earnings	1,000,000	24.63	1,194,000	23.91	194,000	19.40
Total liabilities and equity	$4,060,000	100.00%	$4,994,000	100.00%	934,000	23.00%
Statement of operations:						
Sales (net)	$9,000,000	100.00%	$8,100,000	100.00%	(900,000)	−10.00%
Cost of goods sold	6,296,000	69.96	5,265,000	65.00	(1,031,000)	−16.38
Gross margin	2,704,000	30.04	2,835,000	35.00	131,000	4.84
General expense	2,044,000	22.71	2,005,000	24.75	(39,000)	−1.91
Depreciation	300,000	3.33	300,000	3.70	0	0
Operating income	360,000	4.00	530,000	6.54	170,000	47.22
Interest expense	50,000	0.56	40,000	0.49	(10,000)	−20.00
Income taxes (40%)	124,000	1.38	196,000	2.42	72,000	58.06
Net income	$ 186,000	2.07%	$ 294,000	3.63%	108,000	58.06%

NA means not applicable.

Additional information about Retail Company is as follows:

- The new bank loan, obtained on July 1 of the current year, requires maintenance of a 2:1 current ratio.

- Principal of $100,000 plus interest on the 10 percent long-term note obtained several years ago in the original amount of $800,000 is due each January 1.

- The company has never paid dividends on its common stock and has no plans for a dividend.

7.59   Expenditure   Analysis.   Expenditure analysis is used when fraud has been discovered or strongly suspected, and the information to calculate a suspect's income and expenditures can be obtained (e.g., asset and liability records, bank ac- counts). Expenditure analysis consists of establishing the suspect's known expenditures for all purposes for the relevant period, subtracting all known sources of funds (e.g., wages, gifts, inheritances, bank balances, and the like), and calling the difference the expenditures financed by unknown sources of income.

FORENSIC ACCOUNTING CONSULTING ENGAGEMENT 1

You have been hired by the law firm of Gleckel and Morris. The lawyers have been retained by Blade Manufacturing Company in a case involving a suspected kickback by a purchasing employee, E. J. Cunningham.

EXHIBIT 7.58–2   RETAIL COMPANY

	Prior Year	Current Year	Percent Change
Balance sheet ratios:			
Current ratio	4.57	2.0	−56.34%
Days' sales in receivables	18.40	16.44	−10.63
Doubtful accounts ratio	0.0800	0.0750	−6.25
Days' sales in inventory	85.77	132.65	54.66
Debt/equity ratio	0.35	0.56	40.89
Operations ratios:			
Receivables turnover	19.57	21.89	11.89
Inventory turnover	4.20	2.71	−35.34
Cost of goods sold/sales	69.96%	65.00%	−7.08
Gross margin %	30.04%	35.00%	16.49
Return on equity	6.61%	9.80%	48.26

Cunningham is suspected of taking kickbacks from Mason Varner, a salesman for Tanco Metals. He has denied the charges, but Lanier Gleckel, the lawyer in charge of the case, is convinced the kickbacks have occurred.

Gleckel filed a civil action and subpoenaed Cunningham's books and records, including his last year's bank statements. The beginning bank balance January 1 was $3,462, and the ending bank balance December 31 was $2,050. Over the intervening 12 months, Cunningham's gross salary was $3,600 per month, with a net of $2,950. His wife doesn't work at a paying job. His house payments were $1,377 per month. In addition, he paid $2,361 per month on a new Mercedes 500 SEL and paid a total of $9,444 last year toward a new Nissan Maxima (including $5,000 down payment). He also purchased new state-of-the-art audio and video equipment for $18,763, with no down payment, and total payments on the equipment last year of $5,532. A reasonable estimate of his household expenses during the period is $900 per month ($400 for food, $200 for utilities, and $300 for other items).

Required:
Using expenditure analysis, calculate the amount of income, if any, from "unknown sources."

7.60   Net Worth Analysis.   Net worth analysis is used when fraud has been discovered or strongly suspected, and the information to calculate a suspect's net worth can be obtained (e.g., asset and liability records, bank accounts). The procedure is to calculate the person's change in net worth (excluding changes in market values of assets), and to identify the known sources of funds to finance the changes. Any difference between the change in net worth and the known sources of funds is called "funds from unknown sources," which might be ill-gotten gains.

FORENSIC ACCOUNTING CONSULTING ENGAGEMENT 2

C. Nero has worked for Bonne Consulting Group (BCG) as the executive secretary for administration for nearly 10 years. His dedication has earned him a reputation as an outstanding employee and has resulted in increasing responsibilities. C. Nero is a suspect in fraud.

This is the hindsight story. During Nero's first five years of employment, BCG subcontracted all of its feasibility and marketing studies through Jackson & Company. This relationship was terminated because Jackson & Company merged with a larger, more expensive consulting group. At the time of termination, Nero and his supervisor were forced to select a new firm to conduct BCG's market research. However, Nero never informed the accounting department that the Jackson & Company account had been closed.

Since his supervisor allowed Nero to sign the payment voucher for services rendered, Nero was able to continue to process checks made payable to Jackson's account. Nero was trusted to be the only signature authorizing payments less than $10,000. The accounting department continued to write the checks and Nero took responsibility for delivering them. Nero opened a bank account in a nearby city under the name of Jackson & Company, where he made the deposits.

Required:
C. Nero's financial records have been obtained by subpoena. You have been hired to estimate the amount of loss by estimating Nero's "funds from unknown sources" that financed his comfortable life style. A summary of the data obtained from Nero's records is in Exhibit 7.60–1.

EXHIBIT 7.60-1	NERO'S RECORDS

	Year One	Year Two	Year Three
Assets:			
Residence	$100,000	$100,000	$100,000
Stocks and bonds	30,000	30,000	42,000
Automobiles	20,000	20,000	40,000
Certificate of deposit	50,000	50,000	50,000
Cash	6,000	12,000	14,000
Liabilities:			
Mortgage balance	90,000	50,000	—
Auto loan	10,000	—	—
Income:			
Salary		34,000	36,000
Other		6,000	6,000
Expenses:			
Scheduled mortgage payments		6,000	6,000
Auto loan payments		4,800	—
Other living expenses		20,000	22,000

Hint:
Set up a working paper like this:

	End Year 1	End Year 2	End Year 3
Assets (list)			
Liabilities (list)			
Net worth (difference)			
Change in net worth			
Add total expenses			
= Change plus expenses			
Subtract known income			
= Funds from unknown sources			

DISCUSSION CASES

General Instructions For Cases 7.61–7.66

These cases are designed like the ones in the chapter. They give the problem, the method, the paper trail, and the amount. Your assignment is to write the "audit approach" portion of the case, organized around these sections:

Objective: Express the objective in terms of the facts supposedly asserted in financial records, accounts, and statements. (Refer to the "assertions" of existence, completeness, valuation, rights and obligations, presentation, and disclosure.)

Control: Write a brief explanation of desirable controls, missing controls, and especially the kinds of "deviations" that might arise from the situation described in the case. (Refer to the general and application controls.)

Test of controls: Write some procedures for getting evidence about existing controls, especially procedures that could discover deviations from controls. If there are no controls to test, then there are no procedures to perform; go then to the next section. An audit "procedure" should instruct someone about the source(s) of evidence and the work to do.

Audit of balance: Write some procedures for getting evidence about the existence, completeness, valuation, ownership, or disclosure assertions identified in your objective section above.

Discovery summary: Write a short statement about the discovery you expect to accomplish with your procedures.

7.61   Employee Embezzlement via Cash Disbursements and Inventory.   Follow the instructions at the beginning of this Discussion Cases section. Write the "audit approach" section like the cases in this chapter.

Stealing Was Easy

Problem: Cash embezzlement, inventory and expense overstatement.

Method: Lew Marcus was the only bookkeeper at the Ace Plumbing Supply Company. He ordered the supplies and inventory, paid the bills, collected the cash receipts and checks sent by customers, and reconciled the bank statements. The company had about $11 million in sales, inventory of $3 million, and expenses that generally ran about $6–7 million each year. Nobody checked Lew's work, so sometimes when he received a bill for goods from a supplier (say, for $8,000) he would make an accounting entry for $12,000 debit to inventory, write an $8,000 check to pay the bill, then write a $4,000 check to himself. The check to Lew was not recorded, and he removed it from the bank statement when he prepared the bank reconciliation. The owner of the business considered the monthly bank reconciliation a proper control activity.

Paper Trail: No perpetual inventory records were kept, and no periodic inventory count was taken. The general ledger contained an inventory control account balance that was reduced by 60 percent of the amount of each sale of plumbing fixtures (estimated cost of sales). The bank statements and reconciliations were in a file. The statements showed the check number and amount of Lew's checks to himself, but the checks themselves were missing. The checks to vendors were in the amounts of their bills, but the entries in the cash disbursements journal showed higher amounts.

Amount: Over an eight-year period, Lew embezzled $420,000.

7.62   Employee Embezzlement via Cash Receipts and Payment of Personal Expenses. Follow the instructions at the beginning of this Discussion Cases section. In this case, you can assume you have received the informant's message. Write the "audit approach" section like the cases in the chapter.

THE EXTRA BANK ACCOUNT

Problem: Cash receipts pocketed and personal expenses paid from business account.

Method: The Ourtown Independent School District had red tape about school board approval of cash disbursements. To get around the rules, and to make timely payment of selected bills possible, the superintendent of schools had a school bank account that was used in the manner of a petty cash fund. The board knew about it and had given blanket approval in advance for its use to make timely payment of minor school expenses. However, the board never reviewed the activity in this account. The business manager had sole responsibility for the account, subject to the annual audit. The account got money from transfers from other school accounts and from deposit of cafeteria cash receipts. The superintendent did not like to be bothered with details, and he often signed blank checks so the business manager would not need to run in for a signature all the time. The business manager sometimes paid her personal American Express credit card bills, charged personal items to the school's VISA account, and pocketed some cafeteria cash receipts before deposit.

Paper Trail: An informant called the state education audit agency and told the story that this business manager had used school funds to buy hosiery. When told of this story, the superintendent told the auditor to place no credibility in the informant, who is "out to get us." The business manager had in fact used the account to write unauthorized checks to "cash," put her own American Express bills in the school files (the school district had a VISA card, not American Express), and signed on the school card for gasoline and auto repairs during periods of vacation and summer when school was not in session. (As for the hosiery, she purchased $700 worth with school funds one year.) The superintendent was genuinely unaware of the misuse of funds.

Amount: The business manager had been employed for six years, was trusted, and embezzled an estimated $25,000.

7.63   Employee Embezzlement via Padded Payroll. In this case, your assignment is to analyze the payroll register and see if you can identify any of the ghosts. (This register is short, and you can try to do the analysis visually. However, when available, you can manipulate it in a computer file.)

GHOST RIDERS ON THE PAYROLL

Problem: Embezzlement with fictitious people on the payroll.

Method: Joe Don had responsibility for preparing personnel files for new hires, approval of wages, verification of time cards, and distribution of payroll checks. He "hired" fictitious employees, faked their records, and ordered checks through the payroll system.

Paper Trail: The payroll department produces a payroll register listing various items of information about employees. A selection from the register is in Exhibit 7.63–1. Reading the columns from left to right, it shows the employee identification number, employee name, employees' section number (retail store location), Social Security number,

E X H I B I T 7.63–1 **PAYROLL REGISTER**

I.D. No.	Social Sec. Name	Sect.	Number	Address
5592	Annalee, Michele	1990	455411471	6205193611
8961	Avondale, Richard	1990	435315873	4723265701
186	Bryce, Sharon	1990	449435042	2763431893
3553	Gorman, Thalia	1990	459497264	1565644635
6521	Gordon, Marshall	1990	463355479	8999781365
6999	Harvey, Kevin	1990	396546363	7409894998
8920	Mazzini, Virgil	1990	461785493	2012719362
4534	Paperton, Karen	1990	453491250	6371802086
6204	Peterman, Jennifer	1990	473600914	7818539686
5481	Brione, Kimberly	2000	461635205	5622472908
5363	Brione, Douglas	2000	137567089	4286008036
7891	Jones, Jonothan	2000	464373412	3890567269
9491	Jones, Michael	2000	464373413	3890567269
527	Jones, Thomas	2000	464373413	4609659041
4042	Bull, Lisa	2000	466471495	2797567256
6041	Bushman, Jolle	2000	451355503	9103080617
590	Camp, Liana	2000	455690418	4237338557
3054	Cantraz, Luan	2000	460594645	7894813997
8063	Churchman, Matt	2000	466232740	6977367072
2964	Allford, Eric	2010	444782904	2935968014
9293	Altzheimer, Jeff	2010	453493495	6349921488
6729	Ameston, Jackie	2010	483889548	2722529584
3154	Arrgon, Mary	2010	452535653	8213209536
852	Bulling, John	2010	325462648	5587231055
7219	Chidid, Adam	2010	124491704	7443759037
9346	Chu, Song	2010	465350881	2171962355
5261	Cooker, Scott	2010	459983822	4634865235
4987	Coolman, Maury	2010	458531820	1291047566
1667	Daughterford, Debby	2010	461478070	8223680929
6145	Butterby, Laura	2020	462237424	3463748143
9265	Butterby, Leigh	2020	462236725	3463748143
1231	Butterby, L.A.	2020	462236726	3463748143
6919	Cevil, John	2020	453454988	9781429093
6840	Chung, Hihnno	2020	483113789	4888874664
7489	Cordon, Andy	2020	497605588	5129368143
9111	Coward, Clay	2020	452639707	49242627
4873	Cranehook, Mary	2020	275643410	1622537823
9362	Diercheski, Ward	2020	460496149	7641205905
378	Fineman, Bryan	2020	459679356	8703966421
4613	Dahmer, Jeff	2025	135635583	6947113473
5361	Defard, Joseph	2025	221156649	6947113473
3276	Dellinger, John	2025	764669984	6947113473
3493	Dalton, Jane	2025	681623358	6947113473
8857	Rosingale, Patricia	2025	460654900	6609741958
7103	Ruhle, Mabry	2025	397804404	6940593886
7559	Ruffinio, Jill	2025	461394849	2874916590
8494	Rummsfell, Judith	2025	466539183	4621454720
43	Smith, Michael	2025	442641436	6504510060
1948	Shultze, Robert	2025	457020330	9202701679

and bank addresses (account numbers for electronic funds transfer).

Amount: Joe Don stole $160,000 over a three-year period.

Required:

Analyze the payroll register in Exhibit 7.63–1 and identify the questionable employees who might be ghosts on the payroll.

7.64 Employee Embezzlement: Medical Claims Fraud.   Follow the instructions at the beginning of this Discussion Cases section. Write the "audit approach" section like the cases in the chapter.

DOCTOR! DOCTOR?

Problem: Fictitious medical benefit claims were paid by the company, which self-insured up to $50,000 per employee. The expense account that included legitimate and false charges was "employee medical benefits."

Method: As manager of the claims payment department, Martha Lee was considered one of Beta Magnetic's best employees. She never missed a day of work in 10 years, and her department had one of the company's best efficiency ratings. Controls were considered good, including the verification by a claims processor that: (1) the patient was a Beta employee, (2) medical treatments were covered in the plan, (3) the charges were within approved guidelines, (4) the cumulative claims for the employee did not exceed $50,000 (if over $50,000 a claim was submitted to an insurance company), and (5) the calculation for payment was correct. After verification processing, claims were sent to the claims payment department to pay the doctor directly. No payments ever went directly to employees. Martha Lee prepared false claims on real employees, forging the signature of various claims processors, adding her own review approval, naming bogus doctors who would be paid by the payment department. The payments were mailed to various post office box addresses and to her husband's business address.

Nobody ever verified claims information with the employees. The employees received no reports of medical benefits paid on their behalf. While the department had performance reports by claims processors, these reports did not show claim-by-claim details. No one verified the doctors' credentials.

Paper Trail: The falsified claims forms were in Beta's files, containing all the fictitious data on employee names, processor signatures, doctors' bills, and phony doctors and addresses. The canceled checks were returned by the bank and were kept in Beta's files, containing "endorsements" by the doctors. Martha Lee and her husband were somewhat clever: They deposited the checks in various banks in accounts opened in the names and identification of the "doctors."

Martha Lee did not stumble on the paper trail. She drew the attention of an auditor who saw her take her 24 claims processing employees out to an annual staff appreciation luncheon in a fleet of stretch limousines.

Amount: Over the last seven years, Martha Lee and her husband stole $3.5 million, and, until the last, no one noticed anything unusual about the total amount of claims paid.

7.65   Financial Reporting: Overstated Inventory and Profits.   Follow the instructions at the beginning of this Discussion Cases section. Write the "audit approach" section like the cases in the chapter, and also recalculate the income (loss) before taxes using the correct inventory figures. (Assume the correct beginning inventory two years ago was $5.5 million.)

THE PHANTOM OF THE INVENTORY

Problem: Overstated physical inventory caused understated cost of goods sold and overstated net income, current assets, total assets, and retained earnings.

Method: All Bright Company manufactured lamps. Paul M, manager of the State Street plant, was under pressure to produce profits so the company could maintain its loans at the bank. The loans were secured by the inventory of 1,500 types of finished goods, work in process, and parts used for making lamps (bases, shades, wire, nuts, bolts, and so on). Paul arranged the physical inventory counting procedures and accompanied the external audit team while the external auditors observed the count and made test counts after the company personnel had recorded their counts on tags attached to the inventory locations. At the auditors' request, Paul directed them to the "most valuable" inventory for their test counts, although he did not show them all of the most valuable types. When the auditors were looking the other way, Paul raised the physical count on inventory tags the auditors did not include in their test counts. When everyone had finished each floor of the multistory warehouse, all the tags were gathered and sent to data processing for computer compilation and pricing at FIFO cost.

Paper Trail: All Bright had no perpetual inventory records. All the record of the inventory quantity and pricing was in the count tags and the priced compilation, which was produced by the data processing department six weeks later. The auditors traced their test counts to the compilation and did not notice the raised physical quantities on the inventory types they did not test count. They also did not notice some extra (fictitious) tags Paul had handed over to data processing.

Amount: Paul falsified the inventory for three years before the company declared bankruptcy. Over that period, the inventory was overstated by $1 million (17 percent, two years ago), $2.5 million (31 percent, one year ago), and $3 million (29 percent, current year). The financial statements showed the following (dollars in 000):

	Two Years Ago	One Year Ago	Current Year
Sales	$25,000	$29,000	$40,500
Cost of goods sold	(20,000)	(22,000)	(29,000)
Expenses	(5,000)	(8,000)	(9,000)
Income (loss) before taxes	—	$ (1,000)	$ 2,500
Ending inventory	$ 6,000	$ 8,000	$10,200
Other current assets	9,000	8,500	17,500
Total assets	21,000	21,600	34,300
Current liabilities	5,000	5,500	13,000
Long-term debt*	5,500	6,600	9,300
Stockholder equity	10,500	9,500	12,000

*Secured by inventory pledged to the bank.

7.66   Is This the Perfect Crime? Embezzlers often try to cover up by removing canceled checks they made payable to themselves or endorsed on the back with their own names. Missing canceled checks are a signal (red flag). However, people who reconcile bank accounts may not notice missing checks if the bank reconciliation is performed using only the numerical listing printed in the bank statement. Now consider the case of *truncated bank statements*, when the bank does not even return the canceled checks to the payor. *All* the checks are "missing," and the bank reconciler has no opportunity to notice anything about canceled checks.

Required:
Consider the following story of a real embezzlement. List and explain the ways and means you believe someone might detect it. Think first about the ordinary everyday control activities. Then, think about extensive detection efforts assuming a tip or indication of a possible fraud has been received. Is this a "perfect crime?"

*****

This was the ingenious embezzler's scheme: (a) He hired a print shop to print a private stock of Ajax Company checks in the company's numerical sequence. (b) In his job as an accounts payable clerk, he intercepted legitimate checks written by the accounts payable department and signed by the Ajax treasurer, then destroyed them. (c) He substituted the same-numbered check from the private stock, payable to himself in the same amount as the legitimate check, and he "signed" it with a rubber stamp that looked enough like the Ajax Company treasurer's signature to fool the paying bank. (d) He deposited the money in his own bank account. The bank statement reconciler (a different person) was able to correspond the check numbers and amounts listed in the cleared items in the bank statement to the recorded cash disbursement (check number and amount), thus did not notice the trick. The embezzler was able to process the vendor's "past due"

notice and next month statement with complete documentation, enabling the Ajax treasurer to sign another check the next month paying both the past due balance and current charges. The embezzler was careful to scatter the double-expense payments among numerous accounts (telephone, office supplies, inventory, etc.), so the double-paid expenses did not distort any accounts very much. As time passed, the embezzler was able to recommend budget figures that allowed a large enough budget so his double-paid expenses in various categories did not often pop up as large variances from the budget.

7.67   Bank Reconciliation. Chapter 7 covers a wide range of fraud topics. The audit of bank reconciliations is in Chapter 8. Discussion Case 9.63 deals with a manipulated bank reconciliation and refers to Exhibit 7–3 in Chapter 7. You may wish to use Case 8.59 as an assignment for Chapter 7.

7.68   SAS 82 Review. Management fraud (fraudulent financial reporting) is not the expected norm, but it happens from time to time. In the U.S., several cases have been widely publicized. They happen when motives and opportunities overwhelm managerial integrity.

a. What distinguishes management fraud from a defalcation?

b. What are an auditor's responsibilities under GAAS to detect management fraud?

c. What are some characteristics of management fraud an auditor should consider to fulfill the responsibilities under GAAS?

d. What factors might an auditor notice that should heighten the concern about the existence of management fraud?

e. Under what circumstances might an auditor have a duty to disclose management's frauds to parties other than the company's management and its board of directors?

(AICPA adapted)

APPENDIX 7A

DETAILS OF VARIOUS AUDIT STANDARDS CONCERNING ERRORS, ILLEGAL ACTS, FRAUD, ABUSE, INEFFICIENCY

AMERICAN INSTITUTE OF CPAS (GAAS)

SAS 82 (AU 316)—Consideration of Fraud in a Financial Statement Audit. Numerous aspects of responsibility regarding fraud risk assessment, reasonable assurance of material fraud detection, overall audit responses, specific procedural responses, documentation, and reports to management and the board of directors include the following:

1. Assess the risk of material misstatement of financial statements due to fraud by fraudulent financial reporting (management fraud) and by misappropriation of assets (employee fraud).
2. Consider this risk assessment at the beginning and throughout the audit in designing audit procedures to be performed.
3. Inquire of management its understanding regarding risk of fraud in the company and (*a*) whether any frauds are known to have occurred, and (*b*) whether any fraud risk factors have been identified.
4. Document the fraud risk assessment in the audit working papers, including (*a*) risk factors identified, and (*b*) the auditors' overall and/or specific responses.
5. Pay attention to well-known fraud risk factors. (Many of them are explained in Chapter 7).
6. Pay attention to information that indicates financial stress of employees or adverse relations between the company and its employees (but no requirement to plan the audit to discover such information).
7. Determine whether the company has specific controls that mitigate identified fraud risks or whether specific control deficiencies exacerbate these risks.
8. Consider the effectiveness of clients' programs that include steps to prevent, detect, and deter fraud. Ask persons overseeing such programs whether they have identified any fraud risk factors.
9. Decide whether the fraud risk assessment calls for (*a*) an overall response, and/or (*b*) a response to a particular account balance or class of transactions:

   (*a*) Overall Response
      (i)   Exercise professional skepticism.
      (ii)   Assign personnel with appropriate knowledge, skill, and ability.
      (iii) Study more carefully management's selection and application of accounting principles.
      (iv)   Be sensitive to management's ability to override controls related to fraud risk factors.
      (v)   Alter audit procedures with regard to nature (obtain more reliable or additional corroborative information), timing (closer to year-end), and extent (larger sample sizes or more extensive analytical procedures).

   (*b*) Specific Procedural Response
      (i)   Perform procedures on a surprise or unannounced basis (e.g., visits, inventory observation).
      (ii)   Observe inventory-taking close to year-end.
      (iii) Add oral contacts to the written confirmation procedure.
      (iv)   Review and investigate in detail the client's quarter- and year-end adjusting entries.
      (v)   Investigate unusual transactions near year-end for the possibility of related parties and sources of financial resources that support such transactions.
      (vi)   Perform substantive analytical procedures at a detailed level.
      (vii) Conduct interviews with people in fraud risk areas.
      (viii) Coordinate audit work with other independent auditors, if any.
      (ix)   Perform additional work on specialists' assumptions, methods, and findings.
      (x)   Confirm sales contract terms with customers.
      (xi)   Conduct inventory observations carefully (e.g., surprise basis, multiple locations on sample date, open boxes, assay quality of substances).

10. Consider whether discovered misstatements indicate fraud and evaluate implications even of immaterial misstatements (but no requirement to determine an *intent* element of fraud).
11. When the possibility of material fraud exists, review the audit plan, discuss further investigation with a higher level of management, and attempt to obtain additional evidence.
12. When fraud is detected, consider the implications for the integrity of managers and employees and the possible effect on the audit. [SAS 47 amendment prompted by SAS 82]

13. Withdraw from the engagement if fraud risk is significant and management cooperation is unsatisfactory, and communicate the reasons for withdrawal to the audit committee of the board of directors.
14. When evidence of fraud exists, tell management (appropriate higher level) even about inconsequential matters, and tell the audit committee about fraud involving senior managers.
15. Disclose possible fraud in limited circumstances by:

  - Complying with legal and regulatory requirements (including reporting a change of auditors on SEC Form 8-K, reporting control matters and disagreements according to Item 304 of SEC Regulation S-K).
  - Responding to a successor auditor's inquiries (SAS 84).
  - Responding to a subpoena.
  - Communicating with a funding or other agency when required in audits of entities that receive governmental financial assistance.

  External auditors are *not* responsible for:

  - Determining the element of intent in a possible fraud situation.
  - Authenticating documents (lack of training).
  - Finding intentional misstatements concealed by collusion and falsified documents when using procedures designed to find unintentional misstatements (**Collusion** is the circumstance in which two or more people conspire to conduct fraudulent activity in violation of an organization's internal controls.) [SAS 1, AU 230 amendment prompted by SAS 82]
  - Obtaining *absolute* assurance that material misstatements in financial statements will be detected.
  - Insuring or guaranteeing that all material misstatements will be discovered. [SAS 1, AU 230 amendment prompted by SAS 82]
  - General reporting of frauds to outside agencies or parties.
  - Planning the audit to discover information that indicates particular employees' financial stress or adverse relationships between the company and its employees.

SAS 54 (AU 317)—*Illegal Acts by Clients.* Auditors have these responsibilities for the far-removed illegal acts:

1. Be aware of the types of illegal acts that might occur in the organization under audit and the "signals" of them.
2. Perform audit procedures when specified information indicates that possible illegal acts may have a material indirect effect on financial statements.
3. Make inquiries about management's policies and procedures for compliance with laws and regulations.
4. Obtain written management representations concerning the absence of violations of laws and regulations.
5. Consider both the quantitative and qualitative materiality of known and suspected illegal acts.
6. Consider the implications of illegal acts for other aspects of the audit, specifically the reliability of management representations.
7. Assure that the company's audit committee is informed about illegal acts known to the auditor, except those that are clearly inconsequential. (When senior management is involved, auditors should communicate directly with the audit committee.)
8. Evaluate the adequacy of financial statement disclosure regarding illegal acts.
9. Withdraw from the engagement if management will not accept a qualified, adverse, or disclaimed opinion regarding statement presentation problems, and communicate the reasons in writing to the board of directors.
10. Withdraw from the engagement if management does not take remedial action the auditor considers necessary.
11. Disclose illegal acts to outside agencies in limited circumstances by:

  - Reporting a change of auditors on SEC Form 8-K.
  - Responding to a successor auditor's inquiries (SAS 84).
  - Responding to a subpoena.
  - Communicating with a funding or other agency when required in audits of entities that receive governmental financial assistance.

External auditors are *not* responsible for:

- Final determination that a particular act is illegal (lack of legal, judicial expertise.)
- Assuring that illegal acts will be detected or that related contingent liabilities will be disclosed.
- Designing audit procedures to detect illegal acts in the absence of specific information brought to the auditors' attention.
- General reporting of illegal acts to outside agencies or parties.

SAS 61 (AU 380)—Communication with Audit Committees. External auditors are required to make oral or written communications on several topics, including:

1. Internal controls.
2. Material misstatements in financial statements.
3. Selection or changes in significant accounting policies.
4. Accounting for significant unusual transactions.
5. Effect of controversial accounting policies.
6. Accounting estimates.
7. Significant audit adjustments.
8. Disagreements with management on significant accounting and auditing matters.
9. Management's consultation with other accountants (possible "opinion shopping").
10. Serious difficulties dealing with management (e.g., delays, evidence availability) when conducting the audit.

THE INSTITUTE OF INTERNAL AUDITORS

Statement on Internal Auditing Standards No. 3: Deterrence, Detection, Investigation, and Reporting of Fraud. SIAS 3 acknowledges the concerns about fraud and gives internal auditors these points of guidance regarding responsibilities to:

1. Exercise due professional care and be alert to signs of wrongdoing, errors and omissions, inefficiency, waste, ineffectiveness, and conflicts of interest.
2. Consider the possibility of noncompliance with policies, procedures, laws, and regulations.
3. Inform management of suspected wrongdoing.
4. Review the systems used to safeguard assets from various types of losses, including those resulting from theft and improper or illegal activities.
5. Be aware of signs and indicators of fraud.
6. If significant control weaknesses are detected, conduct additional tests directed toward identification of other indicators of fraud.
7. Assist fraud investigations conducted by lawyers, investigators, security personnel, and other specialists.
8. Report fraud findings to management, the board of directors, or the audit committee of the board, being careful not to report to persons who might be involved in a fraud scheme.

U.S. GENERAL ACCOUNTING OFFICE (GAGAS)

GAO Field Work Standards for Financial Audits: Auditors should design audits to accomplish the following:

1. Provide reasonable assurance of detecting irregularities [frauds] material to the financial statements.
2. Provide reasonable assurance of detecting material misstatements resulting from direct-effect illegal acts.
3. Be aware of the possibility of [indirect-effect] illegal acts. If information comes to attention, apply specific audit procedures to ascertain whether an illegal act has occurred.
4. Provide reasonable assurance of detecting material misstatements resulting from noncompliance with provisions of contracts or grants. If information comes to attention, apply specific audit procedures to ascertain whether the noncompliance has occurred.

GAO Third Field Work Standard for Performance Audits: Auditors should design audits to accomplish the following:

5. Provide reasonable assurance about compliance with laws, regulations, and other compliance requirements.
6. Be alert to indications of illegal acts or abuse.

Aspects of responsibility under these Generally Accepted Government Auditing Standards for detecting and reporting errors, irregularities [frauds], and illegal acts include the following:

7. Be aware of characteristics and types of potential material irregularities [frauds].
8. Understand the relevant laws and regulations, perhaps consulting with attorneys.
9. Exercise due care in pursuing indications of irregularities [frauds] and illegal acts so as not to interfere with future investigations or legal proceedings.
10. Under required circumstances, report indications of irregularities [frauds] to law enforcement or regulatory authorities.
11. Be aware of characteristics and types of potential noncompliance with contracts and grants.
12. Be alert to situations or transactions that could indicate illegal acts or abuse (although "abuse" is so subjective that auditors are not expected to provide reasonable assurance of detecting it).

APPENDIX 7B PROFESSIONAL STANDARDS AND PRACTICES FOR CERTIFIED FRAUD EXAMINERS (JULY 1, 1991)

I. GENERAL STANDARDS

A. Independence and Objectivity

CFEs are responsible for maintaining independence in attitude and appearance, approaching and conducting fraud examinations in an objective and unbiased manner, and assuring that examining organizations they direct are free from impairments to independence.

B. Qualifications

CFEs must possess skills, knowledge, abilities, and appearance needed to perform examinations proficiently and effectively. CFEs responsible for directing fraud examinations must assure they are performed by personnel who collectively possess the skills and knowledge necessary to complete examinations in accordance with these Standards. CFEs must maintain their qualifications by fulfilling continuing education requirements and adhering to the Code of Ethics of the Association of Certified Fraud Examiners.

C. Fraud Examinations

CFEs must conduct fraud examinations using due professional care, with adequate planning and supervision to provide assurance that objectives are achieved within the framework of these Standards. Evidence is to be obtained in an efficient, thorough, and legal manner; and reports of the results of fraud examinations must be accurate, objective, and thorough.

D. Confidentiality

CFEs are responsible for assuring they and the examining organizations they direct exercise due care to prevent improper disclosure of confidential or privileged information.

II. SPECIFIC STANDARDS

A. Independence and Objectivity

1. *Attitude and Appearance*

Independence of attitude requires impartiality and fairness in conducting examinations and in reaching resulting conclusions and judgments. CFEs must also be sensitive to the appearance of independence so that conclusions and judgments will be accepted as impartial by knowledgeable third parties. CFEs who become aware of a situation or relationship that could be perceived to impair independence, whether or not actual impairment exists, should inform management immediately and take steps to eliminate the perceived impairment, including withdrawing from the examination, if necessary.

2. *Objectivity*

To assure objectivity in performing examinations, CFEs must maintain an independent mental attitude, reach judgments on examination matters without undue influence from others, and avoid being placed in positions where they would be unable to work in an objective professional manner.

3. *Organizational Relationship*

The CFE's reporting relationship should be such that the attitude and appearance of independence and objectivity are not jeopardized. Organizational independence is achieved when the CFE's function has a mandate to conduct independent examinations throughout the organization, or by a reporting relationship high enough in the organization to assure independence of action.

B. Qualifications

1. *Skills, Knowledge, Abilities, and Experience*

CFEs cannot be expected to have an expert level of skill and knowledge for every circumstance that might be encountered in a fraud examination. Nevertheless, CFEs must have sufficient skill and knowledge to recognize when additional training or expert guidance is required. It is the responsibility of a CFE to assure that necessary skills, knowledge, ability, and experience are acquired or available before going forward with a fraud examination.

CFEs must be skilled in obtaining information from records, documents, and people; in analyzing and evaluating information and drawing sound conclusions; in communicating the results of fraud examinations, both orally and in writing; and in serving as an expert witness when appropriate.

CFEs must be knowledgeable in investigative techniques, applicable laws and rules of evidence, fraud auditing, criminology, and ethics.

2. *Continuing Education*

CFEs are required to fulfill continuing education requirements established by the Association of Certified Fraud Examiners. Additionally, CFEs are responsible for securing other education necessary for specific fraud examinations and related fields in which they are individually involved.

3. *Code of Ethics*

CFEs are to adhere to the Code of Professional Ethics of the Association of Certified Fraud Examiners.

C. **Fraud Examinations**

1. *Due Professional Care*

Due professional care is defined as exercising the care and skill expected of a prudent professional in similar circumstances. CFEs are responsible for assuring that there is sufficient predication for beginning a fraud examination; that said examinations are conducted with diligence and thoroughness; that all applicable laws and regulations are observed; that appropriate methods and techniques are used; and that said examinations are conducted in accordance with these Standards.

2. *Planning and Supervision*

CFEs must plan and supervise fraud examinations to assure that objectives are achieved within the framework of these Standards.

3. *Evidence*

CFEs must collect evidence, whether exculpatory or incriminating, that supports fraud examination results and will be admissible in subsequent proceedings, by obtaining and documenting evidence in a manner to ensure that all necessary evidence is obtained and the chain of custody is preserved.

4. *Reporting*

CFE reports of the results of fraud examinations, whether written or verbal, must address all relevant aspects of the examination, and be accurate, objective, and understandable.

In rendering reports to management, clients, or others, CFEs shall not express judgments on the guilt or innocence of any person or party, regardless of the CFE's opinion of the preponderance of evidence. CFEs must exercise due professional care when expressing other opinions related to an examination, such as the likelihood that a fraud has or has not occurred, and whether or not internal controls are adequate.

D. **Confidentiality**

CFEs, during fraud examinations, are often privy to highly sensitive and confidential information about organizations and individuals. CFEs must exercise due care so as not to purposefully or inadvertently disclose such information except as necessary to conduct the examination or as required by law.

Source: Association of Certified Fraud Examiners, 716 West Avenue, Austin, Texas, 78701.

APPENDIX 7C   SOCIAL SECURITY NUMBER TABLE

(1)	(2)	(3)	(4)	(5)	(6)
		Highest Group Numbers			
Area Number	Odd less than 10	Even 10 and above	Even less than 10	Odd greater than 10	State or Territory
000	None	None	None	None	Not Assigned
001–003	09	94	None	None	New Hampshire
004–007	09	98	02	None	Maine
008–009	09	84	None	None	Vermont
010–029	09	84	None	None	Massachusetts
030–034	09	82	None	None	Massachusetts
035–037	09	68	None	None	Rhode Island
038–039	09	66	None	None	Rhode Island
040–049	09	98	02	None	Connecticut
050–119	09	90	None	None	New York
120–134	09	88	None	None	New York
135–158	09	98	06	None	New Jersey
159–184	09	80	None	None	Pennsylvania
185–211	09	78	None	None	Pennsylvania
212–216	09	98	08	59	Maryland
217–220	09	98	08	57	Maryland
221–222	09	92	None	None	Delaware
223–231	09	98	08	87	Virginia
232	09	98	08	47	North Carolina West Virginia
233–236	09	98	08	47	West Virginia
237–246	09	98	08	95	North Carolina
247–251	09	98	08	99	South Carolina
252–260	09	98	08	99	Georgia
261–267	09	98	08	99	Florida
268–272	09	98	06	None	Ohio
273–302	09	98	04	None	Ohio
303–309	09	98	08	23	Indiana
310–317	09	98	08	17	Indiana
318–361	09	98	None	None	Illinois
362–386	09	98	08	25	Michigan
387–397	09	98	08	21	Wisconsin
398–399	09	98	08	19	Wisconsin
400–407	09	98	08	57	Kentucky
408-415	09	98	08	89	Tennessee
416–424	09	98	08	51	Alabama
425–428	09	98	08	89	Mississippi
429–431	09	98	08	99	Arkansas
432	09	98	08	97	Arkansas
433–439	09	98	08	99	Louisiana
440–441	09	98	08	15	Oklahoma
442–448	09	98	08	13	Oklahoma
449–467	09	98	08	99	Texas
468–472	09	98	08	39	Minnesota
473–477	09	98	08	37	Minnesota
478–485	09	98	08	29	Iowa
486–500	09	98	08	17	Missouri
501	09	98	08	27	North Dakota
502	09	98	08	25	North Dakota
503–504	09	98	08	31	South Dakota
505–508	09	98	08	41	Nebraska
509–515	09	98	08	19	Kansas

(1)	(2)	(3)	(4)	(5)	(6)
	Highest Group Numbers				
Area Number	Odd less than 10	Even 10 and above	Even less than 10	Odd greater than 10	State or Territory
516	09	98	08	35	Montana
517	09	98	08	33	Montana
518–519	09	98	08	59	Idaho
520	09	98	08	41	Wyoming
521–524	09	98	08	99	Colorado
525	09	98	08	99	New Mexico
526–527	09	98	08	99	Arizona
528–529	09	98	08	99	Utah
530	09	98	08	99	Nevada
531–539	09	98	08	45	Washington
540–544	09	98	08	59	Oregon
545–573	09	98	08	99	California
574	09	98	08	31	Alaska
575–576	09	98	08	89	Hawaii
577-579	09	98	08	31	District of Columbia
580	09	98	08	33	Puerto Rico Virgin Islands
581–584	09	98	08	99	Puerto Rico
585	09	98	08	99	New Mexico
586	09	98	08	43	Guam Amer. Samoa N. Mariana Is. Philippines
587	09	98	08	87	Mississippi
588	None	None	None	None	Mississippi
589–595	09	98	08	95	Florida
596–599	09	64	None	None	Puerto Rico
600–601	09	98	08	99	Arizona
602–620	09	98	08	21	California
621–626	09	98	08	19	California
627–645	09	72	None	None	Texas
646–647	09	54	None	None	Utah
648–649	09	22	None	None	New Mexico
650–653	09	16	None	None	Colorado
654–658	09	None	None	None	South Carolina
659–665	01	None	None	None	Louisiana
666					Not Mentioned
667–675	09	None	None	None	Georgia
676–679	None	None	None	None	Arkansas
680	09	24	None	None	Nevada
681–690	None	None	None	None	North Carolina
691–699	None	None	None	None	Virginia
700–723	09	18	None	None	RR Retirement
724	09	28	None	None	RR Retirement
725–726	09	18	None	None	RR Retirement
727	09	10	None	None	RR Retirement
728	09	14	None	None	RR Retirement
729–749					Not Assigned
750–751	None	None	None	None	Hawaii
752–755	None	None	None	None	Mississippi
756–763	None	None	None	None	Tennessee
764	03	None	None	None	Arizona
765	01	None	None	None	Arizona
766–999					Not Assigned

TECHNICAL NOTES

AREA NUMBERS: Since 1972 the Social Security Administration has assigned area numbers to the zip code for the applicant's return address. Therefore, the area number might or might not signify the state or territory of birth or location at the time a social security number was issued. To find state and territory area number assignments, go to www.ssa.gov/foia/stateweb.html.

GROUP NUMBERS: The data in this appendix is up to date as of October 2000. To find the current highest group numbers, go to www.ssa.gov/foia/highgroup.htm.

RAILROAD (RR) RETIREMENT: Numbers issued to railroad employees were discontinued 1 July 1963.

OTHER: Numbers in areas 574, 580, and 586 were also assigned to Southeast Asia refugees during the period April 1975 through November 1979.

For general information about Social Security, go to www.ssa.gov.

Chapter 8

Revenue and Collection Cycle

Professional Standards References

Compendium Section	Document Reference	Topic
AU 311	SAS 77	*Planning and Supervision*
AU 312	SAS 47	*Audit Risk and Materiality in Conducting an Audit*
AU 313	SAS 45	*Substantive Tests Prior to the Balance Sheet Date*
AU 316	SAS 82	*Consideration of Fraud in a Financial Statement Audit*
AU 319	SAS 78	*Internal Control in a Financial Statement Audit*
AU 326	SAS 80	*Evidential Matter*
AU 329	SAS 56	*Analytical Procedures*
AU 330	SAS 67	*The Confirmation Process*
AU 333	SAS 85	*Management Representations*
AU 339	SAS 41	*Working Papers*

Learning Objectives

This chapter contains a concise overview of a cycle for processing customer orders and making sales, delivering goods and services to customers, accounting for customer accounts receivable, collecting and depositing cash received from customers, and reconciling bank statements. A series of short cases is used to show the application of audit procedures in situations where errors and frauds might be discovered. The chapter contains special technical notes on the existence assertion, using confirmations, auditing bank reconciliations, and preparing a schedule of interbank transfers and the proof of cash. After completing this chapter, you should be able to:

1. Describe the revenue and collection cycle, including typical source documents and controls.

2. Give examples of detail test of controls procedures for auditing control over customer credit approval, delivery, accounts receivable accounting, cash receipts accounting, and bank statement reconciliation.

3. Explain the importance of the existence assertion for the audit of cash and accounts receivable, and describe some procedures for obtaining evidence about the existence of assets.

4. Identify and describe considerations for using confirmations in the audit of cash and accounts receivable.

5. Design and perform substantive audit procedures for the audit of a bank statement reconciliation, and tell how auditors can search for lapping and kiting.

6. Prepare a schedule of interbank transfers and a proof of cash.

7. Describe some common errors and frauds in the revenue and collection cycle, and design some audit and investigation procedures for detecting them.

REVENUE AND COLLECTION CYCLE: TYPICAL ACTIVITIES

LEARNING OBJECTIVE
1. Describe the revenue and collection cycle, including typical source documents and controls.

The basic activities in the revenue and collection cycle are: (1) receiving and processing customer orders, including credit granting; (2) delivering goods and services to customers; (3) billing customers and accounting for accounts receivable; (4) collecting and depositing cash received from customers; and (5) reconciling bank statements. Exhibit 8–1 shows the activities and transactions involved in a revenue and collection cycle. As you follow the exhibit, you can track some of the highlighted elements of a control system.

Sales and Accounts Receivable

Authorization

Exhibit 8–2 represents a computerized system for processing customer orders. The customers' orders go in one end, and the shipping orders and invoices come out the other end. Since various authorizations are imbedded in a computer system, access to the master file for additions, deletions, and other changes must be limited to responsible people. If these controls fail, orders might be processed for fictitious customers, credit might be approved for bad credit risks, and shipping documents (packing slips) might be created for goods that do not exist in the inventory.

Customer orders, shipping documents, and invoices should be numbered in a numerical sequence so the system can check the sequence and determine whether any transactions have not been completed (completeness objective of control).

EXHIBIT 8–1   REVENUE AND COLLECTION CYCLE

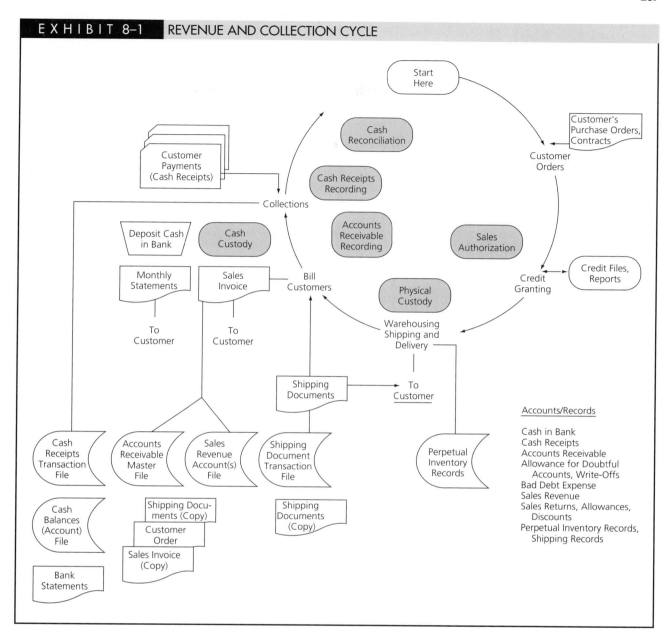

Another authorization in the system is the price list master file. It contains the product unit prices for billing customers. Persons who have power to alter this file have the power to authorize price changes and customer billings.

AUDITING INSIGHT

PRICE MANIPULATION

The company's computer programmer was paid off by a customer to cause the company to bill the customer at prices lower than list prices. The programmer wrote a subroutine that was invoked when the billing system detected the customer's regular code number. This subroutine instructed the computer billing system to reduce all unit prices 9.5 percent. The company relied on the computer billing system, and nobody ever rechecked the actual prices billed.

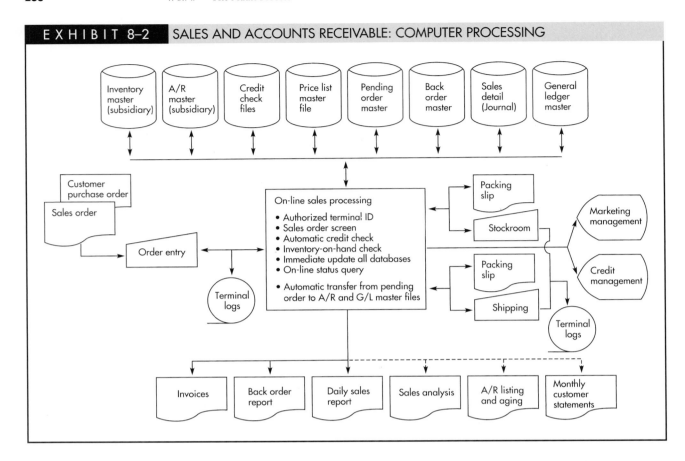

EXHIBIT 8–2   SALES AND ACCOUNTS RECEIVABLE: COMPUTER PROCESSING

Custody

Physical custody of inventory goods starts with the storeroom or warehouse where inventory is kept. Custody is transferred to the shipping department upon the authorization of the shipping order that permits storekeepers to release goods to the shipping area.

"Custody" of accounts receivable records themselves implies the power to alter them directly or enter transactions to alter them (e.g., transfers, returns and allowance credits, write-offs). Personnel with this power have a combination of authorization and recording responsibility.

Recording

When delivery or shipment is complete, the system finished the transaction by filing a shipment record and preparing a final invoice for the customer (which is recorded as sales revenue and accounts receivable). Any personnel who have the power to enter or alter these transactions or to intercept the invoice that is supposed to be mailed to the customer have undesirable combinations of authorization, custody, and recording responsibilities; they can "authorize" transaction changes and record them by making entries in systems under their control.

Periodic Reconciliation

The most frequent reconciliation is the comparison of the sum of customers' unpaid balances with the accounts receivable control account total. This reconciliation is accomplished by preparing a trial balance of the accounts receivable (a list of customers and amounts), adding it, and comparing the total to the control account balance. Internal auditors can perform periodic comparison of the customers' balances by sending confirmations to the customers. (Refer to the special note on confirmations later in this chapter.)

Cash Receipts and Cash Balances

Authorization

Cash can be received in several ways—over the counter, through the mail, by electronic funds transfer, and by receipt in a "lockbox." In a lockbox arrangement, a fiduciary (e.g., a bank) opens the box, lists the receipts, deposits the money, and sends the remittance advices (stubs showing the amount received from each customer) to the company. Authorization is important for approving customers' discounts and allowances. Exhibit 8–3 shows some cash receipts processing procedures in a manual accounting setting. You can see the "approval of discounts" noted in Exhibit 8–3.

Custody

Someone always gets the cash and checks in hand and thus has custody of the physical cash for a time. Since this initial custody cannot be avoided, it is always good control to prepare a list of the cash receipts as early in the process as possible, then separate the actual cash from the bookkeeping documents. The cash goes to the cashier or treasurer's

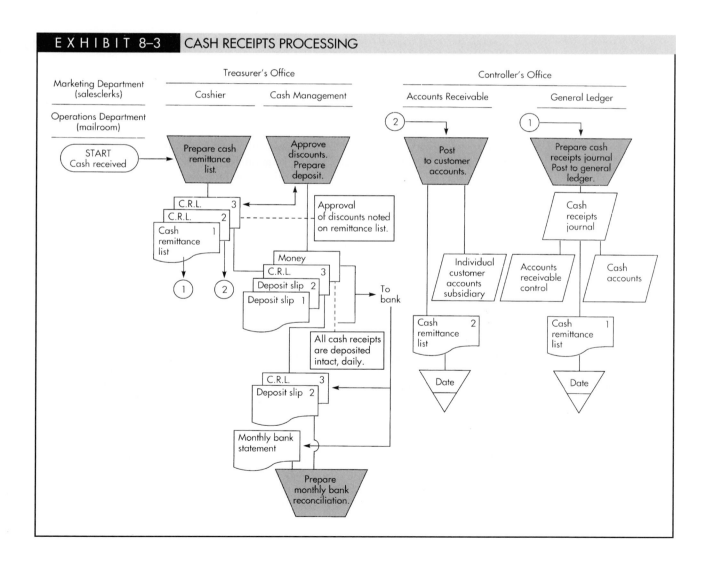

EXHIBIT 8–3 CASH RECEIPTS PROCESSING

CAREFUL RECONCILIATION (REFER TO EXHIBIT 8–3)

Suppose the cashier who prepares the remittance list had stolen and converted Customer A's checks to personal use. It might work for a short time until Customer A complained that the company had not given credit for payments. The cashier knows this. So, the cashier later puts Customer B's check in the bank deposit, but shows Customer A on the remittance list; thus, the accountants give Customer A credit. So far, so good for preventing Customer A's complaint. But now Customer B needs to be covered. This "lapping" of customer payments to hide an embezzlement can be detected by a bank reconciliation comparison of the checks deposited (Customer B) with the remittance credit recorded (Customer A).

office, where a bank deposit is prepared and the money is sent to the bank. The list goes to the accountants, who record the cash receipts. (This list may be only a stack of the remittance advices received with the customers' payments. You have prepared a "remittance advice" each time you write the "amount enclosed" on the top part of your credit card billing, tear it off, and enclose it with your check.)

Recording

The accountants who record cash receipts and credits to customer accounts should not handle the cash. They should use the remittance list to make entries to the cash and accounts receivable control accounts and to the customers' accounts receivable subsidiary account records. A good error-checking activity is to have control account and subsidiary account entries made by different people, then later the accounts receivable entries and balances can be compared (reconciled) to determine whether they agree in total. Some computerized accounting programs post the customers' accounts automatically by keying on the customer identification number, and agreement is controlled by the computer program.

Periodic Reconciliation

Bank account reconciliations should be prepared carefully. Deposit slips should be compared to the details on cash remittance lists, and the total should be traced to the general ledger entries. Likewise, paid checks should be traced to the cash disbursements listing (journal). This care is required to establish that all the receipts recorded in the books were deposited and that credit was given to the right customer. (Refer to the special note on auditing bank reconciliations later in this chapter.)

SHIPPING EMPLOYEE CAUGHT BY COMPUTER!

A customer paid off a shipping department employee to enter smaller quantities than actually shipped on the packing slip and bill of lading. This caused the customer's invoices to be understated. Unknown to the employee, a computer log recorded all the entries that altered the original packing slip record. An alert internal auditor noticed the pattern of "corrections" made by the shipping employee. A trap was laid by initiating fictitious orders for this customer, and the employee was observed making the alterations.

R E V I E W
CHECKPOINTS

8.1 What is the basic sequence of activities and accounting in a revenue and collection cycle?

8.2 What purpose is served by prenumbering sales orders, shipping documents, and sales invoices?

8.3 Why is controlled access to computer terminals and master files (such as credit files and price lists) important in a control system?

8.4 Why should a list of cash remittances be made and sent to the accounting department? Wouldn't it be easier to send the cash and checks to the accountants so they can enter the credits to customers' accounts accurately?

Audit Evidence in Management Reports and Data Files

Computer processing of revenue and cash receipts transactions enables management to generate several reports that can provide important audit evidence. Auditors should obtain and use these reports.

Pending Order Master File

This file contains sales transactions that were started in the system but are not yet completed, thus not recorded as sales and accounts receivable. Old orders may represent shipments that actually were made, but for some reason the shipping department did not enter the shipping information (or entered an incorrect code that did not match the pending order file). The pending orders can be reviewed for evidence of the *completeness* of recorded sales and accounts receivable.

Credit Check Files

The computer system may make automatic credit checks, but up-to-date maintenance of the credit information is very important. Credit checks on old or incomplete information are not good credit checks. A sample of the files can be tested for current status. Alternatively, the company's records on updating the files can be reviewed for evidence of updating operations.

Price List Master File

The computer system may produce customer invoices automatically; but, if the master price list is wrong, the billings will be wrong. The computer file can be compared to an official price source for *accuracy*. (The company should perform this comparison every time the prices are changed.)

Sales Detail (Sales Journal) File

This file should contain the *detail sales entries*, including the shipping references and dates. The file can be scanned for entries without shipping references (fictitious sales?) and for match of recording dates with shipment dates (sales recorded before shipment?). This file contains the population of debit entries to the accounts receivable.

AUDITING INSIGHT

PEAKS AND VALLEYS

During the year-end audit, the independent auditors reviewed the weekly sales volume reports classified by region. They noticed that sales volume was very high in Region 2 the last two weeks of March, June, September, and December. The volume was unusually low in the first two weeks of April, July, October, and January. In fact, the peaks far exceeded the volume in all the other six regions. Further investigation revealed that the manager in Region 2 was holding open the sales recording at the end of each quarterly reporting period in an attempt to make the quarterly reports look good.

Sales Analysis Reports

A variety of sales analyses may be produced. Sales that are classified by product lines are information for the business segment disclosures. Sales classified by sales employee or region can show unusually high or low volume that might bear further investigation if error is suspected.

Accounts Receivable Aged Trial Balance

This list of customers' accounts receivable balances is the accounts receivable. If the control account total is larger than the sum in the trial balance, too bad. A receivable amount that cannot be identified with a customer cannot be collected! The trial balance is used as the population for selecting accounts for confirmation. (See the special note on the existence assertion and the special note on using confirmations later in this chapter.) The aging information is used in connection with assessing the allowance for doubtful accounts. (An aged trial balance is in Exhibit 8–8.)

Cash Receipts Journal

The cash receipts journal contains all the detail entries for cash deposits and credits to various accounts. It contains the population of credit entries that should be reflected in the credits to accounts receivable for customer payments. It also contains the adjusting and correcting entries that can result from the bank account reconciliation. These entries are important because they may signal the types of accounting errors or manipulations that happen in the cash receipts accounting.

REVIEW
CHECKPOINTS

8.5 What computer-based files could an auditor examine to find evidence of unrecorded sales? Of inadequate credit checks? Of incorrect product unit prices?

8.6 Suppose you selected a sample of customers' accounts receivable and wanted to find supporting evidence for the entries in the accounts. Where would you go to vouch the debit entries? What would you expect to find? Where would you go to vouch the credit entries? What would you expect to find?

CONTROL RISK ASSESSMENT

Control risk assessment is important because it governs the nature, timing, and extent of substantive audit procedures that will be applied in the audit of account balances in the revenue and collection cycle. These account balances (listed in the corner of Exhibit 8–1) include:

Cash in bank.

Accounts receivable.

Allowance for doubtful accounts.

Bad debts expense.

Sales revenue.

Sales returns, allowances, and discounts.

Control Considerations

Controls for proper segregation of responsibilities should be in place and operating. By referring to Exhibit 8–1, you can see that proper segregation involves different people and different departments performing the sales and credit authorization; custody of goods and cash; record keeping for sales, receivables, and inventory; and accounts receivable bank account reconciliation duties. Combinations of two or more of these responsibilities in one person, one office, or one computerized system may open the door for errors and frauds.

A common feature of cash management is to require that persons who handle cash be insured under a fidelity bond. A **fidelity bond** is an insurance policy that covers most kinds of cash embezzlement losses. Fidelity bonds do not prevent or detect embezzlement, but the failure to carry the insurance exposes the company to complete loss when embezzlement occurs. Auditors may recommend fidelity bonding to companies that do not know about its coverage.

In addition, the control system should provide for detail error-checking activities. For example: (1) policy should provide that no sales order should be entered without a customer order; (2) a credit-check code or manual signature should be recorded by an authorized means; (3) access to inventory and the shipping area should be restricted to authorized persons; (4) access to billing terminals and blank invoice forms should be restricted to authorized personnel; (5) accountants should be under orders to record sales and accounts receivable when all the supporting documentation of shipment is in order, and care should be taken to record sales and receivables as of the date the goods and services were shipped and the cash receipts on the date the payments were received; (6) customer invoices should be compared with bills of lading and customer orders to determine that the customer is sent the goods ordered at the proper location for the proper prices, and that the quantity being billed is the same as the quantity shipped; (7) pending order files should be reviewed frequently to avoid failure to bill and record shipments; and (8) bank statements should be reconciled in detail monthly.

Information about a company's controls often is gathered by completing an internal control questionnaire. A selection of other questionnaires for both general (manual) controls and computer controls over cash receipts and accounts receivable is in Appendix 8A. You can study these questionnaires for details of desirable control activities. They are organized under headings that identify the important control objectives—environment, validity, completeness, authorization, accuracy, classification, accounting/posting, and proper period recording.

Another way to obtain general information about controls is called a "walk-through," or a "sample of one." In this work, the auditors take a single example of a transaction and "walk it through" from its initiation to its recording in the accounting records. The revenue and collection cycle walk-through involves following a sale from the initial customer order through credit approval, billing, and delivery of goods, to the entry in the sales journal and subsidiary accounts receivable records, then its subsequent collection and cash deposit. Sample documents are collected, and employees in each department are questioned about their specific duties. The walk-through, combined with inquiries, can contribute evidence about appropriate separation of duties, which might be a sufficient basis for assessing control risk slightly below the maximum. However, a walk-through is too limited in scope to provide evidence of whether the client's control activities were operating effectively during the period under audit. Usually, a larger sample of transactions for detail testing of control performance is necessary to justify a low control risk assessment based on actual control performance evidence.

Detail Test of Controls Audit Procedures

An organization should have input, processing, and output control activities in place and operating to prevent, detect, and correct accounting errors. Exhibit 8–4 puts these in the perspective of revenue cycle activity with examples of specific objectives. This exhibit takes control objectives out of the abstract and expresses them in specific examples related to controlling sales accounting.

Auditors can perform detail test of controls audit procedures to determine whether company personnel are actually performing properly controls that are said to be in place. A **detail test of control procedure** consists of (1) identification of the data population from which a sample of items will be selected for audit and (2) an expression of the action that will be taken to produce relevant evidence. In general, the *actions* in detail test of control audit procedures involve vouching, tracing, observing, scanning, and recalcu-

EXHIBIT 8–4	INTERNAL CONTROL OBJECTIVES: REVENUE CYCLE (SALES)

General Objectives	Examples of Specific Objectives
1. Recorded sales are *valid* and documented.	Customer purchase orders support invoices.
	Bills of lading or other shipping documentation exist for all invoices.
	Recorded sales in sales journal supported by invoices.
2. Valid sales transactions are recorded and *none omitted*.	Invoices, shipping documents, and sales orders are prenumbered and the numerical sequence is checked.
	Overall comparisons of sales are made periodically by a statistical or product-line analysis.
3. Sales are *authorized* according to company policy.	Credit sales approved by credit department.
	Prices used in preparing invoices are from authorized price schedule.
4. Sales invoices are *accurately* prepared.	Invoice quantities compared to shipment and customer order quantities.
	Prices checked and mathematical accuracy independently checked after invoice prepared.
5. Sales transactions are properly *classified*.	Sales to subsidiaries and affiliates classified as intercompany sales and receivables.
	Sales returns and allowances properly classified.
6. Sales transaction *accounting and posting* is proper.	Credit sales posted to customers' individual accounts.
	Sales journal posted to general ledger account.
	Sales recognized in accordance with generally accepted accounting principles.
7. Sales transactions are recorded in the *proper period*.	Sales invoices recorded on shipment date.

AUDITING INSIGHT

FICTITIOUS REVENUE

A San Antonio computer peripheral equipment company was experiencing slow sales, so the sales manager entered some sales orders for customers who had not ordered anything. The invoices were marked "hold," while the delivery was to a warehouse owned by the company. The rationale was that these customers would buy the equipment eventually, so why not anticipate the orders! (However, it's a good idea not to send them the invoices until they actually make the orders, hence the "hold.") The "sales" and "receivables" were recorded in the accounts, and the financial statements contained overstated revenue and assets.

lating. If personnel in the organization are not performing their control activities very well, auditors will need to design substantive audit procedures to try to detect whether control failures have produced materially misleading account balances.

Test of controls audit procedures can be used to audit the accounting for transactions in two directions. This dual-direction testing involves samples selected to obtain evidence about control over *completeness* in one direction and control over *validity* in the other direction. The completeness direction determines whether all transactions that occurred were recorded (none omitted), and the validity direction determines whether recorded transactions actually occurred (were valid). An example of the completeness direction is the examination of a sample of shipping documents (from the file of all shipping documents) to determine whether invoices were prepared and recorded. An example of the validity direction is the examinations of a sample of sales invoices (from the file representing all recorded sales) to determine whether supporting shipping documents exist to verify the fact of an actual shipment. The content of each file is compared with the other. The example is illustrated in Exhibit 8–5. (The A-2-a and A-1-a codes correspond to the test of controls procedures in Exhibit 8–6.)

Exhibit 8–6 contains a selection of test of controls audit procedures. Many of these procedures can be characterized as steps taken to verify the content and character of sample documents from one file with the content and character of documents in another file. These steps are designed to enable the audit team to obtain objective evidence about the *effectiveness* of controls and about the *reliability* of accounting records.

Exhibit 8–6 shows the control objectives tested by the audit procedures. Thus, the test of controls procedures produce evidence that helps auditors determine whether the specific control objectives listed in Exhibit 8–4 were achieved.

EXHIBIT 8–5   DUAL DIRECTION OF TEST AUDIT SAMPLES

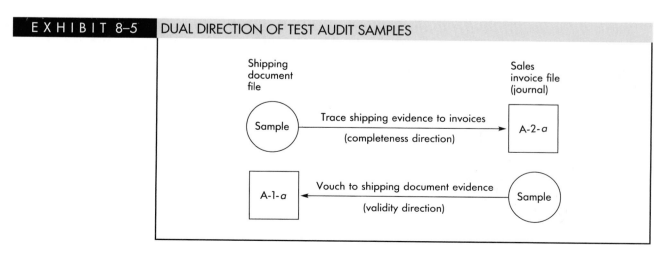

EXHIBIT 8–6 TEST OF CONTROLS AUDIT PROCEDURES FOR SALES, CASH RECEIPTS, AND RECEIVABLES

Control Objective	
A. Sales	
1. Select a sample of recorded sales invoices from the sales journal.	
a. Vouch to supporting shipping documents	Validity
b. Determine whether credit was approved	Authorization
c. Vouch prices to the approved price list	Authorization
	Accuracy
d. Compare the quantity billed to the quantity shipped	Accuracy
e. Recalculate the invoice arithmetic	Accuracy
f. Compare the shipment date with the invoice record date	Proper period
g. Trace the invoice to posting in the general ledger control account	Acctg/posting
and in the correct customer's account	Acctg/posting
h. Note the type of product shipping and determine proper classification	
in the right product-line revenue account	Classification
2. Select a sample of shipping documents from the shipping department file.	
a. Trace shipments to recorded sales invoices	Completeness
3. Scan recorded sales invoices for missing numbers in sequence.	Completeness
B. Cash Receipts	
1. Select a sample of recorded cash receipts.	
a. Vouch them to deposits in the bank statement	Validity
b. Vouch discounts taken by customers to proper approval or policy,	Authorization
recalculate discounts	Accuracy
c. Recalculate the cash summarized for a daily deposit or posting	Accuracy
d. Trace the deposit to the right cash account	Classification
e. Compare the date of receipt to the recording date	Proper period
f. Trace the receipts to postings in the correct customers' accounts	Acctg/posting
2. Select a sample of daily cash reports or another source of original cash records.	
a. Trace to the cash receipts journal	Completeness
C. Accounts Receivable	
1. Select a sample of customers' accounts.	
a. Vouch debits in them to supporting sales invoices	Validity
b. Vouch credits in them to supporting cash receipts documents and	
approved credit memos	Validity
2. Select a sample of credit memos.	
a. Review for proper approval	Authorization
b. Trace to posting in customers' accounts	Acctg/posting
3. Scan the accounts receivable control account for postings from sources other than	Validity
the sales and cash receipts journals (e.g., general journal adjusting entries,	Authorization
credit memos). Vouch a sample of such entries to supporting documents.	Accuracy
	Proper period
	Classification

Summary: Control Risk Assessment

The audit manager must evaluate the evidence obtained from an understanding of internal control and from test of controls audit procedures. The initial process of obtaining an understanding of the company's controls and the later process of obtaining evidence from actual test of controls are two of the phases of control risk assessment work.

If the control risk is assessed very low, the substantive audit procedures on the account balances can be limited in cost-saving ways. For example, the accounts receivable confirmations can be sent on a date prior to the year-end, and the sample size can be fairly small.

On the other hand, if tests of controls reveal weaknesses (such as posting sales without shipping documents, charging customers the wrong prices, and recording credits to customers without supporting credit memos), the substantive procedures will need to be designed to lower the risk of failing to detect material misstatement in the account balances. For example, the confirmation procedure may need to be scheduled on the year-end date with a large sample of customer accounts. Descriptions of major deficiencies, control weaknesses, and inefficiencies may be incorporated in a letter to the client describing "reportable conditions."

R E V I E W
CHECKPOINTS

8.7 What account balances are included in a revenue and collection cycle?

8.8 What specific control activities (in addition to separation of duties and responsibilities) should be in place and operating in a control system governing revenue recognition and cash accounting?

8.9 What is a "walk-through" of a sales transaction? How can the walk-through work complement the use of an internal control questionnaire?

8.10 What are the two important characteristics of a detail test of control procedure? What "actions" are typically contemplated by such a procedure?

8.11 What is "dual direction test of controls sampling?"

SPECIAL NOTE: THE EXISTENCE ASSERTION

LEARNING OBJECTIVE

3. Explain the importance of the existence assertion for the audit of cash and accounts receivable, and describe some procedures for obtaining evidence about the existence of assets.

When considering assertions and obtaining evidence about accounts receivable and other assets, auditors must put emphasis on the existence and rights (ownership) assertions. This emphasis on existence is rightly placed because companies and auditors often have gotten into malpractice trouble by giving unqualified reports on financial statements that overstated assets and revenues and understated expenses. For example, credit sales recorded too early (fictitious sales?) result in overstated accounts receivable and overstated sales revenue; failure to amortize prepaid expense results in understated expenses and overstated prepaid expenses (current assets).

Discerning the population of assets to audit for existence and ownership is easy because the company has asserted their existence by putting them on the balance sheet. The audit procedures described in the following sections can be used to obtain evidence about the existence and ownership of accounts receivable and other assets.

Recalculation

Think about the assets that depend largely on calculations. They are amenable to auditors' recalculation procedures. Expired prepaid expenses are recalculated, using auditors' vouching of basic documents, such as loan agreements (prepaid interest), rent contracts (prepaid rent), and insurance policies (prepaid insurance). Goodwill and deferred expenses are recalculated by using original acquisition and payment document information and term (useful life) estimates. A bank reconciliation is a special kind of calculation, and the company's reconciliation can be audited. (See the special note on auditing a bank reconciliation later in this chapter.)

Physical Observation

Inventories and fixed assets can be inspected and counted. Titles to autos, land, and buildings can be vouched, sometimes using public records in the county clerk's office. Petty cash and undeposited receipts can be observed and counted, but the cash in the bank cannot. Securities held as investments can be inspected if held by the company.

Confirmation

Letters of confirmation can be sent to banks and customers, asking for a report of the balances owed the company. Likewise, if securities held as investments are in the custody of banks or brokerage houses, the custodians can be asked to report the names, numbers, and quantity of the securities held for the company. In some cases, inventories held in public warehouses or out on consignment can be confirmed with the other party. (Refer to the special note on confirmations later in this chapter.)

Verbal Inquiry

Inquiries to management usually do not provide very convincing evidence about existence and ownership. However, inquiries always should be made about the company's agreements to maintain compensating cash balances (may not be classifiable as "cash" among the current assets), about pledge or sale of accounts receivable with recourse in connection with financings, and about pledge of other assets as collateral for loans.

Examination of Documents (Vouching)

Evidence of ownership can be obtained by studying the title documents for assets. Examination of loan documents may yield evidence of the need to disclose assets pledged as loan collateral.

Scanning

Assets are supposed to have debit balances. A computer can be used to scan large files of accounts receivable, inventory, and fixed assets for uncharacteristic credit balances. Usually, such credit balances reflect errors in the record keeping—customer overpayments, failure to record purchases of inventory, depreciation of assets more than cost. The names of debtors can be scanned for officers, directors, and related parties, amounts that need to be reported separately or disclosed in the financial statements.

Analytical Procedures

A variety of analytical comparisons might be employed, depending on the circumstances and the nature of the business. Comparisons of asset and revenue balances with recent history might help detect overstatements. Such relationships as receivables turnover, gross margin ratio, and sales/asset ratios can be compared to historical data and industry statistics for evidence of overall reasonableness. Account interrelationships also can be used in analytical review. For example, sales returns and allowances and sales commissions generally vary directly with dollar sales volume, bad debt expense usually varies directly with credit sales volume, and freight expense varies with the physical sales volume. Accounts receivable write-offs should be compared with earlier estimates of doubtful accounts.

AUDITING INSIGHT

SIMPLE ANALYTICAL COMPARISON

The auditors prepared a schedule of the monthly credit sales totals for the current and prior years. They noticed several variations, but one, in November of the current year, stood out in particular. The current-year credit sales were almost twice as large as any prior November. Further investigation showed that a computer error had caused the November credit sales to be recorded twice in the control accounts. The accounts receivable and sales revenue were materially overstated as a result.

R E V I E W
CHECKPOINTS

8.12 Why is it important to place emphasis on the existence and rights (ownership) assertions when auditing cash and accounts receivable?

8.13 Which audit procedures are usually the most useful for auditing the existence and rights assertions? Give some examples.

SPECIAL NOTE: USING CONFIRMATIONS

LEARNING OBJECTIVE

4. Identify and describe considerations for using confirmations in the audit of cash and accounts receivable.

This special note gives some details about using confirmations in the audit of cash and accounts receivable. In general, the use of confirmations for cash balances and trade accounts receivable is considered a required generally accepted audit procedure (SAS 67, AU 330). However, auditors may decide not to use them if suitable alternative procedures are available and applicable in particular circumstances. Auditors should document justifications for the decision not to use confirmations for trade accounts receivable in a particular audit. Justifications include: (1) receivables are not material; (2) confirmations would be ineffective, based on prior years' experience or knowledge that responses could be unreliable; and (3) analytical procedures and other substantive test of details procedures provide sufficient, competent evidence.

Confirmation of Cash and Loan Balances

The standard bank confirmation form, approved by the AICPA, the American Bankers Association, and the Bank Administration Institute, is shown in Exhibit 8–7. This form is used to obtain bank confirmation of deposit and loan balances. (Other confirmation letters are used to obtain confirmation of contingent liabilities, endorsements, compensating balance agreements, lines of credit, and other financial instruments and transactions.) A word of caution is in order: While financial institutions may note exceptions to the information typed in a confirmation and may confirm items omitted from it, the AICPA warns auditors that sole reliance on the form to satisfy the completeness assertion, insofar as cash and loan balances are concerned, is unwarranted. Officers and employees of financial institutions cannot be expected to search their information systems for balances and loans that may not be immediately evident as assets and liabilities of the client company. However, it is a good idea to send confirmations on accounts the company represents as closed during the year to get the bank to confirm zero balances. (If a bank confirms a nonzero balance, the auditors have evidence that some asset accounting is omitted in the company records.)

Confirmation of Accounts and Notes Receivable

Confirmations provide evidence of existence and, to a limited extent, of valuation of accounts and notes receivable. The accounts and notes to be confirmed should be documented in the working papers with an aged trial balance. (An aged trial balance is

AUDITING INSIGHT

A DECISION NOT TO USE ACCOUNTS RECEIVABLE CONFIRMATIONS

Sureparts Manufacturing Company sold all its production to three auto manufacturers and six after-market distributors. All nine of these customers typically paid their accounts in full by the 10th of each following month. The auditors were able to vouch the cash receipts for the full amount of the accounts receivable in the bank statements and cash receipts records in the month following the Surepart year-end. Confirmation evidence was not considered necessary in these circumstances.

EXHIBIT 8-7　BANK CONFIRMATION

C-22

STANDARD FORM TO CONFIRM ACCOUNT
BALANCE INFORMATION WITH FINANCIAL INSTITUTIONS

Kingston Company
CUSTOMER NAME

FINANCIAL INSTITUTION'S NAME AND ADDRESS

We have provided to our accountants the following information as of the close of business on

Dec. 31   19 01

First National Bank
Main Street
Chicago, Illinois

regarding our deposit and loan balances. Please confirm the accuracy of the information, noting any exceptions to the information provided. If the balances have been left blank, please complete this form by furnishing the balance in the appropriate space below.* Although we do not request nor expect you to conduct a comprehensive, detailed search of your records, if during the process of completing this confirmation additional information about other deposit and loan accounts we may have with you comes to your attention, please include such information below. Please use the enclosed envelope to return the form directly to our accountants.

1. At the close of business on the date listed above, our records indicated the following deposit balance(s):

ACCOUNT NAME	ACCOUNT NO.	INTEREST RATE	BALANCE*
Kingston Company	146-2013	none	$506,100

2. We were directly liable to the financial institution for loans at the close of business on the date listed above as follows:

ACCOUNT NO./ DESCRIPTION	BALANCE*	DATE DUE	INTEREST RATE	DATE THROUGH WHICH INTEREST IS PAID	DESCRIPTION OF COLLATERAL
042743	$750,000	6-30-02	11%	NA	Unsecured

Larry Lancaster
(Customer's Authorized Signature)

December 29, 2001
(Date)

The information presented above by the customer is in agreement with our records. Although we have not conducted a comprehensive, detailed search of our records, no other deposit or loan accounts have come to our attention except as noted below.

Alfred E. Newman
(Financial Institution Authorized Signature)

January 15, 2002
(Date)

Assistant Vice President
(Title)

EXCEPTIONS AND OR COMMENTS

PLEASE RETURN THIS FORM DIRECTLY TO OUR ACCOUNTANTS:

Anderson, Olds, Watershed
Rush Street
Chicago, Illinois

* Ordinarily, balances are intentionally left blank if they are not available at the time the form is prepared.

Approved 1990 by American Bankers Association, American Institute of Certified Public Accountants, and Bank Administration Institute. Additional forms available from: AICPA—Order Department, P.O. Box 1003, NY, NY 10108-1003

D451 5951

---

shown in Exhibit 8–8, annotated to show the auditors' work.) Accounts for confirmation can be selected at random or in accordance with another plan consistent with the audit objectives. Statistical methods may be useful for determining the sample size. Audit software can be used to access computerized receivables files, select, and even to print the confirmations.

Two widely used confirmation forms are *positive confirmations* and *negative confirmations*. An example of a positive confirmation is shown in Exhibit 8–9. A variation of the positive confirmation is the *blank form*. A blank confirmation does not contain the balance; customers are asked to fill it in themselves. The blank positive confirmation may produce better evidence because the recipients need to get the information directly from their own records instead of just signing the form and returning it with no exceptions noted. (However, the effort involved may cause a lower response rate.)

The negative confirmation form for the same request shown in Exhibit 8–9 is in Exhibit 8–10. The positive form asks for a response. The negative form asks for a response

EXHIBIT 8–8   ACCOUNTS RECEIVABLE AGED TRIAL BALANCE

```
D-2                          KINGSTON COMPANY              Prepared   PD
PG. 1 OF 15               ACCOUNTS RECEIVABLE              Date    1-12-02
                           December 31, 2001               Reviewed Terri Tough
                                                            Date    1-17-02
```

	Current	30–60 Days	61–90 Days	Over 90 Days	Total	Jan. 2002 Collection Current	Past Due
Able Hardware	12,337 ✗				12,337 ✗PC "	12,337	
Baker Supply	712				712	712	
Charley Company	1,486 ✗	420 ✗			1,906 ✗PC	1,486	420
Dogg General Store				755	755		
Welsch Windows			531 ✗		531 ✗ NC		531
Zlat Stuff Place				214	214		214
Balance per books	335,000	30,000	20,000	15,000	400,000	320,000	25,000
Billing errors	(11,000)		(1,000)		(12,000) ①		
Adjusted balance	324,000	30,000	19,000	15,000	388,000		

✗ Traced to accounts receivable subsidiary ledger.

PC Positive confirmation mailed Jan. 4. Replies D-2.3

NC Negative confirmation mailed Jan. 4. Replies D-2.4

" No reply to positive confirmation, vouched charges to invoices.

Ɔ Traced to general ledger control account.

① Billing error adjustment explained on working paper D-2.2

Note: See D-2.2 for analysis of doubtful accounts and our test
      of reasonableness

---

only if something is wrong with the balance; thus, lack of response to negative confirmations is considered evidence of propriety.

The positive form is used when individual balances are relatively large or when accounts are in dispute. Positive confirmations may ask for information about either the account balance or specific invoices, depending on knowledge about how customers maintain their accounting records. The negative form is used mostly when inherent risk and control risk are considered low, when a large number of small balances is involved, and when the client's customers can be expected to consider the confirmations properly. Frequently, both forms are used by sending positive confirmations on some customers' accounts and negative confirmations on others.

Getting confirmations delivered to the intended recipient is a problem that requires auditors' careful attention. Auditors need to control the confirmations, including the addresses to which they are sent. Experience is full of cases where confirmations were mailed to company accomplices, who provided false responses. The auditors should carefully consider features of the reply, such as postmarks, fax and telegraph responses, letterhead, electronic mail, telephone, or other characteristics that may give clues to indicate false responses. Auditors should follow up electronic and telephone responses to determine their origin (e.g., returning the telephone call to a known number, looking up telephone numbers to determine addresses, or using a criss-cross directory to determine the location of a respondent). Furthermore, the lack of response to a negative

EXHIBIT 8–9   POSITIVE CONFIRMATION LETTER

D-2.3

KINGSTON COMPANY
Chicago, Illinois

January 5, 2002

Charley Company
Lake and Adams
Chicago, Illinois

Our auditors, Anderson, Olds, and Watershed, are making their regular audit of our financial statements. Part of this audit includes direct verification of customer balances.

PLEASE EXAMINE THE DATA BELOW CAREFULLY AND EITHER CONFIRM ITS ACCURACY OR REPORT ANY DIFFERENCES DIRECTLY TO OUR AUDITORS USING THE ENCLOSED REPLY ENVELOPE.

This is not a request for payment. Please do not send your remittance to our auditors.

Your prompt attention to this confirmation request will be appreciated.

Samuel Carboy
Samuel Carboy, Controller

The balance due Kingston Company as of December 31, 2001, is $1,906. This balance is correct except as noted below:

It's correct. Will send payment as soon

as possible.

Date: *Jan. 7, 2002*   By: *P. "Charley" O'Quirk*

Title: *President*

confirmation is no guarantee that the intended recipient received it unless the auditor carefully controlled the mailing.

The **response rate** for positive confirmations is the proportion of the number of confirmations returned to the number sent, generally after the audit team prompts recipients with second and third requests. Research studies have shown response rates ranging from 66 to 96 percent. Recipients seem to be able to detect account misstatements to varying degrees. Studies have shown **detection rates** (the ratio of the number of exceptions reported to auditors to the number of account errors intentionally reported to customers) ranging from 20 to 100 percent. Negative confirmations seem to have lower detection rates than positive confirmations. Also, studies show somewhat lower detection rates for misstatements favorable to recipients (i.e., an accounts receivable understatement). Overall, positive confirmations appear to be more effective than negative confirmations; but results depend on the type of recipients, the size of the account, and the type of account being confirmed. Effective confirmation practices depend on attention to these factors and on prior years' experience with confirmation results on a particular client's accounts.

Effective confirmation also depends on using a "bag of tricks" to boost the response rate. Often, auditors merely send out a cold, official-looking request in a metered mail envelope and expect customers to be happy to respond. However, the response rate can be increased by using: (1) a postcard sent in advance, notifying that a confirmation is coming; (2) special delivery mail; (3) first-class stamp postage (not metered); and (4) an

EXHIBIT 8–10   NEGATIVE CONFIRMATION LETTER

KINGSTON COMPANY
Chicago, Illinois

January 5, 2002

Charley Company
Lake and Adams
Chicago, Illinois

Our auditors, Anderson, Olds, and Watershed, are making their regular audit of our financial statements. Part of this audit includes direct verification of customer balances.

   PLEASE EXAMINE THE DATA BELOW CAREFULLY AND COMPARE THEM TO YOUR RECORDS OF YOUR ACCOUNT WITH US. IF OUR INFORMATION IS NOT IN AGREEMENT WITH YOUR RECORDS, PLEASE STATE ANY DIFFERENCES ON THE REVERSE SIDE OF THIS PAGE, AND RETURN DIRECTLY TO OUR AUDITORS IN THE RETURN ENVELOPE PROVIDED. IF THE INFORMATION IS CORRECT, NO REPLY IS NECESSARY.

   This is not a request for payment. Please do not send your remittance to our auditors.

   Your prompt attention to this confirmation request will be appreciated.

Samuel Carboy
Samuel Carboy, Controller

As of December 31, 2001, balance due to Kingston Company: $1,906
Date of Origination: November and December, 2001
Type: Open trade account

---

envelope imprinted "Confirmation Enclosed: Please Examine Carefully." These devices increase the cost of the confirmation procedure, but the benefit is a better response rate.[1]

   The audit team should try to obtain replies to all positive confirmations by sending second and third requests to nonrespondents. If there is no response or if the response specifies an exception to the client's records, the auditors should carry out document vouching procedures to audit the account. These alternative procedures include the *vouching direction* of finding sales invoice copies, shipping documents, and customer orders that signal the existence of sales charges. They also are used to find evidence of customers' payments in subsequent cash receipts.

   When sampling is used, all accounts in the sample should be audited. It is improper to substitute an easy-to-audit customer account not in the sample for one that does not respond to a confirmation request.

   Confirmation of receivables may be performed at a date other than the year-end. When confirmation is done at an interim date, the audit firm is able to spread work throughout the year and avoid the pressures of overtime that typically occur around December 31. Also, the audit can be completed sooner after the year-end date if confirmation has been done earlier. The primary consideration when planning confirmation of

---

[1] AICPA, *Confirmation of Accounts Receivable*, Auditing Procedures Study (New York, 1996), chap. 3. See also: Paul Caster, "The Role of Confirmations as Audit Evidence," *Journal of Accountancy*, Febrauary 1992, pp. 73–76.

accounts before the balance sheet date is the client's internal control over transactions affecting receivables. When confirmation is performed at an interim date, the following additional procedures should be considered:

1. Obtain a summary of receivables transactions from the interim date to the year-end date.
2. Obtain a year-end trial balance of receivables, compare it to the interim trial balance, and obtain evidence and explanations for large variations.
3. Consider the necessity for additional confirmations as of the balance sheet date if balances have increased materially.

One final note about confirmations: Confirmations of accounts, loans, and notes receivable may not produce sufficient evidence of ownership by the client (rights assertion). Debtors may not be aware that the auditor's client sold the accounts, notes, or loans receivable to financial institutions or to the public (collateralized securities). Auditors need to perform additional inquiry and detail procedures to get evidence of the ownership of the receivables and the appropriateness of disclosures related to financing transactions secured by receivables.

Summary: Confirmations

Confirmations of loans, accounts receivable, and notes receivable are required, unless auditors can justify substituting other procedures in the circumstances of a particular audit. The bank confirmation is a standard positive form. Confirmations for accounts and notes receivable can be in positive or negative form, and the positive form may be a blank confirmation.

Auditors must take care to control confirmations to ensure that responses are received from the real debtors and not from persons who can intercept the confirmations to give false responses. Responses by fax, telegraph, electronic mail, telephone, or other means not written and signed by a recipient should be followed up to determine their genuine origins. Second and third requests should be sent to prompt responses to positive confirmations, and auditors should audit nonresponding customers by alternative procedures. Accounts in a sample should not be left unaudited (e.g., "They didn't respond"), and easy-to-audit accounts should not be substituted for hard-to-audit ones in a sample. Various "tricks" can be used to raise the response rate.

Confirmations yield evidence about *existence* and gross *valuation*. However, the fact that a debtor admits to owing the debt does not mean the debtor can pay. Other procedures must be undertaken to audit the *collectibility* of the accounts. Nevertheless, confirmations can give some clues about collectibility when customers tell about balances in dispute. Confirmations of accounts, notes, and loans receivable should not be used as the only evidence of the ownership (*rights* assertions) of these financial assets.

R E V I E W
CHECKPOINTS

8.14 List the information a CPA should solicit in a standard bank confirmation inquiry sent to an audit client's bank.

8.15 Distinguish between "positive" and "negative" confirmations. Under what conditions would you expect each type of confirmation to be appropriate?

8.16 Distinguish between confirmation "response rate" and confirmation "detection rate."

8.17 What methods can be used to increase the response rate for receivables confirmations?

8.18 What are some of the justifications for not using confirmations of accounts receivable on a particular audit?

8.19 What special care should be taken with regard to examining the sources of accounts receivable confirmation responses?

SPECIAL NOTE: AUDIT OF BANK RECONCILIATIONS WITH ATTENTION TO LAPPING AND KITING

LEARNING OBJECTIVE

5. Design and perform substantive audit procedures for the audit of a bank statement reconciliation, and tell how auditors can search for lapping and kiting.

The company's bank reconciliation is the primary means of valuing cash in the financial statements. The amount of cash in the bank is almost always different from the amount in the general ledger (financial statements), and the reconciliation purports to explain the difference. The normal procedure is to obtain the company-prepared bank reconciliation and audit it. Auditors should not perform the company's control function of preparing the reconciliation.

A client-prepared bank reconciliation is shown in Exhibit 8–11. The bank balance is confirmed and cross-referenced to the bank confirmation working paper (Exhibit 8–7). The reconciliation is recalculated, the outstanding checks and deposits in transit are footed, and the book balance is traced to the trial balance (which has been traced to the general ledger). The reconciling items should be vouched to determine whether outstanding checks really were not paid and that deposits in transit actually were mailed before the reconciliation date. The auditors' information source for vouching the bank reconciliation items is a **cutoff bank statement**, which is a complete bank statement including all paid checks and deposits slips. The client requests the bank to send this bank statement directly to the auditor. It is usually for a 10- to 20-day period following the reconciliation date. (It also can be the next regular monthly statement, received directly by the auditors.)

EXHIBIT 8–11 | **BANK RECONCILIATION**

```
                            KINGSTON COMPANY
        C-2           BANK RECONCILIATION-FIRST NATIONAL BANK        Prepared  G.D. 1/10/02
                            General Account                          Reviewed  PRA 1/10/02
                               12/31/01
                          (Prepared by client)

Balance per bank statement                              506,100  c
Add:
    Deposit in transit as of 12/31/01                    51,240  n
Deduct outstanding checks:                              557,340
        Date      No.    Payee
        --------  ----   ------------------------

        12/10/00  842    Ace Supply Company           500  X
        11/31/01  1280   Ace Supply Company         1,800  ✓
        12/15/01  1372   Northwest Lumber Co.      30,760  ✓
        12/28/01  1412   Gibson & Johnson           7,270  X
        12/30/01  1417   First National payroll    20,000  ✓
        12/30/01  1418   Ace Supply Company         2,820  ✓
        12/30/01  1419   Windy City Utilities       2,030  ✓
        12/30/01  1420   Howard Hardware Supply     8,160  ✓
                                                  -------
Balance per book                                   73,340
                                                  -------
                                                  484,000  f
                                                  -------
                                                  -------
```

Note: *Obtained cutoff bank statement 1/9/02* (C-23)   (T/B-1)

f *Footed*

c *Confirmed by bank, standard bank confirmation* (C-22)

n *Vouched to cutoff bank statement, deposit recorded by bank on 1/3/02. Vouched to duplicate deposit slip validaged 1/3/02*

✓ *Vouched to paid check cleared with cutoff bank statement.*

X *Vouched to statement from attorneys.*

X *Amount in dispute per controller.*

The vouching of outstanding checks and deposits in transit is a matter of comparing checks that cleared in the cutoff bank statement with the list of outstanding checks for evidence that all checks that were written prior to the reconciliation date were on the list of outstanding checks. The deposits shown in transit should be recorded by the bank in the first business days of the cutoff period. If recorded later, the inference is that the deposit may have been made up from receipts of the period after the reconciliation date. For large outstanding checks not clearing in the cutoff period, vouching may be extended to other documentation supporting the disbursement. These procedures are keyed and described by tick marks in Exhibit 8–11.

Accounts Receivable Lapping

When the business receives many payments from customers, a detailed audit should include comparison of the checks listed on a sample of deposit slips (from the reconciliation month and other months) to the detail of customer credits listed on the day's posting to customer accounts receivable (daily remittance list or other record of detail postings). This procedure is a test for accounts receivable lapping. It is an attempt to find credits given to customers for whom no payments were received on the day in question.

Check Kiting

Auditors also should be alert to the possibility of a company's practice of illegal "kiting." **Check kiting** is the practice of building up balances in one or more bank accounts based on uncollected (float) checks drawn against similar accounts in other banks. Kiting involves depositing money from one bank account to another, using a *hot check*. The depository bank does not know the check is on insufficient funds, but the deficiency is covered by another hot check from another bank account before the first check clears. Kiting is the deliberate floating of funds between two or more bank accounts. By this method, a bank customer uses the time required for checks to clear to obtain an unauthorized loan without any interest charge.

Professional money managers working for cash-conscious businesses try to have minimal unused balances in their accounts, and their efforts sometimes can look like check kites. Tight cash flows initiate kites, and intent to kite is the key for criminal charges. Kites evolve to include numerous banks and numerous checks. The more banks and broader geographical distance, the harder a perpetrator finds it to control a kite scheme.

The transactions described next illustrate a simple kite scheme. The transactions are shown in Exhibit 8–12.

Start with no money in the First National Bank and none in the Last National Bank. Run the kite quickly from July 3 (Monday) through July 12 (next Wednesday)—taking advantage of the holiday and the weekend to float the hot checks.

A. Deposit a $15,000 check drawn on First National Bank to the Last National account. Simultaneously, deposit a $10,000 check drawn on Last National Bank to the First National account. Do not record the deposits and disbursements in the general ledger.

B. Deposit an $11,000 check drawn on First National Bank to the Last National account. Simultaneously, deposit a $13,000 check drawn on Last National Bank to the First National account. Do not record the deposits and disbursements in the general ledger.

C. Purchase an $8,000 certified check from First National Bank to make a down payment on a Mercedes automobile. Record the check in the general ledger.

D. The first transfer checks (part A) clear each bank.

| EXHIBIT 8–12 | | ILLUSTRATIVE CHECK KITING TRANSACTIONS | | | | |

			First National Bank		Last National Bank	
Index	Date	Transaction	At Bank (1)	Actual (2)	At Bank (1)	Actual (2)
A	July 3	1st transfer	—	($15,000)	$15,000	$15,000
A	July 3	1st transfer	$10,000	$10,000	—	($10,000)
		Balances	$10,000	($ 5,000)	$15,000	$ 5,000
B	July 5	2nd transfer	—	($11,000)	$11,000	$11,000
B	July 5	2nd transfer	$13,000	$13,000	—	($13,000)
		Balances	$23,000	($ 3,000)	$26,000	$ 3,000
C	July 6	Mercedes Pmt	($ 8,000)	($ 8,000)		
		Balances	$15,000	($11,000)	$26,000	$ 3,000
D	July 7	1st trf clear	($15,000)		($10,000)	
E	July 7	3rd transfer	—	($16,000)	$16,000	$16,000
E	July 7	3rd transfer	$14,000	$14,000	—	($14,000)
		Balances	$14,000	($13,000)	$32,000	$ 5,000
F	July 8	Pay travel	—	($14,000)	—	($32,000)
		Balances	$14,000	($27,000)	$32,000	($27,000)
G	July 10	2nd trf clear	($11,000)		($13,000)	
G	July 12	3rd trf clear	($16,000)		($14,000)	
G	July 12	Travel clear	($14,000)		($32,000)	
			($27,000)		($27,000)	

[1] "At Bank" means the bank's records of deposits received and checks paid (cleared).

[2] "Actual" means the amounts the general ledger would have shown had the transfers been recorded.

E. Deposit a $16,000 check drawn on First National Bank to the Last National account. Simultaneously, deposit a $14,000 check drawn on Last National Bank to the First National account. Do not record the deposits and disbursements in the general ledger.

F. Write checks for $14,000 drawn on First National Bank and $32,000 drawn on Last National Bank payable to a travel agent, and take a long trip (preferably to a country with no extradition treaty!).

G. When the checks are presented to the banks for payment, the accounts are empty. A total of $79,000 was kited, of which $25,000 cleared during the kite period (the first transfers in A), so the "take" was $54,000. The criminals got the Mercedes ($8,000) and the vacation funds ($46,000).

These are some characteristic signs of check kiting schemes:

- Frequent deposits and checks in same amounts.
- Frequent deposits and checks in round amounts.
- Frequent deposits with checks written on the same (other) banks.
- Short time lags between deposits and withdrawals.
- Frequent ATM account balance inquiries.
- Many large deposits made on Thursday or Friday to take advantage of the weekend.
- Large periodic balances in individual accounts with no apparent business explanation.
- Low average balance compared to high level of deposits.
- Many checks made payable to other banks.
- Bank willingness to pay against uncollected funds.
- "Cash" withdrawals with deposit checks drawn on another bank.
- Checks drawn on foreign banks with lax banking laws and regulations.

Auditors can detect the above signs of check kiting by reviewing bank account activity. The only trouble is that criminal check kiters often destroy the banking documents. If a company cannot or will not produce its bank statements, with all deposit slips and canceled checks, the auditors should be wary.

If these cash transfers are recorded in the books, a company will show the negative balances that result from checks drawn on insufficient funds. However, perpetrators may try to hide the kiting by not recording the deposits and checks. Such maneuvers may be detectable in a bank reconciliation audit.

Summary: Bank Reconciliations, Lapping, and Kiting

The combination of all the procedures performed on the bank reconciliation provides evidence of existence, valuation, and proper cutoff of the bank cash balances. Auditors use a cutoff bank statement to obtain independent evidence of the proper listing of outstanding checks and deposits in transit on a bank reconciliation.

Additional procedures can be performed to try to detect attempts at lapping accounts receivable collections and kiting checks. For lapping, these procedures include auditing the details of customer payments listed in bank deposits in comparison to details of customer payment postings (remittance lists). For kiting, these procedures include being alert to the signs of kites and preparing a schedule of interbank transfers and a proof of cash.

R E V I E W
CHECKPOINTS

8.20 What is a cutoff bank statement? How is it used by auditors?

8.21 What is "lapping"? What procedures can auditors employ for its detection?

8.22 What is "check kiting"? How might auditors detect kiting?

BANK TRANSFER SCHEDULE AND "PROOF OF CASH"

LEARNING OBJECTIVE

6. Prepare a schedule of interbank transfers and a proof of cash.

Auditors usually prepare a schedule of interbank transfers to determine whether transfers of cash from one bank to another were recorded properly (correct amount and correct date). Assume the facts given in the preceding kiting illustration, and the following: (1) the First National Bank account is the company's general bank account, and the Last National Bank account is the payroll account, (2) the company pays its payroll on the 15th and 30th days of each month, and (3) the company transfers the net amount of each payroll from the general account to the payroll account. A "schedule of interbank transfers" prepared from the recorded entries in the general ledger would look like the one in Panel A in Exhibit 8–13.

However, we know that the managers performed a check kite and did not record several transfers between these accounts. Auditors should review the bank statements, and find the other transfers, and put them on the schedule (shown in Panel B in Exhibit 8–13). Panel B shows how the auditors can document the unrecorded transfers.

Auditors can use another method to discover unrecorded cash transactions. It is called a "proof of cash." You may have studied this method in your intermediate accounting course under the name of "four-column bank reconciliation." The proof of cash is a reconciliation in which the bank balance, the bank report of cash deposited, and the bank report of cash paid are all reconciled to the company's general ledger. Exhibit 8–14 illustrates a proof of cash. The illustration assumes some bank reconciliation information,

EXHIBIT 8–13 — ILLUSTRATION OF INTERBANK TRANSFER SCHEDULE

Check Number	Bank	Amount	Date per Books	Date per Bank	Bank	Date per Books	Date per Bank
PANEL A							
7602	1st Nat'l	$24,331	Jul 14	Jul 18	Last Nat'l	Jul 14	Jul 14
8411	1st Nat'l	$36,462	Jul 28	Aug 1	Last Nat'l	Jul 28	Jul 28
PANEL B							
6722	1st Nat'l	$15,000	none	Jul 7	Last Nat'l	none	Jul 3
11062	Last Nat'l	$10,000	none	Jul 7	1st Nat'l	none	Jul 3
6793	1st Nat'l	$11,000	none	Jul 10	Last Nat'l	none	Jul 5
11097	Last Nat'l	$13,000	none	Jul 10	1st Nat'l	none	Jul 5
6853	1st Nat'l	$16,000	none	Jul 12	Last Nat'l	none	Jul 7
11106	Last Nat'l	$14,000	none	Jul 12	1st Nat'l	none	Jul 7

The *Disbursing Account* spans Bank/Amount/Date per Books/Date per Bank; the *Receiving Account* spans the remaining Bank/Date per Books/Date per Bank.

EXHIBIT 8–14 — ILLUSTRATION OF PROOF OF CASH—FIRST NATIONAL BANK

	Balance June 30	Deposits	Payments	Balance July 31
Bank statement amounts	$264,322	$398,406	$390,442	$272,286
Deposits in transit				
June 30	76,501	(76,501)		
July 31		79,721		79,721
Outstanding checks				
June 30	(89,734)		(89,734)	
July 31			62,958	(62,958)
Unrecorded bank interest (recorded in the next month)				
June 30	(162)	162		
July 31		(155)		(155)
Unrecorded service charges (recorded in the next month)				
June 30	118		118	
July 31			(129)	129
Unrecorded transfers received from Last National Bank		(37,000)		(37,000)
Unrecorded transfers to Last National Bank			(42,000)	42,000
General ledger amounts	$251,045	$364,633	$321,655	$294,023

Month of July spans the Deposits and Payments columns.

some transaction activity, and the unrecorded transfers for the First National Bank account used in the previous illustrations of kiting and interbank transfers. (Changing the kiting illustration: the bank accounts did not start with zero balances.)

The proof of cash attempt to reconcile the deposits and payments reported by the bank to the deposits and payments recorded in the general ledger will reveal the unrecorded transfers. The amounts will not reconcile until the auditors inspect the bank statement and find the bank amounts that are not in the general ledger. (Likewise, the attempt to reconcile the July 31 bank balance will show a $5,000 difference, which is explained by the $37,000 unrecorded deposits and the $42,000 unrecorded payments.)

8.23 How does a schedule of interbank transfers show improper cash transfer transactions?

8.24 How can a "proof of cash" reveal unrecorded cash deposit and cash payment transactions?

AUDIT CASES: SUBSTANTIVE AUDIT PROCEDURES

LEARNING OBJECTIVE

7. Describe some common errors and frauds in the revenue and collection cycle, and design some audit and investigation procedures for detecting them.

The audit procedures to gather evidence on the assertions in account balances are called "substantive procedures." Some amount of substantive audit procedures must be performed in all audits. Auditors should not place total reliance on controls to the exclusion of other procedures. Substantive audit procedures differ from test of controls audit procedures in their basic purpose. Substantive procedures are designed to obtain direct evidence about the dollar amounts in account balances, while test of controls procedures are designed to obtain evidence about the company's performance of its own control activities. Sometimes an audit procedure can be used for both purposes and then it is called a **dual-purpose procedure**.

The goal in performing substantive procedures is to detect evidence of errors and frauds, if any exist in the accounts as material overstatements or understatements of account balances. The remainder of this part of the chapter, uses a set of cases that contain specific examples of test of controls and substantive audit procedures (recalculation, observation, confirmation, inquiry, vouching, tracing, scanning, and analysis). The case stories are better than listing schemes and detection procedures in the abstract. (A selection of detail substantive procedures for cash and accounts receivable is in Appendix 8B.)

If errors and frauds exist in account balances, they are characterized by these features:

Method: A cause of the misstatement (accidental error or fraud attempt), which usually is made easier by some kind of failure of controls.

Paper trail: A set of telltale signs of erroneous accounting, missing or altered documents, or a "dangling debit" (the false or erroneous debit that results from an overstatement of assets).

Amount: The dollar amount of overstated assets and revenue, or understated liabilities and expenses.

The cases follow a standard format which first tells about an error or fraud situation in terms of the method, paper trail, and the amount. The first part of each case gives you the "inside story" that auditors seldom know before they perform the audit work. The next part is an "audit approach" section, which tells about the audit objective (assertion), controls, test of controls, and audit of balances (substantive procedures) that could be considered in an approach to the situation. The audit approach section presumes that the auditors do not know everything about the situation. The audit approach section contains these parts:

AUDITING INSIGHT

DUAL-PURPOSE NATURE OF ACCOUNTS RECEIVABLE CONFIRMATIONS

Accounts receivable confirmation is a substantive procedure designed to obtain evidence of the existence and gross amount (valuation) of customers' balances directly from the customer. If such confirmations show numerous exceptions, auditors would be concerned with the controls over the details of sales and cash receipts transactions even if previous control evaluations seemed to show little control risk.

Audit objective: A recognition of a *financial statement assertion* for which evidence needs to be obtained. The assertions are about existence of assets, liabilities, revenues, and expenses; their valuation; their complete inclusion in the account balances; the rights and obligations inherent in them; and their proper presentation and disclosure in the financial statements.

Control: A recognition of the control activities that *should be* used in an organization to prevent and detect errors and frauds.

Test of controls: Ordinary and extended procedures *designed to produce evidence about the effectiveness of the controls* that should be in operation.

Audit of balances: Ordinary and extended *substantive procedures designed to find signs of errors and frauds* in account balances and classes of transactions.

At the end of the chapter, some similar discussion cases are presented, and you can write the audit approach to test your ability to design audit procedures for the detection of errors and frauds. Appendix 8B contains two substantive audit programs for reference.

CASE 8.1
THE CANNY CASHIER

PROBLEM

Cash embezzlement caused overstated accounts receivable, overstated customer discounts expense, and understated cash sales. Company failed to earn interest income on funds "borrowed."

METHOD

D. Bakel was the assistant controller of Sports Equipment, Inc. (SEI), an equipment retailer. SEI maintained accounts receivable for school districts in the region, otherwise customers received credit by using their own credit cards.

Bakel's duties included being the company cashier, who received all the incoming mail payments on school accounts and the credit card account and all the cash and checks taken over the counter. Bakel prepared the bank deposit (and delivered the deposit to the bank), listing all the checks and currency, and also prepared a remittance worksheet (daily cash report) that showed amounts received, discounts allowed on school accounts, and amounts to credit to the accounts receivable. The remittance worksheet was used by another accountant to post credits to the accounts receivable. Bakel also reconciled the bank statement. No one else reviewed the deposits or the bank statements except the independent auditors.

Bakel opened a bank account in the name of Sport Equipment Company (SEC), after properly incorporating the company in the secretary of state's office. Over-the-counter cash and checks and school district payments were taken from the SEI receipts and deposited in the SEC account. (None of the customers noticed the difference between the rubber stamp endorsements for the two similarly named corporations, and neither did the bank.) SEC kept the money awhile, earning interest, then Bakel wrote SEC checks to SEI to replace the "borrowed" funds, in the meantime taking new SEI receipts for deposit to SEC.

Bakel also stole payments made by the school districts, depositing them to SEC. Later, Bakel deposited SEC checks in SEI, giving the schools credit, but approved an additional 2 percent discount in the process. Thus, the schools received proper credit later, and SEC paid less by the amount of the extra discounts.

PAPER TRAIL

SEI's bank deposits systematically showed fairly small currency deposits. Bakel was nervous about taking too many checks, so cash was preferred. The deposit slips also listed the SEC checks because bank tellers always compare the deposit slip listing to the checks submitted. The remittance worksheet showed different details: Instead of showing SEC checks, it showed receipts from school districts and currency, but not many over-the-counter checks from customers.

The transactions became complicated enough that Bakel had to use the microcomputer in the office to keep track of the school districts that needed to get credit. There were no vacations for this hardworking cashier because the discrepancies might be noticed by a substitute, and Bakel needed to give the districts credit later.

AMOUNT

Over a six-year period, Bakel built up a $150,000 average balance in the Sport Equipment Company (SEC) account, which earned a total of $67,500 interest that should have been earned by Sports Equipment, Inc. (SEI). By approving the "extra" discounts, Bakel skimmed 2 percent of $1 million in annual sales, for a total of $120,000. Since SEI would have had net income before taxes of about $1.6 million over this six years (about 9 percent on the sales dollar), Bakel's embezzlement took about 12.5 percent of the income.

AUDIT APPROACH

OBJECTIVE

Obtain evidence to determine whether the accounts receivable recorded on the books represent claims against real customers in the gross amounts recorded.

CONTROL

Authorization related to cash receipts, custody of cash, recording cash transactions, and bank statement reconciliation should be separate duties designed to prevent errors and frauds. Some supervision and detail review of one or more of these duties should be performed as a next-level control designed to detect errors and frauds, if they have occurred. For example, the remittance worksheet should be prepared by someone else, or at least the discounts should be approved by the controller; the bank reconciliation should be prepared by someone else.

Bakel had all the duties. (While recording was not actually performed, Bakel provided the source document—the remittance worksheet—the other accountant used to make the cash and accounts receivable entries.) According to the company president, the "control" was the diligence of "our" long-time, trusted, hard-working assistant controller. Note: An auditor who "thinks like a crook" to imagine ways Bakel could commit errors or fraud could think of this scheme for cash embezzlement and accounts receivable lapping.

TEST OF CONTROLS

Since the "control" purports to be Bakel's honest and diligent performance of the accounting and control activities that might have been performed by two or more people, the test of controls is an audit of cash receipts transactions as they relate to accounts receivable credit. The dual-direction samples and procedures are these:

Validity direction: Select a sample of customer accounts receivable, and vouch payment credits to remittance worksheets and bank deposits, including recalculation of discounts allowed in comparison to sales terms (2 percent), classification (customer name) identification, and correspondence of receipt date to recording date.

Completeness direction: Select a sample of remittance worksheets (or bank deposits), vouch details to bank deposit slips (trace details to remittance worksheets if the sample is bank deposits), and trace forward to complete accounting posting in customer accounts receivable.

AUDIT OF BALANCE

Since there is a control risk of incorrect accounting, perform the accounts receivable confirmation as of the year-end date. Confirm a sample of school district accounts, using positive confirmations. Blank confirmations may be used. Since there is a control risk, the "sample" may be all the accounts, if the number is not too large.

As prompted by notice of an oddity (noted in the discovery summary below), use the telephone book, chamber of commerce directory, local criss-cross directory, and a visit to the secretary of state's office to determine the location and identity of Sport Equipment Company.

DISCOVERY SUMMARY

The test of controls samples showed four cases of discrepancy, one of which is shown below.

The auditors sent positive confirmations on all 72 school district accounts. Three of the responses stated the districts had paid the balances before the confirmation date. Follow-up procedures on their accounts receivable credit in the next period showed they had received credit in remittance reports, and the bank deposits had shown no checks from the districts but had contained a check from Sports Equipment Company.

Investigation of SEC revealed the connection of Bakel, who was confronted and then confessed.

Bank Deposit Slip				
Jones	25			
Smith	35			
Hill District	980			
Sport Equipment	1,563			
Currency	540			
Deposit	3,143			

Cash Remittance Report				
Name	Amount	Discount	AR	Sales
Jones	25	0	0	25
Smith	5	0	0	35
Hill Dist.	980	20	1,000	0
Marlin Dist.	480	20	500	0
Waco Dist.	768	32	800	0
Currency	855	0	0	855
Totals	3,143	72	2,300	915

CASE 8.2
THE TAXMAN ALWAYS RINGS TWICE

PROBLEM

Overstated receivables for property taxes in a school district because the tax assessor stole some taxpayers' payments.

METHOD

J. Shelstad was the tax assessor-collector in the Ridge School District, serving a large metropolitan area. The staff processed tax notices on a computer system and generated 450,000 tax notices each October. An office copy was printed and used to check off "paid" when payments were received. Payments were processed by computer, and a master file of "accounts receivable" records (tax assessments, payments) was kept on the computer hard disk.

Shelstad was a good personnel manager, who often took over the front desk at lunchtime so the teller staff could enjoy lunch together. During these times, Shelstad took payments over the counter, gave the taxpayers a counter receipt, and pocketed some of the money, which was never entered in the computer system.

Shelstad resigned when he was elected to the Ridge school board. The district's assessor-collector office was eliminated upon the creation of a new countywide tax agency.

PAPER TRAIL

The computer records showed balances due from many taxpayers who had actually paid their taxes. The book of printed notices was not marked "paid" for many taxpayers who had received counter receipts. These records and the daily cash receipts reports (cash receipts journal) were available at the time the independent auditors performed the most recent annual audit in April. When Shelstad resigned in August, a power surge permanently destroyed the hard disk receivables file, and the cash receipts journals could not be found.

The new county agency managers noticed that the total of delinquent taxes disclosed in the audited financial statements was much larger than the total turned over to the country attorney for collection and foreclosure.

AMOUNT

Shelstad had been the assessor-collector for 15 years. The "good personnel manager" pocketed 100–150 counter payments each year, in amounts of $500–$2,500, stealing about $200,000 a year for a total of approximately $2.5 million. The district had assessed about $800–$900 million per year, so the annual theft was less than 1 percent. Nevertheless, the taxpayers got mad.

AUDIT APPROACH

OBJECTIVE

Obtain evidence to determine whether the receivables for taxes (delinquent taxes) represent genuine claims collectible from the taxpayers.

CONTROL

The school district had a respectable system for establishing the initial amounts of taxes receivable. The professional staff of appraisers and the independent appraisal review board established the tax base for each property. The school board set the price (tax rate). The computer system authorization for billing was validated on these two inputs.

The cash receipts system was well designed, calling for preparation of a daily cash receipts report (cash receipts journal that served as a source input for computer entry). This report was always reviewed by the "boss," Shelstad.

Unfortunately, Shelstad had the opportunity and power to override the controls and become both cash handler and supervisor. Shelstad made the decisions about sending delinquent taxes to the county attorney for collection, and the ones known to have been paid but stolen were withheld.

TEST OF CONTROLS

The auditors performed dual-direction sampling to test the processing of cash receipts.

Validity direction: Select a sample of receivables from the computer hard disk, and vouch (1) charges to the appraisal record, recalculating the amount using the authorized tax rate and (2) payments, if any, to the cash receipts journal and bank deposits. (The auditors found no exceptions.)

Completeness direction: Select a sample of properties from the appraisal rolls, and determine that tax notices had been sent and tax receivables (charges) recorded in the computer file. Select a sample of cash receipts reports, vouch them to bank deposits of the same amount and date, and trace the payments forward to credits to taxpayers' accounts. Select a sample of bank deposits, and trace them to cash receipts reports of the same amount and date. In one of these latter two samples, compare the details on bank deposits to the details on the cash receipts reports to determine whether the same taxpayers appear on both documents. (The auditors found no exceptions.)

AUDIT OF BALANCE

Confirm a sample of unpaid tax balances with taxpayers. Response rates may not be high, and follow-up procedures determining the ownership (county title files) may need to be performed, and new confirmations may need to be sent.

Determine that proper disclosure is made of the total of delinquent taxes and the total of delinquencies turned over to the county attorney for collection proceedings.

DISCOVERY SUMMARY

Shelstad persuaded the auditors that the true "receivables" were the delinquencies turned over to the county attorney. The confirmation sample and other work was based on this population. Thus, confirmations were not sent to fictitious balances that Shelstad knew had been paid, and the auditors never had the opportunity to receive "I paid" complaints from taxpayers.

The new managers of the countywide tax district were not influenced by Shelstad. They questioned the discrepancy between the delinquent taxes in the audit report and the lower amount turned over for collection. Since the computer file was not usable, the managers had to use the printed book of tax notices, where paid accounts had been marked "paid." (Shelstad had not marked the stolen ones "paid" so the printed book would agree with the computer file.) Tax due notices were sent to the taxpayers with unpaid balances, and they began to show up bringing their counter receipts and loud complaints.

In a fit of audit overkill, the independent auditors had earlier photocopied the entire set of cash receipts reports (cash journal), and they were then able to determine that the counter receipts (all signed by Shelstad) had not been deposited or entered. Shelstad was prosecuted and sentenced to a jail term.

CASE 8.3
BILL OFTEN, BILL EARLY

PROBLEM

Overstated sales and receivables, understated discounts expense, and overstated net income resulted from recording sales too early and failure to account for customer discounts taken.

METHOD

McGossage Company experienced profit pressures for two years in a row. Actual profits were squeezed in a recessionary economy, but the company reported net income decreases that were not as severe as other companies in the industry.

Sales were recorded in the grocery products division for orders that had been prepared for shipment but not actually shipped until later. Employees backdated the shipping documents. Gross profit on these "sales" was about 30 percent. Customers took discounts on payments, but the company did not record them, leaving the debit balances in the customers' accounts receivable instead of charging them to discounts and allowances expense. Company accountants were instructed to wait 60 days before recording discounts taken.

The division vice president and general manager knew about these accounting practices, as did a significant number of the 2,500 employees in the division. The division managers were under orders from headquarters to achieve profit objectives they considered unrealistic.

PAPER TRAIL

The customers' accounts receivable balances contained amounts due for discounts the customers already had taken. The cash receipts records showed payments received without credit for discounts. Discounts were entered monthly by a special journal entry.

The unshipped goods were on the shipping dock at year-end with papers showing earlier shipping dates.

AMOUNT

As misstatements go, some of these were on the materiality borderline. Sales were overstated 0.3 percent and 0.5 percent in the prior and current year, respectively. Accounts receivable were overstated 4 percent and 8 percent. But the combined effect was to overstate the division's net income by 6 percent and 17 percent. Selected data were:

| | One Year Ago* | | Current Year* | |
	Reported	Actual	Reported	Actual
Sales	$330.0	$329.0	$350.0	$348.0
Discounts expense	1.7	1.8	1.8	2.0
Net income	6.7	6.3	5.4	4.6

*Dollars in millions.

AUDIT APPROACH

OBJECTIVE

Obtain evidence to determine whether sales were recorded in the proper period and whether gross accounts receivable represented the amounts due from customers at year-end. Obtain evidence to determine whether discounts expense was recognized in the proper amount in the proper period.

CONTROL

The accounting manual should provide instructions to record sales on the date of shipment (or when title passes, if later). Management subverted this control procedure by having shipping employees date the shipping papers incorrectly.

Cash receipts procedures should provide for authorizing and recording discounts when they are taken by customers. Management overrode this control instruction by giving instructions to delay the recording.

TEST OF CONTROLS

Questionnaires and inquiries should be used to determine the company's accounting policies. It is possible that employees and managers would lie to the auditors to conceal the policies. It is also possible that pointed questions about revenue recognition and discount recording policies would elicit answers to reveal the practices. *For detail procedures:* Select a sample of cash receipts, examine them for authorization, recalculate the customer discounts, trace them to accounts receivable input for recording of the proper amount on the proper date. Select a sample of shipping documents and vouch them to customer orders, then trace them to invoices and to recording in the accounts receivable input with proper amounts on the proper date. These tests follow the *tracing direction*—starting with data that represent the beginning of transactions (cash receipts, shipping) and tracing them through the company's accounting process.

AUDIT OF BALANCE

Confirm a sample of customer accounts. Use analytical relationships of past years' discount expense to a relevant base (sales, sales volume) to calculate an overall test of the discounts expense.

DISCOVERY SUMMARY

The managers lied to the auditors about their revenue and expense timing policies. The sample of shipping documents showed no dating discrepancies because the employees had inserted incorrect dates. The analytical procedures on discounts did not show the misstatement because the historical relationships were too erratic to show a deficient number (outlier). However, the sample of cash receipts transactions showed that discounts were not calculated and recorded at time of receipt. Additional inquiry led to discovery of the special journal entries and knowledge of the recording delay. Two customers in the sample of 65 confirmations responded with exceptions that turned out to be unrecorded discounts.

Two other customers in the confirmation sample complained that they did not owe for late invoices on December 31. Follow-up showed the shipments were goods noticed on the shipping dock. Auditors taking the physical inventory noticed the goods on the shipping dock during the December 31 inventory taking. Inspection revealed the shipping documents dated December 26. When the auditors traced these shipments to the sales recording, they found them recorded "bill and hold" on December 29. (These procedures were performed and the results obtained by a successor audit firm in the third year!)

CASE 8.4
THANK GOODNESS IT'S FRIDAY

PROBLEM

Overstated sales caused overstated net income, retained earnings, current assets, working capital, and total assets. Overstated cash collections did not change the total current assets or total assets, but it increased the amount of cash and decreased the amount of accounts receivable.

METHOD

Alpha Brewery Corporation generally has good control policies and activities related to authorization of transactions for accounting entry, and the accounting manual has instructions for recording sales transactions in the proper accounting period. The company regularly closes the accounting process each Friday at 5 P.M. to prepare weekly management reports. The year-end date (cutoff date) is December 31, and, this year, December 31 was a Monday. However, the accounting was performed through Friday as usual, and the accounts were closed for the year on January 4.

PAPER TRAIL

All the entries were properly dated after December 31, including the sales invoices, cash receipts, and shipping documents. However, the trial balance from which the financial statements were prepared was dated December 31, (this year). Nobody noticed the slip of a few days because the Friday closing was normal.

AMOUNT

Alpha recorded sales of $672,000 and gross profit of $268,800 over the January 1–4 period. Cash collections on customers' accounts were recorded in the amount of $800,000.

AUDIT APPROACH

OBJECTIVE

Obtain evidence to determine the existence, completeness, and valuation of sales for the year ended December 31, and cash and accounts receivable as of December 31.

CONTROL

The company had in place the proper instructions to people to date transactions on the actual date on which they occurred and to enter sales and cost of goods sold on the day of shipment and to enter cash receipts on the day received in the company offices. An accounting supervisor should have checked the entries through Friday to make sure the dates corresponded with the actual events, and that the accounts for the year were closed with Monday's transactions.

TEST OF CONTROLS

In this case, the auditors need to be aware of the company's weekly routine closing and the possibility that the intervention of the December 31 date might cause a problem. Asking the question: "Did you cut off the accounting on Monday night this week?" might elicit the "Oh, we forgot!" response. Otherwise, it is normal to sample transactions around the year-end date to determine whether they were recorded in the proper accounting period.

The procedure: Select transactions 7–10 days before and after the year-end date, and inspect the dates on supporting documentation for evidence of accounting in the proper period.

AUDIT OF BALANCE

The audit for sales overstatement is partly accomplished by auditing the cash and accounts receivable at December 31 for overstatement (the dangling debit location). Confirm a sample of accounts receivable. If the accounts are too large, the auditors expect the debtors to say so, thus leading to detection of sales overstatements.

Cash overstatement is audited by auditing the bank reconciliation to see whether deposits in transit (the deposits sent late in December) actually cleared the bank early in January. Obviously, the

January 4 cash collections could not reach the bank until at least Monday, January 7. That's too long for a December 31 deposit to be in transit to a local bank.

The completeness of sales recordings is audited by selecting a sample of sales transactions (and supporting shipping documents) in the early part of the next accounting period (January next year). One way this year's sales could be incomplete would be to postpone recording December shipments until January, and this procedure will detect them if the shipping documents are dated properly.

The completeness of cash collections (and accounts receivable credits) are audited by auditing the cash deposits early in January to see whether there is any sign of holding cash without entry until January.

In this case, the existence objective is more significant for discovery of the problem than the completeness objective. After all, the January 1–4 sales, shipments, and cash collections did not "exist" in December this year.

DISCOVERY SUMMARY

The test of controls sample from the days before and after December 31 quickly revealed the problem. Company accounting personnel were embarrassed, but there was no effort to misstate the financial statements. This was a simple error. The company readily made the following adjustment:

	Debit	Credit
Sales	$672,000	
Inventory	403,200	
Accounts receivable	800,000	
Accounts receivable		$672,000
Cost of goods sold		403,200
Cash		800,000

REVIEW CHECKPOINTS

8.25 What are the goals of dual-direction sampling in regard to an audit of the accounts receivable and cash collection system?

8.26 In the case of The Canny Cashier, name one bank reconciliation control activity that could have revealed signs of the embezzlement.

8.27 What feature(s) of a cash receipts internal control system would be expected to prevent the cash receipts journal and recorded cash sales from reflecting more than the amount shown on the daily deposit slip?

8.28 In the case of The Taxman Always Rings Twice, what information could have been obtained from confirmations directed to the real population of delinquent accounts?

8.29 In the case of Bill Often, Bill Early, what information might have been obtained from inquiries? From detail test of controls procedures? From observations? From confirmations?

8.30 With reference to the case of Thank Goodness It's Friday, what contribution could an understanding of the business and the management reporting system have made to discovery of the open cash receipts journal cutoff error?

SUMMARY

The revenue and collection cycle consists of customer order processing, credit checking, shipping goods, billing customers and accounting for accounts receivable, and collecting and accounting for cash receipts. Companies reduce control risk by having a suitable separation of authorization, custody, recording, and periodic reconciliation duties. Error-checking activities of comparing customer orders and shipping documents are important for billing customers the right prices for the delivered quantities. Otherwise, many things could go wrong—ranging from making sales to fictitious customers or customers with bad credit to erroneous billings for the wrong quantities at the wrong prices at the wrong time.

Cash collection is a critical point for asset control. Many cases of embezzlement occur in this process. Illustrative cases in the chapter tell the stories of some of these cash embezzlement schemes, including the practice of "lapping" accounts receivable.

Three topics have special technical notes in the chapter. The *existence assertion* is very important in the audit of cash and receivables assets because misleading financial statements often contain overstated assets and revenue. The *use of confirmations* gets a special section because auditors frequently use confirmations to obtain evidence of asset existence from outside parties, such as customers who owe on accounts receivable. The *audit of bank reconciliations* is covered in the context of an audit opportunity to recalculate the amount of cash for the financial statements and to look for signs of accounts receivable lapping and check kiting. The *schedule of interbank transfers* and the *proof of cash* methods are tools auditors can use to find unrecorded cash transactions.

MULTIPLE-CHOICE QUESTIONS FOR PRACTICE AND REVIEW

8.31   Which of the following would be the best protection for a company that wishes to prevent the "lapping" of trade accounts receivable?
    a. Segregate duties so that the bookkeeper in charge of the general ledger has no access to incoming mail.
    b. Segregate duties so that no employee has access to both checks from customers and currency from daily cash receipts.
    c. Have customers send payments directly to the company's depository bank.
    d. Request that customer's payment checks be made payable to the company and addressed to the treasurer.

8.32   Which of the following internal control activities will most likely prevent the concealment of a cash shortage from the improper write-off of a trade account receivable?
    a. Write-off must be approved by a responsible officer after review of credit department recommendations and supporting evidence.
    b. Write-offs must be supported by an aging schedule showing that only receivables overdue several months have been written off.
    c. Write-offs must be approved by the cashier who is in a position to know if the receivables have, in fact, been collected.
    d. Write-offs must be authorized by company field sales employees who are in a position to determine the financial standing of the customers.

8.33   Auditors sometimes use comparisons of ratios as audit evidence. For example, an unexplained decrease in the ratio of gross profit to sales may suggest which of the following possibilities?
    a. Unrecorded purchases.
    b. Unrecorded sales.
    c. Merchandise purchases being charged to selling and general expense.
    d. Fictitious sales.

8.34   An auditor is auditing sales transactions. One step is to vouch a sample of debit entries from the accounts receivable subsidiary ledger back to the supporting sales invoices. What would the auditor intend to establish by this step?
    a. Sales invoices represent bona fide sales.

b. All sales have been recorded.

c. All sales invoices have been properly posted to customer accounts.

d. Debit entries in the accounts receivable subsidiary ledger are properly supported by sales invoices.

8.35 To conceal defalcations involving receivables, the auditor would expect an experienced bookkeeper to charge which of the following accounts?

a. Miscellaneous income.

b. Petty cash.

c. Miscellaneous expense.

d. Sales returns.

8.36 Which of the following would the auditor consider to be an incompatible operation if the cashier receives remittances?

a. The cashier prepares the daily deposit.

b. The cashier makes the daily deposit at a local bank.

c. The cashier posts the receipts to the accounts receivable subsidiary ledger cards.

d. The cashier endorses the checks.

8.37 The audit working papers often include a client-prepared, aged trial balance of accounts receivable as of the balance sheet date. The aging is best used by the auditor to

a. Evaluate internal control over credit sales.

b. Test the accuracy of recorded charge sales.

c. Estimate credit losses.

d. Verify the existence of the recorded receivables.

8.38 Which of the following might be detected by an auditor's cutoff review and examination of sales journal entries for several days prior to the balance sheet date?

a. Lapping year-end accounts receivable.

b. Inflating sales for the year.

c. Kiting bank balances.

d. Misappropriating merchandise.

8.39 Confirmation of individual accounts receivable balances directly with debtors will, of itself, normally provide evidence concerning the

a. Collectibility of the balances confirmed.

b. Ownership of the balances confirmed.

c. Existence of the balances confirmed.

d. Internal control over balances confirmed.

8.40 Which of the following is one of the better auditing procedures that might be used by an auditor to detect kiting between intercompany banks?

a. Review composition of authenticated deposit slips.

b. Review subsequent bank statements.

c. Prepare a schedule of the bank transfers.

d. Prepare a year-end bank reconciliation.

8.41 Which of the following is the best reason for prenumbering in numerical sequence such documents as sales orders, shipping documents, and sales invoices?

a. Enables company personnel to determine the accuracy of each document.

b. Enables personnel to determine the proper period recording of sales revenue and receivables.

c. Enables personnel to check the numerical sequence for missing documents and unrecorded transactions.

d. Enables personnel to determine the validity of recorded transactions.

8.42 When a sample of customer accounts receivable are selected for the purpose of vouching debits therein for validity evidence, the auditors will vouch them to

a. Sales invoices with shipping documents and customer sales invoices.

b. Records of accounts receivable write-offs.

c. Cash remittance lists and bank deposit slips.

d. Credit files and reports.

8.43 In the audit of cash and accounts receivable, the most important emphasis should be on the

a. Completeness assertions.

b. Existence assertion.

c. Obligations assertions.

d. Presentation and disclosure assertion.

8.44 When accounts receivable are confirmed at an interim date, the auditors need not be concerned with

a. Obtaining a summary of receivables transactions from the interim date to the year-end date.

b. Obtaining a year-end trial balance of receivables, comparing it to the interim trial balance, and obtaining evidence and explanations for large variations.

c. Sending negative confirmations to all the customers as of the year-end date.

d. Considering the necessity for some additional confirmations as of the balance sheet date if balances have increased materially.

8.45 The negative request form of accounts receivable confirmation is useful particularly when the

Assessed level of control risk relating to receivables is	Number of small balances is	Proper consideration by the recipient is
a. Low	Many	Likely
b. Low	Few	Unlikely
c. High	Few	Likely
d. High	Many	Likely

(AICPA adapted)

8.46 When an auditor selects a sample of shipping documents and takes the tracing direction of a test to find the related sales invoice copies, the evidence is relevant for deciding
   a. Shipments to customers were invoiced.
   b. Shipments to customers were recorded as sales.
   c. Recorded sales were shipped.
   d. Invoiced sales were shipped.

(AICPA adapted)

8.47 Immediately upon receipt of cash, a responsible employee should
   a. Record the amount in the cash receipts journal.
   b. Prepare a remittance listing.
   c. Update the subsidiary accounts receivable records.
   d. Prepare a deposit slip in triplicate.

(AICPA adapted)

8.48 Upon receipt of customers' checks in the mail room, a responsible employee should

prepare a remittance listing that is forwarded to the cashier. A copy of the listing should be sent to the
   a. Internal auditor to investigate the listing for unusual transactions.
   b. Treasurer to compare the listing with the monthly bank statement.
   c. Accounts receivable bookkeeper to update the subsidiary accounts receivable records.
   d. Entity's bank to compare the listing with the cashier's deposit slip.

(AICPA adapted)

8.49 Cash receipts from sales on account have been misappropriated. Which of the following acts would conceal this defalcation and be least likely to be detected by an auditor?
   a. Understating the sales journal.
   b. Overstating the accounts receivable control account.
   c. Overstating the accounts receivable subsidiary ledger.
   d. Understating the cash receipts journal.

(AICPA adapted)

8.50 Which of the following internal control activities most likely would deter tapping of collections from customers?
   a. Independent internal verification of dates of entry in the cash receipts journal with dates of daily cash summaries.
   b. Authorization of write-offs of uncollectible accounts by a supervisor independent of credit approval.
   c. Segregation of duties between receiving cash and posting the accounts receivable ledger.
   d. Supervisory comparison of the daily cash summary with the sum of the cash receipts journal entries.

(AICPA adapted)

EXERCISES AND PROBLEMS

8.51   Cash Receipts: Control Objectives and Control Examples.   Prepare a table similar to Exhibit 8–4 (Internal Control Objectives) for cash receipts.

8.52   Internal Control Questionnaire for Book Buy-Back Cash Fund.   Taylor, a CPA, has been engaged to audit the financial statements of University Books, Incorporated. University Books maintains a large, revolving cash fund exclusively for the purpose of buying used books

from students for cash. The cash fund is active all year because the nearby university offers a large variety of courses with varying starting and completion dates throughout the year.

Receipts are prepared for each purchase. Reimbursement vouchers periodically are submitted to replenish the fund.

Required:
Construct an internal control questionnaire to be used in evaluating the system of internal control

over University Books' buying back books using the revolving cash fund. The internal control questionnaire should elicit a yes or no response to each question. *Do not discuss the internal controls over books that are purchased.*

(AICPA adapted)

8.53   Test of Controls Audit Procedures for Cash Receipts.   You are the in-charge auditor examining the financial statements of the Gutzler Company for the year ended December 31. During late October you, with the help of Gutzler's controller, completed an internal control questionnaire and prepared the appropriate memoranda describing Gutzler's accounting procedures. Your comments relative to cash receipts are as follows:

All cash receipts are sent directly to the accounts receivable clerk with no processing by the mail department. The accounts receivable clerk keeps the cash receipts journal, prepares the bank deposit slip in duplicate, posts from the deposit slip to the subsidiary accounts receivable ledger, and mails the deposit to the bank.

The controller receives the validated deposit slips directly (unopened) from the bank. She also receives the monthly bank statement directly (unopened) from the bank and promptly reconciles it.

At the end of each month, the accounts receivable clerk notifies the general ledger clerk by journal voucher of the monthly totals of the cash receipts journal for posting to the general ledger.

Each month, with regard to the general ledger cash account, the general ledger clerk makes an entry to record the total debits to Cash from the cash receipts journal. In addition, the general ledger clerk, on occasion, makes debit entries in the general ledger Cash account from sources other than the cash receipts journal; for example, funds borrowed from the bank.

Certain standard auditing procedures listed below already have been performed by you in the audit of cash receipts:

All columns in the cash receipts have been totaled and cross-totaled.

Postings from the cash receipts journal have been traced to the general ledger.

Remittance advices and related correspondence have been traced to entries in the cash receipts journal.

Required:

Considering Gutzler's internal control over cash receipts and the standard auditing procedures already performed, list all other auditing procedures that should be performed to obtain sufficient audit evidence regarding cash receipts control and give the reasons for each procedure. Do not discuss the procedures for cash disbursements and cash balances. Also, do not discuss the extent to which any of the procedures are to be performed. Assume adequate controls exist to ensure that all sales transactions are recorded. Organize your answer sheet as follows:

Other Audit Procedure	Reason for Other Audit Procedures

(AICPA adapted)

Cash: Substantive Audit Procedures

8.54   Procedures for Auditing a Client's Bank Reconciliation.   Auditors normally will find the items lettered A–F in a client-prepared bank reconciliation.

GENERAL COMPANY
Bank Reconciliation
1st National Bank
September 30

A.	Balance per bank		$28,375
B.	Deposits in transit		
	Sept 29	$4,500	
	Sept 30	1,525	6,025
			34,400
C.	Outstanding checks:		
	# 988 Aug 31	$2,200	
	#1281 Sept 26	675	
	#1285 Sept 27	850	
	#1289 Sept 29	2,500	
	#1292 Sept 30	7,255	(11,450)
			20,950
D.	Customer note collected by the bank:		(3,000)
E.	Error: Check #1282, written on Sept 26 for $270 was erroneously charged by bank as $720; bank was notified Oct 2		450
F.	Balance per books		$20,400

Required:

Assume these facts: On October 11, the auditor received a cutoff bank statement dated October 7. The Sept 30 deposit in transit; the outstanding checks #1281, #1285, #1289, and #1292; and the correction of the bank error regarding check #1282 appeared on the cutoff bank statement.

a. For each of the lettered items A–F above, select one or more of the procedures 1–10 below which you believe the auditor should perform to obtain evidence about the item. These procedures may be selected once, more than once, or not at all. Be prepared to explain the reasons for your choices.

1. Trace to cash receipts journal.

2. Trace to cash disbursements journal.

3. Compare to the September 30 general ledger.

4. Confirm directly with the bank.

5. Inspect bank credit memo.

6. Inspect bank debit memo.

7. Ascertain reason for unusual delay, if any.

8. Inspect supporting documents for reconciling items that do not appear on the cutoff bank statement.

9. Trace items on the bank reconciliation to the cutoff bank statement.

10. Trace items on the cutoff bank statement to the bank reconciliation.

b. Auditors ordinarily foot a client-prepared bank reconciliation. If the auditors had performed this recalculation on the bank reconciliation shown above, what might they have found? Be prepared to discuss any findings.

(AICPA adapted)

8.55   Proof of Cash.   You can use the computer-based *Electronic Workpapers* on the course website to prepare the proof of cash required in this problem.

The auditors of Steffey, Ltd., decided to study the cash receipts and disbursements for the month of July of the current year under audit. They obtained the bank reconciliations and the cash journals prepared by the company accountants. They showed the following:

June 30: Bank balance $355,001; deposits in transit $86,899; outstanding checks $42,690; general ledger cash balance $399,210.

July: Cash receipts journal $650,187; cash disbursements journal $565,397.

July 31: Bank balance $506,100; deposits in transit $51,240; outstanding checks $73,340; general ledger cash balance $484,000. Bank statement record of deposits: $835,846; of payments: $684,747.

Required:

Prepare a four-column proof of cash (see Exhibit 8–14 for an example) covering the month of July of the current year. Identify problems, if any.

Receivables and Revenues: Substantive Audit Procedures

8.56   Confirmation of Trade Accounts Receivable.   King, CPA, is auditing the financial statements of Cycle Company, a client that has receivables from customers arising from the sale of goods in the normal course of business. King is aware that the confirmation of accounts receivable is a generally accepted auditing procedure.

Required:

a. Under what circumstances could King justify omitting the confirmation of Cycle's accounts receivable?

b. In designing confirmation requests, what factors are likely to affect King's assessment of the reliability of confirmations that King sends?

c. What alternative procedures could King consider performing when replies to positive confirmation requests are not received.

8.57   Audit Objectives and Procedures for Accounts Receivable.   In the audit of trade accounts receivable, auditors develop specific audit assertions related to the receivables. They then design specific substantive (balance-audit) procedures to obtain evidence about each of these assertions. Here is a selection of accounts receivable assertions:

a. Accounts receivable represent all amounts owed to the client company at the balance sheet date.

b. The client company has legal right to all accounts receivable at the balance sheet date.

c. Accounts receivable are stated at net realizable value.

d. Accounts receivable are properly described and presented in the financial statements.

Required:

For each of these assertions, select the audit procedure (below) that is best suited for the audit program. Select only one procedure for each audit objective. A procedure may be selected once or not at all.

1. Analyze the relationship of accounts receivable and sales and compare with relationships for preceding periods.

2. Perform sales cutoff tests to obtain assurance that sales transactions and corresponding entries for inventories and cost of goods sold are recorded in the same and proper period.

3. Review the aged trial balance for significant past due accounts.

4. Obtain an understanding of the business purpose of transactions that resulted in accounts receivable balances.

5. Review loan agreements for indications of whether accounts receivable have been factored or pledged.

6. Review the accounts receivable trial balance for amounts due from officers and employees.

7. Analyze unusual relationships between monthly accounts receivable and monthly accounts payable balances.

(AICPA adapted)

DISCUSSION CASES

8.58 Interbank Transfers. You can use the computer-based *Electronic Workpapers* on the course website to prepare the schedule of interbank transfers required in this problem.

EverReady Corporation is in the home building and repair business. Construction business has been in a slump, and the company has experienced financial difficulty over the past two years. Part of the problem lies in the company's desire to avoid laying off its skilled crews of bricklayers and cabinetmakers. Meeting the payroll has been a problem.

The auditors are engaged to audit the 2001 financial statements. Knowing of EverReady's financial difficulty and its business policy, the auditors decided to prepare a schedule of interbank transfers covering the 10 days before and after December 31, which is the company's balance sheet date.

First, the auditors used the cash receipts and disbursements journals to prepare part of the schedule shown in Exhibit 8.58–1 below. They obtained the information for everything except the dates of deposit and payment in the bank statements (disbursing date per bank, and receiving date per bank). They learned that EverReady always transferred money to the payroll account at 1st National Bank from the general account at 1st National Bank. This transfer enabled the bank to clear the payroll checks without delay. The only bank accounts in the EverReady financial statements are the two at 1st National Bank.

Next, the auditors obtained the December 2001 and January 2002 bank statements for the general and payroll accounts at 1st National Bank. They recorded the bank disbursement and receipt dates in the schedule of interbank

---

EXHIBIT 8.58–1   SCHEDULE OF INTERBANK TRANSFERS

C-5

EVERREADY CORPORATION
Schedule of Interbank Transfers
December 31, 2001

Prepared _____
Date _____
Reviewed _____
Date _____

| | *Disbursing Account* | | | | *Receiving Account* | | | |
Check #	Bank	Amount	Date per Books	Date per Bank	Bank	Date per Books	Date per Bank
1417	1st Nat'l	9,463√	24-Dec	24-Dec μ	1st Nat Payroll	24-Dec τ	24-Dec ν
1601	1st Nat'l	11,593√	31-Dec b	31-Dec μ	1st Nat Payroll	31-Dec τ	31-Dec ν
1982	1st Nat'l	9,971√	08-Jan	08-Jan μ	1st Nat Payroll	08-Jan τ	08-Jan ν

√ Traced from cash disbursements journal.

b Check properly listed as outstanding on bank reconciliation.

μ Vouched to check cleared in bank statement.

τ Traced from cash receipts journal.

ν Vouched deposit cleared in bank statement.

Note: We scanned the cash disbursements and cash receipts journals for checks to and deposits from other bank accounts.

transfers. For each transfer, these dates are identical because the accounts are in the same bank. An alert auditor noticed that the 1st National Bank general account bank statement also contains deposits received from Citizen National Bank and canceled check number 1799 dated January 5 payable to Citizen National Bank. This check cleared the 1st National Bank account on January 8 and was marked "transfer of funds." This led to new information.

New Information

Asked about the Citizen National Bank transactions, EverReady's chief financial officer readily admitted the existence of an off-books bank account. He explained that it was used for financing transactions in keeping with normal practice in the construction industry. He gave the auditors the December and January bank statements for the account at Citizen National Bank. In it, the auditors found the following:

Citizen National Bank

Check #	Payable to	Amount	Dated	Cleared Bank
4050	1st National	10,000	23-Dec	29-Dec
4051	Chase Bank	12,000	28-Dec	31-Dec
4052	1st National	12,000	30-Dec	05-Jan
4053	Chase Bank	14,000	4-Jan	07-Jan
4054	1st National	20,000	8-Jan	13-Jan

Deposits

Received from	Amount	Dated
Chase Bank	11,000	22-Dec
Chase Bank	15,000	30-Dec
1st National	10,000	05-Jan
Chase Bank	12,000	07-Jan

When asked about the Chase Bank transactions, EverReady's chief financial officer admitted the existence of another off-books bank account, which he said was the personal account of the principal stockholder. He explained that the stockholder often used it to finance EverReady's operations. He gave the auditors the December and January bank statements for this account at Chase Bank; in it, the auditors found the following:

Chase Bank

Check #	Payable to	Amount	Dated	Cleared Bank
2220	Citizen Bank	11,000	22-Dec	28-Dec
2221	Citizen Bank	15,000	30-Dec	05-Jan
2222	Citizen Bank	12,000	7-Jan	12-Jan

Deposits

Received from	Amount	Dated
Citizen Bank	12,000	28-Dec
Citizen Bank	14,000	04-Jan

An abbreviated calendar for the period is in Exhibit 8.58–2.

Required:

a. Complete the Schedule of Interbank Transfers (working paper C-5, Exhibit 8.58–1) by entering the new information.

b. What is the actual cash balance for the four bank accounts combined, considering only the amounts given in this case information, as of December 31, 2001 (before any of the December 31 payroll checks are cashed by employees)? As of January 8, 2002 (before any of the January 8 payroll checks are cashed by

EXHIBIT 8.58–2 CALENDAR

	S	M	T	W	T	F	S
December 2001	20	21	22	23	24	25	26
	27	28	29	30	31		
January 2002						1	2
	3	4	5	6	7	8	9
	10	11	12	13	14	15	16

employees)? (Hint: Prepare a schedule of bank and actual balances.)

8.59 Manipulated Bank Reconciliation.
You can use the computer-based *Electronic Workpapers* on the textbook website to prepare the bank reconciliation solution.

Caulco, Inc., is the audit client. You have obtained the client-prepared bank reconciliation as of February 28 (below).

Required:
Check #2231 was the first check written in February. All earlier checks cleared the bank, some in the January bank statement and some in the February bank statement.

Assume that the only February-dated canceled checks returned in the March bank statement are #2239 and #2240, showing the amounts listed in the February bank reconciliation. They cleared the bank on March 3 and March 2, respectively. The first deposit on the March bank statement was $1,097.69, credited on March 3. Assume further that all checks entered in Caulco's cash disbursements journal through February 29 have either cleared the bank or are listed as outstanding checks in the February bank reconciliation.

Examine the February bank statement in Exhibit 7–3 (Chapter 7). Determine whether anything is wrong with the bank statement and the bank reconciliation. If anything is wrong, prepare a corrected reconciliation and explain the problem.

CAULCO, INC.
Bank Reconciliation
February 28

Balance per bank $7,374.93
Deposit in transit 1,097.69
Outstanding checks

#	Date	Payee	Amount	
2239	Feb 26	Alpha Supply	500.00	
2240	Feb 28	L.C. Stateman	254.37	
Total outstanding				(754.37)
General ledger balance Feb. 28				$7,718.25

8.60 Overstated Sales and Accounts Receivable.
This case is designed like the ones in the chapter. Your assignment is to write the "audit approach" portion of the case, organized around these sections:

Objective: Express the objective in terms of the facts supposedly asserted in financial records, accounts, and statements.

Control: Write a brief explanation of desirable controls, missing controls, and especially the kinds of "deviations" that might arise from the situation described in the case.

Test of controls: Write some procedures for getting evidence about existing controls, especially procedures that could discover deviations from controls. If there are no controls to test, then there are no procedures to perform; go then to the next section. A "procedure" should instruct someone about the source(s) of evidence to tap and the work to do.

Audit of balance: Write some procedures for getting evidence about the existence, completeness, valuation, ownership, or disclosure assertions identified in your objective section above.

Discovery summary: Write a short statement about the discovery you expect to accomplish with your procedures.

Ring Around the Revenue

Problem: Sales were recorded early, sometimes at fictitiously high prices, overstating sales revenue, accounts receivable, and income.

Method: Mattox Toy Manufacturing Company had experienced several years of good business. Income had increased steadily, and the common stock was a favorite among investors. Management had confidently predicted continued growth and prosperity. But business turned worse instead of better. Competition became fierce.

In earlier years, Mattox had accommodated a few large retail customers with the practice of field warehousing coupled with a "bill and hold" accounting procedure. These large retail customers executed noncancellable written agreements, asserting their purchase of toys and their obligation to pay. The toys were not actually shipped because the customers did not have available warehouse space. They were set aside in segregated areas on the Mattox premises and identified as the customers' property. Mattox would later drop-ship the toys to various retail locations upon instructions from the customers. The "field warehousing" was explained as Mattox serving as a temporary warehouse and storage location for the customers' toys. In the related bill and hold accounting procedure, Mattox prepared invoices billing the customers, mailed the invoices to the customers, and recorded the sales and accounts receivable.

When business took the recent downturn, Mattox expanded its field warehousing and its bill and hold accounting practices. Invoices were recorded for customers who did not execute the written agreements used in previous arrangements. Some customers signed the noncancellable written agreements with clauses permitting subsequent inspection, acceptance, and determination of discounted prices. The toys were not always set aside in separate areas, and this failure later gave shipping employees problems with identifying shipments of toys that had been "sold" earlier and those that had not.

Mattox also engaged in over billing. Customers who ordered closeout toys at discounted prices were billed at regular prices, even though the customers' orders showed the discounted prices agreed by Mattox sales representatives.

In a few cases, the bill and hold invoices and the closeout sales were billed and recorded in duplicate. In most cases, the customers' invoices were addressed and mailed to specific individuals in the customers' management instead of the routine mailing to the customers' accounts payable departments.

Paper trail: The field warehousing arrangements were well known and acknowledged in the Mattox accounting manual. Related invoices were stamped "bill and hold." Customer orders and agreements were attached in a document file. Sales of closeout toys also were stamped "close-out," indicating the regular prices (basis for salespersons' commissions) and the invoice prices. Otherwise, the accounting for sales and accounts receivable was unexceptional. Efforts to record these sales in January (last month of the fiscal year) caused the month's sales revenue to be 35 percent higher than the January of the previous year.

In the early years of the practice, inventory sold under the field warehousing arrangements (both regular and close-out toys) was segregated and identified. The shipping orders for these toys left the "carrier name" and "shipping date" blank, even though they were signed and dated by a company employee in the spaces for the company representative and the carrier representative signature.

The lack of inventory segregation caused problems for the company. After the fiscal year-end, Mattox solved the problem by reversing $6.9 million of the $14 million bill and hold sales. This caused another problem because the reversal was larger than the month's sales, causing the sales revenue for first month of the next year to be a negative number!

Amount: Company officials' reasons for the validity of recognizing sales revenue and receivables on the bill and hold procedure and field warehousing were persuasive. After due consideration of the facts and circumstances, the company's own accountants agreed that the accounting practices appropriately accounted for revenue and receivables.

Mattox's abuse of the practices caused financial statements to be materially misstated. In January of the year in question, the company overstated sales by about $14 million, or 5 percent of the sales that should have been recorded. The gross profit of $7 million on these sales caused the income to be overstated by about 40 percent.

8.61   CAATS Application—Receivables Confirmation. You are using computer audit software to prepare accounts receivable confirmations during the annual audit of the Eastern Sunrise Services Club. The company has the following data files:

Master file—debtor credit record.

Master file—debtor name and address.

Master file—account detail:

   Ledger number.

   Sales code.

   Customer account number.

   Date of last billing.

   Balance (gross).

Discount available to customer (memo account only).

Date of last purchase.

The discount field represents the amount of discount available to the customer if the customer pays within 30 days of the invoicing date. The discount field is cleared for expired amounts during the daily updating. You have determined that this is properly executed.

Required:

List the information from the data files shown above that you would include on the confirmation requests. Identify the file from which the information can be obtained.

8.62   Rock Island Quarry—Evidence Collection in an Online System.   Your firm has audited the Rock Island Quarry Company for several years. Rock Island's main revenue comes from selling crushed rock to construction companies from several quarries owned by the company in Illinois and Iowa. The rock is priced by weight, quality, and crushed size.

Past Procedure:

Trucks owned by purchasing contractors or by Rock Island needed to display a current certified empty weight receipt or be weighed in. The quarry yard weighmaster recorded the empty weight on a handwritten "scale ticket" along with the purchasing company name, the truck number, and the date. After the truck was loaded, it was required to leave via the scale where the loaded weight and rock grade were recorded on the "scale tickets." The scale tickets were sorted weekly by grade and manually recorded on a summary sheet that was forwarded to the home office. Scale tickets were prenumbered and an accountant in the home office checked the sequence for missing numbers.

Revenue (and receivables) audit procedures involved evaluating the controls at selected quarries (rotated each year) and vouching a statistical sample of weight tickets to weekly summaries. Weekly summaries were traced through pricing and invoicing to the general ledger on a sample basis, and general ledger entries were vouched back to weekly summaries on a sample basis. Few material discrepancies were found.

New Procedures.

At the beginning of the current year, Rock Island converted to a local area network of personal computers to gather the information formerly entered manually on the "scale ticket." This conversion was done with your knowledge but without your advice or input. Now, all entering trucks must weigh in. The yard weighmaster enters NEW on the terminal keyboard, and a form appears on the screen that is similar to the old scale ticket, except the quarry number, transaction number, date, and incoming empty weight are automatically entered. Customer and truck numbers are keyed in. After the weigh-in, the weighmaster enters HOLD through the terminal. The weight ticket record is stored in the computer until weigh-out.

When a truck is loaded and stops on the scale, the weighmaster enters OLD and a directory of all open transactions appears on the screen. The weighmaster selects the proper one and enters OUT. The truck out-weight and the rock weight are computed and entered automatically. The weighmaster must enter the proper number for the rock grade. The weighmaster cannot change any automatically entered field. When satisfied that the screen weight ticket is correct, the weighmaster enters SOLD and the transaction is automatically transmitted to the home office computer, and the appropriate accounting database elements are updated. One copy of a scale ticket is printed and given to the truck driver. No written evidence of the sale is kept by Rock Island.

Required:

It is now midyear for Rock Island and you are planning for this year's audit.

a. What control procedures (manual and computer) should you expect to find in this system for recording quarry sales?

b. The computer programs that process the rock sales and perform the accounting reside at the home office and at the quarries. What implications does this have on your planned audit procedures?

c. What are you going to do to gather substantive audit evidence now that there are no written "scale tickets"?

APPENDIX 8A   INTERNAL CONTROLS

APPENDIX 8A–1   INTERNAL CONTROL QUESTIONNAIRE—CASH RECEIPTS PROCESSING

Environment:
1. Are receipts deposited daily, intact, and without delay?
2. Does someone other than the cashier or accounts receivable bookkeeper take the deposits to the bank?
3. Are the duties of the cashier entirely separate from record keeping for notes and accounts receivable? From general ledger record keeping?
4. Is the cashier denied access to receivables records or monthly statements?

Validity objective:
5. Is a bank reconciliation performed monthly by someone who does not have cash custody or record keeping responsibility?
6. Are the cash receipts journal entries compared to the remittance lists and deposit slips regularly?

Completeness objective:
7. Does the person who opens the mail make a list of cash received (a remittance list)?
8. Are currency receipts controlled by mechanical devices? Are machine totals checked by the internal auditor?
9. Are prenumbered sales invoice or receipts books used? Is the numerical sequence checked for missing documents?

Authorization objective:
10. Does a responsible person approve discounts taken by customers with payments on account?

Accuracy objective:
11. Is a duplicate deposit slip retained by the internal auditor or someone other than the employee making up the deposit?
12. Is the remittance list compared to the deposit by someone other than the cashier?

Classification objective:
13. Does the accounting manual contain instructions for classifying cash receipts credits?

Accounting and Posting objective:
14. Does someone reconcile the accounts receivable subsidiary to the control account regularly (to determine whether all entries were made to customers' accounts)?

Proper period objective:
15. Does the accounting manual contain instructions for dating cash receipts entries the same day as the date of receipt?

APPENDIX 8A-2   INTERNAL CONTROL QUESTIONNAIRE—SALES

Environment:

1. Is the credit department independent of the marketing department?
2. Are sales of the following types controlled by the same procedures described below? Sales to employees, COD sales, disposals of property, cash sales, and scrap sales.

Validity objective:

3. Is access to sales invoice blanks restricted?
4. Are prenumbered bills of lading or other shipping documents prepared or completed in the shipping department?

Completeness objective:

5. Are sales invoice blanks prenumbered?
6. Is the sequence checked for missing invoices?
7. Is the shipping document numerical sequence checked for missing bills of lading numbers?

Authorization objective:

8. Are all credit sales approved by the credit department prior to shipment?
9. Are sales prices and terms based on approved standards?
10. Are returned sales credits and other credits supported by documentation as to receipt, condition, and quantity, and approved by a responsible officer?

Accuracy objective:

11. Are shipped quantities compared to invoice quantities?
12. Are sales invoices checked for error in quantities, prices, extensions and footing, freight allowances, and checked with customers' orders?
13. Is there an overall check on arithmetic accuracy of period sales data by a statistical or product-line analysis?
14. Are periodic sales data reported directly to general ledger accounting independent of accounts receivable accounting?

Classification objective:

15. Does the accounting manual contain instructions for classifying sales?

Accounting and Posting objective:

16. Are summary journal entries approved before posting?

Proper period objective:

17. Does the accounting manual contain instructions to date sales invoices on the shipment date?

APPENDIX 8A–3   INTERNAL CONTROL QUESTIONNAIRE—ACCOUNTS AND NOTES RECEIVABLE

Environment:

1. Are customers' subsidiary records maintained by someone who has no access to cash?
2. Is the cashier denied access to the customers' records and monthly statements?
3. Are delinquent accounts listed periodically for review by someone other than the credit manager?
4. Are written-off accounts kept in a memo ledger or credit report file for periodic access?
5. Is the credit department separated from the sales department?
6. Are notes receivable in the custody of someone other than the cashier or accounts receivable record keeper?
7. Is custody of negotiable collateral in the hands of someone not responsible for handling cash or keeping records?

Validity objective:

8. Are customers' statements mailed monthly by the accounts receivable department?
9. Are direct confirmations of accounts and notes obtained periodically by the internal auditor?
10. Are differences reported by customers routed to someone outside the accounts receivable department for investigation?
11. Are returned goods checked against receiving reports?

Completeness objective:

(Refer to completeness questions in the sales and cash receipts questionnaires.)

12. Are credit memo documents prenumbered and the sequence checked for missing documents?

Authorization objective:

13. Is customer credit approved before orders are shipped?
14. Are write-offs, returns, and discounts allowed after discount date subject to approval by a responsible officer?
15. Are large loans or advances to related parties approved by the directors?

Accuracy objective:

16. Do the internal auditors confirm customer accounts periodically to determine accuracy?

Classification objective:

17. Are receivables from officers, directors, and affiliates identified separately in the accounts receivable records?

Accounting and Posting objective:

18. Does someone reconcile the accounts receivable subsidiary to the control account regularly?

Proper period objective:

(Refer to proper period objective questions in the sales and cash receipts questionnaires.)

APPENDIX 8A–4   SALES AND ACCOUNTS RECEIVABLE COMPUTER CONTROLS

- Each terminal performs only designated functions. For example, the terminal at the shipping dock cannot be used to enter initial sales information or to access the payroll database.
- An identification number and password (issued on an individual person basis) is required to enter the sale and each command that a subsequent action has been completed. Unauthorized entry attempts are logged and immediately investigated. Further, certain passwords have "read only" (cannot change any data) authorization. For example, the credit manager can determine the outstanding balance of any account or view on-line "reports" summarizing overdue accounts receivable, but cannot enter credit memos to change the balances.
- All input information is immediately logged to provide restart processing should any terminal become inoperative during the processing.
- A transaction code calls up on the terminals a full screen "form" that appears to the operator in the same format as the original paper documents. Each clerk must enter the information correctly or the computer will not accept the transaction. This is called **on-line input validation** and utilizes validation checks, such as missing data, check digit, and limit tests.
- All documents prepared by the computer are numbered, and the number is stored as part of the sales record in the accounts receivable database.
- A daily search of the pending order database is made by the computer, and sales orders outstanding more than seven days are listed on the terminal in marketing management.

APPENDIX 8B   SUBSTANTIVE AUDIT PROGRAMS

APPENDIX 8B–1   AUDIT PROGRAM—SELECTED SUBSTANTIVE PROCEDURES—CASH

1. Obtain confirmations from banks (standard bank confirmation).
2. Obtain reconciliations of all bank accounts.
   a. Trace the bank balance on the reconciliation to the bank confirmation.
   b. Trace the reconciled book balance to the general ledger.
   c. Recalculate the arithmetic on client-prepared bank reconciliations.
3. Review the bank confirmation for loans and collateral.
4. Ask the client to request cutoff bank statements to be mailed directly to the audit firm.
   a. Trace deposits in transit on the reconciliation to bank deposits early in the next period.
   b. Trace outstanding checks on the reconciliation to checks cleared in the next period.
5. Prepare a schedule of interbank transfers for a period of 10 business days before and after the year-end date. Document dates of book entry transfer and correspondence with bank entries and reconciliation items, if any.
6. Count cash funds in the presence of a client representative. Obtain a receipt for return of the funds.
7. Obtain written client representations concerning compensating balance agreements.

APPENDIX 8B–2   AUDIT PROGRAM FOR ACCOUNTS AND NOTES RECEIVABLE AND REVENUE: SELECTED SUBSTANTIVE PROCEDURES

A. Accounts and Notes Receivable.
   1. Obtain an aged trial balance of individual customer accounts. Recalculate the total and trace to the general ledger control account.
   2. Send confirmations to all accounts over $X. Select a random sample of all remaining accounts for confirmation.
      a. Investigate exceptions reported by customers.
      b. Perform alternative procedures on accounts that do not respond to positive confirmation requests.
         (1) Vouch cash receipts after the confirmation date for subsequent payment.
         (2) Vouch sales invoices and shipping documents.
   3. Evaluate the adequacy of the allowance for doubtful accounts.
      a. Vouch a sample of current amounts in the aged trial balance to sales invoices to determine whether amounts aged current should be aged past due.
      b. Compare the current-year write-off experience to the prior-year allowance.
      c. Vouch cash receipts after the balance sheet date for collections on past-due accounts.
      d. Obtain financial statements or credit reports and discuss with the credit manager collections on large past-due accounts.
      e. Calculate an allowance estimate using prior relations of write-offs and sales, taking under consideration current economic events.
   4. Review the bank confirmations, loan agreements, and minutes of the board for indications of pledged, discounted, or assigned receivables.
   5. Inspect or obtain confirmation of notes receivable.
   6. Recalculate interest income and trace to the income account.
   7. Obtain written client representations regarding pledge, discount, or assignment of receivables, and about receivables from officers, directors, affiliates, or other related parties.
   8. Review the adequacy of control over recording of all charges to customers (completeness)—audited in the sales transaction test of controls audit program.

B. Revenue
   1. Select a sample of recorded sales invoices and vouch to underlying shipping documents.
   2. Select a sample of shipping documents and trace to sales invoices.
   3. Obtain production records of physical quantities sold and calculate an estimate of sales dollars based on average sale prices.
   4. Compare revenue dollars and physical quantities with prior-year data and industry economic statistics.
   5. Select a sample of sales invoices prepared a few days before and after the balance sheet date and vouch to supporting documents for evidence of proper cutoff.

Chapter 9
Acquisition and Expenditure Cycle

Professional Standards References

Compendium Section	Document Reference	Topic
AU 311	SAS 77	Planning and Supervision
AU 312	SAS 47	Audit Risk and Materiality in Conducting an Audit
AU 313	SAS 45	Substantive Tests Prior to the Balance Sheet Date
AU 316	SAS 82	Consideration of Fraud in a Financial Statement Audit
AU 319	SAS 78	Internal Control in a Financial Statement Audit
AU 326	SAS 80	Evidential Matter
AU 9326		Interpretation 3: Completeness Assertion
AU 329	SAS 56	Analytical Procedures
AU 331	SAS 1	Inventories
AU 333	SAS 85	Management Representations
AU 334	SAS 45	Related Parties
AU 9334		Interpretation 6: Nature and Extent of Procedures for Related Party Transactions
AU 336	SAS 73	Using the Work of a Specialist
AU 339	SAS 41	Working Papers
AU 901	SAS 1	Public Warehouses—Controls and Auditing Procedures for Goods Held

Learning Objectives

This chapter contains a concise overview of a cycle for the acquisition of goods (inventory) and services (expenses), and the expenditure of cash (cash disbursements) in connection with paying for the purchases and acquisitions. A series of short cases is used to show the application of audit procedures in situations where errors and frauds might be discovered. After completing this chapter, you should be able to:

1. Describe the acquisition and expenditure cycle, including typical source documents and controls.

2. Give examples of detail test of controls procedures for auditing the controls over purchase of inventory and services, and disbursement of cash.

3. Explain the importance of the completeness assertion for the audit of accounts payable liabilities, and list some procedures for a "search for unrecorded liabilities."

4. Identify and describe considerations involved in the audit observation of physical inventory taking.

5. Specify some ways fraud can be found in accounts payable and cash disbursements.

6. Describe some common errors and frauds in the acquisition and expenditure cycle, and design some audit and investigation procedures for detecting them.

ACQUISITION AND EXPENDITURE CYCLE: TYPICAL ACTIVITIES

LEARNING OBJECTIVE
1. Describe the acquisition and expenditure cycle, including typical source documents and controls.

The basic acquisition and expenditure activities are (1) purchasing goods and services and (2) paying the bills. Exhibit 9–1 shows the activities and transactions involved in an acquisition and expenditure cycle. The exhibit also lists the accounts and records typically found in this cycle. As you follow the exhibit, you can track the elements of a control system described in the sections below.

Authorization

Purchases are requested (requisitioned) by people who know the needs of the organization. A purchasing department seeks the best prices and quality and issues a purchase order to a selected vendor. Obtaining competitive bids is a good practice because it tends to produce the best prices and involves several legitimate suppliers in the process.

Cash disbursements are authorized by an accounts payable department's assembly of purchase orders, vendor invoices, and internal receiving reports to show a valid obligation to pay. This assembly of supporting documents is called a **voucher** (illustrated in Exhibit 9–1). Accounts payable obligations usually are recorded when the purchaser receives the goods or services ordered.

AUDITING INSIGHT

TOO MUCH TROUBLE

A trucking company self-insured claims of damage to goods in transit, processed claims vouchers, and paid customers from its own bank accounts. Several persons were authorized to sign checks. One person thought it "too much trouble" to stamp the vouchers PAID and said: "That's textbook stuff anyway." Numerous claims were recycled to other check signers, and $80,000 in claims were paid in duplicate before the problem was discovered.

EXHIBIT 9-1 · ACQUISITION AND EXPENDITURE CYCLE

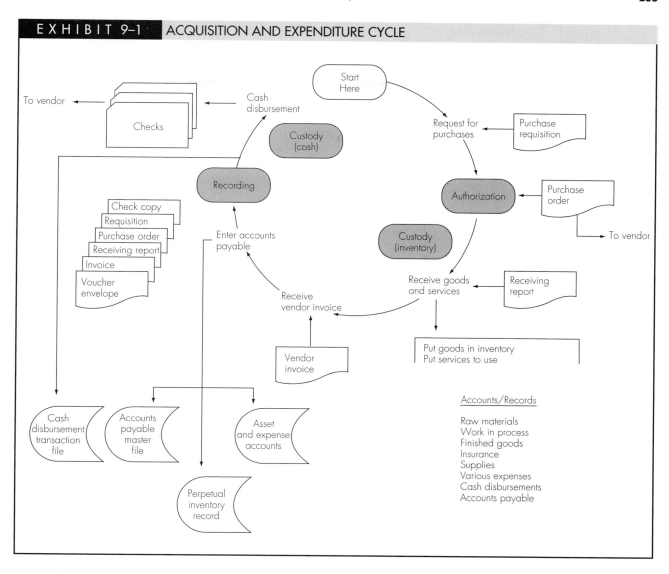

A person authorized by the management or the board of directors signs checks. A company may have a policy to require two signatures on checks over a certain amount (e.g., $1,000). Vouchers should be marked "paid" or otherwise stamped to show that they have been processed completely so they cannot be paid a second time.

Custody

A receiving department inspects the goods received for quantity and quality (producing a *receiving report*), and then puts them in the hands of other responsible persons (e.g., inventory warehousing). Services are not "received" in this manner, but responsible persons accept them. Cash "custody" rests largely in the hands of the person or persons authorized to sign checks.

Another aspect of "custody" involves access to blank documents, such as purchase orders, receiving reports, and blank checks. If unauthorized persons can obtain blank copies of these internal business documents, they can forge a false purchase order to a fictitious vendor, forge a false receiving report, send a false invoice from a fictitious supplier, and prepare a company check to the fictitious supplier, thereby accomplishing an embezzlement.

Recording

When the purchase order, vendor's invoice, and receiving report are in hand, accountants enter the accounts payable with debits to proper inventory and expense accounts and with a credit to accounts payable. When checks are prepared, entries are made to debit the accounts payable and credit cash.

Periodic Reconciliation

A periodic comparison or reconciliation of existing assets to recorded amounts is not shown in Exhibit 9–1, but it occurs in several ways, including: physical inventory-taking to compare inventory on hand to perpetual inventory records, bank account reconciliation to compare book cash balances to bank cash balances, preparation of an accounts payable trial balance to compare the detail of accounts payable to the control account, and internal audit confirmation of accounts payable to compare vendors' reports and monthly statements to recorded liabilities.

AUDIT EVIDENCE IN MANAGEMENT REPORTS AND DATA FILES

Computer processing of acquisition and payment transactions enables management to generate several reports that can provide important audit evidence. Auditors should obtain and use these reports.

Open Purchase Orders

Purchase orders are "open" from the time they are issued until the goods and services are received. They are held in an "open purchase order" file. Generally, no liability exists to be recorded until the transactions are complete. However, auditors may find evidence of losses on purchase commitments in this file, if market prices have fallen below the purchase price shown in purchase orders.

Unmatched Receiving Reports

Liabilities should be recorded on the date the goods and services are received and accepted by the receiving department or by another responsible person. Sometimes, however, vendor invoices arrive later. In the meantime, the accounts payable department holds the receiving reports "unmatched" with invoices, awaiting enough information to record an accounting entry. Auditors can inspect the "unmatched receiving report" file to determine whether the company has material unrecorded liabilities on the financial statement date.

AUDITING INSIGHT

THINKING AHEAD

Lone Moon Brewing purchased bulk aluminum sheets and manufactured its own cans. To assure a source of raw materials supply, the company entered into a long-term purchase agreement for 6 million pounds of aluminum sheeting at 40 cents per pound. At the end of this year, 1.5 million pounds had been purchased and used, but the market price had fallen to 32 cents per pound. Lone Moon was on the hook for a $360,000 (4.5 million pounds × 8 cents) purchase commitment in excess of current market prices.

Unmatched Vendor Invoices

Sometimes, vendor invoices arrive in the accounts payable department before the receiving activity is complete. Such invoices are held "unmatched" with receiving reports, awaiting information that the goods and services were actually received and accepted. Auditors can inspect the "unmatched invoice file" and compare it to the "unmatched receiving report" file to determine whether liabilities are unrecorded. Systems failures and human coding errors can cause "unmatched" invoices and related "unmatched" receiving reports to sit around unnoticed when all the information for recording a liability is actually in hand.

Accounts Payable Trial Balance

This trial balance is a list of payable amounts by vendor, and the sum should agree with the accounts payable control account. (Some organizations keep records by individual invoices instead of vendor names, so the trial balance is a list of unpaid invoices. The sum still should agree with the control account balance.) The best kind of trial balance for audit purposes is one that contains the names of all the vendors with whom the organization has done business, even if their balances are zero. The audit "search for unrecorded liabilities" should emphasize the small and zero balances, especially for regular vendors, because these may be the places where liabilities are unrecorded.

A "voucher" or similar document should support all paid and unpaid accounts payable. A "voucher" is a cover sheet, folder, or envelope that contains all the supporting documents—purchase requisition (if any), purchase order (if any), vendor invoice, receiving report (if any), and check copy (or notation of check number, date, and amount), as shown in Exhibit 9–1.

Purchases Journal

A listing of all purchases may or may not be printed out. It may exist only in a computer transaction file. In either event, it provides raw material for (1) computer-audit analysis of purchasing patterns, which may exhibit characteristics of errors and frauds, and (2) sample selection of transactions for detail test of controls audit of supporting documents for validity, authorization, accuracy, classification, accounting/posting, and proper period recording. (A company may have already performed analyses of purchases, and auditors can use these for analytical evidence, provided the analyses are produced under reliable control conditions.)

Inventory Reports (Trial Balance)

Companies can produce a wide variety of inventory reports useful for analytical evidence. One is an item-by-item trial balance that should agree with a control account (if balances are kept in dollars). Auditors can use such a trial balance (1) to scan for unusual conditions (e.g., negative item balances, overstocking, and valuation problems) and (2) as a population for sample selection for a physical inventory observation. The scanning and sample selection may be computer-audit applications on a computer-based inventory report file.

Cash Disbursements Report

The cash disbursements process will produce a cash disbursements journal, sometimes printed out, sometimes maintained only on a computer file. This journal should contain the date, check number, payee, amount, account debited for each cash disbursement, and a cross-reference to the voucher number (usually the same as the check number). This journal is a population of cash disbursement transactions available for sample selection for detail test of controls audit of supporting documents in the voucher for validity, authorization, accuracy, classification, accounting/posting, and proper period recording.

9.1 What is a voucher?

9.2 How can the situation in which the same supporting documents are used for a duplicate payment be prevented?

9.3 Where could an auditor look to find evidence of losses on purchase commitments? Unrecorded liabilities to vendors?

9.4 List the main supporting source documents used in an acquisition and expenditure cycle.

9.5 List the management reports and data files that can be used for audit evidence. What information in them can be useful to auditors?

CONTROL RISK ASSESSMENT

LEARNING OBJECTIVE

2. Give examples of detail test of controls procedures for auditing the controls over purchase of inventory and services, and disbursement of cash.

Control risk assessment is important because it governs the nature, timing, and extent of substantive audit procedures that will be applied in the audit of account balances in the acquisition and expenditure cycle. These account balances include:

Inventory.

Accounts and notes payable.

Cash disbursements part of cash balance auditing.

Various expenses:

Administrative: supplies, legal fees, and audit fees, taxes.

Selling: commissions, travel, delivery, repairs, and advertising.

Manufacturing: maintenance, freight-in, utilities.

Control Considerations

Control procedures for proper segregation of responsibilities should be in place and operating. By referring to Exhibit 9–1, you can see that proper segregation involves different people and different departments performing the purchasing, receiving, and cash disbursement authorization; custody of inventory and cash; record keeping for purchases and payments; and reconciliation of assets, cash, and accounts payable. Combinations of two or more of these responsibilities in one person, one office, or one computerized system may open the door for errors and frauds.

In addition, the control system should provide for detail control checking activities. For example: (1) Purchase requisitions and purchase orders should be signed or initialed

---

AUDITING INSIGHT

PURCHASE ORDER SPLITTING

The school district authorized its purchasing agent to buy supplies in amounts of $1,000 or less without getting competitive bids for the best price. The purchasing agent wanted to favor local businesses instead of large chain stores, so she broke up the year's $350,000 supplies order into numerous $900–$950 orders, paying about 12 percent more to local stores than would have been paid to the large chains.

by authorized personnel. (Computer-produced purchase orders should come from a system whose master file specifications for reordering and vendor identification are restricted to changes only by authorized persons.) (2) Inventory warehouses should be under adequate physical security (storerooms, fences, locks, and the like). (3) Accountants should be under orders to record accounts payable only when all the supporting documentation is in order; and care should be taken to record purchases and payables as of the date goods and services were received, and to record cash disbursements on the date the check leaves the control of the organization. (4) Vendor invoices should be compared to purchase orders and receiving reports to determine that the vendor is charging the approved price and that the quantity being billed is the same as the quantity received.

Information about the control system often is gathered initially by completing an Internal Control Questionnaire. A selection of questionnaires for both general (manual) controls and computer controls is in Appendix 9A. These questionnaires can be studied for details of desirable control activities. They are organized under headings that identify the important control objectives—environment, validity, completeness, authorization, accuracy, classification, accounting/posting, and proper period recording.

Detail Test of Controls Audit Procedures

An organization should have detail controls in place and operating to prevent, detect, and correct accounting errors. Exhibit 9–2 puts controls in the perspective of purchasing activity with examples of specific objectives. You should study this exhibit carefully. It expresses the general control objectives in specific examples related to purchasing.

EXHIBIT 9–2	INTERNAL CONTROL OBJECTIVES (PURCHASES)

General Objectives	Examples of Specific Objectives
1. Recorded purchases are *valid* and documented.	Recorded vouchers in the voucher register supported by completed vouchers.
	Voucher for purchases of inventory (or fixed assets) supported by vendor invoices, receiving reports, purchase orders, and requisitions (or approved capital budget).
2. Valid purchase transactions are recorded and *none omitted*.	Requisitions, purchase orders, receiving reports, and vouchers are prenumbered and numerical sequence is checked.
	Overall comparisons of purchases are made periodically by statistical or product-line analysis.
3. Purchases are *authorized* according to company policy.	All purchase orders are supported by requisitions from proper persons (or approved capital budgets).
	Purchase made from approved vendors or only after bids are received and evaluated.
4. Purchase orders are *accurately* prepared.	Completed purchase order quantities and descriptions independently compared to requisitions and vendors' catalogs.
5. Purchase transactions are properly *classified*.	Purchase from subsidiaries and affiliates classified as intercompany purchases and payables.
	Purchase returns and allowances properly classified.
	Purchases for repairs and maintenance segregated from purchases of fixed assets.
6. Purchase transaction *accounting* and *posting* is complete and proper.	Account distribution on vouchers proper and reviewed independent of preparation.
	Freight-in included as part of purchase and added to inventory (or fixed assets) costs.
7. Purchase transactions are recorded in the *proper period*.	Perpetual inventory and fixed asset records updated as of date goods are received.

| E X H I B I T   9–3 | TEST OF CONTROLS AUDIT PROCEDURES FOR PURCHASES, CASH DISBURSEMENTS, AND ACCOUNTS PAYABLE |

	Control Objective
A. Purchases	
1. Select a sample of receiving reports:	
a. Vouch to related purchase orders	Authorization
b. Trace to inventory record posting of additions.	Completeness
B. Cash Disbursements and Other Expenses	
1. Select a sample of vouchers recorded in a purchase journal and cash disbursements in a cash journal.	
a. Vouch supporting documentation for evidence of accurate mathematics, correct classification, proper approval, and proper date of entry.	Accuracy Classification Authorization Proper period
b. Trace recorded debits to general and subsidiary ledger accounts.	Acctg/posting
2. Select a sample of recorded expenses from various accounts and vouch them to (a) canceled checks, and (b) supporting documentation.	Validity Classification

Auditors can perform detail test of controls audit procedures to determine whether company personnel actually are performing controls that are said to be in place and operating properly. A **detail test of control procedure** consists of (1) identification of the data population from which a sample of items will be selected for audit and (2) an expression of the action that will be taken to produce relevant evidence. In general, the actions in detail test of control audit procedures involve vouching, tracing, observing, scanning, and recalculating. If personnel in the organization are not performing their control activities very well, auditors will need to design substantive audit procedures to try to detect whether control failures have produced materially misleading account balances. Exhibit 9–3 contains a selection of detail test of controls audit procedures for controls over purchase, cash disbursement, and accounts payable transactions.

Detail Test of Controls for Inventory Records

Many organizations have material investments in inventories. In many engagements, auditors need to determine whether they can rely on the accuracy of perpetual inventory records. Tests of controls over accuracy involve tests of the additions (purchases) to the inventory detail balances and tests of the reductions (issues) of the item balances. Exhibit 9–4 pictures the "direction of the test" for detail test of controls audit procedures. The samples from the source documents (receiving reports, issues documents) meet the completeness direction requirement to determine whether everything received was recorded as an addition and whether everything issued was recorded as a reduction of the balance. The sample from the perpetual inventory records meets the validity direction requirement to determine whether everything recorded as an addition or reduction is supported by receiving reports and issue documents. (The symbols A-1-a, A-2-a, A-3-a, and A-3-b are cross-references to the procedures in Exhibit 9–5). Exhibit 9–5 is similar to Exhibit 9–3 in that it contains a selection of detail test of controls audit procedures for controls over perpetual inventory records.

Summary: Control Risk Assessment

The audit manager or senior accountant in charge of the audit should evaluate the evidence obtained from an understanding of the internal control system and from the test of controls audit procedures. If the control risk is assessed very low, the substantive audit

EXHIBIT 9–4	DUAL DIRECTION OF TEST AUDIT SAMPLES

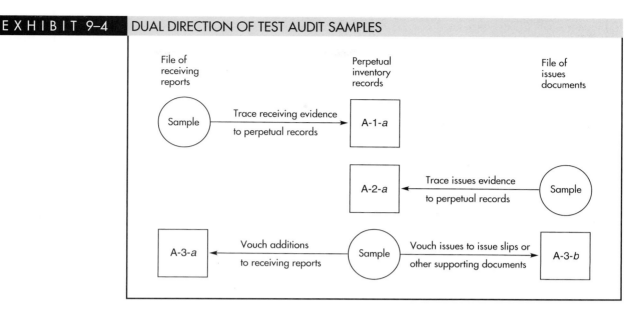

procedures on the account balances can be limited in cost-saving ways. For example, the inventory observation test-counts can be performed on a date prior to the year-end, and the sample size can be fairly small. On the other hand, if tests of controls reveal weaknesses, the substantive procedures will need to be designed to lower the risk of failing to detect material misstatement in the account balances. For example, the inventory observation may need to be scheduled on the year-end date with the audit team making a large number of test counts. Descriptions of major deficiencies, control weaknesses, and inefficiencies may be incorporated in a letter to the client describing "reportable conditions."

EXHIBIT 9–5	TEST OF CONTROLS AUDIT PROCEDURES FOR INVENTORY RECORDS

	Control Objective
A. Inventory Receipts and Issues	
1. Select a sample of receiving reports:	
a. Trace to perpetual inventory record entry of receipt.	Authorization Completeness
2. Select a sample of sales invoices, bills of lading or other shipping documents, or production requisitions:	
a. Trace to perpetual inventory record entry of issue.	Authorization Completeness
3. Select a sample of inventory item perpetual records:	
a. Vouch additions to receiving reports.	Validity
b. Vouch issues to invoices, bills of lading or other shipping documents, or production requisitions.	Validity
B. Cost of Sales	
1. With the sample of issues in A-2 above:	
a. Review the accounting summary of quantities and prices for mathematical accuracy.	Accuracy
b. Trace posting of amounts to general ledger.	Completeness
2. Obtain a sample of cost of goods sold entries in the general ledger and vouch to supporting summaries of finished goods issues.	Validity
3. Review (recalculate) the appropriateness of standard costs, if used, to price inventory issues and cost of goods sold. Review the disposition of variances from standard costs.	Accuracy

R E V I E W
CHECKPOINTS

9.6 What are the primary functions that should be segregated in the acquisition and expenditure cycle?

9.7 What feature of the acquisition and expenditure control would be expected to prevent an employee's embezzling cash through creation of fictitious vouchers?

9.8 How could an auditor determine whether the purchasing agent had practiced "purchase order splitting"?

9.9 Describe the two general characteristics of a test of controls audit procedure.

9.10 How is the information from the shipping department, receiving department, and warehouse used to update perpetual inventory records?

9.11 How would a low combined inherent and control risk affect substantive audit procedures in the inventory area? What about a high combined inherent and control risk?

SPECIAL NOTE: THE COMPLETENESS ASSERTION

LEARNING OBJECTIVE

3. Explain the importance of the completeness assertion for the audit of accounts payable liabilities, and list some procedures for a "search for unrecorded liabilities."

When considering assertions and obtaining evidence about accounts payable and other liabilities, auditors must put emphasis on the completeness assertion. (For asset accounts, the emphasis is on the existence assertion.) This emphasis on completeness is rightly placed because companies typically are less concerned about timely recording of expenses and liabilities than they are about timely recording of revenues and assets. Of course, generally accepted accounting principles require timely recording of liabilities and their associated expenses.

Evidence is much more difficult to obtain to verify the completeness assertion than the existence assertion. Auditors cannot rely entirely on a management assertion of completeness, even in combination with a favorable assessment of control risk (AU 9326). Substantive procedures—tests of details or analytical procedures—ought to be performed. **The search for unrecorded liabilities** is the set of procedures designed to yield audit evidence of liabilities that were not recorded in the reporting period. Such a search normally should be performed up to the report date in the period following the audit client's balance sheet date.

The following is a list of procedures useful in the search for unrecorded liabilities. The audit objective is to search all the places where evidence of them might exist. If these procedures reveal none, the auditors can conclude that all material liabilities are recorded.

1. Scan the open purchase order file at year-end for indications of material purchase commitments at fixed prices. Obtain current prices and determine whether any adjustments for loss and liability for purchase commitments are needed.

2. List the unmatched vendor invoices and determine when the goods were received, looking to the unmatched receiving report file and receiving reports prepared after the year-end. Determine which invoices, if any, should be recorded.

3. Trace the unmatched receiving reports to accounts payable entries, and determine whether ones recorded in the next accounting period need to be adjusted to report them in the current accounting period under audit.

4. Select a sample of cash disbursements from the accounting period following the balance sheet date. Vouch them to supporting documents (invoice, receiving report) to determine whether the related liabilities were recorded in the proper accounting period.

5. Trace the liabilities reported by financial institutions to the accounts.

6. Study IRS examination reports for evidence of income or other taxes in dispute, and decide whether actual or estimated liabilities need to be recorded.

7. Confirm accounts payable with vendors, especially regular suppliers showing small or zero balances in the year-end accounts payable. These are the ones most likely to be understated. (Vendors' monthly statements controlled by the auditors also may be used for this procedure.) Be sure to verify the vendors' addresses so confirmations will not be misdirected, perhaps to conspirators in a scheme to understate liabilities.

8. Study the accounts payable trial balance for indications of dates showing fewer payables than usual recorded near the year-end. (A financial officer may be stashing vendor invoices in a desk drawer instead of recording them.)

9. Review the lawyers' responses to requests for information about pending or threatened litigation, and for unasserted claims and assessments. The lawyers' information may signal the need for contingent liability accruals or disclosures.

10. Use a checklist of accrued expenses to determine whether the company has been conscientious about expense and liability accruals; including accruals for wages, interest, utilities, sales and excise taxes, payroll taxes, income taxes, real property taxes, rent, sales commissions, royalties, and warranty and guarantee expense.

11. When auditing the details of sales revenue, pay attention to the terms of sales to determine whether any amounts should be deferred as unearned revenue. Inquiries directed to management about terms of sales can be used to obtain initial information, such as inquiries about customers' rights of cancellation or return.

12. Confirm life insurance policies with insurance companies to ask whether the company has any loans against the cash value of the insurance. In this confirmation, request the names of the beneficiaries of the policies. If the insurance is for the benefit of a party other than the company, the beneficiaries may be creditors on unrecorded loans. Make inquiries about the business purpose of making insurance proceeds payable to other parties.

13. Review the terms of debt due within one year but classified long-term because the company plans to refinance it on a long-term basis. Holders of the debt or financial institutions must have shown (preferably in writing) a willingness to refinance the debt before it can be classified long-term. Classification cannot be based solely on management's expressed intent to seek long-term financing.

14. Apply analytical procedures appropriate in the circumstances. In general, accounts payable volume and period-end balances should increase when the company experiences increases in physical production volume or engages in inventory stockpiling. Some liabilities may be functionally related to other activities; for example, sales taxes are functionally related to sales dollar totals, payroll taxes to payroll totals, excise taxes to sales dollars or volume, income taxes to income.

AUDITING INSIGHT

ADVERTISED SALES RETURN PRIVILEGE

This advertisement appeared in popular magazines.

THE 1956 THUNDERBIRD—authentic die-cast replica of the classic T-Bird described as America's finest production sports car ever! Send no money now. You will be billed for a deposit of $24 and four equal monthly installments of $24 each.

RETURN ASSURANCE POLICY: If you wish to return any Franklin Mint Precision Models purchase, you may do so within 30 days of your receipt of that purchase for replacement, credit, or refund.

9.12 Describe the purpose and give examples of audit procedures in the "search for unrecorded liabilities."

9.13 Explain the difference in approach in confirmation of accounts receivable and accounts payable.

9.14 In substantive auditing, why is the emphasis on the completeness assertion for liabilities instead of on the existence assertion as in the audit of assets?

Special Note: Physical Inventory Observation

The audit procedures for inventory and related cost of sales accounts frequently are extensive in an audit engagement. A 96-page AICPA auditing procedure study entitled *Audit of Inventories* (AICPA, 1986) describes many facets of inherent risk, control risk, and the process of obtaining evidence about inventory financial statement assertions. Inventories often are the largest current asset.

A *material error or fraud* in inventory has a pervasive effect on financial statements. Misstatements in inventory cause misstatements in current assets, working capital, total assets, cost of sales, gross margin, and net income. While analytical procedures can help indicate inventory presentation problems, the auditors' best opportunity to detect inventory errors and frauds is the physical observation of the client's inventory count taken by company personnel. (Auditors *observe* the inventory taking and make test counts, but they seldom actually *take* (count) the entire inventory.) Auditing standards express the requirement for inventory observation in SAS 1, AU 331:

> Observation of inventories is a generally accepted auditing procedure. . . . When inventory quantities are determined solely by means of a physical count...it is ordinarily necessary for the independent auditor to be present at the time of count and, by suitable observation, tests, and inquiries, satisfy himself respecting the methods of inventory-taking and the reliance which may be placed upon the client's representation about the quantities and physical condition of the inventories.

The remainder of this special note gives details about auditors' observation of physical inventory taking. The first task is to review the client's inventory-taking instructions. The instructions should include the following:

1. Names of client personnel responsible for the count.
2. Dates and times of inventory taking.
3. Names of client personnel who will participate in the inventory taking.
4. Instructions for recording accurate descriptions of inventory items, for count and double-count, and for measuring or translating physical quantities (such as counting by measures of gallons, barrels, feet, dozens).
5. Instructions for making notes of obsolete or worn items.
6. Instructions for the use of tags, punched cards, count sheets, computers, or other media devices and for their collection and control.
7. Plans for shutting down plant operations or for taking inventory after store closing hours, and plans for having goods in proper places (such as on store shelves instead of on the floor, or of raw materials in a warehouse rather than in transit to a job).
8. Plans for counting or controlling movement of goods in receiving and shipping areas if those operations are not shut down during the count.
9. Instructions for computer compilation of the count media (such as tags, count sheets) into final inventory listings or summaries.

10. Instructions for pricing the inventory items.
11. Instructions for review and approval of the inventory count; notations of obsolescence or other matters by supervisory personnel.

These instructions characterize a well-planned counting operation. As the plan is carried out, the independent auditors should be present to hear the count instructions being given to the client's count teams and to observe the instructions being followed.

Many physical inventories are counted at the year-end when the auditor is present to observe. The auditors can perform dual-direction testing by (1) selecting inventory items from a perpetual inventory master file, going to the location, and obtaining a test count, which produces evidence for the existence assertion; and (2) selecting inventory from locations on the warehouse floor, obtaining a test count, and tracing the count to the final inventory compilation, which produces evidence for the completeness assertion. If the company does not have perpetual records and a file to test for existence, the auditors must be careful to obtain a record of all the counts and use it for the existence-direction tests.

Physical Inventory Not on Year-End Date

Clients sometimes count the inventory before or after the balance sheet date. When the auditors are present to make their physical observation, they follow the procedures outlined above for observation of the physical count. However, with a time period intervening between the count date and the year-end, additional roll forward or rollback-auditing procedures must be performed on purchase, inventory addition, and issue transactions during that period. The inventory on the count date is reconciled to the year-end inventory by appropriate addition or subtraction of the intervening receiving and issue transactions.

Cycle Inventory Counting

Some companies count inventory on a cycle basis or use a statistical counting plan but never take a complete count on a single date. In these circumstances, the auditors must understand the cycle or sampling plan and evaluate its appropriateness. In this type of situation, the auditors are present for some counting operations. Only under unusual circumstances and as an "extended procedure" are auditors present every month (or more

INVENTORY COUNT AND MEASUREMENT CHALLENGES

Examples	Challenges
Lumber.	Problem identifying quality or grade.
Piles of sugar, coal, scrap steel.	Geometric computations, aerial photos.
Items weighed on scales.	Check scales for accuracy.
Bulk materials (oil, grain, liquids in storage tanks).	Climb the tanks. Dip measuring rods. Sample for assay or chemical analysis.
Diamonds, jewelry.	Identification and quality determination problems. Ask a specialist.
Pulp wood.	Quantity measurement estimation. Aerial photos.
Livestock.	Movement not controllable. Count critter's legs and divide by four (two, for chickens).

Source (adapted): AICPA, *Audit of Inventories*, Auditing Procedure Study (1986), p.28.

frequently) to observe all counts. Businesses that count inventory in this manner purport to have accurate perpetual records and carry out the counting as a means of testing the records and maintaining their accuracy.

The auditors must be present during some counting operations to evaluate the counting plans and their execution. The procedures for an annual count enumerated above are utilized, test counts are made, and the audit team is responsible for a conclusion concerning the accuracy (control) of perpetual records.

Auditors Not Present at Client's Inventory Count

This situation can arise on a first audit when the audit firm is appointed after the beginning inventory already has been counted. The auditors must review the client's plan for the already completed count as before. Some test counts of current inventory should be made and traced to current records to make a conclusion about the reliability of perpetual records. If the actual count was recent, intervening transaction activity might be reconciled back to the beginning inventory.

However, the reconciliation of more than a few months' transactions to unobserved beginning inventories might be very difficult. The auditors may employ procedures utilizing such interrelationships as sales activity, physical volume, price variation, standard costs, and gross profit margins for the decision about beginning inventory reasonableness. Nevertheless, much care must be exercised in "backing into" the audit of a previous inventory.

Inventories Located off the Client's Premises

The auditors must determine where and in what dollar amounts inventories are located off the client's premises, in the custody of consignees, or in public warehouses. If amounts are material and if control is not exceptionally strong, the audit team may wish to visit these locations and conduct on-site test counts. However, if amounts are not material and/or if related evidence is adequate (such as periodic reports, cash receipts, receivables records, shipping records) and if control risk is low, then direct confirmation with the custodian may be considered sufficient competent evidence of the existence of quantities (*SAS 1*, AU 901).

Inventory Existence and Completeness

The physical observation procedures are designed to audit for existence and completeness (physical quantities) and valuation (recalculation of appropriate FIFO, LIFO, or other pricing at cost, and lower-of-cost-or-market write-down of obsolete or worn inventory). After the observation is complete, auditors should have sufficient competent evidence of the following physical quantities and valuations:

- Goods in the perpetual records but not owned were excluded from the inventory compilation.
- Goods on hand were counted and included in the inventory compilation.
- Goods consigned-out or stored in outside warehouses (goods owned but not on hand) were included in the inventory compilation.
- Goods in transit (goods actually purchased and recorded but not yet received) were added to the inventory count and included in the inventory compilation.
- Goods on hand already sold (but not yet delivered) were not counted and were excluded from the inventory compilation.
- Goods consigned-in (goods on hand but not owned) were excluded from the inventory compilation.

AUDITING INSIGHT

INVENTORY—A RIPE FIELD FOR FRAUD

These problems have arisen in companies' inventory frauds:

- Auditors were fooled as a result of taking a small sample for test-counting, thus missing important information.
- Companies included inventory they pretended to have ordered.
- Auditors permitted company officials to follow them and notice their test counts. Then the managers falsified counts for inventory the auditors did not count.
- Shipments between plants (transfers) were reported as inventory at both plant locations.
- Auditors spotted a barrel whose contents management had valued at thousands of dollars, but it was filled with sawdust. The auditors required management to exclude the value from the inventory, but it never occurred to them that they had found one instance in an intentional and pervasive overstatement fraud.
- Auditors observed inventory at five store locations and told the management in advance of the specific stores. Management took care not to make fraudulent entries in these five stores, instead making fraudulent adjustments in many of the other 236 stores.
- After counting an inventory of computer chips, the auditors received a call from the client's controller: "Just hours after you left the plant, 2,500 chips arrived in a shipment in transit." The auditors included them in inventory but never checked to see whether the chips were real.

An accounting firm advised its audit personnel:

- Focus test counts on high-value items, and sample lower-value items. Test-count a sufficient dollar amount of the inventory.
- If all locations will not be observed, do not follow an easily predictable pattern. Advise client personnel as late as possible of the locations we will visit.
- Be skeptical of large and unusual test count differences or of client personnel making notes or displaying particular interest in our procedures and test counts.
- Be alert for inventory not used for some time, stored in unusual locations, showing signs of damage, obsolescence, or excess quantities.
- Ensure that interplant movements (transfers) are kept to an absolute minimum. Obtain evidence that any items added to inventory after the count is completed are proper and reasonable (i.e., exist in stated quality and quantity).

Source: *The Wall Street Journal* and Grant Thornton.

REVIEW
CHECKPOINTS

9.15 What characteristics do auditors look for in the review of a client's inventory-taking instructions?

9.16 Explain dual-direction sampling in the context of inventory test counts.

9.17 What procedures are employed to audit inventory when the physical inventory is taken on a cycle basis or on a statistical plan, but never a complete count on a single date?

9.18 What could be happening when a client's managers take notes of auditors' test counts while an inventory is being counted?

9.19 What are some characteristics of obsolete or slow-moving inventory?

Special Note: Finding Fraud Signs in Accounts Payable

LEARNING OBJECTIVE

5. Specify some ways fraud can be found in accounts payable and cash disbursements.

Fraudsters can have a field day generating false payments through a company's accounts payable and cash disbursements systems. A common scheme is to send false invoices on the letterhead of a fictitious vendor to the company and have an insider manipulate supporting documents or controls to make payment. Sometimes, a company's own employees engage in unauthorized "business" as suppliers to their employers.

These frauds can proceed undetected for a long time as long as auditors and managers do not try to find the signs and signals they leave behind. In an accounts payable audit for fraud signs ("red flags"), auditors can try several kinds of searches and matches in the company's records.

- *Look for photocopies of invoices in the files.* Fraudsters alter real invoices for false or duplicate payments and make photocopies to hide whiteout and cut-and-paste changes.
- *Look for a vendor's invoices submitted in numerical order.* False vendors sometimes use the same pad of prenumbered invoices (standard office supply store printing) to send bills to the company. Either the company is the vendor's only customer, or the company is a victim of a false billing scheme.
- *Look for a vendor's invoice amounts always in round numbers.* Prices, shipping charges, and taxes too often come in penny amounts to expect a vendor's invoices always to round to even dollars.
- *Look for a vendor's invoices always slightly lower than a review threshold.* Insiders know that a company gives special attention and approval to invoices over a specified dollar amount (e.g., $10,000). Therefore, the fraudster always avoids invoices that are too large.
- *Look for vendors with post office box addresses.* While many businesses use post office box addresses for receiving payments, invoices should also show a street address location.
- *Look for vendors with no listed telephone number.* Legitimate businesses normally do not hide behind unlisted telephone numbers. Also, cheap fraudsters sometimes do not buy a phone line for their false companies.
- *Match vendor and employee addresses.* Match vendor and employee telephone numbers. Many companies have policies that their employees cannot also be vendors. Insiders (employees) often know how to circumvent controls, and their business with the employer may be suspicious.
- *Look for multiple vendors at the same address and telephone.* Many invoices from the same location, especially invoices for different kinds of products and services, may simply come from a front organization conducting a false invoice scheme. However, legitimate suppliers often operate under several company names and conduct business from the same location.

Audit Cases: Substantive Audit Procedures

LEARNING OBJECTIVE

6. Describe some common errors and frauds in the acquisition and expenditure cycle, and design some audit and investigation procedures for detecting them.

The audit of account balances consists of procedural efforts to detect errors and frauds that might exist in the balances, thus making them misleading in financial statements. If such misstatements exist, the following features characterize them:

Method: A cause of the misstatement (accidental error or fraud attempt), which usually is made easier by some kind of failure of controls.

Paper trail: A set of telltale signs of erroneous accounting, missing or altered documents, or a "dangling debit" (the false or erroneous debit that results from an overstatement of assets).

Amount: The dollar amount of overstated assets and revenue, or understated liabilities and expenses.

The cases in this section tell about an error or fraud situation in terms of the method, the paper trail, and the amount. The first part of each case gives you the "inside story" that auditors seldom know before they perform the audit work. The next part is an "audit approach" section, which tells about the audit objective (assertion), controls, test of controls, and test of balances (substantive procedures) that could be considered in an approach to the situation. The audit approach section presumes that the auditors do not know everything about the situation. The audit approach part of each case contains these parts:

Audit objective: A recognition of a financial statement *assertion* for which evidence needs to be obtained. The assertions are about existence of assets, liabilities, revenues, and expenses; their valuation; their complete inclusion in the account balances; the rights and obligations inherent in them; and their proper presentation and disclosure in the financial statements.

Control: recognition of the control activities that *should be* used in an organization to prevent and detect errors and frauds.

Test of controls: Ordinary and extended procedures *designed to produce evidence about the effectiveness of the controls* that should be in operation.

Audit of balance: Ordinary and extended *substantive procedures designed to find signs of errors and frauds* in account balances and classes of transactions.

At the end of the chapter, some similar discussion cases are presented, and you can write the audit approach to test your ability to design audit procedures for the detection of errors and frauds. Appendix 9B contains three substantive audit programs for reference.

CASE 9.1
PRINTING (COPYING) MONEY

PROBLEM

Improper expenditures for copy services charged to motion picture production costs.

METHOD

Argus Productions, Inc., a motion picture and commercial production company, assigned M. Welby the authority and responsibility for obtaining copies of scripts used in production. Established procedures permitted Welby to arrange for outside script copying services, receive the copies, and approve the bills for payment. In effect, Welby was the "purchasing department" and the "receiving department" for this particular service. To a certain extent, Welby was also the "accounting department" by virtue of approving bills for payment and coding them for assignment to projects. Welby did not make the actual accounting entries or sign the checks.

M. Welby set up a fictitious company under the registered name of Quickprint Company with himself as the incorporator and stockholder, complete with a post office box number, letterhead stationery, and nicely printed invoices, but no printing equipment. Legitimate copy services were "subcontracted" by Quickprint with real printing businesses, which billed Quickprint. Welby then prepared Quickprint invoices billing Argus, usually at the legitimate

shop's rate, but for a few extra copies each time. Welby also submitted Quickprint bills to Argus for fictitious copying jobs on scripts for movies and commercials that never went into production. As the owner of Quickprint, Welby endorsed Argus' checks with a rubber stamp and deposited the money in the business bank account, paid the legitimate printing bills, and took the rest for personal use.

PAPER TRAIL

Argus' production cost files contained all the Quickprint bills, sorted under the names of the movie and commercial production projects. Welby even created files for proposed films that never went into full production, and thus should not have had script-copying costs. There were no copying service bills from any shop other than Quickprint Company.

AMOUNT

M. Welby conducted this fraud for five years, embezzling $475,000 in false and inflated billings. (Argus' net income was overstated a modest amount because copying costs were capitalized as part of production cost, then amortized over a two-to-three-year period.)

AUDIT APPROACH

OBJECTIVE

Obtain evidence of the valid existence (occurrence) and valuation of copying charges capitalized as film production cost.

CONTROL

Management should assign the authority to request copies and the purchasing authority to different responsible employees. Other persons also should perform the accounting, including coding cost assignments to projects. Managerial review of production results could result in notice of excess costs.

The request for the quantity (number) of copies of a script should come from a person involved in production who knows the number needed. This person also should sign off for the receipt (or approve the bill) for this requested number of copies, thus acting as the "receiving department." This procedure could prevent waste (excess cost), especially if the requesting person were also held responsible for the profitability of the project.

A company agent always performs actual purchasing, and in this case, the agent was M. Welby. Purchasing agents generally have latitude to seek the best service at the best price, with or without bids from competitors. A requirement to obtain bids is usually a good idea, but much legitimate purchasing is done with sole-source suppliers without bid.

Someone in the accounting department should be responsible for coding invoices for charges to authorized projects, thus making it possible to detect costs charged to projects not actually in production.

Someone with managerial responsibility should review project costs and the purchasing practices. However, this is an expensive use of executive time. It was not spent in the Argus case. Too bad.

TEST OF CONTROLS

In gaining an understanding of the control structure, auditors could learn of the trust and responsibility vested in M. Welby. Since the embezzlement was about $95,000 per year, the total copying cost under Welby's control must have been around $1 million or more. (It might attract unwanted attention to inflate a cost more than 10 percent.)

Controls were very weak, especially in the combination of duties performed by Welby and in the lack of managerial review. For all practical purposes, there were no controls to test, other than to see whether Welby had approved the copying cost bills and coded them to active projects. This provides an opportunity, since proper classification is a control objective.

Procedures: Select a sample of project files, and vouch costs charged to them to support in source documents (validity direction of the test). Select a sample of expenditures, and trace them to the project cost records shown coded on the expenditures (completeness direction of the test).

AUDIT OF BALANCE

Substantive procedures are directed to obtaining evidence about the existence of film projects, completeness of the costs charged to them, valuation of the capitalized project costs, rights in copyright and ownership, and proper disclosure of amortization methods. The most important procedures are the same as the test of controls procedures; thus, when performed at the year-end date on the capitalized cost balances, they are dual-purpose audit procedures.

Either of the procedures described above, as test of controls procedures should show evidence of projects that had never gone into production. (Auditors should be careful to obtain a list of actual projects before they begin the procedures.) Chances are good that the discovery of bad project codes with copying cost will reveal a pattern of Quickprint bills.

Knowing that controls over copying cost are weak, auditors could be tipped off to the possibility of a Welby-Quickprint connection. Efforts to locate Quickprint should be taken (telephone book, chamber of commerce, other directories). Inquiry with the state secretary of state for names of the Quickprint incorporators should reveal Welby's connection. The audit findings can then be turned over to a trained investigator to arrange an interview and confrontation with M. Welby.

DISCOVERY SUMMARY

In this case, internal auditors performed a review of project costs at the request of the manager of production, who was worried about profitability. They performed the procedures described above, noticed the dummy projects and the Quickprint bills, investigated the ownership of Quickprint, and discovered Welby's association. They had first tried to locate Quickprint's shop but could not find it in telephone, chamber of commerce, or other city directories. They were careful not to direct any mail to the post office box for fear of alerting the then-unknown parties involved. A sly internal auditor already had used a ruse at the post office and learned that Welby rented the box, but they did not know whether anyone else was involved. Alerted, the internal auditors gathered all the Quickprint bills and determined the total charged for nonexistent projects. Carefully, under the covert observation of a representative of the local district attorney's office, Welby was interviewed and readily confessed.

CASE 9.2
REAL CASH PAID TO PHONY DOCTORS

PROBLEM

Cash disbursement fraud. Fictitious medical benefit claims were paid by the company, which self-insured up to $50,000 per employee. The expense account that included legitimate and false charges was "employee medical benefits."

METHOD

As manager of the claims payment department, Martha Lee was considered one of Beta Magnetic's best employees. She never missed a day of work in 10 years, and her department had one of the company's best efficiency ratings. Controls were considered good, including the verification by a claims processor that (1) the patient was a Beta employee, (2) medical treatments were covered in the plan, (3) the charges were within approved guidelines, (4) the cumulative claims for the employee did not exceed $50,000 (if over $50,000 a claim was submitted to an insurance company), and (5) the calculation for payment was correct. After verification processing, claims were sent to the claims payment department to pay the doctor directly. No payments ever went directly to employees. Martha Lee prepared false claims on real employees, forging the signature of various claims processors, adding her own review approval, naming bogus doctors who would be paid by the payment department. The payments were mailed to various post office box addresses and to her husband's business address.

Nobody ever verified claims information with the employee. The employees received no reports of medical benefits paid on their behalf. While the department had performance reports by claims processors, these reports did not show claim-by-claim details. No one verified the credentials of the doctors.

PAPER TRAIL

The falsified claims forms were in Beta's files, containing all the fictitious data on employee names, processor signatures, doctors' bills, and phony doctors and addresses. The canceled checks were returned by the bank and were kept in Beta's files, containing "endorsements" by the doctors. Martha Lee and her husband were somewhat clever: They deposited the checks in various banks in accounts opened in the names and identification of the "doctors."

Martha Lee did not stumble on the paper trail. She drew the attention of an auditor who saw her take her 24 claims processing employees out to an annual staff appreciation luncheon in a fleet of stretch limousines.

AMOUNT

Over the last seven years, Martha Lee and her husband stole $3.5 million, and, until the last, no one noticed anything unusual about the total amount of claims paid.

AUDIT APPROACH

OBJECTIVE

Obtain evidence to determine whether employee medical benefits "existed" in the sense of being valid claims paid to valid doctors.

CONTROL

The controls are good as far as they go. The claims processors used internal data in their work—employee files for identification, treatment descriptions submitted by doctors with comparisons to plan provisions, and mathematical calculations. This work amounted to all the approval necessary for the claims payment department to prepare a check.

No controls connected the claims data with outside sources, such as employee acknowledgment or doctor investigation.

TEST OF CONTROLS

The processing and control work in the claims processing department can be audited for deviations from controls.
Procedure: Select a sample of paid claims and reperform the claims processing procedures to verify the employee status, coverage of treatment, proper guideline charges, cumulative amount less than $50,000, and accurate calculation. However, this procedure would not help answer the question: "Does Martha Lee steal the money to pay for the limousines?"

"Thinking like a crook," points out the holes in the controls. Nobody seeks to verify data with external sources. However, an auditor must be careful in an investigation not to cast aspersions on a manager by letting rumors start by interviewing employees to find out whether they actually had the medical claim paid on their behalf. If money is being taken, the company check must be intercepted in some manner.

AUDIT OF BALANCE

The balance under audit is the sum of the charges in the employee medical benefits expense account, and the objective relates to the valid existence of the payments.

Procedure: The first procedure can be as follows: Obtain a list of doctors paid by the company and look them up in the state medical society directory. Look up their addresses and determine whether they are valid business addresses. You might try comparing claims processors' signatures on various forms, but this is hard to do and requires training. An extended procedure would be as follows: Compare the doctors' addresses to addresses known to be associated with Martha Lee and other claims processing employees.

DISCOVERY SUMMARY

The comparison of doctors to the medical society directory showed eight "doctors" who were not licensed in the current period. Five of these eight had post office box addresses, and discrete inquiries and surveillance showed them rented to Martha Lee. The other three had the same mailing address as her husband's business. Further investigation, involving the district attorney and police, was necessary to obtain personal financial records and reconstruct the thefts from prior years.

CASE 9.3
RECEIVING THE MISSING OIL

PROBLEM

Fuel oil supplies inventory and fuel expense inflated because of short shipments.

METHOD

Johnson Chemical started a new contract with Madden Oil Distributors to supply fuel oil for the plant generators on a cost-plus contract. Madden delivered the oil weekly in a 5,000-gallon truck and pumped it into Johnson's storage tanks. Johnson's receiving employees were supposed to observe the pumping and record the quantity on a receiving report, which was then forwarded to the accounts payable department, where it was held pending arrival of Madden's invoice. The quantities received then were compared to the quantities billed by Madden before a voucher was approved for payment and a check prepared for signature by the controller. Since it was a cost-plus contract, Madden's billing price was not checked against any standard price.

Madden's driver rather easily fooled the receiving employees. He mixed sludge with the oil; the receiving employees did not take samples to check for quality. He called out the storage tank content falsely (e.g., 1,000 gallons on hand when 2,000 were actually in the tank); the receiving employees did not check the gauge themselves; and the tank truck was not weighed at entry and exit to determine the amount delivered. During the winter months, when fuel oil use was high, Madden ran in extra trucks more than once a week, but pumped nothing when the receiving employees were not looking. Quantities "received" and paid during the first year of the contract were in gallons (see table below):

Jan.	31,000	May	18,000	Sep	21,000
Feb.	28,000	June	14,000	Oct.	23,000
Mar.	23,000	July	15,000	Nov.	33,000
Apr	19,000	Aug.	14,000	Dec.	36,000

PAPER TRAIL

The Johnson receiving reports all agreed with the quantities billed by Madden. Each invoice had a receiving report attached in the Johnson voucher files. Even though Madden had many trucks, the same driver always came to the Johnson plant, as evidenced by his signature on the receiving report (along with the Johnson company receiving employees' initials). Madden charged $1.80 per gallon, making the charges for the 275,000 gallons a total of $495,000 for the year. Last year, Johnson paid a total of $360,000 for 225,000 gallons, but nobody made a complete comparison with last year's quantity and cost.

AMOUNT

During the first year, Madden shorted Johnson on quantity by 40,000 gallons (loss = 40,000 × $1.80 = $72,000) and charged 20 cents per gallon more than competitors (loss = 235,000 gallons × $0.20 = $47,000) for a total overcharge of $119,000, not to mention the inferior sludge mix occasionally delivered.

AUDIT APPROACH

OBJECTIVE

Obtain evidence to determine whether all fuel oil billed and paid was actually received in the quality expected at a fair price.

CONTROL

Receiving employees should be provided the tools and techniques they need to do a good job. Scales at the plant entrance could be used to weigh the trucks in and out and determine the amount of fuel oil delivered. (The weight per gallon is a well-known measure.) They could observe the quality of the oil by taking samples for simple chemical analysis.

Instructions should be given to teach the receiving employees the importance of their job so they can be conscientious. They should have been instructed and supervised to read the storage tank gauges themselves instead of relying on Madden's driver.

Lacking these tools and instructions, they were easy marks for the wily driver.

TEST OF CONTROLS

The control activity supposedly in place was the receiving report on the oil delivered. A procedure to (1) take a sample of Madden's bills, and (2a) compare quantities billed to quantities received, and (2b) compare the price billed to the contract would probably not have shown anything unusual (unless the auditor became suspicious of the same driver always delivering to Johnson).

The information from the "understanding the control system" phase would need to be much more detailed to alert the auditors to the poor receiving practices.
Procedure: Make inquiries with the receiving employees to learn about their practices and work habits.

AUDIT OF BALANCE

The balances in question are the fuel oil supply inventory and the fuel expense.

The inventory is easily audited by reading the tank storage gauge for the quantity. The price is found in Madden's invoices.

However, a lower-of-cost-or-market test requires knowledge of market prices of the oil. Since Johnson Chemical apparently has no documentation of competing prices, the auditor will need to make a few telephone calls to other oil distributors to get the prices. Presumably, the auditors would learn that the price is approximately $1.60 per gallon.

The expense balance can be audited like a cost of goods sold number. With knowledge of the beginning fuel inventory, the quantity "purchased," and the quantity in the ending inventory, the fuel oil expense quantity can be calculated. This expense quantity can be priced at Madden's price per gallon.

Analytical procedures applied to the expense should reveal the larger quantities used and the unusual pattern of deliveries, leading to suspicions of Madden and the driver.

DISCOVERY SUMMARY

Knowing the higher expense of the current year and the evidence of a lower market price, the auditors obtained the fuel oil delivery records from the prior year. They are shown below, and the numbers in parentheses are the additional gallons delivered in the current year.

Having found a consistent pattern of greater "use" in the current year, with no operational explanation, the auditors took to the field. With the cooperation of the receiving employees, the auditors read the storage tank measure before the Madden driver arrived. They hid in an adjoining building and watched (and filmed) the driver call out an incorrect reading, pump the oil, sign the receiving report, and depart. Then they took samples. These observations were repeated for three weeks. They saw short deliveries, tested inferior products, and built a case against Madden and the driver.

Jan.	28,000 (3,000)	May	13,000 (5,000)	Sep.	15,000 (6,000)
Feb.	24,000 (4,000)	June	11,000 (3,000)	Oct.	20,000 (3,000)
Mar.	20,000 (3,000)	July	10,000 (5,000)	Nov.	28,000 (5,000)
Apr.	17,000 (2,000)	Aug.	9,000 (5,000)	Dec.	30,000 (6,000)

CASE 9.4
RETREAD TIRES

PROBLEM

Inventory and income overstated by substitution of retread tires valued for inventory at new tire prices.

METHOD

Ritter Tire Wholesale Company had a high-volume truck and passenger car tire business in Austin, Texas (area population 750,000). J. Lock, the chief accountant, was a longtime trusted employee who had supervisory responsibility over the purchasing agents as well as general accounting duties. Lock had worked several years as a purchasing agent before moving into the accounting job. In the course of normal operations, Lock often prepared purchase orders; but the manufacturers were directed to deliver the tires to a warehouse in Marlin (a town of 15,000 population 100 miles northeast of Austin). Ritter Tire received the manufacturers' invoices, which Lock approved for payment. Lock and an accomplice (brother-in-law) sold the tires from the Marlin warehouse and pocketed the money. At night, Lock moved cheaper retreaded tires into the Ritter warehouse so spaces would not seem to be empty. As chief accountant, Lock could override controls (e.g., approving invoices for payment with-

out a receiving report), and T. Ritter (president) never knew the difference because the checks presented for signature were not accompanied by the supporting documents.

PAPER TRAIL

Ritter Tire's files were well organized. Each check copy had supporting documents attached (voucher, invoice, receiving report, purchase order), except the misdirected tire purchases had no receiving reports. These purchase orders were all signed by Lock, and the shipping destination on them directed delivery to the Marlin address. There were no purchase requisition documents because "requisitions" were in the form of verbal requests from salespersons.

There was no paper evidence of the retreaded tires because Lock simply bought them elsewhere and moved them in at night when nobody else was around.

AMOUNT

Lock carried out the scheme for three years, diverting tires that cost Ritter $2.5 million, which Lock sold for $2.9 million. (Lock's cost of retread tires was approximately $500,000.)

AUDIT APPROACH

OBJECTIVE

Obtain evidence of the existence and valuation of the inventory. (President Ritter engaged external auditors for the first time in the third year of Lock's scheme after experiencing a severe cash squeeze.)

CONTROL

Competent personnel should perform the purchasing function. Lock and the other purchasing agents were competent and experienced. They prepared purchase orders authorizing the purchase of tires. (The manufacturers required them for shipments.)

A receiving department prepared a receiving report after counting and inspecting each shipment by filling in the "quantity column" on a copy of the purchase order. (A common form of receiving report is a "blind" purchase order that has all the purchase information except the quantity, which is left blank for the receiving department to fill in after an independent inspection and count.) Receiving personnel made notes if the tires showed blemishes or damage.

As chief accountant, Lock received the invoices from the manufacturers and approved them for payment after comparing the quantities with the receiving report and the prices with the purchase order. The checks for payment were produced automatically on the microcomputer accounting system when Lock entered the invoice payable in the system. The computer software did not void transactions for lack of a receiving report reference because many other expenses legitimately had no receiving reports.

The key weakness in the control system was the fact that no one else on the accounting staff had the opportunity to notice missing receiving reports in vouchers that should have had them, and Ritter never had the vouchers when checks were signed. Lock was a trusted employee.

TEST OF CONTROLS

Because the control activities for crosschecking the supporting documents were said to have been placed in operation, the external auditors can test the controls.

Procedure: Select a sample of purchases (manufacturers' invoices payable entered in the microcomputer), and (1) study the related purchase order for (i) valid manufacturer name and address; (ii) date; (iii) delivery address; (iv) unit price, with reference to catalogs or price lists; (v) correct arithmetic; and (vi) approval signature. Then (2) compare purchase order information to the manufacturers' invoice; and (3) compare the purchase order and invoice to the receiving report for (i) date, (ii) quantity and condition, (iii) approval signature, and (iv) location.

AUDIT OF BALANCE

Ritter Tire did not maintain perpetual inventory records, so the inventory was a "periodic system" whereby the financial statement inventory figure was derived from the annual physical inventory count and costing compilation. The basic audit procedure was to observe the count by taking a sample of locations on the warehouse floor, recounting the employees' count, controlling the count sheets, and inspecting the tires for quality and condition (related to proper valuation). The auditors kept their own copy of all the count sheets with their test count notes and notes identifying tires as "new" or "retread." (They took many test counts in the physical inventory sample as a result of the test of controls work, described below.)

DISCOVERY SUMMARY

Forty manufacturers' invoices were selected at random for the test of controls procedure. The auditors were good. They had reviewed the business operations, and Ritter had said nothing about having operations or a warehouse in Marlin, although a manufacturer might have been instructed to "drop ship" tires to a customer there. The auditors noticed three missing receiving reports, all of them with purchase orders signed by Lock and requesting delivery to the same Marlin address. They asked Lock about the missing receiving reports, and got this response: "It happens sometimes. I'll find them for you tomorrow." When Lock produced the receiving reports, the auditors noticed they were in a current numerical sequence (dated much earlier), filled out with the same pen, and signed with an illegible scrawl not matching any of the other receiving reports they had seen.

The auditors knew the difference between new and retread tires when they saw them, and confirmed their observations with employees taking the physical inventory count. When Lock priced the inventory, new tire prices were used, and the auditors knew the difference.

Ritter took the circumstantial evidence to a trained investigator who interviewed the manufacturers and obtained information about the Marlin location. The case against Lock led to criminal theft charges and conviction.

R E V I E W   C H E C K P O I N T S

9.20 Why is a "blind purchase order" used as a receiving report document?

9.21 The cases on Printing (Copying) Money, on Real Cash Paid to Phony Doctors, and on Retread Tires all included fictitious people, businesses, and locations. Where can an auditor obtain information about them?

9.22 How can analytical procedures be used for discovery of excess costs (Receiving the Missing Oil) or understated expenses?

9.23 Give some examples of "receiving departments."

9.24 How can it help an auditor to know the physical characteristics of inventoried assets? (Refer to Retread Tires.)

9.25 Why is "professional skepticism" important for auditors? Give two case examples.

9.26 What evidence could the "verbal inquiry" audit procedure produce in Printing (Copying) Money? Receiving the Missing Oil? Retread Tires?

SUMMARY

The acquisition and expenditure cycle consists of purchase requisitioning, purchase ordering, receiving goods and services, recording vendors' invoices and accounting for accounts payable, and making cash disbursements. Companies reduce control risk by having a suitable separation of authorization, custody, recording, and periodic reconciliation duties. Error-checking procedures of comparing purchase orders and receiving reports to vendor invoices are important for recording proper amounts of accounts payable liabilities. Having a separation of duties between preparing cash disbursement checks and actually signing them provides supervisory control. Otherwise, many things could go wrong, ranging from processing false or fictitious purchase orders to failing to record liabilities for goods and services received.

Three topics have special technical notes in the chapter. The *completeness assertion* is very important in the audit of liabilities because misleading financial statements often have involved unrecorded liabilities and expenses. The "search for unrecorded liabilities" is an important set of audit procedures. The *physical inventory observation* audit work gets a special section because actual contact with inventories provides auditors with direct eyewitness evidence of important tangible assets. The short section on *finding fraud in accounts payable* suggests some methods for trying to find signs that might indicate false payments to fictitious vendors.

Cash disbursement is a critical point for asset control. Many cases of embezzlement occur in this process. Illustrative cases in the chapter tell the stories of some of these schemes, mostly involving payment of fictitious charges to dummy companies set up by employees.

MULTIPLE-CHOICE QUESTIONS FOR PRACTICE AND REVIEW

9.27 When verifying debits to the perpetual inventory records of a nonmanufacturing company, an auditor would be most interested in examining a sample of purchase
  a. Approvals.
  b. Requisitions.
  c. Invoices.
  d. Orders.

9.28 Which of the following is an internal control weakness for a company whose inventory of supplies consists of a large number of individual items?
  a. Supplies of relatively little value are expensed when purchased.
  b. The cycle basis is used for physical counts.
  c. The warehouse manager is responsible for maintenance of perpetual inventory records.
  d. Perpetual inventory records are maintained only for items of significant value.

9.29 An effective internal control that protects against the preparation of improper or inaccurate cash disbursements would be to require that all checks be
  a. Signed by an officer after necessary supporting evidence has been examined.
  b. Reviewed by the treasurer before mailing.
  c. Sequentially numbered and accounted for by internal auditors.

  d. Perforated or otherwise effectively canceled when they are returned with the bank statement.

9.30 A client's purchasing system ends with the recording of a liability and its eventual payment. Which of the following best describes the auditor's primary concern with respect to liabilities resulting from the purchasing system?
  a. Accounts payable are not materially understated.
  b. Authority to incur liabilities is restricted to one designated person.
  c. Acquisition of materials is not made from one vendor or one group of vendors.
  d. Commitments for all purchases are made only after established competitive bidding procedures are followed.

9.31 Which of the following is an internal control activity that could prevent a paid disbursement voucher from being presented for payment a second time?
  a. Vouchers should be prepared by individuals who are responsible for signing disbursement checks.
  b. Disbursement vouchers should be approved by at least two responsible management officials.
  c. The date on a disbursement voucher should be within a few days of the date the voucher is presented for payment.
  d. The official signing the check should compare the check with the voucher

and should stamp "paid" on the voucher documents.

9.32 Which of the following procedures would best detect the theft of valuable items from an inventory that consists of hundreds of different items selling for $1 to $10 and a few items selling for hundreds of dollars?
a. Maintain a perpetual inventory of only the more valuable items with frequent periodic verification of the accuracy of the perpetual inventory record.
b. Have an independent CPA firm prepare an internal control report on the effectiveness of the controls over inventory.
c. Have separate warehouse space for the more valuable items with frequent periodic physical counts and comparison to perpetual inventory records.

9.33 Budd, the purchasing agent of Lake Hardware Wholesalers, has a relative who owns a retail hardware store. Budd arranged for hardware to be delivered by manufacturers to the retail store on a COD basis, thereby enabling his relative to buy at Lake's wholesale prices. Budd was probably able to accomplish this because of Lake's poor internal control over
a. Purchase requisitions.
b. Cash receipts.
c. Perpetual inventory records.
d. Purchase orders.

9.34 Which of the following is the best audit procedure for determining the existence of unrecorded liabilities?
a. Examine confirmation requests returned by creditors whose accounts appear on a subsidiary trial balance of accounts payable.
b. Examine a sample of cash disbursements in the period subsequent to year-end.
c. Examine a sample of invoices a few days prior to and subsequent to the year-end to ascertain whether they have been properly recorded.
d. Examine unusual relationships between monthly accounts payable and recorded purchases.

9.35 When evaluating inventory controls with respect to segregation of duties, a CPA would be least likely to
a. Inspect documents.
b. Make inquiries.
c. Observe procedures.
d. Consider policy and procedure manuals.

9.36 An auditor will usually trace the details of the test counts made during the observation of the physical inventory taking to a final inventory compilation. This audit procedure is undertaken to provide evidence that items physically present and observed by the auditor at the time of the physical inventory count are
a. Owned by the client.
b. Not obsolete.
c. Physically present at the time of the preparation of the final inventory schedule.
d. Included in the final inventory schedule.

9.37 Which of the following procedures is least likely to be performed before the balance sheet date?
a. Observation of inventory.
b. Review of internal control over cash disbursements.
c. Search for unrecorded liabilities.
d. Confirmation of receivables.

9.38 The physical count of inventory of a retailer was higher than shown by the perpetual records. Which of the following could explain the difference?
a. Inventory items had been counted but the tags placed on the items had not been taken off the items and added to the inventory accumulation sheets.
b. Credit memos for several items returned by customers had not been recorded.
c. No journal entry had been made on the retailer's books for several items returned to its suppliers.
d. An item purchased "FOB shipping point" had not arrived at the date of the inventory count and had not been reflected in the perpetual records.

9.39 From the auditor's point of view, inventory counts are more acceptable prior to the year-end when
a. Internal control is weak.
b. Accurate perpetual inventory records are maintained.
c. Inventory is slow moving.
d. Significant amounts of inventory are held on a consignment basis.

9.40 To determine whether accounts payable are complete, an auditor performs a test to verify that all merchandise received is recorded. The population for this test consists of all

a. Vendors' invoices.
b. Purchase orders.
c. Receiving reports.
d. Canceled checks.

(AICPA adapted)

9.41 Which of the following client internal control activities most likely addresses the completeness assertion for inventory?
a. The work-in-process account is periodically reconciled with subsidiary inventory records.
b. Employees responsible for custody of finished goods do not perform the receiving function.
c. Receiving reports are prenumbered and the numbering sequence is checked periodically.
d. There is a separation of duties between the payroll department and inventory accounting personnel.

(AICPA adapted)

9.42 When auditing inventories, an auditor would least likely verify that
a. All inventory owned by the client is on hand at the time of the count.
b. The client has used proper inventory pricing.
c. The financial statement presentation of inventories is appropriate.
d. Damaged goods and obsolete items have been properly accounted for.

(AICPA adapted)

9.43 A client maintains perpetual inventory records in quantities and in dollars. If the assessed level of control risk is high, an auditor would probably
a. Apply gross profit tests to ascertain the reasonableness of the physical counts.
b. Increase the extent of tests of controls relevant to the inventory cycle.
c. Request the client to schedule the physical inventory count at the end of the year.

d. Insist that the client perform physical counts of inventory items several times during the year.

(AICPA adapted)

9.44 An auditor selected items for test counts while observing a client's physical inventory. The auditor then traced the test counts to the client's inventory listing. This procedure most likely obtained evidence concerning management's assertion of
a. Rights and obligations.
b. Completeness.
c. Existence or occurrence.
d. Valuation.

(AICPA adapted)

9.45 Which of the following audit procedures probably would provide the most reliable evidence concerning the entity's assertion of rights and obligations related to inventories?
a. Trace test counts noted during the entity's physical count to the entity's summarization of quantities.
b. Inspect agreements to determine whether any inventory is pledged as collateral or subject to any liens.
c. Select the last few shipping advices used before the physical count and determine whether the shipments were recorded as sales.
d. Inspect the open purchase order file for significant commitments that should be considered for disclosure.

(AICPA adapted)

9.46 An auditor most likely would analyze inventory turnover rates to obtain evidence concerning management's assertions about
a. Existence or occurrence.
b. Rights and obligations.
c. Presentation and disclosure.
d. Valuation or allocation.

(AICPA adapted)

EXERCISES AND PROBLEMS

Test of Controls Audit Procedures

9.47 **Payable ICQ Items: Control Objectives, Test of Controls Procedures, and Possible Errors or Frauds.** Listed below is a selection of items from the internal control questionnaires.

1. Are invoices, receiving reports, and purchase orders reviewed by the check signer?

2. Are checks dated in the cash disbursements journal with the date of the check?

3. Are quantity and quality of goods received determined at time of receipt by receiving personnel independent of the purchasing department?

4. Are vendors' invoices matched against purchase orders and receiving reports before a liability is recorded?

Required:

For each one:

a. Identify the control objective to which it applies.

b. Specify one test of controls audit procedure an auditor could use to determine whether the control was operating effectively.

c. Using your business experience, your logic or your imagination, or both, give an example of an error or fraud that could occur if the control was absent or ineffective.

d. Write a *substantive audit procedure* that could find errors or frauds that might result from the absence or ineffectiveness of the control items.

9.48   Test of Controls Procedures for Cash Disbursements.   The Runge Controls Corporation manufactures and markets electrical control systems: temperature controls, machine controls, burglar alarms, and the like. Electrical and semiconductor parts are acquired from outside vendors, and systems are assembled in Runge's plant. The company incurs other administrative and operating expenditures. Liabilities for goods and services purchased are entered in a vouchers payable journal, at which time the debits are classified to the asset and expense accounts to which they apply.

The company has specified control activities for approving vendor invoices for payment, for signing checks, for keeping records, and for reconciling the checking accounts. The procedures appear to be well specified and placed in operation.

You are the senior auditor on the engagement, and you need to specify a program (list) of test of controls procedures to audit the effectiveness of the controls over cash disbursements.

Required:

Using the seven general internal control objectives, specify two or more test of controls procedures to audit the effectiveness of typical control activities. (*Hint:* From one sample of recorded cash disbursements, you can specify procedures related to several objectives. See Exhibit 9–3 for examples of test of controls procedures over cash disbursements.) Organize your list according to the example shown below for the "completeness" objective.

Completeness Objective	Test of Controls Program
All valid cash disbursements are recorded and none are omitted.	Determine the numerical sequence of checks issued during the period and scan the sequence for missing numbers.
	Scan the accounts payable records for amounts that appear to be too long outstanding (indicating liabilities for which payment may have been made but not recorded properly).

(AICPA adapted)

Liabilities: Substantive Procedures

9.49   Unrecorded Liabilities Procedures.
You were in the final stages of your audit of the financial statements of Ozine Corporation for the year ended December 31, 2001, when you were consulted by the corporation's president. The president believes there is no point to your examining the 2002 voucher register and testing data in support of 2002 entries. He stated: (1) bills pertaining to 2001 that were received too late to be included in the December voucher register were recorded as of the year-end by the corporation by journal entry; (2) the internal auditor made tests after the year-end; and (3) he would furnish you with a letter certifying that there were no unrecorded liabilities.

Required:

a. Should your procedures for unrecorded liabilities be affected by the fact that the client made a journal entry to record 2001 bills that were received later? Explain.

b. Should your test for unrecorded liabilities be affected by the fact that a letter is obtained in which a responsible management official certifies that to the best of his knowledge all liabilities have been recorded? Explain.

c. Should your test for unrecorded liabilities be eliminated or reduced because of the internal audit work? Explain.

d. What sources, in addition to the 2002 voucher register, should you consider to locate possible unrecorded liabilities?

(AICPA adapted)

9.50   Accounts Payable Confirmations.
Clark and his partner, Kent, both CPAs, are planning their audit program for the audit of accounts payable on the Marlboro Corporation's annual audit. Saturday afternoon they reviewed the thick file of last year's working papers, and they both remembered too well the six days they spent last year on accounts payable.

Last year, Clark had suggested that they mail confirmations to 100 of Marlboro's suppliers. The company regularly purchases from about 1,000 suppliers and these account payable balances fluctuate widely, depending on the volume of purchase and the terms Marlboro's purchasing agent is able to negotiate. Clark's sample of 100 was designed to include accounts with large balances. In fact, the 100 accounts confirmed last year covered 80 percent of the total accounts payable.

Both Clark and Kent spent many hours tracking down minor differences reported in confirmation responses. Nonresponding accounts were investigated by comparing Marlboro's balance with monthly statements received from suppliers.

Required:

a. Identify the accounts payable audit objectives that the auditors must consider in determining the audit procedures to be performed.

b. Identify situations when the auditors should use accounts payable confirmations, and discuss whether they are required to use them.

c. Discuss why the use of large dollar balances as the basis for selecting accounts payable for confirmation might not be the most effective approach, and indicate a more effective sample selection procedure that could be followed when choosing accounts payable for confirmation.

9.51   Search for Unrecorded Liabilities. Marsh, CPA, is the independent auditor for Compufast Corporation (Compufast). Compufast sells personal computers, peripheral equipment (printers, data storage), and a wide variety of programs for business and games. From experience on Compufast's previous audits, Marsh knew that the company's accountants were very much concerned with timely recording of revenues and receivables and somewhat less concerned with keeping up-to-date the records of accounts payable and other liabilities. Marsh knew that the control environment was strong in the asset area and weak in the liability area.

Required

Make a list of substantive audit procedures Marsh and the audit staff can perform to obtain reasonable assurance that Compufast's unrecorded liabilities are discovered and adjusted in the financial statements currently under audit.

Inventory: Substantive Procedures

9.52   Inventory Count Observation: Planning and Substantive Audit Procedures. Sammy Smith is the partner in charge of the audit of Blue Distributing Corporation, a wholesaler that owns one warehouse containing 80 percent of its inventory. Sammy is reviewing the working papers that were prepared to support the firm's opinion on Blue's financial statements. Sammy wants to be certain essential audit procedures are well documented in the working papers.

Required:

a. What evidence should Sammy expect to find that the audit observation of the client's physical count of inventory was well planned and that assistants were properly supervised?

b. What substantive audit procedures should Sammy find in the working papers that document management's assertions about existence

and completeness of inventory quantities at the end of the year? (Refer to Appendix 9B–1 for procedures.)

(AICPA adapted)

9.53   Sales/Inventory Cutoff. Your client took a complete physical inventory count under your observation as of December 15 and adjusted the inventory control account (perpetual inventory method) to agree with the physical inventory. Based on the count adjustments as of December 15 and after review of the transactions recorded from December 16 to December 31, you are almost ready to accept the inventory balance as fairly stated.

However, your review of the sales cutoff as of December 15 and December 31 disclosed the following items not previously considered:

		Date		
				Credited to
Sales				Inventory
Cost	Price	Shipped	Billed	Control
$28,400	$36,900	12/14	12/16	12/16
39,100	50,200	12/10	12/19	12/10
18,900	21,300	1/2	12/31	12/31

Required:

What adjusting journal entries, if any, would you make for each of these items? Explain why each adjustment is necessary.

(AICPA adapted)

9.54   Statistical Sampling Used to Estimate Inventory. ACE Corporation does not conduct a complete annual physical count of purchased parts and supplies in its principal warehouse but, instead, uses statistical sampling to estimate the year-end inventory. Ace maintains a perpetual inventory record of parts and supplies. Management believes that statistical sampling is highly effective in determining inventory values and is sufficiently reliable so a physical count of each item of inventory is unnecessary.

Required:

a. List at least 10 normal audit procedures that should be performed to verify physical quantities whenever a client conducts a periodic physical count of all or part of its inventory (see Appendix 9B–1 for procedures).

b. Identify the audit procedures you should use that *change or are in addition* to normal required audit procedures (in addition to those listed in your solution to part [a]) when a client utilizes statistical sampling to determine inventory value and does not conduct a 100 percent annual physical count of inventory items.

(AICPA adapted)

9.55 Inventory Procedures Using Computer-assisted Audit Tools and Techniques (CAATTs). You are conducting an audit of the financial statements of a wholesale cosmetics distributor with an inventory consisting of thousands of individual items. The distributor keeps its inventory in its own distribution center and in two public warehouses. A perpetual inventory computer database is maintained on a computer disk. The database is updated at the end of each business day. Each individual record of the perpetual inventory database contains the following data:

Item number.

Location of item.

Description of item.

Quantity on hand.

Cost per item.

Date of last purchase.

Date of last sale.

Quantity sold during year.

You are planning to observe the distributor's physical count of inventories as of a given date. You will have available a computer disk file, provided by the client, of the above items taken from their database as of the date of the physical count. Your firm has a computer audit program that will be ideal for analyzing the inventory records.

Required:

List the basic inventory auditing procedures and, for each, describe how the use of the general-purpose audit software package and the disk file of the perpetual inventory database might be helpful to the auditor in performing such auditing procedures. (See Appendix 9B–1 for substantive audit procedures for inventory.)

Organize your answer as follows:

Basic Inventory Auditing Procedures	How Audit Software and Copy of the Inventory Data File Might Be Helpful
Conduct an observation of the company's physical count.	Determining which items are to be test counted by selecting a random sample of a representative number of items from the inventory file as of the date of the physical count.

(AICPA adapted)

9.56 CAATTs Application—Inventory. Your client, Boos & Becker, Inc., is a medium-sized manufacturer of products for the leisure time activities market (camping equipment, scuba gear, bows and arrows, and the like). During the past year, a computer system was installed and inventory records of finished goods and parts were converted to computer processing. Each record of the inventory master file contains the following information:

Item or part number.

Description.

Size.

Quantity on hand.

Cost per unit.

Total value of inventory on hand at cost.

Date of last sale or usage.

Quantity used or sold this year.

Reorder point (quantity).

Economic order quantity.

Code number of major vendor.

Code number of secondary vendor.

In preparation for year-end inventory, the client has two identical sets of preprinted, inventory cards prepared from the master file. One set is for the client's inventory counts, and the other is for your use to make audit test counts. The following information has been punched into the cards and printed on their face:

Item or part number.

Description.

Size.

Unit of measure code.

In taking the year-end count, the client's personnel will write the actual counted quantity on the face of each card. When all counts are complete, the counted quantity will be processed against the master file, and quantity-on-hand figures will be adjusted to reflect the actual count. A computer listing will be prepared to show any missing inventory count cards and all quantity adjustments of more than $100 in value. Client personnel will investigate these items and will make all required adjustments. When adjustments have been completed, the final year-end balances will be computed and posted to the general ledger.

Your firm has available an audit software package that will run on the client's computer and can process both cards and disk master files.

Required:

a. In general and without regard to the facts above, discuss the nature of computer audit software packages and list the various audit uses of such packages.

b. List and describe at least five ways a computer audit software package can be used to assist in all aspects of the audit of the inventory of Boos & Becker, Inc. (For example, the package can be used to read the inventory master file and list items and parts with a high unit cost or total value. Such items can be included in the test counts to increase the dollar coverage of the audit verification.) *Hint:* Think of the normal audit procedures in gathering evidence on inventory when the client makes a periodic count, then think of how the CAATTs could help in this particular client situation.

(AICPA adapted)

9.57   Peacock Company: Incomplete Flowchart of Inventory and Purchasing Control Procedures.   Peacock Company is a wholesaler of soft goods. The inventory is composed of approximately 3,500 different items. The company employs a computerized batch processing system to maintain its perpetual inventory records. The system is run each weekend so the inventory reports are available on Monday morning for management use. The system has been functioning satisfactorily for the past 15 months, providing the company with accurate records and timely reports.

The preparation of purchase orders is automatic as a part of the inventory system to ensure that the company will maintain enough inventory to meet customer demand. When an item of inventory falls below a predetermined level, a record of the inventory items is written. This record is used in conjunction with the vendor file to prepare the purchase orders.

Exception reports are prepared during the update of the inventory and the preparation of the purchase orders. These reports list any errors or exceptions identified during the processing. In addition, the system provides for management approval of all purchase orders exceeding a specified amount. Any exceptions or items requiring management approval are handled by supplemental runs on Monday morning and are combined with the weekend results.

A system flowchart of Peacock Company's inventory and purchase order procedure is presented in Exhibit 9.57–1.

Required:

a. The illustrated system flowchart (Exhibit 9.57–1) of Peacock Company's inventory and purchase order system was prepared before the system was fully operational. Several steps that are important to the successful operations of the system were inadvertently omitted from the chart. Now that the system is operating effectively, management wants the system documentation complete and would like the flowchart corrected. Describe the steps that have been omitted and indicate where the omissions have occurred. The flowchart does not need to be redrawn.

b. In order for Peacock's inventory/purchase order system to function properly, control activities should be included in the system. Describe the type of controls Peacock Company should use in its system to assure proper functioning, and indicate where these activities would be placed in the system.

DISCUSSION CASES

9.58   Inventory Evidence and Long-Term Purchase Contracts.   During the audit of Mason Company, Inc., for the calendar year 2001, you noticed that the company produces aluminum cans at the rate of about 40 million units annually. On the plant tour, you noticed a large stockpile of raw aluminum in storage. Your inventory observation and pricing procedures showed this stockpile to be the raw materials inventory of 400 tons valued at $240,000 (LIFO cost). Inquiry with the production chief yielded the information that 400 tons was about a four-month supply of raw materials.

Suppose you learn that Mason had executed a firm long-term purchase contract with All Purpose Aluminum Company to purchase raw materials on the following schedule:

Delivery Date	Quantity (Tons)	Total Price
January 30, 2002	500	$300,000
June 30, 2002	700	420,000
December 30, 2002	1,000	500,000

Because of recent economic conditions, principally a decline in the demand for raw aluminum and a consequent oversupply, the price stood at 40 cents per pound as of January 15, 2002.

EXHIBIT 9.57–1   PEACOCK COMPANY—INVENTORY AND PURCHASE

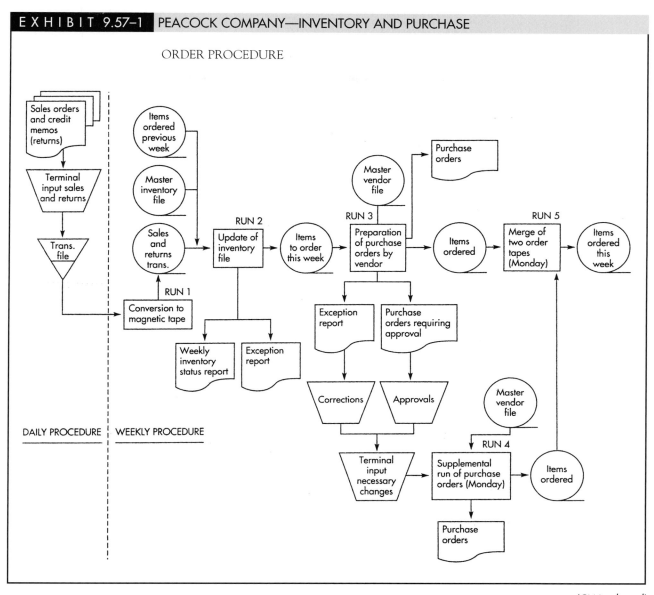

ORDER PROCEDURE

(CMA adapted)

Commodities experts predict that this low price will prevail for 12 to 15 months or until there is a general economic recovery.

Required:

a. Describe the procedures you would employ to gather evidence about this contract (including its initial discovery).

b. What facts recited in the problems are ones that you would have to discover for yourself in an audit?

c. Discuss the effect this contract has on the financial statements.

9.59   Fictitious Vendors, Theft, and Embezzlement.   This case is designed like the ones in

the chapter. It gives the problem, the method, the paper trail, and the amount. Your assignment is to write the "audit approach" portion of the case, organized around these sections:

Objective: Express the objective in terms of the facts supposedly asserted in financial records, accounts, and statements.

Control: Write a brief explanation of desirable controls, missing controls, and especially the kinds of "deviations" that might arise from the situation described in the case.

Test of controls: Write some procedures for getting evidence about existing controls, especially procedures that could discover deviations from controls. If there are no controls to test, then there are no procedures to perform; go then to the next section. A "procedure" should instruct someone about the source(s) of evidence to tap and the work to do.

Audit of balance: Write some procedures for getting evidence about the existence, completeness, valuation, ownership, or disclosure assertions identified in your objective section above.

Discovery summary: Write a short statement about the discovery you expect to accomplish with your procedures.

Purchasing Stars

Problem: Kickbacks taken on books or supplies inventory purchases caused inflated inventory, cost of goods sold, and expenses.

Method: Bailey Books, Inc., is a retail distributor of upscale books, periodicals, and magazines. Bailey has 431 retail stores throughout the southeastern states. Three full-time purchasing agents work at corporate headquarters. They are responsible for purchasing all the inventory at the best prices available from wholesales suppliers. They can

purchase with or without obtaining competitive bids. The three purchasing agents are: R. McGuire in charge of purchasing books, M. Garza in charge of purchasing magazines and periodicals, and L. Collins (manager of purchasing) in charge of ordering miscellaneous items, such as paper products and store supplies.

One of the purchasing agents is suspected of taking kickbacks from vendors. In return, Bailey is thought to be paying inflated prices, which first go to inventory and then to cost of goods sold and other expense accounts as the assets are sold or used.

L. Collins is the manager in charge. Her duties do not include audit or inspection of the performance of the other two purchasing agents. No one audits or reviews Collins's performance.

Paper trail: The purchasing system is computerized, and detail records are retained. An extract from these records is in Exhibit 9.59–1.

Amount: This kickback scheme has been going on for two or three years. Several hundred thousand dollars may have been overpaid by Bailey Books.

EXHIBIT 9.59–1   SUMMARY OF PURCHASING ACTIVITY

BAILEY BOOKS, INCORPORATED
Selected Purchases 1999–2001

Vendor	Items Purchased	1999	2000	2001	Date of Last Bid	Percent of Purchases Bid (3-yr. Period)
Armour	Books	683,409	702,929	810,100	12/01/01	87%
Burdick	Sundries	62,443	70,949	76,722	—	—
Canon	Magazines	1,404,360	1,947,601	2,361,149	11/03/01	94
DeBois, Inc.	Paper	321,644	218,404	121,986	06/08/01	57
Elton Books	Books	874,893	781,602	649,188	07/21/01	91
Fergeson	Books	921,666	1,021,440	1,567,811	09/08/01	88
Guyford	Magazines	2,377,821	2,868,988	3,262,490	10/08/01	81
Hyman, Inc.	Supplies	31,640	40,022	46,911	10/22/01	—
Intertec	Books	821,904	898,683	949,604	11/18/01	86
Jerrico	Paper	186,401	111,923	93,499	10/04/01	72
Julian-Borg	Magazines	431,470	589,182	371,920	02/07/01	44
King Features	Magazines	436,820	492,687	504,360	11/18/01	89
Lycorp	Sundries	16,280	17,404	21,410	—	—
Medallian	Books	—	61,227	410,163	12/15/01	99
Northwood	Books	861,382	992,121	—	12/07/00	—
Orion Corp.	Paper	86,904	416,777	803,493	11/02/00	15
Peterson	Supplies	114,623	—	—	N/A	N/A
Quick	Supplies	—	96,732	110,441	11/03/01	86
Robertson	Books	2,361,912	3,040,319	3,516,811	12/01/01	96
Steele	Magazines	621,490	823,707	482,082	11/03/01	90
Telecom	Sundries	81,406	101,193	146,316	—	—
Union Bay	Books	4,322,639	4,971,682	5,368,114	12/03/01	97
Victory	Magazines	123,844	141,909	143,286	06/09/01	89
Williams	Sundries	31,629	35,111	42,686	—	—

APPENDIX 9A   INTERNAL CONTROLS

APPENDIX 9A–1   PURCHASING AND ACCOUNTS PAYABLE

Environment:

1. Is the purchasing department independent of the accounting department, receiving department, and shipping department?
2. Are receiving report copies transmitted to inventory custodians? To purchasing? To the accounting department?

Validity objective:

3. Are vendors' invoices matched against purchase orders and receiving reports before a liability is recorded?

Completeness objective:

4. Are the purchase order forms prenumbered and the numerical sequence checked for missing documents?
5. Are receiving report forms prenumbered and the numerical sequence checked for missing documents?
6. Is the accounts payable department notified of goods returned to vendors?
7. Are vendors' invoices listed immediately upon receipt?
8. Are unmatched receiving reports reviewed frequently and investigated for proper recording?

Authorization objective:

9. Are competitive bids received and reviewed for certain items?
10. Are all purchases made only on the basis of approved purchase requisitions?
11. Are purchases made for employees authorized through the regular purchases procedures?
12. Are purchase prices approved by a responsible purchasing officer?
13. Are all purchases, whether for inventory or expense, routed through the purchasing department for approval?
14. Are shipping documents authorized and prepared for goods returned to vendors?
15. Are invoices approved for payment by a responsible officer?

Accuracy objective:

16. Are quantity and quality of goods received determined at the time of receipt by receiving personnel independent of the purchasing department?
17. Are vendors' monthly statements reconciled with individual accounts payable accounts?
18. In the accounts payable department, are invoices checked against purchase orders and receiving reports for quantities, prices, and terms?

Classification objective:

19. Does the chart of accounts and accounting manual give instructions for classifying debit entries when purchases are recorded?

Accounting and Posting objective:

20. Is the accounts payable detail ledger balanced periodically with the general ledger control account?

Proper period objective:

21. Does the accounting manual give instructions to date purchase/payable entries on the date of receipt of goods?

APPENDIX 9A–2   CASH DISBURSEMENTS PROCESSING

Environment:

1. Are persons with cash custody or check-signing authority denied access to accounting journals, ledgers, and bank reconciliations?
2. Is access to blank checks denied to unauthorized persons?
3. Are all disbursements except petty cash made by check?
4. Are check signers prohibited from drawing checks to cash?
5. Is signing blank checks prohibited?
6. Are voided checks mutilated and retained for inspection?

Validity objective:

7. Are invoices, receiving reports, and purchase orders reviewed by the check signer?
8. Are the supporting documents stamped "paid" (to prevent duplicate payment) before being returned to accounts payable for filing?
9. Are checks mailed directly by the signer and not returned to the accounts payable department for mailing?

Completeness objective:

10. Are blank checks prenumbered and the numerical sequence checked for missing documents?

Authorization objective:

11. Do checks require two signatures? Is there dual control over machine signature plates?

Accuracy objective:

12. Are bank accounts reconciled by personnel independent of cash custody or record keeping?

Classification objective:

13. Does the chart of accounts and accounting manual give instructions for determining debit classifications of disbursements not charged to accounts payable?
14. Is the distribution of charges double-checked periodically by an official? Is the budget used to check on gross misclassification errors?
15. Are special disbursements (e.g., payroll and dividends) made from separate bank accounts?

Accounting and Posting objective:

16. Is the bank reconciliation reviewed by an accounting official with no conflicting cash receipts, cash disbursements, or record keeping responsibilities?
17. Do internal auditors periodically conduct a surprise audit of bank reconciliations?

Proper period objective:

18. Are checks dated in the cash disbursements journal with the date of the check?

APPENDIX 9A–3   ACQUISITION AND EXPENDITURE COMPUTER CONTROLS

- Each terminal performs only designated functions. For example, the receiving clerk's terminal cannot accept a purchase order entry.
- An identification number and password (used on an individual basis) is required to enter the nonautomatic purchase orders, vendors' invoices, and the receiving report information. Further, certain passwords have "read only" authorization. These are issued to personnel authorized to determine the status of various records, such as an open voucher, but not authorized to enter data.
- All input immediately is logged to provide restart processing should any terminal become inoperative during the processing.
- The transaction codes call up a full screen "form" on the terminals that appears to the operators in the same format as the original paper documents. Each clerk must enter the information correctly (online input validation) or the computer will not accept the data.
- All printed documents are computer numbered and the number is stored as part of the record. Further, all records in the open databases have the vendor's number as the primary search and matching field key. Of course, status searches could be made by another field. For example, the inventory number can be the search key to determine the status of a purchase of an item in short supply.
- A daily search of the open databases is made. Purchases outstanding for more than 10 days and the missing "document" records are printed out on a report for investigation of the delay.
- The check signature is printed, using a signature plate that is installed on the computer printer only when checks are printed. A designated person in the treasurer's office maintains custody of this signature plate and must take it to the computer room to be installed when checks are printed. This person also has the combination to the separate document storage room where the blank check stock is kept and is present at all check printing runs. The printed checks are taken immediately from the computer room for mailing.

APPENDIX 9A–4   INVENTORY TRANSACTION PROCESSING

Environment:
1. Are perpetual inventory records kept for raw materials? Supplies? Work in process? Finished goods?
2. Are perpetual records subsidiary to general ledger control accounts?
3. Do the perpetual records show quantities only? Quantities and prices?
4. Are inventory records maintained by someone other than the inventory stores custodian?
5. Is merchandise or materials on consignment-in (not the property of the company) physically segregated from goods owned by the company?

Validity objective:
6. Are additions to inventory quantity records made only on receipt of a receiving report copy?
7. Do inventory custodians notify the records department of additions to inventory?

Completeness objective:
8. Are reductions of inventory record quantities made only on receipt of inventory issuance documents?
9. Do inventory custodians notify inventory records of reductions of inventory?

Authorization objective:
   Refer to question 6 above (additions).
   Refer to question 8 above (reductions).

Accuracy objective:
10. If standard costs have been used for inventory pricing, have they been reviewed for current applicability?

Classification objective:
11. Are periodic counts of physical inventory made to correct errors in the individual perpetual records?

Accounting and Posting objective:
12. Is there a periodic review for overstocked, slow-moving, or obsolete inventory? Have any adjustments been made during the year?
13. Are perpetual inventory records kept in dollars periodically reconciled to general ledger control accounts?

Proper period objective:
14. Does the accounting manual give instructions to record inventory additions on the date of the receiving report?
15. Does the accounting manual give instructions to record inventory issues on the issuance date?

APPENDIX 9B   SUBSTANTIVE AUDIT PROGRAMS

APPENDIX 9B–1   AUDIT PROGRAM FOR INVENTORY AND COST OF GOODS SOLD

A. **Inventory**
  1. Conduct an observation of the company's physical inventory count. Count a sample of inventory items and trace these counts to the final inventory compilation.
  2. Select a sample of inventory items. Vouch unit prices to vendors' invoices or other cost records. Recalculate the multiplication of unit times price.
  3. Scan the inventory compilation for items added from sources other than the physical count and items that appear to be large round numbers or systematic fictitious additions.
  4. Recalculate the extensions and footings of the final inventory compilation for clerical accuracy. Reconcile the total to the adjusted trial balance.
  5. For selected inventory items and categories, determine the replacement cost and the applicability of lower-of-cost-or-market valuation.
  6. Determine whether obsolete or damaged goods should be written down:
     a. Inquire about obsolete, damaged, unsalable, slow-moving, and overstocked inventory.
     b. Scan the perpetual records for slow-moving items.
     c. During the physical observation, be alert to notice damaged or scrap inventory.
     d. Compare the listing of obsolete, slow-moving, damaged, or unsalable inventory from last year's audit to the current inventory compilation.
  7. At year-end, obtain the numbers of the last shipping and receiving documents for the year. Use these to scan the sales, inventory/cost of sales, and accounts payable entries for proper cutoff.
  8. Read bank confirmations, debt agreements, and minutes of the board, and make inquiries about pledge or assignment of inventory to secure debt.
  9. Inquire about inventory out on consignment and about inventory on hand which is consigned-in from vendors.
  10. Confirm or inspect inventories held in public warehouses.
  11. Recalculate the amount of intercompany profit to be eliminated in consolidation.
  12. Obtain written client representations concerning pledge of inventory as collateral, intercompany sales, and other related party transactions.

B. **Cost of Sales**
  1. Select a sample of recorded cost of sales entries and vouch to supporting documentation.
  2. Select a sample of basic transaction documents (such as sales invoices, production reports) and determine whether the related cost of goods sold was figured and recorded properly.
  3. Determine whether the accounting costing method used by the client (such as FIFO, LIFO, standard cost) was applied properly.
  4. Compute the gross margin rate and compare to prior years.
  5. Compute the ratio of cost elements (such as labor, material) to total cost of goods sold and compare to prior years.

APPENDIX 9B–2 AUDIT PROGRAM FOR ACCOUNTS PAYABLE

1. Obtain a trial balance of recorded accounts payable as of year-end. Foot it and trace the total to the general ledger account. Vouch a sample of balances to vendors' statements. Review the trial balance for related-party payables.
2. When concerned about the possibility of unrecorded payables, send confirmations to creditors, especially those with small or zero balances and those with whom the company has done significant business.
3. Conduct a search for unrecorded liabilities by examining open vouchers, vendors' invoices and statements received, and cash payments made for a period after year-end.
4. Inquire about terms that justify classifying payables as long term instead of current.
5. For estimated liabilities, such as warranties, determine and evaluate the basis of estimation, and recalculate the estimate.
6. Obtain written client representations about related-party payables and pledges of assets as collateral for liabilities.

APPENDIX 9B–3 AUDIT PROGRAM FOR PREPAID, DEFERRED, AND ACCRUED EXPENSES

1. Obtain a schedule of all prepaid expenses, deferred costs, and accrued expenses.
2. Determine whether each item is properly allocated to the current or future accounting periods.
3. Select significant additions to deferred and accrued amounts, and vouch them to supporting invoices, contracts, or calculations.
4. Determine the basis for deferral and accrual, and recalculate the recorded amounts.
5. Study the nature of each item, inquire of management, and determine whether the remaining balance will be recovered from future operations.
6. In other audit work on income and expenses, be alert to notice items that should be considered prepaid, deferred, or accrued, and allocated to current or future accounting periods.
7. Scan the expense accounts in the trial balance and compare to prior year. Investigate unusual difference that may indicate failure to account for a prepaid or accrual item.
8. Study each item to determine the proper current or noncurrent balance sheet classification.

Chapter 10
Production and Payroll Cycle

Professional Standards References

Compendium Section	Document Reference	Topic
AU 311	SAS 77	*Planning and Supervision*
AU 312	SAS 47	*Audit Risk and Materiality in Conducting an Audit*
AU 316	SAS 82	*Consideration of Fraud in a Financial Statement Audit*
AU 317	SAS 54	*Illegal Acts by Clients*
AU 319	SAS 78	*Internal Control in a Financial Statement Audit*
AU 326	SAS 80	*Evidential Matter*
AU 329	SAS 56	*Analytical Procedures*
AU 339	SAS 41	*Working Papers*

Learning Objectives

In the production and payroll cycle, materials, labor, and overhead are converted into finished goods and services. This chapter breaks the production and payroll cycle into two sections. Part I covers the production cycle, dealing with inventory valuation, depreciation, and cost of goods sold accounting. The audit of payrolls and labor cost accounting is in Part II. A few short cases are used to show the application of audit procedures in situations where errors and frauds might be discovered. After completing this chapter, you should be able to:

1. Describe the production cycle, including typical source documents and controls.

2. Give examples of detail test of controls procedures for auditing the controls over conversion of materials and labor in a production process.

3. Describe some common errors and frauds in the accounting for production costs and related cost of goods sold, and design some audit and investigation procedures for detecting them.

4. Describe the payroll cycle, including typical source documents and controls.

5. Give examples of detail test of controls procedures for auditing the controls over payroll.

6. Describe some common errors and frauds in payroll, and design some audit and investigation procedures for detecting them.

PART I: PRODUCTION CYCLE TYPICAL ACTIVITIES

LEARNING OBJECTIVE

1. Describe the production cycle, including typical source documents and controls.

The basic production activities start with production planning, including inventory planning and management. Production planning can range from use of a sophisticated computerized long-range plan with just-in-time (JIT) inventory management to a simple ad hoc method ("Hey, Joe, we got an order today. Go make 10 units!") Exhibit 10–1 shows the activities and accounting involved in a production cycle. As you follow the exhibit, you can track the elements of a control system described in the sections below.

Most businesses try to estimate or forecast sales levels and seasonal timing, and they try to plan facilities and production schedules to meet customer demand. As shown in Exhibit 10–1, the production cycle interacts with the acquisition cycle and the payroll cycle (later in this chapter) for the acquisition of fixed assets, materials, supplies, overhead, and labor.

The physical output of a production cycle is inventory (starting with raw materials, proceeding to work in process, then to finished goods). Exhibit 10–1 shows the connection of inventory to the revenue and collection cycle in terms of orders and deliveries.

Most of the "transactions" in a production cycle are cost accounting allocations, unit cost determinations, and standard cost calculations. These are internal transactions produced entirely within the company's accounting system. Exhibit 10–1 shows the elements of depreciation cost calculation, cost of goods sold determination, and job cost analysis as examples of these transactions.

Authorization

The overall production authorization starts with production planning, which usually is based on a **sales forecast**. Production planning interacts with inventory planning to produce **production orders**. These production orders specify the materials and labor required and the timing for the start and end of production. Managers in the sales/marketing department and production department usually sign off their approval on plans and production orders.

Authorization also can include plans and approvals for subcontracting (outsourcing) work to other companies. The process of taking bids and executing contracts can be a

EXHIBIT 10-1   PRODUCTION CYCLE

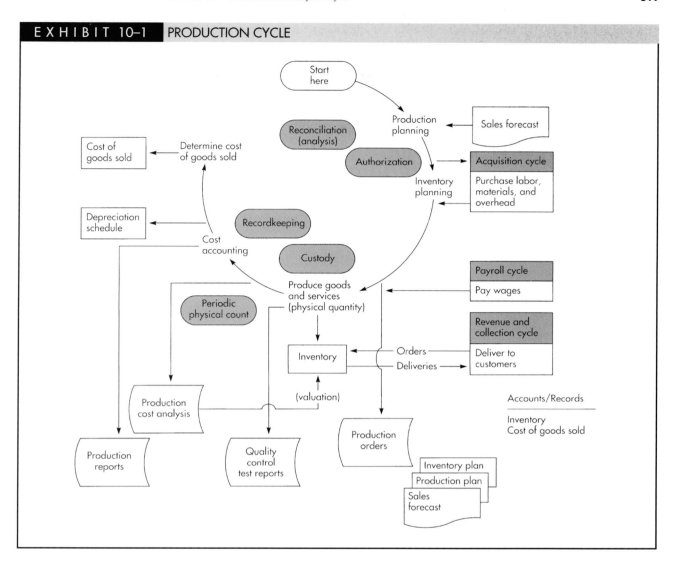

part of the planning-authorization system. In modern management terminology, many of these arrangements are the "strategic alliances" you see announced in the newspapers.

The production order usually includes a **bill of materials** (a specification of the materials authorized for the production). This bill of materials is the source of authorization for the preparation of **materials requisitions**, and these requisitions are the authorization for the inventory custodian to release raw materials and supplies to the production personnel. These documents are the inventory record keepers' authorizations to update the raw materials inventory files to record the reductions of the raw materials inventory.

Later, when production is complete, the production reports, along with the physical units and the quality control test reports, are the authorizations for the finished goods inventory custodian to place the units in the finished goods inventory. These same documents are the inventory record keepers' authorization to update the inventory record files to record the additions to the finished goods inventory.

Custody

Supervisors and workers have physical custody of materials and labor while the production work is performed. They can requisition materials from the raw materials inventory, assign people to jobs, and control the pace of work. In a sense, they have custody of a "moving inventory." The work in process (an inventory category) is literally "moving" and changing form in the process of being transformed from raw materials into finished goods.

Control over this custody is more difficult than control over a closed warehouse full of raw materials or finished goods. Control can be exercised by holding supervisors and workers accountable for the use of materials specified in the production orders, for the timely completion of production, and for the quality of the finished goods. This accountability can be achieved with good cost accounting, cost analysis, and quality control testing.

Record Keeping (Cost Accounting)

When production is completed, production orders and the related records of material and labor used are sent forward to the cost accounting department. Since these accounting documents may come from the production workers, the effective separation of the record keeping function depends upon its receiving independent notices from other places, especially notifications of materials issued from the inventory custodian and the labor costs assigned by the payroll department.

The cost accounting department produces analyses of cost-per-unit, standard cost, and variances. Cost accounting also may determine the allocation of overhead to production in general, to production orders, and to finished units. Depending on the design of the company's cost accounting system, these costs are used in inventory valuation and ultimately in determination of the cost of goods sold. In many cases, the cost accounting department also is responsible for calculating the depreciation of fixed assets and the amortization of intangibles.

AUDITING INSIGHT

OVERHEAD ALLOCATION

The cost accounting department at Pointed Publications, Inc., routinely allocated overhead to book printing runs at the rate of 40 percent of materials and labor cost. The debit was initially to the finished books inventory, while the credit went to an "overhead allocated" account that was offset against other entries in the cost of goods sold calculation, which included all the actual overhead incurred. During the year, 10 million books were produced and $40 million of overhead was allocated to them. The auditors noticed that actual overhead expenditures were $32 million, and 3 million books remained in the ending inventory.

The finding resulted in the conclusion that the inventory was overstated by $2.4 million, the cost of goods sold was understated by $2.4 million, and the income before taxes was overstated by 8.2 percent.

	Company Accounting	Proper Accounting
Books produced	10 million	10 million
Labor and materials cost	$100 million	$ 100 million
Overhead allocated	$ 40 million	$ 32 million
Cost per book	$ 14 00	$ 13.20
Cost of goods sold:		
Labor and materials cost	$100 million	$ 100 million
Overhead allocated to books	$ 40 million	
Overhead incurred	32 million	32 million
Overhead credited to cost	(40 million)	
Ending inventory	(42 million)	(39.6 million)
Total cost of goods sold	$ 90 million	$ 92.4 million

Periodic Reconciliation

The function of periodic reconciliation generally refers to comparison of actual assets and liabilities to the amounts recorded in the company accounts (e.g., comparing the physical count of inventory to the perpetual inventory records, comparing vendors' monthly statements to the recorded accounts payable). Exhibit 10–1 shows the periodic reconciliation of physical inventory to recorded amounts. The work-in-process inventory also can be observed, although the "count" of partially completed units is very judgmental. It can be valued at the cost of labor, materials, and overhead assigned to its stage of completion.

Most other periodic reconciliations in the production cycle take the form of analyses of internal information. These analyses include costing the production orders, comparing the cost to prior experience or to standard costs, and determining lower-of-cost-or-market (LCM) valuations. In a sense, the LCM calculations are a "reconciliation" of product cost to the external market price of product units.

R E V I E W
CHECKPOINTS

10.1 What are the functions normally associated with the production and conversion cycle?

10.2 Why is an understanding of the production process, including the related data processing and cost accounting, important to auditors evaluating the control system as part of their assessment of control risk?

10.3 Describe a "walk-through" of a production transaction from production orders to entry in the finished goods perpetual inventory records. What document copies would be collected? What controls noted? What duties separated?

10.4 Describe how the separation of (1) authorization of production transactions, (2) recording of these transactions, and (3) physical custody of inventories can be specified among the production, inventory, and cost accounting departments.

10.5 What features of the cost accounting system would be expected to prevent the omission of recording materials used in production?

AUDIT EVIDENCE IN MANAGEMENT REPORTS AND FILES

Most production accounting systems produce timely reports managers need to supervise and control production. Auditors can use these reports as supporting evidence for assertions about work-in-process and finished goods inventories and about cost of goods sold. Auditors should obtain and use these reports.

Sales Forecast

Management's sales forecast provides the basis for several aspects of business planning, notably the planning of production and inventory levels. If the auditors want to use the forecast for substantive audit decisions, some work to obtain assurance about its reasonableness needs to be performed. In addition, some work on the mechanical accuracy of the forecast should be performed to avoid an embarrassing reliance on faulty calculations.

Forecasts can be used in connection with knowing management's plans for the year under audit, most of which will have already passed when the audit work begins. It will help the auditors understand the nature and volume of production orders and the level

THE SALY FORECAST

The auditors were reviewing the inventory items that had not been issued for 30 days or more, considering the need to write some items down to market lower than cost. The production manager showed them the SALY forecast that indicated continuing need for the materials in products that are expected to have reasonable demand. The auditors agreed that the forecasts supported the prediction of future sales of products at prices that would cover the cost of the slow-moving material items.

Unfortunately, they neglected to ask the meaning of SALY in the designation of the forecast. They did not learn that it means "Same As Last Year." It is not a forecast at all. The products did not sell at the prices expected, and the company experienced losses the following year that should have been charged to cost of goods sold earlier.

of materials inventory. Forecasts of the following year can be used in connection with valuing the inventory at lower-of-cost-or-market (e.g., slow-moving and potentially obsolete inventory), which influences the amount of cost of goods sold shown in the financial statements. Special care must be taken with using the forecast for the next year in connection with inventory valuation because an overly optimistic forecast can lead to a failure to write down inventory, accelerate the depreciation of fixed assets, and account for more cost of goods sold.

Production Plans and Reports

Based on the sales forecast, management should develop a plan for the amount and timing of production. The production plan provides general information to the auditors, but the production orders and inventory plan associated with the production plan are even more important. The production orders carry the information about requirements for raw materials, labor, and overhead, including the requisitions for purchase and use of materials and labor. These documents are the initial authorizations for control of the inventory and production.

Production reports record the completion of production quantities. When coupled with the related cost accounting reports, they are the company's record of the cost of goods placed into the finished goods inventory. In most cases, auditors will audit the cost reports in connection with determining the cost valuation of inventory and cost of goods sold.

R E V I E W
CHECKPOINTS

10.6 When auditors want to use a client's sales forecast for general familiarity with the production cycle or for evaluation of slow-moving inventory, what kind of work should be done on the forecast?

10.7 If the actual sales for the year are substantially lower than the sales forecasted at the beginning of the year, what potential valuation problems might arise in the production cycle accounts?

10.8 What production cycle documentation supports the valuation of manufactured finished goods inventory?

10.9 What problems may be caused by the client's use of the same production estimates as the previous year?

CONTROL RISK ASSESSMENT

LEARNING OBJECTIVE

2. Give examples of detail test of controls procedures for auditing the controls over conversion of materials and labor in a production process.

Control risk assessment is important because it governs the nature, timing, and extent of substantive audit procedures that will be applied in the audit of account balances in the production cycle. These account balances include:

Inventory:
 Raw materials.
 Work in process.
 Finished goods.
Cost of goods sold.

With respect to inventory valuation, this chapter points out the cost accounting function and its role in determining the cost valuation of manufactured finished goods.

Control Considerations

Control procedures for proper segregation of responsibilities should be in place and operating. By referring to Exhibit 10–1, you can see that proper segregation involves authorization (production planning and inventory planning) by persons who do not have custody, recording, or cost accounting and reconciliation duties. Custody of inventories (raw materials, work in process, and finished goods) is in the hands of persons who do not authorize the amount or timing of production or the purchase of materials and labor, or perform the cost accounting record keeping, or prepare cost analyses (reconciliations). Cost accounting (a recording function) is performed by persons who do not authorize production or have custody of assets in the process of production. Combinations of two or more of the duties of authorization, custody, and cost accounting in one person, one office, or one computerized system may open the door for errors and frauds.

In addition, the controls should provide for detail control checking activities. For example: (1) production orders should contain a list of materials and their quantities, and they should be approved by a production planner/scheduler; (2) materials requisitions should be compared in the cost accounting department with the list of materials on the production order, and the materials requisitions should be signed by the production operator and the materials inventory storekeeper; (3) labor time records on jobs should be signed by production supervisors, and the cost accounting department should reconcile these cost amounts with the labor report from the payroll department; (4) production reports of finished units should be signed by the production supervisor and finished goods inventory custodian then forwarded to cost accounting. These control operations track

---

AUDITING INSIGHT

OVERCHARGING THE GOVERNMENT

Government contracting periodically gets in the news in exposés of companies charging unrelated costs to government contracts of various kinds (e.g., defense production, research contracts). Although the production plans and orders do not specify allowable costs for building the company baseball field or paying for the president's kennel fees while on business trips, costs like these have found their way into government contract reimbursement claims. Government contract auditors have found them, and companies have incurred penalties and requirements to reimburse the costs wrongly charged. Some companies summarily fire cost accountants who engage in cost manipulation on government contracts (McDonnell Douglas Company). Other organizations suffer in the glare of adverse publicity (Northrop Corporation, Massachusetts Institute of Technology, Stanford University).

the raw materials and labor from start to finish in the production process. With each internal transaction, the responsibility and accountability for assets are passed from one person or location to another.

Complex computer systems to manage production and materials flow may be found in many companies. Even though the technology is complex, the basic management and control functions of ensuring the flow of labor and materials to production and the control of waste should be in place. Manual signatures and paper production orders and requisitions may not exist. They may all be imbedded in computer-controlled manufacturing systems.

Internal Control Questionnaire

Information about the production cycle control often is gathered initially by completing an internal control questionnaire (ICQ). An ICQ for general (manual) controls is in Appendix 10A–1. You can study this questionnaire for details of desirable control activities. It is organized with headings that identify the important control objectives—environment, validity, completeness, authorization, accuracy, classification, accounting/posting, and proper period recording.

Detail Test of Controls Audit Procedures

An organization should have detail control activities in place and operating to prevent, detect, and correct accounting errors. Exhibit 10–2 puts controls in the perspective of production activity with examples of specific objectives. This exhibit expresses the general control objectives in specific examples related to production.

Auditors can perform detail test of controls audit procedures to determine whether company personnel are actually performing controls that are said to be in place and operating properly. A **detail test of control procedure** consists of (1) identification of the data population from which a sample of items will be selected for audit and (2) an expression of the action that will be taken to produce relevant evidence. In general, the actions in detail test of control audit procedures involve vouching, tracing, observing, scanning, and recalculating. If personnel in the organization are not performing their control activities very well, auditors will need to design substantive audit procedures to try to detect whether control failures have produced materially misleading account balances.

E X H I B I T 10–2 INTERNAL CONTROL OBJECTIVES (Production Cycle)

General Objectives	Examples of Specific Objectives
1. Recorded production transactions are *valid* and documented.	Cost accounting separated from production, payroll, and inventory control.
	Material usage reports compared to raw material stores issue slips.
	Labor usage reports compared to job time tickets.
2. Valid production transactions are recorded and *none omitted*.	All documents prenumbered and numerical sequence reviewed.
3. Production transactions are *authorized*.	Material usage and labor usage prepared by foreman and approved by production supervisor.
4. Production job cost transactions computations contain *accurate* figures.	Job cost sheet entries reviewed by person independent of preparation.
	Costs of inventory used and labor used reviewed periodically.
5. Labor and materials are *classified* correctly as direct or indirect.	Production foreman required to account for all material and labor used as direct or indirect.
6. Production *accounting and posting* is complete.	Open job cost sheets periodically reconciled to the work-in process inventory accounts.
7. Production transactions are recorded in the *proper period*.	Production reports of material and labor used prepared weekly and transmitted to cost accounting.
	Job cost sheets posted weekly and summary journal entries of work in process and work completed prepared monthly.

Exhibit 10–3 contains a selection of detail test of controls audit procedures for auditing controls over the accumulation of costs for work-in-process inventory. This is the stage of "inventory" while it is in the production process. Upon completion, the accumulated costs become the cost valuation of the finished goods inventory. The illustrative procedures presume the existence of production cost reports that are updated as production takes place, labor reports that assign labor cost to the job, materials-used and materials requisitions charging raw materials to the production order, and overhead allocation calculations. Some or all of these documents may be in the form of computer records.

Direction of the Test of Controls Procedures

The test of controls procedures in Exhibit 10–3 are designed to test the production accounting in two directions. One is the *completeness direction*, in which the control performance of audit interest is the recording of all the production that was ordered to be started. Exhibit 10–4 shows that the sample for this direction is taken from the population of production orders found in the production-planning department. The procedures trace the cost accumulation forward into the production cost reports in the cost accounting department. The procedures keyed in the boxes (5-*a, b, c, d*) are cross-references to the procedures in Exhibit 10–3. A potential finding with these procedures is the cancellation of some production because of technical or quality problems, which should result in write-off or scrap of some partially completed production units.

The other direction is the *validity direction* of the test. The control performance of interest is the proper recording of work in process and finished goods in the general ledger. Exhibit 10–5 shows that the sample for this test is from the production reports (quantity and cost) *recorded in the inventory accounts*. From these basic records the recorded costs can be recalculated, vouched to labor reports, compared to the payroll, and vouched to records of material used and overhead incurred. The procedures keyed in the boxes (2-*a, b, c, d, e, f*) are cross-references to the procedures in Exhibit 10–3. A potential finding with these procedures is improper valuation of the recorded inventory cost.

EXHIBIT 10–3   TEST OF CONTROLS AUDIT PROCEDURES FOR WORK-IN-PROCESS INVENTORY

	Control Objective
1. Reconcile the open production cost reports to the work-in-process inventory control account.	Completeness
2. Select a sample of open and closed production cost reports:	
a. Recalculate all costs entered.	Accuracy
b. Vouch labor costs to labor reports.	Validity
c. Compare labor reports to summary of payroll	Acctg/posting
d. Vouch material costs to issue slips and materials-used reports.	Validity
e. Vouch overhead charges to overhead analysis schedules.	Accuracy
f. Trace selected overhead amounts from analysis schedules to cost allocations and to invoices or accounts payable vouchers.	Validity
3. Select a sample of issue slips from the raw materials stores file:	
a. Determine if a matching requisition is available for every issue slip.	Completeness
b. Trace materials-used reports into production cost reports.	Completeness
4. Select a sample of clock timecards from the payroll file. Trace to job time tickets, labor reports, and into production cost reports.	Completeness
5. Select a sample of production orders:	
a. Determine whether production order was authorized	Authorization
b. Match to bill of materials and manpower needs.	Completeness
c. Trace bill of materials to material requisitions, material issue clips, materials-used reports, and into production cost reports.	Completeness
d. Trace manpower needs to labor reports and into production cost reports.	Completeness

EXHIBIT 10–4 TEST OF PRODUCTION COST CONTROLS: COMPLETENESS DIRECTION

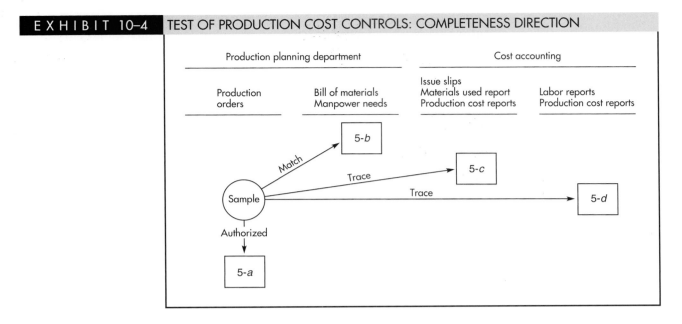

EXHIBIT 10–5 TEST OF PRODUCTION COST CONTROLS: VALIDITY DIRECTION

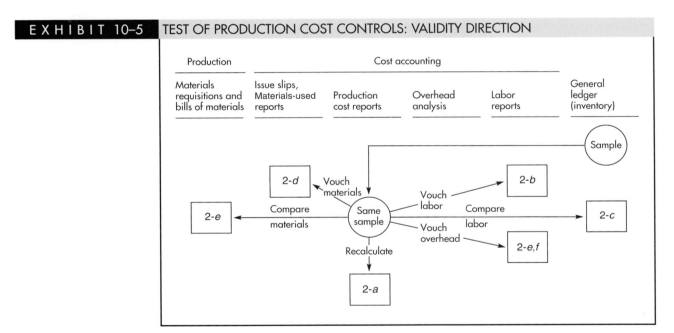

Summary: Control Risk Assessment

The audit manager or senior accountant in charge of the audit should evaluate the evidence obtained from an understanding of the internal control system and from the test of controls audit procedures. If the control risk is assessed very low, the substantive audit procedures on the account balances can be limited in cost-saving ways. For example, the inventory valuation substantive tests can be limited in scope (i.e., smaller sample size), and overall analytical procedures can be used with more confidence in being able to detect material misstatements not otherwise evident in the accounting details.

On the other hand, if tests of controls reveal weaknesses, depreciation calculation errors, and cost accumulation errors, the substantive procedures will need to be designed to lower the risk of failing to detect material misstatements in the inventory and cost of

AUDITING INSIGHT

IMPROPER PRODUCTION LOSS DEFERRALS

According to the SEC, Litton Corporation incurred cost overruns on its shipbuilding contracts and postponed writing off a $128 million cost overrun by classifying it as an asset for financial reporting purposes. If it had been written off timely, the net income of $1 million for the year would have become a substantial loss. Litton wrote off the $128 million later.

* * * * *

According to the SEC, International Systems & Controls Corporation (ISC) recorded and reported cost overruns on fixed price contracts, claims for price escalation, and kickback arrangements with suppliers as unbilled receivables. Additional uncollectible contract costs, which indicated losses on fixed price contracts, were buried in other unrelated contracts. ISC used the unbilled receivables account as a dumping ground for improper and questionable payments on the contracts. It tried to show them as legitimate reimbursable contract costs to avoid (a) writing them off as expense and (b) showing the true nature of the items. ISC used the unbilled receivables account to record cost overruns on fixed price contracts, misrepresenting them as payments due from the owner, but the contract did not provide for any such payments.

Source: I. Kellog, *How to Find Negligence and Misrepresentation in Financial Statements.*

goods sold account balances. For example, the depreciation cost may need to be completely recalculated and reviewed again by the auditors. A large number of inventoried production reports may need to be selected for valuation calculations. Cost overruns will need to be investigated with reference to contract terms to determine whether they should be carried as assets (e.g., inventory or unbilled receivables) or written off. Descriptions of major deficiencies, control weaknesses, and inefficiencies may be incorporated in a letter to the client describing "reportable conditions."

Computerized production cycle records are encountered frequently. Their complexity may range from simple batch systems, which automate the data processing, to transaction-driven integrated systems, which capture the production progress directly from automated devices on the production line. Computer audit techniques, such as test data, frequently are employed to audit controls in such systems, and generalized audit software may be employed to match data on different files.

REVIEW CHECKPOINTS

10.10 What are the primary functions that should be segregated in the production cycle?

10.11 Describe the two general characteristics of a test of controls audit procedure.

10.12 How does the production order document (or computer record) provide a control over the quantity of materials used in production?

10.13 Where might an auditor find accounting records of cost overruns on contracts? Of improper charges? Of improperly capitalized inventory?

10.14 Evaluate the following statement made by an auditing student: "I do not understand cost accounting; therefore, I want to get a job with an auditing firm where I will only have to know financial accounting."

10.15 From what population of documents would an auditor sample to determine whether all authorized production was completed and placed in inventory or written off as scrap? To determine whether finished goods inventory was actually produced and properly costed?

AUDIT CASES: SUBSTANTIVE AUDIT PROCEDURES

LEARNING OBJECTIVE

3. Describe some common errors and frauds in the accounting for production costs and related cost of goods sold, and design some audit and investigation procedures for detecting them.

The audit of account balances consists of procedural efforts to detect errors and frauds that might exist in the balances, thus making them misleading in financial statements. If such misstatements exist, they are characterized by the following features:

Method: A cause of the misstatement (accidental error or fraud attempt), which is usually made easier by some kind of failure of controls.

Paper trail: A set of telltale signs of erroneous accounting, missing, or altered documents, or a "dangling debit" (the false or erroneous debit that results from an overstatement of assets).

Amount: The dollar amount of overstated assets and revenue, or understated liabilities and expenses.

Each of the two cases in this section contains an audit approach that may enable auditors to detect misstatements in account balances. Each application of procedures consists of these elements:

Audit objective: A recognition of a financial statement *assertion* for which evidence needs to be obtained. The assertions are about existence of assets, liabilities, revenues, and expenses; their valuation; their complete inclusion in the account balances; the rights and obligations inherent in them; and their proper presentation and disclosure in the financial statements.

Control: A recognition of the control activities that *should be* used in an organization to prevent and detect errors and frauds.

Test of controls: Ordinary and extended procedures designed to produce *evidence about the effectiveness of the controls* that should be in operation.

Audit of balance: Ordinary and extended *substantive procedures designed to find signs of errors and frauds* in account balances and classes of transactions.

The two cases first set the stage with a story about an error or fraud—its method, paper trail (if any), and amount. The first part of each case gives you the "inside story," which auditors seldom know before they perform the audit work. The second part of each case, under the heading of the "audit approach," tells a structured story about the audit objective, desirable controls, test of control procedures, audit of balance procedures, and discovery summary. At the end of the chapter, some similar discussion cases are presented, and you can write the audit approach to test your ability to design audit procedures for the detection of errors and frauds.

CASE 10.1
UNBUNDLED BEFORE ITS TIME

PROBLEM

Production "sold" as finished goods before actual unit completion caused understated inventory, overstated cost of goods sold, overstated revenue, and overstated income.

METHOD

Western Corporation assembled and sold computer systems. A system production order consisted of hardware and peripheral equipment specifications and software specifications with associated performance criteria. Customer contracts always required assembly to specifications, installation, hardware testing, software installation, and software testing, after which the customer could accept the finished installation and pay the agreed price for the entire package. Completion of an order usually took three to eight months.

For internal accounting purposes, Western "unbundled" the hardware and software components of the customer orders. Production orders were split between the two components. Standard production processing and cost accounting were performed as if the two components were independent orders. When the hardware was installed and tested (with or without customer acceptance), Western recorded part of the contract price as sales revenue and the related cost of goods sold. The amount "due from customers" was carried in an asset account entitled Unbilled Contract Revenue. No billing statement was sent to the customer at this time.

When the software component was completed, installed, tested, and accepted, the remainder of the contract price was recorded as revenue, and the cost of the software was recorded as cost of goods sold. A billing statement was sent to the customer. The Unbilled Contract Revenue, which now matched the customer's obligation, was moved to Accounts Receivable.

During the time either or both of the order components were in process (prior to installation at the customer's location), accumulated costs were carried in a work-in-process inventory account.

PAPER TRAIL

Customer orders and contracts contained all the terms relating to technical specifications, acceptance testing, and the timing of the customer's obligation to pay. Copies of the technical specification sections of the contracts were attached to the separate hardware and software production orders prepared and authorized in the production-planning department. During production, installation, and testing, each of these production orders served as the basis for the

production cost accumulation and the subsidiary record of the work-in-process inventory. At the end, the production report along with the accumulated costs became the production cost report and the supporting documentation for the cost of goods sold entry.

AMOUNT

Western Corporation routinely recorded the hardware component of contracts too early, recognizing revenue and cost of goods sold that should have been postponed until later when the customer accepted the entire system. In the last three years, the resulting income overstatement amounted to 12 percent, 15 percent, and 19 percent of the reported operating income before taxes.

AUDIT APPROACH

OBJECTIVE

Obtain evidence of the actual occurrence of cost of goods sold transactions, thereby yielding evidence of the completeness of recorded inventory.

CONTROL

The major control lies in the production planning department approval of orders that identify a total unit of production (in this case, the hardware and software components combined). Nothing is wrong with approving separate orders for efficiency of production, but they should be cross-referenced so both production personnel and the cost accounting department can see them as separate components of the same order unit.

TEST OF CONTROLS

While the company conducted a large business, it had relatively few production orders (200–250 charged to cost of goods sold during each year). A sample of completed production orders should be taken and vouched to the underlying customer orders and contracts. The purpose of this procedure includes determining the validity of the production orders in relation to customer orders and determining whether the cost of goods sold was recorded in the proper period. (Procedures to audit the accuracy and completeness of the cost accumulation also are carried out on this sample.)

Even though the auditors can read the customer contracts, inquiries should be made about the company's standard procedures for the timing of revenue and cost of goods sold recognition.

AUDIT OF BALANCES

The sample of completed production orders taken for the test of controls also can be used in a "dual purpose test" to audit the details of

the cost of goods sold balance. In connection with the balance audit, the primary points of interest are the existence/occurrence and completeness of the dollar amounts accumulated as cost of the contracts and the proper cutoff for recording the cost.

The existence of the Unbilled Contract Revenue asset account in the general ledger should raise a red flag. Such an account always means that management has made an estimate of a revenue amount that has not been determined according to contract and has not yet been billed to the customer in accordance with contract terms. Even though the revenue is "unbilled," the related cost of goods sold still should be in the Cost of Goods Sold account. While accounting theory and practice permit recognizing unbilled revenue in certain cases (e.g., percentage of completion for construction contracts), the accounting has been known to harbor abuses in some cases.

DISCOVERY SUMMARY

When the company decided to issue stock to the public, a new audit firm was engaged. These auditors performed the dual purpose procedures outlined above, made the suggested inquiries, and investigated the Unbilled Contract Revenue account. They learned about management's unbundling policy and insisted that the policy be changed to recognize revenue only when all the terms of the contract were met. (The investigation yielded the information about prior years' overstatements of revenue, cost of goods sold, and income.) Part of the reason for insisting on the change of policy was the finding that Western did not have a very good record of quality control and customer acceptance of software installation. Customer acceptance was frequently delayed several months while systems engineers debugged software. On several occasions, Western solved the problems by purchasing complete software packages from other developers.

CASE 10.2
WHEN IN DOUBT, DEFER!

PROBLEM

SaCom Corporation deferred costs under the heading of work in process, defense contract claims, and R&D test equipment, thus overstating assets, understating cost of goods sold, and overstating income. Disclosure of the auditor's fees was manipulated and understated.

METHOD

SaCom manufactured electronic and other equipment for private customers and government defense contracts. Near the end of the year, the company used a journal entry to remove $170,000 from cost of goods sold and to defer it as tooling, leasehold improvements, and contract award and acquisition costs.

The company capitalized certain expenditures as R&D test equipment ($140,000) and as claims for reimbursement on defense contracts ($378,000).

In connection with a public offering of securities, the auditors billed SaCom $125,000 for professional fees. The underwriters objected. The auditors agreed to forgive $70,000 of the fees, and SaCom agreed to pay higher fees for work the following year (150 percent of standard billing rates). SaCom disclosed audit fees in the registration statement in the amount of $55,000. This amount was paid from the proceeds of the offering.

PAPER TRAIL

The $170,000 deferred costs consisted primarily of labor costs. The company altered the labor time records in an effort to provide substantiating documentation. The auditors knew about the alterations. The cost was removed from jobs that were left with too little labor cost in light of the work performed on them.

The R&D test equipment cost already had been charged to cost of goods sold with no notice of deferral when originally recorded. Deferral was accomplished with an adjusting journal entry. The company did not have documentation for the adjusting entry, except for an estimate of labor cost (44 percent of all labor cost in a subsidiary was capitalized during the period).

The claim for reimbursement on defense contracts did not have documentation specifically identifying the costs as being related to the contract. (Auditors know that defense department auditors insist on documentation and justification before approving such a claim.)

The audit fee arrangement was known to the audit firm, and it was recorded in an internal memorandum.

AMOUNT

SaCom reported net income of about $542,000 for the year, an overstatement of approximately 50 percent.

AUDIT APPROACH

OBJECTIVE

Obtain evidence of the validity of production costs deferred as tooling, leasehold improvements, contract award and acquisition costs, R&D test equipment, and claims for reimbursement on defense contracts.

CONTROL

The major control lies in the requirement to document the validity of cost deferral journal entries.

TEST OF CONTROLS

The test of controls procedure is to select a sample of journal entries, suspect ones in this case, and vouch them to supporting documentation. Experience has shown that nonstandard adjusting journal entries are the source of accounting errors and frauds more often than standard repetitive accounting for systematic transactions. This phenomenon makes the population of adjusting journal entries a ripe field for control and substantive testing.

AUDIT OF BALANCES

The account balances created by the deferral journal entries can be audited in a "dual purpose procedure" by auditing the supporting documentation. These balances were created entirely by the journal entries, and their "existence" as legitimate assets, deferrals, and reimbursement claims depends on the believability of the supporting explanations. In connection with the defense contract claim, auditors can review it with knowledge of the contract and the extent of documentation required by government contract auditors. (As a separate matter, the auditors could "search for unrecorded liabilities," but they already know about the deferred accounting fees, anyway.)

DISCOVERY SUMMARY

By performing the procedures outlined above, the manager and senior and staff accountants on the engagement discovered all the questionable and improper accounting. However, the partners in the firm insisted on rendering unqualified opinions on the SaCom financial statements without adjustment. One partner owned 300 shares of the company's stock in the name of a relative (without the consent or knowledge of the relative). Another audit partner later arranged a bank loan to the company to get $125,000 to pay past-due audit fees. This partner and another, and both their wives, guaranteed the loan. (When the bank later disclosed the guarantee in a bank confirmation obtained in the course of a subsequent SaCom audit, the confirmation was removed from the audit working paper file and destroyed.)

The SEC investigated, and, among other things, barred the audit firm for a period (about six months) from accepting new audit clients who would file financial statements with the SEC. The SEC also barred the partners involved in supervising various portions of the audit work from involvement with new audit clients for various periods of time. (Adapted: ASR 196.)

R E V I E W
CHECKPOINTS

10.16 In a production situation similar to the Western Corporation in the Unbundled Before Its Time case, what substantive audit work should be done on a sample of completed production orders (cost reports) recorded as cost of goods sold?

10.17 What red flag is raised when a company has an Unbilled Contract Revenue account in its general ledger?

10.18 Why should auditors always select the client's adjusting journal entries for detail audit?

10.19 Is there anything wrong about auditors helping clients obtain bank loans to pay their accounting firm's fees?

PART II: PAYROLL CYCLE TYPICAL ACTIVITIES

LEARNING OBJECTIVE
4. Describe the payroll cycle, including typical source documents and controls.

Every company has a payroll. It may include manufacturing labor, research scientists, administrative personnel, or all of these. Payroll can take different forms. Personnel management and the payroll accounting cycle not only include transactions that affect the

EXHIBIT 10–6 PAYROLL CYCLE

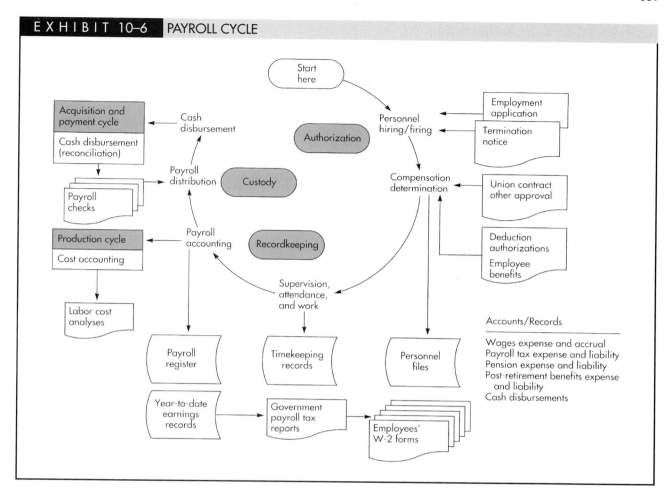

wage and salary accounts but also the transactions that affect pension benefits, deferred compensation contracts, compensatory stock option plans, employee benefits (such as health insurance), payroll taxes, and related liabilities for these costs.

Exhibit 10–6 shows a payroll cycle. It starts with hiring (and firing) people and determining their wage rates and deductions, then proceeds to attendance and work (timekeeping), and ends with payment followed by preparation of governmental (tax) and internal reports.

One of these internal reports is a report of labor cost to the cost accounting department, thus linking the payroll cycle with cost accounting in the production cycle. Five functional responsibilities should be performed by separate people or departments. They are:

- Personnel and Labor Relations—hiring and firing (Authorization).
- Supervision—approval of work time (Authorization).
- Timekeeping and Cost Accounting—payroll preparation and cost accounting (Authorization).
- Payroll Accounting—check preparation and related payroll reports (Record keeping).
- Payroll Distribution—actual custody of checks and distribution to employees (Custody of cash).

The elements that follow are part of the payroll control system.

Authorization

A **personnel or labor relations department** that is independent of the other functions should have transaction initiation authority to add new employees to the payroll, to delete terminated employees, to obtain authorizations for deductions (such as insurance, saving bonds, withholding tax exemptions on federal form W-4), and to transmit authority for pay rate changes to the payroll department.

Authorization also takes place in the **supervision** function. All pay base data (hours, job number, absences, time off allowed for emergencies, and the like) should be approved by an employee's immediate supervisor.

Authorization is also a feature of the **timekeeping and cost accounting** function. Data on which pay is based (such as hours, piece-rate volume, incentives) should be accumulated independent of other functions.

Custody

The main feature of custody in the payroll cycle is the possession of the paychecks, cash, or electronic transfer codes used to pay people. (Electronic transfer codes refer to the practice by some organizations of transferring pay directly into employees' bank accounts.) A **payroll distribution** function should control the delivery of pay to employees so that unclaimed checks, cash, or incomplete electronic transfers are not returned to persons involved in any of the other functions.

Elements of custody of important documents are in the **supervision** function and in the **timekeeping** function. Supervisors usually have access to time cards or time sheets that provide the basis for payment to hourly workers. Likewise, the timekeeping devices (e.g., time clocks, supervisory approval of time cards or time sheets, electronic punch-in systems) have a type of custody of employees' time-base for payroll calculations.

Record keeping

The **payroll accounting** function should prepare individual paychecks, pay envelopes, or electronic transfers using rate and deduction information supplied by the personnel function and base data supplied by the timekeeping–supervision functions. Persons in charge of the authorization and custody functions should not also prepare the payroll. They might be tempted to pay fictitious employees.

Payroll accounting maintains individual year-to-date earnings records and prepares the state and federal tax reports (income tax and Social Security withholding, unemployment tax reports, and annual W-2 forms). The payroll tax returns (e.g., federal Form 941 that reports taxes withheld, state and federal unemployment tax returns) and the annual W-2 report to employees are useful records for audit recalculation and overall testing (analytical) procedures. They should correspond to company records. Most company employees responsible for these reports are reluctant to manipulate them.

AUDITING INSIGHT

APPROVAL OF FICTITIOUS OVERTIME

A supervisor at Austin Stoneworks discovered that she could approve overtime hours even though an employee had not worked 40 regular time hours. She made a deal with several employees to alter their work timecards and split the extra payments. Over a six-year period, the supervisor and her accomplices embezzled $107,000 in excess payments.

The employees' time cards were not reviewed after being approved by the supervisor. The company's payroll computer program did not have a valid data combination test that paid overtime only after 40 regular time hours were paid.

AUDITING INSIGHT

NOT ENOUGH CONTROL, NO FEEDBACK, BYE-BYE MONEY

Homer had been in payroll accounting for a long time. He knew it was not uncommon to pay a terminated employee severance benefits and partial pay after termination. Homer received the termination notices and the data for the final paychecks. But Homer also knew how to keep the terminated employee on the payroll for another week, pay a full week's compensation, change the electronic transfer code, and take the money for himself. The only things he could not change were the personnel department's copy of the termination notices, the payroll register, and the individual employee pay records used for withholding tax and W-2 forms.

Fortunately, nobody reconciled the cost accounting labor charges to the payroll. The supervisors did not get a copy of the payroll register for post-payment approval, so they did not have any opportunity to notice the extra week. Nobody ever reviewed the payroll with reference to the termination notices. Former employees never complained about more pay and withholding reported on their W-2s than they actually received.

Homer and his wife Marge retired comfortably to a villa in Spain on a nest egg that had grown to $450,000. After his retirement, the company experienced an unexpected decrease in labor costs and higher profits.

Periodic Reconciliation

The payroll bank account can be reconciled like any other bank account. Otherwise, there is not much to count or observe in payroll to accomplish a traditional reconciliation—comparing "real payroll" to recorded wage cost and expense. However, one kind of reconciliation in the form of feedback to the **supervision** function can be placed in operation. Some companies send to each supervisor a copy of the payroll register, showing the employees paid under the supervisor's authority and responsibility. The supervisor gets a chance to reapprove the payroll after it is completed. This gives the opportunity to notice whether any persons not approved have been paid and charged to the supervisor's accountability.

The payroll report sent to cost accounting can be reconciled to the labor records used to charge labor cost to production. The cost accounting function should determine whether the labor paid is the same as the labor cost used in the cost accounting calculations.

Employees on Fixed Salary

The functional duties and responsibilities described above relate primarily to nonsalaried (hourly) employees. For salaried employees, the system is simplified by not having to collect timekeeping data. In nonmanufacturing businesses, the cost accounting operations may be very simple or even nonexistent. The relative importance of each of these five areas should be determined for each engagement in light of the nature and organization of the company's operations.

REVIEW CHECKPOINTS

10.20 What functional responsibilities are associated with the payroll cycle?

10.21 Describe a "walk-through" of the payroll transaction flow from hiring authorization to payroll check disbursement. What document copies would be collected? What controls noted?

10.22 In a payroll system, which duties should be separated?

10.23 What features of a payroll system could be expected to prevent or detect payment of a fictitious employee? Omission of payment to an employee?

AUDIT EVIDENCE IN MANAGEMENT REPORTS AND FILES

Payroll systems produce numerous reports. Some are internal reports and bookkeeping records. Others are government tax reports. Auditors should obtain and use these reports.

Personnel Files

The personnel and labor relations department keeps individual employee files. The contents usually include an employment application, a background investigation report, a notice of hiring, a job classification with pay rate authorization, and authorizations for deductions (e.g., health insurance, life insurance, retirement contribution, union dues, W-4 form for income tax exemptions). When employees retire, quit, or are otherwise terminated, appropriate notices of termination are filed. These files contain the raw data for important pension and post-retirement benefit accounting involving an employee's age, tenure with the company, wage record, and other information used in actuarial calculations.

A personnel file should establish the reality of a person's existence and employment. The background investigation report (prior employment, references, Social Security number validity check, credentials investigation, perhaps a private investigator's report) is important for employees in such sensitive areas as accounting, finance, and asset custody positions. One of the primary system controls is capable personnel. Experience is rich with errors and frauds perpetrated by people who falsify their credentials (identification, college degrees, prior experience, criminal records, and the like).

Timekeeping Records

Employees paid by the hour or on various incentive systems require records of time, production, piecework, or other measures of the basis for their pay. (Salaried employees do not require such detail records.) Timekeeping or similar records are collected in a variety of ways. The old-fashioned time clock is still used. It accepts an employee's time card and imprints the time when work started and ended. More sophisticated computer systems perform the same function without the paper time card. Production employees may clock in for various jobs or production processes in the system for assigning labor cost to various stages of production. These records are part of the cost accounting for production labor.

Supervisors should approve timekeeping records. This approval is a sign that employees actually worked the hours (or produced the output) reported to the payroll department. The payroll department should find a supervisor's signature or initials on the documents used as the basis for periodic pay. In computer systems, this approval may be automatic by virtue of the supervisory passwords used to input data into a computerized payroll system.

AUDITING INSIGHT

WHERE DID HE COME FROM?

The controller defrauded the company for several million dollars. As it turned out, he was no controller at all. He didn't know a debit from a credit. The fraudster had been fired from five previous jobs where money had turned up missing. He was discovered one evening when the president showed up unexpectedly at the company and found a stranger in the office with the controller. The stranger was doing all of the accounting for the bogus controller.

Source: Association of Certified Fraud Examiners, "Auditing for Fraud."

Payroll Register

The payroll "register" is a special journal. It typically contains a row for each employee with columns for the gross regular pay, gross overtime pay, income tax withheld, Social Security and Medicare tax withheld, other deductions, and net pay. The net pay amount usually is transferred from the general bank account to a special imprest payroll bank account. The journal entry for the transfer of net payroll, for example, is:

Payroll Bank Account	25,774	
General Bank Account		25,774

The payroll check amounts are accumulated to create the payroll posting to the general ledger, like this example:

Wages Clearing Account	40,265	
Employee Income Taxes Payable		7,982
Employee Social Security Payable		3,080
Health Insurance Premium Payable		2,100
Life Insurance Premium Payable		1,329
Payroll Bank Account		25,774

The payroll register is the primary original record for payroll accounting. It contains the implicit assertions that the employees are real company personnel (existence assertion), they worked the time or production for which they were paid (rights/ownership assertion), the amount of the pay is calculated properly (valuation assertion), and all the employees were paid (completeness assertion). The presentation and disclosure assertion depends on the labor cost analysis explained below.

Payroll department records also contain the canceled checks (or a similar electronic deposit record). The checks will contain the employees' endorsements on the back.

Labor Cost Analysis

The cost accounting department can receive its information in more than one way. Some companies have systems that independently report time and production work data from the production floor directly to the cost accounting department. Other companies let their cost accounting department receive labor cost data from the payroll department. When the data is received independently, it can be reconciled in quantity (time) or amount (dollars) with a report from the payroll department. This is a type of reconciliation to make sure the cost accounting department is using actual payroll data and that the payroll department is paying only for work performed.

AUDITING INSIGHT

LOOK AT THE ENDORSEMENTS

An assistant accountant was instructed to "look at" the endorsements on the back of a sample of canceled payroll checks.

She noticed three occurrences of the payee's signature followed by a second signature. Although scrawled almost illegibly, the second signatures were identical and were later identified as the payroll accountant's handwriting. The payroll accountant had taken unclaimed checks and converted (stolen) them. When cashing these "third-party checks," banks and stores had required the payroll accountant to produce identification and endorse the checks that already had been "endorsed" by the employee payee.

The Lesson: Second endorsements are a red flag.

The cost accounting department (or a similar accounting function) is responsible for the "cost distribution." This is the most important part of the presentation and disclosure assertion with respect to payroll. The cost distribution is an assignment of payroll to the accounts where it belongs for internal and external reporting. Using its input data, the cost accounting department may make a distribution entry like this:

Production Job A	14,364	
Production Job B	3,999	
Production Process A	10,338	
Selling Expense	8,961	
General and Administrative Expense	2,603	
Wages Clearing Account		40,265

Payroll data flows from the hiring process, through the timekeeping function, into the payroll department, then to the cost accounting department, and finally to the accounting entries that record the payroll for inventory cost determination and financial statement presentation. The same data is used for various governmental and tax reports.

Governmental and Tax Reports

Payroll systems have complications introduced by the federal income and Social Security tax laws. Several reports are produced. These can be used by auditors in tests of controls and substantive test of the balances produced by accumulating numerous payroll transactions.

Year-to-Date Earnings Records

The year-to-date (YTD) earnings records are the cumulative subsidiary records of each employee's gross pay, deductions, and net pay. Each time a periodic payroll is produced, the YTD earnings records are updated for the new information. The YTD earnings records are a subsidiary ledger of the wages and salaries cost and expense in the financial statements. Theoretically, like any subsidiary and control account relationship, their sum (e.g., the gross pay amounts) should be equal to the costs and expenses in the financial statements. The trouble with this reconciliation idea is that there are usually many payroll cost/expense accounts in a company's chart of accounts. The production wages may be scattered about in several different accounts, such as inventory (work in process and finished goods), selling, general, and administrative expenses.

However, these YTD records provide the data for periodic governmental tax forms. They can be reconciled to the tax reports.

Government Payroll Tax Report

Federal Form 941 is the payroll tax report that summarizes a total amount paid to employees during each three-month period. It also summarizes the income tax withheld and

---

AUDITING INSIGHT

BEWARE THE "CLEARING ACCOUNT"

"Clearing accounts" are temporary storage places for transactions awaiting final accounting. Like the Wages Clearing Account illustrated in the entries above, all clearing accounts should have zero balances after the accounting is completed.

A balance in a clearing account means that some amounts have not been classified properly in the accounting records. If the Wages Clearing Account has a debit balance, some labor cost has not been properly classified in the expense accounts or cost accounting classifications. If the Wages Clearing Account has a credit balance, the cost accountant has assigned more labor cost to expense accounts and cost accounting classifications than the amount actually paid.

provides a place to calculate the Social Security and Medicare taxes due (employee and employer shares). This is a quarterly report, although employer's deposits of withheld taxes into government accounts may be required more often according to IRS regulations. The YTD records provide the data for Form 941, but the form itself does not list individual employees and their amounts of earnings and taxes. If this report is filed electronically, the basic report data are available in magnetic form.

Federal Form 940 is the employer's annual federal unemployment (FUTA) tax return. It requires a report of the total amount (but not the detail by employee) of wages subject to the unemployment tax, calculation of the tax, and payment. State unemployment tax returns may differ from state to state. Some states require a schedule showing each employee's name, Social Security identification number, and amount of earnings. These details can be compared to the company's YTD earnings records.

Companies in financial difficulty have been known to try to postpone payment of employee taxes withheld. However, the consequences can be serious. IRS can and will padlock the business and seize the assets for nonpayment. After all, the withheld taxes belong to the employees' accounts with the government, and the employers are obligated to pay over the amounts withheld from employees along with a matching share for the Social Security and Medicare tax.

Employee W-2 Reports

The W-2 is the annual report of gross salaries and wages and the income, Social Security, and Medicare taxes withheld. Copies are filed with the Social Security Administration and IRS, and copies are sent to employees for use in preparing their income tax returns. The W-2s contain the annual YTD accumulations for each employee. They also contain the employees' address and Social Security identifying number. Auditors can use the name, address, Social Security number, and dollar amounts in certain procedures (described later) to obtain evidence about the existence of the employees. The W-2s can be reconciled to the payroll tax reports.

REVIEW CHECKPOINTS

10.24 What important information can be found in employees' personnel files?

10.25 What is important about background checks using the employment applications submitted by prospective employees?

10.26 What payroll cycle documentation supports the validity and accuracy of payroll transactions?

10.27 Which government tax returns can be reconciled in total with employees' year-to-date earnings records? Reconciled in total, but not in detail?

10.28 What is the purpose of examining endorsements on the back of payroll checks?

CONTROL RISK ASSESSMENT

LEARNING OBJECTIVE

5. Give examples of detail test of controls procedures for auditing the controls over payroll.

The major risks in the payroll cycle are:

- Paying fictitious "employees" (invalid transactions, employees do not exist).
- Overpaying for time or production (inaccurate transactions, improper valuation).
- Incorrect accounting for costs and expenses (incorrect classification, improper or inconsistent presentation and disclosure).

The assessment of payroll system control risk normally takes on added importance because most companies have fairly elaborate and well-controlled personnel and payroll functions. The transactions in this cycle are numerous during the year yet result in small amounts in balance sheet accounts at year-end. Therefore, in most audit engagements, the review of controls and test of controls audit of transaction details constitute the major portion of the evidence gathered for these accounts. On most audits, the substantive audit procedures devoted to auditing the payroll-related account balances are very limited.

Control Considerations

Control procedures for proper segregation of responsibilities should be in place and operating. By referring to Exhibit 10–6, you can see that proper segregation involves authorization (personnel department hiring and firing, pay rate and deduction authorizations) by persons who do not have payroll preparation, paycheck distribution, or reconciliation duties. Payroll distribution (custody) is in the hands of persons who do not authorize employees' pay rates or time, nor prepare the payroll checks. Record keeping is performed by payroll and cost accounting personnel who do not make authorizations or distribute pay. Combinations of two or more of the duties of authorization, payroll preparation and record keeping, and payroll distribution in one person, one office, or one computerized system may open the door for errors and frauds.

In addition, the control system should provide for detail control checking activities. For example: (1) periodic comparison of the payroll register to the personnel department files to check hiring authorizations and terminated employees not deleted, (2) periodic rechecking of wage rate and deduction authorizations, (3) reconciliation of time and production paid to cost accounting calculations, (4) quarterly reconciliation of YTD earnings records with tax returns, and (5) payroll bank account reconciliation.

Computer-Based Payroll

Complex computer systems to gather payroll data, calculate payroll amounts, print checks, and transfer electronic deposits are found in many companies. Even though the technology is complex, the basic management and control functions of ensuring a flow of data to the payroll department should be in place. Various paper records and approval signatures may not exist. They may all be imbedded in computerized payroll systems.

Internal Control Questionnaire

Information about the payroll cycle control often is gathered initially by completing an internal control questionnaire (ICQ). An ICQ for general (manual) controls is in Appendix 10A–2. You can study this questionnaire for details of desirable control activities. It is organized with headings that identify the important control objectives—environment, validity, completeness, authorization, accuracy, classification, accounting/posting, and proper period recording.

Detail Test of Controls Audit Procedures

An organization should have detail control activities in place and operating to prevent, detect, and correct accounting errors. Exhibit 10–7 puts controls in the perspective of the payroll functions with examples of specific objectives. You should study this exhibit carefully. It expresses the general control objectives with specific examples related to payroll.

Auditors can perform detail test of controls audit procedures to determine whether controls that are said to be in place and operating actually are being performed properly by company personnel. A **detail test of control procedure** consists of (1) identification of the data population from which a sample of items will be selected for audit and (2) an expression of the action that will be taken to produce relevant evidence. In general, the actions in detail test of control audit procedures involve vouching, tracing, observing, scanning, and recalculating. If personnel in the organization are not performing their control activities very well, auditors will need to design additional procedures to try to detect whether control failures have produced payments to fictitious employees, overpayments for time or production, or incorrect accounting for costs and expenses.

EXHIBIT 10–7   CONTROL OBJECTIVES (Personnel and Payroll Cycle)

General Objectives	Examples of Specific Objectives
1. Recorded payroll transactions are *valid* and documented.	Payroll accounting separated from personnel and timekeeping.
	Time cards indicate approval by supervisor's signature.
	Payroll files compared to personnel files periodically.
2. Valid payroll transactions are recorded and *none are omitted*.	Employees' complaints about paychecks investigated and resolved (written records maintained and reviewed by internal auditors).
3. Payroll names, rates, hours, and deductions are *authorized*.	Names of new hires or terminations reported immediately in writing to payroll by the personnel department.
	Authorization for deductions kept on file.
	Rate authorized by union contract, agreement, or written policy and approved by personnel officer.
4. Payroll computations contain *accurate* gross pay, deductions, and net pay.	Payroll computations checked by person independent of preparation.
	Totals of payroll register reconciled to totals of payroll distribution by cost accounting.
5. Payroll transactions are *classified* correctly as direct or indirect labor or other expenses.	Employee classification reviewed periodically.
	Overall charges to indirect labor compared to direct labor and total product costs periodically.
6. Payroll transaction *accounting and posting* is complete.	Details of employee withholding reconciled periodically to liability control accounts and tax returns.
	Employee tax expense and liabilities prepared in conjunction with payroll.
7. Payroll costs and expenses are recorded in the *proper period*.	Month-end accruals reviewed by internal auditors.
	Payroll computed, paid, and recorded in timely manner.

Exhibit 10–8 contains a selection of detail test of controls audit procedures for auditing controls over payroll. Most of the illustrative procedures involve manual records, and B-5 refers to computerized systems.

Direction of the Test of Controls Procedures

The test of controls procedures in Exhibit 10–8 are designed to test the payroll accounting in two directions. One is the *completeness direction*, in which the control performance of audit interest is the matching of personnel file content to payroll department files and the payroll register. Exhibit 10–9 shows that the sample for this direction is taken from the population of personnel files. The procedures trace the personnel department authorizations to the payroll department files (procedure A-1-c).

AUDITING INSIGHT

COVERT SURVEILLANCE

This sounds like spy work, and it indeed has certain elements of it.

Auditors can test controls over employees' clocking into work shifts by making personal observations of the process—observing whether anybody clocks in with two time cards or with two or more electronic entries, or leaves the premises after clocking in.

The auditors need to be careful not to make themselves obvious. Standing around in a manufacturing plant at 6 A.M. in the standard blue pinstripe suit uniform is as good as printing "Beware of Auditor" on your forehead. People then will be on their best behavior, and you will observe nothing unusual.

Find an unobtrusive observation post. Stay out of sight. Use a video camera. Get a knowledgeable office employee to accompany you to interpret various activities. Perform an observation that has a chance of producing evidence of improper behavior.

EXHIBIT 10–8   TEST OF CONTROLS AUDIT PROCEDURES FOR PAYROLL

Control	Objective
A. Personnel Files and Compensation Documents	
1. Select a sample of personnel files:	
a. Review personnel files for complete information on employment date, authority to add to payroll, job classification, wage rate, and authorized deductions.	Authorization Classification Authorization
b. Trace pay rate to union contracts or other rate authorization. Trace salaries to directors' minutes for authorization.	Authorization
c. Trace pay rate and deduction information to payroll department files used in payroll preparation.	Completeness
2. Obtain copies of pension plans, stock options, profit sharing, and bonus plans. Review and extract relevant portions that relate to payroll deductions, fringe benefit expenses, accrued liabilities, and financial statement disclosure.	Validity Completeness Authorization Accuracy Acctg/posting
B. Payroll	
1. Select a sample of payroll register entries.	
a. Vouch employee identification, pay rate, and deductions to personnel files or other authorizations.	Authorization Validity
b. Vouch hours worked to clock time cards and supervisor's approval	Authorization Accuracy
c. Recalculate gross pay, deductions, net pay.	Accuracy
d. Recalculate a selection of periodic payrolls.	Accuracy
e. Vouch to canceled payroll check. Examine employees' endorsement.	Validity
2. Select a sample of clock time cards. Note supervisor's approval and trace to periodic payroll registers.	Authorization Completeness
3. Vouch a sample of periodic payroll totals to payroll bank account transfer vouchers and vouch payroll bank account deposit slip for cash transfer.	Acctg/posting
4. Trace a sample of employees' payroll entries to individual payroll records maintained for tax reporting purposes. Reconcile total of employees' payroll records with payrolls paid for the year.	Completeness Accuracy
5. Review computer-printed error messages for evidence of the use of check digits, valid codes, limit tests, and other input, processing, and output application controls. Investigate correction and resolution of errors.	Accuracy Validity
6. Trace payroll information to management reports and to general ledger account postings.	Acctg/posting
7. Obtain control of a periodic payroll and conduct a surprise distribution of paychecks.	Validity
C. Cost Distribution Reports	
1. Select a sample of cost accounting analysis of payroll.	
a. Reconcile periodic totals with payroll payments for the same periods.	Completeness
b. Vouch to time records.	Validity
2. Trace cost accounting labor cost distributions to management reports and postings in general ledger and subsidiary account(s).	Acctg/posting Classification
3. Select a sample of labor cost items in (a) ledger accounts and/or (b) management reports. Vouch to supporting cost accounting analyses.	Validity

The other direction is the *validity direction* of the test. The control performance of interest is the preparation of the payroll register. Exhibit 10–9 shows that the sample for this test is from the completed payroll registers. The individual payroll calculations are vouched to the personnel files (procedure B-1-a).

AUDITING INSIGHT

OVERT SURVEILLANCE

Surprise Payroll Distribution

Auditors may perform a surprise observation of a payroll distribution in connection with tests for overstatement. Such an observation involves taking control of paychecks and accompanying a company representative as the distribution takes place. The auditor is careful to see that each employee is identified and that only one check is given to each individual. Unclaimed checks are controlled, and in this manner the auditor hopes to detect any fictitious persons on the payroll. Auditors need to be extremely careful to notice any duplication of employee identification or instance of one person attempting to pick up two or more checks.

EXHIBIT 10-9	DUAL DIRECTION TEST OF PAYROLL CONTROLS

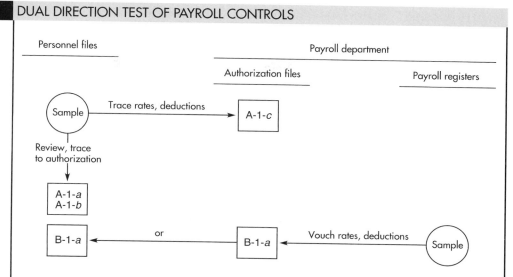

Summary: Control Risk Assessment

The audit manager or senior accountant in charge of the audit should evaluate the evidence obtained from an understanding of the internal control system and from the test of controls audit procedures. If the control risk is assessed very low, the substantive audit procedures on the account balances can be limited in cost-saving ways. As examples: a surprise payroll distribution may be considered unnecessary; the auditors may decide it is appropriate to place considerable reliance on management reports generated by the payroll system.

On the other hand, if tests of controls reveal weaknesses, improper segregation of duties, inaccurate cost reports, inaccurate tax returns, or lax personnel policies, then substantive procedures will need to be designed to lower the risk of failing to detect material misstatements in the financial statements. The problem in payroll is that the payments to fictitious employees and fraudulent overtime payments do not normally misstate the financial statements as long as the improper payments are expensed. (The losses are expensed, as they should be!) The only misstatement is failing to distinguish and disclose "payroll fraud losses" from legitimate wages expense and cost of goods sold, but such losses are usually immaterial in a single year's financial statements. Nevertheless, auditors habitually perform procedures designed to find payroll fraud. It is more of a service to clients than a crucial part of the effort to detect material misstatements in financial statements.

R E V I E W
CHECKPOINTS

10.29 What are the most common errors and frauds in the personnel and payroll cycle? Which control characteristics are auditors looking for to prevent or detect these errors and frauds?

10.30 What's wrong with an auditor standing by the plant gate and time clock at starting time to observe employees checking in for work shifts?

10.31 How can an auditor determine whether the amount of labor cost charged to production was actually paid to employees?

10.32 Why might an auditor conduct a surprise observation of a payroll distribution? What should be observed?

AUDIT CASES: SUBSTANTIVE AUDIT PROCEDURES

LEARNING OBJECTIVE

6. Describe some common errors and frauds in payroll, and design some audit and investigation procedures for detecting them.

The audit of account balances consists of procedural efforts to detect errors and frauds that might exist in the balances, thus making them misleading in financial statements. If such misstatements exist, they are characterized by the following features:

Method: A cause of the misstatement (accidental error or fraud attempt), which usually is made easier by some kind of failure of controls.

Paper trail: A set of telltale signs of erroneous accounting, missing or altered documents, or a "dangling debit" (the false or erroneous debit that results from an overstatement of assets).

Amount: The dollar amount of overstated assets and revenue, or understated liabilities and expenses.

Each of the two cases in this section contains an audit approach that may enable auditors to detect errors and frauds. Each application of procedures consists of these elements:

Audit objective: A recognition of a financial statement *assertion* for which evidence needs to be obtained. The assertions are about existence of assets, liabilities, revenues, and expenses; their valuation; their complete inclusion in the account balances; the rights and obligations inherent in them; and their proper presentation and disclosure in the financial statements.

Control: A recognition of the control activities that *should be* used in an organization to prevent and detect errors and frauds.

Test of controls: Ordinary and extended procedures designed to produce *evidence about the effectiveness of the controls* that should be in operation.

Audit of balance: Ordinary and extended *substantive procedures designed to find signs* of errors and frauds in account balances and classes of transactions.

The two cases first set the stage with a story about an error or fraud—its method, paper trail (if any), and amount. The first part of each case gives you the "inside story," which auditors seldom know before they perform the audit work. The second part of each case, under the heading of the "audit approach," tells a structured story about the audit objective, desirable controls, test of control procedures, audit of balance procedures, and discovery summary. At the end of the chapter, some similar discussion cases are presented, and you can write the audit approach to test your ability to design audit procedures for the detection of errors and frauds.

CASE 10.3
TIME CARD FORGERIES

PROBLEM

False claims for work time caused the overpayment of wages.

METHOD

A personnel-leasing agency assigned Nurse Jane to work at County Hospital. She claimed payroll hours on agency time cards, which showed approval signatures of a hospital nursing shift supervisor. The shift supervisor had been terminated by the hospital several months prior to the periods covered by the time cards in question. Nurse Jane worked one or two days per week but submitted time cards for a full 40-hour workweek.

The leasing agency paid Nurse Jane, then billed County Hospital for the wages and benefits. Supporting documents were submitted with the leasing agency's bills.

PAPER TRAIL

Each hospital workstation keeps ward shift logs, which are sign-in sheets showing nurses on duty at all times. Nurses sign in and sign out when going on and going off duty.

County Hospital maintains personnel records showing, among other things, the period of employment of its own nurses, supervisors, and other employees.

AMOUNT

Nurse Jane's wages and benefits were billed to the hospital at $22 per hour. False time cards overcharging about 24 extra hours per week cost the hospital $528 per week. Nurse Jane was assigned to County Hospital for 15 weeks during the year, so she caused overcharges of about $7,900. However, she told three of her crooked friends about the procedure, and they overcharged the hospital another $24,000.

AUDIT APPROACH

AUDIT OBJECTIVE

Obtain evidence to determine whether wages were paid to valid employees for actual time worked at the authorized pay rate.

CONTROL

Control activities should include a hiring authorization putting employees on the payroll. When leased employees are used, this authorization includes contracts for nursing time, conditions of employment, and terms including the contract reimbursement rate. Control records of attendance and work should be kept (ward shift log). Supervisors should approve time cards or other records used by the payroll department to prepare paychecks.

In this case, the contract with the leasing agency provided that approved time cards had to be submitted as supporting documentation for the agency billings.

TEST OF CONTROLS

Although the procedures and documents for control were in place, the controls did not operate because nobody at the hospital ever compared the ward shift logs to time cards, and nobody examined the supervisory approval signatures for their validity. The scam was easy in the leasing agency situation because the nurses submitted their own time cards to the agency for payment. The same scam might be operated by the hospital's own employees if they, too, could write their time cards and submit them to the payroll department.

Auditors should make inquiries (e.g., internal control questionnaire) about the error-checking activities performed by hospital accounting personnel. Test of control audit procedures are designed to determine whether control procedures are followed properly by the organization. Since the comparison and checking activities were not performed, there is nothing to test.

However, the substantive tests described below are identical to the procedures that could be called "tests of controls," but in this case they are performed to determine whether nurses were paid improperly (a substantive purpose).

AUDIT OF BALANCES

Select a sample of leasing agency billings and their supporting documentation (time cards). Vouch rates billed by the agency to the contract for agreement to proper rate. Vouch time claimed to hospital work attendance records (ward shift logs). Obtain handwriting examples of supervisors' signatures and compare them to the approval signatures on time cards. Use personnel records to determine whether supervisors were actually employed by the hospital at the time they approved the time cards. Use available work attendance records to determine whether supervisors were actually on duty at the time they approved the time cards.

DISCOVERY SUMMARY

The auditors quickly found that Nurse Jane (and others) had not signed-in on ward shift logs for days they claimed to have worked. Further investigation showed that the supervisors who supposedly signed the time cards were not even employed by the hospital at the time their signatures were used for approvals. Handwriting comparison showed that the signatures were not written by the supervisors.

The leasing agency was informed and refunded the $31,900 overpayment proved by the auditors. The auditors continued to comb the records for more! (Adapted from vignette published in *Internal Auditor*.)

CASE 10.4
CLEVERLY HIDDEN PAYCHECKS

PROBLEM

Embezzlement with fictitious people on the payroll.

METHOD

Betty Ruth processed personnel files for RD-Mart, a large retail chain of clothing stores with about 6,400 employees in 233 store locations. She created fictitious files for fictitious employees and notified the outside payroll processing service of their names, addresses, social security numbers, salaries, and deductions. The payroll service prepared the paychecks and delivered them to Martha Lee in the accounting department. Martha Lee placed the paychecks in overnight express envelopes for delivery to the managers at RD-Mart's 46 stores in the Southeast Region. However, Martha Lee first removed the fictitious paychecks. (Betty Ruth and Martha Lee were long-time high school friends and conspirators in the fraud.)

Martha Lee hired a print shop to print a private stock of checks on the RD-Mart payroll bank account. These checks looked exactly like the real payroll checks and were in the payroll service's numerical sequence. After removing the paychecks payable to the fictitious employees, Martha Lee and Betty Ruth selected the checks with the same numbers from their private stock. They then made the checks payable to themselves in the proper net amount and deposited them in their own bank accounts. For a signature, they bought a rubber stamp that looked enough like the RD-Mart machine signature to fool the bank.

PAPER TRAIL

Payroll creates a large paper trail with individual earnings records, W-2 tax forms, payroll deductions for taxes and insurance, and Form 941 payroll tax reports. Betty Ruth's fictitious employees were included in all these reports. Their W-2 forms were mailed to a variety of addresses—some to post office box numbers (rented by Martha Lee), and some to the conspirators' own addresses. (The conspirators even prepared federal income tax returns for the ghosts.)

RD-Mart's payroll bank account was truncated; that is, the bank submitted a statement showing the check number and amount of each paycheck but did not return the canceled checks. The bank reconciler (a person in the treasurer's office) was able to correspond the cleared check numbers and amounts to the payroll service report of check numbers and amounts. Nobody in the RD-Mart offices saw the canceled checks made payable to Betty Ruth and Martha Lee.

AMOUNT

The conspirators embezzled about $200,000 each year (one $340 weekly gross paycheck alternating among 11–12 of the Southeast Region stores all year). This was about two-tenths of 1 percent of the total RD-Mart payroll cost.

AUDIT APPROACH

OBJECTIVE

Obtain evidence of the existence and validity of payroll transactions.

CONTROL

Different people should be responsible for hiring (preparing personnel files), approving wages, preparing paychecks, and distributing the checks. This segregation of duties was evident in the RD-Mart offices. The company had prescribed activities for authorizing personnel hires, personnel file preparation, paycheck production, and check delivery. However, the store managers did not receive any detail reports of employees paid, so they had no post-payment opportunity to review their own payrolls.

TEST OF CONTROLS

Audit for transaction authorization and validity. A sample taken from the payroll service payroll registers can be vouched to personnel files. Since Betty Ruth had prepared authentic personnel files, this procedure will not show any exceptions. Likewise, a selection of personnel files traced to the payroll reports would show that all the people were paid.

AUDIT OF BALANCE

The "balance" to audit is the accumulated total of payroll transactions. Analytical procedures will not show the total out of line with history because the fraud is small in relation to total payroll. The audit procedure to determine existence of the people is a surprise payroll distribution. A small selection of stores might not include one with a fictitious employee at the time of the observation. (Betty Ruth might be smart enough to "fire" the fictitious employees when the auditors are expected.)

If the intent is to search for fictitious employees, several computer-based screening methods can be employed: (1) run all the employee Social Security numbers through a program designed to find unissued numbers, (2) run a test to report all employees using the same address or telephone number, (3) run a report of employees who elect minimum insurance or pension deductions, (4) run a report of all employees using P.O. box addresses, (5) examine these reports to determine whether employees appear on one or more of them. If "suspects" appear, request the bank to send copies of the front and back of the canceled payroll checks.

DISCOVERY SUMMARY

The computer-generated search procedures turned up 300 suspect employees, of which 22 turned out to be the conspirators' ghosts. (They were ones with false Social Security numbers whose addresses were the same as Betty Ruth's and Martha Lee's homes.) The auditors requested these checks from the bank and quickly found the names on the checks not the same as the names in the payroll register. They identified the conspirators. Further investigation and covert observation of Martha Lee removing the paychecks established guilt. Further investigation by the district attorney obtained their bank accounts and revealed the deposits of the ill-gotten embezzlement gains.

R E V I E W
CHECKPOINTS

10.33 What good are control documents and control activities if company personnel do not use them to prevent, detect, and correct payroll errors and frauds?

10.34 How can an auditor find out whether payroll control documents were used and control activities were performed by client personnel?

10.35 Specify some methods an auditor can use to search for fictitious employees in a large company's payroll.

10.36 What difference is there, if any, between tests of controls and tests (audit) of balances in the payroll area?

SUMMARY

The production and payroll cycle consists of two closely related parts. Production involves production planning, inventory planning, acquisition of labor, materials, overhead (acquisition and payment cycle), custody of assets while work is in process and when finished products are stored in inventory, and cost accounting. Payroll is a part of every business and an important part of every production cycle. Management and control of labor costs are important. The payroll cycle consists of hiring, rate authorization, attendance and work supervision, payroll processing, and paycheck distribution.

Production and payroll information systems produce many internal documents, reports, and files. A dozen or more of these sources of audit information are described in the chapter. This cycle is characterized by having mostly internal documentation as evidence and having relatively little external documentary evidence. Aside from the physical inventory in the production process, the accounts in the production and payroll cycle are intangible. They cannot be observed, inspected, touched, or counted in any meaningful way. Most audit procedures for this cycle are analytical procedures and dual-purposes procedures that test both the company's control activities and the existence, valuation, and completeness assertions made by accumulating the results of numerous labor and overhead transactions.

Companies reduce control risk by having a suitable separation of authorization, custody, recording, and periodic reconciliation duties. Error-checking procedures of analyzing production orders and finished production cost reports are important for proper determination of inventory values and proper valuation of cost of goods sold. Otherwise, many things could go wrong, ranging from overvaluing the inventory to understating costs of production by deferring costs that should be expensed.

Cost accounting is a central feature of the production cycle. Illustrative cases in the chapter tell the stories of financial reporting manipulations and the audit procedures that will detect them.

Payroll accounting is a critical operation for expenditure control. Many cases of embezzlement occur in this process. Illustrative cases in the chapter tell the stories of some fictitious employee and false time embezzlements and thefts.

MULTIPLE-CHOICE QUESTIONS FOR PRACTICE AND REVIEW

10.37 When an auditor tests a company's cost accounting system, the auditor's procedures are primarily designed to determine that
   a. Quantities on hand have been computed based on acceptable cost accounting techniques that reasonably approximate actual quantities on hand.
   b. Physical inventories are in substantial agreement with book inventories.
   c. The system is in accordance with generally accepted accounting principles and is functioning as planned.
   d. Costs have been properly assigned to finished goods, work in process, and cost of goods sold.

10.38 The auditor tests the quantity of materials charged to work in process by vouching these quantities to
   a. Cost ledgers.
   b. Perpetual inventory records.
   c. Receiving reports.
   d. Material requisition.

10.39 Effective internal control over the payroll function should include procedures that segregate the duties of making salary payments to employees and
   a. Controlling unemployment insurance claims.
   b. Maintaining employee personnel records.
   c. Approving employee fringe benefits.
   d. Hiring new employees.

10.40 Which of the following is the best way for an auditor to determine that every name on a company's payroll is that of a bona fide employee presently on the job?
   a. Examine personnel records for accuracy and completeness.
   b. Examine employees' names listed on payroll tax returns for agreement with payroll accounting records.

   c. Make a surprise observation of the company's regular distribution of paychecks.
   d. Control the mailing of annual W-2 tax forms to employee addresses in their personnel files.

10.41 It would be appropriate for the payroll accounting department to be responsible for which of the following functions?
   a. Approval of employee time records.
   b. Maintenance of records of employment, discharges, and pay increases.
   c. Preparation of periodic governmental reports of employees' earnings and withholding taxes.
   d. Temporary retention of unclaimed employee paychecks.

10.42 One of the auditor's objectives in observing the actual distribution of payroll checks is to determine that every name on the payroll is that of a bona fide employee. The payroll observation is an auditing procedure that is generally performed for which of the following reasons?
   a. The generally accepted auditing standards require the auditor to perform the payroll observation.
   b. The various phases of payroll work are not sufficiently segregated to afford effective internal control.
   c. The independent auditor uses personal judgment and decides to observe the payroll distribution on a particular audit.
   d. The generally accepted auditing standards are interpreted to mean that payroll observation is expected on an audit unless circumstances dictate otherwise.

10.43 During the year, a bookkeeper perpetrated a theft by preparing erroneous W-2 forms. The bookkeeper's FICA withheld was overstated by $500 and the FICA withheld from all other employees was understated. Which of the following is an audit procedure that would detect such a fraud?

a. Multiplication of the applicable FICA rate by the individual gross taxable earnings.

b. Utilizing Form W-4 and withholding charts to determine whether deductions authorized per pay period agree with amounts deducted per pay period.

c. Footing and cross footing the payroll register followed by tracing postings to the general ledger.

d. Vouching cancelled checks to federal tax Form 941.

10.44 A common audit procedure in the audit of payroll transactions involves vouching selected items from the payroll journal to employee time cards that have been approved by supervisory personnel. This procedure is designed to provide evidence in support of the audit proposition that

a. Only bona fide employees worked and their pay was properly computed.

b. Jobs on which employees worked and their pay was properly computed.

c. Internal controls relating to payroll disbursements are operating effectively.

d. All employees worked the number of hours for which their pay was computed.

10.45 To minimize the opportunities for fraud, unclaimed cash payroll should be

a. Deposited in a safe deposit box.

b. Held by the payroll custodian.

c. Deposited in a special bank account.

d. Held by the controller.

10.46 An effective client internal control activity to prevent lack of agreement between the cost accounting for labor cost and the payroll paid is

a. Reconciliation of totals on production job time tickets with job reports by the employees responsible for the specific jobs.

b. Verification of agreement of production job time tickets with employee clock cards by a payroll department employee.

c. Preparation of payroll transaction journal entries by an employee who reports to the personnel department director.

d. Custody of pay rate authorization forms by the supervisor of the payroll department.

(AICPA adapted)

10.47 The purpose of segregating the duties of hiring personnel and distributing payroll checks is to separate the

a. Authorization of transactions from the custody of related assets.

b. Operational responsibility from the record-keeping responsibility.

c. Human resources function from the controllership function.

d. Administrative controls from the internal accounting controls.

(AICPA adapted)

10.48 Effective internal control activities over the payroll function may include

a. Reconciliation of totals on job time tickets with job reports by employees responsible for those specific jobs.

b. Verification of agreement of job time tickets with employee clock card hours by a timekeeping department employee.

c. Preparation of payroll transaction journal entries by an employee who reports to the supervisor of the personnel department.

d. Custody of rate authorization records by the supervisor of the payroll department.

(AICPA adapted)

10.49 Which of the following activities most likely would be considered a weakness in an entity's internal control over payroll?

a. A voucher for the amount of the payroll is prepared in the general accounting department based on the payroll department's payroll summary.

b. Payroll checks are prepared by the accounts payable department and signed by the treasurer.

c. The employee who distributes payroll checks returns unclaimed payroll checks to the payroll department.

d. The personnel department sends employees' termination notices to the payroll department.

(AICPA adapted)

10.50 An auditor most likely would assess control risk at the maximum if the payroll department supervisor is responsible for

a. Examining authorization forms for new employees.

b. Comparing payroll registers with original batch transmittal data.

c. Authorizing payroll rate changes for all employees.

d. Hiring all subordinate payroll department employees.

(AICPA adapted)

10.51 Which of the following departments most likely would approve changes in pay rates and deductions from employee salaries?
   a. Personnel.
   b. Treasurer.
   c. Controller.
   d. Payroll.

(AICPA adapted)

10.52 Matthew Corp. has changed from a system of recording time worked on clock cards to a computerized payroll system in which employees record time in and out with magnetic cards. The computer system automatically updates all payroll records. Because of this change
   a. A generalized computer audit program must be used.
   b. Part of the audit trail is altered.
   c. The potential for payroll-related fraud is diminished.
   d. Transactions must be processed in batches.

(AICPA adapted)

10.53 Effective control over the cash payroll function would mandate which of the following?
   a. The payroll clerk should fill the envelopes with cash and a computation of the net wages.
   b. Unclaimed payroll envelopes should be retained by the paymaster.
   c. Each employee should be asked to sign a receipt.
   d. A separate checking account for payroll should be maintained.

(AICPA adapted)

10.54 A large retail enterprise has established a policy that requires the paymaster to deliver all unclaimed payroll checks to the internal audit department at the end of each payroll distribution day. This policy was most likely adopted to
   a. Assure that employees who were absent on a payroll distribution day are not paid for that day.
   b. Prevent the paymaster from cashing checks that are unclaimed for several weeks.
   c. Prevent a bona fide employee's check from being claimed by another employee.
   d. Detect any fictitious employee who may have been placed on the payroll.

(AICPA adapted)

10.55 An auditor will ordinarily ascertain whether payroll checks are properly endorsed during the audit of
   a. Clock cards.
   b. The voucher system.
   c. Cash in bank.
   d. Accrued payroll.

(AICPA adapted)

10.56 In determining the effectiveness of an entity's policies and procedures relating to the existence or occurrence assertion for payroll transactions, an auditor most likely would inquire about and
   a. Observe the segregation of duties concerning personnel responsibilities and payroll disbursement.
   b. Inspect evidence of accounting for prenumbered payroll checks.
   c. Recompute the payroll deductions for employee fringe benefits.
   d. Verify the preparation of the monthly payroll account bank reconciliation.

(AICPA adapted)

EXERCISES AND PROBLEMS

Production and Conversion Cycle

10.57   ICQ Items: Possible Error or Fraud Due to Weakness.   Refer to the internal control questionnaire (Appendix 10A–1) and assume the answer to each question is "no." Prepare a table matching questions to errors or frauds that could occur because of the absence of the control. Your column headings should be:

Question	Possible Error or Fraud Due to Weakness

10.58 Test of Controls Audit Procedures Related to Controls and Objectives. Each of the following test of control audit procedures might be performed during the audit of the controls in the production and conversion cycle. For each procedure: (a) identify the internal control procedure (strength) being tested, and (b) identify the internal control objective(s) being addressed.

1. Balance and reconcile detail production cost sheets to the work-in-process inventory control account.

2. Scan closed production cost sheets for missing numbers in the sequence.

3. Vouch a sample of open and closed production cost sheet entries to (a) labor reports and (b) issue slips and materials-used reports.

4. Locate the material issue forms. Are they prenumbered? Kept in a secure location? Available to unauthorized persons?

5. Select several summary journal entries in the work-in-process inventory: (a) vouch to weekly labor and material reports and to production cost sheets, and (b) trace to control account.

6. Select a sample of the material issue slips in the production department file. Examine for:

   a. Issue date and materials used report date.
   b. Production order number.
   c. Foreman's signature or initials.
   d. Name and number of material.
   e. Raw material stores clerk's signature or initials.
   f. Matching material requisition in raw material stores file. Note date of requisition.

7. Determine by inquiry and inspection if cost clerks review dates on report of units completed for accounting in the proper period.

10.59 Control over Departmental Labor Cost in a Job-Cost System. The Brown Printing Company accounts for the services it performs on a job-cost basis. Most jobs take a week or less to complete and involve two or more of Brown's five operating departments. Actual costs are accumulated by job. To ensure timely billing, however, the company prepares sales invoices based on cost estimates.

Recently, several printing jobs have incurred losses. To avoid future losses, management has decided to focus on cost control at the department level. Since labor is a major element of cost, management has proposed the development of a department labor cost report. This report will originate in the payroll department as part of the biweekly payroll and then go to an accounting clerk for comparison to total labor cost estimates by department. If the actual total department labor costs in a payroll are not much more than the estimated total departmental labor cost during that period, the accounting clerk will send the report to the department foreman. If the accounting clerk concludes that a significant variance exists, the report will be sent to the assistant controller. The assistant controller will investigate the cause, when time is available, and recommend corrective action to the production manager.

Required:

Evaluate the proposal:

a. Give at least three common aspects of control with which the department labor cost report proposal complies. Give an example from the case to support each aspect cited.

b. Give at least three common aspects of control with which the departmental labor cost report proposal does not comply. Give an example from the case to support each aspect cited.

(CIA adapted)

Payroll Cycle

10.60 Payroll Audit Procedures, Computers, and Sampling. You are the senior auditor in charge of the annual audit of Onward Manufacturing Corporation for the year ending December 31. The company is of medium size, having only 300 employees. All 300 employees are union members paid by the hour at rates set forth in a union contract, a copy of which is furnished to you. Job and pay rate classifications are determined by a joint union–management conference, and a formal memorandum is placed in each employee's personnel file.

Every week, clock cards prepared and approved in the shop are collected and transmitted to the payroll department. The total of labor hours is summed on an adding machine and entered on each clock card. Batch and hash totals are obtained for the following: (1) labor hours and (2) last four digits of Social Security numbers. These data are keyed into a disk file, batch balanced, and converted to tape storage for batch processing. The clock cards (with cost classification data) are sent to the cost accounting department.

The payroll system is computerized. As each person's payroll record is processed, the Social Security number is matched to a table (in a separate master file) to obtain job classification and pay rate data; then the pay rate is multiplied by the number of hours and the check is printed. (Ignore payroll deductions for the following requirements.)

Required:

a. What audit procedures would you recommend to obtain evidence that payroll data are accurately totaled and transformed into machine-readable records? What deviation rate might you expect? What tolerable deviation rate would you set? What "items" would you sample? What factors should be considered in setting the size of your sample?

b. What audit procedures would you recommend to obtain evidence that the pay rates are appropriately assigned and used in figuring gross pay? In what way, if any, would these procedures be different if the gross pay were calculated by hand instead of on a computer?

10.61 ICQ Items: Errors that Could Occur from Control Weaknesses. Refer to the internal control questionnaire on a payroll system (Appendix 10A–2) and assume the answer to each question is "no." Prepare a table matching the questions to errors or frauds that could occur because of the absence of the control. Your column headings should be:

Question	Possible Error or Fraud Due to Weakness

10.62 ICQ Items: Control Objectives, Test of Controls Procedures, and Possible Errors or Frauds. Listed below is a selection of items from the payroll processing internal control questionnaire in Appendix 10A–2.

1. Are names of terminated employees reported in writing to the payroll department?

2. Are authorizations for deductions, signed by the employees, on file?

3. Is there a timekeeping department (function) independent of the payroll department?

4. Are timekeeping and cost accounting records (such as hours, dollars) reconciled with payroll department calculations of hours and wages?

Required:
For each question above:

a. Identify the control objective to which the question applies.

b. Specify one test of controls audit procedure an auditor could use to determine whether the control was operating effectively (see Exhibit 10–8 for procedures).

c. Using your business experience, your logic, and/or your imagination, give an example of an error or fraud that could occur if the control were absent or ineffective.

d. Write a substantive audit procedure that could find errors or frauds that might result from the absence or ineffectiveness of the control items.

10.63 Major Risks in Payroll Cycle. Prepare a schedule of the major risks in the payroll cycle. Identify the control objectives and the financial statement assertions related to each. Lay out a three-column schedule like this:

Payroll Cycle Risk	Control Objective	Assertion

10.64 Payroll Authorization in a Computer System. Two accountants were discussing control procedures and test of control auditing for payroll systems. The senior accountant in charge of the engagement said: "It is impossible to determine who authorizes transactions when the payroll account is computerized."

Required:
Evaluate the senior accountant's statement about control in a computerized payroll system. List the points in the flow of payroll information where authorization takes place.

10.65 Payroll Processed by a Service Bureau. Assume that you are the audit senior conducting a review of the payroll system of a new client. In the process of interviewing the payroll department manager, she makes the following statement: "We don't need many controls since our payroll is done outside the company by Automated Data Processing, a service bureau."

Required:
Evaluate the payroll department manager's statement and describe how a service bureau affects an auditors' review of controls.

DISCUSSION CASES

10.66 Croyden Factory, Inc.: Evaluation of Payroll Control Weaknesses. A CPA's audit working papers contain a narrative description of a segment of the Croyden Factory, Inc., payroll system as follows:

Narrative:

The internal control system with respect to the personnel department functions well under good control.

At the beginning of each workweek, payroll clerk no. 1 reviews the payroll department files to determine the employment status of factory employees. Clerk no. 1 then prepares clock time cards and distributes them as each individual arrives at work. Later, after the weekly paychecks are prepared, this payroll clerk, who also is responsible for custody of the check signature stamp machine, verifies the identity of each payee before delivering signed checks to the foreman.

EXHIBIT 10.67–1 DIAGRAM OF PAYROLL TEST OF CONTROLS

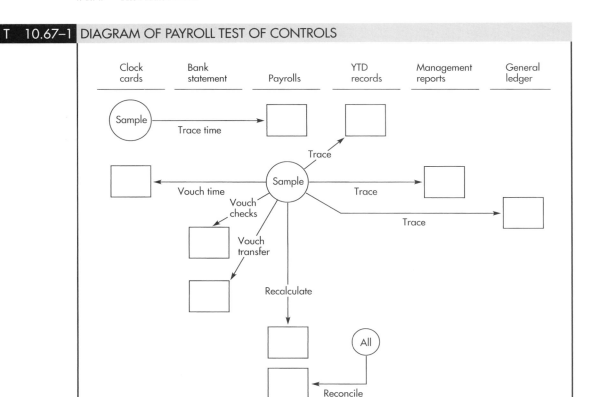

At the end of each workweek, the foreman distributes payroll checks for the preceding workweek. Concurrent with this activity, the foreman reviews the current week's employee timecards, notes the regular and overtime hours worked on a summary form, and initials the clock time cards. The foreman then delivers all time cards and unclaimed payroll checks to payroll clerk no. 2.

Required:

a. Based on the narrative what weaknesses do you notice in the system of internal control?

b. Based on the narrative, what inquiries should be made with respect to clarifying the existence of possible additional weaknesses in the system of internal control?

Note: Do not discuss the internal control system of the personnel department.

(AICPA adapted)

10.67   Payroll Test of Controls.   The diagram in Exhibit 10.67–1 describes several payroll test of control procedures. It shows the direction of the tests, leading from samples of clock cards, payrolls, and cumulative year-to-date earnings records to blank squares.

Required:

For each blank square in Exhibit 10.67–1, write a payroll test of controls procedure and describe

the evidence it can produce. (*Hint*: Refer to Exhibit 10–8.)

10.68   Cost Accounting Test of Controls.
The diagram in Exhibit 10.68–1 describes several cost accounting test of control procedures. It shows the direction of the tests, leading from samples of cost accounting analyses, management reports, and the general ledger to blank squares.

Required:

For each blank square in Exhibit 10.68–1, write a cost accounting test of controls procedure and describe the evidence it can produce. (*Hint*: Refer to Exhibit 10–8.)

Instructions for Discussion Cases 10.69–10.70.

These cases are designed like the ones in the chapter. They give the problem, the method, the paper trail, and the amount. Your assignment is to write the "audit approach" portion of the case, organized around these sections:

Objective: Express the objective in terms of the facts supposedly asserted in financial records, accounts, and statements.

Control: Write a brief explanation of desirable controls, missing controls, and especially the kinds of "deviations" that might arise from the situation described in the case.

EXHIBIT 10.68–1 DIAGRAM OF COST ACCOUNTING TEST OF CONTROLS

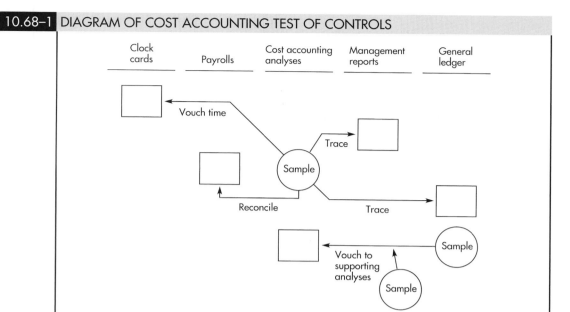

Test of controls: Write some procedures for getting evidence about existing controls, especially procedures that could discover deviations from controls. If there are no controls to test, then there are no procedures to perform; go then to the next section. A "procedure" should instruct someone about the source(s) of evidence to tap and the work to do.

Audit of balance: Write some procedures for getting evidence about the existence, completeness, valuation, ownership, or disclosure assertions identified in your objective section above.

Discovery summary: Write a short statement about the discovery you expect to accomplish with your procedures.

10.69   Inventory and Deferred Cost Overstatement.   Follow the instructions above. Write the "audit approach" section like the cases in the chapter.

Toying Around With the Numbers

Problem: Mattel, Inc., a manufacturer of toys, failed to write off obsolete inventory, thereby overstating inventory, and improperly deferred tooling costs, both of which understated cost of goods sold and overstated income.

Method: "Excess" inventory was identified by comparing types of toys (wheels, general toys, dolls, games), parts, and raw materials with the forecasted sales or usage, Lower-of-cost-or-market (LCM) determinations then were made to calculate the obsolescence write-off. Obsolescence was expected, and the target for the year was $700,000. The first comparison computer run showed $21 million "excess" inventory! The com-

pany "adjusted" the forecast by increasing the quantities of expected sales for many toy lines. (Forty percent of items had forecasted sales greater than the recent actual sales experience.) Another "adjustment" was to forecast toy closeout sales not at reduced prices but at regular price. Also, certain parts were labeled "interchangeable" without the normal reference to a new toy product. These "adjustments" to the forecast reduced the "excess" inventory exposed to LCM valuation and write-off.

The cost of setting up machines, preparing dies, and other preparations for manufacture are "tooling costs." They benefit the lifetime run of the toy manufactured. The company capitalized them as prepaid expenses and amortized them in the ratio of current-year sales to expected product lifetime sales (much like a natural resource depletion calculation). To get the amortization cost lower, the company transferred unamortized tooling costs from toys with low forecasted sales to ones with high forecasted sales. This caused the year's amortization ratio to be smaller, the calculated cost write-off lower, and the cost of goods sold lower than it should have been.

Paper trail: The computer forecast runs of expected usage of interchangeable parts provided a space for a reference to the code number of the new toy where the part would be used. Some of these references contained the code number of the part itself, not a new toy. In other cases, the forecast of toy sales and parts usage contained the quantity on hand, not a forecast number.

In the tooling cost detail records, unamortized cost was classified by lines of toys (similar to classifying asset cost by asset name or description). Unamortized balances were carried forward to the next year. The company changed the classifications shown at the prior year-end to other toy lines that had no balances or different balances. In other words, the balances of unamortized cost at the end of the prior year did not match the beginning balances of the current year, except that the total prepaid expense amount was the same.

Amount: For lack of obsolescence write-offs, inventory was overstated $4 million. The company recorded a $700,000 obsolescence write-off. It should have been about $4.7 million, as later determined.

The tooling cost manipulations overstated the prepaid expense by $3.6 million.

The company reported net income (after taxes) of $12.1 million in the year before the manipulations took place. If pretax income were in the $20–$28 million range in the year of the misstatements, the obsolescence and tooling misstatements alone amounted to about 32 percent income overstatement.

10.70   Payroll in the Blue Sky.

Problem: SueCan Corporation deferred costs under the heading of defense contract claims for reimbursement and deferred tooling labor costs, thus overstating assets, understating cost of goods sold, and overstating income.

Method: SueCan manufactured electronic and other equipment for private customers and government defense contracts. Near the end of the year, the company used a journal entry to remove $110,000 from cost of goods sold and defer it as deferred tooling cost. This $110,000 purported to be labor cost associated with preparing tools and dies for long production runs.

The company opened a receivables account for "cost overrun reimbursement receivable" as a claim for reimbursement on defense contracts ($378,000).

Paper trail: The company altered the labor time records for the tooling costs in an effort to provide substantiating documentation. Company employees prepared new work orders numbered in the series used late in the fiscal year and attached labor time records dated much earlier in the year. The production orders originally charged with the labor cost were left completed but with no labor charges!

The claim for reimbursement on defense contracts did not have documentation specifically identifying the labor costs as being related to the contract. There were no work orders. (Auditors know that defense department auditors insist on documentation and justification before approving such a claim.)

Amount: SueCan reported net income of about $442,000 for the year, an overstatement of approximately 60 percent.

APPENDIX 10A   INTERNAL CONTROLS

APPENDIX 10A–1   PRODUCTION AND COST ACCOUNTING TRANSACTION PROCESSING

Environment:

1. Is access to blank production order forms denied to unauthorized persons?
2. Is access to blank bills of materials and manpower needs forms denied to unauthorized persons?
3. Is access to blank material requisitions forms denied to unauthorized persons?

Validity objective:

4. Are material requisitions and job time tickets reviewed by the production supervisor after the foreman prepares them?
5. Are the weekly direct labor and materials-used reports reviewed by the production supervisor after preparation by the foreman?

Completeness objective:

6. Are production orders prenumbered and the numerical sequence checked for missing documents?
7. Are bills of materials and manpower needs forms prenumbered and the numerical sequence checked for missing documents?
8. Are material requisitions and job time tickets prenumbered and the numerical sequence checked for missing documents?
9. Are inventory issue slips prenumbered and the numerical sequence checked for missing documents?

Authorization objective:

10. Are production orders prepared by authorized persons?
11. Are bills of materials and manpower needs prepared by authorized persons?

Accuracy objective:

12. Are differences between inventory issue slips and materials-used reports recorded and reported to the cost accounting supervisor?
13. Are differences between job time tickets and the labor report recorded and reported to the cost accounting supervisor?
14. Are standard costs used? If so, are they reviewed and revised periodically?
15. Are differences between reports of units completed and products-received reports recorded and reported to the cost accounting supervisor?

Classification objective:

16. Does the accounting manual give instructions for proper classification of cost accounting transactions?

Accounting and Posting objective:

17. Are summary entries reviewed and approved by the cost accounting supervisor?

Proper period objective:

18. Does the accounting manual give instructions to date cost entries on the date of use? Does an accounting supervisor review monthly, quarterly, and year-end cost accruals?

APPENDIX 10A–2 PAYROLL PROCESSING

Environment:
1. Are all employees paid by check?
2. Is a special payroll bank account used?
3. Are payroll checks signed by persons who do not prepare checks nor keep cash funds or accounting records?
4. Is the payroll bank account reconciled by someone who does not prepare, sign, or deliver paychecks?
5. Are payroll department personnel rotated in their duties? Required to take vacations? Bonded?
6. Is there a timekeeping department (function) independent of the payroll department?

Validity objective:
7. Are names of terminated employees reported in writing to the payroll department?
8. Is the payroll compared to personnel files periodically?
9. Are checks distributed by someone other than the employee's immediate supervisor?
10. Are unclaimed wages deposited in a special bank account or otherwise controlled by a responsible officer?
11. Do internal auditors conduct occasional surprise distributions of paychecks?

Completeness objective:
12. Are names of newly hired employees reported in writing to the payroll department?
13. Are blank payroll checks prenumbered and the numerical sequence checked for missing documents?

Authorization objective:
14. Are all wage rates determined by contract or approved by a personnel officer?
15. Are authorizations for deductions, signed by the employees, on file?
16. Are time cards or piecework reports prepared by the employee approved by his or her supervisor?
17. Is a time clock or other electromechanical or computer system used?
18. Is the payroll register sheet signed by the employee preparing it and approved prior to payment?

Accuracy objective:
19. Are timekeeping and cost accounting records (such as hours, dollars) reconciled with payroll department calculations of hours and wages?
20. Are payrolls audited periodically by internal auditors?

Classification objective:
21. Do payroll accounting personnel have instructions for classifying payroll debit entries?

Accounting and Posting objective:
22. Are individual payroll records reconciled with quarterly tax reports?

Proper period objective:
23. Are monthly, quarterly, and annual wage accruals reviewed by an accounting officer?

Chapter 11
Finance and Investment Cycle

Professional Standards References

Compendium Section	Document Reference	Topic
AU 316	SAS 82	*Consideration of Fraud in a Financial Statement Audit*
AU 317	SAS 54	*Illegal Acts by Clients*
AU 319	SAS 78	*Internal Control in a Financial Statement Audit*
AU 326	SAS 80	*Evidential Matter*
AU 332	SAS 92	*Auditing Investments, Hedging Activities, and Investments in Securities*
AU 334	SAS 45	*Related Parties*
AU 9334		*Interpretation: Related Party Transactions with a Component*
AU 339	SAS 41	*Working Papers*
AU 342	SAS 57	*Auditing Accounting Estimates*
AU 9342		*Interpretation: Fair Value Disclosures*

Learning Objectives

The finance and investment cycle comprehends a company's ways and means of planning for capital requirements and raising the money by borrowing, selling stock, and entering into acquisitions and joint ventures. The finance part of the cycle deals with obtaining money for the company through stock or debt issues for investment in necessary resources. The investment portion of the cycle deals with the disposition of these funds for investments in property, plant, and equipment (PP&E), marketable securities, joint ventures and partnerships, and subsidiaries. After completing this chapter, you should be able to:

1. Describe the finance and investment cycle, including typical source documents and controls.

2. Give examples of test of controls procedures for obtaining information about the controls over debt and owner equity transactions and investment transactions.

3. Describe some common errors and frauds in the accounting for capital transactions and investments, and design some audit and investigation procedures for detecting them.

FINANCE AND INVESTMENT CYCLE: TYPICAL ACTIVITIES

LEARNING OBJECTIVE

1. Describe the finance and investment cycle, including typical source documents and controls.

The finance and investment cycle contains a large number of accounts and records, ranging across tangible (e.g., property, plant and equipment) and intangible (e.g., goodwill, patents) assets, long-term liabilities, deferred credits, stockholders' equity, gains and losses, expenses, and income taxes. The major accounts and records are listed in Exhibit 11–1. These include some of the more complicated topics in accounting—equity method accounting for investments, consolidation accounting, goodwill, income taxes, and financial instruments, to name a few. It is not the purpose of this chapter to explain the accounting for these balances and transactions. The chapter concentrates on a few important aspects of auditing them.

Exhibit 11–1 shows a skeleton outline of the finance and investment cycle. Its major functions are financial planning and raising capital; interacting with the acquisition and expenditure, production and payroll, and revenue and collection cycles; and entering into mergers, acquisitions, and other investments.

Financing Transactions: Debt and Stockholder Equity Capital

Transactions in debt and stockholder equity capital are normally few in number but large in monetary amount. The highest levels of management handle them. The control-related duties and responsibilities reflect this high-level attention.

Authorization

Financial planning starts with the chief financial officer's (CFO's) cash flow forecast. This forecast informs the board of directors and management of the business plans, the prospects for cash inflows, and the needs for cash outflows. The cash flow forecast usually is integrated with the capital budget, which contains the plans for asset purchases and business acquisitions. A capital budget approved by the board of directors constitutes the authorization for major capital asset acquisitions (acquisition cycle) and investments.

The board of directors authorizes sales of capital stock and debt financing transactions usually. All the directors must sign registration documents for public securities offerings. However, authority normally is delegated to the CFO to complete such transactions as periodic renewals of notes payable and other ordinary types of financing transactions without specific board approval of each transaction. Auditors should expect to find the authorizing signatures of the chief executive officer (CEO), CFO, chair of the board of directors, and perhaps other high-ranking officers on financing documents.

EXHIBIT 11–1   FINANCE AND INVESTMENT CYCLE

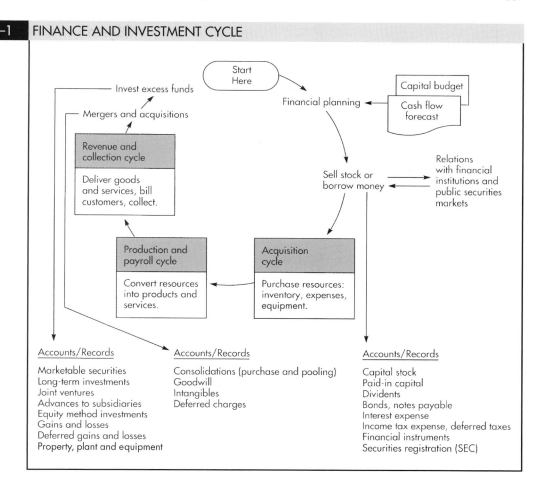

Many financing transactions are "off the balance sheet." Companies can enter into obligations and commitments that are not required to be recorded in the accounts. Examples of such authorizations include: leases, endorsements on discounted notes or on other companies' obligations, letters of credit, guarantees, repurchase or remarketing agreements, commitments to purchase at fixed prices, commitments to sell at fixed

AUDITING INSIGHT

THE FRAUD LOSSES HAPPENED LAST YEAR!

Retained earnings is usually not a very interesting capital account. It cannot be bought, sold, or stolen, but it can be the final resting place for some important accounting decisions.

AM International was the victim of a massive management fraud engineered by high-level executives and put over for awhile on the independent auditors and on everybody else. Reportedly, over $75 million in assets did not exist, even though they were reported in the audited financial statements.

After the corrupt management was terminated, the new management concluded that the losses resulting from the fraud should be a prior period adjustment to retained earnings and prior income statements in the amount of $250 million, counting the fictitious assets and the adverse impact of the events on the company's business. They wanted to start with a new, clean slate.

The argument was that the accounting errors occurred in earlier years, and all the related losses should be placed in the accounting for those years. Do you agree with this prior period adjustment accounting for this situation?

prices, and certain kinds of stock options. They cause problems in financial reporting and disclosure.

Custody

In large companies, custody of stock certificate books is not a significant management problem. Large companies employ banks and trust companies to serve as registrars and transfer agents. A registrar keeps the stockholder list and, from time to time, determines the shareholders eligible to receive dividends (stockholders of record on a dividend record date) and those entitled to vote at the annual meeting. A transfer agent handles the exchange of shares, cancelling the shares surrendered by sellers and issuing new certificates to buyers. The same bank or trust company usually provides both services.

Small companies often keep their own stockholder records. A stock certificate book looks like a checkbook. It has perforated stubs for recording the number of shares, the owner's name and other identification, and the date of issue. Actual unissued share certificates are attached to the stubs, like blank checks in a checkbook. The missing certificates are the ones outstanding in the possession of owners. Custody of the stock certificate book is important because the unissued certificates are like money or collateral. If improperly removed, they can be sold to buyers who think they are genuinely issued or can be used as collateral with unsuspecting lenders.

Lenders have custody of debt instruments (e.g., leases, bonds, and notes payable). A CFO may have copies, but they are merely convenience records. However, when a company repurchases its debt instruments, these come into the custody of trustees or company officials, usually the CFO. Until they are cancelled and destroyed, it is possible to misuse them by improperly reselling them to unsuspecting investors.

Record keeping

Records of notes and bonds payable are maintained by the accounting department and the CFO or controller. The record keeping procedures should be similar to those used to account for vendor accounts payable: payment notices from lenders are compared to the accounting records, due dates are monitored, interest payments are set up in vouchers for payment, and accruals for unpaid interest are made on financial reporting dates. If the company has only a few bonds and notes outstanding, no subsidiary records of notes are kept. All the information is in the general ledger accounts. (Companies with a large number of bonds and notes may keep control and subsidiary accounts, as is done for accounts receivable.) When all or part of the notes become due within the next year, the CFO and controller have the necessary information for properly classifying current and long-term amounts.

Another class of credit balances is treated here under the heading of "record keeping," for which the functions of authorization, custody, and reconciliation are not easy to describe. They are the "calculated liabilities and credits"—lease obligations, deferred income taxes, pension and post-retirement benefit liabilities, and foreign currency translation gains and losses, to name a few. These are accounting creations, calculated according to accounting rules and using basic data from company plans and operations. Management usually enjoys considerable discretion in structuring leases, tax strategies, pension plan and employee benefit terms, foreign holdings, and the like. These accounting calculations often involve significant accounting estimates made by management. Company accountants try to capture the economic reality of these calculated liabilities by following generally accepted accounting principles.

Periodic Reconciliation

A responsible person should periodically inspect the stock certificate book to determine whether the only missing certificates are the ones known to be outstanding in the possession of bona fide owners. If necessary, officials in very small companies can confirm the ownership of shares with the holders of record. Reports with similar information content can be obtained from registrars and transfer agents to verify that the company's record of the number of shares outstanding agrees with the registrars' number. (Without this reconciliation, counterfeit shares handled by the transfer agent and recorded by the registrar might go unnoticed.)

A trustee having duties and responsibilities similar to those of registrars and transfer agents can handle ownership of bonds. Confirmations and reports from bond trustees can be used to reconcile the trustee's records to the company's records.

Investing Transactions: PP&E, Investments and Intangibles

Company investments can take many shapes. For example, the company must ensure that there are adequate resources in terms of property, plant, and equipment (PP&E) to support operations. If a grocery chain is opening a new store, the company must invest not only in the land and building, but also the equipment (e.g., forklifts, refrigerators, cash registers) to support the store's operations. Investment in intangible assets may be in the form of purchased assets (e.g., patents, trademarks) or in the form of accounting allocations (e.g., goodwill, deferred charges). Finally, a company can have a large variety or a limited set of types of investments in marketable securities. While the sections below are phrased in the context of a manufacturing or service company, financial institutions (banks, thrifts), investment companies (mutual funds, small business investment companies—SBICs), and insurance companies have more elaborate systems for managing their investments and intangibles.

Authorization

The board of directors or its investment committee should approve all investment policies. It is not unusual to find board or executive committee approval required for major individual investment transactions. However, auditors should expect to find a great deal of variation across companies about the nature and amount of transactions that must have specific high-level approval.

Custody

Custody depends on the nature of the assets. For equipment purchases, a receiving department inspects the equipment received for quantity and quality (producing a *receiving report*), and then puts the equipment in the hands of other responsible persons. To be honest, custody of land and equipment does not represent a significant risk to either the company or the auditor. Thieves may have significant difficulties trying to hook up the company's building to the back of their pickup truck.

AUDITING INSIGHT

THE LITTLE LEASE THAT COULD

The Park 'N Fly commuter airline was struggling. According to its existing debt covenants, it could not incur any more long-term liabilities. The company needed a new airplane to expand its services, so it "rented" one. The CFO pointed out that the deal for the $12 million airplane was a noncancellable operating lease because: (1) Park 'N Fly does not automatically own the plane at the end of the lease; (2) the purchase option of $1,500,000 is no bargain; (3) the lease term of 133 months is 74 percent, not 75 percent, of the estimated 15-year economic life; and (4) the present value of the lease payments of $154,330 per month, discounted at the company's latest borrowing rate of 14 percent, is $10.4 million, which is less than the 90 percent of fair value (0.90 × $12 million = $10.8 million) criterion in the FASB pronouncements.

The CFO did not record a long-term lease obligation (liability). Do you agree with this accounting conclusion?

Negotiable certificates, such as stocks and bonds, are a different matter. The actual certificates may be kept in a brokerage account in a "house name" (the brokerage company), and, in this case, "custody" rests with the company official who is authorized to order the buy, sell, and delivery transactions. Other negotiable certificates (such as titles to real estate) may be in the actual possession of the owner (client company). If the company keeps them, they should be in a safe or a bank safe-deposit box. Only high-ranking officers (e.g., CFO, CEO, president, chair of board) should have combinations and keys.

Other kinds of investments do not have formal negotiable certificates, and "custody" may take the form of "management responsibility" instead of actual physical handling. Examples are joint ventures and partnerships in which the client company is a partner. Venture and partnership agreements are evidence of these investments, but they usually are merely filed with other important documents. Misuse of them is seldom a problem because they are not readily negotiable. Real custody rests with management's supervision and monitoring the venture or partnership operations.

Having "custody" of most intangibles is like trying to keep Jell-O in your pocket—good in theory but messy in practice. However, patents, trademarks, copyrights, and similar legal intangible rights may be evidenced in legal documents and contracts. These seldom are negotiable, and they usually are kept in ordinary company files. Accounting intangibles like goodwill and deferred charges (deferred tax credits and pension obligations on the liability side) are in the custody of the accountants who calculate them.

AUDITING INSIGHT

CLASSIFY THE DEBITS CORRECTLY

Invoices for expensive repairs were not clearly identified, so the accounts payable accountants entered the debits that should have been repairs and maintenance expense as capitalized assets. This initially understated expenses and overstated income by $125,000 one year, although the incorrectly capitalized expenses were written off as depreciation in later years.

Company managers may be assigned responsibility to protect exclusive rights granted by various intangibles.

Record keeping

The procedures for purchase of most investments involve the voucher system described in the acquisition and expenditure cycle. Authorization by the board of directors or other responsible officials is the approval for the accounting department to prepare the voucher and the check. The treasurer or CFO signs the check for the investment.

The record keeping for many kinds of investments and intangibles can be complicated. The complications arise not so much from the original recording of transactions but from the maintenance of the accounts over time. This is the place where complex accounting standards for marketable securities, equity method accounting, consolidations, goodwill, intangibles amortization and valuation, deferred charges, deferred taxes, pension and post-retirement benefit liabilities, and various financial instruments enter the picture. High-level accountants who prepare financial statements get involved with the accounting rules and the management estimates required to account for such investments and intangibles. Management plans and estimates of future events and interpretations of the accounting standards often become elements of the accounting maintenance of these balances. These decisions are ripe areas for overstatement of assets, understatement of liabilities, and understatement of expenses.

The cost accounting department may be charged with the responsibility of preparing a schedule of the depreciation of buildings and equipment. In many companies, such schedule is long and complicated, involving large dollar amounts of asset cost and calculated depreciation expense. It is not unusual to find the amount of depreciation expense exceeding a company's net income. (In the statement of cash flows, the depreciation added back to calculate the cash flow from operations can be larger than the net income carried forward from the income statement.) An abbreviated illustration of a schedule of property, plant, and equipment (PP&E) and depreciation is in the table below.

PP&E AND DEPRECIATION

	Asset Cost (000s)				Accumulated Depreciation (000s)			
Description	Beginning Balance	Added	Sold	Ending Balance	Beginning Balance	Added	Sold	Ending Balance
Land	10,000			10,000				
Bldg 1	30,000			30,000	6,857	857		7,714
Bldg 2		42,000		42,000		800		800
Computer A	5,000		5,000	0	3,750	208	3,958	0
Computer B		3,500		3,500		583		583
Press	1,500			1,500	300	150		450
Auto 1	15		15	0	15		15	0
Auto 2		22		22		2		2
Total	46,515	45,522	5,015	87,022	10,922	2,600	3,973	9,549

AUDITING INSIGHT

GAAP AND REGULATORY DEPRECIATION

U.S. West took a $5.4 billion pretax charge against earnings, wiping out over one-third of the shareholders' equity. In stock trading, U.S. West's share price increased 4 percent. Wall Street sent two messages: (1)the company should be rewarded for honest bookkeeping, and (2)its bookkeeping has not been very honest in recent years.

U.S. West changed its depreciation accounting for telecommunications equipment from the long lives required by rate regulation agencies to the shorter useful lives appropriate under GAAP. U.S. West reportedly got tired of reporting phony net earnings required by regulators and decided to report GAAP depreciation in its public financial statements. (The company must still use the regulatory depreciation when reporting to the rate regulation agencies.)

Other telecommunications companies are waiting for the regulators to approve the more appropriate depreciation deductions. However, the capital markets clearly approve of U.S. West's new depreciation bookkeeping.
THE LESSON: Auditors should consider carefully the rational basis for useful lives clients incorporate in depreciation calculations.

Source: *Forbes.*

Periodic Reconciliation

A periodic comparison or reconciliation of existing assets to recorded amounts occurs in several ways, including periodic inspection of equipment to compare to detail equipment records. Equipment reports (or *fixed asset reports*) are similar to inventory reports because they show the details of equipment in control accounts. The reports can be used for scanning and sample selection, much like the inventory reports. The information for depreciation calculation (cost, useful life, method, salvage) can be used for the audit of depreciation on a sample basis or by computer applications to recalculate all the depreciation.

The most significant reconciliation opportunity in the investments in marketable securities is the inspection and count of negotiable securities certificates. This reconciliation is similar to a physical inventory in that it consists of an inspection of certificates on hand, along with comparison to the information recorded in the accounts. (When a brokerage firm holds the securities, the "inspection" is accomplished with a written confirmation.)

A securities count is not a mere handling of bits of paper. A securities count "inventory" should include a record of the name of the company represented by the certificate, the interest rate for bonds, the dividend rate for preferred stocks, the due date for bonds, the serial numbers on the certificates, the face value of bonds, the number or face amount of bonds and stock shares, and notes on the name of the owner shown on the face of the

AUDITING INSIGHT

THE SIGN OF THE CREDIT BALANCE

Auto Parts & Repair, Inc., kept perpetual inventory records and equipment records on a computer system. Because of the size of the files (8,000 parts in various locations and 1,500 asset records), the company never printed reports for visual inspection. Auditors ran a computer-audit "sign test" on inventory balances and equipment net book balances. The test called for a printed report for all balances less than zero. The auditors discovered 320 negative inventory balances caused by failure to record purchases and 125 negative net asset balances caused by depreciating assets more than their cost.

AUDITING INSIGHT

A NEW MEANING FOR "RECYCLING"

Something strange must have happened on the way to the dump. Hundreds of issues of long-term bonds were redeemed early and presented to Citicorp's Citibank in New York, acting as agent for the issues, according to the FBI. Many of the bonds still had not reached the maturity date marked on them. Citibank sent about $1 billion of cancelled U.S. corporate bonds to a landfill dump in New Jersey. But in the past year, some of those bonds have been turning up at banks in Europe and the United States. The banks have had a disturbing surprise: The bonds are worthless, though they still might look genuine to a layman or even to some bankers.

An FBI spokesman says a defunct company in New Jersey is being investigated. The company had a contract to destroy the bonds.

Note: Companies obtain a "destruction certificate" when bonds and stock certificates are canceled. The certificate obtained by Citibank apparently was fraudulent.

Source: The Wall Street Journal.

certificate or on the endorsements on the back (should be the client company). Companies should perform this reconciliation reasonably often and not wait for an annual visit by the independent auditors. A securities count in a financial institution that holds thousands of shares in multimillion-dollar asset accounts is a major undertaking.

When auditors perform the securities inspection and count, all this information should be recorded in the audit working papers. Existence is established by inspecting the securities, ownership is established by viewing the client name as owner, valuation evidence is added by finding the cost and market value. If a security certificate is not available for inspection, it may be pledged as collateral for a loan and in the hands of a creditor. It can be confirmed or inspected (if the extended procedure of visiting the creditor is necessary). The pledge as collateral may be important for a footnote disclosure. A securities count and reconciliation is important for management and auditors because companies have been known to try to substitute others' securities for missing ones. If securities have been sold, then replaced without any accounting entries, the serial numbers will show that the certificates recorded in the accounts are not the same as the ones on hand.

REVIEW CHECKPOINTS

11.1 Do you believe losses hidden by fraudulent overstatement of assets should be corrected with prior period adjustment accounting after discovery?

11.2 What is a "destruction certificate"?

11.3 When a management carefully crafts a lease agreement to barely fail the tests for lease capitalization and liability recognition, do you believe auditors should insist on capitalization anyway?

11.4 What would constitute the authorization for notes payable? What documentary evidence could auditors examine as evidence of this authorization?

11.5 What features of a client's capital stock are of importance in the audit?

11.6 What procedures can auditors employ in the audit of investment securities to obtain the names of the issuers, the number of shares held, certificate numbers, maturity value, and interest and dividend rates?

11.7 Describe the procedures and documentation of a controlled count of client's investment securities. What information should be included in an audit working paper?

CONTROL RISK ASSESSMENT

LEARNING OBJECTIVE

2. Give examples of test of controls procedures for obtaining information about the controls over debt and owner equity transactions and investment transactions.

In the finance and investment cycle, auditors look for control activities, such as authorization, custody, record keeping, and periodic reconciliation. They especially look for information about the level of management involved in these functions. Tests of controls generally amount to inquiries and observations related to these features. Samples of transactions for detail tests of control performance are not normally a part of the control risk assessment work as they can be in the revenue and collection cycle, in the acquisition and expenditure cycle, and in the production and payroll cycle. Because finance and investment transactions are usually individually material, each transaction usually is audited in detail. Reliance on control does not normally reduce the extent of substantive audit work on finance and investment cycle accounts. However, lack of control can lead to performance of significant extended procedures.

Control Considerations

Control procedures for suitable handling of responsibilities should be in place and operating. By referring to the discussion accompanying Exhibit 11–1, you can tell that these responsibilities are basically in the hands of senior management officials. You also can tell that different companies may have widely different policies and procedures.

It is hard to have a strict segregation of functional responsibilities when the principal officers of a company authorize, execute, and control finance and investment activities. It is not very realistic to maintain that a CEO can authorize investments but cannot have access to stockholder records, securities certificates, and the like. Real segregation of duties can be found in middle management and lower ranks, but it is hard to create and enforce in upper-level management.

In light of this problem of control, a company should have compensating control procedures. A **compensating control** is a control feature used when a company does not specify standard control procedure (such as strict segregation of functional responsibilities). In the area of finance and investment, the compensating control feature is the involvement of two or more persons in each kind of important functional responsibility.

If involvement by multiple persons is not specified, then oversight or review can be substituted. For example, the board of directors can authorize purchase of securities or creation of a partnership. The CFO or CEO can carry out the transactions, have custody of certificates and agreements, manage the partnership or the portfolio of securities, oversee the record keeping, and make the decisions about valuations and accounting (authorizing the journal entries). These are normal management activities, and they combine several responsibilities. The compensating control can exist in the form of periodic reports to the board of directors, oversight by the investment committee of the board, and internal audit involvement in making a periodic reconciliation of securities certificates in a portfolio with the amounts and descriptions recorded in the accounts.

Control over Accounting Estimates

An **accounting estimate** is an approximation of a financial statement element, item, or account. Estimates often are included in basic financial statements because (1) the measurement of some amount of valuation is uncertain, perhaps depending upon the outcome of future events, or (2) relevant data cannot be accumulated on a timely, cost-effective basis (SAS 57, AU 342). Some examples of accounting estimates in the finance and investment cycle are shown in the box below.

A client's management is responsible for making estimates and should have a process and controls designed to reduce the likelihood of material misstatements in them. According to auditing standards (SAS 57, AU 342), specific relevant aspects of such controls include:

FINANCE AND INVESTMENT CYCLE ESTIMATES

Plant and Equipment: Useful lives; salvage values.

Financial instruments: Valuation of securities; classification into held-to-maturity, available-for-sale, and trading securities investment portfolios; probability of a correlated hedge; sales of securities with puts and calls; investment model assumptions.

Accruals: Compensation in stock option plans, actuarial assumptions in pension costs.

Leases: Initial direct costs, executory costs, residual values, capitalization interest rate.

Rates: Imputed interest rates on receivables and payables.

Other: Losses and net realizable value on segment disposal and business restructuring, fair values in nonmonetary exchanges, fair values assigned to debt and equity securities.

- Management communication of the need for proper accounting estimates.
- Accumulation of relevant, sufficient, and reliable data for estimates.
- Preparation of estimates by qualified personnel.
- Adequate review and approval by appropriate levels of authority.
- Comparison of prior estimates with subsequent results to assess the reliability of the estimation outcomes.
- Consideration by management of whether particular accounting estimates are consistent with the company's operational plans.

Auditors' test of controls over the production of estimates amounts to inquiries and observations related to the features listed immediately above. Such inquiries are: Who prepares estimates? When are they prepared? What data are used? Who reviews and approves the estimates? Have you compared prior estimates with subsequent actual events? Observations include: study of data documentation, study of comparisons of prior estimates with subsequent actual experience, study of intercompany correspondence concerning estimates and operational plans.

The audit of a valuation estimate starts with the test of controls, much of which has a bearing on the substantive quality of the estimation process and of the estimate itself. Further substantive audit work includes procedures to determine whether (a) the valuation principles are acceptable under GAAP, (b) the valuation principles are consistently applied, (c) the valuation principles are supported by the underlying documentation, and (d) the method of estimation and the significant assumptions are properly disclosed according to GAAP.

Control Risk Assessment for Notes Payable

From the preceding discussion, you can tell that test of controls audit procedures take a variety of forms—inquiries, observations, study of documentation, comparison with related data, and detail audit of some transactions. The detail audit of transactions, however, is a small part of the test of controls because of the nature of the finance and investment transactions, their number (few), and their amount (large). However, some companies have numerous debt financing transactions, and a more detailed approach to control risk assessment can be used, including the selection of a sample of transactions for control risk assessment evidence.

An internal control questionnaire for notes payable is in Appendix 11A. It illustrates typical questions about the control objectives. These inquiries give auditors insights into the client's specifications for review and approval of major financing transactions, the system of accounting for them, and the provision for error-checking review activities.

EXHIBIT 11–2	TEST OF CONTROLS AUDIT PROCEDURES FOR NOTES PAYABLE

	Control Objective
1. Read directors' and finance committee's minutes for authorization of financing transactions (such as short-term notes payable, bond offerings).	Authorization
2. Select a sample of paid notes:	
a. Recalculate interest expense for the period under audit.	Accuracy
b. Trace interest expense to the general ledger account.	Completeness
c. Vouch payment to canceled checks.	Validity
3. Select a sample of notes payable:	
a. Vouch to authorization by directors or finance committee.	Authorization
b. Vouch cash receipt to bank statement.	Validity

Auditors can select a sample of notes payable transactions for detail test of controls, provided that the population of notes is large enough to justify sample-based auditing. Exhibit 11–2 lists a selection of such procedures, with notation of the relevant control objectives shown on the right.

Summary: Control Risk Assessment

The audit manager or senior accountant in charge of the audit should evaluate the evidence obtained from an understanding of the internal control system and from test of controls audit procedures. These procedures can take many forms because management systems for finance and investment accounts can vary a great deal among clients. The involvement of senior officials in a relatively small number of high-dollar transactions makes control risk assessment a process tailored specifically to the company's situation. Some companies enter into complicated financing and investment transactions, while others keep to the simple transactions.

In general, substantive audit procedures on finance and investment accounts are not limited in extent. Auditors often perform substantive audit procedures on 100 percent of these transactions and balances. The number of transactions is usually not large, and the audit cost is not high for complete coverage. Nevertheless, control deficiencies and unusual or complicated transactions can cause auditors to adjust the nature and timing of audit procedures. Complicated financial instruments, pension plans, exotic equity securities, related party transactions, and nonmonetary exchanges of investment assets call for procedures designed to find evidence of errors and frauds in the finance and investment accounts. The next section deals with some of the finance and investment cycle assertions, and it has some cases for your review.

REVIEW CHECKPOINTS

11.8 What is a compensating control? Give some examples for finance and investment cycle accounts.

11.9 What are some of the specific relevant aspects of management's control over the production of accounting estimates? What are some inquiries auditors can make?

11.10 When a company has produced an estimate of an investment valuation based on a nonmonetary exchange, what source of comparative information can an auditor use?

11.11 Generally, how much emphasis is placed on adequate internal control in the audit of long-term debt? Of capital stock? Of paid-in capital? Of retained earnings?

AUDITING INSIGHT

AN ESTIMATED VALUATION BASED ON FUTURE DEVELOPMENT

Gulf & Western Industries (G&W) sold 450,000 shares of Pan American stock from its investment portfolio to Resorts International (Resorts). Resorts paid $8 million plus 250,000 shares of its unregistered common stock. G&W recorded the sale proceeds as $14,167,500, valuing the unregistered Resorts stock at $6,167,500, which was approximately 67 percent of the market price of Resorts stock at the time ($36.82 per share). G&W reported a gain of $3,365,000 on the sale.

Four years later, Resorts stock fell to $2.63 per share. G&W sold its 250,000 shares back to Resorts in exchange for 1,100 acres of undeveloped land on Grand Bahamas Island. For its records, Resorts got a broker-dealer's opinion that its 250,000 shares were worth $460,000. For property tax assessment purposes, the Bahamian government valued the undeveloped land at $525,000.

G&W valued the land on its books at $6,167,500, which was the previous valuation of the Resorts stock. The justification was an appraisal of $6,300,000 based on the estimated value of the 1,100 acres when ultimately developed (i.e., built into an operating resort and residential community). However, G&W also reported a loss of $5,527,000 in its tax return (effectively valuing the land at $640,500).

The SEC accused G&W of failing to report a loss of $5.7 million in its financial statements. Do you think the loss should have appeared in the G&W income statement?

Source: I. Kellog, *How to Find Negligence and Misrepresentation in Financial Statements.*

ASSERTIONS, SUBSTANTIVE PROCEDURES, AND AUDIT CASES

LEARNING OBJECTIVE

3. Describe some common errors and frauds in the accounting for capital transactions and investments, and design some audit and investigation procedures for detecting them.

This part of the chapter covers the audit of various account balances and transactions. It is presented in two sections—financing activities (such as owners' equity, long-term liabilities and related accounts), and investing activities (PP&E, investments and intangibles). This chapter provides some assertions and procedures related to accounts in each portion of the financing and investing cycle. As in previous chapters, some cases illustrating errors and frauds are used to describe useful audit approaches.

Financing Activities: Assertions and Audit Procedures

Long-Term Liabilities and Related Accounts

Assertions.   The primary audit concern with the verification of long-term liabilities is that all liabilities are recorded and that the interest expense is properly paid or accrued. Therefore, the assertion of *completeness* is paramount. Alertness to the possibility of unrecorded liabilities during the performance of procedures in other areas frequently will uncover liabilities that have not been recorded. For example, when property, plant, and equipment are acquired during the year under audit, auditors should inquire about the source of funds for financing the new asset.

Management makes assertions about existence, completeness, rights and obligations, valuation, and presentation and disclosure. Typical specific assertions relating to long-term liabilities include:

1. All material long-term liabilities are recorded.
2. Liabilities are properly classified according to their current or long-term status. The current portion of long-term debt is properly valued and classified.
3. New long-term liabilities and debt extinguishments are properly authorized.
4. Terms, conditions, and restrictions relating to noncurrent debt are adequately disclosed.
5. Disclosures of maturities for the next five years and the capital and operating lease disclosures are accurate and adequate.

AUDITING INSIGHT

ENVIRONMENTAL LIABILITIES

The clock is ticking for corporations that missed the SEC's wake-up call to keep investors better informed about environmental liabilities. Companies may awaken to SEC enforcement actions, shareholder lawsuits, even criminal prosecution.

The focus on environmental disclosure is fairly recent—and it is gathering steam. Estimates of the nation's cost of hazardous waste cleanup range up to $1 trillion, but most shareholders have no idea the amounts specific companies must pay. Corporate annual reports tell very little.

Companies must disclose any environmental trends or uncertainties they expect to have a material impact. The SEC is particularly interested in appropriate accounting and disclosure if a company is designated a "potentially responsible party" under the Superfund laws. (Auditors can identify such companies in a national "potentially responsible party" database.)

Source: *New York Times.*

---

6. All important contingencies are either accrued in the accounts or disclosed in footnotes.

An illustrative program of substantive audit procedures for notes payable and long-term debt is in Appendix 11B–2.

Audit Procedures.   When auditing long-term liabilities, auditors usually obtain independent written *confirmations* for notes and bonds payable. In the case of notes payable to banks, the *standard bank confirmation* may be used. The amount and terms of bonds payable, mortgages payable, and other formal debt instruments can be confirmed by requests to holders or a trustee. The confirmation request should include questions not only of amount, interest rate, and due date but also about collateral, restrictive covenants, and other items of agreement between lender and borrower. Confirmation requests should be sent to lenders with whom the company has done business in the recent past, even if no liability balance is shown at the confirmation date. Such extra coverage is a part of the search for unrecorded liabilities.

Confirmation and inquiry procedures may be used to obtain responses on a class of items loosely termed "off-balance sheet information." Within this category are: terms of loan agreements, leases, endorsements, guarantees, and insurance policies (whether issued by a client insurance company or owned by the client). Among these items is the difficult-to-define set of "commitments and contingencies" that often pose evidence-gathering problems. Some common types of commitments are shown in Exhibit 11–3.

Footnote disclosure should be considered for the types of commitments shown in Exhibit 11–3. Some of them can be estimated and valued and, thus, can be recorded in the

---

EXHIBIT 11–3   OFF-BALANCE SHEET COMMITMENTS

Type of Commitment	Typical Procedures and Sources of Evidence
1. Repurchase or remarketing agreements.	1. Vouching of contracts, confirmation by customer, inquiry of client management.
2. Commitments to purchase at fixed prices.	2. Vouching of open purchase orders, inquiry of purchasing personnel, confirmation by supplier.
3. Commitments to sell at fixed prices.	3. Vouching of sales contracts, inquiry of sales personnel, confirmation by customer.
4. Loan commitments (as in a savings and loan assocation).	4. Vouching of open commitment file, inquiry of loan officers.
5. Lease commitments.	5. Vouching of lease agreement, confirmation with lessor or lessee.

accounts and shown in the financial statements themselves (such as losses on fixed-price purchase commitments and losses on fixed-price sales commitments).

Interest expense generally is related item by item to interest-bearing liabilities. Based on the evidence of long-term liability transactions (including those that have been retired during the year), the related interest expense amounts can be recalculated. The amount of debt, the interest rate, and the time period are used to determine whether the interest expense and accrued interest are properly recorded. By comparing the audit results to the recorded interest expense and accrued interest accounts, auditors may be able to detect: (1) greater expense than their calculations show, indicating some interest paid on debt unknown to them, possibly an unrecorded liability; (2) lesser expense than their calculations show, indicating misclassification, failure to accrue interest, or an interest payment default; or (3) interest expense equal to their calculations. The first two possibilities raise questions for further study, and the third shows a correct correlation between debt and debt-related expense.

Several types of deferred credits depend on calculations for their existence and valuation. Examples include: (1) deferred profit on installment sales involving the gross margin and the sale amount; (2) deferred income taxes and investment credits involving tax-book timing differences, tax rates, and amortization methods; and (3) deferred contract revenue involving contract provisions for prepayment, percentage-of-completion revenue recognition methods, or other terms unique to a contract. All of these features are incorporated in calculations that auditors can check for accuracy.

Owners' Equity

Assertions.   Management makes assertions about the existence, completeness, rights and obligations, valuation, and presentation and disclosure of owners' equity. Typical specific assertions include:

1. The number of shares shown as issued is in fact issued.
2. No other shares (including options, warrants, and the like) have been issued and not recorded or reflected in the accounts and disclosures.
3. The accounting is proper for options, warrants, and other stock issue plans, and related disclosures are adequate.
4. The valuation of shares issued for noncash consideration is proper, in conformity with accounting principles.
5. All owners' equity transactions have been authorized by the board of directors.

An illustrative program of substantive audit procedures for owners' equity is in Appendix 11B–1.

Audit Procedures.   Owners' equity transactions usually are well documented in minutes of the meetings of the board of directors, in proxy statements, and in securities offering registration statements. Transactions can be vouched to these documents, and the cash proceeds can be traced to the bank accounts.

Capital stock may be subject to confirmation when independent registrars and transfer agents are employed. Such agents are responsible for knowing the number of shares authorized and issued and for keeping lists of stockholders' names. The basic information about capital stock—such as number of shares, classes of stock, preferred dividend rates, conversion terms, dividend payments, shares held in the company name, expiration dates, and terms of warrants and stock dividends and splits—can be confirmed with the independent agents. The auditors' own inspection and reading of stock certificates, charter authorizations, directors' minutes, and registration statements can corroborate many of those items. However, when the client company does not use independent agents, most audit evidence is gathered by vouching stock record documents (such as certificate book stubs). When circumstances call for extended procedures, information on outstanding stock in very small corporations having only a few stockholders may be confirmed directly with the holders.

11.12 What are some of the typical assertions found in owners' equity descriptions and account balances?

11.13 What are some of the typical assertions found in the long-term liability accounts?

11.14 How can confirmations be used in auditing stockholder capital accounts? In auditing notes and bonds payable?

11.15 What information about capital stock could be confirmed with outside parties? How could this information be corroborated by the auditors?

11.16 Define and give five examples of "off-balance sheet information." Why should auditors be concerned with such items?

11.17 If a company does not monitor notes payable for due dates and interest payment dates in relation to financial statement dates, what misstatements can appear in the financial statements?

Investing Activities: Assertions and Audit Procedures

Derivative Investments, Hedging Activities, and Investments in Securities (SAS 92)

Assertions.   Companies can have a wide variety of investments and relationships with affiliates. Investments accounting may be on the market value method, cost method, equity method, or full consolidation, depending on the nature, size, and influence represented by the investment. Purchase-method consolidations usually create problems of accounting for the fair value of acquired assets and the related goodwill.

Specific assertions typical of variety of an investment account balances are these:

1. Investment securities are on hand or are held in safekeeping by a trustee.
2. The accounting for investment cost and value is appropriate.
3. Controlling investments are accounted for by the equity method.
4. Investment income has been received and recorded.
5. Investments are adequately classified and described in the balance sheet, including disclosures of restrictions, pledges, and liens.
6. Risk related to investment securities (especially derivative securities) has been properly disclosed.

An illustrative program of substantive audit procedures for investments and related accounts is in Appendix 11B–3. Part C of this program covers portfolio classification, fair value determination, and evidence about impairment.

Audit Procedures.   Unlike the current assets accounts, which are characterized by numerous small transactions, the noncurrent investment accounts usually consist of a few large entries. The effect on the auditors' consideration of the control environment is concentration on the authorization of transactions, since each individual transaction is likely to be material in itself and the authorization will give significant information about the proper classification and accounting method. The controls usually are not reviewed, tested, and evaluated at an interim date but are considered along with the year-end procedures when the transactions and their authorizations are audited.

The practice of obtaining independent written confirmation from outside parties is fairly limited in the area of investments, intangibles, and related income and expense accounts. Securities held by trustees or brokers should be confirmed, and the confirmation request should seek the same descriptive information as that obtained in a physical inspection by the auditor.

AUDITING INSIGHT

TROUBLE SPOTS IN AUDITS OF INVESTMENTS AND INTANGIBLES

- Valuation of investments at cost, market, or value impairment that is other than temporary.
- Determination of significant influence relationship for equity method investments.
- Proper determination of goodwill in purchase-method consolidations. Reasonable amortization life for goodwill.
- Capitalization and continuing valuation of intangibles and deferred charges.
- Propriety, effectiveness, and risk disclosure of derivative securities used as a hedge of exposure to changes in fair value (*fair value hedge*), variability in cash flows (*cash flow hedge*), or fluctuations in foreign currency.
- Determination of the fair value of derivatives and securities, including valuation models and the reasonableness of key assumptions.
- Realistic distinctions of research, feasibility, and production milestones for capitalization of software development costs.
- Adequate disclosure of restrictions, pledges, or liens related to investment assets.

Investment costs should be vouched to brokers' reports, monthly statements, or other documentary evidence of cost. At the same time, the amounts of sales are traced to gain or loss accounts, and the amounts of sales prices and proceeds are vouched to the brokers' statements. Auditors should determine what method of cost-out assignment was used (i.e., FIFO, specific certificate, or average cost) and whether it is consistent with prior-years' transactions.

Market valuation of securities is required for securities classified in trading portfolios and available-for-sale portfolios. While a management may assert that an investment valuation is not impaired, subsequent sale at a loss before the end of audit field work will indicate otherwise. Auditors should review investment transactions subsequent to the balance sheet date for this kind of evidence about value impairment.

By consulting quoted market values of securities, auditors can calculate market values and determine whether investments should be written down. If quoted market values are not available, financial statements related to investments must be obtained and analyzed for evidence of basic value. If such financial statements are unaudited, evidence indicated by them is considered to be extremely weak.

Income amounts can be verified by consulting published dividend records for quotations of dividends actually declared and paid during a period (e.g., Moody's and Standard & Poor's dividend records). Since auditors know the holding period of securities, dividend income can be calculated and compared to the amount in the account. Any difference could indicate a cutoff error, misclassification, defalcation, or failure to record a dividend receivable. In a similar manner, application of interest rates to bond or note investments produces a calculated interest income figure (making allowance for amortization of premium or discount if applicable).

Inquiries should deal with the nature of investments and the reasons for holding them, especially derivative securities used for hedging activities. The classification will affect the accounting treatment of market values and the unrealized gains and losses on investments. Due to the complexity of *SFAS 133* (*Accounting for Derivative Securities and Hedging Activities*), auditors may need *special skills or* knowledge to understand client hedging transactions, to ensure that effective controls are in place to monitor them, and to audit the transactions.

When *equity method accounting* is used for investments, auditors will need to obtain financial statements of the investee company. These should be audited statements. Inability to obtain financial statements from a closely held investee may indicate that the client investor does not have the significant controlling influence required by *APB*

Opinion No. 18 (SAS 81, AU 332). When available, these statements are used as the basis for recalculating the amount of the client's share of income to recognize in the accounts. In addition, these statements may be used to audit the disclosure of investees' assets, liabilities, and income presented in footnotes (a disclosure recommended when investments accounted for by the equity method are material).

PP&E and Intangible Assets

Assertions.   Management makes assertions about existence, completeness, rights and obligations, valuation, and presentation and disclosure. Typical specific assertions relating to PP&E and intangible assets include:

1. All property, plant and equipment are recorded.
2. Expenditures for repairs and maintenance segregated from purchases of buildings or equipments.
3. Purchases of new property, plant, and equipment are properly authorized.
4. Freight-in is included as part of purchase and added to equipment costs.
5. Equipment detail records updated as of date goods are received.
6. Purchased goodwill is properly valued.
7. Capitalized intangible costs relate to intangibles acquired in exchange transactions.
8. Research and development costs are properly classified.
9. Amortization and depreciation expenses are properly calculated.

An illustrative program of substantive audit procedures for property, plant and equipment and intangible assets can be found in Appendix 11B–4.

Audit Procedures.   The two primary means of gathering evidence supporting management's assertions with respect to property, plant and equipment are *physical observation* and *vouching*. The principal goal of the physical inspection of PP&E is to determine actual *existence* and condition of the property. The inspection of equipment should be compared to detail PP&E records. The cost of newly acquired real and personal property can be vouched to invoices or other documents of purchase, and title documents (such as on land, buildings) may be inspected. The auditor should also prepare or obtain a schedule of casualty insurance on buildings and equipment, and determine the adequacy of insurance in relation to asset market values. Inadequate insurance and self-insurance should be *disclosed* in the notes to the financial statements.

The depreciation schedule is audited by *recalculating* the depreciation expense, using the company's methods, estimates of useful life, and estimates of residual value. The asset acquisition and disposition information in the schedule gives the auditors some points of departure for auditing the asset additions and disposals. When the schedule covers hundreds of assets and numerous additions and disposals, auditors can (a) use computer auditing methods to recalculate the depreciation expense and (b) use sampling to choose additions and disposals for test of controls and substantive audit procedures. The beginning balances of assets and accumulated depreciation should be traced to the prior year's audit working papers. This schedule can be made into an audit working paper and placed in the auditor's files for future reference.

With respect to intangible assets, official documents of patents, copyrights, and trademark rights can be *inspected* to see that they are in the name of the client. Amortization of goodwill and other intangibles should be *recalculated*. Similar to depreciation expense, this expense owes its existence to a calculation, and recalculation based on audited costs and rates is sufficient audit evidence.

Company counsel can be queried about knowledge of any lawsuits or defects relating to patents, copyrights, trademarks, or trade names. This confirmation can be sought by a specific request in the attorney's letter. Questions about lawsuits challenging patents, copyrights, or trade names may produce early knowledge of problem areas for further investigation. Likewise, discussions and questions about research and development successes and failures may alert the audit team to problems of valuation of intangible assets and related amortization expense. Responses to questions about licensing of patents can be used in the audit of related royalty revenue accounts. Royalty income from patent licenses received from a single licensee may be confirmed. However, such income amounts usually are audited by vouching the licensee's reports and the related cash receipt.

Vouching may be extensive in the areas of research and development (R&D) and deferred software development costs. The principal evidence problem is to determine whether costs are properly classified as assets or as R&D expense. Recorded amounts generally are selected on a sample basis, and the purchase orders, receiving reports, payroll records, authorization notices, and management reports are compared to them. Some R&D costs may resemble non-R&D cost (such as supplies, payroll costs), so auditors must be very careful in the vouching to be alert for costs that appear to relate to other operations.

Merger and acquisition transactions should be reviewed in terms of the appraisals, judgments, and allocations used to assign portions of the purchase price to tangible assets, intangible assets, liabilities, and goodwill. In the final analysis, nothing really substitutes for the inspection of transaction documentation, but verbal inquiries may help auditors to understand the circumstances of a merger.

R E V I E W
CHECKPOINTS

11.18 What are some of the typical assertions found in PP&E, investments and intangibles accounts?

11.19 What procedures do auditors employ to obtain evidence of the cost of investments? Of investment gains and losses? Of investment income?

11.20 What are some of the "trouble spots" for auditors in the audits of investments and intangibles?

11.21 What items in a client's PP&E and depreciation schedules give auditors points of departure (assertions) audit procedures?

Audit Cases Related to the Financing and Investing Cycle

The cases begin with a description containing these elements:

Method: A cause of the misstatement (mistaken estimate or judgment, accidental error or fraud attempt), which usually is made easier by some kind of failure of controls.

Paper trail: A set of telltale signs of erroneous accounting, missing or altered documents, or a "dangling debit" (the false or erroneous debit that results from an overstatement of assets).

Amount: The dollar amount of overstated assets and revenue, or understated liabilities and expenses.

Each of the cases in this section contains an audit approach that may enable auditors to detect misstatements in account balances. Each application of procedures consists of these elements:

Audit objective: A recognition of a financial statement *assertion* for which evidence needs to be obtained. The assertions are about the existence of assets, liabilities, revenues, and expenses; their valuation; their complete inclusion in the account balances; the rights and obligations inherent in them; and their proper presentation and disclosure in the financial statements.

Control: A recognition of the control activities that *should be* used in an organization to prevent and detect errors and frauds.

Test of controls: Ordinary and extended procedures *designed to produce evidence about the effectiveness of the controls* that should be in operation.

Audit of balance: Ordinary and extended *substantive procedures designed to find signs of* mistaken accounting estimates, errors, and frauds in account balances and classes of transactions.

The cases first set the stage with a story about an accounting estimate, error, or fraud—its method, paper trail (if any), and amount. The first part of each case gives you the "inside story," which auditors seldom know before they perform the audit work. The second part of each case, under the heading of the "audit approach," tells a structured story about the audit objective, desirable controls, test of control procedures, audit of balance procedures, and discovery summary. At the end of the chapter, some similar discussion cases are presented, and you can write the audit approach to test your ability to design audit procedures for the detection of mistaken accounting estimates, errors, and frauds. Some substantive balance-audit programs are in Appendix 11B.

CASE 11.1
UNREGISTERED SALE OF SECURITIES

PROBLEM

A.T. Bliss & Company (Bliss) sold investment contracts in the form of limited partnership interests to the public. These "securities" sales should have been under a public registration filing with the SEC, but they were not.

METHOD

Bliss salesmen contacted potential investors and sold limited partnership interests. The setup deal called for these limited partnerships to purchase solar hot water heating systems for residential and commercial use from Bliss. All the partnerships entered into arrangements to lease the equipment to Nationwide Corporation, which then rented the equipment to end users. The limited partnerships were, in effect, financing conduits for obtaining investors' money to pay for Bliss's equipment. The investors depended on Nationwide's business success and ability to pay under the lease terms for their return of capital and profit.

PAPER TRAIL

Bliss published false and misleading financial statements, which used a non-GAAP revenue recognition method and failed to disclose cost of goods sold. Bliss overstated Nationwide's record of equipment installation and failed to disclose that Nationwide had little cash flow from end users (resulting from rent-free periods and other inducements). Bliss knew—and failed to disclose to prospective investors—the fact that numerous previous investors had filed petitions with the U.S. tax court to contest the disallowance by the IRS of all their tax credits and benefits claimed in connection with their investments in Bliss's tax-sheltered equipment lease partnerships.

AMOUNT

Not known, but all the money put up by the limited partnership investors was at risk largely not disclosed to the investors.

AUDIT APPROACH

AUDIT OBJECTIVE

Obtain evidence to determine whether capital fund-raising methods comply with U.S. securities laws and whether financial statements and other disclosures are not misleading.

CONTROL

Management should employ experts—attorneys, underwriters, and accountants—who can determine whether securities and investment contract sales do or do not require registration.

TEST OF CONTROLS

Auditors should learn the business backgrounds and securities-industry expertise of the senior managers. Study the minutes of the board of directors for authorization of the fund-raising method. Obtain and study opinions rendered by attorneys and underwriters about the legality of the fund-raising methods. Inquire about management's interaction with the SEC in any presale clearance. (The SEC will give advice about the necessity for registration.)

AUDIT OF BALANCES

Auditors should study the offering documents and literature used in the sale of securities to determine whether financial information is

being used properly. In this case, the close relationship with Nationwide and the experience of earlier partnerships give reasons for extended procedures to obtain evidence about the representations concerning Nationwide's business success (in this case, lack of success).

DISCOVERY SUMMARY

The auditors gave unqualified reports on Bliss's materially misstated financial statements. They apparently did not question the legality of the sales of the limited partnership interests as a means of raising capital. They apparently did not perform procedures to verify representations made in offering literature respecting Bliss or Nationwide finances. Two partners in the audit firm were enjoined from violations of the securities laws. They resigned from practice before the SEC and were ordered not to perform any attest services for companies making filings with the SEC. (Source: SEC Litigation Release 10274, AAER 20, AAER 21.) They later were expelled from the AICPA for failure to cooperate with the Professional Ethics Division in its investigation of alleged professional ethics violations. (Source: The CPA Letter.)

CASE 11.2
OFF-BALANCE SHEET INVENTORY FINANCING

PROBLEM

Verity Distillery Company used the "product repurchase" ploy to convert its inventory to cash, failing to disclose the obligation to repurchase it later. Related party transactions were not disclosed.

METHOD

Verity's president incorporated the Veritas Corporation, making himself and two other Verity officers the sole stockholders. The president arranged to sell $40 million of Verity's inventory of whiskey in the aging process to Veritas, showing no gain or loss on the transaction. The officers negotiated a 36-month loan with a major bank to get the money Veritas used for the purchase, pledging the inventory as collateral. Verity pledged to repurchase the inventory for $54.4 million, which amounted to the original $40 million plus 12 percent interest for three years.

PAPER TRAIL

The contract of sale was in the files, specifying the name of the purchasing company, the $40 million amount, and the cash consideration. Nothing mentioned the relation of Veritas to the officers. Nothing mentioned the repurchase obligation. However, the sale amount was unusually large.

AMOUNT

The $40 million amount was 40 percent of the normal inventory. Verity's cash balance was increased 50 percent. While the current asset total was not changed, the inventory ratios (e.g., inventory turnover, days' sales in inventory) were materially altered. Long-term liabilities were understated by not recording the liability. The ploy was actually a secured loan with inventory pledged as collateral, but this reality was neither recorded nor disclosed. The total effect would be to keep debt off the books, to avoid recording interest expense, and later to record inventory at a higher cost. Subsequent sale of the whiskey at market prices would not affect the ultimate income results, but the unrecorded interest expense would be buried in the cost of goods sold. The net income in the first year when the "sale" was made was not changed, but the normal relationship of gross margin to sales was distorted by the zero-profit transaction.

	Before Transaction	Recorded Transaction	Should Have Recorded
Assets	$530	$530	$570
Liabilities	390	390	430
Stockholder equity	140	140	140
Debt/equity ratio	2.79	2.79	3.07

AUDIT APPROACH

AUDIT OBJECTIVE

Obtain evidence to determine whether all liabilities are recorded. Be alert to undisclosed related party transactions.

CONTROL

The relevant control in this case would rest with the integrity and accounting knowledge of the senior officials who arranged the transaction. Authorization in the board minutes might detail the arrangements; but, if they wanted to hide it from the auditors, they also would suppress the telltale information in the board minutes.

TEST OF CONTROLS

Inquiries should be made about large and unusual financing transactions. This might not elicit a response because the event is a sales transaction, according to Verity. Other audit work on controls in the revenue and collection cycle might turn up the large sale. Fortunately, this one sticks out as a large one.

AUDIT OF BALANCES

Analytical procedures to compare monthly or seasonal sales probably will identify the sale as large and unusual. This identification should lead to an examination of the sales contract. Auditors should discuss the business purpose of the transaction with knowledgeable officials. If being this close to discovery does not bring out an admission of the loan and repurchase arrangement, the auditors nevertheless should investigate further. Even if the "customer" name were not a giveaway, a quick inquiry at the state secretary of state office for corporation records (online in some databases) will show the names of the officers, and the auditors will know the related party nature of the deal. A request for the financial statements of Veritas should be made.

DISCOVERY SUMMARY

The auditors found the related party relationship between the officers and Veritas. Confronted, the president admitted the attempt to make the cash position and the debt/equity ratio look better than they were. The financial statements were adjusted to reflect the "should have recorded" set of figures shown above.

CASE 11.3
GO FOR THE GOLD

PROBLEM

Assets in the form of mining properties were overstated through a series of "flip" transactions involving related parties.

METHOD

In 1989 Alta Gold Company was a public "shell" corporation that was purchased for $1,000 by the Blues brothers.

Operating under the corporate names of Silver King and Pacific Gold, the brothers purchased numerous mining claims in auctions conducted by the U.S. Department of the Interior. They invested a total of $40,000 in 300 claims. Silver King sold limited partnership interests in its 175 Nevada silver claims to local investors, raising $20 million to begin mining production. Pacific Gold then traded its 125 Montana gold mining claims for all the Silver King assets and partnership interests, valuing the silver claims at $20 million. (Silver King valued the gold claims received at $20 million as the fair value in the exchange.) The brothers then put $3 million obtained from dividends into Alta Gold, and, with the aid of a bank loan, purchased half of the Silver King gold claims for $18 million. The Blues brothers then obtained another bank loan of $38 million to merge the remainder of Silver King's assets and all of Pacific Gold's mining claims by purchase. They paid off the limited partners. At the end of 1989, Alta Gold had cash of $16 million and mining assets valued at $58 million, with liabilities on bank loans of $53 million.

PAPER TRAIL

Alta Gold had in its files the partnership offering documents, receipts, and other papers showing partners' investment of $20 mil-

lion in the Silver King limited partnerships. The company also had Pacific Gold and Silver King contracts for the exchange of mining claims. The $20 million value of the exchange was justified in light of the limited partners' investments.

Appraisals in the files showed one appraiser's report that there was no basis for valuing the exchange of Silver King claims, other than the price limited partner investors had been willing to pay. The second appraiser reported a probable value of $20 million for the exchange based on proved production elsewhere, but no geological data on the actual claims had been obtained. The $18 million paid by Alta to Silver King also had similar appraisal reports.

AMOUNT

The transactions occurred over a period of 10 months. The Blues brothers had $37 million cash in Silver King and Pacific Gold, as well as the $16 million in Alta (all of which was the gullible bank's money, but the bank had loaned to Alta with the mining claims and production as security). The mining claims that had cost $40,000 were now in Alta's balance sheet at $58 million, the $37 million was about to flee, and the bank was about to be left holding the bag containing 300 mining claim papers.

AUDIT APPROACH

OBJECTIVE

Obtain evidence of the existence, valuation, and rights (ownership) in the mining claim assets.

CONTROL

Alta Gold, Pacific Gold, and Silver King had no control system. The Blues brothers, including the hiring of friendly appraisers, engineered all transactions. The only control that might have been effective was at the bank in the loan-granting process, but the bank failed.

TEST OF CONTROLS

The only vestige of control could have been the engagement of competent, independent appraisers. Since the auditors will need to use (or try to use) the appraisers' reports, the procedures involve investigating the reputation, engagement terms, experience, and independence of the appraisers. The auditors can use local business references, local financial institutions that keep lists of approved appraisers, membership directories of the professional appraisal associations, and interviews with the appraisers themselves.

AUDIT OF BALANCES

The procedures for auditing the asset values include analyses of each of the transactions through all their complications, including

obtaining knowledge of the owners and managers of the several companies and the identities of the limited partner investors. If the Blues brothers have not disclosed their connection with the other companies (and perhaps with the limited partners), the auditors will need to inquire at the secretary of state's offices where Pacific Gold and Silver King are incorporated and try to discover the identities of the players in this flip game. Numerous complicated premerger transactions in small corporations and shells often signal manipulated valuations.

Loan applications and supporting papers should be examined to determine the representations made by Alta in connection with obtaining the bank loans. These papers may reveal some contradictory or exaggerated information.

Ownership of the mining claims might be confirmed with the Department of Interior auctioneers or be found in the local county deed records (spread all over Nevada and Montana).

DISCOVER SUMMARY

The inexperienced audit staff was unable to unravel the Byzantine exchanges, and they never questioned the relation of Alta to Silver King and Pacific Gold. They never discovered the Blues brothers' involvement in the other side of the exchange, purchase, and merger transactions. They accepted the appraisers' reports because they had never worked with appraisers before and thought all appraisers were competent and independent. The bank lost $37 million. The Blues brothers changed their names.

CASE 11.4
AMORTIZE BANG THE DRUM SLOWLY

PROBLEM

Net asset values (unamortized costs of films) were overstated by taking too little amortization expense.

METHOD

Candid Production Company was a major producer of theatrical movies. The company usually had 15–20 films in release at theaters across the nation and in foreign countries. Movies also produced revenue from video licenses and product sales (T-shirts, toys, and the like).

Movie production costs are capitalized as assets, and then amortized to expense as revenue is received from theater and video sales and from other sources of revenue. The amortizaton depends on the total revenue forecast and the current-year revenue amount. As the success or failure of a movie unfolds at the box office, revenue estimates are revised. (The accounting amortization is very similar to depletion of a mineral resource, which depends upon estimates of recoverable minerals and current production).

Candid Production was not too candid. For example, its film of Bang the Drum Slowly was forecast to produce $50 million total revenue over six years, although the early box office returns showed only $10 million in the first eight months in the theaters. (Revenue will decline rapidly after initial openings, and video and other revenue depend on the box office success of a film.)

Accounting "control" with respect to film cost amortization resides in the preparation and revision of revenue forecasts. In this case, they were overly optimistic, slowing the expense recognition and overstating assets and income.

PAPER TRAIL

Revenue forecasts are based on many factors, including facts and assumptions about number of theaters, ticket prices, receipt sharing agreements, domestic and foreign reviews, and moviegoer tastes. Several publications track the box office records of movies. You can see them in newspaper entertainment sections and in industry trade publications. Of course, the production companies themselves are the major source of the information. However, company records also show the revenue realized from each movie. Revenue forecasts can be checked against actual experience, and the company's history of forecasting accuracy can be determined by comparing actual to forecast over many films and many years.

AMOUNT

Over a four-year period, Candid Productions postponed recognition of a $20 million amortization expense, thus inflating assets and income.

AUDIT APPROACH

OBJECTIVE

Obtain evidence to determine whether revenue forecasts provide a sufficient basis for calculating film cost amortization and net asset value of films.

CONTROL

Revenue forecasts need to be prepared in a controlled process that documents the facts and underlying assumptions built into the forecast. Forecasts should break down the revenue estimate by years, and the accounting system should produce comparable actual revenue data so forecast accuracy can be assessed after the fact. Forecast revisions should be prepared in as much detail and documentation as original forecasts.

TEST OF CONTROLS

The general procedures and methods used by personnel responsible for revenue forecasts should be studied (inquiries and review of documentation), including their sources of information both internal and external. Procedures for review of mechanical aspects (arithmetic) should be tested: Select a sample of finished forecasts and recalculate the final estimate.

Specific procedures for forecast revision also should be studied in the same manner. A review of the accuracy of forecasts on other movies with hindsight on actual revenues helps in a circumstantial way, but past accuracy on different film experiences may not directly influence the forecasts on a new, unique product.

AUDIT OF BALANCE

The audit of amortization expense concentrates on the content of the forecast itself. The preparation of forecasts used in the amortization calculation should be studied to distinguish underlying reasonable expectations from "hypothetical assumptions." A hypothetical assumption is a statement of a condition that is not necessarily expected to occur, but nonetheless is used to prepare an estimate. For example, a hypothetical assumption is like an "if-then" statement: "If Bang the Drum Slowly sells 15 million tickets in the first 12 months of release, then domestic revenue and product sales will be $40 million, and foreign revenue can eventually reach $10 million." Auditors need to assess the reasonableness of the basic 15 million-ticket assumption. It helps to have some early actual data from the film's release in hand before the financial statements need to be finished and distributed. For actual data, industry publications ought to be reviewed, with special attention to competing films and critics' reviews (yes, movie reviews!).

DISCOVERY SUMMARY

The auditors were not skeptical enough about optimistic revenue forecasts, and they did not weigh unfavorable actual/forecast history comparisons heavily enough. Apparently, they let themselves be convinced by exuberant company executives that the movies were comparable with Gone with the Wind! The audit of forecasts and estimates used in accounting determinations is very difficult, especially when company personnel have incentives to hype the numbers, seemingly with conviction about the artistic and commercial merit of their productions. The postponed amortization expense finally came to roost in big write-offs when the company management changed.

R E V I E W
CHECKPOINTS

11.22 What unfortunate lesson did the auditors learn from the situation in Case 11.1 (Unregistered Sale of Securities)?

11.23 What should an auditor do when violation of U.S. securities laws is suspected?

11.24 How could auditors discover the off-balance sheet financing described in Case 11.2 (Off-Balance Sheet Inventory Financing)?

11.25 What effect can related party transactions have in some cases of asset valuation? (Refer to Go for the Gold.)

SUMMARY

The finance and investment cycle contains a wide variety of accounts—capital stock, dividends, long-term debt, interest expense, income tax expense and deferred taxes, financial instruments, PP&E, marketable securities, equity method investments, related gains and losses, consolidated subsidiaries, goodwill, and other intangibles. These accounts involve some of the most technically complex accounting standards. They create most of the difficult judgments for financial reporting.

Senior officials generally authorize and maintain control of transactions in these accounts. Therefore, internal control is centered on the integrity and accounting knowledge of these officials. The procedural controls over details of transactions are not very effective because the senior managers can override them and order their own desired accounting presentations. As a consequence, auditors' work on the assessment of control risk is directed toward the senior managers, the board of directors, and their authorizations and design of finance and investment deals.

This chapter ends the book's coverage of audit applications for various cycles and their accounts.

MULTIPLE-CHOICE QUESTIONS FOR PRACTICE AND REVIEW

11.26 Jones was engaged to examine the financial statements of Gamma Corporation for the year ended June 30. Having completed an examination of the investment securities, which of the following is the best method of verifying the accuracy of recorded dividend income?

a. Tracing recorded dividend income to cash receipts records and validated deposit slips.

b. Utilizing analytical review techniques and statistical sampling.

c. Comparing recorded dividends with amounts appearing on federal information Form 1099.

d. Comparing recorded dividends with a standard financial reporting service's record of dividends.

11.27 When a large amount of negotiable securities is held by the client, auditors need to plan to guard against

a. Unauthorized negotiation of the securities before they are counted.

b. Unrecorded sales of securities after they are counted.

c. Substitution of securities already counted for other securities that should be on hand but are not.

d. Substitution of authentic securities with counterfeit securities.

11.28 In connection with the audit of an issue of long-term bonds payable, the auditor should

a. Determine whether bondholders are persons other than owners, directors, or officers of the company issuing the bond.

b. Calculate the effective interest rate to see if it is substantially the same as the rates for similar issues.

c. Decide whether the bond issue was made without violating state or local law.

d. Ascertain that the client has obtained the opinion of counsel on the legality of the issue.

11.29 Which of the following is the most important audit consideration when examining the stockholders' equity section of a client's balance sheet?

a. Changes in the capital stock account are verified by an independent stock transfer agent.

b. Stock dividends and stock splits during the year under audit were approved by the stockholders.

c. Stock dividends are capitalized at par or stated value on the dividend declaration date.

d. Entries in the capital stock account can be traced to resolutions in the minutes of the board of directors' meetings.

11.30 If the auditor discovers that the carrying amount of a client's investments is overstated because of a loss in value that is other than a temporary decline in market value, the auditor should insist that

a. The approximate market value of the investments be shown in parentheses on the face of the balance sheet.

b. The investments be classified as long term for balance sheet purposes with full disclosure in the footnotes.

c. The loss in value be recognized in the financial statements.

d. The equity section of the balance sheet separately shows a charge equal to the amount of the loss.

11.31 The primary reason for preparing a reconciliation between interest-bearing obligations outstanding during the year and interest expense in the financial statements is to

a. Evaluate internal control over securities.

b. Determine the validity of prepaid interest expense.

c. Ascertain the reasonableness of imputed interest.

d. Detect unrecorded liabilities.

11.32   The auditor should insist that a representative of the client be present during the inspection and count of securities to
a. Lend authority to the auditor's directives.
b. Detect forged securities.
c. Coordinate the return of all securities to proper locations.
d. Acknowledge the receipt of securities returned.

11.33   When independent stock transfer agents are not employed and the corporation issues its own stock and maintains stock records, canceled stock certificates should
a. Be defaced to prevent reissuance and attached to their corresponding stubs.
b. Not be defaced, but segregated from other stock certificates and retained in a canceled certificates file.
c. Be destroyed to prevent fraudulent reissuance.
d. Be defaced and sent to the secretary of state.

11.34   When a client company does not maintain its own capital stock records, the auditor should obtain written confirmation from the transfer agent and registrar concerning
a. Restrictions on the payment of dividends.
b. The number of shares issued and outstanding.
c. Guarantees of preferred stock liquidation value.
d. The number of shares subject to agreements to repurchase.

(AICPA adapted)

11.35   All corporate capital stock transactions should ultimately be traced to the:
a. Minutes of the board of directors.
b. Cash receipts journal.
c. Cash disbursements journal.
d. Numbered stock certificates.

11.36   A corporate balance sheet indicates that one of the corporate assets is a patent. An auditor will most likely obtain evidence of this patent by obtaining a written representation from
a. A patent attorney.
b. A regional state patent office.
c. The patent inventor.
d. The patent owner.

11.37   An audit program for the examination of the retained earnings account should include a step that requires verification of the (choose two steps)
a. Market value used to charge retained earnings to account for a two-for-one stock split.
b. Approval of the adjustment to the beginning balance as a result of a write-down of an account receivables.
c. Authorization for both cash and stock dividends.
d. Gain or loss resulting from disposition of treasury shares.

11.38   When an entity uses a trust company as custodian of its marketable securities, the possibility of concealing fraud most likely would be reduced if the
a. Trust company has no direct control with the entity employees responsible for maintaining investment accounting records.
b. Securities and registered in the name of the trust company, rather than the entity itself.
c. Interest and dividend checks are mailed directly to an entity employee who is authorized to sell securities.
d. Trust company places the securities in a bank safe-deposit vault under the custodian's exclusive control.

(AICPA adapted)

11.39   An auditor would most likely verify the interest earned on bond investments by
a. Vouching the receipt and deposit of interest checks.
b. Confirming the bond interest rate with the issuer of the bonds.
c. Recomputing the interest earned on the basis of face amount, interest rate, and period held.
d. Testing internal controls relevant to cash receipts.

(AICPA adapted)

11.40   A client has a large and active investment portfolio that is kept in a bank safe-deposit box. If the auditor is unable to count securities at the balance sheet date, the auditor most likely will
a. Request the bank to confirm to the auditor the contents of the safe-deposit box at the balance sheet date.
b. Examine supporting evidence for transactions occurring during the year.
c. Count the securities at a subsequent date and confirm with the bank

whether securities were added or removed since the balance sheet date.

d. Request the client to have the bank seal the safe-deposit box until the auditor can count the securities at a subsequent date.

(AICPA adapted)

11.41 An auditor testing long-term investments would ordinarily use analytical procedures to ascertain the reasonableness of the

a. Existence of unrealized gains or losses.

b. Completeness of recorded investment income.

c. Classification as available-for-sale or trading securities.

d. Valuation of trading securities.

(AICPA adapted)

11.42 In auditing for unrecorded long-term bonds payable, an auditor most likely will

a. Perform analytical procedures on the bond premium and discount accounts.

b. Examine documentation of assets purchased with bond proceeds for liens.

c. Compare interest expense with the bond payable amount of reasonableness.

d. Confirm the existence of individual bondholders at year-end.

(AICPA adapted)

11.43 An auditor's program to examine long-term debt most likely would include steps that require

a. Comparing the carrying amount of held-to-maturity securities with its year-end market value.

b. Correlating interest expense recorded for the period with outstanding debt.

c. Verifying the existence of the holders of the debt by direct confirmation.

d. Inspecting the accounts payable subsidiary ledger for unrecorded long-term debt.

(AICPA adapted)

11.44 Which of the following questions would an auditor most likely include on an internal control questionnaire for notes payable?

a. Are assets that collateralize notes payable critically needed for the entity's continued existence?

b. Are two or more authorized signatures required on checks that repay notes payable?

c. Are the proceeds from notes payable used for the purchase of noncurrent assets?

d. Are direct borrowings on notes payable authorized by the board of directors?

(AICPA adapted)

11.45 An auditor's purpose in reviewing the renewal of a note payable shortly after the balance sheet date most likely is to obtain evidence concerning management's assertions about

a. Existence or occurrence.

b. Presentation and disclosure.

c. Completeness.

d. Valuation or allocation.

(AICPA adapted)

EXERCISES AND PROBLEMS

11.46 ICQ for Equity Investments. Cassandra Corporation, a manufacturing company, periodically invests large sums in marketable equity securities. The investment policy is established by the investment committee of the board of directors. The treasurer is responsible for carrying out the investment committee's directives. All securities are stored in a bank safe-deposit vault.

Your internal control questionnaire with respect to Cassandra's investments in equity securities contains the following three questions:

1. Is investment policy established by the investment committee of the board of directors?

2. Is the treasurer solely responsible for carrying out the investment committee's directive?

3. Are all securities stored in a bank safe-deposit vault?

Required:

In addition to the above three questions, what questions should your internal control questionnaires include with respect to the company's investment in marketable equity securities? (*Hint:* Prepare questions to cover the control objectives—validity, completeness, authorization, accuracy, classification, accounting/posting, and proper period.)

(AICPA adapted)

11.47 Held-to-Maturity Investment Securities.
You are engaged in the audit of the financial statements of Bass Corporation for the year ended December 31, and you are about to begin an audit of the held-to-maturity investment securities. Bass's records indicate that the company owns various bearer bonds, as well as 25 percent of the outstanding common stock of Commercial Industrial, Inc. You are satisfied with evidence that supports the presumption of significant influence over Commercial Industrial, Inc. The various securities are at two locations as follows:

1. Recently acquired securities are in the company's safe in the custody of the treasurer.

2. All other securities are in the company's bank safe-deposit box.

All securities in Bass's portfolio are actively traded in a broad market.

Required:

a. Assuming that the system of internal control over securities is satisfactory, what are the objectives (specific assertions) for the audit of the held-to-maturity securities?

b. What audit procedures should you undertake with respect to obtaining audit evidence for the existence and cost valuation of Bass's securities in the held-to-maturity classification?

c. What audit procedures should you undertake with respect to obtaining audit evidence against Bass's investment in Commercial Industrial, Inc.?

d. What audit procedures should you undertake with respect to obtaining audit evidence about the classification of held-to-maturity securities in the Bass portfolio? (*Hint:* Review the audit program in Appendix 11B–3.)

e. Suppose the held-to-maturity portfolio (excluding the investment in Commercial Industrial, Inc.) is carried at cost in the amount of $3,450,000. What audit procedures should you undertake with respect to obtaining audit evidence about the market (fair) value of this portfolio?

f. Suppose the auditor determines that the held-to-maturity portfolio (excluding the investment in Commercial Industrial, Inc.) has an aggregate market (fair) value of $2,970,000. What audit procedures should you undertake with respect to obtaining audit evidence regarding a value impairment that might be "other than temporary?" (*Hint:* Review the audit program in Appendix 11B–3.)

(AICPA adapted)

11.48 Securities Examination and Count.
You are in charge of the audit of the financial statements of the Demot Corporation for the year ended December 31. The corporation has had the policy of investing its surplus funds in marketable securities. Its stock and bond certificates are kept in a safe-deposit box in a local bank. Only the president and the treasurer of the corporation have access to the box.

You were unable to obtain access to the safe-deposit box on December 31 because neither the president nor the treasurer was available. Arrangements were made for your assistant to accompany the treasurer to the bank on January 11 to examine the securities. Your assistant has never examined securities that were being kept in a safe-deposit box and requires instructions. Your assistant should be able to inspect all securities on hand in an hour.

Required:

a. List the instructions that you should give to your assistant regarding the examination of the stock and bond certificates kept in the safe-deposit box. Include in your instructions the details of the securities to be examined and the reasons for examining these details.

b. After returning from the bank, your assistant reports that the treasurer had entered the box on January 4 to remove an old photograph of the corporation's original building. The photograph was loaned to the local chamber of commerce for display purposes. List the additional audit procedures that are required because of the treasurer's action.

(AICPA adapted)

11.49 Audit Objectives and Procedures for Investments.
In the audit of investment securities, auditors develop specific audit assertions related to the investments. They then design specific substantive (balance-audit) procedures to obtain evidence about each of these assertions. Here is a selection of investment securities assertions:

a. Investments are properly described and classified in the financial statements.

b. Recorded investments represent investments actually owned at the balance sheet date.

c. Investments are properly valued at the lower of cost or market (fair value) at the balance sheet date.

Required:

For each of these assertions, select the audit procedure (below) that is best suited for the audit program. Select only one procedure for each audit objective. A procedure may be selected once or not at all.

1. Trace opening balances in the general ledger to prior year's audit working papers.

2. Determine whether employees who are authorized to sell investments have access to cash.

3. Examine supporting documents for a sample of investment transactions to verify that prenumbered documents are used.

4. Determine whether any other-than-temporary impairments in the carrying value of investments have been properly recorded.

5. Verify that transfers from the trading portfolio current to the held-to-maturity investment portfolio have been properly recorded.

6. Obtain positive confirmations as of the balance sheet date of investments held by independent custodians.

7. Trace investment transactions to minutes of the Board of Directors meetings to determine that transactions were properly authorized.

(AICPA adapted)

11.50   Intangibles.   Sorenson Manufacturing Corporation was incorporated on January 3, 2000. The corporation's financial statements for its first year's operations were not examined by a CPA. You have been engaged to audit the financial statements for the year ended December 31, 2001, and your work is substantially completed.

A partial trial balance of the company's accounts is given below:

SORENSON MANUFACTURING
CORPORATION
Trial Balance
at December 31, 2001

	Trial Balance	
	Debit	Credit
Cash	$11,000	
Accounts receivable	42,500	
Allowance for doubtful accounts		$ 500
Inventories	38,500	
Machinery	75,000	
Equipment	29,000	
Accumulated depreciation		10,000
Patents	85,000	
Leasehold improvements	26,000	
Prepaid expenses	10,500	
Organization expenses	29,000	
Goodwill	24,000	
Licensing Agreement No. 1	50,000	
Licensing Agreement No. 2	49,000	

The following information relates to accounts which may yet require adjustment:

1. Patents for Sorenson's manufacturing process were purchased January 2, 2001, at a cost of $68,000. An additional $17,000 was spent in December 2001 to improve machinery covered by the patents and charged to the Patents account. The patents had a remaining legal term of 17 years.

2. On January 3, 2000, Sorenson purchased two licensing agreements, which at that time were believed to have unlimited useful lives. The balance in the Licensing Agreement No. 1 account included its purchase price of $48,000 and $2,000 in acquisition expenses. Licensing Agreement No. 2 also was purchased on January 3, 2000, for $50,000, but it has been reduced by a credit of $1,000 for the advance collection of revenue from the agreement.

In December 2000, an explosion caused a permanent 60 percent reduction in the expected revenue-producing value of Licensing Agreement No. 1, and, in January 2001, a flood caused additional damage, which rendered the agreement worthless.

A study of Licensing Agreement No. 2 made by Sorenson in January 2001 revealed that its estimated remaining life expectancy was only 10 years as of January 1, 2001.

3. The balance in the Goodwill account includes $24,000 paid December 30, 2000, for an advertising program, which it is estimated will assist in increasing Sorenson's sales over a period of four years following the disbursement.

4. The Leasehold Improvement account includes: (a) the $15,000 cost of improvements with a total estimated useful life of 12 years which Sorenson, as tenant, made to leased premises in January 2000; (b) movable assembly line equipment costing $8,500, which was installed in the leased premises in December 2001; and (c) real estate taxes of $2,500 paid by Sorenson which, under the terms of the lease, should have been paid by the landlord. Sorenson paid its rent in full during 2001. A 10-year nonrenewable lease was signed January 3, 2000, for the leased building that Sorenson used in manufacturing operations.

5. The balance in the Organization Expenses account includes preoperating costs incurred during the organizational period.

Required:
Prepare adjusting entries as necessary.

(AICPA adapted)

11.51   Long-Term Financing Agreement.
You have been engaged to audit the financial statements of Broadwall Corporation for the year ended December 31, 2001. During the year, Broadwall obtained a long-term loan from a local

bank pursuant to a financing agreement, which provided that the:

1. Loan was to be secured by the company's inventory and accounts receivable.

2. Company was to maintain a debt-to-equity ratio not to exceed 2:1.

3. Company was not to pay dividends without permission from the bank.

4. Monthly installment payments were to commence July 1, 2001.

In addition, during the year, the company also borrowed, on a short-term basis, from the president of the company, substantial amounts just prior to the year-end.

Required:

a. For the purposes of your audit of the financial statements of Broadwall Corporation, what procedures should you employ in examining the described loans? Do not discuss internal control.

b. What are the financial statement disclosures that you should expect to find with respect to the loan from the president?

11.52   Bond Indenture Covenants.   The following covenants are extracted from the indenture of a bond issue. The indenture provides that failure to comply with its terms in any respect automatically advances the due date of the loan to the date of noncompliance (the regular date is 20 years hence). Give any audit steps or reporting requirements you believe should be taken or recognized in connection with each of the following:

1. "The debtor company shall endeavor to maintain a working capital ratio of 2:1 at all times, and, in any fiscal year following a failure to maintain said ratio, the company shall restrict compensation of officers to a total of $500,000. Officers for this purpose shall include chairman of the board of directors, president, all vice presidents, secretary, and treasurer."

2. "The debtor company shall keep all property which is security for this debt insured against loss by fire to the extent of 100 percent of its actual value. Policies of insurance comprising this protection shall be filed with the trustee."

3. "The debtor company shall pay all taxes legally assessed against property which is security for this debt within the time provided by law for payment without penalty and shall deposit receipted tax bills or equally acceptable evidence of payment of same with the trustee."

(AICPA adapted)

11.53   Common Stock and Treasury Stock Audit Procedures.   You are the continuing auditor of Sussex, Inc., and are beginning the audit of the common stock and treasury stock accounts. You have decided to design substantive audit procedures with reliance on internal controls.

Sussex has no-par, no-stated-value common stock, and acts as its own registrar and transfer agent. During the past year, Sussex both issued and reacquired shares of its own common stock, some of which the company still owned at year-end. Additional common stock transactions occurred among the shareholders during the year.

Common stock transactions can be traced to individual shareholders' accounts in a subsidiary ledger and to a stock certificate book. The company has not paid any cash or stock dividends. There are no other classes of stock, stock rights, warrants, or option plans.

Required:

What substantive audit procedures should you apply in examining the common stock and treasury stock accounts? Organize your answer as a list of audit procedures organized by the financial statement assertions. (See Appendix 11B–1 for examples of substantive procedures for owners' equity.)

(AICPA adapted)

11.54   Stockholders' Equity.   You are a CPA engaged in an audit of the financial statements of Pate Corporation for the year ended December 31. The financial statements and records of Pate Corporation have not been audited by a CPA in prior years.

The stockholders' equity section of Pate Corporation's balance sheet at December 31 follows:

Stockholders' equity:	
Capital stock—10,000 shares of $10 par value authorized; 5,000 shares issued and outstanding	$ 50,000
Capital contributed in excess of par value of capital stock	32,580
Retained earnings	47,320
Total stockholders' equity	$129,900

Pate Corporation was founded in 1985. The corporation has 10 stockholders and serves as its own registrar and transfer agent. There are no capital stock subscription contracts in effect.

Required:

a. Prepare the detailed audit program for the examination of the three accounts composing the stockholders' equity section of Pate Corporation's balance sheet. Organize the audit program under broad financial statement

EXHIBIT 11.55–1 FIXED ASSETS AND DEPRECIATION

| | Asset Cost (000s) | | | | Accumulated Depreciation (000s) | | | |
Description	Beginning Balance	Added	Sold	Ending Balance	Beginning Balance	Added	Sold	Ending Balance
Land	10,000			10,000				
Bldg 1	30,000			30,000	6,857	857		7,714
Bldg 2		42,000		42,000		800		800
Computer A	5,000		5,000	0	3,750	208	3,958	0
Computer B		3,500		3,500		583		583
Press	1,500			1,500	300	150		450
Auto 1	15		15	0	15		15	0
Auto 2		22		22		2		2
Total	46,515	45,522	5,015	87,022	10,922	2,600	3,973	9,549

assertions. (Do not include in the audit program the audit of the results of the current year's operations.)

b. After every other figure on the balance sheet has been audited, it might appear that the retained earnings figure is a balancing figure and requires no further audit work. Why don't auditors audit-retained earnings as they do the other figures on the balance sheet? Discuss.

(AICPA adapted)

11.55 Audit the PP&E and Depreciation Schedule. Bart's Company has prepared the PP&E and depreciation schedule shown in Exhibit 11.55–1. The following information is available:

- The land was purchased eight years ago when Building 1 was erected. The location was then remote but now is bordered by a major freeway. The appraised value is $35 million.
- Building 1 has an estimated useful life of 35 years and no residual value.
- Building 2 was built by a local contractor this year. It also has an estimated useful life of 35 years and no residual value. The company occupied it on May 1 this year.
- The Computer A system was purchased January 1 six years ago, when the estimated useful life was eight years with no residual value. It was sold on May 1 for $500,000.
- The Computer B system was placed in operation as soon as the Computer A system was sold. It is estimated to be in use for six years with no residual value at the end.
- The company estimated the useful life of the press at 20 years with no residual value.
- Auto 1 was sold during the year for $1,000.
- Auto 2 was purchased on July 1. The company expects to use it five years and then sell it for $2,000.
- All depreciation is calculated on the straight-line method using months of service.

Required:

a. Audit the depreciation calculations. Are there any errors? Put the errors in the form of an adjusting journal entry, assuming 90 percent of the depreciation on the buildings and the press has been charged to cost of goods sold and 10 percent is still capitalized in the inventory, and the other depreciation expense is classified as general and administrative expense.

b. List two audit procedures for auditing the additions to PP&E.

c. What will an auditor expect to find in the "gain and loss on sale of assets" account? What amount of cash flow from investing activities will be in the statement of cash flows?

11.56 Property and Equipment Assertions and Substantive Audit Procedures. This question contains three items that are management assertions about property and equipment. Listed below them are several substantive audit procedures for obtaining evidence about management's assertions.

Assertions

1. The entity has legal right to property and equipment acquired during the year.

2. Recorded property and equipment represent assets that actually exist at the balance sheet date.

3. Net property and equipment are properly valued at the balance sheet date.

Audit Procedures

a. Trace opening balances in the summary schedules to the prior year's audit working papers.

b. Review the provision for depreciation expense and determine whether depreciable lives and methods used in the current year are consistent with those used in the prior year.

c. Determine whether the responsibility for maintaining the property and equipment records is segregated from the responsibility for custody of property and equipment.

d. Examine deeds and title insurance certificates.

e. Perform cutoff tests to verify that property and equipment additions are recorded in the proper period.

f. Determine whether property and equipment is adequately insured.

g. Physically examine all major property and equipment additions.

Required:

For each of the three assertions (1, 2, 3) select the one best substantive audit procedure (a, b, c, d, e, f, g) for obtaining competent evidence. A procedure may be selected only once, or not at all.

(AICPA adapted)

11.57   Assertion and Substantive Balance-Audit Procedures for Property, Plant, and Equipment (PP&E).   Listed below are the five general assertions that can be applied to the audit of a company's PP&E, including assets the company has constructed itself.

> Existence or occurrence
> Completeness
> Valuation or allocation
> Rights and obligations
> Presentation and disclosure

Required:

For each of the balance-audit procedures listed below, (a) cite one assertion most closely related to the evidence the procedure will produce (the primary assertion), and (b) where appropriate, cite one or more other assertions that are also related to the evidence the procedure will produce (the secondary assertion(s)).

1. For major amounts charged to PP&E and a sample of smaller charges, examine supporting documentation for expenditure amounts, budgetary approvals, and capital work orders.

2. For a sample of capitalized PP&E, examine construction work orders in detail.

3. For a sample of construction work orders, vouch time and material charges to supporting payroll and material usage records. Review the reasonableness of the hours worked, the work description, and the material used.

4. Evaluate the policy and procedures for allocating overhead to the work orders and recalculate their application.

5. Determine whether corresponding retirements of replaced PP&E have occurred and properly entered in the detail records.

6. Select major additions for the year and a random sample of other additions, and inspect the physical assets.

7. Discuss plant operations with responsible operating personnel. Inquire about capitalization policies and the use of leased assets.

8. Vouch a sample of charges in the Repairs account and determine whether they are proper repairs and not capital items.

9. Review the useful lives, depreciation methods, and salvage values for reasonableness. Recalculate depreciation.

10. Obtain written management representations about assets pledged as security for loans.

11. Study loan documents for terms and security of loans obtained for purchase of PP&E.

12. Study lease agreements to determine proper GAAP accounting for lease obligations.

13. Inspect title documents for automotive and real estate assets.

14. Study insurance policies to determine whether PP&E is adequately insured for casualty loss.

15. Analyze the productive economic use of PP&E to determine whether any other-than-temporary impairment is evident.

(AICPA adapted)

11.58   CAATTs Application—PP&E.   You are supervising the audit field work of Sparta Springs Company and need certain information from Sparta's equipment records, which are maintained on computer disk. The particular information is (1) net book value of assets so that your assistant can reconcile the subsidiary ledger to the general ledger control accounts (the general ledger contains an account for each asset type at each plant location), and (2) sufficient data to enable your assistant to find and inspect selected assets. Record layout of the master file:

> Asset number.
> Description.
> Asset type.
> Location code.
> Year acquired.
> Cost.

Accumulated depreciation, end of year (includes accumulated depreciation at the beginning of the year plus depreciation for year to date).

> Depreciation for the year to date.
> Useful life.

Required:

a. From the data file described above, list the information needed to verify correspondence of the subsidiary detail records with the general ledger accounts. Does this work complete the audit of PP&E?

b. What additional data are needed to enable your assistant to inspect the assets?

Discussion Cases

11.59 Intercompany and Interpersonal Investment Relations. You have been engaged to audit the financial statements of Hardy Hardware Distributors, Inc., as of December 31. In your review of the corporate nonfinancial records, you have found that Hardy Hardware owns 15 percent of the outstanding voting common stock of Hardy Products Corporation. Upon further investigation, you learn that Hardy Products Corporation manufactures a line of hardware goods, 90 percent of which is sold to Hardy Hardware.

Mr. James L. Hardy, president of Hardy Hardware, has supplied you with objective evidence that he personally owns 30 percent of the Hardy Products voting stock and the remaining 70 percent is owned by Mr. John L. Hardy, his brother and president of Hardy Products. James L. Hardy also owns 20 percent of the voting common stock of Hardy Hardware Distributors, another 20 percent is held by an estate of which James and John are beneficiaries, and the remaining 60 percent is publicly held. The stock is listed on the American Stock Exchange.

Hardy Hardware consistently has reported operating profits greater than the industry average. Hardy Products Corporation, however, has a net return on sales of only 1 percent. The Hardy Products investment always has been reported at cost, and no dividends have been paid by the company. During the course of your conversations with the Hardy brothers, you learn that you were appointed as auditor because the brothers had a heated disagreement with the former auditor over the issues of accounting for the Hardy Products investment and the prices at which goods have been sold to Hardy Hardware.

For Discussion:

a. Identify the issues in this situation as they relate to (1) conflicts of interest and (2) controlling influences among individuals and corporations.

b. Should the investment in Hardy Products Corporation be accounted for on the equity method?

c. What evidence should the auditor seek with regard to the prices paid by Hardy Hardware for products purchased from Hardy Products Corporation?

d. What information would you consider necessary for adequate disclosure in the financial statements of Hardy Hardware Distributors?

Instructions for Discussion Cases 11.60–11.62

These cases are designed like the ones in the chapter. They give the problem, the method, the paper trail, and the amount. Your assignment is to write the "audit approach" portion of the case, organized around these sections:

Objectives: Express the objective in terms of the facts supposedly asserted in financial records, accounts, and statements.

Control: Write a brief explanation of control considerations, especially the kinds of manipulations that might arise from the situation described in the case.

Test of controls: Write some procedures for getting evidence about existing controls, especially procedures that could discover management manipulations. If there are no controls to test, then there are no procedures to perform; go then to the next section. A "procedure" should instruct someone about the source(s) of evidence to tap and the work to do.

Audit of balance: Write some procedures for getting evidence about the existence, completeness, valuation, ownership, or disclosure assertions identified in your objective section above.

Discovery summary: Write a short statement about the discovery you expect to accomplish with your procedures.

11.60 Related Party Transaction "Goodwill." Write the "audit approach" section like the cases in the chapter.

Hide the Loss Under the Goodwill

Problem: A contrived amount of goodwill was used to overstate assets and disguise a loss on discontinued operations.

Method: Gulwest Industries, a public company, decided to discontinue its unprofitable line of business of manufacturing sporting ammunition. Gulwest had capitalized the startup cost of the business, and, with its discontinuance, the $7 million deferred cost should have been written off.

Instead, Gulwest formed a new corporation named Amron and transferred the sporting ammunition assets (including the $7 million deferred cost) to it in exchange for all the Amron stock. In the Gulwest accounts, the Amron investment was carried at $2.4 million, which was the book value of the assets transferred (including the $7 million deferred cost).

In an agreement with a different public company (Big Industrial), Gulwest and Big created another company (BigShot Ammunition). Gulwest transferred all the Amron assets to BigShot in exchange for (1)common and preferred stock of Big, valued at $2 million, and (2)a note from BigShot in the amount of $3.4 million. Big Industrial thus acquired 100 percent of the stock of BigShot. Gulwest management reasoned that it had "given" Amron stock valued at $2.4 million to receive stock and notes valued at $5.4 million, so the difference must be goodwill. Thus, the Gulwest accounts carried amounts for Big Industrial Stock ($2 million) BigShot Note Receivable ($3.4 million), and Goodwill ($7 million).

Paper trail: Gulwest directors included in the minutes an analysis of the sporting ammunition business's lack of profitability. The minutes showed approval of a plan to dispose of the business, but they did not use the words "discontinue the business." The minutes also showed approval of the creation of Amron, the deal with Big Industrial along with the formation of BigShot, and the acceptance of Big's stock and BigShot's note in connection with the final exchange and merger.

Amount: As explained above, Gulwest avoided reporting a write-off of $7 million by overstating the value of the assets given in exchange for the Big Industrial stock and the BigShot Ammunition note.

11.61   Related Party Transaction Valuation. Follow the instructions preceding Case 11.60. Write the audit approach section like the cases in the chapter.

In Plane View

Problem: Whiz Corporation overstated the value of stock given in exchange for an airplane and, thereby, understated its loss on disposition of the stock. Income was overstated.

Method: Whiz owned 160,000 shares of Wing Company stock, carried on the books as an investment in the amount of $6,250,000. Whiz bought a used airplane from Wing, giving in exchange (1)$480,000 cash and (2)the 160,000 Wing shares. Even though the quoted market value of the Wing stock was $2,520,000, Whiz valued the airplane received at $3,750,000, indicating a stock valuation of $3,270,000. Thus, Whiz recognized a loss on disposition of the Wing stock in the amount of $2,980,000.

Whiz justified the airplane valuation with another transaction. On the same day it was purchased Whiz sold the airplane to the Mexican subsidiary of one of its subsidiary companies (two layers down; but Whiz owned 100 percent of the first subsidiary, which in turn owned 100 percent of the Mexican subsidiary). The Mexican subsidiary paid Whiz with US$25,000 cash and a promissory note for US$3,725,000 (market rate of interest).

Paper trail: The transaction was within the authority of the chief executive officer, and company policy did not require a separate approval by the board of directors. A contract of sale and correspondence with Wing detailing the terms of the transaction were in the files. Likewise, a contract of sale to the Mexican subsidiary, along with a copy of the deposit slip, and a memorandum of the promissory note was on file. The note itself was kept in the company vault. None of the Wing papers cited a specific price for the airplane.

Amount: Whiz overvalued the Wing stock and justified it with a related party transaction with its own subsidiary company. The loss on the disposition of the Wing stock was understated by $750,000.

11.62   Loss Deferral on Hedged Investments. This case contains complexities that preclude writing the entire audit approach according to the instructions preceding Case 11.60. Instead, respond to these requirements:

a. What is the objective of the audit work on the investment account described in the Sharp Hedge Clippers case?

b. What is your conclusion about the propriety of deferring the losses on the hedged investments sales and the futures contracts? About the proper carrying amount of the investment in the balance sheet?

c. Do you believe the successor auditors were independent? Competent? Discuss the practice of "shopping around" for an unqualified audit report.

Sharp Hedge Clippers

Problem: Southeastern Savings & Loan Company (Southeastern) overstated its assets and income by improperly deferring losses on hedged investment transactions.

Method: In the course of its normal operations, Southeastern held investments in 15 percent and 16 percent GNMA certificates. Fearing an increase in interest rates and a consequent loss in the market value of these investments, Southeastern sought to hedge by selling futures contracts for U.S. Treasury bonds. If market interest rates increased, the losses in the GNMA investments would be offset by gains in the futures contracts.

However, interest rates declined, and Southeastern was caught in an odd market quirk. The value of the GNMAs increased with the lower interest rates, but not very much. (GNMAs are certificates in pools of government-backed mortgages, which pass through the interest and principle collections to the certificate holders.) As interest rates declined, the market perceived that the underlying mortgages would be paid off more quickly, that investors would receive all their proceeds earlier than previously expected, and that they would need to reinvest their money at the now-lower interest rates. Consequently, the 15 percent and 16 percent GNMAs held by Southeastern began trading as if the expected maturity were 4–5 years instead of the previously expected 8–12 years, which means that their prices did not rise as much as other interest-sensitive securities. On the other hand, the U.S. Treasury bonds with fixed maturity dates fell in price, and the futures hedge generated large losses.

Southeastern sold its 15 percent and 16 percent GNMAs and realized a $750,000 gain. Before and after these sales, the company purchased 8.0–12.5 percent GNMAs. The goal was to be invested in substantially different securities, ones that had a market return and the normal 8–12-year expected life payout. Later, Southeastern closed out its Treasury bond futures and realized a loss of $3.7 million. Still later, Southeastern sold GNMA futures contracts to hedge the investment in the 8.0–12.5 percent GNMA investments. The net loss of about $3 million was deferred in the balance sheet, instead of being recognized as a loss in the income statement.

Paper trail/accounting principles: The accounting for these transactions is complex and requires some significant judgments. In general, no gain or loss is recognized when the security sold is simultaneously replaced by the same or substantially the same security (a "wash" transaction), provided that any loss deferral does not result in carrying the investment at an amount greater than its market value. When a futures hedge is related to the securities sold, gains and losses on the futures contracts must be recognized when the hedged securities are sold, unless the sale of the hedged securities is part of a wash sale.

The significant accounting judgment is the identification of the disposition and new investment as a wash transaction. In turn, this requires a determination of whether the sale and reinvestment is "simultaneous" and involves "substantially the same security."

The "paper trail" is littered with information relevant to these judgments:

Criterion	Southeastern Transaction
Timing:	
Simultaneous sale/purchase or purchase/sale.	Some of the 15 percent and 16 percent GNMAs were sold six weeks after the 8.0–11.5 percent GNMAs were purchased.
Substantial similarity:	
Same issuer.	Both the securities sold and the securities purchased were GNMAs.
Similar market yield.	The yields on the two different GNMA series differed by about 3 percentage points.
Similar contractual maturity date.	The contractual maturity dates were the same.
Similar prospects for redemption.	The market priced the 15 percent and 16 percent GNMAs sold as though payback would occur in 4–5 years and the 8.0–12.5 percent GNMAs as though payback would occur in 8–12 years.
Carrying value:	
Asset carrying amount, including any deferred loss, shall not exceed securities' market value.	Asset value in financial statements exceeded the market value.

Paper trail/auditor involvement: Southeastern's independent auditors concluded that the losses should not be deferred. Southeastern fired the auditors and reported the disagreement in the 8-K reported filed with the SEC. After consulting other auditors, who agreed with the former auditors, Southeastern finally found a CPA firm whose local partners would give an unqualified audit report on financial statements containing the deferral.

In February, the auditors who disagreed with the deferral were fired. The new auditors were hired on February 18 to audit the financial statements for the year ended the previous December 31. The unqualified audit report was dated March 28, 39 days after the new auditors were engaged by Southeastern's audit committee.

The new auditors were well aware of the accounting judgments required. They knew the former auditors and another CPA firm had concluded that the losses should not be deferred. They saw memoranda of the disagreement and the conclusion in the predecessor's working papers. They spoke with the predecessor partner on the engagement.

APPENDIX 11A Internal Controls

APPENDIX 11A-1 Internal Control Questionnaire: Notes Payable

Environment:

1. Are notes payable records kept by someone who cannot sign notes or checks?

Validity objective:

2. Are paid notes canceled, stamped "paid," and filed?

Completeness objective:

3. Is all borrowing authorization by the directors checked to determine whether all notes payable are recorded?

Authorization objective:

4. Are direct borrowings on notes payable authorized by the directors? By the treasurer or by the chief financial officer?
5. Are two or more authorized signatures required on notes?

Accuracy objective:

6. Are bank due notices compared with records of unpaid liabilities?

Classification objective:

7. Is sufficient information available in the accounts to enable financial statement preparers to classify current and long-term debt properly?

Accounting and Posting objective:

8. Is the subsidiary ledger of notes payable periodically reconciled with the general ledger control account(s)?

Proper period objective:

9. Are interest payments and accruals monitored for due dates and financial statement dates?

APPENDIX 11A-2 PP&E and Related Transactions Processing

Environment

1. Are detailed property records maintained for the various assets included in PP&E?

Validity objective:

2. Is the accounting department notified of actions of disposal, dismantling, or idling productive asset? For terminating a lease or rental?
3. Are assets inspected periodically and physically counted?

Completeness objective:

4. Is casualty insurance carried? Is the coverage analyzed periodically? When was the last analysis?
5. Are property tax assessments periodically analyzed? When was the last analysis?

Authorization objective:

6. Are capital expenditure and leasing proposals prepared for review and approval by the board of directors or by responsible officers?
7. When actual expenditures exceed authorized amounts, is the excess approved?

Accuracy objective:

8. Is there a uniform policy for assigning depreciation rates, useful lives, and salvage values?
9. Are depreciation calculations checked by internal auditors or other officials?

Classification objective:

10. Does the accounting manual contain policies for capitalization of assets and expensing repair and maintenance?

Accounting and Posting objective:

11. Are subsidiary records periodically reconciled to the general ledger accounts?
12. Are memorandum records of leased assets maintained?

Proper period objective:

13. Does the accounting manual give instructions for recording PP&E additions on a proper date of acquisition?

APPENDIX 11A–3   Selected Computer Questionnaire Items: General and Application Controls (PP&E)

General controls:

1. Are computer operators and programmers excluded from participating in the input and output control functions?
2. Are programmers excluded from operating the computer?
3. Is there a database administrator who is independent of computer operations, systems, programming, and users?
4. Are computer personnel restricted from initiating, authorizing, or entering transactions or adjustments to the general ledger master database or the subsidiary ledger master database?
5. Is access to the computer room restricted to authorized personnel?
6. Is online access to data and programs controlled through the use of department account codes, personal ID numbers, and passwords?
7. Are systems, programs, and documentation stored in a fireproof area?
8. Can current files, particularly master files, be reconstructed from files stored in an off-site location?

PP&E application controls:

1. Is terminal entry of asset data done on the basis of up-to-date written instructions?
2. Are important asset data fields subject to input validation tests—missing data tests, limit and range tests, check digits, valid codes, and so forth?
3. Does the computer print an input error report? Is this returned to the accounting department for correction of errors?
4. Is an accounting department person assigned the responsibility for promptly correcting errors in asset input data and recentering the data for the inclusion with the next batch?
5. Are batch control totals used to reconcile computer-processed asset output to input control data?
6. Is asset computer output reviewed for reasonableness, accuracy, and legibility by the computer department personnel and the asset accounting personnel?

APPENDIX 11B   Substantive Audit Programs

APPENDIX 11B-1   Audit Program for Owners' Equity

1. Obtain an analysis of owners' equity transactions. Trace additions and reductions to the general ledger.
   a. Vouch additions to directors' minutes and cash receipts.
   b. Vouch reductions to directors' minutes and other supporting documents.
2. Read the directors' minutes for owners' equity authorization. Trace to entries in the accounts. Determine whether related disclosures are adequate.
3. Confirm outstanding common and preferred stock with stock registrar agent.
4. Vouch stock option and profit-sharing plan disclosures to contracts and plan documents.
5. Vouch treasury stock transactions to cash receipts and cash disbursement records and to directors' authorization. Inspect treasury stock certificates.
6. When the company keeps its own stock records:
   a. Inspect the stock record stubs for certificate numbers and number of shares.
   b. Inspect the unissued certificates.
   c. Obtain written client representations about the number of shares issued and outstanding.

APPENDIX 11B-2   Audit Program for Notes Payable and Long-Term Debt

1. Obtain a schedule of notes payable and other long-term debt (including capitalized lease obligations) showing beginning balances, new notes, repayment, and ending balances. Trace to general ledger accounts.
2. Confirm liabilities with creditor: amount, interest rate, due date, collateral, and other terms. Some of these confirmations may be standard bank confirmations.
3. Review the standard bank confirmation for evidence of assets pledged as collateral and for unrecorded obligations.
4. Read loan agreements for terms and conditions that need to be disclosed and for pledge of assets as collateral.
5. Recalculate the current portion of long-term debt and trace to the trial balance, classified as a current liability.
6. Study lease agreements for indications of need to capitalize leases. Recalculate the capital and operating lease amounts for required disclosures.
7. Recalculate interest expense on debts and trace to the interest expense and accrued interest accounts.
8. Obtain written representations from management concerning notes payable, collateral agreements, and restrictive covenants.

APPENDIX 11B–3 Audit Program for Investments and Related Accounts

A. **Investments and related accounts.**
 1. Obtain a schedule of all investments, including purchase and disposition information for the period. Reconcile with investment accounts in the general ledger.
 2. Inspect or confirm with a trustee or broker the name, number, identification, interest rate, and face amount (if applicable) of securities held as investments.
 3. Vouch the cost of recorded investments to brokers' reports, contracts, canceled checks, and other supporting documentation.
 4. Vouch recorded sales to brokers' reports and bank deposit slips, and recalculate gain or loss on disposition.
 5. Recalculate interest income and look up dividend income in a dividend reporting service (such as Moody's or Standard & Poor's annual dividend record).
 6. Obtain market values of investments and determine whether any write-down or write-off is necessary. Scan transactions soon after the client's year-end to see if any investments were sold at a loss. Recalculate the unrealized gains and losses required for fair value securities accounting.
 7. Read loan agreements and minutes of the board, and inquire of management about pledge of investments as security for loans.
 8. Obtain audited financial statements of joint ventures, investee companies (equity method of accounting), subsidiary companies, and other entities in which an investment interest is held. Evaluate indications of significant controlling influence. Determine proper balance sheet classification. Determine appropriate consolidation policy in conformity with accounting principles.
 9. Obtain written representations from the client concerning pledge of investment assets as collateral.

B. **Intangibles and related expenses.**
 1. Review merger documents for proper calculation of purchased goodwill.
 2. Inquire of management about legal status of patents, leases, copyrights, and other intangibles.
 3. Review documentation of new patents, copyrights, leaseholds, and franchise agreements.
 4. Vouch recorded costs of intangibles to supporting documentation and cancelled check(s).
 5. Select a sample of recorded R&D expenses. Vouch to supporting documents for evidence of proper classification.
 6. Recalculate amortization of goodwill, patents, and other intangibles.

C. **Investments in debt and equity securities.**
 1. Determine the proper classification of securities in the categories of held-to-maturity, available-for-sale, and trading securities.
   a. Inquire about management's intent regarding classifications.
   b. Study written records of investment strategies.
   c. Review records of past investment activities and transactions.
   d. Review instructions to portfolio managers.
   e. Study minutes of the investment committee of the board of directors.
 2. Determine whether facts support management's intent to hold securities to maturity.
   a. Determine the company's financial position, working capital requirements, results of operations, debt agreements, guarantees, and applicable laws and regulations.
   b. Study the company's cash flow forecasts.
   c. Obtain written management representations confirming proper classification with regard to intent and ability.
 3. Determine an audit valuation of fair value, where appropriate.
   a. Obtain published market quotations.
   b. Obtain market prices from broker-dealers who are market makers in particular securities.
   c. Obtain valuations from expert specialists.
   d. Determine whether proprietary market valuation models are reasonable and the data and assumptions in them are appropriate.
 4. Determine whether value impairments are "other than temporary," considering evidence of the following:
   a. Fair market is materially below cost.
   b. The value decline is due to specific adverse conditions.
   c. The value decline is industry or geographically specific.
   d. Management does not have both the intent and ability to hold the security long enough for a reasonable hope of value recovery.
   e. The fair value decline has existed for a long time.
   f. A debt security has been downgraded by a rating agency.
   g. The financial condition of the issuer has deteriorated.
   h. Dividends of interest payments have been reduced or eliminated.

APPENDIX 11B–4   Audit Program for PP&E and Related Accounts

A. Property, Plant, and Equipment
1. Summarize and foot detail asset subsidiary records and reconcile to general ledger control account(s).
2. Select a sample of detail asset subsidiary records:
   a. Perform a physical observation (inspection) of the assets recorded.
   b. Inspect title documents, if any.
3. Prepare, or have client prepare, a schedule of asset additions and disposals for the period:
   a. Vouch to documents indicating proper approval.
   b. Vouch costs to invoices, contracts, or other supporting documents.
   c. Determine whether all costs of shipment, installation, testing, and the like have been properly capitalized.
   d. Vouch proceeds (on dispositions) to cash receipts or other asset records.
   e. Recalculate gain or loss on dispositions.
   f. Trace amounts to detail asset records and general ledger control account(s).
4. Prepare an analysis of assets subject to investment tax credit for correlation with tax liability audit work.
5. Observe a physical inventory taking of the assets and compare with detail assets records.
6. Obtain written representation from management regarding pledge of assets as security for loans and leased assets.

B. Depreciation
1. Analyze depreciation expense for overall reasonableness with reference to costs of assets and average depreciation rates.
2. Prepare, or have client prepare, a schedule of accumulated depreciation showing beginning balance, current depreciation, disposals, and ending balance. Trace to depreciation expense and asset disposition analyses. Trace amounts to general ledger account(s).
3. Recalculate depreciation expense and trace to general ledger account(s).

C. Other Accounts
1. Analyze insurance for adequacy of coverage.
2. Analyze property taxes to determine whether taxes due on assets have been paid or accrued.
3. Recalculate prepaid and/or accrued insurance and tax expenses.
4. Select a sample of rental expense entries. Vouch to rent/lease contracts to determine whether any leases qualify for capitalization.

Select a sample of repair and maintenance expense entries and vouch them to supporting invoices for evidence of property that should be capitalized.

D. Intangibles and related expenses.
1. Review merger documents for proper calculation of purchased goodwill.
2. Inquire of management about legal status of patents, leases, copyrights, and other intangibles.
3. Review documentation of new patents, copyrights, leaseholds, and franchise agreements.
4. Vouch recorded costs of intangibles to supporting documentation and cancelled check(s).
5. Select a sample of recorded R&D expenses. Vouch to supporting documents for evidence of proper classification.
6. Recalculate amortization of goodwill, patents, and other intangibles.

Chapter 12

Completing the Audit

Professional Standards References

Compendium Section	Document Reference	Topic
AU 313	SAS 45	*Substantive Tests Prior to the Balance Sheet Date*
AU 316	SAS 82	*Consideration of Fraud in a Financial Statement Audit*
AU 326	SAS 80	*Evidential Matter*
AU 329	SAS 56	*Analytical Procedures*
AU 333	SAS 85	*Management Representations*
AU 333	SAS 89	*Audit Adjustments*
AU 9333		*Interpretation: Violations of Laws and Regulations; When Current Management Not Present*
AU 337	SAS 12	*Inquiry of a Client's Lawyer Concerning Litigation*
AU 337C	SAS 12	*American Bar Association Statement of Policy Regarding Lawyers' Responses to Auditors' Requests for Information*
AU 9337		*Interpretations: Inquiry of a Client's Lawyer*
AU 342	SAS 57	*Auditing Accounting Estimates*
AU 390	SAS 46	*Consideration of Omitted Procedures after the Report Date*
AU 530	SAS 1	*Dating the Independent Auditor's Report*
AU 560	SAS 1	*Subsequent Events*
AU 561	SAS 1	*Subsequent Discovery of Facts Existing at the Date of the Auditor's Report*
AU 9561		*Interpretation: Subsequent Discovery When Auditor Has Resigned or Been Discharged*
AU 711	SAS 37	*Filings under Federal Securities Statutes*
AU 9711		*Interpretation: Subsequent Events Procedures for Shelf Registration Statements Updated After the Original Effective Date*

Learning Objectives

This chapter covers the process of completing the fieldwork and gathering up the loose ends of the audit. The following principal items are covered:

- Completing the audit of revenue and expense.
- Consideration of contingencies and obtaining letters from the client's lawyers.
- Obtaining written client representations.
- Final wrap-up of the audit (audit review).
- Events subsequent to the balance sheet date and events subsequent to the audit report date.

Your learning objectives relative to these topics are to be able to:

1. Describe the related balance sheet account group where the audit of the major revenue and expense accounts normally is associated.

2. Describe the use of analytical procedures to audit revenue and expense accounts.

3. Explain the use of the client representation letter and the attorney's letter as an audit is completed.

4. Describe the reasons written client representations are obtained and list the four items that are included without regard to a materiality criterion.

5. Explain the final audit steps involving adjusting entries, second-partner review, and the management letter.

6. Given a set of facts and circumstances, classify a subsequent event by type and describe the proper treatment in the financial statements.

7. Specify the sequence of decisions and actions auditors must consider upon discovery (after the issuance of the report) (1) of information about facts that may have existed at the date of the auditors' report or (2) that one or more auditing procedures were omitted.

AUDIT OF REVENUE AND EXPENSE

LEARNING OBJECTIVE
1. Describe the related balance sheet account group where the audit of the major revenue and expense accounts normally is associated.

As the fieldwork nears its end, the major revenue and expense accounts will have been audited in connection with related balance sheet accounts. Now auditors need to consider other revenue and expense accounts. The broad financial statement assertions are the bases for specific assertions and audit objectives for these accounts. Typical specific assertions for the revenue and expense accounts are:

1. Revenue accounts represent all the valid transactions recorded correctly in the proper account, amount, and period.
2. The accounting for consignments and goods sold with rights of return are in conformity with accounting principles.
3. Expense accounts represent all the valid expense transactions recorded correctly in the proper account, amount, and period.
4. Revenues, expenses, cost of goods sold, and extraordinary, unusual, or infrequent transactions are adequately classified and disclosed.

Revenue

The types of revenue and related topics already audited, either in whole or in part, at the completion stage of the engagement are shown in Exhibit 12–1. To the extent these revenue items already have been audited in tandem with their related balance sheet accounts, the working papers should show cross-reference indexing to the revenue account in the trial balance.

EXHIBIT 12-1   AUDIT OF VARIOUS REVENUE ACCOUNTS

Revenue and Related Topics	Related Accounts	Related Cycles
Sales and sales returns	Receivables	Revenue/Collection
Lease revenue	PP&E, Receivables	Revenue/Collection
Franchise revenue	Receivables, Intangibles	Revenue/Collection
		Finance/Investment
Long-term sales contracts	Revenue, Receivables	Revenue/Collection
Product line reporting	Revenue, Receivables	Revenue/Collection
Accounting policy disclosure	Revenue, Receivables	Revenue/Collection
Dividends and interest	Receivables, Investments	Finance/Investment
Gain, loss on asset disposals	PP&E, Receivables and Investments	Production
		Finance/Investment
Rental revenue	Receivables, Investments	Finance/Investment
Royalty and license fees	Receivables, Investments	Finance/Investment

Audit Procedures

LEARNING OBJECTIVE

2. Describe the use of analytical procedures to audit revenue and expense accounts.

Auditors can use analytical procedures to compare the revenue accounts and amounts to prior year data and to multiple-year trends to notice any unusual fluctuations. Comparisons also should be made to budgets, monthly internal reports, and forecasts to ascertain whether events have occurred that require explanation or analysis by management. These explanations would then be subjected to audit. For example, a sales dollar increase may be explained as a consequence of a price increase that can be corroborated by reference to price lists used in the test of controls audit of sales transactions.

All "miscellaneous" or "other" revenue accounts and all "clearing" accounts with credit balances should be analyzed. **Account analysis** in this context refers to the identification of each important item and amount in the account followed by *document vouching* and *inquiry* to determine whether amounts should be classified elsewhere. All clearing accounts should be eliminated and the amounts classified as revenue, deferred revenue, liabilities, deposits, or contra-assets.

Miscellaneous revenue and other suspense accounts can harbor many accounting errors. Proceeds from sale of assets, insurance premium refunds, insurance proceeds, and other receipts simply may be credited to such an account. Often, such items reveal unrecorded asset disposals, expiration of insurance recorded as prepaid, or other asset losses covered by insurance. Appendix 12A–1 lists common audit procedures for revenue accounts.

Unusual Transactions

Significant audit evidence and reporting problems can arise with transactions designed by management to manufacture earnings. Frequently, such transactions are run through a complicated structure of subsidiaries, affiliates, and related parties. Generally, the amounts of revenue are large. The transactions themselves may not be concealed, but certain guarantees may have been made by management and not revealed to the auditors. The timing of the transactions may be arranged carefully to provide the most favorable income result.

Controversies have arisen in the past over revenue recognized on the construction percentage-of-completion method, over sales of assets at inflated prices to management-controlled dummy corporations, over sales of real estate to independent parties with whom the seller later associates for development of the property (making guarantees on indemnification for losses), and over disclosure of revenues by source. These revenue issues pose a combination of evidence-gathering problems and reporting-disclosure problems.

AUDITING INSIGHT

UNUSUAL REVENUE TRANSACTIONS

Merger

National Fried Chicken, Inc., a large fast-food franchiser, began negotiations in August to purchase State Hot Dog Company, a smaller convenience food chain. At August 1, 20X1, State's net worth was $7 million, and National proposed to pay $8 million cash for all the outstanding stock. In June 20X2, the merger was consummated and National paid $8 million, even though State's net worth had dropped to $6 million. Consistent with prior years, State lost $1 million in the 10 months ended June 1; as in the past, the company showed a net profit of $1.5 million for June and July. At June 1, 20X2, the fair value of State's net assets was $6 million, and National accounted for the acquisition as a purchase, recording $2 million goodwill. National proposed to show in consolidated financial statements the $1.5 million of post-acquisition income and $50,000 amortization of goodwill.

Audit Resolution. The auditors discovered that the purchase price was basically set at 16 times expected earnings and that management had carefully chosen the consummation date to maximize goodwill (and reportable net income after amortization in fiscal 20X2). The auditors required that $1 million of "goodwill" be treated as prepaid expenses which expired in the year ended July 31, 20X2, so that bottom-line income would be $500,000.

* * * * *

Real Estate Deal

In August, a company sold three real estate properties to BMC for $5,399,000 and recognized profit of $550,000. The agreement that covered the sale committed the company to use its best efforts to obtain permanent financing and to pay underwriting costs for BMC. The agreement provided BMC with an absolute guarantee against loss from ownership and a commitment by the company to complete construction of the properties.

SEC Resolution (ARS 153). The terms of this agreement made the recognition of profit improper because the company had not shifted the risk of loss to BMC.

* * * * *

Real Estate Development, Strings Attached

In December 20X1, Black Company sold one-half of a tract of undeveloped land to Red Company in an arm's-length transaction. The portion sold had a book value of $1.5 million, and Red Company paid $2.5 million in cash. Red Company planned to build and sell apartment houses on the acquired land. In January 20X2, Black and Red announced a new joint venture to develop the entire tract. The two companies formed a partnership, each contributing its one-half of the total tract of land. They agreed to share equally in future capital requirements and profits or losses.

Audit Resolution. The $1 million profit from the sale was not recognized as income in Black's 20X1 financial statements but, instead, was classified as a deferred credit. Black's investment in the joint venture was valued at $1.5 million. Black's continued involvement in development of the property and the uncertainty of future costs and losses were cited as reasons.

Expenses

Although many major expense items will have been audited in connection with other account groupings, numerous minor expenses may still remain unaudited. As a brief review, the major expenses shown in Exhibit 12–2 may have been audited in whole or in part as the audit nears its end.

EXHIBIT 12–2	AUDIT OF VARIOUS EXPENSE ACCOUNTS

Expenses and Related Topics	Related Accounts	Related Cycles
Bad debt expense	Receivables	Revenue/Collection
Sales commissions	Payroll, Sales Revenues	Revenue/Collection
		Payroll
Purchases, cost of goods sold	Inventories	Acquisition/Expenditure
Inventory valuation losses	Inventories	Acquisition/Expenditure
Warranty and guarantee expense	Inventories, Liabilities	Acquisition/Expenditure
Royalty and license expense	Inventories, PP&E	Acquisition/Expenditure
		Production
Marketing and product R&D	Investments, Intangibles	Acquisition/Expenditure
		Production
Depreciation expense	PP&E	Finance/Investment
Property taxes, insurance	PP&E, Liabilities	Production
	Acquisition/Expenditure	
Lease and rental expense	PP&E	Production
Repairs and maintenance	PP&E, Liabilities	Finance/Investment
		Acquisition/Expenditure
Legal, professional fees	Liabilities	Acquisition/Expenditure
Interest expense	Liabilities	Acquisition/Expenditure
Pension, retirement benefits	Payroll	Payroll
Salaries, compensation	Payroll	Payroll
Investment value losses	Investments	Finance/Investment
Rental property expenses	Investments	Finance/Investment
Amortization of intangibles	Intangible Assets	Finance/Investment

Like the revenue accounts mentioned in the previous section, if audit work is complete for expense accounts, the working papers should show cross-reference indexing from the working papers to the trial balance. Some of the expenses may not have been audited completely (such as property tax expense), and some finishing touch vouching of supporting documents may be required.

Audit Procedures

Several minor expenses, such as office supplies, telephone, utilities, and similar accounts, are not audited until late in the engagement. Generally, the dollar amounts in these accounts are not material (taken singly), and the relative risk is small that they might be misstated in such a way as to create misleading financial statements. Auditors usually audit these kinds of accounts with substantive **analytical procedures**. These procedures include making a list of the expenses with comparative balances from one or more prior periods. The dollar amounts are then reviewed for unusual changes (or lack of unusual changes if reasons for change are known). This analysis of comparative balances may be enough to decide whether the amounts are fairly presented.

On the other hand, questions may be raised and additional evidence sought. In this case, auditors may *vouch* some expenses to supporting documents (invoices and canceled checks). Some documentary vouching evidence already may be available about these minor expenses. If the auditors performed detail test of controls procedures on a sample of expenditure transactions in the acquisition and expenditure cycle audit program, a few expense transactions were selected for testing the client's compliance with control objectives (validity, completeness, authorization, accuracy, classification, accounting/posting, and proper period). This evidence should be used.

Analytical comparisons to budgets, forecasts, and other internal reports also may be made. Variations from budget already may have been subject to management explanation, or the auditors may need to investigate variations.

All "miscellaneous" or "other" expense accounts and "clearing" accounts with debit balances should be *analyzed* by listing each important item on a working paper and *vouching* them to supporting documents. Miscellaneous and other expenses may include abandonments of property, items not deductible for tax purposes, or payments that should be classified in other expense accounts. Clearing accounts should be analyzed and items therein classified according to their nature or source so all clearing account balances are removed and accounted for properly.

Advertising expense, travel, entertainment expense, and contributions are accounts that typically are *analyzed* in detail. These accounts are particularly sensitive to management policy violations and income tax consequences. Travel, entertainment, and contributions must be documented carefully to stand the IRS auditor's examination. Questionable items may have an effect on the income tax expense and liability.

Appendix 12A–2 lists common audit procedures for expense accounts.

R E V I E W
CHECKPOINTS

12.1 Certain revenue and expense accounts usually are audited in conjunction with related balance sheet accounts. For the following revenue and expense accounts, list the most likely related balance sheet accounts: Lease Revenue, Franchise Revenue, Royalty and License Revenue, Depreciation Expense, Repairs and Maintenance Expense, Interest Expense.

12.2 Why are many of the revenue and expense accounts only audited by analytical procedures and not by other procedures?

12.3 Why can "unusual revenue transactions" cause significant audit evidence and reporting problems?

12.4 What procedures can be used to obtain information about the material accuracy of balances in minor expense accounts?

A SEQUENCE OF AUDIT EVENTS

LEARNING OBJECTIVE

3. Explain the use of the client representation letter and the attorney's letter as an audit is completed.

Based on the material presented on the organization of audits, you can easily visualize some audit work being done at an interim period sometime before a balance sheet date followed by completion of the work on the balance sheet date. True, much audit work is done months before the balance sheet date, with auditors working for a time, leaving the client's offices, and then returning for the year-end work. Actually, auditors may not even do any work on the balance sheet date itself, but they always perform evidence-gathering *after that date*—sometimes as much as several months afterwards.[1]

Interim and Final Audit Work in Independent Auditing

In the "interim" audit work period, the auditors evaluate internal control with questionnaires, flowcharts, and/or written narratives; identify strengths and weaknesses; and complete the test of controls part of the audit. Some test of controls procedures usually are performed at interim, and tentative judgments about control risk for certain transaction cycles are made early. Also, auditors can apply audit procedures for substantive audit of balances as of an interim date, and in this way a significant amount of recalculating, vouching, tracing, observing, and confirming can be performed early.

When the audit team returns after year-end and receives the final unaudited financial statements (or trial balance) prepared by the client personnel, they can start where they left off at interim and complete the work on control risk assessment and audit of

---

[1] Public companies must file annual reports with the U.S. Securities and Exchange Commission (SEC) within 90 days after the balance sheet date. Thus, audit field work is completed and audit reports are dated for these companies up to 90 days after a company's fiscal year-end.

balances. However, the procedures of obtaining the attorney's letter and the written client representations are deferred until the end of fieldwork. These written representations are dated at the end of the field work (audit report date) because the auditors are responsible for determining whether important events that occurred after the balance sheet date are properly entered in the accounts or disclosed in the financial statement notes.

Contingencies and Attorneys' Letters

For auditors, an "uncertainty" is essentially synonymous with an accounting "contingency," which is defined in *FASB Statement No. 5 (SFAS 5)*:

> A contingency is . . . an existing condition, situation, or set of circumstances involving uncertainty as to possible gain ("gain contingency") or loss ("loss contingency") to an enterprise that will ultimately be resolved when one or more future events occur or fail to occur. Resolution of the uncertainty may confirm the acquisition of an asset or the reduction of a liability or the loss or impairment of an asset or the incurrence of a liability. . . .

Auditing standards define uncertainty in these terms (SAS 58, AU 508): (1) Uncertainties include, but are not limited to, contingencies covered by *FASB Statement No. 5*, and (2) an uncertainty is a matter that is expected to be resolved at a future date, at which time sufficient evidential matter concerning its outcome will be . . . available. When deciding upon the type and content of an audit report, auditors are supposed to consider both the potential materiality of a contingency loss and the probability of its occurrence.

In response to one of the most common contingencies (the uncertain outcome of litigation pending against the company), one of the most important confirmations is the response known as the *attorney's representation letter*. FASB *Statement of Financial Accounting Standards No. 5, (Accounting for Contingencies)*, defines pending litigation, claims, assessments, and the "probable," "reasonably possible," and "remote" likelihood that future events (such as court judgment) could confirm a loss from an existing contingency. *SFAS 5* sets forth standards for accrual and disclosure of litigation, claims, and assessments in financial statements.

SAS 12 (AU 337, *Inquiry of a Client's Lawyer Concerning Litigation, Claims, and Assessments*) is the auditors' counterpart of SFAS 5. This SAS requires auditors to make certain inquiries designed to elicit the information on which accounting in conformity with SFAS 5 can be determined. Exhibit 12–3 is an example of a letter the auditor would request the *client* to send to all lawyers who had performed work for the client during the period under audit. The *client* must make this request because it informs the lawyer that his or her client is waiving the attorney-client privilege and giving the lawyer permission to give information to the auditors.

As implied by the client's letter to the lawyers in Exhibit 12–3, questions about contingencies, litigation, claims, and assessments should be directed not only to attorneys but also to management because an auditor has the right to expect to be informed by management about all material contingent liabilities. Audit procedures useful in this regard include the following:

- Inquire and discuss with management the policies and procedures for identifying, evaluating, and accounting for litigation, claims, and assessments.
- Obtain from management a description and evaluation of litigation, claims, and assessments.
- Examine documents in the client's possession concerning litigation, claims, and assessments, including correspondence and invoices from lawyers.
- Obtain assurance from management that it has disclosed all material unasserted claims the lawyer has advised them are probable of litigation.
- Read minutes of meetings of stockholders, directors, and appropriate committees.
- Read contracts, loan agreements, leases, and correspondence from taxing or other governmental agencies.
- Obtain information concerning guarantees from bank confirmations.

EXHIBIT   12–3   SAMPLE AUDIT INQUIRY TO LEGAL COUNSEL*

Oxford Company
Oxford, Mississippi
March 1, 2002

Grisham and Scruggs, Attorneys-at-:Law
Jackson, Mississippi

In connection with an examination of our financial statements at December 31, 2001, and for the year then ended, management of the Oxford Company has prepared, and furnished to our auditors, Anderson, Olds, and Watershed, a description and evaluation of certain contingencies, including those set forth below involving matters with respect to which you have been engaged and to which you have devoted substantive attention on behalf of Oxford in the form of legal consultation and representation. The contingencies are regarded by management of Oxford as material for this purpose. Your response should include matters that existed at December 31, 2001, and during the period from that date to the date of your response.

Pending or Threatened Litigation (excluding unasserted claims):

* * * * *

(Management's list of litigation; nature; progress of case; management responses or intended responses; and evaluation of likelihood of unfavorable outcome and estimate of potential loss.)

Please furnish our auditors such explanation, if any, that you consider necessary to supplement the foregoing information, including an explanation of those matters about which your views may differ from those stated and an identification of the omission of any pending or threatened litigation, claims, and assessment or a statement that the list of such matters is complete.

Unasserted Claims and Assessments:

* * * * *

(Management's list of unasserted claims and assessments; nature of case; management-intended responses if a claim is asserted; and evaluation of likelihood of unfavorable outcome and estimate of amount or range of potential loss.)

Please furnish to our auditors such explanation, if any, you consider necessary to supplement the foregoing information, including an explanation of those matters on which your views may differ from those stated.

* * * * *

We understand that whenever, in the course of performing legal services for us with respect to a matter recognized to involve an unasserted possible claim or assessment that may call for financial statement disclosure, if you have formed a professional conclusion that we should disclose or consider disclosure concerning such possible claim or assessment, as a matter of professional responsibility to us, you will so advise us and consult with us concerning the question of such disclosure and the applicable requirements of Statement of Financial Accounting Standards No. 5. Please specifically confirm to our auditors that our understanding is correct.

Please specifically identify the nature of and reasons for any limitation on your response.

Sincerely,
Julian Grace
Vice President of Finance

---

* Adapted from Appendix to *SAS 12*, AU 337A.

The attorney's letter serves as a major means to learn of material contingencies. Even so, a devious or forgetful management or a careless attorney may fail to tell the auditor of some important factor or development. Auditors must be alert and sensitive to all possible contingencies so they can ask the right questions at the right time.

Audit uncertainties include not only lawsuits but also such things as the value of fixed assets held for sale (e.g., a whole plant or warehouse facility) and the status of the assets involved in foreign expropriations. Auditors may perform procedures in accordance with generally accepted auditing standards, yet the uncertainty and lack of evidence may persist. The problem is that it is impossible to obtain audit "evidence" about the future. Auditors have a natural conservative tendency to look out for adverse contingencies. However, potentially favorable events also should be investigated and disclosed (such as the contingency of litigation for damages wherein the client is the plaintiff). In an effort to assist management in observing the law and to provide adequate disclosure of information in financial statements, the auditor should be alert to all types of contingencies.

When significant uncertainties about future events exist about such matters as tax deficiency assessments, contract disputes, recoverability of asset cost, lawsuits, and other

AUDITING STANDARDS

INTERPRETING THE LAWYERS' LETTERS

Lawyers take great care making responses to clients' requests for information to be transmitted to auditors. This care causes problems of interpretation for auditors. The difficulty arises over lawyers' desire to preserve attorney-client privileged information yet cooperate with auditors and the financial reporting process that seeks full disclosure.

The American Bar Association policy statement (AU 337C) observes:

> The public interest in protecting the confidentiality of lawyer-client communications is fundamental. . . . disclosure to a third party [auditor] may result in a loss of the confidentiality essential to maintain the privilege. . . . [open disclosure] would inevitably discourage management from discussing potential legal problems with counsel for fear such discussion might become public and precipitate a loss to or potential liability of the business enterprise and its stockholders that might otherwise not materialize.

Consequently, lawyers' responses to auditors may contain vague and ambiguous wording. Auditors need to determine whether a contingency is "remote" (*FASB Statement No. 5*). The following lawyer responses can be properly interpreted to mean "remote," even though the word is not used (AU 9337):

- We are of the opinion that this action will not result in any liability to the company.
- It is our opinion that the possible liability to the company in this proceeding is nominal in amount.
- We believe the company will be able to defend this action successfully.
- We believe that the plaintiff's case against this company is without merit.
- Based on the facts known to us, after a full investigation, it is our opinion that no liability will be established against the company in these suits.

However, auditors should view the following response phrases as unclear—providing no information—about the probable, reasonably possible, or remote likelihood of an unfavorable outcome for a litigation contingency (adapted from AU 9337):

- We believe the plaintiff will have serious problems establishing the company's liability; nevertheless, if the plaintiff is successful, the damage award may be substantial.
- It is our opinion, the company will be able to assert meritorious defenses. ["Meritorious," in lawyer language, apparently means "the judge will not summarily throw out the defenses."]
- We believe the lawsuit can be settled for less than the damages claimed.
- We are unable to express an opinion on the merits of the litigation, but the company believes there is absolutely no merit.
- In our opinion, the company has a substantial chance of prevailing. ["Substantial chance," "reasonable opportunity," and similar phrases indicate uncertainty of success in a defense.]

important contingencies, they should be explained clearly and completely in footnotes to the financial statements. These disclosures are as much a part of management's responsibility as the balance sheet, income statement, and cash flow statement. Also, management must record estimates of loss amounts, when estimates of probable loss can be made (*SFAS 5*).

Uncertainty situations may cause audit reports to be qualified for departures from GAAP, if (1) management's disclosure of the uncertainty is inadequate, (2) management uses inappropriate accounting principles to account for the uncertainty, or (3) management makes unreasonable accounting estimates in connection with the effects of the uncertainty. If management or its attorneys fail to provide adequate information about lawsuit contingencies, auditors consider the scope of the audit limited. A serious audit scope limitation requires a qualification in the audit report or a disclaimer of opinion.

Auditing Insight

Room for Improvement in Litigation Contingency Disclosures

Research on 126 lawsuits lost by public companies examined the disclosures about the suits in prior years' financial statements. The contingencies involved material, uninsured losses. Subsequent failure in the defense indicates the contingencies to have been "reasonably possible," calling for SFAS 5 disclosure. For the 126 cases, wide disclosure diversity existed. As indicated in the table below, the majority of cases carried satisfactory disclosure while the lawsuits were in progress, but a significant minority did not.

	Number	Percent
Satisfactory disclosure:		
Disclosure conceded the possibility of liability	60	47.6%
Disclosure included an estimate of the related liability	5	4.0
Disclosure along with recorded liability	7	5.6
Total	72	57.2%
Unsatisfactory disclosure:		
No mention of the litigation	45	35.7%
Litigation mentioned but with a strong disclaimer of liability	9	7.1
Total	54	42.8%

Among the types of lawsuits covered in the 126 cases, the ones dealing with securities law violations had the highest frequency of satisfactory disclosure (8 out of 11, 73 percent). The ones dealing with fraud or misrepresentation had the lowest frequency of satisfactory disclosure (2 out of 8, or 25 percent).

Speculations about the reasons company officials and attorneys have difficulty providing auditors with appropriate information include:

- High level of emotion surrounding the lawsuits.
- Fear that financial statement disclosure will be construed as an admission of guilt.
- The legal framework for evaluating litigation outcomes varies significantly from the framework used by auditors.
- More appropriate channels exist for disclosure of litigation information [e.g., business press].
- SFAS 5 disclosure requirements are viewed as only a guide and, therefore, need not be taken literally.

Source: "Disclosure of Litigation Contingencies Faulted," *Journal of Accountancy.*

Management Representations

LEARNING OBJECTIVE

4. Describe the reasons written client representations are obtained and list the four items that are included without regard to a materiality criterion.

Management makes numerous responses to auditors' inquiries during the course of an audit. Many of these responses are very important. To the extent that additional evidence is obtainable through other procedures, auditors should corroborate these representations.

In addition, SAS 85, AU 333 (*Management Representations*), requires that auditors obtain *written representations* on matters of audit importance. The written representations take the form of a letter on the client's letterhead, addressed to the auditor, signed by responsible officers (normally the chief executive officer [CEO], chief financial officer [CFO], and other appropriate managers), and dated as of the date of the auditor's report. Thus, the letter, referred to as the "management's rep letter" in practice, covers events and representations running beyond the balance sheet date up to the end of all important field work. These written representations, however, are not substitutes for corroborating evidence obtainable by applying other auditing procedures.

In most cases, the written client representations are merely more assertions, like the ones already in the financial statements (perhaps more detailed, in some cases). In this context, they are not "evidence" for auditors. They are not good defenses against

| EXHIBIT   12–4 | ILLUSTRATIVE REPRESENTATION LETTER* |

Auditee Letterhead   (Same date as audit report)

To Independent Auditor:

   In connection with your examination of the (identification of financial statements) of (name of client) as of (date) and for the (period of examination) for the purpose of expressing an opinion about whether the financial statements present fairly the financial position, results of operations, and cash flows of (name of client) in conformity with generally accepted accounting principles, we confirm, to the best of our knowledge and belief, the following representations made to you during your examination.

1. We are responsible for the fair presentation in the financial statements of financial position, results of operations, and cash flows, and we believe our financial statements are fairly presented in conformity with generally accepted accounting principles.
2. We have made available to you all the financial records and related data.
3. We have made available to you all the minutes of the meetings of stockholders, directors, and committees of directors.
4. We know of no frauds involving management, employees who have significant roles in internal control, or other frauds that could have a material effect on the financial statements.
5. There are no material transactions that have not been properly recorded in the accounting records.
6. We have no plans or intentions that may materially affect the carrying value or classification of assets and liabilities.
7. We believe that the effects of any uncorrected financial statement misstatements aggregated by your firm during the current engagement and pertaining to the latest period presented are immaterial, both individually and in the aggregate, to the financial statements taken as a whole. We have attached a summary of the uncorrected misstatements to this letter.
8. We have no knowledge of any:
   a. Communications from regulatory agencies concerning noncompliance with or deficiencies in financial reporting practices.
   b. Violations or possible violations of laws or regulations whose effects should be considered for disclosure in the financial statements.
   c. Unasserted claims or assessments that our lawyer has advised us are probable of assertion and must be disclosed in accordance with Statement of Financial Accounting Standards No. 5.

_____

Name of CEO and Title

_____

Name of CFO and Title

* Modified from Appendix to AU 333.

criticisms for failing to perform audit procedures independently. ("Management told us in writing that the inventory costing method was FIFO and adequate allowance for obsolescence was provided," is not a good excuse for failing to get the evidence from the records and other sources!) However, in some cases, the written management representations are the only available evidence about important matters of management intent. For example: (1)"We will discontinue the parachute manufacturing business, wind down the operations, and sell the remaining assets" (i.e., accounting for discontinued operations); and (2)"We will exercise our option to refinance the maturing debt on a long-term basis" (i.e., classifying maturing debt as long term).

   One of the major purposes of the management representation letter is to impress upon the management its primary responsibility for the financial statements. These representations also may establish an auditor's defenses if a question of management integrity arises later. If the management lies to the auditors, the management representation letter captures the lies in writing. Auditors draft the management representation letter to be prepared on the client's letterhead paper for signature by company representatives. This draft is reviewed with senior client personnel, then finalized. (A sample letter is in Exhibit 12–4.)

   The management representation letter generally deals only with material matters. Notwithstanding, auditing standards provide that the following four representations must appear in the letter without limitation based on materiality:

1. Management's acknowledgment of its responsibility for fair presentation of financial statements in conformity with generally accepted accounting principles.

2. Availability of all financial records and related data.

3. Completeness of the minutes of meetings of stockholders, directors, and important committees.

4. Information concerning fraud involving (i)management, (ii)employees who have significant roles in internal control, or (iii)cases where the fraud could have a material effect on the financial statements.

SAS 85 (AU 333) contains a list of several other items and discussions of other points that may be included. Exhibit 12–4 contains a sample representation letter. Management's refusal to furnish a representation the auditor considers essential constitutes a scope limitation, which requires a qualification in the audit report (SAS 85, AU 333) or a disclaimer of opinion (AU 9333).

Summary of Audit Correspondence

Many types of formal correspondence have been mentioned in this book. Since you are learning the final procedures to complete the audit, this is a good place to summarize these various correspondence items. Exhibit 12–5 is a summary of audit correspondence. The management letter will be covered later in this chapter.

12.5 What is the purpose of a client representation letter? What representations would you request management to make in a client representation letter with respect to responsibility for financial statements? To availability of financial records? To completeness of the minutes of directors' meetings? To information about frauds?

12.6 Why are written client representations and lawyers' letters obtained near the end of the audit field work and dated on or near the audit report date?

12.7 In addition to the attorney's letter, what other procedures can be used to gather evidence regarding contingencies?

12.8 The following was included in a letter auditors received from the client's lawyers, in response to a letter sent to them similar to Exhibit 12–3: "Several agreements and contracts to which the company is a party are not covered by this response since we have not advised or been consulted in their regard." How might the auditor's report be affected by such a statement in a letter from the client's counsel regarding a pending lawsuit against a client? Explain.

12.9 Why might companies and auditors experience difficulty making appropriate disclosures about litigation contingencies?

12.10 Give some examples of uncertainties that might cause auditors to be careful obtaining evidence about management's disclosures and monetary estimates of probable loss in accordance with *FASB Statement No. 5 (Accounting for Contingencies)*.

FINAL WRAP-UP

LEARNING OBJECTIVE

5. Explain the final audit steps involving adjusting entries, second-partner review, and the management letter.

Several items must be completed before an audit can be considered finished. The client must approve of the proposed adjusting entries and the financial statement notes, and the audit work must be reviewed.

Client Approval of Adjusting Entries and Financial Statement Disclosure

The financial statements, including the notes to the financial statements, are the responsibility of management, although auditors frequently draft them. The adjusting

EXHIBIT 12–5			**AUDIT CORRESPONDENCE**	

Type	From	To	Time	Reference
Engagement letter (acceptance)	Auditor (Client)	Client (Auditor)	Before engagement	SAS 83 AU 310
Internal control deficiencies	Auditor	Client	Interim or after audit	SAS 60 AU 325
Confirmations (replies)	Client (Third parties)	Third parties (Auditor)	Throughout the audit	SAS 67 AU 330
Lawyer's letter (reply)	Client (Attorney)	Attorney (Auditor)	Near end of audit	SAS 12 AU 337
Management rep letter	Client	Auditor	End of field work	SAS 85 AU 333
Management letter	Auditor	Client	After audit	none
Communication with client audit committee	Auditor	Directors	Before, during, or after an audit	SAS 61 AU 380

entries shown in Exhibit 12–6 are labeled *proposed* to indicate this responsibility of management. A formal list of all approved adjusting entries should be given to the client so that formal entries can be made in the accounting records to bring them into balance with the financial statements.

In a like manner, approval of all disclosures in notes must be obtained from the client. The notes considered necessary usually are drafted as *proposed notes* by auditors performing the audit procedures. They must be considered carefully by the audit manager and partner before being presented to the client management for acceptance as the company's disclosures.

Exhibit 12–6 is a summary worksheet ("score sheet") showing the end-of-audit consideration of proposed adjusting journal entries. Auditors can prepare this summary to see how the proposed adjustments affect the financial statements. This review helps auditors decide which adjustments must be made to support an unqualified audit report and which adjustments may be waived. A *waived adjustment* is a proposed adjustment on which the auditors decide not to insist because it does not have a material effect on the financial position and results of operations.

In Exhibit 12–6 the illustrative proposed adjustments are: (1) recording checks written and mailed but not recorded in the books; (2) reversing recorded sales for goods shipped after the balance sheet date, and reversing the 60 percent cost of goods sold; (3) writing off obsolete and damaged inventory; (4) recording the amounts found in the search for unrecorded liabilities; (5) correcting a depreciation calculation error; (6) reclassifying the current portion of long-term debt from the long-term classification; and (7) recording a tax refund asset for overpaid income taxes (could be a debit to tax liability if all the taxes for the year had not already been paid). Some summary effects on income, current assets, current liabilities, and working capital are appended to the bottom of the exhibit.

Working Paper and Report Review

The audit supervisor makes a final review to ensure that all accounts on the trial balance have a working paper reference index (an indication the audit work has been finished for that account) and that all procedures in the audit program are "signed off" with a date and initials.

The working papers of the audit staff are reviewed soon after being completed by the audit supervisor and sometimes by the audit manager. This review is to ensure that all tick-mark notations are clear, that all procedures performed are adequately documented, and that all necessary procedures were performed with due professional care.

The review by the audit manager and engagement partner will focus more on the overall scope of the audit. At this stage, audit standards require the application of

EXHIBIT 12–6 PROPOSED ADJUSTING JOURNAL ENTRIES
(ILLUSTRATIVE SCORESHEET WORKING PAPER)

	INCOME STATEMENT		BALANCE SHEET	
	Debit	Credit	Debit	Credit
(1) Unrecorded cash disbursements:				
Accounts payable			$ 42,000	
Cash				$ 42,000
(2) Improper sales cutoff:				
Sales	$13,000			
Inventory			$ 7,800	
Cost of goods sold (60%)		$ 7,800		
Accounts receivable				$ 13,000
(3) Inventory write-off:				
Cost of goods sold	$21,000			
Inventory				$ 21,000
(4) Unrecorded liabilities:				
Utilities expense	$ 700			
Commissions expense	$ 3,000			
Wages	$ 2,500			
Accounts payable				$ 700
Accrued expenses payable				$ 5,500
(5) Depreciation calculation error:				
Accumulated depreciation			$ 17,000	
Depreciation expense		$17,000		
(6) Reclassify current portion of long-term debt:				
Notes payable			$ 50,000	
Current portion of debt				$ 50,000
(7) Income tax @ 40%:				
Income tax refund receivable			$ 6,160	
Income tax expense		$ 6,160		
	$40,200	$30,960	$122,960	$132,200
Net income change		($ 9,240)		
Current assets change				($ 62,040)
Current liabilities change				$ 14,200
Working capital change				($ 76,240)

analytical procedures to complete the final review of the financial statements. The audit manager and engagement partner are very involved with the planning of the audit, and they perform some of the field work on difficult areas. However, they are usually not involved in preparing the detail working papers. Even though the working papers are reviewed by the onsite audit supervisor, the review by the partner who is going to sign the audit report is essential. Review "to-do lists" are prepared during these reviews citing omissions or deficiencies that must be cleared before the final work is completed.

Audit firms vary in their treatment of the "to-do lists." Some firms prefer to destroy the lists after the work is performed and documented in the working papers. After all, they want to "clean up" the working papers, and the to-do lists were merely notes directing the staff to tie a neat ribbon around any loose ends or difficult issues. Other firms prefer to keep the lists as signed off and cross-referenced for the work performed. They believe that the lists are "working papers" that show evidence of careful review and completion of the audit. Sometimes, retained to-do lists backfire on auditors by showing questions raised but not resolved.

The working papers and financial statements, including footnotes, are given a final review on large engagements by a partner not responsible for client relations. This **second-partner review** ensures that the quality of audit work and reporting is in keeping with the quality standards of the audit firm.

The final audit time budget reports must be prepared and the working papers prepared for storage. At the completion of the field work, performance evaluation reports of the staff auditors usually are prepared by the audit supervisor.

Management Letter

During the audit work (especially the evaluation of the control system and assessment of the control risk), matters are noted that can be made as recommendations to the client. When field work is completed, and in some cases after the audit report is delivered, these items are evaluated and written in a letter (commonly referred to as the **management letter**) to be sent to the client. One firm calls this communication a letter of *client advisory comments* and characterizes it as a voluntary and constructive dimension of an audit designed to provide clients with an important value-added service. The firm encourages consulting and tax professionals to participate with the auditors in preparing the letter.

The management letter is not required by professional standards and should not be confused with the communication of control-related matters, which is required by auditing standards.

Management letters are a service provided as a by-product of the audit. The management letter is an excellent opportunity to develop rapport with the client and to make the client aware of other business services offered by the accounting firm. Wallace read over 100 management letters and concluded that CPA firms frequently miss opportunities to impress clients with their wide range of services.[2] Many of the letters failed to "sell." A brief management letter formulated along the lines of her suggestions is shown in Exhibit 12–7.

REVIEW CHECKPOINTS

12.11 What are review "to-do" lists? Cite several items that such lists might contain. Why must such lists be cleared before the field work is considered completed?

12.12 What is a good reason for keeping the "to-do list" in the audit working paper files?

12.13 Describe a "second-partner review." What is its purpose?

12.14 What is a management letter? Is a management letter required by generally accepted auditing standards?

12.15 Which CPA firm personnel should participate in preparing a management letter at the end of an audit? How can well-prepared management letters lead to additional client services besides audit engagements?

12.16 Why are auditors' drafts of adjusting entries and note disclosures always labeled "proposed" near the end of the audit? Why shouldn't auditors just write them in final form and give them to the client?

EVENTS SUBSEQUENT TO THE BALANCE SHEET DATE

LEARNING OBJECTIVE
6. Given a set of facts and circumstances, classify a subsequent event by type and describe the proper treatment in the financial statements.

Certain material events that occur *after the balance sheet date but before the end of field work* (thus, before issuance of the audit report) require disclosure in the financial statements and related notes. Auditors (and management) are responsible for gathering evidence on these subsequent events and evaluating the proposed disclosure. Material subsequent events have been classified into two types, which are disclosed differently. The first type (Type I) requires adjustment of the dollar amounts in the financial statements and appropriate disclosures (financial statement notes), while the second (Type II) requires note disclosure and sometimes pro forma financial statements.

[2] W.A. Wallace, "More Effective Management Letters," *CPA Journal*.

EXHIBIT   12–7 | MANAGEMENT LETTER

Anderson, Olds, & Watershed
Certified Public Accountants
Chicago, Illinois

April 1, 2002

Mr. Brandon Lucious, Chairman
Oxford Company
Oxford, Mississippi

Dear Mr. Lucious:

During our audit of the Oxford Company financial statements for the year ended December 31, 2001, we observed certain matters we believe should be brought to your attention. Our audit work was not designed to be a study of the overall efficiency and economy of the management and operation of Oxford Company, but ordinary audit procedures nevertheless enabled us to notice some actions that could enhance the profitability of the Company.

Summary

When we audited the physical inventory and compared the quantities actually on hand to the quantities shown in the perpetual inventory records, we noted several shortages. Follow-up with your warehouse personnel revealed that the "shortages" were usually in the assembly department, where numerous items of custom lawn maintenance equipment were being assembled for customers prior to delivery. The removal of the inventory from the records was routinely entered when the assembled equipment was delivered. These procedures eventually maintained the records accurately, but the delay in posting the inventory records has resulted in lost sales and some customer dissatisfaction with the custom-assembly service.

The Problem

The warehouse personnel remove parts according to the specification of custom-assembly work orders, moving the parts to the assembly area. If another customer orders these parts soon thereafter, the inventory records show them on hand, and the new customer is told that the order can be filled. Shortly thereafter, warehouse personnel find that the parts are actually not on hand, and the customer is disappointed when informed of a delay. Sales department personnel confirmed that several (20–25 during the last six months) withdrew their orders and bought the parts from a competitor. They estimated that approximately $25,000 was lost in sales during the last six months, amounting to about $9,000 in lost profits.

Custom-Assembly Losses

The inventory "shortages," noticed by warehouse personnel when they try to fill new orders, causes another difficulty. People spend extra time looking around for the parts, and usually their inquiries reach the assembly area, where workers leave their jobs unfinished while trying to help locate the "missing" parts. This helpfulness causes assembly jobs to be delayed, customers get dissatisfied, and, in one case, a customer refused to pay because of late delivery. This one case resulted in lost profits of $10,000 because the equipment had to be disassembled and returned to the inventory.

Recommendation

We discussed the following recommendation with Mr. Troy Anderson in the warehouse, and he agrees that it can be a practical solution. We recommend that you design a form for "Work in Progress," which will be used to make accounting and inventory entries to remove parts from the main inventory as soon as they are transferred to the assembly area. At that stage, the cost would be classified as "work in progress," which will be entered in cost of goods sold as soon as the assembly is completed and the goods are delivered. Judging from our limited knowledge of the extent of the problem during the year under audit, we estimate that you might produce $20,000–$30,000 additional profit per year, while development and use of the form should cost about $3,000.

Conclusion

AO&W has expertise in system development and operation in our management services department, and we will be happy to assist you in reviewing a new form and a systems plan for your implementation. If you wish to discuss this matter further, please inform Mr. Matt Rothgangel.

Very truly yours,
Anderson, Olds, & Watershed

Type I: Adjustment of Dollar Amounts Required

This type of subsequent event provides new information regarding a financial condition that *existed at the date of the balance sheet.* The subsequent event information affects the numbers and requires adjustment of amounts in the financial statements for the period under audit.

The following examples of Type I subsequent events are in *SAS 1* (AU 560):

- A loss on uncollectible trade accounts receivable as a result of bankruptcy of a major customer. (The customer's deteriorating financial condition existed prior to the balance sheet date.)
- The settlement of litigation for an amount different than estimated (assuming the litigation had taken place prior to the balance sheet date).

Type II: No Adjustment of Financial Statements, but Disclosure Required

The second type of subsequent event involves occurrences that had both their cause and manifestation arising *after the balance sheet date*. Recall that the auditor's responsibility for adequate disclosure runs to the date marking the end of the field work.[3] Consequently, even for events that occurred after the balance sheet date and are not of the first type requiring financial statement adjustment, auditors must consider their importance and may insist that disclosure be made.

Type II events that occur after the balance sheet date may be of such magnitude that disclosure is necessary to keep the financial statements from being misleading as of the report date. Disclosure normally is in a narrative note. Occasionally, however, an event may be so significant that the best disclosure would be pro forma financial data. **Pro forma financial data** is the presentation of the financial statements "as if" the event had occurred on the date of the balance sheet. Such pro forma data are given in a note disclosure. For example, in addition to historical financial statements, pro forma financial data may be the best way to show the effect of a business purchase or other merger or the sale of a major portion of assets. However, a Type II subsequent event involving stock dividends requires retroactive restatement of the earnings per share computations on the income statement.[4]

Examples of Type II subsequent events in *SAS 1* (AU 560) are:

- Loss on an uncollectible trade receivable resulting from a customer's fire or flood loss subsequent to the balance sheet date (as contrasted with a customer's slow decline into bankruptcy cited as a Type I event above).
- Sale of a bond or capital stock issue.
- Settlement of litigation when the event giving rise to the claim took place after the balance sheet date.
- Loss of plant or inventories as a result of fire or flood.

The aspect of retroactive recognition of the effect of stock dividends and splits is an exception that may be explained briefly with an example. The problem is one of timing and one of informative communication to financial statement users. When the financial statements reach the users, the stock dividend or split will have been completed, and to report financial data as if it had not occurred might be considered misleading.

Dual Dating in the Audit Report

Dual dating refers to dating the audit report as of the end of field work along with an additional later date attached to disclosure of a significant Type II subsequent event. Sometimes after completion of field work but before issuance of the report, a significant event comes to the audit team's attention.

The purpose of dual dating is twofold: (1) to provide a means of inserting important information in the financial statement footnote disclosures learned after field work is complete and (2) to inform users that the auditor takes full responsibility for all subsequent events only up to the end of field work and for the specifically identified later event. However, responsibility is not taken for other events that may have occurred after the end of field work.

---

[3] In connection with a registration statement filed under the Securities Act of 1933, responsibility runs to the effective date of the registration statement.

[4] AICPA, *APB Opinion No. 15*, "Earnings per Share" (AC 2011A.04).

The company approved on February 15 a two-for-one stock split to be effective on that date. The fiscal year-end was the previous December 31, and the financial statements as of December 31 showed 50 million shares authorized, 10 million shares issued and outstanding, and earnings per share of $3.

Audit Resolution. Note disclosure was made of the split and of the relevant dates. The equity section of the balance sheet showed 100 million shares authorized, 20 million shares issued and outstanding. The income statement reported earnings per share of $1.50. Earnings per share of prior years were adjusted accordingly. The note disclosed comparative earnings per share on the predividend shares. The audit report was dated February 1, with a dual date of February 15 for the note disclosure.

Actually, dual dating in the audit report is not required. Dual dating is used to cut off the subsequent event procedural responsibility at the earlier date.

Audit Program for the Subsequent Period

Some audit procedures performed in the period subsequent to the balance sheet date may be part of the audit program for determining cutoff and proper valuation of balances as of the balance sheet date (Part A in Exhibit 12–8). However, the procedures specifically designed for gathering evidence about the two types of subsequent events are different and are added to the rest of the audit program (Part B in Exhibit 12–8).

The auditing procedures for subsequent events constitute a large part of the **S-1 review**, which is the audit for subsequent events contemplated by the Securities Act of 1933 respecting the auditor's responsibility running to the effective date of a registration statement. In addition to the procedures in Exhibit 12–8, Part B, auditors should read the entire prospectus and other portions of the registration statement and make inquiries and obtain written representations. (Refer to SAS 37, AU 711, "Filings under Federal Securities Statutes.") Notwithstanding the fact that the subsequent event procedures listed in Exhibit 12–8(B) are set out by the AICPA in an authoritative pronouncement, auditors must be careful to see that the execution of them will stand the test of a reasonable critical review. In addition, auditors must be careful to apply procedures that are not on the list if circumstances indicate matters that should be investigated further.

R E V I E W
CHECKPOINTS

12.17 What are the two types of "subsequent events?" In which way(s) are they treated differently in the financial statements?

12.18 What treatment is given stock dividends and splits that occur after the balance sheet date but before the audit report is issued? Explain.

12.19 What is the purpose of "dual dating" an audit report?

12.20 Generally, what additional actions should auditors take in the period between the audit report date and the effective date of a registration statement?

RESPONSIBILITIES AFTER THE AUDIT REPORT HAS BEEN ISSUED

The next two topics do not deal with responsibilities or concerns during the audit, but with responsibilities after the audit is completed and the report has been issued. They are covered here because they are related to subsequent event responsibilities. The topics are (1) subsequent discovery of facts existing at the date of the audit report and (2) consid-

| EXHIBIT 12–8 | AUDITING PROCEDURES FOR THE PERIOD SUBSEQUENT TO THE BALANCE SHEET DATE |

A. Procedures performed in connection with other audit programs.
  1. Use a cutoff bank statement to:
      a. Examine checks paid after year-end that are, or should have been, listed on the bank reconciliation.
      b. Examine bank posting of deposits in transit listed on the bank reconciliation.
  2. Vouch collections on accounts receivable in the month following year-end for evidence of existence and collectibility of the year-end balances.
  3. Trace cash disbursements of the month after year-end to accounts payable for evidence of any liabilities unrecorded at year-end.
  4. Vouch write-downs of PP&E after year-end for evidence that such valuation problems existed at the year-end date.
  5. Vouch sales of investment securities, write-downs, or write-offs in the months after the audit date for evidence of valuation at the year-end date.
  6. Vouch and trace sales transactions in the month after year-end for evidence of proper sales and cost of sales cutoff.
B. Auditing procedures for subsequent events.
  1. Read the latest available interim financial statements, compare them with the financial statements being reported on, and make any other comparisons considered appropriate in the circumstances.
  2. Inquire of officers and other executives having responsibility for financial and accounting matters about whether the interim statements have been prepared on the same basis as that used for the statements under examination.
  3. Inquire of and discuss with officers and other executives having responsibility for financial and accounting matters (limited where appropriate to major locations):
      a. Whether any substantial contingent liabilities or commitments existed at the date of the balance sheet being reported on or at the date of inquiry.
      b. Whether there was any significant change in the capital stock, long-term debt, or working capital to the date of inquiry.
      c. The current status of items in the financial statements being reported on that were accounted for on the basis of tentative, preliminary, or inconclusive data.
      d. Whether any unusual adjustments have been made during the period from the balance sheet date to the date of inquiry.
  4. Read the available minutes of meetings of stockholders, directors, and appropriate committees; inquire about matters dealt with at meetings for which minutes are not available.
  5. Request that the client send a letter to legal counsel inquiring about litigation, claims, and assessments, with the reply to be sent directly to the auditor.
  6. Obtain a letter of representation, dated as of the date of the auditor's report, from appropriate officials, generally the chief executive officer and chief financial officer, about whether any events occurred subsequent to the date of the financial statements that, in the officer's opinion, would require adjustment or disclosure in these statements.
  7. Make such additional inquiries or perform such procedures as considered necessary and appropriate to dispose of questions that arise in carrying out the foregoing procedures, inquiries, and discussions.

LEARNING OBJECTIVE

7. Specify the sequence of decisions and actions auditors must consider upon discovery (after the issuance of the report) (1) of information about facts that may have existed at the date of the auditors' report. Or (2) that one or more auditing procedures were omitted.

eration of the omission of audit procedures discovered after the report date. The most important thing to remember is that auditors have an active, procedural responsibility for discovering Type I and Type II subsequent events and for their proper disclosure, but they are not required to perform procedures after the audit report date. However, auditors have responsibilities once they become aware of the facts or omitted procedures.

Subsequent Discovery of Facts Existing at the Date of the Auditor's Report

Auditing standards actually deal with two subsequent things: (a) *events* that occur after the balance sheet date and (b) *knowledge* gained after the audit report date of events that occurred or conditions that existed on or before the audit report date. The subsequent event or subsequently acquired knowledge may arise (1) before the end of audit field work, (2) after the end of field work but before issuance of the report, or (3) after the audit report is issued. Exhibit 12–9 shows a time continuum of these combinations with a key to the auditing standards sections that deal with them.

Auditors are under no obligation to continue performing any auditing procedures past the report date (except when engaged on an SEC registration statement). However, when they happen to learn of facts that are important, they have the obligation to (1) determine whether the information is reliable and (2) determine whether the facts existed at the date of the report. When both of these conditions are affirmed and the auditors believe persons are relying on the report, steps should be taken to withdraw the

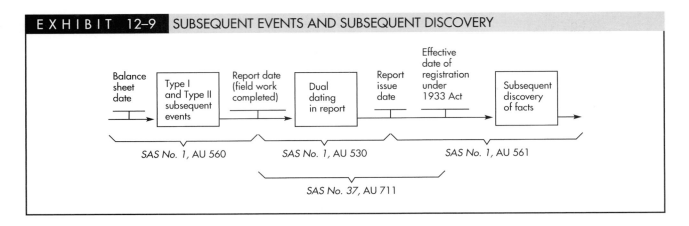

EXHIBIT 12-9   SUBSEQUENT EVENTS AND SUBSEQUENT DISCOVERY

AUDITING INSIGHT

NOTIFICATION OF AUDIT REPORT WITHDRAWAL

Kendall Square Research Corporation restated its 1992 financial results with substantial downward revisions after their auditors withdrew support for the accuracy of the figures. Kendall shares plummeted $3.75 (33%) to $7.50.

Kendall apparently booked 1992 sales of supercomputers to customers who did not have the ability to make payment. The problems involved early revenue recognition issues. More than half of the company's reported sales were not legitimate. The 1992 sales of $20.5 million were restated to $16.3 million, and the reported loss of $12.7 million was restated to a $17.2 million loss.

The company's auditors "withdrew its report" on Kendall's 1992 financial statements—meaning investors should no longer rely on the figures previously reported.

Source: *The Wall Street Journal.*

---

first report, issue a new report, and inform persons currently relying on the financial statements. These measures are facilitated by cooperation on the part of the client. However, the auditors' duty to notify the public that an earlier report should not be relied on is not relieved by client objections.[5]

The sequence of decisions is explained in Exhibit 12–10. Basically, the decisions relate to the importance and impact of the information, the cooperation of the client in taking necessary action, and the actions to be taken. Sometimes, auditors "withdraw" an audit report, as illustrated in the box below.

Consideration of Omitted Procedures after the Report Date

Although auditors have no responsibility to continue to review their work after the audit report has been issued, the report and working papers may be subjected to post issuance review by an outside peer review or the firm's internal inspection program.[6] A **peer review** is a quality assurance review by another auditing firm of an audit firm's quality control policies and procedures and the compliance thereof. Firms belonging to the

---

[5] The discussion here is cast in terms of subsequent discovery of facts while the auditor remains engaged by the client. However, the responsibilities to determine whether the subsequent information is reliable and whether the facts existed at the date of the already-issued report remain in force even when the auditor has resigned from the engagement or has been fired by the client (AU 9561).

[6] See *Statement on Auditing Standards No. 25,* "The Relationship of Generally Accepted Auditing Standards to Quality Control Standards" (AU 161), and related Quality Control Standards regarding the quality control function of monitoring.

EXHIBIT 12–10   SUBSEQUENT DISCOVERY OF FACTS EXISTING AT THE DATE OF THE AUDITOR'S REPORT

```
                          ┌─────────┐
                          │  START  │
                          └────┬────┘
                               │
                    ┌──────────┴──────────┐
                    │ Auditor becomes     │
                    │ aware of facts that │
                    │ may have existed    │
                    │ at the report date  │
                    │ which may affect    │
                    │ the audit report.   │
                    └──────────┬──────────┘
                               │
                      ┌────────┴────────┐
                      │ Consult         │
                      │ legal counsel.  │
                      └────────┬────────┘
                               │
                         ◇ Did
                     reliable facts        No        ┌──────┐
                     exist at report  ─────────────► │ STOP │
                         date? ◇                      └──────┘
                               │ Yes
                         ◇ Would
                       facts have           No        ┌──────┐
                      affected audit  ─────────────► │ STOP │
                         report? ◇                    └──────┘
                               │ Yes
                         ◇ Are
                        persons             No        ┌──────┐
                     currently relying ────────────► │ STOP │
                      on the audit                    └──────┘
                         report? ◇
                               │ Yes
                    ┌──────────┴──────────┐
                    │ Advise client to    │
                    │ make appropriate    │
                    │ discolosures of     │
                    │ facts and their     │
                    │ impact.             │
                    └──────────┬──────────┘
                               │
                         ◇ Did                         ┌──────────────────┐
                        client make        No          │ Notify each      │
                       appropriate   ─────────────────►│ member of board  │
                       disclosure? ◇                    │ of directors,    │
                               │                        │ consult legal    │
                               │ Yes                    │ counsel as to    │
                          ┌────┴────┐                   │ course of action,│
                          │  STOP   │                   │ and notify       │
                          └─────────┘                   │ persons relying. │
                                                        └──────────────────┘
```

Source: *The CPA Journal*, March 1984, p.38. Copyright ©1984 by the New York Society of Certified Public Accountants.

AICPA Division for Firms are required to have a peer review every three years. Such post issuance review may reveal that a situation exists in which an audit was not performed in accordance with generally accepted auditing standards.

Statement on Auditing Standards No. 46 (AU 390), "Consideration of Omitted Procedures after the Report Date," provides guidance for such situations. The sequence of decisions is presented in Exhibit 12–11. Because of legal implications of some of the actions

EXHIBIT 12–11   CONSIDERATION OF OMITTED PROCEDURES AFTER THE REPORT DATE

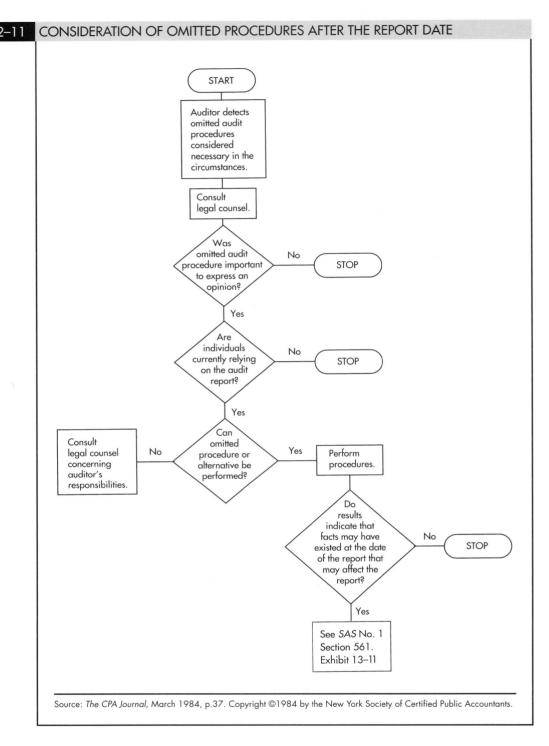

proposed, consultation with the firm's attorney is advised. The relevance of the omitted procedure (and the evidence the auditors failed to obtain) should be measured against the auditors' present ability to support the previously expressed opinion. It may be that, after a review of the working papers and discussions with audit staff personnel, other procedures may be shown to have produced the evidence needed. In such circumstances, the omitted procedure is not considered to impair the report.

However, if the other procedures did not produce sufficient, competent evidence, and, therefore, the previously expressed opinion cannot be supported, further action is necessary. As with subsequent discovery of facts, the next step is to determine whether the auditors' report is still being relied on. If reliance is still possible, the omitted procedure (or alternative procedures) should be undertaken promptly to provide a basis for the audit opinion. If such work reveals facts that existed at the date of the original report, then the actions related to subsequent discovery of facts (Exhibit 12–10) must be taken.

R E V I E W
CHECKPOINTS

12.21 What is the difference between a "subsequent event" and a "subsequent discovery of fact existing at the report date?" Describe the auditors' responsibility for each.

12.22 If, subsequent to issuance of a report, the audit partner discovers information that existed at the report date and materially affects the financial statements, what actions should the partner take if the client consents to disclose the information? What action should be taken if the client (including the board of directors) refuses to make disclosure?

12.23 What are the steps an auditor should take if, after the report has been issued, someone discovers that an important audit procedure was omitted?

SUMMARY

This chapter covers several aspects of completing an audit. As the work draws to a close, several income and expense accounts may remain to be audited. Analytical comparisons of their balances with prior years and current expectations accomplishes this auditing in most cases. Large and significant revenues and expenses usually have already been audited in connection with the audit of other accounts in the cycles. At this late stage in the audit, it is always a good idea to "step back" and review large and unusual revenue and gain transactions recorded near the end of the year. These often have been the vehicles for income statement manipulation. Some examples are given in the chapter.

Two of the most important topics for the audit completion work involve the client's written representation letter and the lawyer's letter. These submissions to the auditors are virtually required for an unqualified audit report. Without them, the audit scope is considered limited. Several requirements for the client representation letter are specified in the chapter. A special insert describes particular problems interpreting lawyers' letters. Information from lawyers is especially important for getting evidence about litigation contingencies and their disclosure according to *SFAS 5*. Some descriptive research on *SFAS 5* disclosure experience is briefed to emphasize the difficulties faced by managers and auditors.

The chapter contains explanations of proposed adjusting journal entries, working paper review, and the management letter. All that remains is the audit report itself.

"Subsequent events" topics end the chapter with explanations of: (1)procedural responsibility for events following the balance sheet date; (2)the dual-dating alternative for reporting on events that occur between the end of field work and the delivery of the report; (3)auditors' discovery, after a report has been delivered, of facts that existed at the balance sheet date; and (4)auditors' finding, after a report has been delivered, that one or more audit procedures they thought were performed were not actually performed. These topics close the text coverage of audit field work. Now you are ready to practice auditing.

MULTIPLE-CHOICE QUESTIONS FOR PRACTICE AND REVIEW

12.24 When auditing the year-end balance of interest-bearing notes payable, the auditors are most likely to audit at the same time the company's

a. Interest income.

b. Interest expense.

c. Amortization of goodwill.

d. Royalty revenue.

12.25 The main purpose of a written management representation letter is to

a. Shift responsibility for financial statements from the management to the auditor.

b. Provide a substitute source of evidence for detail procedures auditors would otherwise perform.

c. Provide management a place to make assertions about the quantity and valuation of the physical inventory.

d. Impress upon management its ultimate responsibility for the financial statements and disclosures.

12.26 Which one of these procedures or sources is not used to obtain evidence about contingencies?

a. Scan expense accounts for credit entries.

b. Obtain a representation letter from the client's attorney.

c. Read the minutes of the board of directors' meetings.

d. Examine terms of sale in sales contracts.

12.27 A Type I subsequent event involves subsequent information about a condition that existed at the balance sheet date. Subsequent knowledge of which of the following would cause the company to adjust its December 31 financial statements?

a. Sale of an issue of new stock for $500,000 on January 30.

b. Settlement of a damage lawsuit for a customer's injury sustained February 15 for $10,000.

c. Settlement of litigation in February for $100,000 that had been estimated at $12,000 in the December 31 financial statements.

d. Storm damage of $1 million to the company's buildings on March 1.

12.28 A. Griffin audited the financial statements of Dodger Magnificat Corporation for the year ended December 31, 2001. She completed the audit field work on January 30, and later learned of a stock split voted by the board of directors on February 5. The financial statements were changed to reflect the split, and she now needs to dual-date the audit report before sending it to the company. Which of the following is the proper form?

a. December 31, 2001, except as to Note X which is dated January 30, 2002.

b. January 30, 2002, except as to note X that is dated February 5, 2002.

c. December 31, 2001, except as to Note X which is dated February 5, 2002.

d. February 5, 2002, except for completion of field work for which the date is January 30, 2002.

12.29 In connection with a company's filing a registration statement under the 1933 Securities Act, auditors have a responsibility to perform procedures to find subsequent events until

a. The year-end balance sheet date.

b. The audit report date.

c. The date the registration statement and audit report are delivered to the U.S. Securities and Exchange Commission.

d. The "effective date" of the registration statement, when the securities can be offered for sale.

12.30 The auditing standards regarding "subsequent discovery of facts that existed at the balance sheet date" refers to knowledge obtained after

a. The date the audit report was delivered to the client.

b. The audit report date.

c. The company's year-end balance sheet date.

d. The date interim audit work was complete.

12.31 Which two of the following is not required by U.S. auditing standards?

a. Management representation letter.

b. Lawyer's letter.

c. Management letter.

d. Engagement letter.

12.32 Which of these persons generally does not participate in writing the management letter (client advisory comments)?

a. Client's outside attorneys.

b. Client's accounting and production managers.

c. Audit firm's audit team on the engagement.

d. Audit firm's consulting and tax experts.

12.33 Hall accepted an engagement to audit the year 1 financial statements of XYZ Company. XYZ completed the preparation of the year 1 financial statements on February 13, year 2, and Hall began the fieldwork on February 17, year 2. Hall completed the fieldwork on March 24, year 2, and completed the report on

March 28, year 2. The client's representation letter normally would be dated
a. February 13, year 2
b. February 17, year 2.
c. March 24, year 2.
d. March 28, year 2.

(AICPA adapted)

12.34 At which point in an ordinary sales transaction of a wholesaling business is a lack of specific authorization of least concern to the auditor in the conduct of sales?
a. Granting of credit.
b. Shipment of goods.
c. Determination of discounts.
d. Selling of goods for cash.

(AICPA adapted)

12.35 Which of the following controls most likely would be effective in offsetting the tendency of sales personnel to maximize sales volume at the expense of high bad debt write-offs?
a. Employees responsible for authorizing sales and bad debt write-offs are denied access to cash.
b. Shipping documents and sales invoices are matched by an employee who does not have authority to write off bad debts.
c. Employees involved in the credit-granting function are separated from the sales function.
d. Subsidiary accounts receivable records are reconciled to the control account by an employee independent of the authorization of credit.

(AICPA adapted)

12.36 Which of the following internal control activities most likely would assure that all billed sales are correctly posted to the accounts receivable ledger?
a. Daily sales summaries are compared to daily postings to the accounts receivable ledger.
b. Each sales invoice is supported by a prenumbered shipping document.
c. The accounts receivable ledger is reconciled daily to the control account in the general ledger.
d. Each shipment on credit is supported by a prenumbered sales invoice.

(AICPA adapted)

12.37 Which of the following controls most likely would help ensure that all credit sales transactions of an entity are recorded?

a. The billing department supervisor sends copies of approved sales orders to the credit department for comparison to authorized credit limits and current customer account balances.
b. The accounting department supervisor independently reconciles the accounts receivable subsidiary ledger to the accounts receivable control account monthly.
c. The accounting department supervisor controls the mailing of monthly statements to customers and investigates any differences reported by customers.
d. The billing department supervisor matches prenumbered shipping documents with entries in the sales journal.

(AICPA adapted)

12.38 A client has a large and active investment portfolio that is kept in a bank safe-deposit box. If the auditor is unable to count the securities at the balance sheet date, the auditor most likely will
a. Request the bank to confirm to the auditor the contents of the safe-deposit box at the balance sheet date.
b. Examine supporting evidence for transactions occurring during the year.
c. Count the securities at a subsequent date and confirm with the bank whether securities were added or removed since the balance sheet date.
d. Request the client to have the bank seal the safe-deposit box until the auditor can count the securities at a subsequent date.

(AICPA adapted)

12.39 A charge in the subsequent period to a notes receivable account from the cash disbursements journal should alert the auditor to the possibility that a
a. Contingent asset has come into existence in the subsequent period.
b. Contingent liability has come into existence in the subsequent period.
c. Provision for contingencies is required.
d. Contingent liability has become a real liability and has been settled.

(AICPA adapted)

12.40 Which of the following procedures should an auditor ordinarily perform regarding subsequent events?
a. Compare the latest available interim financial statements with the financial statements being audited.

b. Send second requests to the client's customers who failed to respond to initial accounts receivable confirmation requests.

c. Communicate material weaknesses in internal control to the client's audit committee.

d. Review the cutoff bank statements for several months after the year-end.

(AICPA adapted)

12.41 Which of the following procedures would an auditor most likely perform to obtain evidence about the occurrence of subsequent events?

a. Recomputing a sample of large-dollar transactions occurring after year-end for arithmetic accuracy.

b. Investigating changes in shareholders' equity occurring after year-end.

c. Inquiring of the entity's legal counsel concerning litigation, claims, and assessments arising after year-end.

d. Confirming bank accounts established after year-end.

(AICPA adapted)

12.42 The primary reason an auditor requests letters of inquiry be sent to a client's attorneys is to provide the auditor with

a. The probable outcome of asserted claims and pending or threatened litigation.

b. Corroboration of the information furnished by management about litigation, claims, and assessments.

c. The attorney's opinions of the client's historical experiences in recent similar litigation.

d. A description and evaluation of litigation, claims, and assessments that existed at the balance sheet date.

(AICPA adapted)

12.43 The scope of an audit is not restricted when an attorney's response to an auditor as a result of a client's letter of audit inquiry limits the response to

a. Matters to which the attorney has given substantive attention in the form of legal representation.

b. An evaluation of the likelihood of an unfavorable outcome of the matters disclosed by the entity.

c. The attorney's opinion of the entity's historical experience in recent similar litigation.

d. The probable outcome of asserted claims and pending or threatened litigation.

(AICPA adapted)

Exercises and Problems

12.44   Management Representation Letter. Hart, an assistant accountant with the firm of Better & Best, CPAs, is auditing the financial statements of Tech Consolidated Industries, Inc. The firm's audit program calls for the preparation of a written client (management) representation letter.

Required:

a. In an audit of financial statements, in what circumstances is the auditor required to obtain a management representation letter?

b. What are the purposes of obtaining the letter?

c. To whom should the representation letter be addressed and as of what date should it be dated?

d. Who should sign the letter and what would be the effect of their refusal to sign the letter?

e. In what respects may an auditor's other responsibilities be relieved by obtaining a management representation letter?

(AICPA adapted)

12.45   Management Representation Letter Omissions. During the audit of the annual financial statements of Amis Manufacturing, Inc., the company's president, Vance Molar, and Wayne Dweebins, the engagement partner, reviewed matters that were supposed to be included in a written representation letter. Upon receipt of the following representation letter, Dweebins contacted Molar to state that it was incomplete.

To John & Wayne, CPAs:

In connection with your examination of the balance sheet of Amis Manufacturing, Inc., as of December 31, 2001, and the related statements of income, retained earnings, and cash flows for the year then ended, for the purpose of expressing an opinion on whether the financial statements present fairly the financial position, results of operations, and cash flows of Amis Manufacturing, Inc., in conformity with generally accepted accounting principles, we confirm, to the best of our knowledge and belief, the following representations made to you during your audit. There were no:

- Plans or intentions that may materially affect the carrying value or classification of assets or liabilities.

- Communications from regulatory agencies concerning noncompliance with, or deficiencies in, financial reporting practices.

- Agreements to repurchase assets previously sold.

- Violations or possible violations of laws or regulations whose effects should be considered for disclosure in the financial statements or as a basis for recording a loss contingency.

- Unasserted claims or assessments that our lawyer has advised are probable of assertion that must be disclosed in accordance with *Statement of Financial Accounting Standards No. 5.*

- Capital stock purchase options or agreements or capital stock reserved for options, warrants, conversions, or other requirements.

- Compensating balance or other arrangements involving restrictions on cash balances.

Vance Molar, President

Amis Manufacturing, Inc.

March 14, 2002.

Required:

Identify the other matters that Molar's representation letter should specifically confirm.

(AICPA adapted)

12.46   Client Request for Lawyer's Letter.
Cole & Cole, CPAs are auditing the financial statements of Consolidated Industries Co. for the year ended December 31, 2001. On May 6, 2002, C.R. Brown, Consolidated's Chief Financial Officer, gave Cole a draft of an inquiry letter for Cole's review before mailing it to J.J. Young, Consolidated's outside counsel. This letter is intended to elicit the lawyer's responses to corroborate information furnished to Cole by management concerning pending and threatened litigation, claims, and assessments, and unasserted claims and assessments.

Required:

Describe the omissions, ambiguities, and inappropriate statements and terminology in Brown's letter below. Remember, this is Brown's letter requesting a response to the auditors, but it must request responses in the manner most useful to the auditors. (*Hint:* Look for 10 or more items.)

(AICPA adapted)

* * * CLIENT'S LAWYER
LETTER REQUEST * *

May 6, 2002
J.J. Young, Attorney at Law
123 Main Street, Anytown, USA

Dear J.J. Young:

In connection with an audit of our financial statements at December 31, 2001, and for the year then ended, management of the Company has prepared, and furnished to our auditors, Cole & Cole, CPAs, a description and evaluation of certain contingencies, including those set forth below involving matters with respect to which you have been engaged and to which you have devoted substantive attention on behalf of the Company in the form of legal consultation or representation. Your response should include matters that existed at December 31, 2001. Because of the confidentiality of all these matters, your response may be limited.

In November 2001, an action was brought against the Company by an outside salesman alleging breach of contract for sales commissions and asking an accounting with respect to claims for fees and commissions. The causes of action claim damages of $3,000,000, but the Company believes it has meritorious defenses to the claims. The possible exposure of the Company to a successful judgment on behalf of the plaintiff is slight.

In July 1994, an action was brought against the Company by Industrial Manufacturing Company (Industrial) alleging patent infringement and seeking damages of $20,000,000. The action in U.S. District Court resulted in a decision on October 16, 2001, holding that the Company infringed seven Industrial patents and awarded damages of $14,000,000. The Company vigorously denies these allegations and has filed an appeal with the U.S. Court of Appeals. The appeal process is expected to take approximately two years, but there is some chance that Industrial may ultimately prevail.

Please furnish to our auditors such explanation, if any, that you consider necessary to supplement this information, including an explanation of those matters as to which your views may differ from those stated, and an identification of the omission of any pending or threatened litigation, claims, and assessments or a statement that the list of such matters is complete. Your response may be quoted or referred to in the financial statements without further correspondence with you.

You also consulted on various other matters considered to be pending or threatened litigation. However, you may not comment on these matters because publicizing them may alert potential plaintiffs to the strengths of their cases. In addition, various other matters probable of assertion that have some chance of an unfavorable outcome, as of December 31, 2001, are presently considered unasserted claims and assessments.

Respectfully,
C.R. Brown
Chief Financial Officer

12.47 Subsequent Events and Contingent Liabilities. Crankwell, Inc., is preparing its annual financial statements and annual report to stockholders. Management wants to be sure that all of the necessary and proper disclosures are incorporated into the financial statements and the annual report. Two classes of items that have an important bearing on the financial statements are subsequent events and contingent liabilities. The financial statements could be materially inaccurate or misleading if proper disclosure of these items is not made.

Required:

a. With respect to subsequent events:

(1) Define what is meant by a "subsequent event."

(2) Identify the two types of subsequent events and explain the appropriate financial statement presentation of each type.

(3) What are the procedures that should be performed to ascertain the occurrence of subsequent events?

b. With respect to contingent liabilities:

(1) Identify the essential elements of a contingent liability.

(2) Explain how a contingent liability should be disclosed in the financial statements.

c. Explain how a subsequent event may relate to a contingent liability. Give an example to support your answer.

(CMA adapted)

12.48 Subsequent Events Procedures. You are in the process of "winding up" the field work on Top Stove Corporation, a company engaged in the manufacture and sale of kerosene space heating stoves. To date there has been every indication that the financial statements of the client present fairly the position of the company at December 31 and the results of its operations for the year then ended. Top Stove had total assets at December 31 of $4 million and a net profit for the year (after deducting federal and state income taxes) of $285,000. The principal records of the company are a general ledger, cash receipts record, voucher register, sales register, check register, and general journal. Financial statements are prepared monthly. Your field work will be completed on February 20, and you plan to deliver the report to the client by March 12.

Required:

a. Write a brief statement about the purpose and period to be covered in a review of subsequent events.

b. Outline the program you would follow to determine what transactions involving material amounts, if any, have occurred since the balance sheet date.

(AICPA adapted)

12.49 Subsequent Events—Cases. In connection with your examination of the financial statements of Olars Manufacturing Corporation for the year ended December 31, your post-balance sheet audit procedures disclosed the following items:

1. January 3: The state government approved a plan for the construction of an express highway. The plan will result in the appropriation of a portion of the land area owned by Olars Manufacturing Corporation. Construction will begin late next year. No estimate of the condemnation award is available.

2. January 4: The funds for a $25,000 loan to the corporation made by Mr. Olars on July 15 were obtained by him with a loan on his personal life insurance policy. The loan was recorded in the account Loan Payable to Officers. Mr. Olars's source of the funds was not disclosed in the company records. The corporation pays the premiums on the life insurance policy, and Mrs. Olars, wife of the president, is the owner and beneficiary of the policy.

3. January 7: The mineral content of a shipment of ore en route on December 31 was determined to be 72 percent. The shipment was recorded at year-end at an estimated content of 50 percent by a debit to Raw Material Inventory and a credit to Accounts Payable in the amount of $20,600. The final liability to the vendor is based on the actual mineral content of the shipment.

4. January 15: A series of personal disagreements have arisen between Mr. Olars, the president, and Mr. Tweedy, his brother-in-law, the treasurer. Mr. Tweedy resigned, effective immediately, under an agreement whereby the corporation would purchase his 10 percent stock ownership at book value as of December 31. Payment is to be made in two equal amounts in cash on April 1 and October 1. In December, the treasurer had obtained a divorce from Mr. Olars's sister.

5. January 31: As a result of reduced sales, production was curtailed in mid-January and

some workers were laid off. On February 5, all the remaining workers went on strike. To date the strike is unsettled.

Required:

Assume that the above items came to your attention prior to completion of your audit work on February 15. For each of the above items:

a. Give the audit procedures, if any, which would have brought the item to your attention. Indicate other sources of information that may have revealed the item.

b. Discuss the disclosure that you would recommend for the item, listing all details that should be disclosed. Indicate those items or details, if any, which should not be disclosed. Give your reasons for recommending or not recommending disclosure of the items or details.

(AICPA adapted)

12.50   Subsequent Discovery of Fact.   On June 1, Albert Faultless of A.J. Faultless & Co., CPAs, noticed some disturbing information about his client, Hopkirk Company. A story in the local paper mentioned the indictment of Tony Baker, whom A.J. knew as the assistant controller at Hopkirk. The charge was mail fraud. A.J. made discreet inquiries with the controller at Hopkirk's headquarters and learned that Baker had been speculating in foreign currency futures. In fact, part of Baker's work at Hopkirk involved managing the company's foreign currency. Unfortunately, Baker had violated company policy, lost a small amount of money, then decided to speculate some more, lost some more, and eventually lost $7 million in company funds.

The mail fraud was involved in his attempt to cover his activity until he recovered the original losses. Most of the events were in process on March 1, when A.J. had signed and dated the unqualified report on Hopkirk's financial statements for the year ended on the previous December 31.

A.J. determined that the information probably would affect the decisions of external users and advised Hopkirk's chief executive to make the disclosure. She flatly refused to make any disclosure, arguing that the information was immaterial. On June 17, A.J. provided the subsequent information in question to a news reporter, and it was printed in *The Wall Street Journal* along with a statement that the financial statements and accompanying audit report could not be relied on.

Required:

Evaluate the actions of Faultless & Co., CPAs, with respect to the subsequent information discovered. What other action might Faultless & Co. have taken? What are the possible legal effects of the firm's actions, if any?

12.51   Omitted Audit Procedures.   The following are independent situations that have occurred in your audit firm, Arthur Hurdman (AH):*

1. During the internal inspection review by the regional office of AH, one of your clients, Wildcat Oil Suppliers, was selected for review. The reviewers questioned the thoroughness of inventory obsolescence procedures, especially in light of the depressed state of the oil exploration industry at the time. They felt that specific procedures, which they considered appropriate, were not performed by your audit team.

2. Top Stove, one of your clients, installed a microcomputer in July of 2001 to process part of the accounting transactions. You completed the audit of Top Stove's December 31, 2001 statements on February 15, 2002. During the April 2002 review work on Top Stove's first-quarter financial information, you discovered that during the audit of the 2001 statements only the manual records were investigated in the search for unrecorded liabilities.

Required:

a. Without regard to the specific situation given, answer the following questions:

(1) What are the proper steps auditors should take if it is discovered, after the report date, that an auditing procedure was omitted?

(2) How are auditors' decisions affected if, after review of the work papers, they determine that other audit procedures produced the necessary sufficient, competent evidence?

(3) If in subsequently applying the omitted procedure, the auditors become aware of material new information that should have been disclosed in the financial statements, how should they proceed?

b. Describe the proper action to take in each situation above, given the additional information provided below:

Case 1: You made a thorough consideration of the scope of the audit of Wildcat Oil Suppliers, and you made a detailed review of the working papers. You have concluded that compensating procedures were conducted sufficient to support the valuation of inventory.

Case 2: Your subsequent investigation of the microcomputer records of Top Stove revealed that material liabilities were not recorded as of December 31.

---

*Situation derived from examples given in Thomas R. Weirich and Elizabeth J. Ringelberg, "Omitted Audit Procedures," *CPA Journal.*

12.52   Second Partner Review and Dating. You have been assigned to perform a review of a correspondent CPA firm's audit of Oxford Millwork Company for the calendar year ending December 31. In the audited financial statements of Oxford Millwork Company, you find the following representations:

Common stock, $10 par value,
100,000 shares outstanding,
400,000 shares authorized
(Note 1) $1,000,000

Note 1: Subsequent event (dated January 20). The board of directors approved a three-for-one stock dividend effective January 20. At the effective date, the par value of outstanding common stock is $3 million.

You have reviewed the correspondent CPA firm's audit report and found the opinion dated "January 15, 2002, except as to Note 1 which is dated January 20, 2002."

Required:

a. What is the purpose of a second partner review?

b. What is the purpose of dual dating?

c. What recommendations would you make to the CPA firm concerning presentation of the subsequent event?

DISCUSSION CASES

12.53   Lawyer's Letter Responses. Omega Corporation is involved in a lawsuit brought by a competitor for patent infringement. The competitor is asking $14 million actual damages for lost profits and unspecified punitive damages. The lawsuit has been in progress for 15 months, and Omega has worked closely with its outside counsel preparing its defense. Omega recently requested its outside attorneys with the firm of Wolfe & Goodwin to provide information to the auditors.

The managing partner of Wolfe & Goodwin asked four different lawyers who have worked on the case to prepare a concise response to the auditors. They returned these:

1. The action involves unique characteristics wherein authoritative legal precedents bearing directly on the plaintiff's claims do not seem to exist. We believe the plaintiff will have serious problems establishing the Omega's liability; nevertheless, if the plaintiff is successful, the damage award may be substantial.

2. In our opinion, Omega will be able to defend this action successfully, and, if not, the possible liability to Omega in this proceeding is nominal in amount.

3. We believe the plaintiff's case against Omega is without merit.

4. In our opinion, Omega will be able to assert meritorious defenses and has a reasonable chance of sustaining an adequate defense, with a possible outcome of settling the case for less than the damages claimed.

Required:

a. Interpret each of the four responses separately. Decide whether each is (1) adequate to conclude the likelihood of an adverse outcome is "remote," requiring no disclosure in financial statements, or (2) too vague to serve as adequate information for a decision, requiring more information from the lawyers or from management.

b. What kind of response do you think the auditors would get if they asked the plaintiff's counsel about the likely outcome of the lawsuit? Discuss.

12.54   Accounting for a Contingency—Lawyer's Letter Information. Central City was involved in litigation brought by MALDEF (Mexican-American Legal Defense Fund) over the creation of single-member voting districts for city council positions. The auditor was working on the financial statements for the year ended December 31, 2001, and had almost completed the field work by February 12, 2002.

The court had heard final arguments on February 1 and rendered its judgment on February 10. The ruling was in favor of MALDEF and required the creation of certain single-member voting districts. While this ruling itself did not impose a monetary loss on Central City, the court also ruled that MALDEF would be awarded a judgment of court costs and attorney fees to be paid by Central City.

Local newspaper reports stated that MALDEF would seek a $250,000 recovery from the city. The auditor obtained a lawyer's representation letter dated February 15 that stated the following:

In my opinion, the court will award some amount for MALDEF's attorney fees. In regard to your inquiry about an amount or range of possible loss, I estimate that such an award could be anywhere from $30,000 to $175,000.

Required:

a. What weight should be given to the newspaper report of the $250,000 amount MALDEF might ask? What weight should be given to the attorney's estimate?

b. How should this subsequent event be reflected in the 2001 financial statements of Central City? As an accounting adjustment of the amounts presented (Type I)? As a disclosure in the 2001 statements with accounting for the amounts in the 2002 financial statements (Type II)?

12.55 Deciding Whether to Waive Proposed Adjusting Journal Entries. This case invites discussion of the issue of *waiving* proposed adjusting journal entries. Auditors know individually material proposed adjustments when they see them. However, when two or more proposed adjustments have offsetting effects, the decision of whether to require all of them is not simple. The difficulty is compounded when client managers resist accepting some or all of the adjustments the auditors think should be entered in the accounts and financial statements. Auditors get stuck between the opposing force of professional standards and the dogma that the financial statements are management's responsibility. The primary issue is the process of considering these pressures while analyzing the effects of proposed adjustments in the aggregate as well as individually.

Four cases are presented. The proposed adjustments either increase or decrease four elements of the income statement. For all the cases, the company's unaudited net income is $490,000. Assume that the auditors are firmly convinced that the overall materiality for the income is $50,000 (this much unaudited misstatement can remain in the reported audited income and the financial statements will not be considered materially misleading). Assume also that this $50,000 materiality

determination arises from the auditors' firm conviction that the reported income can be misstated by 10 percent and yet not be considered materially misleading.

The requirement for this discussion case is somewhat oversimplified because it asks you to make decisions using only one criterion—the effect of your decisions on the company's reported income. This limitation ignores other effects such as the financial ratios that would be different when adjustments are or are not waived. Nevertheless, the income effect criterion is a starting point for the "waive or not-waive" decisions.

Required:

a. For each case (1,2,3,4) taken alone, decide whether either of the *material* proposed adjustments (B = increase or decrease in cost of goods sold, and D = increase in other expenses) can be waived.

b. While you may have already considered the *immaterial* proposed adjustments (A = increase or decrease in sales revenue, and C = increase or decrease in depreciation expense), decide whether any *combination* of the proposed adjustments (A,B,C,D) can be waived.

(*Hint:* For each case, set up a columnar worksheet with rows labeled for each of the proposed adjustments (A,B,C,D) and columns for various combinations of waive and not-waive choices. Calculate the income after adjustment(s), then calculate the amount and percentage of unadjusted income, using the now-adjusted income as a base for the percentage. Suggestion: Start with the case of waiving one material adjustment and not-waiving any of the others.)

Proposed Adjustments	Increase (Decrease) Income Before Taxes			
	Case 1	Case 2	Case 3	Case 4
A. Sales revenue	$ (13,000)	$ 13,000	$ 13,000	$(13,000)
B. Cost of goods sold	$ (91,000)	$ (91,000)	$ 91,000	$ 91,000
C. Depreciation expense	$ (40,000)	$ 40,000	$ 40,000	$(40,000)
D. Other expenses	$ (81,000)	$ (81,000)	$(81,000)	$(81,000)
Effect on income	$(225,000)	$(119,000)	$ 63,000	$(43,000)
% effect on income	−46%	−24%	+13%	−9%

Appendix 12A   Substantive Audit Programs

APPENDIX 12A–1   AUDIT PROGRAM FOR REVENUES

1. Obtain analyses of sales, cost of goods sold, and gross profit by product line, department, division, or location.
   a. Trace amounts to the general ledger.
   b. Compare the analyses to prior years, inquire for explanations of significant variations, and investigate them.
   c. Determine one or more standard markup percentages and calculate expected gross profits. Inquire for explanations of significant variations compared to actual amounts in the accounts. Investigate the explanations.
2. Coordinate procedures for audit of revenue with evidence obtained in other audit programs:

Revenues	Other Audit Programs
Sales and sales returns	Accounts receivable; Sales control; Cash receipts control
Lease revenue	PP&E; Accounts receivable
Long-term sales contracts	Accounts receivable; Inventory
Dividends and interest	Accounts receivable; Investments
Rental revenue	Accounts receivable; Investments
Royalties, license fees	Accounts receivable; Investments
Franchise revenue	Accounts receivable; Intangibles
Gain/loss on asset sales	PP&E; Investments; Accounts receivable

3. Scan the revenue accounts for large and unusual items and for debit entries. Vouch items to supporting documentation.
4. Obtain written management representation about terms of sales, rights of return, consignments, and extraordinary, unusual, or infrequent transactions.

APPENDIX 12A–2   AUDIT PROGRAM FOR EXPENSES

1. Obtain schedules of expense accounts comparing the current year with one or more prior years.
   a. Trace amounts to the general ledger.
   b. Compare the current expenses to prior years, inquire for explanations of significant variations, and investigate them.
   c. Be alert to notice significant variations that could indicate failure to defer or accrue expenses. Inquire for explanations of significant variations. Investigate the explanations.
2. Compare the current expenses to the company budget, if any. Inquire and investigate explanations for significant variances.
3. Coordinate procedures for audit of expenses with evidence obtained in other audit programs:

Expenses	Other Audit Programs
Purchases, Cost of goods sold	Acquisition control; Cash disbursement control; Inventory
Inventory valuation losses	Inventory
Warranty and guarantee expense	Cash disbursement control; Inventory; Accounts payable
Royalty and license expense	Cash disbursement control; Inventory; PP&E; Accounts payable
Marketing, product R&D expense	Cash disbursement control; Investments; Intangibles
Investment value losses	Investments
Rental property expenses	Cash disbursement control; Investments
Amortization of intangibles	Intangibles
Bad debt expense	Accounts receivable
Depreciation expense	PP&E
Property taxes, insurance	Prepaid expenses; PP&E; Accounts payable
Lease and rental expense	Cash disbursements control; PP&E
Repairs and maintenance	PP&E; Accounts payable
Interest expense	Long-term liabilities
Pension and retirement benefits	Liabilities; Payroll
Salaries, compensation	Payroll
Sales commissions	Payroll

4. Prepare analyses of sensitive expense accounts, such as legal and professional fees, travel and entertainment, repairs and maintenance, taxes, and others unique to the company. Vouch significant items therein to supporting invoices, contracts, reimbursement forms, tax notices, and the like for proper support and documentation.
5. Scan the expense accounts for large and unusual items and for credit entries. Vouch items to supporting documentation.
6. Obtain written management representations about long-term purchase commitments, contingencies, and extraordinary, unusual, or infrequent transactions.

Module A

Assurance and Other Public Accounting Services

Professional Standards References

Compendium Section	Document Reference	Topic
		Attestation Engagements
AT 101	SSAE 10	*Attest Engagements*
AT 201	SSAE 10	*Agreed Upon Procedures Engagements*
AT 301	SSAE 10	*Financial Forecasts and Projections*
AT 401	SSAE 10	*Reporting on ProForma Financial Information*
AT 501	SSAE 10	*Reporting on an Entity's Internal Control over Financial Reporting*
AT 601	SSAE 10	*Compliance Attestation*
AT 701	SSAE 10	*Management's Discussion and Analysis*
		Review and Compilation of Unaudited Financial Statements
AR 100	SSARS 1	*Compilation and Review of Financial Statements*
AR 100	SSARS 8	*Amendment to Statement on Standards for Accounting and Review Services No. 1, Compilation and Review of Financial Statements.*
AR 200	SSARS 2	*Reporting on Comparative Financial Statements*
AR 300	SSARS 3	*Compilation Reports on Financial Statements Included in Certain Prescribed Forms*
AR 400	SSARS 4	*Communications Between Predecessor and Successor Accountants*
AR 600	SSARS 6	*Reporting on Personal Financial Statements Included in Written Personal Financial Plans*
AU 722	SAS 71	*Interim Financial Information*
		Special Reports
AU 324	SAS 70	*Reports on the Processing of Transactions by Service Organizations*
AU 324	SAS 88	*Service Organizations and Reporting on Consistency*
AU 544	SAS 1	*Lack of Conformity with GAAP—Regulated Companies*
AU 623	SAS 62	*Special Reports*
AU 9623		*Interpretation: Reporting on Supplementary Current-Value Information*
AU 625	SAS 50	*Reports on the Application of Accounting Principles*

Learning Objectives

CPAs enjoy a high level of trust and a high reputation for objectivity in the eyes of business people and the public in general. The reputation has its foundation in the long history of CPAs serving as intermediaries who lend credibility to information. CPAs in public practice offer numerous assurance and attestation services on information other than audited financial statements. These services grow from consumer demand for association by an objective expert. Naturally, business, government, and the public want the credibility that goes along with CPAs' association. This chapter covers several areas of public accounting practice related to accountants' association with information other than complete, audited historical financial statements. CPAs often perform work and give reports in these areas of practice:

- Assurance engagements.
- Attestation engagements.
- Unaudited Financial Statements: Review and Compilation.
- Special Reports.

This module is broken into four parts. The first part defines and further explores assurance services. The second part of the module is devoted to (non-audit) attestation engagements. The third part deals with reviews and compilations of unaudited financial statements. The module concludes with other topics, including special and restricted use reports. Your learning objectives related to these topics are to be able to:

1. Define, explain and give examples of assurance services.

2. Define, explain and give examples of attestation engagements.

3. Write appropriate reports for review and compilation of unaudited financial statements, given specific fact circumstances.

4. Define, explain, and give examples of "special reports."

ASSURANCE SERVICES

LEARNING OBJECTIVE
1. Define, explain and give examples of assurance services.

As traditional audit service revenues plateaued over the past decade, the American Institute of Certified Public Accountants (AICPA) identified alternative (i.e., non-audit) **assurance service** engagements for CPAs. The material in this section is adapted and condensed from the report of the AICPA Special Committee on Assurance Services, which can be found in far greater detail on the AICPA web site (www.aicpa.org).

Why Develop New Assurance Service Products?

Leaders in the auditing profession say that CPAs' nationwide business revenues from their accounting and auditing practices was about $7 billion annually from 1990–1997. Since consulting and tax practice revenues increased during this period, CPAs saw the accounting and auditing segment of practice become a smaller proportion of the total business. Like other businesses, CPA firms are interested in growth–increases in revenue and profits, staff size, and service variety. Now CPAs see opportunities to expand the accounting and auditing segment of their practices by offering assurance services that are natural extensions of the well-regarded audit and attest services.

The AICPA Special Committee on Assurance Services (SCAS) identified eight megatrends that can affect CPAs' business. Each one presents opportunities for assurance service products, and each one also harbors business risks. Consider the bright side—the opportunities.

- *Information technology* promises vast data bases and easy user access. CPAs can offer services related to database content and design.

- *Competition* among CPA and non-CPA service providers sometimes may favor CPAs because of their reputations for expertise in internal control and measurement methods.

- *Corporate structure changes* that encourage outsourcing and temporary ventures create (a) needs for corporate partners' assurance of other partners' accountability, and (b) services for which the CPAs can be the outsource providers (e.g., internal audit, pension plan administration).

- *Accountability*—the interlocking responsibilities among business and not-for-profit organizations, management, government (Congress, legislatures, regulators), and societal interest groups (e.g., environmentalists, educators, capital market participants)—will arise from various arrangements for grants, ventures, alliances, and similar arrangements wherein participants will seek assurance about other participants' performance and accomplishments.

- *Investment capital* is already becoming institutionalized in large mutual funds, and many more individuals are managing their assets in defined contribution retirement plans. Services related to evaluating mutual fund managers' performance, giving investment advice to corporations and individuals, and managing pension plans fall within many CPAs' financial expertise.

- *Aging of the U.S. population* overlaps with other trends and suggests needs for CPAs' advisory expertise in connection with retirement benefit plans, Social Security financing, school financing, medical services, and the efficiency, effectiveness, and accomplishment of all these issues that affect an older population.

- *Globalization* of trade and cross-border activities can involve CPAs in creating common standards for accounting reports and other forms of information flow (e.g., data bases) as well as services in foreign regulations and taxation.

- *Education*, in light of the problems in the United States, may move away from public schools and thus create needs in private schools (competing for students) for educational outcome measurement, teacher evaluation, institutional certification, and job simplification and automation—all of which CPAs may learn to provide.

Definition

The SCAS presented a concise definition for assurance services:

> Assurance services are independent professional services that improve the quality of information, or its context, for decision makers.

Although this definition is so broad that a large class of activities can fit within it, the definition contains some boundaries. While attestation and audit services are highly structured and intended to be useful for large groups of decision makers (e.g., investors, lenders), assurance services are more customized and intended to be useful to smaller, targeted groups of decision makers. In this sense, assurance services bear resemblance to consulting services. The major elements, and boundaries, of the definition are these:

- *Independence.* CPAs want to preserve their attestation and audit reputations and competitive advantages by preserving integrity and objectivity when performing assurance services.

- *Professional Services.* Virtually all work performed by CPAs (accounting, auditing, data management, taxation, management, marketing, finance) is defined as "professional services" as long as it involves some element of judgment based in education and experience.

- *Improving the Quality of Information.* The emphasis is on "information"—CPAs' traditional stock in trade. CPAs can enhance quality by assuring users about the reliability and relevance of information, and these two features are closely related to the familiar credibility-lending products of attestation and audit services.

- *Improving the Context of Information.* "Context" is relevance in a different light. For assurance services, improving the context of information refers to improving its usefulness when targeted to particular decision makers in the surroundings of particular decision problems. CPAs will need time and experience in various assurance services to develop more fully this concept of context.
- *For Decision Makers.* They are the "consumers" for assurance services, and they personify the consumer focus of new and different professional work. They may or may not be the "client" that pays the fee, and they may or may not be one of the parties to an assertion or other information. The decision makers are the beneficiaries of the assurance services. Depending upon the assignment, decision makers may be a very small, targeted group (e.g., managers of a data base) or a large targeted group (e.g., potential investors interested in a mutual fund manager's performance).

While there are seemingly unlimited assurance opportunities, assurance service engagements proposed to date include CPA WebTrust, CPA SysTrust, CPA ElderCare Services, and CPA Performance View. These four assurance services are described in the following sections.

CPA WebTrust

E-commerce, the sale of goods and services via the Internet, is exploding. According to the estimates of Forrester Research, Inc. (www.forrester.com), a market research company that specializes in information technology and e-commerce, buyers and sellers will exchange well over $100 billion by the end of year 2001. Although the growth of e-commerce is impressive, security issues, both real and perceived, have prevented many potential customers from purchasing over the Internet. Many customers and business owners still distrust the Internet as a medium of conducting business. Indeed, a general lack of security is the number one reason given by non-buyers for not purchasing products online, as well as the number one concern among current online buyers. Specifically, prospective buyers have expressed concerns about ascertaining whether an e-commerce company is authentic (*authentication*), whether the company is trustworthy (*transaction integrity*, i.e., whether the company will do what it says it will do), and whether the company will safeguard their personal information (*information security*). Customers also like to be reassured that they can get their products, services, and warranty service on warranty items on a timely basis. Despite growing familiarity with doing business on the Internet, these security issues are not likely to diminish.

AICPA/CICA WebTrust originated in the AICPA's special committee on assurance services to respond to the customers' concerns about Internet security. AICPA/CICA WebTrust, as its name suggests, is a CPA-provided (or CA-provided (Canadian Chartered Accountant)) assurance service to determine if the website meets certain criteria and WebTrust principles. If the site meets the criteria, the AICPA/CICA WebTrust seal is prominently displayed on the company's website. Generally speaking, the WebTrust practitioner must address the following principles:

- *Privacy.* The client website must disclose and adhere to its privacy practices. The principle is designed to protect a consumer's personal information.
- *Security.* The client website must disclose and adhere to specific security practices that limit access to the website and its data. For example, the WebTrust practitioner must determine if the execution of encryption, digital IDs, and socket securing are consistent with the site's stated practices.
- *Business Practices / Transaction Integrity.* Business practice disclosure requires the site to reveal how it will handle on-line transactions, such as noting how long it takes to fulfill an order. Transaction integrity requires transaction identification, validation,

EXHIBIT A–1	EXAMPLE WEBTRUST REPORT

Independent Auditor's Report

To the Management of E*TRADE Group Inc.

We have examined the assertion by the management of E*TRADE Group, Inc. (E*TRADE) regarding the disclosure of its electronic commerce business and information privacy practices on its Web site and the effectiveness of its controls over transaction integrity and information protection for electronic commerce (insofar as it relates to investing in stocks, bonds and mutual funds at www.etrade.com) based on the AICPA/CICA WebTrust Criteria, during the period September 5, 1998 through August 4, 2000.

These electronic commerce disclosures and controls are the responsibility of E*TRADE management. Our responsibility is to express an opinion on management's assertion based on our examination.

Our examination was conducted in accordance with attestation standards established by the American Institute of Certified Public Accountants and, accordingly, included (1) obtaining an understanding of E*TRADE's electronic commerce business and information privacy practices and its controls over the processing of e-commerce transactions and the protection of related private customer information, (2) selectively testing transactions executed in accordance with disclosed business practices, (3) testing and evaluating the operating effectiveness of the controls, and (4) performing such other procedures as we considered necessary in the circumstances. We believe that our examination provides a reasonable basis for our opinion.

Because of inherent limitations in controls, error or fraud may occur and not be detected. Furthermore, the projection of any conclusions, based on our findings, to future periods is subject to the risk that (1) changes made to the system or controls, (2) changes in processing requirements, or (3) changes required because of the passage of time, or (4) degree of compliance with the policies or procedures may alter the validity of such conclusions.

In our opinion during the period September 5, 1998 through August 4, 2000 E*TRADE, in all material respects—

> Disclosed its business and information privacy practices for e-commerce transactions and executed transactions in accordance with its disclosed practices,

> Maintained effective controls to provide reasonable assurance that customers' orders placed using e-commerce were completed and billed as agreed,

> Maintained effective controls to provide reasonable assurance that private customer information obtained as a result of e-commerce was protected from uses not related to E*TRADE's business based on the AICPA/CICA Web Trust Criteria.

The CPA WebTrust Seal of assurance on E*TRADE's Web site for e-commerce constitutes a symbolic representation of the contents of this report and it is not intended, nor should it be construed, to update this report or provide any additional assurance.

This report does not include any representation as to the quality of E*TRADE's goods or services nor their suitability for any customer's intended purpose.

Deloitte & Touche
Certified Public Accountants
San Jose, California
August 5, 2000

---

accuracy, completeness, and timeliness, with disclosure of terms and billing elements (for instance, sending the customer a confirming email after the order is placed).

- *Availability*. The availability principle requires the website to disclose its hours of operation and to establish effective controls to provide reasonable assurance that the website is available during those hours. For example, the website may need to provide alternative arrangements should the website's service be interrupted for a prolonged period of time.
- *Non-Repudiation*. Non-repudiation refers to validating the authenticity of the website, usually through a digital certificate.

WebTrust practitioners can issue opinions and corresponding seals on individual principles or a combination of the principles. An actual WebTrust report is reproduced in Exhibit A–1.

While initially conceived as a B2C (business to customer) service, the WebTrust program has been expanded to include transactions in the business-to-business market (B2B).

CPA SysTrust

For significant customer-supplier business relationships (B2B (business-to-business)), company computers are often directly linked to each other through Internet-based *virtual private networks* (VPNs). Purchase orders for goods are made via computer and payment is made automatically through electronic funds transfer (EFT) directly to the vendor's bank. The benefit of such a relationship is an increase in the timeliness of the process—transactions that once took several weeks to complete manually (from customer purchase order generation to final payment being deposited to the supplier's bank account) now take only as long as it takes to ship and receive the goods. However, just as Internet customers are wary of purchasing online, business customers are often cautious about entering into such relationships with other businesses. Another joint product of the American Institute of Certified Public Accountants (AICPA) and the Canadian Institute of Chartered Accountants (CICA), SysTrust is a professional service to provide assurance on the reliability of *systems*. While CPA WebTrust focuses on external (Internet) systems, CPA SysTrust instead focuses on internal systems as a means of increasing the comfort of management, customers, and business partners with the client systems. The SysTrust service is based upon four principles:

- *Availability*. The availability principle requires that the system be available for operation and use during agreed upon times and have effective controls to provide reasonable assurance that the system is available during those hours.
- *Security*. The security principle requires that the client system disclose and adhere to specific security practices that limit unauthorized access to the system and its data.
- *Integrity*. The integrity principle requires that system processing be complete, accurate, timely, and authorized.
- *Maintainability*. The system can be updated when required in a manner that continues to provide for system availability, security, and integrity.

The SysTrust practitioner must evaluate, test, and report on the entity's system reliability against each of the principles. With the AICPA's vision of continuous, *real-time assurance* of informational databases and systems just around the corner, the development of this service is considered to be "a fundamental building block" in the process.

CPA ElderCare Services

Given improved healthcare and the aging of the "baby boomer" generation, the U.S. population's average age is growing at a significant rate. The SCAS proposes taking advantage of this demographic by advocating ElderCare Services as a new assurance growth area. The SCAS defines CPA ElderCare as

> . . . a service designed to provide assurance to family members that care goals are achieved for elderly family members no longer able to be totally independent. The service will rely on the expertise of other professionals, with the CPA serving as the coordinator and assurer of quality of services based on criteria and goals set by the client. The purpose of the service is to provide assurance in a professional, independent, and objective manner to third parties (children, family members or other concerned parties) that the needs of the elderly person to whom they are attached are being met.

In other words, CPAs can ensure that people's parents or grandparents are adequately being taken care of by third-party providers. Some of the procedures that the CPA can perform toward this end would include:

- Providing financial services, such as paying bills, estate planning, and supervising investments.
- Ensuring that third-party caregivers are meeting agreed-upon performance criteria.
- Handling unusual or unexpected situations, such as home maintenance and repair or medical emergencies.

The SCAS believes that "CPAs can provide a valuable service to family members by providing assurance that care goals are achieved for elderly family members no longer able to be totally independent."

CPA Performance View

Performance measurement has been defined as "the identification of critical success factors that lead to measures that can be tracked over time to assess progress made in achieving specific targets linked to an entity's vision." Developed jointly by the American Institute of Certified Public Accountants (AICPA) and the Canadian Institute of Chartered Accountants (CICA), CPA Performance View identifies and measures key activities that are critical to the company. Rather than relying strictly on historical financial information, CPA Performance View uses non-financial information, such as customer satisfaction, employee training and satisfaction, and product quality, to identify "critical decision points that can lead to organizational change, better performance, and increased revenue for an organization."

REVIEW CHECKPOINTS

A.1. In what ways are assurance services similar in general to attestation services (including audits of financial statements)?

A.2 What are the five major elements of the broad definition of assurance services?

A.3 Why do you think the AICPA is so interested in developing CPAs' expertise in assurance services?

A.4 Briefly describe the four assurance engagements proposed by the SCAS in terms of services provided and intended customers.

ATTESTATION ENGAGEMENTS

LEARNING OBJECTIVE
2. Define, explain and give examples of attestation engagements

Attestation Engagements

While the majority of this textbook is devoted to auditing financial statements, the audit service is really a subset of a larger group of services referred to as *attestation services*. An **attestation engagement** is defined as:

> An engagement in which a practitioner is engaged to issue or does issue a report on subject matter or an assertion about the subject matter, that is the responsibility of another party.

In an audit, the *subject matter* is the client's financial statements. In the wider perspective of attestation engagements, subject matter is typically *financial statement-related* (but need not be). For example, attestation engagements include:

- Agreed-upon procedures engagements (AT 201).
- Financial forecasts and projections (AT 301).
- Reporting on pro forma financial information (AT 401).
- Reporting on an entity's internal control over financial reporting (AT 501).
- Compliance attestation (AT 601).
- Management's discussion and analysis (AT 701).

We briefly discuss these types of attestation engagements in the following sections.

Applying Agreed-Upon Procedures (AT 201)

Clients sometimes engage auditors to perform a specified set of procedures—the *agreed-upon procedures*—to examine a particular element, account, or item in financial statements or to perform a special engagement. Such work should not be considered an audit because the specified set of agreed-upon procedures is usually not sufficient to be an audit in accordance with generally accepted auditing standards. Agreed-upon procedures engagements have a *limited scope*, so the second and third GAAS field work standards (control risk assessment and overall sufficient competent evidence for an opinion) and the GAAS reporting standards do not apply.

According to attestation standards for agreed-upon procedures engagements, auditors must reach a clear understanding with the client and the report users about the users' needs and the procedures to be performed. Reports are supposed to be restricted to the specified users who participate in, and take responsibility for, defining the work on the engagement.

A report on an agreed-upon procedures engagement is quite different from the standard audit report. In particular, the report should identify the specified users and describe in detail the procedures the users decided were necessary; state that the work is not an audit or review that results in an overall opinion or assurance; describe each of the agreed-upon procedures and the specific audit findings related to each. No overall "opinion" or "negative assurance" is given as a conclusion to the report.

Financial Forecasts and Projections (AT 301) and Pro Forma Financial Information (AT 401)

Prospective financial information (PFI) is financial information representing the financial position, results of operations, and cash flows for some period of time *in the future*. For example, a **financial projection** is PFI based on the occurrence of one or more hypothetical events that change existing business structure (e.g., possible addition of a new distribution center—should the entity continue to distribute goods from only one distribution center?) Similarly, a **financial forecast** is PFI based on expected conditions and courses of action (e.g., no new distribution center). In contrast, **pro forma financial information** shows the effect of a proposed or consummated transaction on the historical financial statements "as if" that transaction had occurred by a specific date, usually *in the past*.

In many cases, the company is negotiating directly with a single user (*limited use*) who has requested prospective financial information for use in economic decisions. Any PFI can be used for limited purposes. In other instances, the company may be preparing financial statements that it intends to present to a large number of users (*general use*), none of whom it is negotiating with at the current time.

The financial information may contain amounts similar to historical financial statements (*single-point estimates*) or *ranges of amounts*. If ranges are used, care should be taken to indicate that the endpoints of this range do not represent "best" and "worst" case scenarios. In addition, the PFI should disclose the significant accounting policies and procedures used to generate the statements. If the basis in the PFI is different from that used in the historical financial statements, a reconciliation of the two bases must be shown. In addition, the client must disclose all significant assumptions used to prepare prospective financial statements, indicate that actual events or conditions may not be consistent with these assumptions, and, for financial projections, indicate the limited usefulness of the projection.

To perform an attestation engagement on either prospective information or pro forma information, the CPA must evaluate the preparation of the financial information, evaluate the support underlying the assumptions, and evaluate the presentation of the information. To accomplish these objectives, the CPA must (1) obtain knowledge about client's business, accounting principles, and factors affecting the events and transactions in question, (2) obtain an understanding of the process through which the information was developed (e.g., has all relevant information been considered in developing assumptions?), (3) evaluate the assumptions (and their underlying support) used to prepare the information, (4) identify key factors affecting the information, and (5) evaluate the preparation and presentation of the financial (e.g., consistency with AICPA guidelines).

Reporting on an Entity's Internal Control over Financial Reporting (AT 501)

Managements and boards of directors have been encouraged to make public reports on internal control, and auditors have been encouraged by the SEC to become associated with such reports. Many annual reports by public companies contain a "report from management" that includes assertions and commentary about internal control. The attestation standards govern accountants' reports on clients' internal control (*SSAE 10*, AT 501). These standards specify that accountants' public reports can be issued only when management issues a separate written report containing assertions about its internal control. In such a case, the accountant's report is an opinion on the fair presentation of management's assertions. (You can no doubt see the analogy to the independent auditor's audit opinion on management's assertions in financial statements.)

An internal control examination is an attestation engagement, which is much like an audit because it produces an opinion. These conditions must be met before an accountant can conduct an examination:

- Management accepts responsibility for the effectiveness of its internal control.
- Management's evaluation of control is based on reasonable criteria (e.g., the COSO Report, see Chapter 6).
- Management's evaluation of control can be supported by sufficient evidence.
- Management presents a written assertion about the effectiveness of its internal control

An internal control examination is similar to an audit. The work must be in accordance with the attestation standards, which bear many points of similarity to generally accepted auditing standards (refer to Chapter 2 for a direct comparison). An examination of management's assertion about the effectiveness of internal control involves (*SSAE 10*, AT 501):

- Planning the engagement.
- Obtaining an understanding of the internal control.
- Evaluating the design effectiveness of internal control activities.
- Testing and evaluating the operating effectiveness of internal control activities.
- Forming an opinion about the fair presentation of management's assertion regarding internal control effectiveness.

Audit procedures for testing and evaluating design and operating effectiveness are very similar to the procedures described in Chapter 6 and other chapters in this textbook. They include inquiries, document examination, observation, and reperformance (test of detail controls) performed on samples of transactions. The standard "unqualified" report is shown in Exhibit A–2.

Compliance Attestation (AT 601)

Often, management must report to a third party its compliance with contractual obligations. Clients may have restrictive covenants in loan agreements. Lenders may require a periodic report on whether the client has complied with such contractual agreements. Contractual agreements could include: dividend limitations, loan limitations, prescribed debt/equity ratios, and limitations on geographic operations. Governmental agencies must comply with applicable laws and regulations.

For a compliance attestation engagement, three conditions must first be met: (1) management accepts responsibility for compliance, (2) management's evaluation of compliance is capable of evaluation and measurement against reasonable criteria, and (3) sufficient evidence must be available to support management's evaluation. Management *may either* make an assertion that the entity is in compliance in a written report or as a written representation to the CPA. The CPA then *examines* or performs *agreed-upon procedures* that evaluate the management's written assertion about the entity's compliance against the reasonable criteria.

Attestation standards direct attestors to consider inherent risk, control risk, and detection risk in connection with compliance. These considerations are very similar to the

E X H I B I T   A–2   STANDARD INTERNAL CONTROL REPORT (*SSAE 10*, AT 501)

Report Title	Independent Accountant's Report
Introductory Paragraph	We have examined management's assertion concerning maintenance of effective internal control over financial reporting as of December 31, 200X, included in the accompanying management report.
Scope Paragraph	Our examination was made in accordance with standards established by the American Institute of Certified Public Accountants, and, accordingly, included obtaining an understanding of the internal control over financial reporting, testing and evaluating the design and operating effectiveness of the internal control, and such other procedures as we considered necessary in the circumstances. We believe that our examination provides a reasonable basis for our opinion.
Inherent Limitations Paragraph	Because of inherent limitations in any internal control, errors or frauds may occur and not be detected. Also, projections of any evaluation of the internal control over financial reporting to future periods are subject to the risk that the internal control may become inadequate because of changes in conditions, or that the degree of compliance with the policies or procedures may deteriorate.
Opinion Paragraph	In our opinion, management's assertion that the company maintained effective internal control over financial reporting as of December 31, 200X is fairly stated, in all material respects, based upon suitable control criteria [may cite the COSO report on Internal Control—Integrated Framework].
Signature	/s/ Accountant's Signature
Date	January 15, 200Y

risk elements in financial statement audits. However, consideration of materiality in compliance engagements may be difficult—sometimes monetary measures can be applied and sometimes they cannot. Nevertheless, risk and materiality are as important in compliance attestation as they are in financial statement audits.

Exercise of due care and professional skepticism about noncompliance are prerequisites for a compliance examination. Otherwise, the major steps are these:

- Understand the specific compliance requirements; assess planning materiality.
- Plan the engagement; assess inherent risk.
- Understand relevant controls over compliance; assess control risk with or without tests of controls; design tests of compliance with detection risk in mind.
- Obtain sufficient evidence of compliance with specific requirements, including a written letter of management representations. (This work is the substantive procedures in a compliance examination.)
- Consider subsequent events—subsequent information that bears on the management assertion and subsequent events of noncompliance after the assertion date.
- Form an opinion and write the report.

These standards call for work that is directly parallel to the work in financial statement audits, placing CPAs on familiar ground. The standard unqualified report (Exhibit A–3) is likewise very similar to the standard audit report. Attestors can write the unqualified report, or if findings dictate, prepare (1) a report modified to disclose a noncompliance event, (2) a qualified report stating material noncompliance, or (3) an adverse report stating that the entity is not in compliance.

Similar assurance may be given with regard to federal and state regulatory requirements. Examples include limitations on investments for mutual funds or state insurance department regulations about the nature of insurance company investments. Regulatory agencies may seek to have auditors sign assertions in prescribed report language that goes beyond acceptable professional reporting responsibilities and involve auditors in areas outside their function and responsibility. In such cases, auditors should insert additional

---

EXHIBIT A–3   STANDARD UNQUALIFIED COMPLIANCE ATTESTATION REPORT

Independent Accountant's Report

To the Agency

    We have examined the Agency's compliance with Department of Employment Regulation JR-52 during the year ended December 31, 200X. Management is responsible for the Agency's compliance with Regulation JR-52. Our responsibility is to express an opinion on the Agency's compliance based on our examination.

    Our examination was made in accordance with standards established by the American Institute of Certified Public Accountants and, accordingly, included examining, on a test basis, evidence about the Agency's compliance with Regulation JR-52 and performing such other procedures as we considered necessary in the circumstances. We believe that our examination provides a reasonable basis for our opinion. Our examination does not provide a legal determination on the Agency's compliance with specified requirements.

    In our opinion, the Agency complied, in all material respects, with Regulation JR-52 for the year ended December 31, 200X.

/s/ Name and signature
Report date

---

wording in the prescribed report language or write a completely revised report that reflects adequately their position and responsibility.

Management's Discussion and Analysis (AT 701)

Accountants can also examine or review the Management's Discussion and Analysis (MD&A) section usually accompanying the audited financial statements in corporate annual reports. Under existing audit standards (*SAS No. 8*, "Other Information in Documents Containing Audited Financial Statements"), auditors are required to read the MD&A section to ensure that the information accompanying the audited financial statements is consistent with the audited financial statements. The attestation engagement allows auditors to undertake engagements to additionally audit or review the MD&A section. The performance of the attestation engagement and subsequent reporting responsibilities are similar to other attestation engagements.

R E V I E W
CHECKPOINTS

A.5 What is attestation? Provide some examples of attestation engagements.

A.6 Identify several points on which a compliance attestation engagement and an audit of financial statements are similar.

UNAUDITED FINANCIAL STATEMENTS

LEARNING OBJECTIVE

3. Write appropriate reports for review and compilation of unaudited financial statements, given specific fact circumstances.

Many CPA firms perform bookkeeping, financial statement preparation, and financial statement review to help small businesses prepare financial communications. A subset of attestation engagements, these services are collectively referred to as *accounting and review services*. The Accounting and Review Services Committee has continuing responsibility to develop and issue pronouncements of standards concerning the services and reports an accountant may render in connection with unaudited financial statements. This committee issues *Statements on Standards for Accounting and Review Services (SSARS)*. SSARS apply to work on unaudited financial statements of nonpublic companies. Auditing standards (SAS), in comparison, apply to work on all audited financial statements (both public and nonpublic companies) and to work on unaudited financial statements of public companies. According to SSARS, a public company is one (1) whose securities trade in a public market—stock exchange, over-the-counter, and locally quoted markets, (2) which files with a regulatory agency in preparation for sale of securities in a public market, or (3) a subsidiary, joint venture, or other entity controlled by a company meeting either criterion (1) or (2). All other organizations are considered nonpublic.

Review Services

The *review services* explained in this section apply specifically to accountants' work on the *unaudited* financial statements of *nonpublic* companies. In a **review services engagement**, an accountant performs some procedures to achieve a level of assurance. This level is not the same that could be attained by performing an audit in accordance with GAAS. According to *SSARS 1* (AR 100), the objective of a review of financial statements is

> to achieve, through the performance of inquiry and analytical procedures, a reasonable basis for expressing limited assurance that there are no material modifications that should be made to the statements in order for them to be in conformity with generally accepted accounting principles or, if applicable, with another comprehensive basis of accounting.

Review work on unaudited financial statements consists primarily of inquiry and analytical procedures. The information gained thereby is similar to audit evidence, but the recommended limitation on procedures (listed below) does not suggest performance of typical auditing procedures of assessing control risk, conducting physical observation of tangible assets, sending confirmations, or examining documentary details of transactions.

- *Obtain* an understanding with management about the nature and limitations of a review engagement (engagement letter).
- *Obtain* knowledge of the client's business. Know the accounting principles of the client's industry. Understand the client's organization and operations.
- *Inquire* about the accounting system and bookkeeping procedures.
- *Perform analytical procedures* to identify relationships and individual items that appear to be unusual.
- *Inquire* about actions taken at meetings of stockholders, directors, and other important executive committees.
- *Read* (study) the financial statements for indications that they conform with generally accepted accounting principles.
- *Obtain reports* from other accountants who audit or review significant components, subsidiaries, or other investees.
- *Inquire* of officers and directors about:
    Conformity with generally accepted accounting principles.
    Consistent application of accounting principles.
    Changes in the client's business or accounting practices.
    Matters about which questions have arisen as a result of applying other procedures (listed above).
    Events subsequent to the date of the financial statements.
- *Perform any other procedures considered necessary* if the financial statements appear to be incorrect, incomplete, or otherwise unsatisfactory.
- *Prepare working papers* showing the matters covered by the inquiry and analytical procedures, especially the resolution of unusual problems and questions.
- *Obtain a written representation letter* from the owner, manager, or chief executive officer and from the chief financial officer.

Given the limited procedures performed (basically inquiry of management and analytic procedures) a review service does not provide a basis for expressing an *opinion* on financial statements. In a standard unqualified report for an audit engagement, the auditor provides **positive assurance** ("In our opinion, the accompanying financial statements present fairly, in all material respects, . . . in conformity with accounting principles generally accepted in the United States")—a forthright and factual statement of the CPA's opinion based on an audit (SAS 58, AU 508) that the financial statements are fairly presented. For engagements less than an audit, practitioners do not provide positive assurance. For example, a *negative assurance* conclusion typical in the review report on unaudited financial statements, reads like this: "Based on our review, *we are not aware of any material modifications* that should be made to the accompanying financial statements in order for them to be in conformity with accounting principles generally accepted in the United States" (*SSARS 1*, AR 100). This conclusion is called **negative assurance** because it uses the phrase "we are not aware" to give assurance about conformity with GAAP. While auditing standards prohibit the use of negative assurance in reports on audited financial statements (because it is considered too weak a conclusion for the audit effort (SAS 26, AU 504)), negative assurance is permitted in reviews of unaudited financial statements, in letters to underwriters, and in reviews of interim financial information.

Each page of the financial statements should be marked "See accountant's review report." The report on a complete review services engagement should include the following:

- Statement that a review service was performed in accordance with *Statements on Standards for Accounting and Review Services* issued by the AICPA.
- Statement that all information included in the financial statements is the representation of the management or owners of the business.
- Statement that a review consists primarily of inquiries of company personnel and analytical procedures applied to financial data.
- Statement that a review service is substantially less in scope than an audit, and an opinion on financial statements is not expressed. (This is a disclaimer of any audit opinion.)
- Statement that the accountant is not aware of any material modifications that should be made or, if aware, a disclosure of departure(s) from generally accepted accounting principles. (This is a negative assurance.)

An accountant who is not independent may not issue a review services report. An example of a review report is in Exhibit A–4.

Reviews of Interim Financial Information

Accounting principles do not require interim financial information as a basic and necessary element of financial statements conforming to GAAP. When interim information is presented, however, it should conform to the accounting principles in *APB Opinion No.*

EXHIBIT A–4   REVIEW REPORT

Board of Directors,
Children's Shoe House, Inc.:

We have reviewed the accompanying balance sheet of Children's Shoe House, Inc., as of January 31, 2002 and 2001, and the related statements of income, retained earnings and cash flows for the years then ended in accordance with Statements on Standards for Accounting and Review Services issued by the American Institute of Certified Public Accountants. All information included in these financial statements is the representation of the management of Children's Shoe House, Inc.

A review consists principally of inquiries of company personnel and analytical procedures applied to financial data. It is substantially less in scope than an audit in accordance with generally accepted auditing standards, the objective of which is the expression of an opinion regarding the financial statements taken as a whole. Accordingly, we do not express such an opinion.

Based on our review, we are not aware of any material modifications that should be made to the accompanying financial statements in order for them to be in conformity with generally accepted accounting principles.

Tosh & Company
February 25, 2002

28. The SEC, on the other hand, requires the presentation of interim information as supplementary information outside the basic financial statements. Thus, interim information is voluntary insofar as FASB is concerned but required insofar as the SEC is concerned. Likewise, auditing standards do not require auditors' reviews of interim information presented voluntarily by nonpublic companies, but the SEC requires reviews (but ordinarily without an explicit report) of interim information presented pursuant to its rules.

A *review* of interim financial information differs considerably from an audit. According to *SAS 71 (AU 722),* the objective of a review of interim financial information is to give the accountant a basis for reporting whether material modifications should be made for such information to conform to *APB 28.* In this respect the interim information review is very similar to a review of unaudited financial statements of a nonpublic company. The interim information review does not require a complete assessment of internal control risk each quarter nor the gathering of sufficient, competent evidential matter on which to base an opinion on interim financial information. The nature, timing, and extent of review procedures explained below presume that the reviewer has a knowledge base of the company from the audit of the most recent annual financial statements.

Review procedures consist mainly of inquiry and analytical procedures. *SAS 71 (AU 722)* suggests the following:

- *Inquire* about the internal control system:

    Obtain an understanding of the system.

    Determine whether there have been any significant changes in the system used to produce interim information.

- *Perform analytical procedures* to identify relationships and individual items that appear to be unusual.

- *Read the minutes* of stockholder, board of director, and board committee meetings to identify actions or events that may affect interim financial information.

- *Read* (study) the interim financial information and determine whether it conforms with generally accepted accounting principles.

- *Obtain reports* from other accountants who perform limited reviews of significant components, subsidiaries, or other investees.

- *Inquire* of officers and executives about:

    Conformity with generally accepted accounting principles.

    Consistent application of accounting principles.

    Changes in the client's business or accounting practices.

    Matters about which questions have arisen as a result of applying other procedures (listed above).

    Events subsequent to the date of the interim information.

- *Obtain written representations* from management about interim information matters.

Review procedures should be performed at or near the date of the interim information. Starting the engagement prior to the cutoff date will give auditors a chance to deal with problems and questions without undue deadline pressures.

The accountant needs to acquire a sufficient knowledge of the client's business, just as if the engagement were a regular audit. Knowledge of strengths and weaknesses in the internal control system and of problem accounting areas obtained during the most recent audit is very useful in judging the extent of review procedures. Basically, the extent of review procedures depends on the accountant's professional judgment about problem areas in the system of internal control, the severity of unique accounting principles problems, and the errors that have occurred in the past. With knowledge of these areas, the accountant can direct and fine-tune the review procedures in the interest of improving the quality of the interim information.

EXHIBIT A–5	REPORT ON INTERIM INFORMATION IN A COMPANY'S QUARTERLY REPORT

Independent Accountant's Report
The Board of Directors and Stockholders,
Fine Devices, Inc.:

We have reviewed the unaudited condensed balance sheets of Fine Devices, Inc., at April 28, 2002, and April 29, 2001, the related unaudited consolidated statements of income for the three- and six-month periods ended April 28, 2002, and April 29, 2001, and the unaudited consolidated statements of cash flows for the six-month periods ending April 28, 2002, and April 29, 2001. This financial information is the responsibility of the company's management.

We conducted our review in accordance with standards established by the American Institute of Certified Public Accountants. A review of interim financial information consists principally of applying analytical procedures to financial data and making inquiries of persons responsible for financial and accounting matters. It is substantially less in scope than an examination in accordance with generally accepted auditing standards, the objective of which is the expression of an opinion regarding the financial statements taken as a whole. Accordingly, we do not express such an opinion.

Based on our review, we are not aware of any material modifications that should be made to the accompanying financial information for it to be in conformity with generally accepted accounting principles.

Ernest & Somebody
Certified Public Accountants
May 16, 2002

An accountant may report on interim information presented separately from audited financial statements, provided that a review has been satisfactorily completed. The basic content of the report is (*SAS 71, AU 722*):

- A title that includes the word *independent.*
- Identification of the interim information.
- A statement that the information is the responsibility of management.
- A statement that a review was made in accordance with standards established by the AICPA.
- A description of the review procedures.
- A statement that a review is substantially less in scope than an audit in accordance with GAAS.
- A disclaimer of opinion on the interim information.
- Negative assurance about the need for any material modifications.
- Accountant's signature and date of the report.
- Each page should be marked "unaudited."

A report on reviewed interim information presented in a quarterly report (not within an annual report) is shown in Exhibit A–5.

When the interim information is presented in a note to audited annual financial statements filed with the SEC as required supplemental information and when it is presented voluntarily under GAAP and the client has requested a review, the auditors give the standard audit report without mentioning the reviewed interim information, unless there is a reason to take exception. Under this exception basis of reporting, interim information is mentioned in a modified standard audit report only in case the information is omitted (SEC registrants only), a review cannot be completed (SEC registrants only), it departs from *APB 28* principles, management indicates the auditor performed procedures without also saying the auditor expresses no opinion, or management fails to label interim information in the note to annual audited financial statements as "unaudited."

Auditors need to be careful about the publication of interim reports. They need to inform management that listing the CPA's name anywhere in the interim publication creates an "association of a CPA with financial statements." This identification may suggest to readers that the CPA offers assurance, even though no report is in the publication along with the interim information. Showing the CPA's name triggers the association, and the requirement of the fourth GAAS reporting standard is applicable—requiring a review report. Management can avoid the need to include the CPA's report by (1) simply omitting any mention of the CPA in the interim publication, or (2) inserting a sentence saying: "The financial information in this interim report was prepared by management without audit by independent public accountants (naming the CPA is optional) who do not express an opinion thereon."

Compilation Services

Compilation is a synonym for an older term—*write-up work*. Both terms refer to an accountant helping a client "write up" the financial information in the form of financial statements. A **compilation service** is accounting work in which an accountant performs few, if any, procedures, and it is substantially less than a review service. The objective of a compilation of financial statements, according to *SSARS 1* (AR 100) is:

> to present in the form of financial statements information that is the representation of the management or owners without undertaking to express any assurance about any need for material modifications or about conformity with generally accepted accounting principles or, if applicable, another comprehensive basis of accounting.

In a compilation service, an accountant should obtain an engagement letter, understand the client's business and applicable accounting standards, read (study) the financial statements looking for obvious clerical or accounting principle errors, and follow up on information that is incorrect, incomplete, or otherwise unsatisfactory. The accountant is not required to assess control risk or to perform any other evidence-gathering procedures (e.g., observation, confirmation, document examination, inquiry, analytical procedures).

In a compilation engagement, given the very limited procedures performed, the accountant explicitly states that *no opinion* and *no assurance* is expressed (basically issuing a *disclaimer of opinion*), thus taking no responsibility for a report on the fair presentation of financial statements in conformity with GAAP. The conclusion sentence in the compilation report on unaudited financial statements specifically states: "We have not audited or reviewed the accompanying financial statements and, accordingly, do not express an opinion or any other form of assurance on them" (SSARS 1, AR 100). An accountant who is not independent can issue the report, provided the lack of independence is disclosed in the report.

Each page of the financial statements should be marked "See accountant's compilation report." The report should contain the following (see Exhibit A–6):

- Statement that a compilation service has been performed in accordance with *Statements on Standards for Accounting and Review Services* issued by the AICPA.
- Statement that financial statement information is the representation of the management or owner(s) of the business.
- Statement that the financial statements have not been audited or reviewed and the accountant does not express an opinion or any other form of assurance on them.

Three kinds of reports on compiled financial statements can be given: First, the management or owners may not want to present all the footnote disclosures required by GAAP (believing such disclosures are not needed for their purposes). An accountant can issue a compilation report that notifies users of the omission and states that if they were included, they might influence users' conclusions about the business. Second, the management or owners may engage an accountant who is not independent. This accountant can issue a compilation report stating the lack of independence. Third, the management or owners can also choose to present GAAP financial statements complete with all the disclosures required by GAAP. Exhibit A–6 shows a compilation report modified for these first two matters. With the passage of SSAR No. 8 (2000), accountants can perform compilation engagements in which no compilation report is necessary. Instead of issuing

EXHIBIT A–6	COMPILATION REPORT MODIFIED FOR OMISSION OF GAAP DISCLOSURES AND ACCOUNTANT'S LACK OF INDEPENDENCE

President and Sole Stockholder,
Petro-Chem Producing Corporation:

We have compiled the accompanying balance sheets of Petro-Chem Producing Corporation as of August 31, 2002 and 2001, and the related statements of income, retained earnings, and cash flows for the years then ended, in accordance with Statements on Standards for Accounting and Review Services issued by the American Institute of Certified Public Accountants.

A compilation is limited to presenting in the form of financial statements information that is the representation of management. We have not audited or reviewed the accompanying financial statements and, accordingly, we do not express an opinion or any other form of assurance on them.

Management has elected to omit all the disclosures required by generally accepted accounting principles. If the omitted disclosures were included in the financial statements, they might influence users' conclusions about the company's financial position, results of operations, and cash flows. Accordingly, these financial statements are not designed for persons who are not informed about such matters.

We are not independent with respect to Petro-Chem Producing Corporation.

Tosh & Company
October 20, 2002

a compilation report, accountants have the option of documenting an understanding with client (through an engagement letter) regarding the services to be performed and the limitations on the use of those financial statements.

Other Review and Compilation Topics

Additional *SSARS* statements explain standards for review and compilation engagements and reports that differ from audit standards. These topics point out some of the different problems in dealing with unaudited financial statements.

Comparative Financial Statements

SSARS 2 (AR 200), "Reporting on Comparative Financial Statements," deals with reporting variations that turn out to be rather complex. The complexity arises from the several possible combinations of prior and current services. The sections below contribute some organization to the technical details found in *SSARS 2*.

Same or Higher Level of Service. These combinations are (in prior-year/current-year order): (1) compilation followed by compilation, (2) compilation followed by review, and (3) review followed by review. The essence of comparative reporting is to report on the current service and update the report on the statements of the prior period. Examples of report language are given in *SSARS 2* (AR 200). The higher level of service when the current-year work is an audit is governed by auditing standards, not by *SSARS*. (See *SAS 26*, AU 504.)

When the current-year service is being performed by a successor accountant, he or she cannot update the predecessor's report. In this case, the successor can request the predecessor to reissue the prior report and distribute it along with the current report (in which case the predecessor must decide whether to reissue, as guided by *SSARS 2*). Alternatively, the successor can simply write in the current report a paragraph describing the predecessor's report on the prior period. The paragraph (1) states that prior-period financials were compiled or reviewed by other accountants, (2) gives the date of the previous report, (3) describes the compilation disclaimer or review report negative assurance rendered last year, and (4) describes any modifications written in the prior-year report. (See AR 200 for examples.)

Lower Level of Service. These combinations are (in prior-year/current-year order): (1) review followed by compilation, (2) audit followed by compilation, and (3) audit followed by review. The essence of comparative reporting is to report on the current service and *reissue* (not *update*) the report on the statements of the prior period. The underlying theory calling for reissuance in such cases is that an accountant cannot update a previous report when currently performing a lesser level of work.

The alternative to reissuing and reprinting a prior report is to write into the current report a paragraph describing the report on the prior-year financial statements. The paragraph (1) states the prior-period financials were reviewed or audited by the same or other (predecessor) accountants, (2) gives the date of the previous report, (3) describes the type of service previously rendered (review or audit), (4) describes the review report negative assurance or the type of audit opinion previously rendered, (5) explains any modifications or opinion qualifications expressed last year, and (6) in the case of a prior-year audit, states that no auditing procedures were performed after the date of the previous audit report, and in the case of a prior-year review, states that no review procedures were subsequently performed. Example reports are given in *SSARS 2* (AR 200).

When the current-year service is being performed by a successor accountant, the predecessor can be asked to reissue the prior report (subject to decisions to do so, AR 200). When the predecessor's report is not presented, the descriptive paragraph about the report can be added to the current-year report.

Prescribed Forms

Industry trade associations, banks, government agencies, and regulatory agencies often use *prescribed forms* (standard preprinted documents) to specify the content and measurement of accounting information required for special purposes. Such forms may not request disclosures required by GAAP or may specify measurements that do not conform to GAAP.

When such forms are compiled (not when reviewed) by an accountant, the compilation report does not need to call attention to GAAP departures or GAAP disclosure deficiencies. The presumption is that the organization that prescribed the form knew what it was doing and does not need to be informed of the ways the form calls for GAAP departures. The reporting obligation is satisfied by adding the following paragraph (*SSARS 3*, AR 300) to the standard compilation disclaimer:

> The financial statements are presented in accordance with the requirements of (name of trade association, bank, agency, or other body), which differ from generally accepted accounting principles. Accordingly, these financial statements are not designed for those who are not informed about such differences.

However, departures from the information specified by a prescribed form should be treated in the report as the accountant otherwise would treat GAAP departures—by disclosing them in the body of the accountant's report. Likewise, GAAP departures that are not specified in the prescribed form should still be treated as GAAP departures.

Communications between Predecessors and Successors

In the case of audits, successor auditors are required to make certain inquiries of predecessor auditors when a new client is obtained (SAS 84, AU 315). However, in compilation and review work, successor accountants are not required to communicate with predecessor accountants.

Nevertheless, *SSARS 4* (AR 400) gives advice to accountants who decide to talk to the predecessor. The standard suggests that inquiries may be a good idea: if the successor does not know much about the new client, if the change in accountants occurred long after the end of the client's fiscal year (hinting at problems between the client and the predecessor), and if the client is one who changes accountants frequently. When inquiries are made, the successor must obtain the client's permission for the predecessor to disclose confidential information. Otherwise, *SSARS 4* gives advice about inquiries that will give the successor a chance to learn about problem areas. When the successor makes inquiries and the client gives the predecessor permission, the predecessor is required to respond.

Personal Financial Plans

Personal financial planning is a big source of business for CPA firms. Most personal financial plan documentation includes personal financial statements. Ordinarily, an accountant associated with such statements would need to give the standard compilation report (disclaimer), which seems rather awkward in a personal financial planning engagement when the client is the only one using the statements. SSARS 6 (AR 600) exempts such personal financial statements from the SSARS 1 reporting requirement. However, the following report must be given, with each page of the financial report marked "See accountant's report":

> The accompanying Statement of Financial Condition of Rooster Cogburn, as of December 31, 2001, was prepared solely to help you develop your personal financial plan. Accordingly, it may be incomplete or contain other departures from generally accepted accounting principles and should not be used to obtain credit or for any purposes other than developing your financial plan. We have not audited, reviewed, or compiled the statement.

A Note on GAAP Departures and Rule of Conduct 203

An accountants' report of known GAAP departures must be treated carefully in review and compilation reports. SSARS interpretations (AR 9100) carefully point out that the conclusion that "the financial statements are not in conformity with GAAP" is not appropriate in review and compilation reports because it is an adverse opinion that should be based only on audit evidence. Review and compilation engagements are not audits, and the adverse opinion sentence cannot be given. After all, both the review and compilation reports contain disclaimers of any audit-based opinion.

However, as in audit reports, the accountant can and should add an explanatory paragraph pointing out known departures from GAAP, including omitted disclosures. This paragraph is placed after the normal standard report that gives the disclaimer on compiled financial statements, but the standard disclaimer is still given. In the case of a review report, the knowledge of GAAP departures means that the accountant must take exception to the departure in the negative assurance sentence, like this: "Based on our review, with the exception of the matter described in the following paragraph, we are not aware of any material modifications that should be made. . . ."

Rule 203 of the AICPA Code of Conduct is explicitly worded to cover the negative assurance given in the standard review report. (The application of this rule in audits is explained in Chapter 3.) In review engagements, justifiable departures from official pronouncements are treated the same as they are in audits. The accountant adds a paragraph explaining the reason why adherence to an official pronouncement would cause financial statements to be misleading, and the departure necessary in the circumstances, then the negative assurance paragraph is written in its standard, unmodified wording (AR 9100).

However, the situation is different in a compilation engagement because the accountant is giving neither an opinion nor a negative assurance. When compiled financial statements contain a known departure from an official pronouncement, the compilation report with its unmodified disclaimer is presented as usual. Then, an explanatory paragraph is added, pointing out the departure and the financial effects, if known. If the accountant believes the GAAP departure causes the financial statements to be misleading, he or she can refuse to give the compilation report and resign from the engagement.

R E V I E W
CHECKPOINTS

A.7 In what area(s) of practice are the Accounting and Review Service Committee pronouncements applicable?

A.8 In what respects is a review of interim financial information similar to a review of the unaudited annual financial statements of a nonpublic company?

A.9 Is interim financial information required to be presented in order for annual financial statements to be in conformity with GAAP? In conformity with SEC filing requirements?

A.10 When interim information is presented in a note to annual financial statements, under what circumstances would an audit report on the annual financial statements be modified with respect to the interim financial information?

A.11 What is the difference between a review service engagement and a compilation service engagement regarding historical financial statements? Compare both of these to an audit engagement.

SPECIAL REPORTS

LEARNING OBJECTIVE

4. Define, explain, and give examples of "Special Reports."

Auditors may perform a variety of services *acting in the capacity of auditor* that require a report, other than the traditional audit report. Such services involve special reports issued in connection with:

- Engagements to report on specified elements, accounts, or items of a financial statement (SAS 62, AU 623).
- Engagements reporting on other comprehensive bases of accounting (OCBOA) (SAS 62).
- Engagements reporting on the application of accounting principles (SAS 50).
- Engagements reporting on service organizations (SAS 88).

Specified Elements, Accounts, or Items (*SAS 62*)

Special engagements with limited objectives enable auditors to provide needed services to clients. Auditors may be requested to render special reports on such things as rentals, royalties, profit participations, or a provision for income taxes. The first AICPA reporting standard does not apply because the specified element, account, or item does not purport to be a financial statement of financial position or results of operations. The second AICPA reporting standard (consistency) applies only if the element, account, or item is measured according to some provision of generally accepted accounting principles.

The auditor's report on element, accounts, or items is very similar to the standard auditor's report. A GAAS audit is performed, but instead of financial statements, specified elements, accounts, or items are audited. The auditor expresses an opinion on whether the account, element, or item is fairly stated in accordance with GAAP. Exhibit A–7

EXHIBIT A–7   REPORT ON A FINANCIAL ELEMENT (UNRESTRICTED SCOPE)

Independent Auditor's Report
To ABC Company Board of Directors:

We have audited the accompanying schedule of accounts receivable of ABC Company as of December 31, 2002. This schedule is the responsibility of the Company's management. Our responsibility is to express an opinion on this schedule based on our audit.

(Standard scope paragraph here,
referring to the accounts receivable schedule)

In our opinion, the schedule of accounts receivable referred to above presents fairly, in all material respects, the accounts receivable of ABC Company as of December 31, 2002, in conformity with generally accepted accounting principles.

/s/ Auditor signature

January 21, 2003

contains an illustrative report on a company's accounts receivable. If an adverse or disclaimer is issued for the financial statements taken as a whole, the auditor may not accept engagement.

Other Comprehensive Bases of Accounting (OCBOA)

For a long time, a small war has been waged over the "Big GAAP-Little GAAP" controversy. Many accountants have been dismayed by the complexity of generally accepted accounting principles and have openly questioned their relevance to small businesses with uncomplicated operations. They believe that business managers and users of the financial statements care little about accounting for such things as pension obligations, capitalized leases, deferred taxes, and similar complicated topics. They characterize such topics as "standards overload" that may be necessary for "big business" but are largely superfluous for "small business."

For a while, the "little GAAP" advocates lobbied for formal GAAP exemptions for small businesses. They actually won some battles. For example, earnings per share is a FASB requirement only for public companies. However, resistance arose in the counterargument that there was a danger of creating "second-class GAAP" for small business while reserving "real GAAP" for big companies. Bankers and other users of financial statements were not nearly so eager to have "little GAAP" financial statements as some accountants wanted them to be. Anyway, many small businesses aspire to be large businesses, and their managers may not want to be stigmatized by "little GAAP" beginnings.

The little GAAP fallback position has been the accounting known as "other comprehensive bases of accounting" (OCBOA). The Private Companies Practice Section (PCPS) of the AICPA Division for Firms has promoted OCBOA to its members as a way of accomplishing "little GAAP." The position is that OCBOA financial statements can be less expensive to produce and easier to interpret than full GAAP statements. Surveys report that 50 percent of OCBOA financial statements are on the "tax basis of accounting," and 49 percent are on the "cash basis." However, PCPS also notes that OCBOA is only appropriate when it meets user needs.

OCBOA Statements

Companies that are not subject to SEC regulations and filing requirements can choose to present financial information in accordance with a comprehensive basis of accounting other than GAAP. A comprehensive basis in this context refers to a coherent accounting treatment in which substantially all the important financial measurements are governed by criteria other than GAAP. Some examples include: (1) insurance company statements conforming to state regulatory agency accounting rules, (2) tax basis accounting, (3) cash basis accounting, and (4) some other methods, such as constant-dollar, price-level-adjusted financial statements, and current-value financial statements.

SAS 62 warns that OCBOA financial statements should not use the titles normally associated with GAAP statements, such as "balance sheet," "statement of financial position," "statement of operations," "income statement," and "statement of cash flows." Even the titles are said to suggest GAAP financial statements. Instead, OCBOA statements should use titles like the ones shown in the box on the next page.

OCBOA statements can be audited, reviewed, or compiled like any other financial statements. All the general and field work auditing standards and the standards for review and compilation apply, just like they apply for GAAP financial statements. The reporting standards regarding consistency, adequate disclosure, and report responsibility (fourth reporting standard) also apply to OCBOA statements. Disclosure requirements are not reduced by OCBOA. However, the first reporting standard, which requires the audit report statement on whether the financial statements are presented in conformity with GAAP, is handled differently.

SOME APPROPRIATE OCBOA FINANCIAL STATEMENT TITLES

Statement of Assets and Liabilities—Regulatory Basis.
Statement of Assets and Liabilities—Cash Basis.
Statement of Admitted Assets, Liabilities, and Surplus—Statutory Basis Required by the Insurance Department of the State of (name).
Statement of Assets, Liabilities, and Capital—Income Tax Basis.
Statement of Income—Regulatory Basis.
Statement of Revenue and Expenses—Income Tax Basis.
Statement of Revenue Collected and Expenses Paid—Cash Basis.
Statement of Changes in Partners' Capital Accounts—Income Tax Basis

---

EXHIBIT   A–8   **SPECIAL REPORT ON NON-GAAP COMPREHENSIVE BASIS**

Independent Auditors' Report
To Natalia National Bank Association (Trustee)
and the Unit Holders of the Mega Offshore Trust:

We have audited the accompanying statements of assets, liabilities, and trust corpus—cash basis, of the Mega Offshore Trust as of December 31, 2001 and 2000, and the related statements of changes in trust corpus—cash basis, for each of the three years in the period ended December 31, 2001. These financial statements are the responsibility of the Company's management. Our responsibility is to express an opinion on these financial statements based on our audits.

(Standard scope paragraph here)

As described in Note 2, these financial statements were prepared on the cash receipts and disbursements basis of accounting, which is a comprehensive basis of accounting other than generally accepted accounting principles.

In our opinion, the financial statements referred to above present fairly, in all material respects, the assets, liabilities, and trust corpus arising from cash transactions of the Mega Offshore Trust as of December 31, 2001 and 2000, and the related changes in trust corpus arising from cash transactions for each of the three years in the period ended December 31, 2001, on the basis of accounting described in Note 2.

/s/ Auditor signature
March 18, 2002

Note 2 describes a cash basis of accounting and concludes:

This basis for reporting royalty income is considered to be the most meaningful because distributions to the Unit holders for a month are based on net cash receipts for such month. However, it will differ from the basis used for financial statements prepared in accordance with generally accepted accounting principles because, under such accounting principles, royalty income for a month would be based on net proceeds for such month without regard to when calculated or received.

When a non-GAAP accounting method is used, the first reporting standard is satisfied by a sentence in the report that presents the OCBOA basis of accounting, and the opinion sentence refers to the OCBOA instead of to GAAP. Disclosures in the financial statements should (1) contain an explanation of the OCBOA, and (2) describe in general how the OCBOA differs from GAAP, but (3) the differences do not have to be quantified—that is, the OCBOA does not need to be reconciled to GAAP with dollar amounts. For all practical purposes, the GAAP criteria are replaced by criteria applicable to the OCBOA. An example of a special report on cash basis statements is in Exhibit A–8.

GAAP, Other Than Historical Cost

You should be aware that GAAP sometimes is not historical cost. The prime examples are market value accounting for the assets in defined benefit pension plans, investment companies (e.g., venture capital companies, small business investment companies,

OPINION PARAGRAPH ON LIQUIDATION BASIS STATEMENTS

In our opinion, the financial statements referred to above present fairly, in all material respects, the financial position of USA Liquidating Corporation at December 31, 2001, and the excess of revenues over costs and expenses and its cash flows for the year then ended, in conformity with generally accepted accounting principles for a company in liquidation.

mutual funds), and personal financial statements (e.g., individual or family). In these cases, current value accounting is GAAP. The audit report on such financial statements gives an opinion that they are "in conformity with generally accepted accounting principles." No mention is made of an OCBOA, because the current value accounting is GAAP and not an OCBOA. Indeed, if such financial statements are prepared using the normal historical cost accounting, they contain departures from GAAP, and a qualified audit opinion should be given.

Another informally recognized basis of accounting that has no formal body of rules is "liquidation basis accounting." Some mention is made of this basis in the literature, but you will not find much official guidance. Nevertheless, auditors sometimes give reports on liquidation basis financial statements without referring to it as an OCBOA. (Be aware, however, that this type of opinion is not illustrated in any SAS. It was invented in practice.)

Reporting on the Application of Accounting Principles (SAS 50)

The subject of "reporting on the application of accounting principles" touches a sensitive nerve in the public accounting profession. It arose from clients' *shopping* for an auditor who would agree to give an unqualified audit report on a questionable accounting treatment. "Shopping" often involved auditor–client disagreements, after which the client said: "If you won't agree with my accounting treatment, then I'll find an auditor who will." These disagreements often involved early revenue recognition and unwarranted expense or loss deferral. A few cases of misleading financial statements occurred after shopping resulted in clients' switching to more agreeable auditors. However, the practice is not entirely undesirable, because "second opinions" on complex accounting matters often benefit from consultation with other CPAs.

The auditing standard entitled "Reporting on the Application of Accounting Principles" (SAS 50, AU 625) established procedures for dealing with requests for consultation from parties other than an auditor's own clients. These parties can include other companies (nonclients who are shopping), attorneys, investment bankers, and perhaps other people. SAS 50 is applicable in these situations:

- When preparing a written report or giving oral advice on specific transactions, either completed or proposed.
- When preparing a written report or giving oral advice on the type of audit opinion that might be rendered on specific financial statements.
- When preparing a written report on hypothetical transactions.

The standard does not apply to conclusions about accounting principles offered in connection with litigation support engagements or expert witness work, nor does it apply to advice given to another CPA in public practice. It also does not apply to an accounting firm's expressions of positions in newsletters, articles, speeches, lectures, and the like, provided that the positions do not give advice on a specific transaction or apply to a specific company.

Written reports are not required. However, a written report or oral advice should include these elements:

- Description of the engagement and a statement that it was performed in accordance with standards (SAS 50).
- Description of the transactions and circumstances.
- Statement of the advice—the conclusion about appropriate accounting principles or the type of audit report, including reasons for the conclusions, if appropriate.
- Statement that a company's management is responsible for proper accounting treatments, in consultation with its own auditors.
- Statement that any differences in facts, circumstances, or assumptions might change the conclusions.

The purpose of the SAS 50 standards is to impose some discipline on the process of shopping/consultation and to erect a barrier in the way of some companies' quest for a willing accountant.

Special Reports: Service Organizations

Occasionally, some clients' transactions are handled by a service organization—another business that executes or records transactions on behalf of the client. Examples of service organizations include computer data processing service centers, trust departments of banks, insurers that maintain the accounting records for ceded insurance (reinsurance transactions), mortgage bankers and savings and loan associations that service loans for owners, and transfer agents that handle the shareholder accounting for mutual and money market investment funds. An auditor may need information about the service organization's control over their mutual client's transactions. However, the auditor may not have access to do the work when the service organization is not an audit client. This situation is described in Exhibit A–9.

In such situations, all the parties concerned—the user auditor and its client organization, and the service auditor and its client (the service organization)—cooperate to try to enable the user auditor to obtain enough information about controls that affect the audit client's transactions. Certain special-purpose reports on internal accounting control (described more fully in SAS 70, AU 324) can be relied on by the user auditor in connection with the assessment of control risk of the client organization. The reports provide opinions about the service organization's controls as they are applied to the

EXHIBIT A-9   SPECIAL CONTROL REPORTS: SERVICE ORGANIZATION CONTROLS

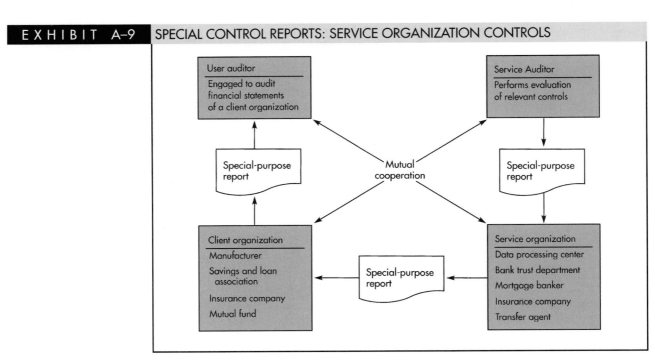

client organization's transactions. Ordinarily, service auditors' reports are not public reports on internal controls. Mainly only auditors use them.

A.12 Why does OCBOA exist? Can OCBOA financial statements be audited?

A.13 What are some examples of OCBOA? Of entities for which current value is GAAP?

A.14 Why might "opinion shopping" be suspect? Beneficial?

A.15 What must a CPA do when reporting on the application of accounting principles?

SUMMARY

CPAs have a strong reputation for integrity, objectivity, and competence. Many forms of services, in addition to audits of historical financial statements, have arisen or have been proposed. For example, the AICPA has devoted much recent attention to potentially lucrative assurance engagements. Managers of companies often develop innovative financial presentations, and they want to give the public some assurance about them, so they engage auditors. Regulators also often become interested in CPAs' communication of information and press for attestation involvement. Guided by the general attestation standards, auditing standards, and accounting and review services standards, CPAs offer services and render reports in several areas.

Unaudited financial statements have been around for a long time. Work on them is known in public practice as *review* and *compilation*. The difference lies in the amount of work performed and the level of assurance given in an accountant's report. Review engagements involve less work than an audit, and the report gives a low level of negative assurance instead of an audit opinion. Compilation engagements are merely writing up the financial statements, which is less work than a review, and the report gives no assurance in the form of an outright disclaimer.

Another type of review is accountants' review of interim financial information (e.g., quarterly financial reports). This review is technically similar to a review of unaudited financial statements, and the report on free-standing interim financial statements gives the negative assurance.

Not everyone wants to produce financial statements fully in conformity with generally accepted accounting principles. Managers have the option to prepare their statements for public use on an "other comprehensive basis of accounting" (OCBOA). Auditors can audit and report on such financial statements. This track gives managers an opportunity to avoid the complications of many of the GAAP rules. OCBOA audits and reporting are in the auditing standards under the heading of "special reports." Other kinds of special audit reports can be given on particular elements, accounts, or items in a financial statement.

A special kind of engagement can result in a report on a company's internal control. This report is a positive assurance report on the internal control system. Regulators in the SEC and federal banking agencies have been interested in management reports and audit reports on internal control. This topic of reporting on internal control spills over into auditing standards designed to require auditors to report internally to managers and the board of directors in a company about internal control deficiencies and relations with management in connection with the annual audit.

MULTIPLE-CHOICE QUESTIONS FOR PRACTICE AND REVIEW

A.16 Practice in connection with unaudited historical-cost financial statements is conducted by
 a. International accounting firms only.
 b. Regional- and local-size CPA firms.
 c. Local-size CPA firms only.
 d. All CPA firms.

A.17 The official Statements on Standards for Accounting and Review Services are applicable to practice with
 a. Audited financial statements of public companies.
 b. Unaudited financial statements of public companies.
 c. Unaudited financial statements of nonpublic companies.
 d. Audited financial statements of nonpublic companies.

A.18 A review service engagement for an accountant's association with unaudited financial statements involves
 a. More work than a compilation, and more than an audit.
 b. Less work than an audit, but more than a compilation.
 c. Less work than a compilation, but more than an audit.
 d. More work than an audit, but less than a compilation.

A.19 When an accountant is not independent, the following report can nevertheless be given:
 a. Compilation report.
 b. Standard unqualified audit report.
 c. Examination report on a forecast.
 d. Review report on unaudited financial statements.

A.20 An accountant is permitted to express "negative assurance" in which of the following types of reports?
 a. Standard unqualified audit report on audited financial statements.
 b. Compilation report on unaudited financial statements.
 c. Review report on unaudited financial statements.
 d. Adverse opinion report on audited financial statements.

A.21 When a company's financial statements in a review or compilation engagement contain a known material departure, acceptable to the CPA, from a FASB Statement on Financial Accounting Standards, the accountant's report can

 a. Make no mention of the departure in a compilation report because it contains an explicit disclaimer of opinion.
 b. Express the adverse conclusion: "The accompanying financial statements are not presented in conformity with generally accepted accounting principles."
 c. Explain the departure as necessary to make the statements not misleading, then give the standard compilation report disclaimer.
 d. Explain the departure as necessary to make the statements not misleading, then give the standard review report negative assurance.

A.22 When interim financial information is presented in a note to annual financial statements, the standard audit report on the annual financial statements should
 a. Not mention the interim information unless there is an exception the auditor needs to include in the report.
 b. Contain an audit opinion paragraph that specifically mentions the interim financial information if it is not in conformity with GAAP.
 c. Contain an extra paragraph that gives negative assurance on the interim information, if it has been reviewed.
 d. Contain an extra explanatory paragraph if the interim information note is labeled "unaudited."

A.23 According to auditing standards, financial statements presented on another comprehensive basis of accounting should not
 a. Contain a note describing the other basis of accounting.
 b. Describe in general how the other basis of accounting differs from generally accepted accounting principles.
 c. Be accompanied by an audit report that gives an unqualified opinion with reference to the other basis of accounting.
 d. Contain a note with a quantified dollar reconciliation of the assets based on the other comprehensive basis of accounting with the assets based on generally accepted accounting principles.

A.24 For which two of the following reports is an expression of negative assurance not permitted?
 a. A review report on unaudited financial statements.
 b. An audit report on financial statements prepared on a comprehensive basis of accounting other than GAAP.

  c. An examination report on a financial forecast.

  d. A review report on interim financial information.

A.25 In a current-value presentation of the balance sheet of a manufacturing company

  a. The basis of valuation must always be explained in notes to the financial statements.

  b. The basis of valuation is well known as a "comprehensive basis of accounting other than GAAP."

  c. An auditor can attest to the fair presentation of financial position in conformity with GAAP.

  d. The company must follow the AICPA guides for presentation of a financial forecast.

EXERCISES AND PROBLEMS

A.26   **Errors in an Accountant's Review Report.**   Jordan & Stone, CPAs, audited the financial statements of Tech Company, a nonpublic entity, for the year ended December 31, 2001, and expressed an unqualified opinion. For the next year ended December 31, 2002, Tech issued comparative financial statements. Jordan & Stone reviewed Tech's 2002 financial statements and Kent, an assistant on the engagement, drafted the accountants' review report (below). Stone, the engagement supervisor, decided not to reissue the prior year's audit report, but instructed Kent to include a separate paragraph in the current year review report describing the responsibility assumed for the prior year audited financial statements. This is an appropriate reporting procedure.

Stone reviewed Kent's draft and indicated in the Supervisor's Review Notes below that the draft contained several deficiencies.

Required:

These Supervisor's Review Notes may or may not be correct. For each item 1–13, indicate whether Stone is correct ("C") or incorrect ("I") in the criticism of Kent's draft.

1. The report should contain no reference to the prior year's audited financial statements in the first (introductory) paragraph.

2. All the current-year basic financial statements are not properly identified in the first (introductory) paragraph.

3. The report should contain no reference to the American Institute of Certified Public Accountants in the first (introductory) paragraph.

4. The accountant's review and audit responsibilities should follow management's responsibilities in the first (introductory) paragraph.

5. The report should contain no comparison of the scope of a review to an audit in the second (scope) paragraph.

6. Negative assurance should be expressed on the current year's reviewed financial statements in the second (scope) paragraph.

7. The report should contain a statement that no opinion is expressed on the current year's financial statements in the second (scope) paragraph.

8. The report should contain a reference to "conformity with generally accepted accounting principles" in the third paragraph.

9. The report should not express a restriction on the distribution of the accountant's review report in the third paragraph.

10. The report should not contain a reference to "material modifications" in the third paragraph.

11. The report should contain an indication of the type of opinion expressed on the prior year's audited financial statements in the fourth (separate) paragraph.

12. The report should give an indication that no auditing procedures were performed after the date of the report on the prior year's financial statements in the fourth (separate) paragraph.

13. The report should not contain a reference to "updating the prior year's auditor's report for events and circumstances occurring after that date" in the fourth (separate) paragraph.

Accountant's Review Report—Kent's Draft

We have reviewed and audited the accompanying balance sheets of Tech Co. as of December 31, 2002 and 2001, and the related statements of income, retained earnings, and cash flows for the years then ended, in accordance with Statements on Standards for Accounting and Review Services issued by the American Institute of Certified Public Accountants and generally accepted auditing standards. All information included in these financial statements is the representation of the management of Tech Company.

A review consists principally of inquiries of company personnel and analytical procedures applied to financial data. It is substantially less in scope than an audit in accordance with generally accepted auditing standards, the objective of which is the expression of an opinion regarding the financial statements taken as a whole.

Based on our review, we are not aware of any material modifications that should be made to the accompanying financial statements. Because of the inherent limitations of a review engagement, this report is intended for the information of management and should not be used for any other purpose.

The financial statements for the year ended December 31, 2001, were audited by us and our report was dated March 2, 2002. We have no responsibility for updating that report for events and circumstances occurring after that date.

Jordan and Stone, CPAs
March 1, 2002

(AICPA adapted)

A.27 Review of Forecast Assumptions. You have been engaged by the Dodd Manufacturing Corporation to attest to the reasonableness of the assumptions underlying its forecast of revenues, costs, and net income for the next calendar year, 2002. Four of the assumptions are shown below.

a. The company intends to sell certain real estate and other facilities held by Division B at an aftertax profit of $600,000; the proceeds of this sale will be used to retire outstanding debt.

b. The company will call and retire all outstanding 9 percent subordinated debentures (callable at 108). The debentures are expected to require the full call premium given present market interest rates of 8 percent on similar debt. A rise in market interest rates to 9 percent would reduce the loss on bond retirement from the projected $200,000 to $190,000.

c. Current labor contracts expire on September 1, 2002, and the new contract is expected to result in a wage increase of 5.5 percent. Given the forecasted levels of production and sales, aftertax operating earnings would be reduced approximately $50,000 for each percentage-point wage increase in excess of the expected contract settlement.

d. The sales forecast for Division A assumes that the new Portsmouth facility will be complete and operating at 40 percent of capacity on February 1, 2002. It is highly improbable that the facility will be operational before January of 2002. Each month's delay would reduce sales of Division A by approximately $80,000 and operating earnings by $30,000.

Required:
For each assumption, state the evidence sources and procedures you would use to determine the reasonableness.

A.28 Compilation and Review Procedures. The items numbered 1 through 10 below are procedures an accountant may consider in review engagements and compilation engagements on the annual financial statements of nonpublic entities (performed in accordance with AICPA Statements on Standards for Accounting and Review Services). For each item (taken separately), tell whether the item is (a) required in all review engagements, (b) not required in review engagements, (c) required in all compilation engagements, (d) not required in compilation engagements. For each item, give two responses (a,b,c,d)—one regarding review engagements, and the other regarding compilation engagements.

1. The accountant should establish an understanding with entity management regarding the nature and limitations of the services to be performed.

2. The accountant should make inquiries concerning actions taken at the board of directors' meetings.

3. The accountants, as the entity's successor accountant, should communicate with the predecessor account to obtain access to the predecessor's working papers.

4. The accountant should obtain a level of knowledge of the accounting principles and practices of the entity's industry.

5. The accountant should obtain an understanding of the entity's internal control.

6. The accountant should perform analytical procedures designed to identify relationships that appear to be unusual.

7. The accountant should make an assessment of control risk.

8. The accountant should obtain a letter from the entity's attorney to corroborate the information furnished by management concerning litigation.

9. The accountant should obtain a management representation letter from the entity.

10. The accountant should study the relationship of the financial statement elements that would be expected to conform to a predictable pattern.

(AICPA adapted)

A.29 Compilation Presentation Alternatives. Jimmy C operates a large service station, garage, and truck stop on Interstate 95 near Plainview. His brother, Bill, has recently joined as a partner, even though he still keeps a small CPA practice. One slow afternoon, they were discussing financial statements with Bert, the local CPA who operates the largest public practice in Plainview.

Jimmy: The business is growing, and sometimes I need to show financial statements to parts suppliers and to the loan officers at the bank.

Bert: That so.

Jimmy: Yea-boy, and they don't like the way I put 'em together.

Bert: That so.

Bill: Heck, Jimmy, I know all about that. I can compile a jim-dandy set of financial statements for us.

Jimmy: What does Jim Dan over at the cafe have to do with it?

Bert: Never mind, Jimmy. Bill can't do compiled financial statements for you. He's not independent.

Jimmy: I know. Momma didn't let him outa the house 'til he was 24. The neighbors complained.

Bert: That so.

Bill: Shucks.

Jimmy: But Bert, those fellas are always asking me about accounting policies, contingencies, and stuff like that. Said something about "footnotes." I don't want to fool with all that small print.

Required:

Think about the financial disclosure problems of Jimmy and Bill's small business. What kinds of compiled financial statements can be prepared for them and by whom?

A.30   Negative Assurance in Review Reports. One portion of the report on a review services engagement is the following:

Based on my review, I am not aware of any material modifications that should be made to the accompanying financial statements in order for them to be in conformity with accounting principles generally accepted in the United States.

Required:

a. Is this paragraph a "negative assurance" given by the CPA?

b. Why is "negative assurance" generally prohibited in audit reports?

c. What justification is there for permitting "negative assurance" in a review services report on unaudited financial statements and on interim financial information?

A.31   Deficiencies in an Internal Control Communication. Land & Hale, CPAs, are auditing the financial statements of Marlowe Company, a nonpublic entity, for the year ended December 31, 2001. Land, the engagement supervisor, anticipates expressing an unqualified opinion on May 20, 2002 at the end of the field work.

Wood, an assistant on the engagement, drafted the auditor's communication of internal control matters that Land plans to send to Marlowe's board of directors with the May 20 audit report.

Land reviewed Wood's draft (follows item 15) and indicated in the Supervisor's Review Notes certain deficiencies.

Required:

These Supervisor's Review Notes may or may not be correct. For each item 1–15, indicate whether Land is correct ("C") or incorrect ("I") in the criticism of Wood's draft. (Hint: Refer to SAS 60 for details not in the textbook chapter.)

In the 1st paragraph

1. There should be no reference to "our audit of the financial statements."

2. The report should indicate that providing assurance is not the purpose of our consideration of the internal control system.

3. The reference to "our assessment of control risk" at the end of the paragraph should have been a reference to "the assertions of management in the financial statements."

4. There should be a reference to "conformity with generally accepted accounting principles."

In the 2nd paragraph

5. There should be no reference to deficiencies because such reference is inconsistent with the expression of an unqualified opinion on the financial statements.

6. When deficiencies (reportable conditions) are noted, the report should include a description of the assessed level of control risk.

In the 3rd paragraph

7. The definition of "material weakness" is incorrect. A material weakness is a reportable condition.

8. The report should indicate that the auditor assumes no responsibility for errors or frauds resulting from the deficiencies (reportable conditions) identified in the report.

9. The report should refer to detection by the entity's employees at the end of the paragraph, not detection by the auditors.

In the 4th paragraph

10. The report should indicate that our consideration of the internal control system is expected to disclose all reportable conditions.

11. It is inappropriate to state that "none of the reportable conditions . . . is believed to be a material weakness."

In the final paragraph

12. The restriction on the report's distribution is inadequate because management ordinarily would receive the report.

13. The report should indicate that the financial statement audit resulted in an unqualified opinion.

14. The report should indicate that the auditor is not responsible to update the report for events or circumstances occurring after the date of the report.

Dating the report

15. The report may not be dated before the auditor's report on the financial statements.

Independent Auditor's Report

To the Board of Directors of
Marlowe Company:

In planning and performing our audit of the financial statements of Marlowe Company for the year ended December 31, 2001, we considered its internal control system to determine our auditing procedures for the purpose of expressing our opinion on the financial statements and to provide assurance on the internal control system. However, we noted certain matters involving internal control and its operations that we consider to be reportable conditions under standards established by the American Institute of Certified Public Accountants. Reportable conditions involve matters coming to our attention relating to significant deficiencies in the design or operation of the internal control system that, in our judgment, could adversely affect the organization's ability to record, process, summarize, and report financial data consistent with our assessment of control risk.

We noted that deficiencies in the internal control design included inadequate provisions for the safeguarding of assets, especially concerning cash receipts and inventory stored at remote locations. Additionally, we noted failures in the operation of the internal controls. Reconciliations of subsidiary ledgers to control accounts were not timely prepared and senior employees in authority intentionally overrode the internal control procedures concerning cash payments to the detriment of the overall objectives of control.

A material weakness is not necessarily a reportable condition, but is a design defect in which the internal control elements do not reduce to a relatively low level the risk that errors or frauds in amounts that would be material in relation to the financial statements being audited may occur and not be detected by the auditors during the audit.

Our consideration of the internal control system will not necessarily disclose all matters of internal control that might be reportable conditions and, accordingly, will not necessarily disclose all reportable conditions that are also considered to be material weaknesses as defined above. However, none of the reportable conditions described above is believed to be a material weakness.

This report is intended solely for the information and use of the Board of Directors of Marlowe Co. Accordingly, it is not intended to be distributed to stockholders, management, or those who are not responsible for these matters.

Land & Hale, CPAs
May 4, 2002

(AICPA adapted)

A.32   Reporting on an Other Comprehensive Basis of Accounting.   The report abstracted below is an actual report on a pension fund that refers to a statutory basis of accounting (OCBOA) as well as to generally accepted accounting principles (GAAP).

Required:

a. What is the purpose of the third paragraph (#3) in relation to the fourth paragraph (#4)? [Hint: Consider the fourth GAAS reporting standard.]

b. What is the message in the fourth paragraph (#4)? What is the name for the message under GAAS?

c. What is the message in the fifth paragraph (#5)? What is the name for the message under GAAS?

Report of Independent Auditors

Board of Trustees
The Church Pension Fund

[#1: Standard introductory paragraph here]
[#2: Standard scope paragraph here]

(#3) As described in the Financial Review under the heading "Accounting Principles and Practices," the accompanying financial statements have been prepared on the basis of accounting practices prescribed by the New York Insurance Department, whose statutory accounting practices vary from generally accepted accounting principles for defined benefit pension plans, principally with respect to the valuation of bonds and the computation of pension obligations.

(#4) In our opinion, for the reasons set forth in the preceding paragraph, the financial statements referred to above are not intended to and do not present fairly, in conformity with certain generally accepted accounting principles for defined benefit pension plans, the assets and liabilities of The Fund at March 31, 2002 and 2001, or the changes in funded reserve for the years then ended.

(#5) Also, in our opinion, the financial statements referred to above present fairly, in all material respects, the assets and liabilities of The Fund at March 31, 2002 and 2001, and the changes in its funded reserve for the year then ended, in conformity with accounting practices prescribed or permitted by the New York Insurance Department.

/s/ Auditor signature
New York, New York
June 8, 2002

REPORT-WRITING CASES

These cases require a written report. The *Electronic Workpapers* on the textbook website has four ASCII files (filenames AUDIT, REVIEW, COMPILE, and INTERIM) containing the standard reports for these services. These can be used as the starting place for the report-writing requirements in these cases. You can read this file into many word processing programs to make your report-writing task easier and more professional.

A.33   Prepare a Compilation Report.   You have been engaged by the Coffin Brothers to compile their financial schedules from books and records maintained by James Coffin. The brothers own and operate three auto parts stores in Central City. Even though their business is growing, they have not wanted to employ a full-time bookkeeper. James specifies that all he wants is a balance sheet, a statement of operations, and a statement of cash flows. He does not have time to write up footnotes to accompany the statement.

James directed the physical count of inventory on June 30 and adjusted and closed the books on that date. You find that he actually is a good accountant, having taken some night courses at the community college. The accounts appear to have been maintained in conformity with generally accepted accounting principles. At least you have noticed no obvious errors.

Required:
You are independent with respect to the Coffin brothers and their Coffin Auto Speed Shop business. Prepare a report on your compilation services engagement.

A.34   Reporting on Comparative Unaudited Financial Statements.   Anson Jones, CPA, performed a review service for the Independence Company in 2002. He wants to present comparative financial statements. However, the 2001 statements were compiled by Able and Associates, CPAs, and Able does not want to cooperate with Jones by reissuing the prior year compilation report. Jones has no indication that any adjustments should be made to either the 2002 or 2001 statements, which are to be presented with all necessary disclosures. However, he does not have time to perform a review of the 2001 statements. He completed his work on January 15, 2000, for the statement dated December 31, 2002.

Required:
Write Jones' review report and include the paragraph describing the report on the 2001 statements.

A.35   Erroneous Reporting on Interim Financial Information.   The following report (see the box below) was prepared by Baker & Baker, CPAs, on the interim financial information of Micro Mini Company. The interim financial information was presented in the first quarterly report for the three-month period ended March 31, 2002. No comparative quarterly information of the first quarter of the prior year was presented. Baker & Baker completed a review in accordance with standards established by the AICPA and found that, to the best of their knowledge, the information was presented in conformity with FASB requirements. In an audit report dated January 21, 2002, Baker & Baker had given a standard unqualified audit report on Micro Mini's 2001 and 2000 annual financial statements.

Required:
a. Review the report and list, with explanation, the erroneous portions in it.

b. Rewrite the report.

Report of Independent Auditors
The Board of Directors and Stockholders,
Micro Mini Company:

We have made a review of the balance sheet of Micro Mini Company at March 31, 2002, the related statement of income for the three-month period ended March 31, 2002, and the statement of cash flows for the three-month period ended March 31, 2002, in accordance with standards established by the American Institute of Certified Public Accountants.

A review of interim financial information consists principally of obtaining an understanding of the system for the preparation of the interim financial information, applying analytical review procedures to financial data, and making inquiries to persons responsible for financial and accounting matters.

In our opinion, the accompanying interim financial information presents fairly, in all material respects, the financial position of Micro Mini Company at March 31, 2002, and the results of its operations and its cash flows for the three-month period then ended in conformity with generally accepted accounting principles.

Baker & Baker, CPAs
March 31, 2002

A.36 Report on Comprehensive Basis Other Than GAAP. The Brooklyn Life Insurance Company prepares its financial statements on a statutory basis in conformity with the accounting practices prescribed and permitted by the Insurance Department of the State of New York. This statutory basis produces financial statements that differ materially from statements prepared in conformity with generally accepted accounting principles. On the statutory basis, for example, agents' first-year commissions are expensed instead of being partially deferred, and equity securities are reported at market value lower than cost, even if a "permanent impairment" of value is not evident.

The company engaged its auditors, Major and Major Associates, to audit the statutory basis financial statements and report on them. Footnote 10 in the statements contains a narrative description and a numerical table explaining the differences between the statutory basis and GAAP accounting. Footnote 10 also reconciles the statutory basis assets, liabilities, income, expense, and net income (statutory basis) to the measurements that would be obtained using GAAP.

Required:

Write the audit report appropriate in the circumstances. The year-end date is December 31, 2001, and the audit field work was completed on February 20, 2002. (The company plans to distribute this report to persons other than the department of insurance regulators, so the auditors will need to follow *SAS 1*, AU 544.)

A. 37 Internet Exercise—CPA WebTrust. The AICPA recently launched a new assurance service entitled CPA WebTrust. Access the CPA WebTrust site (www.cpawebtrust.org) to answer the following questions:

a. What is CPA WebTrust?

b. Why is CPA WebTrust needed?

c. How does an Internet user know that a website has received the CPA WebTrust service?

d. Where can a person obtain copies of the CPA WebTrust standards?

Module B

Professional Ethics

Professional Standards References

Compendium Section	Document Reference	Topic
AU 220	SAS 1	*Independence*
AU 9326	SAS 26	*Interpretation: Evidential Matter Relating to Income Tax Accruals*
QC 20	SQCS 2	*System of Quality Control for a CPA Firm's Accounting and Auditing Practice*
ET 51-57		*Principles of Professional Conduct*
ET 91-92		*Definitions and Applicability of Rules*
ET101-191		*Rules of Conduct, Interpretations, and Rulings on Independence, Integrity, and Objectivity*
ET201-291		*Rules of Conduct, Interpretations, and Rulings on General and Technical Standards*
ET301-391		*Rules of Conduct, Interpretations, and Rulings on Responsibilities to Clients*
ET501-591		*Rules of Conduct, Interpretations, and Rulings on Other Responsibilities and Practices*
ETAppendix A		*Resolution Designating Bodies to Promulgate Technical Standards (Rules 201, 202, and 203)*
ETAppendix B		*Resolution Concerning Form of Organization and Name (Rule 505)*
BL100-900		*Bylaws of the AICPA*
ISB 1		*Independence Discussion with Audit Committees*
ISB 2		*Certain Independence Implications of Audits of Mutual Funds and Related Entities*
ISB 3		*Employment with Audit Clients*

Learning Objectives

Previous chapters have focused on the theory and practice of auditing. This module tells you about the regulation of accountants and accounting practice. Regulation and discipline depend on published codes of ethics and on effective enforcement practices. Your objectives in this module on professional ethics are to be able to:

1. Understand general ethics and a series of steps for making ethical decisions.

2. Reason through an ethical decision problem using the imperative, utilitarian, and generalization principles of moral philosophy.

3. With reference to AICPA, SEC, and ISB rules, analyze fact situations and decide whether an accountant's conduct does or does not impair independence or damage integrity.

4. With reference to AICPA rules on topics other than independence, analyze fact situations and decide whether an accountant's conduct does or does not conform to the AICPA Rules of Conduct.

5. Name and explain the various professional associations and government agencies that enforce rules of conduct and explain the types of penalties they can impose on accountants.

GENERAL ETHICS

LEARNING OBJECTIVE

1. Understand general ethics and a series of steps for making ethical decisions.

What is ethics? Wheelwright defined ethics as "that branch of philosophy which is the systematic study of reflective choice, of the standards of right and wrong by which it is to be guided, and of the goods toward which it may ultimately be directed."[1] In this definition, you can detect three key elements: (1) ethics involves questions requiring reflective choice (*decision problems*), (2) ethics involves guides of right and wrong (*moral principles*), and (3) ethics is concerned with the consequences (*goods*) of decisions.

What is an ethical problem? A *problem situation* exists when you must make a choice among alternative actions, and the right choice is not absolutely clear. An *ethical problem situation* may be described as one in which the choice of alternative actions affects the well-being of other persons.

What is ethical behavior? You can find two standard philosophical answers to this question: (1) ethical behavior is that which produces the greatest good, and (2) ethical behavior is that which conforms to moral rules and principles. The most difficult problem situations arise when two or more rules conflict or when a rule and the criterion of "greatest good" conflict.

Why does an individual or group need a code of ethical conduct? While it has been said that a person should be upright and not be *kept* upright, a code serves a useful purpose as a reference and a benchmark for individuals. A code makes explicit some of the criteria for conduct peculiar to the profession. Therefore, codes of professional ethics provide some direct solutions that may not be available in general ethics theories. Furthermore, an individual is better able to know what the profession expects. From the viewpoint of the organized profession, a code is a public declaration of principled conduct, and it is a means of facilitating *enforcement* of standards of conduct. Practical enforcement and professionwide internal discipline are impossible if members are not first notified of the standards.

While one of the main purposes of ethics is to guide the actions of decision makers, the role of decision maker does not fully describe a professional person's entire obligation. Each person acts not only as an individual but also as a member of a profession and as a member of society. Hence, accountants and auditors are also *spectators* (observing the decisions of colleagues), *advisers* (counseling with co-workers), *instructors* (teaching

---

[1] Philip Wheelwright, *A Critical Introduction to Ethics,* 3d ed. (Indianapolis, Ind.: Odyssey Press, 1959).

accounting students or new employees on the job), *judges* (serving on disciplinary committees of a state society, a state board of accountancy, or the AICPA), and *critics* (commenting on the ethical decisions of others). All of these roles are important in the practice of professional ethics.

AN ETHICAL DECISION PROCESS

In considering general ethics, your primary goal is to arrive at a set of acceptable methods for making ethical decisions. Consequently, an understanding of some of the general principles of ethics can contribute background for a detailed consideration of the behavior directed by the AICPA Code of Professional Conduct and other ethics rules.

In the earlier definition of ethics, one of the key elements was *reflective choice*. It involves an important sequence of events beginning with the recognition of a decision problem. Collection of evidence, in the ethics context, refers to thinking about rules of behavior and outcomes of alternative actions. The process ends with analyzing the situation and taking an action. Ethical decision problems almost always involve projecting yourself into the future to live with your decisions. Professional ethics decisions usually turn on these questions: "What written and unwritten rules govern my behavior?" and "What are the possible consequences of my choices?" *Principles* of ethics can help you think about these two questions in real situations.

A good way to approach ethical decision problems is to think through several steps:

1. Define all the facts and circumstances known at the time you need to make the decision. They are the "who, what, where, when, and how" dimensions of the situation. Identify the actor who needs to decide what to do.

   Example: Kathy (the chief financial officer) ordered Jorge (a staff accountant) to "enhance" the financial statements in a loan application to Spring National Bank by understating the allowance for uncollectible accounts receivable, saying, "It's an estimate anyway and we need the loan for a short time to keep from laying off loyal employees." What should Jorge do?

2a. Since ethical decision problems are defined in terms of their effects on *people*, identify the people involved in the situation or affected by the situation. These are the "stakeholders," but be careful not to expand the number of stakeholders beyond the bounds of reasonable analysis.

   Example: The stakeholders include the direct participants—Kathy, Jorge, Luis (Spring National Bank's loan officer)—and some indirect participants—bank stockholders, loyal employees. Other people may be affected, but identifying them probably will not improve the analysis—Jorge's mother, citizens who depend upon the solvency of the banking system as a whole, taxpayers who eventually need to bail out the insolvent banking system, and others.

2b. Identify and describe the stakeholders' rights and obligations in general and to each other.

   Example: Obligations—Kathy and Jorge should be professionally honest (truthtellers via financial statements), Kathy should not put pressure on Jorge to cut corners with financial statements, Luis should make careful loan approval decisions. Rights—Jorge should not be subject to pressures to cut corners with "enhanced financial statements," Luis should receive information that is not materially misstated or manipulated. (Some rights of employees and bank stockholders could also be identified.)

3. Specify the actor's major alternative decision actions and their consequences (good, bad, short-run, long-run).

   Example: Jorge can: (1) Follow orders—Kathy is happy, Jorge keeps his job, Luis gets fooled and approves the loan, the employees keep their jobs, the company fails, the bank loses, the employees are laid off anyway, Kathy and Jorge get prosecuted for making false statements to a federal institution, they go to federal prison. (2) Refuse to "enhance" the financial statements—Kathy is not happy, Jorge gets fired (and finds a better job), Kathy prepares the financial statements herself, etc. (3) Jorge tries to persuade Kathy of the potential problems—Kathy agrees and Luis refuses the loan (and gets praise from the bank president), and the company must find another way to survive, or Luis approves the loan anyway and the bank takes the risk; or Kathy does not agree, and Jorge must again face alternatives (1) and (2) anyway.

In addition to weighing the consequences, Jorge should also consider general and professional rules. If Jorge is a CPA, some of the relevant professional rules relate to maintaining integrity (AICPA rule 102), application of accounting standards (AICPA rule 203), and the prohibition of discreditable acts (AICPA rule 501). Jorge needs to decide whether to follow rules or balance the expected consequences in the particular situation.

4. As the actor, Jorge must choose one of the alternative decision actions and justify it by presenting a convincing argument for its superiority. Jorge can base the argument on rules, consequences, or a combination of both.

PHILOSOPHICAL PRINCIPLES IN ETHICS

LEARNING OBJECTIVE
2. Reason through an ethical decision problem using the imperative, utilitarian, and generalization principles of moral philosophy.

We could skip a discussion of ethical theories if we were willing to accept a simple rule: "Let **conscience** be your guide." Such a rule is appealing because it calls on an individual's own judgment, which may be based on wisdom, insight, adherence to custom, or an authoritative code. However, it might also be based on caprice, immaturity, ignorance, stubbornness, or misunderstanding. The problem with using *conscience* as a guide is that it tells you about a wrong decision *after* you act!

In a similar manner, reliance on the opinions of others or on the weight of opinion of a particular social group is not always enough. Another person or a group of persons may perpetuate a custom or habit that is wrong. (Think about the signboard that proclaimed: "Wrong is wrong, even if everybody is doing it.") To adhere blindly to custom or to group habits is to abdicate individual responsibility. Titus and Keeton summarized this point succinctly: "Each person capable of making moral decisions is responsible for making his own decisions. The ultimate locus of moral responsibility is in the individual."[2] Thus, the function of ethical *principles* is not to provide a simple and sure rule but to provide some guides for your individual decisions and actions.

Consider Jorge's problem in light of the *imperative*, the *utilitarian*, and the *generalization* principles.

The Imperative Principle

The imperative principle directs a decision maker to act according to the requirements of an ethical rule. Strict versions of imperative ethics maintain that a decision should be made without trying to predict whether an action will probably create the greatest balance of good over evil. Ethics in the imperative sense are a function of moral rules and principles and do not involve a situation-specific calculation of the consequences.[3]

The philosopher Immanuel Kant (1724–1804) was perhaps the foremost advocate of the imperative school. Kant was unwilling to rely solely on decision makers' inclinations and values for decisions in various circumstances. He strongly preferred rules without exceptions to the varied and frequently inconsistent choices of individuals. He maintained

---

[2] Harold H. Titus and Morris Keeton, *Ethics for Today*, 4th ed. (New York: American Book–Stratford Press, 1966), p. 131.
[3] I. Kant, *Foundations of the Metaphysics of Morals*, trans. Lewis W. Beck (Indianapolis, Ind.: Bobbs-Merrill, 1959; originally published in 1785).

that *reason* and the strict *duty to be consistent* governed the formulation of his first law of conduct: "Act only on that maxim whereby you can at the same time will that it should become a universal law." (Act only as you think everyone should act all the time.) This law of conduct is Kant's first formulation of his **categorical imperative**, meaning that it specifies an *unconditional obligation*. One such maxim (rule), for example, is: "Lying is wrong."

Suppose you believe that Jorge (from the example given earlier) should agree with Kathy and do everything she asked for "enhancing the financial statements," thus participating in a lie (knowingly misrepresenting the facts about the allowance for uncollectible accounts receivable). The Kantian test of the morality of such a lie is: Can this maxim be a moral rule which should be followed without exception by all persons who have the opportunity to fool a bank loan officer for a good cause (avoiding the layoffs of loyal employees)? In order for all persons to follow a rule, all persons must know about it, and when everyone knows that the rule is to fool bank officers when they think they have good reasons, then no one should be fooled by accepting loan application financial statements without question.

A lie succeeds only when the hearer of it does not know it is a lie. The nature of the universal rule is universal knowledge of it. Therefore, any manner of lying is bound to fail the test because no one would believe the speaker of the lie. Thus, lying is wrong because, when made universal, no one could be believed and virtually all common communication would become impossible.

So, should Jorge refuse in such a way that Luis ultimately refuses to approve the loan, thus carrying out the action that may result in employee layoffs and economic hardship? Kant maintained that motive and duty alone define a moral act, not the consequences of the act. This reasoning places the highest "value" on the duty to be consistent and a lower "value" on the fate of the employees.

The general objection to the imperative principle is the belief that so-called universal rules always turn out to have exceptions. The general response to this objection is that if the rule is stated properly to include the exceptional cases, the principle is still valid. The problem with this response, however, is that human experience is complicated, and extremely complex universal rules would have to be constructed to try to cover all possible cases.[4]

One value of the Kantian categorical imperative with its emphasis on universal, unconditional obligations is that it lets you know when you are faced with an ethical decision problem. When only one rule derived from the categorical imperative is applicable, you may have no trouble following it. When two rules or two duties are in conflict, a serious problem exists. Think about Jorge and his decision problem. One of his rules is "Live up to all your professional duties not to knowingly misrepresent facts." Another is the duty to "Be loyal to your employer." Jorge may see these two to be in conflict. Such conflicts of rules and duties create difficult problems because adherence to one means breaking the other.

The Kantian imperative theory, however, does not provide an easy way to make the decision. Someone who is rule-bound may find himself or herself in a dilemma. This kind of dilemma prompts people to look for ways to weigh the consequences of actions, and one way is described by the principle of utilitarianism discussed in the next section

Most professional codes of ethics have characteristics of the imperative type of theory. As a general matter, professionals are expected to act in a manner in conformity with the rules. However, society frequently questions not only conduct itself but the rules on which conduct is based. Thus, a dogmatic imperative approach to ethical decisions may not be completely sufficient for the maintenance of professional standards. Society may question the rules, and conflicts among them are always possible. A means of estimating the consequences of alternative actions may be useful.

---

[4] Several rules in the AICPA Rules of Conduct are explicitly phrased. to provide for exceptions to the general rules, notably Rules 203 and 301. Imperative rules also seem to generate borderline cases, so the AICPA Ethics Division issues *interpretations* and *rulings* to explain the applicability of the rules.

AUDITING INSIGHT

BALANCING ACT

Consolidata, Inc., was a tax client of Alexander Grant & Company, CPAs (AG). Consolidata prepared payrolls for 38 customers, received the customers' money, then paid the payrolls. AG learned that Consolidata was in serious financial difficulty and advised the company to inform its customers, but company officials did not do so. When AG learned that the company's officers and directors had resigned, AG telephoned 12 Consolidata customers who were also AG clients, told them of the situation, and advised them not to entrust further payroll funds to Consolidata. The 12 were spared the risk of losing their money, and Consolidata went out of business one month later.

Consolidata accused AG of breach of contract for breaking an obligation of confidentiality required by the AICPA Code of Professional Conduct. One SEC attorney said she thought AG should have alerted all 38 customers, not just the 12 AG clients. Accountants and SEC officials viewed the situation as a balancing of confidentiality (AICPA rule) against the public interest (Consolidata customers who needed a warning).

The Principle of Utilitarianism

The principle of utilitarianism maintains that the ultimate criterion of an ethical decision is the balance of good over evil consequences produced by an action.[5] The emphasis in utilitarianism is on the consequences of action, rather than on following some rules. The criterion of producing the greater good is made an explicit part of the decision process. While the *principle* is very useful, be sure to notice that it does not specify the *values* that enable you to figure the good or evil of an action.

In **act-utilitarianism,** the center of attention is the individual act as it is affected by the specific circumstances of a situation. An act-utilitarian's ethical problem may be framed in this way: "What effect will my doing this act in this situation have on the general balance of good over evil?" This theory admits general guides such as: "Telling the truth is probably always for the greatest good." However, the emphasis is always on the specific situation, and decision makers must determine whether they have independent grounds for thinking that the greatest general good will result from not telling the truth in a particular case.

The general difficulty with act-utilitarianism is that it seems to permit too many exceptions to well-established rules. By focusing attention on individual acts, the long-run effect of setting examples for other people appears to be ignored. If an act-utilitarian decision is to break a moral rule, then the decision's success usually depends on everyone else's adherence to the rule. For example, to benefit from tax evasion for a good reason depends on everyone else not having an equally good reason for not paying their taxes.

Rule-utilitarianism, on the other hand, emphasizes the centrality of rules for ethical behavior while still maintaining the criterion of the greatest universal good. This kind of utilitarianism means that decision makers must first determine the rules that will promote the greatest general good for the largest number of people. The initial question is not which *action* has the greatest utility, but which *rule.* Thus, the rule-utilitarian's ethical decision problem can be framed as follows: "What effect will everyone's doing this kind of act in this kind of situation have on the general balance of good over evil?" The principle of utility becomes operative not only in determining a particular action to take in a specific decision situation in which rules conflict but also in establishing the rules in the first place.

---

[5] J. S. Mill, *Utilitarianism,* ed. Oskar Piest (Indianapolis, Ind.: Bobbs-Merrill, 1957; originally published in 1861).

AUDITING INSIGHT

SERVICE VERSUS INDEPENDENCE

For many years, a national CPA firm had encouraged its professionals to become active members of the boards of directors of corporations. The purpose was to provide expertise to businesses in the metropolitan area and to enable the accounting firm to become well known and well respected. The firm changed its policy to *prohibit* such service after it had the opportunity to obtain some of these corporations as audit clients, but it was forced to refuse or delay the CPA-client relationship. The firm's audit independence was considered impaired when a member of the firm had served in a director or management capacity during the period covered by the financial statements the corporations wanted the firm to audit. The generalization test was: If members of the firm serve on the boards of directors of all corporations that may become audit clients, none of these corporations can be accepted as audit clients—a result that is undesirable.

The statement of the rule-utilitarian's problem may be given a very commonsense expression: "What would happen if everybody acted this way?" In this form, the question is known as *generalization*.

The Generalization Argument

For all practical purposes, the **generalization argument** may be considered a judicious combination of the imperative and utilitarian principles. Stated succinctly, the argument is: "If all relevantly similar persons acting under relevantly similar circumstances were to act in a certain way and the consequences would be undesirable, then no one ought to act in that way without a reason."[6] A more everyday expression of the argument is the question: "What would happen if everyone acted in that certain way?" If the answer to the question is that the consequences would be undesirable, then your conclusion, according to the generalization test, is that the way of acting is unethical and ought not be done.

The key ideas in the generalization test are *similar persons* and *similar circumstances*. These features provide the needed flexibility to consider the many variations that arise in real problem situations. They also demand considerable judgment in determining whether persons and circumstances are genuinely different or are just arbitrarily rationalized as different so that a preconceived preference can be "explained" as right.

Jorge's problem as a professional accountant and as an employee arose when Kathy asked him to "enhance the financial statements," and he saw the enhancement as a lie. His generalization question may be something like this: "What if all accountants fudged financial statements and fooled loan officers when their companies needed to obtain loans?" Most people will see an easy answer—the result would be undesirable (because it might succeed often and cause considerable losses to banks along with other undesirable personal consequences for the actors, in addition to the problem of having broken a rule that requires truth-telling).

Another kind of conflict subject to the generalization test is illustrated by a CPA firm's desire for service and need for independence (see the box above).

This brief review of principles in ethics provides some guide to the ways many people approach difficult decision problems. The greatest task is to take general notions of ethics—the imperative, utilitarianism, and generalization—and apply them to a real decision. Their application through codes of professional conduct is a challenge.

---

[6] Marcus G. Singer, *Generalization in Ethics* (New York: Atheneum Publishers, 1961, 1971), esp. pp. 5, 10–11, 61, 63, 73, 81, 105–22.

B.1 What *roles* must a professional accountant be prepared to occupy in regard to ethical decision problems?

B.2 When might the rule "Let conscience be your guide" not be sufficient basis for your personal ethics decisions? For your professional ethics decisions?

B.3 Assume that you accept the following ethical rule: "Failure to tell the whole truth is wrong." In the textbook illustration about Jorge's problem with Kathy's instructions, what would this rule require Jorge to do? Why is an unalterable rule like this classified as an element of *imperative* ethical theory?

B.4 How does *utilitarian* ethics differ from *imperative* ethics?

EMPHASIS ON INDEPENDENCE AND INTEGRITY

In 1999 and 2000 the ethics pot was boiling with profession-wide concerns about the principles and rules on auditor independence and integrity. Regulators at the U.S. Securities and Exchange Commission, CPAs in public practice, and a wide variety of investors and analysts were worried about the nature of auditors' practices and about public perceptions of audits. They all believed that the fate of accountants' business practices and the public faith in financial reports and securities markets hung in the balance. As a consequence, three rule-making agencies became very active in the independence and integrity arena.

Independence in Triplicate

Three agencies produce rules about auditor independence—the U.S. Securities and Exchange Commission (SEC), the AICPA Professional Ethics Executive Committee (PEEC), and the Independence Standards Board (ISB).

The SEC has federal statutory authority to define auditor independence for the purpose of (1) protecting the reliability and integrity of the financial statements of public companies, and (2) promoting investor confidence in financial statements and the securities markets. The SEC's jurisdiction covers only public companies that are required by federal securities laws to file financial statements audited by independent accountants. About 16,500 companies file such financial statements in the United States.

The PEEC is the AICPA committee that makes and enforces all the rules of conduct for CPAs who are AICPA members. It makes independence rules applicable not only for public companies but also for all audits (thousands of audits of nonpublic companies, not-for-profit organizations, and government units over and above the 16,500 public companies). To help overcome potential conflicts of rules the PEEC expressed this policy (May 2000): ISB independence standards are authoritative for all audits *unless* PEEC expressly announces disagreement, and ISB standards will supercede existing AICPA rules as they apply to a particular topic. Since the ISB accepts SEC rules, this policy also means that the AICPA PEEC accepts SEC rules in place of its own *unless* PEEC expressly disagrees (and then perhaps different rules might apply only to auditors of nonpublic companies and other organizations, but such a conflict is not very likely).

The ISB was created in 1997, and it is located and funded in the SEC Practice Section of the AICPA Division for Firms. The ISB and the SEC cooperate to make private-sector independence rules applicable to auditors of public companies (the same jurisdiction as the SEC). The ISB goals are to (1) serve the public interest and (2) promote investors' confidence in the securities markets. In the beginning, the ISB ruled that its starting point for a body of independence rules was the SEC's then-existing independence rules.

American Institute of Certified Public Accountants

The AICPA Code of Professional Conduct contains two basic sections. The first section is the Principles of Professional Conduct—a set of six positive essays expressing the profession's high ideals. These headlines introduce the six essays:

I. **Responsibilities.** In carrying out their responsibilities as professionals, members should exercise sensitive professional and moral judgments in all their activities.

II. **The public interest.** Members should accept the obligation to act in a way that will serve the public interest, honor the public trust, and demonstrate commitment to professionalism.

III. **Integrity.** To maintain and broaden public confidence, members should perform all professional responsibilities with the highest sense of integrity.

IV. **Objectivity and independence.** A member should maintain objectivity and be free of conflicts of interest in discharging professional responsibilities. A member in public practice should be independent in fact and appearance when providing auditing and other attestation services.

V. **Due care.** A member should observe the profession's technical and ethical standards, strive continually to improve competence and quality of services, and discharge professional responsibility to the best of the member's ability.

VI. **Scope and nature of services.** A member in public practice should observe the Principles of the Code of Professional Conduct in determining the scope and nature of services to be provided.

These principals reflect high ideals about moral judgment, commitment to the public interest, and skillful performance. The sixth one (VI) refers to the issue of balancing audit firms' commitment to clients (giving business advice and consulting) and commitment to the public (giving opinions on financial statements).

The second section contains the enforceable Rules of Conduct. Below you will find the two rules (Rule 101 and Rule 102) on independence and objectivity. We emphasize these two rules here because we will also study the SEC and ISB rules at the same time. The PEEC also publishes "Interpretations of Rules of Conduct," which are detailed explanations of specific rules necessary to help members understand particular applications. The AICPA PEEC interpretations on independence and objectivity are in Appendix BA (We put the details in the Appendix so we can move more directly to the details of the SEC and ISB rules in this section.) The AICPA PEEC also publishes "rulings" on the applicability of rules in specific situations. (The full text of the interpretations and rulings are available at the AICPA website www.aicpa.org.)

Rule 101 itself has no substantive content. It "hooks" the interpretations that are explained in Appendix BA. The fundamental thrust of these interpretations is that auditors preserve independence by (a) avoiding financial connections that make it appear that the auditor's wealth depends upon the outcome of the audit, and (b) avoiding managerial connections that make it appear that the auditors are involved in management decisions for the audit client (thus auditing their own work). You need to study these interpretations to understand the details of the AICPA independence requirements. The "body designated by Council" to produce them is the AICPA PEEC.

AICPA RULE OF CONDUCT

Rule 101: Independence

A member in public practice shall be independent in the performance of professional services as required by standards promulgated by bodies designated by Council.

AICPA RULE OF CONDUCT

Rule 102: Integrity and Objectivity

In the performance of any professional service, a member shall maintain objectivity and integrity, shall be free of conflicts of interest, and shall not knowingly misrepresent facts or subordinate his or her judgment to others.

Rule 102 applies not only to AICPA members in public practice but also to AICPA members working in government and industry (MIGIs). (Jorge—the staff accountant in the decision process illustration given earlier in this module—is a MIGI.) The rule requires integrity and objectivity in all kinds of professional work—tax practice and consulting practice as well as audit practice for public accountants—and all kinds of accounting work performed by AICPA members employed in corporations, not-for-profit organizations, governments, and individual practices. In addition to integrity and objectivity, Rule 102 emphasizes (a) being free from conflicts of interest between CPAs and others, (b) knowing the truth but misrepresenting facts in reports and discussions, and (c) letting other people dictate or influence the CPA's judgment and professional decisions. The interpretations in Appendix BA tell more of the details about these features of the rule.

U.S. Securities and Exchange Commission

The SEC issued its comprehensive independence rule in November 2000. The first premise is that *independence in fact* is a mental state of objectivity and lack of bias. The second premise is that *independence in appearance* depends on whether a reasonable investor, with knowledge of all relevant facts and circumstances, can conclude that the auditor is *not* capable of exercising objective and impartial judgment. Hence, an auditor's independence depends upon auditors both having the proper mental state and passing the appearance test.

In a preface to the rule, the SEC wrote four principles for determining whether an accountant is independent of an audit client. They are factors the SEC will first consider when making independence determinations in controversial cases. Accountants may *not* be independent if they have a relationship that:

- creates a mutual or conflicting interest between the accountant and the audit client.
- places the accountant in the position of auditing his or her own work.
- results in the accountant acting as management or an employee of the audit client.
- places the accountant in a position of being an advocate for the audit client.

The most significant categories addressed by the SEC rules are in the areas of financial and employment relationships, non-audit services (e.g., taxation, consulting), and disclosure of fees. The following discussion is a simplification of the lengthy SEC rules. The full text of the rules is in the SEC website at www.sec.gov.)

Financial Employment Relationships

The SEC independence rules relating to financial relationships are very similar to the AICPA Interpretations explained in Appendix BA in the Rule 101 and Rule 102 series. (Students who wish to know all about the minor differences can study the full text of the rules in the SEC website at www.sec.gov.)

However, the November 2000 SEC rules enacted a significant difference in the application of the rules to audit firm personnel and family members. You will notice in

SEC Definitions

Audit Engagement Team
All partners, principals, shareholders, and professional employees participating in an audit, review, or attestation engagement of an audit client, including those conducting concurring or second partner reviews and all persons who consult with others on the audit engagement team during the audit, review, or attestation engagement regarding technical or industry-specific issues, transactions, or events.

Chain of Command
All persons who: (1) Supervise or have direct management responsibility for the audit, including at all successively senior levels through the accounting firm's chief executive; (2) Evaluate the performance or recommend the compensation of the audit engagement partner; or (3) Provide quality control or other oversight of the audit.

Authors' Note: These definitions essentially include all the audit firm's professionals who work on a particular audit client or are involved in the audit in some direct way through influence on the audit partner or post-audit quality control monitoring.

SEC Definitions

Covered Persons in the Firm

The following partners, principals, shareholders, and employees of an accounting firm:
(1) On the audit engagement team,
(2) In the chain of command,
(3) Any other partner, principal, shareholder, or managerial employee of the accounting firm who has provided ten or more hours of non-audit services to the audit client for the period beginning on the date such services are provided and ending on the date the accounting firm signs the report on the financial statements for the fiscal year during which those services are provided, or who expects to provide ten or more hours of non-audit services to the audit client on a recurring basis, and
(4) Any other partner, principal, or shareholder from an office of the accounting firm in which the lead audit engagement partner primarily practices in connection with the audit.

Authors' Note: In essence the "covered persons" are the firm's professionals closely connected to the audit engagement and the firm's owners who are located in the office where the lead engagement partner practices. However, the SEC added the category of owners and manager-level professionals who provide non-audit (tax, consulting) services for the audit client. Therefore, almost everyone who provides services of any type for an audit client must observe the independence rules.

Appendix BA, Interpretation 101-9, the set of family members the AICPA considers when attributing financial and managerial interests to auditors. The SEC narrowed this set by enacting the definitions explained in the boxes above. (No doubt the AICPA will accept and adopt these definitions at some later date.) The SEC defined *the audit engagement team, the chain of command, covered persons, immediate family members,* and *close family members.*

In most cases related to financial relationships, the SEC rules apply to the audit engagement team, the chain of command, covered persons and immediate family members.

So what do all these definitions mean for applying the independence rules? For most practical purposes, the SEC rules are almost the same as the AICPA interpretations in Appendix BA, and the people who cannot have the financial and managerial relationships

SEC Definitions

Immediate Family Members
A person's spouse, spousal equivalent (i.e., cohabitant), and dependents.

Close Family Members
A person's spouse, spousal equivalent, parents (including adoptive parents and step-parents), dependents (i.e., people who received half or more support), nondependent children (including step-children), and brothers and sisters.

Authors' Note: The SEC rule narrows the specifications of family members. In Appendix BA, Interpretation 101-9, the AICPA included in the "close family members" category the grandchildren, grandparents, parents-in-law, and the spouses of each of these. (The AICPA will probably adopt the SEC categories at a later date.)

therein prohibited are the audit engagement team, the people in the chain of command, the covered persons in the firm, and the immediate family members.

The close family members definition comes into play in connection with (a) ownership or control of an audit client—for example, the audit firm's independence is impaired when a close family member of a covered person in the firm owns 5 percent or more of an audit client's stock or controls an audit client; and close family members are important in connection with (b) employment with an audit client—for example, the audit firm's independence is impaired when a close family member works in an accounting or financial reporting role at an audit client or was in such a role during any period covered by an audit for which the covered person in the firm is a covered person. (The close family member cannot work in such jobs as a member of the board of directors, chief executive officer, president, chief financial officer, chief operating officer, general counsel, chief accounting officer, controller, director of internal audit, director of financial reporting, treasurer, vice president of marketing).

Nonaudit Services

The SEC is very concerned about the fact and appearance of independence when audit firms perform consulting services for audit clients. An apparent anxiety about auditors' objectivity and lack of bias underlies this concern—considering the possibility of human frailty to give in to a client's improper financial reporting for the sake of preserving lucrative consulting work. The SEC's concern in this regard is controversial, but nevertheless, the SEC independence rules prohibit or place restrictions on the following nine types of nonaudit services provided to audit clients. (No such restrictions apply to these services when they are performed for clients who are not audit clients.)

- Bookkeeping or other services related to the audit client's accounting records or financial statements (including maintaining or preparing the accounting records, preparing the financial statements, or preparing or originating source data underlying the financial statements; *except* in emergency situations).

- Financial information systems design and implementation (including operating or supervising the client's information system, designing or implementing a hardware or software system that generates information that is significant to the client's financial statements *unless* the audit client's management takes full and complete responsibility for all design, implementation, internal control, and management decisions about the hardware and software).

- Appraisal or valuation services or fairness opinions (including any such service material to the financial statements where the auditor might audit the results of the audit firm's own work; *but* the audit firm's valuation experts may audit actuarial calculations, perform tax-oriented valuations, and perform nonfinancial valuations for audit clients).

- Actuarial services (including determination of actuarial liabilities *unless* the audit client management first uses its own actuaries and accepts responsibility for significant actuarial methods and assumptions).

- Internal audit services (including internal audit services amounting to more than 40 percent of the total hours expended on the audit client's internal audit activities related to the client's internal accounting controls, financial systems, or financial statements for companies with more than $200 million in total assets; or any kind of internal audit services *unless* the audit client's management appoints an internal audit director who has complete authority to be responsible for all aspects of the internal audit function from beginning to end).

- Management functions (including acting temporarily or permanently as a director, officer, or employee of an audit client, or performing any decision-making, supervisory, or ongoing monitoring function for the audit client).

- Human resources (including all aspects of executive search activities, reference checking, status and compensation determination, and hiring advice).

- Broker-dealer services (including acting as a broker-dealer, promoter, or underwriter, on behalf of an audit client, making investment decisions or otherwise having discretionary authority over investments, executing a transaction to buy or sell investments, or having custody of assets).

- Legal services (including any service under circumstances in which the person providing the service must be admitted to practice before the courts of a U.S. jurisdiction).

Disclosures About Fees

The SEC believes that people who use financial statements and audit reports can be enlightened with information about auditors' fee arrangements with clients. Hence, SEC rules require that companies (not auditors) disclose the following in proxy statements delivered to their shareholders:

- Total audit fees to the audit firm for the annual audit and the reviews of quarterly financial information.

- Total fees to the audit firm for consulting services on financial information systems design and implementation.

- Total fees to the audit firm for all other consulting and advisory work (over and above the audit fees and the information systems fees above).

- Tell whether the audit committee or the board of directors considered the audit firm's information systems work and other consulting work to be compatible with maintaining the auditor's independence.

- If greater than 50 percent, tell the percentage of the audit hours performed by persons other than the principal accountant's full-time, permanent employees. (This disclosure refers to "leased employees" in an "alternative practice structure" arrangement. Please refer to AICPA Interpretation 101-14 in Appendix BA.)

Independence Standards Board

From its creation in 1997 through December 2000, the ISB issued three standards and three interpretations.

ISB Interpretation 99-1: Assisting clients with Implementation of FAS 133 (Derivatives)

The ISB's first pronouncement (March 1999) drew attention to auditor's work that might produce an auditor's product that the auditor would then audit! Accounting for derivatives according to FAS 133 is very complicated, and many audit clients seek assistance from their auditors. Interpretation 99-1 rules that such assistance is permitted, and independence is not impaired, so long as the auditors (1) do not prepare accounting entries, (2) do not compute derivative values (even with a firm-developed valuation model), and (3) do not take responsibility for valuation assumptions and inputs. These three features are the essence of accounting for derivatives, and the client must perform them. The auditors can give advice and then audit the client's results.

ISB Standard No.1: Independence Discussions with Audit Committees (June 1999)

ISB 1 requires that the audit firm each year:

- Disclose in writing to the audit client's board of directors and its audit committee all relationships between the auditor and the company the auditor thinks may be reasonably related to consideration of the auditor's independence.
- Confirm to the board of directors that, in the auditor's professional judgment, the audit firm is independent in accordance with SEC rules.
- Discuss its independence with the audit committee or with the board of directors.

This rule is imposed on auditors. However, its intent is to ensure that public company audit clients' audit committees and boards of directors consider their auditors' independence at least once each year. If the discussion is not held, auditors are supposed to withhold the audit report.

ISB Interpretation 00-1 (February 2000) added to ISB No. 1 the requirement that when more than one auditor is involved in the audit of a consolidated group of companies, the primary auditor is the firm that must produce the required disclosures and conduct the discussion, but any other auditors ("secondary auditors") of public companies in the consolidation must also comply with respect to their audit clients. ISB Interpretation 00-2 (July 2000) amended Interpretation 00-1 with the requirement that the primary audit firm must disclose all the relationships of domestic and foreign audit firms involved in the audit and describe the other auditors' relationships, if possible.

ISB Standard No. 2: Certain Independence Implications of Audits of Mutual Funds and Related Entities (December 1999, Amended July 2000)

An investment company "complex" can consist of several related entities involved in mutual fund management—the fund sponsor, banks, broker-dealers, investment advisers, insurance companies, trustees, transfer agents, and "sister funds" (other mutual funds in the same family). Imagine a complex consisting of TruFund (sponsor); the sister funds TrufundDiversified, TruFundIndex, and TruFundInternational; Faithful & Co. (broker-dealer); BigBank (transfer agent); and Big Deal Investment Management (investment advisers).

When auditing one mutual fund in the complex (e.g., TruFundDiversified) or when auditing a nonfund entity (e.g., Faithful & Co.), the audit firm, the audit engagement team, and the persons in the chain of command (refer to the SEC definitions above) must be independent of all the entities in the complex. This independence refers to all the financial, employment, and non-audit services explained above in the SEC rules.

ISB No.2 rules that independence is not impaired: (1) when anyone in the audit firm who is not on the audit engagement team and not in the chain of command holds investments in nonclient sister funds, and (2) when anyone who is not on the audit engagement team or in the chain of command, including firm owners and their immediate family members, hold investments in audit client mutual funds through their employment benefit plans. The first exception means that owners and employees in the audit firm who are not connected with the audit of TruFundDiversified can own shares in TruFundInternational (sister fund that is not an audit client). The second exception means, for example, that the husband of the partner in charge of the TruFundDiversified audit can own shares in TruFundIndex (also an audit client, but not led by the partner-wife) so long as the shares are acquired in connection with his employment benefit plan at AnyCompany (the husband's employer).

ISB Standard No. 3: Employment with Audit Clients (July 2000)

This standard deals with the threat to audit independence when audit firm professionals consider or take jobs with audit clients. The threat is that the auditor considering a job offer from a client might not perform audit work properly while on the audit team. Likewise, after the professional takes a job with the audit client, he or she might improperly influence the audit performed by former colleagues in the audit firm.

The audit firm's independence is considered impaired unless it undertakes certain safeguards. The safeguards are these:

- Audit professionals must report to the firm conversations with an audit client about possible employment, then the audit firm must:

  (1) remove the person from the audit engagement team, and

  (2) review the person's audit work to date to determine whether he or she exercised proper skepticism while on the audit.

- When a former owner or professional employee of the firm joins an audit client within one year after leaving the firm and this person has significant interaction with the continuing audit engagement team, then the audit firm must perform additional review of the next annual audit. The purpose of the review is to determine whether:

  (1) the former firm professional circumvented the audit because of familiarity with design, approach, and strategy , and

  (2) the remaining members of the audit engagement team maintained objectivity when auditing the work and representations of the former firm professional.

In addition for persons who leave the audit firm to take client employment, the audit firm must (1) liquidate former owners' capital balances, (2) settle all material retirement account balances unless the payments are fixed as to timing and amount (but the former professional does not have to liquidate balances held under a defined contribution retirement plan), (3) settle all immaterial retirement account balances when in the five years following separation from the audit firm the former professional becomes a client officer named in a proxy statement or annual report filed with the SEC. This last requirement dictates complete separation of financial connections with the audit firm when the person becomes a highly ranked officer in a public company.

The potential problems involved in audit firm owners or professional employees taking jobs with audit clients is one of the topics that ought to be discussed with the client's audit committee or board in accordance with ISB Standard No. 1.

ISB Exposure Draft on a Conceptual Framework for Auditor Independence (November 2000)

ISB wants to have a coherent framework for independence standards. Hence, the *conceptual framework* is under discussion. Since the framework is a work-in-process, we mention it in this textbook only to note that it proposes a model of elements for independence deliberations and standards-setting. The essential elements are (a) suggestions for auditors' assessment of *independence risk*, (b) consideration of *threats* to independence, (c) implementation of independence *safeguards* and (d) analysis of the *costs and benefits* of independence requirements. Perhaps you noticed that the language of threats and safeguards has already entered the literature in ISB No.3 above (because an earlier draft of the conceptual framework was already in the hands of ISB members!).

R E V I E W
CHECKPOINTS

B.5 In regard to making rules about independence, what are the jurisdictions of the (a) AICPA PEEC, (b) SEC, (c) ISB?

B.6 Yolanda is the executive in charge of the Santa Fe office of SIDA&Co, an international-size audit firm. Yolanda is responsible for the practice in all areas of audit, tax, and consulting, but she does not serve as a field audit partner or a reviewer. Javier is the partner in charge of the Besame, Inc. audit (an SEC filing). Is SIDA&Co independent if Yolanda owns common stock of Besame? Is SIDA&Co independent if Yolanda's brother owns 10 shares of the common stock of Besame?

B.7 Can audit managers on the audit engagement team who are also attorneys admitted to the State Bar assist in the defense of a lawsuit against an audit client for product liability defects?

B.8 Why do you think the SEC requires companies to disclose fees paid to independent accounting firms for audit and consulting services? What must be disclosed?

B.9 What do the SEC disclosure rules and ISB Standard No.1 have in common in connection with auditors' relations with an audit client's board of directors and its audit committee?

B.10 What is the perceived independence problem concerning members of an audit engagement team entertaining employment offers from audit clients?

B.11 Reference: You can use numerous short questions at the end of the chapter to review the application of rules.

AICPA Rules of Conduct: General and Technical Standards, Responsibilities to Clients, and Other Responsibilities

Now that we have dealt with the emphasis on independence, we can turn to the other AICPA rules of conduct. Nine such rules are in sections 200, 300, and 500. The box below shows the organization of these rules.

AICPA Rules of Conduct

Section 100: Independence, Integrity, and Objectivity.
    Rule 101: Independence.
    Rule 102: Integrity and Objectivity.

Section 200: General and Technical Standards.
    Rule 201: General Standards.
    Rule 202: Compliance with Standards.
    Rule 203: Accounting Principles.

Section 300: Responsibilities to Clients.
    Rule 301: Confidential Client Information.
    Rule 302: Contingent Fees.

Section 400: (No title or rules are in the 400 series.)

Section 500: Other Responsibilities and Practices.
    Rule 501: Acts Discreditable.
    Rule 502: Advertising and Other Forms of Solicitation.
    Rule 503: Commissions and Referral Fees.
    Rule 504: (No Rule 504.)
    Rule 505: Form of Practice and Name.

> ## AICPA Rule of Conduct
>
> ### General Standards
>
> **Rule 201:** A member shall comply with the following standards and with any interpretations thereof by bodies designated by Council:
>
> **A.** *Professional competence.* Undertake only those professional services that the member or the member's firm can reasonably expect to be completed with professional competence.
>
> **B.** *Due professional care.* Exercise due professional care in the performance of professional services.
>
> **C.** *Planning and supervision.* Adequately plan and supervise the performance of professional services.
>
> **D.** *Sufficient relevant data.* Obtain sufficient relevant data to afford a reasonable basis for conclusions or recommendations in relation to any professional services performed.

Analysis and Interpretation

Rule 201 is a comprehensive statement of general standards accountants are expected to observe in all areas of practice. This is the rule that enforces the various series of professional standards. The AICPA Council has authorized the following committees and boards to issue standards enforceable under Rule 201: Auditing Standards Board, (auditing standards and attestation standards), Accounting and Review Services Committee, Tax Executive Committee, and Consulting Services Executive Committee. (AICPA Council has not authorized the Personal Financial Planning Committee to issue Rule 201 standards.)

Rule 201 effectively prohibits the acceptance of any engagement that the CPA knows he or she cannot handle. Such engagements may involve audits that require extensive capability with computers—knowledge the auditor may lack—or consulting services in areas unknown to the practitioner. This rule covers all areas of public accounting practice

AUDITING INSIGHT

AUDITOR'S DOWNFALL

MIAMI: Mr. G, former partner of a large CPA firm, surrenders today to begin a 12- year prison term.

As auditor of ESM, Mr. G knowingly approved the company's false financial statements for five years, allowing the massive fraud to continue, ultimately costing investors $320 million.

Just days after being promoted to partner, two ESM officers told him about an accounting ruse that was hiding millions of dollars in losses. He had missed it in two previous audits. They said: "It's going to look terrible for you, a new partner."

Mr. G didn't want to face his superiors at the firm with the admission of the failed audits. He decided to go along with ESM because he thought the company could make up the losses and get everybody out of it.

Mr. G: "I never evaluated a criminal side to what I was doing. It was a professional decision, a judgment decision that it would eventually work itself out. It's the only thing I never discussed with my wife."

ESM loaned Mr. G $200,000 to help out with his financial problems. "I never related my actions to the money. I just didn't want to face up that I had missed it originally."

On being prepared for prison: "I don't know. What can I bring, a typewriter, computer? I'd like to read and work on things."

Source: The Wall Street Journal

AICPA RULE OF CONDUCT

Compliance with Standards

Rule 202: A member who performs auditing, review, compilation, management consulting, tax, or other professional services shall comply with standards promulgated by bodies designated by Council.

---

except personal financial planning and business valuation. Of course, a CPA may have to do some research to learn more about a unique problem or technique and may need to engage a colleague as a consultant.

Analysis and Interpretation

Rule 202 requires adherence to duly promulgated technical standards in all areas of professional service. These areas include the ones cited in the rule—auditing, review and compilation (unaudited financial statements), consulting, tax or "other" professional services. The "bodies designated by Council" are the Auditing Standards Board, the Accounting and Review Services Committee, the Tax Executive Committee, and the Consulting Services Executive Committee. The practical effect of Rule 202 is to make noncompliance with all technical standards (in addition to the Rule 201 general standards) subject to disciplinary proceedings. Therefore, failure to follow auditing standards, accounting and review standards, tax standards, and consulting standards, is a violation of Rule 202.

You should realize that the AICPA Council has not authorized its Personal Financial Planning Committee to issue standards enforceable under rule 202. This committee has published a series of statements on Personal Financial Planning standards to guide CPAs in financial planning work. The introduction to these statements includes this warning: "Statements on Personal Financial Planning are published for the guidance of members of the Institute and do not constitute enforceable standards. . . . they depend for their authority on the general acceptability of the opinions expressed." Apparently, the AICPA does not wish to make standards in the complicated area of financial planning subject to the discipline available through Rule 202. Improper practice, however, can be governed under other rules, notable Rule 501 (Acts Discreditable) discussed later.

AICPA RULE OF CONDUCT

Accounting Principles

Rule 203: A member shall not (1) express an opinion or state affirmatively that the financial statements or other financial data of any entity are presented in conformity with generally accepted principles or (2) state that he or she is not aware of any material modifications that should be made to such statements or data in order for them to be in conformity with generally accepted accounting principles, if such statements or data contain any departure from an accounting principle promulgated by bodies designated by Council to establish such principles that has a material effect on the statements or data taken as a whole. If, however, the statements or data contain such a departure and the member can demonstrate that due to unusual circumstances the financial statements or data would otherwise have been misleading, the member can comply with the rule by describing the departure, its approximate effects, if practicable, and the reasons why compliance with the princple would result in a misleading statement.

Analysis and Interpretation

AICPA Council has designated three rule-making bodies to pronounce accounting principles under Rule 203. The FASB and its predecessors are designated to pronounce standards in general. Therefore, Rule 203 requires adherence to Accounting Research Bulletins of the Committee on Accounting Procedure (issued before 1959), Opinions of the Accounting Principles Board (1959–1973), and statements and interpretations of financial accounting standards adopted by the Financial Accounting Standards Board (1973 to present). Council has also designated the Governmental Accounting Standards Board (GASB) to pronounce accounting standards for state and local government entities. In 1999, AICPA Council designated the Federal Accounting Standards Advisory Board (FASAB) as the body authorized to establish generally accepted accounting principles for federal government units. FASAB issues the Statements of Federal Financial Accounting Standards.

You may wonder about the two parts at the beginning of Rule 203: "(1) express an opinion or state affirmatively . . . , or (2) state that he or she is not aware of any material modifications. . . . " These two parts are intended to cover two types of attestation reports regarding the conformity of financial statements or other data with generally accepted accounting principles, the first part refers to *opinions* on financial statement and other data—for example, the standard unqualified audit report on audited financial statements. The second part refers to reports in which *negative assurance* is permitted—for example, the review report on unaudited financial statements.

Rule 203 requires adherence to official pronouncements of accounting principles, with the important exception in unusual circumstances where adherence would *create* misleading statements. The rule itself admits that unusual circumstances may exist, permits CPAs to decide for themselves the applicability of official pronouncements, and places on them the burden of an ethical decision. The rule is not strictly imperative because it allows CPAs to exercise a utilitarian calculation for special circumstances. Rule 203 requires adherence to official pronouncements *unless* such adherence would be misleading. The consequences of misleading statements to outside decision makers would be financial harm, so presumably the greater good would be realized by explaining a departure and thereby "breaking the rule of officially promulgated accounting principles." (An example of such a report is shown in Chapter 3).

AICPA RULE OF CONDUCT

Confidential Client Information

Rule 301: A member in public practice shall not disclose any confidential information without the specific consent of the client.

This rule shall not be construed (1) to relieve a member of his or her professional obligations under Rules 202 and 203, (2) to affect in any way the member's obligation to comply with a validly issued and enforceable subpoena or summons, or to prohibit a member's compliance with applicable laws and government regulations, (3) to prohibit review of a member's professional practice under AICPA or state CPA society or Board of Accountancy authorization, or (4) to preclude a member from initiating a complaint with or responding to any inquiry made by, the ethics division or trial board of the Institute or a duly constituted investigative or disciplinary body of a state CPA society or Board of Accountancy.

Members of any of the bodies identified in (4) above and members involved with professional practice reviews identified in(3) above shall not use to their own advantage or disclose any member's confidential client information that comes to their attention in carrying out those activities. This prohibition shall not restrict members' exchange of information in connection with the investigative or disciplinary proceedings described in (4) above or the professional practice reviews described in (3) above.

Members in government and industry (MIGIs) can also be subject to Rule 203. Working as management accountants, MIGIs produce financial statements and sign written management representation letters for their external auditors. They also present financial statements to regulatory authorities and creditors. MIGIs generally "report" that the company's financial statements conform to GAAP, and this report is taken as an expression of opinion (or negative assurance) of the type governed by Rule 203. The result is that MIGIs who present financial statements containing any undisclosed departures from official pronouncements face disciplinary action for violating the rule.

Analysis and Interpretation

Confidential information is information that should not be disclosed to outside parties unless demanded by a court or an administrative body having subpoena or summons power. *Privileged* information is information that cannot even be demanded by a court. Common-law privilege exists for husband-wife and attorney-client relationships. Physician-patient and priest-penitent relationships have obtained the privilege through state statutes. No accountant-client privilege exists under federal law, and no state-created privilege has been recognized in federal courts. In all the recognized privilege relationships, the professional person is obligated to observe the privilege, which can be waived only by the client, patient, or penitent. (These persons are said to be the holders of the privilege.)

The rules of privileged and confidential communication are based on the belief that they facilitate a free flow of information between parties to the relationship. The nature of accounting services makes it necessary for the accountant to have access to information about salaries, products, contracts, merger or divestment plans, tax matters, and other data required for the best possible professional work. Managers would be less likely to reveal such information if they could not trust the accountant to keep it confidential. If accountants were to reveal such information, the resultant reduction of the information flow might be undesirable, so no accountants should break the confidentiality rule without a good reason.

The AICPA interprets exception 4 in Rule 301 (referring to complaints made to a recognized investigative or disciplinary body) to apply only to investigative or disciplinary bodies under its jurisdiction, namely the AICPA Professional Ethics Division and the ethics enforcement committees in the various state societies of CPAs and also to state Boards of Accountancy. Thus, the ethics and law enforcement agencies in the U.S. Securities and Exchange Commission, the Internal Revenue Service, and such other agencies as the U.S. Department of Justice, Federal Trade Commission, EEOC, and local police and district attorneys are not within the exception. Voluntary disclosure to these agencies is not explicitly permitted under Rule 301.

Difficult problems arise over auditors' obligations to "blow the whistle" about clients' shady or illegal practices. Auditing standards deal with this problem: If a client refuses to accept an audit report that has been modified because of inability to obtain sufficient competent evidence about a suspected illegal act, failure to account for or disclose properly a material amount connected with an illegal act, or inability to estimate amounts involved in an illegal act, the audit firm should withdraw from the engagement and give the reasons in writing to the board of directors. In such an extreme case, the withdrawal amounts to whistle blowing, but the action results from the client's decision not to disclose the information. For all practical purposes, information is not considered confidential if disclosure of it is necessary to make financial statements not misleading.

Auditors are not, in general, legally *obligated* to blow the whistle on clients. However, circumstances may exist where auditors are legally *justified* in making disclosures to a regulatory agency or a third party. Such circumstances include: (1) when a client has intentionally and without authorization associated or involved a CPA in its misleading conduct, (2) when a client has distributed misleading draft financial statements prepared by a CPA for internal use only, or (3) when a client prepares and distributes in an annual report or prospectus misleading information for which the CPA has not assumed any responsibility.[7] In addition, the Private Securities Litigation Reform Act of 1995 imposed another report-

---

[7] C. Chazen, R. L. Miller, and K. I. Solomon, "When the Rules Say: 'See Your Lawyer,'" *Journal of Accountancy.*

ing requirement in connection with clients' illegal acts. Refer to the Chapter 7 explanation of auditors' responsibility to report to the board of directors and to the U.S. Securities and Exchange Commission (SEC) if the board does not report illegal acts to the SEC.

CPAs should not view Rule 301 on confidential information as an excuse for inaction where action may be appropriate to right a wrongful act committed or about to be committed by a client. In some cases, auditors' inaction may be viewed as part of a conspiracy or willingness to be an accessory to a wrong. Such situations are dangerous and potentially damaging. A useful initial course of action is to consult with an attorney about possible legal pitfalls of both whistle blowing and silence. Then, decide for yourself.

Purchase, Sale, or Merger of a Practice

Accountants can permit other accountants to review confidential working papers and other information about clients in connection with arrangements to sell or merge an accounting practice. The AICPA advises accountants to have an agreement between themselves that extends the confidentiality safeguard to the prospective purchasing accountant as it existed with the original accountant.

AUDITING INSIGHT

IRS INFORMANT

James C, CPA, was in hot water with the IRS. To get relief, he agreed to tell IRS about tax cheating by his clients. After all, some of them were practicing tax evasion, and James C knew about it.

Steven N, a client said: "It's every taxpayer's worst nightmare. I relied on my trusted accountant to keep me out of trouble with the IRS. James C often sat in my living room. We treated him like family. I even gave him power of attorney to represent me before the IRS."

But Steve N had skimmed untaxed income from his restaurant business and was indicted for tax evasion. An AICPA spokesman said: "The accountant's job is to point out errors to the client—not to the IRS."

Postscript: The Missouri State Board of Accountancy revoked James C's CPA certificate, saying: "His action is not only at odds with the role of the CPA, but acts to undermine the very foundation of the professional relationship between an accountant and client. Such duplicity cannot and will not be condoned."

Post Postscript: The U.S Senate considered a bill making it a crime for federal agents to offer forgiveness of taxes to induce CPAs to inform on their clients. The U.S. Justice Department dropped the tax evasion charges against Steven N.

Source: *The Wall Street Journal.*

AICPA RULE OF CONDUCT

Contingent Fees

Rule 302: A member in public practice shall not
(1) Perform for a contingent fee any professional services for, or receive such a fee from, a client for whom the member of the member's firm performs
    (*a*) an audit or review of a financial statement; or
    (*b*) a compilation of a financial statement when the member expects, or reasonably might expect, that a third party will use the financial statement and the member's compilation report does not disclose a lack of independence; or
    (*c*) an examination of prospective financial information; or
(2) Prepare an original or amended tax return or claim for a tax refund for a contingent fee for any client.

Analysis and Interpretation

A **contingent fee** is a fee established for the performance of any service in an arrangement in which no fee will be charged unless a specific finding or result is attained, or the fee otherwise depends on the result of the service. (Fees are not contingent if they are fixed by a court or other public authority or, in tax matters, determined as a result of the findings of judicial proceedings or the findings of government agencies; nor are fees contingent when they are based on the complexity or time required for the work.) Under Rule 302, CPAs can charge contingent fees for such work as representing a client in an IRS tax audit and certain other tax matters, achieving goals in a consulting service engagement, or helping a person obtain a bank loan in a financial planning engagement. CPAs can charge contingent fees like investment bankers in merger deals and lawyers in injury lawsuits.

Rule 302 permits CPAs to receive contingent fees *except* from clients for whom the CPAs perform attest services, where users of financial information may be relying on the CPAs' work. The prohibitions in item 1 (*a*), 1 (*b*), and 1 (*c*) all refer to attest engagements in which independence is required. Acceptance of contingent fee arrangements during the period in which the member or the member's firm is engaged to perform any of these attestations or during the period covered by any historical financial statements involved in any of these engagements is considered an impairment of independence.

Rule 302 also prohibits contingent fees in connection with everyday tax practice of preparing original or amended tax returns. This prohibition arose from an interesting conflict of government agencies. The FTC wanted to see contingent fees permitted, but the IRS objected on the grounds that such fees might induce accountants and clients to "play the audit lottery"—understating tax improperly in the hope of escaping audit. The IRS asserted that if the AICPA permitted such contingent fees, then the IRS would make its own rules prohibiting them. The FTC agreed that the AICPA rule could contain this prohibition.

AICPA Rule of Conduct

Responsibilities to Colleagues

In light of the numbering system for the Rules of Conduct, you might wonder why no rule is numbered in the 400 series and why no rules deal directly with such responsibilities. The last rule in this section (Rule 401, which basically prohibited competition by one member for the clients and practice of another) was repealed by vote of the AICPA membership in 1979. The rule then was being challenged by the U.S. Department of Justice as an unwarranted restraint on competition. The AICPA simply has not changed the numbering system.

AICPA Rule of Conduct

Acts Discreditable

Rule 501: A member shall not commit an act discreditable to the profession.

Analysis and Interpretation

Rule 501 may be called the *moral clause* of the code, but it is only occasionally the basis for disciplinary action. Penalties normally are invoked automatically under the AICPA Bylaws, which provide for expulsion of members found by a court to have committed any fraud, filed false tax returns, been convicted of any criminal offense, or found by the AICPA Trial Board to have been guilty of an act discreditable to the profession.

AICPA interpretations consider discreditable acts to include these:

- Withholding a client's books and records and important working papers when the client has requested their return.
- Being found guilty by a court or administrative agency to have violated employment antidiscrimination laws, including ones related to sexual and other forms of harassment.
- Failing to follow government audit standards and guides in governmental audits when the client or the government agency expects such standards to be followed.
- Soliciting or disclosing CPA Examination questions and answers from the closed CPA Examination.
- Failing to file tax returns or remit payroll and other taxes collected for others (e.g., employee taxes withheld).
- Making, or permitting others to make, false and misleading entries in records and financial statements.

This last item is specifically applicable to members in government and industry (MIGIs) as well as members in public practice. Any management accountant who participates in the production of false and misleading financial statements commits a discreditable act.

AUDITING INSIGHT

DISCREDITABLE ACT

The Enforcement Committee found that Respondent drew a gun from his desk drawer during a dispute with a client in his office in contravention of Secion 501.41 [discreditable acts prohibition] of the [Texas] Rules of Professional Conduct. Respondent agreed to accept a private reprimand to be printed . . . in the Texas State Board Report.

Source: Texas State Board Report

AICPA RULE OF CONDUCT

Advertising and Other Forms of Solicitation

Rule 502: A member in public practice shall not seek to obtain clients by advertising or other forms of solicitation in a manner that is false, misleading, or deceptive. Solicitation by the use of coercion, overreaching or harassing conduct is prohibited.

Analysis and Interpretation

Rule 502 permits advertising with only a few limitations. The current rule applies only to CPAs practicing public accounting and relates to their efforts to obtain clients. Basic guidelines about advertising include:

- Advertising may not create false or unjustified expectations of favorable results.
- Advertising may not imply the ability to influence any court, tribunal, regulatory agency, or similar body or official.
- Advertising may not contain a fee estimate when the CPA knows it is likely to be substantially increased, unless the client is notified.

- Advertising may not contain any other representation likely to cause a reasonable person to misunderstand or be deceived.

Advertising consists of messages designed to attract business that are broadcast widely to an undifferentiated audience (e.g., print, radio, television, billboards). The guidelines basically prohibit false, misleading, and deceptive messages.

Solicitation, on the other hand, generally refers to direct contact (e.g., in person, mail, telephone) with a specific potential client. In regard to solicitation, Rule 502 basically prohibits, extreme bad behavior (*coercion, overreaching,* or *harassing conduct*).

Most CPAs carry out only modest advertising efforts, and many do no advertising at all. Public practice is generally marked by decorum and a sense of good taste. However, there are exceptions, and they tend to get much attention—most of it disapproving—from other CPAs and the public in general. The danger in bad advertising lies in getting the image of a professional huckster, which may backfire on efforts to build a practice.

Solicitation

Many CPAs abhor *solicitation* and many state boards of accountancy try to prohibit direct, uninvited approaches to prospective clients, especially when the client already has a CPA. Nevertheless, the U.S. Supreme Court struck down the Florida solicitation prohibition, declaring it to be an infringement of personal and business rights to free speech and due process *(Edenfield* v. *Fane,* no. 91.1594, April 26, 1993). Fane moved to Florida and conducted face-to-face meetings to obtain clients. The Florida board of accountancy brought suit to enforce its anti-solicitation rule. The Florida board lost in court. At present, some state boards try to discourage solicitation with restrictive rules they hope will not run afoul of the Supreme Court decision. Some state boards are trying to get anti-solicitation rules into their state laws where they think they will be shielded from the

---

AICPA Rule of Conduct

Commissions and Referral Fees

Rule 503:

A. Prohibited Commissions

   A member in public practice shall not for a commission recommend or refer to a client any product or service, or for a commission recommend or refer any product or service to be supplied by a client, or receive a commission, when the member or the member's firm also performs for that client.

   (a) an audit or review of a financial statement; or

   (b) a compilation of a financial statement when the member expects, or reasonably might expect, that a third party will use the financial statement and the member's compilation report does not disclose a lack of independence; or

   (c) an examination of prospective financial information.

   This prohibition applies during the period in which the member is engaged to perform any of the services listed above and the period covered by any historical financial statements involved in such listed services.

B. Disclosure of Permitted Commission

   A member in public practice who is not prohibited by this rule from performing services for or receiving a commission and who is paid or expects to be paid a commission shall disclose that fact to any person or entity to whom the member recommends or refers a product or service to which the commission relates.

C. Referral Fees

   Any member who accepts a referral fee for recommending or referring any service of a CPA to any person or entity or who pays a referral fee to obtain a client shall disclose such acceptance or payment to the client.

U.S. Supreme Court. How do things stand now: Solicitation is legal, but be aware that your local state board may have rules or laws prohibiting it.

Engagements Obtained Through Third Parties

CPAs sometimes hire marketing firms to obtain clients. In years past, this arrangement was designed to avoid direct involvement in advertising and solicitation efforts that might violate Rule 502. The AICPA permits such arrangements, but warns that all such "practice development" activity is subject to Rule 502 because members cannot do through others things they are prohibited from doing themselves.

Analysis and Interpretation

A **commission** is generally defined as a percentage fee charged for professional services in connection with executing a transaction or performing some other business activity. Examples are insurance sales commissions, real estate sales commissions, and securities sales commissions. CPAs can earn commissions except in connection with any client for whom the CPA performs attest services.

Part A of Rule 503 treats commissions as an impairment of independence just like Rule 302 treats contingent fees. When a CPA is involved in an attest engagement with a client, the CPA cannot receive a commission from anyone for (1) referring a product or service *to* the client, or (2) referring to someone else a product or service supplied *by* the client. It does not matter which party actually pays the commission.

Part B of Rule 503 permits commissions, provided the engagement does not involve attestation of the types cited in Part A of the rule. This permission is tempered by the requirement that the CPA must *disclose* to clients an arrangement to receive a commission.

Most of the commission fee activity takes place in connection with personal financial planning services. CPAs often recommend insurance and investments to individuals and families. Some critics point out that clients cannot always trust commission agents (e.g., insurance salespersons, securities brokers) to have their best interests in mind when their own compensation depends on clients' buying the product that produces commissions for themselves. They make the point that "fee-only" planning advisers, who do not work on commission, are more likely to have the best interest of the clients in mind, directing them to investment professionals who handle a wide range of alternatives. In light of these matters, some CPAs make it a point to provide financial planning services on a fee-only basis.

Part C of Rule 503 deals with **referral fees**, which are: (a) fees a CPA receives for recommending another CPA's services and (b) fees a CPA pays to obtain a client. Such fees may or may not be based on a percentage of the amount of any transaction. Referral involves the practices of sending business to another CPA and paying other CPAs or outside agencies for drumming up business. Some CPAs have hired services that solicit clients on their behalf, paying a fixed or percentage fee. These arrangements are frowned upon by many CPAs, but they are permitted. However, CPAs must *disclose* such fees to clients.

AICPA RULE OF CONDUCT

Form of Organization and Name

Rule 505: A member may practice public accounting only in a form of organization permitted by law or regulation whose characteristics conform to resolutions of Council.

A member shall not practice public accounting under a firm name that is misleading. Names of one or more past owners may be included in the firm name of a successor organization.

A firm may not designate itself as "Member of the American Institute of Certified Public Accountants" unless all of its CPA owners are members of the Institute.

Analysis and Interpretation

Rule 505 allows CPAs to practice public accounting in any form of organization permitted by a state board of accountancy and authorized by law. Organization forms include proprietorship, partnership, limited partnership, limited liability partnership (LLP), professional corporation (PC), limited liability corporation (LLC), and ordinary corporation (INC). You may have noticed that the large international accounting firms now place "LLP" after their firm names. Many smaller accounting firms place "PC" in their names.

However, AICPA Council limits this privilege of organizational form by expressing certain requirements for ownership and control, especially regarding non-CPAs who have ownership interests in an organization that practices public accounting. (See the Council resolution provisions in the box at the bottom of this page.) The purpose of the Council resolution is to conform the operations of an accounting organization as closely as possible to the traditional accounting firm and to ensure control of professional services in the hands of CPAs.

CPAs in public practice cannot use misleading firm names. For example, suppose CPAs Jack and Tim, who are not in partnership together, agree to share expenses for office support, advertising, and continuing education. Jack cannot call himself "Jack, Louwers & Associates" because this name suggests a partnership where there is none.

The last paragraph of Rule 505 permits a mixed accounting organization consisting of CPA and non-CPA owners to designate itself "Member of AICPA" if all the CPA owners are actually AICPA members. (People who are not CPAs, including owners of CPA firms, are not eligible to be members of the AICPA)

Other Interpretations

A member who practices public accounting can also participate in the operation of another business organization (e.g., a consulting or tax preparation firm) that offers professional services of the types offered by public accounting firms. If this business is one permitted to practice public accounting under state law, the member is also considered to be in the practice of public accounting in it and must observe all the rules of conduct. Also, members can be passive owners (investors) in accounting services organizations that are not permitted to practice public accounting under a state's laws and regulations.

CPAs who work in alternative practice structures (APS) occupy an odd position. They can prepare compiled (unaudited) financial statements, which is considered a form of public accounting practice. In such a case, a CPA employee of the APS "PublicCo" must take final responsibility for the accountant's compilation report and must sign it with his or her own personal name (not the name of "PublicCo").

COUNCIL RESOLUTION CONCERNING FORM OF ORGANIZATION AND NAME

(Excerpts)

The characteristics of an accounting organization under Rule 505 are as follow:

- A majority (50+ %) ownership and voting rights must belong to CPAs.
- Non-CPA owners must be active in the firm, not passive investors.
- A CPA must have ultimate responsibility for the firm's services.
- Non-CPA owners can use titles such as "principal, owner, officer, member, shareholder," but cannot hold out to be a CPA.
- Non-CPA owners must abide by the AICPA Code of Professional Conduct.
- Non-CPA owners must hold a bachelor degree, and after the year 2010 must have 150 semester hours of college education.
- Non-CPA owners must complete the same continuing education requirements as CPAs who are members of the AICPA.
- Non-CPA owners are not eligible to be members of the AICPA.

AICPA RULES AND ETHICAL PRINCIPLES

Specific rules in the AICPA Rules of Conduct may not necessarily be classified under one of the ethics principles. Decisions based on a rule may involve imperative, utilitarian, or generalization considerations, or elements of all three. The rules have the form of imperatives because that is the nature of a code. However, elements of utilitarianism and generalization seem to be apparent in the underlying rationale for most of the rules. If this perception is accurate, then these two principles may be utilized by auditors in difficult decision problems where adherence to a rule could produce an undesirable result.

REVIEW
CHECKPOINTS

B.12 What ethical responsibilities do members of the AICPA have for acts of nonmembers who are under their supervision (e.g., recent college graduates who are not yet CPAs)?

B.13 What rules of conduct apply specifically to members in government and industry (MIGIs)?

B.14 What provisions of the AICPA Council Resolution on form of organization place control of accounting services in the hands of CPAs?

B.15 Reference: You can use numerous short questions at the end of the chapter to review the application of rules.

REGULATION AND QUALITY CONTROL

LEARNING OBJECTIVE

5. Name and explain the various professional associations and government agencies that enforce rules of conduct and explain the types of penalties they can impose on accountants.

As a CPA, you will be expected to observe rules of conduct published in several codes of ethics. If you join the AICPA and a state society of CPAs and practice before the U.S. Securities and Exchange Commission (SEC), you will be subject to the following:

Source of Rules of Conduct	Applicable to
State Board of Accountancy	Persons licensed by the state to practice accounting.
American Institute of CPAs	Members of AICPA.
State Society of CPAs	Members of state society of CPAs.
U.S. Securities and Exchange Commission	Persons who practice before the SEC as accountants and auditors for SEC-registered companies.

If you are an internal auditor, you will be expected to observe the rules of conduct of the Institute of Internal Auditors. As a management accountant, you will be expected to observe the Institute of Management Accountants' standards of ethical conduct for management accountants. Certified Fraud Examiners are expected to observe the Association of Certified Fraud Examiners' Code of Ethics.

Regulation and *professional ethics* go hand in hand. Codes of ethics provide the underlying authority for regulation. Quality control practices and disciplinary proceedings provide the mechanisms of self-regulation. **Self-regulation** refers to the quality control reviews and disciplinary actions conducted by fellow CPAs—professional peers.

Self-Regulatory Discipline

Individual persons (not accounting firms) are subject to the rules of conduct of state CPA societies and the AICPA only if they choose to join these organizations. The AICPA and most of the state societies have entered into a Joint Ethics Enforcement Program (JEEP), wherein complaints against CPAs can be referred by the AICPA to the state societies or by the state societies to the AICPA. Both organizations have ethics committees to hear complaints. They can (*a*) acquit an accused CPA, (*b*) find the CPA in violation of rules and issue a Letter of Required Corrective Action (LCRA), and (*c*) refer serious cases to

---

AUDITING INSIGHT

FRAUD EXAMINER EXPELLED FOR FRAUD

Curtis C was expelled by the board of regents at its regular meeting on August 4. Mr. C, formerly an internal auditor employed by the City of S___, was a member from February 1992 until his expulsion. He was the subject of an investigation by the trial board for falsifying information.

Mr. C wrongfully represented himself as a certified internal auditor, when in fact he did not hold the CIA designation. Such conduct is in violation of Article 1.A.4 of the CFE Code of Professional Ethics.

L. Jackson Shockey, CFE, CPA, CISA, chairman of the board of regents, said: "We are saddened that a member has been expelled for such conduct. However, in order to maintain the integrity of the CFE program, the trial board vigorously investigates violations of the Code of Professional Ethics. When appropriate, the board of regents will not hesitate to take necessary action."

Source: *CFE News.*

---

an AICPA Trial Board. The LRCA ordinarily admonishes the CPA and requires specific continuing education courses to bring the CPA up to date in technical areas. These committees do not have authority to take action that affects a CPA's membership in the AICPA or in a state society (i.e., suspension or expulsion).

The trial board panel has the power to: (1) acquit the CPA, (2) admonish the CPA, (3) suspend the CPA's membership in the state society and the AICPA for up to two years, or (4) expel the CPA from the state society and the AICPA. The AICPA Bylaws (not the Code of Professional Conduct) provide for automatic expulsion of CPAs judged to have committed a felony, failed to file their tax returns, or aided in the preparation of a false and fraudulent income tax return. The trial board panels are required to publish the names of the CPAs disciplined in their proceedings. Published details about these disciplinary actions are in the AICPA website at www.aicpa.org/pubs/cpaltr/index.htm.

The AICPA also has a *settlement offer* procedure designed to impose penalties for rule violations. When the preliminary investigation of a complaint against a CPA shows clear evidence of a violation, the AICPA can (*a*) proceed with the full investigation and documentation leading to a trial board hearing or (*b*) offer the CPA the opportunity to plead and accept the penalties proposed by the Professional Ethics Executive Committee. The penalties are typically the same ones that would result from a trial board panel hearing—resignation, CPE requirement, and suspension or termination of membership with publication—but the lengthy process of investigation, documentation, and formal hearing is not carried out. When a CPA agrees, the penalty is presented to the Joint Trial Board for endorsement. The settlement offer procedure is a means of closing cases without the time-consuming investigation and trial board hearing that burdens both the CPA and the AICPA Professional Ethics Division.

The expulsion penalty, while severe, does not prevent a CPA from continuing to practice accounting. Membership in the AICPA and state societies, while beneficial, is not required. However, a CPA must have a valid state license in order to practice. State boards of accountancy are the agencies that can suspend or revoke the license to practice.

Public Regulation Discipline

State boards of accountancy are government agencies consisting of CPA and non-CPA officeholders. They issue licenses to practice accounting in their jurisdictions. Most state laws require a license to use the designation *CPA* or *Certified Public Accountant* and limit the attest (audit) function to licenseholders.

AUDITING INSIGHT

AICPA JOINT TRIAL BOARD ACTION

At a meeting of a hearing panel of the joint trial board in D_____, Michigan, Willie M of D_____ was suspended from membership in the AICPA and the Michigan Association of CPAs for one year for violating the Rules of Conduct. The violations involved his undertaking an engagement which he or his firm could not reasonably expect to complete with professional competence, permitting his name to be associated with financial statements so as to imply that he was acting as an independent accountant without complying with generally accepted auditing standards and statements on auditing standards, and expressing an opinion that financial statements conformed with GAAP when they contained material departures therefrom. In addition to the suspension, he was required to complete 64 hours of CPE and to submit a list of engagements which his firm will be performing within the next year, from which two engagements will be selected by the AICPA and the Michigan Association of CPAs for their review.

Mr. M, who was present at the hearing, did not request a review of the decision which, therefore, became effective.

Source: *The CPA Letter.* (www.aicpa.org/pubs/capltr/index.htm)

State boards have rules of conduct and trial board panels. They can admonish a licenseholder; but, more importantly, they can suspend or revoke the license to practice. Suspension and revocation are severe penalties because a person no longer can use the CPA title and cannot sign audit reports. When candidates have successfully passed the CPA examination and are ready to become CPAs, some state boards administer an ethics examination or an ethics course intended to familiarize new CPAs with the state rules.

The SEC also conducts public regulation disciplinary actions. Its authority comes from its rules of practice, of which Rule 102(e) provides that the SEC can deny, temporarily or permanently, the privilege of practice before the SEC to any person found to have engaged in unethical or improper professional conduct. When conducting a "Rule 102(e) proceeding," the SEC acts in a quasi-judicial role as an administrative agency.

The SEC penalty bars an accountant from signing any documents filed by an SEC-registered company. The penalty effectively stops the accountant's SEC practice. In a few severe cases, Rule 102(e) proceedings have resulted in settlements barring not only the individual accountant but also the accounting firm or certain of its practice offices from accepting new SEC clients for a period of time.

The Internal Revenue Service (IRS) can also discipline accountants as a matter of public regulation. The IRS can suspend or disbar from practice before the IRS any CPA shown to be incompetent or disreputable or who refuses to comply with tax rules and regulations. The IRS can also levy monetary fines for improper practices.

R E V I E W
CHECKPOINTS

B.16 What organizations and agencies have rules of conduct you must observe when practicing public accounting? Internal auditing? Management accounting? Fraud examination?

B.17 What penalties can be imposed by AICPA and the state societies on CPAs in their "self-regulation" of ethics code violators?

B.18 What penalties can be imposed by public regulatory agencies on CPAs who violate rules of conduct?

Summary

This module begins with philosophers' considerations of moral philosophy, explains the AICPA Rules of Conduct, and the SEC and ISB rules related to auditors' independence. The module ends with the agencies and organizations that enforce the rules governing CPAs' behavior.

Professional ethics for accountants is not simply a matter covered by a few rules in a formal Code of Professional Conduct. Concepts of proper professional conduct permeate all areas of practice. Ethics and its accompanying disciplinary potential are the foundation for public accountants' self-regulatory efforts.

Your knowledge of philosophical principles in ethics—the imperative, the utilitarian, and generalization—will help you make decisions about the AICPA, SEC, and ISB rules. This structured approach to thoughtful decisions is important not only when you are employed in public accounting but also when you work in government, industry, and education. The ethics rules may appear to be restrictive, but they are intended for the benefit of the public as well as for the discipline of CPAs.

Public accountants must be careful in all areas of practice. As an accountant, you must not lose sight of the nonaccountants' perspective. No matter how complex or technical a decision may be, a simplified view of it always tends to cut away the details of special technical issues to get directly to the heart of the matter. A sense of professionalism coupled with a sensitivity to the effect of decisions on other people are invaluable in the practice of accounting and auditing.

Multiple-Choice Questions for Practice and Review

B.19 Auditors are interested in having independence in appearance because
  a. They want to impress the public with their independence in fact.
  b. They want the public at large to have confidence in the profession.
  c. They need to comply with the standards of field work of GAAS.
  d. Audits should be planned and assistants, if any, need to be properly supervised.

B.20 If a CPA says she always follows the rule that requires adherence to FASB pronouncements in order to give a standard unqualified audit report, she is following a philosophy characterized by
  a. The imperative principle in ethics.
  b. The utilitarian principle in ethics.
  c. The generalization principle in ethics.
  d. Reliance on her inner conscience.

B.21 Which of the following agencies makes independence rules for the auditors of public companies?
  a. Financial Accounting Standards Board (FASB)
  b. U.S. General Accounting Office (GAO)
  c. Independence Standards Board (ISB)
  d. AICPA Accounting and Review Services Committee (ARSC)

B.22 Audit independence *in fact* is most clearly lost when
  a. An audit firm audits competitor companies in the same industry (e.g., Coke and Pepsi)
  b. An auditor agrees to the client's financial vice-president's argument that deferring losses on debt refinancings is in accordance with generally accepted accounting principles.
  c. An audit team fails to discover the client's misleading omission of disclosure about permanent impairment of asset values.
  d. An audit firm issues a standard unqualified report, but the reviewing partner fails to notice that the assistant's observation of inventory was woefully incomplete.

B.23 AICPA members who work in industry and government (MIGIs) must always uphold which two of the following AICPA rules of conduct?
  a. Rule 101—Independence
  b. Rule 102—Integrity and Objectivity
  c. Rule 301—Confidential Client Information
  d. Rule 501—Acts Discreditable

B.24 An audit firm's independence is not impaired when members of the audit engagement team perform for an audit client

a. Preparation of special purchase orders for active plutonium in secure national defense installations.

b. Operational internal audit assignments under the directions of the client's Director of Internal Auditing.

c. Sixty percent of the out-sourced internal audit work on the client's financial accounting control monitoring.

d. Preparation of actuarial assumptions used by the client's actuaries for life insurance actuarial liability determination.

B.25 When the audit firm audits FUND-A in a mutual fund complex which has sister funds FUND-B and FUND-C, independence for the audit of FUND-A is not impaired when

a. Manager-level professionals located in the office where the engagement audit partner is located but who are not on the engagement team own shares in FUND-B, which is not an audit client.

b. The wife of the FUND-A audit engagement partner owns shares in FUND-C (an audit client of another of the firm's offices) and these shares are held through the wife's employee benefit plan funded by her employer, the AllSteelFence Company.

c. Both (a) and (b) above.

d. Neither (a) nor (b) above.

B.26 Which of the following is true?

a. Members of an audit engagement team cannot speak with audit client officers about employment possibilities with the client while the audit work is in progress.

b. Audit team members who leave the audit firm for employment with audit clients offer audit efficiencies (next year) because they are very familiar with the firm's audit programs.

c. Audit team partners who leave the audit firm for employment with audit clients can retain variable annuity retirement accounts established in the person's former firm retirement plan.

d. The audit firm must discuss with the audit client's board or its audit committee the independence implications of the client having hired the audit engagement team manager as its financial vice-president.

B.27 Which of the following "bodies designated by Council" have been authorized

to promulgate General Standards enforceable under Rule 201 of the AICPA Code of Professional Conduct?

a. AICPA Division of Professional Ethics.

b. Financial Accounting Standards Board.

c. Government Accounting Standards Board.

d. Accounting and Review Services Committee.

B.28 Which of the following "bodies designated by Council" have been authorized to promulgate accounting principles enforceable under Rule 203 of the AICPA Code of Professional Conduct?

a. Auditing Standards Board.

b. Federal Accounting Standards Advisory Board.

c. Consulting Services Executive Committee.

d. Accounting and Review Services Committee.

B.29 Phil Greb has a thriving practice in which he assists attorneys to prepare litigation dealing with accounting and auditing matters. Phil is "practicing public accounting" if he

a. Uses his CPA designation on his letterhead and business card.

b. Is in partnership with another CPA.

c. Practices in a professional corporation with other CPAs.

d. Never lets his clients know that he is a CPA.

B.30 The AICPA removed its general prohibition of CPAs taking commissions and contingent fees because:

a. CPAs prefer more price competition to less.

b. Commissions and contingent fees enhance audit independence.

c. Nothing is inherently wrong about the form of fees charged to non-audit clients.

d. Objectivity is not always necessary in accounting and auditing services.

B.31 CPA Brevard is the auditor of Ajax Corporation. Her audit independence will not be considered impaired if she

a. Owns $1,000 worth of Ajax stock.

b. Has a husband who owns $1,000 worth of Ajax stock.

c. Has a sister who is the financial vice president of Ajax.

d. Owns $1,000 worth of the stock of Pericles Corporation, which is controlled by Ajax as a result of Ajax's ownership of 40 percent of Pericles' stock, and Pericles contributes 3 percent of the total assets and income in Ajax's financial statements.

B.32 When a client's financial statements contain a material departure from a *FASB Statement on Accounting Standards* and the CPA believes the departure is necessary to make the statements not misleading

   a. The CPA must qualify the audit report for a departure from GAAP.

   b. The CPA can explain why the departure is necessary, then give an unqualified opinion paragraph in the audit report.

   c. The CPA must give an adverse audit report.

   d. The CPA can give the standard unqualified audit report with an unqualified opinion paragraph.

B.33 Which of the following would *not* be considered confidential information obtained in the course of an engagement for which the client's consent would be needed for disclosure:

   a. Information about whether a consulting client has paid the CPA's fees on time.

   b. The actuarial assumptions used by a tax client in calculating pension expense.

   c. Management's strategic plan for next year's labor negotiations.

   d. Information about material contingent liabilities relevant for audited financial statements.

B.34 Which of the following would probably not be considered an "act discreditable to the profession":

   a. Numerous moving traffic violations.

   b. Failing to file the CPA's own tax return.

   c. Filing a fraudulent tax return for a client in a severe financial difficulty.

   d. Refusing to hire Asian-Americans in an accounting practice.

B.35 According to the AICPA Code of Conduct, which of the following acts is generally forbidden to CPAs in public practice?

   a. Purchasing bookkeeping software from a hi-tech development company and reselling it to tax clients.

   b. Being the author of a "TaxAid" newsletter promoted and sold by a publishing company.

   c. Having a commission arrangement with an accounting software developer to receive 4 percent of the price of programs recommended and sold to audit clients.

   d. Engaging in a marketing firm to obtain new financial planning clients for a fixed fee of $1,000 for each successful contact.

B.36 A CPAs legal license to practice public accounting can be revoked by the:

   a. American Institute of Certified Public Accountants.

   b. State Society of CPAs.

   c. Auditing Standard Board.

   d. State board of accountancy.

B.37 An auditor's independence would not be considered impaired if he had:

   a. Owned common stock of the audit client but sold it before the company became a client.

   b. Sold short the common stock of an audit client while working on the audit engagement.

   c. Served as the company's treasurer for six months during the year covered by the audit but resigned before the company became a client.

   d. Performed the bookkeeping and financial statement preparation for the company, which had no accounting personnel and the president had no understanding of accounting principles.

B.38 When a CPA knows that a tax client has skimmed cash receipts and not reported the income in the federal income tax return but signs the return as a CPA who prepared the return, the CPA has violated the following AICPA Rule of Conduct:

   a. Rule 301—Confidential Client Information.

   b. Rule 102—Integrity and Objectivity.

   c. Rule 101—Independence.

   d. Rule 203—Accounting Prinicples.

EXERCISES AND PROBLEMS

B.39 **SEC Independence Rules.** Is independence impaired on these SEC filing audits according to SEC independence rules?

   a. CPA Yolanda is the SIDA&Co engagement partner on the Casa Construction Company (CCC) audit supervised from the Santa Fe office of the firm. Yolanda owns 100 shares of CCC.

b. CPA Yolanda sold the 100 CCC shares to CPA Javier, who is another partner in the Santa Fe office but who is not involved in the CCC audit.

c. CPA Javier transferred ownership of the 100 CCC shares to his wife.

d. CPA Javier's wife gave the shares to their 12 year-old son.

e. CPA Javier's son sold the shares to Javier's father.

f. CPA Javier's father was happy to combine the 100 CCC shares with shares he already owned because now he owns 25 percent of CCC and can control many decisions of the board of directors.

g. CPA Javier's father declared personal bankruptcy and sold his CCC stock. CCC then hired him to fill the newly created position of director of financial reporting.

B.40   SEC Independence and Nonaudit Services.   Is independence impaired on these SEC filing audits according to SEC independence rules regarding non-audit services?

a. CPA Neuman is a staff assistant II auditor on the Section Co. audit. Upon the completion of audit field work in January, Neuman drafted the balance sheet, income statement, statement of cash flows, and notes for review by the engagement partner before the audit report was finalized.

b. CPA Arens is a manager in the firm's consulting division. She spent 100 hours with the Section Co. audit client on an accounts payable information system study which involved selecting the preferred software and supervising Section Co.'s employees in startup operations.

c. CPA Churchill, working in the audit firm's asset valuation consulting division located in Chicago, prepared for Section Co. an appraisal of the fair value of assets purchased in Section's merger with the Group Co. These valuations were then audited by the engagement team located in Dallas in connection with the purchase accounting for the merger.

d. CPA Jack is the engagement partner on the Section Co. audit, and he is also an actuarial consultant in the firm's consulting division. He personally audited the client's post-employment benefits calculations which had been prepared by Section's actuaries.

e. Section Co. appointed its own employee, CIA Leslie, to be Director of Internal Auditing with complete responsibility for planning,

management, and review of all internal audit work. Leslie engaged Section's independent audit firm to supply staff to perform all the operational audit studies of efficiency and effectiveness in Section's domestic subsidiary companies. The audit firm used half of these same staff professionals to work on the audit of Section's financial statement audit.

f. CPA Norgaard is the partner in charge of the Dallas office where the Section Co. audit is managed (by engagement partner Jack). She has no direct role on the audit engagement team. However, Section relies on Norgaard to prepare the confidential papers for the board of directors' stock options, and she signs the release forms for option grants.

g. CPA Loebbecke works in the executive search department of the audit firm's consulting division, located in New York City. In connection with Section Co.'s hiring its new Vice President—Marketing, Loebbecke checked the references on the lead candidate Smith and performed a thorough background investigation that led to the firm's advice that Smith was the best person for the appointment. Section Co. board members investigated other candidates, then hired Smith in Dallas without further interaction with Loebbecke.

h. Section Co. completed a private placement of long-term bonds during the year under audit. The bonds were distributed to 40 qualified-exempt investors through the brokerage firm of Amalgamated Exchange, Inc., which is 50 percent owned by the audit firm and 50 percent owned by Merril Lynch Investment Corporation

i. The audit firm's tax consulting division prepared Section Co.'s export-import tax reports, which involved numerous interpretations of complicated export-import tax law provisions.

B.41   Independence, Integrity, and Objectivity Cases.   For each case, state whether the action or situation shows violation of the AICPA Code of Professional Conduct, explain why, and cite the relevant rule or interpretation.

a. CPA R. Stout performs the audit of the local symphony society. Because of her good work, she was elected an honorary member of the board of directors.

b. CPA N. Wolfe practices management consulting in the area of computer information systems under the firm name of Wolfe & Associates. The "associates" are not CPAs, and the firm is not an "accounting firm." However, Wolfe shows "CPA" on business cards and uses these credentials when dealing with clients.

c. CPA Archie Goodwin performs significant day-to-day bookkeeping services for Harper Corporation and supervises the work of the one part-time bookkeeper employed by Marvin Harper. This year, Marvin wants to engage CPA Goodwin to perform an audit.

d. CPA H. Poirot bought a home in 1989 and financed it with a mortgage loan from Farraway Savings and Loan. Farraway was merged into Nearby S&L, and Poirot became the manager in charge of the Nearby audit.

e. Poirot inherited a large sum of money from old Mr. Giraud in 2000. Poirot sold his house, paid off the loan to Nearby S&L, and purchased a much larger estate, a mansion in fact. Nearby S&L provided the financing.

f. Poirot and Ms. Lemon (a local real estate broker) formed a partnership to develop apartment buildings. Ms. Lemon is a 20 percent owner and managing partner. Poirot and three partners in the accounting firm are limited partners. They own the remaining 80 percent of the partnership but have no voice in everyday management. Ms. Lemon obtained permanent real estate financing from Nearby S&L.

g. Ms. Lemon won the lottery and purchased part of the limited partners' interests. She now owns 90 percent of the partnership and remains general partner while the CPAs remain limited partners with the 10% interest.

h. CPA Shultz purchased a variable annuity insurance contract that offered her the option to choose the companies in which this contract will invest. At Schultz's direction the insurance company purchased common stock in one of her audit clients.

B.42   Independence, Integrity, and Objectivity Cases.   For each case, state whether the action or situation shows violation of the AICPA Code of Professional Conduct, explain why, and cite the relevant rule or interpretation.

a. Your client, Contrary Corporation, is very upset over the fact that your audit last year failed to detect an $800,000 inventory overstatement caused by employee theft and falsification of the records. The board discussed the matter and authorized its attorneys to explore the possibility of a lawsuit for damages.

b. Contrary Corporation filed a lawsuit alleging negligent audit work, seeking $1 million in damages.

c. In response to the lawsuit by Contrary, you decided to start litigation against certain officers of the company alleging management fraud and deceit. You are asking for a damage judgment of $500,000.

d. The Allright Insurance Company paid Contrary Corporation $700,000 under fidelity bonds covering the employees involved in the inventory theft. Both you and Contrary Corporation have dropped your lawsuits. However, under subrogation rights, Allright has sued your audit firm for damages on the grounds of negligent performance of the audit.

e. Your audit client, Science Tech, Inc., installed a cost accounting system devised by the consulting services department of your firm. The system failed to account properly for certain product costs (according to management), and the system had to be discontinued. Science Tech management was very dissatisfied and filed a lawsuit demanding return of the $10,000 consulting fee. The audit fee is normally about $50,000, and $10,000 is not an especially large amount for your firm. However, you believe that Science Tech management operated the system improperly. While you are willing to do further consulting work at a reduced rate to make the system operate, you are unwilling to return the entire $10,000 fee.

f. A group of dissident shareholders filed a class-action lawsuit against both you and your client, Amalgamated, Inc., for $30 million. They allege there was a conspiracy to present misleading financial statements in connection with a recent merger.

g. CPA Anderson, a shareholder in the firm of Anderson, Olds, and Watershed, P.C. (a professional accounting corporation), owns 25 percent of the common stock of Dove Corporation (not a client of AO&W). This year, Dove purchased a 32 percent interest in Tale Company and is accounting for the investment using the equity method of accounting. The investment amounts to 11 percent of Dove's consolidated net assets. Tale Company has been an audit client of AO&W for 12 years.

h. CPAs Richard and Ellery are the father-and-son partners in Queens', LLP. They have a joint private investment in ownership of 12 percent of the voting common stock of Hydra Corporation, which is not an audit client of Queens', LLP. However, their audit client, Sabrina Company, owns 46 percent of Hydra, and this investment accounts for 20 percent of Sabrina's assets (using the equity method of accounting).

i. Durkin & Panzer, CPAs, regularly perform the audit of the First National Bank, and the firm is preparing for the audit of the financial statements for the year ended December 31, 2001.

1. Two directors of the First National Bank became partners in D&P, CPAs, on July 1,

2001, resigning their directorship on that date. They will not participate in the audit.

2. During 2001, the former controller of the First National Bank, now a partner of D&P, was frequently called on for assistance regarding loan approvals and the bank's minimum checking account policy. In addition, he conducted a computer feasibility study for First National.

(AICPA adapted)

j. The Cather Corporation is indebted to a CPA for unpaid fees and has offered to give the CPA unsecured interest-bearing notes. Alternatively, Cather Corporation offered to give two shares of its common stock, after which 10,002 shares would be outstanding.

(AICPA adapted)

k. Johnny Keems is not yet a CPA but is doing quite well in this first employment with a large CPA firm. He's been on the job two years and has become a "heavy junior." If he passes the CPA exam in November, he will be promoted to senior accountant. This month, during the audit of Row Lumber Company, Johnny told the controller about how he is remodeling an old house. The controller likes Johnny and had a load of needed materials delivered to the house, billing Johnny at a 70 percent discount—a savings over the normal cash discount of about $300. Johnny paid the bill and was happy to have the materials that he otherwise could not afford on his meager salary.

l. Groaner Corporation is in financial difficulty. You are about to sign the report on the current audit when your firm's office manager informs you the audit fee for last year has not yet been paid.

m. CPA Lily Rowan prepared Goodwin's tax return this year. Last year, Goodwin prepared the return and paid too much income tax because the tax return erroneously contained "income" in the amount of $300,000 from an inheritance received when dear Aunt Martha died. This year, the inherited property was sold for $500,000. Goodwin argued with Rowan, who agreed to omit the sale of the property and the $200,000 gain this year on the grounds that Goodwin had already overpaid tax last year and this omission did not make things even.

n. CPA D. Watson is employed by Baker Street Company as its chief accountant. M. Lestrade, also a CPA and the financial vice-president of Baker, owns a trucking company that provides shipping services to Baker in a four-state area. The trucking company needs to buy 14 new trailers, and Lestrade authorized a payment to finance the purchase in the amount of $750,000. The related document cited repayment in terms of reduced trucking charges for the next seven years. M. Lestrade created the journal entry for this arrangement, charging the $750,000 to prepaid expenses. Watson and Lestrade signed the representation letter to Baker's external auditors and stated that Baker had no related party transactions that were not disclosed to the auditors.

B.43   General and Technical Rule Cases. For each case, state whether the action or situation shows violation of the AICPA Code of Professional Conduct, explain why, and cite the relevant rule or interpretation.

a. CPA J. Cheese became the new auditor for the Python Insurance Company. Cheese knew a great deal about insurance accounting, but he had never conducted an audit of an insurance company. Consequently, he hired CPA T. Gilliam, who had six years' experience with the State Department of Insurance Audit. Gilliam managed the audit and Cheese was the partner in charge.

b. CPA M. Palin practices public accounting and is also a director of Comedy Company. Palin's firm performs consulting and tax services for Comedy. Palin prepared unaudited financial statements on Comedy's letterhead and submitted them to First National Bank in support of a loan application. Palin's accounting firm received a fee for this service.

c. CPA E. Idle audited the financial statements of Monty Corporation and gave an unqualified report. Monty is not a public company, so the financial statements did not contain the SEC-required reconciliation of deferred income taxes.

d. CPA G. Chapman audited the financial statement of BTV. Ltd. These financial statements contain capitalized leases that do not meet FASB criteria for capitalization. They resemble more closely the criteria for operating leases. The effect is material—adding $4 million to assets and $3.5 million to liabilities. However, BTV has a long experience with acquiring such property as its own assets after the "lease" terms end. Chapman and the BTV management believe the financial statements should reflect the operating policy of the management instead of the technical requirements of the FASB. Consequently, the audit report explains the accounting and gives an unqualified opinion.

B.44   Responsibilities to Clients' Cases. For each case, state whether the action or situation shows violation or potential for violation of the

AICPA Code of Professional Conduct, explain why, and cite the relevant rule or interpretation.

a. CPA Sally Colt has discovered a way to eliminate most of the boring work of processing routine accounts receivable confirmations by contracting with the Cohen Mail Service. After the auditor has prepared the confirmations, Cohen will stuff them in envelopes, mail them, receive the return replies, open the replies, and return them to Sally.

b. Cadentoe Corporation, without consulting its CPA, has changed its accounting so that it is not in conformity with generally accepted accounting principles. During the regular audit engagement, the CPA discovers the statements based on the accounts are so grossly misleading that they might be considered fraudulent. CPA Cramer resigns the engagement after a heated argument. Cramer knows that the statements will be given to Saul Panzer, his friend at the Last National Bank, and knows that Saul is not a very astute reader of complicated financial statements. Two days later, Panzer calls Cramer and asks some general questions about Cadentoe's statements and remarks favorably on the very thing that is misrepresented. Cramer corrects the erroneous analysis, and Panzer is very much surprised.

c. A CPA who had reached retirement age arranged for the sale of his practice to another certified public accountant. Their agreement called for the review of all working papers and business correspondence by the accountant purchasing the practice.

d. Martha Jacoby, CPA, withdrew from the audit of Harvard Company after discovering irregularities in Harvard's income tax returns. One week later, Ms. Jacoby was telephoned by Jake Henry, CPA, who explained that he had just been retained by Harvard Company to replace Ms. Jacoby. Mr. Henry asked Ms. Jacoby why she withdrew from the Harvard engagement. She told him.

e. CPA Wallace has as audit clients two companies—Willingham Corporation owned by J. Willingham and Ward Corporation owned by B. Ward. Willingham Corp. sells a large proportion of its products to Ward Corp., which amounts to 60 percent of Ward Corp.'s purchases in most years. J. Willingham and B. Ward themselves as individuals are also Wallace's tax clients. This year, while preparing B. Ward's tax return, Wallace discovered information that suggested Ward Corporation is in a failing financial position. Thereupon in consideration of the fact that the companies and individuals are mutual clients, Wallace discussed Ward Corporation's financial difficulties with J. Willingham.

f. Amos Fiddle, CPA, prepared an uncontested claim for a tax refund on Faddle Corporation's amended tax return. The fee for the service was 30 percent of the amount the IRS rules to be a proper refund. The claim was for $300,000.

g. After Faddle had won a $200,000 refund and Fiddle collected the $60,000 fee, Jeremy Faddle, the president, invited Amos Fiddle to be the auditor for Faddle Corporation.

h. Burgess Company engaged CPA Kim Philby to audit Maclean Corporation in connection with a possible initial public offering (IPO) of stock registered with the SEC. Burgess Company established a holding company named Cairncross Inc. and asked Philby to issue an engagement letter addressed to Cairncross stating that Cairncross would receive the audit report. Cairncross has no assets, and Philby agreed to charge a fee for the audit of Maclean only if the IPO is successful.

B.45   Other Responsibilities and Practices Cases. For each case, state whether the action or situation shows violation or potential for violation of the AICPA Code of Professional Conduct, explain why, and cite the relevant rule or interpretation.

a. CPA R. Stout completed a review of the unaudited financial statements of Wolfe Gifts. Ms. Wolfe was very displeased with the report. An argument ensued, and she told Stout never to darken her door again. Two days later, she telephoned Stout and demanded he return: (1) Wolfe's cash disbursement journal, (2) Stout's working paper schedule of adjusting journal entries, (3) Stout's inventory analysis working papers, and (4) all other working papers prepared by Stout. Since Wolfe had not yet paid her bill, Stout replied that state law gave him a lien on all the records and he would return them as soon as she paid his fee.

b. CPA May teaches a CPA review course at the university. He needs problem and question material for students' practice, but the CPA examination questions and answers are no longer published. He pays $5 to students who take the exam for each question they can "remember" after taking the examination.

c. CPA Panzer has been invited to conduct a course in effective tax planning for the City Chamber of Commerce. The C. of C. president said a brochure would be mailed to members giving the name of Panzer's firm, his educational background and degrees held, professional society affiliations, and testimonials from participants in the course held last year comparing his excellent performance with other CPAs who have offered competing courses in the city.

d. CPA Philby is a member of the state bar. Her practice is a combination of law and accounting, and she is heavily involved in estate planning engagements. Here is her letterhead: Member, State Bar of —, and Member, AICPA.

e. The CPA firm of Burgess & Maclean has made a deal with Brit & Company, a firm of management consulting specialists, for mutual business advantage. B&M agreed to recommend Brit to clients who need management consulting services. Brit agreed to recommend B&M to clients who need improvements in their accounting systems. During the year, both firms would keep records of fees obtained by these mutual referrals. At the end of the year, Brit and B&M would settle the net differences based on a referral rate of 5 percent of fees.

f. Jack Robinson and Archie Robertson (both CPAs) are not partners, but they have the same office, the same employees, a joint bank account, and they work together on audits. A letterhead they use shows both their names and the description "Members, AICPA."

g. CPA Dewey retired from the two-person firm of Dewey & Cheatham. One year later, D&C merged practices with Howe & Company, to form a regional firm under the name of Dewey, Cheatham, & Howe Company.

B.46   AICPA Independence and Other Services.   AICPA Interpretation 101-3 (Performance of Other Services: www.aicpa.org) cites several "other services" that do and do not impair audit independence. Go to the AICPA website, and find whether the items below impair independence ("yes") or do not impair independence ("no") when performed for audit clients.

a. Post client-approved entries to a client's trail balance.

b. Authorize client's customer credit applications.

c. Use CPA's data processing facilities to prepare client's payroll and generate checks for the client treasurer's signature.

d. Sign the client's quarterly federal payroll tax return.

e. Advise client management about the application or financial effect of provisions in a employee benefit plan contract.

f. Have emergency signature authority to co-sign cash disbursement checks in connection with a client's hospital benefit plan.

g. As an investment advisory service, provide analyses of a client's investments in comparison to benchmarks produced by unrelated third parties.

h. Take temporary custody of a client's investment assets each time a purchase is made as a device to reduce cash float expense.

DISCUSSION CASES

B.47   General Ethics.   Is there any moral difference between a disapproved action in which you are caught and the same action that never becomes known to anyone else? Do many persons in business and professional society make a distinction between these two circumstances? If you respond that *you* do (or do not) perceive a difference while *persons in business and professional society* do not (or do), then how do you explain the differences in attitudes?

B.48   Competition and Audit Proposals.   Accounting firms are often asked to present "proposals" to companies' boards of directors. These "proposals" are comprehensive booklets, accompanied by oral presentations, telling about the firm's personnel, technology, special qualifications, and expertise in hopes of convincing the board to award the work to the firm.

Dena has a new job as staff assistant to Michael, chairman of the board of Granof Grain Company. The company has a policy of engaging new auditors every seven years. The board will hear oral proposals from 12 accounting firms. This is the second day of the three-day meeting. Dena's job is to help evaluate the proposals. Yesterday, the proposal by Anderson, Olds, and Watershed was clearly the best.

Then Dena sees Michael's staff chief slip a copy of the AOW written proposal into an envelope. He tells Dena to take it to a friend who works for Hunt and Hunt, a CPA firm scheduled to make its presentation tomorrow. He says: "I told him we'd let him glance at the best proposal." Michael is absent from the meeting and will not return for two hours.

What should Dena do? What should CPA Hunt do if he receives the AOW proposal, assuming he has time to modify the Hunt and Hunt proposal before tomorrow's presentation?

B.49   Engagement Timekeeping Records.   A time budget is always prepared for audit engagements. Numbers of hours are estimated for various segments of the work—for example, internal control evaluation, cash, inventory, report review, and the like. Audit supervisors expect the work segments to be completed "within budget," and staff accountants' performance is evaluated in part on ability to perform audit work efficiently within budget.

Sara is an audit manager who has worked hard to get promoted. She hopes to become a partner in two or three years. Finishing audits on time weighs heavily on her performance evaluation. She assigned the cash audit work to Ed, who has worked for the firm for 10 months. Ed hopes to get a promotion and salary raise this year. Twenty hours were budgeted for the cash work. Ed is efficient, but it took 30 hours to finish because the company had added seven new bank accounts. Ed was worried about his performance evaluation, so he recorded 20 hours for the cash work and put the other 10 hours under the internal control evaluation budget.

What do you think about Ed's resolution of his problem? Was his action a form of lying? What would you think of his action if the internal control evaluation work was presently "under budget" because it was not yet complete, and another assistant was assigned to finish that work segment later?

B.50   Audit Overtime.   All accountants' performance evaluations are based in part on their ability to do audit work efficiently and within the time budget planned for the engagement. New staff accountants, in particular, usually have some early difficulty learning speedy work habits, which demand that no time be wasted.

Elizabeth started work for Anderson, Olds, and Watershed in September. After attending the staff training school, she was assigned to the Rising Sun Company audit. Her first work assignment was to complete the extensive recalculation of the inventory compilation, using the audit test counts and audited unit prices for several hundred inventory items. Her time budget for the work was six hours. She started at 4 P.M. and was not finished when everyone left the office at 6 P.M. Not wanting to stay downtown alone, she took all the necessary working papers home. She resumed work at 8 P.M and finished at 3 A.M. The next day, she returned to the Rising Sun offices, put the completed working papers in the file, and recorded six hours in the time budget/actual schedule. Her supervisor was pleased, especially about her diligence in taking the work home.

What do you think about Elizabeth's diligence and her understatement of the time she took to finish the work? What would you think of the case if she had received help at home from her husband Paul? What would you think of the case if she had been unable to finish and had left the work at home for her husband to finish while he took off a day from his job interviews?

B.51   Conflict of Client's Interests.   Jon Williams, CPA, has found himself in the middle of the real-life soap opera "Taxing Days of Our Lives."

The cast of characters:

Oneway Corporation is Jon's audit and tax client. The three directors are the officers and also the only three stockholders, each owning exactly one-third of the shares.

President Jack founded the company and is now nearing retirement. As an individual, he is also Jon's tax client.

Vice President Jill manages the day-to-day operations. She has been instrumental in enlarging the business and its profits. Jill's individual tax work is done by CPA Phil.

Treasurer Bill has been a long-term, loyal employee and has been responsible for many innovative financial transactions and reports of great benefit to the business. He is Jon's close personal friend and also an individual tax client.

The conflict:

President Jack discussed with CPA Jon the tax consequences to him as an individual of selling his one-third interest in Oneway Corporation , to Vice President Jill. Later, meeting with Bill to discuss his individual tax problems, Jon learns that Bill fears that Jack and Jill will make a deal, put him in a minority position, and force him out of the company. Bill says: "Jon, we have been friends a long time. Please keep me informed about Jack's plans, even rumors. My interest in Oneway Corporation represents my life savings and my resources for the kid's college. Remember, you're little Otto's godfather."

Thinking back, Jon realized that Vice President Jill has always been rather hostile. Chances are that Phil would get the Oneway engagement if Jill acquires Jack's shares and controls the corporation. Nevertheless, Bill will probably suffer a great deal if he cannot learn about Jack's plans, and Jon's unwillingness to keep him informed will probably ruin their close friendship.

Later, on dark and stormy night:

Jon ponders the problem. "Oneway Corporation is my client, but a corporation is a fiction. Only a form. The stockholders personify the real entity, so they are collectively my clients, and I can transmit information among them as though they were one person. Right? On the other hand, Jack and Bill engage me for individual tax work, and information about one's personal affairs is really no business of the other. What to do? What to do?"

Required:

Give Jon advice about alternative actions, considering the constraints of the AICPA Code of Conduct.

B.52   Managerial Involvement and Audit Independence.   CPA P. Marlowe is the partner in charge of the audit practice in the midsize CPA firm of Marlowe & Chandler, PC. CPA R. Chandler is the overall managing partner of the firm. They founded the firm 20 years ago. CPA Marlowe is also a member of the board of directors of the Hobart Arms Hotel Corporation, one of the firm's tax clients. Hobart wanted to acquire the Bristol Apartment Company, and the Los Angeles National Bank insisted on an independent audit of Hobart's financial statements in connection with its loan application for $3 million. Marlowe & Chandler knew they were not independent for this audit because of Marlowe's position on the board.

To solve this problem, Hobart engaged Wilde & Associates, LLP to perform the audit. The Wilde firm was not very large, so the following arrangement was made: CPA Wilde was the partner in charge of the audit, CPA Linda (a Wilde professional) was the manager of the audit, and CPAs Lacosta and Martinez were the staff assistants. Lacosta and Martinez were employed by Marlowe & Chandler, and they were loaned to Wilde & Associates for the purpose of staffing the Hobart audit. They performed almost all the detail field work.

Wilde & Associates, LLP completed the audit and delivered an unqualified audit report. Fees were paid to Wilde & Associates for the work of its professionals. Fees were billed separately by Marlowe & Chandler, PC for the work performed by Lacosta and Martinez, and Hobart paid these directly to Marlowe & Chandler.

Required:

Analyze this situation. Do you see any lack of independence in connection with the audit? Discuss.

APPENDIX BA   AICPA INTERPRETATIONS OF THE RULES OF CONDUCT

This appendix contains the AICPA interpretations on independence and objectivity rules as they stood in early 2001. You should study them in conjunction with the SEC definitions and rules in the module. Some numbers in the sequence of interpretations are missing because interpretations were withdrawn long ago.

INTERPRETATIONS OF RULE 101—INDEPENDENCE

These interpretations cover 13 detail topics that define many parameters of independence. They are applicable to AICPA members in public practice (i.e., CPA firms).

Interpretation 101-1: General independence.

INTERPRETATION 101-1

Independence will be considered to be impaired if, for example, a member had any of the following transactions, interests, or relationships:

A. During the period of a professional engagement, or at the time of expressing an opinion, a member or a member's firm:
1. Had or was committed to acquire any direct or material indirect financial interest in the enterprise.
2. Was a trustee of any trust or executor or administrator of any estate if such trust or estate had or was committed to acquire any direct or material indirect financial interest in the enterprise.
3. Had any joint, closely held business investment with the enterprise or with any officer, director, or principal stockholder thereof that was material in relation to the member's net worth or to the net worth of the member's firm.
4. Had any loan to or from the enterprise or any officer, director, or principal stockholder of the enterprise except as specifically permitted in Interpretation 101-5.

B. During the period covered by the financial statements, during the period of the professional engagement, or at the time of expressing an opinion, a member or a member's firm:
1. Was connected with the enterprise as a promoter, underwriter, or voting trustee, as a director or officer, or in any capacity equivalent to that of a member of management or of an employee.
2. Was a trustee for any pension or profit-sharing trust of the enterprise.

The above examples are not intended to be all-inclusive.

Section A

Interpretation 101-1, Section A, deals with the financial interests in a client. Note that the "period covered by the financial statements" is not relevant to this section as it is in Section B. A member may divest a prohibited financial interest before the first work on a new client begins, after which it is improper to reinvest when the engagement will continue for future years. Any direct financial interest (e.g., common stock, preferred stock, bonds) is prohibited. This requirement is the strictest one in the code. The words of the rule offer no exceptions. Indirect financial interests, on the other hand, are allowed up to the point of *materiality* (with reference to the member's wealth). This provision permits members to have some limited business transactions with clients so long as they do not reach material proportions. Items 2, 3, and 4 of Interpretation 101-1(A) define certain specific types of prohibited and allowed indirect financial interests.

    Item 101-1.A.4 prohibits most loans from audit clients. The only loans permitted are "grandfathered loans," and "other permitted loans." The discussion below on these topics is from Interpretation 101-5 "Loans from financial institution clients and related terminology."

GRANDFATHERED LOANS

CPA's independence is not impaired by holding certain specified types of loans from clients if: (a) the loans were obtained before January 1,1992; (b) loans were obtained from a financial institution before it became a client for services requiring independence; (c) loans were obtained from a financial institution for which independence was not required but were later sold to a client for which independence is required; or (d) loans were obtained from a financial institution client before the CPA became a "member" subject to the independence rules. These grandfathered loans must at all times be current under all their terms, and the terms shall not be renegotiated. The specific types of loans that can be grandfathered are home mortgages, loans not material to the CPA's net worth, and secured loans for which the collateral value must exceed the balance of the loan at all times.

OTHER PERMITTED LOANS

Independence is not considered impaired by a member obtaining these kinds of personal loans from attest clients: (a) auto loans and leases collateralized by the automobile, (b) insurance policy loans based on policy surrender value, (c) loans collateralized by cash deposits at the same financial institution, and (d) credit card balances and cash advances of $5,000 or less. Thus, an individual involved in the audit of a bank can have an auto loan at the bank, borrow money secured by cash in a certificate of deposit, and have the bank's credit card with a balance of less than $5,000. (The SEC rule cites a $10,000 limit for credit card balances.) For insurance company clients, the CPA can borrow against the cash surrender value of a life insurance policy. However, notice that these loans are limited to personal loans, with the unwritten understanding that they are for personal convenience, not large loans for business purposes.

Section B

Section B of the interpretation prohibits activities that amount to the ability to make decisions for the client—to act as management, broadly defined. The appearance of independence is impaired if such a connection existed at any time during the *period covered by the financial statements*, regardless of whether the association was terminated prior to the beginning of the audit work. The presumption is that members cannot be independent and objective when attesting to decisions in which they took part or with which they appeared to be connected.

Interpretation 101-2. Former practitioners and firm independence.

Independence problems do not end when owners (partners, shareholders) and professional employees retire, resign, or otherwise leave an accounting firm. A former owner can cause independence to be impaired under the circumstances shown in the interpretation of Rule 101 in connection with his or her association with a client of the former firm. However, the problems are solved and independence is not impaired if: (1) the person's retirement benefits are fixed, (2) the person is no longer active in the accounting firm (sometimes retired owners remain "active"), and (3) the former owner is not held out to be associated with the accounting firm. (ISB Standard No. 3 also speaks to the topic of employment with audit clients, as discussed in the module.)

Interpretation 101-3. Performance of other services.

If a CPA performs the bookkeeping and makes accounting or management decisions for a company and the management of the company does not know enough about the financial statements to take primary responsibility for them, the CPA cannot be considered independent for audit and other attest services. The problem in this situation is the appearance of the CPA having both prepared the financial statements or other data and given an audit report or other attestation on his or her own work. In the final analysis, the management must be able to say, "These are our financial statements (or other data); we made the choices of accounting principles; we take primary responsibility for them." The auditors cannot authorize transactions, have control of assets, sign checks or reports, prepare source documents, supervise the client's personnel, or serve as the client's registrar, transfer agent, or general counsel.

Interpretation 101-4. Honorary directorships and trusteeships of not-for-profit organizations.

Ordinarily, independence is impaired if a CPA serves on an organization's board of directors. However, members can be honorary directors of such organizations as charity hospitals, fund drives, symphony orchestra societies, and similar not-for-profit organizations so long as: (1) the position is purely honorary, (2) the CPA is identified as an honorary director on letterheads and other literature, (3) the only form of participation is the use of the CPA's name, and (4) the CPA does not vote with the board or participate in management functions. When all these criteria are satisfied, the CPA/board member can perform audit and attest services because the appearances of independence will have been preserved.

Interpretation 101-6. Effect of actual or threatened litigation on independence.

Independence can be threatened by appearances of a CPA trying to serve his or her own best interests. This condition can arise when a CPA and a client move into an adversary relationship instead of the cooperative relationship needed in an attest engagement. CPAs are considered not independent when (1) company management threatens or actually starts a lawsuit against the CPA alleging deficiencies in audit or other attestation work and (2) the CPA threatens or starts litigation against the company management alleging fraud or deceit. Such cases may be rare, but the AICPA has provided auditors a way out of the difficult audit situation by this rule requiring them to declare "nonindependence" and the ability to give only a disclaimer on financial statements or other data. Essentially the CPA–client relationship ends, and the litigation begins a new relationship.

Interpretation 101-8. Effect on independence of financial interests in nonclients having investor or investee relationships with a member's client.

In this context "investor" and "investee" have the same meaning as in the accounting rules about accounting for investments on the equity method (APB Opinion No. 18). The investor is the party that has significant influence over a business, and the investee is the business in which the investor has the significant influence.

When the CPA's client is the investor, a CPA's direct or material indirect financial interest in a nonclient investee impairs the CPA's independence. The reasoning for the basic rule is that the client investor, through its ability to influence a nonclient investee, can increase or decrease the CPA's financial stake in the investee by an amount material to the CPA, and, therefore, the CPA may not appear to be independent.

When a CPA has an investment in a nonclient investor: (a) independence is impaired with respect to a client investee that is material in the financial statements of the investor when the CPA has any direct or material indirect financial interest in the nonclient investor; (b) independence is not impaired with respect to a client investee that is not material in the financial statements of the investor, even if the CPA's investment is material to the CPA, as long as the CPA does not have significant influence over the actions of the nonclient investor; but (c) independence is impaired with respect to a client investee that is not material in the financial statements of the investor when the CPA has a large enough investment to give the CPA a significant influence over the actions of the nonclient investor, which then can influence (manage) affairs of the client investee. The reasoning underlying the independence impairment conclusions in these relationships is that the CPA occupies a position similar to being a member of management of the client investee.

Interpretation 101-9. Meaning of certain independence terminology and the effect of family relationships on independence.

Beware! The AICPA interpretation explained here covers a larger set of owners, professional employees, and family members than the SEC rule in the module. (Refer to the module for the SEC definitions of *audit engagement team*, *covered persons in the firm*, *immediate family members*, and *close family members*) In all likelihood, the AICPA will change its interpretation to match the SEC. However, for purposes of Rule 101, the AICPA interpretation defines the terms *member* and *member's firm* to include:

- All partners or shareholders (owners) in the accounting firm
- All professional employees participating in the engagement, including audit, tax. and management consulting personnel.
- All other manager-level employees located in a firm office that does a significant part of the audit.
- Any CPA firm person formerly employed by or connected with the audit client in a managerial capacity (see Interpretation 101-1-B) unless the person (a) is disassociated from the client and (b) does not participate in the engagement.
- Any CPA firm professional (e.g., partner, manager, staff) who is associated with the client in a managerial capacity (see Interpretation 101-1-B) and is located in an office of the CPA firm that does a significant part of the engagement.

Financial interests of spouses and dependent persons (whether related or not) and some financial interests of close relatives are attributed to a member. (Close relatives include nondependent children, grandchildren, stepchildren, brothers, sisters, parents, grandparents, parents-in-law, and the spouses of each of these.) When these people are involved closely enough with the audit client, independence is considered impaired.

Employment relations of spouses, dependent persons, and close relatives can be attributed to a member. When these people can exercise significant influence over the operating, financial, or accounting policies of the client (e.g., as financial officer, treasurer), independence is often considered impaired. When these people hold positions that are "audit sensitive" (e.g., cashier, internal auditor, accounting supervisor, purchasing agent, inventory warehouse supervisor), independence is often considered impaired.

So, what financial and employment interests in clients can relatives have, yet not create independence problems on an engagement? These relations appear to be "safe": (a) financial interests attributed to manager-level members located in offices not involved in the engagement, (b) financial interests attributed to staff below the manager level provided the staff person is not on the engagement itself, (c) employment relationships attributed to partners (owners) who are not located in an office that performs the engagement, (d) employment relationships attributed to managers located anywhere provided they do not work on the engagement, (e) former managerial relationships (Interpretation 101-1-B) by partners, managers, and staff, provided they are now disassociated from the client and do not participate in the engagement, and (f) current managerial relationships (Interpretation 101-1-B) by managers and staff, provided they do not participate in the engagement and are located in an office that does not do a significant part of the engagement.

The AICPA and SEC rules express minimum criteria relating to independence. CPA firms can make more limiting rules. You will learn a CPA firm's particular rules if you take employment with one of them.

Interpretation 101-10. Effect on independence of relationships with entities included in governmental financial statements.

Governments often operate with a primary government (e.g., city council, county government) and component units (e.g., city transit authority, county library corporation). Basically, the auditor must be independent of the primary government (e.g., city council) and the component unit (e.g., transit authority) when auditing the primary government (city's general-purpose financial statements). However, if the auditor is not independent with respect to one component (e.g., county library corporation), but audits another (e.g., county flood-control district), independence is required only with respect to the entity audited (the flood-control district) and the primary government. The lack of independence with respect to the library corporation does not impair independence with respect to the flood-control district. However, because of the lack of independence in one component, this auditor is not independent with respect to the audit of the county itself (the primary government).

Interpretation 101-11. Independence and attest engagements.

Independence is required for attestation engagements (governed by Statements on Standards for Attestation Engagements, dealing with assertions other than financial statements) when a report lends credibility to assertions made by other parties. The basic requirement for independence in Rule 101 and its interpretations apply to the professional team members who work on the engagement.

Interpretation 101-12. Independence and cooperative arrangements with clients.

Material cooperative arrangements with clients impair independence. Cooperative arrangements are joint participation in a business activity. Examples include: joint ventures to develop or market products, marketing a package of client and CPA services, one party working to market the products or services of the other.

Interpretation 101-13. Extended audit services.

For all practical purposes, this interpretation legitimizes a client company's internal audit outsourcing to the CPA firm that performs the annual audit for the same client company. Internal auditors view themselves as professionals committed to providing business services in alliance with and for the benefit of management. When CPAs who are the independent auditors of a company also perform the internal auditing ("extended audit services") as a consulting service, the question of independence arises.

The AICPA Code of Conduct considers independence impaired if the CPA firm appears to outside observers to be working in the capacity of management or employees of the client. Of course, these features are common for internal auditors—a company's Director of Internal Auditing is a member of management, and the internal audit staff members are employees.

To get around this appearance problem and preserve audit independence, the AICPA interpretation requires that the client company acknowledge responsibility for and assign a senior manager to control the internal audit function—planning the internal audit assignments, evaluating internal audit reports, and evaluating the adequacy of the internal audit work. Essentially, the employees of the CPA firm can be consultants and staff assistants, but they cannot take over the internal audit management functions. The CPAs lose independence if they perform ordinary control activities, choose control strategies for implementation, report to the board on behalf of management, prepare transaction documentation, have custody of assets, or use management titles or appear in an employee directory.

Note that the SEC rules in the module track very closely the spirit of this AICPA interpretation. In addition, the SEC considers independence questionable when a CPA firm conducts more than 40 percent of the internal audit work for a client (for clients with more than $200 million assets).

Interpretation 101-14. Effect of alternative practice structures on the applicability of independence rules.

The topic of alternative practice structures (APS) arises from an accounting practice organization not in the traditional mold of CPA firms. In the 1990s some companies (e.g., American Express Tax and Business Services) and some "consolidators" (e.g., Century Business Services) started buying CPA firms and using them to provide tax, personal financial planning, and consulting services to customers. The former owners and professional employees of the CPA firm became employees of the purchaser. These companies and consolidators typically are public companies with stock trading in public markets. Stand-alone CPA firms that offer audit services cannot be organized as public companies.

So what happened to the audit practice of a CPA firm purchased by "Public Co"? The CPA owners can create another CPA firm ("NewFirm") to conduct audits. NewFirm may have some separate owners and employees, but to have enough resources and people it usually pays PublicCo for office space, equipment, and the like, and it "leases" professional employees from PublicCo (often the same professionals formerly employed in the original CPA firm). All the people in NewFirm, whether employed directly by NewFirm or leased from PublicCo, are subject to all the independence requirements.

In addition, officers in PublicCo who can exert influence over NewFirm and its employees are subject to all the AICPA independence requirements. This extension makes direct supervisors in PublicCo (e.g., the CEO of the Professional Services Division to whom the CPAs in NewFirm report and who controls performance evaluation, promotion, and compensation) subject to the same restrictions as CPAs in the NewFirm practice. Also, indirect superiors up the line (e.g., an officer to whom the PublicCo CEO of Professional Services reports) cannot have material financial and influential relationships with NewFirm's audit clients. Also, NewFirm is not independent for audit purposes to audit PublicCo or any of its subsidiaries or any company that owns a material investment in PublicCo (as a parent company or investor with significant influence).

You can notice in the SEC rules concerning disclosure the requirement to tell the percentage of audit hours performed by persons other than the accountant's full-time permanent employees. The APS arrangement is the reason for this disclosure requirement.

INTERPRETATIONS OF RULE 102—INTEGRITY AND OBJECTIVITY

Rule 102 is generally applicable to AICPA members working in government and industry (MIGIs) as well as to members in public practice (CPA firms). As a group, these are the interpretations of Rule 102:

- Interpretation 102-1. Knowing misrepresentations in the presentation of financial statements or records.
- Interpretation 102-2: Conflicts of interest.
- Interpretation 102-3: Obligations of a member to his or her employer's external accountant.
- Interpretation 102-4: Subordination of judgment by a member.
- Interpretation 102-5: Members performing educational services.
- Interpretation 102-6: Professional services involving client advocacy

ANALYSIS

The AICPA Rules of Conduct make a fine distinction between independence and integrity-objectivity. The spirit of the rules is that integrity and objectivity are required in connection with all professional services, and, in addition, independence is required for audit and attest services. In this context, integrity and objectivity are the larger concepts, and "independence" is a special condition largely defined by the matters of appearance specified in the interpretations of Rule 101. Conflicts of interest cited in Rule 102 refer to the need to avoid having business interests in which the accountant's personal financial relationships or the accountant's relationships with other clients might tempt the accountant to fail to serve the best interests of a client or the public that uses the results of the engagement. Some examples of conflicts of interest are these:

- CPA is engaged to perform litigation support services for a plaintiff in a lawsuit filed against a client.
- In a personal financial planning engagement, CPA recommends client investment in a business in which the CPA has a financial interest.
- CPA provides tax services for several members of a family who have opposing interests.
- CPA performs management consulting for a client and also has a financial or managerial interest in a major competitor.
- CPA serves on a city Board of Tax Appeals, which hears matters involving clients.
- CPA refers a tax client to an insurance broker, who refers clients to the CPA under an exclusive agreement.
- CPA charges a contingent fee to a client for expert witness litigation support services when the fee can be affected by the opinion the CPA expresses.

The phrases "shall not knowingly misrepresent facts" and "shall not subordinate his or her judgment to others" emphasize conditions people ordinarily identify with the concepts of integrity and objectivity. Accountants who know about a client's lies in a tax return, about false journal entries, about material misrepresentations in financial statements, and the like have violated both the spirit and the letter of Rule 102. However, in tax practice, an accountant can act as an advocate to resolve doubt in favor of a taxpayer-client as long as the tax treatment has a reasonable or justifiable basis.

Rule 102 is applicable to members employed in government and industry (MIGIs). (Jorge—the staff accountant in the decision process illustration given earlier in this module—is a MIGI.) The prohibition of misrepresentations in financial statements applies to the management accountants who prepare companies' statements. MIGIs should not subordinate their professional judgment to superiors who try to produce materially misleading financial statements and fool their external auditors. MIGIs must be candid and not knowingly misrepresent facts or fail to disclose material facts when dealing with their employer's external auditor. MIGIs cannot have conflicts of interest in their jobs and their outside business interests that are not disclosed to their employers and approved. The importance of integrity and objectivity for MIGIs cannot be overemphasized. Too often, CPAs relate the Code of Professional Conduct only to CPAs in public practice.

Rule 102 has two other applications. One concerns serving as a client advocate, which occurs frequently in taxation and rate regulation practice and also in supporting clients' positions in FASB and SEC proceedings. Client advocacy in support or advancement of client positions is acceptable only so long as the member acts with integrity, maintains objectivity, and does not subordinate judgment to others. (Accountants-as-advocates do not adopt the same attitude as defense attorneys in a courtroom) The other application is directed specifically at your college professors: They are supposed to maintain integrity and objectivity, be free of conflicts of interest, and shall not knowingly misrepresent facts to students.

Module C

Legal Liability

Professional Standards References

Learning Objectives

The previous module on professional ethics dealt mainly with accountants' *self-regulation.* This module focuses on *public regulation* enforced by the SEC and the state and federal court systems. The discussion will help you understand accountants' legal liability for professional work. Your learning objectives are to be able to:

1. Identify and describe accountants' exposure to lawsuits and loss judgments.

2. Identify and describe aspects of accountants' "liability crisis" and the post-1994 relief developments.

3. Specify the characteristics of accountants' liability under common law, and cite some specific case precedents.

4. Describe the SEC activities and literature involved in the regulation of accounting.

5. Identify the "forms" used in SEC regulation of securities sales and periodic reporting.

6. Specify the civil and criminal liability provisions of the Securities Act of 1933, compare the civil liability to common law, and cite some specific cases.

7. Specify the civil and criminal liability provisions of the Securities and Exchange Act of 1934, compare the civil liability to common law, and cite some specific cases.

THE LEGAL ENVIRONMENT

LEARNING OBJECTIVE

1. Identify and describe accountants' exposure to lawsuits and loss judgments.

Accountants are potentially liable for monetary damages and even subject to criminal penalties, including fines and jail terms, for failure to perform professional services properly. They can be sued by clients, clients' creditors, investors, and the government. Exposure to large lawsuit claims is possible through *class actions* permitted under federal rules of court procedure in the United States. In a class action suit, a relatively small number of aggrieved plaintiffs with small individual claims can bring suit for large damages in the name of an extended class. After a bankruptcy, for example, 40 bondholders who lost $40,000 might decide to sue, and they can sue on behalf of the entire class of bondholders for *all* their alleged losses (say $40 million). Lawyers will take such suits on a contingency fee basis (a percentage of the judgment, if any). The size of the claim and the zeal of the lawyers make the class action suit a serious matter.

Audit Responsibilities

Many users of audit reports expect auditors to detect fraud, theft, and illegal acts, and to report them publicly. Auditors take responsibility for detecting material misstatements in financial statements; but they are very cautious about taking responsibility for detecting all manner of fraud, and are especially cautious about accepting a public reporting responsibility. Fraud and misleading financial statements loom large among the concerns of financial statement users. They are afraid of *information risk,* and they want it to be reduced, even eliminated. Some of their expectations are very high, and for this reason an *expectation gap* often exists between the diligence users expect and the diligence auditors are able to accept.

The audit responsibility for detection of fraud in financial statements is a complex topic, and Chapter 7 (Fraud Awareness Auditing) is devoted entirely to it. Auditors take some responsibility but not as much as many users expect. This disparity leads to lawsuits, even when auditors have performed well.

Tort Reform

Legal defense expenses and liabilities for large damage awards consume approximately 10 percent of audit service revenues of the large CPA firms. The profession considers the

United States tort liability system a "crisis of expanding liability exposure" in need of reform. In the early 1990s, federal agencies collected $2 billion from accountants, lawyers, and other professionals for malpractice in savings and loan institutions, including $981 million from four of the Big 5 accounting firms.

The AICPA and many state societies of CPAs have targeted two features of tort liability for change. They are (1) joint and several liability, and (2) the privity rule governing liability to third parties.

Joint and several liability is a doctrine that allows a successful plaintiff to recover the full amount of a damage award from the defendants who have money or insurance. Often in cases of business failures, the auditors are the only parties with "deep pockets" of resources to pay damages. Thus, when a group of defendants (auditors, management, a client company) are found liable for damages, the accountants pay the entire amount even though they may be only partially at fault. Tort reform seeks to replace this doctrine with a rule of "**proportionate liability**." Under this rule, a defendant is required to pay a proportionate share of the court's damage award, depending upon the degree of fault determined by a judge and jury (e.g., 20 percent, 30 percent, but not 100 percent).

Proportionate liability was largely accomplished at the Federal level in 1995 with the passage of the Private Securities Litigation Reform Act. Civil lawsuits for damages now are governed by these proportionate liability terms:

- The total responsibility for loss is divided among all parties responsible for the loss. This is the main proportionate liability feature.
- However, if other defendants are insolvent, a solvent defendant's liability is extended to 50 percent more than the proportion found at trial. (For example, if an accounting firm is found 20 percent responsible for a loss and the company and its managers are insolvent, the accounting firm will have to pay 30 percent of the loss, but not 100 percent as before.)
- Then the exception to compensate smaller investors is that all defendants remain jointly and severally liable to plaintiffs who have net worth of less than $200,000 and lost 10 percent or more of the net worth in the case.
- Only the defendants who knowingly committed a violation of securities laws remain jointly and severally liable for all the plaintiffs' damages. (This is the imposition of penalty for actively participating in an actual fraud.)

The main objective of the Private Securities Litigation Reform Act is to discourage lawsuit abuse in the form of "strike suits." These lawsuits typically arose when a company's stock price declined significantly on some bad news, oftentimes merely the market's recognition of changes in the business or the company's future prospects. Class action lawsuits alleging fraud brought on behalf of the shareholders then consumed considerable managerial time and expense in defense. All such claims must now cite examples of a strong inference of a defendant's fraudulent intent—not only an allegation that permits a discovery fishing expedition and an out-of-court monetary settlement just to end a lawsuit.

The Private Securities Litigation Reform Act deals only with lawsuits in the federal courts. So, clever lawyers learned to file these class action lawsuits in state courts that followed joint and several liability doctrines—lawsuit business as usual! To counter this perceived evasion of the federal law, Congress enacted in 1998 the Securities Litigation Uniform Standards Act. Its most significant provision requires that class action lawsuits with 50 or more parties must be filed in the federal courts.

The privity rule is a matter of contract law. Essentially, strict **privity** is the relationship of parties who enter into a contract together. (You may know this concept as "privity of contract.") The parties in a contract owe each other duties of nonnegligent care. One party can be liable to the other(s) for ordinary negligence. The parties to a contract always have the right to sue each other on grounds of negligence and breach of contract. In accounting services, the primary contractual relationship is between the accountant and the client, and they always have standing to sue each other. Indeed, a significant proportion of lawsuits involve clients and accountants suing each other.

However, the problem for accountants involves the ability of parties ("third parties") who are not in the direct contractual relationship to have standing to sue the accountants. These parties include investors, creditors, and others who use financial statements for business decisions. Various states and the federal courts have different views of the rights of third parties to sue accountants. These views are covered more thoroughly in the box below and the more liberal of them makes accountants vulnerable to lawsuits based on negligence brought by users of financial statements. The position of the AICPA and the state societies of CPAs favors a privity rule that permits third party negligence suits against accountants only when the accountant knows and understands that the financial statements are intended for use by particular third parties for particular purposes, and the accountant shows this understanding through some form of direct contact and communication with the particular party. This position on privity is intended to reduce accountants' exposure to lawsuits by reducing the number of parties who have rights to sue accountants for negligent performance.

AUDITING INSIGHT

THREE DEGREES OF ACCOUNTANTS' LIABILITY EXPOSURE

Accountants' liability exposure depends on courts' common law theories about the third parties who are permitted to sue them for negligence. The states differ, some taking each of the paths described below.

[handwritten: Primary beneficiary]

Limited Exposure. The New York case of *Credit Alliance* v. *Arthur Andersen* (1986) led the way for limiting accountants' exposure. The court held that accountants are not liable for negligence to third parties unless (1) the accountants were aware that a particular third party intended to rely on the audit opinion and the financial statements; (2) the third party was specifically identified, and (3) some action by the accountants showed they acknowledged the third party's identification and intent to rely on the opinion and financial statements. For example, an auditor can be subject to negligence claims from a bank when the client told the auditor about using the financial statements in a loan application to that bank, and the auditor included the name of the bank and acknowledged its intended use of the financial statements in the engagement letter. Several states follow this view.

Restatement of Torts. The *restatement of torts* is a general legal doctrine. It extends liability for ordinary negligence to "foreseen" third parties not explicitly known to the accountants. Under this approach, accountants may be subject to negligence claims if they know that an audit report and financial statements will be delivered to unidentified investors and creditors. Specific acknowledgement is not required. The accountants must only be aware that the audit report and financial statements will be used by some third party. For example, an auditor can be subject to negligence claims from a bank when the client told the auditor about using the financial statements to obtain a specific loan from that bank *and also liable* to a different bank if the client used the financial statements to obtain a similar loan. A majority of states follow the restatement of torts view.

Reasonably Foreseeable Users. This approach follows the decision in the *Rosenblum* v. *Adler* decision briefed later in this chapter. It holds the broadest liability exposure because it allows potential liability for negligence to all third parties who are reasonably foreseeable users of audit reports and financial statements. The privity concept is virtually abandoned. For example, a client may tell its auditor nothing about an intended use of the audit report and financial statements, but the auditor can be liable to banks, creditors, investors, and others because the auditor can "reasonably foresee" that the client wants the audited financial statements for the purpose of helping these users make financial decisions about the company. Two state courts (Mississippi and Wisconsin) are said to apply this broad concept for negligence actions. However, it still applies in cases of fraud.

R E V I E W
CHECKPOINTS

C.1 What are class action lawsuits, and why should auditors be concerned about them?

C.2 What two principle elements of "tort reform" are favored by the accounting profession? Describe them. What

changes were made by the Private Securities Litigation Reform Act?

C.3 What new requirement was enacted in the Securities Litigation Uniform Standards Act that reinforced the Private Securities Litigation Reform Act?

LITIGATION REFORM AND ACCOUNTANTS' RELIEF

LEARNING OBJECTIVE

2. Identify and describe aspects of accountants' "liability crisis" and the post-1994 relief developments.

After 1994, accountants' perception of the "liability exposure crisis" eased considerably. Five statutory and judicial developments made lawsuits against auditors more difficult for plaintiffs to argue and sustain.

- The U.S. Supreme Court ruled that accountants are not subject to civil RICO complaints unless they actually participated in the management or operation of a corrupt business. The important requirement is "active participation," and negligence in an audit or advisory capacity is not enough to subject public accountants to RICO. (RICO is the Racketeer Influenced and Corrupt Organization Act originally intended to combat organized crime in businesses and other organizations. Before this Supreme Court ruling, lawyers used it to hook auditors and subject them to threats of characterization as "racketeers" and imposition of treble damages under the law.)

- The Private Securities Litigation Reform Act raised the plaintiffs' pleading standards in cases against auditors and public accountants. No longer are allegations of negligence or "involvement" enough. Plaintiffs must allege a strong inference of accountants' fraud and even their participation in some misconduct in an organization. These allegations are hard to make at the beginning of a lawsuit.

- The Private Securities Litigation Reform Act adopted the doctrine of proportionate liability. Now, even when plaintiffs successfully sue accountants, chances are they will obtain judgment for only part of their losses (instead of all losses under the joint and several liability doctrine). This limitation reduces plaintiff lawyers' ability to win the full amount of losses and reduces their economic incentives to sue accountants.

- The Securities Litigation Uniform Standards Act limited lawyers' strategy of filing most class action lawsuits in state courts (where joint and several liability still prevails in some jurisdictions) by requiring that large class actions (50 or more parties) be filed in Federal courts where the Private Securities Litigation Reform Act dictates damages determined according to proportionate liability rules.

- The U.S. Supreme Court in another case limited the extent to which the doctrine of "aiding and abetting" could be used against accountants. "Aiding and abetting" means that plaintiffs could argue that the accountants' negligence or failure to find fraud and illegal acts amounted to complicity in a management's strategy to mislead investors and creditors, hence accountants could be found liable for losses.

Altogether, these developments meant that including the public accountants and auditors in a lawsuit for investment losses became less attractive in terms of monetary recovery. Therefore, with less economic incentive, lawyers are less likely to pursue the accountants with the vigor the system previously allowed.

The next parts of this chapter cover accountants' legal liabilities under common law and statutory law. Common law is all the cases and precedents that govern judges' decisions in lawsuits for monetary damages. Common law is "common knowledge" in the sense that judges tend to follow the collective wisdom of past cases decided by themselves and other judges. Common law is not enacted in statutes by a legislature. In contrast, statutory law is all the provisions enacted by a legislature.

C.4 Before 1994, what were the threats auditors faced in class action lawsuits claiming investors' losses and fault on the accountants' part?

C.5 What developments after 1994 reduced public accountants' and auditors' liability exposure?

C.6 Why do these developments limiting accountants' liability exposure seem to work in the arena of securities litigation?

LIABILITY UNDER COMMON LAW

LEARNING OBJECTIVE

3. Specify the characteristics of accountants' liability under common law, and cite some specific case precedents.

Legal liabilities of professional accountants may arise from lawsuits brought on the basis of the law of contracts or as tort actions for negligence. **Breach of contract** is a claim that accounting or auditing services were not performed in the manner agreed. This basis is most characteristic of lawsuits involving public accountants and their clients. **Tort** actions cover other civil complaints (e.g., fraud, deceit, injury), and such actions are normally initiated by users of financial statement.

Suits for civil damages under common law usually result when someone suffers a financial loss after relying on financial statements later found to be materially misleading. In the popular press, such unfortunate events are called *audit failures*. However, a distinction should be made between a business failure and an audit failure. A **business failure** is an audit client's bankruptcy or other serious financial difficulty. Business failures arise from many kinds of adverse economic events. An **audit failure** is an auditor's faulty performance, a failure to conduct an audit in accordance with generally accepted auditing standards (GAAS), with the result that misleading financial statements get published.

Characteristics of Common-Law Actions

Lawsuit plaintiffs generally assert all possible causes of action, including breach of contract, tort, deceit, fraud, and whatever else may be relevant to the claim.

Burden of Proof on the Plaintiff

Actions brought under common law place most of the burdens of affirmative proof on the plaintiff, who must prove: (1) he or she was damaged or suffered a loss, (2) the necessary privity or beneficiary relationship, (3) the financial statements were materially misleading or the accountant's advice was faulty, (4) he or she relied on the statements or advice, (5) they were the direct cause of the loss, and (6) the accountant was negligent, grossly negligent, deceitful, or otherwise responsible for damages. In a subsequent section dealing with the securities acts, you will see how the statutes shift some of these burdens of affirmative proof to the professional accountant.

Clients may bring a lawsuit for breach of contract. The relationship of direct involvement between parties to a contract is known as **privity**. When privity exists, a plaintiff usually need only show that the defendant accountant was negligent and did not perform in accordance with the terms of the contract. (**Ordinary negligence**—a lack of reasonable care in the performance of professional accounting tasks—is usually meant when the word negligence stands alone.) If the plaintiffs prove negligence, the accountant may be liable, provided the client has not been involved in some sort of contributory negligence in the dispute.

LEGAL PRECEDENT

Smith v. *London Assur. Corp* (1905)

This was the first American case involving an auditor. The auditor sued for an un-paid fee, and the company counterclaimed for a large sum that had been embezzled by one of its employees, which they claimed would not have occurred except for the auditor's breach of contract. The evidence indicated that the auditors indeed failed to audit cash accounts at one branch office as stipulated in an engagement contract. The court recognized the auditors as skilled professionals and held them liable for embezzlement losses that could have been prevented by nonnegligent performance under the contract.

Seventy years ago, parties other than contracting clients had a hard time succeed-ing in lawsuits against auditors. Other parties not in privity had no cause of action for breach of contract. However, the court opinion in the case known as *Ultramares* ex-pressed the view that, if negligence were so great as to constitute **gross negligence**—lack of even minimum care in performing professional duties, indicating reckless disregard for duty and responsibility—grounds might exist for concluding that the ac-countant had engaged in *constructive fraud.* Actual fraud is characterized as an inten-tional act designed to deceive, mislead, or injure the rights of another person. **Constructive fraud,** however, may not have the same element of intent, but the result is the same—to deprive or injure another unsuspecting party.

LEGAL PRECEDENT

Ultramares Corp. v. *Touche* (1931)

The *Ultramares* decision stated criteria for an auditor's liability to third parties for deceit (a tort action). To prove deceit: (1) a false representation must be shown, (2) the tort-feasor must possess **scienter**—either knowledge of falsity or insuffi-cient basis of information, (3) an intent to induce action in reliance must be shown, (4) the damaged party must show justifiable reliance on the false repre-sentation, and (5) there must have been a resulting damage. The court held that an accountant could be liable when he did not have sufficient information (au-dit evidence) to lead to a sincere or genuine belief. An audit report is deceitful when the auditor purports to speak from knowledge when he has none. The court also wrote that the degree of negligence might be so gross, however, as to amount to a constructive fraud. Then the auditor could be liable in tort to a third-party beneficiary.

Fraud is a basis for liability in tort, so parties not in privity with the accountant may have causes of action when negligence is gross enough to amount to constructive fraud. These other parties include primary beneficiaries, actual foreseen and limited classes of persons, and all other injured parties.

LEGAL PRECEDENT

State Street Trust Co. v. Ernst (1938)

Accountants, however, may be liable to third parties, even without deliberate or active fraud. A representation certified as true to the knowledge of accountants when knowledge there is none, a reckless misstatement, or an opinion based on grounds so flimsy as to lead to the conclusion that there was no genuine belief in its truth, are all sufficient upon which to base liability. A refusal to see the obvious, a failure to investigate the doubtful, if sufficiently gross, may furnish evidence leading to an inference of fraud so as to impose liability for losses suffered by those who rely on the balance sheet. Heedlessness and reckless disregard of consequences may take the place of deliberate intention. In this connection we are to bear in mind the principle already stated, that negligence or blindness, even when not equivalent to fraud, is nonetheless evidence to sustain an inference of fraud. At least this is so if the negligence is gross.

Primary beneficiaries are third parties for whose primary benefit the audit or other accounting service is performed. Such a beneficiary will be identified to, or reasonably foreseeable by, the accountant prior to or during the engagement, and the accountant will know that his or her work will influence the primary beneficiary's decisions. For example, an audit firm may be informed that the report is needed for a bank loan application at the First National Bank. Many cases indicate that proof of ordinary negligence may be sufficient to make accountants liable for damages to primary beneficiaries.

LEGAL PRECEDENT

Fleet National Bank v. *Gloucester Co.* (1994)

Accountants owe a duty to a limited class of third parties who rely on audited financial statements. Fleet Bank relied on financial statements audited by Tonneson when making loans to Gloucester. The court applied the *Restatement of Torts* to identify Fleet Bank as a primary beneficiary of the audit contract. These points were made: (1) Tonneson knew about the bank's loans to Gloucester, (2) Tonneson reviewed the loan agreements, (3) Tonneson knew the loan agreements required submission of audited financial statements, and (4) Tonneson believed and expected Gloucester would give the audited financial statements to the bank.

Accountants may also be liable to **foreseeable beneficiaries**—creditors, investors, or potential investors who rely on accountants work. If the accountant is reasonably able to *foresee* a limited class of potential users of his or her work (e.g., local banks, regular suppliers), liability may be imposed for ordinary negligence. This, however, is an uncertain area, and liability in a particular case depends entirely on the unique facts and circumstances. Beneficiaries of these types and all other injured parties may recover damages if they are able to show that an accountant was grossly negligent and perpetrated a constructive fraud.

LEGAL PRECEDENT

Rosenblum, Inc. v. Adler (1983)

Giant Stores Corporation acquired the retail catalog showroom business owned by Rosenblum, giving stock in exchange for the business. Fifteen months after the acquisition, Giant Stores declared bankruptcy. Its financial statements had been audited and had received unqualified opinions on several prior years. These financial statements turned out to be misstated because Giant Stores had manipulated its books.

In finding for the plaintiffs on certain motions, the New Jersey Supreme Court held: Independent auditors have a duty of care to all persons whom the auditor should reasonably foresee as recipients of the statements from the company for proper business purposes, provided that the recipients rely on those financial statements. . . . It is well recognized that audited financial statements are made for the use of third parties who have no direct relationship with the auditor. . . . Auditors have responsibility not only to the client who pays the fee but also to investors, creditors, and others who rely on the audited financial statements.

[The case went back to the trial court for further proceedings.]

Accountants' Defenses

Accountants can defend a common-law action by presenting arguments and evidence to mitigate the plaintiff's claims and evidence. In particular, an accountant can offer evidence to show: (1) the plaintiff did not suffer a real loss; (2) the plaintiff has no standing to sue because of lack of privity or lack of a known third-party or foreseeable user status; (3) the financial statement misstatements were not material or the accountant's advice was not faulty; (4) the plaintiff did not rely on the financial statements but on some other source of information; (5) even if the plaintiff used the financial statements, the loss was caused by some other events beyond the accountant's scope of responsibility; and (6) the accountant's work was performed in accordance with professional standards (e.g., GAAS for audits of financial statements). In addition, accountants can defend themselves on the ground of **contributory negligence.** If the plaintiff (usually a client in the contributory negligence defense situation) was also negligent and failed to heed advice or made the situation worse, the accountant may be able to avoid liability by not being the real cause of the loss.

LEGAL PRECEDENT

Gilbert Wegad v. Howard Street Jewelers (1992)

Howard Street Jewelers retained CPA Wegad to compile financial statements. Wegad noticed unexplained cash shortages and informed the client of the possibility that someone was stealing from the store. The court found Wegad negligent, but it also ruled that the client's contributory negligence barred recovery. The accountant's failure to report shortages completely did not insulate the company which consistently left the company's cash unattended and fully accessible to all employees and customers.

Liability in Compilation and Review Services

You may find it easy to think about common-law liability in connection with *audited* financial statements. Do not forget, however, that accountants also render compilation and review services and are associated with *unaudited* financial information. People expect public accountants to perform these services in accordance with professional standards, and courts can impose liability for accounting work found to be substandard. Accountants have been assessed damages for work on such statements, as shown in the *1136 Tenants' Corporation* v. *Max Rothenberg & Co.* case. The *Bank of Tokyo* v. *Friedman* case shows how courts can interpret the professional relationship of accountants and clients. Approximately 11 percent of losses in the AICPA professional liability insurance plan involve compilation and review engagements involving unaudited financial statements.

LEGAL PRECEDENT

1136 Tenants' Corp. v. *Max Rothenberg & Co.* (1967)

Despite defendant's claims to the contrary, the court found that he was engaged to audit and not merely write up plaintiff's books and records. The accountant had, in fact, performed some limited auditing procedures including preparation of a worksheet entitled "Missing Invoices 1/1/63–12/31/63." These were items claimed to have been paid but were not. The court held that even if accountants were hired only for write-up work, they had a duty to inform plaintiffs of any circumstances that gave reason to believe that a fraud had occurred (e.g., the record of "missing invoices"). The plaintiffs recovered damages of about $237,000.

LEGAL PRECEDENT

Bank of Tokyo v. *Friedman* (1993)

The accounting firm (Friedman) performed bookkeeping and review services for Globe Office Supply. Bank of Tokyo made loans to Globe based on unaudited financial statements prepared by Friedman. Globe became bankrupt, and the court ruled that Friedman was a de facto employee of Globe serving in the capacity of an internal accountant and not an independent accountant.

One significant risk is that the client may fail to understand the nature of the service being given. Accountants should use a conference and an engagement letter to explain clearly that a compilation service ("write-up") involves little or no investigative work, and it is lesser in scope than a review service. Similarly, a review service should be explained in terms of being less extensive than a full audit service. Clear understandings at the outset can enable accountants and clients to avoid later disagreements.

Yet, even with these understandings, public accountants cannot merely accept client-supplied information that appears to be unusual or misleading. A court has held that a public accountant's preparation of some erroneous and misleading journal entries without sufficient support was enough to trigger common-law liability for negligence, even though the accountant was not associated with any final financial statements. AICPA standards for compilations require accountants to obtain additional information if client-supplied accounting data is incorrect, incomplete, or otherwise unsatisfactory. Courts might hold accountants liable for failure to obtain additional information in such circumstances.

When financial statements are reviewed, accountants' reports declare: "Based on our review, we are not aware of any material modifications that should be made to the accompanying financial statements in order for them to be in conformity with generally accepted accounting principles." Courts can look to the facts of a case and rule on whether the review was performed properly. Some courts might decide an accountant's review was substandard if necessary adjustments or "material modifications" should have been discovered. These risks tend to induce more work by accountants beyond superficially looking-it-over and inquiry procedures.

Accountants do not lose all the lawsuits based on unaudited financial statements. The *Iselin* v. *Landau* case turned on the nature of the report on reviewed financial statements.

LEGAL PRECEDENT

Iselin v. *Landau* (1987)

The decision created an attitude more favorable for CPAs' review work on unaudited financial statements. William Iselin & Company sued the Mann Judd Landau (MJL) accounting firm, claiming damages for having relied on financial statements reviewed by MJL. Iselin had used the financial statements of customers for its factoring-financing business. A customer had gone bankrupt and Iselin's loans became worthless, A New York appeals court dismissed the case, saying that third parties (Iselin) cannot rely on reviewed financial statements as they can on audited financial statements to assure themselves that a company is financially healthy. The court observed that MJL expressed no opinion on the reviewed financial statements. The Iselin attorney was reported to have observed: "Accountants and their clients will find that reviews are useless, since no one can rely on them."

REVIEW CHECKPOINTS

C.7 What must be proved by the plaintiff in a common-law action seeking recovery of damages from an independent auditor of financial statements? What must the defendant accountant do in such a court action?

C.8 What legal theory is derived from the *Ultramares* decision? Can auditors rely on the *Ultramares* decision today?

C.9 Define and explain *privity, primary beneficiary*, and *foreseeable beneficiary* in terms of the degree of negligence on the part of an accountant that would trigger the accountant's liability.

C.10 What proportion of lawsuits against accountants relate to compilation and review (unaudited financial statements) practice?

LIABILITY UNDER STATUTORY LAW

Several federal statutes provide sources of potential liability for accountants, including: Federal False Statements Statute, Federal Mail Fraud Statute, Federal Conspiracy Statute, Securities Act of 1933 ("Securities Act"), and Securities and Exchange Act of 1934 ("Exchange Act"). The securities acts contain provisions defining certain civil and criminal liabilities of accountants. Because a significant segment of accounting practice is under the jurisdiction of the securities acts, the following discussion will concentrate on duties and liabilities under these laws. First, however, you should become familiar with the scope and function of the securities acts and the Securities and Exchange Commission (SEC).

Federal securities regulation in the United States was enacted in 1933 not only as a reaction to the events of the early years of the Great Depression but in the spirit of the

New Deal era and as a culmination of attempts at "blue-sky" regulation by the states.[1] The Securities Act of 1933 and the Securities and Exchange Act of 1934 require disclosure of information needed for informed investment decisions. The securities acts and the SEC operate for the protection of investors and for the facilitation of orderly capital markets. Even so, no federal government agency, including the SEC, rules on the quality of investments. The securities acts have been characterized as "truth-in-securities" law. Their spirit favors the otherwise uninformed investing public, while *caveat vendor* is applied to the issuer—let the *seller* beware of violations.

Regulation of Accounting Standards

LEARNING OBJECTIVE

4. Describe the SEC activities and literature involved in the regulation of accounting.

Both the Securities Act (1933) and the Exchange Act (1934) give the SEC power to establish accounting rules and regulations. **Regulation S-X** contains accounting requirements for audited annual and unaudited interim financial statements filed under both the Securities Act and the Exchange Act. Equally important, **Regulation S-K** contains requirements relating to all other business, analytical, and supplementary financial disclosures. In general, Regulation S-X governs the content of the financial statements themselves, and Regulation S-K governs *all other disclosures* in financial statement footnotes and other places in reports required to be filed.

For more than 70 years, the SEC has followed a general policy of relying on the organized accounting profession to establish generally accepted accounting principles (GAAP). However, the SEC makes its influence and power known in the standard-setting process. Its chief accountant monitors the development of FASB standards, meets with FASB staff, and decides whether a proposed pronouncement is reasonable. The SEC view is communicated to the FASB, and the two organizations try to work out major differences before a new *Statement on Financial Accounting Standards (SFAS)* is made final. Usually the two bodies reach agreement.

In the past, however, the SEC itself has made a few accounting rules because: (1) the SEC could act faster when an emerging problem needed quick attention, and (2) the SEC thought GAAP was deficient and wanted to prod the FASB to act. Consequently, GAAP and Regulation S-X differ in a few respects, but not many. Examples where Regulation S-X requires more than GAAP include nonequity classification of redeemable preferred stock, separate presentation of some income tax details, and additional disclosures about compensating balances, inventories, and long-term debt maturities. Otherwise, "SEC accounting" is not fundamentally different from GAAP accounting. The spirit of the force and effect of accounting principles and the respective roles of FASB and SEC are explained by an early SEC policy statement as follows:[2]

1. When financial statements filed with the commission are prepared according to principles that have no authoritative support, *they will be presumed to be misleading. Other disclosures or footnotes will not cure this presumption.*

2. When financial statements involve a principle on which the commission disagrees but has promulgated no explicit rules or regulations, and the principle has substantial authoritative support, *then supplementary disclosures will be accepted in lieu of correction of the statements.*

3. When financial statements involve a principle that (*a*) has authoritative support in general, but (*b*) the commission has ruled against its use, then *the statements will be presumed misleading. Supplementary disclosures will not cure this presumption.*

The biggest difference between SEC practice and other accounting practice involves the disclosures required by Regulation S-K. These requirements are detailed, and

---

[1] The term *blue sky* comes from a state judge's remark during a securities fraud case. He said: "There securities have no more substance than a piece of the blue sky."

[2] *Accounting Series Release No. 4* (1983). Also, *Accounting Series Release No. 150* (1973) affirmed that pronouncements of the FASB will be considered to constitute substantial authoritative support of accounting principles, standards, and practices (FRR No. 1, Section 101).

accountants must be well aware of them. In many respects, Regulation S-K goes beyond GAAP because FASB pronouncements usually do not specify as much detail about footnote disclosures. Also, accountants must keep up to date on the SEC's **Financial Reporting Releases** (FRR), which express new rules and policies about disclosure. Finally, accountants must keep up to date on the SEC's **Staff Accounting Bulletins** (SAB), which are unofficial but important interpretations of Regulation S-X and Regulation S-K.

Integrated Disclosure System

Under the integrated disclosure system, companies must give annual reports to shareholders, file annual reports on Form 10-K (discussed later), and file registration statements (also discussed later) when securities are offered to the public. However, companies can prepare the annual report to shareholders in conformity with Regulation S-X and Regulation S-K, and use it to provide most of the other information required for the Form 10-K annual report. Some companies can also use these reports as the basic reports required in a Securities Act registration statement because the integrated disclosure system basically has made the 10-K requirements the same as the registration statement disclosure requirements.

The integrated disclosure system simplifies and coordinates various reporting requirements. It also has the not-too-subtle effect of making most of Regulation S-X and Regulation S-K required in annual reports to shareholders, making them GAAP for companies that want to obtain the benefits of integration.

Regulation of Auditing Standards

In contrast to its concern for the quality of accounting principles, the SEC's involvement in auditing standards and procedural matters has been minimal since the developments of the McKesson and Robbins affair. Following an investigation of the *McKesson* case, the SEC ruled that auditors' reports must state that an audit was performed in accordance with "generally accepted auditing standards." At that time (1938), the 10 standards had not yet been issued by the AICPA. They were written and adopted soon afterward.

LEGAL PRECEDENT

McKesson & Robbins, Inc.

An SEC investigation resulted in these conclusions expressed in *Accounting Series Release No. 19* (1940): First, the auditors failed to employ that degree of vigilance, inquisitiveness, and analysis of the evidence available that is necessary in a professional undertaking and is recommended in all well-known and authoritative works on auditing. Meticulous verification was not needed to discover the inventory fraud. Second, although the auditors are not guarantors and should not be responsible for detecting all fraud, the discovery of gross overstatements in the accounts is a major purpose in an audit, despite the fact that every minor defalcation might not be disclosed.

The SEC's chief accountant also monitors the development of auditing standards by the AICPA Auditing Standards Board (ASB). A member of the chief accountant's staff attends ASB meetings, analyzes new proposals, and decides whether an issue of relevance to SEC-registered public companies is involved. The chief accountant discusses differences of opinion with the ASB, and the two try to work them out. Ordinarily, the SEC does not get as involved with technical auditing standards and ASB proceedings as it does with accounting standards and FASB proceedings. The SEC has rules about audit reports that correspond with generally accepted auditing standards (GAAS), but the SEC has no body of technical rules similar to the *Statements on Auditing Standards*.

C.11 What is Regulation S-X? Regulation S-K? Financial Reporting Releases? Staff Accounting Bulletins?

C.12 How does the SEC's integrated disclosure systems simplify and coordinate various SEC report filings?

Regulation of Securities Sales

LEARNING OBJECTIVE

5. Identify the "forms" used in SEC regulation of securities sales and periodic reporting.

For the most part, the Securities Act (1933) regulates the issue of securities, and the Exchange Act (1934) regulates trading in securities. Neither these securities laws nor the SEC approves or guarantees investments. The laws and the SEC's regulation concentrate on *disclosure of information* to investors, who have the responsibility for judging investment risk and reward potential. The Securities Act provides that no person may lawfully buy, sell, offer to buy, or offer to sell any security by the means of interstate commerce unless a registration statement is "effective" (a legal term meaning, essentially, "filed and accepted"). This prohibition should be interpreted literally: *No person can buy or sell any security* by means of *interstate commerce* (e.g., telephone, mail, highway, national bank) unless a registration statement is effective.

While this filing requirement is all-encompassing, other sections of the Securities Act offer exemptions. In general, Section 3 exempts from registration (but not from antifraud provisions): government securities, short-term obligations maturing within nine months, charitable and educational institutions, securities of businesses subject to regulation by the Interstate Commerce Commission, and intrastate issues sold by local companies to state residents. SEC rules also exempt small issues on the grounds that a sufficiently broad public interest is not involved. Section 4 exempts from registration (but not from antifraud provisions) certain specified *transactions*, principally any transaction *not* involving a "public offering," and transactions by any person who is *not* an issuer, underwriter, or dealer (e.g., a small investor).

In a spirit of deregulation, the SEC has made it easier for companies to offer securities to the public. **Regulation D** provides for offerings without registration of: (1) up to $1 million in a 12-month period by nonpublic companies, with no limit on the number of purchasers; (2) up to $5 million in a 12-month period to fewer than 35 nonaccredited investors or an unlimited number of accredited investors; and (3) an unlimited amount to an unlimited number of accredited investors. In essence, Regulation D expanded the concept of "nonpublic offering" to include deals involving accredited investors, who are presumed to have the financial knowledge and ability to take care of themselves. However, the regulation requires certain kinds of minimum disclosures, even though formal filing of a registration statement is not required.

The general point concerning the Securities Act is that *all* sales must be registered, except those exempted by Sections 3 and 4 or by other regulations (including Regulation D). One fine point of the law is that *offerings* are registered, but specific securities are not. This means that a corporation holding treasury stock, or a large shareholder (10 percent or more), must consult the law before selling large holdings. Even if the shares held were acquired in an earlier registration, subsequent sales may have to be registered anew.

A registration statement must be filed and must be effective before a sale is lawful. The SEC has adopted a series of forms for use in registrations. The forms most commonly used for general public offerings are Forms S-1, S-2, and S-3. These forms are related to the integrated disclosure system discussed earlier. They are not sets of "forms" like an income tax return, however. A "registration form" is a list of financial statement and disclosure requirements cross-referenced to Regulation S-X and Regulation S-K.

AUDITING INSIGHT

ENTHUSIASM FOR PRIVATE STOCK OFFERINGS

Ariad Pharmaceuticals, Inc., raised $46 million in a private stock sale. Specialists in small-company finance say the sale is a sign of growing interest in private financings that could benefit many companies.

Ariad's stock was offered to only a small number of wealthy investors. They had to attest that they have a net worth of at least $1 million (excluding homes) or otherwise met government tests [SEC Regulation D] aimed at protecting small investors. Ariad obtained about 21 percent from institutional investors and the rest from individuals.

Many companies prefer to sell stock privately to avoid the need for public disclosure about proprietary technology or trade practices.

Source: The Wall Street Journal

GENERAL SEC DEFINITIONS

Nonpublic Offering ("Private Placement"). Sales of securities to a small number of persons or institutional investors (usually not more than 35), who can demand and obtain sufficient information without the formality of SEC registration.

Nonpublic Company. Company with less than $10 million in assets and fewer than 500 shareholders. Not required to register and file reports under the Exchange Act.

Accredited Investors. Financial institutions, investment companies, large tax-exempt organizations, directors and executives of the issuer, and individuals with net worth of $1 million or more or income of $200,000 or more.

These forms are filed electronically using the SEC's "EDGAR" system. You can find the documents through the SEC web page on the Internet at www.sec.gov. (EDGAR stands for *Electronic Data Gathering, Analysis, and Retrieval* system. The SEC accepts many documents only in electronic filing form, although some specialized paper filings are still accepted.)

Form S-1 is the general registration form. It is available to all issuers, but issuers who do not qualify for Forms S-2 or S-3 must use it. A certain set of financial statements and disclosures (Part I) in an S-1 is known as the *prospectus* which must be distributed to all purchasers. Investors can obtain the complete S-1, containing all the required information, in the EDGAR system.

Form S-2 is a simplified optional registration form that can be used by well-known companies. In this context, "well-known companies" are ones that have made timely reports under the Exchange Act for 36 months. The company can incorporate by reference the financial information that appears in the annual report to shareholders (or in the annual report on Form 10-K) without actually reprinting it in the registration statement. In a sense, in Form S-2 the SEC recognizes that the financial information investors need for informed decisions is "out there" and the issuer does not need to print it again in the registration statement—only refer to it, and investors can find it in the EDGAR system.

Form S-3 is the most simplified optional registration form, and it can be used by large, well-known companies. In this context, the SEC defines "large" in terms of the dollar value of stock trading in the market and the annual trading volume in number of shares exchanged. This form represents the SEC's acknowledgment of "efficient markets" for widely distributed information. Part I (the prospectus) can be concise—containing information about the terms of the securities being offered, the purpose and use of proceeds, the risk factors, and some other information about the offering. The remainder of the financial information is incorporated by reference, and also incorporated by reference is all the other information in required public filings—therefore, the device of referring to information available elsewhere is maximized in Form S-3.

Another often-used registration is Form SB-1. Small businesses (less than $25 million public market value) can use it for initial public offerings up to $10 million. It is not as complicated or extensive as Form S-1.

SECURITIES ACT (1933) REGISTRATION FORMS

Form S-1   General registration form available to all companies.
Form S-2   Registration form for small well-known companies.
Form S-3   Registration form for large well-known companies.
Form SB-1   Registration form for relatively small public offerings.

Regulation of Periodic Reporting

The Exchange Act primarily regulates daily trading in securities and requires registration of most companies whose securities are traded in interstate commerce. Companies having total assets of $10 million or more and 500 or more stockholders are required to register under the Exchange Act. The purpose of these size and share criteria is to define securities in which there is a significant public interest. (From time to time, these criteria may be changed.)

For auditors and accountants, the most significant aspect of the Exchange Act is the requirement for annual reports, quarterly reports, and periodic special reports. These reports are referred to by the form numbers 10-K, 10-Q, and 8-K, respectively. Under the integrated disclosure system, a company's regular annual report to shareholders may be filed as a part of the 10-K to provide part or all of the information required by law. The 10-Q quarterly report is filed after each of the first three fiscal quarters, and its contents are largely financial statement information. Form 8-K, the "special events report," is required whenever certain significant events occur, such as changes in control and legal proceedings. These 8-K reports are "filed" with the SEC but are not usually sent to all shareholders and creditors. They can be obtained from the SEC and, therefore, are considered publicly available information. Frequently, 8-Ks consist of news releases distributed by the company.

One of the events considered significant for an 8-K report is a change of auditors. Companies that change auditors must report that the change was approved by the board of directors. Companies must also tell the SEC about disagreements, if any, with the former auditors about accounting principles or audit procedures.

EXCHANGE ACT (1934) PERIODIC REPORTS

Form 10-K   Annual report.
Form 10-Q   Quarterly report.
Form 8-K   Periodic report of selected special events.

In the past, some auditor changes have occurred for the purpose of getting an auditor who will agree with management's treatment of a troublesome revenue recognition or expense deferral treatment. Such changes are suspect, and a few of them have turned out to be cases of audit failure on the part of the new auditor. Thus, auditor changes in the context of a disagreement with management are supposed to be of interest to investors. Whenever a company changes auditors, the company must report the fact and state whether there has been any disagreement with the auditors concerning matters of accounting principles, financial statement disclosure, or auditing procedure. At the same time, the former auditor must submit a letter stating whether the auditor agrees with the explanation and, if the auditor disagrees, giving particulars. These documents are available to the public, and their purpose is to make information available about client-auditor conflicts that might have a bearing on financial presentations and consequent investment decisions. Reported disagreements have included disputes over recoverability of asset cost, revenue recognition timing, expense recognition timing, amounts to be reported as liabilities, and necessity for certain auditing procedures. These disclosures must also provide information about "opinion shopping" consultations with a new auditor.

AUDITING INSIGHT

FORMER CLIENT FAILED TO DISCLOSE DISPUTE IN 8-K

The accounting firm told the SEC (in the required accountant's letter) that a former client incorrectly reported no disagreements preceding the firm's dismissal as the company's auditor. The disagreement involved the company's wish to capitalize the cost of moving an acquired company's headquarters to another city in the accounting for the acquisition. The accounting firm believed the costs were expenses of the period and not related to the acquisition.

  Note: Another accounting firm, however, agreed with the company's preferred accounting. The company dismissed the former firm and hired as auditor the one that agreed.

Source: Accounting Today.

R E V I E W
CHECKPOINTS

C.13 What is Regulation D?

C.14 What is a registration of a public offering of securities? What is the use of the Forms S-1, S-2, S-3, and SB-1?

C.15 What is a "nonpublic offering" (private placement) of securities? What are "accredited investors" and how

are they related to nonpublic offerings?

C.16 What are the 10-K, 10-Q, and 8-K reports? To which securities act do they relate? How has the 8-K report been used to strengthen the independent auditor's position?

LIABILITY PROVISIONS: SECURITIES ACT OF 1933

LEARNING OBJECTIVE

6. Specify the civil and criminal liability provisions of the Securities Act of 1933, compare the civil liability to common law, and cite some specific cases.

Section 11 of the Securities Act is of great interest to auditors because it alters significantly the duties and responsibilities otherwise required by common law. This section contains the principal criteria defining civil liabilities under the statute. Portions of Section 11 pertinent to auditors' liability are discussed next.

Section 11—General Liability

The Securities Act (1933) is applicable only when a company files a registration statement (e.g., S-1, S-2, S-3, SB-1) to issue securities. Excerpts from Section 11 are shown in the box on page 524. The sections that follow explain the practical meaning of the legal language.

> # SECTION 11, SECURITIES ACT OF 1933
>
> **Section 11(*a*):** . . . any person acquiring such security [in a registered offering] . . . may sue:
>
> Every person who signed the registration statement.
>
> Every person who was a director of . . . or partner in, the issuer.
>
> Every accountant, engineer, or appraiser.
>
> Every underwriter with respect to such security.
>
> If such person acquired the security after the issuer has made generally available to its security holders an earnings statement covering a period of at least 12 months beginning after the effective date of the registration statement, then the right of recovery . . . shall be conditioned on proof that such person acquired the security relying upon . . . the registration statement . . .
>
> **Section 11(*b*):** Notwithstanding the provisions of subsection (*a*), no person, other than the issuer, shall be liable as provided therein who shall sustain the burden of proof
>
> > that (A) as regards any part of the registration statement *not purporting to be made on the authority of an expert*, . . . he had, after reasonable investigation, reasonable ground to believe . . . that the statements therein were true and that there was no omission to state a material fact . . .
> >
> > and (B) as regards any part of the registration statement *purporting to be made upon his authority as an expert* . . . he had, after reasonable investigation, reasonable ground to believe . . . that the statements therein were true and that there was no omission to state a material fact . . .
> >
> > and (C) as regards any part of the registration statement *purporting to be made on the authority of an expert (other than himself)* . . . he had no reasonable ground to believe . . . that the statements were untrue or that there was an omission to state a material fact. . . .
>
> **Section 11 (*c*):** In determining, for the purpose of . . . subsection (*b*) of this section, what constitutes reasonable investigation and reasonable ground for belief, the standards of reasonableness shall be that required of a prudent man in the management of his own property. . . .
>
> **Section 11(*e*):** . . . if the defendant proves that any portion or all of such damages [claimed in a lawsuit] represents other than the depreciation in value of such security resulting from such part of the registration statement, with respect to which his liability is asserted, not being true or omitting to state a material fact required to be stated therein . . . such portion of or all such damages shall not be recoverable.

In Section 11(*b*)(B), the accountant is considered the "expert" on the financial statements covered by the audit report and, therefore, must perform a reasonable investigation—an audit in accordance with GAAS using due professional care. Read carefully again Section 11(*b*)C; all other people who might be included in a registration legal action do *not* need to prove that they made a "reasonable investigation" of the financial statements, since they relied on the authority of the expert (the accountant who provided the audit report). Thus, the other parties would like the accountant to expand the audit report to cover as much as possible, while the accountant must be careful to specify exactly which statements, including footnotes, are covered by the audit report.

The effect of Section 11 is to shift the major burdens of affirmative proof from the injured plaintiff to the expert accountant. Recall that under the common law, the *plaintiff* had to allege and prove damages, misleading statements, reliance, direct cause, and negligence. Under Section 11, the plaintiff still must show that he or she was damaged and

EXHIBIT   C–1   COMPARISON OF COMMON-LAW AND STATUTORY LITIGATION

Under Common Law	Under Securities Act (1933) Section 11	Under Exchange Act (1934) Section 10(*b*)
Plaintiff		
Proves damages or loss.	Same as common law.	Same as common law.
Proves necessary privity or beneficiary relationship.	Any purchaser may sue the accountant.	Any purchaser or seller may sue the accountant.
Alleges, shows evidence, and the court decides whether financial statements were misleading.	Same as common law.	Same as common law.
Proves reliance on misleading statements.	Not required.*	Same as common law.
Proves misleading statements the direct cause of loss.	Not required.*	Same as common law.
Proves the requisite degree of negligence by the accountant.	Not required.	Must allege and prove the accountant knew about the scheme or device to defraud.
Defendant Accountant		
Offers evidence to counter above, such as: no privity, statements not misleading, and that the audit was conducted in accordance with GAAS with due care.†	Must prove a reasonable investigation was performed (due diligence).†	Must prove acted in good faith and had no knowledge of the misleading statements.†

*Proof of purchaser's reliance may be required if a 12-month earnings statement had been issued.

†Upon failing to prove a proper audit, due diligence, or good faith, the accountant may try to prove that the plaintiff's loss was caused by something other than the misleading financial statements, for example, actions by the plaintiff such as contributory negligence or loss from some other cause.

must allege and show proof that financial statements in the registration statement were materially misleading, but here the plaintiff's duties essentially are ended. Exhibit C–1 summarizes these common-law and statutory duties.

Privity Not Required

The plaintiff does not have to be in privity with the auditor. Section 11 provides that *any purchaser* may sue the accountant. The purchaser-plaintiff does not need to prove he or she relied on the financial statements in the registration statement. In fact, the purchaser may not have even read them.[3] The purchaser is not required to show that the misleading statements caused an unwise decision and a loss.

Section 11 was written with the protection of the investing public in mind, not the protection of the expert auditor. The first significant court case under Section 11 was *Escott et al.* v. *BarChris Construction Corporation et al.* The ruling in this case was that the auditors did not conduct a reasonable investigation and, thus, did not satisfy Section 11(*b*)(B).

Section 11(*a*) Exemption

Financial reporting has changed since 1933. The SEC now requires some larger companies to present interim financial statements and encourages the presentation of forecasts. To remove the legal liability barrier to auditor association with such information, the

---

[3] This matter of reliance is modified by Section 11(a) to the extent that when enough time has elapsed and the registrant has filed an income statement covering a 12-month period beginning after the effective date, then the plaintiff must prove that he or she purchased after that time in reliance on the registration statement. However, the plaintiff may prove reliance without proof of actually having read the registration statement.

LEGAL PRECEDENT

Escott v. BarChris Construction Corp. (1968)

The court ruled that the auditors were the only experts under Section 11 and specifically ruled that the attorneys were not considered experts. In individual findings against all defendants (except the auditors), the court generally ruled that they had not conducted reasonable investigations to form a bases for belief and that they had not satisfied the diligence requirement, *except to the extent that they had relied upon the portions of the prospectus expertised by the auditors* [a lesser diligence requirement under Section 11(b)(C)]. The court ruled that the auditors had also failed to perform a diligent and reasonable investigation [Section 11(b)(B)]. The court found that the auditor had spent "only" 20.5 hours on the subsequent events review, had read no important documents, and "He asked questions, he got answers that he considered satisfactory, and he did nothing to verify them. . . . He was too easily satisfied with glib answers to his inquiries" The court also said: "Accountants should not be held to a standard higher than that recognized in their profession. I do not do so here. The senior accountant's review did not come up to that standard. He did not take some of the steps which [the] written program prescribed. He did not spend an adequate amount of time on a task of this magnitude."

SEC has exempted auditors from Section 11 liability related to interim information and has enacted a "safe harbor" with respect to forecasts. A **safe harbor** means that plaintiffs in a lawsuit must show that the auditor did not act in good faith when reporting on a forecast, effectively placing the burden of proof on the plaintiff.

Statute of Limitations

Section 13 of the Securities Act defines the statute of limitations in such a way that suit is barred if not brought within one year after discovery of the misleading statement or omission, or in any event if not brought within three years after the public offering. These limitations and the reliance limitation related to a 12-month earnings statement restrict auditors' liability exposure to a determinable time span. Oftentimes, the statute of limitations is the best defense available to auditors.

Due Diligence Defense

Section11 also states the means by which auditors can avoid liability. Section 11(b) describes the "due diligence" defense. If the auditor can prove that a *reasonable examination* was performed, then the auditor is not liable for damages. Section 11(c) states the standard of reasonableness to be that degree of care required of a prudent person in the management of his or her own property. In a context more specific to auditors, a reasonable investigation can be shown by the conduct of an audit in accordance with generally accepted auditing standards in both form and substance.

Section 11(b) also gives a diligence defense standard for portions of a registration statement made on the authority of an expert. Any person who relies on an "expert" is not required to conduct a reasonable investigation of his or her own, but only to have no reasonable grounds for disbelief. Thus, the auditor who relies on the opinion of an actuary or engineer need not make a personal independent investigation of that expert's areas. Similarly, any officer, director, attorney, or underwriter connected with a registration has a far lesser diligence duty for any information covered by an auditor's expert opinion. In the *BarChris* judgment, officers, attorneys, and underwriters were found lacking in diligence except with respect to audited financial statements.

Causation Defense

Section 11(*e*) defines the last line of defense available to an auditor when lack of diligence has been proved. This defense is known as *causation defense*. Essentially, if auditors can prove that all or part of the plaintiff's damages were caused by something other than the misleading and negligently prepared registration statement, then all or part of the damages will not have to be paid. This defense may create some imaginative "other reasons." In the *BarChris* case, at least one plaintiff had purchased securities *after* the company had gone bankrupt. The presumption that the loss in this instance resulted from events other than the misleading registration statement is fair, but this claim was settled out of court, so there is no judicial determination for reference.

Section 17—Antifraud

Section 17 of the Securities Act is the antifraud section. The wording and intent of this section is practically identical to Section 10(*b*) and Rule 10*b*-5 under the Exchange Act. The difference between the two acts is the Securities Act reference to "offer or sale" and the Exchange Act reference to "use of securities exchanges." The pertinent portion of Section 17 is below.

SECTION 17, SECURITIES ACT OF 1933

Section 17(*a*): It shall be unlawful for any person in the offer or sale of any securities by the use of any means or instruments of transportation in interstate commerce or by the use of the mails, directly or indirectly—(1) to employ any device, scheme, or artifice to defraud, or (2) to obtain money or property by means of any untrue statement of a material fact or any omission to state a material fact . . . (3) to engage in any transaction, practice, or course of business which operates or would operate as a fraud or deceit upon the purchaser.

Section 24—Criminal Liability

Section 24 sets forth the criminal penalties imposed by the Securities Act. Criminal penalties are characterized by monetary fines or prison terms, or both. They key words in Section 24 are *willful* violation and *willfully* causing misleading statements to be filed.

SECTION 24, SECURITIES ACT OF 1933

Section 24. Any person who willfully violates any of the provisions of this title, or the rules and regulations promulgated by the commission under authority thereof, or any person who willfully, in a registration statement filed under this title, makes any untrue statement of a material fact or omits to state any material fact required to be stated therein or necessary to make the statements therein not misleading, shall upon conviction be fined not more than $10,000 or imprisoned not more than five years, or both.

LEGAL PRECEDENT

United States v. *Benjamin* (1964)

The judgment in this case resulted in conviction of an accountant for willingly conspiring by use of interstate commerce to sell unregistered securities and to defraud in the sale of securities, in violation of Section 24 of the 1933 Securities Act. The accountant had prepared "pro forma" balance sheets and claimed that use of the words *pro forma* absolved him of responsibility. He also claimed he did not know his reports would be used in connection with securities sales. The court found otherwise, showing that he did in fact know about the use of his reports and that certain statements about asset values and acquisitions were patently false and the accountant knew they were false. The court made two significant findings: (1) that the willfulness requirements of Section 24 may be proved by showing that due diligence would have revealed the false statements and (2) that use of limiting words such as "pro forma" do not justify showing false ownership of assets in any kind of financial statements.

REVIEW
CHECKPOINTS

C.17 How does Section 11 of the Securities Act (1933) change the legal environment that previously existed under common law?

C.18 What must be proved by the plaintiff in a suit under Section 11 of the Securities Act (1933) seeking recovery of damages from an independent auditor of financial statements? What must the defendant auditor do in such a court action?

C.19 Why should officers, directors, and underwriters want auditors to include under the audit opinion such information as the plan for use of the proceeds of an offering, the description of the organization and business, the description of physical properties, and other quasi-financial information, such as plant floor space and sales order backlog?

C.20 What liability exposure for accountants is found in Section 17 of the Securities Act (1933)? In Section 24 of the Securities Act (1933)?

C.21 With reference to the *BarChris* decision, what lessons might be learned about the force and effect of generally accepted auditing standards?

LIABILITY PROVISIONS: SECURITIES AND EXCHANGE ACT OF 1934

LEARNING OBJECTIVE

7. Specify the civil and criminal liability provisions of the Securities and Exchange Act of 1934, compare the civil liability to common law, and cite some specific cases.

Section 10 of the Exchange Act is used against accountants quite frequently. Like Section 17 of the Securities Act, Section 10 is a general antifraud section. The law itself states Section 10(*b*) as shown below.

SECTION 10, SECURITIES AND EXCHANGE ACT OF 1934

Section 10. It shall be unlawful for any person, directly or indirectly, by use of any means or instrumentality of interstate commerce or of the mails, or of any facility of any national securities exchange . . . (*b*) to use or employ, in connection with the purchase or sale of any security registered on a national securities exchange or any securities not so registered, any manipulative or deceptive device or contrivance in contravention of such rules and regulations as the commission may prescribe as necessary or appropriate in the public interest or for the protection of investors.

Rule 10*b*-5—Antifraud

Rule 10*b*-5 made under the SEC's authority to make administrative rules related to the statute, is more explicit than Section 10.

RULE 10*b*-5, SECURITIES AND EXCHANGE ACT OF 1934

Rule 10*b*-5. Employment of Manipulative and Deceptive Devices. It shall be unlawful for any person, directly or indirectly, by the use of any means or instrumentality of interstate commerce, or of the mails, or of any facility of any national securities exchange,

1. To employ any device, scheme, or artifice to defraud.
2. To make any untrue statement of material fact or to omit to state a material fact necessary in order to make the statements made, in the light of the circumstances under which they were made, not misleading.
3. To engage in any act, practice, or course of business which operates or would operate as a fraud or deceit upon any person in connection with the purchase or sale of any security.

An important point about Rule 10*b*-5 liability is that plaintiffs must prove **scienter**–that an accountant acted with intent to deceive—to impose liability under the rule. Mere negligence is not enough cause for liability. (The U.S. Supreme Court ruled in 1980 that the SEC when bringing a case must prove scienter under 10(*b*) of the Exchange Act and 17*a*-1 of the Securities Act, but need not prove scienter for 17*a*-2, 3 of the Securities Act.) The basic comparison of Section 10(*b*) with common law and with Section 11 of the Securities Act is shown in Exhibit C–1.

LEGAL PRECEDENT

Ernst & Ernst v. *Hochfelder* (U.S. Supreme Court, 1976)

The decision in this case established precedent for plaintiff's needs to allege and prove scienter—intent to deceive—to impose Section 10(*b*) liability under the Exchange Act. The point of law at issue in the case was whether negligent conduct alone is sufficient. "Scienter" refers to a mental state embracing intent to deceive, manipulate or defraud. Section 10(*b*) makes unlawful the use or employment of any manipulative or deceptive device or contrivance in contravention of Securities and Exchange Commission rules. The respondents (Hochfelder) specifically disclaimed any allegations of fraud or intentional misconduct on the part of Ernst & Ernst, but they wanted to see liability under 10(*b*) imposed for negligence.

The Court reasoned that Section 10(*b*) in its reference to "employment of any manipulative and deceptive device" meant that intention to deceive, manipulate, or defraud is necessary to support a private cause of action under Section 10(*b*), and negligent conduct is not sufficient. This decision is considered a landmark for accountants because it relieved them of liability for negligence under Section 10(*b*) of the Exchange Act and its companion SEC Rule 10*b*-5. Mere negligence is not enough. However, reckless professional work might yet be a sufficient basis for 10(*b*) liability even though scienter is not clearly established.

Section 18—Civil Liability

Section 18 sets forth the pertinent civil liability under the Exchange Act.

> ### SECTION 18, SECURITIES AND EXCHANGE ACT OF 1934
>
> **Section 18(a):** Any person who shall make or cause to be made any statement . . . which . . . was at the time and in the light of the circumstances under which it was made false or misleading with respect to any material fact shall be liable to any person (not knowing that such statement was false or misleading) who, in reliance upon such statement, shall have purchased or sold a security at a price which was affected by such statement, for damages caused by such reliance, unless the person sued shall prove that he acted in good faith and had no knowledge that such statement was false or misleading.

Good Faith Defense

Under Rule 10b-5 and Section 18, a plaintiff must prove reliance on misleading statements and damages caused thereby—the same requirement as under common law. As a defense, the auditor must then prove action in good faith and no knowledge of the misleading statement. This requirement appears to be the *Ultramares* rule written into statute, to the extent that proving good faith is equivalent to showing that any negligence was no greater than ordinary negligence. (A note on the *Ultramares* decision was presented earlier in this module.)

Section 32—Criminal Liability

Section 32 states the criminal penalties for violation of the Exchange Act. Like Section 24 of the Securities Act, the critical test is whether the violator acted "willfully and knowingly."

> ### SECTION 32, SECURITIES AND EXCHANGE ACT OF 1934
>
> **Section 32(a):** Any person who willfully violates any provision of this title, or any rule or regulation thereunder . . . or any person who willfully and knowingly makes, or causes to be made, any statement . . . which . . . was false or misleading with respect to any material fact, shall upon conviction be fined not more than $1,000,000, or imprisoned not more than ten years, or both . . . but no person shall be subjected to imprisonment under this section for the violation of any rule or regulation if he proves that he had no knowledge of such rule or regulation.

The defendant accountants in the *Continental Vending* case (*United States* v. *Simon*) and in *United States* v. *Natelli* were charged with violation of Section 32.

> ### LEGAL PRECEDENT
>
> *United States* v. *Simon* (popularly known as the "Continental Vending" case, 1969)
>
> The circumstances were judged to be evidence of willful violation of the Exchange Act. Generally accepted accounting principles were viewed by the judge as a persuasive but not necessarily conclusive criteria for financial reporting.
>
> In affirming the conviction, the appeals court stated that it should be the auditor's responsibility to report factually whenever corporate activities are carried out for the benefit of the president of the company and when "looting" has occurred.

LEGAL PRECEDENT

United States v. *Natelli* (popularly known as the "National Student Marketing" case, 1975)

Circumstances and actions on the part of accountants were construed to amount to willful violation of the Exchange Act.

The court stated: "It is hard to probe the intent of a defendant. . . . When we deal with a defendant who is a professional accountant, it is even harder at times to distinguish between simple errors of judgment and errors made with sufficient criminal intent to support a conviction, especially when there is no financial gain to the accountant other than his legitimate fee."

Nevertheless, the court affirmed one accountant's conviction by the lower trial court because of this apparent motive and action to conceal the effect of some accounting adjustments. A footnote in particular, as it was written, failed to reveal what it should have revealed—the write-off of $1 million of "sales" (about 20 percent of the amount previously reported) and the large operating income adjustment ($210,000 compared to $388,031 originally reported). The court concluded that the concealment of the retroactive adjustments to the company's 1968 revenues and earnings were properly found to have been intentional for the very purpose of hiding earlier errors.

R E V I E W
CHECKPOINTS

C.22 What liability exposure for accountants is found in Section 10(*b*) of the Exchange Act (1934)? In Section 18 of the Exchange Act (1934)? In Section 32 of the Exchange Act (1934)?

C.23 With reference to the *Continental Vending* case (*U.S.* v. *Simon*), what lesson might be learned abut the force and effect of generally accepted accounting principles?

C.24 In what form of the law will you find provisions for criminal penalties? For civil remedies?

EXTENT OF LIABILITY

You may be interested in knowing about who suffers exposure and penalties in lawsuits—the accounting firm, partners, managers, senior accountants, staff assistants, or all of these. Most lawsuits center attention on the accounting firm and on the partners and managers involved in the audit or other accounting work. However, court opinions have cited the work of senior accountants, and there is no reason that the work of new staff assistant accountants should not come under review. All persons involved in professional accounting are exposed to potential liability.

Statement on Auditing Standards No. 22 (AU 311), "Planning and Supervision," offers some important thoughts for accountants who question the validity of some of the work. Accountants can express their own positions and let the working paper records show the nature of the disagreement and the resolution of the question. SAS 22 (Planning and Supervision) expressed the appropriate action as follows:

> The auditor with final responsibility for the examination [partner in charge of the audit] and assistants should be aware of the procedures to be followed when differences of opinion concerning accounting and auditing issues exist among firm personnel involved in the examination. Such procedures should enable an assistant to document his disagreement with the conclusions reached if,

after appropriate consultation, he believes it necessary to disassociate himself from the resolution of the matter. In this situation, the basis for the final resolution should also be documented.

SUMMARY

Starting in the 1970s and extending through the 1980s and 1990s, litigation against accountants became a serious financial issue for accounting firms. Damage claims of hundreds of millions of dollars were paid by CPA firms and their insurers. Insurance became expensive. The Laventhol & Horwath CPA firm declared bankruptcy. Accountants were not alone in this rash of litigation, which affected manufacturers, architects, doctors, and people in many other walks of life. The AICPA joined with other interest groups pushing for "tort reform" of various types (e.g., limitation of damages, identification of liability) in an effort to stem the tide.

Accountants' liability to clients and third parties under common law expanded. Seventy years ago, a strict privity doctrine required other parties to be in a contract with and known to the accountant before they could sue for damages based on negligence. Of course, if an accountant was grossly negligent in such a way as to amount to constructive fraud, liability existed as it would for anyone who committed a fraud. Over the years, the privity doctrine was modified in many jurisdictions, leading to liability for ordinary negligence to primary beneficiaries (known users) of the accountants' work product, then to liability based on ordinary negligence to foreseen and foreseeable beneficiaries (users not so easily known). While the general movement has been to expand accountants' liability for ordinary negligence, some state courts have held closer to the privity doctrine of the past. The treatment can vary from state to state.

The Securities Act of 1933 changed the CPA's obligations. Under common law, a plaintiff suing an accountant had to bring all the proof of the accountant's negligence to the court and convince the judge or jury. In the case of a public offering of securities registered in a registration statement filed under the Securities Act, the plaintiff only needs to show evidence of a loss and that the financial statements were materially misleading. Case rested. Then, the accountant shoulders the burden of proof of showing that the audit was performed properly or that the loss resulted from some other cause. The burden of proof was shifted from the plaintiff to the defendant. The Securities and Exchange Act of 1934 added a continuing exposure to liability for the periodic audited reports companies are required to file. However, the Exchange Act requirements of proof closely resemble the common-law requirements. The securities acts also impose criminal penalties in some cases.

After 1994, accountants obtained considerable relief. The federal Private Securities Litigation Reform Act and the Securities Litigation Uniform Standards Act forced many class action lawsuits into federal courts where rules of proportionate liability prevail in place of the onerous doctrine of joint and several liability. Some court decisions limited the causes of action against accountants to cases where they were actively involved in fraud and illegal acts instead of merely auditors who failed to find evidence of management misdeeds. These developments meant that plaintiffs' lawyers might now expect to recover less money from accountants, therefore making them less attractive lawsuit targets.

MULTIPLE-CHOICE QUESTIONS FOR PRACTICE AND REVIEW

C.25   From the accountants' point of view, which one of these is a preferable provision for imposition of civil liability in a lawsuit against an accountant for financial damages?

a. Joint and several liability.
b. Reasonable forseeable users approach to privity.
c. Forseen third parties approach to privity.
d. Proportionate liability.

C.26 If an auditor lost a civil lawsuit for damages, and the court found total losses of $5 million, and the auditor was found 30 percent at fault, and the auditor was the only solvent defendant, and the court followed Private Securities Litigation Reform Act rules of proportionate liability, the court would order the auditor to pay
   a. $ 5,000,000
   b. -0-
   c. $2,250,000
   d. $1,500,000

C.27 Suppose the auditor in the question above participated knowingly in commission of violations of securities laws (along with managers and directors of the audit client), then the court would order the auditor to pay
   a. $ 5,000,000
   b. -0-
   c. $2,250,000
   d. $1,500,000

C.28 When a client sues an accountant for failure to perform consulting work properly, the accountants' best defense is probably based on the idea of
   a. Lack of privity of contract.
   b. Contributory negligence on the part of the client.
   c. Lack of any measurable dollar amount of damages.
   d. No negligence on the part of the consultant.

C.29 When creditors who relied upon a company's audited financial statements lose money after a customer (the auditor's client) goes bankrupt, the plaintiff creditors in a lawsuit for damages must show in a court that follows the limited exposure (*Credit Alliance*) privity doctrine
   a. The auditors knew and specifically acknowledged identification of the creditors.
   b. The auditors could reasonably forsee them as beneficiaries of the audit because companies such as this client use financial statements to get credit from vendors.
   c. They were forseen users of the audited financial statements because they were vendors of long standing.
   d. All of the above.

C.30 When CPAs agree to perform a compilation or review of unaudited financial statements, the best way to avoid clients' misunderstanding the nature of the work is to describe it completely in

   a. An engagement letter.
   b. An audit report.
   c. A report to the clients' board of directors at the close of the engagement.
   d. A management letter to the board of director's audit committee.

C.31 The securities acts (Securities Act–1933 and Exchange Act–1934) contain
   a. Civil liability provisions applicable to auditors.
   b. Criminal liability provisions applicable to auditors.
   c. a but not b
   d. Both a and b

C.32 The SEC relies on the accounting profession to pronounce accounting principles (GAAP) but applies the concept *authoritative support* to determine whether financial statements are presented in conformity with GAAP. In this regard, SEC follows a policy
   a. When financial statements apply accounting on which the SEC disagrees but has no explicit rules to prohibit use, supplementary disclosures are accepted instead of corrections to the financial statements.
   b. When financial statements apply accounting on which the SEC disagrees and has explicit rules to prohibit use, supplementary disclosures are accepted instead of corrections to the financial statements.
   c. When financial statements apply accounting that has authoritative support below the level of FASB standards but with which the SEC disagrees and has explicit rules to prohibit use, supplementary disclosures are accepted instead of corrections to the financial statements.
   d. Both b and c.

C.33 Abrazame Corporation cannot sell voting common stock in this circumstance without filing an appropriate registration statement.
   a. A $1 million initial offering to FaithFul&Co's brokerage customers located in any of the 50 states.
   b. $4 million initial offering to 30 nonaccredited investors and 100 accredited investors.
   c. $6 million initial offering to 40 nonaccredited investors and 100 accredited investors.
   d. $120 million to 40 accredited investors.

C.34 Under the Securities and Exchange Act of 1934, companies are required to report to the public about the event of changing auditors on

a. Form 10-K.
b. Form S-1.
c. Form 10-Q.
d. Form 8-K.

C.35 Section 11(*b*) of the Securities Act (1933) provides that people can be sued and may be liable for investors' losses in connection with a public securities offering under one of these circumstances.

a. The chair of the board of directors performed a reasonable investigation of facts in connection with writing the section in the registration statement concerning the specification of the use of the proceeds of the offering.

b. A consulting engineer performed a reasonable investigation and reported in the registration statement on the feasibility of construction of a roadway to be financed with the offering proceeds.

c. The president of the issuing company had no reason to doubt the report of the consulting engineer, although the president did not perform separate reasonable investigation of her own.

d. The officers of the issuing company were relieved that the independent auditors did not make an issue about the excessive valuation of inventory held to support construction in progress.

C.36 In comparison to the burdens of affirmative proof required of plaintiffs in civil lawsuits against independent auditors under the common law, Section 10(*b*) of the Securities and Exchange Act of 1934

a. Is the same regarding plaintiffs' need to prove damages or losses.

b. Is the same regarding plaintiffs' need to establish privity or beneficiary relationship with the auditors.

c. Does not require that plaintiffs prove their reliance on misleading financial statements.

d. Does not require that plaintiffs prove that relying on the misleading financial statement caused their losses.

C.37 The management accountants employed by Robbins, Inc., wrongfully charged executives' personal expenses to the overhead on a government contract. Their activities can be characterized as

a. Errors in the application of accounting principles.

b. Irregularities of the type independent auditors should plan an audit to detect.

c. Irregularities of the type independent auditors have no responsibility to plan an audit to detect.

d. Illegal acts of a type independent auditors should be aware might occur in government contract business.

C.38 Good Gold Company sold $20 million of preferred stock. The company should have registered the offering under the Securities Act of 1933 if it were sold to

a. 150 accredited investors.
b. One insurance company.
c. 30 investors all resident in one state.
d. Diverse customers of a brokerage firm.

C.39 When a company registers a security offering under the Securities Act of 1933, the law provides an investor with

a. An SEC guarantee that the information in the registration statement is true.

b. Insurance against loss from the investment.

c. Financial information about the company audited by independent CPAs.

d. Inside information about the company's trade secrets.

C.40 A group of investors sued Anderson, Olds, and Watershed, CPAs, for alleged damages suffered when the company in which they held common stock went bankrupt. To avoid liability under the common law, AOW must prove which of the following?

a. The investors actually suffered a loss.

b. The investors relied on the financial statements audited by AOW.

c. The investors' loss was a direct result of their reliance on the audited financial statements.

d. The audit was conducted in accordance with generally accepted auditing standards and with due professional care.

C.41 The Securities and Exchange Commission document that governs accounting in financial statements filed with the SEC is:

a. Regulation D.
b. Form 8-K.
c. Form SB-1.
d. Regulation S-X.

C.42 Able Corporation plans to sell $12 million common stock to investors. The company can do so without filing a S-1 registration statement under the Securities Act (1933) if Able sells the stock:

a. To an investment banker who then sells it to investors in its national retail network.

b. To no more than 75 investors solicited at random.

c. Only to accredited investors.

d. Only to 35 accredited investors and an unlimited number of unaccredited investors.

C.43   A "public company" subject to the periodic reporting requirements of the Exchange Act (1934) must file an annual report with the SEC known as the

a. Form 10-K.

b. Form 10-Q.

c. Form 8-K.

d. Form S-3.

C.44   When investors sue auditors for damages under Section 11 of the Securities Act (1933), they must allege and prove.

a. Scienter on the part of the auditor.

b. The audited financial statements were materially misleading.

c. They relied on the misleading audited financial statements.

d. Their reliance on the misleading financial statements was the direct cause of their loss.

DISCUSSION CASES

C.45   Common-Law Responsibility for Errors and Fraud.   Huffman & Whitman (H&W), a large regional CPA firm, was engaged by the Ritter Tire Wholesale Company to audit its financial statements for the year ended January 31. H&W had a busy audit engagement schedule from December 31 through April 1, and they decided to audit Ritter's purchase vouchers and related cash disbursements on a sample basis. They instructed staff accountants to select a random sample of 130 purchase transactions and gave directions about the important deviations, including missing receiving reports. Boyd, the assistant in charge, completed the working papers, properly documenting the fact that 13 of the purchases in the sample had been recorded and paid without the receiving report (required by stated internal control procedures) being included in the file of supporting documents. Whitman, the partner in direct charge of the audit, showed the findings to Lock, Ritter's chief accountant. Lock appeared surprised but promised that the missing receiving reports would be inserted into the files before the audit was over. Whitman was satisfied, noted in the work papers that the problem was solved, and did not say anything to Huffman about it.

Unfortunately, H&W did not discover the fact that Lock was involved in a fraudulent scheme in which he diverted shipments to a warehouse leased in his name and sent the invoices to Ritter for payment. He then sold the tires for his own profit. Internal auditors discovered the scheme during a study of slow-moving inventory items. Ritter's inventory was overstated by about $500,000 (20 percent)—the amount Lock has diverted.

Required:

a. With regard to the 13 missing receiving reports, does a material weakness in internal control exist? If so, does Huffman & Whitman have any further audit responsibility? Explain.

b. Was the audit conducted in a negligent manner?

C.46   Common-Law Responsibility for Errors and Fraud.   Herbert McCoy is the president of McCoy Forging Corporation. For the past several years, Donovan & Company, CPAs, has done the company's compilation and some other accounting and tax work. McCoy decided to have an audit. Moreover, McCoy had recently received a disturbing anonymous letter that stated: "Beware, you have a viper in your nest. The money is literally disappearing before your very eyes! Signed: A friend." He told no one about the letter.

McCoy Forging engaged Donovan & Company, CPAs, to render an opinion on the financial statements for the year ended June 30. McCoy told Donovan he wanted to verify that the financial statements were "accurate and proper." He did not mention the anonymous letter. The usual engagement letter providing for an audit in accordance with generally accepted auditing standards (GAAS) was drafted by Donovan & Company and signed by both parties.

The audit was performed in accordance with GAAS. The audit did not reveal a clever defalcation plan. Harper, the assistant treasurer, was siphoning off substantial amounts of McCoy Forging's money. The defalcations occurred both before and after the audit. Harper's embezzlement was discovered by McCoy's new internal auditor in October, after Donovan had delivered the audit report. Although the scheme was fairly sophisticated, it could have been detected if Donovan & Company had performed additional procedures. McCoy Forging demands reimbursement from Donovan for the entire amount of the embezzlement, some $40,000 of which occurred before the audit and $65,000 after. Donovan has denied any liability and refuses to pay.

Required:

Discuss Donovan's responsibility in this situation. Do you think McCoy Forging could prevail in whole or in part in a lawsuit against Donovan under common law? Explain your conclusions.

(AICPA adapted)

C.47 Common-Law Liability Exposure. A CPA firm was engaged to examine the financial statements of Martin Manufacturing Corporation for the year ending December 31. Martin needed cash to continue its operations and agreed to sell its common stock investment in a subsidiary through a private placement. The buyers insisted that the proceeds be placed in escrow because of the possibility of a major contingent tax liability that might result from a pending government claim against Martin's subsidiary. The payment in escrow was completed in late November. The president of Martin told the audit partner that the proceeds from the sale of the subsidiary's common stock, held in escrow, should be shown on the balance sheet as an unrestricted current account receivable. The president was of the opinion that the government's claim was groundless and that Martin needed an "uncluttered" balance sheet and a "clean" auditor's opinion to obtain additional working capital from lenders. The audit partner agreed with the president and issued an unqualified opinion on the Martin financial statements, which did not refer to the contingent liability and did not properly describe the escrow arrangement.

The government's claim proved to be valid, and, pursuant to the agreement with the buyers, the purchase price of the subsidiary was reduced by $450,000. This adverse development forced Martin into bankruptcy. The CPA firm is being sued for deceit (fraud) by several of Martin's unpaid creditors who extended credit in reliance on the CPA firm's unqualified opinion on Martin's financial statements.

Required:

a. What deceit (fraud) do you believe the creditors are claiming?

b. Is the lack of privity between the CPA firm and the creditors important in this case?

c. Do you believe the CPA firm is liable to the creditors? Explain.

(AICPA adapted)

C.48 Common-Law Liability Exposure. Risk Capital Limited, a Delaware corporation, was considering the purchase of a substantial amount of treasury stock held by Florida Sunshine Corporation, a closely held corporation. Initial discussions with the Florida Sunshine Corporation began late in 2001.

Wilson and Wyatt, Florida Sunshine's accountants, regularly prepared quarterly and annual unaudited financial statements. The most recently prepared financial statements were for the year ended September 30, 2001.

On November 15, 2001, after extensive negotiations, Risk Capital agreed to purchase 100,000 shares of no par, class A capital stock of Florida Sunshine at $12.50 per share. However, Risk Capital insisted on audited statements for calendar year 2001. The contract that was made available to Wilson and Wyatt specifically provided:

Risk Capital shall have the right to rescind the purchase of said stock if the audited financial statements of Florida Sunshine for the calendar year 2001 show a material adverse change in the financial condition of the corporation.

The audited financial statements furnished to Florida Sunshine by Wilson and Wyatt showed no such material adverse change. Risk Capital relied on the audited statements and purchased the treasury stock of Florida Sunshine. It was subsequently discovered that, as of the balance sheet date, the audited statements were incorrect and that in fact there had been a material adverse change in the financial condition of the corporation. Florida Sunshine is insolvent, and Risk Capital will lose virtually its entire investment.

Risk Capital seeks recovery against Wilson and Wyatt.

Required:

Assuming that only ordinary negligence is proved, will Risk Capital prevail:

a. Under a theory of limited exposure to third parties (*Credit Alliance v. Arthur Andersen*)?

b. Under the theory of restatement of torts, (*Rosenblum v. Adler*)?

C.49 Common-Law Liability Exposure. Smith, CPA, is the auditor for Juniper Manufacturing Corporation, a privately owned company that has a June 30 fiscal year. Juniper arranged for a substantial bank loan, which depended on the bank receiving, by September 30, audited financial statements showing a current ratio of at least 2 to 1. On September 25, just before the audit report was to be issued, Smith received an anonymous letter on Juniper's stationery indicating that a five-year lease by Juniper, as lessee, of a factory building that was in the financial statements as an operating lease was in fact a capital lease. The letter stated that Juniper had a secret written agreement with the lessor modifying the lease and creating a capital lease.

Smith confronted the president of Juniper, who admitted that a secret agreement existed but said it was necessary to treat the lease as an operating lease to meet the current ratio requirement of the pending loan and that nobody would ever discover the secret agreement with the lessor. The president said that, if Smith did not issue his report by September 30, Juniper would sue Smith for substantial damages that would result from not getting the loan. Under this pressure and because the working papers contained a copy of the five-year lease agreement supporting the operating lease treatment, Smith issued his report with an unqualified opinion on September 29. In spite of the fact that the loan was received, Juniper went bankrupt. The bank is suing Smith to recover its losses on the loan and the lessor is suing Smith to recover uncollected rents.

Required:

Answer the following, setting forth reasons or any conclusions stated:

a. Is Smith liable to the bank?

b. Is Smith liable to the lessor?

c. Was Smith independent?

(AICPA adapted)

C.50   Liability in a Review Engagement. Mason & Dilworth, CPAs, were the accountants for Hotshot Company, a closely held corporation owned by 30 residents of the area. M&D had been previously engaged by Hotshot to perform some compilation and tax work. Bubba Crass, Hotshot's president and holder of 15 percent of the stock, said he needed something more than these services. He told Mason, the partner in charge, that he wanted financial statements for internal use, primarily for management purposes, but also to obtain short-term loans from financial institutions. Mason recommended a "review" of the financial statements. Mason did not prepare an engagement letter.

During the review work, Mason had some reservations about the financial statements. Mason told Dilworth at various times he was "uneasy about certain figures and conclusions," but he would "take Crass's word about the validity of certain entries since the review was primarily for internal use in any event and was not an audit."

M&D did not discover a material act of fraud committed by Crass. The fraud would have been detected had Mason not relied so much on the unsupported statements made by Crass concerning the validity of the entries about which he had felt so uneasy.

Required:

a. What potential liability might M&D have to Hotshot Company and other stockholders?

b. What potential liability might M&D have to financial institutions that used the financial statements in connection with making loans to Hotshot Company?

(AICPA adapted)

C.51   Common-Law and Section 10(*b*) Liability Exposure. Butler Manufacturing Corporation raised capital for a plant expansion by borrowing from a bank and making a stock offering. Butler engaged Weaver, CPA, to audit its December 2001 financial statements. Butler told Weaver that the financial statements would be given to Union Bank and certain other named banks and also included in a registration statement for the stock offering.

In performing the audit, Weaver did not confirm accounts receivable and therefore failed to discover a material overstatement of accounts receivable. Also, Weaver was aware of pending class action product liability lawsuit that was not disclosed in Butler's financial statements. Despite being advised by Butler's legal counsel that Butler's potential liability under the lawsuit would result in material losses, Weaver issued an unqualified opinion on Butler's financial statements.

In May 2002, Union Bank relied on the financial statements and Weaver's opinion to grant Butler a $500,000 loan.

Butler raised additional funds in November 2002 with a $14,000,000 unregistered offering of preferred stock. This offering was sold directly by the company to 40 nonaccredited private investors during a one-year period.

Shortly after obtaining the Union Bank loan, Butler experienced financial problems but was able to stay in business because of the money raised by the stock offering. Butler lost the product liability suit. This resulted in a judgment Butler could not pay. Butler also defaulted on the Union Bank loan and was involuntarily petitioned into bankruptcy. This caused Union Bank to sustain a loss and Butler's stockholders' investments also became worthless.

Union Bank sued Weaver for negligence and common-law fraud. The stockholders who purchased Butler's stock through the offering sued Weaver, alleging fraud under Section 10(*b*) and Rule 10*b*-5 of the Securities and Exchange Act of 1934.

These transactions took place in a jurisdiction providing for accountant's liability for negligence to known and intended users of financial statements.

Required:

Answer the following questions and give the reasons for your conclusions:

a. Will Union Bank be successful in its suit against Weaver for (1) negligence? (2) common-law fraud?

b. Will the stockholders who purchased Butler's stock through the offering succeed against Weaver under the anti-fraud provisions of Section 10(*b*) and Rule 10*b*-5 of the Securities Exchange Act of 1934 ?

(AICPA adapted)

C.52   Regulation D Exemption. One of your firm's clients, Fancy Fashions, Inc., is a highly successful, rapidly expanding company. It is owned predominantly by the Munster family and key corporate officials. Although additional funds would be available on a short-term basis from its bankers, this would only represent a temporary solution of the company's need for capital to finance its expansion plans. In addition, the interest rates being charged are not appealing. Therefore, John Munster, Fancy's chairman of the board, in consultation with the other shareholders, has decided to explore the possibility of raising additional equity capital of approximately $15 million to $16 million. This will be Fancy's first public offering to investors, other than the Munster family and the key management personnel.

At a meeting of Fancy's major shareholders, its attorneys and a CPA from your firm spoke about the advantages and disadvantages of "going public" and registering a stock offering. One of the shareholders suggested that Regulation D under the Securities Act of 1933 might be a preferable alternative.

Required:

a. Assume Fancy makes a public offering for $16 million and, as a result, more than 1,000 persons own shares of the company. What are the implications with respect to the Securities Exchange Act of 1934?

b. What federal civil and criminal liabilities may apply in the event that Fancy sells the securities without registration and a registration exemption is not available?

c. Discuss the exemption applicable to offerings under Regulation D, in terms of the two kinds of investors, and how many of each can participate.

(AICPA adapted)

C.53   Section 11 of Securities Act (1933)—Liability Exposure. The Chriswell Corporation decided to raise additional long-term capital by issuing $20 million of 12 percent subordinated debentures to the public. May, Clark, & Company, CPAs, the company's auditors, were engaged to examine the June 30, 2002, financial statements, which were included in the bond registration statement.

May, Clark, & Company completed its examination and submitted an unqualified auditor's report dated July 15, 2002. The registration statement was filed and became effective on September 1, 2002. On August 15, one of the partners of May, Clark, & Company called on Chriswell Corporation and had lunch with the financial vice president and the controller. He questioned both officials on the company's operations since June 30 and inquired whether there had been any material changes in the company's financial position since that date. Both officers assured him that everything had proceeded normally and that the financial condition of the company had not changed materially.

Unfortunately, the officers' representation was not true. On July 30, a substantial debtor of the company failed to pay the $400,000 due on its account receivable and indicated to Chriswell that it would probably be forced into bankruptcy. This receivable was shown as a collateralized loan on the June 30 financial statements. It was secured by stock of the debtor corporation, which had a value in excess of the loan at the time the financial statements were prepared but was virtually worthless at the effective date of the registration statement. This $400,000 account receivable was material to the financial condition of Chriswell Corporation, and the market price of the subordinated debentures decreased by nearly 50 percent after the foregoing facts were disclosed.

The debenture holders of Chriswell are seeking recovery of their loss against all parties connected with the debenture registration.

Required:

Is May, Clark, & Company liable to the Chriswell debenture holders under Section 11 of the Securities Act (1933)? Explain. (*Hint:* Review the *BarChris* case in this chapter.)

(AICPA adapted)

C.54   Rule 10*b*-5—Liability Exposure under the Exchange Act (1934). Gordon & Groton, CPAs, were the auditors of Bank & Company, a brokerage firm and member of a national stock exchange. G&G examined and reported on the financial statements of Bank, which were filed with the Securities and Exchange Commission.

Several of Bank's customers were swindled by a fraudulent scheme perpetrated by Bank's president, who owned 90 percent of the voting stock of the company. The facts establish that Gordon & Groton were negligent in the conduct of the audit but neither participated in the fraudulent scheme nor knew of its existence.

The customers are suing G&G under the antifraud provisions of Section 10(*b*) and Rule 10*b*-5 of the Exchange Act (1934) for aiding and abetting the fraudulent scheme of the president. The customers' suit for fraud is predicated exclusively on the negligence of G&G in failing to conduct a proper audit, thereby failing to discover the fraudulent scheme.

Required:

Answer the following, setting forth reasons for any conclusions stated:

a. What is the probable outcome of the lawsuit?

b. What might be the result if plaintiffs had sued under a common-law theory of negligence? Explain.

(AICPA adapted)

C.55   Independence, Exchange Act (1934), Private Securities Litigation Reform Act.   Andersen-Olds & Watershed (AOW) has been the independent auditor for Accord Corporation since 1990. Accord is a public company obligated to file periodic reports under the Exchange Act (1934).

Beginning in January 2000, the AOW litigation support consulting division performed a special engagement for Accord. The work involved a lawsuit Accord filed against Civic Company for patent infringement on microchip manufacturing processes. AOW personnel compiled production statistics—costs and lost profits—under various volume assumptions, then testified in court about the losses to Accord that resulted from Civic's improper use of patented processes. The amounts at issue were very large, with claims of $50 million for lost profits and a plea for $150 million punitive damages. Accord won a court judgment for a total

of $120 million, and Civic has appealed the damage award. The case remained pending throughout 2000 and 2001. By March 1, 2000, AOW had billed Accord $265,000 for the litigation support work.

In December 2000, AOW started the audit work on Accord's financial statements for the fiscal year that would end January 30, 2001. During this work, AOW auditors found that Accord's management and board of directors did not fully disclose the stage of the appeal of the Civic case; and in addition had improperly deferred a material loss on new product start-up costs as an element of its inventory and had accrued sales revenue for promotional chip sales that carried an unconditional right of return. As partner in charge of the engagement, D. Ward agreed with the company president that the accounting and disclosure were suitable to protect Accord's shareholders from adverse business developments, and he issued a standard unqualified audit report that was included in the company's 10-K annual report filed with the SEC and dated April 1, 2001.

AOW then billed Accord for the $200,000 audit fee and sent a reminder for payment of the $265,000 consulting fee, both billings dated April 2, 2001.

Required:

a. Was AOW independent for the audit of Accord for the fiscal year ended January 30, 2001? Explain.

b. Did Ward and AOW follow generally accepted auditing standards in the audit? Cite any specific standards that might have been violated and explain your reasoning.

c. Did Ward and AOW violate any section(s) of the Exchange Act (1934)? Explain.

d. Did Ward and AOW violate any Part(s) of the Private Securities Litigation Reform Act?

Module D

Operational Auditing:
Governmental and Internal Audits

Professional Standards References

Compendium Section	Document Reference	Topic
AU 322	SAS 65	Auditor's Consideration of Internal Audit Function in an Audit of Financial Statements
AU 801	SAS 74	Compliance Auditing Consideration in Audits of Governmental Entities and Recipients of Governmental Financial Assistance
	SIAS 1	Control: Concepts and Responsibilities
	SIAS 2	Communicating Results
	SIAS 3	Deterrence, Detection, Investigation, and Reporting of Fraud
	SIAS 4	Quality Assurance
	SIAS 5	Internal Auditors' Relationships with Independent Outside Auditors
	SIAS 6	Audit Working Papers
	SIAS 7	Communicating with the Board of Directors
	SIAS 8	Analytical Auditing Procedures
	SIAS 9	Risk Assessment
	SIAS 10	Evaluating the Accomplishment of Established Objectives and Goals for Operations or Programs
	SIAS 11	1992 Omnibus Statement
	SIAS 12	Planning the Audit Assignment
	SIAS 13	Follow-up in the Performance of Audit Work
	SIAS 14	Glossary
	SIAS 15	Supervision
	SIAS 16	Auditing Compliance with Policies, Plans, Procedures, Laws, Regulations, and Contracts
	SIAS 17	Assessment of Performance of External Auditors
	SIAS 18	Use of Outside Providers
ET101.12		Ethics Interpretation 101-10. The Effect on Independence of Relationships with Entities Included in the Governmental Financial Statements
ET501.04		Ethics Interpretation 501-3. Failure to Follow Standards and/or Procedures . . . in Governmental Audits
ET501.06		Ethics Interpretation 501-5. Failure to Follow Requirements of Governmental Bodies . . . in Attest or Similar Services

Learning Objectives

This module introduces governmental and internal auditing in the context of operational auditing. These fields differ in important respects from financial statement auditing practiced by independent CPAs in public accounting, However, you will find that all the fields of auditing share many similarities. The explanations and examples in this module will help you understand the working environment, objectives, and procedures that characterize governmental and internal auditing. Your learning objectives are to be able to:

1. Describe the governmental and internal audit institutions (IIA, GAO), and tell how governmental and internal audit work interacts with independent audits.

2. Define governmental auditing and internal auditing.

3. Compare aspects of governmental, internal, and external auditors' independence problems.

4. Specify the elements of expanded scope auditing in both governmental and internal audit practice.

5. Describe the coverage of governmental and internal audit standards.

6. Describe the Single Audit Act of 1984 in relation to audits of governmental fund recipients.

7. Describe risk-based auditing (RBA) in governmental and internal audits.

8. Explain the function of standards and measurements in economy and efficiency and program results audits.

9. List and explain several features and requirements in internal audit and governmental audit reports.

"EXTERNAL," GOVERNMENTAL, AND INTERNAL AUDITS

LEARNING OBJECTIVE
1. Describe the governmental and internal audit institutions (IIA, GAO), and tell how governmental and internal audit work interacts with independent audits.

Governmental and internal auditing is an extensive subject. This module explains some of the main features. Even though points of similarity and difference in comparison to "external" auditing would be useful, space does not permit presentation of a detailed comparison. Many such similarities and differences will be apparent, however, when you study this module.

Perhaps you have already noticed the reference to "external" auditing. Ordinarily you can refer to governmental, internal, and independent auditors—the latter referring to CPAs in public practice. Yet, labels are potentially confusing. Many governmental and internal auditors are CPAs, and they take pride in their independence in mental attitude. For purposes of this module, therefore, "external" auditing will be used to refer to auditing performed by CPAs in public accounting firms and thereby distinguish public practice from governmental and internal practice.

Internal Auditing

Internal auditing is practiced by auditors employed by an organization, such as a bank, hospital, city government, or industrial company. The Institute of Internal Auditors (IIA) is the international organization that governs the standards, continuing education, and general rules of conduct for internal auditors as a profession. (The IIA Standards for the practice of internal auditing are summarized in Appendix DA.) The IIA also sponsors research and development of practices and procedures designed to enhance the work of internal auditors wherever they are employed. For example, the IIA actively provides courses in numerous internal audit and investigation subjects and promotes its massive, multivolume *Systems Auditability and Control* guide for dealing with computerized information systems.

The IIA also controls the Certified Internal Auditor (CIA) program. This certification is a mark of professional achievement that has gained widespread acceptance throughout the world. To become a CIA, a candidate must hold a college degree and pass an examination on internal auditing and related subjects. Candidates must also have two years of audit experience (internal audit or public accounting audit) obtained before or after passing the examination. Holders of masters' degrees need only one year of experience. You can sit for the CIA exam while you are still in school. For more details, consult the IIA's website (www.theiia.org).

Governmental Auditing

The governmental auditors discussed in this module are persons employed by the U.S. General Accounting Office (GAO), which is an accounting, auditing, and investigating agency of the U.S. Congress. The GAO audits the departments, agencies, and programs of the federal government to determine whether the laws passed by the U.S. Congress are followed and to determine whether programs are being implemented with economy and efficiency and achieving desired results. The U.S. Congress always receives a copy of the GAO reports.

The GAO is headed by the U.S. Comptroller General. In one sense, GAO auditors are the highest level of internal auditors for the federal government as a whole. State and federal agencies and other local governmental units use the GAO *Generally Accepted Government Auditing Standards* (GAGAS) to guide their audits. These standards are published in a book with a yellow cover and, thus, are referred to as the "Yellow Book."

Many states also have audit agencies similar to the GAO. They answer to state legislatures and perform the same types of work described herein as GAO auditing. In another sense, GAO and similar state agencies are really external auditors with respect to government agencies they audit because they are organizationally independent.

Many government agencies have their own internal auditors and inspectors general. Well-managed local governments also have internal audit departments. For example, most federal agencies (Department of Defense, Department of Human Resources, Department of the Interior), state agencies (education, welfare, controller) and local governments (cities, counties, tax districts) have internal audit staffs. In the private sector, some huge industrial companies have revenues and assets as large as some governments, and the corporate internal auditors are in a position relative to such a company as a whole as the GAO is to the federal government. Both in matters of scale and the positions they occupy, governmental and internal auditors have much in common. The discussion in this chapter combines and compares their activities.

Interaction with External Auditors

External auditors often find themselves working with internal auditors on an independent audit of a company's financial statements. They also often take engagements to perform audits in accordance with GAGAS. The AICPA auditing and attestation standards contain three statements dealing with these interactions.

Considering the Internal Audit Function in an Independent Audit of Financial Statements (*SAS 65*, AU 322)

External auditors consider the internal audit function in two contexts: (1) internal audit is part of a company's control system, and external auditors must understand how it operates to gain an understanding of the company's controls (second GAAS field work standard) and (2) internal auditors may help the external auditors gather evidence about internal control and about balances in accounts (third GAAS field work standard). External auditors can make their audits more efficient by utilizing the work of a company's internal auditors and, thereby, avoiding duplication of effort.

External auditors must obtain an understanding of a company's internal audit department and its program of work. This task is part of the understanding of the entire control system. If a preliminary review of the internal audit function shows that the internal auditors have developed, monitored, and made recommendations about internal controls, the external auditors will probably decide that it will be efficient to use internal audit information to reduce their own work on the audit. When this decision is made, the external auditors are obligated to investigate the *competence* and *objectivity* of the internal auditors. These investigations become a part of the external auditors' work program.

Internal auditors' competence is investigated by obtaining evidence about their educational and experience qualifications, their certification (CIA) and continuing education status, the department's policies and procedures for work quality and for making personnel assignments, the supervision and review activities, and the quality of reports and working paper documentation. This evidence enables the external auditors to make an evaluation of internal auditors' performance.

Internal auditors' objectivity is investigated by learning about their organizational status and lines of communication in the company. The theory is that objectivity is enhanced when the internal auditors are responsible to high levels of management and can report directly to the audit committee of the board of directors. Objectivity is questioned when the internal auditors report to divisional management, line managers, or other persons with a stake in the outcome of their findings. Objectivity is especially questioned when managers have some power over the pay or job tenure of the internal auditors. Likewise, objectivity is questioned when individual internal auditors have relatives in audit-sensitive areas or are scheduled to be promoted to positions in the activities under internal audit review.

Favorable conclusions about competence and objectivity enable external auditors to accept the internal auditors' documentation and work on review, assessment, and monitoring of a company's internal control activities. This information, combined with other evidence obtained through the external auditors' own work, leads to an assessment of control risk used in the remainder of the external audit planning.

Competent, objective internal auditors may also have performed some external audit-like procedures to obtain evidence about the dollar balances in accounts (substantive procedures). For example, they often confirm accounts receivable and make observations during interim counts of physical inventory. By relying in part on this work, external auditors may be able to relax the nature, timing, or extent of their own procedures in the same areas. Be careful to note, however, that this utilization of internal auditors' work cannot be a complete substitute for the external auditors' own procedures and evidence related to accounting judgments and material financial statement balances.

The external auditors cannot share responsibility for audit decisions with the internal auditors and must supervise, review, evaluate, and test the work performed by the internal auditors. This requirement applies both to the work of obtaining an understanding of the internal control system and the work of using internal auditors' evidence about financial statement balances.

Compliance Auditing Considerations in Audits of Governmental Entities and Recipients of Governmental Financial Assistance (*SAS 74*, AU 801)

When independent CPAs in public practice take engagements to audit government units or financial assistance recipients, they are supposed to conduct the work in accordance with GAGAS. In fact, failure to follow GAGAS in such engagements is an "act discreditable to the profession" (ET 501.04, ET 501.06). The GAO GAGAS and the Single Audit Act of 1984 (covered later) require auditors to test and report on an entity's compliance with laws and regulations. This work is known as *compliance auditing* and it has a special relevance in government-standard audit engagements.

The *compliance* in *compliance auditing* refers to governmental managers' obligations to follow the laws and regulations applicable to their organizations (e.g., purchasing regulations, eligibility requirements, debt limitations, and the like). Such entities are subject to many laws and regulations, and the recipients of audit reports are eager to know whether they have been followed.

Management is responsible for enforcing compliance—identifying the laws and regulations, establishing controls to ensure compliance, and monitoring compliance. External auditors enter the scene in the capacity of professionals engaged to audit financial statements and also to attest to management's compliance assertions. *SAS 74* does not require procedures beyond those required to accomplish an external audit of financial statements, including the audit responsibilities regarding errors, frauds, and direct-effect illegal acts. (Refer to the coverage of *SAS 82*—Consideration of Fraud in a Financial Statement Audit, and *SAS 54*—Illegal Acts—briefed in the Chapter 7 appendices.)

SAS 74 provides general guidance about the applicability of *SAS 54*, mentions audits in accordance with government auditing standards, places federal audit requirements in perspective, and warns auditors to have a good understanding with the management about the terms of the engagement (i.e., compliance audit in accordance with government auditing standards along with the audit of financial statements). However, technical standards for the performance of other compliance engagements are not in the SAS series; they are considered under the heading of "attestation standards" in Statement on Standards for Attestation Engagements (SSAE 3).

R E V I E W
CHECKPOINTS

D.1 What special professional certification is available for internal auditors? For GAO auditors?

D.2 What must external auditors do to use the work of internal auditors in the audit of a company's financial statements?

D.3 Who is responsible for enforcing compliance with laws and regulations in business and governmental administration?

DEFINITIONS AND OBJECTIVES

LEARNING OBJECTIVE

2. Define governmental auditing and internal auditing.

The Institute of Internal Auditors (IIA) defined internal auditing and stated its objective as follows:

> Internal auditing is an independent, objective, assurance and consulting activity designed to add value and improve an organization's operations. It helps an organization accomplish its objectives by bringing a systematic, disciplined approach to evaluate and improve effectiveness of risk management, control, and governance processes.

Operational Auditing

Internal auditors perform audits of financial reports for internal use, much like external auditors audit financial statements distributed to outside users. Thus, some internal auditing work is similar to the auditing described elsewhere in this textbook. However, some internal auditing activity is known as **operational auditing.** Operational auditing (also known as **performance auditing** and as **management auditing**) refers to auditors' study of business operations for the purpose of making recommendations about economic and efficient use of resources, effective achievement of business objectives, and compliance with company policies. The goal of operational auditing is to help managers discharge their management responsibilities and improve profitability. Operational auditing, thus, is included in the definition of internal auditing given above. In a similar context, an AICPA committee defined operational auditing performed by independent CPA firms as a distinct type of consulting service having the goal of helping a client improve the use of its capabilities and resources to achieve its objectives. So, internal auditors consider operational auditing an integral part of internal auditing, and external auditors define it as a type of consulting service offered by public accounting firms.

Independence

LEARNING OBJECTIVE

3. Compare aspects of governmental, internal and external auditors' independence problems.

Internal auditors hold independence, and the objectivity thus obtained, as a goal. Although internal auditors cannot be disassociated from their employers in the eyes of the public, they seek operational and reporting independence. Operationally, internal auditors should be independent when obtaining evidence in the sense of being free from direction or constraint by the managers of the business unit under audit (program, division, subsidiary, for example). Independence and objectivity are enhanced by having the authority and responsibility to report to a high executive level and to the audit committee of the board of directors. Their goal is a measure of practical independence from the control or direct influence of operating managers whose functions, operations, and results they may be assigned to audit. Practical independence enables internal auditors to be objective in reporting findings without having to fear for their jobs. (See the IIA Code of Ethics in Appendix DB.)

Government auditors, like external and internal auditors, hold independence as a goal. GAO standards speak to substantive issues of integrity and objectivity as well as to the independence-damaging appearance of financial and managerial involvement. Government auditors must be aware that such personal factors as preconceived ideas about programs, political or social convictions, and loyalty to a level of government may impair the integrity and objectivity that is the foundation of real independence. Like internal auditors, government auditors must be wary of external sources of independence impairment, such as interference by higher-level officials and threats to job security.

Organizational separation from such influences is essential for independence so auditors can report directly to top management without fear of job or compensation retribution. Auditors of governmental units are presumed independent when they are (1) free from sources of personal impairment, (2) free from sources of external impairment, (3) organizationally independent, (4) independent under AICPA Code of Professional Conduct rules, (5) elected or appointed and reporting to a legislative body of government, or (6) auditing in a level or branch of government other than the one to which they are normally assigned.

On any particular assignment, governmental auditors may perform services for the benefit of several interested parties—the management of the auditee, officials of the agency requiring the audit, officials of one or more agencies that fund the auditee's programs, members and committees of local governments, a state legislature or the U.S. Congress, and the public. GAO standards provide that all such parties should receive the audit report unless laws or regulations restrict public distribution (e.g., for reasons of national security). In contrast, standard audit reports on financial statements given by independent external auditors are addressed to the client and distributed only by the client to whomever the client wishes (except in the case of SEC-registered companies where the law requires the reports to be filed for public inspection).

From time to time, the GAO has independence problems. An editorialist wrote: "GAO has been functioning lately not as Congress's watchdog, but as its lapdog." These are strong words! They were prompted by several events in which GAO was reportedly "bullied" and its work restricted by a member of Congress who requested a report on a controversial foreign aid issue. In another case, congressmen forbade the GAO to follow its normal procedure requiring prerelease discussion of the report with the managers of a controversial agency. In the same case, the auditor in charge of the work had reportedly denounced certain policies of the agency regarding a controversial social issue. These examples illustrated some of the difficulties involved in GAO independence issues.

LEARNING OBJECTIVE

4. Specify the elements of expanded scope auditing in both governmental and internal audit practice.

Scope of Service

The stated objective of internal auditing is phrased in terms of service to "the organization," not just to management or some narrow internal interest group. Internal auditors, exercising their objectivity, function for the benefit of the whole organization—whether it is

AUDITING INSIGHT

INTERNAL AUDITORS PRODUCE INTEREST INCOME

During an audit of the cash management operations at branch offices, internal auditors found that bank deposits were not made until several days after cash and checks were received. Company policy was to complete the bookkeeping before making the deposit.

The auditors showed branch managers a cost-efficient way to capture the needed bookkeeping information that would permit release of the cash and checks. Management agreed to implement the timely deposit of checks and transfer to headquarters through an electronic funds transfer system from local banks to the headquarters bank, performing the bookkeeping afterward.

The change resulted in additional interest income in the first year in the amount of $150,000.

represented by the board of directors, the chief executive officer, the chief financial officer, or other executives. The services provided by internal auditors include (1) audits of financial reports and accounting control systems; (2) reviews of control systems that ensure compliance with company policies, plans, and procedures and with laws and regulations; (3) appraisals of the economy and efficiency of operations; and (4) reviews of effectiveness in achieving program results in comparison to established objectives and goals. Internal auditors often make recommendations that result in additional profits or cost savings for their companies. In this capacity, they function like management consultants.

The U.S. General Accounting Office has a concept of *expanded-scope services*. The GAO emphasizes the accountability of public officials for the efficient, economical, and effective use of public funds and other resources. The GAO defines and describes expanded-scope governmental auditing in terms of *two types of government audits* that can be performed as follows:

1. Financial Statement Audits.
   a. Financial statement audits determine (1) whether the financial statements of an audited entity present fairly the financial position, results of operations, and cash flows or changes in financial position in conformity with generally accepted accounting principles, (2) whether the entity has complied with laws and regulations for transactions and events that may have a material effect on the financial statements, and (3) whether internal controls over financial reporting and safeguarding assets are designed and implemented to achieve control objectives.

2. Performance Audits.
   a. Economy and efficiency audits include determining (1) whether the entity is acquiring, protecting, and using its resources (such as personnel, property, and space) economically and efficiently; (2) the causes of inefficiencies or uneconomical practices; and (3) whether the entity has complied with laws and regulations concerning matters of economy and efficiency.
   b. Program audits include determining (1) the extent to which the desired results or benefits established by the legislature or other authorizing body are being achieved; (2) the effectiveness of organizations, programs, activities, or functions; and (3) whether the agency has complied with laws and regulations applicable to the program.

The audit of a governmental organization, program, activity, or function may involve one or both of these two types of audits. GAO standards do not require all engagements to include both types. The scope of the work is supposed to be determined according to the needs of the users of the audit results. However, the GAO requires observance of its standards in audits of governmental units by external auditors as well as by governmental auditors at federal, state, and local levels.

R E V I E W
CHECKPOINTS

D.4 What is operational auditing, and why can it be called a type of consulting service?

D.5 How can internal auditors achieve practical independence?

D.6 What general auditing services do internal auditors provide?

D.7 What general auditing services do governmental auditors provide?

D.8 What factors should governmental auditors consider in determining whether they are independent?

INTERNAL AUDITING STANDARDS

LEARNING OBJECTIVE

5. Describe the coverage of governmental and internal audit standards.

The *Standards for the Professional Practice of Internal Auditing* are issued by the Institute of Internal Auditors (IIA). (See Appendix DA.) The IIA also issues *Statements on Internal Auditing Standards (SIAS)* to provide authoritative interpretations of the standards.

The IIA standards are classified in three major categories:

1. Attribute Standards.
2. Performance Standards.
3. Implementation Standards.

Aptly named, the Attribute Standards address the *characteristics of internal auditors* (independence, objectivity) and organizations performing internal audit activities. Performance Standards relate to the *conduct of internal audit activities* and provide a *measure of quality* against which the performance of internal audit activities can be measured. The Attribute Standards and the Performance Standards are similar to the general standards in GAAS—they apply to internal audit services in general. Implementation Standards, on the other hand, are specific applications of the Attribute and Performance Standards to specific types of engagements (e.g., control self-assessment, compliance auditing, fraud auditing).

Students usually learn AICPA generally accepted auditing standards (GAAS) first, then study other auditing standards. The IIA standards include the spirit of all the general and field work standards of AICPA generally accepted auditing standards. On the assumption that GAAS, including the AICPA *Statements on Auditing Standards*, are familiar, we will look only at the IIA standards that are significantly different.

Internal auditors are expected to comply with the Institute of Internal Auditors' standards of professional conduct (see Appendix DB). The IIA standards require internal auditors to be skilled in dealing with people and in communicating effectively. Such a requirement may be considered implicit in GAAS related to training and proficiency, but little is said in GAAS about effective communication, perhaps because the audit report language is so standardized. External auditors tend to believe the public has the responsibility to learn how to understand their audit reports, while internal auditors believe it is their own responsibility to see that their reports are understood properly.

The IIA standards include a requirement for following up to ascertain that appropriate action is taken on reported audit findings or ascertaining that management or the board of directors has accepted the risk of not taking action on reported findings. AICPA standards have no comparable follow-up requirement.

Many of the IIA standards deal with the organization and management of the internal audit department. CPAs in public practice have similar standards, but their standards are in the AICPA quality control standards, rather than in GAAS. However, observance of quality control standards is considered essential for proper auditing practice in accordance with GAAS. The AICPA quality control standards are "incorporated by reference" in GAAS and enforced through the peer reviews and monitoring activities of accounting firms.

While the four AICPA reporting standards are comprehensive insofar as audit reports on financial statements are concerned, the related IIA standards are very limited. Since the details under this standard are similar to the GAO reporting standards, further explanation will be given later in the discussion of the GAO standards.

GAO GOVERNMENT AUDITING STANDARDS

The *Generally Accepted Government Auditing Standards* (GAGAS) incorporate the AICPA generally accepted auditing standards as well as a number of ideas from the AICPA *Statements on Auditing Standards*. However, GAGAS goes beyond the AICPA standards in several respects. Many external auditors accept engagements to audit federal grants and programs that must follow not only the GAAS but the GAGAS as well. Therefore, these standards are important to independent auditors. Indeed, these government standards control all the government audit work performed by CPA firms.

Government auditing imposes other requirements for expertise. An auditor must be thoroughly familiar with a body of literature that establishes many of the rules and regulations about handling government funds and accounts.[1] A sample of this literature includes the following:

- *Single Audit Act of 1984*: This is the federal law that established uniform requirements for audits of federal financial assistance provided to state and local governments.
- OMB *Circular A-133*: "Audits of States, Local Governments, and Non-profit Organizations." This is the Office of Management and Budget guidance that helps auditors implement the Single Audit Act of 1984 for governmental units and a wide range of nonprofit organizations (e.g., colleges, universities, voluntary health and welfare organizations, hospitals).
- OMB *Circular A-122*: "Cost Principles for Nonprofit Organizations."
- OMB *Circular A-110*: "Uniform Requirements for Grants to Universities, Hospitals and Other Nonprofit Organizations."
- OMB *Circular A-102*: "Uniform Requirements for Grants to State and Local Governments."
- OMB *Circular A-87*: "Cost Principles for State and Local Governments."
- OMB *Circular A-21*: "Cost Principles for Educational Institutions."
- *AICPA Audit and Accounting Guide*: Audits of State and Local Governments."

GAGAS explicitly require review and testing for compliance with applicable laws and regulations. Since most governmental programs are created by regulated grants and operate under laws and regulations, compliance auditing is very important. GAAS also requires such work, especially when noncompliance with laws and regulations could result in errors or frauds that could be material to the financial statements taken as a whole. For the guidance of auditors on governmental engagements, the Auditing Standards Board issued *SAS 74* (AU 801).

GAGAS have more elaborate specifications for working paper documentation that does not need additional supplementation with detailed oral explanations. GAAS requires working papers, but the general spirit of public practice compliance is that such documentation need not be as complete as the GAO standards suggest.

GAGAS reporting standards go considerably beyond the GAAS standards, which require an audit report on financial statements and communications (verbal or written) to the client of reportable conditions regarding internal control deficiencies. The GAO standards require the following written reports in financial statement audits:

---

[1] Extensive government audit literature can be found in two important websites: (1) OMB website <http://www.whitehouse.gov> (search "OMB" in the GO Box), and (2) AICPA website <http://www.AICPA.org/belt/a133.htm>.

1. Audit report on financial statements.
2. A report on the auditee's compliance with applicable laws and regulations, including a report of irregularities, frauds, illegal acts, material noncompliance, and internal control deficiencies.
3. A report on the auditee's internal control and the control risk assessment.

GAGAS contain an elaborate set of guides for reports on performance audits—economy, efficiency, and program results audits. These audits cover such a wide range of subjects (from food programs to military contracts) that no "standard" report is possible. The details of these standards are presented in Appendix DC. These GAO standards are good guides for internal audit reports and for operational audit reports (consulting services engagements) prepared by CPAs in public practice.

R E V I E W
CHECKPOINTS

D.9 What scope of practice is suggested or required by internal audit standards? By GAO standards (GAGAS)?

D.10 Why do GAGAS require a review for compliance with laws and regulations in conjunction with financial audits?

SINGLE AUDIT ACT OF 1984

LEARNING OBJECTIVE

6. Describe the Single Audit Act of 1984 in relation to audits of governmental fund recipients.

The Federal government requires audits of state and local governments that receive federal financial assistance through appropriations, grants, contracts, cooperative agreements, loans, loan guarantees, property, interest subsidies, and insurance. Prior to 1985, state and local governments often were visited by audit teams from several federal agencies. The Single Audit Act of 1984 replaced the system of expensive and duplicative grant-by-grant audits with an organizationwide single audit encompassing all federal funds a governmental unit receives. When a state or local government, university, or community organization receives federal financial assistance from several federal agencies, all these agencies are supposed to rely on the "single audit" report instead of requiring other auditors to enter the same unit to audit various grants.

The act established an annual audit requirement for all governments, agencies, and nonprofit organizations that spend $300,000 or more federal funds. A "single audit," conducted in accordance with GAGAS, covering financial statements, compliance with laws and regulations, and internal control systems, is required. The act does not require expanded scope audits of economy, efficiency, or program results. However, federal agencies may require, and pay for, additional audits of economy, efficiency, and program results to monitor the benefits of federal fund expenditures.

The auditors can be from public accounting firms or from state and local agencies, provided they meet the GAO independence and proficiency requirements. In a single audit, the auditors are supposed to determine and report whether:

1. The financial statements present fairly the financial position and results of operations in accordance with generally accepted accounting principles.
2. The organization has internal control systems to provide reasonable assurance that it is managing federal financial assistance programs in compliance with applicable laws and regulations.
3. The organization has complied with laws and regulations that may have a material effect on its financial statements and on each major federal assistance program.

OMB Circular A-133 imposes additional audit and reporting requirements. These reports are directed toward information about the accountability of agencies that receive federal funds:

• Supplementary schedule of federal financial assistance programs showing expenditures for each program.

- Report of the compliance audit procedures showing the extent of testing and the amount and explanation of questioned expenditures.
- Report on internal control, identifying significant controls designed to provide reasonable assurance that federal programs are being managed in compliance with laws and regulations, and identifying material weaknesses.
- Report of fraud, abuse, or illegal acts that become known to the auditors.

Government audits under the Yellow Book and the Single Audit Act of 1984 (including OMB Circular A-133) are not for the fainthearted! GAO requires auditors to have 24 hours of continuing education in governmental auditing to qualify for planning an audit, conducting field work, and preparing reports. GAO also imposes requirements for continuing education and participation in a peer review program. Most CPAs in public practice have similar continuing education and peer review requirements, though not specific to governmental auditing, in connection with their state licenses and voluntary membership in the AICPA. But the GAO makes the requirements even for CPAs who do not have similar demands from their state boards or who choose not to belong to the AICPA. In this manner, GAO exercises its own control over government audit quality.

Government audits require more work on compliance and reporting on internal control than external auditors normally do in an audit of financial statements of a private business. The reason is the federal government's concern for laws, regulations, and control of expenditures. Over $100 *billion* of federal funds is used by state and local governments for various programs, so the stakes are high.

AUDITING INSIGHT

EXAMPLE OF SCOPE PARAGRAPH OF INDEPENDENT CPA's AUDIT REPORT ON COMPLIANCE WITH LAWS AND REGULATIONS UNDER THE SINGLE AUDIT ACT OF 1984

We conducted our audit in accordance with generally accepted auditing standards, *Generally Accepted Government Auditing Standards* issued by the Comptroller General of the United States, and the provisions of Office of Management and Budget (OMB) Circular A-133, "Audits of States, Local Governments and Nonprofit Institutions." These standards and OMB Circular A-133 require that we plan and perform the audit to obtain reasonable assurance about whether material noncompliance with the requirements referred to above [introductory paragraph] occurred. An audit includes examining, on a test basis, evidence about the Institution's compliance with those requirements. We believe that our audit provides a reasonable basis for our opinion.

R E V I E W CHECKPOINTS	**D.12** What additional requirements for audit field work are imposed by GAGAS and the Single Audit	Act of 1984 in comparison to the AICPA generally accepted auditing standards?

AUDIT APPROACH

LEARNING OBJECTIVE

7. Describe risk-based auditing (RBA) in governmental and internal audits.

The field work in governmental and internal audits can best be described in general terms as an application of a practical method for solving audit problems.

- *Problem recognition.* Ascertain the organization's objectives and its risks. Identify specific objectives and specific risks in detail. Define problem areas or opportunities for improvement. Define program goals.

- *Evidence collection.* Select and perform procedures designed to produce information about management's plans to mitigate risks and achieve effectiveness, efficiency, and program goals.
- *Evidence evaluation.* Evaluate management's risk assessment and risk mitigation activities in terms of effectiveness, efficiency, and goal achievement. Report findings and recommendations specifically in terms of the risks.

Risk-Based Auditing (RBA)

Many internal and governmental auditors are shifting their focus from controls-based auditing to risk-based auditing (RBA). This focus on RBA is consistent with the COSO Report on internal control.

Right now, you should go to Exhibit 6–2 in Chapter 6 and notice the three "objectives categories" cited in the COSO integrated framework. They are (1) effectiveness and efficiency of operations, (2) reliable financial reporting, and (3) compliance with laws and regulations. In Chapter 6, we limited our auditing attention to the reliable financial reporting objective. However, internal and governmental auditors involved in expanded-scope audits pay particular attention to the other two categories—operations and compliance. Also, notice in Exhibit 6–2 and elsewhere in Chapter 6 that *management* has a responsibility for *risk assessment*. In RBA, auditors have responsibilities to study management's risk assessment and to make risk assessments of their own. Now some definitions will help:

- *Risk (SIAS 9).* The probability that an event or action may adversely affect the organization. (Risk in this sense is a type of inherent risk related to the type of organization and its particular activities).
- *Risk Factors (SIAS 9).* Criteria used to identify the relative significance and likelihood that conditions and events may occur that could adversely affect the organization. (Many of these are *red flags* that may exist in the particular industry, in the organization's management, and in the data processing systems).
- *Risk Assessment (SIAS 9).* Systematic process for assessing and integrating professional judgments about probable adverse conditions and events in assigning audit priorities to high-risk estimates.

In RBA, auditors view all activities in the organization first in terms of risks and then in terms of management's plan to mitigate the risks. The departure from controls-based auditing is subtle. In controls-based auditing, auditors first obtain an understanding of controls and assess control risk for particular types of errors and frauds. In RBA, the risks are identified first, then the auditors determine how management plans to mitigate the risk. The three basic ways to mitigate a risk are: (1) avoid it, (2) control it, and (3) share it.

RBA begins with auditors learning about an organization unit's, functions and objectives. Then RBA asks the auditors' important question: "What can go wrong?" The answer reveals the "risk"—the event or action, and its probability, that something may adversely affect the organization. Then the auditing is directed to determining how management plans to mitigate the risk and whether those plans are in place and operating effectively.

An example will help. Consider the cash disbursement activity of a large university that produces 9,000 check payments each month. The amount exposed is large—about $50 million each month. The university managers want to safeguard the cash assets from unauthorized payments. What could go wrong? The list of errors and frauds that can affect cash disbursements is long! One of them is that checks may be produced without official approval. Another is that outsiders may create checks that look like university checks and fool the bank into drawing them on the university account.

So what is the management doing to mitigate this risk of forgery loss? The university can hardly avoid it—check payments must be processed. The university can share it by purchasing fidelity bond and other insurance. Is this enough mitigation effort? Maybe it is for some types of operations, but insurance companies usually require an organization to try to avoid loss by having controls. Auditors now get to the study of controls, but it is a very focused study directed to the particular forgery loss risk. The audit question is not the general "Are controls adequate?" but instead the very focused question "Are controls over invalid payments (forgeries) adequate when considered in conjunction with the insurance policies?"

Suppose these auditors find that one of the prevention controls is a "positive pay" arrangement with the bank. In a positive pay control activity, the university gives the bank a computer file listing all the checks properly produced by the legitimate university system. The bank compares every university check presented for payment and pays only the checks on the list. This control, in conjunction with other approval activities, may constitute appropriate mitigation, and the auditors can perform test of control procedures to determine (*a*) whether the production of the positive pay file itself is controlled, and (*b*) whether any unauthorized or forged checks were paid by the bank despite these controls.

Consider another more extensive scenario of an audit assignment in an organization's purchasing activity. Assume that the auditors learn through inquiry that the purchasing objectives are: Provide the right materials to the assembly line, from the right vendors, at the right price, in the right quantities, of the right quality, in the right locations, at the right time. "What can go wrong?" Surely you can see now that the question elicits "risks" of adverse effects related to materials, vendors, prices, quantities, qualities, locations, and timing. These objectives and their attendant risks move the auditors beyond the limits of financial reporting to the operational and compliance aspects of internal and governmental auditing.

Emphasis on Management Risk Mitigation Controls

Auditors classify controls in two broad categories: management controls and accounting transaction processing control activities. **Management control** has been defined as *the plan of organization and all methods and procedures that are concerned mainly with operational efficiency and adherence to managerial policies and usually relate only indirectly to financial records.* This management function is directly associated with the responsibility for managing risks and achieving the organization's objectives. It is the starting point for establishing accounting control of transactions. Management control sets the stage for detailed accounting control.

Another aspect of control is **internal accounting control** activities. They are the plan of organization and risk mitigation activities designed to prevent, detect, and correct accounting errors that may occur and get recorded in ledger accounts and financial statements.

In connection with governmental and internal audits, auditors are very concerned with the management risk mitigation activities because they directly affect economy, efficiency, and program results. Management control is a broad concept involving all management activities, such as responsibilities for production, quality control, transportation, research and development, personnel relations, and many other areas. The focus is not limited to accounting-related activities.

For now, you should think of accounting controls as being very specific and accounting-related and of management risk mitigation controls as being more general and management-related. Some examples illustrating the contrast are in Exhibit D–1.

One key question is: How can you cope with the need to study and evaluate management risk mitigation? Answer: It is not easy! You need to rely on knowledge of marketing, management, production, finance, statistics, business law, economics, taxation, operations research, political science, physical sciences, and other subjects. These are some of the nonaccounting courses you can take in your college curriculum.

Such studies are important because they serve as a foundation for organizing your early practical experiences and your development of a common sense of business management.

EXHIBIT D–1	ACCOUNTING AND MANAGEMENT RISK MITIGATION CONTROLS

Transaction Processing Control Activities	Management Risk Mitigation Activities
Cash	
Establish a control total of cash receipts as soon as they are received, so subsequent deposits, journal entries, and ledger entries can be compared to the total.	Prepare timely forecasts of cash flow and provide for temporary borrowing to cover need, or for temporary investment to generate interest income.
Accounts Receivable	
Reconcile customers' subsidiary ledger accounts with the control account total to control bookkeeping accuracy.	Prepare an aged trial balance of customer receivables for the credit manager's collection efforts.
Inventory	
Assign physical control responsibility to a storekeeper to safeguard inventory from theft or other unauthorized removal.	Coordinate inventory purchases with sales and production forecasts so stockout losses and inventory carrying cost can be optimized.

You can expect very little to be routine in a study and evaluation of management risk mitigation, and that is what makes governmental and internal audit assignments such exciting challenges.

AUDIT PROCEDURES—ECONOMY, EFFICIENCY, AND PROGRAM RESULTS AUDITS

LEARNING OBJECTIVE

8. Explain the function of standards and measurements in economy and efficiency and program results audits.

The general evidence-gathering procedures in governmental and internal audits are about the same as the ones used by external auditors in the audit of financial statements. These procedures are explained in more specific terms in other chapters in this textbook. However, the audit *problems* are usually different in audits of economy, efficiency, and program results.

Governmental and internal auditors must be as objective as possible when developing conclusions about efficiency, economy, and program results. This objectivity is achieved by (1) finding *standards* for evaluation and (2) using *measurements* of actual results, so (3) the actual results can be *compared* to the standards. Finding standards and deciding on relevant measurements takes imagination. Sawyer presented two examples, one rather routine and the other very unusual, to illustrate the role of standards and measurements.[2]

Routine Problem. Evaluate the promptness with which materials pass through a receiving inspection before being accepted and placed in inventory.

- *Source of a Standard.* Management policy about acceptable delay between date of receipt and date of inspection approval.
- *Measurement Unit.* Number of days between date of receipt and date of inspection approval.
- *Audit Procedures.* Select a sample of inspection reports and record the two relevant dates and the number of elapsed days. Develop descriptive statistics of the sample data. Compare these measurements to the management policy standard. Report the findings and conclusions.

---

[2] Lawrence B. Sawyer, *Sawyer's Internal Auditing* (Altamonte Springs, Fla.: The Institute of Internal Auditors, 1988), pp. 229–30.

Unusual Problem. Determine whether the company's test pilots are reporting aircraft defects properly.

- *Background Information.* Test pilots fill out check sheets as they fly, recording such things as pressure instrument readings under various flight conditions. If a reading is outside acceptable limits, the pilot is supposed to prepare a report, which will trigger an investigation of the reason for the unacceptable instrument reading.

- *Source of a Standard.* Engineering specifications of acceptable limits for pressure readings under specific flight conditions. For example, the fuel pressure at 20,000 feet and a power setting of 85 percent should be between 90 and 100 pounds.

- *Measurement Unit.* Number of times an instrument reading is reported improperly by a test pilot.

- *Audit Procedures.* Select a sample of check sheets and related test pilot reports. Compare each instrument reading on the check sheet to the engineering specifications. Read the test pilot's reports and look for no unfavorable mention of acceptable readings and for appropriate mention of unacceptable readings. Tally and describe all report deficiencies. Summarize the findings and report the conclusions. (Notice that the procedure involves reading the test pilot's reports for two possible deficiencies—inappropriate reporting of acceptable readings as well as failure to report unacceptable readings.)

When dealing with standards, measurements, and comparisons, auditors must keep *inputs* and *outputs* in perspective. Evidence about inputs—personnel hours and cost, materials quantities and cost, asset investment—are most important in connection with reaching financial audit conclusions. For economy, efficiency, and program results conclusions, however, output measurements are equally important. Management has the responsibility for devising information systems to measure output. Such measurements should correspond to program objectives set forth in laws, regulations, administrative policies, legislative reports, or other such sources. Auditors must realize that output measurements are usually not expressed in financial terms; for example, water quality improvement, educational progress, weapons effectiveness, materials-inspection time delays, and test pilot reporting accuracy.

Many economy and efficiency audits and most program results audits are *output-oriented.* Auditors need to be careful not to equate program activity with program success without measuring program results. These features are significantly different from auditors' roles with respect to financial statement audits where the primary concern is with reporting on the accounting for inputs.

R E V I E W
CHECKPOINTS

D.12 What is a practical method an auditor can use for solving internal and governmental audit problems?

D.13 What is "risk" with regard to risk-based auditing (RBA)?

D.14 What is the basic question for the risk-based audit approach with regard to an organization's functions and objectives?

D.15 What are the three ways a management can mitigate a risk?

D.16 What can go wrong in the management of a purchasing activity with regard to the objective of wanting to assure that the right quantities of materials are delivered to the assembly line at the right time?

D.17 What is management risk mitigation control? What does it accomplish?

D.18 How can governmental and internal auditors try to achieve objectivity when developing conclusions about economy, efficiency, or program results?

REPORTING

Internal audit and governmental audit reports are not standardized like external auditors' reports on financial statements. Each report is different because internal auditors and governmental auditors need to communicate findings on a variety of assignments and audit objectives. The key criterion for an internal audit report is *clear and concise communication* of findings and recommendations. The government auditing standards emphasize *accountability* by requiring reports on errors, irregularities, fraud, abuse, and internal control.

Internal Audit Report

The reporting stage is the internal auditors' opportunity to capture management's undivided attention. To be effective, a report cannot be unduly long, tedious, technical, or laden with minutiae. It must be accurate, concise, clear, and timely. It must speak directly to the risks the auditors studied. Internal audit reports are usually considered "open" until a formal written reply to the recommendations is received from the management of the audited unit or department. This reply, which goes to the same people who receive the audit report (e.g., the audit committee), indicates which recommendations were implemented and which were not. Only after the written response is received is the audit considered "closed."

Internal audit standards do not offer a detail checklist of report content. Standard 2400 (Appendix DA) simply states: "Internal auditors should communicate the engagement results promptly." However, the detail government auditing standards for performance audit reports (Appendix DC) give a number of requirements, most of which can be applied in internal audit reports.

GAO Audit Reports

GAGAS has two sets of reporting standards—one for financial audits and another for performance audits.

Financial audit reports start with an audit report like the external auditors' standard report, except that the description of the audit in the scope paragraph must include a citation of generally accepted *government* auditing standards (GAGAS). The report on financial statements contains an opinion regarding conformity with generally accepted accounting principles, just like the reports independent auditors in public practice give on nongovernmental organizations. In addition, GAGAS includes reports on internal control and on tests of compliance with laws and regulations as part of the financial reporting requirements. The detail financial reporting standards are in Appendix DC.

Performance audit reports are altogether different from financial audit reports. Like internal auditors, the GAO objective is clear communication for the purpose of making recommendations and improving operations. Hence, GAGAS performance audit reporting standards require timely, well-written communications of findings and recommendations for action. The managers of an audited entity are expected to respond to the report, and this response is usually included in the final version of the report. Unlike internal audit reports, most GAO reports are available to the public and can be requested from the Government Printing Office. (A sample of a few titles is in Chapter 1.)

However, performance audits have another side. GAGAS requires the reports to tell about illegal acts, abuse of public money and property, noncompliance with laws and regulations, and internal control weaknesses. These matters reflect negatively on an organization's management. On the other hand, GAGAS also requires reporting on noteworthy accomplishments to give management credit where credit is due and to make such information available to other managers. The detail performance audit reporting standards are in Appendix DC.

R E V I E W
CHECKPOINTS

D.19 What are the major differences between independent auditors' reports on financial statements and internal and governmental reports on efficiency, economy, and program results audits?

D.20 Why do you think the GAGAS reporting standards permit performance audit reports to include "views of responsible officials of the audited program concerning the auditors' findings, conclusions, and recommendations?"

SUMMARY

Governmental and internal auditing standards include the essence of the AICPA generally accepted auditing standards (GAAS) and go much further by expressing standards for audits of economy, efficiency, and program results. In addition, the internal auditing standards contain many guides for the management of an internal audit department within a company.

All auditors hold independence as a primary goal, but internal auditors must look to an internal organization independence from the managers and executives whose areas they audit. Governmental auditors must be concerned about factual independence with regard to social, political, and level-of-government influences.

Governmental auditing is complicated by the special context of audit assignments intended to accomplish accountability by agencies that handle federal funds—grants, subsidies, entitlement programs, and the like. The requirements of the GAO Standards and the Single Audit Act of 1984 impose on the audit function the responsibility for compliance audit work designed to determine agencies' observance of laws and regulations, of which there are many. Auditors must report not only on financial statements but also on internal control, violations of laws and regulations, fraud, abuse, and illegal acts. These elements are all part of the federal oversight of federal spending, facilitated by auditors.

Audit engagements are an application of a practical problem-solving method—essentially a fact-finding approach. Auditors start the work with an understanding of the audit objectives involved in the assignment and carry them out through a risk-based audit approach (RBA), which includes the audit or management's risk mitigation activities and reports of the audit conclusions and recommendations. Auditors try to achieve objectivity by determining appropriate standards for economy, efficiency, and program results, by measuring their evidence, and by comparing their measurements to the standards in order to reach objective conclusions.

Governmental and internal audit reports are not standardized like the GAAS reports on audited financial statements. Auditors must be very careful that their reports communicate their conclusions and recommendations in a clear and concise manner. The variety of assignments and the challenge of reporting in such a free-form setting contribute to making governmental auditing, internal auditing, and consulting services exciting fields for career opportunities.

MULTIPLE-CHOICE QUESTIONS FOR PRACTICE AND REVIEW

D.21 Governmental auditor's independence and objectivity are enhanced when they report the results of an audit assignment directly to

a. Managers of the government agency under audit and in which they are employed.

b. The audit committee of directors of the agency under audit.

c. Political action committees of which they are members.

d. The Congressional committee that ordered the audit.

D.22   In all audits of governmental units performed according to GAGAS, the most important work is
a. Compliance auditing.
b. Obtaining a sufficient understanding of internal control.
c. Documentation of the audit in working papers.
d. Exit interviews with managers in the government unit.

D.23   Which of the following is considered different and more limited in objectives than the others?
a. Operational auditing.
b. Performance auditing.
c. Management auditing.
d. Financial statement auditing.

D.24   A typical objective of an operational audit is for the auditor to
a. Determine whether the financial statements fairly present the company's operations.
b. Evaluate the feasibility of attaining the company's operational objectives.
c. Make recommendations for achieving company objectives.
d. Report on the company's relative success in attaining profit maximization.

D.25   A government auditor assigned to audit the financial statements of the state highway department would not be considered independent if the auditor
a. Also held a position as a project manager in the highway department.
b. Was the state audit official elected in a general statewide election with responsibility to report to the legislature.
c. Normally works as a state auditor employed in the department of human services.
d. Was appointed by the state governor with responsibility to report to the legislature.

D.26   Government auditing can extend beyond audits of financial statements to include audits of an agency's efficient and economical use of resources and
a. Constitutionality of laws and regulations governing the agency.
b. Evaluation of the personal managerial skills shown by the agency's leaders.
c. Correspondence of the agency's performance with public opinion regarding the social worth its mission.
d. Evaluations concerning the agency's achievements of the goals set by the legislature for the agency's activities.

D.27   Which of the following best describes how the detailed audit program of the external auditor who is engaged to audit the financial statements of a large publicly held company compares with the audit client's comprehensive internal audit program?
a. The comprehensive internal audit program covers areas that would normally not be reviewed by an external auditor.
b. The comprehensive internal audit program is more detailed although it covers fewer areas than would normally be covered by an external auditor.
c. The comprehensive internal audit program is substantially identical to the audit program used by an external auditor because both review substantially identical areas.
d. The comprehensive internal audit program is less detailed and covers fewer areas than would normally be reviewed by an external auditor.

D.28   Which of the following would you not expect to see in an auditor's report(s) on the financial statements of an independent government agency?
a. A statement that the audit was conducted in accordance with generally accepted government audit standards.
b. A report on the agency's compliance with applicable laws and regulations.
c. Commentary by the agency's managers on the audit findings and recommendations.
d. A report on the agency's internal control structure.

D.29   The federal Single Audit Act of 1984 requires auditors to determine and report several things about state and local governments that receive federal funds. Which of the following is not normally required to be reported?
a. An opinion on the fair presentation of the financial statements in accordance with generally accepted accounting principles.
b. A report on the government's internal control related to federal funds.
c. The government's performance in meeting goals set in enabling legislation.
d. A report on the government's compliance with applicable laws and regulations.

D.30   When performing risk-based auditing (RBA), internal auditors first

a. Study and evaluate internal controls to determine whether the activity faces any special risks.

b. Evaluate managers' risk assessments and risk mitigation activity in terms of the operational effectiveness of their risk mitigation controls.

c. Develop their own perceptions of the risks that may affect the operations of an activity.

d. Interview managers to determine their perception of risks they face in the operations of the activity.

D.31 In government performance auditing, which of the following is the least important consideration when performing the field work?

a. Determining the applicable generally accepted government accounting principles pronounced by the GASB.

b. Defining problem areas or opportunities for improvement and defining program goals.

c. Selecting and performing procedures designed to obtain evidence about operational problems and production output.

d. Evaluating evidence in terms of economy, efficiency, and achievement of program goals.

D.32 Which of the following is the least important consideration for a government auditor who needs to be objective when auditing and reporting on an agency's achievement of program goals?

a. Measure the actual output results of agency activities.

b. Compare the agency's actual output results to quantitative goal standards.

c. Perform a comprehensive review of management controls.

d. Determine quantitative standards that describe goals the agency was supposed to achieve.

D.33 When an external auditor obtains an understanding of a client's internal control in connection with the annual audit of financial statements, the external auditor must at a minimum obtain information and evaluate

a. The competence and objectivity of the internal auditors.

b. The education, experience, and certification of the internal auditors.

c. The employment of internal auditors' relatives in management positions.

d. The internal audit department and its program of work.

D.34 Compliance auditing in audits performed under the Single Audit Act of 1984 in accordance with GAGAS is necessary for an auditor's

a. Report on the auditee's internal control, including reportable conditions and material weaknesses.

b. Opinion on the auditee's observance, or lack thereof, of applicable laws and regulations.

c. Opinion on the auditee's financial statements.

d. Report of a supplementary schedule of federal assistance programs and amounts.

EXERCISES AND PROBLEMS

D.35 **Identification of Audits and Auditors.** Audits may be characterized as (*a*) financial statement audits, (*b*) compliance audits, (*c*) economy and efficiency audits, and (*d*) program results audits. The work can be done by independent (external) auditors, internal auditors, or governmental auditors (including IRS auditors and federal bank examiners). Below is a list of the purpose or products of various audit engagements. [Students may need to refer to Chapter 1.]

1. Analyze proprietary schools' spending to train students for oversupplied occupations.

2. Determining the fair presentation in conformity with GAAP of an advertising agency's financial statements.

3. Study of the Department of Defense's expendable launch vehicle program.

4. Determination of costs of municipal garbage pickup services compared to comparable service subcontracted to a private business.

5. Audit of tax shelter partnership financing terms.

6. Study of a private aircraft manufacturer's test pilot performance in reporting on the results of test flights.

7. Periodic U.S. Comptroller of Currency examination of a national bank for solvency.

8. Evaluation of the promptness of materials inspection in a manufacturer's receiving department.

9. Report on the need for the States to consider reporting requirements for chemical use data.

10. Rendering a public report on the assumptions and compilation of a revenue forecast by a sports stadium/racetrack complex.

Required:
Prepare a three-column schedule showing (1) each of the engagements listed above; (2) the type of audit (financial statement, compliance, economy and efficiency, or program results); and (3) the kind of auditors you would expect to be involved.

D.36   Organizing a Risk Analysis.   You are the director of internal auditing of a large municipal hospital. You receive monthly financial reports prepared by the accounting department, and your review of them has shown that total accounts receivable from patients has steadily and rapidly increased over the past eight months.

Other information in the reports shows the following conditions:

a. The number of available hospital beds has not changed.

b. The bed occupancy rate has not changed.

c. Hospital billing rates have not changed significantly.

d. The hospitalization insurance contracts have not changed since the last modification 12 months ago.

Your internal audit department audited the accounts receivable 10 months ago. The working paper file for that assignment contains financial information, a record of the risk analysis, documentation of the study and evaluation of management and internal risk mitigation controls, documentation of the evidence-gathering procedures used to produce evidence about the validity and collectibility of the accounts, and a copy of your report which commented favorably on the controls and collectibility of the receivables.

However, the current increase in receivables has alerted you to a need for another audit, so things will not get out of hand. You remember news stories last year about the manager of the city water system who got into big trouble because his accounting department double-billed all the residential customers for three months.

Required:
You plan to perform a risk analysis to get a handle on the problem, if indeed a problem exists. Write a memo to your senior auditor listing at least eight questions he should use to guide and direct the risk analysis. (*Hint:* The questions used last year were organized under these headings: (1) Who does the accounts receivable accounting? (2) What data processing procedures and policies are in effect? and (3) How is the accounts receivable accounting done? This time, you will add a fourth category: What financial or economic events have occurred in the last 10 months?)

(CIA adapted)

D.37   Study and Evaluation of Management Control.   The study and evaluation of management risk mitigation control in a governmental or internal audit is not easy. First, auditors must determine the risks and the controls subject to audit. Then, they must find a standard by which performance of the control can be evaluated. Next, they must specify procedures to obtain the evidence on which an evaluation can be based. Insofar as possible, the standards and related evidence must be quantified.

Students working on this case usually do not have the experience or theoretical background to figure out control standards and audit procedures, so the description below gives certain information (*in italics*) that internal auditors would know about or be able to figure out on their own. Fulfilling the requirement thus amounts to taking some information from the scenario below and figuring out other things by using accountants' and auditors' common sense.

The Scenario: Ace Corporation ships building materials to more than a thousand wholesale and retail customers in a five-state region. The company's normal credit terms are net/30 days, and no cash discounts are offered. Fred Clark is the chief financial officer, and he is concerned about risks related to maintaining control over customer credit. In particular, he has stated two management control principles for this purpose.

1. Sales are to be billed to customers accurately and promptly. *Fred knows that errors will occur but thinks company personnel ought to be able to hold quantity, unit price, and arithmetic errors down to 3 percent of the sales invoices. He considers an invoice error of $1 or less not to matter.* He believes prompt billing is important since customers are expected to pay within 30 days. *Fred is very strict in thinking that a bill should be sent to the customer one day after shipment.* He believes he has staffed the billing department well enough to be able to handle this workload. The relevant company records consist of an accounts receivable control account; a subsidiary ledger of customers' accounts in which charges are entered by billing (invoice) date and credits are

entered by date of payment receipts; a sales journal that lists invoices in chronological order; and a file of shipping documents cross-referenced by the number on the related sales invoice copy kept on file in numerical order.

2. Accounts receivable are to be aged and followed up to ensure prompt collection. *Fred has told the accounts receivable department to classify all the customer accounts in categories of (a) current, (b) 31–59 days overdue, (c) 60–90 days overdue, and (d) more than 90 days overdue. He wants this trial balance to be complete and to be transmitted to the credit department within five days after each month-end. In the credit department, prompt follow-up means sending a different (stronger) collection letter to each category, cutting off credit to customers over 60 days past due (putting them on cash basis), and giving the over-90-days accounts to an outside collection agency. These actions are supposed to be taken within five days after receipt of the aged trial balance.* The relevant company records, in addition to the ones listed above, consist of the aged trial balance, copies of the letters sent to customers, copies of notices of credit cutoff, copies of correspondence with the outside collection agent, and reports of results—statistics of subsequent collections.

Required:

Take the role of a senior internal auditor. You are to write a memo to the internal audit staff to inform them about comparison standards for the study and evaluation of these two management control policies. You also need to specify two or three procedures for gathering evidence about performance of the controls. The body of your memo should be structured as follows:

1. Control: Sales are billed to customers accurately and promptly.
   a. Accuracy.
      (1) Policy standard . . .
      (2) Audit procedures . . .
   b. Promptness.
      (1) Policy standard . . .
      (2) Audit procedures . . .
2. Control: Accounts receivable are aged and followed up to ensure prompt collection.
   a. Accounts receivable aging.
      (1) Policy standard . . .
      (2) Audit procedures . . .
   b. Follow-up prompt collection.
      (1) Policy standard . . .
      (2) Audit procedures . . .

D.38   Analytical Audit of Inventory.   External auditors usually calculate inventory turnover (cost of goods sold for the year divided by average inventory) and use the ratio as a broad indication of inventory age, obsolescence, or overstocking. External auditors are interested in evidence relating to the material accuracy of the financial statements taken as a whole. Internal auditors, on the other hand, calculate turnover by categories and classes of inventory to detect problem areas that might otherwise get overlooked. This kind of detailed analytical audit might point to conditions of buying errors, obsolescence, overstocking, and other matters that could be changed to save money.

The data shown in Exhibit D38–1 are turnover, cost of sales, and inventory investment data for a series of four history years and the current year. In each of the history years, the external auditors did not recommend any adjustments to the inventory valuations.

Required:

Calculate the current year inventory turnover ratios. Interpret the ratio trends and point out what conditions might exist, and write a memo to the vice president for production explaining your findings and the further investigation that can be conducted.

D.39   CPA Involvement in an Expanded-Scope Audit   A public accounting firm received an invitation to bid for the audit of local food commodity distribution program funded by the U.S. Department of Agriculture. The audit is to be conducted in accordance with the audit standards published by the General Accounting Office (GAO). The accountants have become familiar with the GAGAS standards and recognize that they incorporate the AICPA generally accepted auditing standards (GAAS).

The public accounting firm has been engaged to perform the audit of the program, and the audit is to encompass both financial and performance audits that constitute the expanded scope of a GAGAS audit.

Required (See Appendix DC):

a. The accountants should perform sufficient audit work to satisfy the financial and compliance element of GAGAS. What is the objective of such audit work?

b. The accountants should be aware of general and specific kinds of uneconomical or inefficient practices in such a program. What are some examples?

c. What might be some standards and sources of standards for judging program results?

EXHIBIT D.38–1	INVENTORY DATA

	Inventory Turnover				Current-Year Inventory (000)	
	20X1	20X2	20X3	20X4	Beginning	Ending
Total inventory	2.1	2.0	2.1	2.1	$3,000	$2,917
Material and parts	4.0	4.1	4.3	4.5	1,365	620
Work in process	12.0	12.5	11.5	11.7	623	697
Finished products:						
Computer games	6.0	7.0	10.0	24.0	380	500
Floppy disk drives	8.0	7.2	7.7	8.5	64	300
Semiconductor parts	4.0	3.5	4.5	7.0	80	400
Electric typewriters	3.0	2.5	2.0	1.9	488	400

ADDITIONAL INFORMATION

	Current Year (000)				
	Transfers	Sales	Cost of Goods Sold	Gross Profit	Compared to 20X4
Materials and parts	$3,970*	NA	NA	NA	
Work in process	7,988†	NA	NA	NA	
Computer games	2,320‡	$2,000	$2,200	$<200>	Sales volume declined 60%§
Floppy disk drives	2,236‡	3,000	2,000	1,000	Sales volume increased 35%
Semiconductor parts	2,720‡	4,000	2,400	1,600	Sales volume increased 40%
Electric typewriters	712‡	1,000	800	200	Sales volume declined 3%

NA means not applicable.
* Cost of materials transferred to Work in Process.
† Cost of materials, labor, and overhead transferred to Finished Goods.
‡ Cost of goods transferred from Work in Process to Finished Product Inventories.
§ Selling prices also were reduced and the gross margin declined.

DISCUSSION CASES

D.40   Auditing the Effectiveness of a Loan Program.   The Office of Economic Opportunity (OEO) designed Special Impact programs to have a major impact on unemployment, dependency, and community tensions in urban areas with large concentrations of low-income residents or in rural areas having substantial migration to such urban areas. The purpose of these experimental programs—combining business, community, and manpower development—is to offer poor people an opportunity to become self-supporting through the free enterprise system. The programs are intended to create training and job opportunities, improve the living environment, and encourage development of local entrepreneurial skills.

One area chosen to participate in the Special Impact Program was Bedford-Stuyvesant. The Bedford-Stuyvesant program was the first and largest such program to be sponsored by the federal government. It has received more than $30 million in federal funds from its inception through the current year. Another $7.7 million was obtained from private sources, such as the Ford Foundation and the Astor Foundation.

Problems:

Bedford-Stuyvesant is a five-square-mile area with a population of 350,000 to 400,000 in New York City's borough of Brooklyn. This area has serious problems of unemployment and underemployment and inadequate housing.

Bedford-Stuyvesant's problems are deep seated and have resisted rapid solution. They stem primarily from the fact that local residents, to a considerable degree, lack the education and training required for the jobs available elsewhere in the city and from the lack of jobs in the area. Unemployment and underemployment, in turn, reduce buying power, which has a depressing effect on the area's economy.

The magnitude of the Bedford-Stuyvesant problems is indicated by the following data disclosed by the U.S. census:

1. Of the total civilian labor force, 8.9 percent were unemployed, compared with unemployment rates of 7.1 percent for New York City and 6.8 percent for the New York Standard Metropolitan Statistical Area (SMSA).

2. Per capita income was $7,106, compared with $10,720 for New York City and $13,909 for the SMSA.

3. Families below the poverty level made up 24.8 percent of the population, compared with 11.4 percent in New York City and 9.2 percent in the SMSA.

4. Families receiving public assistance made up 25.4 percent of the population, compared with 9.6 percent in New York City and 7.5 percent in the SMSA.

A number of factors serve to aggravate the area's economic problems and make them more difficult to solve. Some of these are:

1. A reluctance of industry to move into New York City.

2. A net outflow of industry from New York City.

3. High city taxes and a high crime rate.

4. A dearth of local residents possessing business managerial experience.

The area's housing problems resulted from the widespread deterioration of existing housing and are, in part, a by-product of below-average income levels resulting from unemployment and underemployment. They were aggravated by a shortage of mortgage capital for residential housing associated with a lack of confidence in the area on the part of financial institutions, which, as discussed later, seems to have been somewhat overcome.

Bedford-Stuyvesant was the target of several "special impact" programs. Included were programs designed to stimulate private business, to improve housing, to establish community facilities, and to train residents in marketable skills. There were two programs to stimulate private business: a program to loan funds to local businesses and a program to attract outside businesses to the area.

Under the business loan program begun five years ago, the sponsors proposed to create jobs and stimulate business ownership by local residents. At first, investments in local businesses were made only in the form of loans. Later, the sponsors adopted a policy of making equity investments in selected companies to obtain for the sponsors a voice in management. Equity investments totaling about $159,000 were made in four companies.

Loans were to be repaid in installments over periods of up to 10 years, usually with a moratorium on repayment for six months or longer. Repayment was to be made in cash or by applying subsidies allowed by the sponsors for providing on-the-job training to unskilled workers. Loans made during the first two years of the program were interest free. Later, the sponsors revised the policy to one of charging below-market interest rates. Rates charged were from 3 to 6.5 percent. This policy change was made to (1) emphasize to borrowers their obligations to repay the loan and (2) help the sponsors monitor borrowers' progress toward profitability.

Prospective borrowers learned of the loan program through (1) information disseminated at neighborhood centers, (2) advertisements on radio and television and in a local newspaper, and (3) word of mouth. Those who wished to apply for loans were required to complete application forms providing information relating to their education, business and work experience, and their personal financial statements and references. The sponsors set up a management assistance division, which employed consultants to supplement its internal marketing assistance efforts and to provide management, accounting, marketing, legal, and other assistance to borrowers.

The sponsors proposed to create at least 1,700 jobs during the first four years of the loan program by making loans to some 73 new and existing businesses.

Required:

Put yourself in the position of the GAO manager in charge of all audits pertaining to the Office of Economic Opportunity. The New York City field office has been assigned the job of conducting a detailed review of the Special Impact program described above. Prepare a memo to the New York City field office in which you indicate, in as great detail as is possible from the information provided, the specific steps they should perform in conducting an evaluation of the program effectiveness of the Special Impact Loan Program.

D.41 Operational Audit: Customer Complaints. Danny Deck, the director of internal auditing for the Rice Department Stores, was working in his office one Thursday when Larry McMurray, president of the company, burst in to tell about a problem. According to Larry: "Customer complaints about delays in getting credit for merchandise returns are driving Sally Godwin up the wall! She doesn't know what to do because she has no control over the processing of credit memos."

Sally is the manager in charge of customer relations, and she tries to keep everybody happy. Upon her recommendation, the company adopted an advertising motto: "Satisfaction Guaranteed and Prompt Credit When You Change Your Mind." The motto is featured in newspaper ads and on large banners in each store.

Danny performed a preliminary review and found the following:

1. Sally believes customers will be satisfied if they receive a refund check or notice of credit on account within five working days.

2. The chief accountant described the credit memo processing procedure as follows: When a customer returns merchandise, the sales clerks give a smile, a "returned merchandise receipt," and a promise to send a check or a notice within five days. The store copy of the receipt and the merchandise is sent to the purchasing department, where buyers examine the merchandise for quality or damage to decide whether to put it back on the shelves, return it to the vendor, or hold it for the annual rummage sale. The buyers then prepare a brief report and send it with the returned merchandise receipt to the customer relations department for approval. The buyer's report is filed for reference and the receipt, marked for approval in Sally's department, is sent to the accounting department. The accounting department sorts the receipts in numerical order, checking the numerical sequence, and files them in readiness for the weekly batch processing of transactions other than sales and cash receipts, both of which are processed daily. When the customer has requested a cash refund, the checks and canceled returned merchandise receipts are approved by the treasurer, who signs and mails the check. When the credit is on a customer's charge account, it is shown on the next monthly statement sent to the customer.

3. The processing in each department takes two or three days.

Required:

a. Analyze the problem. How much time does it take the company to process the merchandise returns?

b. Formulate a recommendation to solve the problem. Write a brief report explaining your recommendation.

D.42 GAO Auditor Independence. The GAO reporting standards for performance audits state that each report should include "recommendations for action to correct the problem areas and to improve operations." For example, an audit of the Washington Metropolitan Area Transit Authority found management decision deficiencies affecting some $230 million in federal funds. The GAO auditors recommended that the transit authority could improve its management control over railcar procurement through better enforcement of contract requirements and development of a master plan to test cars.

Suppose the transit authority accepted and implemented specific recommendations made by the GAO auditors. Do you believe these events would be enough to impair the independence of the GAO auditors in a subsequent audit of the transit authority? Explain and tell if it makes any difference to you whether the same or different person performs both the first and subsequent audits.

D.43 Using the Work of Internal Auditors. North, CPA, is planning an independent audit of the financial statements of General Company. In determining the nature, timing and extent of the auditing procedures, North is considering General's internal audit function, which is staffed by Tyler.

Required:

a. In what ways may the internal auditor's work be relevant to North, the independent auditor?

b. What factors should North consider and what inquiries should North make in deciding whether to use Tyler's internal audit work?

(AICPA adapted)

D.44 Efficiency Standards.   The U.S. Postal Service (USPS) advertises prompt delivery schedules for express mail (overnight delivery) and priority mail (2–3 day delivery). The USPS knows various risks that may arise to thwart their work of timely (as advertised) delivery but believes that systems and controls are in place and operating to mitigate the risks. The USPS advertised that 94 percent of express mail and 87 percent of priority mail was delivered on time from the time the mail was postmarked to the time it reached the destination post office. However, a consulting firm studied the USPS operations and determined that the express mail arrived at the recipients' addresses 81 percent of the time (not 94 percent) and the priority mail arrived timely 75 percent of the time (not 87 percent).

Required:

What can account for the difference in these performance statistics between the USPS delivery rates and the consultant's rates? (*Hint:* Think in terms of orientation to customers and standards for measuring performance.)

D.45   Costs and Benefits of on Control. Module D teaches that managers can mitigate risk three ways—avoid it, control it, and share it. Actually, another way is available—accept it and live with it! This "acceptance" comes in the form of deciding that the costs of unavoidable risks that remain after buying insurance (or some other form of sharing it) should not exceed the benefits of the control (e.g., profits, losses prevented). Problem 6.54 in Chapter 6 contains some cost-benefit scenarios for analysis.

APPENDIX DA   STANDARDS FOR THE PROFESSIONAL PRACTICE OF INTERNAL AUDITING*

ATTRIBUTE STANDARDS

1000—Purpose, Authority, and Responsibility
The purpose, authority, and responsibility of the internal audit activity should be formally defined in a charter, consistent with the *Standards*, and approved by the board.

1100—Independence and Objectivity
The internal audit activity should be independent, and internal auditors should be objective in performing their work.

1110—Organizational Independence
The chief audit executive should report to a level within the organization that allows the internal audit activity to fulfill its responsibilities.

> 1110.A1—The internal audit activity should be free from interference in determining the scope of internal auditing, performing work, and communicating results.

1120—Individual Objectivity
Internal auditors should have an impartial, unbiased attitude and avoid conflicts of interest.

1130—Impairments to Independence or Objectivity
If independence or objectivity is impaired in fact or appearance, the details of the impairment should be disclosed to appropriate parties. The nature of the disclosure will depend upon the impairment.

> 1130.A1—Internal auditors should refrain from assessing specific operations for which they were previously responsible. Objectivity is presumed to be impaired if an auditor provides assurance services for an activity for which the auditor had responsibility within the previous year.

> 1130.A2—Assurance engagements for functions over which the chief audit executive has responsibility should be overseen by a party outside the internal audit activity.

1200—Proficiency and Due Professional Care
Engagements should be performed with proficiency and due professional care.

1210—Proficiency
Internal auditors should possess the knowledge, skills, and other competencies needed to perform their individual responsibilities. The internal audit activity collectively should possess or obtain the knowledge, skills, and other competencies needed to perform its responsibilities.

> 1210.A1—The chief audit executive should obtain competent advice and assistance if the internal audit staff lacks the knowledge, skills, or other competencies needed to perform all or part of the engagement.

> 1210.A2—The internal auditor should have sufficient knowledge to identify the indicators of fraud but is not expected to have the expertise of a person whose primary responsibility is detecting and investigating fraud.

1220—Due Professional Care
Internal auditors should apply the care and skill expected of a reasonably prudent and competent internal auditor. Due professional care does not imply infallibility.

> 1220.A1—The internal auditor should exercise due professional care by considering the:
> - Extent of work needed to achieve the engagement's objectives.
> - Relative complexity , materiality, or significance of matters to which assurance procedures are applied.
> - Adequacy and effectiveness of risk management, control, and governance processes.
> - Probability of significant errors, irregularities, or noncompliance.
> - Cost of assurance in relation to potential benefits.

> 1220.A2—The internal auditor should be alert to the significant risks that might affect objectives, operations, or resources. However, assurance procedures alone,

even when performed with due professional care, do not guarantee that all significant risks will be identified.

1230—Continuing Professional Development

Internal auditors should enhance their knowledge, skills, and other competencies through continuing professional development.

1300—Quality Assurance and Improvement Program

The chief audit executive should develop and maintain a quality assurance and improvement program that covers all aspects of the internal audit activity and continuously monitors its effectiveness. The program should be designed to help the internal auditing activity add value and improve the organization's operations and to provide assurance that the internal audit activity is in conformity with the Standards and the Code of Ethics.

1310—Quality Program Assessments

The internal audit activity should adopt a process to monitor and assess the overall effectiveness of the quality program. The process should include both internal and external assessments.

1311—Internal Assessments

Internal assessments should include:

- Ongoing reviews of the performance of the internal audit activity; and
- Periodic reviews performed through self-assessment or by other persons within the organization, with knowledge of internal auditing practices and the *Standards*.

1312—External Assessments

External assessments, such as quality assurance reviews, should be conducted at least once every five years by a qualified, independent reviewer or review team from outside the organization.

1320—Reporting on the Quality Program

The chief audit executive should communicate the results of external assessments to the board.

1330—Use of "Conducted in Accordance with the Standards"

Internal auditors are encouraged to report that their activities are "conducted in accordance with the *Standards for the Professional Practice of Internal Auditing*." However, internal auditors may use the statement only if assessments of the quality improvement program demonstrate that the internal audit activity is in compliance with *Standards*.

1340—Disclosure of Noncompliance

Although the internal audit activity should achieve full compliance with the *Standards* and internal auditors with the *Code of Ethics*, there may be instances in which full compliance is not achieved. When noncompliance impacts the overall scope or operation of the internal audit activity, disclosure should be made to senior management and the board.

PERFORMANCE STANDARDS

2000—Managing the Internal Audit Activity

The chief audit executive should effectively manage the internal audit activity to ensure it adds value to the organization.

2010—Planning

The chief audit executive should establish risk-based plans to determine the priorities of the internal audit activity, consistent with the organization's goals.

> **2010.A1**—The internal audit activity's plan of engagements should be based on a risk assessment, undertaken at least annually. The input of senior management and the board should be considered in this process.

2020—Communication and Approval

The chief audit executive should communicate the internal audit activity's plans and resource requirements, including significant interim changes, to senior management and to the board for review and approval. The chief audit executive should also communicate the impact of resource limitations.

2030—Resource Management

The chief audit executive should ensure that internal audit resources are appropriate, sufficient, and effectively deployed to achieve the approved plan.

2040—Policies and Procedures

The chief audit executive should establish policies and procedures to guide the internal audit activity.

2050—Coordination

The chief audit executive should share information and coordinate activities with other internal and external providers of relevant assurance and consulting services to ensure proper coverage and minimize duplication of efforts.

2060—Reporting to the Board and Senior Management

The chief audit executive should report periodically to the board and senior management on the internal audit activity's purpose, authority, responsibility, and performance relative to its plan. Reporting should also include significant risk exposures and control issues, corporate governance issues, and other matters needed or requested by the board and senior management.

2100—Nature of Work

The internal audit activity evaluates and contributes to the improvement of risk management, control and governance systems.

2110—Risk Management

The internal audit activity should assist the organization by identifying and evaluating significant exposures to risk and contributing to the improvement of risk management and control systems.

2110.A1—The internal audit activity should monitor and evaluate the effectiveness of the organization's risk management system.

2110.A2—The internal audit activity should evaluate risk exposures relating to the organization's governance, operations, and information systems regarding the:

- Reliability and integrity of financial and operational information.
- Effectiveness and efficiency of operations.
- Safeguarding of assets.
- Compliance with laws, regulations, and contracts.

2120—Control

The internal audit activity should assist the organization in maintaining effective controls by evaluating their effectiveness and efficiency and by promoting continuous improvement.

2120.A1—Based on the results of the risk assessment, the internal audit activity should evaluate the adequacy and effectiveness of controls encompassing the organization's governance, operations, and information systems. This should include:

- Reliability and integrity of financial and operational information.
- Effectiveness and efficiency of operations.
- Safeguarding of assets.
- Compliance with laws, regulations, and contracts.

2120.A2—Internal auditors should ascertain the extent to which operating and program goals and objectives have been established and conform to those of the organization.

2120.A3—Internal auditors should review operations and programs to ascertain the extent to which results are consistent with established goals and objectives to determine whether operations and programs are being implemented or performed as intended.

2120.A4—Adequate criteria are needed to evaluate controls. Internal auditors should ascertain the extent to which management has established adequate criteria to determine whether objectives and goals have been accomplished. If adequate, internal auditors should use such criteria in their evaluation. If inadequate, internal auditors should work with management to develop appropriate evaluation criteria.

2130—Governance

The internal audit activity should contribute to the organization's governance process by evaluating and improving the process through which (1) values and goals are established and communicated, (2) the accomplishment of goals is monitored, (3) accountability is ensured, and (4) values are preserved.

2130.A1

Internal auditors should review operations and programs to ensure consistency with organizational values.

2200—Engagement Planning

Internal auditors should develop and record a plan for each engagement.

2201—Planning Considerations

In planning the engagement, internal auditors should consider:

- The objectives of the activity being reviewed and the means by which the activity controls its performance.
- The significant risks to the activity, its objectives, resources, and operations and the means by which the potential impact of risk is kept to an acceptable level.

- The adequacy and effectiveness of the activity's risk management and control systems compared to a relevant control framework or model.
- The opportunities for making significant improvements to the activity's risk management and control systems.

2210—Engagement Objectives

The engagement's objectives should address the risks, controls, and governance processes associated with the activities under review.

> 2210.A1—When planning the engagement, the internal auditor should identify and assess risks relevant to the activity under review. The engagement objectives should reflect the results of the risk assessment.

> 2210.A2—The internal auditor should consider the probability of significant errors, irregularities, noncompliance, and other exposures when developing the engagement objectives.

2220—Engagement Scope

The established scope should be sufficient to satisfy the objectives of the engagement.

> 2220.A1—The scope of the engagement should include consideration of relevant systems, records, personnel, and physical properties, including those under the control of third parties.

2230—Engagement Resource Allocation

Internal auditors should determine appropriate resources to achieve engagement objectives. Staffing should be based on an evaluation of the nature and complexity of each engagement, time constraints, and available resources.

2240—Engagement Work Program

Internal auditors should develop work programs that achieve the engagement objectives. These work programs should be recorded.

> 2240.A1—Work programs should establish the procedures for identifying, analyzing, evaluating, and recording information during the engagement. The work program should be approved prior to the commencement of work, and any adjustments approved promptly.

2300—Performing the Engagement

Internal auditors should identify, analyze, evaluate, and record sufficient information to achieve the engagement's objectives.

2310—Identifying Information

Internal auditors should identify sufficient, reliable, relevant, and useful information to achieve the engagement's objectives.

2320—Analysis and Evaluation

Internal auditors should base conclusions and engagement results on appropriate analyses and evaluations.

2330—Recording Information

Internal auditors should record relevant information to support the conclusions and engagement results.

> 2330.A1—The chief audit executive should control access to engagement records. The chief audit executive should obtain the approval of senior management and/or legal counsel prior to releasing such records to external parties, as appropriate.

> 2330.A2—The chief audit executive should develop retention requirements for engagement records. These retention requirements should be consistent with the organization's guidelines and any pertinent regulatory or other requirements.

2340—Engagement Supervision

Engagements should be properly supervised to ensure objectives are achieved, quality is assured, and staff is developed.

2400—Communicating Results

Internal auditors should communicate the engagement results promptly.

2410—Criteria for Communicating

Communications should include the engagement's objectives and scope as well as applicable conclusions, recommendations, and action plans.

> 2410.A1—The final communication of results should, where appropriate, contain the internal auditor's overall opinion.

> 2410.A2—Engagement communications should acknowledge satisfactory performance.

2420—Quality of Communications

Communications should be accurate, objective, clear, concise, constructive, complete, and timely.

2421—Errors and Omissions

If a final communication contains a significant error or omission, the chief audit executive should communicate corrected information to all individuals who received the original communication.

2430—Engagement Disclosure of Noncompliance with the *Standards*

When noncompliance with the *Standards* impacts a specific engagement, communication of the results should disclose the:

- *Standard*(s) with which full compliance was not achieved,
- Reason(s) for noncompliance, and
- Impact of noncompliance on the engagement.

2440—Disseminating Results

The chief audit executive should disseminate results to the appropriate individuals.

2440.A1—The chief audit executive is responsible for communicating the final results to individuals who can ensure that the results are given due consideration.

2500—Monitoring Progress

The chief audit executive should establish and maintain a system to monitor the disposition of results communicated to management.

2500.A1—The chief audit executive should establish a follow-up process to monitor and ensure that management actions have been effectively implemented or that senior management has accepted the risk of not taking action.

2600—Management's Acceptance of Risks

When the chief audit executive believes that senior management has accepted a level of residual risk that is unacceptable to the organization, the chief audit executive should discuss the matter with senior management. If the decision regarding residual risk is not resolved, the chief audit executive and senior management should report the matter to the board for resolution.

APPENDIX DB   THE INSTITUTE OF INTERNAL AUDITORS, CODE OF ETHICS*

INTRODUCTION

The purpose of The Institute's *Code of Ethics* is to promote an ethical culture in the profession of internal auditing.

> *Internal auditing is an independent, objective assurance and consulting activity designed to add value and improve an organization's operations. It helps an organization accomplish its objectives by bringing a systematic, disciplined approach to evaluate and improve the effectiveness of risk management, control, and governance processes.*

A code of ethics is necessary and appropriate for the profession of internal auditing, founded as it is on the trust placed in its objective assurance about risk management, control, and governance. The Institute's *Code of Ethics* extends beyond the definition of internal auditing to include two essential components:

1. Principles that are relevant to the profession and practice of internal auditing;
2. Rules of Conduct that describe behavior norms expected of internal auditors. These rules are an aid to interpreting the Principles into practical applications and are intended to guide the ethical conduct of internal auditors.

The *Code of Ethics* together with The Institute's *Professional Practices Framework* and other relevant Institute pronouncements provide guidance to internal auditors serving others. "Internal auditors" refers to Institute members, recipients of or candidates for IIA professional certifications, and those who provide internal auditing services within the definition of internal auditing.

APPLICABILITY AND ENFORCEMENT

This *Code of Ethics* applies to both individuals and entities that provide internal auditing services.

For Institute members and recipients of or candidates for IIA professional certifications, breaches of the *Code of Ethics* will be evaluated and administered according to The Institute's Bylaws and Administrative Guidelines. The fact that a particular conduct is not mentioned in the Rules of Conduct does not prevent it from being unacceptable or discreditable, and therefore, the member, certification holder, or candidate can be liable for disciplinary action.

PRINCIPLES

Internal auditors are expected to apply and uphold the following principles:

Integrity

The integrity of internal auditors establishes trust and thus provides the basis for reliance on their judgment.

Objectivity

Internal auditors exhibit the highest level of professional objectivity in gathering, evaluating, and communicating information about the activity or process being examined. Internal auditors make a balanced assessment of all the relevant circumstances and are not unduly influenced by their own interests or by others in forming judgments.

Confidentiality

Internal auditors respect the value and ownership of information they receive and do not disclose information without appropriate authority unless there is a legal or professional obligation to do so.

Competency

Internal auditors apply the knowledge, skills, and experience needed in the performance of internal auditing services.

RULES OF CONDUCT

1. **Integrity**
   Internal auditors:
   1.1. Shall perform their work with honesty, diligence, and responsibility.
   1.2. Shall observe the law and make disclosures expected by the law and the profession.
   1.3. Shall not knowingly be a party to any illegal activity, or engage in acts that are discreditable to the profession of internal auditing or to the organization.
   1.4. Shall respect and contribute to the legitimate and ethical objectives of the organization.

2. **Objectivity**
   Internal auditors:
   2.1. Shall not participate in any activity or relationship that may impair or be presumed to impair their unbiased assessment. This participation includes those activities or relationships that may be in conflict with the interests of the organization.
   2.2 Shall not accept anything that may impair or be presumed to impair their professional judgment.
   2.3 Shall disclose all material facts known to them that, if not disclosed, may distort the reporting of activities under review.

3. **Confidentiality**
   Internal auditors:
   3.1 Shall be prudent in the use and protection of information acquired in the course of their duties.
   3.2 Shall not use information for any personal gain or in any manner that would be contrary to the law or detrimental to the legitimate and ethical objectives of the organization.

4. **Competency**
   Internal auditors:
   4.1. Shall engage only in those services for which they have the necessary knowledge, skills, and experience.
   4.2 Shall perform internal auditing services in accordance with the *Standards for the Professional Practice of Internal Auditing.*
   4.3 Shall continually improve their proficiency and the effectiveness and quality of their services.

Appendix DC · Abridged Summary of GAO Government Auditing Standards (1994 Revision)

Scope of Audit Work

Audits may have a combination of financial and performance audit objectives, or may have objectives limited to only some aspects of one audit type. Auditors should follow the appropriate generally accepted government audit standards (GAGAS) that are applicable to the individual objectives of the audit.

1. Financial Statement Audits.
   a. Financial statement audits provide reasonable assurance about (1) whether the financial statements of an audited entity present fairly the financial position, results of operation, and cash flows or changes in financial position in conformity with generally accepted accounting principles, (2) whether the entity has adhered to specific financial compliance requirements [i.e., laws and regulations], and (3) whether the entity's internal control over financial reporting and safeguarding assets is suitably designed and implemented.
2. Performance Audits.
   a. Economy and efficiency audits include determining (1) whether the entity is acquiring, protecting, and using its resources (such as personnel, property, and space) economically and efficiently, (2) the causes of inefficiencies or uneconomical practices, and (3) whether the entity has complied with laws and regulations concerning matters of economy and efficiency.
   b. Program audits include determining (1) the extent to which the desired results or benefits established by the legislature or other authorizing body are being achieved, (2) the effectiveness of organizations, programs, activities, or functions, and (3) whether the agency has complied with laws and regulations applicable to the program.

General Standards

1. *Qualifications:* The staff assigned to conduct the audit should collectively possess adequate professional proficiency for the tasks required.
2. *Independence:* In all matters relating to the audit work, the audit organization and the individual auditors, whether government or public, must be free from personal and external impairments to independence, should be organizationally independent, and should maintain an independent attitude and appearance.
3. *Due professional care:* Due professional care should be used in conducting the audit and in preparing related reports.
4. *Quality Control:* Each audit organization conducting audits in accordance with these standards should have an appropriate internal quality control system in place and undergo an external quality control review.

Financial Audits

Field Work Standards for Financial Audits

1. The GAGAS standards of field work incorporate the AICPA standards of field work for financial audits (GAAS) and prescribe supplemental standards to satisfy the unique needs of government financial audits.
2. The work is to be properly planned, and auditors should consider materiality, among other matters, in determining the nature, timing, and extent of auditing procedures and in evaluating the results of those procedures. Auditors should follow up on known material findings and recommendations from previous audits.
3. Auditors should design the audit to provide reasonable assurance of detecting (1) irregularities that are material to the financial statements, (2) material misstatements resulting from direct and material illegal acts, and (3) material misstatements resulting from noncompliance with provisions of contract or grant agreements. Auditors should be aware of the possibility that indirect illegal acts may have occurred.

4. The auditors' understanding of internal control shall include matters of internal controls over safeguarding assets from unauthorized acquisition, use, or disposition. Preventing and detecting material misappropriations is an objective of safeguard controls, and understanding the control is essential to planning an audit.

5. A record of the auditors' work should be retained in the form of working papers, which should contain sufficient information to enable an experienced auditor having no previous connection with the audit to ascertain from them the evidence that supports the auditors' significant conclusions and judgments.

Reporting Standards for Financial Audits

1. The GAGAS financial reporting standards incorporate the AICPA standards of reporting for financial audits (GAAS) and prescribe supplemental standards to satisfy the unique needs of governmental financial audits.

2. Auditors should communicate certain information related to the conduct and reporting of the audit to the audit committee or the individuals with whom they have contracted for the audit. [This "certain information" includes auditors' responsibilities for testing internal control and reporting on compliance with laws and regulations, and the nature of control and compliance testing required by laws and regulations in the circumstances.]

3. Audit reports should state that the audit was made in accordance with generally accepted government auditing standards (GAGAS).

4. The report on financial statements should either (1) describe the scope of the auditors' testing of compliance with laws and regulations and internal controls and present the results of those tests, or (2) refer to separate reports containing that information. Auditors should report irregularities, illegal acts, other material noncompliance, and reportable conditions in internal control. In some circumstances, auditors should report irregularities and illegal acts directly to parties external to the audited entity.

5. If certain information is prohibited from general disclosure, the audit report should state the nature of the information omitted and the requirement that makes the omission necessary.

6. Written audit reports are to be submitted by the audit organization to the appropriate officials of the auditee and to the appropriate officials of the organizations requiring or arranging for the audits, including external funding organizations, unless legal restrictions prevent it. Copies of the reports should also be sent to other officials who have legal oversight authority or who may be responsible for acting on audit findings and recommendations and to others authorized to receive such reports. Unless restricted by law or regulation, copies should be made available for public inspection.

PERFORMANCE AUDITS

Field Work Standards for Performance Audits

1. Work is to be adequately planned.

2. Staff are to be properly supervised.

3. When laws, regulations, and other compliance requirements are significant to audit objectives, auditors should design the audit to provide reasonable assurance about compliance with them. In all performance audits, auditors should be alert to situations or transactions that could be indicative of illegal acts or abuse.

4. Auditors should obtain an understanding of management controls that are relevant to the audit. When management controls are significant to audit objectives, auditors should obtain sufficient evidence to support judgments about these controls.

5. Sufficient, competent, and relevant evidence is to be obtained to afford a reasonable basis for the auditors' findings and conclusions. A record of the auditors' work should be retained in the form of working papers, which should contain sufficient information to enable an experienced auditor having no previous connection with the audit to ascertain from them the evidence that supports the auditors' significant conclusions and judgments.

Reporting Standards for Performance Audits

1. Auditors should prepare written audit reports communicating the results of each audit.
2. Auditors should issue the reports to make the information available for timely use by management, legislative officials, and other interested parties.
3. The report should include statements about the:
   a. audit objectives and the audit scope and methodology.
   b. significant audit findings, and where applicable, the auditors' conclusions.
   c. recommendations for actions to correct problem areas and to improve operations.
   d. audit's performance in accordance with generally accepted government auditing standards.
   e. significant instances of noncompliance and abuse that were found during or in connection with the audit. In some circumstances, auditors should report illegal acts directly to parties external to the audited entity.
   f. scope of the auditors' work on management controls and any significant weaknesses found during the audit.
   g. views of responsible officials of the audited program concerning the auditors' findings, conclusions, and recommendations, as well as corrections planned.
   h. noteworthy accomplishments, particularly when management improvements in one area may be applicable elsewhere.
   i. significant issues needing further audit work to the auditors responsible for planning future audit work.
   j. information prohibited from general disclosure. [The audit report should state the nature of the information omitted and the requirement that makes the omission necessary.]
4. The report should be complete, accurate, objective, convincing, and as clear and concise as the subject matter permits.
5. Written audit reports are to be submitted by the audit organization to the appropriate officials of the auditee, and to the appropriate officials of the organizations requiring or arranging for the audits, including external funding organizations, unless legal restrictions prevent it. Copies of the reports should also be sent to other officials who have legal oversight authority or who may be responsible for acting on audit findings and recommendations and to others authorized to receive such reports. Unless restricted by law or regulation, copies should be made available for public inspection.

Module E

An Introduction to Audit Sampling

Professional Standards References

Learning Objectives

Audit sampling relies heavily on the concepts of materiality and risk—audit risk, inherernt risk, control risk, and detection risk. Audit sampling is not an *audit procedure*; it is a *method* of organizing the application of audit procedures and a *method* of organizing auditors' thoughts for decision making. After you study Module E, you should be able to:

1. Define and explain the terms unique to audit sampling, including the fundamental technical differences between statistical sampling and nonstatistical sampling.

2. Identify audit work considered to be audit sampling and distinguish it from work not considered to be audit sampling.

3. Develop a simple audit program for a test of controls audit of a clients's internal control activities, including:
   a. Specify objectives, deviation conditions, populations, and sampling units.

   b. Determine sample size and select sampling units.
   c. Evaluate evidence from a test of controls audit.

4. Develop a simple audit program for an account balance audit considering the influence of risk and tolerable misstatement, including:
   a. Specify objectives and define a population for data.
   b. Determine sample size and select sampling units.
   c. Evaluate monetary misstatement evidence from a balance audit sample.

INTRODUCTION TO AUDIT SAMPLING

LEARNING OBJECTIVE

1. Define and explain the terms unique to audit sampling, including the fundamental technical differences between statistical sampling and nonstatistical sampling.

Generally accepted auditing standards define **audit sampling** as the *application of an audit procedure to less than 100 percent of the items within an account balance or class of transactions for the purpose of evaluating some characteristic of the balance or class* (SAS 39, AU 350). You have already seen the sampling idea incorporated in the explanation of test of controls audit procedure, which was defined as a two-part statement consisting of: (1) an identification of the data population from which a *sample* of items will be selected for audit and (2) an expression of an action taken to produce relevant evidence. To understand the definition of audit sampling, you must keep the following definitions in mind: **Audit procedure** refers to actions described as general audit procedures (recalculation, physical observation, confirmation, verbal inquiry, document examination, scanning, and analytical procedures). An **account balance** refers to a control account made up of many constituent items (for example, an accounts receivable control account representing the sum of customers' accounts, an inventory control account representing the sum of various goods in inventory, a sales account representing the sum of many sales invoices, or a long-term debt account representing the sum of several issues of outstanding bonds). A **class of transactions** refers to a group of transactions having common characteristics, such as cash receipts or cash disbursements, but which are not simply added together and presented as an account balance in financial statements.

Other definitions: A **population** is the set of all the items that constitute an account balance or class of transactions. Each of the items is a **population unit**; and when an auditor selects a sample, each item selected is called a *sampling unit*. A **sampling unit** can be a customer's account, an inventory item, a debt issue, a cash receipt, a canceled check, and so forth. A **sample** is a set of sampling units.

Sampling and the Extent of Auditing

Three aspects of auditing procedures are important—their nature, timing, and extent. **Nature** refers to the seven general procedures (recalculation, physical observation,

EXHIBIT E-1	TWO KINDS OF AUDIT PROGRAMS: TWO PURPOSES FOR AUDIT SAMPLING

Test of Controls Audit Program	Balance-Audit Program
Purpose Obtain evidence about client's transaction processing control performance	**Purpose** Obtain evidence about client's financial statement assertions
Validity Completeness Authorization Accuracy Classification Accounting/Posting Proper periods	Existence/Occurrence Completeness Valuation Rights and obligations (ownership and ownership) Presentation and disclosure
Sample Usually from a class of transactions (population) such as:	**Sample** Usually from items in an asset or liability balance (population) such as:
Cash receipts Cash disbursements Purchases (inventory additions) Inventory issues Sales on credit Expense details Welfare payments (eligibility)	Accounts receivable Loans receivable Inventory Small tool fixed assets Depositors' savings accounts Accounts payable Unexpired magazine subscriptions

confirmation, verbal inquiry, document examination, scanning, and analytical procedures). Timing is a matter of *when* procedures are performed. More will be said about timing later in this module. Audit sampling is concerned primarily with matters of **extent**—the *amount* of work done when the procedures are performed. In the context of auditing standards, nature and timing relate most closely to the *competence* of evidential matter, while extent relates most closely to the *sufficiency* (sample size) of evidential matter.

Exhibit E–1 (above) shows that audit sampling can be performed in two audit programs for two different purposes. Sampling in the test of controls program is for the purpose of obtaining evidence about a client's control activity performance. Sampling in the balance-audit program is for the purpose of obtaining direct evidence about management's financial statement assertions.

Inclusions and Exclusions Related to Audit Sampling

LEARNING OBJECTIVE

2. Identify audit work considered to be audit sampling and distinguish it from work not considered to be audit sampling.

Look again at the audit sampling definition and to that part about auditing sampling being "for the purpose of evaluation some characteristics of the balance or class." An application of audit procedures is considered audit sampling if and only if the auditors' objective is to reach a conclusion about the entire account balance or transaction class (the population) on the basis of the evidence obtained from the audit of a sample drawn from the balance or class. If the entire population is audited, or if the purpose is only to gain general familiarity, the work is not considered to be audit sampling.

Perhaps the distinction between audit sampling and other methods can be perceived more clearly in terms of the following work that is not considered audit sampling according to the standards expressed in *SAS 39* (AU 350):

- Complete (100 percent) audit of all the elements in a balance or class, by definition, does not involve sampling.

- Analytical procedures, in the nature of overall comparisons, ratio calculations, and the like, are normally not applied on a sample basis.
- A **walk-through**—following one or a few transactions through the accounting and control systems to obtain a general understanding of the client's system—is not audit sampling because the objective is not to reach a conclusion about a balance or class.
- Several procedures (for example, verbal inquiry of employees, obtaining written representations, obtaining inquiry responses in the form of answers on an internal control questionnaire, scanning accounting records for unusual items, and observation of personnel and procedures) do not lend themselves to sampling method.

Several procedures are typically used in audit sampling applications. They are recalculation, physical observation of tangible assets, confirmation, and document examination. These procedures most often are applied to the audit of details of transactions and balances.

Why Auditors Sample

Auditors utilize audit sampling when (1) the nature and materiality of the balance or class does not demand a 100 percent audit, (2) a decision must be made about the balance or class, and (3) the time and cost to audit 100 percent of the population is too great. So, auditors use sampling because they need to perform efficient audits on a timely basis and cannot do so by auditing 100 percent. The two sampling designs used by auditors are *statistical sampling* and *nonstatistical sampling*.

Statistical Sampling

Auditors define **statistical sampling** as *audit samping that uses the laws of probability for selecting and evaluating a sample from a population for the purpose of reaching a conclusion about the population*. The essential points of this definition are: (1) A statistical sample is selected at random, and (2) statistical calculations are used to measure and express the results. Both conditions are necessary for a method to be considered statistical sampling rather than nonstatistical sampling.

AUDITING INSIGHT

WHEN TO USE STATISTICAL SAMPLING

Random numbers can be associated with population items.
Objective results that can be defended mathematically are desired.
Auditors have insufficient knowledge about the population to justify a basis for a nonstatistical sample.
A representative (random) sample is required.

Advantages of Statistical Sampling

Requires a precise and definite approach to the audit problem.
Incorporates evaluation that calculates a direct relation between the sample results and the entire population under audit.
Requires auditors to specify, and even quantify, particular judgments on risk and materiality.
Does not eliminate or reduce auditors' professional judgment.

A **random sample** is a set of sampling units so chosen that each population item has an *equal likelihood* of being selected in the sample. You can use a random sample in a "nonstatistical sampling" design. However, you cannot use statistical calculations with a nonrandom sample. The mathematical laws of probability are not applicable for nonrandom samples, and basing such calculations on a nonrandom sample is wrong.

A statistical calculation of sample size in advance is *not* necessary for a method to be considered statistical sampling. You can use a "magic number"—any sample size you wish. However, a preliminary estimate of sample size can be calculated using statistical models. A sampling method is *statistical* by virtue of random selection of the sample couples with statistical calculation of the results, not because statistical calculations are used to predetermine a sample size.

Nonstatistical Sampling

A good definition of **nonstatistical sampling** is *audit sampling in which auditors do not utilize statistical calculations to express the results*. The sample selection technique can be random sampling or some other selection technique not based on mathematical randomness. Auditors say that nonstatistical sampling involves "consideration of sampling risk in evaluating an audit sample without using statistical theory to measure that risk." "Consideration" in this context means "giving sampling risk some thoughtful attention" without direct knowledge or measurement of its magnitude.

AUDITING INSIGHT

WHEN TO USE NONSTATISTICAL SAMPLING

- Association of population items with random numbers is difficult and expensive.
- Strictly defensible results based on mathematics are not necessary.
- Auditors have sufficient knowledge about the population to justify a basis for a nonstatistical sample with expectation of a reasonable conclusion about the population.
- A representative (random) sample is not required; for example, because an efficient nonstatistical sample of large items leaves an immaterial amount unaudited.
- The population is known to be diverse with some segments especially error-prone.

Advantages of Nonstatistical Sampling

- Permits a less rigidly defined approach to unique problems that might not fit into a statistical method.
- Permits the auditors to reapply evaluation judgments based on factors in addition to the sample evidence.
- Permits auditors to be vague and less than definite about, and omit quantification of, particular judgments on risk and materiality.
- Permits auditors to assert standards of subjective judgment.

Sampling and Nonsampling Risk

Be careful not to confuse sampling and nonsampling risk with statistical and nonstatistical sampling. They are not related. When auditors perform procedures on a sample basis and obtain sufficient evidence, *a conclusion about the population characteristic can still be wrong*. For example, suppose an auditor selected 100 sales invoices for audit and found no errors or misstatements in any of them. The conclusion that a significant incidence of errors and misstatements does not exist in the entire population of sales invoices from which the sample was drawn might be wrong. How, you ask? Simple: The sample might not reflect the actual condition of the population. No matter how randomly or carefully the sample was selected, it might not be a good representation of the extent of errors and misstatements actually in the population.

Sampling risk is defined as *the probability that an auditor's conclusion based on a sample might be different from the conclusion based on an audit of the entire population*. You could audit a sample of sales invoices and decide, based on the sample, that the population of sales invoices contained few errors. However, suppose some auditors with more time could audit *all* the sales invoices and find a large number of errors. In such a case, your sample-based decision will be proved wrong. Your sample apparently did not represent the population very well. Sampling risk expresses the probability of making a wrong decision based on sample evidence, and it *exists in both statistical sampling methods*. You cannot escape it in audit sampling. With statistical sampling, you can measure it, and you can control it by auditing sufficiently large samples. With nonstatistical sampling, you can "consider" it without measuring it. However, considering sampling risk without measuring it requires experience and expertise.

Nonsampling risk is *all risk other than sampling risk*. You need to refer to the audit risk model to grasp the breadth of this definition:

$$\textbf{Risk Model: } AR = IR \times CR \times DR$$

Nonsampling risk can arise from:

- Misjudging the inherent risk (IR). An auditor who mistakenly believes few material misstatements occur in the first place will tend to do less work and, therefore, might fail to detect problems.
- Misjudging the control risk (CR). An auditor who is too optimistic about the ability of controls to prevent, detect, and correct errors will tend to do less work, with the same results as misjudging the inherent risk.
- Poor choice of procedures and mistakes in execution—related to detection risk (DR). Auditors can select procedures inappropriate for the objective (e.g., confirming recorded accounts receivable when the objective is to find unrecorded accounts receivable), can fail to recognize errors when vouching supporting documents, or can sign off as having performed procedures when the work actually was not done.

Nonsampling risk also is a possibility of making a wrong decision. *It exists both in statistical and nonstatistical sampling*. The problem is that nonsampling risk cannot be measured. Auditors control it—and believe it is reduced to a negligible level—through adequate planning and supervision of audit engagements and personnel, by having policies and procedures for quality control of their auditing practices, and by having internal monitoring and external peer review of their own quality control systems.

One other distinction is important: External critics (judges, juries, peer reviewers) have few grounds for criticizing auditors who fall victim to sampling risk, provided that an audit sampling application is planned and executed reasonably well. Auditors are more open to criticism and fault-finding when erroneous audit decisions result from nonsampling risk.

Sampling Methods and Applications

Audit sampling is concerned with the amount of work performed and the sufficiency of audit evidence obtained. Audit sampling terminology contains many new concepts and definitions. The ones presented above, however, are general and apply to all phases of audit sampling. You need to know them so you can "speak the language."

Auditors design audit samples to deal with (1) auditing control for the purpose of assessing control risk and (2) auditing account balances for the purpose of getting direct evidence about financial statement assertions (see Exhibit E–1).

AUDITING INSIGHT

MANIFESTATIONS OF NONSAMPLING RISK

- *Performing inappropriate procedures*: Auditors based the evaluation of inventory obsolescence on forecasted sales without adequately evaluating the forecast assumptions.
- *Failure to consider test results adequately*: Auditor did not adequately investigate discrepancies in inventory counts and pricing, failing to draw the appropriate conclusions.
- *Neglecting the importance of analytical procedures*: Auditor might have discovered client's failure to eliminate the intercompany profits if year-to-year product mix, gross profit, and recorded eliminations had been studied.
- *Failure to maintain control over audit procedures*: Auditors' loose attitude permitted client employees to tamper with records selected for confirmation.
- *Lack of professional skepticism*: Auditors accepted client's unsupported verbal representations instead of gathering independent evidence.

R E V I E W
CHECKPOINTS

E.1 Why do auditors sample?

E.2 What are the primary distinctions between statistical and nonstatistical sampling?

E.3 What is nonsampling risk? Give some examples.

E.4 What are test controls audit procedures in general? What purpose do they serve?

E.5 Why must an audit sample be representative of the population from which it is drawn?

E.6 What transaction processing control objectives should be achieved by a company's control system?

E.7 What two types of auditing programs are ordinarily used as written plans for audit procedures?

TEST OF CONTROLS FOR ASSESSING CONTROL RISK

LEARNING OBJECTIVE

3. Develop a simple audit program for a test of controls audit of a client's internal control activities.

Auditors must assess the control risk to determine the nature, timing, and extent of other audit procedures. Final evaluations of internal control are based on evidence obtained in the review and testing phases of an evaluation. Auditors' assessments of control risk always depend entirely on the circumstances in each specific situation. The judgments are usually very specific. For example, an auditor might learn that a company's validity control activity to prevent fictitious sales is to require the bookkeeper to match a shipping order with each sales invoice before recording a sale—good control, as specified. Now suppose the test of control audit procedure of selecting recorded sales invoices and vouching them to shipping orders shows a number of mistakes (invoices without supporting shipping orders)—poor control, as performed. Sales might be overstated. One way to take this control deficiency into account is to perform more extensive work on accounts receivable using confirmation and inquiries and analytical procedures related to collectibility. (If sales are overstated, one result could be overstatement of receivables—the debit side of the accounting entry.)

The example above related a specific control (the validity-related control activity of matching sales invoices with shipping orders) to a specific set of other audit procedures directed toward a possible problem (overstatement of sales and receivables). In a more general sense, auditors reach judgments about control risk along the lines shown in Exhibit E–2 (on page 584). Some situations may call for a nonquantitative expression, and auditors sometimes need a quantitative expression. The quantitative ranges overlap so

EXHIBIT E–2	AUDITORS' ASSESSMENT OF CONTROL RISK

Evaluation of Internal Control	Expression of Control Risk	
	Qualitative	Quantitative
Excellent—as specified and in compliance	Low	0.10–0.45
Good—lacks something in specification or compliance	Moderate	0.40–0.70
Deficient—weakness in specification or compliance or both	Slightly Below Maximum	0.60–0.95
Little or no control	Maximum	1.00

you will not get the idea that auditors really can put exact numbers on these kinds of evaluations.

Audit sampling can be used as a method and plan for performing the test of controls audit procedures. The application of sampling in test of controls auditing is a structured, formal approach embodied in seven steps. The seven-step framework helps auditors plan, perform, and evaluate test of controls audit work. It also helps auditors accomplish an eighth step—careful documentation of the work—by showing each of the seven areas to be described in the working papers. The first seven steps are:

1. Specify the audit objectives.
2. Define the deviation conditions.
3. Define the population.
4. Determine the sample size.
5. Select the sample.
6. Perform the test of controls procedures.
7. Evaluate the evidence.

Plan the Procedures

The first three steps are planning steps that represent the **problem-recognition** phase of the sampling method. When a client describes the control system, the implicit assertion is: "These controls work; people perform the control activities and achieve the control objectives." The auditors' question (problem) is: "Is it so? Are the validity (and other) control objectives achieved satisfactorily?"

Test of controls audit work is always directed toward producing evidence of the client's performance of its own control activities. Thus, auditors' procedures should produce evidence about the client's achievement of the seven control objectives.

1. Specify the Audit Objectives

Take a control activity under the *validity* objective as an example—namely, the client's requirement that a shipping order be matched with a sales invoice before a valid sale is recorded. The specific objective of an auditor's test of controls audit procedure would be: *Determine whether recorded sales invoices are supported by matched shipping orders*. The audit procedure itself would be: *Select a sample of recorded sales invoices and vouch them to supporting shipping orders*.

The client's matching of sales invoices to shipping orders in the example is a **key control**—it is *important*. Auditors should identify and audit only the key controls. Incidental controls that are not important will not be relied on to reduce control risk and need not be audited for compliance. Auditing them for compliance just wastes time if they really do not have much effect on the control risk assessment.

2. Define the Deviation Conditions

The terms **deviation, error, occurrence,** and **exception** are synonyms in test of controls sampling. They all refer to a departure from a prescribed internal control activity in a particular case; for example, an invoice is recorded with no supporting shipping order (bill of lading). Defining the deviation conditions at the outset is important, so the auditors doing the work will know a deviation when they see one. As an assistant accountant, you would prefer to be instructed: "Select a sample of recorded sales invoices, vouch them to supporting shipping orders, and document cases where the shipping order is missing" instead of "Check recorded sales invoices for any mistakes." The latter instruction does not define the deviation condition well enough. Clear and precise definitions of deviations help auditors avoid the nonsampling risk of simply failing to notice deviations in documents they audit.

The example we are using is oversimplified. However, this vouching procedure for compliance evidence can be used to obtain evidence about several control objectives at the same time. The invoice can be compared to the shipping order for evidence of actual shipment (*validity*), reviewed for credit approval (*authorization*), prices compared to the price list (*authorization* and *accuracy*), quantity billed compared to quantity shipped (*accuracy*), recalculated (arithmetic *accuracy*), compared for correspondence of shipment date and record date (*proper period*), and traced to postings in the general ledger and subsidiary accounts (*accounting/postings*). Exhibit E–3 shows these deviation conditions laid out in a working paper designed to record the results of a test of controls audit of a sample of sales invoices.

EXHIBIT E–3   TEST OF CONTROLS AUDIT DOCUMENTATION

Index *M 10.3*

By *J C*   Date *11-11-01*
Review *G.D.*   Date *11-15-01*

KINGSTON COMPANY
Test of Controls Over Recorded Sales
December 31, 2001

Invoice number	Date	Amount	Bill of lading	Credit approved	Approved prices	Quantities match	Arithmetic accurate	Dates match	Posted to customer
35000	Mar. 30	$ 3,000							
35050	Mar. 31	$ 800			X				
35100	Apr. 2	$ 1,200					Y		
35150	Apr. 3	$ 1,500			Y				
35200	Apr. 5	$ 400							
35250	Apr. 6	$ 300	X			X	Y	X	
32100	Jan. 3	$ 1,000							
32150	Jan. 4	$ 200							
34850	Mar. 25	Missing	X	X	X	X	X	X	
34900	Mar. 26	$ 100			Y				
34950	Mar. 27	$ 200							
Sample = 200		$98,000							
Uncorrected deviations			4	9	5	6	3	7	0

X = Uncorrected deviation.
Y = Deviation occurred but was detected and corrected later.

Time for some more terminology: Test of controls audit sampling also is called **attribute sampling.** Attribute sampling is audit sampling in which auditors look for the *presence* or *absence* of a control condition. In response to the audit question: "For each sales invoice in the sample, can a matched shipping order be found?" The answer can be only yes or no. With this definition, auditors can count the number of deviations and use the count when evaluating the evidence.

3. Define the Population

The specification of test of controls audit objectives and the definition of deviation conditions usually define the **population** which is the set of all items in the balance or class of transactions. In the example case, the population consists of all the recorded sales invoices, and each invoice is a **population unit.** In **classical attribute sampling,** a *sampling unit* is the same thing as a *population unit.*

Population definition is important because audit conclusions can be made only about the population from which the sample was selected. For example, evidence from a sample of recorded sales invoices (the population for our illustrative procedure) *cannot* be used for a conclusion about *completeness.* Controls related to the completeness objective (in this case, control over failure to record an invoice for goods shipped) can only be audited by sampling from a population representing goods shipped (the shipping order file) and not by sampling from the population of recorded invoices.

A complicating factor in population definition is the timing of the audit work. Test of controls audit procedures ideally should be applied to transactions executed throughout the period under audit because auditors want to reach a conclusion about control risk during the entire period. However, auditors often perform test of controls procedures at an **interim date**—a date some weeks or months before the client's year-end date—and at that time the entire population (say, recorded sales invoices for the year) will not be available for audit. Nothing is wrong with doing the work at an interim date, but auditors cannot ignore the remaining period between the interim date and the year-end. Strategies for considering control in the period after the interim date are explained later.

Another complicating factor in population definition is the need to determine the correspondence of the physical representation of the population to the population itself. The **physical representation of the population** is the *auditor's frame of reference for selecting a sample.* It can be a journal listing of recorded sales invoices, a file drawer full of invoice copies, a magnetic disk file of invoices, or another physical representation. The sample actually will be selected from the physical representation, so it must be complete

AUDITING INSIGHT

A BALANCE-AUDIT APPLICATION OF ATTRIBUTE SAMPLING

Previous presentations have said that attribute test of controls samples *usually* are drawn from a class of transactions to obtain evidence about compliance with control objectives. Attribute sample also can be used sometimes for balance-audit purposes. This example suggests an attribute sample to obtain evidence about an ownership (rights) financial statement assertion.

Question: A lessor is in the business of leasing autos, large trucks, tractors, and trailers. Is it necessary for the auditors to examine the titles to all the equipment?

Answer: It is not necessary, unless some extraordinary situation or circumstance is brought to light, for the auditors to examine titles to all equipment. Random test verification of title certificates or proper registration of vehicles should be made.

Source: *AICPA Technical Practice Aids.*

and correspond with the actual population. The physical representation of the recorded sales invoice population as a list in a journal is fairly easy to visualize. However, an auditor should make sure that periodic listings (e.g., monthly sales journals) are added correctly and posted to the general ledger sales accounts. Now, a selection of individual sales invoices from the sales journal is known to be from the complete population of recorded sales invoices.

Perform the Procedures

LEARNING OBJECTIVE

3b. Determine sample size and select sampling units.

The next three performance steps represent the **evidence-collection** phase of the sampling method. These steps are performed to get the evidence.

The sample size determination and sample selection steps explained in this section might be considered planning steps, but since they require a little more action, they also can be considered performance. The distinction is not crucial. They are merely the next things to do.

4. Determine the Sample Size

Sample size—the number of population units to audit—should be determined thoughtfully. Some auditors operate on the "magic number theory" (e.g., select 30). Be careful, however, because a magic number may or may not satisfy the need for enough evidence. A magic number might also be too large. Auditors must consider four influences on sample size: *sampling risk, tolerable deviation rate, expected population deviation rate,* and *population size*.

Sampling Risk. Earlier, sampling risk was defined as the probability that an auditor's conclusion based on a sample might be different from the conclusion based on an audit of the entire population. In other words, when using evidence from a sample, an auditor might reach a wrong conclusion. He or she might decide that (1) control risk is very low when, in fact, it is not, or (2) control risk is very high when, in fact, it is not so bad. The more you know about a population (from a larger sample), the less likely you are to reach a wrong conclusion. Thus, the larger the sample, the lower the sampling risk of making either of the two decision errors. More will be said about these risks in the section on evaluation.

In terms of our example, the important sampling risk is the probability that the sample will reveal few or no recorded sales invoices without supporting shipping orders when, in fact, the population contains many such deviations. This result leads to the erroneous conclusion that the control worked well. The probability of finding few or no deviations when many exist is reduced by auditing a larger sample. Thus, sample size varies inversely with the amount of sampling risk an auditor is willing to take.

Tolerable Deviation Rate. Auditors should have an idea about the correspondence of rates of deviation in the population with control risk assessments. Perfect control compliance is not necessary, so the question is: What rate of deviation in the population signals control risk of 10 percent? 20 percent? 30 percent? and so forth, up to 100 percent? Suppose an auditor believes $90,000 of sales invoices could be exposed to control deviations without causing a minimum material misstatement in the sales and accounts receivable balances. If the total gross sales is $8.5 million, this judgment implies a **tolerable deviation rate** of about 1 percent ($90,000/$8.5 million). Since this 1 percent rate marks the *minimum* material misstatement, it indicates a *low control risk* (say, 0.05), and it justifies a great deal of reliance on internal control in the audit of the sales and accounts receivable balances.

This calculation creates a direct association of the 1 percent tolerable deviation rate with the lowest control risk ($CR = 0.05$), but what can auditors say about higher control risks (e.g., $CR = 0.10, 0.20$, etc.)? Answer: The higher control risks can be identified by direct association with higher tolerable deviation rates. For example: Tolerable deviation of 2 percent identifies $CR = 0.10$, tolerable deviation of 4 percent identifies

$CR = 0.20$, and so forth. The table below shows this series of identifications.[1] When an auditor says "I will test controls to a 10 percent tolerable deviation rate," the auditor is also saying "I plan to assess control risk at 0.50." At the beginning of planning, therefore, auditors can consider more than one tolerable deviation rate, recognizing that the acceptance of a single tolerable deviation rate dictates the planned assessed control risk level.

	Control Risk		Tolerable Deviation Rate
Qualitative		Quantitative	
		0.05	1%
		0.10	2
Low control risk		0.20	4
		0.30	6
		0.40	8
Moderate control risk		0.50 ←	10
		0.60	12
Control risk slightly		0.70	14
below the maximum		0.80	16
		0.90	18
Maximum control risk		1.00	20

directly related

Since sample size varies inversely with the tolerable deviation rate, the auditor who wants to assess control risk at 0.05 (tolerable rate = 1 percent) will need to audit a larger sample of sales transactions than another auditor who is willing to assess control risk at 0.50 (tolerable rate = 10 percent). The desired control risk level and its tolerable rate is a matter of auditor choice.

The tolerable rate is not a fixed rate until the auditor decides what control risk assessment suits the audit plan. It then becomes a decision criterion involved in the sampling application. Some auditors express the tolerable rate as a number (necessary for statistical calculation of sample size), while others do not put a number on it. Module A contains more explanation about the determination of various tolerable rates.

Expected Population Deviation Rate. Auditors usually know or suspect some control performance conditions. Sometimes they have last year's audit experience with the client; sometimes they have information from a predecessor auditor. They have information about the client's personnel, the working conditions, and the general control environment. This knowledge contributes to an **expectation about the population deviation rate,** which is an *estimate of the ratio the number of expected deviations to population size.* Suppose the auditors discovered 1 percent deviation in last year's audit. The expected population deviation rate could then be 1 percent. Auditors can also stipulate a zero expected deviation rate, which will produce a minimum sample size for audit.

The expected rate is important in a commonsense perspective. If auditors had reason to expect more deviations than they could tolerate, there would be no reason to perform any test of controls audit procedures. Thus, the expected rate must be less than the tolerable rate. Also, the closer the expected rate is to the tolerable rate, the larger the sample will need to be to reach a conclusion that deviations do not exceed the tolerable rate. Consequently, the sample size varies directly with the expected deviation rate (especially in terms of larger samples when the expected rate nears the tolerable rate).

Population Size. Common sense probably tells you that samples should be larger for bigger populations (a direct relationship). Strictly speaking, your common sense is accurate. As

---

[1] The association of tolerable deviation rates with control risks starts at 1 percent for $CR = 0.05$; then the tolerable deviation rate increases 1 percent for each 0.05 increment in control risk. Accounting firms have a variety of policies. Some start with a 1 percent minimum tolerable deviation for the lowest control risk level, others start with higher rates.

EXHIBIT E–4	SAMPLE SIZE RELATIONSHIPS: TEST OF CONTROLS AUDITING

	Predetermined Sample Size Will Be		
Sample Size Influence	High Rate or Large Population	Low Rate or Small Population	Sample Size Relationship
a. Acceptable sampling risk.	Smaller	Larger	Inverse
b. Tolerable deviation rate.	Smaller	Larger	Inverse
c. Expected population deviation rate.	Larger	Smaller	Direct
d. Population size.	Larger*	Smaller*	Direct

*Effect on sample size is quite small for populations of 1,000 or more.

a practical matter, however, an appropriate sample size for a population of 100,000 units may be only 2 or 3 sampling units larger than an appropriate sample size for a 10,000-unit population. Not much difference! The power of the mathematics of probability is at work.

The preceding discussion of sample size determinants is intended to give you a general understanding of the four influences on sample size. These influences are applicable to both statistical and nonstatistical sampling. A summary is presented in Exhibit E–4. For further information about how to calculate a sample size, refer to Module F.

5. Select the Sample

Auditing standards express two requirements for samples: (1) Sampling units must be selected from the population to which an audit conclusion will apply, ideally from transactions executed throughout the period under audit, and (2) a sample must be representative of the population from which it is drawn. In this context, a **representative sample** is one that *mirrors the characteristics of the population*. Auditors, however, cannot guarantee representativeness. After all, that is what sampling risk is all about—the probability that the sample might not mirror the population well enough.

Auditors can try to attain representativeness by selecting random samples. A sample is considered **random** if *each unit in the population has an equal probability of being included in the sample*. Intentional or accidental exclusion of a segment population can render a sample nonrepresentative. A popular way to select random samples is to associate each population unit with a unique number (easily done if the population units are prenumbered documents), then obtain a selection of random numbers to identify the sample units. You can use a printed random number table or a computerized random number generator to obtain a list of random numbers. This method is known as **unrestricted random selection.**

Another popular method is called **systematic random selection**. You need to know the population size and have a predetermined sample size to use it. The process is: (1) obtain a random starting place in the physical representation (list of sales invoices recorded in a sales journal, for example) and select that unit, then (2) count through the file and select every k^{th} unit, where k = Population size ÷ Sample size. For example, if 10,000 invoices, numbered from 32071 to 42070, were issued, and you want a sample of 200, first use a random number table to get a starting place, say at invoice #35000, then select every k^{th} = 10,000 ÷ 200, = 50th invoice. So the next would be #35050, then #35100 . . . , then #42050, then #32100, #32150, and so on. (At the end of the list, you cycle back through the invoices #32071 through #34940.) Most systematic samples are selected using five or more random starts. (See the example in Exhibit E–3.)

Sample selection is the first step where a distinction between statistical and nonstatistical audit sampling is crucial. *For statistical sampling evaluation, the sample must be random.*

In nonstatistical plans, auditors sometimes use sample selection methods whose randomness and representativeness cannot be evaluated easily. **Haphazard selection** refers to any *unsystematic way of selecting sample units*; for example, closing your eyes and dipping into a file drawer of sales invoices to pick items. The problem is that you may pick only the dog-eared ones that stick out, and they may be different from most of the other invoices in the drawer. Also, you cannot describe your method so someone else can **replicate** it—*reperform your selection procedure and get the same sample units*. Some auditors describe haphazard sampling as a method of choosing items without any special reason for including or excluding items, thus obtaining a representative sample. However, haphazard selection should be considered only as a last resort because it is hard to document and impossible to replicate.

Another method is **block sampling**, which is the practice of *choosing segments of contiguous transactions*; for example, choosing the sales invoices processed on randomly chosen days, say February 3, July 17, and September 29. Implicitly, the block sampling auditor has defined the population unit as a business day (260 to 365 of them in a year) and has selected three—not much of a sample. Block sampling is undesirable because it is hard to get a representative sample of blocks efficiently. When you have enough blocks, you have a huge number of invoices to audit.

6. Perform the Test of Controls Procedures.

Now you are ready to obtain the evidence. A **test of controls audit program** consists of procedures designed to produce evidence about the effectiveness of client's internal control performance. The test of controls procedures listed in the box on page 591 can be performed to determine how well the client's control activities were followed on the transactions that affect accounts receivable. After each action part of a procedure, the parenthetical note tells you the control objective the auditor is testing.

REVIEW
CHECKPOINTS

E.8 In test controls auditing, why is it necessary to define a control deviation in advance? Give seven examples of control deviations.

E.9 Which judgments must an auditor make when deciding on a sample size for test of controls audit sampling?

Describe the influence of each judgment on sample size.

E.10 What criterion must be met if a sample is to be considered random?

E.11 Name and describe four sample selection methods.

Evaluate the Evidence (Step 7)

LEARNING OBJECTIVE
3c. Evaluate evidence from a test of controls audit.

The final step represents the **evidence evaluation** phase of the sampling method. First, you *recognized the problem* as the task of determining whether each specified key control activity worked satisfactorily. Then you *gathered relevant compliance evidence*. Now you need to *evaluate* the evidence and *make justifiable decisions* about the control risk.

Test of controls audit sampling is undertaken to provide evidence of whether a client's internal control activities are being performed satisfactorily. Compliance evidence, therefore, is very important for the conclusion about control risk. When auditors evaluate sample-based compliance evidence, they run the sampling risks of making one of two decision errors: assessing the control risk too low, or assessing the control risk too high. These two decision errors are related to the idea of sampling risk presented earlier.

The **risk of assessing the control risk too low** is the probability that the compliance evidence in the sample indicates low control risk when the actual (but unknown) degree of compliance does not justify such a low control risk assessment. Assessing the control risk too low can lead to auditors' failure to do additional work that should be done. Assessing the control risk too low creates a threat to the *effectiveness* of the audit.

The **risk of assessing the control risk too high** is the probability that the compliance evidence in the sample indicates high control risk when the actual (but unknown)

TEST OF CONTROLS AUDITING

1. Select a sample of recorded sales invoices and:
   a. Determine whether a shipping document is attached (evidence of *validity*).
   b. Determine whether credit was approved (evidence of *authorization*).
   c. Determine whether product prices on the invoice agree with the approved price list (evidence of *authorization* and *accuracy*).
   d. Compare the quantity billed to the quantity shipped (evidence of *accuracy*).
   e. Recalculate the invoice arithmetic (evidence of *accuracy*).
   f. Compare the shipment date with the invoice record date (evidence of *proper period*).
   g. Trace the invoice to posting in the general ledger control account and in the correct customer's account (evidence of *accounting/posting*).
   h. Note the type of product shipped and determine proper classification in the right product-line revenue account (evidence of *classification*).
2. Select a sample of shipping orders and:
   a. Trace them to recorded sales invoices (evidence of *completeness*).
   b. The procedures in 1b, 1c, 1d, 1e, 1f, 1g and 1h also could be performed on the sales invoices produced by this sample. However, the work need not be duplicated.
3. Select a sample of recorded cash receipts and:
   a. Vouch them to deposits in the bank statement (evidence of *validity*).
   b. Vouch discounts taken by customers to proper approval or policy (evidence of *authorization*).
   c. Recalculate the cash summarized for a daily deposit or posting (evidence of *accuracy*).
   d. Trace the deposit to the right cash account (evidence of *classification*).
   e. Compare the date of receipt to the recording date (evidence of *proper period*).
   f. Trace the receipts to postings in the correct customer's accounts (evidence of *accounting/posting*).
4. Select a sample of daily cash reports or another source of original cash records and:
   a. Trace to the cash receipts journal (evidence of *completeness*).
   b. The procedures in 3b, 3c, 3d, 3e, and 3f also could be performed on this cash receipts sample. However, the work need not be duplicated.
5. Scan the accounts receivable for posting from sources other than the sales and cash receipts journals (e.g., general journal adjusting entries, credit memos). Vouch a sample of such entries to supporting documents (evidence of *validity, authorization, accuracy,* and *classification*).

This program describes the **nature** of the procedures. Each is a specific application of one of the general procedures.

degree of compliance would justify a *lower* control risk assessment. Assessing the control risk too high tends to trigger more audit work than was planned originally. Assessing the control risk too high threatens the *efficiency* of the audit.

Audit efficiency is certainly important, but audit effectiveness is considered more important. For this reason, auditing standards require auditors to allow for a low level of risk of assessing the control risk too low, especially when this decision error could cause an auditor to do significantly less work on the related account balances. These risks and

| EXHIBIT E–5 | THE TEST OF CONTROLS AUDIT SAMPLING DECISION MATRIX |

		Unknown Actual Deviation Rate	
Decision Alternatives (based on sample evidence)		Less than Tolerable Rate	Greater than Tolerable Rate
The population deviation rate is less than the tolerable rate, so the control is performed satisfactorily.		Correct decision	Control risk too low decision error.
The population deviation rate is greater than the tolerable rate, so the control is **not** performed satisfactorily.		Control risk too high decision error.	Correct decision.

decisions are illustrated in Exhibit E–5. Keeping these risks in mind, the evaluation of evidence consists of calculating the sample deviation rate, comparing it to the tolerable rate, and following up all the deviations discovered.

Calculate the Sample Deviation Rate

The first piece of hard evidence is the sample deviation rate. Suppose an auditor selected 200 recorded sales invoices and vouched them to shipping documents (bills of lading), finding 4 without shipping documents. The sample deviation rate is $4 \div 200 = 2$ percent. This is the best single-point estimate of the actual, but unknown, deviation rate in the population. However, you cannot say that the deviation rate in the population is *exactly* 2 percent. Chances are the sample is not *exactly* representative, so the actual but unknown population deviation rate could be lower or higher.

Judge the Deviation Rate in Relation to the Tolerable Rate and the Risk of Assessing the Control Risk Too Low

Suppose the auditor in the example believed the tolerable rate was 8 percent to justify a control risk assessment of $CR = 0.40$. In a nonstatistical sampling application, this auditor is supposed to think about the sample deviation rate (2 percent) in relation to the tolerable rate (8 percent), and he or she is supposed to think about the risk (of assessing control risk too low) that the actual, but unknown, deviation rate in the population exceeds 8 percent. The decision in a nonstatistical evaluation depends on the auditor's experience and expertise. In our example, a nonstatistical auditor might conclude that the population deviation rate probably does not exceed 8 percent because the sample deviation rate of 2 percent is so much lower.

In a statistical sample evaluation, an auditor does things that are more explainable in a textbook. He or she establishes decision criteria by (1) assigning a number to the risk of assessing the control risk too low, say 10 percent, and (2) assigning a number to the tolerable rate, say 8 percent. Then a statistical table is used to calculate a **sampling error-adjusted upper limit** which is the *sample deviation rate adjusted upward to allow for the idea that the actual population rate could be higher.* In this example, the adjusted limit (call it CUL for "computed upper limit) can be calculated to be 4 percent. This finding can be interpreted to mean: "The probability is 10 percent that the actual but unknown population deviation rate is greater than 4 percent." The decision criterion was: "The actual but unknown population deviation rate needs to be 8 percent or lower, with 10 percent risk of assessing the control risk too low." So the decision criterion is satisfied, and the control risk assessment (0.40) associated with the 8 percent tolerable rate can be justified.[2]

---

[2] Changing the example to suppose 11 deviations were found creates a problem for the nonstatistical sampler. He or she must think harder about the evidence (a 5.5 percent sample rate) in relation to the tolerable rate (8 percent) and acceptable risk. The statistical sampler can measure the CUL at 8.3 percent, which is greater than the 8 percent tolerable rate at 10 percent risk. The control fails the decision criterion test. Module A contains more information about making these calculations using statistical tables and formulas.

Follow Up All the Deviations

All the evaluation described so far has been mostly *quantitative* in nature, involving counts of deviations, deviation rates, and tolerable rate and risk judgment criteria. *Qualitative* evaluation is also necessary in the form of following up all the deviations to determine their nature and cause. A single deviation can be the tip of the iceberg—the telltale sign of a more pervasive deficiency. Auditors are obligated by the standard of due audit care to investigate known deviations so nothing important and within grasp will be overlooked.

The qualitative evaluation is sometimes called **error analysis** because each deviation from a prescribed client control activity is investigated to determine its nature, cause, and probable effect on financial statements. The analysis is essentially judgmental and involves auditors' determination of whether the deviation is (1) a pervasive error in principle made systematically on all like transactions or just a mistake on the particular transaction; (2) a deliberate or intentional control breakdown, rather than unintentional; (3) a result of misunderstanding of instructions or careless inattention to control duties; or (4) directly or remotely related to a money amount measurement in the financial statements. You can see that different qualitative perceptions of the seriousness of a deviation would result from error-analysis findings.

When the decision criteria are not satisfied and the preliminary conclusion is that the control risk is higher than the planned assessed control risk, the auditors need to decide what to do next. The deviation follow-up can give auditors comfort for deciding to do more account balance audit work by changing the nature, timing, and extent of other audit procedures; that is, by not limiting the work in reliance on the client's particular internal control activities. If the audit manager hesitates to make this commitment to do more audit work, he or she can enlarge the sample and perform the test of controls audit procedures on more sample units in hopes of deciding that the control risk is actually lower. However, when faced with the preliminary "nonreliance" decision, you should never manipulate the quantitative evaluation by raising the tolerable rate or the risk of assessing the control risk too low. Supposedly, these two decision criteria were carefully determined in the planning stage, so now only new information would be a good basis for easing them.

Timing of Test of Controls Audit Procedures

Earlier in the module you learned that auditors can perform the test of controls audit procedures at an *interim date*—a date some weeks or months before the client's year-end date. When test of controls auditing is timed early, an audit manager must decide what to do about the remaining period (e.g., the period October through December after doing test of controls auditing in September for a December 31 year-end audit).

The decision turns on several factors: (1) The results of the work at interim might, for example, indicate poor control performance and high control risk; (2) inquiries made after interim may show that a particular control activity has been abandoned or improved; (3) the length of the remaining period may be short enough to forgo additional work or long enough to suggest a need for continuing the test of controls audit; (4) the dollar amounts affected by the control activity may have been much larger or much smaller than before; (5) evidence obtained about control as a byproduct of performing substantive procedures covering the remaining period may show enough about control performance that separate work on the control activity performance might not be necessary; or (6) work performed by the company's internal auditors might be relied on with respect to the remaining period.

Depending on the circumstances indicated by these sources of information, an audit manager can decide to: (1) continue the test of controls audit work because knowledge of the state of control performance is necessary to justify restriction of other audit work or (2) stop further test of controls audit work because (*a*) compliance evidence derived from other procedures provides sufficient evidence or (*b*) information shows the control has failed, control risk is high, and other work will not be restricted. Whatever the final judgment, considerations of audit effectiveness and efficiency should always be uppermost in the audit manager's mind.

E.12 Why should auditors be more concerned in test of controls auditing with the risk of assessing the control risk too low than with the risk of assessing the control risk too high?

E.13 What important decision must be made when test of controls auditing is performed and control risk is evaluated at an interim date several weeks or months before the client's fiscal year-end-date?

SUBSTANTIVE PROCEDURES FOR AUDITING ACCOUNT BALANCES

LEARNING OBJECTIVE
4. Develop a simple audit program for an account balance audit considering the influence of risk and tolerable misstatement.

When audit sampling is used for auditing the assertions in account balances, the main feature of interest is the *monetary amount* of the population units, not the presence or absence of control deviations, as is the case with attribute sampling. Test of controls auditing is a part of the evaluation of internal control. **Substantive tests of details auditing** is the *performance of procedures to obtain direct evidence about the dollar amounts and disclosures in the financial statements.*

Substantive-purpose procedures include (1) analytical procedures and (2) test (audit) of details of transactions and balances. Analytical procedures involve overall comparisons of account balances with prior balances, financial relationships, nonfinancial information, budgeted or forecasted balances, and balances derived from estimates calculated by auditors. Analytical procedures are usually not applied on a sample basis. So, substantive-purpose procedures for auditing details are the normal procedures used in account balance audit sampling.

Risk Model Expansion

Up to now you have worked with a conceptual risk model that had a single term for "detection risk" (DR.) The detection risk is actually a combination of two risks: **Analytical procedures risk (AP)** is the probability that analytical procedures will fail to detect material errors, and the **risk of incorrect acceptance (RIA)** is the probability that test-of-detail procedures will *fail* to detect material errors.[3] The two types of procedures are considered independent, so detection risk is DR = AP × RIA, and the expanded risk model is:

$$AR = IR \times CR \times AP \times RIA$$

This model is still a conceptual tool, The expansion of it did not make auditing any less professional. It can now be used to help you understand some elements of sampling for auditing the details of account balances. First, recognize that auditors exercise professional judgment in assessing the inherent risk (IR), control risk (CR), analytical procedures risk (AP), *and* the audit risk (AR). If these four risks are given, you can then manipulate the model to express the risk of incorrect acceptance (RIA):

$$RIA = \frac{AR}{IR \times CR \times AP}$$

---

[3] In the auditing standards, the RIA has another name—"TD," meaning "test of details" risk (*SAS 39, AU 350*)

EXHIBIT E-6	THE ACCOUNT BALANCE AUDIT SAMPLING DECISION MATRIX

	Unknown Actual Account Balance Is	
Decision Alternatives (based on sample evidence)	Materially* Accurate	Materially* Misstated
The book value of the account is materially accurate.	Correct decision.	Incorrect acceptance.
The book value of the account is materially misstated.	Incorrect rejection.	Correct decision.

*Materially in this context refers to the "tolerable misstatement" assigned to the account balance.

With AR, IR, and AP held constant, RIA varies *inversely* with CR; that is, the higher the control risk (CR), the lower the acceptable risk of incorrect acceptance (RIA), and vice versa.

More about Sampling Risk

Substantive-purpose procedures are performed to produce the evidence necessary to enable an auditor to decide whether an account balance is or is not fairly presented in conformity with GAAP. Thus, auditors run the sampling risks of making one of two decision errors. The **risk of incorrect acceptance (RIA)** represents the decision to accept a balance as being materially accurate when, in fact (unknown to the auditor), the balance is *materially misstated*. The other decision error risk is the **risk of incorrect rejection,** and represents the decision that a balance is materially misstated when, in fact, it *is*. These sampling risk relationships are shown in Exhibit E–6.

Incorrect Acceptance

The risk of incorrect acceptance is considered the more important of the two decision error risks. When an auditor decides an account book balance is materially accurate (hence, needs no adjustment or change), the audit work on that account is considered finished, the decision is documented in the working papers, and the audit team proceeds to work on other accounts. When the account is, in fact, materially misstated, an unqualified opinion on the financial statements may be unwarranted. Incorrect acceptance damages the *effectiveness* of the audit.

Incorrect Rejection

When an auditor decides an account book balance is materially misstated, some more audit work on that account is performed to determine the amount of an adjustment to recommend. The risk, however, is that the book balance really is a materially accurate representation of the (unknown) actual value. At this point, the event of *incorrect rejection* is about to be realized, and the audit manager may be inclined to recommend an adjustment that is not needed.

However, incorrect rejection is not considered to be as serious an error as incorrect acceptance. When auditors first begin to think a balance may contain a material misstatement, efforts will be made to determine why the misstatement occurred and to estimate the amount. Thus, *more* evidence will be sought by the audit team or provided by the client. The data will be reviewed for a source of systematic error. The amounts of discovered misstatements will be analyzed carefully. Client personnel may be assigned to do a complete analysis to determine a more accurate account balance.

If the initial decision was, in fact, a decision error of incorrect rejection, this other work should allow the auditors to determine whether the recorded amount is really misstated or the sample was not representative. Hence, incorrect rejection is not considered as serious as incorrect acceptance because steps will be taken to determine the amount of misstatement and the erroneous decision has a chance to be reversed. Incorrect rejection thus affects the *efficiency* of an audit by causing unnecessary work.

Materiality and Tolerable Misstatement

Determining a threshold for the materiality of misstatements in financial statements is a tough problem under any circumstances. Audit sampling for the substantive audit of particular account balances adds another wrinkle. Auditors also must decide on an amount of **tolerable misstatement** which is a judgment of the *maximum monetary misstatement that may exist in an account balance or class of transactions without causing the financial statements to be materially misstated.* Audit risk (AR in the risk model for a particular account), therefore, is the risk that all the audit work on an account balance will not result in discovery of actual misstatement equal to the tolerable misstatement when this much or more misstatement exists in an account.

Auditors must judge the materiality of misstatement overall, then assign a part of that amount to all the account(s) and account groupings. Suppose, for purposes of illustration, an audit manager decided that an income-before-taxes misstatement of $71,000 would be material. Using the "top-down approach," he or she needs to decide where parts of this *allowable misstatement* can exist, so the audit work can be directed to the important areas. Suppose the manager can justify allocating $10,000 to sales, $46,000 to cost of goods sold, and $15,000 to expenses. The allocations suggest that each of these accounts and account groups could be overstated (or understated) by these amounts. Even if all the misstatements were in the same direction, they would still only add up to the $71,000 considered material.

If sales are overstated, chances are that the accounts receivable is overstated. The audit manager can reason that the material amount assigned to sales also can be assigned to the accounts receivable audit work. Now, suppose the manager decides that a good way to audit for sales overstatement is to audit the receivables for overstatement. If the receivables are audited with allowance for $10,000 of misstatement, that will take care of part of the audit for sales overstatement. This $10,000 is the **tolerable misstatement** planned for the audit of the accounts receivable on a sample basis.

SAMPLING STEPS FOR ACCOUNT BALANCE AUDIT

Audit sampling for the audit of account balances is structured much like the steps you studied in connection with test of controls audit sampling. As the steps are explained, an example related to auditing receivables is used. Remember, the example used with regard to test of controls sampling was the audit of a control activity designed to prevent the recording of sales invoices without shipping documents. Now we move on to the next stage of work that can produce independent evidence of sales overstatement resulting from a breakdown of the control or from other causes. The seven-step framework explained in the next sections helps auditors plan, perform, and evaluate account balance detail audit work. It also helps auditors accomplish an eighth step—careful documentation of the work—by showing each of the seven areas to be described in the working papers. The first seven steps are:

1. Specify the audit objectives.
2. Define the population.
3. Choose an audit sampling method.
4. Determine the sample size.
5. Select the sample.
6. Perform the substantive-purpose procedures.
7. Evaluate the evidence.

Plan the Procedures

LEARNING OBJECTIVE

4a. Specify objectives and define a population for data.

The three planning steps represent the **problem-recognition** phase of the sampling method. When a client presents the financial statements, the assertions include (for example): "The trade accounts receivable exist and are bona fide obligations owed to the company" (ownership); "All the accounts receivable are recorded" (*completeness*); "They are stated at net realizable value" (*valuation*); and "They are properly *classified as current assets, presented, and disclosed* in conformity with GAAP." Each assertion represents a hypothesis (problem) to be tested; for example, "The trade accounts receivable exist as bona fide obligations owed to the company." A test of this hypothesis is the objective. The set of recorded accounts receivable is the population of data.

1. Specify the Audit Objectives

When performing accounts receivable confirmation on a sample basis, the specific objective is to decide whether the client's assertions about *existence, rights (ownership)*, and *valuation* are materially accurate. In this context, the auditing is viewed as **hypothesis testing**—the auditors hypothesize that *the book value is materially accurate about existence, ownership, and valuation*. The evidence will enable them to accept or reject the hypothesis. The audit objective is to determine the monetary misstatement found by comparing the recorded balances to the balances determined from the evidence.

Accountants can use similar sampling methods for **dollar-value estimation objective,** which is the job of *helping a client obtain an estimate of an amount*. Examples include estimation of inventory LIFO indexes and data or current cost accounting information. In dollar-value estimation, the objective is to develop a basic measurement, not to audit the balance or amount. Audit sampling, in the following discussion, adopts the objective of hypothesis testing.

2. Define the Population

Auditors need to be sure the definition of the population matches the objectives. Defining the population as the recorded accounts receivable balances suits the objective of obtaining evidence about existence, ownership, and valuation. This definition also suits the related objective of obtaining evidence about sales overstatement. In the case of accounts receivable, each customer's account balance is a population unit. However, if the objectives were to obtain evidence about completeness and sales understatement, the *recorded* accounts receivable would be the wrong population.

Ordinarily, the sampling unit is the same as the population unit. Sometimes, however, it is easier to define the sampling unit as a smaller part of a population unit. For example, if the client's accounting system keeps track of individual invoices charged to customers, an auditor might want to audit a sample of invoices by confirming them with customers instead of working with each customer's balance.

Since a sample will be drawn from a physical representation of the population (e.g., a printed trial balance or magnetic disk file of customers' accounts), the auditors must determine whether it is complete. Footing the trial balance and reconciling it to the control account total will accomplish the job.

Auditing standards require auditors to use their judgment to determine whether any population units should be removed from the population and audited separately (not sampled) because taking sampling risk (risk of incorrect acceptance or incorrect rejection) with respect to them is not justified. Suppose the accounts receivable in our example amounted to $400,000, but six of the customers had balances of $10,000 or more, for a sum of $100,000. The next largest account balance is less than $10,000. The six accounts are considered **individually significant items** because each of them exceeds the tolerable misstatement amount, and they should be removed from the population and audited completely.

In the jargon of audit sampling related to account balances, *subdividing* the population is known as **stratification**. The total population is subdivided into subpopulations by account balance size. For example, a small number of accounts totaling $75,000 may be

AUDITING INSIGHT

STRATIFICATION EXAMPLE

The stratification below subdivides the population into a first set of six individually significant accounts and four strata, which each have approximately one fourth ($75,000) of the remaining dollar balance. You can see the typical situation in which the accounts of smaller value are more numerous.

The example also shows one kind of allocation of a sample size of 90 to four strata. When each stratum get one fourth of the sample size, the sample is skewed toward the higher-value accounts: The second stratum has 23 in the sample out of 80 in the stratum, and the fifth stratum has 23 out of 910 in the stratum.

Stratum	Book Value	Number	Amount	Sample
1	Over $10,000	6	$100,000	6
2	$625–$9,999	80	75,068	23
3	$344–$624	168	75,008	22
4	$165–$343	342	75,412	23
5	$1–$164	910	74,512	23
		1,506	$400,000	96

This kind of stratification takes care of the normal situation in which the variability of the account balances and errors in them tend to be larger in the high-value accounts than in the low-value accounts. As a consequence, the sample includes a larger proportion of the high-value accounts (23/80) and a smaller portion of the low-value accounts (23/910).

identified as the first (large balance) stratum when four strata are defined. Three more strata may be defined, each containing a total of approximately $75,000 of the recorded balances, but each made up of a successively larger *number* of customer accounts whose average balance is successively smaller. Stratification can be used to increase *audit efficiency* (smaller total sample size).[4]

3. Choose an Audit Sampling Method
You already have been introduced to statistical and nonstatistical sampling methods. At this point, an auditor must decide which to use. If he or she chooses statistical sampling, another choice needs to be made. In statistical sampling, **classical variables sampling** methods that utilize *normal distribution theory* are available. Probability proportionate to size sampling (PPS) (or **dollar-unit sampling**), which utilizes *attribute sampling theory*, also can be used. Some of the technical characteristics of the statistical methods are explained more fully in Module G.

The calculation examples shown later in this module use the difference and ratio methods of classical variables sampling. These calculations are relatively simple and illustrate the points adequately. However, PPS sampling is used more often in practice. The PPS calculations are a little more complex, and, used here, they would complicate the illustrations unnecessarily. PPS calculations are covered in Module G.

Perform the Procedures

LEARNING OBJECTIVE

4*b*. Determine sample size and select sampling units.

The next three steps represent the **evidence-collection** phase of the sampling method. These steps are performed to get the evidence.

---

[4] Automotic stratification is obtained when auditors use probability proportionate to size (PPS). This method is explained in Module G.

Figuring sample size for account balance auditing requires consideration of several influences. The main reason for figuring a sample size in advance is to help guard against underauditing (not obtaining enough evidence) and overauditing (obtaining more evidence than needed). Another important reason is to control the cost of the audit. An arbitrary sample size *could* be used to perform the accounts receivable confirmation procedures; but, if it turned out to be too small, sending and processing more confirmations might be impossible before the audit report deadline. Alternative procedures then could become costly and time-consuming. A predetermined sample size is not as important in other situations where the auditors can increase the sample simply by choosing more items available for audit in the client's office.

4. Determine the Sample size

Whether using statistical or nonstatistical sampling methods, auditors first need to establish *decision criteria* for the risk of incorrect acceptance, the risk of incorrect rejection, and the tolerable misstatement. Also, auditors need to estimate the expected dollar amount of misstatement and the variability within the population. The three decision criteria and the estimated misstatement and variability information should be determined before any evidence is obtained from a sample.

a. Risk of Incorrect Acceptance (RIA). This risk can be assessed in terms of the audit risk model. An acceptable risk of incorrect acceptance depends on the assessments of inherent risk, control risk, and analytical procedures risk. The risk of incorrect acceptance varies *inversely* with the combined product of the other risks. The larger the combined product of the other risks, the smaller is the acceptable risk of incorrect acceptance.

Suppose, for example, two different auditors independently assess the client's control risk and their own analytical procedures and arrive at the following conclusions. Assume both auditors believe an appropriate audit risk—AR—is 0.05:

Auditor A believes the inherent risk is high (IR = 1.0), the control risk is moderate (CR = 0.50), and analytical procedures will not be performed (AP = 1.0). Audit procedures need to be so planned that the risk of incorrect acceptance will be about 10 percent.

$$RIA = \frac{AR}{IR \times CR \times AP} = \frac{0.05}{1.0 \times 0.50 \times 1.0} = 0.10$$

Auditor B believes the inherent risk is high (IR = 1.0), the control risk is very low (CR = 0.20), and analytical procedures will not be performed (AP = 1.0). Audit procedures need to be so planned that the risk of incorrect acceptance will be about 25 percent.

$$RIA = \frac{AR}{IR \times CR \times AP} = \frac{0.05}{1.0 \times 0.20 \times 1.0} = 0.25$$

Use the model with caution. The lesson you should learn from these examples is that auditor A's account balance sampling work must provide less risk that that of auditor B. Since *sample size varies inversely with the risk of incorrect acceptance,* auditor A's sample will be larger. In fact, when the control risk is lower, as in auditor B's evaluation, the acceptable risk of incorrect acceptance (RIA) is higher. Thus, auditor B's sample of customers' accounts receivable can be smaller than auditor A's sample.

b. Risk of Incorrect Rejection. Like the risk of incorrect acceptance, the risk of incorrect rejection exists both in statistical and nonstatistical sampling applications. It can be controlled, usually by auditing a larger sample. So, sample size varies inversely with the risk of incorrect rejection. The determination of the risk of incorrect rejection in a cost trade-off analysis is discussed in Module G.

c. Tolerable Misstatement. The tolerable misstatement—part of the overall materiality of misstatements—also must be considered in nonstatistical as well as statistical sampling applications. In statistical sampling, tolerable misstatement must be expressed as a dollar

EXHIBIT E–7	SAMPLE SIZE RELATIONSHIPS: AUDIT OF ACCOUNT BALANCES

		Predetermined Sample Size Will Be		
	Sample Size Influence	High Rate or Large Amount	Low Rate or Small Amount	Sample Size Relation
a.	Risk of incorrect acceptance.	Smaller	Larger	Inverse
b.	Risk of incorrect rejection.	Smaller	Larger	Inverse
c.	Tolerable misstatement.	Smaller	Larger	Inverse
d.	Expected misstatment.	Larger	Smaller	Direct
e.	Population variability.	Larger	Smaller	Direct
f.	Population size.	Larger	Smaller	Direct

amount. The sample size varies inversely with the amount of the tolerable misstatement for an account. The greater the tolerable misstatement, the smaller the sample size needed.

d. Expected Dollar Misstatement. Auditors need to estimate an "expected dollar misstatement" amount. The estimate may be based on last year's audit findings or on other knowledge of the accounting system. Expectations of dollar misstatement have the effect of reducing the allowable tolerable misstatement. The more dollar misstatement expected, the less "tolerable misstatement cushion" remains. Sample sizes should be larger when more dollar misstatement is expected. So, sample size varies directly with the amount of expected dollar misstatement.

e. Variability within the Population. Auditors using nonstatistical sampling must take into account the degree of dispersion among unit values in a population. The typical skewness of some accounting populations needs to be taken into account. **Skewness** is the concentration of a large proportion of the dollar amount in an account in a small number of the population items. In our illustration, $100,000 (25 percent) of the total accounts receivable is in 6 customers' accounts while the remaining $300,000 is in 1,500 customers' accounts.

As a general rule, auditors should be careful about populations whose unit values range widely, say from $1 to $10,000. Obtaining a *representative sample* in such a case, as you might imagine, would take a larger sample than if the range of the unit values were only from $1 to $500. Sample size should vary directly with the magnitude of the variability of population unit values. Populations with high variability should be stratified, as previously shown in the stratification example.

Auditors using classical sampling methods must obtain an estimate of the population **standard deviation**, which is a measure of the population variability. When using PPS sampling, the variability is taken into account with the expected dollar misstatement, and no separate estimate of a standard deviation needs to be made.

These five influences, plus the influence of population size on sample size, are summarized in Exhibit E–7.

5. Select the Sample

As was the case with test of controls audit samples, account balance samples must be representative. Nothing is new about the selection methods. You can use unrestricted random selection and systematic selection to obtain the random samples necessary for statistical applications. Haphazard and block selection methods have the same drawbacks as they have in test of controls audit samples.

6. Perform the Substantive-Purpose Procedures

The basic assertions in a presentation of accounts receivable are that they *exist as* claims against real customers, they are *complete* (no receivables are unrecorded), the company has the *right* to collect the money, they are *valued* properly at net realizable value, and

AUDITING INSIGHT

PRELIMINARY SAMPLE SIZE GUIDANCE

The AICPA has drafted some guidance for nonstatistical sample size calculations. It uses an "assurance factor" that is based on an underlying statistical concept. (In Module G this "assurance factor" is called the "Poisson Risk Factor.") The guidance defines sample size as:

$$\text{Sample size} = \frac{\text{Population Recorded Amount}}{\text{Tolerable Misstatement}} \times \text{Assurance Factor}$$

The assurance factors are based on the audit risk model, which does not take into account the risk of incorrect rejection or the expected dollar misstatement; and, this sample size formula assumes the auditors will use a stratified sample selection method (explained in terms of PPS Sampling in Module G). These things should be taken into account subjectively, insofar as modifying the sample size produced by the formula is concerned. The assurance factors are:

When: Combined Control and Inherent Risk (CR × IR) are:	And When Other, Analytical Procedures Risk (AP) is:			
	1.0	0.75	0.50	0.35
1.00	3.0	2.7	2.3	2.0
0.75	2.7	2.4	2.1	1.6
0.50	2.3	2.1	1.6	1.2
0.35	2.0	1.6	1.2	1.0

NOTE: The underlying Audit Risk (AR) = 0.05.
Examples:

$$\text{Sample size} = \frac{\$300,000}{\$10,000} \times 3.0 = 90$$

$$\text{Sample size} = \frac{\$300,000}{\$10,000} \times 1.6 = 48$$

they are *presented and disclosed properly in conformity with GAAP*. A **substantive-purpose audit program** consists of account balance-related procedures designed to produce evidence about these assertions. The substantive-purpose procedures usually performed on a sample basis are listed in the box below.

ACCOUNT BALANCE AUDITING

1. Obtain an aged trial balance of the receivables. Select a sample of the current accounts, and audit their aging accuracy.
2. Select a sample of customer accounts and send positive confirmations.
   a. Investigate exceptions reported by customers.
   b. Follow up nonrespondents by vouching sales charges and cash receipts to supporting documents.
   c. Vouch balances to subsequent cash received in payment.
3. Select a sample of past due accounts.
   a. Discuss collectibility with the credit manager.
   b. Obtain credit reports and financial statements for independent analysis of large overdue accounts.

The confirmation procedures should be performed for all the sampling units. The other procedures should be performed as necessary to complete the evidence relating to existence and gross valuation. The important thing is to audit *all* the sample units. You cannot simply discard one that is hard to audit in favor of adding to the sample a customer whose balance is easy to audit. This action might bias the sample. Sometimes, however, you will be unable to audit a sample unit. Suppose a customer did not respond to the confirmation requests, sales invoices supporting the balance could not be found, and no payment was received after the confirmation date. Auditing standards contain the following guidance (SAS 39, Au 350):

- If considering the entire balance to be misstated will not alter your evaluation conclusion, then you do not need to work on it any more. Your evaluation conclusion might be to *accept the book value*, as long as the account is not big enough to change the conclusion. Your evaluation conclusion already might be to *reject the book value*, and considering another account misstated just reinforces the decision.

- If considering the entire balance to be misstated would change an *acceptance* decision to a *rejection* decision, you need to do something about it. Since the example seems to describe a dead end, you may need to select more accounts (expand the sample), perform the procedures on them (other than confirmation), and reevaluate the results.

R E V I E W
CHECKPOINTS

E.14 Write the expanded risk model. What risk is implied for "test of detail risk" when: inherent risk = 1.0, control risk = 0.40, analytical procedures risk = 0.60, audit risk = 0.048, tolerable misstatement = $10,000, and the estimated standard deviation in the population = $25?

E.15 When auditing account balances, why is an incorrect acceptance decision considered more serious than an incorrect rejection decision?

E.16 What should be the relationship between tolerable misstatement in the audit of an account balance and the amount of monetary misstatement considered material to the overall financial statements?

E.17 What general set of audit objectives can you use as a frame of reference to be specific about the particular objectives for the audit of an account balance?

E.18 What audit purpose is served by stratifying an account balance population and by removing some units from the population for 100 percent audit attention?

E.19 What is the influence on dollar-value variables sample sizes of the risk of incorrect acceptance? Of the risk of incorrect rejection? Of the tolerable misstatement? Of the population variability and the population size?

Evaluate the Evidence (Step 7)

LEARNING OBJECTIVE
4c. Evaluate monetary misstatement evidence from a balance audit sample.

The final step represents the **evidence evaluation** and decision-making phase of the sampling method. Your decisions about existence, ownership, and valuation need to be *justifiable* by sufficient, competent quantitative and qualitative evidence. You should be concerned first with *quantitative* evaluation of the evidence. *Qualitative follow-up* is also important and is discussed later. The basic steps in quantitative evaluation are these:

- Figure the total amount of actual monetary misstatement found in the sample. This amount is the **known misstatement**.

- Project the known misstatement to the population. The projected amount is the **likely misstatement**

- Compare the likely misstatement (also called the "projected misstatement") to the tolerable misstatement for the account and consider the **risk of incorrect acceptance** that likely misstatement is calculated to be less than tolerable misstatement even though the actual misstatement in the population is greater; or the **risk of incorrect**

EXHIBIT E–8   HYPOTHETICAL SAMPLE DATA

Sample Item	Audited Amount	Recorded Amount	Difference* (Audited − Recorded)
1	$691	$691	$0
6	372	508	−136
23	136	141	−5
50	62	62	0
90	135	130	+5
Totals	$18,884	$19,289	$−405
Averages:			
Audited amount	$209.82		
Recorded amount		$214.32	
Difference			$−4.50

*A negative difference is an account *overstatement,* and a positive difference is an account *understatement.*

rejection that likely misstatement is calculated to be greater than tolerable misstatement, even though the actual misstatement in the population is smaller.

Amount of Known Misstatement
Now you need some illustrative numbers. Hypothetical audit evidence from a sample is shown in Exhibit E–8. The example cited earlier said total accounts receivable is $400,000, and $100,000 of the total is in six large balances, which are to be audited separately. The remainder is in 1,500 customer accounts whose balances range from $1 to $9,999. Suppose the audit team selected 90 of these accounts and applied the confirmation or vouching procedures to each of them. The evidence showed −$405 of actual misstatement representing overstatement of the recorded amounts (Exhibit E–8). This amount is the *known misstatement* for this sample of 90 customer accounts.

Project the Known Misstatement to the Population
To make a decision about the population, the known misstatement in the sample must be *projected to the population*. The key requirement for projecting the known misstatement to the population is that *the sample must be representative*. If the sample is not representative, a projection produces a nonsense number. Take an extreme example: Remember that all of the six largest accounts ($100,000 in total) were audited. Suppose one of them contained a $600 disputed amount. Investigation showed the customer was right, management agreed, so the $600 is the amount of known misstatement. If an auditor takes this group of six accounts as being representative of the population, projecting the $100 average misstatement to 1,506 accounts ($100 × 1,506) would project a total misstatement of $150,600, compared to the recorded accounts receivable total of $400,000. This projection is neither reasonable nor appropriate. The 6 large accounts are not representative of the entire population of 1,506 accounts. Nothing is wrong with the calculation method. The nonrepresentative "sample" is the culprit in this absurd result.

A projection based on a sample applies only to the population from which the sample was drawn. Consider the sample of 90 accounts from the population of 1,500. The average difference is $4.50 (overstatement of the recorded amount), so the projected **likely misstatement** is $6,750 (overstatement), provided the sample is representative. This projection method is called the **average difference method,** expressed in equation form as:

$$\text{Projected likely misstatement (Average difference method)} = \left[\frac{\begin{array}{c}\text{Dollar amount of}\\\text{misstatement in the sample}\end{array}}{\begin{array}{c}\text{Number of}\\\text{sampling units}\end{array}}\right] \times \left[\begin{array}{c}\text{Number of}\\\text{population}\\\text{units}\end{array}\right]$$

In the example:

$$\text{Projected likely misstatement (Average difference method)} = \frac{\$405}{90} \times 1{,}500 = \$6{,}750 \text{ (overstatement)}$$

How can you tell whether a sample is representative? You cannot guarantee representativeness, but you can try to attain it by selecting a random sample and by carefully subdividing (stratifying) the population according to an important characteristic, such as the size of individual customers' balances. When the population is stratified, each stratum is more homogeneous according to account size than the population as a whole, and the known misstatement in each can be projected.

You also can inspect the sample to see whether it shows the characteristics of the population. In the example, for instance, the average recorded amount of the population is $200 ($300,000 ÷ 1,500); the average in the illustrative unstratified sample is $214.32 (a little high). You also can look to see whether the sample contains a range of recorded amounts similar to the population that ranged from $1 to $9,999. With statistics, you can calculate the standard deviation of the sample recorded amounts and compare it to the standard deviation of the population.

Another projection method takes into account the fact that the average recorded account balance in the sample may turn out to be quite different from the population average. If you have reason to believe that the size of misstatement amounts is directly related to the size of the customers' accounts (e.g., larger receivables balances have larger differences), you can project using the **ratio method,** expressed in equation form as:

$$\text{Projected likely misstatement (Ratio method)} = \left[\frac{\begin{array}{c}\text{Dollar amount of}\\\text{misstatement in the sample}\end{array}}{\begin{array}{c}\text{Recorded amount}\\\text{in the sample}\end{array}}\right] \times \left[\begin{array}{c}\text{Recorded amount}\\\text{in the}\\\text{population}\end{array}\right]$$

In the example:

$$\text{Projected likely misstatement (Ratio method)} = \frac{\$405}{\$19{,}289} \times 300{,}000 = \$6{,}299 \text{ (overstatement)}$$

The first term in this equation is the *ratio of misstatement to recorded amount.* So the representativeness of the ratio is crucial. Auditors must be very careful to discern the representativeness of the average difference and the ratio. They also need to be very careful about the adequacy of the sample size. You can see that small samples which produce large or small dollar differences can distort both the average difference and the ratio, thus distorting the projected likely misstatement. One way to exercise care is to take the sampling risks into account.

Consider Sampling Risks
The risks of making wrong decisions (incorrect acceptance or incorrect rejection) exist in both nonstatistical and statistical sampling. The smaller the sample, the greater both

AUDITING INSIGHT

STRATIFICATION CALCULATION EXAMPLE

Projected Likely Misstatement: Average Difference Method

Stratification of population is said to be more *efficient* because you can usually calculate a smaller projected likely misstatement with the same sample size that would have been used in an unstratified sample (as illustrated in this module), or you can usually calculate the same projected likely misstatement with a smaller stratified sample. The example below illustrates a typical situation of finding larger misstatements in the larger accounts, resulting in a projected likely misstatement smaller than the $7,350 illustrated in the module for an unstratified sample ($600 in the six largest customer plus $6,750 projected from the sample of 90 from the other 1,500 customers).

The calculation of projected likely misstatements (PLM), using the difference method, is applied separately to each stratum. Then, the amounts are added to get the whole sample result.

Stratum	Number	Account	Sample	Misstatement*	PLM
1	6	$100,000	6	$ −600	$ −600
2	80	75,068	23	$ −274	$ −953
3	168	75,008	22	$ −66	−504
4	342	75,412	22	−88	−1,368
5	910	75,512	23	23	910
	1,506	$400,000	96	$−1,005	$−2,515

*A negative misstatement indicates *overstatement* of the book value, and a positive misstatement indicates *understatement*.

risks. Common sense tells you the less you know about a population because of a small sample, the more risk you run of making a wrong decision.

The problem is to consider the risk that the projected likely misstatement ($6,750 overstatement for the sample of 90 accounts in the example using the average difference method) could have been obtained even though the actual total misstatement in the population is *greater* than the tolerable misstatement ($10,000 in the example). Auditing guidance suggests you can use your experience and professional judgment to consider the risk. If the projected likely misstatement is considerably less than tolerable misstatement, chances are good that the total actual misstatement in the population is not greater than tolerable misstatement. However, when projected likely misstatement is close to tolerable misstatement (say, $6,750, compared to $10,000), the chance is not so good, and the risk of incorrect acceptance might exceed the acceptable risk (RIA) an auditor initially established as a decision criterion.

A similar situation exists with respect to the risk of incorrect rejection. Suppose the sample results had produced a projected likely misstatement of $15,000 overstatement. Now the question is: "What is the risk that this result was obtained even though the actual misstatement in the population is $10,000 or less?" Again, the judgment depends on the size of the sample and the kinds and distribution of misstatements discovered.

Auditors take the rejection decision as a serious matter and conduct enough additional investigation to determine the amount and adjustment required. Hence, the risk of incorrect rejection is mitigated by additional work necessary to determine the amount and nature of an adjustment. In the example, if the sample of 90 customers' accounts had shown total misstatement of $900 (yielding the $15,000 projected misstatement using the average difference method), most auditors would consider the evidence insufficient to propose a significant adjustment. (Incidentally, however, correction of the $900 should not by itself be a sufficient action to satisfy the auditors.)

When using nonstatistical sampling, auditors utilize their experience and expertise to take risks into account. Statistical samplers can add statistical calculations to these considerations of sampling risk. Further explanation of statistical calculations is in Module G.

Qualitative Evaluation

The numbers are not enough. Auditors are required to follow up each monetary difference to determine whether it arose from (a) misunderstanding of accounting principles, (b) simple mistakes or carelessness, (c) an intentional fraud, or (d) management override of internal control. Auditors also need to relate the differences to their effect on other amounts in the financial statements. For example, overstatements in accounts receivable may indicate overstatement of sales revenue.

Likewise, you should not overlook the information that can be obtained in account balance auditing about the performance of internal control activities—the dual-purpose characteristic of auditing procedures. Deviations (or absence of deviations) discovered when performing substantive procedures can help confirm or contradict an auditor's previous conclusion about control risk. If many more monetary differences arise than expected, the control risk conclusion may need to be revised, and more account balance auditing work may need to be done.

Knowledge of the source, nature, and amount of monetary differences is very important. Such knowledge is required to explain the situation to management and to direct additional work to areas where adjustments are needed. The audit work is not complete until the qualitative evaluation and follow-up is finished.

Evaluate the Amount of Misstatement

Auditing standards require the aggregation of *known misstatement* and *projected likely misstatement* (SAS 47, AU 312). The aggregation is the sum of (a) known misstatement in the population units identified for 100 percent audit (in the example, the six accounts totaling $100,000, with $600 overstatement discovered), and (b) the projected likely misstatement for the population sampled (in the example, the $6,750 overstatement projected using the average difference method). The theory underlying (b) is that the projected likely misstatement is the best single estimate of the amount that would be determined if *all* the accounts in the sampled population had been audited. You can see the importance of sample representativeness in this regard. This aggregation ($7,350 overstatement in the example) should be judged in combination with other misstatements found in the audit of other account balances to determine whether the financial statements taken as a whole need to be adjusted and, if so, in what amount.

The evaluation of amounts is not over yet, however. One thing that *cannot* be said about the projected likely misstatement is that it is the exact amount that would be found if all the units in the population were audited. The actual amount might be more or less, and the problem arises from **sampling error**—the amount by which a projected likely misstatement amount could differ from an actual (unknown) total misstatement as a result of the sample not being exactly representative. Of course, auditors are most concerned with the possibility that the actual total misstatement might be considerably larger than the projected likely misstatement.

This sampling phenomenon gives rise to the concept of **possible misstatement** (the third kind, in addition to known and likely misstatement), which is interpreted in auditing standards as the *further misstatement remaining undetected* in the units not selected in the sample (SAS 47, AU 312). Nonstatistical auditors resort to experience and professional judgment to consider additional possible misstatement. Statistical auditors, however, can utilize some statistical calculations to measure possible misstatement.

Timing of Substantive Audit Procedures

Account balances can be audited, at least in part, at an interim date. When this work is done before the company's year-end-date, auditors must extend the interim-date audit conclusion to the balance sheet date. The process of *extending the audit conclusion*

AUDITING INSIGHT

BALANCE-AUDIT SAMPLING FAILURE

The company owned surgical instruments that were loaned and leased to customers. The auditors decided to audit the existence of the assets by confirming them with the customers who were supposed to be holding and using them. From the population of 880 instruments, the auditors selected 8 for confirmation, using a sampling method that purported to produce a representative selection.

Two confirmations were never returned, and the auditors did not follow up on them. One returned confirmation said the customer did not have the instrument in question, and the auditors were never able to find it. Nevertheless, the auditors concluded that the $3.5 million recorded amount of the surgical instrument assets was materially accurate.

Judges who heard complaints on the quality of the audit work concluded that it was not performed in accordance with generally accepted auditing standards (GAAS) because the auditors did not gather sufficient evidence concerning the existence and valuation of the surgical instruments. GAAS requires auditors to project the sample findings to the population. The auditors did not do so. They never calculated (nonstatistical) the fact that ($1,368,750) of the asset amount could not be confirmed or found to exist. The sample of the eight was woefully inadequate both in sample size and in the proportionately large number of exceptions reported. There was a wholly insufficient statistical basis for concluding that the account was fairly stated under generally accepted accounting principles.

Source: U.S. Securities and Exchange Commission, *Administrative Proceeding File No. 3-6579.*

amounts to nothing more (and nothing less) than performing substantive-purpose audit procedures on the transactions in the remaining period and on the year-end balance to produce sufficient competent evidence for a decision about the year-end balance.

Substantive procedures must be performed to obtain evidence about the balance after the interim date. You cannot audit a balance (say, accounts receivable) as of September 30, then without further work accept the December 31 balance. Internal control must be well specified and performed adequately. If the company's internal control over transactions that produce the balance under audit is not particularly strong, you should time the substantive detail work at year-end instead of at interim.

If rapidly changing business conditions might predispose managers to misstate the accounts (try to slip one by the auditors), the work should be timed at year-end. In most cases, careful *scanning of transactions* and *analytical procedure comparisons* should be performed on transactions that occur after the interim date.

As an example, accounts receivable confirmation can be done at an interim date. Subsequently, efforts must be made to ascertain whether controls continued to be reliable. You must scan the transactions of the remaining period, audit any new large balances, and update work on collectibility, especially with analysis of cash received after the year-end.

Audit work is performed at interim for two reasons: (1) to spread the accounting firms' workload so not all the work on clients is crammed into December and January, and (2) to make the work efficient and enable companies to report audited financial results soon after the year-end. Some well-organized companies with well-planned audits report their audited figures as early as five or six days after their fiscal year-ends.

REVIEW CHECKPOINTS

E.20 What kind of evidence evaluation consideration should an auditor give to the dollar amount of a population unit that cannot be audited?

E.21 What are the three basic steps in quantitative evaluation of monetary amount evidence when auditing an account balance?

E.22 What are two methods of projecting the known misstatement to the population?

E.23 What are some of the signs that an unstratified random sample is actually representative of the population from which it was drawn?

E.24 The projected likely misstatement may be calculated, yet further (possible) misstatement might remain unde-

tected in the population. How can auditors take the further (possible) misstatement into consideration when completing the quantitative evaluation of monetary evidence?

E.25 What additional considerations are in order when auditors plan to audit account balances at an interim date several weeks or months before the client's fiscal year-end date?

SUMMARY

Audit sampling is explained in this module as an organized method to make decisions. Two kinds of decisions are shown—assessment of control risk and the decision about whether financial statement assertions in an account balance are fairly presented. The method is organized by two kinds of audit programs to guide the work on these two decisions—the test of controls audit program and the balance-audit program. The audit sampling itself can be attribute sampling for test of controls, and balance-audit (variables) sampling for auditing the assertions in an account balance.

Audit sampling is a method of organizing the application of audit procedures and a disciplined approach to decision problems. Both types of sampling are explained in basic terms of planning the audit procedures, performing the audit procedures, and evaluating the evidence produced by the audit procedures. The latter process is reinforced with some difference and ratio projections of misstatement amounts. Mathematical consideration of sampling error ("possible misstatement," "further misstatement remaining undetected") is covered in Module G.

Risk in audit decisions is explained in the context of nonsampling and sampling risk, with sampling risk further subdivided into two types of decision errors: (1) assessing control risk too low and incorrect acceptance of a balance and (2) assessing control risk too high and incorrect rejection of an account balance. The first pair damages the effectiveness of audits, and the second pair damages the efficiency of audits.

Dollar-valued materiality is incorporated in the balance-audit sampling in terms of the tolerable misstatement assigned to the audit of a particular account. The connection of tolerable misstatement to the tolerable deviation rate in test of controls sampling is covered in Module F.

Audit programs for test of controls procedures and balance-audit procedures are illustrated. Separate sections explain the application of procedures at an interim date. Thus, the module covers the nature, timing, and extent of audit procedures. One of the goals of this module is to enable students to be able to understand these procedural programs in the context of audit sampling.

MULTIPLE-CHOICE QUESTIONS FOR PRACTICE AND REVIEW

E.26 In an *audit sampling* application, an auditor
   a. Performs procedures on all items in a balance and makes a conclusion about the whole balance.
   b. Performs procedures on less than 100 percent of the items in a balance and formulates a conclusion about the whole balance.
   c. Performs procedures on less than 100 percent of the items in a class of transactions for the purpose of becoming familiar with the client's accounting system.
   d. Performs analytical procedures on the client's unaudited financial statements when planning the audit.

E.27   Auditors consider *statistical sampling* to be characterized by the following:
   a. Representative sample selection and nonmathematical consideration of the results.
   b. Carefully biased sample selection and statistical calculation of the results.
   c. Representative sample selection and statistical calculation of the results.
   d. Carefully biased sample selection and nonmathematical consideration of the results.

E.28   In audit sampling applications, *sampling risk* is
   a. Characteristics of statistical sampling applications but not of nonstatistical applications.
   b. The probability that the auditor will fail to recognize erroneous accounting in the client's documentation.
   c. Probability that accounting errors will rise in transactions and enter the accounting system.
   d. The probability that an auditor's conclusion based on a sample might be different from the conclusion based on an auditor of the entire population.

E.29   When auditing the client's performance of control to accomplish the *completeness* objective related to ensuring that all sales are recorded, auditors should draw sample items from
   a. The sales journal list of recorded sales invoices.
   b. The file of shipping documents.
   c. The file of customer order copies.
   d. The file of receiving reports for inventory additions.

E.30   Nelson Williams was considering the sample size needed for a selection of sales invoices for the test of controls audit of the LoHo Company's internal controls. He presented the following information for two alternative cases:

	Case A	Case B
Acceptable risk of assessing control risk too high	High	Low
Acceptable risk of assessing control risk too low	High	Low
Tolerable deviation rate	High	Low
Expected population deviation rate	Low	High

Nelson should expect the sample size for Case A to be:
   a. Smaller than the sample size for Case B.
   b. Larger than the sample size for Case B.
   c. The same as the sample size for Case B.
   d. Not determinable relative to the Case B sample size.

E.31   Nelson next considered the sample size needed for a selection of customers' accounts receivable for the substantive audit of the total accounts receivable. He presented the following information for two alternative cases:

	Case X	Case Y
Acceptable risk of incorrect acceptance	Low	High
Acceptable risk of incorrect rejection	Low	High
Tolerable dollar misstatement in the account	Small	Large
Expected dollar misstatement in the account	Large	Small
Estimate of population variability	Large	Small

Nelson should expect the sample size for Case X to be
   a. Smaller than the sample size for Case Y.
   b. Larger than the sample size for Case Y.
   c. The same as the sample size for Case Y.
   d. Not determinable relative to the Case Y sample size.

E.32   Which of the following should be considered an audit *procedure* for obtaining evidence:
   a. An audit sampling application in accounts receivable selection.
   b. The accounts receivable exist and are valued properly.
   c. Sending a written confirmation on a customer's account balance.
   d. Nonstatistical consideration of the amount of difference reported by a customer on a confirmation response.

E.33   When calculating the total amount of misstatement relevant to the analysis of an account balance, an auditor should add to the misstatement discovered in individually significant items the following:
   a. The projected likely misstatement and the additional possible misstatement estimate.
   b. The known misstatement in the sampled items.
   c. The known misstatement in the sampled items, the projected likely misstatement, and the additional possible misstatement estimate.
   d. The additional possible misstatement estimate.

E.34 Eddie audited the LoHo Company's inventory on a sample basis. She audited 120 items from an inventory compilation list and discovered net overstatement of $480. The audited items had a book (recorded) value of $48,000. There were 1,200 inventory items listed, and the total inventory book amount was $490,000. Which two of these calculations are correct:

a. Known misstatement of $4,800 using the difference method.
b. Projected likely misstatement of $480 using the ratio method.
c. Projected likely misstatement of $4,900 using the ratio method.
d. Projected likely misstatement of $4,800 using the difference method.

E.35 Steve Katchy audited the client's accounts receivable, but he could not get any good information about customer #102's balance. The customer responded to the confirmation saying, "Our system does not provide detail for such a response." The sales invoice and shipping document papers have been lost, and the customer has not yet paid. Steve should

a. Get another customer's account to consider in the sample.
b. Treat customer 102's account as being entirely wrong (overstated), if doing so will not affect his audit conclusion about the receivables taken altogether.
c. Require adjustment of the receivables to write off customer 102's balance.
d. Treat customer 102's account as accurate because there is no evidence saying it is fictitious.

E.36 The risk of incorrect acceptance in balance-audit sampling and the risk of assessing control risk too low in test of controls sampling both relate to

a. Effectiveness of an audit.
b. Efficiency of an audit.
c. Control risk assessment decisions.
d. Evidence about assertions in financial statements.

E.37 An advantage of statistical sampling is that it helps an auditor

a. Eliminate nonsampling risk.
b. Reapply evaluation judgments based on factors in addition to the sample evidence.
c. Be precise and definite in the approach to an audit problem.
d. Omit quantification of risk and materiality judgments.

E.38 To determine the sample size for a balance-audit sampling application, an auditor should consider the tolerable misstatement, the risk of incorrect acceptance, the risk of incorrect rejection, the population size, and the

a. Expected monetary misstatement in the account.
b. Overall materiality for the financial statements taken as a whole.
c. Risk of assessing control risk too low.
d. Risk of assessing control risk too high.

E.39 An advantage of statistical over nonstatistical sampling methods in tests of controls is that the statistical methods

a. Afford greater assurance than a nonstatistical sample of equal size.
b. Provide an objective basis for quantitatively evaluating sample risks.
c. Can more easily convert the sample into a dual-purpose test useful for substantive testing.
d. Eliminate the need to use judgment in determining appropriate sample sizes.

(AIPCA adapted)

E.40 An advantage of statistical sampling over nonstatistical sampling is that statistical sampling helps an auditor to

a. Minimize the failure to detect errors and fraud.
b. Eliminate the risk of nonsampling errors.
c. Reduce the level of audit risk and materiality to a relatively low amount.
d. Measure the sufficiency of the evidential matter obtained.

(AIPCA adapted)

E.41 A principal advantage of statistical methods of attribute sampling over nonstatistical methods is that they provide a scientific basis for planning the

a. Risk of assessing control risk too low.
b. Tolerable rate.
c. Expected population deviation rate.
d. Sample size.

(AIPCA adapted)

E.42 The risk of incorrect acceptance and the likelihood of assessing control risk too low relate to the

a. Effectiveness of the audit.
b. Efficiency of the audit.
c. Preliminary estimates of materiality levels.
d. Tolerable misstatement.

(AIPCA adapted)

E.43 The likelihood of assessing control risk too high is the risk that the sample selected to test controls

a. Does not support the auditor's planned assessed level of control risk when the true operating effectiveness of internal control justifies such an assessment.

b. Contains misstatements that could be material to the financial statements when aggregated with misstatements in other account balances of transactions classes.

c. Contains proportionately fewer deviations from prescribed internal controls than exist in the balance or class or as whole.

d. Does not support the tolerable misstatement for some or all of management's assertions.

(AIPCA adapted)

E.44 While performing a substantive test of details during an audit, the auditor determined that the sample results supported the conclusion that the recorded account balance was materially misstated. It was, in fact, not materially misstated. This situation illustrates the risk of

a. Incorrect rejection.
b. Incorrect acceptance.
c. Assessing control risk too low.
d. Assessing control risk too high.

(AIPCA adapted)

E.45 Which of the following courses of action would an auditor most likely follow in planning a sample of cash disbursements if the auditor is aware of several unusually large cash disbursements?

a. Increase the sample size to reduce the effect of the unusually large disbursements.
b. Continue to draw new samples until all the unusually large disbursements appear in the sample.
c. Set the tolerable rate of deviation at a lower level than originally planned.
d. Stratify the cash disbursements population so that the unusually large disbursements are selected.

(AIPCA adapted)

Exercises and Problems

E.46 Sampling and Nonsampling Audit Work. The accounting firm of Mason & Jarr performed the work described in each separate case below. The two partners are worried about properly applying standards regarding audit sampling. They have asked your advice.

Required:
Write a report addressed to them, stating whether they did or did not observe the essential elements of audit sampling standards in each case:

a. Mason selected three purchase orders for raw materials from the LIZ Corporation files. He started at this beginning point in the accounting process and traced each one through the accounting system. He saw the receiving reports, purchasing agent's approvals, receiving clerks' approvals, the vendors' invoices (now stamped PAID), the entry in the cash disbursement records, and the canceled checks. This work gave him a firsthand familiarity with the cash disbursement system, and he felt confident about understanding related questions in the internal control questionnaire completed later.

[handwritten: not audit sampling]

b. Jarr observed the inventory taking at SER Corporation. She had an inventory list of the different inventory descriptions with the quantities taken from the perpetual inventory records. She selected the 200 items with the largest quantities and counted them after the client's shop foreman had completed his count. She decided not to check out the count accuracy on the other 800 items. The shop foreman miscounted in 16 cases. Jarr concluded the rate of miscount was 8 percent, so as many as 80 of the 1,000 items might be counted wrong. She asked the foreman to recount everything.

[handwritten: is auditing but sampling, but it is done incorrectly]

c. CSR Corporation issued seven series of short-term commercial paper notes near the fiscal year-end to finance seasonal operations. Jarr confirmed the obligations under each series with the independent trustee for the holders, studied all seven indenture agreements, and traced the proceeds of each issue to the cash receipts records.

[handwritten: not audit sampling]

d. At the completion of the EH&R Corporation audit, Mason obtained written representations, as required by auditing standards, from the president, the chief financial officer, and the controller. He did not ask the chief accountant at headquarters or the plant controllers in the three divisions for written representations.

[handwritten: not audit sampling]

e. Jarr audited the Repairs and Maintenance account of the Kerr Corporation by vouching all the entries over $5,000 to supporting documents—a total of $278,000. She considered the sum of all the remaining items ($75,000, a material amount) in relation to the prior year's

[handwritten: sampling but not done properly]

similar total of $56,000 and decided not to perform any additional procedures.

E.47 Test of Controls Audit Procedure Objectives and Control Deviations. This exercise asks you to specify test of controls audit procedure objectives and define deviations in connection with planning the test of controls audit of Tordik Company's internal controls.

Required:

a. For each control cited below, state the objective of an auditor's test of controls audit procedure.

b. For each control cited below, state the definition of a deviation from the control.

1. The credit department supervisor reviews each customer's order and approves credit by making a notation on the order.

2. The billing department must receive written notice from the shipping department of actual shipment to a customer before a sale is recorded. The sales record date is supposed to be the shipment date.

3. Billing clerks carefully look up the correct catalog list prices for goods shipped and calculate and recheck the amounts billed on invoices for the quantities of goods shipped.

4. Billing clerks review invoices for intercompany sales and mark each one with the code "9," so they will be posted to intercompany sales accounts.

E.48 Timing of Test of Controls Audit Procedures. Auditor Hill was auditing the authorization control over cash disbursements. She selected cash disbursement entries made throughout the year and vouched them to paid invoices and canceled checks bearing the initials and signatures of people authorized to approve the disbursements. She performed the work on September 30, when the company had issued checks numbered from 43921 to 52920. Since 9,000 checks had been issued in nine months, she reasoned that 3,000 more could be issued in the three months before the December 31 year-end. About 12,000 checks had been issued last year. She wanted to take one sample of 100 disbursements for the entire year, so she selected 100 random numbers in the sequence 43921 to 55920. She audited the 80 checks in the sample that were issued before September 30, and she held the other 20 randomly selected check numbers for later use. She found no deviations in the sample of 80—a finding that would, in the circumstances, cause her to assign a low (20 percent) control risk to the probability that the system would permit improper charges to be hidden away in expense and purchase/inventory accounts.

Required:

Take the role of Hill and write a memo to the audit manager (dated October 1) describing the audit team's options with respect to evaluating control performance for the remaining period, October through December.

E.49 Evaluation of Quantitative Test of Controls Evidence. Assume you audited control compliance in the Brighter Image Company for the deviations related to a random selection of sales transactions, as shown below. For different sample sizes, the number of deviations was as follows:

	Sample Sizes				
	30	60	80	90	120
Missing sales invoice	0	0	0	0	0
Missing bill of lading	0	0	0	0	0
No credit approval	0	3	6	8	10
Wrong prices used	0	0	0	0	2
Wrong quantity billed	1	2	4	4	4
Wrong invoice arithmetic	0	0	0	0	1
Wrong invoice date	0	0	0	0	0
Posted to wrong account	0	0	0	0	0

	Sample Sizes				
	160	220	240	260	300
Missing sales invoice	0	0	0	0	0
Missing bill of lading	1	2	2	3	3
No credit approval	14	17	23	26	31
Wrong prices used	4	8	9	9	12
Wrong quantity billed	5	5	5	5	5
Wrong invoice arithmetic	2	2	2	2	3
Wrong invoice date	2	2	2	2	2
Posted to wrong account	0	0	0	0	0

Required:

For each deviation and each sample, calculate the rate of deviation in the sample (sample deviation rate).

E.50 Stratification Calculation of Projected Likely Misstatement Using the Ratio Method. The stratification calculation example in the module shows the results of calculating the projected likely misstatement using the difference method. Assume the results shown in Exhibit E.50–1 (on the next page) were obtained from a stratified sample.

Required:

Apply the ratio calculation method to each stratum to calculate the projected likely misstatement (PLM). What is PLM for the entire sample?

E.51 Projected Likely Misstatement. When Marge Simpson, CPA, audited the Candle Company inventory, a random sample of inventory

EXHIBIT E.50-1

		Sample Results			
Stratum	Population Size	Recorded Amount	Sample	Recorded Amount	Misstatement Amount*
1	6	$100,000	6	$100,000	$ −600
2	80	75,068	23	21,700	−274
3	168	75,008	22	9,476	−66
4	342	75,412	22	4,692	−88
5	910	74,512	23	1,973	23
	1,506	$400,000	96	$137,841	$−1,005

*A negative misstatement indicates overstatement of the book value, and a positive misstatement indicates understatement.

types was chosen for physical observation and price testing. The sample size was 75 different types of candle and candle-making inventory. The entire inventory contained 1,740 types, and the amount in the inventory control account was $1,660,000. Simpson already had decided that a misstatement as much as $60,000 in the account would not be material. The audit work revealed the following eight errors in the sample of 75.

Book Value	Audit Value	Error Amount
$6,000.00	6,220.00	$220.00
155.00	145.00	(10.00)
652.50	315.00	(337.50)
834.40	534.50	(299.90)
167.80	156.30	(11.50)
783.30	125.00	(658.30)
133.30	142.20	8.90
938.70	398.70	(540.00)
$9,665.00	$8,036.70	$(1,628.30)

The negative difference indicates overstatement of the recorded amount.

Required:

a. Calculate the projected likely misstatement using the difference method. Discuss the decision choice of accepting or rejecting the $1,660,000 book value (recorded amount) without adjustment.

b. Refer to the box explaining the AICPA "Preliminary Sample Size Guidance" about sample size calculation in the module. What analytical procedures risk (AP) and combined Control-Inherent Risk (CR-IR) did Marge use to figure a sample size of 75?

E.52   Sample-Based Audit of an Accounts Receivable Balance.   The Cooperative Electric Company serves commercial customers in a central state geographical area. Hammer & Wimsey, CPAs has performed the audit for several years. This year, your assistant prepared the following summary of the accounts receivable confirmation procedure results. The customer receivables were confirmed as of the December 31 fiscal year-end, and these data were compiled after the assistant completed the work on February 25.

	Number of Customers	Dollar Amounts Recorded	Dollar Amounts Audited
Total accounts receivable	2,000	$2,000,000	NA
Sample selection	200	$284,000	see below
Selected for positive confirmation requests	54	$260,000	see next
Replies to positive confirmation requests:			
No exception	44	$213,000	$213,000
Exceptions resolved, no adjustment	6	$30,000	$30,000
Exceptions with potential adjustments	2	$10,000	$8,000
No response	2	$7,000	NA
Selected for negative confirmation requests	140	$20,000	see next
No replies to negatives	120	$15,000	$15,000
Exceptions resolved, no adjustment	12	$2,000	$2,000
Exceptions with potential adjustments	8	$3,000	$2,700
Selected but client asked us not to confirm	6	$4,000	NA

When submitting the work, your assistant said: "The confirmation results turned out about the same as last year. I found only $2,300 real error of overstatement, and it seemed to come from the facts that the accounting department recorded eight prompt payment discounts late and charged two small retail stores at the manufacturing company rates. Since the amount we planned for tolerable misstatement for the accounts receivable is $70,000, the $2,000,000 recorded amount looks OK without adjustment. And, you'll be glad to know that I finished this work ten hours under budget."

Required:

a. Evaluate the assistant's conclusions. Do you have any suggestions about work the assistant should have performed?

b. You notice that the average recorded amount of the customer accounts selected in the sample was $1,420, which is considerably larger than the $1,000 average across all 2,000 customer accounts. Using the ratio method, calculate the projected likely misstatement (PLM) evident in the assistant's confirmation results summary.

c. Should you agree with the assistant and close the work on the $2,000,000 recorded amount of accounts receivable (i.e., accept the recorded amount as materially accurate)?

E.53 Sample-Based Audit of an Inventory Balance. The law firm of Spade & Associates (Spade) hired D. Sayers to review the audit work Hammer & Wimsey, CPAs (H&W) completed last year for Golden Sound and Records Company (Golden). Specifically, the attorneys engaged Sayers to determine whether the audit of the Golden inventory of sound equipment, tapes, and CDs conformed to generally accepted auditing standards. After Golden declared bankruptcy three months ago (eight months after the latest audited financial statements were issued), stockholders sued Golden alleging distribution of misleading financial statements, and H&W hired Spade to prepare a defense in case H&W were included later in the lawsuit. The latest year was the first time Golden had been audited.

Golden's business has grown rapidly. The company had 40 stores two years ago, opened 36 more last year, and added 23 more (for a total of 99) during the year of the inventory audit in question. The records showed the growth of the business in the inventory:

	Two Years Ago June 30	Last Year June 30	Audited Year June 30
Sound equipment	$5,800,000	$10,000,000	$12,200,000
Tapes and CDs	$2,200,000	$ 6,800,000	$ 9,000,000
Total inventory	$8,000,000	$16,800,000	$21,200,000
Number of stores	40	76	99
Average equipment	$ 145,000	$ 131,579	$ 123,232
Average tapes, CDs	$ 55,000	$ 89,474	$ 90,909

Sayers reviewed the H&W working papers and wrote this summary: In April of the year under audit, Bobby Earl (H&W audit manager on the Golden engagement) met with Golden's managers and discussed the program for taking the physical inventory as of June 30. Mikki LaTouche (Golden's chief financial officer) suggested that the auditors' inventory observation be conducted at the big-city stores in the area where Golden had started business. According to LaTouche: "These stores are well-stocked with a representative selection of all the types of equipment and musical releases available across all the stores. The store managers are well-acquainted with the inventory and can conduct an accurate counting with experienced store employees. The newer stores carry less stock, and the managers are relatively new to their jobs. You'll get a more accurate inventory-taking observation in these stores." Earl

agreed and noted in the conference memorandum in the working papers that the prospect of sending auditors to distant stores in the Midwestern and Southeastern states (where Golden had established new stores in the past year or so) would be very costly in terms of auditors' time and travel expenses. Together, LaTouche and Earl selected eight of the stores in the Western Region. Earl supervised experienced audit teams as they observed the inventory-taking at these eight stores. The auditors observed that the Golden store managers gave good instructions to the inventory-takers and that the count records were in good order. Test-counts showed only minor mistakes, which the managers promptly and courteously corrected. Everyone was interested in making an accurate count because Golden had no reliable perpetual inventory records, and the financial statement figure for inventory was determined by this physical inventory-taking. In fact, Earl wrote in the internal control letter to the board of directors and in the management letter addressed to the CFO the observation that Golden needed to establish reliable inventory records for physical control and profit enhancement. The auditors determined inventory amounts in the eight stores as shown below. Using the total inventory of $1,712,700 in these stores, Earl divided by eight to find the average per store, then multiplied by 99, and projected the total inventory in the amount of $21,194,663. Since this figure was only $5,337 less than the book value of inventory in the general ledger, Earl and the reviewing partner passed further work and incorporated the $21,200,000 inventory in the financial statements, along with a standard unqualified audit report.

GOLDEN SOUND AND RECORDING COMPANY
Inventory Observation (excerpts) June 30

Store Location	Inventory
Los Angeles #1	$238,300
Los Angeles #3	$212,500
San Diego #2	$206,800
San Diego #4	$195,400
Las Vegas #1	$223,200
Sacramento	$211,900
San Francisco #1	$240,000
Phoenix	$184,600
Total audit observation	$1,712,700

Required:

Complete Sayers' engagement by evaluation the H&W conduct of the inventory portion of the Golden audit. Specify the applicable auditing standards and tell whether H&W did or did not conform to them. (*Hint:* Since this chapter covers audit sampling topics, your evaluation will include observations about the sample-based inventory audit.)

Module F

Test of Controls with Attribute Sampling

Professional Standards References

Compendium Section	Document Reference	Topic
AU 312	SAS 47	*Audit Risk and Materiality in Conduction an Audit*
AU 319	SAS 78	*Internal Control in a Financial Statement Audit*
AU 350	SAS 39	*Audit Sampling*
AU 9350		*Interpretations: Audit Sampling*

Learning Objectives

Module F contains more mathematical-statistical details related to the test of controls sampling introduced in Module E. In fact, Module F is a technical appendix on test of controls sampling. In Module F, you will find more specific explanation of how to do statistical sampling in the test of controls phase of the control risk assessment work. After studying this module in conjunction with Module E, you should be able to:

1. Explain the role of professional judgment in assigning numbers to risk of assessing control risk too low, risk of assessing control risk too high, and tolerable deviation rate.

2. Use statistical tables or calculations to determine test of controls sample sizes.

3. Calculate the effect on test of controls sample sizes of subdividing a population into two relevant populations.

4. Use your imagination to overcome difficult sampling unit selection problems.

5. Use evaluation tables or calculations to compute statistical results (CUL, the computed upper limit) for evidence obtained with detail test of controls procedures.

6. Use the discovery sampling evaluation table for assessment of audit evidence.

7. Choose a test of controls sample size among several equally acceptable alternatives.

RISK AND RATE QUANTIFICATIONS

LEARNING OBJECTIVE
1. Explain the role of professional judgment in assigning numbers to risk of assessing control risk too low, risk of assessing control risk too high, and tolerable deviation rate.

The quantification of sampling risk is an exercise of professional judgment. When using statistical sampling methods, auditors must quantify the two risks of decision error. The risk of assessing control risk too low is generally considered more important than the risk of assessing control risk too high. Auditors must also exercise professional judgment to determine the extent of deviation allowable (tolerable rate) for each level of control risk.

Risk of Assessing Control Risk Too Low: A Professional Judgment

Assessing control risk too low causes auditors to rely on control too much (overreliance) and audit the related account balances less than is necessary. The *risk* in "*risk* of assessing control risk too low" relates to the *effect* of the erroneous control evaluation. This effect is produced in the substantive audit by influencing the sample size for auditing the account balances related to the controls being evaluated. (Refer to Exhibit F–2.)

Internal control is evaluated, and control risk is assessed in relation to particular account balances. For example, auditors will evaluate control over the processing of sales and cash receipts transactions because these are the transactions that produce the debits and credits to the customer accounts receivable. Some other examples are shown in Exhibit F–1. The ultimate purpose of the control risk assessment is to decide how much work to do when auditing the general ledger accounts—for example, cash accounts receivable, inventory, sales revenue, expenses. The question of "how much work" relates directly to the sample size of the general ledger account details to audit—for example, how many bank accounts to reconcile, how many customer accounts receivable to confirm, how many inventory items to count and recalculate for correct costing. The control risk assessment provides supporting information for the balance-audit work. We will proceed using the audit of accounts receivable as an example.

When planning the audit of the accounts receivable balance, auditors make judgments and estimates of the overall risk of failing to detect material misstatements in the balance (AR, audit risk related to the receivables audit), the probability that errors entered the accounts (IR, inherent risk), and the effectiveness of their analytical procedures for detecting material errors in the receivables (AP, analytical procedures risk). At this

| EXHIBIT F–1 | EXAMPLES OF CLASSES OF TRANSACTIONS FLOWING INTO GENERAL LEDGER BALANCES |

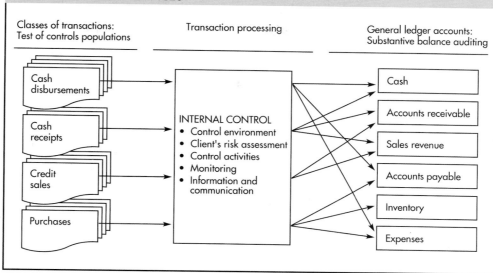

| EXHIBIT F–2 | CONTROL RISK INFLUENCE ON SUBSTANTIVE BALANCE-AUDIT SAMPLE SIZE |

Control Risk Categories	(1) Possible Control Risk Assessments (CR)	(2) Related Risk of Incorrect Acceptance (RIA)*	(3) Number of Balance Items to Select for Substantive Audit
Low control risk	0.10	0.50	51
	0.20	0.25	81
	0.30	0.167	96
Moderate control risk	0.40	0.125	107
	0.50	0.10	117
	0.60	0.083	125
	0.70	0.071	130
Control risk slightly below the maximum	0.80	0.0625	136
	0.90	0.0556	140
Maximum control risk	1.00	0.05	143

*Assuming AR = 0.05, IR = 1.0. Therefore, RIA = 0.05/(1.0 × CR × 1.0).

stage, the remaining elements of the risk model are the control risk (CR) and the substantive sample risk of incorrect acceptance (RIA). The internal control evaluation task is directed to assessing the control risk, and the risk of incorrect acceptance is then derived using the expanded risk model: RIA = AR/(IR × CR × AP).[1]

Since control risk is the *probability* that the client's controls will fail to detect material misstatements, provided any enter the accounting system in the first place, control risk itself can take values ranging from very low probability (say, 0.10) to maximum probability (1.0). Using the audit risk model (SAS 39, AU 350), there is a risk of incorrect acceptance (RIA) for every possible control assessment (CR). These RIAs affect the sample sizes for the substantive audit work on the account balances.

Exhibit F–2 shows a range of possible control risk assessments in column (1). To their left are some labels commonly used in public accounting practice. (CPA firms deal with

[1] In the auditing standards, the RIA has another name—"TD," meaning "Test of details risk" (*SAS 39, AU 350*).

a few control risk categories instead of a full range of control risk probabilities.[2]) Column (2) contains the risks of incorrect acceptance (RIA) derived from the audit risk model for the balance-audit substantive sample, and column (3) shows the substantive sample sizes based on these RIAs. The sample sizes in column (3) are the *substantive balance-audit sample sizes* (e.g., number of customer accounts, number of inventory items), not the test of controls samples. (The actual calculation of these substantive sample sizes is explained in Module G.)

These relationships are evident in Exhibit F–2: (1) for higher control risk, the related RIA is lower; (2) for lower RIAs, the substantive samples are larger; and (3) therefore, the higher the control risk, the larger the substantive sample size required for the audit of the related balance sheet account. These are the relationships suggested by the second AICPA field work standard—that is, the understanding of internal control and the assessment of control risk is for the purpose of planning the nature, timing, and *extent* of substantive tests to be performed.

We may have lost track of the subject of this discussion—it is about judging the acceptable risk of assessing control risk too low (RACRTL) in the test of controls sample. CPA firms almost always use a RACRTL of 10 percent. This is an arbitrary policy that eases the burden of the number of judgments auditors need to make. The implication is that auditors are willing to take 1 chance in 10 of assessing control risk too low and suffer the consequences of auditing a substantive sample smaller than they would have audited had the decision error not been made. However, a more logical derivation of an acceptable RACRTL is available.

For convenience, this RACRTL-determination method will be called *Roberts' method*, named after Professor Roberts, who explained it.[3] According to Roberts, auditors should decide an amount of **incremental risk of incorrect acceptance** (e.g., 0.01) they are willing to add in the substantive sample as a result of assessing control risk too low. With reference to Exhibit F–2, this means, for instance, if the auditors would accept 0.05 RIA figured using the SAS 39 risk model when control risk is actually 1.0, they also would accept the risk (RACRTL) of erroneously assessing control risk lower, audit a smaller substantive sample, and incur 0.06 RIA, instead. In equation form, one way to express Robert' method is:

$$\text{Incremental RIA} = \text{RACRTL} \times \left(\begin{array}{c} \text{RIA at assessed} \\ \text{control risk} \end{array} - \begin{array}{c} \text{RIA at maximum} \\ \text{control risk} \end{array} \right)$$

and, RIA at maximum control risk is the "worst case control assessment," therefore:

$$\text{RACRTL} = \dfrac{\text{Incremental RIA}}{\left(\begin{array}{c} \text{RIA at assessed} \\ \text{control risk} \end{array} - \begin{array}{c} \text{RIA at maximum} \\ \text{control risk} \end{array} \right)}$$

but with a maximum RACRTL of 50 percent, because there is no use in performing a sampling application that has less than a 50-50 chance of being correct. For example, the RACRTL for control risk = 0.20 would be:

$$\text{RACRTL} = \frac{0.01}{(0.25 - 0.05)} = 0.05, \text{ or } 5\%$$

and the RACRTL for control risk = 0.80 would be:

$$\text{RACRTL} = \frac{0.01}{(0.0625 - 0.05)} = 0.80, \text{ or } 80\%, \text{ but maximum} = 0.50, \text{ or } 50\%$$

---

[2] CPA firms that use quantitative test of controls sampling policies have quantified probabilities underlying their categories, and they fall in the ranges indicated in Exhibit F–2.

[3] Donald M. Roberts, *Statistical Auditing* (New York: American Institute of Certified Public Accountants, 1978), p. 145.

Roberts' method is not in generally accepted auditing standards, and auditors have no standards concerning an "incremental risk of incorrect acceptance." Audit guidance suggests that the RACRTL should be low because the test of controls evidence is important for assessing control risk below the maximum (1.0). For example, assessing control risk at 0.20 instead of 0.50 lowers the substantive sample by 36 items. (117 − 81, as shown in Exhibit F–2.)

However, at the higher control risk levels, it is *not* very important because assessing control risk too low (say, at 0.80 instead of 1.0) makes only a small difference in the size of the subsequent substantive sample (143 − 136 = 7 sampling units in the example in Exhibit F–2). Thus, it makes only a small difference in the additional risk incurred by auditing a smaller substantive sample.

Roberts' method makes sense by effectively saying: "At the lower control risk levels, the acceptable RACRTL should be small because assessing control risk quite low makes a big difference in the substantive sample size and, hence, in the risk of incorrect acceptance in the substantive balance-audit work; but at the higher control risk levels, the acceptable RACRTL can be high because assessing control risk slightly too low does not affect the substantive sample size and risk of incorrect acceptance very much."

One further note on Roberts' method as it is illustrated above: The incremental risk of incorrect acceptance is another auditor judgment. It can be larger or smaller than 0.01. No official pronouncement or research analysis defines this additional risk. Also, the "worst case" of the RIA at control risk = 1.0 was chosen merely for illustration because it is conservative (producing lower RACRTLs than any other "worst case").

Risk of Assessing Control Risk Too High: A Professional Judgment

Auditors usually do not say much about the acceptable risk of assessing control risk too high (RACRTH). As a result, test of controls sampling, as explained in *SAS 39* (AU 350) and in this book, has a potentially serious drawback. The methods concentrate on controlling for the RACRTL to avoid erroneous decisions that might reduce the *effectiveness* of audits. Erroneous decisions leading to assessing control risk too high also should be avoided in the interest *of* audit *efficiency*.

For the following explanation, you need to be introduced to the concept of the computed upper limit (CUL). The **CUL** is a statistical estimate of the population deviation rate computed from the test of controls sample evidence. It consists of the actual sample deviation rate (number of deviations found in the sample divided by the test of controls sample size) plus a statistical allowance for sampling error. The CUL is similar to the upper confidence limit of a statistical confidence interval. (You probably studied confidence intervals in your statistics course.) It is used in statistical evaluation of test of controls sample results as the estimate of the population deviation rate. It is compared to the tolerable deviation rate when auditors assess the control risk.

If the number of deviations in a test of controls sample causes the CUL to be higher than the tolerable deviation rate, when the population deviation rate is actually equal to or lower than the tolerable deviation rate, the auditors may assess control risk too high. This causes them to perform more substantive audit work on the related account balance than they would have performed had they obtained better information about the control risk.

Take, for example, a test of controls sample of 77 sales invoices. The problem is this: Suppose the sample size of 77 invoices were based on a zero expected population deviation rate and a 3 percent tolerable rate, with 10 percent risk of assessing the control risk too low (RACRTL).

Finding no deviations in the sample would yield a CUL of 3 percent, and finding one or more deviations would yield a CUL of 5 percent or more. For all practical purposes, zero is a maximum *acceptance number*.

The probability of finding one or more deviations when the actual population deviation rate is 3 percent is 0.90. Thus, the risk of assessing the control risk too high is 90 percent.

You can compute the risk of assessing the control risk too high for the case where finding one deviation is important by using this formula:

Risk of assessing control risk too high = Probability that one or more deviations will be found in a sample of size n ($=77$) for a given population deviation rate ($=3\%$)

$$= 1 - (1 - \text{Rate})^n$$
$$= 1 - (1 - 0.03)^{77}$$
$$= 0.90$$

The 90 percent risk is high. This situation illustrates a pitfall in using relatively small samples. Statistically, finding even one deviation can cause a sample evaluation (CUL) to exceed the tolerable rate when the sample is based on zero expected deviations. In fact, this can happen even when the population deviation rate is *less* than the tolerable rate. Using the formula above, the risk of assessing the control risk too high is 79 percent if the population deviation rate is 2 percent, 54 percent if the population rate is 1 percent, and 7 percent if the population rate is 0.1 percent.

The only way to guard against the control-risk-too-high decision error is to audit a larger sample. This strategy permits discovery of one or more exceptions without making CUL exceed your tolerable rate. The concept is that even a good control can have a few deviations.

For example, instead of selecting 77 items where discovery of one deviation would indicate ineffective control performance, select 130 invoices where discovery of one deviation still leaves the CUL equal to the tolerable rate at 3 percent. Now the risk of assessing the control risk too high has been reduced to a risk less than 90 percent because you have the flexibility to find one deviation without exceeding the 3 percent tolerable rate criterion. Larger samples would reduce the risk even further, which is a *benefit*. The *cost* of reducing the risk of assessing the control risk too high is the cost of auditing more sampling units.

Tolerable Deviation Rate: A Professional Judgment

Auditors should have an idea about the correspondence of rates of deviation in the population with control risk assessments. Perfect control compliance is not necessary, so the question is: What rate of deviation in the population signals control risk of 10 percent? 20 percent? 30 percent? and so forth, up to 100 percent? You can answer these questions two ways:

1. Simply assign a range of deviation rates to the range of control risk probabilities in a way that makes some common sense. As you can see in Exhibit F–3, the tolerable deviation rate (TDR) of 1% signals control risk (CR) of 0.05, TDR = 2% signals CR = 0.10, and so forth up to TDR = 20% signals CR = 1.0. Auditors have used this particular assignment in practice.
2. Instead of always starting the assignment with TDR = 1% signals CR = 0.05, apply the "smoke-fire" concept to derive the TDR starting anchor (at CR = 0.05) by relating the balance-audit materiality concepts to the test of controls problem.

The simple assignment is easy and automatic. The remainder of this section explains the situation-specific application of the **smoke-fire concept.** To begin, remember the *top-down approach* for materiality determination and the allocation of *tolerable misstatement* to various accounts. Here we will use an example of test of controls over sales transactions, leading to the balance-audit of the accounts receivable.

EXHIBIT F–3	ILLUSTRATIVE CONTROL RISK AND TOLERABLE RATE RELATIONSHIPS

Tolerable Rate	Control Risk	Control Risk
1% (anchor)	0.05	
2	0.10	
3	0.20	Low control risk.
6	0.30	
8	0.40	
10	0.50	Moderate control risk.
12	0.60	
14	0.70	Control risk slightly below maximum.
16	0.80	
18	0.90	
20	1.00 →	Maximum control risk.

Note: The tolerable rate increases 1 percentage point for each additional 0.05 control risk in this example. This association corresponds to the AICPA *Audit Sampling Guide* suggestions.

Assume that tolerable dollar misstatement of $30,000 is allocated to the audit of accounts receivable for possible overstatement. This allocation is relevant to the audit of control over sales transactions because uncorrected errors in sales transactions misstate the financial statements by remaining uncorrected in the accounts receivable balance. In other words, we test the controls over sales transaction processing to determine the control risk relevant to our audit of the accounts receivable balance. Therefore, if sales transactions are in error by $30,000 or more, the accounts receivable balance *may* be materially misstated.

However, a deviation in a sales transaction (e.g., one unsupported by shipping documents) does not necessarily mean the transaction amount is totally in error. After all, missing paperwork may be the only problem. Perhaps a better example is a mathematical accuracy deviation: If a sales invoice is computed incorrectly to charge the customer $2,000 instead of $1,800, there is a 100 percent control deviation (the inaccuracy), but it does not describe a 100 percent dollar misstatement of the transaction. Therefore, more than $30,000 in sales transactions can be "exposed" to control deviation without generating $30,000 dollar misstatement in the sales and the accounts receivable balances. This "exposure" is sometimes called the **smoke-fire concept,** meaning that there can be more exposure to error (smoke) than actual error (fire), just as in a conflagration.

Smoke-fire thinking produces a multiplier to apply to the tolerable dollar misstatement assigned to the account balance, $30,000 in our example. We know that a multiplier of 1 is not reasonable (i.e., $30,000 on invoices with deviations produces $30,000 of misstatement in the accounts receivable), and a multiplier of 100 or 200 is probably also not reasonable (too large). Some auditors say a multiplier of 3 is reasonable, having no other basis than a mild conservatism. Some CPA firms have sampling policies with implicit multipliers that range from 3 to 14. For our example, a multiplier of 3 has the practical effect of producing the conclusion that $90,000 on sales invoices could be exposed to control deviations. If the total gross sales on all invoices is $8.5 million, the implied **tolerable deviation rate** is $90,000/$8.5 million = 0.0106, or approximately 1 percent.

This 1 percent tolerable deviation rate now represents a theoretical *anchor*. It is the deviation rate that marks *low control risk* (say, 0.05 control risk). When this tolerable deviation rate seems too low for practical audit work, auditors can "accept" a higher tolerable rate. The only thing that happens is that auditors are implicitly saying that a *higher control risk assessment* is ultimately satisfactory for the audit of the account balance. Higher tolerable rates signal greater control risk in this scheme of thinking, like the example in Exhibit F–3.

The point in this demonstration of smoke-fire and tolerable rate thinking is to show that *tolerable rate* is a decision criterion that helps auditors assess a control risk. The *association* of tolerable rates with different control risks is the important point. To achieve a low control risk assessment (e.g., 10 percent), the sample size of transactions will be very large, but the sample size required to obtain a moderate control risk assessment (e.g., 50 percent) can be much smaller. Therefore, sample size varies inversely with the tolerable rate—the lower the rate (and the lower the "planned assessed control risk"), the larger the sample size.

The audit strategy is to think about the audit plan, including a consideration of the sample size of balances the team wants to audit. For example, Exhibit F–2, column 3, shows various numbers of customer accounts, and suppose the audit manager plans to select 107 for confirmation and other procedures. This decision suggests that control risk needs to be as good as 40 percent (Exhibit F–2, column 1), and the tolerable rate for this assessment is 8 percent (Exhibit F–3). Thus the auditors need to select a sample of sales transactions for test of controls audit sufficient to justify a decision about an 8 percent tolerable rate.

R E V I E W
CHECKPOINTS

F.1 If inherent risk (IR) is assessed as 0.90 and the detection risk (DR) implicit in an audit plan is 0.10, what audit risk (AR) is implied when the assessed level of control risk is 0.10? 0.50? 0.70? 0.90? and 1.0?

F.2 What is the logic underlying Roberts' method of figuring the risk of assessing control risk too low (RACRTL)? Explain.

F.3 What general considerations are important when an auditor decides on an acceptable risk of assessing control risk too low?

F.4 What considerations are important when an auditor decides on an acceptable risk of assessing control risk too high? What is the probability of finding one or more deviations in a sample of 100 if the population deviation rate is actually 2 percent?

F.5 What is the probability of finding one or more deviations in a sample of 100 units if the deviation rate in the population is only 0.5 percent?

F.6 What is the connection between possible assessments of control risk and a judgment about tolerable rate, both considered prior to performing test of controls audit procedures?

F.7 What is the connection between tolerable dollar misstatement assigned for the substantive audit of a balance and tolerable deviation rate used in a test of controls sample?

F.8 What professional judgment and estimation decisions must be made by auditors when applying statistical sampling in test of controls audit work?

SAMPLE SIZE DETERMINATION

LEARNING OBJECTIVE

2. Use statistical tables or calculations to determine test of controls sample sizes.

You can use the evaluation tables in Appendix FB to calculate (predetermine) a sample size. The basic idea is to get a sample size you can evaluate using the same table.

Using Tables

Here is an example of using Appendix FB.1 to predetermine a test of controls sample size. The illustration below is a portion of Appendix FB.1.

1. Assume that your RACRTL is 5 percent, so you are in Appendix FB.1 instead of Appendix FB.2 (where the RACRTL is 10 percent).

2. Assume that you might find 1 control deviation in any sample of transactions.

3. Assume that your tolerable deviation rate (TDR) is 10 percent.
4. Figure sample size:
   a. Find the column for 1 deviation
   b. Read down to the cell in the table that is the upper limit closest to TDR = 10 (percent).
   c. Read to the left to find the sample size (45).[4]

Illustration from Appendix FB.1
Evaluation Table
RACRTL = 5%

Sample Size	Number of Deviations		
	0	①	2
25	11.3	17.6	
30	9.5	14.9	19.6
35	8.3	12.9	17.0
40	7.3	11.4	15.0
㊺	6.5	10.2	13.4
50	5.9	9.2	12.1
55	5.4	8.4	11.1

This process reads the table backwards—starting with RACRTL and a number of deviations to find the sample size. After performing the actual audit work, you can use Appendix FB.1 to calculate the upper limit (CUL). For example, if you audit 45 transactions and (1) find no deviations, your CUL (reading to the right from the sample of 45) is 6.5 percent, (2) find 1 deviation, your CUL is 10.2 percent, or (3) find 2 deviations, your CUL is 13.4 percent.

Using Calculations

Another device for calculating sample sizes is a *Poisson risk factor* equation. These risk factors are in Appendix FD. Without going into the underlying mathematics, the sample size calculation is:

$$\text{Sample size } (n) = \frac{\text{Poisson risk factor for number of deviations, RACRTL}}{\text{Tolerable deviation rate}}$$

An example of using the Poisson Risk Factors for sample size determination is next. The illustration below is a portion of Appendix FD.

1. Assume that your RACRTL is 5 percent, so you need to find the column for 5%.
2. Assume that you think you might find 1 control deviation in any sample of transactions.
3. Assume that your tolerable deviation rate (TDR) is 10 percent.
4. Figure the sample size:
   a. Find the row for 1 deviation.

---

[4] If you are dealing with a population with fewer than 1,000 units, you can adjust the sample size determined in the table or by calculation like this:

$$n = \frac{n'}{1 + (n'/N)}$$

where

n' = Sample size found in Appendix FB
N = Population size
n = Sample size adjusted for population size

When an adjusted sample is audited, the resultant CUL calculation needs to be adjusted: (1) Calculate the difference between CUL in the evaluation table and the actual sample deviation rate (CUL = x/n); (2) multiply this difference by $1/(1 + n/N)$; then (3) add the result from (2) to the actual sample deviation rate to get the adjusted CUL.

   b. Read across the cell in the table that is under the 5% RACRTL column to find
       the Poisson Risk Factor (4.75).
   c. Divide the factor (4.75) by the TDR (0.10) to calculate the sample size (48,
       after rounding up from 47.5).

This sample size is slightly different from the one figured using the Appendix FB.1
table (45) in the previous illustration. The reason lies in some rounding in the factors.

Illustration from Appendix FD
Poisson Risk Factors

Number of Deviations	Risk of Assessing Control Risk Too Low		
	6%	(5%)	4%
0	2.81	3.00	3.22
1	4.52	4.75	5.01
2	6.04	6.30	6.60
3	7.48	7.76	8.09
4	8.86	9.16	9.51
5	10.20	10.52	10.89

The Poisson risk factor equation is not any easier than using the tables, but it has the
advantage of supplying factors for all the RACRTLs from 50 percent to 1 percent. You
are not limited to RACRTLs of 5 percent and 10 percent like you are with the Appendix FB tables.

R E V I E W
CHECKPOINTS

F.9 What facts, estimates, and judgments
do you need to figure a test of controls
sample size using the Appendix FB tables? What other relevant judgment is
not used?

F.10 Test yourself to see whether you can
get the sample size of 70 from Appendix FB with these specifications:
RACRTL = 5 percent, tolerable deviation rate = 9 percent, expected
number of deviations = 2.

F.11 What facts, estimates, and judgments
do you need to figure a test of controls sample size using the Appendix
FD Poisson risk factors? What other
relevant judgment is not used?

F.12 Test yourself to see whether you can
get the sample size of 70 using the
Poisson risk factor equation with
these specifications: RACRTL = 5
percent, tolerable deviation rate = 9
percent, expected number of deviations = 2.

MORE ABOUT DEFINING POPULATIONS: STRATIFICATION

LEARNING OBJECTIVE

3. Calculate the effect on
test of controls sample
sizes of subdividing a population into two relevant
populations.

Auditors can exercise flexibility when defining populations. Accounting populations are
often **skewed**, meaning that *much of the dollar value in a population is in a small number of
population units*. For example, the **"80/20 rule"** is that *80 percent of the value tends to be in
20 percent of the units*. Many inventory and accounts receivable populations have this
skewness. Sales invoice, cash receipt, and cash disbursement populations may be skewed,
but usually not as much as inventory and receivables balances.

   Theoretically, a company's control activities should apply to small-dollar as well as to
large-dollar transactions. Nevertheless, many auditors believe evidential matter is better
when more dollars are covered in the test of controls part of the audit. This inclination
can be accommodated in a sampling plan by subdividing (stratifying) a population according to a relevant characteristic of interest. For example, sales transactions might be

subdivided into foreign and domestic; accounts receivable might be subdivided into sets of customers with balances of $5,000 or more and those with smaller balances; payroll transactions might be subdivided into supervisory payroll (salaried) and hourly payroll.

Nothing is wrong with this kind of stratification. However, you must remember that (1) an audit conclusion based on a sample applies only to the population from which the sample was drawn and (2) the sample should be representative—random for statistical sampling. If 10,000 invoices represent 2,000 foreign sales and 8,000 domestic sales, and you want to subdivide the population this way, you will have two populations. You can establish decision criteria of acceptable risk of assessing control risk too low and tolerable deviation rate for each population. You also can estimate an expected number of deviations in a sample for each one. Suppose your specifications are these:

	Foreign	Domestic
Risk of assessing control risk too low	5%	10%
Tolerable deviation rate	5%	5%
Expected sample deviations	2	1
Then, sample size (Appendix FD)	126	78

As long as you evaluate the two samples separately, everything is fine. However, you cannot add the two samples together and evaluate the combination in terms of the whole sales invoice population. Why? Because the "sample" of 204 is not random. Each foreign sales invoice had a 126/2,000 chance of being in the sample, and each domestic sales invoice had a 78/8,000 chance. Each invoice did not have an equal likelihood. Therefore, the sample of 204 is not random (even though the separate samples of 126 and 78 are random), and it should not be taken as representative of the whole population of 10,000 sales invoices.

If the population had not been stratified but treated as one population of 10,000 invoices, and the criteria had been RACRTL = 5 percent, tolerable deviation rate = 5 percent, expected number of deviations = 1, the sample size would be 95. Subdividing a population subject to test of controls sampling in two has the practical effect of doubling the extent of sampling.

A LITTLE MORE ABOUT SAMPLING UNIT SELECTION METHODS

LEARNING OBJECTIVE

4. Use your imagination to overcome difficult sampling unit selection problems.

Audit sampling can be wrecked on the shoals of auditors' impatience. Planning an imaginative selection method takes a little time, and auditors are sometimes in a big hurry to grab some units and audit them. A little imagination goes a long way. For example, suppose an auditor of a newspaper publishing client needs to audit the controls over the completeness of billings—specifically, the control activity designed to ensure that customers were billed for classified ads printed in the paper. You have seen classified ad sections, so you know they consist of different size ads, and you know that ad volume is greater on weekends than on weekdays. How can you get a random sample that can be considered representative of the printed ads?

The newspaper pages of printed ads defines the population. You probably cannot obtain a population count (size) of the number of ads. However, you know that paper was printed on 365 days of the year, and the ad manager can probably show you a record of the number of pages of classified ads printed each day. Using this information, you can determine the number of ad pages for the year, say 5,000. For a sample of 100 ads, you can choose 100 random numbers between 1 and 5,000 to obtain a random page. Then you can choose a random number between 1 and 10 to identify one of the 10 columns on the page, and another random number between 1 and 500 (the number of lines on a page). The column-line coordinate identifies an ad on the random day. (This method *approximates* randomness because larger ads are more likely to be chosen than smaller ads. In fact, the selection method probably approximates a sample selection stratified by the size of the ads.)

You can judge the representativeness by noticing the size of the ads selected. Also, since you will know the number of Friday-Saturday-Sunday pages (say, 70 percent of the total, or 3,500 pages), you can expect about 70 of the ads to come from week-end days.

Random Number Table

The simplest, although most time consuming, sampling unit selection device is a table of random digits. (See Appendix FA.) This table contains rows and columns of digits from 0 to 9 in random order. When items in the population are associated with numbers in the table, the choice of a random number amounts to choice of a sampling unit, and the resulting sample is random. Such a sample is called an **unrestricted random sample.** For example, in a population of 10,000 sales invoices, assume the first invoice in the year was 32071 and the last one was 42070. By obtaining a random start in the table and proceeding systematically through it, 100 invoices may be selected for audit.[5] Assume that a random start is obtained at the five-digit number in the second row, fifth column—number 29094—and that the reading path in the table is down to the bottom of the column, then to the top of the next column, and so on. The first usable number and first invoice is 40807, the second is 32146, and so forth. Note that several of the random numbers were skipped because they do not correspond with the invoice number sequence.[6] A page of random digits like the one in Appendix FA can be annotated and made into your sample selection working paper to document the selection, as shown in Exhibit F–4.

Systematic Random Selection

Another selection method used commonly in auditing because of its simplicity and relative ease of application is **systematic selection.** This method is employed when direct association of the population with random numbers is cumbersome. Systematic selection consists of (*a*) dividing the population size by the sample size, obtaining a quotient *k* (a "skip interval"); (*b*) obtaining a random start in the population file; and (*c*) selecting every *k*th unit for the sample. A file of credit records provides a good example.

These may be filed alphabetically with no numbering system. Therefore, to select 50 from a population of 5,000, first find $k = 5,000/50 = 100$, then obtain a random start in the set of physical files and pull out every 100th one, progressing systematically to the end of the file and returning to the beginning of the file to complete the selection. This method only approximates randomness, but the approximation can be improved by taking more than one random start in the process of selection. When more than one start is used, the interval *k* is changed. For example, if five starts are used, then every 500th item would be selected. Five random starts give you five systematic passes through the population, and each pass produces 10 sampling items, for a total of 50.

Auditors usually require five or more random starts. You can see that when the number of random starts equals the predetermined sample size, the "systematic" method becomes the same as the unrestricted random selection method. Multiple random starts are a good idea because a population may have a nonrandom order that could be imbedded in a single-start systematic method.

---

[5] A random start in a table may be obtained by poking a pencil at the table, or by checking the last four digits on one of your $100 bills to give row and column coordinates for a random start.

[6] Most auditors will not allow the same sample item to appear twice in a selection—duplicate selections are counted only once. Strictly speaking, this amounts to *sampling without replacement* and the hypergeometric probability distribution is appropriate instead of the binomial distribution. The binomial probabilities are exact only when each sample item is *replaced* after the selection, thus giving it an equally likely chance of appearing in the sample more than once. For audit purposes, the practice of ignoring the distribution is acceptable because the difference is mathematically insignificant. The evaluation tables in Appendix FB are based on the binomial distribution, with rounding to show one decimal place. In practice, you may use other tables or computer programs that calculate rates to one or two decimal places.

| EXHIBIT F–4 | RANDOM NUMBER TABLE USED AS AUDIT WORKING PAPER |

Index _____

Kingston Company
Random Selection of Sales Invoices
12/31/01

Prepared by _____
Reviewed by _____

Population: 10,000 invoices numbered 32071–42070.
Method: unrestricted selection of 5-digit random invoice numbers.
Random Start: ⟶

32942	95416	42339	59045	26693	49057	87496	20624	14819
07410	99859	83828	21409	29094	65114	36701	25762	12827
59981	68155	45673	76210	58219	45738	29550	24736	09574
46251	25437	69654	99716	11563	08803	86027	51867	12116
65558	51904	93123	27887	53138	21488	09095	78777	71240
99187	19258	86421	16401	19397	83297	40111	49326	81686
35641	00301	16096	34775	21562	97983	45040	19200	16383
14031	00936	81518	48440	02218	04756	19506	60695	88494
60677	15076	92554	26042	23472	69869	62877	19584	39576
66314	05212	67859	89356	20056	30648	87349	20389	53805
20416	87410	75656	64176	82752	63606	37011	57346	69512
28701	56992	70423	62415	40807	98086	58850	28968	45297
74579	33844	33426	07570	00728	07079	19322	56325	84819
62615	52342	82968	75540	80045	53069	20665	21282	07768
93945	06293	22879	08161	01442	75071	21427	94842	26210
75689	76131	96837	67450	44511	50424	82848	41975	71663
02921	16919	35424	93209	52133	87327	95897	65171	20376
14295	34969	14216	03191	61647	30296	66667	10101	63203
05303	91109	82403	40312	62191	67023	90073	83205	71344
57071	90357	12901	08899	91039	67251	28701	03846	94589
78471	57741	13599	84390	32146	00871	09354	22745	65806
89242	79337	59293	47481	07740	43345	25716	70020	54005
14955	59592	97035	80430	87220	06392	79028	57123	52872
42446	41880	37415	47472	04513	49494	08860	08038	43624
18534	22346	54556	17558	73689	14894	05030	19561	56517

Selection path: down each column to bottom, top next right column, then to top of column at left.

◯ *Sampling unit selection.*

AUDITING INSIGHT

DANGER IN SYSTEMATIC SELECTION

Western Productions Company has a stable payroll of 50 hourly employees, paid weekly, for a total of 2,600 pay transactions in the year under audit. The auditors decided to select a systematic sample of 104 paychecks for detail test of controls audit procedures. The skip interval was $k = 2600/104 = 25$. The auditors carefully chose a random start in the first week at #3 on the payroll register (Wyatt Earp) and selected every 25th payroll entry thereafter. They got 52 entries for Wyatt Earp and 52 entries for Bat Masterson. The audit manager was disgusted over the failure to get a representative sample!

Computerized Selection

Most audit organizations have computerized random number generators available to cut short the drudgery of poring over printed random number tables. Such routines can print a tailored series of numbers with relatively brief turnaround time. Even so, some advance planning is required, and knowledge of how a random number table works is useful.

You can also use random number generators in popular electronic spreadsheet programs. These functions take specifications for the number of digits desired in the random number, then generate a list of random numbers in a desired range. A custom list using an electronic spreadsheet or another random number generator can eliminate the problem of numerous discards (unusable numbers) that are encountered in a printed random number table. (Notice the numerous discards skipped in the procedure shown in Exhibit F–4.)

R E V I E W
CHECKPOINTS

F.13 When you subdivide a population into two populations for attribute sampling, how do the two samples compare to the one sample that would be drawn if the population had not been subdivided?

F.14 Are you required to use all five digits of a random number when you have a random number table like the one in Appendix FA?

F.15 What steps are involved in selecting a sample using the systematic random selection method?

STATISTICAL EVALUATION

LEARNING OBJECTIVE

5. Use evaluation tables or calculation to compute statistical results (CUL, the computed upper limit) for evidence obtained with detail test of controls procedures.

To accomplish a statistical evaluation of test of controls audit evidence, you must know the tolerable deviation rate and the acceptable risk of assessing the control risk too low. These are your **decision criteria**—the *standards for evaluation in the circumstances*. You also need to know the size of the sample that was audited and the number of deviations. Now you can use the evaluation tables in Appendix FB or the Poisson risk factors in Appendix FD.

Using Tables

The procedure for using the tables in Appendix FB is to: (1) Find the evaluation table for your acceptable risk of assessing the control risk too low (5% or 10%); (2) Find your sample size in the left margin; (3) Read across to the column for the number of deviations you found in the sample; and (4) the cell value is the sampling error-adjusted upper limit (the *computed upper limit* "CUL"). Try it with a sample of 45 sales transactions in which you found 1 deviation of product pricing, with RACRTL of 5 percent. The probability is 5 percent (the *risk of assessing control risk too low* when you read the 5 percent table) that the population deviation rate is greater than 10.2 percent. If your tolerable deviation rate is 10 percent, you can assess control risk of mispricing invoices and charges to customers at the control risk level identified with TDR = 10 percent. (This method of finding CUL is also illustrated in the box on page 625.)

Using Calculations

Another device for calculating CUL is a *Poisson risk factor* equation. These risk factors are in Appendix AD. Without going into the underlying mathematics, the CUL calculation is:

$$\text{CUL} = \frac{\text{Poisson risk factor for number of deviations, RACRTL}}{\text{Sample size}}$$

For example: The Poisson risk factor for RACRTL = 5 percent and 1 deviation found in a sample is 4.75; thus, with a sample of 45:

$$CUL = \frac{4.75}{45} = .106 \text{ or } 10.6 \text{ percent}$$

Finding the proper Poisson Risk Factors for this CUL calculation is illustrated in the box on page 626. For the number of deviations discovered (1), read to the left to the column for RACRTL = 5%, and find the factor in the cell (4.75). Divide this factor by the sample size (45 in our example) to get the CUL = 10.6 percent.

CULs calculated using the Poisson risk factor equation will not always be exactly the same as those figured using the Appendix FB tables. The tables are rounded differently than the Poisson factors, and this accounts for most of the difference.

The risk factor equation is very easy to use for CUL calculation. You just need to find the right risk factor. It has the advantage of supplying factors for all the RACRTLs from 50 percent to 1 percent. You are not limited to RACRTLs of 5 percent and 10 percent like you are with the Appendix FB tables.

Applying a Decision Rule

After you calculate the CUL, you can compare it to your previously determined tolerable deviation rate (TDR) and apply an appropriate decision rule.

A higher control risk assessment decision is not the same as a "rejection" decision. You just take the CUL derived from your sample and use it to assess the control risk. For example, assume you audited 30 sales transactions (tolerable deviation rate criterion of 8 percent, a risk of assessing control-risk-too-low criterion of 10 percent, and an expectation of zero deviations) to try to evaluate control risk at 0.40 (see Exhibit F–3) and justify the audit of 107 customer accounts in the accounts receivable total (see Exhibit F–2). You can achieve this control risk assessment if you find no deviations in the sample of 30 transactions (see Appendix FB.2). If you find one actual deviation in the sample of 30, your computed upper limit is 12.4 percent (see Appendix FB.2), and according to the decision rule, you should not assess control risk at 0.40. However, you can take CUL = 12.4%, assess a higher control risk (0.60 according to Exhibit F–3), and audit a sample of 125 customer accounts, which is appropriate for control risk of 0.60, instead of the sample of 107 appropriate if control risk had been assessed at 0.40.

AUDITING INSIGHT

TEST OF CONTROLS DECISION RULE

If CUL (computed upper limit) is less than your tolerable deviation rate, you can conclude that the population deviation rate is low enough to meet your tolerable rate decision criterion, and you can assess the control risk at the level associated with the tolerable deviation rate. (Alternatively, you can assess the control risk at the level associated with the CUL.)

If CUL exceeds your tolerable deviation rate, you can conclude that the population deviation rate may be higher than your decision criterion, and you should assess a higher control risk—for example, the control risk associated with the CUL.

The **computed upper limit** is a *statistical calculation that takes sampling error into account.* You know a sample deviation rate (number of actual deviations in the sample ÷ sample size) cannot be expressed as the *exact* population deviation rate. According to common sense and statistical theory, the actual but unknown population rate might be lower or higher. Since auditors are mainly concerned with the risk of assessing control risk too

AUDITING INSIGHT

VOTER PETITION DECLARED VOID

City Clerk Eldon Aldridge used a statistical sampling of 6,637 of the 31,038 signatures submitted by the Save Our Springs Coalition to determine the validity of the petition. In the sample, 5,011 (75.5%) were found to belong to valid, registered voters. Based on this validity percentage, Aldridge determined that the Coalition was 1,455 signatures short of the 24,889 required.

OBSERVATION: The article does not state any risk criteria. Problem F.43 at the end of the chapter asks you to reproduce and explain the city clerk's calculation.

Source: *Austin American Statesman.*

low, the *higher* limit is calculated to show how high the estimated population deviation rate may be.

Auditing standards tell you to "consider the risk that your sample deviation rate can be lower than your tolerable deviation rate for the population, even though the actual population rate exceeds the tolerable rate." In statistical evaluation, you accomplish this consideration by holding the risk of assessing the control risk too low (RACRTL) constant at the acceptable level while computing CUL, then comparing CUL to your tolerable deviation rate (TDR).

The story about the "voter petition declared void" in the box (above) illustrates another use of attribute statistics to estimate a number of valid voter signatures. In this case the attribute of interest was "registered voter."

Example of Satisfactory Results

Suppose you selected 200 recorded sales invoices and vouched them to supporting shipping orders. You found no shipping orders for one invoice. When you followed up, no one could explain the missing documents, but nothing about the sampling unit appeared to indicate a fraud. You have already decided that a 10 percent risk of assessing control risk too low and a 3 percent tolerable deviation rate adequately define your decision criteria for the test of controls audit.

1. Find Appendix FB.2, the evaluation table of 10 percent risk assessing control risk too low.
2. Find the sample size, 200, in the left margin.
3. Read across to the column for 1 deviation.
4. In the cell, you find 2.0 (CUL = 2 percent).

Or, calculate using the Poisson Risk Factor from Appendix FD; CUL = $^{3.89}/_{200}$ = 1.945 percent.

Audit conclusion: The probability is 10 percent that the population deviation rate is greater than 2 percent. This finding (CUL of 2 percent, less than tolerable rate of 3 percent) satisfies your decision criteria, and you can assess control risk as you had originally planned.

Example of Unsatisfactory Results

The situation is the same as above, except you found four invoices with missing shipping orders.

1. Find Appendix FB.2, the evaluation table for 10 percent risk of assessing control risk too low.
2. Find the sample size, 200, in the left margin.
3. Read across to the column for 4 deviations.
4. In the cell, you find 4.0 (CUL = 4 percent).

Or, calculate using the Poisson Risk Factor from Appendix FD, CUL = $^{8.00}/_{200}$ = 4 percent.

Audit conclusion: The probability is 10 percent that the population deviation rate is greater than 4 percent. This CUL finding exceeds your tolerable rate criterion of 3 percent, and you ought to assess a higher control risk than you had originally planned.

DISCOVERY SAMPLING—FISHING FOR FRAUD

LEARNING OBJECTIVE

6. Use the discovery sampling evaluation table for assessment of audit evidence.

Discovery sampling is essentially another kind of sampling design directed toward a specific objective. However, discovery sampling statistics also offer an additional means of evaluating the sufficiency of audit evidence in the event that no deviations are found in a sample.

A discovery sampling table is shown in Appendix FC. A discovery sampling plan deals with this kind of question: *If I believe some important kind of error or fraud might exist in the records, what sample size will I have to audit to have assurance of finding at least one example?* Ordinarily, discovery sampling is used for designing procedures to search for such things as examples of forged checks or intercompany sales improperly classified as sales to outside parties. However, discovery sampling may be used effectively whenever a low deviation rate is expected. Auditors must quantify a desired **probability of at least one occurrence**, which is *1 minus a relevant risk of assessing control risk too low* and must specify a tolerable deviation rate that is called **critical rate of occurrence.** Generally, the critical rate is very low because the deviation is something very sensitive and important, like a sign of a fraud.

The probability in this case represents the desired probability of finding at least one occurrence (example of the deviation) in a sample. In Appendix FC, you can read down a specified critical rate column to the specified probability of at least one occurrence, then read the required sample size in the left column. This discovery sampling table expresses a type of cumulative binomial probability of finding one or more deviations in a sample of a particular size, if the population deviation rate is equal to a given critical occurrence rate.

Suppose that in the test of controls audit of recorded sales, you are especially concerned about finding an example of a deviation if as few as 50 outright fictitious sales (intentional frauds) existed in the population of 10,000 recorded invoices (a critical rate of 0.5 percent). Furthermore, suppose you want to achieve at least 0.99 probability of finding at least one. Appendix FC indicates a required sample of 900 recorded sales invoices. If a sample of this size were audited and no fictitious sales were found, you could conclude that the actual rate of fictitious sales in the population was *less than* 0.5 percent with 0.99 probability of being right.

This feature of discovery sampling evaluation provides the additional means of evaluating the *sufficiency* of audit evidence whenever an attribute sample turns up zero deviations. You can read across from the sample size audited (say, 200) to a probability that in your judgment represents reasonable assurance. Then, reading up the column, you find the critical rate. Suppose 200 sales invoices were audited and no deviations of missing shipping orders were found. The discovery sampling table shows that, if the population deviation rate were 2 percent, the probability of including at least 1 deviation in a sample of 200 is 0.98. None was found, so, with 0.98 probability, you can believe that the occurrence rate of missing shipping orders is 2 percent or less.

F.16 What is the auditing interpretation of the sampling error-adjusted deviation rate (CUL)?

F.17 What is the CUL for these data: sample size audited = 46, actual deviations found = 3, RACRTL = 37 percent?

F.18 What is the proper interpretation of the *probability* in the Discovery Sampling table in Appendix FC?

PUTTING IT ALL TOGETHER

LEARNING OBJECTIVE

7. Choose a test of controls sample size from among several equally acceptable alternatives.

To this point, you have learned some of the theoretical details about defining populations, perceiving control risk (CR) as a probability ranging from low (e.g., 0.10) to high (e.g., 1.0), using smoke/fire multiplier thinking to determine an anchor tolerable deviation rate (TDR), using Roberts' method to calculate the risk of assessing control risk too low (RACRTL), and using tables and Poisson risk factor calculations to determine the test of controls sample size ($n[c]$). You also learned about an assignment of successively higher TDRs to successively higher CRs as a means of associating each control risk level with a tolerable deviation rate.

You also have learned about the *links* that connect test of controls sampling for control risk assessment to substantive sampling for the audit of an account balance. These *links* are: (1) the smoke/fire multiplier judgment that relates tolerable dollar misstatement in the substantive balance-audit sample to the anchor tolerable deviation rate in the test of controls sample and (2) Roberts' method of calculating RACRTL that relates an audit judgment of incremental risk of incorrect acceptance for the substantive balance-audit sample to the risk of incorrect acceptance consequences of assessing control risk too low. There is one more *link:* (3) considering the cost of the substantive balance-audit sample to decide the test of controls sample size and the *planned control risk assessment.* The **planned control risk assessment,** with the emphasis on *planned,* is the auditors' selection of a control risk level for which they *want* to justify a control risk assessment after completing the test of controls audit work. Looking at Exhibit F–5, you can see 10 test of controls sample sizes (column 5), one for each of the possible control risk levels.

Question: Which one should you choose?
Answer: The one for which the total cost is lowest ($1,008 in column 9). Test of control sample = 40. Tolerable deviation rate = 6%. Risk of assessing control risk too low = 9%. (Expected deviation rate = zero.) Planned control risk assessment = 0.30.

| EXHIBIT F–5 | COMBINED COST OF TEST OF CONTROLS AND SUBSTANTIVE SAMPLING |

	(1)	(2)	(3)	(4)	(5) Test of Control	(6) Test of Control	(7) Balance-Audit	(8) Balance-Audit	(9)
Control Risk Categories	CR	TDR	RIA	RACRTL	n[c]	Cost	n[s]	Cost	Total
Low control risk	0.10	2%	0.50	0.02	196	$1,176	51	$ 408	$1,548
Low control risk	0.20	4	0.25	0.05	75	450	81	648	1,098
Low control risk	0.30	6	0.17	0.09	40	240	96	768	1,008
Moderate control risk	0.40	8	0.13	0.13	26	156	107	856	1,012
Moderate control risk	0.50	10	0.10	0.20	16	96	117	936	1,032
Moderate control risk	0.60	12	0.08	0.30	10	60	125	1,000	1,060
Control risk slightly below the maximum	0.70	14	0.07	0.48	5	30	130	1,040	1,070
Control risk slightly below the maximum	0.80	16	0.06	0.50	4	24	136	1,088	1,112
Control risk slightly below the maximum	0.90	18	0.06	0.50	4	24	140	1,120	1,144
Maximum control risk	1.00	20	0.05	0.50	4	24	143	1,144	1,168

Reason: If control risk is assessed at 0.30, as planned, the substantive sample can be 96 items from the related balance, and the total cost will be $1,008, the lowest cost among all the equally effective alternatives.

Let's review Exhibit F–5 more closely. Column *1* contains the range of possible control risk assessments (CR).

Column *2* contains the tolerable deviation rates (TDR), which are based on a smoke-fire multiplier of 8.5, a tolerable misstatement in the balance sheet account (e.g., accounts receivable) of $10,000, and a total of $8.5 million in (sales) transaction subject to test of controls sampling. This multiplier produces an *anchor* TDR = 1 percent at CR = 0.05, and the TDR is stepped up 1 percent for each 0.05 increase in the control risk thereafter (refer to Exhibit F–3).

Column *4* contains the RACRTLs figured using Roberts' method with an incremental risk of incorrect acceptance of 0.01 and the RIAs shown in Column *3*.

Column *5* contains the test of control sample sizes ($n[c]$) calculated with the Poisson risk factor equation (to accommodate the RACRTLs not available in the Appendix FB tables).

For column *6* the cost of the test of controls sample work assumes that each sampling unit costs $6 to audit.

Column *7* contains the substantive balance-audit sample sizes ($n[s]$) derived from several variables (more on this in Module G), including the control risk level in Column *1*.

For column *8*, the cost of the substantive sample work on the balance items assumes that each sampling unit cost $8 to audit.

Column *9* is the sum of column *6* (test of controls sample cost) and column *8* (substantive sample cost).

The choice of a *planned control risk assessment* completes the planning phase for a sample-based detail test of controls. After the sample is audited, statistical evaluation of the evidence is performed to justify a control risk assessment of 0.30 and a substantive audit of 96 balance items, or, if some deviations are found, a higher control risk assessment and the audit of a larger substantive balance-audit sample.

R E V I E W CHECKPOINTS	**F.19** What are the *links* that connect test of controls sample planning with substantive balance-audit sample planning?	**F.20** When you have several alternative test of controls sample sizes to choose from, how do you choose the one to audit?

SUMMARY

Statistical sampling for attributes in test of controls auditing provides quantitative measures of deviation rates and risks of assessing control risk too low. The statistics support the auditors' professional judgments involved in control risk assessment. The most important judgments are the numbers assigned to the tolerable rate of deviation, the risk of assessing control risk too low, and the risk of assessing control risk too high. With these specifications and an estimate of the deviation rate in the population, a preliminary sample size can be predetermined. However, nothing is magic about a predetermined sample size. It will turn out to be too few, just right, or too many, depending on the evidence produced by it and the control risk assessment supported by it.

The easy part of attribute sampling is the statistical evaluation. The hard parts are: (1) specifying the controls for audit and defining deviations, (2) quantifying the decision criteria, (3) using imagination to find a way to select a random sample, and (4) associating the quantitative evaluation with the assessment of control risk. The structure and formality of the steps involved in statistical sampling force auditors to plan the procedures exhaustively. This same structure and formality also contribute to good working paper documentation because they clearly identify the things that should be recorded in the working papers. Altogether, statistical sampling facilitates auditors' plans, procedures, and evaluations of defensible evidence.

MULTIPLE-CHOICE QUESTIONS FOR PRACTICE AND REVIEW

F.21 When auditors plan a test of controls and think about several control risk assessments that *could* be made, they also can think about
a. One relevant tolerable deviation rate.
b. Two relevant tolerable deviation rates.
c. Three relevant tolerable deviation rates.
d. Several relevant tolerable deviation rates.

F.22 When auditors plan a test of controls and decide the *want* to assess one control risk level (say, control risk of 0.40), they should think about decision criteria that include
a. One relevant tolerable deviation rate.
b. Two relevant tolerable deviation rates.
c. Three relevant tolerable deviation rates.
d. Several relevant tolerable deviation rates.

F.23 An audit manager decided the possible control risk assessments listed in the left column could be relevant to the audit plan. What is wrong with the tolerable deviation rates associated with each control risk?

Control Risk	Tolerable Deviation Rate
0.20	0.06
0.50	0.04
0.80	0.02

a. The control risks are too widely spaced, ignoring possible assessments of 0.10, 0.30, 0.40, 0.60, 0.70, 0.90, and 1.00.
b. Nothing is wrong with the tolerable deviation rates associated with the possible control risk assessments.
c. All the tolerable deviation rates are too low.
d. The tolerable deviation rate relationships are reversed because the lowest rate (0.02) should be associated with the lowest risk (0.20) and the highest rate (0.06) should be associated with the highest risk (0.80).

F.24 Hershiser, an audit manager, made the judgments that his test of controls of the company's 50,000 purchase transactions should be based on a tolerable deviation rate of 0.06, a risk of assessing control risk too low of 0.05, and an expected deviation rate of 3 percent. His statistical sample size should be
a. 125.
b. 110.
c. 90.
d. 100.

F.25 K. Gibson, an audit manager, decided the possible control risk assessments listed in the left column were relevant when thinking about control over sales transactions. The sample sizes *for the subsequent substantive audit of the customer accounts receivable* are shown to the right of each control risk. What *risk of assessing control risk too low* (RACRTL) could be assigned for tests of controls at each control risk level?

Control Risk	Accounts Receivable Sample	RACRTL
0.20	190	?
0.50	350	?
0.80	390	?
0.90	400	0.10

a. From top to bottom: 5%, 10%, 1%.
b. From top to bottom: 10%, 1%, 5%.
c. From top to bottom: 1%,10%, 5%.
d. From top to bottom: 1%, 5%, 10%.

F.26 Assume that audit manager Lasorda found two deviations in a sample of 90 transactions. The computed upper limit (CUL) at 5 percent risk of assessing control risk too low is
a. 9%.
b. 7%.
c. 6%.
d. 2%.

F.27 The auditing interpretation of the sampling error-adjusted deviation rate (computed upper limit, CUL) in a test of controls sample is

a. The estimated worst likely deviation rate in the population with probability = risk of assessing control risk too low that the actual deviation rate is even higher.

b. The estimated lowest likely deviation rate in the population with probability = risk of assessing control risk too low that the actual deviation rate is even lower.

c. The estimated lowest likely deviation rate in the population with certainty that the actual deviation rate is even lower.

d. The estimated worst likely deviation rate in the population with certainty that the actual deviation rate is even higher.

F.28 If an auditor tested 100 transactions and found one deviation from an important control procedure, the audit conclusion could be that control risk can be assessed at the associated control risk level when

a. The relevant tolerable deviation rate is 0.02.

b. The relevant tolerable deviation rate is 0.03.

c. The relevant tolerable deviation rate is 0.04.

d. More information about decision criteria is available.

F.29 If an auditor calculated a CUL of 5 percent when she had a tolerable deviation rate criterion of 4 percent, both at the same risk of assessing control risk too low,

a. Control risk should be assessed at the level associated with the 4 percent tolerable deviation rate.

b. Control risk should be assessed at the level associated with the 5 percent tolerable deviation rate.

c. Control risk should be assessed at the maximum level (100 percent) because the company's performance failed the test.

d. Control risk should be assessed at the minimum level (10 percent) because the statistics are close enough.

F.30 If an auditor calculated a CUL of 2 percent when she had a tolerable deviation rate criterion of 4 percent, both at the same risk of assessing control risk too low;

a. Control risk should be assessed at the level associated with the 4 percent tolerable deviation rate.

b. Control risk should be assessed at the level associated with the 2 percent tolerable deviation rate.

c. Control risk should be assessed at the maximum level (100 percent) because the company's performance failed the test.

d. Control risk should be assessed at the minimum level (10 percent) because the statistics are close enough.

F.31 What is the evaluation conclusion from a statistical sample of internal control activities when a test of 125 documents shows five deviations if the tolerable deviation rate is 5 percent, the expected population deviation rate is 2 percent, and the allowance for sampling risk is 3 percent?

a. Accept the sample results as suitable support for assessing a low control risk because the tolerable rate less the allowance for sampling risk is less than the expected population deviation rate.

b. Use the evidence to assess a higher control risk than planned because the sample deviation rate plus the allowance for sampling risk exceeds the tolerable deviation rate.

c. Use the evidence to assess a higher control risk than planned because the tolerable deviation rate plus the allowance for sampling risk exceeds the expected population deviation rate.

d. Accept the sample results as suitable support for assessing a low control risk because the sample deviation rate plus the allowance for sampling risk exceeds the tolerable deviation rate.

F.32 An auditor designed a statistical test of controls sample that would provide a 10 percent risk of assessing control risk too low that not more than 7 percent of sales invoices lacked credit approval. From previous audits, the auditor expected about 3 examples of lack of approval in the sample. The auditor selected 90 invoices, and 7 were found to lack credit approval. The achieved (computed) upper limit of the deviation rate was

a. 3.3%.

b. 7.8%.

c. 4.5%.

d. 12.8%.

F.33 Based on the same information in F.32, the allowance for sampling error was

a. 10.0%.

b. 7.8%.

c. 5.0%.

d. 2.2%.

EXHIBIT F.34–1

	Case 1		Case 2		Case 3		Case 4		Case 5	
Sample A or B	A	B	A	B	A	B	A	B	A	B
Number of invoices examined	75	200	150	25	250	100	100	125	225	200
Number of deviations found in sample	1	4	2	0	6	2	1	3	7	4
Percentage (%) of sample invoices with deviations	1.3	2.0	1.3	0.0	2.4	2.0	1.0	2.4	3.1	2.0

EXERCISES AND PROBLEMS

F.34   Deciding the Best Evidence Representation.   Assume you are working on the audit of a small company and are examining purchase invoices for the presence of a "received" stamp. The omission of the stamp is thus a deviation. The population is composed of approximately 4,000 invoices, which were processed by the company during the current year.

You decide that a deviation rate in the population as high as 5 percent would not require any extended audit procedures. However, if the population deviation rate is greater than 5 percent, you would want to assess a higher control risk and do more audit work.

In each case in Exhibit F.34–1, below, write the letter of the sample (A or B) which, in your judgment, provides the better evidence that the deviation rate in the population is 5 percent or less. (Assume that each sample observation is selected at random.)

F.35   Estimating a Frequency.   A local industrial company has two departments. In the larger department, about 45 sales invoices are completed each day; in the smaller department, about 15 invoices are completed each day. About 50 percent of all sales invoices completed in each department specify discounts from the company's list prices. However, the exact percentage varies from day to day. Sometimes it may be higher than 50 percent, sometimes lower.

For a period of one year, and for each department, a member of the audit staff kept track of the number of days on which more than 60 percent of the sales invoices specified discounts. Which department do you think showed the greater number of such days?

a. The larger department.

b. The smaller department.

c. About the same.

F.36   Sample Size Relationships.   For the specifications of acceptable risk of assessing control risk too low, tolerable deviation rate, and expected number of deviations shown below, prepare tables showing the appropriate sample sizes. (Use the Poisson risk factor equation.)

a. Tolerable deviation rate = 0.05. Expected deviations = 0. Acceptable risk of assessing control risk too low = 0.01, 0.05, 0.10.

b. Acceptable risk of assessing control risk too low = 0.10. Expected deviations = 1. Tolerable deviation rate = 0.10, 0.08, 0.05, 0.03, 0.02.

c. Acceptable risk of assessing control risk too low = 0.10. Tolerable deviation rate = 0.10. Expected deviations = 1, 2, 4, 7, 9.

d. Place a second sample size column in *a*, *b*, and *c*, and figure the sample size when the population contains only 500 units.

F.37   Exercises in Sample Selection.

a. Sales invoices beginning with number 0001 and ending with number 5000 are entered in a sales journal. You want to choose 50 invoices for a test of controls. Start at row 5, column 3, of the random number table in Appendix FA and select the first five usable numbers, using the first four digits in the column.

b. There are 9,100 numbered checks in a cash disbursements journal, beginning with number 2220 and ending with number 11319. You want to choose 100 disbursements for a test of controls. Start at row 11, column 1, of the table of random digits in Appendix FA and select the first five usable numbers.

c. During the year, the client wrote 45,200 vouchers. Each month, the numbering series started over with number 00001, prefixed with a number for the month (January = 01, February = 02, and so on), so the voucher numbers had seven digits, the last five of which were in overlapping series. You want to choose 120 vouchers for audit. Evaluate each of the following suggested selection methods:

(1) Choose a month at random and select 120 at random in that month by association with a five-digit random number.

(2) Choose 120 usable seven-digit random numbers.

(3) Select 10 vouchers at random from each month.

d. Explain how you could use systematic sampling to select the first five items in each case above. For case (c), assume the random start is at voucher 03-01102.

F.38   Imagination in Sample Selection.   The text illustrated a problem of selecting a sample of classified ads printed in a newspaper. Auditors often need to be imaginative when figuring out how to obtain a random sample. For each of the cases below, explain how you could select a sample having the best chance of being random.

a. You need a sample of recorded cash disbursements. The client used two bank accounts for general disbursements. Account number 1 was used during January–August and issued checks numbered 3633–6632. Account number 2 was used during May–December and issued checks numbered 0001–6000. (*Hint:* For purposes of random number selection and check identification, convert one of the numerical sequences to a sequence that does not overlap the other.) In Appendix FA, start at row 1, column 2, and select the first five random checks, reading down column 2.

b. You need a sample of purchase orders. The client issued prenumbered purchase orders in the sequence 9000–13999 (5,000 of them). You realize if you just select five-digit random numbers from a table, looking for numbers in this sequence, 95 percent of the random numbers you scan will be discards because a table has 100,000 different five-digit random numbers. (The computer is down today!) How can you fiddle with this sequence to reduce the number of discards? (*Hint:* You can reduce discards to zero.) In Appendix FA, start at row 30, column 3, and select the first five random purchase orders, reading down column 3.

c. You need a sample of perpetual inventory records so you can go to the warehouse and count the quantities while the stock clerks take the physical inventory. The perpetual records have been printed out in a control list showing location, item description, and quantity. You have a copy of the list. It is 75 pages long, with 50 lines to a page (40 lines on the last page). Find an efficient way to select 100 lines for your test of controls audit of the client's counting procedure.

d. You need to determine whether an inventory compilation is complete. You plan to select a sample of physical locations, describe and count the inventory units, and trace the information to the inventory list. The inventory consists of tools, parts, and other hardware material shelved in a large warehouse. The warehouse contains 300 rows of 75-foot-long shelves, each of which has 10 tiers. The inventory is stored on these shelves. Find an efficient way to select 100 sampling units of physical inventory for count and tracing to the inventory listing.

F.39   CUL Calculation Exercises.   Using the Poisson risk factor equation, find the computed upper limit (CUL) for each case below.

	(a)	(b)	(c)
Risk of assessing control risk too low	0.01	0.05	0.10
Sample size	300	300	300
Deviations	6	6	6
Sample deviation rate	—	—	—
Computed upper limit	—	—	—

	(d)	(e)	(f)
Risk of assessing control risk too low	0.05	0.05	0.05
Sample size	100	200	400
Deviations	2	4	8
Sample deviation rate	—	—	—
Computed upper limit	—	—	—

	(g)	(h)	(i)
Risk of assessing control risk too low	0.05	0.05	0.05
Sample size	100	100	100
Deviations	10	6	0
Sample deviation rate	—	—	—
Computed upper limit	—	—	—

F.40   Discovery Sampling.   Using the discovery sampling table in Appendix AC, fill in the missing data in each case:

	(a)	(b)	(c)
Critical rate of occurrence	0.4%	0.5%	1.0%
Required probability	99	99	99
Sample size (minimum)	—	—	—

	(d)	(e)	(f)
Critical rate of occurrence	2.0%	1.0%	0.5%
Required probability	—	—	—
Sample size (minimum)	240	240	240

EXHIBIT F.41–1   RACRTL ASSOCIATED WITH POSSIBLE CONTROL RISK ASSESSMENTS

| | | | RACRTL, given | |
Control Risk Categories	(1) Possible CR Assessments	(2) Related RIA	(3) Incremental RIA 0.01	(4) Incremental RIA 0.02
Low control risk	0.10	0.50		
	0.20	0.25		
	0.30	0.167		
Moderate control risk	0.40	0.125		
	0.50	0.10		
	0.60	0.083		
Control risk slightly below the maximum	0.70	0.071		
	0.80	0.0625		
	0.90	0.0556		
Maximum control risk	1.00	0.05		

Assuming AR = 0.05, IR = 1.0, AP = 1.0. Therefore, RIA = 0.05/(1.0 × CR × 1.0).

	(g)	(h)	(i)
Critical rate of occurrence	—	—	—
Required probability	70	85	95
Sample size (minimum)	300	460	700

F.41   Roberts' Method RACRTL Calculation. Exhibit F.41–1 contains some of the data from Exhibit F–2 in the text.

Required:

a. Complete columns (3) and (4) by calculating the acceptable risk of assessing control risk too low (RACRTL) for incremental risks of incorrect acceptance of 0.01 and 0.02. Let RIA at control risk = 1.0 be the "worst case" point.

b. Discuss the meaning of the difference in the two ranges of RACRTLs.

DISCUSSION CASES

F.42   Tom's Misapplied Application. Tom Barton, an assistant accountant with a local CPA firm, has recently graduated from the Other University. He studied statistical sampling for auditing in college and wants to impress his employers with his knowledge of modern auditing methods.

He decided to select a random sample of payroll checks for the test of controls, using a tolerable rate of 5 percent and an acceptable risk of assessing control risk too low of 5 percent. The senior accountant told Tom that 2 percent of the checks audited last year had one or more errors in the calculation of net pay. Tom decided to audit 100 random checks. Since supervisory personnel had larger paychecks than production workers, he selected 60 of the larger checks and 40 of the others. He was very careful to see that the selections of 60 from the April payroll register and 40 from the August payroll register were random.

The audit of this sample yielded two deviations, exactly the 2 percent rate experienced last year. The first was the deduction of federal income taxes based on two exemptions for a supervisory employee, when his W-4 form showed four exemptions. The other was payment to a production employee at a rate for a job classification one grade lower than his actual job. The worker had been promoted the week before, and Tom found that in the next payroll he was paid at the higher correct rate.

When he evaluated this evidence, Tom decided that these two findings were really not control deviation at all. The withholding of too much tax did not affect the expense accounts, and the proper rate was paid the production worker as soon as the clerk caught up with his change orders. Tom decided that having found zero deviations in a sample of 100, the computed upper limit at 5 percent risk of assessing control risk too low was 3 percent, which easily satisfied his predetermined criterion.

The senior accountant was impressed. Last year he had audited 15 checks from each month, and Tom's work represented a significant time savings. The reviewing partner on the audit was also impressed because he had never thought that statistical sampling could be so efficient, and that was the reason he had never studied the method.

Required:

Identify and explain the mistakes made by Tom and the others.

F.43   Statistical Estimation of the Number of Voters.   The box on page 632 tells about a city clerk's estimation of the number of voter signatures needed on a petition to make the petition complete.

Required:

a. Show calculations to reproduce the city clerk's estimate of 1,455 signatures needed on the petition.

b. Discuss the missing statistical concept in this estimate.

F.44   Determine a Test of Controls Sample Size.   You can use the computer-based *Electronic Workpapers* on the textbook website to complete the worksheet.

N. Wolfe, CPA, is planning the audit of Goodwin Manufacturing Company's inventory. Wolfe plans to audit the inventory by selecting a sample of items for physical observation and counting, followed by price testing. The price testing part of the work takes a large portion of the time on each sampling unit because the company's costing method is complex. The estimated cost of auditing each sampling unit in this substantive balance-audit sample is estimated at $25.

Because this detail substantive work is expensive, Wolfe would like to minimize the sample size by assessing a low control risk. She decided that control over accurate pricing of purchases (additions to the inventory) would be the control attribute most appropriate. The reasoning is that inventory balance misstatements could arise from either or both of miscounting or erroneous pricing and costing calculations. If the basic purchase pricing were accurate, then that would leave the inventory count accuracy and the difficult inventory costing calculations as the remaining source

for error and audit attention. The estimated cost to audit a purchase transaction for pricing accuracy is estimated to be $12. She thinks the client's staff makes few, if any, errors in pricing the purchase transactions.

For the audit of the inventory balance, Wolfe accepted the accounting firm's policy of setting audit risk at 0.05. Since business activity in the client company had been hectic lately, she decided to be conservative and set inherent risk at 1.0. However, certain analytical procedures will be performed by comparing the inventory balance to prior years, the company budget, and certain historical statistics, and these procedures might have a 10 percent chance of detecting material misstatements of the balance.

The book recorded amount of the inventory is $72 million, spread among 3,345 different kinds of inventory items. Purchases for the year amounted to $467 million in about 6,000 separate purchase transactions.

Wolfe believes the inventory balance can be misstated by as much as $2 million without causing the financial statements as a whole to be materially misstated. The overall materiality judgment is $8 million misstatement of operating income before taxes, and $2 million is the amount assigned to the audit of the inventory balance.

The audit staff recently attended a training session where Wolfe learned about the concepts of a smoke/fire multiplier and an incremental risk of incorrect acceptance used to judge the risk of assessing control risk too low. Inventory purchase pricing errors can be numerous, yet not affect the dollar amounts very much, so Wolfe decided that a smoke/fire multiplier of 7 was appropriate. (The firm's policy is to use the multiplier to figure an anchor tolerable deviation rate for control risk = 0.05, and round the anchor up to 1 percent if the

EXHIBIT   F.44–1   **GOODWIN MANUFACTURING COMPANY**

Control Risk Categories	CR	TDR	RIA	RACRTL	Test of Control n[c]	Cost	Balance-Audit n[s]	Cost	Total
Low control risk	0.10						25		
	0.20						46		
	0.30						60		
Moderate control risk	0.40						71		
	0.50						80		
	0.60						87		
Control risk below maximum	0.70						91		
	0.80						96		
	0.90						101		
Maximum risk	1.00						101		

RIA = Risk of incorrect acceptance for the substantive balance-audit sample.

multiplier produces an anchor less than 1 percent. After that, each tolerable deviation rate is 1 percentage point higher for each 0.05 control risk level increment.)

The firm's policy about an incremental risk of incorrect acceptance resulting from assessing control risk too low has not yet been published, but Wolfe thinks that a 0.02 change should not make much difference.

The problem is deciding the size of the test of controls sample for the audit of the purchase-

pricing transactions. Wolfe partially completed the worksheet shown in Exhibit F.44–1. She handed it over to you.

Required:
Copy the worksheet. Complete it and decide the size of the sample for the detail test of accuracy control over the pricing of purchases (additions to the inventory). [Round the risk of incorrect acceptance and risk of assessing control risk too low probabilities to two decimal places.]

APPENDIX FA

TABLE OF RANDOM DIGITS

32942	95416	42339	59045	26693	49057	87496	20624	14819
07410	99859	83828	21409	29094	65114	36701	25762	12827
59981	68155	45673	76210	58219	45738	29550	24736	09574
46251	25437	69654	99716	11563	08803	86027	51867	12116
65558	51904	93123	27887	53138	21488	09095	78777	71240
99187	19258	86421	16401	19397	83297	40111	49326	81686
35641	00301	16096	34775	21562	97983	45040	19200	16383
14031	00936	81518	48440	02218	04756	19506	60695	88494
60677	15076	92554	26042	23472	69869	62877	19584	39576
66314	05212	67859	89356	20056	30648	87349	20389	53805
20416	87410	75646	64176	82752	63606	37011	57346	69512
28701	56992	70423	62415	40807	98086	58850	28968	45297
74579	33844	33426	07570	00728	07079	19322	56325	84819
62615	52342	82968	75540	80045	53069	20665	21282	07768
93945	06293	22879	08161	01442	75071	21427	94842	26210
75689	76131	96837	67450	44511	50424	82848	41975	71663
02921	16919	35424	93209	52133	87327	95897	65171	20376
14295	35469	14216	03191	61647	30296	66667	10101	63203
05303	91109	82403	40312	62191	67023	90073	83205	71344
57071	90357	12901	08899	91039	67251	28701	03846	94589
78471	57741	13599	84390	32146	00871	09354	22745	65806
89242	79337	59293	47481	07740	44345	25716	70020	54005
14955	59592	97035	80430	87220	06392	79028	57123	52872
42446	41880	37415	47472	04513	49494	08860	08038	43624
18534	22346	54556	17558	73689	14894	05030	19561	56517
39284	33737	42512	86411	23753	29690	26096	81361	93099
33922	37329	89911	55876	28379	81031	22058	21487	54613
78355	54013	50774	30666	61205	42574	47773	36027	27174
08845	99145	94316	88974	29828	97069	90327	61842	29604
01769	71825	55957	98271	02784	66731	40311	88495	18821
17639	38284	59478	90409	21997	56199	30068	82800	49692
05851	58653	99949	63505	40209	85551	90729	64938	52403
42396	40112	11469	03476	03328	84238	26570	51790	42122
13318	14192	98167	75631	74141	22369	36757	89117	54998
60571	54786	26281	01855	30706	66578	32019	65884	58485
09531	81853	59334	70929	03544	18150	89541	13555	21168
72865	16829	86542	00396	20363	13010	69645	49608	54738
56324	31093	77924	28622	83543	28912	15059	80192	83964
78192	21626	91399	07235	07104	73652	64425	85149	75409
64666	34767	97298	92708	01994	53188	78476	07804	62404
82201	75694	02808	65983	74373	66693	13094	74183	73020
15360	73776	40914	85190	54278	99054	62944	47351	89098
68142	67957	70896	37983	20487	95350	16371	03426	13895
19138	31200	30616	14639	44406	44236	57360	81644	94761
28155	03521	36415	78452	92359	81091	56513	88321	97910
87971	29031	51780	27376	81056	86155	55488	50590	74514
58147	68841	53625	02059	75223	16783	19272	61994	71090
18875	52809	70594	41649	32935	26430	82096	01605	65846
75109	56474	74111	31966	29969	70093	98901	84550	25769
35983	03742	76822	12073	59463	84420	15868	99505	11426

Source: The Rand Corporation, *A Million Random Digits with 100,000 Normal Deviates* (Glencoe, IL: Free Press, 1955), p. 102.

APPENDIX FB.1   AICPA SAMPLING GUIDE EVALUATION TABLE

STATISTICAL SAMPLE RESULTS EVALUATION TABLE FOR TESTS OF CONTROLS
(Upper limits at 5 percent risk of assessing control risk too low)

Sample Size	Actual Number of Deviations Found										
	0	1	2	3	4	5	6	7	8	9	10
25	11.3	17.6	*	*	*	*	*	*	*	*	*
30	9.5	14.9	19.6	*	*	*	*	*	*	*	*
35	8.3	12.9	17.0	*	*	*	*	*	*	*	*
40	7.3	11.4	15.0	18.3	*	*	*	*	*	*	*
45	6.5	10.2	13.4	16.4	19.2	*	*	*	*	*	*
50	5.9	9.2	12.1	14.8	17.4	19.9	*	*	*	*	*
55	5.4	8.4	11.1	13.5	15.9	18.2	*	*	*	*	*
60	4.9	7.7	10.2	12.5	14.7	16.8	18.8	*	*	*	*
65	4.6	7.1	9.4	11.5	13.6	15.5	17.4	19.3	*	*	*
70	4.2	6.6	8.8	10.8	12.6	14.5	16.3	18.0	19.7	*	*
75	4.0	6.2	8.2	10.1	11.8	13.6	15.2	16.9	18.5	20.0	*
80	3.7	5.8	7.7	9.5	11.1	12.7	14.3	15.9	17.4	18.9	*
90	3.3	5.2	6.9	8.4	9.9	11.4	12.8	14.2	15.5	16.8	18.2
100	3.0	4.7	6.2	7.6	9.0	10.3	11.5	12.8	14.0	15.2	16.4
125	2.4	3.8	5.0	6.1	7.2	8.3	9.3	10.3	11.3	12.3	13.2
150	2.0	3.2	4.2	5.1	6.0	6.9	7.8	8.6	9.5	10.3	11.1
200	1.5	2.4	3.2	3.9	4.6	5.2	5.9	6.5	7.2	7.8	8.4

Note: This table presents upper limits as percentages. This table assumes a large population.
* Over 20 percent.
Source: *Audit Sampling,* Audit and Accounting Guide (New York: AICPA, 1983).

HOW TO USE APPENDIX FB

Appendix FB.1 is for 5 percent RACRTL, and FB.2 for 10 percent RACRTL. These are evaluation tables, primarily useful for finding the computed upper limit (CUL).

1. *Be sure to get into the correct table:* FB.1 is for 5 percent RACRTL; FB.2 is for 10 percent RACRTL.
2. *Find the CUL:* Given a sample size and number of deviations found in the sample, read across to the column headed at the top by the number of deviations, and the cell value is CUL. Example: In the 5 percent RACRTL table (FB.1), a sample of 45 was audited, one deviation was found, and the CUL is 10.2 percent.
3. *Read the table to figure a sample size:* Given the tolerable deviation rate and the expected *number of deviations* in any sample, find the number of deviations column at the top, read down to the deviation rate in a cell, then read across the row to find the sample size. Example: For 5 percent RACRTL, if the number of deviations is 1, and the tolerable deviation rate is 6 percent, the sample size is about 77 (interpolating).

APPENDIX FB.2   AICPA SAMPLING GUIDE EVALUATION TABLE

STATISTICAL SAMPLE RESULTS EVALUATION TABLE FOR TESTS OF CONTROLS
(Upper limits at 10 percent risk of assessing control risk too low)

Sample Size	Actual Number of Deviations Found										
	0	1	2	3	4	5	6	7	8	9	10
20	10.9	18.1	*	*	*	*	*	*	*	*	*
25	8.8	14.7	19.9	*	*	*	*	*	*	*	*
30	7.4	12.4	16.8	*	*	*	*	*	*	*	*
35	6.4	10.7	14.5	18.1	*	*	*	*	*	*	*
40	5.6	9.4	12.8	16.0	19.0	*	*	*	*	*	*
45	5.0	8.4	11.4	14.3	17.0	19.7	*	*	*	*	*
50	4.6	7.6	10.3	12.9	15.4	17.8	*	*	*	*	*
55	4.1	6.9	9.4	11.8	14.1	16.3	18.4	*	*	*	*
60	3.8	6.4	8.7	10.8	12.9	15.0	16.9	18.9	*	*	*
70	3.3	5.5	7.5	9.3	11.1	12.9	14.6	16.3	17.9	19.6	*
80	2.9	4.8	6.6	8.2	9.8	11.3	12.8	14.3	15.8	17.2	18.6
90	2.6	4.3	5.9	7.3	8.7	10.1	11.5	12.8	14.1	15.4	16.6
100	2.3	3.9	5.3	6.6	7.9	9.1	10.3	11.5	12.7	13.9	15.0
120	2.0	3.3	4.4	5.5	6.6	7.6	8.7	9.7	10.7	11.6	12.6
160	1.5	2.5	3.3	4.2	5.0	5.8	6.5	7.3	8.0	8.8	9.5
200	1.2	2.0	2.7	3.4	4.0	4.6	5.3	5.9	6.5	7.1	7.6

Note: this table presents upper limits as percentages. This table assumes a large population.
* Over 20 percent.
Source: *Audit Sampling*, Audit and Accounting Guide (New York: AICPA, 1983).

APPENDIX FC

DISCOVERY SAMPLING TABLE*

	Critical Rate of Occurrence							
Sample Size	.1%	.2%	.3%	.4%	.5%	.75%	1%	2%
50	5%	10%	14%	18%	22%	31%	40%	64%
60	6	11	17	21	26	36	45	70
70	7	13	19	25	30	41	51	76
80	8	15	21	28	33	45	55	80
90	9	17	24	30	36	49	60	84
100	10	18	26	33	40	53	64	87
120	11	21	30	38	45	60	70	91
140	13	25	35	43	51	65	76	94
160	15	28	38	48	55	70	80	96
200	18	33	45	56	64	78	87	98
240	22	39	52	62	70	84	91	99
300	26	46	60	70	78	90	95	99+
340	29	50	65	75	82	93	97	99+
400	34	56	71	81	87	95	98	99+
460	38	61	76	85	91	97	99	99+
500	40	64	79	87	92	98	99	99+
600	46	71	84	92	96	99	99+	99+
700	52	77	89	95	97	99+	99+	99+
800	57	81	92	96	98	99+	99+	99+
900	61	85	94	98	99	99+	99+	99+
1000	65	88	96	99	99	99+	99+	99+
1500	80	96	99	99+	99+	99+	99+	99+
2000	89	99	99+	99+	99+	99+	99+	99+

*Probability, in percent, of including at least one deviation in a sample for populations between 5,000 and 10,000.

HOW TO USE APPENDIX FC

1. *Find the probability, in percent, of including at least one deviation in a sample:* Given a sample size and a critical rate of occurrence, read across from the sample size until you reach the critical rate column, the cell value is the probability. Example: If you take a sample of 400 transactions and believe 0.2 percent (0.002) is a critical rate of occurrence for the population, the probability of finding at least one such occurrence (deviation) is 56 percent.
2. *Find the sample size that will give a stated probability:* Given a critical rate of occurrence criterion, read down the critical rate column until you reach the stated probability, then read across to get the sample size. Example: Given a critical rate of occurrence criterion of 0.75 percent (0.0075) and a desire to have 98 percent probability of finding one example if the population rate is that high, you need to audit a sample of 500.
3. *Evaluate samples in which you found zero deviations:* Given the sample size, read across, and each cell gives the probability of finding one or more deviations; since you found zero, each cell gives the probability that the population deviation rate is less than the critical rate at the top of the column. Example: You audited 80 transactions and found no deviations: the probability is 8 percent that the population deviation rate is less than 0.1 percent; 15 percent that it is less than 0.2 percent; . . . ; 80 percent that it is less than 2 percent.

APPENDIX FD   POISSON RISK FACTORS

Deviations	*Risk of Assessing Control Risk Too Low*							
	50%	49%	48%	47%	46%	45%	44%	43%
0	0.70	0.71	0.73	0.76	0.78	0.80	0.82	0.84
1	1.70	1.71	1.74	1.78	1.81	1.84	1.88	1.91
2	2.70	2.71	2.76	2.80	2.84	2.88	2.93	2.97
3	3.70	3.72	3.77	3.82	3.87	3.92	3.97	4.02
4	4.70	4.72	4.78	4.83	4.89	4.95	5.00	5.06
5	5.70	5.73	5.79	5.85	5.91	5.97	6.04	6.10
6	6.70	6.73	6.80	6.86	6.93	7.00	7.07	7.13
7	7.70	7.74	7.81	7.88	7.95	8.02	8.09	8.17
8	8.70	8.74	8.81	8.89	8.96	9.04	9.12	9.20
9	9.70	9.74	9.83	9.90	9.98	10.06	10.14	10.23
10	10.70	10.75	10.83	10.92	11.00	11.08	11.17	11.26

Deviations	42%	41%	40%	39%	38%	37%	36%	35%
0	0.87	0.89	0.92	0.94	0.97	1.00	1.02	1.05
1	1.95	1.99	2.02	2.06	2.10	2.14	2.18	2.22
2	3.01	3.06	3.11	3.15	3.20	3.25	3.30	3.35
3	4.07	4.12	4.18	4.23	4.28	4.34	4.40	4.45
4	5.12	5.18	5.24	5.30	5.36	5.43	5.48	5.55
5	6.16	6.23	6.29	6.36	6.43	6.49	6.56	6.63
6	7.20	7.27	7.34	7.41	7.49	7.56	7.63	7.71
7	8.24	8.31	8.39	8.47	8.54	8.63	8.70	8.78
8	9.28	9.35	9.43	9.51	9.60	9.68	9.76	9.85
9	10.31	10.39	10.47	10.56	10.65	10.74	10.82	10.91
10	11.34	11.43	11.51	11.60	11.70	11.79	11.88	11.97

Deviations	34%	33%	32%	31%	30%	29%	28%	27%
0	1.08	1.11	1.14	1.17	1.21	1.24	1.27	1.31
1	2.26	2.30	2.35	2.39	2.44	2.49	2.54	2.59
2	3.40	3.45	3.50	3.56	3.62	3.67	3.73	3.79
3	4.51	4.57	4.64	4.70	4.77	4.83	4.90	4.96
4	5.61	5.68	5.75	5.82	5.90	5.96	6.04	6.11
5	6.70	6.78	6.85	6.93	7.01	7.08	7.16	7.25
6	7.79	7.87	7.95	8.03	8.12	8.20	8.28	8.37
7	8.86	8.95	9.03	9.12	9.21	9.30	9.93	9.49
8	9.93	10.02	10.12	10.21	10.31	10.40	10.49	10.59
9	11.00	11.10	11.19	11.29	11.39	11.49	11.59	11.70
10	12.07	12.17	12.26	12.37	12.47	12.57	12.68	12.79

APPENDIX FD   (CONCLUDED)

Deviations	Risk of Assessing Control Risk Too Low							
	26%	25%	24%	23%	22%	21%	20%	19%
0	1.35	1.39	1.43	1.47	1.51	1.56	1.61	1.66
1	2.64	2.70	2.75	2.81	2.87	2.93	3.00	3.06
2	3.86	3.93	3.99	4.06	4.13	4.20	4.28	4.36
3	5.04	5.11	5.19	5.26	5.34	5.43	5.52	5.61
4	6.19	6.28	6.36	6.44	6.53	6.63	6.73	6.82
5	7.34	7.43	7.51	7.61	7.70	7.80	7.91	8.01
6	8.46	8.56	8.65	8.75	8.86	8.96	9.08	9.19
7	9.58	9.69	9.79	9.89	10.00	10.11	10.24	10.35
8	10.70	10.81	10.91	11.02	11.14	11.26	11.38	11.51
9	11.80	11.92	12.03	12.14	12.26	12.39	12.52	12.65
10	12.90	13.03	13.14	13.26	13.38	13.51	13.66	13.79

Deviations	18%	17%	16%	15%	14%	13%	12%	11%
0	1.71	1.77	1.83	1.90	1.97	2.04	2.12	2.21
1	3.13	3.21	3.29	3.38	3.46	3.56	3.66	6.77
2	4.44	4.53	4.63	4.73	4.83	4.94	5.06	5.18
3	5.70	5.80	5.90	6.02	6.13	6.25	6.39	6.53
4	6.92	7.03	7.15	7.27	7.39	7.53	7.67	7.83
5	8.12	8.24	8.36	8.50	8.63	8.77	8.93	9.09
6	9.31	9.43	9.57	9.71	9.85	10.00	10.17	10.34
7	10.48	10.61	10.75	10.90	11.05	11.21	11.38	11.57
8	11.64	11.78	11.92	12.08	12.24	12.41	12.59	12.78
9	12.79	12.93	13.09	13.25	13.41	13.59	13.78	13.99
10	13.93	14.08	14.24	14.42	14.58	14.77	14.97	15.18

Deviations	10%	9%	8%	7%	6%	5%	4%	3%
0	2.31	2.41	2.53	2.66	2.81	3.00	3.22	3.51
1	3.89	4.02	4.17	4.33	4.52	4.75	5.01	5.36
2	5.33	5.47	5.64	5.83	6.04	6.30	6.60	6.98
3	6.69	6.85	7.03	7.24	7.48	7.76	8.09	8.51
4	8.00	8.18	8.38	8.60	8.86	9.16	9.51	9.96
5	9.28	9.47	9.68	9.92	10.20	10.52	10.89	11.37
6	10.54	10.74	10.97	11.22	11.51	11.85	12.24	12.75
7	11.78	11.99	12.23	12.49	12.80	13.15	13.57	14.10
8	13.00	13.22	13.47	13.75	14.07	14.44	14.87	15.42
9	14.21	14.44	14.70	15.00	15.32	15.71	16.16	16.73
10	15.41	15.65	15.92	16.23	16.57	16.97	17.43	18.02

Deviations	2%	1%
0	3.91	4.61
1	5.83	6.64
2	7.52	8.41
3	9.08	10.05
4	10.58	11.61
5	12.03	13.11
6	13.44	14.58
7	14.82	16.00
8	16.17	17.41
9	17.51	18.79
10	18.83	20.15

Module G

Test of Balances with PPS Sampling

Professional Standards References

Compendium Section	Document Reference	Topic
AU 312	SAS 47	*Audit Risk and Materiality in Conducting an Audit*
AU 326	SAS 80	*Evidential Matter*
AU 350	SAS 39	*Audit Sampling*
AU 9350		*Interpretations: Audit Sampling*

Learning Objectives

Module G contains more mathematical-statistical details related to the substantive balance-audit sampling introduced in Module E. In fact, Module G is a technical appendix on account balance audit sampling for monetary evidence. Here you will find more specific explanations of how to do "dollar-unit" statistical sampling. After studying this chapter in conjunction with Module E, you should be able to:

1. Calculate a risk of incorrect acceptance, given judgments about inherent risk, control risk, and analytical procedures risk, using the *SAS 39* audit risk model.

2. Explain the cost trade-off theory for determining a risk of incorrect rejection.

3. Explain the characteristics of probability proportionate to size (PPS) sampling and its relationship to attribute sampling.

4. Calculate a PPS sample size for the audit of the details of an account balance.

5. Describe a method for selecting a PPS sample, define a "logical unit," and explain the stratification effect of PPS selection.

6. Calculate an upper error limit for the evaluation of PPS evidence, and discuss the relative merits of alternatives for determining an amount by which a monetary balance should be adjusted.

AUDIT OF AN ACCOUNT BALANCE

Most of the account balances that appear in financial statements consist of numerous subsidiary accounts, some more numerous than others. Many of these accounts may be audited with sampling methods—auditing less than 100 percent of the subsidiary accounts within a control account balance or financial statement total for the purpose of determining the fair presentation of one or more of the financial statement assertions. Some examples of such accounts include:

- *Cash:* Usually not audited by sampling because there are few accounts. Might be sampled if a company has a large number of bank accounts.
- *Accounts receivable:* Usually audited by sampling when the company has a modest to large number of customers.
- *Inventory:* Usually audited by sampling when the company has a modest to large number of different inventory items.
- *Fixed assets:* Sampling may be used to audit numerous additions or an "inventory-taking" of fixed assets.
- *Accounts payable:* Some sampling used, but normally a judgment sample for missing payables.
- *Notes payable:* Usually not audited by sampling because of small number.

The audit of an account balance with sampling has a different objective than test of controls auditing with attribute sampling. Test of controls sampling has the main objective of producing evidence about the *rate of deviation* from company control activities for the purpose of assessing the control risk. Measuring the dollar effect of control deviations is a secondary consideration. On the other hand, a test of an account balance has the objective of producing direct evidence of dollar amounts of misstatement in the account. This is called dollar-value sampling to indicate that the important unit of measure is dollar amounts. Sometimes, dollar-value sampling is called *variables sampling* just to distinguish it from attributes sampling and the control risk assessment objective.

Auditors use two main types of dollar-value sampling. The one most frequently used in financial auditing is called *probability proportional to size (PPS) sampling*. This method is the subject of Module G. The other method is known as *classical sampling*, a name attached merely to distinguish it from PPS sampling. Classical sampling is not covered in this textbook. The method is called "classical" because it was used before PPS sampling was developed, and because it depends on the well-known statistical mathematics of the normal distribution. PPS sampling, by contrast, does not depend upon the normal distribution statistics.

Before we get to the techniques of PPS sampling, however, two topics need to be expanded—the risk of incorrect acceptance and the risk of incorrect rejection.

RISK OF INCORRECT ACCEPTANCE

LEARNING OBJECTIVE

1. Calculate a risk of incorrect acceptance, given judgments about inherent risk, control risk, and analytical procedures risk, using the SAS 39 audit risk model.

In Module E, you saw the audit risk model expanded to include these terms (SAS 39, AU 350):[1]

$$AR = IR \times CR \times AP \times RIA$$

Dollar-value sampling for account balance auditing is primarily concerned with the risk of incorrect acceptance (RIA) in the SAS 39 risk model. The RIA is also called the *test of details risk* because it is the sampling risk of failing to detect monetary error of a tolerable misstatement magnitude with audit procedures applied to the details (subsidiary units) in a control account. The other elements of the model are products of auditors' professional judgment.

The audit risk (AR) is the overall risk the auditor is willing to take of failing to discover misstatement in the account at least equal to the tolerable misstatement assigned to the account. CPA firms that quantify this risk usually set it at 0.05 or 0.10. Their policies are somewhat arbitrary because there is no overall theory acceptable in the practice world to justify any particular quantification of the audit risk. Five percent and 10 percent just seem to work adequately.

The inherent risk (IR) is the auditors' assessment of general factors relating to the probability of erroneous transactions entering the accounting system in the first place. It is hard to assess, often consisting of auditors' memory of problems in previous audits or other aspects of the knowledge of the business. Some CPA firms have questionnaires to document the findings of the know-the-business procedures and to translate them into an inherent risk assessment. CPA firms that quantify this risk assign values from 0.30 to 1.00. The control risk (CR) is the auditors' assessment of the quality of the client's internal control.

Analytical procedures consist of all evidence-gathering procedures other than direct audit of account details. They are substantive procedures, as are the substantive tests of details, but they are not applied on a sample basis. Thus, there is no mathematical way to measure their risk of failure. The analytical procedures risk in the model (AP) is the auditors' subjective judgment of the probability that these nondetail procedures will fail to detect misstatement in the amount of tolerable misstatement in the account. CPA firms that quantify this risk assign values from 0.30 to 1.0.

These risk elements are considered independent, meaning that their combined risk can be a product (multiplication). While theoretical arguments of the validity of the model rage, several CPA firms have built it into their sampling plans. They determine the risk of incorrect acceptance for a sampling application by first making the AR, IR, CR, and AP judgments and assessments, then calculating the RIA:

$$RIA = \frac{AR}{IR \times CR \times AP}$$

Maximum RIA = 0.50, if the equation produces RIA > 0.50.

---

[1] In the auditing standards, the RIA has another name—"TD," meaning "test of details risk" (*SAS 39*, AU 50).

EXHIBIT G-1   CONTROL RISK INFLUENCE ON SUBSTANTIVE BALANCE-AUDIT SAMPLE SIZE

Control Risk Categories	(1) Possible Control Risk Assessments (CR)	(2) Related Risk of Incorrect Acceptance (RIA)*	(3) Number of Balance Items to Select for Substantive Audit
Low control risk	0.10	0.50	51
	0.20	0.25	81
	0.30	0.167	96
Moderate control risk	0.40	0.125	107
	0.50	0.10	117
	0.60	0.083	125
Control risk slightly below the maximum	0.70	0.071	130
	0.80	0.0625	136
	0.90	0.0556	140
Maximum control risk	1.00	0.05	143

*Assuming $AR = 0.05$, $IR = 1.0$, $AP = 1.0$. Therefore, $RIA = 0.05/(1.0 \times CR \times 1.0)$. Maximum $RIA = 0.50$.
Sample sizes are based on the Poisson risk factor for 1 error.

However, be forewarned: Not all CPA firms or other audit organizations use the model in this fashion. Some quantify RIA for statistical sampling in the context of the client situation without reference to the model. Some say they do sampling without quantifying RIA. Some say they do audit sampling, but not statistical sampling. Some say they do not perform audit sampling (as it is defined in auditing standards, SAS 39, AU 350). Practice varies.

The risk of incorrect acceptance influences statistical sample size calculations, and thus it is a prime determinant of the extent of substantive audit work. Exhibit G–1 is the same as Exhibit F–2 (page 619), presented to emphasize the effect of the audit risk model and its RIA on the substantive balance-audit sample sizes, as affected by the range of possible control risk assessments.

Notice the nonlinear change in sample size in relation to the evenly spaced (linear) control risk levels. From CR = 0.10 to CR = 0.20, the sample size increases by 30 sampling units (81–51), but from CR = 0.90 to CR = 1.00, the sample size increases by only 3 sampling units (143–140). The sample sizes are based on dollar-unit calculations for an account balance of $300,000 with a tolerable misstatement of $10,000.

R E V I E W
CHECKPOINTS

G.1   What is the objective of test of controls auditing with attribute sampling? Test of a balance with dollar-value sampling?

G.2   Does use of the audit risk model to calculate RIA remove audit judgment from the risk determination process?

G.3   Is there any benefit to be gained from using the audit risk model to calculate RIA?

G.4   If audit risk (AR) is 0.015, inherent risk (IR) is 0.50, control risk (CR) is 0.30, and analytical procedures risk (AP) is 0.50, what risk of incorrect acceptance (RIA) is suggested by the expanded risk model?

RISK OF INCORRECT REJECTION

LEARNING OBJECTIVE

2. Explain the cost trade-off theory for determining a risk of incorrect rejection.

The other risk auditors accept in audit sampling is to decide that an account balance is misstated by more than the tolerable misstatement when, in fact, but unknown to the auditors, it is *not* misstated by that much. This can happen when the sample is not actually representative of the population from which it was drawn. An initial incorrect rejection decision will create an audit inefficiency because additional work will be done to determine the amount of an adjustment, and the auditors ordinarily will discover that the recorded amount was not materially misstated all along. The planning goal is to keep the risk of incorrect rejection low and also to keep the cost of the audit work within reasonable bounds. When planning the size of an audit sample, the judgment about the acceptable risk of incorrect rejection amounts to an incremental cost analysis.

You can minimize the risk of incorrect rejection by auditing a large sample—spending time and effort at the beginning with the initial sample size. Alternatively, you can take a smaller sample size and save time and cost; but this strategy will increase the risk of incorrect rejection. Taking more risk of incorrect rejection increases the likelihood of "rejection," in which case you may need to expand the sample or otherwise perform work later that you could have performed at the beginning with the initial sample. Thus, your cost trade-off relationship involves (*a*) the cost saved by taking a smaller initial sample, reduced by (*b*) the probability-weighted expected cost of needing to expand the sample or perform other types of audit procedures. These two elements taken together are the expected cost saving from taking more risk of incorrect rejection. Taking a chance on needing to expand the sample is important only if the cost (per item) is lower in the initial sample and higher (per item) when sample units are added later. (If these costs were equal, you could simply audit sample items one at a time until you reached a justifiable conclusion.)

An efficient risk of incorrect rejection (RIR) can be found by successive trials to maximize the expected cost saving (ECS) for the substantive audit sample. The expected cost saving is:

$$ECS = \text{element } (a) - \text{element } (b)$$

where element (*a*) = $C_1 (n_b - n_a)$:

C_1 is the cost-per-unit of auditing a unit in the initial sample.

n_b is the "base" sample size from which comparisons are made, using a "base" *RIR*.

n_a is an "alternative" sample size using a trial RIR_a greater than RIR_b.

element (*b*) = $C_2 (n_b - n_a) (RIR_a - RIR_b)$

C_2 is the cost-per-unit of auditing when a unit is added to the sample.

RIR_b is the RIR "base" used to calculate the "base sample size."

RIR_a is the risk of incorrect rejection greater than RIR_b and is used to calculate the smaller "alternative sample size" and the incremental risk of incorrect rejection.

The objective of the cost trade-off analysis is to find the alternative risk of incorrect rejection (RIR_a) that will maximize the expected cost savings, expressed altogether as:

$$ECS = C_1 (n_b - \dot{n}_a) - C_2 (n_b - n_a) (RIR_a - RIR_b)$$

For example, consider these data:

C_1 = $10 Cost-per-unit to audit in the initial sample.
C_2 = $15 Cost-per-unit to audit in an expanded sample.
n_b = 222 Customer accounts receivable.
n_a = 90 Customer accounts receivable.
RIR_b = 0.10 "Base" 10 percent risk of incorrect rejection.
RIR_a = 0.50 "Alternative" 50 percent risk of incorrect rejection.

The first question is: "Is the expected cost saving positive or negative?" You must calculate the result:

$$ECS = \$10 (222 - 90) - \$15 (222 - 90) (0.50 - 0.10)$$
$$ECS = \$528$$

The expected cost saving is positive, so a 50 percent risk of incorrect rejection is "better" (more cost efficient) than a 10 percent risk of incorrect rejection in these circumstances. The next question is: "At what risk of incorrect rejection is the expected cost savings maximized?" To answer this question, you must calculate ECS for a range of alternative risks of incorrect rejection (e.g., 0.11, 0.12, 0.13, 0.14, on up to 0.50), and find the RIR_a that produces the largest expected cost savings.

The cost trade-off is based on probabilities, and these sometimes are hard to grasp. The analysis illustrated above shows that a risk of 50 percent can be more efficient than a risk of 10 percent with repeated trials using samples of 90. However, auditors do not perform repeated trials—only one sample of 90 units constitutes the first audit work. An audit manager may prefer to incur the $1,320 additional cost ($10 × 132 units) in the first phase of work to avoid any possibility of additional cost of subsequent work. Cost aside, the auditors may not have time to select and audit additional items before the report deadline. For example, auditors may not have time to mail additional accounts receivable confirmations and wait two weeks for replies. Assessment of the risk of incorrect rejection also depends on the audit manager's preferences for cost certainty and the time deadlines for completing the audit.

Generally accepted auditing standards (GAAS) define the risk of incorrect rejection and mention that it pertains to audit efficiency (SAS 39, AU 350). However, GAAS does not present a model or method for determining or thinking about this risk. GAAS also does not have anything to say about a "base RIR" or an "alternative RIR" used in planning a dollar-value audit sample.

R E V I E W
CHECKPOINTS

G.5 Why is the risk of incorrect acceptance considered more critical than the risk of incorrect rejection in connection with audit decisions about an account balance?

G.6 What considerations are important for determining the risk of incorrect rejection?

G.7 What position is taken in generally accepted auditing standards with respect to the risk of incorrect rejection?

PPS SAMPLING FOR ACCOUNT BALANCE AUDITING

LEARNING OBJECTIVE

3. Explain the characteristics of dollar-unit sampling and its relationship to attribute sampling.

Probability proportional to size (PPS) or dollar-unit sampling (DUS) is a modified form of attributes sampling that permits auditors to reach conclusions about dollar amounts. Variations are called *combined attributes-variables* sampling (CAV), *cumulative monetary amount* sampling (CMA), and *monetary unit* sampling (MUS).

Recall from Module F the discussion of the point that the test of controls audit of a client's control activities based on attribute statistics did not directly incorporate dollar measurements. Hence, conclusions were limited to decisions about the rate of control deviations, which helped auditors assess the control risk. PPS is a sampling plan that attaches dollar amounts to attribute statistics. PPS is used widely by many accounting firms and other audit organizations for account balance auditing (variables sampling).

The unique feature of PPS is its definition of the population as the number of dollars in an account balance or class of transactions. Thus, in our example of auditing accounts receivable with a recorded amount (book value) of $300,000, the population is defined as 300,000 *dollar units*. (In Module E we defined the population as 1,500 *customer accounts* when we used the average difference method to calculate *projected likely misstatement* (PLM), and we defined the population as $300,000 *dollars* when we used the ratio method to calculate PLM.)

With this definition of the population, the audit is theoretically conducted on a sample of *dollar units*, and each of these sampling units is either right or wrong. This is the type of treatment given to control performance in attribute sampling; a control activity is either performed or not performed and auditors find either a deviation or no deviation, thus a *rate* of deviation is the statistical measure. However, PPS sampling adopts a convention for assigning dollar values to the deviations, and we will cover these calculations a little later in this module.

USE OF PROBABILITY PROPORTIONAL TO SIZE (PPS) SAMPLING

All dollar-value sampling methods, including PPS, require basic audit judgments for audit risk (AR), inherent risk (IR), control risk (CR), and analytical procedures risk (AP) for the purpose of deriving the risk of incorrect acceptance (RIA). All these sampling methods, including PPS, require an audit judgment of tolerable dollar misstatement (TM) for the account and an estimate of the misstatement (EM) the auditors think might exist in the account.

PPS has advantages for audit sampling plans, such as:

- PPS does not require an estimate of a statistical standard deviation because the statistical basis is the binomial distribution.
- PPS imposes no requirements for a minimum number of errors.
- PPS sample sizes are usually fairly small and hence efficient.
- PPS sample selection methods accomplish stratification by automatically selecting a large proportion of high-value items.

PPS sampling also has some disadvantages. They include:

- The PPS assignment of dollar amounts to errors is conservative (high) because rigorous mathematical proof of PPS upper error limit calculations has not yet been accomplished.
- PPS is not designed to evaluate financial account understatement very well. (No sampling estimator is considered very effective for understatement error.)
- Expanding a PPS sample is difficult when preliminary results indicate a decision that a balance is materially misstated.

The use of PPS in account balance auditing can be inferred from the advantages and disadvantages indicated above. PPS is clearly the best method to use when auditors expect to find few or no errors, and where the greatest risk of error is the risk that the book value is overstated. In all other situations, such as (1) the expectation of many errors, (2) very little basis to estimate the number of errors, or (3) the expectation of both understatement and overstatement of book values, caution is advised. A careful evaluation of the audit situation and alternative sampling methods is recommended before selecting PPS.

R E V I E W
CHECKPOINTS

G.8 What are some of the other names for types of probability proportional to size sampling (PPS)?

G.9 What is the unique feature of PPS sampling?

G.10 What are the advantages and disadvantages of PPS?

G.11 In what way does PPS sampling resemble attribute sampling for control deviations?

PPS SAMPLE SIZE CALCULATION

LEARNING OBJECTIVE

4. Calculate a PPS sample size for the audit of the details of an account balance.

The basic equation for calculating a PPS sample size is:

$$n = \frac{RA \times RF}{TM}$$

where:

RA = Population recorded amount (book value) of the account balance.
RF = Poisson risk factor appropriate for the risk of incorrect acceptance (RIA) and the expected misstatement (EM) [see Appendix GA].[2]
TM = Tolerable misstatement assigned to the account balance.

The recorded amount (RA) is the book balance of the account under audit—for example, a $300,000 accounts receivable total for 1,500 customers, subject to auditing by sampling. The tolerable misstatement (TM) is the portion of overall materiality assigned to this recorded amount. The assignment of tolerable misstatement was covered in Chapter 4.

Finding the appropriate risk factor can be a little tricky. Part of Appendix GA is identical to Appendix FD in Module F. In Appendix GA, the column labeled RF contains the same risk factors as found in Appendix FD. These are the risk factors (RF) auditors can use to calculate a PPS sample size.

The tricky part comes in making the estimate of the number of errors. A suitable first approximation is to calculate the ratio of estimated misstatement to the recorded amount:

$$\text{EM ratio} = \frac{EM}{RA}$$

For example, suppose the auditors expected that there could be $4,000 misstatement in the $300,000 accounts receivable. The EM ratio is:

$$\text{EM ratio} = \frac{\$4,000}{\$300,000} = 0.0133, \text{ or } 1.3 \text{ percent}$$

The ratio, expressed as a percent, can be used to identify the number of errors shown in the left column of Appendix GA. Since they are whole numbers, you can use the risk factor for 1 error or 2 errors in our example. (The higher number will produce a larger, more "conservative," sample size.) Thus, the PPS sample size for a risk of incorrect acceptance of 0.17:

If Error = 1 is used: If Error = 2 is used:

$$n = \frac{\$300,000 \times 3.21}{\$10,000} = 96 \qquad n = \frac{\$300,000 \times 4.53}{\$10,000} = 136$$

This calculation of sample size holds some dangers. While the calculation controls the risk of incorrect acceptance, the only control over the risk of incorrect rejection lies in the estimated misstatement. If it is underestimated, yet the actual misstatement is less than the tolerable misstatement, the sample could show more error than the auditor allowed when the sample size was calculated (1 or 2 errors), and the evaluation would show evidence for a rejection decision. That is, the evaluation would falsely indicate misstatement larger than the tolerable misstatement. Computer programs are available to accept input of an explicit risk of incorrect rejection judgment as well as an estimated amount of misstatement. Such programs calculate a sample size with direct consideration of the risk of incorrect rejection. (This kind of computer program is beyond the scope of this book.)

REVIEW CHECKPOINTS

G.12 All other factors remaining the same, will PPS sample size be larger, smaller, or the same, for a larger book balance?

G.13 All other factors remaining the same, will PPS sample size be larger, smaller, or the same, for a larger risk of incorrect acceptance?

---

[2] In the AICPA literature, the risk factor is also called the *assurance factor* or the *reliability factor*.

G.14 All other factors remaining the same, will PPS sample size be larger, smaller, or the same, for a larger expected misstatement?

G.15 All other factors remaining the same, will PPS sample size be larger, smaller, or the same, for a larger tolerable misstatement?

SELECTING THE SAMPLE

LEARNING OBJECTIVE

5. Describe a method for selecting a PPS sample, define a "logical unit," and explain the stratification effect of PPS selection.

PPS sampling unit selection is a type of *systematic selection*, very similar to the systematic selection method introduced for attribute sampling in Module F.

However, before sampling is started, auditors usually take some defensive auditing measures. They identify the *individually significant units* in the whole population and remove them for a 100 percent audit. In our example of auditing the $400,000 accounts receivable in the balance sheet of Kingston Company, the auditors can identify the six customer accounts over $10,000 (total amount of $100,000) and set them aside for audit. The cutoff size of $10,000 in this case corresponds to the tolerable misstatement assigned to the accounts receivable audit. By being sure to audit each customer account whose balance exceeds the tolerable misstatement, the auditors guard against the possibility of missing a material misstatement that might exist in a single subsidiary account. This leaves the remaining $300,000 of accounts receivable as the dollar-value population (RA) subject to auditing by sampling.

To carry out a systematic PPS selection, you must calculate the sample size (*n*), then divide the population size (*RA*) by the sample size to get a "skip interval" (*k*):

$$k = \frac{RA}{n}$$

For example, in the audit of the Kingston Company accounts receivable, if the sample size is 96 the skip interval is:

$$k = \frac{\$300,000}{96} = 3,125$$

With one random start, you select every 3,125th dollar unit. Each time a $1 unit is selected, it hooks the *logical unit* that contains it. A **logical unit** is the ordinary accounting subsidiary unit that contains the dollar unit selected in the sample. In this example, the logical unit is a customer's account. Obviously, all customer accounts with balances of $3,125 or more will be selected, and the larger units have a proportionately larger likelihood of selection than the smaller units. These phenomena of the selection method give PPS its high degree of stratification with automatic selection of the high-value logical units. PPS samplers say the PPS selection *hooks* the largest logical units and places them in the sample.

In contrast, an unrestricted sample of the accounts receivable defined as 1,500 logical units (customer accounts) gives each customer an equal likelihood of being selected for the sample. Thus, very large and very small customer balances will be in an unrestricted random sample of customer accounts receivable. On average, the number of dollars of the account balance in such a sample will be smaller than the number hooked in a PPS sample. Indeed, the PPS systematic selection guarantees that all customer accounts larger than the skip interval (k) will be in the sample, but unrestricted random sampling selection of logical units carries no such guarantee. In PPS sampling, each logical unit has a probability of being in the sample in proportion to its size. That is, a $500 customer balance has twice the probability of selection as a $250 customer balance.

A mini-example of PPS selection is shown in the box on the next page.

AUDITING INSIGHT

MINI-EXAMPLE OF PPS SYSTEMATIC SAMPLE SELECTION

Assume Kingston has $30,000 accounts receivable in 15 customer accounts, and you want to select a sample of 10 dollar units, which gives you a skip interval, $k = 30,000/10 = 3,000$.

We still start with a random number between 1 and 3,000, say 722, and this random number identifies the first sampled dollar. (The first one will not necessarily fall in the first account.)

You identify subsequent logical units by creating a cumulative total of the recorded dollars in the subsidiary account balances. Alongside, accumulate the skip interval starting with the random start at 722. The selected dollar units are the 722nd, the 3,722nd, the 6,722nd, and so forth to the end at the 27,722nd. The sample units are the subsidiary accounts that contain the cumulative interval dollar.

Account Number	Account Balance	Cumulative Balance	Cumulative Interval	Sample	Logical Unit
1	$ 750	$ 750	722	Selected	$ 750
2	3,500	4,250	3,722	Selected	3,500
3	1,965	6,215			
4	2,400	8,615	6,722	Selected	2,400
5	949	9,564			
6	563	10,127	9,722	Selected	563
7	1,224	11,351			
8	3,211	14,562	12,722	Selected	3,211
9	2,961	17,523	15,722	Selected	2,961
10	1,622	19,145	18,722	Selected	1,622
11	7,200	26,345	21,722	Selected	7,200
12	1,199	27,544	24,722	Selected*	
13	1,000	28,544	27,722	Selected	1,000
14	500	29,044			
15	956	30,000			
Total of logical units in the sample of 10 dollar units					$23,207

* Two dollar units in the same logical unit.

This is a selection routine for manual application. It may seem complicated at first glance, but it is really not hard to do with a calculator. When populations are on computer files, a routine like this one can be programmed to make the sample selection.

R E V I E W
CHECKPOINTS

G.16 What effect does the identification of individually significant logical units have on the size of the recorded amount population for probability proportional to size sampling (PPS)?

G.17 How does PPS sample selection produce an automatic stratification of choosing the high-value logical units in a control account balance?

G.18 What happens when two dollar units for the sample fall in the same logical unit?

EXPRESS THE ERROR EVIDENCE IN DOLLARS

The problem with attribute sampling is expressing the results in terms of a deviation rate instead of in dollars. In an audit context, expressing results in dollars is more meaningful when the audit objective is a decision about the fair presentation of a balance expressed in dollars. Therefore, PPS sampling adopts some conventions for expressing the error evidence in dollars.

LEARNING OBJECTIVE

6. Calculate an upper error limit for the evaluation of PPS evidence, and discuss the relative merits of alternatives for determining an amount by which a monetary balance should be adjusted.

The first step is determination of an average sampling interval. The **average sampling interval (ASI)** is:

$$ASI = \frac{RA}{n}$$

In our example of the audit of Kingston Company's accounts receivable with a sample of 96 customer accounts:

$$ASI = \frac{\$300,000}{96} = \$3,125$$

Calculate an Upper Error Limit (UEL): The No-Error Case

The upper error limit (UEL) is a quasi-statistical estimate of the greatest amount of dollar error that might exist in an account balance, with a likelihood (risk of incorrect acceptance) that the actual amount of error might be even greater. The easiest UEL calculation arises when the sample is audited and no dollar misstatements are discovered. Then the calculation is:[3]

$$UEL = ASI \times RF$$

In our example, suppose the auditors audited 96 of Kingston's customers' accounts and found nothing wrong, no misstatements and no disputed amounts. If the auditors wish to evaluate the "greatest amount of error that might exist" at a risk of incorrect acceptance of 0.17, they will find the Poisson risk factor for $RIA = 0.17$ and zero errors in Appendix GA, which is 1.77, and calculate the upper error limit:

$$
\begin{aligned}
UEL &= AASI \times RF \\
&= \$3,125 \times 1.77 \\
&= \$5,531
\end{aligned}
$$

This $5,531 is the amount of statistical sampling error when no dollar errors appear in the audited sample.

The risk of incorrect acceptance (RIA) represented by the choice of the Poisson risk factor should be the RIA derived from the risk model the auditor uses to plan the audit work.[4] This RIA is one of the auditors' decision criteria for accepting the book value as materially accurate or for rejecting it as appearing to contain a material misstatement. The calculated upper error limit is similar to an attribute sampling computed upper limit (CUL). The auditor can say: "Based on the quantitative evidence, I estimate the greatest amount of error in the population is UEL [rate of deviation for CUL], with a likelihood of RIA [RACRTL for attribute sampling] that the amount of misstatement error [rate of deviation for attribute sampling] might be greater."

The UEL must have a reference point to mean anything. The reference point is the tolerable misstatement (TM) assigned to the account, and it is the other decision criterion. You can use it with an "upper error limit decision rule," as expressed in the box below.

UPPER ERROR LIMIT DECISION RULE

Using actual sample data, calculate the upper error limit of monetary misstatement. Compare this UEL to the tolerable misstatement (TM) decision criterion amount. If the UEL is larger, make the "rejection" decision. If the UEL is smaller, make the "acceptance" decision.

---

[3] There are other methods for calculating a dollar-unit sampling UEL. They are more complicated and require a computer.

[4] Refer to Exhibit F–5 in Module F to see that the most efficient audit plan called for a control risk assessment of 0.30, which, if achieved, would justify an RIA of 0.17 and a substantive balance-audit sample of 96 customer accounts.

Using this UEL decision rule in our Kingston Company example, where the RIA is 0.17 and the tolerable misstatement is $10,000, the decision is that the evidence shows the $300,000 accounts receivable does not appear to contain a material misstatement. The UEL of $5,531 at $RIA = 0.17$ is less than the tolerable misstatement.

The phenomenon of measuring a UEL amount of misstatement when no errors were found in the sample is a reflection of the partial knowledge given by a sample from the population instead of knowledge of the entire population. Similarly, in attribute sampling for detail test of controls, a CUL greater than zero is expressed even when no deviations are found in a sample. In auditing standards, this kind of measurement of sampling error is called *further misstatement remaining undetected* in the balance (SAS 47, AU 312). Auditors can take it into account by calculating the UEL measurement.

The zero-error UEL measurement is actually a reflection of the *sufficiency* of audit evidence as represented by the size of the sample audited. If the sample size is very small, indicating limited knowledge of the population, the ASI will be large, and the UEL will be high. In these circumstances, the failure of the upper error limit decision rule (i.e., UEL greater than TM) is an indication of not enough evidence (sample size too small).

Calculate an Upper Error Limit (UEL): When Errors Are Found

When a dollar-unit sample is audited, the auditors determine (1) the dollar amount of difference between the book value and the audit value of the logical unit—the account or invoice—that contains the sampled dollar, and (2) the ratio of this difference to the recorded amount of the logical unit. This ratio is called the tainting percentage:

$$\text{Tainting } \% = \frac{\text{Book value} - \text{Audit value}}{\text{Book value}}$$

The tainting percentage is the PPS device for departing from the all-or-nothing, error-no-error measurement of attribute sampling. The theory is that a $1 unit is being audited, but each $1 unit is imbedded in a larger logical unit. A logical unit can be partially in error, and this part is attributed to all the dollars in the unit, including the "sampling unit dollar." Thus, a sampling unit dollar can be wrong in part—the tainting percentage.

Look at the three illustrative errors from the audit of Kingston's accounts receivable in Exhibit G–2. The first account had a book value of $1,000, but the auditors determined that the recorded amount should be $200. The customer's account is overstated by 80 percent (tainted with error), and so is the $1 sampling unit in it. The other two errors reflect 90 percent and 75 percent overstatement errors.

The calculation of UEL when errors are found is a combination of Poisson risk factors (RF), tainting percentages, and the average sampling interval (ASI). Exhibit G–3 shows a UEL calculation assuming an audit of 96 dollar units from Kingston Company's $300,000 accounts receivable when the three errors in Exhibit G–2 were found.

The "basic error," calculated using the RF for the zero-error case, is the underlying sampling error associated with the sample size. It is weighted by a 100 percent tainting under the assumption that the maximum overstatement of a dollar unit is its recorded amount.

EXHIBIT G–2 **THREE ILLUSTRATIVE ERRORS**

Customer	Book Value	Audit Value	Difference	Taint Percent
1425	$1,000	$200	$ 800	80%
310	3,000	300	2,700	90
963	2,000	500	1,500	75

EXHIBIT G–3   UEL CALCULATION (RIA = 0.17)

	Basic Error Likely Error and PGW Factors	×	Tainting Percentage	×	Average Sampling Interval	=	Dollar Measurement	
1. Basic error (0)	1.77		100.00%		$3,125			$ 5,531
2. Most likely error:								
First error	1.00		90.00		3,125		$2,813	
Second error	1.00		80.00		3,125		2,500	
Third error	1.00		75.00		3,125		2,344	
Projected likely misstatement (error)								$ 7,657
3. Precision gap widening:								
First error	0.44		90.00		3,125		1,238	
Second error	0.32		80.00		3,125		800	
Third error	0.27		75.00		3,125		633	
								2,671
Total upper error limit (0.17 risk of incorrect acceptance)								$15,859

Next, the errors are put in descending order of their tainting percentages, the largest first and the smallest last. These are given a "likely error" factor of 1.0. The sum of 1.0 × respective tainting percentages × ASI for the errors is called the "projected likely misstatement." This is the auditor's estimate based on the actual errors discovered ($5,000 = $800 + $2,700 + $1,500) projected to the population as $7,657.

The "precision gap widening" (PGW) is an addition to the sampling error generated by finding errors in the sample. These factors are in Appendix GA. They bear a direct relationship to the Poisson risk (RF) factors in Appendix GA. Each PGW is the difference between the risk factor for the error number and the risk factor for the error number that preceded it minus 1.0 (the risk factor assigned to the actual error). Thus, the PGW for the first error at RIA = 0.17 is 0.44 = 3.21 − 1.77 − 1.00. The use of PGW is shown in Exhibit G–3 and in the box below.

In terms of our UEL decision rule test of the accounts receivable, it appears that Kingston's $300,000 accounts receivable may contain more than $10,000 tolerable misstatement because the UEL of $15,859 is greater than $10,000 at risk of incorrect acceptance of 0.17. In other words, there is a 0.17 probability that overstatement in the receivables exceeds $15,859, when the auditors wanted to achieve a probability of 0.17 that misstatement could exceed only $10,000. We have the "rejection" decision.

AUDITING INSIGHT

PPS EFFECT OF ONE ERROR

The PPS calculation of UEL when an error is discovered involves the actual error amount and its tainting percentage, the average sampling interval (ASI), and an additional provision for sampling error caused by finding the dollar error. For example, consider the first error in the example—a 90 percent tainting overstatement error. This error contributes an additional $4,051 to the UEL, as follows:

Projected likely misstatement	1.00 × 0.90 × $3,125 =	$2,813
Precision gap widening	0.44 × 0.90 × $3,125 =	$1,238
Total effect of the first error		$4,051

Calculate the Projected Likely Misstatement

The whole point of quantitative evidence evaluation is to extend the findings from the sample to the entire population. The first step is to calculate the **projected likely misstatement,** which is the auditors' best estimate of misstatement based on the errors found in the sample. You can see the projected likely misstatement (PLM) of $7,657 in the middle of Exhibit G–3.

Auditors are supposed to think about the amount of PLM in relation to the tolerable misstatement (TM) and consider whether there may be "further misstatement remaining undetected" (SAS 47, AU 312). The difference between UEL and PLM ($8,202 = $15,859 − $7,657) is the PPS quasi-statistical measurement of sampling error and the "further misstatement remaining undetected."

The PLM measurement plays a significant role in the auditors' problem of deciding upon an amount to recommend for adjustment when they have made a "rejection" decision.

Determine the Amount of an Adjustment

The problem of determining the amount to recommend for adjustment is troublesome because auditors usually do not know the exact amount of misstatement in an account. When the evidential base is a random sample, the three measurable aspects of monetary misstatement are: (1) known misstatement, (2) projected likely misstatement, and (3) possible misstatement—the "further misstatement remaining undetected."

Quantitative Considerations

The known misstatement is the sum of the actual dollar error found in the sample. The projected likely misstatement is a calculation based on the known misstatements. Neither of these is affected by the auditors' risk of incorrect acceptance criterion. However, the possible misstatement may be large or small depending upon the RIA specification. This makes "possible misstatement" a slippery concept.

In our example of the audit of Kingston's accounts receivable, we have:

$$\text{Known misstatement} = \$5,000$$
$$\text{Projected likely misstatement} = \$7,657$$
$$\text{Possible misstatement} = \$8,202 \text{ (at RIA} = 0.17)$$

Auditing standards and practice contain no hard and fast rules for determining the amount of adjustment in sampling situations. Several measures of adjustment amounts can be derived from the data. Various sources have suggested the following:

- Adjust the amount of the known misstatement, in this case $5,000. Usually, the actual amount of known misstatement is smaller than the tolerable misstatement. Often, this adjustment is too small and leaves too much potential for remaining error (in this case $10,859 = $15,859 − $5,000) is left unadjusted.
- Adjust the amount of the projected misstatement, in this case $7,657. The point estimate of likely misstatement is considered the best single-value measurement available for recommending an adjustment to a client.
- In addition to adjusting for the projected likely misstatement amount, also adjust the amount of the possible misstatement, in this case another $8,202. This sum is the largest one an auditor can measure using the risk of incorrect acceptance in the audit plan. It contains an element of statistical measurement that auditors and clients may or may not be willing to accept for adjustment purposes.
- Adjust by the amount of tolerable misstatement when the sum of projected and possible misstatement exceeds tolerable misstatement, in this case $10,000. This kind of rule is somewhat arbitrary and is subject to question when the sum exceeds 2 × tolerable misstatement.

AUDITING INSIGHT

STATISTICAL SAMPLING BECOMES A TOOL IN AUDITS OF MULTINATIONAL CONCERNS

The IRS often tries to save resources in audits by projecting tax errors from samples of company data. It does this for travel and entertainment deductions. Now, the IRS is using sampling in challenging prices that a company charges for items sold to foreign subsidiaries. In such cases, the IRS claims that a parent company is avoiding U.S. tax by undercharging its foreign units.

In a tax court dispute, Halliburton Company says the IRS seeks to raise its income by $62.5 million for alleged underbilling; $29.5 million of the amount is from "adjustment for statistical sampling population." The pending case shows that the IRS is using sampling more aggressively.

Source: The Wall Street Journal.

- Adjust by the amount that the sum of projected and possible misstatement exceeds tolerable misstatement, in this case $5,859 ($15,859 − $10,000). The theory here is that the amount of misstatement left in the account balance after adjustment will not exceed tolerable misstatement ($10,000). This measure is somewhat arbitrary.

Statistical projections are used for adjustment recommendations. Not too much is known about CPA firms' use in financial audits, but, as noted in the box below, the Internal Revenue Service uses such measures.

Nonquantitative Considerations

You can see that much latitude exists for determining the amount of an adjustment to recommend. Often the amount recommended for one account depends on adjustment amounts recommended for other accounts. Auditors typically consider the findings in other audit areas when recommending adjustments.

The special characteristics of the accounts also must be considered. For example, in some cases the actual misstatement (overstatement in our Kingston accounts receivable example) may consist of overcharges to customers and undercharges from sales that were underbilled or simply not invoiced to customers (understatements). Management may make a policy decision not to try to recover the underbilled or unbilled amounts, so the audit manager then must deal with all the overstatement error instead of a smaller net overstatement. Other accounts may be different. For example, both overstatements and understatements in an inventory valuation may be adjustable simply by correcting the records, and no one needs to take customer relations into account.

Even though the lack of a definitive rule on "how to figure the amount of an adjustment" has revealed the lack of science in auditing, we can close the discussion with a more definite statement: As a general rule, all actual misstatements discovered in accounts audited completely should be adjusted.

R E V I E W
CHECKPOINTS

G.19 Suppose you have audited a $600,000 recorded amount of inventory with a sample of 100 dollar units and their logical units, and found no errors. What is the UEL at RIA = 0.05? RIA = 0.10? RIA = 0.25? RIA = 0.50?

G.20 What is the risk-related interpretation of each of the UELs you calculated in G.19 above?

G.21 What is the UEL for the audit of 96 dollar units from the $300,000 accounts receivable, given the errors shown in Exhibit G–2, for RIA = 0.48? For RIA = 0.05? What interpretation can you give to these UELs?

G.22 If you had to pick the one best measure for an amount to recommend for adjustment based on a sample, which one would you choose?

G.23 Why do you think the auditing profession has no definite rules for deciding the amount of an adjustment?

Overstatement and Understatement

When both overstatement and understatement errors are discovered, you need to combine them properly. The calculations are not difficult.[5] According to Leslie, Teitlebaum, and Anderson:

1. Calculate separately the *gross projected likely error* ($GPLE_O$) and the *total upper error limit* ($TUEL_O$) for *overstatements*, using an array of error taints only of the overstatement errors, ignoring understatement errors.

2. Calculate separately the *gross projected likely error* ($GPLE_U$) and the *total upper error limit* ($TUEL_U$) for understatements, using an array of error taints only of the understatement errors, ignoring overstatement errors.

3. Calculate the *net projected likely error* (PLE_N) by finding the net amount of the two gross projected likely error amounts, keeping track of whether the net amount is overstatement or understatement.

$$PLE_N = GPLE_O - GPLE_U$$

4. Calculate the *net upper limits* ($NUEL_O$ for overstatement and $NUEL_U$ for understatement) by reducing each *gross upper error limit* (GUEL) by the *gross projected likely error* (GPLE) of the opposite direction of misstatement, that is:

$$NUEL_O = TUEL_O - GUEL_U$$
$$NUEL_U = TUEL_U - GUEL_O$$

The following example uses the overstatement amounts calculated in the preceding Kingston accounts receivable example and some hypothetical understatement amounts.

	Projected Likely Error	Upper Error Limit
Gross errors:		
Overstatements	$7,657	$15,859
Understatements	5,000	10,000
Net errors:		
Overstatements	2,657	10,859
Understatements	NA	2,343

NA means not applicable.

Now you can say that with risk of incorrect acceptance equal to the risk used to calculate both overstatement and understatement estimates: (1) the most likely misstatement amount is PLE_N = $2,657 overstatement, but (2) the misstatement could be between $NUEL_O$ = $10,859 overstatement and $NUEL_U$ = $2,343 understatement. Since tolerable misstatement for the receivables is $10,000, the total $300,000 appears to be misstated because the net upper error limit for overstatement exceeds $10,000.

---

[5] The purpose of these calculations is to take into account both overstatement and understatement errors. It is not valid to (a) net the sample errors themselves and project the net error or (b) net the two total upper error limits to arrive at a net upper error limit. Actually, the calculations are simplifications of more complex calculations, but they will serve in all but the most extreme situations. (Do not use these calculations when the larger of the two total upper error limits exceeds 5 × TM, five times the tolerable misstatement.)

DISCLOSURE OF SAMPLING EVIDENCE

Generally accepted auditing standards do not require independent auditors to disclose anything about their audit sampling applications in their reports on audited financial statements. Auditors' determinations of risk, materiality, tolerable misstatement, sample selection, sample coverage of the population, and other details are private auditor information. Consequently, users of financial reports are unable to judge the appropriateness of auditors' decision criteria and evidence evaluation.

However, the Office of Management and Budget audit report requirements (OMB Circular A-133) include some very interesting sampling disclosures. Among the information required to be reported is a "Schedule of Findings and Questioned Costs" related to government grant programs. The format shown in the box above is an illustration of the OMB requirement for the disclosure of sampling information. The XYZ Organization (e.g., a state agency) uses funds from two federal programs.

This illustration offers some information for statistical analysis. Although the schedule does not tell users whether the sample was random, assume that it was a PPS sample. (The average sampling unit was $307 = \$9,210/30$, whereas the average population item amount was $228 = \$53,330/234$, indicating a PPS-type weighting toward the higher-valued units.)

A report reader could derive the following:

Average sampling interval (ASI) = $53,330/30 = $1,778
Actual errors = one 100% error lack of documentation

AUDITING INSIGHT

XYZ ORGANIZATION

Schedule of Findings and Questioned Costs

	Department of Energy: Heating Assistance for Low-Income Persons	Department of Health and Human Services: ABC Program
Number of items in population	234	1
Number of items tested	30	1
Number of items not in compliance	1	1
Dollar amount of population	$53,330	$2,826
Dollar amount of items tested	$9,210	$2,826
Dollar amount of items not in compliance	$202	$2,826
Amount of questioned costs	$202	$2,176

Department of Energy:

Documentation of verification of low-income status of one grant recipient could not be located. The cost of the assistance may be disallowed.

Department of Health and Human Services:

The organization exceeded the approved advertising budget ($650), received an oral authorization, but did not request a written budget modification ($2,176). The program has agreed to accept the overexpenditure.

Source: CPA firm accounting and auditing bulletin.

The projected likely error (lack of documentation and possible disallowed cost), applying the sample evidence to the whole population is $1,778 = UEL$ weight (1.0) $\times$ tainting percentage (100%) $\times$ ASI ($1,778).

Calculation of the UEL requires an assumption about the risk of incorrect acceptance. Assume that 0.05 is appropriate, then:

	UEL Factor	$\times$	Tainting Percent	$\times$	ASI	=	Dollar Amount
Basic error	3.00		100%		$1,778		$5,334
PLM	1.00		100		1,778		1,778
Precision gap widening (PGW)	0.75		100		1,778		1,334
Upper error limit at 0.05 risk							$8,446

Note: the illustrative disclosure does not suggest that the auditors projected the sample findings to the population. The disclosure suggests that a minor amount of cost ($202) was questioned in the Department of Energy program. However, government auditors, like the IRS auditors cited earlier, will not stop at the seemingly minor amount of actual error discovered in a sample. They want to know the amount that might be wrong with the entire population, and in this case the amount could be large. A sample-based projection might become the basis for a claim for refund of federal funds, then the XYZ Organization can try to defend its proper control and stewardship over federal grants!

SUMMARY

Statistical sampling requires knowledge of the underlying statistical calculations and relationships and a certain amount of faith in the mathematics. Auditors are entitled to hold a statistical result at arm's length and study it for its face validity. However, deciding to disregard an adverse statistical result because it does not give an auditor a good "feeling" is dangerous. Auditors must make decisions about account balances with care and with the best evidential base reasonably obtainable. It is not enough to develop a conclusion about the sampled units from a population. An auditor must project the sample evidence for a conclusion about the whole population—the dollar amount of the account under audit.

Applying statistical sampling is not technically difficult. However, making good sense of the judgments and estimates involved in sampling is hard. These are the facts, estimates, and judgments auditors should use when applying probability proportional to size (PPS) sampling for the substantive audit of an account balance:

Fact

Recorded amount (book value, population value) of the account.

Estimates

Expected dollar misstatement in the account.
Cost of audit procedures in the initial sample.
Cost of audit procedures applied after an initial rejection decision, whether to expand the sample or do other work.

Judgments

Audit risk as it relates to the account.
Inherent risk as it relates to the account.

Control risk as it relates to the controls over transactions that create the account balance (coordinated with the control risk assessment work).

Analytical procedures risk related to other substantive procedures designed to obtain substantive evidence about the account balance.

Risk of incorrect acceptance (derived from the other risk judgments).

Risk of incorrect rejection (derived from the cost relationships).

Tolerable misstatement—the portion of overall materiality assigned to the account.

The chapter incorporates all these elements in the application of dollar-unit sampling. They are used for explanations of procedures for calculating a sample size, selecting a dollar-unit sample, and evaluating the quantitative evidence obtained from a sample. The quantitative evidence measurements are integrated in a discussion of the problem of determining an amount to recommend for adjustment when the evidence is based on a sample.

Audit sampling is not just theory for schoolbooks. IRS auditors, government auditors, and independent auditors who perform audits of government programs all use sampling for regulatory purposes. IRS and government audit applications are illustrated.

MULTIPLE-CHOICE QUESTIONS FOR PRACTICE AND REVIEW

G.24   When audit risk (AR) is 0.015, inherent risk (IR) is 0.50, control risk (CR) is 0.30, and analytical procedures risk (AP) is 0.50, the risk of incorrect acceptance (RIA) is
  a. 0.20.
  b. 0.02.
  c. 2.00.
  d. 0.50.

G.25   Which of the following elements in the audit risk model is a product of the auditors' professional judgment?
  a. Control risk.
  b. Analytical procedures risk.
  c. Test of details risk of incorrect acceptance.
  d. All the above.

G.26   When making a sample-based decision about the dollar amount in an account balance, the incorrect acceptance decision error is considered more serious than the incorrect rejection decision error because
  a. The incorrect rejection decision impairs the efficiency of the audit.
  b. Auditors will do additional work and discover the error of the incorrect decision.
  c. The incorrect acceptance decision impairs the effectiveness of the audit.
  d. Sufficient, competent evidence will not have been obtained.

G.27   "Overauditing" can be defined as
  a. Auditing too small a sample size.
  b. Auditing a larger sample size than necessary.
  c. Taking more risk than is professionally acceptable.

  d. Giving an inappropriate unqualified report on financial statements.

PPS Sampling Questions

G.28   The unique feature of dollar-unit sampling (PPS) insofar as sample design is concerned is
  a. Sampling units are not chosen at random.
  b. A dollar unit selected in a sample is not replaced before the sample selection is completed.
  c. Auditors need not worry about the risk of incorrect acceptance decision error.
  d. The population is defined as the number of $1 units in an account balance or class of transactions.

G.29   When calculating a PPS sample size, an auditor does not need to make a judgment or estimate of
  a. Audit risk.
  b. Tolerable misstatement.
  c. Estimated misstatement.
  d. Standard deviation of misstatement.

G.30   Which of these combinations will produce the largest PPS sample size:

RIA	Errors	Recorded Amount	Tolerable Misstatement
a. 0.03	2	$1,000,000	$50,000
b. 0.03	1	1,000,000	35,000
c. 0.06	0	1,500,000	65,000
d. 0.10	4	1,500,000	65,000

G.31   Which of the following statements is correct about PPS sampling?

    a. The risk of incorrect acceptance must be specified.

    b. Smaller logical units have a greater probability of selection in the sample than larger units.

    c. Each logical unit in the population has an equally likely chance of being selected in the sample.

    d. Projected likely misstatement cannot be calculated in the quantitative evaluation when one or more errors are discovered.

G.32   One of the primary advantages of PPS sampling is the fact that

    a. It is a good method of sampling for evidence of understatement in asset accounts.

    b. The sample selection automatically achieves high-dollar selection and stratification.

    c. The sample selection provides for including a representative number of small-value population units.

    d. Expanding the sample for additional evidence is very easy.

PLM Calculation Questions

G.33   O. Orosco audited the $4.5 million book value inventory of Athletics Corporation. In her sample of 472 of the 4,000 inventory lines she found $17,500 overstatement error. The projected likely misstatement for this sample is

    a. $148,305.

    b. $157,500.

    c. $2,065.

    d. $531,000.

G.34   D. Strawberry audited the $4.5 million book value accounts receivable of Athletics Corporation. In his sample of 472 of the customer accounts, for which the book value total was $500,000, he found $17,500 overstatement. The projected likely misstatement for this sample is

    a. $148,305.

    b. $157,500.

    c. $1,059.

    d. $9,534.

EXERCISES AND PROBLEMS

G.35   Similarity of PPS and Attribute Sampling. The Poisson distribution is an approximation of the binomial distribution that is appropriate for attribute sampling sample size determination and evidence evaluation. The Poisson risk factors have a direct relationship to the computed upper limits that can be calculated using attribute evaluation tables.

Required:
Verify this relationship by finding the computed upper limits for a sample of 100 for the error findings shown below. Use the AICPA Sampling Guide Evaluation Tables in Appendix FB (Module F).

	RACRTL*	Risk Error(s)	Factor	CUL†
a.	0.05	0	3.00	
b.	0.05	1	4.75	
c.	0.05	2	6.30	
d.	0.05	3	7.76	
e.	0.05	9	15.71	
f.	0.10	0	2.31	
g.	0.10	1	3.89	
h.	0.10	2	5.33	
i.	0.10	3	6.69	
j.	0.10	9	14.21	

* Risk of assessing control risk too low.
† From Appendix FB.

G.36   Selecting a PPS Sample. You have been assigned the task of selecting a PPS sample from the Whitney Company's detail inventory records as of September 30. Whitney's controller gave you a list of the 23 different inventory items and their recorded book amounts. The senior accountant told you to select a sample of 10 dollar units and the logical units that contain them.

Required:
Prepare a working paper showing a systematic selection of 10 dollar units and the related logical units. Arrange the items in their numerical identification number order, and take a random starting place at the 1,210th dollar. (Check figure: $23,003 total logical unit amount in the sample.)

ID	Amount	ID	Amount	ID	Amount	ID	Amount
1	$1,750	7	$1,255	13	$937	19	$2,577
2	1,492	8	3,761	14	5,938	20	1,126
3	994	9	1,956	15	2,001	21	565
4	629	10	1,393	16	222	22	2,319
5	2,272	11	884	17	1,738	23	1,681
6	1,163	12	729	18	1,228		

DISCUSSION CASES

G.37   Relation of Dollar-Unit Sample Sizes to Audit Risk Model.   You can use the computer-based *Electronic Workpapers* to prepare a table like the one in Exhibit G–1 in the text.

Prepare tables like the one in Exhibit G–1 under different assumptions for the three combinations given below. Calculate PPS sample sizes using the Poisson risk factors for a dollar value of the balance of $300,000 and a tolerable misstatement of $10,000. Assume zero expected misstatement. (These are the recorded amount and tolerable misstatement underlying Exhibit 15–1.) Round your RIAs to two decimal places to use the Poisson risk factor tables.

1. AR = 0.10, IR = 1.00, AP = 1.00
2. AR = 0.05, IR = 0.50, AP = 1.00
3. AR = 0.05, IR = 1.00, AP = 0.50

Required:
Explain the differences or similarities among the different or same sample sizes produced by your calculations.

G.38   Accounts Receivable Misstatements and Upper Error Limit Calculation.   The auditors mailed positive confirmations on 70 customers' accounts receivable balances. The Company showed 2,356 customers with recorded amounts totaling $19.6 million (control account balance). The auditors received four positive confirmation returns reporting exceptions. Upon follow-up, they found the following:

Account #2333. Recorded amount $8,345. The account was overstated $1,669 because the client made an arithmetic mistake recording a credit memo. The Company issued only 86 credit memos during the year. The auditors examined all of them for the same arithmetic mistake and found no other similar errors.

Account #363. Recorded amount $7,460. The account was overstated $1,865 because the Company sold merchandise to a customer with payment due in six months plus 15 percent interest. The billing clerk made a mistake and recorded the sales price and the unearned interest as the sale and receivable amount. Inquiries revealed that the Company always sold on "payment due immediately" terms but had made an exception for this customer. Numerous sales transactions had been audited in the sales control audit work, and none had shown the extended terms allowed to account #363.

Account #1216. Recorded amount $19,450. The account was overstated $1,945 because an accounting clerk had deliberately misfooted several invoices to create extra charges to a business that competed with his brother's business unrelated to the Company. The accounting clerk had forged the initials of the supervisor who normally reviewed invoices for accuracy. This clerk was a temporary employee. The auditors examined all the invoices for this and other customers processed by this clerk and found no other similar errors.

Account #2003. Recorded amount $9,700. The account was overstated $1,455 because of a fictitious sale submitted by a salesperson, apparently part of an effort to boost third quarter sales and commissions. The auditors learned that the salesperson was employed from August 20 through October 30 before being dismissed as a result of customer complaints. They examined all other unpaid balances attributed to this salesperson and found no other fictitious sales.

Required:

a. Decide which, if any, of the account misstatements should be considered monetary misstatements and included in the calculation of a PPS upper limit.

b. Calculate the upper error limit, and decide whether the evidence from these misstatements indicates that the control account balance is or is not materially misstated. (The tolerable misstatement for the accounts receivable was $1 million, and the auditors had already decided upon a risk of incorrect acceptance criterion of 0.05.)

G.39   Mistakes in an Audit Sampling Application.   This is a CPA examination essay question that contains some very subtle mistaken statements about statistical audit sampling. You will need to be very careful to notice them.

Mead, CPA, was engaged to audit Jiffy Company's financial statements for the year ended August 31. Mead applied sampling procedures.

Required:
Describe each incorrect assumption, statement, and inappropriate application of sampling in Mead's procedures in the story below.

(AICPA adapted)

For the current year Mead decided to use probability-proportional-to-size (PPS) sampling (also known as dollar-unit sampling) to select accounts receivable for balance-audit confirmation because PPS sampling uses each account in the population as a separate sampling unit. Mead expected to discover many overstatements, but presumed that the PPS sample still would be smaller than the corresponding size for classical variables sampling.

Mead reasoned that the PPS sample would automatically result in a stratified sample because each account would have an equal chance of being selected for confirmation. Additionally, the selection of negative (credit) balances would be facilitated without special considerations.

Mead computed the sample size using the risk of incorrect acceptance, the total recorded book amount of the receivables, and the number of misstated accounts allowed. Mead divided the total recorded book amount of the receivables by the sample size to determine the sampling interval. Mead then calculated the standard deviation of the dollar amounts of the accounts selected for evaluation of the receivables.

Mead's calculated sample size was 60 and the sampling interval was determined to be $10,000. However, only 58 different accounts were selected because two accounts were so large that the sampling interval caused each of them to be selected twice. Mead proceeded to send confirmation requests to 55 of the 58 customers. Three accounts originally selected for the sample each had insignificant recorded balances under $20. Mead ignored these three small accounts and substituted the three largest accounts that had not been selected by the random selection procedure. Each of these accounts had balances in excess of $7,000, so Mead sent confirmation requests to these customers.

The confirmation process revealed two differences. One account with an audited amount of $3,000 had been recorded at $4,000. Mead projected this to be a $1,000 misstatement. Another account with an audited amount of $2,000 had been recorded at $1,900. Mead did not count the $100 difference because the purpose of the test was to detect overstatements.

In evaluating the sample results, Mead decided that the accounts receivable balance was not overstated because the projected misstatement was less than the allowance for sampling risk.

G.40 Determining an Efficient Risk of Incorrect Rejection (DUS).

Your audit firm is planning the audit of a company's accounts receivable, which consist of 1,032 customer accounts with a total recorded amount (book value) of $300,000. You have already decided that the accounts receivable can be overstated by as much as $10,000, and the financial statements would not be considered materially misstated. Judging by the experience of past audits on this client, only a negligible amount of misstatement is expected to exist in the account.

Preliminary calculations of sample sizes have been made for several possible control risk levels. These calculations were based on a "base" risk of incorrect rejection of 0.01. Minimum sample sizes based on the alternative risks of incorrect rejection shown below also were calculated.

Audit work on the accounts will cost $8 per sampling unit when the accounts are selected for the initial sample. However, if the sample indicates a rejection (material overstatement) decision, the audit of additional sampling units will cost $19 each.

Control Risk	"Base" Sample	Alternative RIR	Alternative (Minimum) Sample
0.20	80	0.02	41
0.30	96	0.02	53
0.40	107	0.03	62
0.50	116	0.03	68
0.60	122	0.03	74
0.70	128	0.03	78
0.80	133	0.03	82
0.90	137	0.03	86
1.00	141	0.03	89

Required:

For each of the control risk levels shown above, calculate the expected cost savings from auditing the alternative (minimum) sample. Assume that the action in the event of a rejection decision is to expand the work by selecting additional units up to the number in the base sample. Discuss the potential audit efficiencies and possible inefficiencies from beginning the audit work with the alternative (minimum) sample size.

G.41 RIA and Underlying Error Guidance.

In Module E, you will find a box titled "Preliminary Sample Guidance" (page 601). It presents some sample size calculation guidance. The table in the box is reproduced on the next page, but without the Assurance Factors you see on page 601.

Required:

a. Assuming that the Audit Risk (AR) that underlies the assurance factors shown on page 225 is AR = 0.05, enter the RIAs for each combination of CR $\times$ IR and AP shown in the table.

b. What underlying number of errors assumption is built into the guidance on page 000? (*Hint:* Find the Poisson Risk Factors that correspond to the RIAs you entered.)

c. Discuss any problems you might perceive using the guidance (assurance factors) shown on page 601.

When: Combined Control and Inherent Risk (CR × IR) are:	And When Other, Analytical, Procedures Risk (AP) is:			
	1.0	0.75	0.50	0.35
1.00	_____	_____	_____	_____
0.75	_____	_____	_____	_____
0.50	_____	_____	_____	_____
0.35	_____	_____	_____	_____

APPENDIX GA

POISSON RISK FACTORS (FOR CALCULATING UPPER ERROR LIMITS OF OVERSTATEMENT AND UNDERSTATEMENT)

	Risk of Incorrect Acceptance							
	50%		49%		48%		47%	
Errors	RF	PGW	RF	PGW	RF	PGW	RF	PGW
0	0.70	—	0.71	—	0.73	—	0.76	—
1	1.70	0.00	1.71	0.00	1.74	0.01	1.78	0.02
2	2.70	0.00	2.71	0.00	2.76	0.02	2.80	0.02
3	3.70	0.00	3.72	0.01	3.77	0.01	3.82	0.02
4	4.70	0.00	4.72	0.00	4.78	0.01	4.83	0.01
5	5.70	0.00	5.73	0.01	5.79	0.01	5.85	0.02
6	6.70	0.00	6.73	0.00	6.80	0.01	6.86	0.01
7	7.70	0.00	7.74	0.01	7.81	0.01	7.88	0.02
8	8.70	0.00	8.74	0.00	8.81	0.00	8.89	0.01
9	9.70	0.00	9.74	0.00	9.83	0.02	9.90	0.01
10	10.70	0.00	10.75	0.01	10.83	0.00	10.92	0.02
11	11.70	0.00	11.75	0.00	11.84	0.01	11.93	0.01
12	12.70	0.00	12.75	0.00	12.85	0.01	12.94	0.01
13	13.70	0.00	13.76	0.01	13.86	0.01	13.95	0.01
14	14.70	0.00	14.76	0.00	14.86	0.00	14.95	0.00
15	15.70	0.00	15.77	0.01	15.87	0.01	15.96	0.01
16	16.70	0.00	16.77	0.00	16.87	0.00	16.97	0.01
17	17.70	0.00	17.77	0.00	17.88	0.01	17.98	0.01
18	18.70	0.00	18.77	0.00	18.88	0.00	18.99	0.01
19	19.70	0.00	19.78	0.01	19.89	0.01	20.00	0.01
20	20.70	0.00	20.78	0.00	20.90	0.01	21.01	0.01

	Risk of Incorrect Acceptance							
	46%		45%		44%		43%	
Errors	RF	PGW	RF	PGW	RF	PGW	RF	PGW
0	0.78	—	0.80	—	0.82	—	0.84	—
1	1.81	0.03	1.84	0.04	1.88	0.06	1.91	0.07
2	2.84	0.03	2.85	0.04	2.93	0.05	2.97	0.06
3	3.87	0.03	3.92	0.04	3.97	0.04	4.02	0.05
4	4.89	0.02	4.95	0.03	5.00	0.03	5.06	0.04
5	5.91	0.02	5.97	0.02	6.04	0.04	6.10	0.04
6	6.93	0.02	7.00	0.03	7.07	0.03	7.13	0.03
7	7.95	0.02	8.02	0.02	8.09	0.02	8.17	0.04
8	8.96	0.01	9.04	0.02	9.12	0.03	9.20	0.03
9	9.98	0.02	10.06	0.02	10.14	0.02	10.23	0.03
10	11.00	0.02	11.08	0.02	11.17	0.03	11.26	0.03
11	12.01	0.01	12.10	0.02	12.19	0.02	12.28	0.02
12	13.02	0.01	13.12	0.02	13.21	0.02	13.30	0.02
13	14.04	0.02	14.14	0.02	14.23	0.02	14.32	0.02
14	15.05	0.01	15.15	0.01	15.25	0.02	15.35	0.03
15	16.06	0.01	16.16	0.01	16.27	0.02	16.37	0.02
16	17.08	0.02	17.18	0.02	17.26	0.02	17.39	0.02
17	18.09	0.01	18.19	0.01	18.31	0.02	18.42	0.03
18	19.10	0.01	19.21	0.02	19.33	0.02	19.44	0.02
19	20.11	0.01	20.22	0.01	20.34	0.01	20.46	0.02
20	21.12	0.01	21.24	0.02	21.36	0.02	21.48	0.02

APPENDIX GA   (CONTINUED)

	Risk of Incorrect Acceptance							
	42%		41%		40%		39%	
Errors	RF	PGW	RF	PGW	RF	PGW	RF	PGW
0	0.87	—	0.89	—	0.92	—	0.94	—
1	1.95	0.08	1.99	0.10	2.02	0.10	2.06	0.12
2	3.01	0.06	3.06	0.07	3.11	0.09	3.15	0.09
3	4.07	0.06	4.12	0.06	4.18	0.07	4.23	0.08
4	5.12	0.05	5.18	0.06	5.24	0.06	5.30	0.07
5	6.16	0.04	6.23	0.05	6.29	0.05	6.36	0.06
6	7.20	0.04	7.27	0.04	7.34	0.05	7.41	0.05
7	8.24	0.04	8.31	0.04	8.39	0.05	8.47	0.06
8	9.28	0.04	9.35	0.04	9.43	0.04	9.51	0.04
9	10.31	0.03	10.39	0.04	10.47	0.04	10.56	0.05
10	11.34	0.03	11.43	0.04	11.51	0.04	11.60	0.04
11	12.37	0.03	12.46	0.03	12.55	0.04	12.65	0.05
12	13.40	0.03	13.49	0.03	13.59	0.04	13.69	0.04
13	14.43	0.03	14.52	0.03	14.62	0.03	14.72	0.03
14	15.46	0.03	15.55	0.03	15.66	0.04	15.76	0.04
15	16.48	0.02	16.58	0.03	16.69	0.03	16.80	0.04
16	17.50	0.02	17.61	0.03	17.72	0.03	17.83	0.03
17	18.53	0.03	18.64	0.03	18.75	0.03	18.86	0.03
18	19.55	0.02	19.67	0.03	19.78	0.03	19.90	0.04
19	20.58	0.03	20.70	0.03	20.81	0.03	20.93	0.03
20	21.60	0.02	21.72	0.02	21.84	0.03	21.96	0.03

	Risk of Incorrect Acceptance							
	38%		37%		36%		35%	
Errors	RF	PGW	RF	PGW	RF	PGW	RF	PGW
0	0.97	—	1.00	—	1.02	—	1.05	—
1	2.10	0.13	2.14	0.14	2.18	0.16	2.22	0.17
2	3.20	0.10	3.25	0.11	3.30	0.12	3.35	0.13
3	4.28	0.08	4.34	0.09	4.40	0.10	4.45	0.10
4	5.36	0.08	5.43	0.09	5.48	0.08	5.55	0.10
5	6.43	0.07	6.49	0.06	6.56	0.08	6.63	0.08
6	7.49	0.06	7.56	0.07	7.63	0.07	7.71	0.08
7	8.54	0.05	8.63	0.07	8.70	0.07	8.78	0.07
8	9.60	0.00	9.68	0.05	9.76	0.06	9.85	0.07
9	10.65	0.05	10.74	0.06	10.82	0.06	10.91	0.06
10	11.70	0.05	11.79	0.05	11.88	0.06	11.97	0.06
11	12.74	0.04	12.84	0.05	12.93	0.05	13.03	0.06
12	13.78	0.04	13.89	0.05	13.98	0.05	14.09	0.06
13	14.83	0.05	14.93	0.04	15.03	0.05	15.14	0.05
14	15.87	0.04	15.97	0.04	16.08	0.05	16.19	0.05
15	16.91	0.04	17.02	0.05	17.13	0.05	17.24	0.05
16	17.94	0.03	18.06	0.04	18.17	0.04	18.29	0.05
17	18.98	0.04	19.10	0.04	19.21	0.04	19.33	0.04
18	20.02	0.04	20.14	0.04	20.26	0.05	20.38	0.05
19	21.05	0.03	21.18	0.04	21.30	0.04	21.42	0.04
20	22.09	0.04	22.22	0.04	22.34	0.04	22.47	0.05

Appendix GA   (Continued)

	Risk of Incorrect Acceptance							
	34%		33%		32%		31%	
Errors	RF	PGW	RF	PGW	RF	PGW	RF	PGW
0	1.08	—	1.11	—	1.14	—	1.17	—
1	2.26	0.18	2.30	0.19	2.35	0.21	2.39	0.22
2	3.40	0.14	3.45	0.15	3.50	0.15	3.56	0.17
3	4.51	0.11	4.57	0.12	4.64	0.14	4.70	0.14
4	5.61	0.10	5.68	0.11	5.75	0.11	5.82	0.12
5	6.70	0.09	6.78	0.10	6.85	0.10	6.93	0.11
6	7.79	0.09	7.87	0.09	7.95	0.10	8.03	0.10
7	8.86	0.07	8.95	0.08	9.03	0.08	9.12	0.09
8	9.93	0.07	10.02	0.07	10.12	0.09	10.21	0.09
9	11.00	0.07	11.10	0.08	11.19	0.07	11.29	0.08
10	12.07	0.07	12.17	0.07	12.26	0.07	12.37	0.08
11	13.13	0.06	13.23	0.06	13.33	0.07	13.44	0.07
12	14.19	0.06	14.29	0.06	14.40	0.07	14.51	0.07
13	15.25	0.06	15.36	0.07	15.47	0.07	15.58	0.07
14	16.30	0.05	16.41	0.05	16.53	0.06	16.65	0.07
15	17.35	0.05	17.47	0.06	17.59	0.06	17.71	0.06
16	18.41	0.06	18.53	0.06	18.65	0.06	18.77	0.06
17	19.45	0.04	19.58	0.05	19.70	0.05	19.83	0.06
18	20.50	0.05	20.63	0.05	20.76	0.06	20.89	0.06
19	21.55	0.05	21.68	0.05	21.81	0.05	21.94	0.05
20	22.60	0.05	22.73	0.05	22.86	0.05	23.00	0.06

	Risk of Incorrect Acceptance							
	30%		29%		28%		27%	
Errors	RF	PGW	RF	PGW	RF	PGW	RF	PGW
0	1.21	—	1.24	—	1.27	—	1.31	—
1	2.44	0.23	2.49	0.25	2.54	0.27	2.59	0.28
2	3.62	0.18	3.67	0.18	3.73	0.19	3.79	0.20
3	4.77	0.15	4.83	0.16	4.90	0.17	4.96	0.17
4	5.90	0.13	5.96	0.13	6.04	0.14	6.11	0.15
5	7.01	0.11	7.08	0.12	7.16	0.12	7.25	0.14
6	8.12	0.11	8.20	0.12	8.28	0.12	8.38	0.12
7	9.21	0.09	9.30	0.10	9.39	0.11	9.49	0.12
8	10.31	0.10	10.40	0.10	10.49	0.10	10.59	0.10
9	11.39	0.08	11.49	0.09	11.59	0.10	11.70	0.11
10	12.47	0.08	12.57	0.06	12.68	0.09	12.79	0.09
11	13.55	0.08	13.66	0.09	13.77	0.09	13.88	0.09
12	14.63	0.08	14.74	0.08	14.85	0.08	14.97	0.09
13	15.70	0.07	15.81	0.07	15.93	0.08	16.05	0.08
14	16.77	0.07	16.89	0.08	17.01	0.08	17.14	0.09
15	17.84	0.07	17.96	0.07	18.08	0.07	18.21	0.07
16	18.90	0.06	19.02	0.06	19.16	0.08	19.29	0.08
17	19.97	0.07	20.09	0.07	20.23	0.07	20.36	0.07
18	21.03	0.06	21.16	0.07	21.30	0.07	21.44	0.08
19	22.09	0.06	22.22	0.06	22.36	0.06	22.51	0.07
20	23.15	0.06	23.28	0.06	23.43	0.07	23.58	0.07

APPENDIX GA   (CONTINUED)

	Risk of Incorrect Acceptance							
	26%		25%		24%		23%	
Errors	RF	PGW	RF	PGW	RF	PGW	RF	PGW
0	1.35	—	1.39	—	1.43	—	1.47	—
1	2.64	0.29	2.70	0.31	2.75	0.32	2.81	0.34
2	3.86	0.22	3.93	0.23	3.99	0.24	4.06	0.25
3	5.04	0.18	5.11	0.18	5.19	0.20	5.26	0.20
4	6.19	0.15	6.28	0.17	6.36	0.17	6.44	0.18
5	7.34	0.15	7.43	0.15	7.51	0.15	7.61	0.17
6	8.46	0.12	8.56	0.13	8.65	0.14	8.75	0.14
7	9.58	0.12	9.69	0.13	9.79	0.14	9.89	0.14
8	10.70	0.12	10.81	0.12	10.91	0.12	11.02	0.13
9	11.80	0.10	11.92	0.11	12.03	0.12	12.14	0.12
10	12.90	0.10	13.03	0.11	13.14	0.11	13.26	0.12
11	14.00	0.10	14.13	0.10	14.24	0.10	14.37	0.11
12	15.09	0.09	15.22	0.09	15.34	0.10	15.48	0.11
13	16.18	0.09	16.31	0.09	16.43	0.09	16.57	0.09
14	17.27	0.09	17.40	0.09	17.53	0.10	17.67	0.10
15	18.34	0.07	18.49	0.09	18.62	0.09	18.77	0.10
16	19.42	0.08	19.57	0.08	19.71	0.09	19.86	0.09
17	20.50	0.08	20.65	0.08	20.80	0.09	20.95	0.09
18	21.58	0.08	21.73	0.08	21.88	0.08	22.04	0.09
19	22.65	0.07	22.81	0.08	22.96	0.08	23.12	0.08
20	23.73	0.08	23.89	0.08	24.04	0.08	24.20	0.08

	Risk of Incorrect Acceptance							
	22%		21%		20%		19%	
Errors	RF	PGW	RF	PGW	RF	PGW	RF	PGW
0	1.51	—	1.56	—	1.61	—	1.66	—
1	2.87	0.36	2.93	0.37	3.00	.039	3.06	0.40
2	4.13	0.26	4.20	0.27	4.28	0.28	4.36	0.30
3	5.34	0.21	5.43	0.23	5.52	0.24	5.61	0.25
4	6.53	0.19	6.63	0.20	6.73	0.21	6.82	0.21
5	7.70	0.17	7.80	0.17	7.91	0.18	8.01	0.19
6	8.86	0.16	8.96	0.16	9.08	0.17	9.19	0.18
7	0.00	0.14	10.11	0.15	10.24	0.16	10.35	0.16
8	11.14	0.14	11.26	0.15	11.38	0.14	11.51	0.16
9	2.26	0.12	12.39	0.13	12.52	0.14	12.65	0.14
10	13.38	0.12	13.51	0.12	13.66	0.14	13.79	0.14
11	14.50	0.12	14.63	0.12	14.78	0.12	14.92	0.13
12	15.61	0.11	15.75	0.12	15.90	0.12	16.04	0.12
13	16.72	0.11	16.86	0.11	17.02	0.12	17.17	0.13
14	17.82	0.10	17.97	0.11	18.13	0.11	18.28	0.11
15	18.92	0.10	19.07	0.10	19.24	0.11	19.39	0.11
16	20.01	0.09	20.17	0.10	20.36	0.10	20.50	0.11
17	21.11	0.10	21.27	0.10	21.44	0.10	21.61	0.10
18	22.20	0.09	22.36	0.09	22.54	0.10	22.71	0.10
19	23.29	0.09	23.46	0.10	23.64	0.10	23.81	0.10
20	24.37	0.08	24.54	0.08	24.73	0.09	24.91	0.10

APPENDIX GA   (CONTINUED)

	Risk of Incorrect Acceptance							
	18%		17%		16%		15%	
Errors	RF	PGW	RF	PGW	RF	PGW	RF	PGW
0	1.71	—	1.77	—	1.83	—	1.90	—
1	3.13	0.42	3.21	0.44	3.29	0.46	3.38	0.48
2	4.44	0.31	4.53	0.32	4.63	0.34	4.73	0.35
3	5.70	0.26	5.80	0.27	5.90	0.27	6.02	0.29
4	6.92	0.22	7.03	0.23	7.15	0.25	7.27	0.25
5	8.12	0.20	8.24	0.21	8.36	0.21	8.50	0.23
6	9.31	0.19	9.43	0.19	9.57	0.21	9.71	0.21
7	10.48	0.17	10.61	0.18	10.75	0.18	10.90	0.19
8	11.64	0.16	11.78	0.17	11.92	0.17	12.08	0.18
9	12.79	0.15	12.93	0.15	13.09	0.17	13.25	0.17
10	13.93	0.14	14.08	0.15	14.24	0.15	14.42	0.17
11	15.07	0.14	15.23	0.15	15.39	0.15	15.57	0.15
12	16.20	0.13	16.36	0.13	16.54	0.15	16.72	0.15
13	17.33	0.13	17.49	0.13	17.67	0.13	17.86	0.14
14	18.45	0.12	18.62	0.13	18.80	0.13	19.00	0.14
15	19.57	0.12	19.74	0.12	19.93	0.13	20.13	0.13
16	20.68	0.11	20.87	0.13	21.06	0.13	21.26	0.13
17	21.79	0.11	21.98	0.11	22.17	0.11	22.39	0.13
18	22.90	0.11	23.09	0.11	23.29	0.12	23.51	0.12
19	24.00	0.10	24.20	0.11	24.40	0.11	24.63	0.12
20	25.10	0.10	25.30	0.10	25.52	0.12	25.74	0.11

	Risk of Incorrect Acceptance							
	14%		13%		12%		11%	
Errors	RF	PGW	RF	PGW	RF	PGW	RF	PGW
0	1.97	—	2.01	—	2.12	—	2.21	—
1	3.46	0.49	3.56	0.52	3.66	0.54	3.77	0.56
2	4.83	0.37	4.94	0.38	5.06	0.40	5.18	0.41
3	6.13	0.30	6.25	0.31	6.39	0.33	6.53	0.35
4	7.39	0.26	7.53	0.28	7.67	0.28	7.83	0.30
5	8.63	0.24	8.77	0.24	8.93	0.26	9.09	0.26
6	9.85	0.22	10.00	0.23	10.17	0.25	10.34	0.25
7	11.05	0.20	11.21	0.21	11.38	0.21	11.57	0.23
8	12.24	0.19	12.41	0.20	12.59	0.21	12.78	0.21
9	13.41	0.17	13.59	0.18	13.78	0.19	13.99	0.21
10	14.58	0.17	14.77	0.18	14.97	0.19	15.18	0.19
11	15.75	0.17	15.94	0.17	16.14	0.17	16.36	0.18
12	16.90	0.15	17.10	0.16	17.31	0.17	17.54	0.18
13	18.05	0.15	18.26	0.16	18.47	0.16	18.70	0.16
14	19.19	0.14	19.41	0.15	19.63	0.16	19.87	0.17
15	20.33	0.14	20.55	0.14	20.78	0.15	21.02	0.15
16	21.46	0.13	21.69	0.14	21.92	0.14	22.18	0.16
17	22.59	0.13	22.83	0.14	23.07	0.15	2.3.33	0.15
18	23.72	0.13	23.96	0.13	24.21	0.14	24.47	0.14
19	24.84	0.12	25.09	0.13	25.34	0.13	25.61	0.14
20	25.97	0.13	26.21	0.12	26.47	0.13	26.75	0.14

APPENDIX GA   (CONTINUED)

	Risk of Incorrect Acceptance							
	10%		9%		8%		7%	
Errors	RF	PGW	RF	PGW	RF	PGW	RF	PGW
0	2.31	—	2.41	—	2.53	—	2.66	—
1	3.89	0.58	4.02	0.61	4.17	0.64	4.33	0.67
2	5.33	0.44	5.47	0.45	5.64	0.47	5.83	0.50
3	6.69	0.36	6.85	0.38	7.03	0.39	7.24	0.41
4	8.00	0.31	8.18	0.33	8.38	0.35	8.60	0.36
5	9.28	0.28	9.47	0.29	9.68	0.30	9.92	0.32
6	10.54	0.26	10.74	0.27	10.97	0.29	11.22	0.30
7	11.78	0.24	11.99	0.25	12.23	0.26	12.49	0.27
8	13.00	0.22	13.22	0.23	13.47	0.24	13.75	0.26
9	14.21	0.21	14.44	0.22	14.70	0.23	15.00	0.25
10	15.41	0.20	15.65	0.21	15.92	0.22	16.23	0.23
11	16.60	0.19	16.85	0.20	17.13	0.21	17.45	0.22
12	17.79	0.19	18.05	0.20	18.33	0.20	18.66	0.21
13	18.96	0.17	19.23	0.18	19.53	0.20	19.86	0.20
14	20.13	0.17	20.41	0.18	20.72	0.19	21.06	0.20
15	21.30	0.17	21.58	0.17	21.90	0.18	22.25	0.19
16	22.46	0.16	22.75	0.17	23.07	0.17	23.43	0.18
17	23.61	0.15	23.91	0.16	24.24	0.17	24.61	0.18
18	24.76	0.15	25.06	0.15	25.40	0.16	25.78	0.17
19	25.91	0.15	26.22	0.16	26.56	0.16	26.95	0.17
20	27.05	0.14	27.37	0.15	27.72	0.16	28.11	0.16

	Risk of Incorrect Acceptance							
	6%		5%		4%		3%	
Errors	RF	PGW	RF	PGW	RF	PGW	RF	PGW
0	2.81	—	3.00	—	3.22	—	3.51	—
1	4.52	0.71	4.75	0.75	5.01	0.79	5.36	0.85
2	6.04	0.52	6.30	0.55	6.60	0.59	6.98	0.62
3	7.48	0.44	7.76	0.46	8.09	0.49	8.51	0.53
4	8.86	0.38	9.16	0.40	9.51	0.42	9.96	0.45
5	10.20	0.34	10.52	0.36	10.89	0.38	11.37	0.41
6	11.51	0.31	11.85	0.33	12.24	0.35	12.75	0.38
7	12.80	0.29	13.15	0.30	13.57	0.33	14.10	0.35
8	14.07	0.27	14.44	0.29	14.87	0.30	15.42	0.32
9	15.32	0.25	15.71	0.27	16.16	0.29	16.73	0.31
10	16.57	0.25	16.97	0.26	17.43	0.27	18.02	0.29
11	17.80	0.23	18.21	0.24	18.69	0.26	19.30	0.28
12	19.02	0.22	19.45	0.24	19.97	0.25	20.57	0.27
13	20.24	0.22	20.67	0.22	21.18	0.24	21.83	0.26
14	21.44	0.20	21.89	0.22	22.42	0.24	23.08	0.25
15	22.64	0.20	23.10	0.21	23.64	0.22	24.32	0.24
16	23.83	0.19	24.31	0.21	24.86	0.22	25.56	0.24
17	25.02	0.19	25.50	0.19	26.07	0.21	26.78	0.22
18	26.20	0.18	26.70	0.20	27.27	0.20	28.00	0.22
19	27.38	0.18	27.88	0.18	28.47	0.20	29.22	0.22
20	28.55	0.17	29.07	0.19	29.67	0.20	30.42	0.20

APPENDIX GA   *(CONTINUED)*

	Risk of Incorrect Acceptance			
	2%		1%	
Errors	RF	PGW	RF	PGW
0	3.91	—	4.61	—
1	5.83	0.92	6.64	1.03
2	7.52	0.69	8.41	0.77
3	9.08	0.56	10.05	0.64
4	10.58	0.50	11.61	0.56
5	12.03	0.45	13.11	0.50
6	13.44	0.41	14.58	0.47
7	14.82	0.38	16.00	0.42
8	16.17	0.35	17.41	0.41
9	17.51	0.34	18.79	0.38
10	18.83	0.32	20.15	0.36
11	20.13	0.30	21.49	0.34
12	21.42	0.29	22.83	0.34
13	22.71	0.29	24.14	0.31
14	23.98	0.27	25.45	0.31
15	25.24	0.26	26.75	0.30
16	26.50	0.26	28.04	0.29
17	27.74	0.24	29.31	0.27
18	28.98	0.24	30.59	0.28
19	30.22	0.24	31.85	0.26
20	31.43	0.20	33.11	0.26

Module H

Information Systems Auditing

Professional Standards Reference

Learning Objectives

Given its extensive use by clients, auditors must consider clients' computer technology. An auditing text cannot describe fully all the complexities of electronic processing of business transactions, so this module assumes you have had a course in computer concepts and general information processing. The focus of this module is on the examination of the client's computerized information system and its related controls. The module is subdivided into three parts. The first part reviews the basic elements of a computer system and related controls. The second part describes the procedures an information system auditor performs to ensure that the client's information system controls are operating effectively. The module concludes with a discussion of computer fraud and the controls that can be used to prevent it. After you study Module H, you should be able to:

1. List and describe the basic elements of a computerized information system.

2. Explain the difference between auditing around the computer and auditing through the computer; list several techniques auditors can use to perform tests of controls in a computerized information system.

3. Describe the characteristics and control problems of personal computer installations.

4. Define and describe computer fraud and the controls a company can use to prevent it.

ELEMENTS OF A COMPUTER-BASED SYSTEM

LEARNING OBJECTIVE

1. List and describe the basic elements of a computerized information system.

Thomas Watson, former Chairman of IBM, is quoted as saying (in 1943), "I think there is a world market for maybe five computers." Time has proven him to be mistaken about the world market for computers. Today, companies use thousands of different information systems, and rarely are two alike. Auditors must assess the control risk in a client's organization no matter what technology is used for preparing the financial statements. In an electronic environment, auditors must study and test general and application computer controls for compliance with the company's controls (if the detail test of controls is necessary in the circumstances). All auditors should have enough familiarity with computers, electronic transaction processing, and computer controls to be able to complete the audit of simple systems and to work with information system auditors.

A computer-based system includes the following six elements and related controls:

1. *Hardware* refers to the physical equipment or devices that constitute a computer. These may include the central processing unit (CPU), optical readers, tape drives, disk devices, printers, terminals, and other equipment. Modern computer equipment is very reliable. Machine malfunctions that go undetected are relatively rare. You are not expected to be a computer systems engineer, but you should be familiar with some of the hardware controls so you can converse knowledgeably with information system personnel.

    The most important hardware control now incorporated in all computers is a parity check. The **parity check** ensures that the coding of data internal to the computer does not change when it is moved from one internal storage location to another. An additional hardware control commonly found is an **echo check.** It involves a magnetic read after each magnetic write "echoing" back to the sending location and comparing results. Many computers also contain dual circuitry to perform arithmetic operations twice. Auditors (and management) cannot do much about the absence of such controls but should be concerned primarily with operator procedures when such errors occur. Modern computers are largely self-diagnostic. Therefore, written procedures should exist for all computer malfunctions, and all malfunctions should be recorded along with their causes and resolutions.

    Another significant area of auditor interest is *preventative maintenance*. Auditors should determine whether maintenance is scheduled and whether the schedule is followed and documented. Maintenance frequently is under contract with the computer vendor. In such cases, auditors should review the contract as well as the record of regular maintenance work. Other general evidence on hardware reliability may be obtained from a review of operating reports and downtime logs.

2. *Software* includes both systems programs and application programs. System programs perform generalized functions for more than one application. These programs, sometimes referred to as supervisory programs, typically include: "operating systems" (such as *Windows NT, Windows 2000,* and *Linux*), that control, schedule, and maximize efficient use of the hardware; "data management systems," which perform standardized data-handling functions for one or more application programs; and "utility" programs (such as *Norton Utilities*) that can perform basic computer maintenance operations. System programs generally are developed by the hardware supplier or by software development companies. Application (user) programs are sets of computer instructions that perform data processing tasks. These programs (such as *Microsoft Excel*) usually are written within the organization or purchased from an outside supplier. Enterprise resource planning programs (ERPs) such as *SAP/R3, PeopleSoft,* and *J. D. Edwards* are examples of more complex application systems.

3. *Documentation* provides a description of the system and its controls in relation to input, data processing, output, report processing, logic, and operator instructions. Documentation is the means of communicating the essential elements of the data processing system. The following purposes may be served by computer system documentation:

   - Provide for management review of proposed application systems.
   - Provide explanatory materials for users.
   - Instruct new personnel by providing background on previous application systems and serve as a guidelines for developing new applications.
   - Provide the data necessary for answering inquiries about the operation of a computer application.
   - Serve as one source of information for an evaluation of controls.
   - Provide operating instructions.
   - Simplify program revision by providing details of processing logic.
   - Supply basic information for planning and implementing audit software or other auditing techniques.[1]

Auditors review the documentation to gain an understanding of the system and to determine whether the documentation is adequate. Of utmost importance in this area of the review is whether the client has established systems development and documentation standards. Unless written standards exist, it is very difficult to determine whether the systems development controls and the documentation are adequate. The **systems development and documentation standards manual** prepared by management should contain standards that ensure (1) proper user involvement in the systems design and modification process, (2) review of the specifications of the system, (3) approval by user management and data processing management, and (4) controls and auditability.

Armed with the manual describing systems development standards, auditors first evaluate the standards to determine whether they are adequate and then review the documentation to determine whether the standards are followed. This review actually accomplishes a test of controls audit of systems development standards (and controls), as well as provides an understanding of how a particular system works. This kind of work may require the knowledge and skills of an information system auditor.

[1] Gordon B. Davis, Donald L. Adams, and Carol A. Schaller, *Auditing and EDP,* 2nd ed. (New York: AICPA).

DOCUMENTATION AND SYSTEMS DEVELOPMENT: SELECTED QUESTIONNAIRE ITEMS

Development

1. Does a written priority plan exist for development of new systems and changes to old systems?
2. Do the design and development of a new system involve the users as well as computer personnel?
3. Is there a formal review and approval process at the end of each significant phase in developing a new system?

Documentation

4. Do written standards exist for documentation of new systems and for changing documentation when existing systems are revised?
5. Does the following documentation exist for each application?

   - System flowchart.
   - Record layouts.
   - Program edit routines.
   - Program source listing.
   - Operator instructions.
   - Approval and change record.

Auditors are interested in the following elements of the documentation of accounting applications: *application description, problem definition, programs description, acceptance testing records, computer operator instructions, user department manual, change and modification log,* and *listing of controls.* For example, the **application description** usually contains system flowcharts, description of all inputs and outputs, record formats, lists of computer codes, and control features. The application system flowcharts frequently can be adapted to audit working paper flowcharts where the flow of transactions can be followed and control points noted. Copies of record formats of significant master files frequently are obtained for use in computer-assisted audit techniques.

The **program description** should contain a program flowchart, a listing of the program source code (such as COBOL), and a record of all program changes. Auditors should review this documentation to determine whether programmed controls such as input validations exist.

The **acceptance testing records** may contain test data that auditors can use to perform their own test of controls audit procedures. The user's manual should indicate manual procedures and controls in the user departments that submit transactions and receive the output. The log changes and modifications is important to auditors because it should provide assurance that the application systems have been operating as described for the period under review and that all changes and modifications have been authorized.

The *controls section* of the documentation also is very important. Here all the computer controls described in other sections are repeated along with manual controls that affect the application program. Careful review by auditors of this section should provide a complete overview of the entire control over the processing of transactions in a particular application and how the general controls are carried out in the application.

4. *Organizational personnel* manage, design, program, operate, and control data processing systems. However, information-processing systems involve such functions

as systems analysis, programming, data conversion, library functions, and machine operations that are unique; therefore, further separation of duties is recommended. The duties associated with these and other important roles are defined as follows:

- *Systems Analysts* analyze requirements for information, evaluate the existing system, and design new or improved data processing. They also outline the system and prepare specifications that guide the programmers, as well as prepare documentation of the application system. Finally, they often acquire suitable commercial software.

- *Programmers* flowchart and code the logic of the computer programs required by the overall system designed by the systems analyst. They also often prepare documentation of the program.

- *Computer Operators* operate the computer for each accounting application system according to written operating procedures found in the computer operation instructions.

- *Data Conversion Operators* prepare data for machine processing. Previously these individuals operated keypunch machines and produced punched cards; now these operators usually convert visible source data to magnetic tape or disk, use optical-character reading equipment, or use data transmission terminals. In advanced computer systems, the data conversion operators will likely be accounting clerks entering transactions from the accounting department into remote terminals.

- *Librarians* may perform two types of functions in a computer facility—one for system and program documentation and the other for the actual programs and data files. The purpose of the system/program documentation library is to maintain control over documentation of the design and operation stages of computer information systems. The purpose of the program/data library is to maintain control over the data files and programs actually used from day to day. In many systems, this second library function is done automatically with software. The librarian function or librarian software should control access to systems documentation and access to program and data files by using a checkout log (a record of entry and use) or a password to record the use by authorized persons. Someone who possesses both documentation and data files will have enough information to alter data and programs for his or her own purposes.

- The *Control Group* receives input from user departments, logs the input and transfers it to data conversion, reviews documentation sequence numbers, reviews and processes error messages, monitors actual processing, compares control totals to computer output, and distributes output.

Separation of the duties performed by analysts, programmers, and operators is important. The general idea is that anyone who designs a processing system should not do the technical programming work, and anyone who performs either of these tasks should not be the computer operator when "live" data is processed. Persons performing each function should not have access to each other's work, and only the computer operators should have access to the equipment. Computer systems are susceptible to manipulative handling, and the lack of separation of duties along the lines described should be considered a serious weakness in general control.

5. *Data* refers to transactions and related information entered, stored, and processed by the system. Since magnetic storage media can be erased or written over, controls are necessary to ensure that the proper file is being used and that the files and programs are appropriately backed up. **Backup** involves a retention system for files, programs, and documentation so master files can be reconstructed in case of accidental loss and so processing can continue at another site if the computer center is lost to fire or flood. Thus, backup files must be stored offsite, away from the main computer. Some of the more important security and retention control techniques and procedures relating to data are explained next.

- *External Labels* are paper labels on the outside of a file (e.g., portable disk packs, or magnetic tapes). The label identifies the contents, such as "Accounts Receivable Master File," so the probability of using the file inappropriately (e.g., in the payroll run) is minimized.

- *Header and Trailer Labels* are special internal records on magnetic tapes and disks. They are magnetic records on the tape or disk; but, instead of containing data, they hold label information similar to the external file label. Therefore, the header and trailer labels are sometimes called internal labels. Their function is to prevent use of the wrong file during processing. The header label contains the name of the file and relevant identification codes. The trailer label gives a signal that the end of the file has been reached. Sometimes these trailer labels are designed to contain accumulated control totals to serve as a check on loss of data during operation; for example, the number of accounts and the total balance of an accounts receivable file.

- *File Security* is enhanced by many physical devices, such as storage in fireproof vaults, backup in remote locations, and files sorted in computer-readable, printed, or microfilm form. In the majority of cases, the exposure to risk of loss warrants insurance on program and data files.

- *File Retention Practices* are related closely to file security; but, in general, retention may provide the first line of defense against relatively minor loss, while security generally consists of all measures taken to safeguard files against total loss. In essence, the problem is how to reconstruct records and files once they have been damaged. One of the most popular methods is the **grandfather–father–son concept.** This involves the retention of backup files, such as the current transaction file and the prior master file, from which the current master file can be reconstructed. Exhibit H–1 illustrates the file retention plan. Particularly important files may be retained to the great-grandfather generation if considered necessary.

EXHIBIT H–1   GRANDFATHER, FATHER, AND SON FILE RETENTION

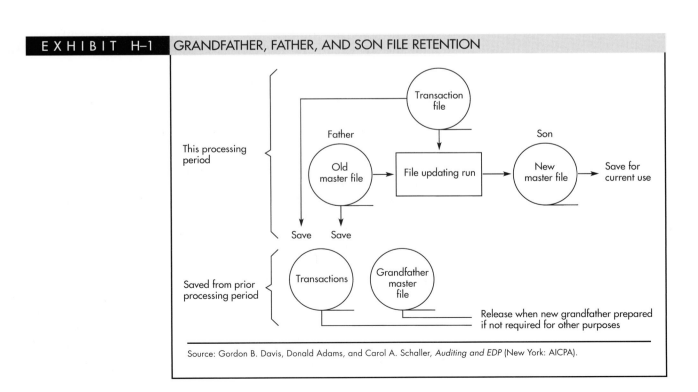

Source: Gordon B. Davis, Donald Adams, and Carol A. Schaller, *Auditing and EDP* (New York: AICPA).

ORGANIZATION AND PHYSICAL ACCESS: SELECTED QUESTIONNAIRE ITEMS

Preliminary

1. Prepare or have the client prepare a "Computer Profile," which should include an organization chart, hardware and peripheral equipment, communication network, major application processes (batch or online), significant input and output files, software used, and a layout of the data center.

Organization

2. Are the following functions performed by different individuals so that proper segregation of duties exists between:
   a. Application programming, computer operation, and control of data files?
   b. Application programming and control and reconciliation of input and output?
   c. Computer employees and users who initiate transactions and authorize changes to master files?
3. Are computer operators rotated periodically from shift to shift?
4. Are programmers and systems analysts rotated periodically from application to application?

Data and Procedural Control

5. Is there a separate group within the computer department to perform control and balancing of input and output?
6. Are there written procedures for setting up input for processing?
7. Is there a formal procedure for distribution of output to user departments?

Access Control

8. Is access to the computer room restricted to authorized personnel?
9. Are operators restricted from access to program and application documentation?
10. Does access to online files require that specific passwords be entered to identify and validate the terminal user?

Disk files are more difficult to reconstruct than tape files because the process of updating old records with new information is "destructive." The old or superseded data on a record are removed (destroyed) when new data are entered in the same place on a disk. One means of reconstruction is to have a disk file "dumped" onto tape periodically (each day or each week). This file copy, along with the related transaction file also retained, can serve as the father to the current disk file (son).

6. *Control Activities* refer to a client's activities designed to ensure the proper recording of transactions and to prevent or detect errors and frauds. Control activities include: (1) *Performance reviews*—management's continuous supervision of operations, (2) *Segregation of duties* designed to reduce opportunities for a person to be in a position to perpetrate and conceal errors and frauds when performing normal duties, (3) *Physical controls* designed to ensure safeguarding and security of assets and records, and (4) *Information processing controls*, including approvals, authorizations, verifications, and reconciliations.

H.1 What does a financial statement auditor need to know about information processing systems? Why?

H.2 What are the six elements of computer-based information system?

H.3 Describe the typical duties of computer personnel. Which duties should be segregated within the computer department?

H.4 Describe the purposes of computer system documentation. Why should the auditor review the computer system documentation?

H.5 What aspects of documentation, file security, and retention control procedures are unique to computer systems?

H.6 What does an auditor need to know about computer hardware controls?

EVALUATION APPROACHES FOR INFORMATION SYSTEM CONTROLS

LEARNING OBJECTIVE

2. Explain the difference between auditing around the computer and auditing through the computer; list several techniques auditors can use to perform tests of controls in a computerized information system.

Auditors can use several methods to evaluate a client's computer information system controls. For example, auditors can conduct audits by **auditing around the computer.** This method treats the computer system as a "black box." Auditors obtain evidence by vouching data from general ledger output to source documents and by tracing from source documents to the general ledger output. They use visible evidence, such as the input source data, the machine-produced error listings, the visible control points (e.g., use of batch totals), and the detailed printed output. When the client uses the computer simply as a calculator and printer, this method may be adequate. Nothing is inherently wrong with auditing around the computer if auditors are satisfied with the control system and are able to gather sufficient evidence. However, auditing around the computer is unacceptable if this approach is used because of lack of auditor expertise.

Exhibit H–2 below shows the scheme of auditing around the computer. The auditors select a sample of source documents for a tracing procedure to test the controls over recording sales transactions. The client's computer system processes the transactions, but the auditors treat it like a "black box," interested only in the correspondence of the input (customer's order, quantity shipped, and amount billed) to the output (debit accounts receivable, credit to sales revenue).

EXHIBIT H–2	EXAMPLE OF AUDITING AROUND THE COMPUTER

In contrast, **auditors can audit through the computer.** The auditors evaluate the client's hardware and software to determine the reliability of operations that cannot be viewed by the human eye. *Auditing through* is common in practice because more and more computer systems do not operate as mere calculators and printers; they have significant controls built into the information processing systems. Thus, ignoring an information system and the controls built into it can amount to ignoring important features of internal control.

Internal control audit objectives do not change when the client operates in an electronic environment. Auditors must still assess control risk. Although the audit of complex information systems usually involves information system auditors with advanced technical proficiency, "general" auditors (and you as a student of auditing) must possess some knowledge of the tools and techniques available in order to coordinate the specialist's work. Auditors also need to know the available techniques so they can advise clients of the control concerns and potential audit aids. Many of the tools and techniques discussed below are designed into the system. Auditors should become more involved in reviewing systems at the development stage to ensure that adequate controls are installed and auditability is possible.

For simple batch systems, adequate evidence of control performance frequently exists in the printed output and logs (thus, *auditing around the computer* is possible). For example, input error reports usually will contain examples of each type of error the edit routines are designed to detect. A sample of each type of error can be traced to the error log maintained by the computer control group and to evidence of correction and resubmission. Likewise, printed documentation may exist of compliance with authorized procedures required for execution of transactions or for changes to master files. However, external auditors occasionally must use the computer as an audit tool to test the controls with the application programs of even simple systems. (Internal auditors more frequently utilize these techniques.) The tools and techniques applicable to auditing in a complex computer environment can be classified as those that (1) operate online on a real-time basis with live data, (2) utilize simulated or dummy data, (3) operate on historical data, and (4) utilize programs analysis techniques.

Techniques Using Live Data

In most cases, these techniques require that special audit modules be designed and coded into programs at the time of development. These *audit hooks* allow auditors to select specific transactions of audit interest before or during processing and save them for subsequent audit follow-up. (Program modules solely for audit or maintenance purposes are called **audit hooks.** The same concepts used for fraudulent purposes are called **trap doors.**) These techniques also enable internal auditors to continuously monitor the information processing system.

Tagging Transactions.
Transactions selected by the auditor are "tagged" with an indicator at input. A computer trail of all processing steps of these transactions in the application system can be printed out or stored in computer files for subsequent evaluation.

Audit-Files (Embedded Audit Modules).
Auditor-selected transactions are written to a special file for later verification. Two methods may be employed. **Systems control audit review file (SCARF)** is a method in which auditors build into the data processing programs special limit, reasonableness, or other audit tests. These tests produce reports of transactions selected according to the auditor's criteria, and the reports are delivered directly to the auditor for review and follow-up. The SCARF procedure is especially attractive to internal auditors. A **sample audit review file (SARF)** technique is similar to SCARF, except that instead of programming auditors' test criteria, a random sampling selection scheme is programmed. Auditors can

review the report of sample transactions after each production run. The SARF method is efficient for producing representative samples of transactions processed over a period by the computer.

Snapshot.

A "picture" of main memory of transactions and database elements is taken before and after computer processing operations have been performed. The picture is then printed out for auditor use. For example, the contents of an accounts receivable balance are saved before a sales transaction is posted, and the contents after posting are saved. These balances, along with the sales transaction, indicate whether update processing was correct. The auditor can trace and verify the accounting process utilizing the results.

Monitoring Systems Activity.

Hardware and software are available to analyze activity within a computer. These monitors are designed to determine computer efficiency. However, they may be applied for financial audit purposes to determine who uses elements of the system and for what operations. For example, a record of passwords used to enter accounting transactions can be captured and compared to the list of personnel authorized to enter these transactions.

Extended Records.

Special programs provide an audit trail of an individual transaction by accumulating the results of all application programs that contributed to the processing of the transaction. The accumulated results are stored either as additional fields of the transaction record or in a separate audit file. For example, the snapshot example of accounts receivable balances before and after update processing could be added to the sales transaction, making an extended transaction record. Thus, auditors can follow the flow of a transaction without reviewing several files at various times and stages of processing.

Techniques Using Simulated or Dummy Data

Auditors often use two methods to test a client computer information system using fictional data: (1) the **test data** approach, and (2) the **integrated test facility (ITF)** approach.

Test Data.

The basic concept of test data is that once a computer is programmed to handle transactions in a certain logical way, it will faithfully handle every transaction exactly the same way. Therefore, the audit team need only prepare a limited number of simulated transactions (some with "errors" and some without) to determine whether each control operates as described in the program documentation.

A set of **test data** contains a sample of one of each possible combination of data fields that may be processed through the real system. Simulated test data can be on tape or disk. Test data also may be entered into an online system through computer terminals. The purpose of using test data is to determine whether controls operate as described in questionnaire responses and program flowcharts. Test transactions may consist of abstractions from real transactions and simulated transactions generated by the auditors' imagination.[2] The auditors must prepare a worksheet listing each transaction and the predicted output based on the program documentation. Then these test transactions must be converted to the normal machine-sensed input form, and arrangements must be made to process the transactions with the actual program used for real transactions.

---

[2] This may be an oversimplification because computer systems may have multiple controls that create thousands of error combinations and possible test transactions. Computerized test data generators are available to help auditors overcome the magnitude of the test data creation task.

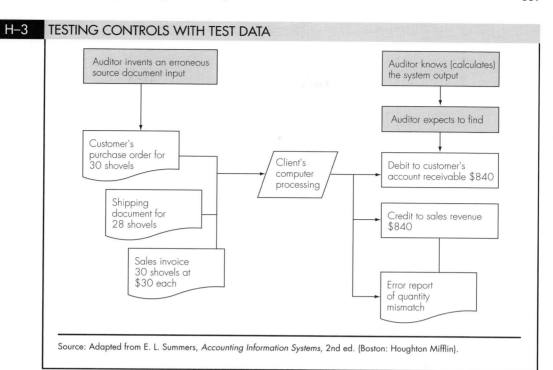

EXHIBIT H–3   TESTING CONTROLS WITH TEST DATA

Source: Adapted from E. L. Summers, *Accounting Information Systems,* 2nd ed. (Boston: Houghton Mifflin).

Auditors must be very familiar with the nature of the business and the logic of the programs to anticipate all data combinations that might exist as transaction input or that might be process-generated. They must be able to assign degrees of audit importance to each kind of error-checking control method. They must ensure that the test data do not get commingled with real transactions and change the actual master files.

Test data are processed at a single point in time with the client program that is supposed to have been used during the period under audit. After the analysis of test output, the audit manager still must make an inference about processing throughout the entire period. In order to do so, he or she must be satisfied by a review of documentation that any program changes have been authorized and correctly made. Some auditors occasionally perform test data procedures on an irregular surprise basis during the year.

Exhibit H–3 shows the scheme of testing controls with test data. (You should compare it to Exhibit H–2, the example of auditing around the computer.) The auditors create source document input that contains one or more error conditions, in this case a shipment of fewer units than the customer ordered. The auditors know the desired outcome—an error message that the quantity shipped and the quantity billed do not match, perhaps with an accounting entry to charge the customer for the shipped quantity. If this result does not appear from the processing of the test data, the auditors can conclude that the processing control over accurate sales recording contains a deficiency (weakness). The auditors are testing the controls embedded in the computer program, and they are using the actual processing program for the test.

Integrated Test Facility (ITF).

The use of an integrated test facility is a technique commonly used by clients' program maintenance personnel, although auditors can use the approach as well. This "minicompany" approach involves creating a dummy department or branch complete with records of employees, customers, vendors, receivables, payables, and other accounts. The ITF has master file records (or database records), carefully coded (such as "99"), included among the real master file records. Simulated transactions (test data) are inserted along with real transactions, and the same application program(s) operate on both the test data and the real transactions. Since the auditor knows what the ITF output should be, the actual

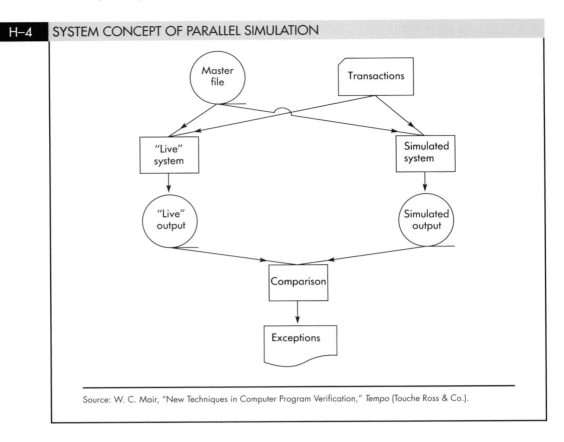

Source: W. C. Mair, "New Techniques in Computer Program Verification," *Tempo* (Touche Ross & Co.).

results of processing (output reports, error reports) can be reviewed to determine whether the application program is functioning properly.

A great deal of care is required when ITF is used because the fictitious master file records, the transactions, and the account outputs are placed in the actual accounting system and in the business records. The account amounts and other output data must be reversed or adjusted out of the financial statements. Also, care must be taken not to damage or misstate any of the real master file records and account balances.

Techniques Using Historical Data

The primary technique used to test program controls using actual historic client data is called *parallel simulation*. In **parallel simulation** the audit team prepares a computer program designed to process client data properly. The result of the auditors' processing of real client data is compared with the result of the real data processed by the actual client program. The concept of this method is illustrated in Exhibit H–4.

To test the controls contained in computer programs, auditors have the options of (1) using the client's real programs, (2) having client personnel write special programs, or (3) writing their own special programs to collect evidence that the controls work. The first option would be used in the test data technique described in the previous section. The second option requires close supervision and testing to ensure that the client's personnel have prepared the audit program correctly. The third option is parallel simulation, and it requires significant programming expertise of the audit staff or close liaison with expert independent programmers.

However, with computerized audit tools and techniques (CAATTs), the parallel simulation option is easier. CAATTs audit software programs consist of numerous prepackaged subroutines that can perform most tasks needed in auditing and business applications. The auditor's programming task consists of writing simple instructions that

AUDITING INSIGHT

PARALLEL SIMULATION

A parallel simulation of a company's sales invoice and accounts receivable processing system revealed that invoices that showed no bill of lading or shipment reference were processed and charged to customers with a corresponding credit to sales. Further audit of the exceptions showed that the real-data processing program did not contain a missing-data test and did not provide error messages for lack of shipping references. This finding led to (1) a more extensive test of the sales invoice population with comparison to shipping documents and (2) a more extensive audit of accounts receivable for customers who were charged with such sales.

call up one or more of the subroutines. Thus, auditors do not need to write complete, complex programs, and the expertise to use most CAATTs software can be acquired in one week of training.

Using the CAATTs program capabilities, an auditor can construct a system of information processing that will accept the same input as the real program, use the same files, and attempt to produce the same results. This simulated system will contain all the controls the auditor believes appropriate, and, in this respect, the thought process is quite similar to the logic that goes into preparing test data. The simulated-system output then is compared to the real-system output for correspondence or difference, and at this point the audit evidence is similar to the evidence obtained by using test data with the real program: Conclusions can be reached about the error-detection capabilities of the real system.

Another way to create a parallel system is to conduct a thorough technical audit of the controls in the client's actual program, then keep a copy of it secure in the auditors' files. Actual client data later can be processed using this audited copy of the client's program (e.g., at times later in the year under audit or in the following year audit). The goal is to determine whether output from the program the client actually used in processing data produces satisfactory accounting output when compared to the output from the auditors' controlled copy of the program. This approach is often called **controlled reprocessing,** and it is a version of parallel simulation. (The method is also called **comparison program utilization.**)

The first audit application of parallel simulation may be very costly, although it probably will be more efficient than auditing without the computer or utilizing test data. Real economies are realized, however, is subsequent audits of the same client.

The audit team must take care to determine that the real transactions selected for processing are "representative." Thus, some exercise in random selection and identification of important transactions may be required in conjunction with parallel processing.

Program Analysis Techniques

Computer technicians use numerous software packages for program documentation, debugging, and analysis. These tools also can be used for audit purposes in certain situations. Programs exist to take the source code (e.g., COBOL) and produce flowcharts or decision tables that can be used to understand the logic of an application program. **Cross-reference** programs provide printed listings of every occurrence of each name used in an application program or a list of every file used in an application system. Auditors can use these listings to follow the flow of transactions and identify significant data files. Auditors can utilize program analysis software to identify potential trapdoors created for fraudulent use.

These advanced computer systems audit tools and techniques are summarized in Exhibit H–5. You should study these audit tools and techniques carefully—especially the purposes, advantages, and disadvantages.

EXHIBIT H-5   ADVANCED INFORMATION SYSTEM AUDIT TOOLS AND TECHNIQUES

Technique	Capability Supplied By	Used By	Data Used	Purpose	Advantages	Disadvantages
Tagging transactions	Vendor or application system designer.	Auditors and managers.	Actual transactions.	Test of controls and substantive audit.	Full range of selectivity.	Adds to overhead of systems, special programming.
Audit files (embedded audit modules)	Systems designer.	Auditors and control personnel.	Actual transactions and system.	Test of controls and substantive audit.	Specified transactions logged for audit review.	Cost subject to manipulation by client.
Snapshot	Systems designer.	Programmers and auditors.	Actual transactions.	Review system, logic.	Aids understanding flow of transaction processing.	Special programming.
Monitoring	Vendor.	Auditors and managers.	Actual systems.	Review actual system activity.	Shows what has happened.	Requires techniques knowledge to interpret.
Computer Assisted Audit Tools and Techniques (CAATTs)	Vendors or audit firm.	Auditors and managers.	Actual transactions.	Test of controls and substantive audit. Perform wide variety of audit procedures.	Retrieves data for audit purposes. Relatively easy to use, not expensive.	Presently limited to types of files that can be accessed.
Simulation	Auditors, internal and external with controlled program copy.	Auditors.	Actual transactions.	Determine accuracy of data processed test of controls audit.	Permits comparison with real processing.	Extensive use can be large consumer of machine resources.
Extended records	Design of client application.	Auditors and managers.	Actual transactions.	Provide complete trail for audit and management purposes.	Provide complete account history.	Costly use of machine resources.
Integrated test facility	Auditors, mostly internal.	Auditors.	Simulated transactions.	Test of controls audit.	Relatively inexpensive.	Must be "backed out" very carefully.
Program analysis techniques	Special software, contractor, or vendor.	Auditors and programmers.	Actual client programs.	Authentication of program, operation.	Gives better understanding of application; gives assurance controls are functioning.	Needs auditor knowledge of programming; may be expensive, useful only in certain circumstances.
Flowchart software	Special software, contractor, or vendor.	Auditors and programmers.	Actual client programs	Check of key points in program execution.	Gives better understanding of application; gives assurance controls are functioning.	Needs auditor knowledge of programming; may be expensive; useful only in certain circumstances.

R E V I E W
CHECKPOINTS

H.7   What is the difference between auditing "through the computer" and auditing "around the computer"?

H.8   Name some advanced control techniques that clients can embed in computer systems.

H.9   What is the difference between the test data technique and the integrated test facility technique?

H.10   "The use of the integrated test facility technique to test the client's application control activities is unprofessional. We don't enter fake transactions into a client's manual system. Why should we do it in their computer system?" Evaluate this position and question posed by an audit partner.

H.11   What is the difference between the computerized test of controls audit procedures of test data and parallel simulation?

H.12   What is "controlled reprocessing"?

PERSONAL COMPUTER ENVIRONMENTS

LEARNING OBJECTIVE
3. Describe the characteristics and control problems of personal computer installations.

Computer activity involving personal computers (PCs) should be included in the assessment of control risk. Since the control objectives do not change, the internal control questionnaires illustrated and the audit techniques discussed in this module are relevant but may have to be tailored to the personal computer or local area network (LAN) installation. The following explanations are designed to assist you in appreciating how the questionnaires, flowcharts, and audit techniques may have to be modified by directing attention to potential problems and controls normally affecting personal computers.

Major Characteristics

Personal computers may be elements of a local area network (LAN) or stand-alone systems doing all the information processing for a business. The control environment, and not the computer technology, is the important aspect for auditors. Many small businesses get along well with computers for accounting purposes by using these resources:

- *Utility programs*. Purchased utility programs are used extensively to enter and change data.
- *Diskettes*. Floppy diskettes are used extensively for accounting file storage.
- *Terminals*. Terminals and minicomputers are used for transaction data entry, inquiry, and other interactive functions.
- *Software packages*. Purchased software packages are used extensively, rather than internally developed application software.
- *Documentation*. Available system, program, operation, and user documentation may be limited or nonexistent.

In a personal computer installation with these limited computer resources, the most significant control weakness is a lack of segregation of duties. This potential weakness may be compounded by the lack of controls in the operating system and application programs. Simply turning on the system may provide access to all the files and programs with no record of usage.

Personal Computer Control Considerations

Most of the control problems can be traced to the lack of segregation of duties and computerized controls. It follows that most of the auditors' control considerations and techniques are designed to overcome these deficiencies. Auditors should consider the entire control system, including manual controls, and look for compensating control strengths

AUDITING INSIGHT

CONTROL PROBLEMS IN PERSONAL COMPUTER ENVIRONMENTS

Lack of Segregation of Accounting Functions

Individual employees may initiate and authorize source documents, enter data, operate the computer, and distribute output reports.

Lack of Segregation of Computer Functions

Small organizations may not separate the functions of programming and operating the computer. Programs and data are often resident on disk at all times and accessible by any operator.

Lack of Physical Computer Security

Computers are often located in the end-user department instead of in a separate secure area. Ease of access and use is desired, and access to hardware, programs, and data files may not be restricted.

Lack of Computer Knowledge

Individuals responsible for data processing sometimes have limited knowledge of computers, relying instead on packaged software and utility programs with convenient user manuals. Computer professionals may be assigned to monitor mainframe systems but not personal computers.

that might offset apparent weaknesses. The various control considerations and techniques are discussed below under heading similar to the general controls discussed previously—organizational, operations and processing, and systems development and modification.

Organizational Control Procedures

The environment in a personal computer or local area network installation is similar to the one-person bookkeeping department because only one or two people perform the systems analysis, design, and programming operations. The main controls involve limiting the concentration of functions (to the extent possible) and establishing proper supervision. The implementation of the other controls discussed below will help offset control weaknesses caused by lack of segregation of duties.

Operational Control

In personal computer and local area network installations, the most important controls are those over online data entry (accounting transactions).

- *Restricting Access to Input Devices.* Terminals may be physically locked and keys controlled. The utilization of various levels of passwords to access files, initiate changes, and invoke programs should be strictly followed. **Automatic terminal logoff** is another effective control that limits unauthorized access by automatically terminating the link between computer and local area network after a specified period of time, preventing unauthorized users from accessing a vacant logged-on terminal.
- *Standard Screens and Computer Prompting.* Computers can be programmed to produce a standard screen format when a particular function is called. The operator must complete all blanks as prompted by the computer, thus ensuring that complete transactions are entered before they are processed.
- *Online Editing and Sight Verification.* The input edit and validation controls discussed previously can be programmed to occur at time of input. In some installations, the data on the screen are not released until the data have been sight-verified and the operator signals the computer to accept the entire screen.

Processing Control

Processing can be controlled by artificially creating the files equivalent to the grandfather–father–son retention concept found in batch systems. The activities to ensure that the data processed are in balance, that an adequate audit trail is maintained, and that recovery is possible include the following:

- *Transaction Logs.* Transaction entry through the terminal should be captured automatically in a computerized log. The transaction logs (for each terminal or each class of terminals) should be summarized into the equivalent of batch totals (counts of transactions, financial totals, or hash totals).
- *Control Totals.* Master files should contain records that accumulate the number of records and financial totals. The update processing automatically should change these control records.
- *Balancing Input to Output.* The summary of daily transactions and the master file control totals from the computer should be balanced to manual control totals maintained by the accounting department. If this external balancing is not feasible, techniques similar to the auditor's analytical procedures can be employed to test for reasonableness.
- *Audit Trail.* The transaction logs and periodic dumps of master files should provide an audit trail and means for recovery. In addition, some computer installations have systems software that can provide a log of all files accessed and all jobs processed.

Systems Development and Modification

The control objectives and activities in personal computer or local area network installations are no different than on a mainframe system, even though the environment is different. Many application programs are purchased from computer manufacturers or software vendors not completely familiar with online control techniques. Purchased programs should be reviewed carefully and tested before acquisition and implementation.

The programming languages most frequently used in personal computers are easily learned, and programming ability may develop within the user group. Most personal computers have "menu-type" instructions that are simple to use without technical training. Further, the programming is in an interpretative language, which means it remains in the computer program library in source code form that is easy to change. Development standards and modification authorization become even more important than in larger systems. Since most programming will be done through terminals, special passwords should be required to access programs and only authorized personnel should have these passwords.

REVIEW
CHECKPOINTS

H.13 Which important duties are generally not segregated in small business computer systems?

H.14 What are the major characteristics and control problems in personal computer and local area network installations?

H.15 What control activities can a company use to achieve control over the operation of a personal computer or local area network-based accounting system?

H.16 What control activities can a company use to achieve control over the computer processing of accounting data on a personal computer or local area network?

COMPUTER ABUSE AND COMPUTER FRAUD

Computer fraud is a matter of concern for managers and investors as well as auditors. Experts in the field have coined two definitions related to computer chicanery: *Computer abuse* is the broad definition, but *computer fraud* is probably the term used more often.

COMPUTER ABUSE AND COMPUTER FRAUD DEFINITIONS

Computer Abuse:
    Any incident associated with computer technology in which a victim suffered or could have suffered a loss and a perpetrator by intention made or could have made a gain. [D. B. Parker, *Crime by Computer* (New York, Charles Scribner's Sons).]

Computer Fraud:
    Fraud is any intentional act designed to deceive or mislead another person with the result of the victim suffering a loss or the perpetrator achieving a gain.
    Computer fraud is any fraud that involves electronic data processing in the perpetration or cover-up of the fraudulent acts.

LEARNING OBJECTIVE
4. Define and describe computer fraud and the controls a company can use to prevent it.

Computer abuse and fraud include such diverse acts as intentional damage or destruction of a computer, use of the computer to assist in a fraud, and use of the mystique of computers to promote business. Perpetrators of the Equity Funding financial fraud used a computer to print thousands of fictitious records and documents that otherwise would have occupied the time of hundreds of clerks. Some services (such as "computerized" dating services) have promoted business on the promise of using computers when none are actually used.

In a business environment auditors and managers are concerned particularly with acts of computer theft or embezzlement of assets or material misstatements in the financial statements. To perpetrate computer frauds, persons must have access to one or more of the following:

- The computer itself, or a terminal.
- Data files.
- Computer programs.
- System information.
- Time and opportunity to convert assets to personal use.

While computer financial frauds range from the crude to the complex, they hit financial institutions with alarming frequency. Moreover, computer financial frauds are frustratingly difficult to detect in the ordinary course of business. The AICPA conducted a study of computer frauds in the banking and insurance industry and found that customer complaints were the leading clues to discovery of fraud, while routine audits were credited with discovery of 18 percent. Auditors have some success, but they are not infallible detectives.

AUDITING INSIGHT

HOW FRAUD IS DETECTED IN FINANCIAL INSTITUTIONS

Customer complaint or inquiry	24%
Accident, tip-off, unusual perpetrator activity	22
Controls	18
Routine audit	18
Nonroutine study	8
Changes in operations, EDP, financial statements	6
Unidentified	5

Source: *Report on the Study of EDP-Related Fraud in the Banking and Insurance Industries* (AICPA).

Control Protection

Organizations can install controls designed to prevent and detect computer frauds and to limit the extent of damage from them. These prevention, detection, and limitation controls are summarized in the box below.

PROTECTING THE COMPUTER FROM FRAUD (SELECTED CONTROLS)

	Objective of Control		
	Prevention	Detection	Limitation
Administrative controls:			
Security checks on personnel	X		
Segregation of duties	X		
Access and execution log records (properly reviewed)		X	
Program testing after modification		X	
Rotation of computer duties		X	X
Transaction limit amounts			X
Physical controls:			
Inconspicuous location	X		
Controlled access	X		
Computer room guard (after hours)	X	X	
Computer room entry log record	X	X	
Preprinted limits on documents (e.g., checks)			X
Data backup storage			X
Technical controls:			
Data encryption	X		
Access control software and passwords	X		
Transaction logging reports		X	
Control totals (financial, hash)	X	X	
Program source comparison (comparing versions of programs)		X	
Range checks on permitted transaction amounts			X
Reasonableness check on permitted transaction amounts			X

Controls can be classified in three different levels: (1) administrative, (2) physical, and (3) technical. The administrative level refers to general controls that affect the management of an organization's computer resources.

The physical controls affect the computer equipment itself and related documents. The "inconspicuous location" control simply refers to placing personal computers, terminals, and data processing centers in places out of the way of casual traffic. Of course, the equipment used daily must be available in employees' workplaces, but access must be controlled to prevent unauthorized persons from simply sitting down and invading the system and its data files.

Technical controls include some matters of electronic wizardry. **Data encryption** techniques convert information to scrambled form or code so it can look like garbled nonsense when transmitted or retrieved from a file. In recent years, industrial spying has increased. Businesses should assume that public and private intelligence services intercept and analyze data submitted by wire and airwaves (e.g., satellite transmission) for the purpose of commercial advantage. Unscrupulous industrial spies may try to break into an organization's computer system, and elaborate password software will be necessary to thwart them. (Hackers have been known to program telephones to call random numbers to find a computer system, then try millions of random passwords to try to get in!) The "programmed range and reasonableness checks" refer to computer monitoring of transaction processing to try to detect potentially erroneous or fraudulent transactions. These are the equivalent of the low-tech imprint you may have seen on some negotiable checks: "Not negotiable if over $500," for example.

AUDITING INSIGHT

TAKE A BYTE OUT OF COMPUTER CRIME

The best way to prevent unauthorized computer access is through user authentication, most commonly accomplished through the use of individual employee passwords. Unfortunately, many employees find it difficult to remember multiple passwords. Some employees post their passwords near their computers where hackers (sometimes posing as pizza delivery persons) can easily find them. Others choose words and phrases that are easy for them to remember. A Chicago computer consultant recently broke into dozens of Chicago-area computers using the password "Bulls." Employees should be encouraged to choose unusual, but memorable passwords, and to change their passwords on a periodic basis.

Embezzlement and Financial Statement Fraud

Computer experts generally agree that an ingenious programmer can commit theft or misappropriation of assets that would be difficult, if not impossible, to detect. Nonetheless, such frauds usually produce an unsupported debit balance in some asset account. For example, someone might manipulate the computer to cause purchased goods to be routed to his own warehouse. In this case, the business inventory balances probably would be overstated. One bank employee caused checking account service charges to be credited to his own account instead of to the appropriate revenue account. In this case, the service charge revenue account would be less than the sum of charges to the checking account customers. Thorough auditing of accounting output records might result in detection of computer-assisted frauds such as these.

Noncomputer auditing methods, as well as some computer-assisted methods, may be employed to try to detect computer frauds. Direct confirmations with independent outside parties, analytical procedures examining the output of the system for expected relationships, and comparison of output with independently maintained files may reveal errors and frauds in computer-produced accounting records. However, all too often auditors and managers are surprised by computer frauds reported to them by conscience-stricken participants, anonymous telephone messages, tragic suicides, or other haphazard means. Nevertheless, auditors working in an electronic environment are expected to possess the expertise required to identify serious information system control weaknesses. When such weaknesses are believed to exist, the best strategy is to use the services of an information system auditor to help plan and execute technical procedures for further study and evaluation of the computer control system.

R E V I E W
CHECKPOINTS

H.17 What are the five things a person must use to commit a computer fraud?

H.18 What physical controls can a company use to protect computer systems from fraud?

H.19 What technical controls can a company use to protect computer systems from fraud?

H.20 What administrative controls can a company use to protect computer systems from fraud?

H.21 What are some ways of limiting damages as a result of computer fraud?

SUMMARY

All auditors should have enough familiarity with computers, electronic transaction processing, and computer controls to be able to audit simple systems and to work with information system auditors on more complex information systems. This module provides insight into element of a computerized information system, its related controls, and the methods used to audit the controls.

The examination of client computer controls can take different forms. Auditors can try to audit "around" the computer, and act like it does not exist except as a very fast and accurate manual accounting processor. They can adopt computer expertise and audit "through" the computer to test its control features. Tests of computer controls described in the module include live data techniques (audit hooks, tagging transactions, SCARF, SARF, snapshot, monitoring systems activity, and extended records), historical data techniques (parallel processing and generalized software applications), simulated data processing (test data and ITF), and program analysis techniques (computerized program flowcharting and cross-reference programs).

The ultimate goal of the computer methods of test of controls auditing is to reach a conclusion about the actual operation of controls in a computer system. This conclusion allows the audit manager to assess the control risk and determine the nature, timing, and extent of substantive audit procedures for auditing the related account balances. This control risk assessment decision is crucial, particularly in computerized information systems, because subsequent work may be performed using data files that are produced by the computerized information system.

Not all businesses use large-scale systems, so this module includes a personal computer and local area network orientation to information processing systems. Their characteristics and typical control problems are described. The module concludes with a section on computer fraud.

MULTIPLE-CHOICE QUESTIONS FOR PRACTICE AND REVIEW

H.22 In a computerized information system, automated equipment controls or hardware controls are designed to
  a. Arrange data in a logical sequential manner for processing purposes.
  b. Correct errors in the computer programs.
  c. Monitor and detect errors in source documents.
  d. Detect and control errors arising from use of equipment.

H.23 A good example of application (user) computer software is
  a. Payroll processing program.
  b. Operating system program.
  c. Data management system software.
  d. Utility programs.

H.24 Which of the following would lessen internal control in a computer system?
  a. The computer librarian maintains custody of computer program instructions and detailed listings.
  b. Computer operators have access to operator instructions and detailed program listing.
  c. The control group is solely responsible for the distribution of all computer output.

  d. Computer programmers write and debug programs that perform routines designed by the systems analyst.

H.25 When an online, real-time (OLRT) computer system is in use, the computer controls can be strengthened by
  a. Providing for the separation of duties between data input and error listing operations.
  b. Attaching plastic file protection rings to reels of magnetic tape before new data can be entered on the file.
  c. Preparing batch totals to provide assurance that file updates are made for the entire input.
  d. Making a validity check of an identification number before a user can obtain access to the computer files.

H.26 A procedural control used in the management of a computer center to minimize the possibility of data or program file destruction through operator error includes
  a. Control figures.
  b. Crossfooting tests.
  c. Limit checks.
  d. External labels.

H.27 An auditor would most likely use computer-assisted audit tools and techniques (CAATTS) to
a. Make copies of client data files for controlled reprocessing.
b. Construct a parallel simulation to test the client's computer controls.
c. Perform tests of a client's hardware controls.
d. Test the operative effectiveness of a client's password access control.

H.28 Which of the following client computer systems generally can be audited without examining or directly testing the computer programs of the system?
a. A system that performs relatively uncomplicated processes and produces detailed output.
b. A system that affects a number of master files and produces a limited output.
c. A system that updates a few master files and produces no other printed output than final balances.
d. A system that performs relatively complicated processing and produces very little detailed output.

H.29 The client's computerized exception reporting system helps an auditor to conduct a more efficient audit because it
a. Condenses data significantly.
b. Highlights abnormal conditions.
c. Decreases the tests of computer controls requirements.
d. Is an efficient computer input control.

H.30 An auditor will use the test data method to gain certain assurances with respect to
a. Input data.
b. Machine capacity.
c. Control procedures contained within the program.
d. General control procedures.

H.31 Assume an auditor estimates that 10,000 cash disbursement checks were issued during the accounting period. If a computer application control, which performs a limit check for each check request, is to be subjected to the auditor's test-data approach, the sample should include
a. Approximately 1,000 test items.
b. A number of test items determined by the auditor to be sufficient under the circumstances.
c. A number of test items under the circumstances.
d. One transaction.

H.32 When auditing a computerized accounting system, which of the following is not true of the test data approach?
a. Client's computer programs process test data under the auditor's control.
b. The test data must consist of all possible valid and invalid conditions.
c. The test data need consist of only those valid and invalid conditions in which the auditor is interested.
d. Only one transaction of each type need be tested.

H.33 An auditor cannot test the reliable operation of computerized control activities by
a. Submission at several different times of test data for processing on the computer program the company uses for actual transaction processing.
b. Manual comparison of detail transactions the internal auditors used to test a program to the program's actual error messages.
c. Programming a model transaction processing system and processing actual client transactions for comparison to the output produced by the client's program.
d. Manual reperformance of actual transaction processing with comparison of results to the actual system output.

H.34 An auditor can get evidence of the proper functioning of password access control to a computer system by
a. Writing a computer program that simulates the logic of a good password control system.
b. Selecting a random sample of the client's completed transactions to check the existence of proper authorization.
c. Attempting to sign onto the computer system with a false password.
d. Obtaining written representations from the client's computer personnel that the password control prevents unauthorized entry.

H.35 Control procedures within the computer system may leave no visible evidence indicating that the procedures were performed. In such instances, the auditor should test these computer controls by
a. Making corroborative inquiries.
b. Observing the separation of duties of personnel.
c. Reviewing transactions submitted for processing and comparing them to related output.
d. Reviewing the run manual.

H.36 Which of the following statements most likely represents a disadvantage for a company that performs its accounting using personal computers?

  a. It is usually difficult to detect arithmetic errors.

  b. Unauthorized persons find it easy to access the computer and alter the data files.

  c. Transactions are coded for account classifications before they are processed on the computer.

  d. Random errors in report printing are rare in packaged software systems.

H.37 Which of the following is true with respect to fraud risk factors in an electronic environment?

  a. Employees are more intelligent in an electronic environment.

  b. Auditors cannot audit the information system during the year.

  c. Larger dollar amounts are involved in an electronic environment.

  d. Employees have greater access to information systems and computer resources in an electronic environment.

EXERCISES AND PROBLEMS

H.38 Audit "around" versus Audit "through" Computers CPAs may audit "around" or "through" computers in the examination of financial statements of clients who utilize computers to process accounting data.

Required:

  a. Describe the auditing approach referred to as auditing "around" the computer.

  b. Under what conditions does the CPA decide to audit "through" the computer instead of "around" the computer?

  c. In auditing "through" the computer, the CPA may use "test data."

   (1) What is the "test data" test of controls audit procedure?

   (2) Why does the CPA use the "test data" procedure?

  d. How can the CPA be satisfied that the client is actually using the computer program tested to process its accounting data?

(AICPA adapted)

H.39 Computer Internal Control Questionnaire Evaluation. Assume that, when conducting procedures to obtain an understanding of Denton Seed Company's internal controls, you checked "No" to the following internal control questionnaire items (selected from those illustrated in the module):

• Does access to online files require specific passwords to be entered to identify and validate the terminal user?

• Does the user establish control totals prior to submitting data for processing? (Order entry application subsystem.)

• Are input control totals reconciled to output control totals? (Order entry application subsystem.)

Required:

Describe the errors and frauds that could occur due to the weaknesses indicated by the lack of controls.

H.40 Check Digit. Suppose that a credit sale was made to John Q. Smyth, customer account number 8149732. The last digit is a check calculated by the "Modulus 11 Prime Number" method. The data entry operator made an error and keyed in the customer as 8419732.

Required: (refer to Chapter 6):

  a. Calculate the check digit for the number that was keyed in.

  b. How would the self-checking number control detect this data input error?

H.41 Explain Computer Control Procedures. At a meeting of the corporate audit committee attended by the general manager of the products division and you, representing the internal audit department, the following dialogue took place:

Jones (committee chair): Mr. Marks had suggested that the internal audit department conduct an audit of the computer activities of the products division.

Smith (general manager): I don't know much about the technicalities of computers, but the division has some of the best computer people in the company.

Jones: Do you know whether the internal controls protecting the system are satisfactory?

Smith: I suppose they are. No one has complained. What's so important about controls anyway, as long as the system works?

Jones turns to you and asks you to explain computer control policies and procedures.

Required:

Address your response to the following points:

a. State the principal objective of achieving control over (1) input, (2) processing, and (3) output.

b. Give at least three methods of achieving control over (1) source data, (2) processing, and (3) output.

H.42   File Retention and Backup.   You have audited the financial statement of the Solt Manufacturing Company for several years and are making preliminary plans for the audit for the year ended June 30. This year, however, the company has installed and used a computer system for processing a portion of its accounting data.

The following output computer files are produced in the daily processing runs:

1. Cash disbursements sequenced by check number.

2. Outstanding payable balances (alphabetized).

3. Purchase journals arranged by (a) account charged and (b) vendor.

Company records, as described above, are maintained on magnetic tapes. All tapes are stored in a restricted area within the computer room. A grandfather–father–son policy is followed in retaining and safeguarding tape files.

Vouchers (with supporting invoices, receiving reports, and purchase order copies) are filed by vendor code. Another purchase order copy and the checks are filed numerically.

Required:

a. Explain the grandfather–father–son policy. Describe how files could be reconstructed when this policy is used.

b. Discuss whether company policies for retaining and safeguarding the tape files provide adequate protection against losses of data.

(AICPA adapted)

H.43   Separation of Duties and General Control Procedures.   You are engaged to examine the financial statements of Horizon Incorporated, which has its own computer installation. During the preliminary understanding phase, you found that Horizon lacked proper segregation of the programming and operating functions. As a result, you intensified the evaluation of the internal control surrounding the computer and concluded that the existing compensating general controls provided reasonable assurance that the objectives of internal control were being met.

Required:

a. In a properly functioning computer environment, how is the separation of the programming and operating functions achieved?

b. What are the compensating general control procedures that you most likely found?

(AICPA adapted)

H.44   Computer Frauds and Missing Control Procedures.   The following are brief stories of actual employee thefts and embezzlements perpetrated using computers.

Required:

What kind of control procedures were missing or inoperative that might have prevented or detected the fraud?

a. An accounts payable terminal operator at a subsidiary company fabricated false invoices from a fictitious vendor, and entered them in the parent company's central accounts payable/cash disbursement system. Five checks totaling $155,000 were issued to the "vendor."

b. A bank provided custodial and recordkeeping services for several mutual funds. A proof-and-control department employee substituted his own name and account number for those of the actual purchasers of some shares. He used the computerized recordkeeping and correction system to conceal and shift balances from his name and account to names and accounts of the real investors when he needed to avoid detection because of missing amounts in the investors' accounts.

c. The university computer system was entered. Vandals changed many students' first name to "Susan," student telephone numbers were changed to the number of the university president, grade point averages were modified, and some academic files were deleted completely.

d. A computer operator at a state-run horse race betting agency set the computer clock back three minutes. After the race was won, he quickly telephoned bets to his girlfriend, an input clerk at the agency, gave her the winning horse and the bet amount, and won every time!

H.45   Computer   Control   Weaknesses. Ajax, Inc., an audit client, recently installed a new computer system to process the shipping, billing, and accounts receivable records more efficiently. During interim work, an assistant completed the review of the accounting system and the internal controls. The assistant determined the following information concerning the new computer systems and the processing and control of shipping notices and customer invoices.

Each major computerized function (i.e., shipping, billing, accounts receivable) is permanently assigned to a specific computer operator who is responsible for making program changes, running the program, and reconciling the computer log. Responsibility for custody and control over the various databases and system documentation is randomly rotated among the computer operators on a monthly basis to prevent any one person from access to the database and documentation at all times. Each computer programmer and computer operator has access to the computer room via a magnetic card and a digital code that is different for each card. The systems analyst and the supervisor of computer operators do not have access to the computer room.

The computer system documentation consists of the following items: program listings, error listings, logs, and database dictionaries. To increase efficiency, batch totals and processing controls are not used in the system.

Ajax ships its products directly from two warehouses, which forward shipping notices to general accounting. There, the billing clerk enters the price of the item and accounts for the numerical sequence of the shipping notices. The billing clerk also prepares daily adding machine tapes of the units shipped and the sales amounts. Shipping notices and adding machine tapes forwarded to the

computer department for processing the computer output consist of:

a. A three-copy invoice that is forwarded to the billing clerk.

b. A daily sales register showing the aggregate totals of units shipped and sales amounts that the computer operator compares to the adding machine tapes.

The billing clerk mails two copies of each invoice to the customer and retains the third copy in an open invoice file that serves as a detail accounts receivable record.

Required:

a. Prepare a list of weaknesses in internal control (manual and computer), and for each weakness, describe one or more recommendations.

b. Suggest how Ajax's computer processing over shipping and billing could be improved through the use of remote terminals to enter shipping notices. Describe appropriate controls for such an online data entry system.

DISCUSSION CASES

H.46   Control Weaknesses and Recommendations—Louisville Sales Corporation. George Beemster, CPA, is examining the financial statements of the Louisville Sales Corporation, which recently installed a computer. The following comments have been extracted from Mr. Beemster's notes on computer operations and the processing and control of shipping notices and customer invoices:

To minimize inconvenience, Louisville converted without changing its existing data processing system, which utilized tabulating equipment. The computer company supervised the conversion and provided training to all computer department employees in systems design, operations, and programming.

Each computer run is assigned to a specific employee who is responsible for making program changes, running the program, and answering questions. This procedure has the advantage of eliminating the need for records of computer operations because each employee is responsible for her or his own computer runs.

At least one computer department employee remains in the computer room during office hours, and only computer department employees have keys to the computer room.

The company considered the desirability of programmed controls but decided to retain the manual controls from its existing system.

Company products are shipped directly from public warehouses, which forward shipping no-

tices to general accounting. There, a billing clerk enters the price of the items and accounts for the numerical sequence of shipping notices from each warehouse. The billing clerk also prepares daily adding machine tapes ("control tapes") of the units shipped and the unit prices.

Shipping notices and control tapes are forwarded to the computer department for input and processing. Extension calculations are made on the computer. Output consists of invoices (in six copies) and a daily sales register. The daily sales register shows the aggregate totals of units shipped and unit prices, which the computer operator compares to the control tapes.

All copies of the invoice are returned to the billing clerk. The clerk mails three copies to the customer, forwards one copy to the warehouse, maintains one copy in a numerical file, and retains one copy in an open invoice file that serves as a detail accounts receivable record.

Required:

Describe the weaknesses in the internal control over information and data flows and the procedures for processing shipping notices and customer invoices. Recommend some improvements in these control policies and procedures. Organize your answer sheet with two columns, one headed "Weaknesses" and the other headed "Recommended Improvements."

(AICPA adapted)

EXHIBIT H.47–1

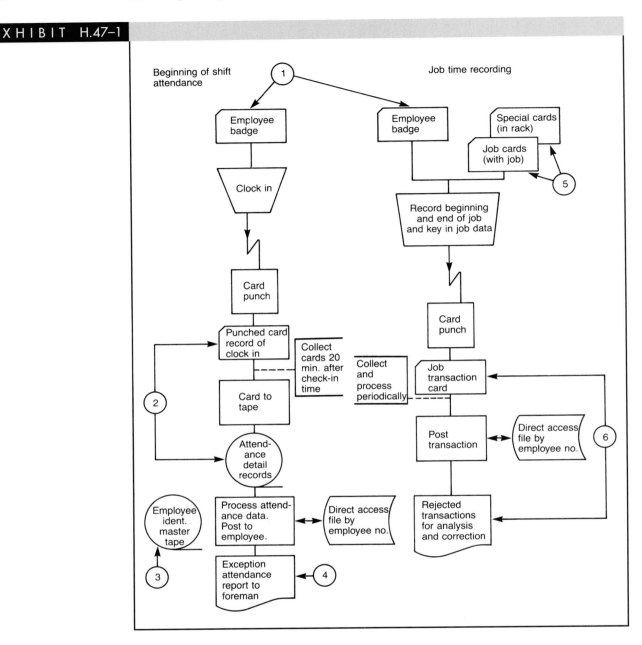

H.47   Flowchart Control Points. Each number of the flowchart in Exhibit H.47–1 locates a control point in the payroll processing system. Make a list of the control points, and for each point, describe the type or kind of internal control procedure that ought to be specified.

H.48   Internal Control Considerations in a Personal Computer Environment.

INTRODUCTION

The second standard of field work requires that an audit include "a sufficient understanding of internal control to plan the audit and to determine the nature, timing, and extent of tests to be performed."

Given the use of personal computers by many businesses, auditors must know about the potential internal control weaknesses inherent in such an environment. Such knowledge is crucial if the auditor is to make a proper assessment of the related control risk and to plan an effective and efficient audit approach.

Required:

In the following case study, assume you are participating in the audit of Chicago Appliance Company and that the background information below has been obtained during the planning phase. You have been asked to (1) consider the potential effects on internal control that have been introduced by the local area network application and (2) assess how those internal control effects may alter the audit plan for the current year.

Background Information

Chicago Appliance is a wholesale distributor of electric appliances. The company's sales in each of the last two years have been approximately $40 million. All accounting applications are handled at the company's corporate office.

Information processing operations have historically centered on an onsite mainframe computer. The computer applications include accounts payable and cash disbursements, payroll, inventory, and general ledger. Accounts receivable and fixed asset records have been prepared manually in the past. Internal controls in all areas have been considered strong in the last few years.

During the past year, financial management decided to automate the processing of sales, accounts receivable, and fixed asset transactions and accounting. Management also concluded that purchasing a personal computer and related available software was more cost effective than increasing the mainframe computer capacity and hiring a second computer operator. The controller and accounting clerks have been encouraged to find additional uses for the personal computer and to "experiment" with it when they are not too busy.

The accounts receivable clerk is enthusiastic about the personal computer (PC), but the fixed asset clerk seems somewhat apprehensive about it because he has no prior experience with computers. The accounts receivable clerk explained that the controller had purchased a "very easy to use" accounts receivable software application program for the PC, which enables her to input the daily information regarding billings and receipts quickly and easily. The controller has added some programming of his own to the software to give it better report-writing features.

During a recent demonstration, the accounts receivable clerk explained that the program required her only to input the customer's name and invoice amount in the case of billings, or the customer's name and check amount in the case of receipts. The computer then automatically updates the respective customer's account balance. At the end of every month, the accounts receivable trial balance is printed and reconciled by the clerk to the general ledger balance, and the controller reviews the reconciliation.

The fixed asset program also was purchased from an outside vendor. The controller indicated that the software package had just recently been put on the market and that it was programmed to compute tax depreciation based on recent changes in the federal tax laws. He also stated that, because of the fixed asset clerk's reluctance to use the computer, he had input all the informa-

tion from the fixed asset manual records. He indicated, however, that the fixed asset clerk would be responsible for the future processing related to the fixed assets files and for generating the month-end and year-end reports used to prepare the related accounting entries.

The various accounts receivable and fixed asset disks are all adequately labeled by the type of program or data file. They are arranged in an organized manner in a disk holder located near the personal computer.

(Adapted from a case contributed by PricezWaterhouseCoopers to The Auditor's Report.)

H.49   Test Data Transactions in a Payroll Processing Program.   You will have to use the computer-based *Electronic Workpapers* on the textbook website to perform a test of the payroll processing program.

The *Electronic Workpapers* contains a simple program that accepts payroll transaction input and calculates an individual's weekly gross and net pay. When you get to the proper place in the program, you will see places to input these data:

Employee identification (Social Security number).

Regular pay rate (round dollars, no cents).

Regular time (hours, 40 or fewer)

Overtime (hours over 40).

Gross earnings to date (gross pay prior to this payroll entry).

According to the client's description of the controls in the system:

1. The program checks for valid employee identification.
2. The regular pay rate is tested for reasonableness.
3. No more than 40 regular-time hours will be accepted by the system.
4. There is a limit on the number of overtime hours that will be paid.
5. Overtime is paid at the rate of 150 percent of the regular pay rate.
6. Social Security and Medicare taxes and federal income tax withholding are calculated automatically according to applicable laws and regulations.

Applicable Laws and Regulations

The minimum wage is $5 per regular hour (assumed for the case). Social Security tax is 6.2 percent on the first $68,400 of gross pay, and Medicare tax is 1.45 percent of all pay. (Assume these regulations for the purpose of this problem.) Federal income tax withholding is assumed to be 23 percent of gross pay. (This assumption is imposed to simplify the case.)

Required:

The payroll calculation program contains control deficiencies. Your job is to identify and describe them. Follow the instructions in the Electronic Workpapers Student Manual and on the disk. Devise and enter test transactions of your own making. Write a memo to the audit partner identifying and describing the control failures in the payroll calculation program.

KEY TERMS

acceptance testing records contain test data that can be used by auditors when performing their own test of controls audit procedures. (Module H)

account analysis identification of each important item and amount in an account followed by document vouching and inquiry to determine whether amounts should be classified elsewhere. (Chapter 12)

account balance a control account made up of many constituent items. (Module E)

account balance audit program a specification (list) of procedures designed to produce evidence about the assertions in financial statements. (Chapter 4)

accounting/posting (as a control objective) a general category concerned with ensuring that the accounting process for a transaction is completely performed and in conformity with GAAP. (Chapter 6)

accounting estimate an approximation of a financial statement element, item, or account made by an organization's management. (Chapters 5, 7, and 11)

accounting system (as element of control) an organization of policies and procedures for recording transactions properly. (Chapter 6)

accredited investors (in SEC Regulation D exempt offerings) financial institutions, investment companies, large tax-exempt organizations, directors and executives of the issuer, and individuals with net worth of $1 million or more or income of $200,000 or more. (Module C)

accuracy (as a control objective) refers to ensuring that dollar amounts are figured correctly. (Chapter 6)

act-utilitarianism (in moral philosophy) emphasis on an individual act as it is affected by the specific circumstances of a situation. (Module B)

adverse opinion the opposite of an unqualified opinion, stating that financial statements are not in conformity with GAAP. (Chapters 2 and 3)

analytical procedures audit evaluation of financial statement accounts by studying and comparing relationships among financial and nonfinancial data. (Chapters 5 and 12)

analytical procedures risk (AP) the probability that analytical procedures will fail to detect material errors. (Module E)

anchoring practice of carrying over preconceived notions about control risk when auditing a client year after year. (Chapter 4)

application controls controls relating to specific computerized accounting applications; for example, programmed validation controls for verifying customers' account numbers and credit limits. (Chapter 6)

application description (in computer system documentation) system flowcharts, description of all inputs and outputs, record formats, lists of computer codes, and control features. (Chapter 6)

associated with financial statements circumstance in which a CPA's name is used in connection with financial statements, or a CPA has prepared the statements, even if the CPA's name is not used in any written report. (Chapter 3)

assurance services independent professional services that improve the quality of information, or its context, for decision makers. (Chapter 1 and Module A)

attest function common reference to independent audits of financial statements, but also refers to review services, association with forecasts and projections, and compilation services where lack of independence is not noted. (Chapter 1 and Module A)

attestation the lending of some credibility to financial or other information by professional auditors who serve as objective intermediaries. (Chapter 1 and Module A)

attestation standards a general set of standards intended to guide attestation work in areas other than audits of financial statements. (Chapter 2)

attribute sampling another name for test of controls audit sampling. (Module E)

audit hooks computer program modules for audit or maintenance purposes. (Module H)

audit objective expression of a financial statement assertion for which evidence needs to be obtained. (Chapters 8, 9, 10, and 11)

audit of balances ordinary and extended substantive procedures designed to find signs of errors and frauds in account balances and classes of transactions. (Chapters 8, 9, 10, and 11)

audit procedure (nature) actions described as the general audit procedures of recalculation, physical observation, confirmation, verbal inquiry, document examination, scanning, and analytical review. (Chapter 4)

audit procedures particular and specialized actions auditors take to obtain evidence in a specific audit engagement. (Chapter 2)

audit program a list of the audit procedures necessary to obtain sufficient, competent evidence that will serve as the basis for the audit report. (Chapter 4)

audit risk (global) the probability that an auditor will give an inappropriate opinion on financial statements. (Chapter 4)

audit risk (account level) probability that an auditor will fail to find misstatement equal to, or greater than, the tolerable misstatement assigned to an account. (Chapter 4)

audit sampling application of an audit procedure to less than 100 percent of the items within an account balance or class of transactions for the purpose of evaluating some characteristic of the balance or class. (Module E)

audit standards   audit quality guides that remain the same through time and for all audits. (Chapter 2)

auditee   the company or other entity whose financial statements are being audited. (Chapter 2)

auditing around the computer   auditors' attempt to isolate the computer system and to find audit assurance by vouching data from output to source documents and by tracing from source documents to output. (Module H)

auditing through the computer   auditors' actual evaluation of the client's hardware and software to determine the reliability of operations that cannot be viewed by the human eye. (Module H)

auditing with the computer   audit techniques such as the use of the client's computer hardware and software to process real or simulated transactions or the use of specialized audit software to perform other audit tasks. (Chapter 4)

authorization (as a control objective)   ensuring that transactions are approved before they are recorded. (Chapter 6)

automatic terminal logoffs   computer control that limits unauthorized access by automatically terminating the link between the microcomputer and the local area network after a specified period of time. (Module H)

average difference method   calculation of projected likely misstatement (PLM) using the average misstatement measure in a sample. (Module E)

average sampling interval (ASI)   the recorded dollar amount of a population being sampled divided by the sample size. (Module G)

backup   a retention system for files, programs, and documentation so that master files can be reconstructed in case of accidental loss and processing can continue at another site if the computer center is lost to fire or flood. (Module H)

batch control totals   totals of dollar numbers, nonsense numbers, or count of documents. (Chapter 6)

batch processing (also serial or sequential processing)   all records to be processed are collected in groups (batches) of like transactions before computer processing. (Chapter 6)

bill of materials   a specification of the materials authorized for production; the source of authorization for the preparation of materials requisitions. (Chapter 10)

block sampling   choosing segments of contiguous transactions for a sampling application. (Module E)

breach of contract   a claim that accounting or auditing services were not performed in the manner agreed. (Module C)

business risk   the risk a company normally experiences that adverse conditions will arise (inflation, competition, loss of business) and create financial difficulty; may also include the probability that good things will happen! (Chapter 1)

capital budget   management document that contains the plans for asset purchases and business acquisitions. (Chapter 12)

cash flow forecast   forecast that informs the board of directors and management of the business plans, the prospects for cash inflows, and the needs for cash outflows. (Chapter 11)

categorical imperative (in moral philosophy)   Kant's specification of an unconditional obligation. (Module B)

Certified Internal Auditors   persons who have met the Institute of Internal Auditors' criteria for professional CIA credentials. (Chapter 7)

chain of custody   the crucial link of the evidence to the suspect, called the "relevance" of evidence by attorneys and judges. (Chapter 7)

check digit   an extra number, precisely calculated, that is tagged onto the end of a basic identification number, such as an employee number. (Chapter 6)

check kiting   the illegal practice of building up apparent balances in one or more bank accounts based on uncollected (float) checks drawn against similar accounts in other banks. (Chapter 8)

class of transactions   a group of transactions having common characteristics, such as cash receipts or cash disbursements, but which are not simply added together and presented as an account balance in financial statements. (Module E)

classification (as a control objective)   ensuring that transactions are recorded in the right accounts, charged or credited to the right customer (including classification of sales to subsidiaries and affiliates), entered in the correct segment product line or inventory description, and so forth. (Chapter 6)

client   person (company, board of directors, agency, or some other person or group) who retains the auditor and pays the fee. (Chapter 2)

collusion   circumstance in which two or more people conspire to conduct fraudulent activity in violation of an organization's internal control policies and procedures. (Chapter 7)

commission   a percentage fee charged for professional services in connection with executing a transaction or performing some other business activity. (Module B)

common law   all the cases and precedents that govern judges' decisions in lawsuits for monetary damages. Common law is "common knowledge" in the sense that judges tend to follow the collective wisdom of past cases decided by themselves and other judges. (Module C)

comparison program utilization (or controlled reprocessing or parallel simulation)   reprocessing live data to test program controls. (Module H)

compensating control   a control feature used when a standard control activity (such as strict segregation of functional responsibilities) is not specified by the company. (Chapter 11)

competent (characteristic of evidence)   evidence that is valid, relevant, and unbiased. (Chapter 2)

compilation service   accountant performs few if any procedures and presents (writes up) management's financial statements with a disclaimer of opinion and no negative assurance. (Module D)

completeness (as a control objective)   ensuring that valid transactions are not omitted entirely from the accounting records. (Chapter 6)

computed upper limit (CUL)   a statistical estimate of the population deviation rate computed from the test of controls sample evidence. (Module F)

computer assisted audit tools and techniques (CAATTs) programs that may be utilized to read, compute, and operate on machine-readable records. (Chapter 4)

conflict of interest any relationship whereby an individual or his or her relative may benefit from a transaction within the individual's business relations where he or she has influenced the transaction or relationship. (Module B)

conscience an inner sense (voice) that informs a person of his or her wrongdoing after an improper action is taken, hence being an insufficient benchmark for making ethical decisions before taking action. (Module B)

constructive fraud lack of even minimum care in performing professional duties—reckless disregard—with the same effect as actual fraud. (Module C)

contingent fee a fee established for the performance of any service in an arrangement in which no fee will be charged unless a specific finding or result is attained, or the fee otherwise depends on the result of the service. (Module B)

contributory negligence a legal defense theory in which the plaintiff's own negligent action bars recovery from a negligent defendant. (Module C)

control environment a set of characteristics that defines good management control features other than accounting policies and control activities. (Chapter 6)

control activities specific error-checking routines performed by company personnel. (Chapter 6)

control risk the probability that a material misstatement (error or fraud) could occur and not be prevented or detected on a timely basis by the company's internal control structure policies and procedures (Chapter 4)

controlled reprocessing (or parallel simulation or comparison program utilization) reprocessing live data to test program controls. (Module H)

critical rate of occurrence a special tolerable deviation rate used in discovery sampling. (Module F)

cross-reference computer program provide printed listings of every occurrence of each name used in an application program or a list of every file used in an application system. (Module H)

cutoff refers to a date, usually the year-end balance sheet date, around which transactions should be recorded in the proper period (year). (Chapter 1)

cutoff bank statement auditors' information source for vouching the bank reconciliation items; a complete bank statement including all paid checks and deposit slips received directly by the auditors. (Chapter 8).

cycle set of accounts and business activities that go together in an accounting system. (Chapter 6)

data encryption conversion of information to scrambled form or code so it can look like garbled nonsense when transmitted or retrieved from a file. (Module H)

data mining (or drilling down) retrieval of information regarding specific transactions from a centralized electronic database. (Chapter 5)

data warehousing the storage of vast quantities of electronic data in a centralized electronic database. (Chapter 5)

decision criteria standards for decision and evaluation in specific circumstances. (Module F)

defalcation another name for employee fraud, embezzlement, and theft (larceny). (Chapter 7)

detail test of control procedure consists of (1)identification of the data population from which a sample of items will be selected for audit and (2)an expression of the action that will be taken to produce relevant evidence. In general, the actions in detail test of control audit procedures involve vouching, tracing, observing, scanning, and recalculating. (Chapters 8, 9, and 10)

detection rate ratio of the number of exceptions reported to auditors to the number of account errors. (Chapter 8)

detection risk the probability that audit procedures will fail to produce evidence of material misstatement, provided any have entered the accounting system in the first place and have not been detected and corrected by the client's control policies and procedures. (Chapter 4)

deviation (as in control failure, also error, occurrence, and exception) refers to a departure from a prescribed internal control activity in a particular case. (Module E)

digitized signature an approved encrypted password that provides authorization for electronic transactions. (Chapter 4)

direct-effect illegal acts violations of laws or government regulations by the company or its management or employees that produce direct and material effects on dollar amounts in financial statements. (Chapter 7)

direct personal knowledge audit evidence obtained by eyewitness and physical inspection. (Chapter 2)

disclaimer of opinion lowest level of assurance; "no assurance." Auditors explicitly state that they give no opinion and no assurance, thus taking no responsibility for a report on the fair presentation of financial statements in conformity with GAAP. (Chapter 3)

drilling down (or data mining) the retrieval of information regarding specific transactions from a centralized electronic database. (Chapter 5)

dual-purpose procedure an audit procedure that simultaneously serves the substantive purpose (obtain direct evidence about the dollar amounts in account balances) and the test of controls purpose (obtain evidence about the company's performance of its own control activities). (Chapters 6 and 8)

echo check a magnetic read after each magnetic write, "echoing" back to the sending location and comparing results. (Module H)

80/20 "rule" the rule of thumb about population skewness that 80 percent of the value tends to be in 20 percent of the units. (Module F)

electronic commerce (EC) the conduct of business through electronic networks, including the Internet. (Chapter 6)

electronic data interchange (EDI) the transmission of information between linked computers. (Chapter 6)

electronic funds transfer (EFT) the transmission of monetary funds through linked computers. (Chapter 6)

embezzlement   a type of fraud involving employees' or nonemployees' wrongfully taking money or property entrusted to their care, custody, and control, often accompanied by false accounting entries and other forms of lying and coverup. (Chapter 7)

emphasis of a matter   one or more paragraphs auditors can add to a report to emphasize something they believe readers should consider important and useful. (Chapter 3)

employee fraud   the use of fraudulent means to take money or other property from an employer. (Chapter 7)

engagement letter   letter from the auditor to the management of an audit client setting forth the terms of the engagement. (Chapter 5)

error (as in **control failure,** also **deviation, occurrence,** and **exception**)   refers to a departure from a prescribed internal control activity in a particular case. (Module E)

error analysis   investigation of each deviation from a prescribed control activity to determine its nature, cause, and probable effect on financial statements. (Module E)

errors (as in **errors and frauds**)   unintentional misstatements or omissions of amounts or disclosures in financial statements. (Chapter 7)

event driven (also **transaction driven**)   information processing system that is started with each transaction event; the individual transaction triggers the processing activity and updates all relevant files. (Chapter 6)

evidence   all the influences upon the minds of auditors which ultimately guide their decisions. (Chapter 2)

exception (as in **control failure,** also **deviation, error,** and **occurrence**)   a departure from a prescribed internal control activity in a particular case. (Module E)

expectation about the population deviation rate   an estimate of the ratio of the number of expected deviations to population size. (Module E)

extending the audit conclusion   performing substantive-purpose audit procedures on the transactions in the remaining period and on the year-end balance to produce sufficient competent evidence for a decision about the year-end balance. (Module E)

extent (of audit procedures)   refers to the amount of work done when the procedures are performed. (Chapter 6)

existence (as a **financial statement assertion**)   management representation that assets, liabilities, equities, revenue, and expenses exist in reality. (Chapter 1)

expanded scope governmental auditing   auditing that goes beyond an audit of financial reports and compliance with laws and regulations to include economy and efficiency and program results audits. (Chapter 1 and Module D)

expert witness   testifying to findings determined during litigation support and testifying as to accounting principles and auditing standards applications. (Chapter 7)

external auditors   independent CPAs who audit financial statements for the purpose of rendering an opinion. (Chapter 7)

external evidence   documentary evidence obtained directly from independent external sources. (Chapter 2)

external-internal evidence   documentary evidence that has originated outside the client's data processing system but which has been received and processed by the client. (Chapter 2)

fidelity bond   an insurance policy that covers most kinds of cash embezzlement losses. (Chapter 8)

financial reporting   broad-based process of providing statements of financial position (balance sheets), statements of results of operations (income statements), statements of changes in financial position (cash flow statements), and accompanying disclosure notes (footnotes) to outside decision makers who have no internal source of information like the management of the company has. (Chapter 1)

Financial Reporting Releases (FRR)   SEC publications of rules and policies about accounting and disclosures. (Module C)

forensic accounting   application of accounting and auditing skills to legal problems, both civil and criminal. (Chapter 7)

foreseeable beneficiaries   creditors, investors, or potential investors who rely on accountant's work. (Module C)

fraud   action of knowingly making material misrepresentations of fact with the intent of inducing someone to believe the falsehood and act upon it and thus suffer a loss or damage. (Chapter 7)

fraud auditing   a pro-active approach to detect financial frauds using accounting records and information, analytical relationships, and an awareness of fraud perpetration and concealment efforts (ACFE). (Chapter 7)

fraud examiners   people engaged specifically for fraud investigation work. (Chapter 7)

fraudulent financial reporting (see also **management fraud**)   intentional or reckless conduct, whether by act or omission, that results in materially misleading financial statements (National Commission on Fraudulent Financial Reporting, 1987). (Chapter 7)

general controls   controls relating to all aspects of computerized information processing activities, such as hardware, segregation of technical responsibilities, file retention and backup. (Chapter 6)

generalization argument (in moral philosophy)   a judicious combination of the imperative and utilitarian principles. (Module B)

government auditors   auditors whose work is governed by the GAO audit standards, whether they be audit employees of governments or public accounting firms engaged to perform government audits. (Chapter 7 and Module D)

gross negligence   lack of even minimum care in performing professional duties, indicating reckless disregard for duty and responsibility. (Module C)

haphazard selection   any unsystematic way of selecting sample units. (Module E)

harmonization   accountants' and regulators' interest in making accounting and auditing standards coordinated, if not uniform, throughout the world. (Chapter 2)

horizontal analysis   study of changes of financial statement numbers and ratios across two or more years. (Chapters 5 and 7)

hypothesis testing auditors hypothesize that an account balance is materially accurate as to existence, ownership, and valuation and test the hypothesis with sample-based evidence. (Module E)

illegal acts violations of laws and regulations that are far removed from financial statement effects. (Chapter 7)

incremental risk of incorrect acceptance the additional risk auditors are willing to add in the substantive sample as a result of assessing control risk too low. (Module F)

individually significant items units in an account balance population that are alone larger than the tolerable misstatement. (Module E)

information risk risk (probability) that the financial statements distributed by a company will be materially false and misleading. (Chapters 1 and 4)

inherent risk probability that material misstatements have occurred in transactions entering the accounting system used to develop financial statements. (Chapter 4)

inspection (as in **test of controls procedures**) auditors look to see whether the documents were marked with an initial, signature, or stamp to indicate they had been checked. (Chapter 6)

integrated test facility (ITF) a technique used to test programmed computer controls by creating a dummy department or branch complete with records of employees, customers, vendors, receivables, payables, and other accounts. (Module H)

integrity ability to act in accordance with the highest moral and ethical values all the time. (Chapter 7)

interim audit work procedures performed several weeks or months before the balance sheet date. (Chapter 5)

interim date a date some weeks or months before the auditee's fiscal year-end. (Chapter 2)

internal accounting control the plan of organization and procedures designed to prevent, detect, and correct accounting errors that may occur and get recorded in ledger accounts and financial statements. (Module D)

internal auditors persons employed within organizations for audit assignments. (Chapters 1, 7, and Module D)

internal auditing (see also **management auditing, operational auditing, performance auditing**) study of business operations for the purpose of making recommendations about the economic and efficient use of resources, effective achievement of business objectives, and compliance with company policies. (Chapter 1 and Module D)

internal control questionnaire a checklist used in a formal interview with knowledgeable managers. (Chapter 6)

internal control consists of a management's control environment, risk assessment, control activities, monitoring, and communication (accounting system). The existence of satisfactory control reduces the probability of errors and frauds in the accounts. (Chapters 2 and 6)

internal evidence documents that are produced, circulated, and finally stored with the client's information system. (Chapter 2)

joint and several liability doctrine that allows a successful plaintiff to recover the full amount of a damage award from the defendants who have money or insurance. (Module C)

known misstatement the actual monetary error found in a sample. (Module E)

larceny simple theft—taking money or property not entrusted into one's care. (Chapter 7)

likely misstatement the projected amount of misstatement in a population based on sample evidence. (Module E)

litigation support consulting in the capacity of helping attorneys document cases and determine damages. (Chapter 7)

logical unit ordinary accounting subsidiary unit that contains the dollar unit selected in a dollar-unit sample. (Module G)

management auditing (see also **internal auditing, operational auditing, performance auditing**) study of business operations for the purpose of making recommendations about the economic and efficient use of resources, effective achievement of business objectives, and compliance with company policies. (Chapter 1 and Module D)

management control the plan of organization and all methods and procedures that are concerned mainly with operational efficiency and adherence to managerial policies and usually relate only indirectly to financial records. (Module D)

management fraud (see also **fraudulent financial reporting**) deliberate fraud committed by management that injures investors and creditors through materially misleading financial statements. (Chapter 7)

management letter auditor's recommendations to the client to add value to the audit in the form of constructive observations and suggestions. (Chapter 12)

material weakness in internal control condition in which the design or operation of internal control does not reduce to a relatively low level the risk that errors or irregularities in amounts that would be material to the financial statements being audited may occur and may not be detected within a timely period by employees in the normal course of performing their assigned functions. (Chapter 6)

materials requisitions requests that create authorizations for the inventory custodian to release raw materials and supplies to the production personnel; documents that are the inventory recordkeepers' authorizations to update the raw materials inventory files to record reductions of the raw materials inventory. (Chapter 10)

mathematical computations (as **audit evidence**) auditors' own calculations. (Chapter 2)

mitigating factors elements of financial flexibility (salability of assets, lines of credit, debt extension, dividend elimination) available as survival strategies in circumstances of going concern uncertainty which may reduce the financial difficulty problems. (Chapter 3)

motive (with reference to fraud) pressure experienced by a person and believed unshareable with friends and confidants. (Chapter 7)

narrative descriptions (internal control documentation) written descriptions of auditors' understanding of a client's control environment, accounting system, and control activities. (Chapter 6)

nature (of audit procedures)   refers to the seven general procedures: recalculation, physical observation, confirmation, verbal inquiry, document examination, scanning, and analytical procedures. (Chapter 6)

negative assurance   "Based on our review, we are not aware of any material modifications that should be made to the accompanying financial statements in order for them to be in conformity with generally accepted accounting principles"; permitted in reviews of unaudited financial statements, letters to underwriters, and reviews of interim financial information. (Module A)

negative confirmation   confirmation letter that requests a reply only if the account balance is considered incorrect. (Chapters 2 and 8)

nonpublic company   company with less than $10 million in assets and fewer than 500 shareholders. Not required to register and file reports under the Exchange Act. (Module G)

nonpublic offering (see also private placement)   sale of securities to a small number of persons or institutional investors (usually not more than 35), who can demand and obtain sufficient information without the formality of SEC registration. (Module C)

nonsampling risk   all risk other than sampling risk. (Module E)

nonstatistical sampling   audit sampling in which auditors do not utilize statistical calculations to express the results. (Module E)

occurrence (as in control failure, also deviation, error, and exception)   refers to a departure from a prescribed internal control activity in a particular case. (Module E)

operational auditing (see also internal auditing, management auditing, performance auditing)   study of business operations for the purpose of making recommendations about the economic and efficient use of resources, effective achievement of business objectives, and compliance with company policies. (Chapter 1 and Module D)

opportunity (with reference to fraud)   an open door for solving the unshareable problem in secret by violating a trust. (Chapter 7)

ordinary negligence   lack of reasonable care in the performance of professional accounting tasks. (Module C)

overaudit   performing more audit work than is necessary. (Chapter 4)

ownership (as a financial statement assertion)   another name for the rights assertion, suggesting auditee's possession of legal title to assets. (Chapter 1)

paper trail   set of telltale signs of erroneous accounting, missing or altered documents, or a "dangling debit" (the false or erroneous debit that results from an overstatement of assets). (Chapters 8, 9, 10, and 11)

parallel simulation (or controlled reprocessing or comparison program utilization)   reprocessing live data to test program controls. (Module H)

parity check   electronic function that ensures the coding of data internal to the computer does not change when it is moved from one internal storage location to another. (Module H)

payroll accounting   preparation of individual paychecks, pay envelopes, or electronic transfers using rate and deduction information supplied by the personnel function and base data supplied by the timekeeping-supervision functions. (Chapter 10)

payroll distribution (as an employer's activity)   control of the delivery of pay to employees so that unclaimed checks, cash, or incomplete electronic transfers are not returned to persons involved in any of the other payroll functions. (Chapter 10)

peer review   study of a firm's quality control policies and procedures followed by a report on a firm's quality of audit practice. (Chapter 2)

performance auditing (see also internal auditing, management auditing, operational auditing)   study of business operations for the purpose of making recommendations about the economic and efficient use of resources, effective achievement of business objectives, and compliance with company policies. (Chapter 1 and Module D)

personnel or labor relations department   function having transaction initiation authority to add new employees to the payroll, delete terminated employees, obtain authorizations for deductions (such as insurance, saving bonds, withholding tax exemptions on federal form W-4), and transmit authority for pay rate changes to the payroll department. (Chapter 10)

physical observation (as an audit procedure)   auditors' actual eyewitness inspection of tangible assets and formal documents. (Chapter 2)

physical representation of the population   auditor's frame of reference for selecting a sample. (Module E)

planned control risk assessment   emphasis on planned; the auditors' selection of a control risk level for which they want to justify a control risk assessment after completing the test of controls audit work. (Module F)

planning materiality   the largest amount of uncorrected dollar misstatement the auditors believe could exist in published financial statements without causing them to be considered materially misleading. (Chapter 4)

planning memorandum   working paper in which auditors summarize the preliminary analytical procedures and the materiality assessment with specific directions about the effect on the audit. (Chapter 5)

population   set of all the items that constitute an account balance or class of transactions. (Module E)

population unit   one item in a population. (Module E)

positive assurance   a forthright and factual statement of the CPA's opinion based on an audit—can be unqualified, qualified, or adverse. (Module A)

positive confirmation   confirmation letter requesting a reply in all cases, whether the account balance is considered correct or incorrect. (Chapters 2 and 8)

possible misstatement   the further misstatement remaining undetected in units not selected in a sample. (Module E)

predication (with reference to fraud examination)   a reason to believe fraud may have occurred. (Chapter 7)

primary beneficiaries   third parties for whose primary benefit an audit or other accounting service is performed. (Module C)

private placement (see also nonpublic offering) sale of securities to a small number of persons or institutional investors (usually not more than 35), who can demand and obtain sufficient information without the formality of SEC registration. (Module C)

privity the relationship of direct involvement between parties to a contract. (Module C)

problem-recognition (as an audit method phase) phase of formulating an audit objective related to a financial assertion. (Module A)

pro forma financial data presentation of financial statements "as if" an event had occurred on the date of the balance sheet. (Module A)

production orders internal documents that specify the materials and labor required and the timing for the start and end of production. (Chapter 10)

program description (in computer program documentation) contains a program flowchart, a listing of the program source code (such as COBOL), and a record of all program changes. (Module H)

program driven information processing system that is started when a specific program is loaded into the computer to process all transactions that fit that program and its related files; characterized by batch processing. (Chapter 6)

projected likely misstatement (PLM) auditors' best estimate of misstatement based on the errors found in a sample. (Modules E and G)

proper period (as a control objective) ensuring the accounting for transactions in the period in which they occur (in accordance with generally accepted accounting principles) related to the cutoff date. (Chapter 6)

proportionate liability a rule requiring a defendant to pay a proportionate share of a court's damage award in a lawsuit depending upon the degree of fault determined by a judge and jury. (Module C)

prospectus set of financial statements and disclosures distributed to all purchasers in an offering registered under the Securities Act of 1933. (Module C)

qualified audit report audit report other than the standard unqualified audit report; contains an opinion paragraph that does not give the assurance that everything in the financial statements is in conformity with GAAP. (Chapter 3)

quality review study of a firm's quality control policies and procedures; an "audit" of a firm's quality of audit practice. (Chapter 2)

random sample set of sampling units chosen so that each population item has an equal likelihood of being selected in a sample. (Module E)

ratio method calculation of projected likely misstatement (PLM) using the measurement of the ratio of known misstatement to book value in the sample. (Module E)

reasonable assurance concept that recognizes that the cost of any entity's internal control should not exceed the benefits that are expected to be derived. (Chapter 6)

referral fees (a) fees a CPA receives for recommending another CPA's services and (b) fees a CPA pays to obtain a client. Such fees may or may not be based on a percentage of the amount of any transaction. (Module B)

registrar fiduciary who keeps the stockholder list and from time to time determines the shareholders eligible to receive dividends (stockholders of record on a dividend record date) and those entitled to vote at the annual meeting. (Chapter 11)

Regulation D (SEC) provides for securities offerings without registration of (1)up to $1 million in a 12-month period by nonpublic companies, with no limit on the number of purchasers, (2)up to $5 million in a 12-month period to fewer than 35 nonaccredited investors or an unlimited number of accredited investors, and (3)an unlimited amount to an unlimited number of accredited investors. (Module C)

Regulation S-K (SEC) contains requirements relating to all business, analytical, and supplementary financial disclosures other than financial statements themselves. (Module C)

Regulation S-X (SEC) contains accounting requirements for audited annual and unaudited interim financial statements filed under both the Securities Act and the Exchange Act. (Module C)

relative risk condition of more or less inherent risk. (Chapter 4)

reperformance (in test of controls procedure) auditors perform again the arithmetic calculations and the comparisons the company people were supposed to have performed. (Chapter 6)

replication process of reperforming a selection procedure and getting the same sample units. (Module E)

reportable condition significant deficiency in the design or operation of a company's internal controls which could adversely affect the organization's ability to record, process, summarize, and report financial data in conformity with GAAP. (Chapter 6)

representative sample sample that mirrors the characteristics of the population. (Module E)

response rate for positive confirmations is the proportion of the number of confirmations returned to the number sent, generally after the audit team prompts recipients with second and third requests. Research studies have shown response rates ranging from 66 to 96 percent. (Chapter 8)

review services accountant performs some procedures lesser in scope than an audit for the purpose of giving a negative assurance report on financial statements. (Module A)

risk model $AR = IR \times CR \times DR$ (Chapter 4); $AR = IR \times CR \times AP \times RIA$. (Module G)

risk of assessing the control risk too high probability that the test of controls (compliance) evidence in the sample indicates high control risk when the actual (but unknown) degree of compliance would justify a lower control risk assessment. (Module E)

risk of assessing the control risk too low probability that the test of controls (compliance) evidence in the sample indicates low control risk when the actual (but unknown) degree of compliance does not justify such a low control risk assessment. (Module E)

risk of incorrect acceptance (RIA) probability that test of detail procedures will fail to detect material errors in an account balance. (Module E)

risk of incorrect rejection probability that test of detail procedures will indicate that a balance is materially misstated when, in fact, it is not. (Module E)

rule-utilitarianism (in moral philosophy) emphasis on the centrality of rules for ethical behavior while still maintaining the criterion of the greatest universal good. (Module B)

S-1 review the audit for subsequent events contemplated by the Securities Act of 1933 respecting the auditor's responsibility running to the effective date of a registration statement. (Chapter 12)

safe harbor plaintiffs in a lawsuit must show that the auditor did not act in good faith, effectively placing the burden of proof on the plaintiff. (Module C)

sales forecast estimated future sales. (Chapter 10)

sample set of sampling units. (Module E)

sample audit review file (SARF) a random sampling selection scheme programmed into the data processing programs to producing representative samples of transactions processed over a period by the computer. (Module H)

sampling error amount by which a projected likely misstatement amount could differ from an actual (unknown) total as a result of the sample not being exactly representative. (Module E)

sampling error-adjusted upper limit sample deviation rate adjusted upward to allow for the idea that the actual population rate could be higher. (Module E)

sampling risk probability that an auditor's conclusion based on a sample might be different from the conclusions based on an audit of the entire population. (Module E)

sampling unit one logical unit from a population, such as a customer's account, an inventory item, a debt issue, a cash receipt, a canceled check, and so forth. (Module E)

scienter person's action with knowing intent to deceive. (Module C)

scope limitation condition in which the auditors are unable to obtain sufficient competent evidence. (Chapter 3)

search for unrecorded liabilities set of procedures designed to yield audit evidence of liabilities that were not recorded in the reporting period. (Chapter 9)

second audit partner one who reviews the work of the audit team. (Chapter 5)

second partner review working papers and financial statements, including footnotes, are given a final review on large engagements by a partner not responsible for client relations. (Chapter 12)

self-checking number a basic code number with its check digit. (Chapter 6)

self-regulation quality control reviews and disciplinary actions conducted by fellow CPAs—professional peers. (Module B)

sequential processing (also called **batch** or **serial processing**) all records to be processed are collected in groups (batches) of like transactions before processing. (Chapter 6)

serial processing (also called **batch** or **sequential processing**) all records to be processed are collected in groups (batches) of like transactions before processing. (Chapter 6)

service organization another business that executes or records transactions on behalf of the client. (Module A)

simple extension calculation of projected likely misstatement based on sample evidence using the difference and ratio methods. (Module G)

skewness concentration of a large proportion of the dollar amount in an account in a small number of the population items. (Module F)

smoke/fire concept means there can be more exposure to error (smoke) than actual error (fire), in analogy to test of controls sampling determination of a tolerable deviation rate. (Module F)

specialists persons skilled in fields other than accounting and auditing who are not members of the audit team. (Chapter 5)

standard deviation a measure of population variability. (Module E)

statistical sampling audit sampling that uses the laws of probability for selecting and evaluating a sample from a population for the purpose of reaching a conclusion about the population. (Module E)

statutory law all the prohibitions enacted by a legislature. (Module C)

Staff Accounting Bulletins (SAB) (SEC) unofficial publications but important interpretations of Regulation S-X and Regulation S-K. (Module C)

stratification relating to account balances and audit sampling, refers to subdividing a population. (Module E)

substantive audit procedures transaction detail audit and analytical procedures designed to detect material misstatements in account balances and footnote disclosures. (Chapters 4 and 6)

substantive-purpose audit program list of account balance-related procedures designed to produce evidence about assertions in financial statements. (Module E)

substantive tests of details auditing performance of procedures to obtain direct evidence about the dollar amounts and disclosures in financial statements. (Module E)

supervision (in payroll processing) authorization of all pay base data (hours, job number, absences, time off allowed for emergencies, etc.) by an employee's immediate supervisor. (Chapter 10)

systematic random sample random sample chosen by calculating a skip interval and selecting every kth population unit in a frame. (Modules E, F, and G)

systems control audit review file (SCARF) method in which auditors build into the data processing programs special limit, reasonableness, or other audit tests for selection of transactions for audit. (Module H)

systems development and documentation standards manual computer documentation containing standards that ensure

(1) proper user involvement in the systems design and modification process, (2) review of the specifications of the system, (3) approval by user management and data processing management, and (4) controls and auditability. (Module H)

tainting percentage   ratio of misstatement in a sampling unit to the recorded amount of the sampling unit. (Module G)

termination letter   letter from a former auditor (fired or resigned) to a former client specifying terms for future services and the auditor's understanding of the circumstances of termination. (Chapter 5)

test data   auditor-produced transactions used to audit programmed control procedures with simulated data. (Module H)

test of controls   ordinary and extended procedures designed to produce evidence about the effectiveness of client controls that should be in operation. (Chapters 6, 8, 9, 10, and 11)

timekeeping   payroll function of producing time cards or time sheets that provide the basis for payment to hourly workers. (Chapter 10)

timing (of audit procedures)   refers to when procedures are performed: at "interim" before the balance sheet date, or at "year-end" shortly before and after the balance sheet date. (Chapter 6 and Module E)

tolerable deviation rate   decision criterion of the frequency of control failure for assessing control risk. (Module E and Module F)

tolerable misstatement   decision criterion of the amount of dollar misstatement that can exist undetected in an account and not cause financial statements to be considered materially misleading. (Chapters 5 and 6 and Module G)

tort   legal action covering civil complaints other than breach of contract; normally initiated by users of financial statements. (Module C)

tracing   auditor selects sample items from basic source documents and proceeds forward through the accounting and control system to find the final recording of the accounting transactions. (Chapter 2)

transaction driven (also event driven)   information processing system that is started with each transaction event; the individual transaction triggers the processing activity and updates all relevant files. (Module G)

transfer agent   fiduciary who handles the exchange of shares, cancelling the shares surrendered by sellers and issuing new certificates to buyers. (Chapter 11)

trap doors   unauthorized computer program modules used for fraudulent purposes. (Module H)

unqualified (audit) report   "good" audit report that makes no mention of accounting or auditing deficiencies. (Chapter 2)

unrestricted random sample   items in a population are associated with numbers in a random number table or computer program for selection of a sample; no population stratification. (Modules E and F)

upper error limit (UEL)   largest amount of monetary misstatement that can be calculated, using the factor for the decision criterion risk of incorrect acceptance. (Module G)

validity (as a control objective)   ensuring that recorded transactions are ones that should have been recorded. (Chapter 6)

verbal and written representations (audit evidence)   responses to audit inquiries given by the client's officers, directors, owners, and employees. (Chapter 2)

vertical analysis   study of financial statement amounts expressed each year as proportions of a base such as sales for the income statement accounts and total assets for the balance sheet accounts. (Chapters 5 and 7)

voucher   an assembly of supporting documents (purchase requisition, purchase order, vendor invoice, receiving report) that shows a valid obligation to pay a vendor for goods or services. (Chapter 9)

vouching   auditor selects sample items from an account and goes backward through the accounting and control system to find the source documentation that supports the item selected. (Chapters 2 and 12)

walk-through   act of following one or a few transactions through the accounting system and control system to obtain a general understanding of the client's systems. (Module E)

white collar crime   misdeeds done by people who wear ties to work and steal with a pencil or a computer terminal. (Chapter 7)

year-end audit work   audit procedures performed shortly before and after the balance sheet date. (Chapter 4)

INDEX

Statements on Internal Auditing Standards
The Institute of Internal Auditors

SIAS No.

1	1983	*Control: Concepts and Responsibilities*
2	1983	*Communicating Results*
3	1985	*Deterrence, Detection, Investigation, and Reporting of Fraud*
4	1986	*Quality Assurance*
5	1987	*Internal Auditors' Relationships with Independent Outside Auditors*
6	1987	*Audit Working Papers*
7	1989	*Communicating with the Board of Directors*
8	1991	*Analytical Auditing Procedures*
9	1991	*Risk Assessment*
10	1991	*Evaluating the Accomplishment of Established Objectives and Goals for Operations or Programs*
11	1992	*Omnibus Statement*
12	1993	*Planning the Audit Assignment*
13	1993	*Follow-up in the Performance of Audit Work*
14	1995	*Glossary*
15	1996	*Supervision*
16	1997	*Auditing Compliance with Policies, Plans, Procedures, Laws, Regulations, and Contracts*
17	1997	*Assessment of Performance of External Auditors*
18	1997	*Use of Outside Service Providers*

Government Auditing Standards (U.S. General Accounting Office)

	1994	*Governmental Auditing Standards (the "Yellow Book")*
GAO/A-GAGAS-1	1999	*Amendment No. 1, Documentation Requirements When Assessing Control Risk at Maximum for Controls Significantly Dependent Upon Computerized Information Systems*
GAO/A-GAGAS-2	1999	*Amendment No. 2, Auditor Communication*

The most current standards can be found at http://www.gao.gov/govaud/ybk01.htm.

Statements on Standards for Accounting and Review Services (AICPA)

SSARS No.

1	1978	*Compilation and Review of Financial Statements*
2	1979	*Reporting on Comparative Financial Statements*
3	1981	*Compilation Reports on Financial Statements Included in Certain Prescribed Forms*
4	1981	*Communications Between Predecessor and Successor Accountants*
6	1986	*Reporting on Personal Financial Statements Included in Written Personal Financial Plans*
7	1992	*Omnibus Statement*
8	2000	*Amendment to Statement on Standards for Accounting and Review Services No. 1, Compilation and Review of Financial Statements.*

Code of Professional Conduct (AICPA)

Article I—Responsibilities
Article II—The Public Interest
Article III—Integrity

Article IV—Objectivity and Independence
Article V—Due Care
Article VI—Scope and Nature of Services

Rule No.

101	*Independence*
102	*Integrity and Objectivity*
201	*General Standards*
202	*Compliance with Standards*
203	*Accounting Principles*
301	*Confidential Client Information*

Rule No.

302	*Contingent Fees*
501	*Acts Discreditable*
502	*Advertising and Other Forms of Solicitation*
503	*Commissions and Referral Fees*
505	*Form of Practice and Name*